Business Law Today, Standard

Text & Summarized Cases
Custom Edition

10th Edition

Roger LeRoy Miller

 CENGAGE
Learning·

Australia • Brazil • Japan • Korea • Mexico • Singapore • Spain • United Kingdom • United States

**Business Law Today, Standard: Text &
Summarized Cases, Custom Edition,
10th Edition**

Senior Project Development Manager:
Linda deStefano

Market Development Manager:
Heather Kramer

Senior Production/Manufacturing Manager:
Donna M. Brown

Production Editorial Manager:
Kim Fry

Sr. Rights Acquisition Account Manager:
Todd Osborne

For product information and technology assistance, contact us at
Cengage Learning Customer & Sales Support, 1-800-354-9706

For permission to use material from this text or product,
submit all requests online at **cengage.com/permissions**
Further permissions questions can be emailed to
permissionrequest@cengage.com

This book contains select works from existing Cengage Learning resources and
was produced by Cengage Learning Custom Solutions for collegiate use. As such,
those adopting and/or contributing to this work are responsible for editorial
content accuracy, continuity and completeness.

Compilation © 2013 Cengage Learning

ISBN-13: 978-1-285-92426-7

ISBN-10: 1-285-92426-6

Cengage Learning
5191 Natorp Boulevard
Mason, Ohio 45040
USA
Cengage Learning is a leading provider of customized learning solutions with
office locations around the globe, including Singapore, the United Kingdom,
Australia, Mexico, Brazil, and Japan. Locate your local office at:
international.cengage.com/region.

Cengage Learning products are represented in Canada by Nelson Education, Ltd.
For your lifelong learning solutions, visit **www.cengage.com/custom.**
Visit our corporate website at **www.cengage.com.**

Printed in the United States of America

Brief Contents

LAW, DIVERSITY, AND BUSINESS: MANAGERIAL IMPLICATIONS

LINKING BUSINESS LAW to . . .

Preface to the Instructor

Today's business and legal environment is changing at a pace never before experienced. In many instances, technology is both driving and facilitating this change. The expanded use of the Internet for both business and personal transactions has led to new ways of doing business in the twenty-first century. Other factors that have affected the legal environment include the recent economic recession and our nation's ongoing struggle to regain financial stability, combat joblessness, and reduce the national debt.

In the midst of this evolving environment, however, one thing remains certain: For those entering the business world, an awareness of business law and the legal environment is critical. *Business Law Today*, Tenth Edition, provides the information your students need in an interesting and contemporary way. The Tenth Edition of *Business Law Today* continues its established tradition of being the most up-to-date text on the market.

I have spent a great deal of effort incorporating the latest legal developments and giving this book a visual appeal that will encourage students to learn the law. The law presented in *Business Law Today* includes new statutes, regulations, and cases, as well as recent developments in cyberlaw.

What's New in the Tenth Edition

Instructors have come to rely on the coverage, accuracy, and applicability of *Business Law Today*. To make sure that the text engages your students' interest, solidifies their understanding of the legal concepts presented, and provides the best teaching tools available, the following items are now offered either in the text or in conjunction with the text.

New *Spotlight Cases* and *Spotlight Case Problems*

For the Tenth Edition of *Business Law Today*, certain cases and case problems have been carefully chosen to spotlight as good teaching cases. **Spotlight Cases** and **Spotlight Case Problems** are labeled either by the name of one of the parties or by the subject involved. Some examples include *Spotlight on Amazon, Spotlight on Apple, Spotlight on the Seattle Mariners, Spotlight on Commercial Speech,* and *Spotlight on Internet Porn.*

Instructors will find these *Spotlight Cases* useful to illustrate the legal concepts under discussion, and students will enjoy studying these cases because they involve interesting and memorable facts.

Suggested answers to all case-ending questions and case problems are included in both the *Instructor's Manual* and the *Answers Manual* for this text.

New Focus on Diversity

This Tenth Edition of *Business Law Today* recognizes the tremendous impact of diversity on the business world and legal environment today. Therefore, the text includes a special new feature entitled **Law, Diversity, and Business: Managerial Implications** that emphasizes diversity issues. These features address important topics such as marriage equality laws, appearance-discrimination legislation, and discriminatory mortgage lending. The new *Law, Diversity, and Business: Managerial Implications* features include the following:

- *Derogatory Trademarks* (Chapter 5)
- *Native Americans and Criminal Justice* (Chapter 6)
- *The Worldwide Lack of Women on Boards of Directors* (Chapter 31)
- *How Should Airlines Deal with "Customers of Size"?* (Chapter 33)

New *Appendix to Chapter 14* Focuses on Reading and Analyzing Contracts

Because reading and analyzing contracts is such a crucial skill for businesspersons, **a special new Appendix to Chapter 14** has been added. This appendix follows the last contracts chapter and explains how to read and analyze a contract. Then, it presents an example of an employee noncompetition and nondisclosure agreement. The sample contract is annotated so that students can quickly see what each contract provision means.

New *Debate This* Feature

To encourage student participation and motivate students to think critically about the rationale underlying the law on a particular topic, a new feature has been created for the Tenth Edition. Entitled *Debate This,* it consists of a brief statement or question concerning the chapter material that can be used to spur lively classroom or small group discussions. It can also be used as a written assignment. This feature follows the *Reviewing* feature (discussed shortly) at the end of each chapter. **Suggested pro and con responses to the *Debate This* features can be found in both the *Instructor's Manual* and the *Answers Manual* for this text.**

New Cases and Case Problems

The Tenth Edition of *Business Law Today* is filled with new cases and case problems. Nearly every chapter features at least one new case and new case problem from 2011 and 2012. Many chapters include two recent case summaries and problems. That means more than 75 percent of the cases are new to this edition.

The new cases have been carefully selected based on these criteria: (1) they illustrate important points of law, (2) they are of high interest to students and instructors, and (3) they are simple enough factually for business law students to understand. I have made it a point to find recent cases that enhance learning. I have also eliminated cases that are too difficult procedurally or factually.

New *Group Projects*

For instructors who want to have their classes perform group projects, each chapter of the Tenth Edition includes a **new *Business Law Critical Thinking Group Assignment.*** Each project begins by describing a business scenario and then requires each group of students to answer a specific question pertaining to the scenario based on the information that they learned in the chapter. These projects may be used in class to spur discussion or as homework assignments.

I have also created **a new *Group Project*** for the end of every unit. These projects require students, as a group, to apply the concepts they learned in the previous chapters. These projects can be useful for reviewing materials in class prior to a test. **Suggested answers to all group assignments are included in both the *Instructor's Manual* and the *Answers Manual* for this text.**

A New Chapter on *Mortgages and Foreclosures after the Recession*

The Tenth Edition includes an entirely new chapter (Chapter 22) entitled **Mortgages and Foreclosures after the Recession.** This chapter examines some of the mortgage-lending practices that contributed to the Great Recession that began in 2008 and discusses the legal reforms enacted in response to it.

New Coverage of Current Significant Topics

To pique student interest from the outset, many chapters in the Tenth Edition open with the latest news related to important legal topics. For example:

• Chapter 2 covers the constitutional challenge to the Obama administration's Patient Protection and Affordable Care Act and the United States Supreme Court's 2012 decision in that matter.
• Chapter 5 discusses the patent infringement lawsuit that Apple, Inc., filed against Samsung for allegedly imitating the iPhone and iPad too closely.
• Chapter 24 mentions the United States Supreme Court's 2012 decision on the extent to which federal law preempts the states from enacting immigration legislation.

Coverage of the latest developments in the topics under discussion is a priority throughout the text.

Practical and Effective Learning Tools

Today's business leaders must often think "outside the box" when making business decisions. For this reason, I have included numerous critical-thinking elements in the Tenth Edition that are designed to challenge students' understanding of the materials beyond simple retention. I have also retained, improved, and streamlined the many practical features of this text to help students learn how the law applies to business.

Highlighted and Numbered *Case Examples*

One of the most appreciated features of *Business Law Today* has always been the highlighted numbered examples that appear throughout the book to illustrate the legal principles under discussion. Further, many instructors use cases to illustrate how the law applies to business. For this reason, the in-text numbered examples have been expanded to include *Case Examples.*

These *Case Examples* are integrated appropriately throughout the text and present the facts, issues, and rulings from actual court cases. These are especially useful to simplify difficult areas of law. Students can read through the case examples and quickly see how courts apply the legal principles under discussion in the real world.

Linking Business Law to . . . Feature

The Tenth Edition of *Business Law Today* also includes a **special feature entitled *Linking Business Law to . . .* [one of the six functional fields of business].** As will be discussed in Chapter 1, the six functional fields of business are *corporate management, production and transportation, marketing, research and development, accounting and finance,* and *human resources management.*

This feature appears in selected chapters to underscore how the law relates to other fields of business. Some of the new *Linking Business Law to . . .* features include:

• *Linking Business Law to Marketing*—Trademarks and Service Marks (Chapter 5)
• *Linking Business Law to Corporate Management*—Quality Control (Chapter 17)
• *Linking Business Law to Corporate Management*—What Can You Do to Prepare for a Chapter 11 Reorganization? (Chapter 21)
• *Linking Business Law to Accounting and Finance*—Sources of Funds (Chapter 29)

Business Application

Many chapters end with a ***Business Application* feature** that focuses on practical considerations related to the chapter's contents. This feature concludes with a **checklist** of tips for the businessperson. For example, these topics include the following:

- *Protecting Your Company against Hacking of Your Bank Accounts* (Chapter 6)
- *How to Choose and Use a Lawyer* (Chapter 8)
- *What Can You Do When a Contract Is Breached?* (Chapter 16)
- *How to Develop a Policy on Employee Use of the Internet and Social Media* (Chapter 24)

Preventing Legal Disputes

The Tenth Edition of *Business Law Today* continues the emphasis on providing practical information in every chapter through a special feature entitled **Preventing Legal Disputes.** These brief, integrated sections offer sensible guidance on steps that businesspersons can take in their daily transactions to avoid legal disputes and litigation in a particular area.

Adapting the Law to the Online Environment

The Tenth Edition contains many new **Adapting the Law to the Online Environment** features, which examine cutting-edge cyberlaw issues coming before today's courts. Here are some examples of these features:

- *Vulgar Facebook Photos Receive First Amendment Protection* (Chapter 2)
- *The Validity of E-Signatures for Online Colleges and Universities* (Chapter 10)
- *The Supreme Court Takes a Stand on Warning Labels for Video Games* (Chapter 17)
- *Live Chatting with Your State's Bankruptcy Court* (Chapter 21)
- *Social Media in the Workplace Come of Age* (Chapter 24)
- *The New Era of Crowdfunding* (Chapter 29)
- *The Justice Department Goes after E-Book Pricing* (Chapter 32)

Each feature concludes with a *Critical Thinking* question that asks the student to analyze some facet of the issues discussed in the feature. **Suggested answers to these questions are included in both the *Instructor's Manual* and the *Answers Manual* for this text.**

Summarized Case Presentation

Each case is presented in a certain format, which begins with the case title and citation (including parallel citations). Whenever possible, a URL that can be used to access the case online appears just below the case citation (a footnote to the URL explains how to find the specific case at that Web site). I then briefly outline the facts of the dispute, the legal issue presented, and the court's decision.

To enhance student understanding, I paraphrase the reason for the court's decision and provide bracketed explanations for any unfamiliar terms. Each case concludes with a question, which may include a *Critical Thinking, What If the Facts Were Different?* or *Why Is This Case Important?* question. *Classic Cases* include a special section entitled *Impact of This Case on Today's Law* to clarify the relevance of the case to modern law. **Suggested answers to all case-ending questions are included in both the *Instructor's Manual* and the *Answers Manual* for this text.**

Critical-Thinking and Legal Reasoning Elements

The chapter-ending materials include a separate section of questions that focus on critical thinking and writing. This section includes the *Business Law Critical Thinking Group Assignment* (discussed previously) and may also include one or more of the following:

- **Critical Legal Thinking** questions require students to think critically about some aspect of the law discussed in the chapter.
- **Business Law Writing** questions require students to compose a written response to a business-oriented critical-thinking question.

- *Case Analysis Questions* are sometimes included to improve students' ability to analyze cases and perform legal reasoning. Students read through a case excerpt that is provided in *Appendix I* at the end of this text, brief the case, and then answer a series of questions relating to the case.

Reviewing . . . Features

Each chapter in this text ends with a *Reviewing . . .* **feature** that helps solidify students' understanding of the chapter materials. Each of these features presents a hypothetical scenario and then asks a series of questions that require students to identify the issues and apply the legal concepts discussed in the chapter. The questions are intended to help students review the chapter materials in a simple and interesting way.

An instructor can use this feature as the basis for a lively in-class discussion or can encourage students to use it for self-study and assessment prior to completing homework assignments.

ExamPrep Sections

Following the chapter summary in every chapter is an *ExamPrep* **section that includes two** *Issue Spotters* **related to the chapter's topics** that facilitate student learning and review of the chapter materials. For this edition, the answers to the *Issue Spotters* are provided in *Appendix E* at the end of this text.

Beyond Our Borders

The *Beyond Our Borders* feature gives students an awareness of the global legal environment by indicating how international laws or the laws of other nations deal with specific legal concepts or topics being discussed in the chapter. This feature always concludes with a *Critical Thinking* question. **Suggested answers to these questions are included in both the *Instructor's Manual* and the *Answers Manual* for this text.**

Landmark in the Law

The *Landmark in the Law* feature discusses a landmark case, statute, or other legal development that has had a significant effect on business law. Each of these features has a section titled *Application to Today's World,* which indicates how the law discussed in the feature affects the legal landscape of today's world.

Sample Answers

Each chapter includes a **Question with Sample Answer** that is answered in *Appendix G* and a **Case Problem with Sample Answer** that is based on an actual case and answered in *Appendix H*. Students can compare their own answers to the answers provided to determine whether they have applied the law correctly and to learn what needs to be included when answering the end-of-chapter *Business Scenarios and Case Problems*.

Ethical Issues

In addition to a full chapter on ethics, chapter-ending ethical questions, and the **Ethical Considerations** in many of the *Critical Thinking* questions in the cases, this text includes a feature called **Ethical Issues**. This feature, which is closely integrated with the text, opens with a question addressing an ethical dimension of the topic being discussed. The feature is designed to make sure that students understand that ethics is an integral part of a business law course.

Business Law Today on the Web

The Web site for the Tenth Edition of *Business Law Today* can be found by going to **www. cengagebrain.com** and entering ISBN 9781133273561. The Web site offers a broad array of teaching/learning resources, including the following:

- *Practice quizzes* for every chapter in this text.
- *Appendix A: How to Brief Cases and Analyze Case Problems*
- *Legal reference materials* including a "Statutes" page that offers links to the full text of selected statutes referenced in the text, a Spanish glossary, and other important legal resources.
- *CourseMate* access can also be purchased by the students, where they will find additional study tools, such as an e-Book, additional quizzes, flashcards, key terms, and PowerPoint slides.

Other Pedagogical Devices within Each Chapter

- *Learning Objectives* (a series of brief questions at the beginning of each chapter provide a framework for the student as he or she reads through the chapter). *For this edition, to facilitate learning, I repeat the Learning Objective question in the margin adjacent to where the question is answered in the text.*
- *Chapter Outline* (an outline of the chapter's first-level headings).
- *Margin definitions.*
- *Margin Quotations.*
- *Exhibits.*
- *Photographs (often with critical-thinking questions) and cartoons.*

Chapter-Ending Pedagogy

- *Reviewing . . .* **feature** (in every chapter).
- *Debate This* (in every chapter).
- *Key Terms* (with appropriate page references).
- *Chapter Summary* (in table format with page references).
- *ExamPrep* (including two *Issue Spotters* for each chapter that are answered in *Appendix E*).
- *For Review* (the questions set forth in the chapter-opening *Learning Objectives* section are presented again to aid students in reviewing the chapter. For this edition, answers to the even-numbered questions for each chapter are provided in Appendix F.).
- *Business Scenarios and Case Problems* (every chapter includes a *Question with Sample Answer* (answered in *Appendix G*), a *Case Problem with Sample Answer* (answered in *Appendix H*), *A Question of Ethics,* and a *Business Law Critical Thinking Group Assignment.* Selected chapters also include a *Spotlight Case Problem.*)

Unit-Ending Pedagogy

Each of the seven units in the Tenth Edition of *Business Law Today* concludes with the following features:

- *Business Case Study with Dissenting Opinion*—This feature focuses on a court case that relates to a topic covered in the unit. It opens with an introductory section, discusses the case background and significance, and then provides excerpts from the court's majority opinion and from a dissenting opinion as well. The case study portion ends with *Questions for Analysis*—a series of questions that prompt the student to think critically about the legal, ethical, economic, international, or general business implications of the case.

- *Business Scenario*—This feature presents a hypothetical business situation and then asks a series of questions about how the law applies to various actions taken by the firm. To answer the questions, the student must apply the laws discussed throughout the unit.
- *Group Project*—The final portion of the unit-ending pedagogy is the new *Group Project* that was discussed earlier in this preface.

Suggested answers to all unit-ending questions are included in both the *Instructor's Manual* and the *Answers Manual* for this text.

Supplemental Teaching Materials

This edition of *Business Law Today* is accompanied by an expansive number of teaching and learning supplements, which are available on the *Instructor's Resource CD-ROM,* or IRCD, as well as on the password-protected portion of the companion Web site. Individually and in conjunction with a number of colleagues, I have developed supplementary teaching materials that I believe are the best available today. The many components of the supplements package are listed below.

Instructor's Resource CD-ROM (IRCD)

The IRCD includes the following supplements:

- *Instructor's Manual* (includes at least one **additional case on point** per chapter, answers to all *Critical Thinking* questions, *Reviewing* features, *Business Law Critical Thinking Group Assignments, Business Case Studies with Dissenting Opinions, Business Scenarios,* and *Group Projects*).
- *Answers Manual* (includes answers to all the *Business Scenarios and Case Problems, Critical Thinking* questions, and unit-ending questions in the text, and **Alternate Problem Sets with Answers**).
- A comprehensive **Test Bank.**
- **Case-Problem Cases.**
- **Case Printouts.**
- **ExamView.**
- **PowerPoint slides.**
- *Instructor's Manual* for the *Drama of the Law* video series.
- *Handbook of Landmark Cases and Statutes in Business Law and the Legal Environment.*
- *Handbook on Critical Thinking in Business Law and the Legal Environment.*
- *A Guide to Personal Law.*

Software, Video, and Multimedia Supplements

- *Business Law Digital Video Library*—Provides access to ninety videos that spark class discussion and clarify core legal concepts. Access is available as an optional package with each new text at no additional cost. You can access the *Business Law Digital Video Library,* along with corresponding *Video Questions,* at **login.cengage.com.**
- **Westlaw®**—Ten free hours on Westlaw are available to qualified adopters.
- *CengageNOW* for *Business Law Today* (at an additional cost)—Arguably the most comprehensive online learning and assessment tool for business law and the legal environment on the market today. For more information, contact your South-Western/Cengage Learning Sales Representative. For a demo of this complete online learning system, go to **www.cengage.com/now.**
- *CourseMate*—Brings business law concepts to life with interactive learning, study, and exam preparation tools that support this printed textbook. Built-in engagement

tracking tools allow you to assess your students' study activities. Additionally, *CourseMate* includes an interactive e-Book, which contains the entire contents of this printed textbook enhanced by the many advantages of a digital environment.

For Users of the Ninth Edition

I thought that those of you who have been using *Business Law Today* would like to know some of the major changes that have been made for the Tenth Edition.

New Features and Special Pedagogy

I have added the following entirely new elements for the Tenth Edition:

* *Law, Diversity, and Business: Managerial Implications* feature in selected chapters.
* *Spotlight Cases* and *Spotlight Case Problems* in selected chapters.
* An *Appendix to Chapter 14* on reading and analyzing contracts.
* A *Debate This* feature in every chapter.
* A *Business Law Critical Thinking Group Assignment* in every chapter.
* A *Group Project* at the end of each unit.
* *Appendix E* (Answers to the *Issue Spotters*), *Appendix F* (Answers to Even-Numbered *For Review* Questions), and *Appendix H* (Sample Answers for *Case Problems with Sample Answer*).

Significantly Revised Chapters

Every chapter of the Tenth Edition has been revised as necessary to incorporate new developments in the law, and to simplify or streamline the presentations. Other major changes and additions made for this edition include the following:

* **Chapter 2 (Constitutional Law)**—This chapter has been thoroughly updated and revised. It opens with a discussion of the constitutional issue raised by the Obama administration's Patient Protection and Affordable Care Act and considers how the United States Supreme Court's decision in the matter will affect business. The privacy concerns raised by social networking Web sites are also discussed. A feature addresses First Amendment rights and postings on Facebook, and another feature examines the legal issues presented by same-sex marriage and marriage equality laws.
* **Chapter 5 (Intellectual Property and Internet Law)**—The materials on intellectual property rights have been thoroughly revised and updated. The chapter incorporates the major changes to patent law made by the America Invents Act, which make the first person to file for a patent application the holder. A new subsection addresses patent infringement lawsuits and high-tech companies, and the suit filed by Apple, Inc., against Samsung over iPhones, iPads, and Android software is discussed. Coverage of domain names and cybersquatting has been updated. Numerous updates and new examples have been added to illustrate how intellectual property laws apply in the digital world. A *Spotlight on Internet Porn* case covers trademark dilution by a porn site using a toymaker's domain name. There is also a discussion of the 2012 United States Supreme Court decision addressing Congress's authority to restore copyright protection to foreign works that were already in the public domain. A *Beyond Our Borders* feature outlines the provisions of a new international treaty to combat global counterfeiting and piracy.
* **Chapter 6 (Criminal Law and Cyber Crime)**—This chapter has been substantially revised to deal with the growing problem of cyber crime, including many types of Internet fraud, identity theft, phishing, and hacking. It also covers some of the difficulties involved in prosecuting cyber crime. The chapter incorporates recent United States Supreme Court decisions on whether police can attach a GPS tracking device to a suspect's vehicle and whether police

officers can be held personally liable for performing an illegal search. New features examine whether a person can be prosecuted for posting fake photos on Facebook and provide guidance on how businesspersons can prevent their bank accounts from being hacked.

- **Chapters 9 through 14 (the Contracts unit)**—The discussion of online contracting and electronic signatures has been merged with the coverage of traditional contracts. More examples, case examples, updates throughout, and streamlined coverage have been added. Numerous *Spotlight Cases* have been added to this unit, including *Spotlight on Amazon, Spotlight on Columbia Pictures, Spotlight on the Improv,* and *Spotlight on PC Magazine.*

- **Chapters 15 through 22 (the Commercial Transactions unit)**—This entire unit deals with commercial transactions and aspects of the Uniform Commercial Code, including sales and lease law, negotiable instruments, banking, secured transactions, and bankruptcy. This edition includes an entirely new chapter on Mortgages and Foreclosures after the Recession (Chapter 22). Chapter 22 provides a timely look at the mortgage crisis, predatory lending practices, and the laws enacted to address some of the problems that became evident during the recession.

- **Chapter 24 (Employment, Immigration, and Labor Law)**—This chapter has been thoroughly revised and updated to include discussions of legal issues facing employers today. A feature covers the use of social media in the workplace, and another feature explains how to develop policies on social media and Internet use. The chapter includes a section on immigration law, a topic of increasing importance to employers, and discusses the United States Supreme Court's decision on whether federal law preempts state immigration laws. The chapter also includes an updated discussion of the Family and Medical Leave Act, employee privacy rights and electronic monitoring of employees—including social media communications—drug testing, rights of union workers, strikes, and lockouts (such as the recent NFL and NBA lockouts).

- **Chapter 25 (Employment Discrimination and Diversity)**—The chapter covering employment discrimination has been significantly updated and now emphasizes diversity. A feature was added on combating appearance-based discrimination. The materials on sexual harassment and retaliation have been revised to incorporate recent case law.

- **Chapters 26 through 31 (the Business Organizations unit)**—This unit has been reworked to simplify and streamline the presentation of the materials and to focus on diversity. Features address whether a person who is not a member of a protected class can sue for discrimination (Chapter 28) and why so few women are included on corporate boards of directors (Chapter 31). Chapter 29 includes a new feature on crowdfunding and a *new Landmark in the Law* feature on the *Citizens United* case. Chapter 30 features cover shareholder access rules and software designed to help corporate officers spot potential embezzlers. Chapter 31 has been substantially reworked to simplify complex materials into basic concepts. The materials on insider trading, Ponzi schemes, and fraud have been updated, new examples have been added, and a new *Spotlight Case* focuses on securities fraud.

- **Chapter 32 (Antitrust Law and Promoting Competition)**—The materials in this chapter have been reworked to focus on overriding principles of antitrust law and provide concrete information. The chapter includes updated figures on interlocking directorates and an updated discussion of global antitrust law. Features cover the Justice Department's concern about pricing of e-books for Kindles and iPads, and whether cable and other TV programmers violate the Sherman Act by bundling services. A *Spotlight Case on the Weyerhaeuser Company* was added.

- **Chapter 33 (Consumer and Environmental Law)**—The chapter has been thoroughly updated and incorporates recent changes to menu labeling requirements, the recent health-care reforms, and new federal credit-card rules. New features have been added on how airlines deal with "customers of size," the new Consumer Privacy Bill of Rights, and the proper way to use credit reporting services.

- **Chapters 35 through 37 (the Property and Its Protection unit)**—These three chapters have been updated to deal with issues surrounding virtual and digital property and social media estate planning. A *Spotlight on Haunted Houses* case appears in Chapter 36.

Acknowledgments

Numerous careful and conscientious users of *Business Law Today* were kind enough to help me revise the book. In addition, the staff at South-Western/Cengage Learning went out of their way to make sure that this edition came out early and in accurate form. In particular, I wish to thank Rob Dewey and Vicky True-Baker for their countless new ideas, many of which have been incorporated into the Tenth Edition. I also extend special thanks to Jan Lamar, my longtime developmental editor, for her many useful suggestions and for her efforts in coordinating reviews and ensuring the timely and accurate publication of all supplemental materials. I am particularly indebted to Lisa Lysne for her support and excellent marketing advice.

My production manager and designer, Bill Stryker, made sure that I came out with an error-free, visually attractive edition. I will always be in his debt. I thank my photo researcher, Ann Hoffman, for providing an amazingly varied number of choices of photographs for this edition. I am also indebted to the staff at Parkwood Composition, the compositor. Their ability to generate the pages for this text quickly and accurately made it possible for me to meet my ambitious printing schedule.

I must especially thank Katherine Marie Silsbee for her management of the project, as well as for the application of her superb research and editorial skills. I also wish to thank William Eric Hollowell, coauthor of the *Instructor's Manual, Study Guide,* and *Test Bank,* for his excellent research efforts. The copyediting services of Pat Lewis were invaluable, and the proofreading by Maggie Jarpey and Sue Bradley will not go unnoticed. I thank, too, Lavina Leed Miller, for her indexing expertise. I also thank Vickie Reierson and Roxanna Lee for their proofreading and other assistance, which helped to ensure an error-free text. Finally, my appreciation goes to Suzanne Jasin for her many special efforts on the projects.

Acknowledgments for Previous Editions

John J. Balek
Morton College, Illinois

John Jay Ballantine
University of Colorado, Boulder

Lorraine K. Bannai
Western Washington University

Marlene E. Barken
Ithaca College, New York

Daryl Barton
Eastern Michigan University

Denise A. Bartles
Missouri Western State University

Merlin Bauer
Mid State Technical College, Wisconsin

Donna E. Becker
Frederick Community College, Maryland

Richard J. Bennet
Three Rivers Community College, Connecticut

Anne Berre
Schreiner University, Texas

Brad Botz
Garden City Community College, Kansas

Teresa Brady
Holy Family College, Philadelphia

Lee B. Burgunder
California Polytechnic University— San Luis Obispo

Bradley D. Childs
Belmont University, Tennessee

Dale Clark
Corning Community College, New York

Peter Clapp
St. Mary's College, Moraga, California

Tammy W. Cowart
University of Texas, Tyler

Stanley J. Dabrowski
*Hudson County Community College,
New Jersey*

Sandra J. Defebaugh
Eastern Michigan University

Patricia L. DeFrain
Glendale College, California

Julia G. Derrick
Brevard Community College, Florida

Joe D. Dillsaver
Northeastern State University, Oklahoma

Claude W. Dotson
Northwest College, Wyoming

Larry R. Edwards
*Tarrant County Junior College,
South Campus, Texas*

Jacolin Eichelberger
Hillsborough Community College, Florida

George E. Eigsti
Kansas City, Kansas, Community College

Florence E. Elliott-Howard
Stephen F. Austin State University, Texas

Tony Enerva
Lakeland Community College, Ohio

Benjamin C. Fassberg
*Prince George's Community College,
Maryland*

Jerry Furniss
University of Montana

Elizabeth J. Guerriero
Northeast Louisiana University

Phil Harmeson
University of South Dakota

Nancy L. Hart
Midland College, Texas

Janine S. Hiller
*Virginia Polytechnic Institute &
State University*

Karen A. Holmes
*Hudson Valley Community College,
New York*

Fred Ittner
College of Alameda, California

Susan S. Jarvis
University of Texas, Pan American

Jack E. Karns
East Carolina University, North Carolina

Sarah Weiner Keidan
Oakland Community College, Michigan

Richard N. Kleeberg
Solano Community College, California

Bradley T. Lutz
Hillsborough Community College, Florida

Darlene Mallick
*Anne Arundel Community College,
Maryland*

John D. Mallonee
Manatee Community College, Florida

Joseph D. Marcus
*Prince George's Community College,
Maryland*

Woodrow J. Maxwell
*Hudson Valley Community College,
New York*

Beverly McCormick
Morehead State University, Kentucky

William J. McDevitt
Saint Joseph's University, Pennsylvania

John W. McGee
Aims Community College, Colorado

James K. Miersma
*Milwaukee Area Technical Institute,
Wisconsin*

Susan J. Mitchell
*Des Moines Area Community College,
Iowa*

Jim Lee Morgan
West Los Angeles College, California

Jack K. Morton
University of Montana

Solange North
Fox Valley Technical Institute, Wisconsin

Jamie L. O'Brien
South Dakota State University

Ruth R. O'Keefe
Jacksonville University, Florida

Robert H. Orr
Florida Community College at Jacksonville

George Otto
Truman College, Illinois

Thomas L. Palmer
Northern Arizona University

David W. Pan
University of Tulsa, Oklahoma

Victor C. Parker, Jr.
North Georgia College and State University

Donald L. Petote
Genessee Community College, New York

Francis D. Polk
Ocean County College, New Jersey

Gregory Rabb
Jamestown Community College, New York

Brad Reid
Abilene Christian University, Texas

Anne Montgomery Ricketts
University of Findlay, Ohio

Donald A. Roark
University of West Florida

Hugh Rode
Utah Valley State College

Dr. William J. Russell
Northwest Nazarene University, Idaho

William M. Rutledge
Macomb Community College, Michigan

Martha Wright Sartoris
*North Hennepin Community College,
Minnesota*

Anne W. Schacherl
Madison Area Technical College, Wisconsin

Edward F. Shafer
Rochester Community College, Minnesota

Lance Shoemaker
West Valley College, California

Lou Ann Simpson
Drake University, Iowa

Denise Smith
Missouri Western State College

Hugh M. Spall
Central Washington University

Catherine A. Stevens
College of Southern Maryland

Maurice Tonissi
*Quinsigamond Community College,
Massachusetts*

James D. Van Tassel
Mission College, California

Russell A. Waldon
College of the Canyons, California

Frederick J. Walsh
Franklin Pierce College, New Hampshire

James E. Walsh, Jr.
Tidewater Community College, Virginia

Randy Waterman
Richland College, Texas

Jerry Wegman
University of Idaho

Edward L. Welsh, Jr.
Phoenix College, Arizona

Clark W. Wheeler
Santa Fe Community College, Florida

Lori Whisenant
University of Houston, Texas

Kay O. Wilburn
The University of Alabama at Birmingham

John G. Williams
Northwestern State University, Louisiana

James L. Wittenbach
University of Notre Dame, Indiana

Joseph Zavaglia, Jr.
Brookdale Community College, New Jersey

I also wish to extend special thanks to the following individuals for their valuable input for the new Chapter 22 and for helping revise Chapter 36:

Robert C. Bird
University of Connecticut

Dean Bredeson
University of Texas at Austin

Corey Ciocchetti
University of Denver

Thomas D. Cavenagh
North Central College, Illinois

Joan Gabel
Florida State University

Eric D. Yordy
Northern Arizona University

Acknowledgments for the Tenth Edition

John Jay Ballantine
University of Colorado, Boulder

Laura Barnard
Lakeland Community College, Ohio

Bonnie S. Bolinger
*Ivy Tech Community College,
Wabash Valley Region, Indiana*

Sandra Defebaugh
Eastern Michigan University

Joseph L. Flack
Washtenaw Community College, Michigan

Mo Hassan
Cabrillo College, California

Andy E. Hendrick
Coastal Carolina University, South Carolina

Diane MacDonald
Pacific Lutheran University, Washington

Susan Mitchell
Des Moines Area Community College, Iowa

Annie Laurie I. Myers
*Northampton Community College,
Pennsylvania*

Jamie L. O'Brien
South Dakota State University

Gerald M. Rogers
Front Range Community College, Colorado

I know that I am not perfect. If you or your students find something you don't like or want me to change, use the "Contact Us" button on this text's Web site. In the alternative, pass along your thoughts to your South-Western/Cengage Learning sales representative. Your comments will help us make *Business Law Today* an even better book in the future.

Roger LeRoy Miller

Dedication

To Debbie and Gary,
Great friends and partners are rare.

R.L.M.

(BackyardProduction/iStockphoto.com)

UNIT 1

The Legal Environment of Business

UNIT CONTENTS

The Legal Environment

(JustASC/Shutterstock.com)

CHAPTER OUTLINE

- Business Activities and the Legal Environment
- Sources of American Law
- The Common Law Tradition
- Classifications of Law

LEARNING OBJECTIVES

The five learning objectives below are designed to help improve your understanding of the chapter. After reading this chapter, you should be able to answer the following questions:

1 What are four primary sources of law in the United States?

2 What is the common law tradition?

3 What is a precedent? When might a court depart from precedent?

4 What is the difference between remedies at law and remedies in equity?

5 What are some important differences between civil law and criminal law?

> "Laws should be like clothes.
> They should be made to fit the people they are meant to serve."
> —Clarence Darrow, 1857–1938 (American lawyer)

I n the chapter-opening quotation, Clarence Darrow asserts that law should be created to serve the public. As you are part of that public, the law is important to you. Those entering the world of business will find themselves subject to numerous laws and government regulations. A basic knowledge of these laws and regulations is beneficial—if not essential—to anyone contemplating a successful career in today's business environment.

Although the law has various definitions, they all are based on the general observation that **law** consists of *enforceable rules governing relationships among individuals and between individuals and their society.* In some societies, these enforceable rules consist of unwritten principles of behavior, while in other societies they are set forth in ancient or contemporary law codes. In the United States, our rules consist of written laws and court decisions created by modern legislative and judicial bodies. Regardless of how such rules are created, they all have one feature in common: *they establish rights, duties, and privileges that are consistent with the values and beliefs of a society or its ruling group.*

Law A body of enforceable rules governing relationships among individuals and between individuals and their society.

In this introductory chapter, we look first at an important question for any student reading this text: How do business law and the legal environment affect business decision making? Next, we describe the basic sources of American law, the common law tradition, and some schools of legal thought. We conclude the chapter with a discussion of some general classifications of law.

Business Activities and the Legal Environment

As those entering the business world will learn, laws and government regulations affect all business activities—hiring and firing decisions, workplace safety, the manufacturing and marketing of products, and business financing, to name just a few. To make good business decisions, a basic understanding of the laws and regulations governing these activities is essential. Moreover, in today's setting, simply being aware of what conduct can lead to legal liability is not enough. Businesspersons must develop critical thinking and legal reasoning skills so that they can evaluate how various laws might apply to a given situation and determine the potential result of their course of action. Businesspersons are also under increasing pressure to make ethical decisions and to consider the consequences of their decisions for stockholders and employees (as will be discussed in Chapter 7).

Many Different Laws May Affect a Single Business Transaction

As you will note, each chapter in this text covers a specific area of the law and shows how the legal rules in that area affect business activities. Although compartmentalizing the law in this fashion facilitates learning, it does not indicate the extent to which many different laws may apply to just one transaction. This is where the critical thinking skills that you will learn throughout this book become important. You need to be able to identify the various legal issues, apply the laws that you learn about, and arrive at a conclusion on the best course of action.

EXAMPLE 1.1   Suppose that you are the president of NetSys, Inc., a company that creates and maintains computer network systems for other business firms. NetSys also markets software for internal computer networks. One day, Janet Hernandez, an operations officer for Southwest Distribution Corporation (SDC), contacts you by e-mail about a possible contract involving SDC's computer network. In deciding whether to enter into a contract with SDC, you need to consider, among other things, the legal requirements for an enforceable contract. Are the requirements different for a contract for services and a contract for products? What are your options if SDC **breaches** (breaks, or fails to perform) the contract? The answers to these questions are part of contract law and sales law.

Breach The failure to perform a legal obligation.

Other questions might concern payment under the contract. How can you guarantee that NetSys will be paid? For example, if SDC pays with a check that is returned for insufficient funds, what are your options? Answers to these questions can be found in the laws that relate to negotiable instruments (such as checks) and creditors' rights. Also, a dispute may arise over the rights to NetSys's software, or there may be a question of liability if the software is defective. There may even be an issue as to whether you and Hernandez had the authority to make the deal in the first place. Resolutions of these questions may be found in the laws that relate to intellectual property, e-commerce, torts, product liability, agency, business organizations, or professional liability. ●

Finally, if any dispute cannot be resolved amicably, then the laws and the rules concerning courts and court procedures spell out the steps of a lawsuit. Exhibit 1.1 on the facing page illustrates the various areas of the law that may influence business decision making.

Exhibit 1.1 Areas of the Law That May Affect Business Decision Making

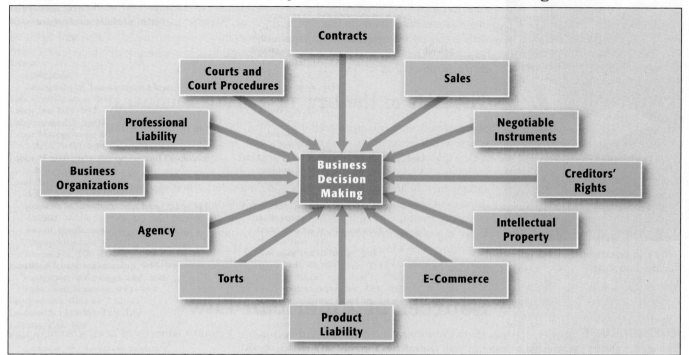

....

**PREVENTING
LEGAL DISPUTES**

To avoid potential legal disputes, be aware of the many different laws that may apply to a single business transaction. Become familiar with the laws that affect your business operations, but always consult an expert. Attorneys must keep up with the myriad rules and regulations that govern the conduct of business in the United States. When you need to choose an attorney, obtain recommendations from friends, relatives, or business associates who have had long-standing relationships with their attorneys. If that fails, contact your local or state bar association, or check FindLaw's online directory (at lawyers.findlaw.com).

Linking Business Law to the Six Functional Fields of Business

In all likelihood, you are taking a business law or legal environment course because you intend to enter the business world, though some of you may also plan to become full-time practicing attorneys. Many of you are taking other business school courses and may therefore be familiar with the functional fields of business listed below:

1. Corporate management.
2. Production and transportation.
3. Marketing.
4. Research and development.
5. Accounting and finance.
6. Human resource management.

(Kzenon/Shutterstock.com)

Why is a basic understanding of the law important?

What are four primary sources of law in the United States?

Primary Source of Law A document that establishes the law on a particular issue, such as a constitution, a statute, an administrative rule, or a court decision.

Secondary Source of Law A publication that summarizes or interprets the law, such as a legal encyclopedia, a legal treatise, or an article in a law review.

Constitutional Law The body of law derived from the U.S. Constitution and the constitutions of the various states.

One of our goals in this text is to show how legal concepts can be useful for managers and businesspersons, whether their activities focus on management, marketing, accounting, or some other field. To that end, numerous chapters, including this chapter, conclude with a special feature called "*Linking Business Law to* [one of the six functional fields of business]." The link between the law and accounting is so significant that it is treated in an entire chapter (Chapter 34).

The Role of the Law in a Small Business

Some of you may end up working in a small business or even owning and running one yourselves. The small business owner/operator is the most general of managers. When you seek additional financing, you become a finance manager. When you "go over the books" with your bookkeeper, you become an accountant. When you decide on a new advertising campaign, you are suddenly the marketing manager. When you hire employees and determine their salaries and benefits, you become a human resources manager.

Just as the functional fields of business are linked to the law, so too are all of these different managerial roles that a small-business owner/operator must perform. Exhibit 1.2 on the facing page shows some of the legal issues that may arise as part of the management of a small business. Large businesses face most of these issues, too.

Sources of American Law

There are numerous sources of American law. **Primary sources of law,** or sources that establish the law, include the following:

- The U.S. Constitution and the constitutions of the various states.
- Statutes, or laws, passed by Congress and by state legislatures.
- Regulations created by administrative agencies, such as the federal Food and Drug Administration.
- Case law (court decisions).

We describe each of these important primary sources of law in the following pages. (See the appendix at the end of this chapter for a discussion of how to find statutes, regulations, and case law.)

Secondary sources of law are books and articles that summarize and clarify the primary sources of law. Legal encyclopedias, compilations (such as *Restatements of the Law,* which summarize court decisions on a particular topic), official comments to statutes, treatises, articles in law reviews published by law schools, and articles in other legal journals are examples of secondary sources of law. Courts often refer to secondary sources of law for guidance in interpreting and applying the primary sources of law discussed here.

Constitutional Law

The federal government and the states have separate written constitutions that set forth the general organization, powers, and limits of their respective governments. **Constitutional law** is the law as expressed in these constitutions.

The U.S. Constitution is the supreme law of the land. As such, it is the basis of all law in the United States. A law in violation of the U.S. Constitution, if challenged, will be declared unconstitutional and will not be enforced, no matter what its source. Because of its paramount importance in the American legal system, we discuss the U.S. Constitution at length in Chapter 2 and present the complete text of the U.S. Constitution in Appendix B.

Exhibit 1.2 Linking Business Law to the Management of a Small Business

Business Organization
What is the most appropriate business organizational form,
and what type of personal liability does it entail?

Taxation
How will the small business be taxed, and are there ways to reduce those taxes?

Intellectual Property
Does the small business have any patents or other intellectual
property that needs to be protected, and if so, what steps should the firm take?

Administrative Law
What types of government regulations apply to the
business, and what must the firm do to comply with them?

Employment
Does the business need an employment manual,
and does management have to explicitly inform employees of their rights?

Contracts, Sales, and Leases
Will the firm be regularly entering into contracts with others,
and if so, should it hire an attorney to review those contracts?

Accounting
Do the financial statements created by an accountant need to be verified for accuracy?

Finance
What are appropriate and legal ways to raise
additional capital so that the business can grow?

The Tenth Amendment to the U.S. Constitution reserves to the states all powers not granted to the federal government. Each state in the union has its own constitution. Unless it conflicts with the U.S. Constitution or a federal law, a state constitution is supreme within that state's borders.

Statutory Law

Statutory Law The body of law enacted by legislative bodies (as opposed to constitutional law, administrative law, or case law).

Laws enacted by legislative bodies at any level of government, such as the statutes passed by Congress or by state legislatures, make up the body of law generally referred to as **statutory law.** When a legislature passes a statute, that statute ultimately is included in

Citation A reference to a publication in which a legal authority—such as a statute or a court decision—or other source can be found.

Ordinance A regulation enacted by a city or county legislative body that becomes part of that state's statutory law.

Uniform Law A model law developed by the National Conference of Commissioners on Uniform State Laws for the states to consider enacting into statute.

Administrative Law The body of law created by administrative agencies in order to carry out their duties and responsibilities.

Administrative Agency A federal or state government agency created by the legislature to perform a specific function, such as to make and enforce rules pertaining to the environment.

the federal code of laws or the relevant state code of laws. Whenever a particular statute is mentioned in this text, we usually provide a footnote showing its **citation** (a reference to a publication in which a legal authority—such as a statute or a court decision—or other source can be found). In the appendix following this chapter, we explain how you can use these citations to find statutory law.

Statutory law also includes local **ordinances**—statutes (laws, rules, or orders) passed by municipal or county governing units to administer matters not covered by federal or state law. Ordinances commonly have to do with city or county land use (zoning ordinances), building and safety codes, and other matters affecting only the local governing unit.

A federal statute, of course, applies to all states. A state statute, in contrast, applies only within the state's borders. State laws thus may vary from state to state. No federal statute may violate the U.S. Constitution, and no state statute or local ordinance may violate the U.S. Constitution or the relevant state constitution.

Uniform Laws   During the 1800s, the differences among state laws frequently created difficulties for businesspersons conducting trade and commerce among the states. To counter these problems, a group of legal scholars and lawyers formed the National Conference of Commissioners on Uniform State Laws (NCCUSL, online at **www.nccusl.org**) in 1892 to draft **uniform laws** ("model statutes") for the states to consider adopting. The NCCUSL still exists today and continues to issue uniform laws: it has issued more than two hundred uniform acts since its inception.

Each state has the option of adopting or rejecting a uniform law. *Only if a state legislature adopts a uniform law does that law become part of the statutory law of that state.* Furthermore, a state legislature may choose to adopt only part of a uniform law or to rewrite the sections that are adopted. Hence, even though many states may have adopted a uniform law, those laws may not be entirely "uniform."

The Uniform Commercial Code (UCC)   One of the most important uniform acts is the Uniform Commercial Code (UCC), which was created through the joint efforts of the NCCUSL and the American Law Institute.[1] The UCC was first issued in 1952 and has been adopted in all fifty states,[2] the District of Columbia, and the Virgin Islands. The UCC facilitates commerce among the states by providing a uniform, yet flexible, set of rules governing commercial transactions. Because of its importance in the area of commercial law, we cite the UCC frequently in this text. We also present excerpts of the UCC in Appendix C. (For a discussion of the creation of the UCC, see the *Landmark in the Law* feature on page 385 in Chapter 15.)

Administrative Law

Another important source of American law is **administrative law**, which consists of the rules, orders, and decisions of administrative agencies. An **administrative agency** is a federal, state, or local government agency established to perform a specific function. Rules issued by various administrative agencies now affect almost every aspect of a business's operations, including the firm's capital structure and financing, its hiring and firing procedures, its relations with employees and unions, and the way it manufactures and markets its products. (See this chapter's *Linking Business Law to Management* feature on page 20.)

---

1. This institute was formed in the 1920s and consists of practicing attorneys, legal scholars, and judges.
2. Louisiana has adopted only Articles 1, 3, 4, 5, 7, 8, and 9.

Enabling Legislation A statute enacted by Congress that authorizes the creation of an administrative agency and specifies the name, composition, purpose, and powers of the agency being created.

Adjudicate To render a judicial decision. Adjudication is the trial-like proceeding in which an administrative law judge hears and resolves disputes involving an administrative agency's regulations.

Administrative Process The procedure used by administrative agencies in administering the law.

Rulemaking The process by which an administrative agency formally adopts a new regulation or amends an old one.

Legislative Rule An administrative agency's rule that carries the same weight as a congressionally enacted statute.

Federal Agencies   At the national level, numerous *executive agencies* exist within the cabinet departments of the executive branch. For example, the Food and Drug Administration is within the U.S. Department of Health and Human Services. Executive agencies are subject to the authority of the president, who has the power to appoint and remove their officers.

There are also major *independent regulatory agencies* at the federal level, including the Federal Trade Commission, the Securities and Exchange Commission, and the Federal Communications Commission. The president's power is less pronounced in regard to independent agencies, whose officers serve for fixed terms and cannot be removed without just cause.

State and Local Agencies   There are administrative agencies at the state and local levels as well. Commonly, a state agency (such as a state pollution-control agency) is created as a parallel to a federal agency (such as the Environmental Protection Agency). Just as federal statutes take precedence over conflicting state statutes, so do federal agency regulations take precedence over conflicting state regulations. Because the rules of state and local agencies vary widely, we focus here exclusively on federal administrative law.

Agency Creation   Because Congress cannot possibly oversee the actual implementation of all the laws it enacts, it must delegate such tasks to others, especially when the legislation involves highly technical matters, such as air and water pollution. Congress creates an administrative agency by enacting **enabling legislation**, which specifies the name, composition, purpose, and powers of the agency being created.

EXAMPLE 1.2   The Federal Trade Commission (FTC) was created in 1914 by the Federal Trade Commission Act.[3] This act prohibits unfair and deceptive trade practices. It also describes the procedures the agency must follow to charge persons or organizations with violations of the act, and it provides for judicial review (review by the courts) of agency orders. Other portions of the act grant the agency powers to "make rules and regulations for the purpose of carrying out the Act," conduct investigations of business practices, obtain reports from interstate corporations concerning their business practices, investigate possible violations of the act, publish findings of its investigations, and recommend new legislation. The act also empowers the FTC to hold trial-like hearings and to **adjudicate** (resolve judicially) certain kinds of disputes involving its regulations. ●

Note that the powers granted to the FTC incorporate functions associated with the legislative branch of government (rulemaking), the executive branch (investigation and enforcement), and the judicial branch (adjudication). Taken together, these functions constitute **administrative process**, which is the administration of law by administrative agencies.

Rulemaking   A major function of an administrative agency is **rulemaking**—formulating new regulations. When Congress enacts an agency's enabling legislation, it confers the power to make **legislative rules**, or substantive rules, which are legally binding on all businesses. The Administrative Procedure Act of 1946 (APA)[4] imposes strict procedural requirements that agencies must follow in legislative rulemaking and other functions. **EXAMPLE 1.3**   The Occupational Safety and Health Act of 1970 authorized the Occupational Safety and Health Administration (OSHA) to develop and issue rules governing safety in the workplace. When OSHA wants to formulate rules regarding safety in the steel industry, it has to follow specific procedures outlined by the APA. ●

---

3. 15 U.S.C. Sections 45–58.
4. 5 U.S.C. Sections 551–706.

Legislative Rules   Legislative rulemaking commonly involves three steps. First, the agency must give public notice of the proposed rulemaking proceedings, where and when the proceedings will be held, the agency's legal authority for the proceedings, and the terms or subject matter of the proposed rule. The notice must be published in the *Federal Register,* a daily publication of the U.S. government. Second, following this notice, the agency must allow ample time for interested parties to comment in writing on the proposed rule. The agency takes these comments into consideration when drafting the final version of the regulation. The third and last step is the drafting of the final rule and its publication in the *Federal Register.* (See the appendix at the end of this chapter for an explanation of how to find agency regulations.)

Interpretive Rules   In addition to making *legislative rules,* which are subject to the procedural requirements of the APA, agencies also issue **interpretive rules**—rules that specify how the agency will interpret and apply its regulations. The APA does not apply to interpretive rulemaking. Interpretive rules are not legally binding on all businesses but simply indicate how an agency plans to interpret and enforce its statutory authority. **EXAMPLE 1.4**   The Equal Employment Opportunity Commission periodically issues interpretive rules indicating how it plans to interpret the provisions of certain statutes, such as the Americans with Disabilities Act. These informal rules provide enforcement guidelines for agency officials. •

Interpretive Rule A nonbinding rule or policy statement issued by an administrative agency that explains how it interprets and intends to apply the statutes it enforces.

Investigation and Enforcement
Agencies have both investigatory and prosecutorial powers. An agency can request that individuals or organizations hand over specified books, papers, electronic records, or other documents. In addition, agencies may conduct on-site inspections, although a search warrant is normally required for such inspections. Sometimes, a search of a home, an office, or a factory is the only means of obtaining evidence needed to prove a regulatory violation. Agencies investigate a wide range of activities, including coal mining, automobile manufacturing, and the industrial discharge of pollutants into the environment.

After investigating a suspected rule violation, an agency may decide to take action against an individual or a business. Most administrative actions are resolved through negotiated settlement at their initial stages without the need for formal adjudication. If a settlement cannot be reached, though, the agency may issue a formal complaint and proceed to adjudication.

Adjudication
Agency adjudication involves a trial-like hearing before an **administrative law judge (ALJ).** Hearing procedures vary widely from agency to agency. After the hearing, the ALJ renders a decision in the case. The ALJ can fine the charged party or prohibit the party from carrying on some specified activity. Either the agency or the charged party may appeal the ALJ's decision to the commission or board that governs the agency. If the party fails to get relief there, appeal can be made to a federal court. If neither side appeals the case, the ALJ's decision becomes final.

Administrative Law Judge (ALJ) One who presides over an administrative agency hearing and has the power to administer oaths, take testimony, rule on questions of evidence, and make determinations of fact.

ETHICAL ISSUE

Do administrative agencies exercise too much authority? Administrative agencies, such as the Federal Trade Commission, combine in a single governmental entity functions normally divided among the three branches of government. They create rules, conduct investigations, and prosecute and pass judgment on violators. Yet administrative agencies' powers often go unchecked by the other branches, causing some businesspersons to suggest that it is unethical for agencies—which are not even mentioned in the U.S. Constitution—to wield so many powers.

Although agency rulemaking must comply with the requirements of the Administrative Procedure Act (APA), the act applies only to legislative, not interpretive, rulemaking. In addition, the APA is largely procedural and aimed at preventing arbitrariness. It does little to ensure that the rules passed by agencies are fair or correct. Even on those rare occasions when an agency's ruling is challenged and later reviewed by a court, the court cannot reverse the agency's decision unless the agency exceeded its authority or acted arbitrarily. Courts typically are reluctant to second-guess an agency's rules, interpretations, and decisions.[5] Moreover, once an agency has final regulations in place, it is difficult to revoke or alter them. President Barack Obama discovered this when he tried to change some of the rules that agencies had put into place in the last few months of the administration of his predecessor, President George W. Bush.

Case Law and Common Law Doctrines

Case Law The rules of law announced in court decisions. Case law interprets statutes, regulations, constitutional provisions, and other case law.

The rules of law announced in court decisions constitute another basic source of American law. These rules of law include interpretations of constitutional provisions, of statutes enacted by legislatures, and of regulations created by administrative agencies. Today, this body of judge-made law is referred to as **case law.** Case law—the doctrines and principles announced in cases—governs all areas not covered by statutory law or administrative law and is part of our common law tradition. We look at the origins and characteristics of the common law tradition in some detail in the pages that follow.

The Common Law Tradition

LEARNING OBJECTIVE 2
What is the common law tradition?

Because of our colonial heritage, much of American law is based on the English legal system. A knowledge of this tradition is crucial to understanding our legal system today because judges in the United States still apply common law principles when deciding cases.

Early English Courts

After the Normans conquered England in 1066, William the Conqueror and his successors began the process of unifying the country under their rule. One of the means they used to do this was the establishment of the king's courts, or *curiae regis.* Before the Norman Conquest, disputes had been settled according to the local legal customs and traditions in various regions of the country. The king's courts sought to establish a uniform set of rules for the country as a whole. What evolved in these courts was the beginning of the **common law**—a body of general rules that applied throughout the entire English realm. Eventually, the common law tradition became part of the heritage of all nations that were once British colonies, including the United States.

Common Law The body of law developed from custom or judicial decisions in English and U.S. courts, not attributable to a legislature.

LEARNING OBJECTIVE 3
What is a precedent? When might a court depart from precedent?

Precedent A court decision that furnishes an example or authority for deciding subsequent cases involving identical or similar facts.

Courts developed the common law rules from the principles underlying judges' decisions in actual legal controversies. Judges attempted to be consistent, and whenever possible, they based their decisions on the principles suggested by earlier cases. They sought to decide similar cases in a similar way and considered new cases with care because they knew that their decisions would make new law. Each interpretation became part of the law on the subject and served as a legal **precedent**—that is, a court decision that furnished an example or authority for deciding subsequent cases involving identical or similar legal principles or facts.

In the early years of the common law, there was no single place or publication where court opinions, or written decisions, could be found. Beginning in the late thirteenth and early fourteenth centuries, however, portions of significant decisions from each year were gathered together and recorded in *Year Books.* The *Year Books* were useful references for lawyers and judges. In the sixteenth century, the *Year Books* were discontinued, and other reports of cases became available. (See the appendix to this chapter for a discussion of how cases are reported, or published, in the United States today.)

---

5. See, for example, *Citizens' Committee to Save Our Canyons v. Krueger,* 513 F.3d 1169 (10th Cir. 2008). See the appendix at the end of this chapter for an explanation of how to read legal citations.

Stare Decisis

The practice of deciding new cases with reference to former decisions, or precedents, eventually became a cornerstone of the English and U.S. judicial systems. The practice forms a doctrine called *stare decisis*[6] ("to stand on decided cases").

Stare Decisis A common law doctrine under which judges are obligated to follow the precedents established in prior decisions.

The Importance of Precedents in Judicial Decision Making

Under the doctrine of *stare decisis,* once a court has set forth a principle of law as being applicable to a certain set of facts, that court and courts of lower rank must adhere to that principle and apply it in future cases involving similar fact patterns. *Stare decisis* has two aspects: (1) decisions made by a higher court are binding on lower courts, and (2) a court should not overturn its own precedents unless there is a strong reason to do so.

Controlling precedents in a *jurisdiction* (an area in which a court or courts have the power to apply the law) are referred to as binding authorities. A **binding authority** is any source of law that a court must follow when deciding a case. Binding authorities include constitutions, statutes, and regulations that govern the issue being decided, as well as court decisions that are controlling precedents within the jurisdiction. United States Supreme Court case decisions, no matter how old, remain controlling until they are overruled by a subsequent decision of the Supreme Court, by a constitutional amendment, or by congressional legislation.

Binding Authority Any source of law that a court *must* follow when deciding a case.

Stare Decisis and Legal Stability   The doctrine of *stare decisis* helps the courts to be more efficient because if other courts have carefully reasoned through a similar case, their legal reasoning and opinions can serve as guides. *Stare decisis* also makes the law more stable and predictable. If the law on a given subject is well settled, someone bringing a case to court can usually rely on the court to make a decision based on what the law has been.

Departures from Precedent   Although courts are obligated to follow precedents, sometimes a court will depart from the rule of precedent. If a court decides that a precedent is simply incorrect or that technological or social changes have rendered the precedent inapplicable, the court may rule contrary to the precedent. Cases that overturn precedent often receive a great deal of publicity.

CASE EXAMPLE 1.5   In *Brown v. Board of Education of Topeka,*[7] the United States Supreme Court expressly overturned precedent when it concluded that separate educational facilities for whites and blacks, which had been upheld as constitutional in numerous previous cases,[8] were inherently unequal. The Supreme Court's departure from precedent in the *Brown* decision received a tremendous amount of publicity as people began to realize the ramifications of this change in the law. ●

Persuasive Authority Any legal authority or source of law that a court may look to for guidance but need not follow when making its decision.

School integration occurred after *Brown v. Board of Education of Topeka.*

(Library of Congress)

When There Is No Precedent

At times, a case may raise issues that have not been raised before in that jurisdiction, so the court has no precedents on which to base its decision. When deciding such cases, called "cases of first impression," courts often look at precedents established in other jurisdictions for guidance. Precedents from other jurisdictions, because they are not binding on the court, are referred to as **persuasive authorities.** A court may also consider other factors, including legal principles and policies underlying previous court decisions or existing statutes, fairness, social values and customs, public policy, and data and concepts drawn from the social sciences.

---

6. Pronounced *stah*ree dih-*si*-sis.
7. 347 U.S. 483, 74 S.Ct. 686, 98 L.Ed. 873 (1954).
8. See *Plessy v. Ferguson,* 163 U.S. 537, 16 S.Ct. 1138, 41 L.Ed. 256 (1896).

ADAPTING THE LAW TO THE ONLINE ENVIRONMENT

HOW THE INTERNET HAS EXPANDED PRECEDENT

The notion that courts should rely on precedents to decide the outcome of similar cases has long been a cornerstone of U.S. law. Nevertheless, the availability of "unpublished opinions" over the Internet has changed what the law considers to be precedent. An *unpublished opinion* is a decision issued by an appellate (reviewing) court that is not intended for publication in a reporter (the bound books that contain court opinions).[a] Courts traditionally did not consider unpublished opinions to be "precedents," binding or persuasive, and often did not allow attorneys to refer to (cite) these decisions in their arguments.

Increased Online Availability of Unpublished Decisions

The number of court decisions not published in printed books has risen dramatically in recent years. Nearly 80 percent of the decisions of the federal appellate courts are unpublished, and the number is equally high in some state court systems. Even though certain decisions are not intended for publication, they are posted ("published") almost immediately in online legal databases, such as Westlaw and Lexis. With the proliferation of free legal databases and court Web sites, the general public also has almost instant access to the unpublished decisions of most courts. This situation has caused many to question why these opinions have no precedential effect.

Prior to the Internet, not considering unpublished decisions as precedent might have been justified on the grounds of fairness. How could lawyers know about decisions if they were not printed in the case reporters? Now that opinions are so readily available on the Web, however, this justification is no longer valid. Moreover, it now seems unfair *not* to consider these decisions as

precedent because they are so publicly accessible. Some claim that unpublished decisions could make bad precedents because these decisions frequently are written by staff attorneys and law clerks, rather than by judges, so the reasoning may be inferior. If the decision is considered merely as persuasive precedent, however, judges who disagree with the reasoning are free to reject the conclusion.

The Federal Rules Now Allow Judges to Consider Unpublished Opinions

The United States Supreme Court made history in 2006 when it announced that it would allow lawyers to cite unpublished decisions in all federal courts. Rule 32.1 of the Federal Rules of Appellate Procedure states that federal courts may not prohibit or restrict the citation of federal judicial opinions that have been designated as "not for publication," "nonprecedential," or "not precedent." The rule applies only to federal courts and only to unpublished opinions issued after January 1, 2007. It does not specify what weight a court must give to its own unpublished opinions or to those from another court.

Basically, Rule 32.1 establishes a uniform rule for all of the federal courts that allows attorneys to cite—and judges to consider as persuasive precedent—unpublished decisions.

Critical Thinking

Only a few states, such as Massachusetts, have followed the federal courts in allowing unpublished decisions to be used as persuasive precedent. The other states claim that doing so would increase the already heavy workload of their courts. Under the current system, a judge who designates an opinion as unpublished does not have to take the time to provide a complete set of facts, references, and views. Does this argument justify the different treatment for unpublished opinions in the state and federal courts? Explain.

---

a. Recently decided cases that are not yet published are also sometimes called *unpublished opinions,* but because these decisions will eventually be printed in reporters, we do not include them here.

Can a court consider unpublished decisions as persuasive precedent? See this chapter's *Adapting the Law to the Online Environment* feature above for a discussion of this issue.

Equitable Remedies and Courts of Equity

Remedy The relief given to an innocent party to enforce a right or compensate for the violation of a right.

A **remedy** is the means given to a party to enforce a right or to compensate for the violation of a right. **EXAMPLE 1.6** Elena is injured because of Rowan's wrongdoing. If Elena files a lawsuit and is successful, a court can order Rowan to compensate Elena for the harm by paying her a certain amount. The compensation is Elena's remedy. ●

LEARNING OBJECTIVE 4
What is the difference between remedies at law and remedies in equity?

The kinds of remedies available in the early king's courts of England were severely restricted. If one person wronged another, the king's courts could award as compensation either money or property, including land. These courts became known as *courts of law,* and the remedies were called *remedies at law.* Even though this system introduced uniformity in the settling of disputes, when a person wanted a remedy other than economic compensation, the courts of law could do nothing, so "no remedy, no right."

Remedies in Equity

Equity is a branch of law, founded on what might be described as notions of justice and fair dealing, that seeks to supply a remedy when no adequate remedy at law is available. When individuals could not obtain an adequate remedy in a court of law, they petitioned the king for relief. Most of these petitions were referred to the *chancellor,* an adviser to the king who had the power to grant new and unique remedies. Eventually, formal chancery courts, or *courts of equity,* were established. Thus, two distinct court systems were created, each having its own set of judges and its own set of remedies. The remedies granted by the chancery courts were called *remedies in equity.*

Plaintiff One who initiates a lawsuit.

Defendant One against whom a lawsuit is brought, or the accused person in a criminal proceeding.

Plaintiffs (those bringing lawsuits) had to specify whether they were bringing an "action at law" or an "action in equity," and they chose their courts accordingly. **EXAMPLE 1.7** A plaintiff might ask a court of equity to order the **defendant** (the person against whom a lawsuit is brought) to perform within the terms of a contract. A court of law could not issue such an order because its remedies were limited to the payment of money or property as compensation for damages. A court of equity, however, could issue a decree for *specific performance*—an order to perform what was promised. A court of equity could also issue an *injunction,* directing a party to do or refrain from doing a particular act. In certain cases, a court of equity could allow for the *rescission* (cancellation) of the contract, thereby returning the parties to the positions that they held prior to the contract's formation. • Equitable remedies will be discussed in greater detail in Chapter 14.

The Merging of Law and Equity

Today, in most states, the courts of law and equity have merged, and thus the distinction between the two courts has largely disappeared. A plaintiff may now request both legal and equitable remedies in the same action, and the trial court judge may grant either form—or both forms—of relief.

► KNOW THIS ◄
Even though courts of law and equity have merged, the principles of equity still apply, and courts will not grant an equitable remedy unless the remedy at law is inadequate.

The distinction between legal and equitable remedies remains significant, however, because a court normally will grant an equitable remedy only when the remedy at law (monetary damages) is inadequate. To request the proper remedy, a businessperson (or her or his attorney) must know what remedies are available for the specific kinds of harms suffered. Exhibit 1.3 below summarizes the procedural differences (applicable in most states) between an action at law and an action in equity.

Exhibit 1.3 Procedural Differences between an Action at Law and an Action at Equity

PROCEDURE	ACTION AT LAW	ACTION IN EQUITY
Initiation of lawsuit	By filing a complaint.	By filing a petition.
Decision	By jury or judge.	By judge (no jury).
Result	Judgment.	Decree.
Remedy	Monetary damages.	Injunction, specific performance, or rescission.

Equitable Principles and Maxims General propositions or principles of law that have to do with fairness (equity).

Equitable Principles and Maxims Over time, the courts have developed a number of **equitable principles and maxims** that provide guidance in deciding whether plaintiffs should be granted equitable relief. Because of their importance, both historically and in our judicial system today, these principles and maxims are set forth in this chapter's *Landmark in the Law* feature below.

Schools of Legal Thought

Jurisprudence The science or philosophy of law.

How judges apply the law to specific cases, including disputes relating to the business world, depends on their philosophical approaches to law, among other things. The study of law, often referred to as **jurisprudence,** includes learning about different schools of legal thought and discovering how each school's approach to law can affect judicial decision making.

Natural Law The oldest school of legal thought, based on the belief that the legal system should reflect universal ("higher") moral and ethical principles that are inherent in human nature.

The Natural Law School Those who adhere to the **natural law** theory believe that a higher, or universal, law exists that applies to all human beings and that written laws should imitate these inherent principles. If a written law is unjust, then it is not a true (natural) law and need not be obeyed.

LANDMARK IN THE LAW
Equitable Principles and Maxims

In medieval England, courts of equity were expected to use discretion in supplementing the common law. Even today, when the same court can award both legal and equitable remedies, it must exercise discretion. Students of business law should know that courts often invoke equitable principles and maxims when making their decisions. Here are some of the most significant equitable principles and maxims:

1. *Whoever seeks equity must do equity.* (Anyone who wishes to be treated fairly must treat others fairly.)
2. *Where there is equal equity, the law must prevail.* (The law will determine the outcome of a controversy in which the merits of both sides are equal.)
3. *One seeking the aid of an equity court must come to the court with clean hands.* (Plaintiffs must have acted fairly and honestly.)
4. *Equity will not suffer a wrong to be without a remedy.* (Equitable relief will be awarded when there is a right to relief and there is no adequate remedy at law.)
5. *Equity regards substance rather than form.* (Equity is more concerned with fairness and justice than with legal technicalities.)
6. *Equity aids the vigilant, not those who rest on their rights.* (Equity will not help those who neglect their rights for an unreasonable period of time.)

The last maxim has come to be known as the *equitable doctrine of laches.* The doctrine arose to encourage people to bring lawsuits while the evidence was fresh. If they failed to do so, they would not be allowed to bring a lawsuit. What constitutes a reasonable time, of course, varies according to the circumstances of the case. Time periods for different types of cases are now usually fixed by *statutes of limitations*—that is, statutes that set the maximum time period during which a certain action can be brought. After the time allowed under a statute of limitations has expired, no action can be brought, no matter how strong the case was originally.

Application to Today's World *The equitable maxims listed above underlie many of the legal rules and principles that are commonly applied by the courts today—and that you will read about in this book. For example, in Chapter 10 you will read about the doctrine of promissory estoppel. Under this doctrine, a person who has reasonably and substantially relied on the promise of another may be able to obtain some measure of recovery, even though no enforceable contract, or agreement, exists. The court will estop (bar, or impede) the one making the promise from asserting the lack of a valid contract as a defense. The rationale underlying the doctrine of promissory estoppel is similar to that expressed in the fourth and fifth maxims listed on the left.*

The natural law tradition is one of the oldest and most significant schools of jurisprudence. It dates back to the days of the Greek philosopher Aristotle (384–322 B.C.E.), who distinguished between natural law and the laws governing a particular nation. According to Aristotle, natural law applies universally to all humankind.

The notion that people have "natural rights" stems from the natural law tradition. Those who claim that certain nations, such as China and North Korea, are depriving many of their citizens of their human rights are implicitly appealing to a higher law that has universal applicability. The question of the universality of basic human rights also comes into play in the context of international business operations. For example, U.S. companies that have operations abroad often hire foreign workers as employees. Should the same laws that protect U.S. employees apply to these foreign employees? This question is rooted implicitly in a concept of universal rights that has its origins in the natural law tradition.

Legal Positivism   In contrast, *positive,* or national, law (the written law of a given society at a particular point in time) applies only to the citizens of that nation or society. Those who adhere to **legal positivism** believe that there can be no higher law than a nation's positive law. According to the positivist school, there is no such thing as "natural rights." Rather, human rights exist solely because of laws. If the laws are not enforced, anarchy will result. Thus, whether a law is morally "bad" or "good" is irrelevant. The law is the law and must be obeyed until it is changed—in an orderly manner through a legitimate lawmaking process.

A judge with positivist leanings probably would be more inclined to defer to an existing law than would a judge who adheres to the natural law tradition.

The Historical School

The **historical school** of legal thought emphasizes the evolutionary process of law by concentrating on the origin and history of the legal system. This school looks to the past to discover what the principles of contemporary law should be. The legal doctrines that have withstood the passage of time—those that have worked in the past—are deemed best suited for shaping present laws. Hence, law derives its legitimacy and authority from adhering to the standards that historical development has shown to be workable.

Followers of the historical school are more likely than those of other schools to adhere strictly to decisions made in past cases.

Legal Realism   In the 1920s and 1930s, a number of jurists and scholars, known as *legal realists,* rebelled against the historical approach to law. **Legal realism** is based on the idea that law is just one of many institutions in society and that it is shaped by social forces and needs. This school holds that because the law is a human enterprise, judges should look beyond the law and take social and economic realities into account when deciding cases. Legal realists also believe that the law can never be applied with total uniformity. Given that judges are human beings with unique experiences, personalities, value systems, and intellects, different judges will obviously bring different reasoning processes to the same case. Female judges, for instance, might be more inclined than male judges to consider whether a decision might have a negative impact on the employment of women or minorities.

Classifications of Law

The law may be broken down according to several classification systems. For example, one classification system divides law into **substantive law** (all laws that define, describe, regulate, and create legal rights and obligations) and **procedural law** (all laws that establish the methods of enforcing the rights established by substantive law).

Legal Positivism A school of legal thought centered on the assumption that there is no law higher than the laws created by a national government. Laws must be obeyed, even if they are unjust, to prevent anarchy.

Historical School A school of legal thought that looks to the past to determine what the principles of contemporary law should be.

Legal Realism A school of legal thought that holds that the law is only one factor to be considered when deciding cases and that social and economic circumstances should also be taken into account.

Substantive Law Law that defines, describes, regulates, and creates legal rights and obligations.

Procedural Law Law that establishes the methods of enforcing the rights established by substantive law.

EXAMPLE 1.8   A state law that provides employees with the right to workers' compensation benefits for any on-the-job injuries they sustain is a substantive law because it creates legal rights (workers' compensation laws will be discussed in Chapter 24). Procedural laws, in contrast, establish the method by which an employee must notify the employer about an on-the-job injury, prove the injury, and periodically submit additional proof to continue receiving workers' compensation benefits. Note that a law concerning workers' compensation may contain both substantive and procedural provisions. •

Other classification systems divide law into federal law and state law or private law (dealing with relationships between persons) and public law (addressing the relationship between persons and their governments). Frequently, people use the term **cyberlaw** to refer to the emerging body of law that governs transactions conducted via the Internet.

Cyberlaw is not really a classification of law, nor is it a new *type* of law. Rather, it is an informal term used to describe traditional legal principles that have been modified and adapted to fit situations that are unique to the online world. Of course, in some areas new statutes have been enacted, at both the federal and state levels, to cover specific types of problems stemming from online communications. Throughout this book, you will read about how the law is evolving to govern specific legal issues that arise in the online context.

Civil Law and Criminal Law

Civil law spells out the rights and duties that exist between persons and between persons and their governments, and the relief available when a person's rights are violated. Typically, in a civil case, a private party sues another private party (although the government can also sue a party for a civil law violation) to make sure that the other party complies with a duty or pays for the damage caused by the failure to comply with a duty.   **EXAMPLE 1.9**   If a seller fails to perform a contract with a buyer, the buyer may bring a lawsuit against the seller. The purpose of the lawsuit will be either to compel the seller to perform as promised or, more commonly, to obtain monetary damages for the seller's failure to perform. •

Much of the law that we discuss in this text is civil law. Contract law, for example, which we will discuss in Chapters 9 through 14, is civil law. The whole body of tort law (see Chapter 4) is civil law. Note that *civil law* is not the same as a *civil law system*. As you will read shortly, a **civil law system** is a legal system based on a written code of laws.

Criminal law has to do with wrongs committed against society for which society demands redress. Criminal acts are proscribed by local, state, or federal government statutes (see Chapter 6 and many of the laws discussed in Chapters 31 through 34). Thus, criminal defendants are prosecuted by public officials, such as a district attorney (D.A.), on behalf of the state, not by their victims or other private parties. Whereas in a civil case the object is to obtain a remedy (such as monetary damages) to compensate the injured party, in a criminal case the object is to punish the wrongdoer in an attempt to deter others from similar actions. Penalties for violations of criminal statutes consist of fines and/or imprisonment—and, in some cases, death. We will discuss the differences between civil and criminal law in greater detail in Chapter 6.

National and International Law

Although the focus of this book is U.S. business law, increasingly businesspersons in this country engage in transactions that extend beyond our national borders. In these situations, the laws

---

Cyberlaw An informal term used to refer to all laws governing electronic communications and transactions, particularly those conducted via the Internet.

What are some important differences between civil law and criminal law?

Civil Law The branch of law dealing with the definition and enforcement of all private or public rights, as opposed to criminal matters.

Civil Law System A system of law derived from Roman law that is based on codified laws (rather than on case precedents).

Criminal Law The branch of law that defines and punishes wrongful actions committed against the public.

A witness points out someone in the courtroom to the judge.

(Junial Enterprises/Shutterstock.com)

of other nations or the laws governing relationships among nations may come into play. For this reason, those who pursue a career in business today should have an understanding of the global legal environment (discussed further in Chapter 8).

National Law

National Law Law that pertains to a particular nation (as opposed to international law).

The law of a particular nation, such as the United States or Sweden, is **national law.** National law, of course, varies from country to country because each country's law reflects the interests, customs, activities, and values that are unique to that nation's culture. Even though the laws and legal systems of various countries differ substantially, broad similarities do exist, as discussed in this chapter's *Beyond Our Borders* feature below.

International Law

International Law The law that governs relations among nations.

In contrast to national law, international law applies to more than one nation. **International law** can be defined as a body of written and unwritten laws

BEYOND OUR BORDERS   National Law Systems

Despite their varying cultures and customs, almost all countries have laws governing torts, contracts, employment, and other areas. Two types of legal systems predominate around the globe today. One is the common law system of England and the United States, which we have discussed elsewhere. The other system is based on Roman civil law, or "code law," which relies on the legal principles enacted into law by a legislature or governing body.

Civil Law Systems

Although national law systems share many commonalities, they also have distinct differences. In a *civil law system*, the primary source of law is a statutory code, and case precedents are not judicially binding, as they normally are in a common law system. Although judges in a civil law system commonly refer to previous decisions as sources of legal guidance, those decisions are not binding precedents (*stare decisis* does not apply).

Exhibit 1.4 below lists some countries that today follow either the common law system or the civil law system. Generally, those countries that were once colonies of Great Britain have retained their English common law heritage. The civil law system, which is used in most continental European nations, has been retained in the countries that were once colonies of those nations. In the United States, the state of Louisiana, because of its historical ties to France, has in part a civil law system, as do Haiti, Québec, and Scotland.

Islamic Legal Systems

A third, less prevalent legal system is common in Islamic countries, where the law is often influenced by *sharia*, the religious law of Islam. Islam is both a religion and a way of life. *Sharia* is a comprehensive code of principles that governs the public and private lives of Islamic persons and directs many aspects of their day-to-day life, including politics, economics, banking, business law, contract law, and social issues.

Although *sharia* affects the legal codes of many Muslim countries, the extent of its impact and its interpretation vary widely. In some Middle Eastern nations, aspects of *sharia* have been codified in modern legal codes and are enforced by national judicial systems.

Critical Thinking
Does the civil law system offer any advantages over the common law system, or vice versa? Explain.

Exhibit 1.4 The Legal Systems of Selected Nations

CIVIL LAW		COMMON LAW	
Argentina	Indonesia	Australia	Nigeria
Austria	Iran	Bangladesh	Singapore
Brazil	Italy	Canada	United Kingdom
Chile	Japan	Ghana	United States
China	Mexico	India	Zambia
Egypt	Poland	Israel	
Finland	South Korea	Jamaica	
France	Sweden	Kenya	
Germany	Tunisia	Malaysia	
Greece	Venezuela	New Zealand	

observed by independent nations and governing the acts of individuals as well as governments. It is a mixture of rules and constraints derived from a variety of sources, including the laws of individual nations, customs developed among nations, and international treaties and organizations. Each nation is motivated not only by the need to be the final authority over its own affairs, but also by the desire to benefit economically from trade and harmonious relations with other nations. In essence, international law is the result of centuries-old attempts to strike a balance between these competing needs.

The key difference between national law and international law is that government authorities can enforce national law. If a nation violates an international law, however, enforcement is up to other countries or international organizations, which may or may not choose to act. If persuasive tactics fail, the only option is to take coercive actions against the violating nation. Coercive actions range from the severance of diplomatic relations and boycotts to, as a last resort, war. We will examine the laws governing international business transactions in later chapters (including all of Chapter 8 and parts of Chapters 15 and 16, which cover contracts for the sale and lease of goods).

Reviewing . . . The Legal Environment

Suppose that the California legislature passes a law that severely restricts carbon dioxide emissions from automobiles in that state. A group of automobile manufacturers files a suit against the state of California to prevent the enforcement of the law. The automakers claim that a federal law already sets fuel economy standards nationwide and that these standards are essentially the same as carbon dioxide emission standards. According to the automobile manufacturers, it is unfair to allow California to impose more stringent regulations than those set by the federal law. Using the information presented in the chapter, answer the following questions.

1. Who are the parties (the plaintiffs and the defendant) in this lawsuit?
2. Are the plaintiffs seeking a legal remedy or an equitable remedy? Why?
3. What is the primary source of the law that is at issue here?
4. Read through the appendix that follows this chapter, and then answer the following question: Where would you look to find the relevant California and federal laws?

DEBATE THIS: Under the doctrine of *stare decisis*, courts are obligated to follow the precedents established in their jurisdiction unless there is a compelling reason not to do so. Should U.S. courts continue to adhere to this common law principle, given that our government now regulates so many areas by statute?

LINKING BUSINESS LAW to Management

Dealing with Administrative Law

Whether you work for a large corporation or own a small business, you will be dealing with multiple aspects of administrative law. Recall from page 8 that administrative law involves all of the rules, orders, and decisions of administrative agencies. All federal, state, and local government administrative agencies create rules that have the force of law. As a manager, you probably will need to pay more attention to administrative rules and regulations than to laws passed by local, state, and federal legislatures.

Federal versus State and Local Agency Regulations

The three levels of government create three levels of rules and regulations though their respective administrative agencies. At the federal level, these include the Food and Drug Administration, the Equal Employment Opportunity Commission, and the Occupational Safety and Health Administration. At the state level, there are often agencies that govern business activities in a manner similar to federal agencies.

As a manager, you will have to learn about agency regulations that pertain to your business activities. It will be up to you, as a manager or small-business owner, to discern which of those regulations are most important and could potentially create the most liability if you violate them.

When Should You Participate in the Rulemaking Process?

All federal agencies and many state agencies invite public comments on proposed rules. Suppose that you manage a large construction company and your state occupational safety agency proposes a new rule requiring every employee on a construction site to wear hearing protection. You believe that the rule will lead to a *less* safe environment because your employees will not be able to communicate easily with one another.

Should you spend time offering comments to the agency? As an efficient manager, you make a trade-off calculation. First, you determine the value of the time that you would spend attempting to prevent or at least alter the proposed rule. Then you compare this implicit cost with your estimate of the potential benefits your company would receive if the rule is *not* put into place.

Be Prepared for Investigations

All administrative agencies have investigatory powers. Agencies' investigators usually have the power to search business premises, although normally they first have to obtain a search warrant. As a manager, you often have the choice of cooperating with agency investigators or providing just the minimum amount of assistance. If your business is routinely investigated, you will often opt for cooperation. In contrast, if your business is rarely investigated, you may decide that the on-site proposed inspection is overreaching. Then you must contact your company's attorney for advice on how to proceed.

If an administrative agency cites you for a regulatory violation, you will probably negotiate a settlement with the agency rather than take your case before an administrative law judge. Again, as a manager, you have to weigh the cost of the negotiated settlement with the potential cost of fighting the enforcement action.

Critical Thinking

Why are owner/operators of small businesses at a disadvantage relative to large corporations when they attempt to decipher complex regulations that apply to their businesses?

Key Terms

Chapter Summary: The Legal Environment

Sources of American Law (See pages 6–11.)	1. *Constitutional law*—The law as expressed in the U.S. Constitution and the various state constitutions. The U.S. Constitution is the supreme law of the land. State constitutions are supreme within state borders to the extent that they do not violate the U.S. Constitution or a federal law. 2. *Statutory law*—Laws or ordinances created by federal, state, and local legislatures and governing bodies. None of these laws can violate the U.S. Constitution or the relevant state constitutions. Uniform laws, when adopted by a state legislature, become statutory law in that state. 3. *Administrative law*—The rules, orders, and decisions of federal or state government administrative agencies. Federal administrative agencies are created by enabling legislation enacted by the U.S. Congress. Agency functions include rulemaking, investigation and enforcement, and adjudication. 4. *Case law and common law doctrines*—Judge-made law, including interpretations of constitutional provisions, of statutes enacted by legislatures, and of regulations created by administrative agencies. The common law—the doctrines and principles embodied in case law—governs all areas not covered by statutory law or administrative law.

The Common Law Tradition (See pages 11–16.)	1. *Common law*—Law that originated in medieval England with the creation of the king's courts, or *curiae regis,* and the development of a body of rules that were common to (or applied in) all regions of the country.
	2. *Stare decisis*—A doctrine under which judges "stand on decided cases"—or follow the rule of precedent—in deciding cases. *Stare decisis* is the cornerstone of the common law tradition.
	3. *Remedies*—A remedy is the means by which a court enforces a right or compensates for a violation of a right. Courts typically grant legal remedies (monetary damages) but may also grant equitable remedies (specific performance, injunction, or rescission) when the legal remedy is inadequate or unavailable.
	4. *Schools of legal thought*—Judges' decision making is influenced by their philosophy of law. The following are four important schools of legal thought, or legal philosophies:
	  a. Natural law tradition—One of the oldest and most significant schools of legal thought. Those who believe in natural law hold that there is a universal law applicable to all human beings and that this law is of a higher order than positive, or conventional, law.
	  b. Legal positivism—A school of legal thought centered on the assumption that there is no law higher than the laws created by the government. Laws must be obeyed, even if they are unjust, to prevent anarchy.
	  c. Historical school—A school of legal thought that stresses the evolutionary nature of law and looks to doctrines that have withstood the passage of time for guidance in shaping present laws.
	  d. Legal realism—A school of legal thought that generally advocates a less abstract and more realistic approach to the law that takes into account customary practices and the circumstances in which transactions take place.

Classifications of Law (See pages 16–19.)	The law may be broken down according to several classification systems, such as substantive or procedural law, federal or state law, and private or public law. Two broad classifications are civil and criminal law, and national and international law. Cyberlaw is not really a classification of law but a term that is used for the growing body of case and statutory law that applies to Internet transactions.

ExamPrep

ISSUE SPOTTERS

1. The First Amendment to the U.S. Constitution provides protection for the free exercise of religion. A state legislature enacts a law that outlaws all religions that do not derive from the Judeo-Christian tradition. Is this law valid within that state? Why or why not? **(See page 6.)**

2. Apples & Oranges Corporation learns that a federal administrative agency is considering a rule that will have a negative impact on the firm's ability to do business. Does the firm have any opportunity to express its opinion about the pending rule? Explain. **(See page 10.)**

—Check your answers to the Issue Spotters against the answers provided in Appendix E at the end of this text.

BEFORE THE TEST

Go to www.cengagebrain.com, enter the ISBN 9781133273561, and click on "Find" to locate this textbook's Web site. Then, click on "Access Now" under "Study Tools," and select Chapter 1 at the top. There, you will find a Practice Quiz that you can take to assess your mastery of the concepts in this chapter, as well as Flashcards, a Glossary of important terms, and Video Questions (when assigned).

For Review

Answers to the even-numbered questions in this For Review section can be found in Appendix F at the end of this text.

1. What are four primary sources of law in the United States?
2. What is the common law tradition?
3. What is a precedent? When might a court depart from precedent?
4. What is the difference between remedies at law and remedies in equity?
5. What are some important differences between civil law and criminal law?

Business Scenarios and Case Problems

1–1 Binding versus Persuasive Authority. A county court in Illinois is deciding a case involving an issue that has never been addressed before in that state's courts. The Iowa Supreme Court, however, recently decided a case involving a very similar fact pattern. Is the Illinois court obligated to follow the Iowa Supreme Court's decision on the issue? If the United States Supreme Court had decided a similar case, would that decision be binding on the Illinois court? Explain. **(See page 12.)**

1–2 Remedies. Arthur Rabe is suing Xavier Sanchez for breaching a contract in which Sanchez promised to sell Rabe a Van Gogh painting for $150,000. **(See page 14.)**

  1. In this lawsuit, who is the plaintiff, and who is the defendant?

  2. If Rabe wants Sanchez to perform the contract as promised, what remedy should Rabe seek?

  3. Suppose that Rabe wants to cancel the contract because Sanchez fraudulently misrepresented the painting as an original Van Gogh when in fact it is a copy. In this situation, what remedy should Rabe seek?

  4. Will the remedy Rabe seeks in either situation be a remedy at law or a remedy in equity?

  5. Suppose that the court finds in Rabe's favor and grants one of these remedies. Sanchez then appeals the decision to a higher court. Read through the subsection entitled "Parties to Lawsuits" in the appendix following this chapter. On appeal, which party in the Rabe-Sanchez case will be the appellant (or petitioner), and which party will be the appellee (or respondent)? **(See page 30.)**

1–3 ❓ **Question with Sample Answer—Sources of Law.** Under a Massachusetts state statute, large wineries could sell their products through wholesalers or to consumers directly, but not both. Small wineries could use both methods.

Family Winemakers of California filed a suit against the state, arguing that this restriction gave small wineries a competitive advantage in violation of the U.S. Constitution. The court agreed that the statute was in conflict with the Constitution. Which source of law takes priority, and why? [*Family Winemakers of California v. Jenkins*, 592 F.3d 1 (1st Cir. 2010)] **(See page 6.)**

—**For a sample answer to Question 1–3, go to Appendix G at the end of this text.**

1–4 Philosophy of Law. After World War II ended in 1945, an international tribunal of judges convened at Nuremberg, Germany. The judges convicted several Nazi war criminals of "crimes against humanity." Assuming that the Nazis who were convicted had not disobeyed any law of their country and had merely been following their government's (Hitler's) orders, what law had they violated? Explain. **(See page 15.)**

1–5 Reading Citations. Assume that you want to read the court's entire opinion in the case of *State v. Allen*, 268 P.3d 1198 (Kan. 2012). Read the section entitled "Finding Case Law" in the appendix that follows this chapter, and then explain specifically where you would find the court's opinion. **(See page 25.)**

1–6 ⚖ **Case Problem with Sample Answer—Law around the World.** Karen Goldberg's husband was killed in a terrorist bombing in Israel. She filed a suit in a U.S. federal court against UBS AG, a Switzerland-based global financial services company. She claimed that UBS aided her husband's killing because it provided services to the terrorists. UBS argued that the case should be transferred to another country. Like many nations, the United States has a common law system. Other nations have civil law systems. What are the key differences between these systems? [*Goldberg v. UBS AG,* 690 F.Supp.2d 92 (E.D.N.Y. 2010)] **(See page 18.)**

—For a sample answer to Problem 1–6, go to Appendix H at the end of this text.

1–7 **Spotlight on AOL—Common Law.** AOL, LLC, mistakenly made public the personal information of 650,000 of its members. The members filed a suit, alleging violations of California law. AOL asked the court to dismiss the suit on the basis of a "forum-selection" clause in its member agreement that designates Virginia courts as the place where member disputes will be tried. Under a decision of the United States Supreme Court, a forum-selection clause is unenforceable "if enforcement would contravene a strong public policy of the forum in which suit is brought." California has declared in other cases that the AOL clause contravenes a strong public policy. If the court applies the doctrine of *stare decisis,* will it dismiss the suit? Explain. [*Doe 1 v. AOL, LLC,* 552 F.3d 1077 (9th Cir. 2009)] **(See page 12.)**

1–8 **A Question of Ethics—*Stare Decisis.*** On July 5, 1884, Dudley, Stephens, and Brooks—"all able-bodied English seamen"—and a teenage English boy were cast adrift in a lifeboat following a storm at sea. They had no water with them in the boat, and all they had for sustenance were two one-pound tins of turnips. On July 24, Dudley proposed that one of the four in the lifeboat be sacrificed to save the others. Stephens agreed with Dudley, but Brooks refused to consent—and the boy was never asked for his opinion. On July 25, Dudley killed the boy, and the three men then fed on the boy's body and blood. Four days later, the men were rescued by a passing vessel. They were taken to England and tried for the murder of the boy. If the men had not fed on the boy's body, they would probably have died of starvation within the four-day period. The boy, who was in a much weaker condition, would likely have died before the rest. [*Regina v. Dudley and Stephens,* 14 Q.B.D. (Queen's Bench Division, England) 273 (1884)] **(See pages 16–17.)**

1. The basic question in this case is whether the survivors should be subject to penalties under English criminal law, given the men's unusual circumstances. You be the judge and decide the issue. Give the reasons for your decision.

2. Should judges ever have the power to look beyond the written "letter of the law" in making their decisions? Why or why not?

Critical Thinking and Writing Assignments

1–9 **Business Law Writing.** John's company is involved in a lawsuit with a customer, Beth. John argues that for fifty years higher courts in that state have decided cases involving circumstances similar to his case in a way that indicates he can expect a ruling in his company's favor. Write at least one paragraph discussing if this is a valid argument. Write another paragraph discussing whether the judge in this case must rule as those other judges did, and why. **(See page 12.)**

1–10 **Business Law Critical Thinking Group Assignment— Court Opinions.** Read through the subsection entitled "Decisions and Opinions" in the appendix following this chapter. **(See page 30.)**

1. One group will explain the difference between a concurring opinion and a majority opinion.

2. Another group will outline the difference between a concurring opinion and a dissenting opinion.

3. A third group will explain why judges and justices write concurring and dissenting opinions, given that these opinions will not affect the outcome of the case at hand, which has already been decided by majority vote.

Appendix to Chapter 1:
Finding and Analyzing the Law

The statutes, agency regulations, and case law referred to in this text establish the rights and duties of businesspersons engaged in various types of activities. The cases presented in the following chapters provide you with concise, real-life illustrations of how the courts interpret and apply these laws. Because of the importance of knowing how to find statutory, administrative, and case law, this appendix offers a brief introduction to how these laws are published and to the legal "shorthand" employed in referencing these legal sources.

Finding Statutory and Administrative Law

When Congress passes laws, they are collected in a publication titled *United States Statutes at Large*. When state legislatures pass laws, they are collected in similar state publications. Most frequently, however, laws are referred to in their codified form—that is, the form in which they appear in the federal and state codes. In these codes, laws are compiled by subject.

United States Code

The *United States Code* (U.S.C.) arranges all existing federal laws of a public and permanent nature by subject. Each of the fifty subjects into which the U.S.C. arranges the laws is given a title and a title number. For example, laws relating to commerce and trade are collected in "Title 15, Commerce and Trade." Titles are subdivided by sections. A citation to the U.S.C. includes title and section numbers. Thus, a reference to "15 U.S.C. Section 1" means that the statute can be found in Section 1 of Title 15. ("Section" may be designated by the symbol §, and "Sections" by §§.) In addition to the print publication of the U.S.C., the federal government also provides a searchable online database of the *United States Code* at **www.gpo.gov** (click on "Libraries" and then "Core Documents of Our Democracy" to find the *United States Code*).

Commercial publications of these laws are available and are widely used. For example, West Group publishes the *United States Code Annotated* (U.S.C.A.). The U.S.C.A. contains the complete text of laws included in the U.S.C., notes of court decisions that interpret and apply specific sections of the statutes, and the text of presidential proclamations and executive orders. The U.S.C.A. also includes research aids, such as cross-references to related statutes, historical notes, and other references. A citation to the U.S.C.A. is similar to a citation to the U.S.C.: "15 U.S.C.A. Section 1."

State Codes

State codes follow the U.S.C. pattern of arranging laws by subject. The state codes may be called codes, revisions, compilations, consolidations, general statutes, or statutes, depending on the state. In some codes, subjects are designated by number. In others, they are designated by name. For example, "13 Pennsylvania Consolidated Statutes Section 1101" means that the statute can be found in Title 13, Section 1101, of the Pennsylvania code. "California Commercial Code Section 1101" means the statute can be found in Section 1101 under the subject heading "Commercial Code" of the California code. Abbreviations may be used. For example, "13 Pennsylvania Consolidated Statutes Section 1101" may be abbreviated

"13 Pa. C.S. § 1101," and "California Commercial Code Section 1101" may be abbreviated "Cal. Com. Code § 1101."

Administrative Rules

Rules and regulations adopted by federal administrative agencies are compiled in the *Code of Federal Regulations* (C.F.R.). Like the U.S.C., the C.F.R. is divided into fifty titles. Rules within each title are assigned section numbers. A full citation to the C.F.R. includes title and section numbers. For example, a reference to "17 C.F.R. Section 230.504" means that the rule can be found in Section 230.504 of Title 17.

Finding Case Law

Before discussing the case reporting system, we need to look briefly at the court system (which will be discussed in detail in Chapter 3). There are two types of courts in the United States: federal courts and state courts. Both the federal and state court systems consist of several levels, or tiers, of courts. *Trial courts,* in which evidence is presented and testimony is given, are on the bottom tier (which also includes lower courts handling specialized issues). Decisions from a trial court can be appealed to a higher court, which commonly would be an intermediate *court of appeals,* or an *appellate court.* Decisions from these intermediate courts of appeals may be appealed to an even higher court, such as a state supreme court or the United States Supreme Court.

State Court Decisions

Most state trial court decisions are not published. Except in New York and a few other states that publish selected opinions of their trial courts, decisions from state trial courts are merely filed in the office of the clerk of the court, where the decisions are available for public inspection. (Increasingly, they can be found online as well.)

Written decisions of the appellate, or reviewing, courts, however, are published and distributed. As you will note, most of the state court cases presented in this book are from state appellate courts. The reported appellate decisions are published in volumes called *reports* or *reporters,* which are numbered consecutively. State appellate court decisions are found in the state reporters of that particular state.

Additionally, state court opinions appear in regional units of the *National Reporter System,* published by West Group. Most lawyers and libraries have the West reporters because they report cases more quickly and are distributed more widely than the state-published reports. In fact, many states have eliminated their own reporters in favor of West's National Reporter System. The National Reporter System divides the states into the following geographic areas: *Atlantic* (A. or A.2d), *North Eastern* (N.E. or N.E.2d), *North Western* (N.W. or N.W.2d), *Pacific* (P., P.2d, or P.3d), *South Eastern* (S.E. or S.E.2d), *South Western* (S.W., S.W.2d, or S.W.3d), and *Southern* (So., So.2d, or So.3d). (The *2d* and *3d* in the abbreviations refer to *Second Series* and *Third Series,* respectively.) The states included in each of these regional divisions are indicated in Exhibit 1A.1 on the following page, which illustrates West's National Reporter System.

After appellate decisions have been published, they are normally referred to (cited) by the name of the case; the volume, name, and page number of the state's official reporter (if different from West's National Reporter System); the volume, name, and page number of the *National Reporter;* and the volume, name, and page number of any other selected reporter. This information is included in the *citation.* (Citing a reporter by volume number, name, and page number, in that order, is common to all citations.) When more than one reporter is cited for the same case, each reference is called a *parallel citation.* Note that some states have adopted a "public domain citation system" that uses a somewhat different format for

Exhibit 1A.1 West's National Reporter System—Regional/Federal

Regional Reporters	Coverage Beginning	Coverage
Atlantic Reporter (A., A.2d, or A.3d)	1885	Connecticut, Delaware, District of Columbia, Maine, Maryland, New Hampshire, New Jersey, Pennsylvania, Rhode Island, and Vermont.
North Eastern Reporter (N.E. or N.E.2d)	1885	Illinois, Indiana, Massachusetts, New York, and Ohio.
North Western Reporter (N.W. or N.W.2d)	1879	Iowa, Michigan, Minnesota, Nebraska, North Dakota, South Dakota, and Wisconsin.
Pacific Reporter (P., P.2d, or P.3d)	1883	Alaska, Arizona, California, Colorado, Hawaii, Idaho, Kansas, Montana, Nevada, New Mexico, Oklahoma, Oregon, Utah, Washington, and Wyoming.
South Eastern Reporter (S.E. or S.E.2d)	1887	Georgia, North Carolina, South Carolina, Virginia, and West Virginia.
South Western Reporter (S.W., S.W.2d, or S.W.3d)	1886	Arkansas, Kentucky, Missouri, Tennessee, and Texas.
Southern Reporter (So., So.2d, or So.3d)	1887	Alabama, Florida, Louisiana, and Mississippi.
Federal Reporters		
Federal Reporter (F., F.2d, or F.3d)	1880	U.S. Circuit Courts from 1880 to 1912; U.S. Commerce Court from 1911 to 1913; U.S. District Courts from 1880 to 1932; U.S. Court of Claims (now called U.S. Court of Federal Claims) from 1929 to 1932 and since 1960; U.S. Courts of Appeals since 1891; U.S. Court of Customs and Patent Appeals since 1929; U.S. Emergency Court of Appeals since 1943.
Federal Supplement (F.Supp. or F.Supp.2d)	1932	U.S. Court of Claims from 1932 to 1960; U.S. District Courts since 1932; U.S. Customs Court since 1956.
Federal Rules Decisions (F.R.D.)	1939	U.S. District Courts involving the Federal Rules of Civil Procedure since 1939 and Federal Rules of Criminal Procedure since 1946.
Supreme Court Reporter (S.Ct.)	1882	United States Supreme Court since the October term of 1882.
Bankruptcy Reporter (Bankr.)	1980	Bankruptcy decisions of U.S. Bankruptcy Courts, U.S. District Courts, U.S. Courts of Appeals, and the United States Supreme Court.
Military Justice Reporter (M.J.)	1978	U.S. Court of Military Appeals and Courts of Military Review for the Army, Navy, Air Force, and Coast Guard.

NATIONAL REPORTER SYSTEM MAP

the citation. For example, in Wisconsin, a Wisconsin Supreme Court decision might be designated "2012 WI 23," meaning that the decision was the twenty-third issued by the Wisconsin Supreme Court in the year 2012. Parallel citations to the *Wisconsin Reports* and West's *North Western Reporter* are still included after the public domain citation.

Consider the following citation: *Goldstein v. Lackard,* 81 Mass.App.Ct. 1112, 961 N.E.2d. 163 (2012). We see that the opinion in this case can be found in Volume 81 of the official *Massachusetts Appellate Court Reports,* on page 1112. The parallel citation is to Volume 961 of the *North Eastern Reporter, Second Series,* page 163. When we present opinions in this text (starting in Chapter 2), in addition to the reporter, we give the name of the court hearing the case and the year of the court's decision. Sample citations to state court decisions are listed and explained in Exhibit 1A.2 on pages 28–29.

Federal Court Decisions

Federal district (trial) court decisions are published unofficially in the *Federal Supplement* (F. Supp. or F.Supp.2d), and opinions from the circuit courts of appeals (federal reviewing courts) are reported unofficially in the *Federal Reporter* (F., F.2d, or F.3d). Cases concerning federal bankruptcy law are published unofficially in West's *Bankruptcy Reporter* (Bankr. or B.R.).

The official edition of United States Supreme Court decisions is the *United States Reports* (U.S.), which is published by the federal government. Unofficial editions of Supreme Court cases include West's *Supreme Court Reporter* (S.Ct.) and the *Lawyers' Edition of the Supreme Court Reports* (L.Ed. or L.Ed.2d). Sample citations for federal court decisions are also listed and explained in Exhibit 1A.2.

Unpublished Opinions

Many court opinions that are not yet published or that are not intended for publication can be accessed through Westlaw® (abbreviated in citations as "WL"), an online legal database. When no citation to a published reporter is available for cases cited in this text, we give the WL citation (such as 2012 WL 573109, which means it was case number 573109 decided in the year 2012). Sometimes, both in this text and in other legal sources, you will see blanks left in a citation. This occurs when the decision will be published, but the particular volume number or page number is not yet available.

Old Cases

On a few occasions, this text cites opinions from old, classic cases dating to the nineteenth century or earlier. Some of these cases are from the English courts. The citations to these cases may not conform to the descriptions given above because they were published in reporters that are no longer used today.

Reading and Understanding Case Law

The cases in this text have been condensed from the full text of the courts' opinions and paraphrased by the authors. For those wishing to review court cases for future research projects or to gain additional legal information, the following sections will provide useful insights into how to read and understand case law.

Case Titles and Terminology

The title of a case, such as *Adams v. Jones,* indicates the names of the parties to the lawsuit. The *v.* in the case title stands for *versus,* which means "against." In the trial court, Adams was the plaintiff—the person who filed the suit. Jones was the defendant. If the case is appealed, however, the appellate court will sometimes place the name of the party

Exhibit 1A.2 How to Read Citations

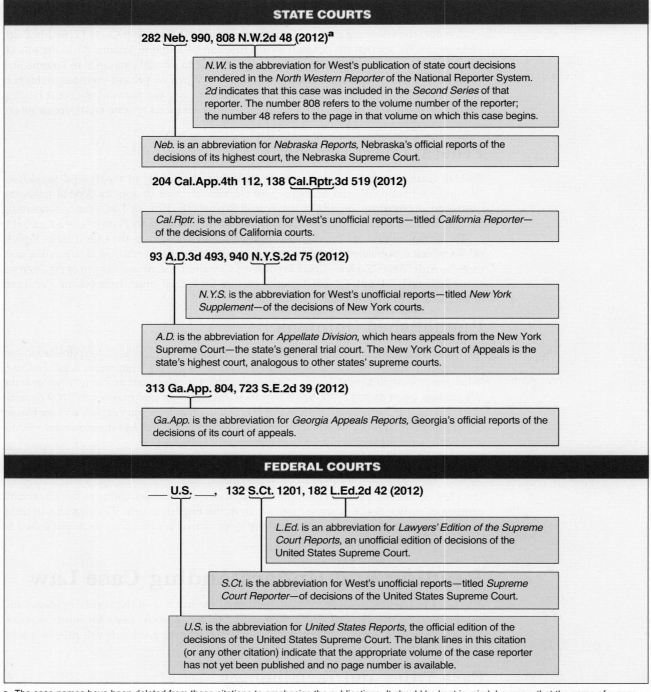

STATE COURTS

282 Neb. 990, 808 N.W.2d 48 (2012)[a]

> *N.W.* is the abbreviation for West's publication of state court decisions rendered in the *North Western Reporter* of the National Reporter System. *2d* indicates that this case was included in the *Second Series* of that reporter. The number 808 refers to the volume number of the reporter; the number 48 refers to the page in that volume on which this case begins.

> *Neb.* is an abbreviation for *Nebraska Reports,* Nebraska's official reports of the decisions of its highest court, the Nebraska Supreme Court.

204 Cal.App.4th 112, 138 Cal.Rptr.3d 519 (2012)

> *Cal.Rptr.* is the abbreviation for West's unofficial reports—titled *California Reporter—* of the decisions of California courts.

93 A.D.3d 493, 940 N.Y.S.2d 75 (2012)

> *N.Y.S.* is the abbreviation for West's unofficial reports—titled *New York Supplement*—of the decisions of New York courts.

> *A.D.* is the abbreviation for *Appellate Division*, which hears appeals from the New York Supreme Court—the state's general trial court. The New York Court of Appeals is the state's highest court, analogous to other states' supreme courts.

313 Ga.App. 804, 723 S.E.2d 39 (2012)

> *Ga.App.* is the abbreviation for *Georgia Appeals Reports,* Georgia's official reports of the decisions of its court of appeals.

FEDERAL COURTS

___ U.S. ___, 132 S.Ct. 1201, 182 L.Ed.2d 42 (2012)

> *L.Ed.* is an abbreviation for *Lawyers' Edition of the Supreme Court Reports*, an unofficial edition of decisions of the United States Supreme Court.

> *S.Ct.* is the abbreviation for West's unofficial reports—titled *Supreme Court Reporter*—of decisions of the United States Supreme Court.

> *U.S.* is the abbreviation for *United States Reports*, the official edition of the decisions of the United States Supreme Court. The blank lines in this citation (or any other citation) indicate that the appropriate volume of the case reporter has not yet been published and no page number is available.

a. The case names have been deleted from these citations to emphasize the publications. It should be kept in mind, however, that the name of a case is as important as the specific page numbers in the volumes in which it is found. If a citation is incorrect, the correct citation may be found in a publication's index of case names. In addition to providing a check on errors in citations, the date of a case is important because the value of a recent case as an authority is likely to be greater than that of older cases from the same court.

Exhibit 1A.2 How to Read Citations, Continued

FEDERAL COURTS (Continued)

668 F.3d 1148 (9th Cir. 2012)

> *9th Cir.* is an abbreviation denoting that this case was decided in the U.S. Court of Appeals for the Ninth Circuit.

___ F.Supp.2d ___ (S.D. Fla. 2012)

> *S.D. Fla.* is an abbreviation indicating that the U.S. District Court for the Southern District of Florida decided this case.

ENGLISH COURTS

9 Exch. 341, 156 Eng.Rep. 145 (1854)

> *Eng.Rep.* is an abbreviation for *English Reports, Full Reprint,* a series of reports containing selected decisions made in English courts between 1378 and 1865.

> *Exch.* is an abbreviation for *English Exchequer Reports*, which includes the original reports of cases decided in England's Court of Exchequer.

STATUTORY AND OTHER CITATIONS

18 U.S.C. Section 1961(1)(A)

> *U.S.C.* denotes *United States Code*, the codification of *United States Statutes at Large*. The number 18 refers to the statute's U.S.C. title number and 1961 to its section number within that title. The number 1 in parentheses refers to a subsection within the section, and the letter A in parentheses to a subsection within the subsection.

UCC 2–206(1)(b)

> *UCC* is an abbreviation for *Uniform Commercial Code*. The first number 2 is a reference to an article of the UCC, and 206 to a section within that article. The number 1 in parentheses refers to a subsection within the section, and the letter b in parentheses to a subsection within the subsection.

Restatement (Third) of Torts, Section 6

> *Restatement (Third) of Torts* refers to the third edition of the American Law Institute's *Restatement of the Law of Torts*. The number 6 refers to a specific section.

17 C.F.R. Section 230.505

> *C.F.R.* is an abbreviation for *Code of Federal Regulations*, a compilation of federal administrative regulations. The number 17 designates the regulation's title number, and 230.505 designates a specific section within that title.

appealing the decision first, so the case may be called *Jones v. Adams.* Because some reviewing courts retain the trial court order of names, it is often impossible to distinguish the plaintiff from the defendant in the title of a reported appellate court decision. You must carefully read the facts of each case to identify the parties.

The following terms and phrases are frequently encountered in court opinions and legal publications. Because it is important to understand what these terms and phrases mean, we define and discuss them here.

Parties to Lawsuits

As mentioned in Chapter 1, the party initiating a lawsuit is referred to as the *plaintiff* or *petitioner,* depending on the nature of the action, and the party against whom a lawsuit is brought is the *defendant* or *respondent.* Lawsuits frequently involve more than one plaintiff and/or defendant. When a case is appealed from the original court or jurisdiction to another court or jurisdiction, the party appealing the case is called the *appellant.* The *appellee* is the party against whom the appeal is taken. (In some appellate courts, the party appealing a case is referred to as the *petitioner,* and the party against whom the suit is brought or appealed is called the *respondent.*)

Judges and Justices

The terms *judge* and *justice* are usually synonymous and are used to refer to the judges in various courts. All members of the United States Supreme Court, for example, are referred to as justices. And justice is the formal title usually given to judges of appellate courts, although this is not always the case. In New York, a justice is a judge of the trial court (which is called the Supreme Court), and a member of the Court of Appeals (the state's highest court) is called a judge. The term *justice* is commonly abbreviated to J., and *justices* to JJ. A Supreme Court case might refer to Justice Sotomayor as Sotomayor, J., or to Chief Justice Roberts as Roberts, C.J.

Decisions and Opinions

Most decisions reached by reviewing, or appellate, courts are explained in written *opinions.* The opinion contains the court's reasons for its decision, the rules of law that apply, and the judgment. When all judges or justices unanimously agree on an opinion, the opinion is written for the entire court and can be deemed a *unanimous opinion.* When there is not unanimous agreement, a **majority opinion** is written. The majority opinion outlines the views of the majority of the judges or justices deciding the case. Sometimes, the majority agrees on the result, but not the reasoning. The opinion joined by the largest number of judges or justices, but less than a majority, is called a **plurality opinion.**

Often, a judge or justice who strongly wishes to make or emphasize a point that was not made or emphasized in the unanimous or majority opinion will write a **concurring opinion.** This means the judge or justice agrees (concurs) with the judgment given in the unanimous or majority opinion but for different reasons. When there is not a unanimous opinion, a **dissenting opinion** presents the views of one or more judges who disagree with the majority's decision. (See the *Unit 1: Business Case Study with Dissenting Opinion* on page 233 for an example of a dissenting opinion.) The dissenting opinion is important because it may form the basis of the arguments used years later in overruling the precedential majority opinion. Occasionally, a court issues a ***per curiam* opinion** (*per curiam* is Latin for "of the court"), which does not indicate which judge or justice authored the opinion.

A Sample Court Case

Knowing how to read and analyze a court opinion is an essential step in undertaking accurate legal research. A further step involves "briefing" the case. Legal researchers routinely brief cases by summarizing and reducing the texts of the opinions to their essential elements. Briefing cases facilitates the development of critical thinking skills that are crucial for businesspersons when evaluating relevant business law. (For instructions on how to brief a case, go to Appendix A at the end of this text.)

Majority Opinion A court opinion that represents the views of the majority (more than half) of the judges or justices deciding the case.

Plurality Opinion A court opinion that is joined by the largest number of the judges or justices hearing the case, but less than half of the total number.

Concurring Opinion A court opinion by one or more judges or justices who agree with the majority but want to make or emphasize a point that was not made or emphasized in the majority's opinion.

Dissenting Opinion A court opinion that presents the views of one or more judges or justices who disagree with the majority's decision.

***Per Curiam* Opinion** A court opinion that does not indicate which judge or justice authored the opinion.

The cases contained within the chapters of this text have already been analyzed and briefed by the authors, and the essential aspects of each case are presented in a convenient format consisting of four basic sections: *Facts, Issue, Decision,* and *Reason,* as shown in Exhibit 1A.3 below, which has also been annotated (see the next page) to illustrate the kind of information that is contained in each section.

Throughout this text, in addition to this basic format, we sometimes include a special introductory section entitled *Historical and Social [Economic, Technological, Political, or other] Setting.* In some instances, a *Company Profile* is included in place of the introductory setting. These profiles provide background on one of the parties to the lawsuit.

Each case is followed by a question or section that is designed to enhance your analysis. *Critical Thinking* sections, such as the one shown in Exhibit 1A.3, present a question about some issue raised by the case. *Why Is This Case Important?* sections explain the significance of the case. *What If the Facts Were Different?* questions alter the facts slightly and ask you to consider how this would change the outcome. A section entitled *Impact of This Case on Today's Law* concludes each of the *Classic Cases* that appear throughout the text to indicate the significance of the case for today's legal landscape.

Exhibit 1A.3 A Sample Court Case

Sample Case

United States v. Jones

1

Supreme Court of the United States **2**

3 ____ U.S.____, 132 S.Ct. 945, 181 L.Ed.2d 911 (2012).
www.supremecourt.gov/opinions/11pdf/10-1259.pdf

Tracking device for automobiles.

(Radoslav Stoilov/Shutterstock.com)

FACTS Antoine Jones owned and operated a nightclub in the District of Columbia and was suspected of drug trafficking. As part of an investigation, the government installed a Global Positioning System (GPS) tracking device underneath a vehicle belonging to Jones's wife. Although it did not have a valid warrant, the government tracked the vehicle for four weeks, ultimately gathering enough evidence of drug trafficking to obtain an indictment. Before the trial, Jones filed a motion to suppress the evidence obtained with the device, arguing that the government had violated his Fourth Amendment rights by subjecting him to an unlawful "search." The district court held that most of the evidence was admissible, and Jones was convicted and sentenced to life in prison. A federal appellate court reversed the conviction, and the government appealed to the United States Supreme Court.

ISSUE Did the government engage in a "search" within the meaning of the Fourth Amendment by installing the GPS tracking device and then monitoring the vehicle's movements?

DECISION Yes. The United States Supreme Court affirmed the judgment of the federal appellate court. The government engaged in a Fourth Amendment "search" by installing and using the tracking device.

REASON The Fourth Amendment prohibits "unreasonable searches and seizures" based on "the right of the people to be secure in their persons, houses, papers, and effects." A vehicle is an "effect," and the government's installation and use of the tracking device constituted a "search." Traditionally, the Supreme Court recognized the Fourth Amendment's close connection to property rights and found a "search" only if the government's conduct would have amounted to trespass under English common law. In 1967, however, the Supreme Court ruled that the Fourth Amendment also protects a person's "reasonable expectation of privacy."

Whether or not Jones had a reasonable expectation of privacy in either the vehicle's undercarriage or its movements on public streets was irrelevant in this situation. The Court reasoned that its precedent on privacy did not eliminate the traditional rule that a common law trespass may also establish a search. In this case, the government engaged in trespass, and therefore a search, by installing the tracking device without consent.

CRITICAL THINKING—Ethical Consideration *Was the government's conduct ethical? Why or why not?*

Continued

Review of Sample Court Case

1 The name of the case is *United States v. Jones*. The government prosecuted Jones in federal court, and now the government is appealing, or challenging, a decision by the U.S. Court of Appeals for the District of Columbia (the federal appellate court).

2 The court deciding this case is the United States Supreme Court.

3 The case citation includes a citation to the *Supreme Court Reporter,* which contains only decisions of the United States Supreme Court. The case can be found in Volume 132 of the *Supreme Court Reporter,* beginning on page 945. The heading also provides a Web address at which you can view the opinion.

4 The *Facts* section identifies the parties, summarizes the relevant facts, and explains the procedural history leading up to the decision being summarized.

5 The *Issue* section presents the central issue(s) that the court must decide. In this case, for example, the United States Supreme Court must determine whether the government's conduct constituted a "search" for purposes of the Fourth Amendment. Most cases address more than one issue, but this textbook's authors have edited many cases to focus on just one issue.

6 The *Decision* section summarizes the court's decision about an issue. The decision reflects the opinion of the judge or, if a panel heard the case, the majority's opinion. For an appellate court case, the *Decision* section will frequently explain whether the appellate court "affirmed" or "reversed" a lower court's ruling. In either situation, the appellate court may remand the case, meaning it sends the case back for further proceedings consistent with its decision.

7 The *Reason* section explains how the court arrived at its decision, summarizing the key legal principles and authorities. In the *Jones* case, for example, the Supreme Court held that the government performed a Fourth Amendment search by installing and using a GPS tracking device. The Court found that a search may occur if the government violates either a reasonable expectation of privacy or a person's property rights.

8 The *Critical Thinking* section raises a question relating to the summarized case. Here, the question concerns an "ethical" consideration. Other cases in this text raise critical thinking questions that focus on diversity, e-commerce, economics, global, legal environment, political, social, or technological issues.

3 CHAPTER

Courts and Alternative Dispute Resolution

(Alina555/iStockphoto.com)

CHAPTER OUTLINE

- The Judiciary's Role in American Government
- Basic Judicial Requirements
- The State and Federal Court Systems
- Following a State Court Case
- The Courts Adapt to the Online World
- Alternative Dispute Resolution

LEARNING OBJECTIVES

The five learning objectives below are designed to help improve your understanding of the chapter. After reading this chapter, you should be able to answer the following questions:

1 What is judicial review? How and when was the power of judicial review established?

2 Before a court can hear a case, it must have jurisdiction. Over what must it have jurisdiction? How are the courts applying traditional jurisdictional concepts to cases involving Internet transactions?

3 What is the difference between a trial court and an appellate court?

4 What is discovery, and how does electronic discovery differ from traditional discovery?

5 What are three alternative methods of resolving disputes?

"An eye for an eye will make the whole world blind."
—Mahatma Gandhi, 1869–1948 (Indian political and spiritual leader)

Every society needs to have an established method for resolving disputes. Without one, as Mahatma Gandhi implied in the chapter-opening quotation, the biblical "eye for an eye" would lead to anarchy. This is particularly true in the business world—almost every businessperson will face a lawsuit at some time in his or her career. For this reason, anyone involved in business needs to have an understanding of court systems in the United States, as well as the various methods of dispute resolution that can be pursued outside the courts.

In this chapter, after examining the judiciary's overall role in the American governmental scheme, we discuss some basic requirements that must be met before a party may bring a lawsuit before a particular court. We then look at the court systems of the United States in some detail and, to clarify judicial procedures, follow a hypothetical case through a state court system. Because Islamic legal systems are prevalent in many parts of the world, some judges in this country have been asked to accept some Islamic law. You will read later in this chapter about this controversy.

60

Throughout this chapter, we indicate how court doctrines and procedures are being adapted to the needs of a cyber age. The chapter concludes with an overview of some alternative methods of settling disputes, including online dispute resolution.

The Judiciary's Role in American Government

As you learned in Chapter 1, the body of American law includes the federal and state constitutions, statutes passed by legislative bodies, administrative law, and the case decisions and legal principles that form the common law. These laws would be meaningless, however, without the courts to interpret and apply them. This is the essential role of the judiciary—the courts—in the American governmental system: to interpret and apply the law. (For a discussion of the impact of increased diversity on our nation's court system, see this chapter's *Law, Diversity, and Business: Managerial Implications* feature on the following page.)

Judicial Review

LEARNING OBJECTIVE 1
What is judicial review? How and when was the power of judicial review established?

Judicial Review The process by which a court decides on the constitutionality of legislative enactments and actions of the executive branch.

As the branch of government entrusted with interpreting the laws, the judiciary can decide, among other things, whether the laws or actions of the other two branches are constitutional. The process for making such a determination is known as **judicial review.** The power of judicial review enables the judicial branch to act as a check on the other two branches of government, in line with the checks-and-balances system established by the U.S. Constitution. (Today, nearly all nations with constitutional democracies, including Canada, France, and Germany, have some form of judicial review.)

The Origins of Judicial Review in the United States

The U.S. Constitution does not mention judicial review, but the concept was not new at the time the nation was founded. Indeed, before 1789 state courts had already overturned state legislative acts that conflicted with state constitutions. Additionally, many of the founders expected the United States Supreme Court to assume a similar role with respect to the federal Constitution. Alexander Hamilton and James Madison both emphasized the importance of judicial review in their essays urging the adoption of the new Constitution. How was the doctrine of judicial review established? See this chapter's *Landmark in the Law* feature on page 63 for the answer.

(Library of Congress)

James Madison (1751–1836) wrote in favor of the states' adopting the new Constitution. What did he think of judicial review?

Jurisdiction The authority of a court to hear and decide a specific case.

Basic Judicial Requirements

Before a court can hear a lawsuit, certain requirements must first be met. These requirements relate to jurisdiction, venue, and standing to sue. We examine each of these important concepts here.

Jurisdiction

In Latin, *juris* means "law," and *diction* means "to speak." Thus, "the power to speak the law" is the literal meaning of the term **jurisdiction.** Before any court can hear a case, it must have jurisdiction over the person (or company) against whom the suit is brought (the defendant) or over the property involved in the suit. The court must also have jurisdiction over the subject matter of the dispute.

LAW, DIVERSITY, AND BUSINESS: MANAGERIAL IMPLICATIONS

INCREASED DIVERSITY IN THE FEDERAL JUDICIARY

The United States Supreme Court first met in 1790, but the first female associate justice—Sandra Day O'Connor—was not appointed until 1981. In the Court's two-hundred-twenty-year history, only three other women have been appointed—Ruth Bader Ginsburg in 1993; Sonia Sotomayor in 2009, who was also the first Hispanic on the Court; and Elena Kagan in 2010. When Kagan joined the Court, for the first time in its history, one-third of the justices were women.

Obama's Judicial Nominations Set a Record for Women and Minorities   As president, Barack Obama moved at a historic pace to diversify the federal judiciary. Nearly three of every four individuals confirmed for the federal bench have been women or members of minority groups. Indeed, he is the first president who has not selected a majority of white males for lifetime judgeships. During the first three years of Obama's presidency, 21 percent of his nominees who were confirmed were African American, 11 percent were Hispanic, and 7 percent were Asian American. Almost half were women.

The Benefits of a More Diverse Judiciary   According to the Alliance for Justice, the more diverse the courts, the more

confidence people have in our judicial system. Having a diverse judiciary enriches the decision-making process.

Does having more women on the bench change the way the law is interpreted? Yes, according to Vanderbilt University law professor Tracey George. She cites research that suggests including a woman in a decision-making group influences the behavior of the rest of the group. In particular, some academic studies have found evidence that in gender discrimination lawsuits, if a three-judge panel of a federal appeals court includes a woman, the court is more likely to rule in favor of the person asserting discrimination.

Business Implications   *A more diverse federal judiciary will mean that managers must be more conscientious about their employment decisions and make sure that they are not motivated by gender or racial discrimination. Business owners and managers should also establish internal decision-making and record-keeping procedures that are fair and neutral, to avoid any appearance of bias at the workplace. If allegations of discrimination arise, managers should promptly investigate and evaluate the company's conduct, and consider the possibility of settling the claim before trial.*

Jurisdiction over Persons or Property

Generally, a court can exercise personal jurisdiction (*in personam* jurisdiction) over any person or business that resides in a certain geographic area. A state trial court, for example, normally has jurisdictional authority over residents (including businesses) in a particular area of the state, such as a county or district. A state's highest court (often called the state supreme court)[1] has jurisdiction over all residents of that state.

A court can also exercise jurisdiction over property that is located within its boundaries. This kind of jurisdiction is known as *in rem* jurisdiction, or "jurisdiction over the thing."   **EXAMPLE 3.1**   A dispute arises over the ownership of a boat in dry dock in Fort Lauderdale, Florida. The boat is owned by an Ohio resident, over whom a Florida court normally cannot exercise personal jurisdiction. The other party to the dispute is a resident of Nebraska. In this situation, a lawsuit concerning the boat could be brought in a Florida state court on the basis of the court's *in rem* jurisdiction. •

Long Arm Statute A state statute that permits a state to exercise jurisdiction over nonresident defendants.

Long Arm Statutes   Under the authority of a state **long arm statute**, a court can exercise personal jurisdiction over certain out-of-state defendants based on activities that took place within the state. Before exercising long arm jurisdiction over a nonresident, however, the court must be convinced that the defendant had sufficient contacts, or *minimum*

---

1. As will be discussed shortly, a state's highest court is frequently referred to as the state supreme court, but there are exceptions. For example, in New York, the supreme court is a trial court.

LANDMARK IN THE LAW
Marbury v. Madison (1803)

The power of judicial review was established in the Supreme Court's decision in the case of *Marbury v. Madison*.[a] Though the decision is widely viewed as a cornerstone of constitutional law, the case had its origins in early U.S. politics. When Thomas Jefferson defeated the incumbent president, John Adams, in the presidential elections of 1800, Adams feared the Jeffersonians' antipathy toward business and toward a strong national government. Adams thus rushed to "pack" the judiciary with loyal Federalists (those who believed in a strong national government) by appointing what came to be called "midnight judges" just before he left office. But Adams's secretary of state (John Marshall) was able to deliver only forty-two of the fifty-nine judicial appointment letters by the time Jefferson took over as president. Jefferson refused to order his secretary of state, James Madison, to deliver the remaining commissions.

Marshall's Dilemma   William Marbury and three others to whom the commissions had not been delivered sought a writ of *mandamus* (an order directing a government official to fulfill a duty) from the United States Supreme Court, as authorized by the Judiciary Act of 1789. As fate would have it, John Marshall had just been appointed as chief justice of the Supreme Court. Marshall faced a dilemma: If he ordered the commissions delivered, the new secretary of state (Madison) could simply refuse to deliver them—and the Court had no way to compel him to act. At the same time, if Marshall simply allowed the new administration to do as it wished, the Court's power would be severely eroded.

Marshall's Decision   Marshall masterfully fashioned his decision to enlarge the power of the Supreme Court by affirming the Court's power of judicial review. He stated, "It is emphatically the province and duty of the Judicial Department to say what the law is. . . . If two laws conflict with each other, the Courts must decide on the operation of each. . . . [I]f both [a] law and the Constitution apply to a particular case, . . . the Court must determine which of these conflicting rules governs the case."

Marshall's decision did not require anyone to do anything. He concluded that the highest court did not have the power to issue a writ of *mandamus* in this particular case. Although the Judiciary Act of 1789 specified that the Supreme Court could issue writs of *mandamus* as part of its original jurisdiction, Article III of the Constitution, which spelled out the Court's original jurisdiction, did not mention writs of *mandamus*. Because Congress did not have the right to expand the Supreme Court's jurisdiction, this section of the Judiciary Act of 1789 was unconstitutional—and thus void. The *Marbury* decision stands to this day as a judicial and political masterpiece.

Application to Today's World   *Since the* Marbury v. Madison *decision, the power of judicial review has remained unchallenged and today is exercised by both federal and state courts. If the courts did not have the power of judicial review, the constitutionality of Congress's acts could not be challenged in court—a congressional statute would remain law unless changed by Congress. The courts of other countries that have adopted a constitutional democracy often cite this decision as a justification for judicial review.*

---

a. 5 U.S. (1 Cranch) 137, 2 L.Ed. 60 (1803).

---

contacts, with the state to justify the jurisdiction.[2] Generally, this means that the defendant must have enough of a connection to the state for the judge to conclude that it is fair for the state to exercise power over the defendant. If an out-of-state defendant caused an automobile accident or sold defective goods within the state, for instance, a court will usually find that minimum contacts exist to exercise jurisdiction over that defendant.

CASE EXAMPLE 3.2   After an Xbox game system caught fire in Bonnie Broquet's home in Texas and caused substantial personal injuries, Broquet filed a lawsuit in a Texas court against Ji-Haw Industrial Company, a nonresident company that made the Xbox components. Broquet alleged that Ji-Haw's components were defective and had caused the fire. Ji-Haw argued that the Texas court lacked jurisdiction over it, but in 2008, a state appellate court held that the Texas long arm statute authorized the exercise of jurisdiction over the out-of-state defendant.[3] ●

---

2. The minimum-contacts standard was established in *International Shoe Co. v. State of Washington*, 326 U.S. 310, 66 S.Ct. 154, 90 L.Ed. 95 (1945).

3. *Ji-Haw Industrial Co. v. Broquet*, 2008 WL 441822 (Tex.App.—San Antonio 2008).

(Jacob Kepler/Bloomberg via Getty Images)

Suppose that a young gamer is injured because Microsoft's Xbox, shown above, released an electrical shock. Who can the parents sue?

Similarly, a state may exercise personal jurisdiction over a nonresident defendant who is sued for breaching a contract that was formed within the state, even when that contract was negotiated over the phone or through correspondence. **EXAMPLE 3.3** Sharon Mills, a California resident, forms a corporation to distribute a documentary film on global climate change. Brad Cole, an environmentalist who lives in Ohio, loans the corporation funds that he borrows from an Ohio bank. A year later, the film is still not completed. Mills agrees to repay Cole's loan in a contract arranged through phone calls and correspondence between California and Ohio. When Mills does not repay the loan, Cole files a lawsuit in an Ohio court. In this situation, the Ohio court can likely exercise jurisdiction over Mills because her phone calls and letters have established sufficient contacts with the state of Ohio. ●

Corporate Contacts   Because corporations are considered legal persons, courts use the same principles to determine whether it is fair to exercise jurisdiction over a corporation.[4] A corporation normally is subject to personal jurisdiction in the state in which it is incorporated, has its principal office, and is doing business. Courts apply the minimum-contacts test to determine if they can exercise jurisdiction over out-of-state corporations.

The minimum-contacts requirement is usually met if the corporation advertises or sells its products within the state, or places its goods into the "stream of commerce" with the intent that the goods be sold in the state. **EXAMPLE 3.4** A business is incorporated under the laws of Maine but has a branch office and manufacturing plant in Georgia. The corporation also advertises and sells its products in Georgia. These activities would likely constitute sufficient contacts with the state of Georgia to allow a Georgia court to exercise jurisdiction over the corporation. ●

Some corporations do not sell or advertise products or place any goods in the stream of commerce. Determining what constitutes minimum contacts in these situations can be more difficult. In the following case, the question before the court was whether a New Jersey firm had minimum contacts with a North Carolina firm.

---

4. In the eyes of the law, corporations are "legal persons"—entities that can sue and be sued. See Chapter 29.

Case 3.1

Southern Prestige Industries, Inc. v. Independence Plating Corp.

Court of Appeals of North Carolina, 690 S.E.2d 768 (2010). www.nccourts.org[a]

(J van der Wolf/Shutterstock.com)

Many parts in these jets must be metal coated.

FACTS Independence Plating Corporation (the defendant) is a New Jersey corporation that provides metal-coating services. Its only office and all of its personnel are located in New Jersey. It does not advertise out of state, but it had a long-standing business relationship with Kidde Aerospace in North Carolina (filing under the name Southern Prestige Industries, Inc.). For almost a year, Independence and Kidde engaged in frequent transactions. On November 18, 2008, Kidde initiated an action for breach of contract in a North Carolina state court, alleging defects in the metal-plating process carried out by Independence. Independence filed a motion to dismiss for lack of personal jurisdiction, which the trial court denied.

---

a. In the right-hand column of the page, click on "Court Opinions." When that page opens, select the year 2010 under the heading "Court of Appeals Opinions." Scroll down to February 2, 2010, and click on the case title under "Unpublished Opinions" to access the opinion. The North Carolina court system maintains this Web site.

Case 3.1—Continued

Independence appealed, arguing that it had insufficient contacts with North Carolina for the state to exercise jurisdiction.

ISSUE   Did Independence Plating Corporation have sufficient minimum contacts with North Carolina for the state to exercise personal jurisdiction?

DECISION   Yes. The North Carolina appellate court affirmed the trial court's decision. Independence had sufficient minimum contacts with North Carolina to satisfy the due process of law requirements necessary for the state to exercise jurisdiction.

REASON   In determining whether minimum contacts existed, the court looked at several factors, including the number of contacts and their nature and quality, as well as the interests of North Carolina, the forum state. In this case, thirty-two separate purchase orders were exchanged between the two parties in a period of less than twelve months. Independence sent invoices totaling more than $21,000, and these invoices were paid from Southern's corporate bank account. "North Carolina has a single 'manifest interest' in providing the plaintiff with 'a convenient forum for redressing injuries inflicted by' [the] defendant, an out-of-state merchant."

CRITICAL THINKING—Ethical Consideration   *Was it fair for the North Carolina courts to require a New Jersey company to litigate in North Carolina? Explain.*

Jurisdiction over Subject Matter

Jurisdiction over subject matter is a limitation on the types of cases a court can hear. In both the federal and state court systems, there are courts of *general* (unlimited) *jurisdiction* and courts of *limited jurisdiction*. An example of a court of general jurisdiction is a state trial court or a federal district court. An example of a state court of limited jurisdiction is a probate court. **Probate courts** are state courts that handle only matters relating to the transfer of a person's assets and obligations after that person's death, including matters relating to the custody and guardianship of children. An example of a federal court of limited subject-matter jurisdiction is a bankruptcy court. **Bankruptcy courts** handle only bankruptcy proceedings, which are governed by federal bankruptcy law (discussed in Chapter 21).

A court's jurisdiction over subject matter is usually defined in the statute or constitution creating the court. In both the federal and state court systems, a court's subject-matter jurisdiction can be limited not only by the subject of the lawsuit but also by the amount in controversy, by whether a case is a felony (a more serious type of crime) or a misdemeanor (a less serious type of crime), or by whether the proceeding is a trial or an appeal.

Probate Court A state court of limited jurisdiction that conducts proceedings relating to the settlement of a deceased person's estate.

Bankruptcy Court A federal court of limited jurisdiction that handles only bankruptcy proceedings, which are governed by federal bankruptcy law.

Original and Appellate Jurisdiction

The distinction between courts of original jurisdiction and courts of appellate jurisdiction normally lies in whether the case is being heard for the first time. Courts having original jurisdiction are courts of the first instance, or trial courts—that is, courts in which lawsuits begin, trials take place, and evidence is presented. In the federal court system, the *district courts* are trial courts. In the various state court systems, the trial courts are known by various names, as will be discussed shortly.

The key point here is that any court having original jurisdiction is normally known as a trial court. Courts having appellate jurisdiction act as reviewing courts, or appellate courts. In general, cases can be brought before appellate courts only on appeal from an order or a judgment of a trial court or other lower court.

Jurisdiction of the Federal Courts

Because the federal government is a government of limited powers, the jurisdiction of the federal courts is limited. Federal courts have subject-matter jurisdiction in two situations.

Federal Questions   Article III of the U.S. Constitution establishes the boundaries of federal judicial power. Section 2 of Article III states that "[t]he judicial Power shall extend to

➤ **KNOW THIS** ◄

Federal courts do not have the power to hear every case. They have jurisdiction to hear a dispute only when it raises a federal question or when the parties are residents of different states (or countries) and the amount involved in the controversy exceeds $75,000.

Federal Question A question that pertains to the U.S. Constitution, an act of Congress, or a treaty and provides a basis for federal jurisdiction in a case.

all Cases, in Law and Equity, arising under this Constitution, the Laws of the United States, and Treaties made, or which shall be made, under their Authority." This clause means that whenever a plaintiff's cause of action is based, at least in part, on the U.S. Constitution, a treaty, or a federal law, then a **federal question** arises, and the federal courts have jurisdiction. Any lawsuit involving a federal question, such as a person's rights under the U.S. Constitution, can originate in a federal court. Note that in a case based on a federal question, a federal court will apply federal law.

Diversity of Citizenship A basis for federal court jurisdiction over a lawsuit between citizens of different states and countries.

Diversity of Citizenship   Federal district courts can also exercise original jurisdiction over cases involving **diversity of citizenship.** The most common type of diversity jurisdiction has two requirements:[5] (1) the plaintiff and defendant must be residents of different states, and (2) the dollar amount in controversy must exceed $75,000. For purposes of diversity jurisdiction, a corporation is a citizen of both the state in which it is incorporated and the state in which its principal place of business is located. A case involving diversity of citizenship can be filed in the appropriate federal district court. If the case starts in a state court, it can sometimes be transferred, or "removed," to a federal court. A large percentage of the cases filed in federal courts each year are based on diversity of citizenship.

As noted, a federal court will apply federal law in cases involving federal questions. In a case based on diversity of citizenship, in contrast, a federal court will apply the relevant state law (which is often the law of the state in which the court sits).

Exclusive versus Concurrent Jurisdiction

Concurrent Jurisdiction Jurisdiction that exists when two different courts have the power to hear a case.

Exclusive Jurisdiction Jurisdiction that exists when a case can be heard only in a particular court or type of court.

Exclusive versus Concurrent Jurisdiction   When both federal and state courts have the power to hear a case, as is true in lawsuits involving diversity of citizenship, **concurrent jurisdiction** exists. When cases can be tried only in federal courts or only in state courts, **exclusive jurisdiction** exists. Federal courts have exclusive jurisdiction in cases involving federal crimes, bankruptcy, patents, and copyrights; in suits against the United States; and in some areas of admiralty law (law governing transportation on the seas and ocean waters). State courts also have exclusive jurisdiction over certain subject matter—for instance, divorce and adoption.

When concurrent jurisdiction exists, a party may bring a suit in either a federal court or a state court. A number of factors can affect the decision of whether to litigate in a federal or a state court, such as the availability of different remedies, the distance to the respective courthouses, or the experience or reputation of a particular judge. For instance, if the dispute involves a trade secret, a party might conclude that a federal court—which has exclusive jurisdiction over copyrights, patents, and trademarks—would have more expertise in the matter.

A resident of another state might also choose a federal court over a state court if he or she is concerned that a state court might be biased against an out-of-state plaintiff. In contrast, a plaintiff might choose to litigate in a state court if it has a reputation for awarding substantial amounts of damages or if the judge is perceived as being pro-plaintiff. The concepts of exclusive and concurrent jurisdiction are illustrated in Exhibit 3.1 on the facing page.

Jurisdiction in Cyberspace

The Internet's capacity to bypass political and geographic boundaries undercuts the traditional basis on which courts assert personal jurisdiction. As already discussed, for a court to compel a defendant to come before it, there must be at least minimum contacts—the

---

5. Diversity jurisdiction also exists in cases between (1) a foreign country and citizens of a state or of different states and (2) citizens of a state and citizens or subjects of a foreign country. These bases for diversity jurisdiction are less commonly used.

Exhibit 3.1 Exclusive and Concurrent Jurisdiction

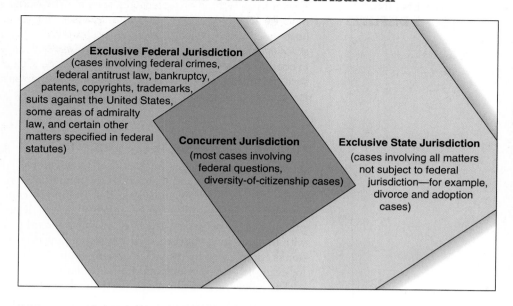

Exclusive Federal Jurisdiction
(cases involving federal crimes, federal antitrust law, bankruptcy, patents, copyrights, trademarks, suits against the United States, some areas of admiralty law, and certain other matters specified in federal statutes)

Concurrent Jurisdiction
(most cases involving federal questions, diversity-of-citizenship cases)

Exclusive State Jurisdiction
(cases involving all matters not subject to federal jurisdiction—for example, divorce and adoption cases)

presence of a salesperson within the state, for example. Are there sufficient minimum contacts if the defendant's only connection to a jurisdiction is an ad on a Web site originating from a remote location?

LEARNING OBJECTIVE 2
Before a court can hear a case, it must have jurisdiction. Over what must it have jurisdiction? How are the courts applying traditional jurisdictional concepts to cases involving Internet transactions?

The "Sliding-Scale" Standard   The courts have developed a standard—called a "sliding-scale" standard—for determining when the exercise of jurisdiction over an out-of-state defendant is proper. In developing this standard, the courts have identified three types of Internet business contacts: (1) substantial business conducted over the Internet (with contracts and sales, for example), (2) some interactivity through a Web site, and (3) passive advertising. Jurisdiction is proper for the first category, improper for the third, and may or may not be appropriate for the second.[6] An Internet communication is typically considered passive if people have to voluntarily access it to read the message, and active if it is sent to specific individuals.

In certain situations, even a single contact can satisfy the minimum-contacts requirement. **CASE EXAMPLE 3.5**   Daniel Crummey purchased a used recreational vehicle (RV) from sellers in Texas after viewing numerous photos of it on eBay. The sellers' statements on eBay claimed that "everything works great on this RV and will provide comfort and dependability for years to come. This RV will go to Alaska and back without problems!" Crummey picked up the RV in Texas, but on the drive home, the RV quit working. He filed a suit in Louisiana against the sellers alleging that the vehicle was defective, but the sellers claimed that the Louisiana court lacked jurisdiction. Because the sellers had used eBay to market and sell the RV to a Louisiana buyer—and had regularly used eBay to sell vehicles to remote parties in the past—the court found that jurisdiction was proper.[7] ●

---

6. For a leading case on this issue, see *Zippo Manufacturing Co. v. Zippo Dot Com, Inc.*, 952 F.Supp. 1119 (W.D.Pa. 1997).

7. *Crummey v. Morgan*, 965 So.2d 497 (La.App.1 Cir. 2007). But note that a single sale on eBay does not necessarily confer jurisdiction. Jurisdiction depends on whether the seller regularly uses eBay as a means for doing business with remote buyers. See *Boschetto v. Hansing*, 539 F.3d 1011 (9th Cir. 2008).

Those of you with an entrepreneurial spirit may be eager to establish Web sites to promote products and solicit orders. Be aware, however, that you can be sued in states in which you have *never* been physically present if you have had sufficient contacts with residents of those states over the Internet. Before you create a Web site that is the least bit interactive, you need to consult an attorney to find out whether you will be subjecting yourself to jurisdiction in every state. Becoming informed about the extent of your potential exposure to lawsuits in various locations is an important part of preventing litigation.

International Jurisdictional Issues   Because the Internet is global in scope, it obviously raises international jurisdictional issues. The world's courts seem to be developing a standard that echoes the minimum-contacts requirement applied by U.S. courts. Most courts are indicating that minimum contacts—doing business within the jurisdiction, for example—are enough to compel a defendant to appear and that a physical presence is not necessary. The effect of this standard is that a business firm has to comply with the laws in any jurisdiction in which it targets customers for its products. This situation is complicated by the fact that many countries' laws on particular issues—free speech, for example—are very different from U.S. laws

   The following case illustrates how federal courts apply a sliding-scale standard to determine if they can exercise jurisdiction over a foreign defendant whose only contact with the United States is through a Web site.

Spotlight on Gucci

Case 3.2
Gucci America, Inc. v. Wang Huoqing
United States District Court, Northern District of California, ____ F.Supp.3d ____ (2011).

Gucci luxury leather products are often counterfeited. Can Gucci sue an Asian company in the United States, nonetheless?

FACTS Gucci America, Inc., is a New York corporation headquartered in New York City. Gucci manufactures and distributes high-quality luxury goods, including footwear, belts, sunglasses, handbags, and wallets, which are sold worldwide. In connection with its products, Gucci uses twenty-one federally registered trademarks (trademark law will be discussed in Chapter 5). Gucci also operates a number of boutiques, some of which are located in California. Wang Huoqing, a resident of the People's Republic of China, operates numerous Web sites. When Gucci discovered that Huoqing's Web sites were selling counterfeit goods—products with Gucci's trademarks but not genuine Gucci articles—it hired a private investigator in San Jose, California, to buy goods from the Web sites. The investigator purchased a wallet that was labeled Gucci but was counterfeit. Gucci filed a trademark infringement lawsuit against Huoqing in a federal district court in California seeking damages and an injunction to prevent further infringement. Huoqing was notified of the lawsuit via e-mail (see the discussion of *service of process* on page 76) but did not appear in court. Gucci asked the court to enter a default judgment—that is, a judgment entered when the defendant fails to appear—but the court first had to determine whether it had personal jurisdiction over Huoqing based on the Internet sales.

ISSUE Can a U.S. federal court exercise personal jurisdiction over a resident of China whose only contact with the United States was through an interactive Web site that advertised and sold counterfeit goods?

DECISION Yes. The U.S. District Court for the Northern District of California held that it had personal jurisdiction over the foreign defendant, Huoqing. The court entered a default judgment against Huoqing and granted Gucci an injunction.

REASON The court reasoned that the due process clause allows a federal court to exercise jurisdiction over a defendant who has had sufficient minimum contacts with the court's forum—the place where the court exercises jurisdiction.

Case 3.2—Continued

Specifically, jurisdiction exists when (1) the nonresident defendant engages in some act or transaction with the forum "by which he purposefully avails himself of the privilege of conducting activities in the forum, thereby invoking the benefits and protections of its laws; (2) the claim must be one which arises out of or results from the defendant's forum-related activities; and (3) exercise of jurisdiction must be reasonable." To determine whether Huoqing had purposefully conducted business activities in Gucci's district, the court used a sliding-scale analysis. Under this analysis, passive Web sites do not create sufficient contacts for such a finding, but interactive sites may

do so. Huoqing's Web sites were fully interactive. In addition, Gucci presented evidence that Huoqing had advertised and sold the counterfeited goods within the court's district, and that he had made one actual sale within the district—the sale to Gucci's private investigator.

WHAT IF THE FACTS WERE DIFFERENT? *Suppose that Gucci had not presented evidence that Huoqing had made one actual sale through his Web site to a resident (the private investigator) of the court's district. Would the court still have found that it had personal jurisdiction over Huoqing? Why or why not?*

Venue

Venue The geographic district in which a legal action is tried and from which the jury is selected.

Jurisdiction has to do with whether a court has authority to hear a case involving specific persons, property, or subject matter. **Venue**[8] is concerned with the most appropriate physical location for a trial. Two state courts (or two federal courts) may have the authority to exercise jurisdiction over a case, but it may be more appropriate or convenient to hear the case in one court than in the other.

Basically, the concept of venue reflects the policy that a court trying a suit should be in the geographic neighborhood (usually the county) where the incident leading to the lawsuit occurred or where the parties involved in the lawsuit reside. Venue in a civil case typically is where the defendant resides, whereas venue in a criminal case normally is where the crime occurred. Pretrial publicity or other factors, though, may require a change of venue to another community, especially in criminal cases when the defendant's right to a fair and impartial jury has been impaired.

EXAMPLE 3.6 Police raid a compound of religious polygamists in Texas and remove many children from the ranch. Authorities suspect that some of the girls were being sexually and physically abused. The raid receives a great deal of media attention, and the people living in the nearby towns are likely influenced by this publicity. In this situation, if the government files criminal charges against a member of the religious sect, that individual may request—and will probably receive—a change of venue to another location. •

Standing to Sue

Standing to Sue The legal requirement that an individual must have a sufficient stake in a controversy before he or she can bring a lawsuit.

Justiciable Controversy A controversy that is not hypothetical or academic but real and substantial; a requirement that must be satisfied before a court will hear a case.

Before a person can bring a lawsuit before a court, the party must have **standing to sue,** or a sufficient "stake" in the matter to justify seeking relief through the court system. In other words, to have standing, a party must have a legally protected and tangible interest at stake in the litigation. The party bringing the lawsuit must have suffered a harm, or have been threatened by a harm, as a result of the action about which she or he has complained. Standing to sue also requires that the controversy at issue be a **justiciable**[9] **controversy**—a controversy that is real and substantial, as opposed to hypothetical or academic. As Chief Justice John Roberts recently noted in a United States Supreme Court decision, a lack of

---

8. Pronounced *ven*-yoo.

9. Pronounced jus-*tish*-uh-bul.

standing is like Bob Dylan's line in the song "Like a Rolling Stone": "When you got nothing, you got nothing to lose."[10]

CASE EXAMPLE 3.7   James Bush visited the office of the Federal Bureau of Investigation (FBI) in San Jose, California, on two occasions. He filled out forms indicating that he was seeking records under the Freedom of Information Act (FOIA—see Chapter 33) regarding a police brutality claim and the FBI's failure to investigate it. Bush later filed a suit against the U.S. Department of Justice in an attempt to compel the FBI to provide the requested records. The court dismissed the lawsuit on the ground that no justiciable controversy existed. Because Bush had not complied with the requirements of the FOIA, the FBI was not obligated to provide any records, and thus there was no actual controversy for the court to decide.[11] •

Note that in some situations a person may have standing to sue on behalf of another person, such as a minor or a mentally incompetent person. **EXAMPLE 3.8**   Three-year-old Emma suffers serious injuries as a result of a defectively manufactured toy. Because Emma is a minor, her parent or legal guardian can bring a lawsuit on her behalf. •

The State and Federal Court Systems

As mentioned earlier in this chapter, each state has its own court system. Additionally, there is a system of federal courts. Even though there are fifty-two court systems—one for each of the fifty states, one for the District of Columbia, plus a federal system—similarities abound. Exhibit 3.2 on the facing page illustrates the basic organizational structure characteristic of the court systems in many states. The exhibit also shows how the federal court system is structured. Keep in mind that the federal courts are not superior to the state courts. They are simply an independent system of courts, which derives its authority from Article III, Sections 1 and 2, of the U.S. Constitution. We turn now to an examination of these court systems, beginning with the state courts.

The State Court Systems

Typically, a state court system will include several levels, or tiers, of courts. As indicated in Exhibit 3.2 on the facing page, state courts may include (1) trial courts of limited jurisdiction, (2) trial courts of general jurisdiction, (3) appellate courts, and (4) the state's highest court (often called the state supreme court). Generally, any person who is a party to a lawsuit has the opportunity to plead the case before a trial court and then, if he or she loses, before at least one level of appellate court. If the case involves a federal statute or a federal constitutional issue, the decision of a state supreme court on that issue may be further appealed to the United States Supreme Court.

The states use various methods to select judges for their courts. Generally, judges are elected, but in some states, they are appointed. Usually, states specify the number of years that a judge will serve. In contrast, as you will read shortly, judges in the federal court system are appointed by the president of the United States and, if confirmed by the Senate, hold office for life—unless they engage in blatantly illegal conduct.

Trial Courts   Trial courts are exactly what their name implies—courts in which trials are held and testimony taken. State trial courts have either general or limited jurisdiction.

---

10. The chief justice stated, "The absence of any substantive recovery means that respondents cannot benefit from the judgment they seek and thus lack Article III standing." He then quoted Bob Dylan's lyrics from "Like a Rolling Stone," on *Highway 61 Revisited* (Columbia Records 1965). This was the first time that a member of the Supreme Court cited rock lyrics in an opinion. See *Sprint Communications Co. v. APCC Services, Inc.*, 554 U.S. 269, 128 S.Ct. 2531, 171 L.Ed.2d 424 (2008).

11. *Bush v. Department of Justice*, 2008 WL 5245046 (N.D.Cal. 2008).

Exhibit 3.2 The State and Federal Court Systems

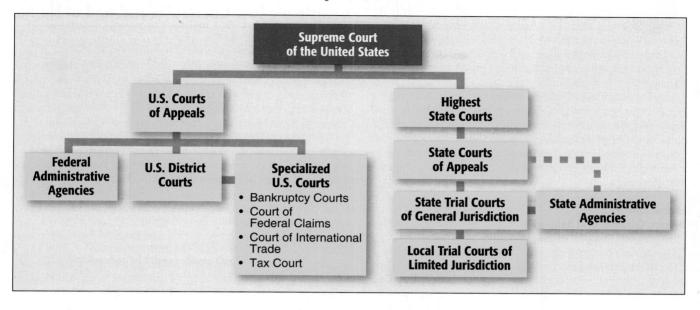

Trial courts that have general jurisdiction as to subject matter may be called county, district, superior, or circuit courts.[12] The jurisdiction of these courts is often determined by the size of the county in which the court sits. State trial courts of general jurisdiction have jurisdiction over a wide variety of subjects, including both civil disputes and criminal prosecutions. (In some states, trial courts of general jurisdiction may hear appeals from courts of limited jurisdiction.)

Some courts of limited jurisdiction are called special inferior trial courts or minor judiciary courts. **Small claims courts** are inferior trial courts that hear only civil cases involving claims of less than a certain amount, such as $5,000 (the amount varies from state to state). Suits brought in small claims courts are generally conducted informally, and lawyers are not required (in a few states, lawyers are not even allowed).

Another example of an inferior trial court is a local municipal court that hears mainly traffic cases. Decisions of small claims courts and municipal courts may sometimes be appealed to a state trial court of general jurisdiction. Other courts of limited jurisdiction as to subject matter include domestic relations or family courts, which handle primarily divorce actions and child-custody disputes, and probate courts, as mentioned earlier. A few states have even established Islamic law courts, which are courts of limited jurisdiction that serve the American Muslim community. (See this chapter's *Beyond Our Borders* feature on the following page for a discussion of the rise of Islamic law courts.)

Appellate, or Reviewing, Courts

Every state has at least one court of appeals (appellate court, or reviewing court), which may be an intermediate appellate court or the state's highest court. About three-fourths of the states have intermediate appellate courts. Generally, courts of appeals do not conduct new trials, in which evidence is submitted to the court and witnesses are examined. Rather, an appellate court panel of three or more judges reviews the record of the case on appeal, which includes a transcript of the trial proceedings, and determines whether the trial court committed an error.

Small Claims Court A special court in which parties can litigate small claims without an attorney.

---

12. The name in Ohio is court of common pleas, and the name in New York is supreme court.

BEYOND OUR BORDERS   Islamic Law Courts Abroad and at Home

As discussed in Chapter 1, Islamic law is one of the world's three most common legal systems, along with civil law and common law systems. In most Islamic countries, the law is based on *sharia*, a system of law derived from the Qur'an and the sayings and doings of Muhammad and his companions. Today, many non-Islamic countries are establishing Islamic courts for their Muslim citizens.

Islamic Law in Britain, Canada, and Belgium

For several years, Great Britain has had councils that arbitrate disputes between British Muslims involving child custody, property, employment, and housing. These councils do not deal with criminal law or with any civil issues that would put *sharia* in direct conflict with British statutory law. Most Islamic law cases involve marriage or divorce. Starting in 2008, Britain officially sanctioned the authority of *sharia* judges to rule on divorce and financial disputes of Muslim couples. Britain now has eighty-five officially recognized *sharia* courts that have the full power of their equivalent courts within the traditional British judicial system.

In Ontario, Canada, a group of Canadian Muslims established a judicial tribunal using *sharia*. To date, this tribunal has resolved only marital disagreements and some other civil disputes. Under Ontario law, the regular judicial system must uphold such agreements as long as they are voluntary and negotiated through an arbitrator. Any agreements that violate Canada's Charter of Rights and Freedoms will not be upheld.

In 2011, Belgium established its first *sharia* court. This court also handles primarily family law disputes for Muslim immigrants in Belgium.

Islamic Law Courts in the United States

The use of Islamic courts in the United States has been somewhat controversial. The legality of arbitration clauses that require disputes to be settled in Islamic courts has been upheld by regular state courts in some states, including Minnesota and Texas.

In the Texas case, an American Muslim couple was married and was issued an Islamic marriage certificate. Years later, a dispute arose over marital property and the nonpayment of a "dowry for the bride." The parties involved had signed an arbitration agreement stating that all claims and disputes were to be submitted to arbitration in front of the Texas Islamic Court. A Texas appeals court ruled that the arbitration agreement was valid and enforceable.[a]

In some other states, however, there has been a public backlash against the use of Islamic courts. For instance, in Detroit, Michigan, which has a large American Muslim population, a controversy over the community's attempt to establish Islamic courts erupted in 2008. In 2011, a law that would prohibit judges from enforcing foreign laws, including *sharia*, was proposed in the Michigan state legislature.

Critical Thinking
One of the arguments against allowing sharia *courts in the United States is that we would no longer have a common legal framework within our society. Do you agree or disagree? Why?*

---

a. *Jabri v. Qaddura*, 108 S.W.3d 404 (Tex.App.— Fort Worth 2003).

Question of Fact In a lawsuit, an issue that involves only disputed facts, and not what the law is on a given point.

Question of Law In a lawsuit, an issue involving the application or interpretation of a law.

LEARNING OBJECTIVE 3
What is the difference between a trial court and an appellate court?

Focus on Questions of Law   Appellate courts generally focus on questions of law, not questions of fact. A **question of fact** deals with what really happened in regard to the dispute being tried—such as whether a party actually burned a flag. A **question of law** concerns the application or interpretation of the law—such as whether flag-burning is a form of speech protected by the First Amendment to the U.S. Constitution. Only a judge, not a jury, can rule on questions of law.

Defer to the Trial Court's Findings of Fact   Appellate courts normally defer (or give weight) to a trial court's findings on questions of fact because the trial court judge and jury were in a better position to evaluate testimony by directly observing witnesses' gestures, demeanor, and nonverbal behavior during the trial. At the appellate level, the judges review the written transcript of the trial, which does not include these nonverbal elements.

An appellate court will challenge a trial court's finding of fact only when the finding is clearly erroneous (that is, when it is contrary to the evidence presented at trial) or when there is no evidence to support the finding.   **EXAMPLE 3.9**   A jury concludes that a manufacturer's product harmed the plaintiff, but no evidence was submitted to the court to support that conclusion. In this situation, the appellate court will hold that the trial court's decision was erroneous. ● The options exercised by appellate courts will be discussed further later in this chapter.

Highest State Courts   The highest appellate court in a state is usually called the supreme court but may be called by some other name. For example, in both New York and Maryland, the highest state court is called the court of appeals. The decisions of each state's highest court are final on all questions of state law. Only when issues of federal law are involved can a decision made by a state's highest court be overruled by the United States Supreme Court.

The Federal Court System

The federal court system is basically a three-tiered model consisting of (1) U.S. district courts (trial courts of general jurisdiction) and various courts of limited jurisdiction, (2) U.S. courts of appeals (intermediate courts of appeals), and (3) the United States Supreme Court.

Unlike state court judges, who are usually elected, federal court judges—including the justices of the Supreme Court—are appointed by the president of the United States and confirmed by the U.S. Senate. All federal judges receive lifetime appointments because under Article III they "hold their offices during Good Behavior."

ETHICAL ISSUE

Can justice be served when courts are underfunded? The economic downturn that started a few years ago has led to massive budget cuts for many of this nation's court systems. In California, for example, which is experiencing unsustainable state government budget deficits, court funding has been reduced by hundreds of millions of dollars. As a consequence, a typical civil lawsuit may take several years to be heard by a court. Nationwide, the American Bar Association found that in the last several years most states have cut court funding by almost 15 percent. Twenty-six states have stopped filling judicial vacancies. Some have even forced judges to take a leave of absence without pay. One municipal court in Ohio stopped accepting new cases because it could not buy paper.

The end result is that the courts are limiting access to the justice system. According to Rebecca Love Kourlis of the Institute for the Advancement of the American Legal System, our traditional idea that everyone has an equal right to justice is being threatened. The American Bar Association reports that its members fear that "the underfunding of our judicial system threatens the fundamental nature of our tripartite system of government." That brings to mind the words of Judge Learned Hand, who said in 1951: "If we are to keep our democracy, there must be one commandment: Thou shalt not ration justice."

U.S. District Courts   At the federal level, the equivalent of a state trial court of general jurisdiction is the district court. There is at least one federal district court in every state. The number of judicial districts can vary over time, primarily owing to population changes and corresponding caseloads. Today, there are ninety-four federal judicial districts. U.S. district courts have original jurisdiction in federal matters. Federal cases typically originate in district courts. Federal courts with original, but special (or limited), jurisdiction include the bankruptcy courts and others shown in Exhibit 3.2 on page 71.

U.S. Courts of Appeals   In the federal court system, there are thirteen U.S. courts of appeals—also referred to as U.S. circuit courts of appeals. The federal courts of appeals for twelve of the circuits, including the U.S. Court of Appeals for the District of Columbia Circuit, hear appeals from the federal district courts located within their respective judicial circuits. The Court of Appeals for the Thirteenth Circuit, called the Federal Circuit, has national appellate jurisdiction over certain types of cases, such as cases involving patent law and cases in which the U.S. government is a defendant.

The decisions of the circuit courts of appeals are final in most cases, but appeal to the United States Supreme Court is possible. Exhibit 3.3 below shows the geographic boundaries of the U.S. circuit courts of appeals and the boundaries of the U.S. district courts within each circuit.

The United States Supreme Court   The highest level of the three-tiered model of the federal court system is the United States Supreme Court. According to the language of Article III of the U.S. Constitution, there is only one national Supreme Court. All other courts in the federal system are considered "inferior." Congress is empowered to create other inferior courts as it deems necessary. The inferior courts that Congress has created include the second tier in our model—the U.S. courts of appeals—as well as the district courts and any other courts of limited, or specialized, jurisdiction.

The United States Supreme Court consists of nine justices. Although the Supreme Court has original, or trial, jurisdiction in rare instances (set forth in Article III, Section 2), most of its work is as an appeals court. The Supreme Court can review any case decided by any of the federal courts of appeals, and it also has appellate authority over some cases decided in the state courts.

Writ of *Certiorari* A writ from a higher court asking a lower court for the record of a case.

Appeals to the Supreme Court   To bring a case before the Supreme Court, a party requests that the Court issue a writ of *certiorari*. A **writ of *certiorari***[13] is an order issued by

13. Pronounced sur-shee-uh-*rah*-ree.

Exhibit 3.3 **Boundaries of the U.S. Courts of Appeals and U.S. District Courts**

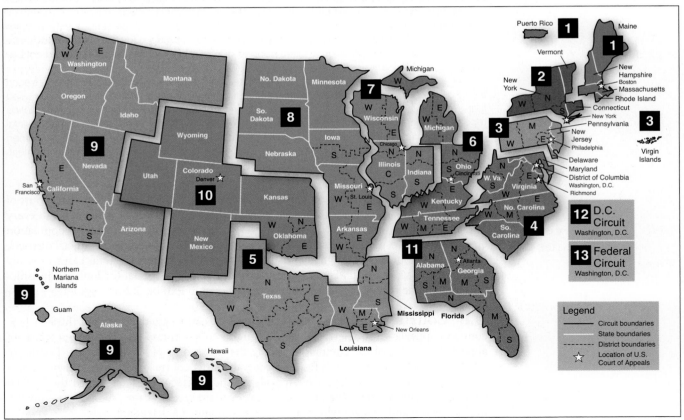

Source: Administrative Office of the United States Courts.

Rule of Four A rule of the United States Supreme Court under which the Court will not issue a writ of *certiorari* unless at least four justices approve of the decision to issue the writ.

the Supreme Court to a lower court requiring that court to send the record of the case for review. Under the **rule of four,** the Court will not issue a writ unless at least four of the nine justices approve. Whether the Court will issue a writ of *certiorari* is entirely within its discretion. The Court is not required to issue one, and most petitions for writs are denied. (Although thousands of cases are filed with the Supreme Court each year, it hears, on average, fewer than one hundred of these cases.)[14] A denial is not a decision on the merits of a case, nor does it indicate agreement with the lower court's opinion. Furthermore, a denial of the writ has no value as a precedent.

Petitions Granted by the Court Typically, the Court grants petitions when cases raise important constitutional questions or when the lower courts are issuing conflicting decisions on a significant issue. The justices, however, never explain their reasons for hearing certain cases and not others, so it is difficult to predict which type of case the Court might select.

Following a State Court Case

"Lawsuit: A machine which you go into as a pig and come out of as a sausage."

Ambrose Bierce, 1842–1914 (American journalist)

To illustrate the procedures that would be followed in a civil lawsuit brought in a state court, we present a hypothetical case and follow it through the state court system. The case involves an automobile accident in which Kevin Anderson, driving a Lexus, struck Lisa Marconi, driving a Hyundai Genesis. The accident occurred at the intersection of Wilshire Boulevard and Rodeo Drive in Beverly Hills, California. Marconi suffered personal injuries and incurred medical and hospital expenses as a result, as well as lost wages for four months. Anderson and Marconi are unable to agree on a settlement, and Marconi sues Anderson. Marconi is the plaintiff, and Anderson is the defendant. Both are represented by lawyers.

Litigation The process of resolving a dispute through the court system.

During each phase of the **litigation** (the process of working a lawsuit through the court system), Marconi and Anderson will have to observe strict procedural requirements. A large body of law—procedural law—establishes the rules and standards for determining disputes in courts. Procedural rules are very complex, and they vary from court to court and from state to state. In addition to the various sets of rules for state courts, the federal courts have their own rules of procedure. Additionally, the applicable procedures will depend on whether the case is a civil or criminal proceeding. Generally, the Marconi-Anderson civil lawsuit will involve the procedures discussed in the following subsections. Keep in mind that attempts to settle the case may be ongoing throughout the trial.

The Pleadings

Pleadings Statements by the plaintiff and the defendant that detail the facts, charges, and defenses of a case.

The complaint and answer (and the counterclaim and reply)—all of which are discussed next—taken together are called the **pleadings.** The pleadings inform each party of the other's claims and specify the issues (disputed questions) involved in the case. The style and form of the pleadings may be quite different in different states.

Complaint The pleading made by a plaintiff alleging wrongdoing on the part of the defendant. When filed with a court, the complaint initiates a lawsuit.

The Plaintiff's Complaint

Marconi's suit against Anderson commences when her lawyer files a **complaint** with the appropriate court. The complaint contains a statement alleging (1) the facts necessary for the court to take jurisdiction, (2) a brief summary of the facts necessary to show that the plaintiff is entitled to relief (a remedy),[15] and

---

14. From the mid-1950s through the early 1990s, the United States Supreme Court reviewed more cases per year than it has in the last few years. In the Court's 1982–1983 term, for example, the Court issued opinions in 151 cases. In contrast, in its 2011–2012 term, the Court issued opinions in only 77 cases.

15. The factual allegations in a complaint must be enough to raise a right to relief above the speculative level. They must plausibly suggest that the plaintiff is entitled to a remedy. See *Bell Atlantic Corp. v. Twombly,* 550 U.S. 544, 127 S.Ct. 1955, 167 L.Ed.2d 929 (2007).

(3) a statement of the remedy the plaintiff is seeking. Complaints may be lengthy or brief, depending on the complexity of the case and the rules of the jurisdiction.

Service of Process   After the complaint has been filed, the sheriff, a county deputy, or another *process server*—that is, one who delivers a complaint and summons—serves a **summons** and a copy of the complaint on defendant Anderson. The summons notifies Anderson that he must file an answer to the complaint with both the court and the plaintiff's attorney within a specified time period (usually twenty to thirty days). The summons also informs Anderson that failure to answer may result in a **default judgment** for the plaintiff, meaning the plaintiff could be awarded the damages sought in her complaint. Service of process is essential in our legal system. No case can proceed to trial unless the plaintiff can prove that he or she has properly served the defendant.

The Defendant's Answer   The defendant's **answer** either admits the statements or allegations set forth in the complaint or denies them and outlines any defenses that the defendant may have. If Anderson admits to all of Marconi's allegations in his answer, the court will enter a judgment for Marconi. If Anderson denies any of Marconi's allegations, the litigation will go forward.

Anderson can deny Marconi's allegations and set forth his own claim that Marconi was negligent and therefore owes him compensation for the damage to his Lexus. This is appropriately called a **counterclaim.** If Anderson files a counterclaim, Marconi will have to answer it with a pleading, normally called a **reply,** which has the same characteristics as an answer.

Anderson can also admit the truth of Marconi's complaint but raise new facts that may result in dismissal of the action. This is called raising an *affirmative defense.* For example, Anderson could assert the expiration of the time period under the relevant *statute of limitations* (a state or federal statute that sets the maximum time period during which a certain action can be brought or rights enforced) as an affirmative defense.

Motion to Dismiss   A **motion to dismiss** requests the court to dismiss the case for stated reasons. Grounds for dismissal of a case include improper delivery of the complaint and summons, improper venue, and the plaintiff's failure to state a claim for which a court could grant relief. For instance, if Marconi had suffered no injuries or losses as a result of Anderson's negligence, Anderson could move to have the case dismissed because Marconi would not have stated a claim for which relief could be granted.

If the judge grants the motion to dismiss, the plaintiff generally is given time to file an amended complaint. If the judge denies the motion, the suit will go forward, and the defendant must then file an answer. Note that if Marconi wishes to discontinue the suit because, for example, an out-of-court settlement has been reached, she can likewise move for dismissal. The court can also dismiss the case on its own motion.

Pretrial Motions

Either party may attempt to get the case dismissed before trial through the use of various pretrial motions. We have already mentioned the motion to dismiss. Two other important pretrial motions are the motion for judgment on the pleadings and the motion for summary judgment.

At the close of the pleadings, either party may make a **motion for judgment on the pleadings,** or on the merits of the case. The judge will grant the motion only when there is no dispute over the facts of the case and the sole issue to be resolved is a question of law. In deciding on the motion, the judge may consider only the evidence contained in the pleadings.

Summons A document informing a defendant that a legal action has been commenced against her or him and that the defendant must appear in court on a certain date to answer the plaintiff's complaint.

Default Judgment A judgment entered by a court against a defendant who has failed to appear in court to answer or defend against the plaintiff's claim.

Answer Procedurally, a defendant's response to the plaintiff's complaint.

Counterclaim A claim made by a defendant in a civil lawsuit against the plaintiff. In effect, the defendant is suing the plaintiff.

Reply Procedurally, a plaintiff's response to a defendant's answer.

Motion to Dismiss A pleading in which a defendant admits the facts as alleged by the plaintiff but asserts that the plaintiff's claim to state a cause of action has no basis in law.

Motion for Judgment on the Pleadings A motion by either party to a lawsuit at the close of the pleadings requesting the court to decide the issue solely on the pleadings without proceeding to trial. The motion will be granted only if no facts are in dispute.

Motion for Summary Judgment A motion requesting the court to enter a judgment without proceeding to trial. The motion can be based on evidence outside the pleadings and will be granted only if no facts are in dispute.

In contrast, in a **motion for summary judgment,** the court may consider evidence outside the pleadings, such as sworn statements (affidavits) by parties or witnesses, or other documents relating to the case. Either party can make a motion for summary judgment. Like the motion for judgment on the pleadings, a motion for summary judgment will be granted only if there are no genuine questions of fact and the sole question is a question of law.

LEARNING OBJECTIVE 4
What is discovery, and how does electronic discovery differ from traditional discovery?

Discovery A method by which the opposing parties obtain information from each other to prepare for trial.

Discovery

Before a trial begins, each party can use a number of procedural devices to obtain information and gather evidence about the case from the other party or from third parties. The process of obtaining such information is known as **discovery.** Discovery includes gaining access to witnesses, documents, records, and other types of evidence.

The Federal Rules of Civil Procedure and similar rules in the states set forth the guidelines for discovery. Generally, discovery is allowed regarding any matter that is not privileged and is relevant to the claim or defense of any party. Discovery rules also attempt to protect witnesses and parties from undue harassment and to safeguard privileged or confidential material from being disclosed. If a discovery request involves privileged or confidential business information, a court can deny the request and can limit the scope of discovery in a number of ways. For instance, a court can require the party to submit the materials to the judge in a sealed envelope so that the judge can decide if they should be disclosed to the opposing party.

Discovery prevents surprises at trial by giving parties access to evidence that might otherwise be hidden. This allows both parties to learn what to expect during a trial before they reach the courtroom. Discovery also serves to narrow the issues so that trial time is spent on the main questions in the case.

Deposition The testimony of a party to a lawsuit or a witness taken under oath before a trial.

Depositions and Interrogatories
Discovery can involve the use of depositions or interrogatories, or both. A **deposition** is sworn testimony by a party to the lawsuit or any witness. The person being deposed (the deponent) answers questions asked by the attorneys, and the questions and answers are recorded by an authorized court official and sworn to and signed by the deponent. (Occasionally, written depositions are taken when witnesses are unable to appear in person.) The answers given to depositions will, of course, help the attorneys prepare for the trial. They can also be used in court to impeach (challenge the credibility of) a party or a witness who changes her or his testimony at the trial. In addition, a witness's deposition can be used as testimony if he or she is not available for the trial.

Interrogatories A series of written questions for which written answers are prepared by a party to a lawsuit, usually with the assistance of the party's attorney, and then signed under oath.

Interrogatories are written questions for which written answers are prepared and then signed under oath. The main difference between interrogatories and written depositions is that interrogatories are directed to a party to the lawsuit (the plaintiff or the defendant), not to a witness, and the party can prepare answers with the aid of an attorney. The scope of interrogatories is broader because parties are obligated to answer the questions, even if that means disclosing information from their records and files.

Requests for Other Information
A party can serve a written request on the other party for an admission of the truth on matters relating to the trial. Any matter admitted under such a request is conclusively established for the trial. For example, Marconi can ask Anderson to admit that he was driving at a speed of forty-five miles an hour. A request for admission saves time at trial because the parties will not have to spend time proving facts on which they already agree.

A party can also gain access to documents and other items not in her or his possession in order to inspect and examine them. Likewise, a party can gain "entry upon land" to inspect the premises. Anderson's attorney, for example, normally can gain permission to inspect and photocopy Marconi's car repair bills.

   When the physical or mental condition of one party is in question, the opposing party can ask the court to order a physical or mental examination, but the court will do so only if the need for the information outweighs the right to privacy of the person to be examined. If the court issues the order, the opposing party can obtain the results of the examination.

Electronic Discovery   Any relevant material, including information stored electronically, can be the object of a discovery request. The federal rules and most state rules now specifically allow all parties to obtain electronic "data compilations." Electronic evidence, or **e-evidence,** includes all types of computer-generated or electronically recorded information, such as e-mail, voice mail, tweets, blogs, spreadsheets, as well as documents and other data stored on computers. E-evidence can reveal significant facts that are not discoverable by other means. For example, computers automatically record certain information about files—such as who created the file and when, and who accessed, modified, or transmitted it—on their hard drives. This information can be obtained only from the file in its electronic format—not from printed-out versions.

E-Discovery Procedures   Amendments to the Federal Rules of Civil Procedure that took effect in 2006 deal specifically with the preservation, retrieval, and production of electronic data. Although traditional means, such as interrogatories and depositions, are still used to find out about the e-evidence, a party must usually hire an expert to retrieve evidence in its electronic format. The expert uses software to reconstruct e-mail exchanges and establish who knew what and when they knew it. The expert can even recover files that the user thought had been deleted from a computer.

Advantages and Disadvantages   Electronic discovery has significant advantages over paper discovery. Back-up copies of documents and e-mail can provide useful—and often quite damaging—information about how a particular matter progressed over several weeks or months. E-discovery can uncover the proverbial smoking gun that will win the lawsuit, but it is also time consuming and expensive, especially when lawsuits involve large firms with multiple offices. Also, many firms are finding it difficult to fulfill their duty to preserve electronic evidence from a vast number of sources. For a discussion of some of the problems associated with preserving electronic evidence for discovery, see this chapter's *Adapting the Law to the Online Environment* feature on the facing page.

Pretrial Conference

Either party or the court can request a pretrial conference, or hearing. Usually, the hearing consists of an informal discussion between the judge and the opposing attorneys after discovery has taken place. The purpose of the hearing is to explore the possibility of a settlement without trial and, if this is not possible, to identify the matters that are in dispute and to plan the course of the trial.

Jury Selection

A trial can be held with or without a jury. The Seventh Amendment to the U.S. Constitution guarantees the right to a jury trial for cases in *federal* courts when the amount in controversy exceeds $20, but this guarantee does not apply to state courts. Most states have similar guarantees in their own constitutions (although the threshold dollar amount is higher than $20). The right to a trial by jury does not have to be exercised, and many cases are tried without a jury. In most states and in federal courts, one of the parties must request a jury in a civil case, or the judge presumes that the parties waive the right.

E-Evidence A type of evidence that consists of all computer-generated or electronically recorded information.

"The judicial system is the most expensive machine ever invented for finding out what happened and what to do about it."

Irving R. Kaufman, 1910–1992 (American jurist)

▶ KNOW THIS ◀
Picking the "right" jury is often an important aspect of litigation strategy, and a number of firms now specialize in jury consulting services.

ADAPTING THE LAW TO THE ONLINE ENVIRONMENT

THE DUTY TO PRESERVE ELECTRONIC EVIDENCE FOR DISCOVERY

Today, less than 0.5 percent of new information is created on paper. Instead of sending letters and memos, people send e-mails and text messages, creating a massive amount of electronically stored information (ESI). The law requires parties to preserve ESI whenever there is a "reasonable anticipation of litigation."

Why Companies Fail to Preserve E-Evidence

Preserving e-evidence can be a challenge, though, particularly for large corporations that have electronic data scattered across multiple networks, servers, desktops, laptops, iPhones, iPads, and other smartphones and tablets. Although many companies have policies regarding back-up of office e-mail and computer systems, these may cover only a fraction of the e-evidence requested in a lawsuit.

Technological advances further complicate the situation. Users of BlackBerrys, for example, can configure them so that messages are transmitted with limited or no archiving rather than going through a company's servers and being recorded. How can a company preserve e-evidence that is never on its servers? In one case, the court held that a company had a duty to preserve transitory "server log data," which exist only temporarily on a computer's memory.[a]

Potential Sanctions and Malpractice Claims

A court may impose sanctions (such as fines) on a party that fails to preserve electronic evidence or to comply with e-evidence requests. A firm may be sanctioned if it provides e-mails without the attachments, does not produce all of the e-discovery requested, overwrites the contents of files, or fails to suspend its automatic e-mail deletion procedures.[b] Sanctions for e-discovery

violations have become increasingly common in recent years.[c] Attorneys who fail to properly advise their clients concerning the duty to preserve e-evidence or who fail to supervise vendors, contract attorneys, or subordinates who work for the clients also often face sanctions and malpractice claims.[d]

Lessons from Intel

A party that fails to preserve e-evidence may even find itself at such a disadvantage that it will settle a dispute rather than continue litigation. For instance, Advanced Micro Devices, Inc. (AMD), sued Intel Corporation, one of the world's largest microprocessor suppliers, for violating antitrust laws. Immediately after the lawsuit was filed, Intel began collecting and preserving the ESI on its servers. Although the company instructed its employees to retain documents and e-mails related to competition with AMD, many employees saved only copies of the e-mails that they had received and not e-mails that they had sent.

In addition, Intel did not stop its automatic e-mail deletion system, causing other information to be lost. In the end, although Intel produced data that were equivalent to "somewhere in the neighborhood of a pile 137 miles high" in paper, its failure to preserve e-discovery led it to settle the dispute.[e]

Critical Thinking

How might a large company protect itself from allegations that it intentionally failed to preserve electronic data?

---

a. See *Columbia Pictures v. Brunnell,* 2007 WL 2080419 (C.D.Cal. 2007).

b. See, for example, *Io Group, Inc. v. GLBT, Ltd,* 2011 WL 4974337 (N.D.Cal. 2011); *E. I. Du Pont de Nemours & Co. v. Kolon Industries, Inc.,* 803 F.Supp.2d 469 (E.D.Va. 2011); *Genger v. TR Investors, LLC,* 26 A.3d 180 (Del.Supr. 2011); *PIC Group, Inc. v. LandCoast Insulation, Inc.,* 2011 WL 2669144 (S.D.Miss. 2011).

c. Elizabeth E. McGinn and Karen M. Morgan, "New Ethical Issues and Challenges in E-Discovery," *New York Law Journal,* October 5, 2011.

d. See, for example, *Surowiec v. Capital Title Agency, Inc.,* 790 F.Supp.2d 997 (D.Ariz. 2011).

e. See *In re Intel Corp. Microprocessor Antitrust Litigation,* 2008 WL 2310288 (D.Del. 2008). See also *Net2Phone, Inc. v. eBay, Inc.,* 2008 WL 8183817 (D.N.J. 2008).

Voir Dire An important part of the jury selection process in which the attorneys question prospective jurors about their backgrounds, attitudes, and biases to ascertain whether they can be impartial jurors.

Before a jury trial commences, a jury must be selected. The jury selection process is known as **voir dire**.[16] During *voir dire* in most jurisdictions, attorneys for the plaintiff and the defendant ask prospective jurors oral questions to determine whether a potential jury member is biased or has any connection with a party to the action or with a prospective witness. In some jurisdictions, the judge may do all or part of the questioning based on written questions submitted by counsel for the parties.

During *voir dire*, a party may challenge a prospective juror *peremptorily*—that is, ask that an individual not be sworn in as a juror without providing any reason. Alternatively, a party

---

16. Pronounced vwahr *deehr.*

may challenge a prospective juror *for cause*—that is, provide a reason why an individual should not be sworn in as a juror. If the judge grants the challenge, the individual is asked to step down. A prospective juror may not be excluded from the jury by the use of discriminatory challenges, however, such as those based on racial criteria or gender.

At the Trial

At the beginning of the trial, the attorneys present their opening arguments, setting forth the facts that they expect to prove during the trial. Then the plaintiff's case is presented. In our hypothetical case, Marconi's lawyer would introduce evidence (relevant documents, exhibits, and the testimony of witnesses) to support Marconi's position. The defendant has the opportunity to challenge any evidence introduced and to cross-examine any of the plaintiff's witnesses.

Motion for a Directed Verdict A motion for the judge to take the decision out of the hands of the jury and to direct a verdict for the party making the motion on the ground that the other party has not produced sufficient evidence to support her or his claim.

Directed Verdicts
At the end of the plaintiff's case, the defendant's attorney has the opportunity to ask the judge to direct a verdict for the defendant on the ground that the plaintiff has presented no evidence that would justify the granting of the plaintiff's remedy. This is called a **motion for a directed verdict** (known in federal courts as a *motion for judgment as a matter of law*). If the motion is not granted (it seldom is granted), the defendant's attorney then presents the evidence and witnesses for the defendant's case. At the conclusion of the defendant's case, the defendant's attorney has another opportunity to make a motion for a directed verdict. The plaintiff's attorney can challenge any evidence introduced and cross-examine the defendant's witnesses.

Closing Arguments and Awards
After the defense concludes its presentation, the attorneys present their closing arguments, each urging a verdict in favor of her or his client. The judge instructs the jury in the law that applies to the case (these instructions are often called *charges*), and the jury retires to the jury room to deliberate a verdict. In the Marconi-Anderson case, the jury will not only decide for the plaintiff or for the defendant but, if it finds for the plaintiff, will also decide on the amount of the **award** (the compensation to be paid to her).

Award The monetary compensation given to a party at the end of a trial or other proceeding.

Posttrial Motions

After the jury has rendered its verdict, either party may make a posttrial motion. If Marconi wins and Anderson's attorney has previously moved for a directed verdict, Anderson's attorney may make a **motion for judgment n.o.v.** (from the Latin *non obstante veredicto*, which means "notwithstanding the verdict"—called a *motion for judgment as a matter of law* in the federal courts). Such a motion will be granted only if the jury's verdict was unreasonable and erroneous. If the judge grants the motion, the jury's verdict will be set aside, and a judgment will be entered in favor of the opposite party (Anderson).

Motion for Judgment N.O.V. A motion requesting the court to grant judgment in favor of the party making the motion on the ground that the jury's verdict against him or her was unreasonable and erroneous.

Alternatively, Anderson could make a **motion for a new trial,** asking the judge to set aside the adverse verdict and to hold a new trial. The motion will be granted if, after looking at all the evidence, the judge is convinced that the jury was in error but does not feel that it is appropriate to grant judgment for the other side. A judge can also grant a new trial on the basis of newly discovered evidence, misconduct by the participants or the jury during the trial, or error by the judge.

Motion for a New Trial A motion asserting that the trial was so fundamentally flawed (because of error, newly discovered evidence, prejudice, or another reason) that a new trial is necessary to prevent a miscarriage of justice.

The Appeal

Assume here that any posttrial motion is denied and that Anderson appeals the case. (If Marconi wins but receives a smaller monetary award than she sought, she can appeal also.) Keep in mind, though, that a party cannot appeal a trial court's decision simply because he

The members of the California Supreme Court, that state's highest court, ready themselves for a hearing. Do all parties to legal disputes have a right to be heard by an appellate court?

(AP Photo/Paul Sakuma)

or she is dissatisfied with the outcome of the trial. A party must have legitimate grounds to file an appeal. In other words, he or she must be able to claim that the lower court committed an error. If Anderson has grounds to appeal the case, a notice of appeal must be filed with the clerk of the trial court within a prescribed time. Anderson now becomes the appellant, or petitioner, and Marconi becomes the appellee, or respondent.

Filing the Appeal   Anderson's attorney files the record on appeal with the appellate court. The record includes the pleadings, the trial transcript, the judge's rulings on motions made by the parties, and other trial-related documents. Anderson's attorney will also provide the reviewing court with a condensation of the record, known as an *abstract,* and a brief. The **brief** is a formal legal document outlining the facts and issues of the case, the judge's rulings or jury's findings that should be reversed or modified, the applicable law, and arguments on Anderson's behalf (citing applicable statutes and relevant cases as precedents).

Marconi's attorney will file an answering brief. Anderson's attorney can file a reply to Marconi's brief, although it is not required. The reviewing court then considers the case.

Brief A written summary or statement prepared by one side in a lawsuit to explain its case to the judge.

Appellate Review   As explained earlier, a court of appeals does not hear evidence. Instead, the court reviews the record for errors of law. Its decision concerning a case is based on the record on appeal, the abstracts, and the attorneys' briefs. The attorneys can present oral arguments, after which the case is taken under advisement.

After reviewing a case, an appellate court has the following options:

1. The court can *affirm* the trial court's decision.
2. The court can *reverse* the trial court's judgment if it concludes that the trial court erred or that the jury did not receive proper instructions.
3. The appellate court can *remand* (send back) the case to the trial court for further proceedings consistent with its opinion on the matter.
4. The court might also affirm or reverse a decision *in part.* For example, the court might affirm the jury's finding that Anderson was negligent but remand the case for further proceedings on another issue (such as the extent of Marconi's damages).

5. An appellate court can also *modify* a lower court's decision. If the appellate court decides that the jury awarded an excessive amount in damages, for example, the court might reduce the award to a more appropriate, or fairer, amount.

Appeal to a Higher Appellate Court
If the reviewing court is an intermediate appellate court, the losing party may decide to appeal to the state supreme court (the highest state court). Such a petition corresponds to a petition for a writ of *certiorari* from the United States Supreme Court. Although the losing party has a right to ask (petition) a higher court to review the case, the party does not have a right to have the case heard by the higher appellate court.

Appellate courts normally have discretionary power and can accept or reject an appeal. Like the United States Supreme Court, state supreme courts generally deny most appeals. If the appeal is granted, new briefs must be filed before the state supreme court, and the attorneys may be allowed or requested to present oral arguments. Like the intermediate appellate court, the supreme court may reverse or affirm the appellate court's decision or remand the case. At this point, the case typically has reached its end (unless a federal question is at issue and one of the parties has legitimate grounds to seek review by a federal appellate court).

Enforcing the Judgment

The uncertainties of the litigation process are compounded by the lack of guarantees that any judgment will be enforceable. Even if a plaintiff wins an award of damages in court, the defendant may not have sufficient assets or insurance to cover that amount. Usually, one of the factors considered before a lawsuit is initiated is whether the defendant has sufficient assets to pay the damages sought, should the plaintiff win the case. What other factors should be considered when deciding whether to bring a lawsuit? See this chapter's *Business Application* feature on page 90 for answers to this question.

The Courts Adapt to the Online World

We have already mentioned that the courts have attempted to adapt traditional jurisdictional concepts to the online world. Not surprisingly, the Internet has also brought about changes in court procedures and practices, including new methods for filing pleadings and other documents and issuing decisions and opinions. Some jurisdictions are exploring the possibility of cyber courts, in which legal proceedings could be conducted totally online.

Electronic Filing

The federal court system has now implemented its electronic filing system, Case Management/Electronic Case Files (CM/ECF), in nearly all of the federal courts. The system is available in federal district, appellate, and bankruptcy courts, as well as the U.S. Court of International Trade and the U.S. Court of Federal Claims. More than 33 million cases are on the CM/ECF system. Users can create a document using conventional document-creation software, save it as a PDF (portable digital file), then log on to a court's Web site and submit the PDF to the court via the Internet. Access to the electronic documents filed on CM/ECF is available through a system called PACER (Public Access to Court Electronic Records), which is a service of the U.S. Judiciary.

More than 60 percent of the states have some form of electronic filing. Some states, including Arizona, California, Colorado, Delaware, Mississippi, New Jersey, New York, and Nevada, offer statewide e-filing systems. Generally, when electronic filing is made available, it is optional. Nonetheless, some state courts have now made e-filing mandatory in certain types of disputes, such as complex civil litigation.

Courts Online

Most courts today have sites on the Web. Of course, each court decides what to make available at its site. Some courts display only the names of court personnel and office phone numbers. Others add court rules and forms. Many appellate court sites include judicial decisions, although the decisions may remain online for only a limited time. In addition, in some states, including California and Florida, court clerks offer **docket** (the court's schedule of cases to be heard) information and other searchable databases online.

Docket The list of cases entered on a court's calendar and thus scheduled to be heard by the court.

Appellate court decisions are often posted online immediately after they are rendered. Recent decisions of the U.S. courts of appeals, for example, are available online at their Web sites. The United States Supreme Court also has an official Web site and publishes its opinions there immediately after they are announced to the public. In fact, even decisions that are designated as "unpublished" opinions by the appellate courts are usually published online (as discussed in the *Adapting the Law to the Online Environment* feature in Chapter 1 on page 13).

Cyber Courts and Proceedings

Someday, litigants may be able to use cyber courts, in which judicial proceedings take place only on the Internet. The parties to a case could meet online to make their arguments and present their evidence. This might be done with e-mail submissions, through video cameras, in designated chat rooms, at closed sites, or through the use of other Internet and social media facilities. These courtrooms could be efficient and economical. We might also see the use of virtual lawyers, judges, and juries—and possibly the replacement of court personnel with computer software.

Already the state of Michigan has passed legislation creating cyber courts that will hear cases involving technology issues and high-tech businesses. The state of Wisconsin has also enacted a rule authorizing the use of videoconferencing in both civil and criminal trials, at the discretion of the trial court.[17] In some situations, a Wisconsin judge can allow videoconferencing even if the parties object, provided that certain operational criteria are met.

The courts may also use the Internet in other ways. For instance, some bankruptcy courts in Arizona, New Mexico, and Nevada recently began offering online chatting at their Web sites, which you will read about in Chapter 23. The model for these online chats came from retailers in the private sector, and chatting may eventually be offered on all federal bankruptcy court Web sites. Other courts are ordering parties to use the Internet as part of their judgments. A Florida county court granted "virtual" visitation rights in a couple's divorce proceedings so that the child could visit with each parent online (through a videoconferencing system or Skype, for instance) during stays at the other parent's residence.

Alternative Dispute Resolution

Litigation is expensive. It is also time consuming. Because of the backlog of cases pending in many courts, several years may pass before a case is actually tried. For these and other reasons, more and more businesspersons are turning to **alternative dispute resolution** (**ADR**) as a means of settling their disputes.

Alternative Dispute Resolution (ADR) The resolution of disputes in ways other than those involved in the traditional judicial process, such as negotiation, mediation, and arbitration.

The great advantage of ADR is its flexibility. Methods of ADR range from the parties sitting down together and attempting to work out their differences to multinational corporations agreeing to resolve a dispute through a formal hearing before a panel of experts. Normally, the parties themselves can control how they will attempt to settle their dispute, what procedures will be used, whether a neutral third party will be present or make a decision, and whether that decision will be legally binding or nonbinding.

17. Wisconsin Statute Section 751.12.

Today, more than 90 percent of cases are settled before trial through some form of ADR. Indeed, most states either require or encourage parties to undertake ADR prior to trial. Many federal courts have instituted ADR programs as well. In the following pages, we examine the basic forms of ADR. Keep in mind, though, that new methods of ADR—and new combinations of existing methods—are constantly being devised and employed.

Negotiation

Negotiation A process in which parties attempt to settle their dispute informally, with or without attorneys to represent them.

The simplest form of ADR is **negotiation,** in which the parties attempt to settle their dispute informally, with or without attorneys to represent them. Attorneys frequently advise their clients to negotiate a settlement voluntarily before they proceed to trial. Parties may even try to negotiate a settlement during a trial or after the trial but before an appeal. Negotiation traditionally involves just the parties themselves and (typically) their attorneys. The attorneys, though, are advocates—they are obligated to put their clients' interests first.

Mediation

Mediation A method of settling disputes outside the courts by using the services of a neutral third party, who acts as a communicating agent between the parties and assists them in negotiating a settlement.

In **mediation,** a neutral third party acts as a mediator and works with both sides in the dispute to facilitate a resolution. The mediator talks with the parties separately as well as jointly and emphasizes their points of agreement in an attempt to help the parties evaluate their options. Although the mediator may propose a solution (called a *mediator's proposal*), he or she does not make a decision resolving the matter. States that require parties to undergo ADR before trial often offer mediation as one of the ADR options or (as in Florida) the only option.

One of the biggest advantages of mediation is that it is not as adversarial as litigation. In a trial, the parties "do battle" with each other in the courtroom, trying to prove each other wrong, while the judge is usually a passive observer. In mediation, the mediator takes an active role and attempts to bring the parties together so that they can come to a mutually satisfactory resolution. The mediation process tends to reduce the hostility between the disputants, allowing them to resume their former relationship without bad feelings. For this reason, mediation is often the preferred form of ADR for disputes involving business partners, employers and employees, or other parties involved in long-term relationships.

LEARNING OBJECTIVE 5
What are three alternative methods of resolving disputes?

EXAMPLE 3.10   Two business partners, Mark Shalen and Charles Rowe, have a dispute over how the profits of their firm should be distributed. If the dispute is litigated, Shalen and Rowe will be adversaries, and their respective attorneys will emphasize how the parties' positions differ, not what they have in common. In contrast, when the dispute is mediated, the mediator emphasizes the common ground shared by Shalen and Rowe and helps them work toward agreement. The two men can work out the distribution of profits without damaging their continuing relationship as partners. •

Arbitration

Arbitration The settling of a dispute by submitting it to a disinterested third party (other than a court), who renders a decision.

In **arbitration,** a more formal method of ADR, an arbitrator (a neutral third party or a panel of experts) hears a dispute and imposes a resolution on the parties. Arbitration differs from other forms of ADR in that the third party hearing the dispute makes a decision for the parties. Exhibit 3.4 on the facing page outlines the basic differences among the three traditional forms of ADR. Usually, the parties in arbitration agree that the third party's decision will be *legally binding,* although the parties can also agree to *nonbinding* arbitration. (Arbitration that is mandated by the courts often is nonbinding.) In nonbinding arbitration, the parties can go forward with a lawsuit if they do not agree with the arbitrator's decision.

In some respects, formal arbitration resembles a trial, although usually the procedural rules are much less restrictive than those governing litigation. In the typical arbitration,

Exhibit 3.4 Basic Differences in the Traditional Forms of Alternative Dispute Resolution

TYPE OF ADR	DESCRIPTION	NEUTRAL THIRD PARTY PRESENT	WHO DECIDES THE RESOLUTION
Negotiation	The parties meet informally with or without their attorneys and attempt to agree on a resolution.	No	The parties themselves reach a resolution.
Mediation	A neutral third party meets with the parties and emphasizes points of agreement to help them resolve their dispute.	Yes	The parties decide the resolution, but the mediator may suggest or propose a resolution.
Arbitration	The parties present their arguments and evidence before an arbitrator at a hearing, and the arbitrator renders a decision resolving the parties' dispute.	Yes	The arbitrator imposes a resolution on the parties that may be either binding or nonbinding.

the parties present opening arguments and ask for specific remedies. Both sides present evidence and may call and examine witnesses. The arbitrator then renders a decision.

The Arbitrator's Decision   The arbitrator's decision is called an *award*. It is usually the final word on the matter. Although the parties may appeal an arbitrator's decision, a court's review of the decision will be much more restricted in scope than an appellate court's review of a trial court's decision. The general view is that because the parties were free to frame the issues and set the powers of the arbitrator at the outset, they cannot complain about the results. A court will set aside an award only in the event of one of the following:

1. The arbitrator's conduct or "bad faith" substantially prejudiced the rights of one of the parties.
2. The award violates an established public policy.
3. The arbitrator exceeded her or his powers—that is, arbitrated issues that the parties did not agree to submit to arbitration.

Arbitration Clauses   Just about any commercial matter can be submitted to arbitration. Frequently, parties include an **arbitration clause** in a contract. The clause provides that any dispute that arises under the contract will be resolved through arbitration rather than through the court system. Parties can also agree to arbitrate a dispute after a dispute arises.

Arbitration Clause A clause in a contract that provides that, in the event of a dispute, the parties will submit the dispute to arbitration rather than litigate the dispute in court.

Arbitration Statutes   Most states have statutes (often based in part on the Uniform Arbitration Act of 1955) under which arbitration clauses will be enforced, and some state statutes compel arbitration of certain types of disputes, such as those involving public employees. At the federal level, the Federal Arbitration Act (FAA), enacted in 1925, enforces arbitration clauses in contracts involving maritime activity and interstate commerce (though its applicability to employment contracts has been controversial, as discussed in a later subsection). Because of the breadth of the commerce clause (see Chapter 2), arbitration agreements involving transactions only slightly connected to the flow of interstate commerce may fall under the FAA.

CASE EXAMPLE 3.11   Buckeye Check Cashing, Inc., cashes personal checks for consumers in Florida. Buckeye would agree to delay submitting a consumer's check for payment if the consumer paid a "finance charge." For each transaction, the consumer signed an agreement that included an arbitration clause. A group of consumers filed a lawsuit claiming that Buckeye was charging an illegally high rate of interest in violation of state law. Buckeye filed a motion to compel arbitration, which the trial court denied, and the case was appealed. The plaintiffs argued that the entire contract—including the arbitration clause—was illegal and therefore arbitration was not required. The United States Supreme Court found that the arbitration provision was *severable,* or capable of being separated, from the rest of the contract. The Court held that when the challenge is to the validity of a contract as a whole, and not specifically to an arbitration clause within the contract, an arbitrator must resolve the dispute. Even if the contract itself later proves to be unenforceable, arbitration will still be required because the FAA established a national policy favoring arbitration and that policy extends to both federal and state courts.[18] ●

   In the following case, the parties had agreed to arbitrate disputes involving their contract, but a state law allowed one party to void a contractual provision that required arbitration outside the state. The court had to decide if the FAA preempted the state law.

18.   *Buckeye Check Cashing, Inc. v. Cardegna,* 546 U.S. 440, 126 S.Ct. 1204, 163 L.Ed.2d 1038 (2006).

Case 3.3

Cleveland Construction, Inc. v. Levco Construction, Inc.

Court of Appeals of Texas, First District, 359 S.W.3d 843 (2012).
law.justia.com[a]

(Bertold Werkmann/Shutterstock.com)
An excavation machine.

FACTS   Cleveland Construction, Inc. (CCI), was the general contractor on a project to build a grocery store in Houston, Texas. CCI hired Levco Construction, Inc., as a subcontractor to perform excavation and grading. The contract included an arbitration provision stating that any disputes would be resolved by arbitration in Ohio. When a dispute arose between the parties, Levco filed a suit against CCI in a Texas state court. CCI sought to compel arbitration in Ohio under the Federal Arbitration Act (FAA), but a Texas statute allows a party to void a contractual provision that requires arbitration outside Texas. The Texas court granted an emergency motion preventing arbitration. CCI appealed.

ISSUE   Does the FAA preempt the Texas statute, which denies enforcement of arbitration clauses that require a party to submit to arbitration outside Texas?

DECISION   Yes. The Texas appellate court reversed the trial court, holding that the FAA preempts the Texas statute.

REASON   The FAA requires courts to enforce valid arbitration agreements, and it "preempts . . . inconsistent state laws . . . under the Supremacy Clause of the United States Constitution." (See page 39 in Chapter 2.) In this case, the Texas statute provided that an agreement to arbitrate was voidable if it required arbitration outside Texas. Thus, if the court applied the Texas statute, it would void the parties' agreement to arbitrate any disputes in Ohio. Voiding the agreement, however, the court found "would undermine the declared federal policy of rigorous enforcement of arbitration agreements." The court ruled that the parties had a valid arbitration agreement, so the FAA preempted the Texas statute.

CRITICAL THINKING—Legal Consideration   *How would business be affected if each state could pass a statute, like the one in Texas, allowing parties to void out-of-state arbitrations?*

---

a. In the search box, type "Cleveland Construction v. Levco Construction" and click on "Search Justia." On the page that opens, click on the link to access this case opinion. Justia Company maintains this Web site.

The Issue of Arbitrability

Notice that in the preceding *Case Example 3.11,* the issue before the United States Supreme Court was *not* the basic controversy (whether the interest rate charged was illegally high) but rather the issue of arbitrability—that is, whether the matter had to be resolved by arbitration under the arbitration clause. Actions over arbitrability often occur when a dispute arises over an agreement that contains an arbitration clause: one party files a motion to compel arbitration, while the other party wants to have the dispute settled by a court, not by arbitration. If the court finds that the dispute is covered by the arbitration clause, it may compel the other party to submit to arbitration, even though his or her claim involves the violation of a statute, such as an employment statute. Usually, if the court finds that the legislature, in enacting the statute, did not intend to prohibit arbitration, the court will allow the claim to be arbitrated.

No party will be ordered to submit a particular dispute to arbitration, however, unless the court is convinced that the party consented to do so.[19] Additionally, the courts will not compel arbitration if it is clear that the prescribed arbitration rules and procedures are inherently unfair to one of the parties.

The terms of an arbitration agreement can limit the types of disputes that the parties agree to arbitrate. When the parties do not specify limits, however, disputes can arise as to whether a particular matter is covered by the arbitration agreement. Then it is up to the court to resolve the issue of arbitrability.

Mandatory Arbitration in the Employment Context

A significant question in the last several years has concerned mandatory arbitration clauses in employment contracts. Many claim that employees' rights are not sufficiently protected when workers are forced, as a condition of being hired, to agree to arbitrate all disputes and thus waive their rights under statutes specifically designed to protect employees. The United States Supreme Court, however, has generally held that mandatory arbitration clauses in employment contracts are enforceable.

CASE EXAMPLE 3.12   In a landmark decision, *Gilmer v. Interstate Johnson Lane Corp.,*[20] the Supreme Court held that a claim brought under a federal statute prohibiting age discrimination (see Chapter 25) could be subject to arbitration. The Court concluded that the employee had waived his right to sue when he agreed, as part of a required registration application to be a securities representative with the New York Stock Exchange, to arbitrate "any dispute, claim, or controversy" relating to his employment. •

Since the *Gilmer* decision, some courts have refused to enforce one-sided arbitration clauses on the ground that they are unconscionable (see Chapter 11).[21] Thus, businesspersons considering using arbitration clauses in employment contracts should be careful that they are not too one sided—especially provisions on how the parties will split the costs of the arbitration procedure.

Private Arbitration Proceedings

In 2011, the Delaware Chancery Court established a new confidential arbitration process, which allows parties to arbitrate their disputes in private. Because many companies are headquartered in Delaware, the court's caseload is heavy, and its influence on the business environment is significant. Delaware's decision to authorize secret arbitration proceedings has been controversial.

EXAMPLE 3.13   Two smartphone makers were the first to use Delaware's confidential arbitration procedures to reach a settlement of their dispute. Skyworks Solutions, Inc.,

KNOW THIS
Litigation—even of a dispute over whether a particular matter should be submitted to arbitration—can be time consuming and expensive.

---

19. See, for example, *Wright v. Universal Maritime Service Corp.,* 525 U.S. 70, 119 S.Ct. 391, 142 L.Ed.2d 361 (1998).
20. 500 U.S. 20, 111 S.Ct. 1647, 114 L.Ed.2d 26 (1991).
21. See, for example, *Macias v. Excel Building Services, LLC,* 767 F.Supp.2d 1002 (N.D.Cal. 2011), citing *Davis v. O'Melveny & Myers, LLC,* 485 F.3d 1066 (9th Cir. 2007), and *Nagrampa v. MailCoups, Inc.,* 469 F.3d 1257 (9th Cir. 2006).

makes technology that transmits signals from smartphones, and Advanced Analogic Technologies, Inc. (AATI), makes power management devices for smartphones. Skyworks had agreed to a merger deal with AATI for $262.5 million, but then backed out, claiming that AATI had not properly accounted for revenue. Both parties filed lawsuits and ended up arbitrating using Delaware's new process. The two reached a settlement to complete the merger for $256 million, without disclosing the details of their agreement. •

Other Types of ADR

The three forms of ADR just discussed are the oldest and traditionally the most commonly used. In recent years, several new types of ADR have emerged. Some parties today are using *assisted negotiation,* in which a third party participates in the negotiation process. The third party may be an expert in the subject matter of the dispute. In *early neutral case evaluation,* the parties explain the situation to an expert, and the expert assesses the strengths and weaknesses of each party's claims. Another form of assisted negotiation is the *mini-trial,* in which the parties present arguments before the third party (usually an expert), who renders an advisory opinion on how a court would likely decide the issue. This proceeding is designed to assist the parties in determining whether they should settle or take the dispute to court.

Other types of ADR combine characteristics of mediation and arbitration. In *binding mediation,* for example, the parties agree that if they cannot resolve the dispute, the mediator may make a legally binding decision on the issue. In *mediation-arbitration,* or "med-arb," the parties agree to attempt to settle their dispute through mediation. If no settlement is reached, the dispute will be arbitrated.

Today's courts are also experimenting with a variety of ADR alternatives to speed up (and reduce the cost of) justice. Numerous federal courts now hold **summary jury trials (SJTs),** in which the parties present their arguments and evidence and the jury renders a verdict. The jury's verdict is not binding, but it does act as a guide to both sides in reaching an agreement during the mandatory negotiations that immediately follow the trial. Other alternatives being employed by the courts include summary procedures for commercial litigation and the appointment of special masters to assist judges in deciding complex issues.

Providers of ADR Services

ADR services are provided by both government agencies and private organizations. A major provider of ADR services is the American Arbitration Association (AAA), which was founded in 1926 and now handles more than 200,000 claims a year in its numerous offices worldwide. Most of the largest U.S. law firms are members of this nonprofit association. Cases brought before the AAA are heard by an expert or a panel of experts in the area relating to the dispute and are usually settled quickly. The AAA has a special team devoted to resolving large, complex disputes across a wide range of industries.

Hundreds of for-profit firms around the country also provide various forms of dispute-resolution services. Typically, these firms hire retired judges to conduct arbitration hearings or otherwise assist parties in settling their disputes. The judges follow procedures similar to those of the federal courts and use similar rules. Usually, each party to the dispute pays a filing fee and a designated fee for a hearing session or conference.

Online Dispute Resolution

An increasing number of companies and organizations offer dispute-resolution services using the Internet. The settlement of disputes in these online forums is known as **online dispute resolution (ODR).** The disputes have most commonly involved disagreements

Summary Jury Trial (SJT) A method of settling disputes by holding a trial in which the jury's verdict is not binding but instead guides the parties toward reaching an agreement during the mandatory negotiations that immediately follow.

Online Dispute Resolution (ODR) The resolution of disputes with the assistance of organizations that offer dispute-resolution services via the Internet.

over the rights to domain names or over the quality of goods sold via the Internet, including goods sold through Internet auction sites.

ODR may be best suited for resolving small- to medium-sized business liability claims, which may not be worth the expense of litigation or traditional ADR. Rules being developed in online forums may ultimately become a code of conduct for everyone who does business in cyberspace. Most online forums do not automatically apply the law of any specific jurisdiction. Instead, results are often based on general, universal legal principles. As with most offline methods of dispute resolution, any party may appeal to a court at any time.

Interestingly, some local governments are using ODR to resolve claims. **EXAMPLE 3.14** New York City has used Cybersettle.com to resolve auto accident, sidewalk, and other personal-injury claims made against the city. Parties with complaints submit their demands, and the city submits its offers confidentially online. If an offer exceeds a demand, the claimant keeps half the difference as a bonus. •

Reviewing . . . Courts and Alternative Dispute Resolution

Stan Garner resides in Illinois and promotes boxing matches for SuperSports, Inc., an Illinois corporation. Garner created the promotional concept of the "Ages" fights—a series of three boxing matches pitting an older fighter (George Foreman) against a younger fighter, such as John Ruiz or Riddick Bowe. The concept included titles for each of the three fights ("Challenge of the Ages," "Battle of the Ages," and "Fight of the Ages"), as well as promotional epithets to characterize the two fighters ("the Foreman Factor"). Garner contacted George Foreman and his manager, who both reside in Texas, to sell the idea, and they arranged a meeting at Caesar's Palace in Las Vegas, Nevada. At some point in the negotiations, Foreman's manager signed a nondisclosure agreement prohibiting him from disclosing Garner's promotional concepts unless they signed a contract. Nevertheless, after negotiations between Garner and Foreman fell through, Foreman used Garner's "Battle of the Ages" concept to promote a subsequent fight. Garner filed a lawsuit against Foreman and his manager in a federal district court in Illinois, alleging breach of contract. Using the information presented in the chapter, answer the following questions.

1. On what basis might the federal district court in Illinois exercise jurisdiction in this case?
2. Does the federal district court have original or appellate jurisdiction?
3. Suppose that Garner had filed his action in an Illinois state court. Could an Illinois state court exercise personal jurisdiction over Foreman or his manager? Why or why not?
4. Assume that Garner had filed his action in a Nevada state court. Would that court have personal jurisdiction over Foreman or his manager? Explain.

DEBATE THIS   In this age of the Internet, when people communicate via e-mail, tweets, FaceBook, and Skype, is the concept of jurisdiction losing its meaning?

BUSINESS APPLICATION

To Sue or Not to Sue?*

Inadvertently or intentionally, wrongs are committed every day in the United States. Sometimes, businesspersons believe that wrongs have been committed against them by other businesspersons, by consumers, or by the government. If you are deciding whether to sue for a wrong committed against you or your business, you must consider many issues.

The Question of Cost

Competent legal advice is not inexpensive. Commercial business law attorneys charge $100 to $600 an hour, plus expenses. It is almost always worthwhile to make an initial visit to an attorney who has skills in the area in which you are going to sue to get an estimate of the expected costs of pursuing redress for your grievance. Note that less than 10 percent of all corporate lawsuits go to trial—the rest are settled beforehand. You may end up settling for far less than you think you are "owed" simply because of the length of time a lawsuit would take and the cost of going to court. And then you might not win, anyway!

Basically, you must do a cost-benefit analysis to determine whether you should sue. Your attorney can give you an estimate of the dollar costs involved in litigating the dispute. Realize, though, that litigation also involves nondollar costs such as time away from your business, stress, inconvenience, and publicity. You can "guess-timate" the benefits by multiplying the probable size of the award by the probability of obtaining that award.

---

*This *Business Application* is not meant to substitute for the services of an attorney who is licensed to practice law in your state.

The Alternatives before You

Negotiation, mediation, arbitration, and other ADR forms are becoming increasingly attractive alternatives to court litigation because they usually yield quick results at a comparatively low cost. Most disputes relating to business can be mediated or arbitrated through the American Arbitration Association (AAA).

There are numerous other ADR providers as well. You can obtain information on ADR from the AAA, courthouses, chambers of commerce, law firms, state bar associations, or the American Bar Association. The Yellow Pages in large metropolitan areas usually list agencies and firms that can help you settle your dispute out of court. You can also locate providers on the Web by using a general search engine and searching for arbitration providers in a specific city.

Checklist for Deciding Whether to Sue

1. *Are you prepared to pay for going to court? Make this decision only after you have consulted an attorney to get an estimate of the costs of litigating the dispute.*
2. *Do you have the patience to follow a court case through the judicial system, even if it takes several years?*
3. *Is there a way for you to settle your grievance without going to court? Even if the settlement is less than you think you are owed, you may be better off settling now for the smaller figure.*
4. *Can you use some form of ADR? Investigate these alternatives— they are usually cheaper and quicker to use than the courts.*

Key Terms

Chapter Summary: Courts and Alternative Dispute Resolution

The Judiciary's Role in American Government (See page 61.)	The role of the judiciary—the courts—in the American governmental system is to interpret and apply the law. Through the process of judicial review—determining the constitutionality of laws—the judicial branch acts as a check on the executive and legislative branches of government.

Basic Judicial Requirements (See pages 61–70.)	1. *Jurisdiction*—Before a court can hear a case, it must have jurisdiction over the person against whom the suit is brought or the property involved in the suit, as well as jurisdiction over the subject matter.
	   a. Limited versus general jurisdiction—Limited jurisdiction exists when a court is limited to a specific subject matter, such as probate or divorce. General jurisdiction exists when a court can hear any kind of case.
	   b. Original versus appellate jurisdiction—Original jurisdiction exists when courts have authority to hear a case for the first time (trial courts). Appellate jurisdiction is exercised by courts of appeals, or reviewing courts, which generally do not have original jurisdiction.
	   c. Federal jurisdiction—Arises (1) when a federal question is involved (when the plaintiff's cause of action is based, at least in part, on the U.S. Constitution, a treaty, or a federal law, for example) or (2) when a case involves diversity of citizenship (citizens of different states, for example) and the amount in controversy exceeds $75,000.
	   d. Concurrent versus exclusive jurisdiction—Concurrent jurisdiction exists when two different courts have authority to hear the same case. Exclusive jurisdiction exists when only state courts or only federal courts have authority to hear a case.
	 2. *Jurisdiction in cyberspace*—Because the Internet does not have physical boundaries, traditional jurisdictional concepts have been difficult to apply in cases involving activities conducted via the Web. Gradually, the courts are developing standards to use in determining when jurisdiction over a Web site owner or operator located in another state is proper.
	 3. *Venue*—Venue has to do with the most appropriate location for a trial, which is usually the geographic area where the event leading to the dispute took place or where the parties reside.
	 4. *Standing to sue*—A requirement that a party must have a legally protected and tangible interest at stake sufficient to justify seeking relief through the court system. The controversy at issue must also be a justiciable controversy—one that is real and substantial, as opposed to hypothetical or academic.

The State and Federal Court Systems (See pages 70–75.)	1. *Trial courts*—Courts of original jurisdiction, in which legal actions are initiated.
	   a. State—Courts of general jurisdiction can hear any case. Courts of limited jurisdiction include domestic relations courts, probate courts, traffic courts, and small claims courts.
	   b. Federal—The federal district court is the equivalent of the state trial court. Federal courts of limited jurisdiction include the U.S. Tax Court, the U.S. Bankruptcy Court, and the U.S. Court of Federal Claims.
	 2. *Intermediate appellate courts*—Courts of appeals, or reviewing courts, which generally do not have original jurisdiction. Many states have an intermediate appellate court. In the federal court system, the U.S. circuit courts of appeals are the intermediate appellate courts.
	 3. *Supreme (highest) courts*—Each state has a supreme court, although it may be called by some other name. Appeal from the state supreme court to the United States Supreme Court is possible only if the case involves a federal question. The United States Supreme Court is the highest court in the federal court system and the final arbiter of the U.S. Constitution and federal law.

Following a State Court Case (See pages 75–82.)	Rules of procedure prescribe the way in which disputes are handled in the courts. Rules differ from court to court, and separate sets of rules exist for federal and state courts, as well as for criminal and civil cases. A civil court case in a state court would involve the following procedures:
	 1. *The pleadings*—
	   a. Complaint—Filed by the plaintiff with the court to initiate the lawsuit. The complaint is served with a summons on the defendant.
	   b. Answer—A response to the complaint in which the defendant admits or denies the allegations made by the plaintiff. The answer may assert a counterclaim or an affirmative defense.
	   c. Motion to dismiss—A request to the court to dismiss the case for stated reasons, such as the plaintiff's failure to state a claim for which relief can be granted.
	 2. *Pretrial motions (in addition to the motion to dismiss)*—
	   a. Motion for judgment on the pleadings—May be made by either party. It will be granted if the parties agree on the facts and the only question is how the law applies to the facts. The judge bases the decision solely on the pleadings.
	   b. Motion for summary judgment—May be made by either party. It will be granted if the parties agree on the facts and the sole question is a question of law. The judge can consider evidence outside the pleadings when evaluating the motion.

Continued

Chapter Summary: Courts and Alternative Dispute Resolution—Continued

Following a State Court Case—Continued	3. *Discovery*—The process of gathering evidence concerning the case. Discovery involves depositions (sworn testimony by a party to the lawsuit or any witness), interrogatories (written questions and answers to these questions made by parties to the action with the aid of their attorneys), and various requests (for admissions, documents, and medical examinations, for example). Discovery may also involve electronically recorded information, such as e-mail, voice mail, word-processing documents, and other data compilations. Although electronic discovery has significant advantages over paper discovery, it is also more time consuming and expensive and often requires the parties to hire experts.
	4. *Pretrial conference*—Either party or the court can request a pretrial conference to identify the matters in dispute after discovery has taken place and to plan the course of the trial.
	5. *Trial*—Following jury selection *(voir dire),* the trial begins with opening statements from both parties' attorneys. The following events then occur:
	  a. The plaintiff's introduction of evidence (including the testimony of witnesses) supporting the plaintiff's position. The defendant's attorney can challenge evidence and cross-examine witnesses.
	  b. The defendant's introduction of evidence (including the testimony of witnesses) supporting the defendant's position. The plaintiff's attorney can challenge evidence and cross-examine witnesses.
	  c. Closing arguments by the attorneys in favor of their respective clients, the judge's instructions to the jury, and the jury's verdict.
	6. *Posttrial motions*—
	  a. Motion for judgment *n.o.v.* ("notwithstanding the verdict")—Will be granted if the judge is convinced that the jury was in error.
	  b. Motion for a new trial—Will be granted if the judge is convinced that the jury was in error. The motion can also be granted on the grounds of newly discovered evidence, misconduct by the participants during the trial, or error by the judge.
	7. *Appeal*—Either party can appeal the trial court's judgment to an appropriate court of appeals. After reviewing the record on appeal, the abstracts, and the attorneys' briefs, the appellate court holds a hearing and renders its opinion.

The Courts Adapt to the Online World (See pages 82–83.)	A number of state and federal courts now allow parties to file litigation-related documents with the courts via the Internet or other electronic means. Nearly all of the federal appellate courts and bankruptcy courts and a majority of the federal district courts have implemented electronic filing systems. Almost every court now has a Web page offering information about the court and its procedures, and increasingly courts are publishing their opinions online. In the future, we may see cyber courts, in which all trial proceedings are conducted online.
Alternative Dispute Resolution (See pages 83–89.)	1. *Negotiation*—The parties come together, with or without attorneys to represent them, and try to reach a settlement without the involvement of a third party. 2. *Mediation*—The parties themselves reach an agreement with the help of a neutral third party, called a mediator. The mediator may propose a solution but does not make a decision resolving the matter. 3. *Arbitration*—A more formal method of ADR in which the parties submit their dispute to a neutral third party, the arbitrator, who renders a decision. The decision may or may not be legally binding, depending on the circumstances. 4. *Other types of ADR*—These include assisted negotiation, early neutral case evaluation, mini-trials, and summary jury trials (SJTs). 5. *Providers of ADR services*—The leading nonprofit provider of ADR services is the American Arbitration Association. Hundreds of for-profit firms also provide ADR services. 6. *Online dispute resolution*—A number of organizations and firms are now offering negotiation, mediation, and arbitration services through online forums. These forums have been a practical alternative for the resolution of domain name disputes and e-commerce disputes in which the amount in controversy is relatively small.

ExamPrep

ISSUE SPOTTERS

1. Sue contracts with Tom to deliver a quantity of computers to Sue's Computer Store. They disagree over the amount, the delivery date, the price, and the quality. Sue files a suit against Tom in a state court. Their state requires that their dispute be submitted to mediation or nonbinding arbitration. If the dispute is not resolved, or if either party disagrees with the decision of the mediator or arbitrator, will a court hear the case? Explain. **(See page 84.)**
2. At the trial, after Sue calls her witnesses, offers her evidence, and otherwise presents her side of the case, Tom has at least two choices between courses of action. Tom can call his first witness. What else might he do? **(See page 80.)**

—Check your answers to the Issue Spotters against the answers provided in Appendix E at the end of this text.

For Review

Answers to the even-numbered questions in this For Review section can be found in Appendix F at the end of this text.

1. What is judicial review? How and when was the power of judicial review established?
2. Before a court can hear a case, it must have jurisdiction. Over what must it have jurisdiction? How are the courts applying traditional jurisdictional concepts to cases involving Internet transactions?
3. What is the difference between a trial court and an appellate court?
4. What is discovery, and how does electronic discovery differ from traditional discovery?
5. What are three alternative methods of resolving disputes?

Business Scenarios and Case Problems

3–1 Standing to Sue. Jack and Maggie Turton bought a house in Jefferson County, Idaho, located directly across the street from a gravel pit. A few years later, the county converted the pit to a landfill. The landfill accepted many kinds of trash that cause harm to the environment, including major appliances, animal carcasses, containers with hazardous content warnings, leaking car batteries, and waste oil. The Turtons complained to the county, but the county did nothing. The Turtons then filed a lawsuit against the county alleging violations of federal environmental laws pertaining to groundwater contamination and other pollution. Do the Turtons have standing to sue? Why or why not? **(See page 69.)**

3–2 Question with Sample Answer—Jurisdiction. Marya Callais, a citizen of Florida, was walking along a busy street in Tallahassee when a large crate flew off a passing truck and hit her. Callais sustained numerous injuries. She incurred a great deal of pain and suffering plus significant medical expenses, and she could not work for six months. She wishes to sue the trucking firm for $300,000 in damages. The firm's headquarters are in Georgia, although the company does business in Florida. In what court may Callais bring suit—a Florida state court, a Georgia state court, or a federal court? What factors might influence her decision? **(See page 69.)**

—For a sample answer to Question 3–2, go to Appendix G at the end of this text.

3–3 Discovery. Advance Technology Consultants, Inc. (ATC), contracted with RoadTrac, LLC, to provide software and client software systems for the products of global positioning satellite (GPS) technology being developed by RoadTrac. RoadTrac agreed to provide ATC with hardware with which ATC's software would interface. Problems soon arose, however, and RoadTrac filed a lawsuit against ATC alleging breach of contract. During discovery, RoadTrac requested ATC's customer lists and marketing procedures. ATC objected to providing this information because RoadTrac and ATC had become competitors in the GPS industry. Should a party to a lawsuit have to hand over its confidential business secrets as part of a discovery request? Why or why not? What limitations might a court consider imposing before requiring ATC to produce this material? **(See page 77.)**

3–4 Case Problem with Sample Answer—Arbitration. Kathleen Lowden sued cellular phone company T-Mobile USA, Inc., contending that its service agreements were not enforceable under Washington state law. Lowden moved to create a class-action lawsuit, in which her claims would extend to similarly affected customers. She contended that T-Mobile had improperly charged her fees beyond the advertised price of service and charged her for roaming calls that should not have been classified as roaming. T-Mobile moved to force arbitration in accordance with provisions that were clearly set forth in the service agreement. The agreement also specified that no class-action lawsuit could be brought, so T-Mobile asked the court to dismiss the class-action request. Was T-Mobile correct that Lowden's only course of action would be to file for arbitration personally? Explain. [*Lowden v. T-Mobile USA, Inc.,* 512 F.3d 1213 (9th Cir. 2008)] **(See page 86.)**

—For a sample answer to Problem 3–4, go to Appendix H at the end of this text.

3–5 Venue. Brandy Austin used powdered infant formula to feed her infant daughter shortly after her birth. Austin claimed that a can of Nestlé Good Start Supreme Powder Infant Formula was contaminated with *Enterobacter sakazakii* bacteria, which can cause infections of the bloodstream and central nervous system, in particular, meningitis (inflammation of the tissue surrounding the brain or spinal cord). Austin filed an action against Nestlé in Hennepin County District Court in Minnesota. Nestlé argued for a change of venue because the alleged tortious action on the part of Nestlé occurred in South Carolina. Austin is a South Carolina resident and gave birth to her daughter in that state. Should the case be transferred to a South Carolina venue? Why or why not? [*Austin v. Nestle USA, Inc.*, 677 F.Supp.2d 1134 (D.Minn. 2009)] **(See page 69.)**

3–6   Arbitration. PRM Energy Systems owned patents licensed to Primenergy, LLC, to use in the United States. Their contract stated that "all disputes" would be settled by arbitration. Kobe Steel of Japan was interested in using the technology represented by PRM's patents. Primenergy agreed to let Kobe use the technology in Japan without telling PRM. When PRM learned about the secret deal, the firm filed a suit against Primenergy for fraud and theft. Does this dispute go to arbitration or to trial? Why? [*PRM Energy Systems v. Primenergy, LLC*, 592 F.3d 830 (8th Cir. 2010)] **(See page 85.)**

3–7   Spotlight on National Football—Arbitration. Bruce Matthews played football for the Tennessee Titans. As part of his contract, he agreed to submit any dispute to arbitration. He also agreed that Tennessee law would determine all matters related to workers' compensation. After Matthews retired, he filed a workers' compensation claim in California. The arbitrator ruled that Matthews could pursue his claim in California but only under Tennessee law. Should this award be set aside? Explain. [*National Football League Players Association v. National Football League Management Council*, 2011 WL 1137334 (S.D.Cal. 2011)] **(See pages 84–87.)**

3–8   Minimum Contacts. Seal Polymer Industries sold two freight containers of latex gloves to Med-Express, Inc., a company based in North Carolina. When Med-Express failed to pay the $104,000 owed for the gloves, Seal Polymer sued in an Illinois court and obtained a judgment against Med-Express. Med-Express argued that it did not have minimum contacts with Illinois and therefore the Illinois judgment based on personal jurisdiction was invalid. Med-Express stated that it was incorporated under North Carolina law, had its principal place of business in North Carolina, and therefore had no minimum contacts with Illinois. Was this statement alone sufficient to prevent the Illinois judgment from being collected against Med-Express in North Carolina? Why or why not? [*Seal Polymer Industries v. Med-Express, Inc.*, 725 S.E.2d 5 (N.C.App. 2012)] **(See pages 62–64.)**

3–9   ◆▶ A Question of Ethics—Agreement to Arbitrate. Nellie Lumpkin, who suffered from dementia, was admitted to the Picayune Convalescent Center, a nursing home. Because of her mental condition, her daughter, Beverly McDaniel, signed the admissions agreement. It included a clause requiring the parties to submit any dispute to arbitration. After Lumpkin left the center two years later, she filed a suit against Picayune to recover damages for mistreatment and malpractice. [*Covenant Health & Rehabilitation of Picayune, LP v. Lumpkin*, 23 So.2d 1092 (Miss. App. 2009)] **(See page 87.)**

1. Is it ethical for this dispute—involving negligent medical care, not a breach of a commercial contract—to be forced into arbitration? Why or why not? Discuss whether medical facilities should be able to impose arbitration when there is generally no bargaining over such terms.

2. Should a person with limited mental capacity be held to the arbitration clause agreed to by her next of kin who signed on her behalf? Why or why not?

Critical Thinking and Writing Assignments

3–10   Business Law Critical Thinking Group Assignment. Assume that a statute in your state requires that all civil lawsuits involving damages of less than $50,000 be arbitrated and allows such a case to be tried in court only if a party is dissatisfied with the arbitrator's decision. The statute also provides that if a trial does not result in an improvement of more than 10 percent in the position of the party who demanded the trial, that party must pay the entire costs of the arbitration proceeding.

1. One group will argue that the state statute violates litigants' rights of access to the courts and to trial by jury.

2. Another group will argue that the statute does not violate litigants' rights of access to the courts.

3. A third group will evaluate how the determination on rights of access would be changed if the statute was part of a pilot program and affected only a few judicial districts in the state.

Torts and Cyber Torts

(Oxford/iStockphoto.com)

LEARNING OBJECTIVES

The five learning objectives below are designed to help improve your understanding of the chapter. After reading this chapter, you should be able to answer the following questions:

1 What is the purpose of tort law? What types of damages are available in tort lawsuits?

2 What are two basic categories of torts?

3 What is defamation? Name two types of defamation.

4 Identify the four elements of negligence.

5 What is meant by strict liability? In what circumstances is strict liability applied?

"Two wrongs do not make a right."
—English Proverb

Tort A wrongful act (other than a breach of contract) that results in harm or injury to another and leads to civil liability.

Torts are wrongful actions (the word *tort* is French for "wrong"). Most of us agree with the chapter-opening quotation—two wrongs do not make a right. Through tort law, society tries to ensure that those who have suffered injuries as a result of the wrongful conduct of others receive compensation from the wrongdoers. Although some torts, such as assault and trespass, originated in the English common law, the field of tort law continues to expand. As technological advances such as the Internet provide opportunities to commit new types of wrongs, the courts are extending tort law to cover these wrongs. For instance, not too long ago, Google announced that it was starting a competing service similar to Facebook's. The unveiling of Google+ was met with praise and some very damning criticisms that turned out to have been initiated by a public relations firm that Facebook regularly used. Was a cyber tort committed? You'll decide later in this chapter.

As you will see in later chapters of this book, many of the lawsuits brought by or against business firms are based on the tort theories discussed in this chapter. Some of the torts examined here can occur in any context, including the business environment. Others, traditionally referred to as **business torts**, involve wrongful interference with the business

Business Tort Wrongful interference with another's business rights and relationships.

95

Cyber Tort A tort committed in cyberspace.

rights of others. Business torts include such vague concepts as *unfair competition* and *wrongfully interfering with the business relations of another.*

Torts committed via the Internet are sometimes referred to as **cyber torts.** We look at how the courts have applied traditional tort law to wrongful actions in the online environment in the concluding pages of this chapter.

The Basis of Tort Law

Two notions serve as the basis of all torts: wrongs and compensation. Tort law is designed to compensate those who have suffered a loss or injury due to another person's wrongful act. In a tort action, one person or group brings a personal suit against another person or group to obtain compensation (monetary **damages**) or other relief for the harm suffered.

Damages A monetary award sought as a remedy for a breach of contract or a tortious action.

The Purpose of Tort Law

LEARNING OBJECTIVE 1
What is the purpose of tort law? What types of damages are available in tort lawsuits?

Generally, the purpose of tort law is to provide remedies for the invasion of various *protected interests.* Society recognizes an interest in personal physical safety, and tort law provides remedies for acts that cause physical injury or interfere with physical security and freedom. Hence, society recognizes an interest in protecting real and personal property. Tort law provides remedies for acts that cause destruction or damage to property. Society also recognizes an interest in protecting certain intangible interests, such as personal privacy, family relations, reputation, and dignity. Consequently, tort law provides remedies for invasion of these interests.

Damages Available in Tort Actions

Because the purpose of tort law is to compensate the injured party for the damage suffered, it is important to have a basic understanding of the types of damages that plaintiffs seek in tort actions.

Compensatory Damages A monetary award equivalent to the actual value of injuries or damage sustained by the aggrieved party.

Compensatory Damages   **Compensatory damages** are intended to compensate or reimburse plaintiffs for actual losses—to make the plaintiffs whole and put them in the same position that they would have been in had the tort not occurred. Compensatory damages awards are often broken down into *special damages* and *general damages.*

Special damages compensate the plaintiff for quantifiable monetary losses, such as medical expenses, lost wages and benefits (now and in the future), extra costs, the loss of irreplaceable items, and the costs of repairing or replacing damaged property. **CASE EXAMPLE 4.1** Seaway Marine Transport operates the *Enterprise,* a large cargo ship with twenty-two hatches for storing coal. When the *Enterprise* moved into position to receive a load of coal on the shores of Lake Erie in Ohio, it struck a land-based coal-loading machine operated by Bessemer & Lake Erie Railroad Company. A federal court found Seaway liable for negligence and awarded $522,000 in special damages to compensate Bessemer for the cost of repairing the damage to the loading machine.[1] •

General damages compensate individuals (not companies) for the nonmonetary aspects of the harm suffered, such as pain and suffering. A court might award general damages for physical or emotional pain and suffering, loss of companionship, loss of consortium (losing the emotional and physical benefits of a spousal relationship), disfigurement, loss of reputation, or loss or impairment of mental or physical capacity.

Punitive Damages Monetary damages that may be awarded to a plaintiff to punish the defendant and deter similar conduct in the future.

Punitive Damages   Occasionally, **punitive damages** may also be awarded in tort cases to punish the wrongdoer and deter others from similar wrongdoing. Punitive damages are appropriate only when the defendant's conduct was particularly egregious (bad)

---

1. *Bessemer & Lake Erie Railroad Co. v. Seaway Marine Transport,* 596 F.3d 357 (6th Cir. 2010).

or reprehensible (unacceptable). Usually, this means that punitive damages are available mainly in intentional tort actions and only rarely in negligence lawsuits (*intentional torts* and *negligence* will be explained later in the chapter). They may be awarded, however, in suits involving *gross negligence,* which can be defined as an intentional failure to perform a manifest duty in reckless disregard of the consequences of such a failure for the life or property of another. (See this chapter's *Business Application* feature on page 122 for steps businesses can take to avoid tort liability and the large damages awards that may go with it.)

Courts exercise great restraint in granting punitive damages to plaintiffs in tort actions because punitive damages are subject to the limitations imposed by the due process clause of the U.S. Constitution (discussed in Chapter 2). The United States Supreme Court has held that a punitive damages award that is grossly excessive furthers no legitimate purpose and violates due process requirements.[2] Consequently, an appellate court will sometimes reduce the amount of punitive damages awarded to a plaintiff because the amount was excessive and thereby violates the due process clause.

Tort Reform

Although tort law performs a valuable function by enabling injured parties to obtain compensation, critics contend that certain aspects of today's tort law encourage too many trivial and unfounded lawsuits, which clog the courts and add unnecessary costs. They say that damages awards are often excessive and bear little relationship to the actual damage suffered, which inspires more plaintiffs to file lawsuits. The result, in the critics' view, is a system that disproportionately rewards a few plaintiffs while imposing a "tort tax" on business and society as a whole. Among other consequences, physicians and hospitals order more tests than necessary in an effort to avoid medical malpractice suits, thereby adding to the nation's health-care costs.

Measures to reduce the number of tort cases include (1) limiting the amount of both punitive damages and general damages that can be awarded, (2) capping the amount that attorneys can collect in contingency fees (attorneys' fees that are based on a percentage of the damages awarded to the client), and (3) requiring the losing party to pay both the plaintiff's and the defendant's expenses.

The Class Action Fairness Act (CAFA) of 2005[3] shifted jurisdiction over large interstate tort and product liability class-action lawsuits (lawsuits filed by a large number of plaintiffs) from the state courts to the federal courts. The intent was to prevent plaintiffs' attorneys from *forum shopping*—looking for a state court known to be sympathetic to their clients' cause and predisposed to award large damages. At the state level, more than thirty states have limited damages, especially in medical malpractice suits.

Classifications of Torts

LEARNING OBJECTIVE 2
What are two basic categories of torts?

There are two broad classifications of torts: *intentional torts* and *unintentional torts* (torts involving negligence). The classification of a particular tort depends largely on how the tort occurs (intentionally or negligently) and the surrounding circumstances. In the following pages, you will read about these two classifications of torts.

Intentional Torts against Persons

Intentional Tort A wrongful act knowingly committed.

Tortfeasor One who commits a tort.

An **intentional tort,** as the term implies, requires *intent.* The **tortfeasor** (the one committing the tort) must intend to commit an act, the consequences of which interfere with the personal or business interests of another in a way not permitted by law. An evil or harmful

---

2. *State Farm Mutual Automobile Insurance Co. v. Campbell,* 538 U.S. 408, 123 S.Ct. 1513, 155 L.Ed.2d 585 (2003).
3. 28 U.S.C. Sections 1453, 1711–1715.

motive is not required—in fact, the person committing the action (the actor) may even have a beneficial motive for committing what turns out to be a tortious act.

In tort law, intent means only that the actor intended the consequences of his or her act or knew with substantial certainty that certain consequences would result from the act. The law generally assumes that individuals intend the *normal* consequences of their actions. Thus, forcefully pushing another—even if done in jest and without any evil motive—is an intentional tort if injury results, because the object of a strong push can ordinarily be expected to fall down.

We now discuss intentional torts against persons, which include assault and battery, false imprisonment, infliction of emotional distress, defamation, invasion of the right to privacy, appropriation, misrepresentation, abusive or frivolous litigation, and wrongful interference.

Assault and Battery

An **assault** is any intentional and unexcused threat of immediate harmful or offensive contact, including words or acts that create in another person a reasonable apprehension of harmful contact. An assault can be completed even if there is no actual contact with the plaintiff, provided the defendant's conduct causes the plaintiff to have a reasonable apprehension of imminent harm. Tort law aims to protect individuals from having to expect harmful or offensive contact.

If the act that created the apprehension is *completed* and results in harm to the plaintiff, it is a **battery,** which is defined as an unexcused and harmful or offensive physical contact *intentionally* performed. **EXAMPLE 4.2** Ivan threatens Jean with a gun and then shoots her. The pointing of the gun at Jean is an assault. The firing of the gun (if the bullet hits Jean) is a battery. • The contact can be harmful, or it can be merely offensive (such as an unwelcome kiss). Physical injury need not occur. The contact can involve any part of the body or anything attached to it—for example, a hat, a purse, or a wheelchair in which one is sitting. The contact can also occur as a result of some force set in motion by the defendant, such as throwing a rock. Whether the contact is offensive or not is determined by the *reasonable person standard.*[4]

If the plaintiff shows that there was contact, and the jury (or judge, if there is no jury) agrees that the contact was offensive, the plaintiff has a right to compensation. A plaintiff may be compensated for the emotional harm resulting from a battery, as well as for physical harm. The defendant may raise a number of legally recognized **defenses** (reasons why plaintiffs should not obtain what they are seeking) that justify his or her conduct, including self-defense and defense of others.

False Imprisonment

False imprisonment is the intentional confinement or restraint of another person's activities without justification. False imprisonment interferes with the freedom to move without restraint. The confinement can be accomplished through the use of physical barriers, physical restraint, or threats of physical force. Moral pressure or threats of future harm do not constitute false imprisonment. It is essential that the person under restraint does not wish to be restrained.

Businesspersons are often confronted with suits for false imprisonment after they have attempted to confine a suspected shoplifter for questioning. Under the "privilege to detain" granted to merchants in most states, a merchant can use *reasonable force* to detain or delay a person suspected of shoplifting the merchant's property. Although the details of the

---

KNOW THIS

In intentional tort actions, the defendant must intend to commit the act, but need not have intended to cause harm to the plaintiff.

Assault Any word or action intended to make another person fearful of immediate physical harm—a reasonably believable threat.

Battery Unexcused, harmful or offensive, physical contact with another that is intentionally performed.

Defense A reason offered and alleged by a defendant in an action or lawsuit as to why the plaintiff should not recover or establish what she or he seeks.

---

4. The reasonable person standard is an objective test of how a reasonable person would have acted under the same circumstances. See "The Duty of Care and Its Breach" later in this chapter.

privilege vary from state to state, generally laws require that any detention be conducted in a *reasonable* manner and for only a *reasonable* length of time. Undue force or unreasonable detention can lead to liability for the business.

Cities and counties may also face lawsuits for false imprisonment if they detain individuals without reason. In the following case, a man sued the County of Los Angeles for false imprisonment.

Case 4.1

Shoyoye v. County of Los Angeles

Court of Appeal of California, Second District, 203 Cal.App.4th 947, 137 Cal.Rptr.3d 839 (2012).

Cities and counties can be sued for false imprisonment.

FACTS   Adetokunbo Shoyoye was lawfully arrested in 2007 when he was at a police station reporting an unrelated incident. The police discovered that he had two outstanding warrants: one for an unpaid subway ticket, and another for grand theft, which was actually issued because a former roommate had stolen his identity and been convicted of grand theft under Shoyoye's name. Shoyoye was incarcerated. Shortly thereafter, he appeared before a magistrate who ordered him released on the first warrant. A few days later, a different court released him on the second warrant.

A Los Angeles County employee mistakenly attached information related to another person—who was scheduled to be sent to state prison for violating his parole—to Shoyoye's paperwork. Subsequently, this erroneous information was entered into the computer system under Shoyoye's name. As a result, instead of being released as ordered, Shoyoye was held in jail for sixteen days, subjected to strip searches, required to wait naked in line to shower in close proximity to other inmates, and shackled. During this time, Shoyoye made numerous attempts to explain to various officials that he was being detained for no reason. He was housed in a large dormitory with hundreds of inmates, many of whom were gang members, and witnessed criminal activity and fights. He feared that he might be sent to prison, be put into "the hole" for discipline, or become a victim of violence. After his release, he sued the County of Los Angeles for, among other things, false imprisonment. A jury awarded him $22,700 in economic damages (for past and future lost earnings and property loss), and $180,000 in noneconomic

damages (for past and future pain and suffering). The County of Los Angeles appealed.

ISSUE   Did the County of Los Angeles wrongfully detain Shoyoye because of its clerical errors?

DECISION   Yes. The reviewing court found that Shoyoye had experienced false imprisonment and held that the jury award for economic damages and noneconomic damages was appropriate under the circumstances.

REASON   "The elements of a tortious claim of false imprisonment are: (1) the non-consensual, intentional confinement of a person, (2) without lawful privilege, and (3) for an appreciable period of time, however brief." The court concluded that the evidence presented at trial "was clearly sufficient to establish these elements." Had any county employees simply looked at the paper file on Shoyoye rather than the computer records, they would have realized that the "hold" on Shoyoye did not pertain to him. The erroneous paperwork on Shoyoye resulted in sixteen days of undeserved detention in a less-than-desirable environment.

CRITICAL THINKING—Ethical Consideration   *Shoyoye asked numerous county employees to verify that he had been wrongfully detained. What obligation did those employees have to attempt to discover "the truth"?*

Intentional Infliction of Emotional Distress

Actionable Capable of serving as the basis of a lawsuit. An actionable claim can be pursued in a lawsuit or other court action.

The tort of *intentional infliction of emotional distress* can be defined as an extreme and outrageous act, intentionally committed, that results in severe emotional distress to another. To be **actionable** (capable of serving as the ground for a lawsuit), the conduct must be so extreme and outrageous that it exceeds the bounds of decency accepted by society.

Outrageous Conduct   Courts in most jurisdictions are wary of emotional distress claims and confine them to truly outrageous behavior. Generally, repeated annoyances (such as those experienced by a person who is being stalked), coupled with threats, are sufficient to support a claim. Acts that cause indignity or annoyance alone usually are not enough.

EXAMPLE 4.3   A father attacks a man who has had consensual sexual relations with the father's nineteen-year-old daughter. The father handcuffs the man to a steel pole and threatens to kill him unless he leaves town immediately. The father's conduct may be sufficiently extreme and outrageous to be actionable as an intentional infliction of emotional distress. ●

Limited by the First Amendment   Note that when the outrageous conduct consists of speech about a public figure, the First Amendment's guarantee of freedom of speech also limits emotional distress claims.   **CASE EXAMPLE 4.4**   *Hustler* magazine once printed a fake advertisement that showed a picture of the Reverend Jerry Falwell and described him as having lost his virginity to his mother in an outhouse while he was drunk. Falwell sued the magazine for intentional infliction of emotional distress and won, but the United States Supreme Court overturned the decision. The Court held that creators of parodies of public figures are protected under the First Amendment from claims of intentional infliction of emotional distress. (The Court applied the same standards that apply to public figures in defamation lawsuits, discussed next.)[5] ●

Defamation

LEARNING OBJECTIVE 3
What is defamation? Name two types of defamation.

Defamation Anything published or publicly spoken that causes injury to another's good name, reputation, or character.

Libel Defamation in writing or another form having the quality of permanence (such as a digital recording).

Slander Defamation in oral form.

As discussed in Chapter 2, the freedom of speech guaranteed by the First Amendment to the U.S. Constitution is not absolute. In interpreting the First Amendment, the courts must balance free speech rights against other strong social interests, including society's interest in preventing and redressing attacks on reputation. (Nations with fewer free speech protections have seen an increase in defamation lawsuits targeting U.S. citizens and journalists as defendants. See this chapter's *Beyond Our Borders* feature on page 102 for a discussion of this trend.)

Defamation of character involves wrongfully hurting a person's good reputation. The law has imposed a general duty on all persons to refrain from making *false,* defamatory *statements of fact* about others. Breaching this duty in writing or some other permanent form (such as a digital recording) constitutes the tort of **libel.** Breaching this duty orally is the tort of **slander.** As you will read later in this chapter, the tort of defamation can also arise when a false statement of fact is made about a person's product, business, or legal ownership rights to property.

Statement of Fact Requirement   Often at issue in defamation lawsuits (including online defamation, discussed later in this chapter) is whether the defendant made a statement of fact or a *statement of opinion.*[6] Statements of opinion normally are not actionable because they are protected under the First Amendment. In other words, making a negative statement about another person is not defamation unless the statement is false and represents something as a fact (for example, "Lane cheats on his taxes") rather than a personal opinion (for example, "Lane is a jerk").

Whether an attorney's statement to a reporter about another attorney constituted fact or opinion was at issue in the following case.

---

5. *Hustler Magazine, Inc. v. Falwell,* 485 U.S. 46, 108 S.Ct. 876, 99 L.Ed.2d 41 (1988). For another example of how the courts protect parody, see *Busch v. Viacom International, Inc.,* 477 F.Supp.2d 764 (N.D.Tex. 2007), involving a fake endorsement of televangelist Pat Robertson's diet shake.

6. See, for example, *Lott v. Levitt,* 469 F.Supp.2d 575 (N.D.Ill. 2007).

Case 4.2

Orlando v. Cole

Appeals Court of Massachusetts,
76 Mass.App.Ct. 1112, 921 N.E.2d 566 (2010).

High school women's basketball remains popular.

FACTS Joseph Orlando, an attorney, was representing a high school student who had sued her basketball coach for sexual assault. The coach, Thomas Atwater, was apparently an acquaintance of Orlando's. Before he had retained an attorney, Atwater approached Orlando and admitted that he had committed the assault. Atwater signed an affidavit to that effect and then made a full confession to the police. A few days later, Orlando spoke to two newspaper reporters, gave them a copy of Atwater's affidavit, and explained the circumstances under which Atwater gave the affidavit. The reporters then asked Garrick Cole, who was now representing Atwater, for comments. Cole responded that the affidavit was "inaccurate" and called Orlando's actions "deceitful" and "fraudulent." The newspaper published an article that quoted both Orlando and Cole, and also indicated that Cole would not say what he thought was inaccurate in the affidavit. Both Orlando's and Cole's comments were reported together in various publications. Orlando sued Cole for slander, alleging that Cole's comments were false, described conduct undertaken by Orlando in his profession and business, and imputed "an unfitness for or a misconduct in his office or employment." Orlando claimed that he had suffered harm to his reputation as an attorney as a result of Cole's comments. The trial court granted Cole's motion to dismiss the complaint, and Orlando appealed.

ISSUE Did Cole's statements that another attorney filed an "inaccurate" affidavit and engaged in "fraudulent" and "deceptive" conduct with regard to a case constitute statements of fact that give rise to a defamation claim?

DECISION Yes. The Appeals Court of Massachusetts reversed the trial court's judgment and held that Cole's statements were "reasonably susceptible of a defamatory connotation [implication]." The appellate court remanded the case to allow for a jury trial.

REASON The reviewing court reasoned that the dismissal was premature because "a statement is defamatory in the circumstances if it discredits a person in the minds of any considerable and respectable class of the community." The terms that Cole had used—"inaccurate," "fraudulent," and "deceitful"—implied professional misconduct. Further, those statements are capable of being proved false in a trial. The comments were not offered simply as opinions, nor did any cautionary language accompany them. They appeared to be based on undisclosed defamatory facts. A jury should be allowed to decide whether defamation had occurred.

CRITICAL THINKING—Legal Consideration   *Orlando sued Cole for slander. Why didn't he sue Cole for libel, given that the comments were reported in various news publications?*

The Publication Requirement   The basis of the tort of defamation is the publication of a statement or statements that hold an individual up to contempt, ridicule, or hatred. *Publication* here means that the defamatory statements are communicated to persons other than the defamed party.   **EXAMPLE 4.5**   If Thompson writes Andrews a private letter falsely accusing him of embezzling funds, the action does not constitute libel. If Peters falsely states that Gordon is dishonest and incompetent when no one else is around, the action does not constitute slander. In neither instance was the message communicated to a third party. ●

The courts have generally held that even dictating a letter to a secretary constitutes publication, although the publication may be privileged (privileged communications will be discussed shortly). Moreover, if a third party overhears defamatory statements by chance, the courts usually hold that this also constitutes publication. Defamatory statements made via the Internet are also actionable, as you will read later in this chapter. Note further that anyone who republishes or repeats defamatory statements is liable even if that person reveals the source of the statements.

BEYOND OUR BORDERS   "Libel Tourism"

As mentioned earlier, U.S. plaintiffs sometimes engage in forum shopping by trying to have their complaints heard by a particular state court that is likely to be sympathetic to their claims. *Libel tourism* is essentially forum shopping on an international scale. Rather than filing a defamation lawsuit in the United States where the freedoms of speech and press are strongly protected, a plaintiff files it in a foreign jurisdiction where there is a greater chance of winning.

The Threat of Libel Tourism

Libel tourism can have a chilling effect on the speech of U.S. journalists and authors because the fear of liability in other nations may prevent them from freely discussing topics of profound public importance. Libel tourism could even increase the threat to our nation's security if it discourages authors from writing about persons who support or finance terrorism or other dangerous activities.

The threat of libel tourism captured media attention when Khalid bin Mahfouz, a Saudi Arabian businessman, sued U.S.

resident Dr. Rachel Ehrenfeld in London, England. Ehrenfeld had written a book on terrorist financing that claimed Mahfouz financed Islamic terrorist groups. Mahfouz filed the case in England because English law assumes that the offending speech is false (libelous), and the author must prove that the speech is true in order to prevail.

The English court took jurisdiction because twenty-three copies of the book had been sold online to residents of the United Kingdom. Ehrenfeld did not go to England to defend herself, and the court entered a judgment of $225,000 against her. She then countersued Mahfouz in a U.S. court in an attempt to show that she was protected under the First Amendment and had not committed libel, but that case was dismissed for lack of jurisdiction.[a]

The U.S. Response

In response to the *Ehrenfeld* case, the New York state legislature enacted the Libel

---

a. *Ehrenfeld v. Mahfouz*, 518 F.3d 102 (2d Cir. 2008).

Terrorism Reform Act in 2008.[b] That act enables New York courts to assert jurisdiction over anyone who obtains a foreign libel judgment against a writer or publisher living in New York State. It also prevents courts from enforcing foreign libel judgments unless the foreign country provides equal or greater free speech protection than is available in the United States and New York. In 2010, the federal government passed similar legislation that makes foreign libel judgments unenforceable in U.S. courts unless they comply with the First Amendment.[c]

Critical Thinking

Why do we need special legislation designed to control foreign libel claims against U.S. citizens? Explain.

---

b. McKinney's Consolidated Laws of New York, Sections 302 and 5304.

c. Securing the Protection of our Enduring and Established Constitutional Heritage Act, 28 U.S.C. Sections 4101–4105.

Damages for Libel   Once a defendant's liability for libel is established, general damages are presumed as a matter of law. As mentioned earlier, general damages are designed to compensate the plaintiff for nonspecific harms such as disgrace or dishonor in the eyes of the community, humiliation, injured reputation, and emotional distress—harms that are difficult to measure. In other words, to recover damages in a libel case, the plaintiff need not prove that she or he was actually harmed in any specific way as a result of the libelous statement.

Damages for Slander   In contrast to cases alleging libel, in a case alleging slander, the plaintiff must prove *special damages* to establish the defendant's liability. In other words, the plaintiff must show that the slanderous statement caused the plaintiff to suffer actual economic or monetary losses. Unless this initial hurdle of proving special damages is overcome, a plaintiff alleging slander normally cannot go forward with the suit and recover any damages. This requirement is imposed in cases involving slander because slanderous statements have a temporary quality. In contrast, a libelous (written) statement has the quality of permanence, can be circulated widely, especially through tweets and blogs, and usually results from some degree of deliberation on the part of the author.

Exceptions to the burden of proving special damages in cases alleging slander are made for certain types of slanderous statements. If a false statement constitutes "slander *per se*," no proof of special damages is required for it to be actionable. The following four types of false utterances are considered to be slander *per se:*

1. A statement that another has a loathsome disease (historically, leprosy and sexually transmitted diseases, but now also including allegations of mental illness).
2. A statement that another has committed improprieties while engaging in a business, profession, or trade.
3. A statement that another has committed or has been imprisoned for a serious crime.
4. A statement that a person (usually only unmarried persons and sometimes only women) is unchaste or has engaged in serious sexual misconduct.

Defenses against Defamation

Truth is normally an absolute defense against a defamation charge. In other words, if the defendant in a defamation suit can prove that his or her allegedly defamatory statements were true, normally no tort has been committed. Other defenses to defamation may exist if the statement is privileged or concerns a public figure. Note that the majority of defamation actions in the United States are filed in state courts, and the states may differ both in how they define defamation and in the particular defenses they allow, such as privilege (discussed next).

Privileged Communications In some circumstances, a person will not be liable for defamatory statements because she or he enjoys a **privilege**, or immunity. Privileged communications are of two types: absolute and qualified.[7] Only in judicial proceedings and certain government proceedings is an absolute privilege granted. Thus, statements made in a courtroom by attorneys and judges during a trial are absolutely privileged, as are statements made by government officials during legislative debate.

In other situations, a person will not be liable for defamatory statements because he or she has a *qualified,* or conditional, privilege. An employer's statements in written evaluations of employees are an example of a qualified privilege. Generally, if the statements are made in good faith and the publication is limited to those who have a legitimate interest in the communication, the statements fall within the area of qualified privilege. **EXAMPLE 4.6** Jorge worked at Facebook for five years and was being considered for a management position. His supervisor, Lydia, wrote a memo about Jorge's performance to those evaluating him for the management position. The memo contained certain negative statements. As long as Lydia honestly believed that what she wrote was true and limited her disclosure to company representatives, her statements would likely be protected by a qualified privilege. •

Public Figures Politicians, entertainers, professional athletes, and other persons who are in the public eye are considered *public figures*. In general, public figures are considered fair game, and false and defamatory statements about them that appear in the media will not constitute defamation unless the statements are made with **actual malice**.[8] To be made with actual malice, a statement must be made *with either knowledge of its falsity or a reckless disregard of the truth.*

Statements about public figures, especially when made via a public medium, are usually related to matters of general interest. They are made about people who substantially affect all of us. Furthermore, public figures generally have some access to a public medium

---

"My initial response was to sue her for defamation of character, but then I realized that I had no character."

Charles Barkley, 1963–present (National Basketball Association player, 1984–2000)

Privilege A special right, advantage, or immunity granted to a person or a class of persons, such as a judge's absolute privilege to avoid liability for defamation over statements made in the courtroom during a trial.

Actual Malice The deliberate intent to cause harm that exists when a person makes a statement with either knowledge of its falsity or reckless disregard of the truth. Actual malice is required to establish defamation against public figures.

---

7. Note that the term *privileged communication* in this context is not the same as privileged communication between a professional, such as an attorney, and his or her client. The latter type of privilege will be discussed in Chapter 34, in the context of the liability of professionals.
8. *New York Times Co. v. Sullivan,* 376 U.S. 254, 84 S.Ct. 710, 11 L.Ed.2d 686 (1964).

Lynne Spears, mother of singer Britney Spears, wrote a "tell all" book entitled *Through the Storm: A Real Story of Fame and Family in a Tabloid World.*

for answering disparaging (belittling, discrediting) falsehoods about themselves, whereas private individuals do not. For these reasons, public figures have a greater burden of proof in defamation cases (they must prove actual malice) than do private individuals.

CASE EXAMPLE 4.7   Lynne Spears, the mother of pop star Britney Spears, wrote a book in which she claimed that Sam Lutfi, Britney's former business manager, contributed to a mental breakdown that Britney experienced in 2008. Among other things, the book stated that Lutfi added psychiatric drugs to Britney's food, disabled her cars and phones, and stole funds from her bank accounts. Lutfi filed a lawsuit for defamation and asserted that Lynne's statements were untrue, disparaging, and made with actual malice. A court found that Lutfi was a public figure but had presented enough evidence in his complaint for the case to go forward to trial. Lynne appealed, but the appellate court affirmed the ruling and refused to dismiss Lufti's complaint.[9] •

Invasion of the Right to Privacy and Appropriation

A person has a right to solitude and freedom from prying public eyes—in other words, to privacy. As discussed in Chapter 2, the Supreme Court has held that a fundamental right to privacy is implied by various amendments to the U.S. Constitution. Some state constitutions also explicitly provide for privacy rights. In addition, a number of federal and state statutes have been enacted to protect individual rights in specific areas. Tort law also safeguards these rights through the torts of *invasion of privacy* and *appropriation*.

Invasion of Privacy   Four acts qualify as an invasion of privacy:

1. *Intrusion into an individual's affairs or seclusion.* Invading someone's home or illegally searching someone's briefcase is an invasion of privacy. The tort has been held to extend to eavesdropping by wiretap, the unauthorized scanning of a bank account, compulsory blood testing, and window peeping. **EXAMPLE 4.8**   A female sports reporter for ESPN was digitally videoed while naked through the peephole in the door of her hotel room. She subsequently won a lawsuit against the man who took the video and posted it on the Internet. •

2. *False light.* Publication of information that places a person in a false light is also an invasion of privacy. For example, writing a story about a person that attributes ideas and opinions not held by that person is an invasion of privacy. (Publishing such a story could involve the tort of defamation as well.) **EXAMPLE 4.9**   An Arkansas newspaper printed an article with the headline "Special Delivery: World's oldest newspaper carrier, 101, quits because she's pregnant!" Next to the article was a picture of a ninety-six-year-old woman who was not the subject of the article (and not pregnant). She sued the paper for false light and won. •

3. *Public disclosure of private facts.* This type of invasion of privacy occurs when a person publicly discloses private facts about an individual that an ordinary person would find objectionable or embarrassing. A newspaper account of a private citizen's sex life or financial affairs could be an actionable invasion of privacy, even if the information revealed is true, because it should not be a matter of public concern.

4. *Appropriation of identity.* Under the common law, using a person's name, picture, or other likeness for commercial purposes without permission is a tortious invasion of privacy. An individual's right to privacy normally includes the right to the exclusive use of her or his identity. **EXAMPLE 4.10**   An advertising agency asks a singer with a distinctive voice and stage presence to do a marketing campaign for a new automobile. The singer rejects the offer. If the agency then uses someone who imitates the singer's voice and dance moves in the ad, this would be actionable as an appropriation of identity. •

---

9. *Lutfi v. Spears,* 2010 WL 4723437 (2010).

Appropriation In tort law, the use by one person of another person's name, likeness, or other identifying characteristic without permission and for the benefit of the user.

Appropriation

Most states today have codified the common law tort of appropriation of identity in statutes that establish the distinct tort of **appropriation** or right of publicity. **CASE EXAMPLE 4.11** Vanna White, the hostess of the popular television game show *Wheel of Fortune,* brought an appropriation action against Samsung Electronics America, Inc. Without White's permission, Samsung had included in one of its advertisements a depiction of a robot dressed in a wig, gown, and jewelry, posed in a scene that resembled the *Wheel of Fortune* set, in a stance for which White is famous. The court held in White's favor, reasoning that Samsung's robot ad left "little doubt" as to the identity of the celebrity whom the ad was meant to depict.[10] ●

States differ as to the degree of likeness that is required to impose liability for appropriation, however. Some courts have held that even when an animated character in a video or a video game is made to look like an actual person, there are not enough similarities to constitute appropriation.

CASE EXAMPLE 4.12 The Naked Cowboy, Robert Burck, has been a street entertainer in New York City's Times Square for years. He performs for tourists wearing only a white cowboy hat, white cowboy boots, and white underwear and carrying a guitar strategically placed to give the illusion of nudity. Burck has become a well-known persona, appearing in television shows, movies, and video games, and has licensed his name and likeness to various companies, including Chevrolet. When Mars, Inc., the maker of M&Ms candy, installed a video on billboards in Times Square that depicted a blue M&M dressed exactly like The Naked Cowboy, Burck sued for appropriation. A federal district court held that Mars's use of a cartoon character dressed in The Naked Cowboy's signature costume did not amount to appropriation by use of Burck's "portrait or picture." (Burck was allowed to continue his lawsuit against Mars for allegedly violating trademark law—to be discussed in Chapter 5.)[11] ●

Fraudulent Misrepresentation

Fraudulent Misrepresentation Any misrepresentation, either by misstatement or by omission of a material fact, knowingly made with the intention of deceiving another and on which a reasonable person would and does rely to his or her detriment.

A misrepresentation leads another to believe in a condition that is different from the condition that actually exists. This is often accomplished through a false or incorrect statement. Although persons sometimes make misrepresentations accidentally because they are unaware of the existing facts, the tort of **fraudulent misrepresentation,** or fraud, involves *intentional* deceit for personal gain. The tort includes several elements:

1. The misrepresentation of facts or conditions with knowledge that they are false or with reckless disregard for the truth.
2. An intent to induce another to rely on the misrepresentation.
3. Justifiable reliance by the deceived party.
4. Damage suffered as a result of the reliance.
5. A causal connection between the misrepresentation and the injury suffered.

Puffery A salesperson's often exaggerated claims concerning the quality of property offered for sale. Such claims involve opinions rather than facts and are not legally binding promises or warranties.

For fraud to occur, more than mere **puffery,** or *seller's talk,* must be involved. Fraud exists only when a person represents as a fact something she or he knows is untrue. For example, it is fraud to claim that a roof does not leak when one knows it does. Facts are objectively ascertainable, whereas seller's talk is not. "I am the best accountant in town" is seller's talk. The speaker is not trying to represent something as fact because the term *best* is a subjective, not an objective, term.[12]

---

10. *White v. Samsung Electronics America, Inc.,* 971 F.2d 1395 (9th Cir. 1992).

11. *Burck v. Mars, Inc.,* 571 F.Supp.2d 446 (S.D.N.Y. 2008). Also see *Kirby v. Sega of America, Inc.,* 144 Cal.App.4th 47, 50 Cal.Rptr.3d 607 (2006).

12. In contracts for the sale of goods, Article 2 of the Uniform Commercial Code distinguishes, for warranty purposes, between statements of opinion (puffery) and statements of fact. See Chapter 17 for a further discussion of this issue.

Statement of Fact versus Opinion

Normally, the tort of misrepresentation or fraud occurs only when there is reliance on a *statement of fact*. Sometimes, however, the tort may involve reliance on a *statement of opinion* if the individual making the statement has a superior knowledge of the subject matter. For instance, when a lawyer makes a statement of opinion about the law in a state in which the lawyer is licensed to practice, a court would construe reliance on that statement to be equivalent to reliance on a statement of fact. We will examine fraudulent misrepresentation in further detail in Chapter 12, in the context of contract law.

Negligent Misrepresentation

Sometimes, a tort action can arise from misrepresentations that are made negligently rather than intentionally. The key difference between intentional and negligent misrepresentation is whether the person making the misrepresentation had actual knowledge of its falsity. Negligent misrepresentation requires only that the person making the statement or omission did not have a reasonable basis for believing its truthfulness. Liability for negligent misrepresentation usually arises when the defendant who made the misrepresentation owed a duty of care to the particular plaintiff to supply correct information. Statements or omissions made by attorneys and accountants to their clients, for example, can lead to liability for negligent misrepresentation.

Abusive or Frivolous Litigation

Persons or businesses generally have a right to sue when they have been injured, but they do not have a right to file meritless lawsuits or use the legal system simply to harass others. Tort law recognizes that people have a right not to be sued without a legally just and proper reason, and therefore it protects individuals from the misuse of litigation. Torts related to abusive litigation include malicious prosecution and abuse of process.

If a person initiates a lawsuit out of malice and without probable cause (a legitimate legal reason), and ends up losing the suit, he or she can be sued for *malicious prosecution*. In some states, the plaintiff (who was the defendant in the first proceeding) must also prove injury beyond the normal costs of litigation, such as lost profits. *Abuse of process* can apply to any person using a legal process against another in an improper manner or to accomplish a purpose for which it was not designed. The key difference between the torts of abuse of process and malicious prosecution is the level of proof required to succeed.

Abuse of process does not require the plaintiff to prove malice or show that the defendant (who was previously the plaintiff) lost in a prior legal proceeding. In addition, an abuse of process claim is not limited to prior litigation. It can be based on the wrongful use of subpoenas, court orders to attach or seize real property, or other types of formal legal process.

Wrongful Interference

Business torts involving wrongful interference are generally divided into two categories: wrongful interference with a contractual relationship and wrongful interference with a business relationship.

Wrongful Interference with a Contractual Relationship

Three elements are necessary for wrongful interference with a contractual relationship to occur:

1. A valid, enforceable contract must exist between two parties.
2. A third party must know that this contract exists.
3. The third party must *intentionally* induce a party to breach the contract.

CASE EXAMPLE 4.13 A landmark case involved an opera singer, Joanna Wagner, who was under contract to sing for a man named Lumley for a specified period of years. A man named Gye, who knew of this contract, nonetheless "enticed" Wagner to refuse to carry out the agreement, and Wagner began to sing for Gye. Gye's action constituted a tort because it wrongfully interfered with the contractual relationship between Wagner and Lumley.[13] (Of course, Wagner's refusal to carry out the agreement also entitled Lumley to sue Wagner for breach of contract.) •

The body of tort law relating to intentional interference with a contractual relationship has expanded greatly in recent years. In principle, any lawful contract can be the basis for an action of this type. The contract could be between a firm and its employees or a firm and its customers. Sometimes, a competitor draws away one of a firm's key employees. To recover damages from the competitor, the original employer must show that the competitor knew of the contract's existence and intentionally induced the breach.

Wrongful Interference with a Business Relationship Businesspersons devise countless schemes to attract customers, but they are prohibited from unreasonably interfering with another's business in their attempts to gain a share of the market. There is a difference between *competitive methods* and *predatory behavior*—actions undertaken with the intention of unlawfully driving competitors completely out of the market.

Attempting to attract customers in general is a legitimate business practice, whereas specifically targeting the customers of a competitor is more likely to be predatory. **EXAMPLE 4.14** A shopping mall contains two athletic shoe stores: Joe's and Ultimate Sport. Joe's cannot station an employee at the entrance of Ultimate Sport to divert customers by telling them that Joe's will beat Ultimate Sport's prices. This type of activity constitutes the tort of wrongful interference with a business relationship, which is commonly considered to be an unfair trade practice. If this activity were permitted, Joe's would reap the benefits of Ultimate Sport's advertising. •

Defenses to Wrongful Interference A person can avoid liability for the tort of wrongful interference with a contractual or business relationship by showing that the interference was justified or permissible.

Bona fide competitive behavior is a permissible interference even if it results in the breaking of a contract. **EXAMPLE 4.15** If Antonio's Meats advertises so effectively that it induces Sam's Restaurant to break its contract with Burke's Meat Company, Burke's will be unable to recover against Antonio's Meats on a wrongful interference theory. After all, the public policy that favors free competition in advertising outweighs any possible instability that such competitive activity might cause in contractual relations. •

Although luring customers away from a competitor through aggressive marketing and advertising obviously interferes with the competitor's relationship with its customers, courts typically allow such activities in the spirit of competition. (For a discussion of Facebook's advertising campaign that alleged sweeping privacy violations by Google's social network, see this chapter's *Adapting the Law to the Online Environment* on the next page.)

⟜ KNOW THIS ⟜

What society and the law consider permissible often depends on the circumstances.

Intentional Torts against Property

Intentional torts against property include trespass to land, trespass to personal property, conversion, and disparagement of property. These torts are wrongful actions that interfere with individuals' legally recognized rights with regard to their land or personal property.

---

13. *Lumley v. Gye,* 118 Eng.Rep. 749 (1853).

ADAPTING THE LAW TO THE ONLINE ENVIRONMENT

FACEBOOK USES PRIVACY CONCERNS TO "SMEAR" GOOGLE

With close to one billion users, Facebook is the largest social network in the world. Although Facebook has had various competitors, none has posed as much of a threat as Google. Several years ago, Google added a social-networking feature called Social Circles that eventually became part of Google+. Today, Google+ has more than 100 million users and is growing faster than Facebook.

Privacy Policies Matter

For many users of social networks, privacy is a major concern. Facebook has faced a number of complaints about its privacy policy and has changed its policy several times to satisfy its critics and to ward off potential government investigations. One of Google's main advertising points has been its social network's ability to keep "conversations" private and limited to as few individuals as users desire.

As the rivalry between Google and Facebook intensified, Facebook hired Burson-Marsteller, a public relations firm, to plant anonymous stories raising questions about Google's privacy policy. Although Facebook later claimed that Burson-Marsteller was only supposed to investigate how Social Circles collected and used data, several influential bloggers reported that they were approached by Burson-Marsteller and asked to publish negative stories about privacy concerns on Social Circles. In some instances, Burson-Marsteller even offered to supply the stories—one would have claimed that Social Circles "enables people to trace their contacts' connections and profile information by crawling and scraping the sites you and your contacts use, such as Twitter, YouTube, and Facebook."

The Campaign Backfires

If Facebook's goal was to discredit Google, the plan failed dramatically. Bloggers across the Web responded with a mixture of derision and amazement. Some pointed out that planting anonymous stories violated Facebook's privacy policy for its own site, while others said that Facebook's effort to attack Google showed that the social-networking giant was running scared. Writing in *Wired* magazine, Steven Levy concluded that "Facebook was running a smear campaign against itself."[a]

Critical Thinking

If you were part of Google's legal team, on what basis might you think that you could sue Facebook and its public relations firm?

---

a. Steven Levy, "Facebook's Stealth Attack on Google Exposes Its Own Privacy Problem," *Wired*, May 12, 2011. See also Sam Gustin, "Burson-Marsteller Deletes Critical Facebook Posts, Spares Google-Smear Flacks," *Wired*, May 13, 2011; David Sarno, "Sibling Rivalry? Facebook vs. Google," *Los Angeles Times*, May 13, 2011; and Barbara Ortutay, "Facebook-Google Rivalry Intensifies with PR Fiasco," *Huffington Post*, May 12, 2011.

The law distinguishes real property from personal property (see Chapters 35 and 36). *Real property* is land and things "permanently" attached to the land. *Personal property* consists of all other items, which are basically movable. Thus, a house and lot are real property, whereas the furniture inside the house is personal property. Cash and stocks and bonds are also personal property.

Trespass to Land

Trespass to Land Entry onto, above, or below the surface of land owned by another without the owner's permission or legal authorization.

A **trespass to land** occurs anytime a person, without permission, enters onto, above, or below the surface of land that is owned by another; causes anything to enter onto the land; or remains on the land or permits anything to remain on it. Actual harm to the land is not an essential element of this tort because the tort is designed to protect the right of an owner to exclusive possession of her or his property.

Common types of trespass to land include walking or driving on someone else's land, shooting a gun over the land, throwing rocks at a building that belongs to someone else, building a dam across a river and thereby causing water to back up on someone else's land, and constructing a building so that part of it is on an adjoining landowner's property.

Trespass Criteria, Rights, and Duties   Before a person can be a trespasser, the real property owner (or other person in actual and exclusive possession of the property) must establish that person as a trespasser. For example, "posted" trespass signs expressly establish as a trespasser a person who ignores these signs and enters onto the property. A guest in your home is not a trespasser—unless she or he has been asked to leave but refuses. Any person who enters onto your property to commit an illegal act (such as a thief entering a lumberyard at night to steal lumber) is established impliedly as a trespasser, without posted signs.

At common law, a trespasser is liable for any damage caused to the property and generally cannot hold the owner liable for injuries sustained on the premises. This common law rule is being abandoned in many jurisdictions in favor of a *reasonable duty of care* rule that varies depending on the status of the parties. For instance, a landowner may have a duty to post a notice that guard dogs patrol the property. Also, under the *attractive nuisance* doctrine, children do not assume the risks of the premises if they are attracted to the property by some object, such as a swimming pool, an abandoned building, or a sand pile. Trespassers normally can be removed from the premises through the use of reasonable force without the owner being liable for assault, battery, or false imprisonment.

Defenses against Trespass to Land   One defense to a claim of trespass to land is to show that the trespass was warranted—for instance, that the trespasser entered the property to assist someone in danger. Another defense is for the trespasser to show that he or she had a license to come onto the land. A *licensee* is one who is invited (or allowed to enter) onto the property of another for the licensee's benefit. A person who enters another's property to read an electric meter, for example, is a licensee. When you purchase a ticket to attend a movie or sporting event, you are licensed to go onto the property of another to view that movie or event.

Note that licenses to enter are *revocable* by the property owner. If a property owner asks a meter reader to leave and the meter reader refuses to do so, the meter reader at that point becomes a trespasser.

Trespass to Personal Property

Trespass to Personal Property
Wrongfully taking or harming the personal property of another or otherwise interfering with the lawful owner's possession of personal property.

Whenever an individual wrongfully takes or harms the personal property of another or otherwise interferes with the lawful owner's possession of personal property, **trespass to personal property** occurs (also called *trespass to chattels* or *trespass to personalty*[14]). In this context, harm means not only destruction of the property, but also anything that diminishes its value, condition, or quality.

Trespass to personal property involves intentional meddling with a possessory interest (the right to possess), including barring an owner's access to personal property. **EXAMPLE 4.16**   Kelly takes Ryan's business law book as a practical joke and hides it so that Ryan is unable to find it for several days before the final examination. Here, Kelly has engaged in a trespass to personal property. (Kelly has also committed the tort of *conversion*—to be discussed next.) ●

A complete defense to a claim of trespass to personal property is to show that the trespass was warranted. Most states, for example, allow automobile repair shops to retain a customer's car (under what is called an *artisan's lien*—see Chapter 21) when the customer refuses to pay for repairs already completed.

---

14. Pronounced *per-sun-ul-tee.*

Conversion

Whenever a person wrongfully possesses or uses the personal property of another without permission, the tort of **conversion** occurs. Any act that deprives an owner of personal property or the use of that property without that owner's permission and without just cause can be conversion. Even the taking of electronic records and data can be a form of conversion.[15]

Often, when conversion occurs, a trespass to personal property also occurs because the original taking of the personal property from the owner was a trespass, and wrongfully retaining it is conversion. Conversion is the civil side of crimes related to theft, but it is not limited to theft. Even if the rightful owner consented to the initial taking of the property, so there was no theft or trespass, a failure to return the personal property may still be conversion. **EXAMPLE 4.17**   Chen borrows Mark's iPad to use while traveling home from school for the holidays. When Chen returns to school, Mark asks for his iPad back. Chen tells Mark that she gave it to her little brother for Christmas. In this situation, Mark can sue Chen for conversion, and Chen will have to either return the iPad or pay damages equal to its replacement value. •

Even if a person mistakenly believed that she or he was entitled to the goods, the tort of conversion may occur. In other words, good intentions are not a defense against conversion. In fact, conversion can be an entirely innocent act. Someone who buys stolen goods, for example, can be liable for conversion even if he or she did not know that the goods were stolen. If the true owner brings a tort action against the buyer, the buyer must either return the property to the owner or pay the owner the full value of the property, despite having already paid the purchase price to the thief. A successful defense against the charge of conversion is that the purported owner does not, in fact, own the property or does not have a right to possess it that is superior to the right of the holder.

Disparagement of Property

Disparagement of property occurs when economically injurious falsehoods are made about another's product or property, not about another's reputation. Disparagement of property is a general term for torts specifically referred to as *slander of quality* or *slander of title*. Publication of false information about another's product, alleging that it is not what its seller claims, constitutes the tort of **slander of quality,** or **trade libel.** To establish trade libel, the plaintiff must prove that the improper publication caused a third party to refrain from dealing with the plaintiff and that the plaintiff sustained economic damages (such as lost profits) as a result.

An improper publication may be both a slander of quality and defamation of character. For example, a statement that disparages the quality of a product may also, by implication, disparage the character of the person who would sell such a product.

When a publication denies or casts doubt on another's legal ownership of any property, and the property's owner suffers financial loss as a result, the tort of **slander of title** may exist. Usually, this is an intentional tort that occurs when someone knowingly publishes an untrue statement about property with the intent of discouraging a third party from dealing with the property's owner. For instance, a car dealer would have difficulty attracting customers after competitors published a notice that the dealer's stock consisted of stolen automobiles.

---

15. See, for example, *Thyroff v. Nationwide Mutual Insurance Co.*, 8 N.Y.3d 283, 864 N.E.2d 1272, 832 N.Y.S.2d 873 (2007).

Unintentional Torts (Negligence)

Negligence The failure to exercise the standard of care that a reasonable person would exercise in similar circumstances.

The tort of **negligence** occurs when someone suffers injury because of another's failure to live up to a required *duty of care*. In contrast to intentional torts, in torts involving negligence, the tortfeasor neither wishes to bring about the consequences of the act nor believes that they will occur. The actor's conduct merely creates a *risk* of such consequences. If no risk is created, there is no negligence. Moreover, the risk must be foreseeable—that is, it must be such that a reasonable person engaging in the same activity would anticipate the risk and guard against it. In determining what is reasonable conduct, courts consider the nature of the possible harm.

LEARNING OBJECTIVE 4
Identify the four elements of negligence.

Many of the actions discussed earlier in the chapter in the section on intentional torts constitute negligence if the element of intent is missing. **EXAMPLE 4.18** Juan walks up to Maya and intentionally shoves her. Maya falls and breaks an arm as a result. In this situation, Juan has committed an intentional tort (assault and battery). If Juan carelessly bumps into Maya, however, and she falls and breaks an arm as a result, Juan's action will constitute negligence. In either situation, Juan has committed a tort. ●

To succeed in a negligence action, the plaintiff must prove each of the following:

1. *Duty.* That the defendant owed a duty of care to the plaintiff.
2. *Breach.* That the defendant breached that duty.
3. *Causation.* That the defendant's breach caused the plaintiff's injury.
4. *Damages.* That the plaintiff suffered a legally recognizable injury.

We discuss each of these four elements of negligence next.

The Duty of Care and Its Breach

Duty of Care The duty of all persons, as established by tort law, to exercise a reasonable amount of care in their dealings with others. Failure to exercise due care, which is normally determined by the reasonable person standard, constitutes the tort of negligence.

Central to the tort of negligence is the concept of a **duty of care.** The basic principle underlying the duty of care is that people in society are free to act as they please so long as their actions do not infringe on the interests of others.

When someone fails to comply with the duty to exercise reasonable care, a potentially tortious act may have been committed. Failure to live up to a standard of care may be an act (setting fire to a building) or an omission (neglecting to put out a campfire). It may be a careless act or a carefully performed but nevertheless dangerous act that results in injury.

Reasonable Person Standard The standard of behavior expected of a hypothetical "reasonable person." It is the standard against which negligence is measured and that must be observed to avoid liability for negligence.

Courts consider the nature of the act (whether it is outrageous or commonplace), the manner in which the act was performed (cautiously versus heedlessly), and the nature of the injury (whether it is serious or slight).

The Reasonable Person Standard Tort law measures duty by the **reasonable person standard.** In determining whether a duty of care has been breached, the courts ask how a reasonable person would have acted in the same circumstances. The reasonable person standard is said to be (though in an absolute sense it cannot be) objective. It is not necessarily how a particular person would act. It is society's judgment on how people *should* act. If the so-called reasonable person existed, he or she would be careful, conscientious, even tempered, and honest.

The courts frequently use this hypothetical reasonable person in decisions relating to other areas of law as well. That individuals are required to exercise a reasonable standard of care in

"Do you have any picture books that could help a child understand tort reform?"

their activities is a pervasive concept in business law, and many of the issues discussed in subsequent chapters of this text have to do with this duty.

In negligence cases, the degree of care to be exercised varies, depending on the defendant's occupation or profession, her or his relationship with the plaintiff, and other factors. Generally, whether an action constitutes a breach of the duty of care is determined on a case-by-case basis. The outcome depends on how the judge (or jury, if it is a jury trial) decides a reasonable person in the position of the defendant would act in the particular circumstances of the case.

ETHICAL ISSUE

Does a pharmacist's duty of care include a duty to warn customers of certain adverse effects when filling prescriptions? Pharmacists typically discuss the potential side effects of prescription medications with the customer when they first fill a prescription. Under what is known as the "learned intermediary doctrine," pharmacists are generally *immune* from liability for any negative effects resulting from medications that were prescribed by the customer's physician (the intermediary). Nevertheless, according to the Nevada Supreme Court, pharmacists may have a duty to warn a customer in some situations, if they are aware of certain customer-specific risks, such as allergies. The case involved a pharmacist at a Walgreen drugstore who filled a prescription for a woman even though the pharmacy's computer indicated that she was allergic to the medication prescribed. The woman subsequently died when her condition worsened. The court concluded that the pharmacist should have either warned the customer or notified the prescribing physician. The court noted, however, that the duty to warn exists only when the pharmacist *knows* of a possible adverse effect for the specific customer.[16]

> "A little neglect may breed great mischief."
>
> Benjamin Franklin, 1706–1790 (American politician and inventor)

Business Invitee A person, such as a customer or a client, who is invited onto business premises by the owner of those premises for business purposes.

The Duty of Landowners

Landowners are expected to exercise reasonable care to protect persons coming onto their property from harm. As mentioned earlier, in some jurisdictions, landowners are held to owe a duty to protect even trespassers against certain risks. Landowners who rent or lease premises to tenants (see Chapter 36) are expected to exercise reasonable care to ensure that the tenants and their guests are not harmed in common areas, such as stairways, entryways, and laundry rooms.

Duty to Warn Business Invitees of Risks   Retailers and other firms that explicitly or implicitly invite persons to come onto their premises are usually charged with a duty to exercise reasonable care to protect those persons, who are considered **business invitees.** **EXAMPLE 4.19** Liz enters a supermarket, slips on a wet floor, and sustains injuries as a result. If there was no sign warning that the floor was wet when Liz slipped, the owner of the supermarket would be liable for damages. A court would hold that the business owner was negligent because the owner failed to exercise a reasonable degree of care in protecting the store's customers against foreseeable risks about which the owner knew or *should have known*. That a patron might slip on the wet floor and be injured was a foreseeable risk, and the owner should have taken care to avoid this risk or to warn the customer of it (by posting a sign or setting out orange cones, for example). •

The landowner also has a duty to discover and remove any hidden dangers that might injure a customer or other invitee. Store owners have a duty to protect customers from potentially slipping and injuring themselves on merchandise that has fallen off the shelves, for instance.

Obvious Risks Are an Exception   Some risks, of course, are so obvious that the owner need not warn of them. For instance, a business owner does not need to warn customers to open a door before attempting to walk through it. Other risks, however, may seem obvious to a business owner but may not be so to someone else, such as a child. In addition, even if a risk is obvious, that does not necessarily excuse a business owner from the duty to protect its customers from foreseeable harm.

---

16. *Klasch v. Walgreen Co.*, 264 P.3d 1155 (Nev. 2011).

CASE EXAMPLE 4.20   Giorgio's Grill in Hollywood, Florida, is a restaurant that becomes a nightclub after hours. At those times, traditionally, as the manager of Giorgio's knew, the staff and customers throw paper napkins into the air as the music played. The napkins land on the floor, but no one picks them up. One night, Jane Izquierdo went to Giorgio's. Although she had been to the club on other occasions and knew about the napkin-throwing tradition, she slipped on a napkin and fell, breaking her leg. She sued Giorgio's for negligence but lost at trial because the jury found that the risk of slipping on the napkins was obvious. A state appellate court reversed, however, holding that the obviousness of a risk does not discharge a business owner's duty to its invitees to maintain the premises in a safe condition.[17] ●

....

PREVENTING LEGAL DISPUTES

It can be difficult to determine whether a risk is obvious. Because you can be held liable if you fail to discover hidden dangers on business premises that could cause injuries to customers, you should post warnings of any conceivable risks on the property. Be vigilant and frequently reassess potential hazards. Train your employees to be on the lookout for possibly dangerous conditions at all times and to notify a superior immediately if they notice something. Remember that a finding of liability in a single lawsuit can leave a small enterprise close to bankruptcy. To prevent potential negligence liability, make sure that your business premises are as safe as possible for all persons who might be there, including children, senior citizens, and individuals with disabilities.

The Duty of Professionals

If an individual has knowledge, skill, or training superior to that of an ordinary person, the individual's conduct must be consistent with that status. Because professionals—such as physicians, dentists, architects, engineers, accountants, and lawyers—are required to have a certain level of knowledge and training, a higher standard of care applies. In determining whether professionals have exercised reasonable care, the law takes their training and expertise into account. Thus, an accountant's conduct is judged not by the reasonable person standard, but by the reasonable accountant standard.

Malpractice Professional misconduct or the lack of the requisite degree of skill as a professional. Negligence — the failure to exercise due care — on the part of a professional, such as a physician, is commonly referred to as malpractice.

If a professional violates her or his duty of care toward a client, the professional may be sued for **malpractice**, which is essentially professional negligence. For example, a patient might sue a physician for *medical malpractice*. A client might sue an attorney for *legal malpractice*. We will discuss the liability of accountants and attorneys in more detail in Chapter 34.

Causation

Another necessary element in a negligence action is *causation*. If a person fails in a duty of care and someone suffers an injury, the wrongful act must have caused the harm for the act to be considered a tort.

Courts Ask Two Questions

In deciding whether there is causation, the court must address two questions:

1. *Is there causation in fact?* Did the injury occur because of the defendant's act, or would it have occurred anyway? If an injury would not have occurred without the defendant's act, then there is causation in fact. **Causation in fact** can usually be determined by the use of the *but for* test: "but for" the wrongful act, the injury would not have occurred. Theoretically, causation in fact is limitless. One could claim, for example, that "but for"

Causation in Fact An act or omission without which an event would not have occurred.

17. *Izquierdo v. Gyroscope, Inc.,* 946 So.2d 115 (Fla.App. 2007).

Proximate Cause Legal cause. It exists when the connection between an act and an injury is strong enough to justify imposing liability.

the creation of the world, a particular injury would not have occurred. Thus, as a practical matter, the law has to establish limits, and it does so through the concept of proximate cause.

2. *Was the act the proximate cause of the injury?* **Proximate cause,** or legal cause, exists when the connection between an act and an injury is strong enough to justify imposing liability. Courts use proximate cause to limit the scope of the defendant's liability to a subset of the total number of potential plaintiffs that might have been harmed by the defendant's actions. **EXAMPLE 4.21** Ackerman carelessly leaves a campfire burning. The fire not only burns down the forest but also sets off an explosion in a nearby chemical plant that spills chemicals into a river, killing all the fish for a hundred miles downstream and ruining the economy of a tourist resort. Should Ackerman be liable to the resort owners? To the tourists whose vacations were ruined? These are questions of proximate cause that a court must decide. ●

Both of these questions regarding causation in fact and proximate cause must be answered in the affirmative for liability in tort to arise. If a defendant's action constitutes causation in fact but a court decides that the action was not the proximate cause of the plaintiff's injury, the causation requirement has not been met—and the defendant normally will not be liable to the plaintiff.

➤ **KNOW THIS** ➤

Proximate cause can be thought of in terms of a question of social policy. Should the defendant be made to bear the loss instead of the plaintiff?

Foreseeability   Questions of proximate cause are linked to the concept of foreseeability because it would be unfair to impose liability on a defendant unless the defendant's actions created a foreseeable risk of injury. Probably the most cited case on proximate cause is the *Palsgraf* case, which is discussed in this chapter's *Landmark in the Law* feature on the facing page. In determining the issue of proximate cause, the court addressed the following question: Does a defendant's duty of care extend only to those who may be injured as a result of a foreseeable risk, or does it also extend to a person whose injury could not reasonably be foreseen?

The Injury Requirement and Damages

For a tort to have been committed, the plaintiff must have suffered a *legally recognizable* injury. To recover damages (receive compensation), the plaintiff must have suffered some loss, harm, wrong, or invasion of a protected interest. Essentially, the purpose of tort law is to compensate for legally recognized injuries resulting from wrongful acts. If no harm or injury results from a given negligent action, there is nothing to compensate—and no tort exists. **EXAMPLE 4.22** If you carelessly bump into a passerby, who stumbles and falls as a result, you may be liable in tort if the passerby is injured in the fall. If the person is unharmed, however, there normally cannot be a suit for damages because no injury was suffered. ●

Compensatory damages are the norm in negligence cases. As noted earlier, a court will award punitive damages only if the defendant's conduct was grossly negligent, reflecting an intentional failure to perform a duty with reckless disregard of the consequences to others.

Injuries from car accidents can cause handicaps that last a lifetime. Do such injuries satisfy the injury requirement for a finding of a negligence tort?

(Joyce Marshall/Fort Worth Star-Telegram/MCT via Getty Images)

Defenses to Negligence

Defendants often defend against negligence claims by asserting that the plaintiffs failed to prove the existence of one or more of the required elements for negligence. Additionally,

LANDMARK IN THE LAW
Palsgraf v. Long Island Railroad Co. (1928)

In 1928, the New York Court of Appeals (that state's highest court) issued its decision in *Palsgraf v. Long Island Railroad Co.*,[a] a case that has become a landmark in negligence law and proximate cause.

The Facts of the Case The plaintiff, Helen Palsgraf, was waiting for a train on a station platform. A man carrying a small package wrapped in newspaper was rushing to catch a train that had begun to move away from the platform. As the man attempted to jump aboard the moving train, he seemed unsteady and about to fall. A railroad guard on the train car reached forward to grab him, and another guard on the platform pushed him from behind to help him board the train. In the process, the man's package fell on the railroad tracks and exploded, because it contained fireworks. The repercussions of the explosion caused scales at the other end of the train platform to fall on Palsgraf, who was injured as a result. She sued the railroad company for damages in a New York state court.

The Question of Proximate Cause At the trial, the jury found that the railroad guards were negligent in their conduct. On appeal, the question before the New York Court of Appeals was whether the conduct of the railroad guards was the proximate cause of Palsgraf's injuries. In other words, did the guards' duty of care extend to Palsgraf, who was outside the zone of danger and whose injury could not reasonably have been foreseen?

The court stated that the question of whether the guards were negligent *with respect to Palsgraf* depended on whether her injury was *reasonably foreseeable* by the railroad guards. Although the guards may have acted negligently with respect to the man boarding the train, this had no bearing on the question of their negligence with respect to Palsgraf. This was not a situation in which a person commited an act so potentially harmful (for example, firing a gun at a building) that he or she would be held responsible for any harm that resulted. The court stated that here "there was nothing in the situation to suggest to the most cautious mind that the parcel wrapped in newspaper would spread wreckage through the station." The court thus concluded that the railroad guards were not negligent with respect to Palsgraf because her injury was not reasonably foreseeable.

Application to Today's World *The Palsgraf case established foreseeability as the test for proximate cause. Today, the courts continue to apply this test in determining proximate cause—and thus tort liability for injuries. Generally, if the victim of a harm or the consequences of a harm done are unforeseeable, there is no proximate cause. Note, though, that in the online environment, distinctions based on physical proximity, such as the "zone of danger" cited by the court in this case, are largely inapplicable.*

a. 248 N.Y. 339, 162 N.E. 99 (1928).

there are three basic *affirmative* defenses in negligence cases (defenses that a defendant can use to avoid liability even if the facts are as the plaintiff states): (1) assumption of risk, (2) superseding cause, and (3) contributory and comparative negligence.

Assumption of Risk A defense to negligence. A plaintiff may not recover for injuries or damage suffered from risks he or she knows of and has voluntarily assumed.

Assumption of Risk A plaintiff who voluntarily enters into a risky situation, knowing the risk involved, will not be allowed to recover. This is the defense of **assumption of risk.** The requirements of this defense are (1) knowledge of the risk and (2) voluntary assumption of the risk. This defense is frequently asserted when the plaintiff is injured during recreational activities that involve known risk, such as skiing and skydiving. Note that assumption of risk can apply not only to participants in sporting events, but also to spectators and bystanders who are injured while attending those events.

The risk can be assumed by express agreement, or the assumption of risk can be implied by the plaintiff's knowledge of the risk and subsequent conduct. Courts do not apply the assumption of risk doctrine in emergency situations, though.

In the following case, the issue was whether a spectator at a baseball game voluntarily assumed the risk of being hit by an errant ball thrown while the players were warming up before the game.

Spotlight on the Seattle Mariners

Case 4.3
Taylor v. Baseball Club of Seattle, L.P.
Court of Appeals of Washington, 132 Wash.App. 32, 130 P.3d 835 (2006).

Many fans arrive at baseball games early so they can watch the players warm up.

FACTS Delinda Middleton Taylor went to a Mariners baseball game at Safeco Field with her boyfriend and two minor sons. Their seats were four rows up from the field along the right field foul line. They arrived more than an hour before the game began so that they could see the players warm up and get their autographs. When she walked in, Taylor saw that Mariners pitcher Freddy Garcia was throwing a ball back and forth with José Mesa right in front of their seats. As Taylor stood in front of her seat, she looked away from the field, and a ball thrown by Mesa got past Garcia and struck her in the face, causing serious injuries. Taylor sued the Mariners for the allegedly negligent warm-up throw. The Mariners filed a motion for a summary judgment in which they argued that Taylor, a Mariners fan, was familiar with baseball and the inherent risk of balls entering the stands, and therefore assumed the risk of her injury. The trial court granted the motion and dismissed Taylor's case. Taylor appealed.

ISSUE Was the risk of injury from an errant baseball thrown during pregame warm-up foreseeable to a reasonable person with Taylor's familiarity with baseball?

DECISION Yes. The state intermediate appellate court affirmed the lower court's judgment. Taylor, as a spectator in an unprotected area of seats, voluntarily undertook the risk associated with being hit by an errant baseball thrown during warm-ups before the start of the game.

REASON The court observed that there was substantial evidence that Taylor was familiar with the game. She was a seasoned Mariners fan, and both of her sons had played baseball for at least six years. "She attended many of her sons' baseball games, she witnessed balls entering the stands, she had watched Mariners' games both at the Kingdome and on television, and she knew that there was no screen protecting her seats, which were close to the field. In fact, as she walked to her seat she saw the players warming up and was excited about being in an unscreened area where her party might get autographs from the players and catch balls." It was not legally relevant that the injury occurred during the pregame warm-up because "it is the normal, every-day practice at all levels of baseball for pitchers to warm up in the manner that led to this incident." The Mariners had satisfied their duty to protect spectators from balls entering the stands by providing a protective screen behind home plate. Taylor chose not to sit in the protected area and thus knowingly put herself at risk.

CRITICAL THINKING—Ethical Consideration *Would the result in this case have been different if Taylor's minor son, rather than Taylor herself, had been struck by the ball? Should courts apply the doctrine of assumption of risk to children? Discuss.*

Superseding Cause
An unforeseeable intervening event may break the connection between a wrongful act and an injury to another. If so, the event acts as a *superseding cause*—that is, it relieves a defendant of liability for injuries caused by the intervening event. **EXAMPLE 4.23**   While riding his bicycle, Derrick negligently hits Julie, who is walking on the sidewalk. As a result of the impact, Julie falls and fractures her hip. While she is waiting for help to arrive, a small plane crashes nearby and explodes, and some of the fiery debris hits her, causing her to sustain severe burns. Derrick will be liable for Julie's fractured hip because the risk of hitting her with his bicycle was foreseeable. Normally, Derrick will not be liable for the burns caused by the plane crash—because the risk of a plane's crashing nearby and injuring Julie was not foreseeable. ●

Contributory Negligence A rule in tort law, used in only a few states, that completely bars the plaintiff from recovering any damages if the damage suffered is partly the plaintiff's own fault.

Contributory and Comparative Negligence
All individuals are expected to exercise a reasonable degree of care in looking out for themselves. In the past, under the common law doctrine of **contributory negligence**, a plaintiff who was also negligent (failed to exercise a reasonable degree of care) could not recover anything from

the defendant. Under this rule, no matter how insignificant the plaintiff's negligence was relative to the defendant's negligence, the plaintiff was precluded from recovering any damages. Today, only a few jurisdictions still hold to this doctrine.

Comparative Negligence A rule in tort law, used in the majority of states, that reduces the plaintiff's recovery in proportion to the plaintiff's degree of fault, rather than barring recovery completely.

In most states, the doctrine of contributory negligence has been replaced by a **comparative negligence** standard. Under this standard, both the plaintiff's and the defendant's negligence are computed, and the liability for damages is distributed accordingly. Some jurisdictions have adopted a "pure" form of comparative negligence that allows the plaintiff to recover, even if the extent of his or her fault is greater than that of the defendant. For example, if the plaintiff was 80 percent at fault and the defendant 20 percent at fault, the plaintiff may recover 20 percent of his or her damages. Many states' comparative negligence statutes, however, contain a "50 percent" rule that prevents the plaintiff from recovering any damages if she or he was more than 50 percent at fault. Under this rule, a plaintiff who is 35 percent at fault could recover 65 percent of his or her damages, but a plaintiff who is 65 percent (more than 50 percent) at fault could recover nothing.

Special Negligence Doctrines and Statutes

There are a number of special doctrines and statutes relating to negligence. We examine a few of them here.

Res Ipsa Loquitur

Res Ipsa Loquitur A doctrine under which negligence may be inferred simply because an event occurred, if it is the type of event that would not occur in the absence of negligence. Literally, the term means "the facts speak for themselves."

Generally, in lawsuits involving negligence, the plaintiff has the burden of proving that the defendant was negligent. In certain situations, however, under the doctrine of *res ipsa loquitur*[18] (meaning "the facts speak for themselves"), the courts may infer that negligence has occurred. Then the burden of proof rests on the defendant—to prove she or he was *not* negligent. This doctrine is applied only when the event creating the damage or injury is one that ordinarily would occur only as a result of negligence.

CASE EXAMPLE 4.24   Mary Gubbins undergoes abdominal surgery and following the surgery has nerve damage in her spine near the area of the operation. She is unable to walk or stand for months, and even after regaining some use of her legs through physical therapy, her mobility is impaired and she experiences pain. In her subsequent negligence lawsuit, Gubbins can assert *res ipsa loquitur,* because the injury would never have occurred in the absence of the surgeon's negligence.[19] ●

Negligence Per Se

Negligence Per Se An action or failure to act in violation of a statutory requirement.

Certain conduct, whether it consists of an action or a failure to act, may be treated as **negligence *per se*** (*per se* means "in or of itself"). Negligence *per se* may occur if an individual violates a statute or ordinance and thereby causes the kind of harm that the statute was intended to prevent. The statute must clearly set out what standard of conduct is expected, when and where it is expected, and of whom it is expected. The standard of conduct required by the statute is the duty that the defendant owes to the plaintiff, and a violation of the statute is the breach of that duty.

CASE EXAMPLE 4.25   A Delaware statute states that anyone "who operates a motor vehicle and who fails to give full time and attention to the operation of the vehicle" is guilty of inattentive driving. Michael Moore was cited for inattentive driving after he collided with Debra Wright's car when he backed a truck out of a parking space. Moore paid the ticket, which meant that he pleaded guilty to violating the statute. The day after the accident, Wright began having back pain, which eventually required surgery. She sued Moore for damages, alleging negligence *per se*. The Delaware Supreme Court ruled that the inattentive driving statute set forth a sufficiently specific standard of conduct to warrant application of negligence *per se*.[20] ●

---

18. Pronounced *rehz ihp*-suh *low*-kwuh-tuhr.
19. *Gubbins v. Hurson*, 885 A.2d 269 (D.C. 2005).
20. *Wright v. Moore*, 931 A.2d 405 (Del.Supr. 2007).

"Danger Invites Rescue" Doctrine   Sometimes, a person who is trying to avoid harm—such as an individual who swerves to avoid a head-on collision with a drunk driver—ends up causing harm to another (such as a cyclist riding in the bike lane) as a result. In those situations, the original wrongdoer (the drunk driver in this scenario) is liable to anyone who is injured, even if the injury actually resulted from another person's attempt to escape harm. The "danger invites rescue" doctrine extends the same protection to a person who is trying to rescue another from harm—the original wrongdoer is liable for injuries to an individual attempting a rescue. The idea is that the rescuer should not be held liable for any damages because he or she did not cause the danger and because danger invites rescue.

EXAMPLE 4.26   Ludley drives down a street but fails to see a stop sign because he is trying to quiet his squabbling children in the car's back seat. Salter, who is standing on the curb, realizes that Ludley is about to hit a pedestrian and runs into the street to push the pedestrian out of the way. If Ludley's vehicle hits Salter instead, Ludley will be liable for Salter's injury, as well as for any injuries the other pedestrian sustained. ● Whether rescuers injure themselves, the person rescued, or even a stranger, the original wrongdoer will still be liable.

Good Samaritan Statutes   Most states have enacted what are called **Good Samaritan statutes.**[21] Under these statutes, someone who is aided voluntarily by another cannot turn around and sue the "Good Samaritan" for negligence. These laws were passed largely to protect physicians and medical personnel who voluntarily render medical services in emergency situations to those in need, such as individuals hurt in car accidents. Indeed, the California Supreme Court has interpreted the state's Good Samaritan statute to mean that only a person who renders medical aid is immune from liability.[22] Thus, only medical personnel and persons rendering medical aid in emergencies are protected in California.

Dram Shop Acts   Many states have also passed **dram shop acts,**[23] under which a tavern owner or bartender may be held liable for injuries caused by a person who became intoxicated while drinking at the bar or who was already intoxicated when served by the bartender. Some states' statutes also impose liability on *social hosts* (persons hosting parties) for injuries caused by guests who became intoxicated at the hosts' homes. Under these statutes, it is unnecessary to prove that the tavern owner, bartender, or social host was negligent. **EXAMPLE 4.27**   Selena hosts a Super Bowl party at which Raul, a minor, sneaks alcoholic drinks. Selena is potentially liable for damages resulting from Raul's drunk driving after the party. ●

Strict Liability

Another category of torts is called **strict liability,** or *liability without fault.* Intentional torts and torts of negligence involve acts that depart from a reasonable standard of care and cause injuries. Under the doctrine of strict liability, liability for injury is imposed for reasons other than fault.

Good Samaritan Statute A state statute stipulating that persons who provide emergency services to, or rescue, someone in peril cannot be sued for negligence unless they act recklessly, thereby causing further harm.

Dram Shop Act A state statute that imposes liability on the owners of bars and taverns, as well as those who serve alcoholic drinks to the public, for injuries resulting from accidents caused by intoxicated persons when the sellers or servers of alcoholic drinks contributed to the intoxication.

LEARNING OBJECTIVE 5
What is meant by strict liability? In what circumstances is strict liability applied?

Strict Liability Liability regardless of fault, which is imposed on those engaged in abnormally dangerous activities, on persons who keep dangerous animals, and on manufacturers or sellers that introduce into commerce defective and unreasonably dangerous goods.

---

21. These laws derive their name from the Good Samaritan story in the Bible. In the story, a traveler who had been robbed and beaten lay along the roadside, ignored by those passing by. Eventually, a man from the country of Samaria (the "Good Samaritan") stopped to render assistance to the injured person.
22. *Van Horn v. Watson,* 45 Cal.4th 322, 197 P.3d 164, 86 Cal.Rptr.3d 350 (2008).
23. Historically, a *dram* was a small unit of liquid, and spirits were sold in drams. Thus, a dram shop was a place where liquor was sold in drams.

Abnormally Dangerous Activities

Strict liability for damages proximately caused by an abnormally dangerous or exceptional activity is one application of this doctrine. Courts apply the doctrine of strict liability in such cases because of the extreme risk of the activity. For instance, even if blasting with dynamite is performed with all reasonable care, there is still a risk of injury. Because of the potential for harm, the person who is engaged in an abnormally dangerous activity—and benefits from it—is responsible for paying for any injuries caused by that activity. Although there is no fault, there is still responsibility because of the dangerous nature of the undertaking.

Other Applications of Strict Liability

The strict liability principle is also applied in other situations. Persons who keep wild animals, for example, are strictly liable for any harm inflicted by the animals. In addition, an owner of domestic animals may be strictly liable for harm caused by those animals if the owner knew, or should have known, that the animals were dangerous or had a propensity to harm others.

A significant application of strict liability is in the area of *product liability*—liability of manufacturers and sellers for harmful or defective products. Liability here is a matter of social policy and is based on two factors: (1) the manufacturer or seller can better bear the cost of injury because it can spread the cost throughout society by increasing prices of goods and services, and (2) the manufacturer or seller is making a profit from its activities and therefore should bear the cost of injury as an operating expense. We will discuss product liability in greater detail in Chapter 17.

Cyber Torts

Torts can also be committed in the online environment. One of the most common types of *cyber torts* is online defamation, as we discuss next. We also discuss how the courts are attempting to address the problems associated with bulk, unsolicited, junk e-mails, or spam.

Identifying the Author of Online Defamation

An initial issue raised by online defamation was simply discovering who was committing it. In the real world, identifying the author of a defamatory remark generally is an easy matter, but suppose that a business firm has discovered that defamatory statements about its policies and products are being posted in an online forum. Such forums allow anyone—customers, employees, or crackpots—to complain about a firm that they dislike while remaining anonymous.

Therefore, a threshold barrier to anyone who seeks to bring an action for online defamation is discovering the identity of the person who posted the defamatory message. An Internet service provider (ISP)—a company that provides connections to the Internet—can disclose personal information about its customers only when ordered to do so by a court. Consequently, businesses and individuals are increasingly bringing lawsuits against "John Does" (John Doe, Jane Doe, and the like are fictitious names used in lawsuits when the identity of a party is not known or when a party wishes to conceal his or her name for privacy reasons). Then, using the authority of the courts, the plaintiffs can obtain from the ISPs the identity of the persons responsible for the defamatory messages.

(AP Photo/Joel Ryan)

Woody Allen sued a clothing company for using his image on the Web. Can the Internet service provider through which the offending ads were directed be held liable?

"Speech is not free when it comes postage due."

Jim Nitchals, 1962–1998
(Spam fighter and computer programmer)

Liability of Internet Service Providers

Recall from the discussion of defamation earlier in this chapter that those who repeat or otherwise disseminate defamatory statements made by others can be held liable for defamation. Thus, newspapers, magazines, and radio and television stations can be subject to liability for defamatory content that they publish or broadcast, even though the content was prepared or created by others. Applying this rule to cyberspace, however, raises an important issue: Should ISPs be regarded as publishers and therefore be held liable for defamatory messages that are posted by their users in online forums or other arenas?

Before 1996, the courts grappled with this question. Then Congress passed the Communications Decency Act (CDA), which states that "[n]o provider or user of an interactive computer service shall be treated as the publisher or speaker of any information provided by another information content provider."[24] Thus, under the CDA, ISPs generally are treated differently from publishers in other media and are not liable for publishing defamatory statements that come from a third party.[25] Although the courts generally have construed the CDA as providing a broad shield to protect ISPs from liability for third-party content, some courts have started establishing some limits to CDA immunity.[26]

The Spread of Spam

Businesses and individuals alike are targets of *spam,* or unsolicited "junk e-mails" that flood virtual mailboxes with advertisements, solicitations, and other messages. Considered relatively harmless in the early days of the Internet, by 2012 spam accounted for roughly 75 percent of all e-mails.

State Regulation of Spam   In an attempt to combat spam, thirty-six states have enacted laws that prohibit or regulate its use. Many state laws that regulate spam require the senders of e-mail ads to instruct the recipients on how they can "opt out" of further e-mail ads from the same sources. For instance, in some states an unsolicited e-mail ad must include a toll-free phone number or return e-mail address that the recipient can use to contact the sender to request that no more ads be e-mailed.

The Federal CAN-SPAM Act   In 2003, Congress enacted the Controlling the Assault of Non-Solicited Pornography and Marketing (CAN-SPAM) Act, which took effect on January 1, 2004. The legislation applies to any "commercial electronic mail messages" that are sent to promote a commercial product or service. Significantly, the statute preempts state antispam laws except for those provisions in state laws that prohibit false and deceptive e-mailing practices.

Generally, the act permits unsolicited commercial e-mail but prohibits certain spamming activities, including the use of a false return address and the inclusion of false, misleading, or deceptive information in e-mail. The statute also prohibits "dictionary attacks"—sending messages to randomly generated e-mail addresses—and the "harvesting" of e-mail addresses from Web sites with specialized software.

CASE EXAMPLE 4.28   In 2007, federal officials arrested Robert Alan Soloway, considered one of the world's most prolific spammers. Soloway, known as the "Spam King," had been using botnets (automated spamming networks—see Chapter 6) to send out hundreds of millions of unwanted e-mails. In 2008, Soloway pleaded guilty to mail fraud and failure to pay taxes.[27] •

---

24. *47 U.S.C. Section 230.*
25. *See, for example, Fair Housing Council of San Fernando Valley v. Roommate.com, LLC, 521 F.3d 1157 (9th Cir. 2008).*
26. *See, for example, Chicago Lawyers' Committee for Civil Rights Under Law, Inc. v. Craigslist, Inc., 519 F.3d 666 (7th Cir. 2008); Anthony v. Yahoo!, Inc., 421 F.Supp.2d 1257 (N.D.Cal. 2006); and Almeida v. Amazon.com, Inc., 456 F.3d 1316 (11th Cir. 2006).*
27. *See www.usdoj.gov/usao/waw/press/2008/mar/soloway.html.*

The U.S. Safe Web Act   After the CAN-SPAM Act prohibited false and deceptive e-mails originating in the United States, spamming from servers located in other nations increased. These cross-border spammers generally were able to escape detection and legal sanctions because the Federal Trade Commission (FTC) lacked the authority to investigate foreign spamming.

Congress sought to rectify the situation by enacting the U.S. Safe Web Act of 2006 (also known as the Undertaking Spam, Spyware, and Fraud Enforcement with Enforcers Beyond Borders Act). The act allows the FTC to cooperate and share information with foreign agencies in investigating and prosecuting those involved in Internet fraud and deception, including spamming and spyware. It also provides ISPs with a "safe harbor" (immunity from liability) for supplying information to the FTC concerning possible unfair or deceptive conduct in foreign jurisdictions.

There is some evidence that the U.S. Safe Web Act—in conjunction with the increased efforts of federal law enforcement and security experts—has been effective. The number of spam messages sent appeared to have decreased somewhat between 2010 and 2011, although spam still flows at a rate of 70 billion messages per day. The Federal Bureau of Investigation has worked with dozens of ISPs to stop some of the automated spamming networks and has also been actively cooperating with other nations, leading to the arrest of several major spammers located in the Netherlands and Russia.

Reviewing . . . Torts and Cyber Torts

Two sisters, Darla and Irene, are partners in an import business located in a small town in Rhode Island. Irene is also campaigning to be the mayor of their town. Both sisters travel to other countries to purchase the goods they sell at their retail store. Irene buys Indonesian goods, and Darla buys goods from Africa. After a tsunami destroys many of the towns in Indonesia to which Irene usually travels, she phones one of her contacts there and asks him to procure some items and ship them to her. He informs her that it will be impossible to buy these items now because the townspeople are being evacuated due to a water shortage. Irene is angry and tells her contact that if he cannot purchase the goods, he should simply take them without paying for them after the town has been evacuated. Darla overhears her sister's instructions and is outraged. They have a falling-out, and Darla decides that she no longer wishes to be in business with her sister. Using the information presented in the chapter, answer the following questions.

1. Suppose that Darla tells several of her friends about Irene's instructing her contact to take goods without paying for them after the tsunami. If Irene files a tort action against Darla alleging slander, will her suit be successful? Why or why not?
2. Now suppose that Irene wins the election and becomes the city's mayor. Darla then writes a letter to the editor of the local newspaper disclosing Irene's misconduct. If Irene accuses Darla of committing libel, what defenses could Darla assert?
3. If Irene accepts goods shipped from Indonesia that were wrongfully obtained, has she committed an intentional tort against property? Explain.
4. Suppose now that Darla was in the store one day with an elderly customer, Betty Green, who was looking for a graduation gift for her granddaughter. When Darla went to the counter to answer the phone, Green continued to wander around the store and eventually went through an open door into the stockroom, where she fell over some boxes on the floor and fractured her hip. Green files a negligence action against the store. Did Darla breach her duty of care? Why or why not?

DEBATE THIS Because of the often anonymous nature of the Internet, defamation has become an outdated legal concept. It's now too difficult to track down the person responsible for the defamatory statement.

BUSINESS APPLICATION

How Important Is Tort Liability to Business?*

Although there are more claims for breach of contract than for any other category of lawsuits, the dollar amount of damages awarded in tort actions is typically much higher than the awards in contract claims. Tort claims are also commonplace for businesses.

Because of the potential for large damages awards for intentional and unintentional acts, businesspersons should take preventive measures to avoid tort liability as much as possible. Remember that injured persons can bring most tort actions against a business as well as against another person. In fact, if given a choice, plaintiffs often sue a business rather than an individual because the business is more likely to have "deep pockets" (the ability to pay large damages awards). Moreover, sometimes businesses can be held liable for torts that individuals cannot.

The Extent of Business Negligence Liability

A business can be exposed to negligence liability in a wide variety of instances. Liability to business invitees is a clear example. A business that fails to warn invitees that its floor is slippery after a rainstorm, or that its parking lot is icy after snow, may be liable to an injured customer. Indeed, business owners can be liable for nearly any fall or other injury that occurs on business premises.

Even the hiring of employees can lead to negligence liability. For example, a business can be liable if it fails to do a criminal background check before hiring a person to supervise a child-care center when an investigation would have revealed that the person had previously been convicted of sexual assault. Failure to

*This *Business Application* is not meant to substitute for the services of an attorney who is licensed to practice law in your state.

properly supervise or instruct employees can also lead to liability for a business.

Liability for Torts of Employees and Agents

A business can also be held liable for the negligence or intentional torts of its employees and agents. As you will learn in Chapters 23, 24, and 25, a business is liable for the torts committed by an employee who is acting within the scope of his or her employment or an agent who is acting with the authority of the business. Therefore, if a sales agent commits fraud while acting within the scope of her or his employment, the business will be held liable.

Checklist for Minimizing Business Tort Liability

1. Constantly inspect the premises and look for areas where customers or employees might trip, slide, or fall. Take corrective action whenever you find a problem.
2. Train employees on the importance of periodic safety inspections and the procedures for reporting unsafe conditions.
3. Routinely maintain all business equipment (including vehicles).
4. Check with your liability insurance company for suggestions on improving the safety of your premises and operations.
5. Make sure that your general liability policy will adequately cover the potential exposure of the business, and reassess your coverage annually.
6. Review the background and qualifications of individuals you are considering hiring as employees or agents.
7. Investigate and review all negligence claims promptly. Most claims can be settled at low cost before a lawsuit is filed.

Key Terms

Chapter Summary: Torts and Cyber Torts

Intentional Torts against Persons (See pages 97–107.)	1. *Assault and battery*—An assault is an unexcused and intentional act that causes another person to be apprehensive of immediate harm. A battery is an assault that results in physical contact. 2. *False imprisonment*—The intentional confinement or restraint of another person's movement without justification. 3. *Intentional infliction of emotional distress*—An extreme and outrageous act, intentionally committed, that results in severe emotional distress to another. 4. *Defamation (libel or slander)*—A false statement of fact, not made under privilege, that is communicated to a third person and that causes damage to a person's reputation. For public figures, the plaintiff must also prove actual malice. 5. *Invasion of the right to privacy*—Includes four acts: wrongful intrusion into a person's private activities; publication of information that places a person in a false light; disclosure of private facts that an ordinary person would find objectionable; and appropriation of identity, which involves the use of a person's name, likeness, or other identifying characteristic, without permission and for a commercial purpose. Most states have enacted statutes establishing appropriation of identity as the tort of *appropriation* or right of publicity. Courts differ on the degree of likeness required. 6. *Misrepresentation (fraud)*—A false representation made by one party, through misstatement of facts or through conduct, with the intention of deceiving another and on which the other reasonably relies to his or her detriment. Negligent misrepresentation occurs when a person supplies information without having a reasonable basis for believing its truthfulness. 7. *Abusive or frivolous litigation*—When a person initiates a lawsuit out of malice and without probable cause, and loses the suit, he or she can be sued for the tort of *malicious prosecution*. When a person uses a legal process against another improperly or to accomplish a purpose for which it was not designed, she or he can be sued for *abuse of process*. 8. *Wrongful interference*—The knowing, intentional interference by a third party with an enforceable contractual relationship or an established business relationship between other parties for the purpose of advancing the economic interests of the third party.
Intentional Torts against Property (See pages 107–110.)	1. *Trespass to land*—The invasion of another's real property without consent or privilege. 2. *Trespass to personal property*—Unlawfully damaging or interfering with the owner's right to use, possess, or enjoy her or his personal property. 3. *Conversion*—Wrongfully taking or using the personal property of another without permission. 4. *Disparagement of property*—Any economically injurious falsehood that is made about another's product or property. The term includes the torts of *slander of quality* and *slander of title*.

Unintentional Torts (Negligence)
(See pages 111–118.)
	1. *Negligence*—The careless performance of a legally required duty or the failure to perform a legally required act. Elements that must be proved are that a legal duty of care existed, that the defendant breached that duty, that the breach caused the plaintiff's injury, and that the plaintiff suffered a legally recognizable injury.
	2. *Defenses to negligence*—The basic affirmative defenses in negligence cases are assumption of risk, superseding cause, and contributory or comparative negligence.
	3. *Special negligence doctrines and statutes*—
	  a. *Res ipsa loquitur*—A doctrine under which a plaintiff need not prove negligence on the part of the defendant because "the facts speak for themselves."
	  b. Negligence *per se*—A type of negligence that may occur if a person violates a statute or an ordinance and the violation causes another to suffer the kind of injury that the statute or ordinance was intended to prevent.
	  c. Special negligence statutes—State statutes that prescribe duties and responsibilities in certain circumstances. Violation of these statutes will impose civil liability. Dram shop acts and Good Samaritan statutes are examples of special negligence statutes.

Strict Liability (See pages 118–119.)	Under the doctrine of strict liability, a person may be held liable, regardless of the degree of care exercised, for damages or injuries caused by her or his product or activity. Strict liability includes liability for harms caused by abnormally dangerous activities, by dangerous animals, and by defective products (product liability).
Cyber Torts (See pages 119–121.)	General tort principles are being extended to cover cyber torts, or torts that occur in cyberspace, such as online defamation. Federal and state statutes may also apply to certain forms of cyber torts. For example, under the federal Communications Decency Act of 1996, Internet service providers (ISPs) are not liable for defamatory messages posted by their subscribers.

ExamPrep

ISSUE SPOTTERS

1. Jana leaves her truck's motor running while she enters a Kwik-Pik Store. The truck's transmission engages and the vehicle crashes into a gas pump, starting a fire that spreads to a warehouse on the next block. The warehouse collapses, causing its billboard to fall and injure Lou, a bystander. Can Lou recover from Jana? Why or why not? **(See pages 111–114.)**
2. A water pipe bursts, flooding a Metal Fabrication Company utility room and tripping the circuit breakers on a panel in the room. Metal Fabrication contacts Nouri, a licensed electrician with five years' experience, to check the damage and turn the breakers back on. Without testing for short circuits, which Nouri knows that he should do, he tries to switch on a breaker. He is electrocuted, and his wife sues Metal Fabrication for damages, alleging negligence. What might the firm successfully claim in defense? **(See pages 112, 115–117.)**

—Check your answers to the Issue Spotters against the answers provided in Appendix E at the end of this text.

BEFORE THE TEST

Go to www.cengagebrain.com, enter the ISBN 9781133273561, and click on "Find" to locate this textbook's Web site. Then, click on "Access Now" under "Study Tools," and select Chapter 4 at the top. There, you will find a Practice Quiz that you can take to assess your mastery of the concepts in this chapter, as well as Flashcards, a Glossary of important terms, and Video Questions (when assigned).

For Review

Answers to the even-numbered questions in this For Review section can be found in Appendix F at the end of this text.

1. What is the purpose of tort law? What types of damages are available in tort lawsuits?
2. What are two basic categories of torts?
3. What is defamation? Name two types of defamation.
4. Identify the four elements of negligence.
5. What is meant by strict liability? In what circumstances is strict liability applied?

Business Scenarios and Case Problems

4–1 Liability to Business Invitees. Kim went to Ling's Market to pick up a few items for dinner. It was a stormy day, and the wind had blown water through the market's door each time it opened. As Kim entered through the door, she slipped and fell in the rainwater that had accumulated on the floor. The manager knew of the weather conditions but had not posted any sign to warn customers of the water hazard. Kim injured her back as a result of the fall and sued Ling's for damages. Can Ling's be held liable for negligence? Discuss. **(See page 112.)**

4–2 Question with Sample Answer—Negligence. Shannon's physician gives her some pain medication and tells her not to drive after taking it because the medication induces drowsiness. In spite of the doctor's warning, Shannon decides to drive to the store while on the medication. Owing to her lack of alertness, she fails to stop at a traffic light and crashes into another vehicle, causing a passenger in that vehicle to be injured. Is Shannon liable for the tort of negligence? Explain. **(See pages 113–114.)**

—For a sample answer to Question 4–2, go to Appendix G at the end of this text.

4–3 Spotlight on Intentional Torts—Defamation. Sharon Yeagle was an assistant to the vice president of student affairs at Virginia Polytechnic Institute and State University (Virginia Tech). As part of her duties, Yeagle helped students participate in the Governor's Fellows Program. The *Collegiate Times*, Virginia Tech's student newspaper, published an article about the university's success in placing students in the program. The article's text surrounded a block quotation attributed to Yeagle with the phrase "Director of Butt Licking" under her name. Yeagle sued the *Collegiate Times* for defamation. She argued that the phrase implied the commission of sodomy and was therefore actionable. What is *Collegiate Times*'s defense to this claim? [*Yeagle v. Collegiate Times*, 497 S.E.2d 136 (Va. 1998)] **(See page 100.)**

4–4 Case Problem with Sample Answer—Libel and Invasion of Privacy. The *Northwest Herald*, a newspaper, received regular e-mail reports from police departments about criminal arrests. When it received a report that Caroline Eubanks had been charged with theft, the *Herald* published the information. Later, the police sent an e-mail that retracted the report about Eubanks. The *Herald* published a correction.

Eubanks filed a suit against the paper for libel and invasion of privacy. Does Eubanks have a good case for either tort? Why or why not? [*Eubanks v. Northwest Herald Newspapers,* 397 Ill. App.3d 746, 922 N.E.2d 1196 (2010)] **(See pages 102–104.)**

—For a sample answer to Problem 4–4, go to Appendix H at the end of this text.

4–5 **Proximate Cause.** Galen Stoller was killed at a railroad crossing when an Amtrak train hit his car. The crossing was marked with a stop sign and a railroad-crossing symbol but there were no flashing lights. Galen's parents filed a suit against National Railroad Passenger Corporation (Amtrak) and Burlington Northern & Santa Fe Railroad Corp alleging negligence in the design and maintenance of the crossing. The defendants argued that Galen had not stopped at the stop sign. Was Amtrak negligent? What was the proximate cause of the accident? [*Henderson v. National Railroad Passenger Corp.,* ___ F.3d ___ (10th Cir. 2011)] **(See page 114.)**

4–6 **Business Torts.** Medtronic, Inc., is a medical technology company that competes for customers with St. Jude Medical S.C., Inc. James Hughes worked for Medtronic as a sales manager. His contract prohibited him from working for a competitor for one year after leaving Medtronic. Hughes sought a position as a sales director for St. Jude. St. Jude told Hughes that his contract with Medtronic was unenforceable and offered him a job. Hughes accepted. Medtronic filed a suit, alleging wrongful interference. Which type of interference was most likely the basis for this suit? Did it occur here? Explain. [*Medtronic, Inc. v. Hughes,* __ N.W.2d __ (Minn.App. 2011)] **(See pages 106–107.)**

4–7 **Intentional Infliction of Emotional Distress.** While living in her home country of Tanzania, Sophia Kiwanuka signed an employment contract with Anne Margareth Bakilana, a Tanzanian living in Washington, D.C. Kiwanuka traveled to the United States to work as a babysitter and maid in Bakilana's house. When Kiwanuka arrived, Bakilana confiscated her passport, held her in isolation, and forced her to work long hours under threat of having her deported. Kiwanuka worked seven days a week without breaks and was subjected to regular verbal and psychological abuse by Bakilana. Kiwanuka filed a complaint against Bakilana for intentional infliction of emotional distress, among other claims. Bakilana argued that Kiwanuka's complaint should be dismissed because the allegations were insufficient to show outrageous intentional conduct that resulted in severe emotional distress. If you were the judge, in whose favor would you rule? Why? [*Kiwanuka v. Bakilana,* 2012 WL 593065 (D.D.C. 2012)] **(See pages 99–100.)**

4–8 ⬌ **A Question of Ethics—Wrongful Interference.** White Plains Coat & Apron Co. and Cintas Corp. are competitors. White Plains had five-year exclusive contracts with some of its customers. As a result of Cintas's soliciting of business, dozens of White Plains' customers breached their contracts and entered into rental agreements with Cintas. White Plains filed a suit against Cintas, alleging wrongful interference. [*White Plains Coat & Apron Co. v. Cintas Corp.,* 8 N.Y.3d 422, 867 N.E.2d 381 (2007)] **(See pages 106–107.)**

1. What are the two policies at odds in wrongful interference cases? When there is an existing contract, which of these interests should be accorded priority? Why?

2. Is a general interest in soliciting business for profit a sufficient defense to a claim of wrongful interference with a contractual relationship? What do you think? Why?

Critical Thinking and Writing Assignments

4–9 💡 **Business Law Critical Thinking Group Assignment.** Assume that your business partner, Gayanne Zokhrabov, was at the train station when a train, traveling at more than 70 mph, hit eighteen-year-old Hiroyuki Joho, who was running across the tracks. The impact killed Joho and flung parts of his body about 100 feet into the air. Some of them landed on Gayanne and knocked her to the ground. As a result, she hurt her shoulder and broke her leg and wrist. She has not been able to work and has hired an attorney to file a negligence lawsuit against Joho's estate. (The attorney believes that Gayanne cannot successfully sue Amtrak because of a lack of proximate cause—it was not reasonably foreseeable that Joho would run across the tracks and his body parts would cause injuries to others.)

1. One group should analyze whether Joho had a *duty* to Gayanne and whether his decision to run in front of the train was a *breach* of that duty because she was in the zone of danger.

2. A second group should consider proximate cause: Was it reasonably foreseeable that a train accident could send Joho's body parts into crowds of waiting passengers?

3. A third group should discuss whether it is ethical to sue the dead man's estate over flying body parts. Further, what impact might the case and the publicity surrounding it have on you and your partner's business reputation?

4–10 **Case Analysis Question.** Go to Appendix I at the end of this text and examine the excerpt of Case No. 1, *Lott v. Levitt.* Review and then brief the case, making sure that your brief answers the following questions.

1. **Issue:** At the center of the dispute in this case was a distinction between what types of speech?

2. **Rule of Law:** What difference does it make what type of speech a particular statement is?

3. **Applying the Rule of Law:** How does a court determine to which type of speech a certain statement belongs?

4. **Conclusion:** In this case, how was the speech at issue classified, and why? What effect did that decision have on the parties' suit?

5 CHAPTER

Intellectual Property and Internet Law

LEARNING OBJECTIVES

The five learning objectives below are designed to help improve your understanding of the chapter. After reading this chapter, you should be able to answer the following questions:

1 What is intellectual property?

2 Why is the protection of trademarks important?

3 How does the law protect patents?

4 What laws protect authors' rights in the works they create?

5 What are trade secrets, and what laws offer protection for this form of intellectual property?

(Login/Shutterstock.com)

"The Internet is just a world passing around notes in a classroom."
—Jon Stewart, 1962–present (American comedian and host of *The Daily Show*)

Intellectual Property Property resulting from intellectual and creative processes.

LEARNING OBJECTIVE 1
What is intellectual property?

Intellectual property is any property resulting from intellectual, creative processes—the products of an individual's mind. Although it is an abstract term for an abstract concept, intellectual property is nonetheless familiar to almost everyone. The information contained in books and computer files is intellectual property. The apps for your iPhone and iPad, the movies you watch, and the music you listen to are all forms of intellectual property. Although the need to protect creative works was first recognized in Article I, Section 8, of the U.S. Constitution (see Appendix B), statutory protection of these rights began in the 1940s and continues to evolve to meet the needs of modern society.

Of significant concern to businesspersons is the need to protect their rights in intellectual property, which may be more valuable than their physical property, such as machines and buildings. Consider, for instance, the importance of intellectual property rights to technology companies, such as Apple, Inc., the maker of the iPhone and iPad. In today's world, intellectual property rights can be a company's most valuable assets, which is why

Apple sued rival Samsung Electronics Company in 2011. Apple claimed that Samsung's Galaxy line of mobile phones and tablets (those that run Google's Android software) copy the look, design, and user interface of Apple's iPhone and iPad. Although Apple is one of Samsung's biggest customers and buys many of its components from Samsung, Apple also needs to protect its iPhone and iPad revenues from competing Android products. You will read about the verdict in this case on pages 139 and 140.

In today's global economy, however, protecting intellectual property in one country is no longer sufficient, and the United States is participating in various international agreements to secure ownership rights in intellectual property in other countries. Because the Internet allows the world to "pass around notes" so quickly, as Jon Stewart joked in the chapter-opening quotation on the facing page, protecting these rights in today's online environment has proved particularly challenging.

Trademarks and Related Property

Trademark A distinctive word, symbol, or design that identifies the manufacturer as the source of particular goods and distinguishes its products from those made or sold by others.

A **trademark** is a distinctive word, symbol, sound, or design that identifies the manufacturer as the source of particular goods and distinguishes its products from those made or sold by others. At common law, the person who used a symbol or mark to identify a business or product was protected in the use of that trademark. Clearly, by using another's trademark, a business could lead consumers to believe that its goods were made by the other business. The law seeks to avoid this kind of confusion. (For information on how companies use trademarks and service marks, see this chapter's *Linking Business Law to Marketing* feature on page 151.)

LEARNING OBJECTIVE 2
Why is the protection of trademarks important?

In the following *Classic Case* concerning Coca-Cola, the defendants argued that the Coca-Cola trademark was not entitled to protection under the law because the term did not accurately represent the product.

✳ Classic Case 5.1

Coca-Cola Co. v. Koke Co. of America

Supreme Court of the United States,
254 U.S. 143, 41 S.Ct. 113, 65 L.Ed. 189 (1920).
www.findlaw.com/casecode/supreme.html[a]

(Rob Wilson / Shutterstock.com)

How is Coca-Cola protected?

COMPANY PROFILE   *John Pemberton, an Atlanta pharmacist, invented a caramel-colored, carbonated soft drink in 1886. His bookkeeper, Frank Robinson, named the beverage Coca-Cola after two of the ingredients, coca leaves and kola nuts. Asa Candler bought the Coca-Cola Company in 1891 and, within seven years, had made the soft drink available throughout the United States and in parts of Canada and Mexico as well. Candler continued to sell Coke aggressively and to open up new markets, reaching Europe before 1910. In doing so, however, he attracted numerous competitors, some of whom tried to capitalize directly on the Coke name.*

FACTS The Coca-Cola Company brought an action in a federal district court to enjoin (prevent) other beverage companies from using the words *Koke* and *Dope* for their products. The defendants contended that the Coca-Cola trademark was a fraudulent representation and that Coca-Cola was therefore not entitled to any help from the courts. By using the Coca-Cola name, the defendants alleged, the Coca-Cola Company represented that the beverage contained cocaine (from coca leaves). The district court granted the injunction, but the federal appellate court reversed. The

---

a. This is the "US Supreme Court Opinions" page within the Web site of the "FindLaw Internet Legal Resources" database. This page provides several options for accessing an opinion. Because you know the citation for this case, you can go to the "Citation Search" box, type in the appropriate volume and page numbers for the *United States Reports* ("254" and "143," respectively, for the *Coca-Cola* case), and click on "Search."

Classic Case 5.1—Continues next page ➡

Classic Case 5.1—Continued

Coca-Cola Company appealed to the United States Supreme Court.

ISSUE   Did the marketing of products called Koke and Dope by the Koke Company of America and other firms constitute an infringement on Coca-Cola's trademark?

DECISION   Yes for Koke, but no for Dope. The United States Supreme Court enjoined the competing beverage companies from calling their products Koke but did not prevent them from calling their products Dope.

REASON   The Court noted that before 1900 the Coca-Cola beverage had contained a small amount of cocaine. This ingredient had been deleted from the formula by 1906 at the latest, however, and the Coca-Cola Company had advertised to the public that no cocaine was present in its drink. Coca-Cola was a widely popular drink "to be had at almost any soda fountain." Because of the public's widespread familiarity with Coca-Cola, the retention of the name (referring to coca leaves and kola nuts) was not misleading: "Coca-Cola probably means to most persons the plaintiff's familiar product to be had everywhere rather than a compound of particular substances." The name *Coke* was found to be so common a term for the trademarked product Coca-Cola that the defendants' use of the similar-sounding *Koke* as a name for their beverages was disallowed. The Court could find no reason to restrain the defendants from using the name *Dope*, however.

WHAT IF THE FACTS WERE DIFFERENT?   *Suppose that Coca-Cola had been trying to make the public believe that its product contained cocaine. Would the result in the case likely have been different? Explain your answer.*

IMPACT OF THIS CASE ON TODAY'S LAW   *In this early case, the United States Supreme Court made it clear that trademarks and trade names (and nicknames for those marks and names, such as "Coke" for "Coca-Cola") that are in common use receive protection under the common law. This holding is significant historically because it is the predecessor to the federal statute later passed to protect trademark rights (the Lanham Act of 1946, discussed below).*

Statutory Protection of Trademarks

Statutory protection of trademarks and related property is provided at the federal level by the Lanham Act of 1946.[1] The Lanham Act was enacted in part to protect manufacturers from losing business to rival companies that used confusingly similar trademarks. The act incorporates the common law of trademarks and provides remedies for owners of trademarks who wish to enforce their claims in federal court. Many states also have trademark statutes.

> ➤ **KNOW THIS** ◄
>
> Trademark dilution laws protect the owners of distinctive marks from unauthorized uses even when the defendant's use involves noncompeting goods or is unlikely to cause confusion.

Trademark Dilution   Before 1995, federal trademark law prohibited only the unauthorized use of the same mark on competing—or on noncompeting but "related"— goods or services. Protection was given only when the unauthorized use would likely confuse consumers as to the origin of those goods and services. In 1995, Congress amended the Lanham Act by passing the Federal Trademark Dilution Act,[2] which allowed trademark owners to bring a suit in federal court for trademark *dilution*.

Trademark dilution laws protect "distinctive" or "famous" trademarks (such as Rolls Royce, McDonald's, Dell, and Apple) from certain unauthorized uses even when the use is on noncompeting goods or is unlikely to confuse. More than half of the states have also enacted trademark dilution laws.

Use of a Similar Mark May Constitute Trademark Dilution
A famous mark may be diluted not only by the use of an *identical* mark but also by the use of

---

1. 15 U.S.C. Sections 1051–1128.
2. 15 U.S.C. Section 1125.

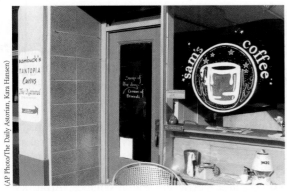

(AP Photo/The Daily Astorian, Kara Hansen)

When an Oregon woman opened this store, its sign read "Sambuck's." On what ground did Starbuck's sue her so that she had to change the store's name?

a *similar* mark, provided that it reduces the value of the famous mark.[3]
CASE EXAMPLE 5.1 A woman opened a coffee shop under the name "Sambuck's Coffeehouse" in Astoria, Oregon, even though she knew that "Starbucks" was one of the largest coffee chains in the nation. When Starbucks Corporation filed a dilution lawsuit, the federal court ruled that use of the "Sambuck's" mark constituted trademark dilution because it created confusion for consumers. Not only was there a "high degree" of similarity between the marks, but also both companies provided coffee-related services through "stand-alone" retail stores. Therefore, the use of the similar mark (Sambuck's) reduced the value of the famous mark (Starbucks).[4] ●

Trademark Registration

Trademarks may be registered with the state or with the federal government. To register for protection under federal trademark law, a person must file an application with the U.S. Patent and Trademark Office in Washington, D.C. A mark can be registered (1) if it is currently in commerce or (2) if the applicant intends to put the mark into commerce within six months.

In special circumstances, the six-month period can be extended by thirty months, giving the applicant a total of three years from the date of notice of trademark approval to make use of the mark and to file the required use statement. Registration is postponed until the mark is actually used. Nonetheless, during this waiting period, the applicant's trademark is protected against any third party who has neither used the mark previously nor filed an application for it. Registration is renewable between the fifth and sixth years after the initial registration and every ten years thereafter (every twenty years for trademarks registered before 1990).

Trademark Infringement

Registration of a trademark with the U.S. Patent and Trademark Office gives notice on a nationwide basis that the trademark belongs exclusively to the registrant. The registrant is also allowed to use the symbol ® to indicate that the mark has been registered. Whenever someone else uses that trademark in its entirety or copies it to a substantial degree, intentionally or unintentionally, the trademark has been *infringed* (used without authorization).

When a trademark has been infringed, the owner has a cause of action against the infringer. To succeed in a lawsuit for trademark infringement, the owner must show that the defendant's use of the mark created a likelihood of confusion about the origin of the defendant's goods or services. The owner need not prove that the infringer acted intentionally or that the trademark was registered (although registration does provide proof of the date of inception of the trademark's use). See this chapter's *Adapting the Law to the Online Environment* feature on the following page for a discussion of how some companies are turning first to Internet forums, before they resort to costly trademark litigation.

The remedy most commonly granted for trademark infringement is an *injunction* to prevent further infringement. Under the Lanham Act, a trademark owner that successfully proves infringement can recover actual damages, plus the profits that the infringer wrongfully received from the unauthorized use of the mark. A court can also order the destruction of any goods bearing the unauthorized trademark. In some situations, the trademark owner may also be able to recover attorneys' fees.

---

3. See *Moseley v. V Secret Catalogue, Inc.*, 537 U.S. 418, 123 S.Ct. 1115, 155 L.Ed.2d 1 (2003).
4. *Starbucks Corp. v. Lundberg*, 2005 WL 3183858 (D.Or. 2005).

Distinctiveness of the Mark

A central objective of the Lanham Act is to reduce the likelihood that consumers will be confused by similar marks. For that reason, only those trademarks that are deemed sufficiently distinctive from all competing trademarks will be protected. (In addition, a trademark may not be derogatory, as the *Law, Diversity, and Business: Managerial Implications* feature on the facing page explains.)

Strong Marks   Fanciful, arbitrary, or suggestive trademarks are generally considered to be the most distinctive (strongest) trademarks. Because they are normally taken from outside the context of the particular product, strong marks provide the best means of distinguishing one product from another. Fanciful trademarks include invented words, such as *Xerox* for one manufacturer's copiers and *Google* for search engines. Arbitrary trademarks use common words that would not ordinarily be associated with the product, such as *Dutch Boy* as a name for paint.

A single letter used in a particular style can be an arbitrary trademark. **CASE EXAMPLE 5.2** Sports entertainment company ESPN, Inc., sued Quiksilver, Inc., a maker of youth-oriented clothing, alleging trademark infringement. ESPN claimed that

ADAPTING THE LAW TO THE ONLINE ENVIRONMENT

USING ONLINE SHAME IN TRADEMARK DISPUTES

Claims of trademark infringement have risen 5 percent each year for the past several years and will exceed four thousand in 2013. Trademark litigation is costly and can drag on for years. Small businesses, particularly start-ups, typically do not have the resources to engage in such lengthy litigation. Yet claims of infringement, even when they seem dubious, must be addressed. Some entrepreneurs are finding that online publicity and the shame it can bring are an effective alternative to going to federal court to resolve trademark disputes.

Can a Company Trademark the Letter "K"?

When Phil Michaelson created the Web site KeepRecipes.com to provide an Internet cookbook where people could collect and share recipes, he never thought the word "Keep" and the letter "K" could be someone's trademarks. On his site, users click on "K," short for "Keep," when they want to save the instructions for a recipe. Nevertheless, AdKeeper, a New York–based service company, immediately sent Michaelson a cease-and-desist letter. AdKeeper claimed that the use of "K" and "Keep," as well as the Web site name KeepRecipes.com, constituted "blatant trademark infringement."

Online Publicity Provides a Solution

Michaelson did not have the resources to engage in a prolonged legal battle with AdKeeper, even though he thought its claims had no merit. Instead, he turned to Chillingeffects.org, a Web site created by several universities to foster lawful online activity. Soon after he described his problem and posted the cease-and-desist letter, several lawyers who deal with Web site issues offered to represent him in his trademark dispute at no charge.

Using Social Media

Other small entrepreneurs facing lawsuits are turning to social media, especially Facebook and Twitter, where large companies' threats to sue small companies for trademark infringement are generally met with displeasure. When the restaurant company Chick-fil-A, Inc., threatened Vermont T-shirt manufacturer Bo Muller-Moore with a lawsuit, he created a Facebook page. Chick-fil-A claimed that Muller-Moore had infringed its trademarked slogan "Eat Mor Chikin" when he used the slogan "Eat More Kale" on his T-shirts—even though Muller-Moore used correct spelling and kale and chicken would seem to be rather different foods. Several thousand supporters regularly look at Muller-Moore's Facebook page and have donated $10,000 for his defense.

Critical Thinking

As social media becomes ever more pervasive in our lives, what do you expect to occur with respect to trademark disputes?

LAW, DIVERSITY, AND BUSINESS: MANAGERIAL IMPLICATIONS

DEROGATORY TRADEMARKS

When determining whether a trademark is sufficiently distinctive to warrant protection, the U.S. Patent and Trademark Office (USPTO) also considers whether the mark might be offensive to any of the diverse groups in our society. Under the Lanham Act, the USPTO must deny registration to trademarks that "may disparage or falsely suggest a connection with persons, living or dead, institutions, beliefs, or national symbols, or bring them into contempt, or derision."[a]

A Disparaging Mark Can Be Costly Sometimes, the USPTO fails to recognize a potentially disparaging mark and approves its registration. Discovering too late that it has chosen the wrong trademark can be very expensive for a business. Biggby Coffee, one of the nation's fastest-growing coffee franchises, spent nearly $1 million to change its name from Beaner's Coffee to Biggby Coffee after it became aware that the word *beaners* is sometimes used as a disparaging term for Hispanic Americans.

Names of Sports Teams One of the most controversial issues involving trademarks has to do with the use of American Indian names and mascots for sports teams. Many Native Americans find the use of these names highly offensive and demeaning. In 1992, seven Native Americans petitioned the Trademark Trial and Appeal Board, which hears appeals of USPTO decisions, and asked it to cancel six trademarks of the Washington Redskins football team

that had been registered since the late 1960s and 1970s. The board agreed that the use of the term *redskins* was offensive and canceled the marks. The team's owner appealed to a federal court, setting off a long-running legal battle that did not end until 2009 when a federal appellate court found that the Native Americans had waited too long to bring their suit. The United States Supreme Court subsequently declined to hear the case.[b]

Native Americans were more successful in their long struggle to end the use of the name *Fighting Sioux* for the University of North Dakota's teams. The National Collegiate Athletic Association (NCAA) had put the University of North Dakota (UND) on a list of schools with names and mascots that it found objectionable. All of the other schools on the list either changed their teams' names or obtained permission from Native Americans to keep them. After several months of debate and controversy, in June 2012, the citizens of North Dakota overwhelming voted to get rid of the UND's team name, and the state's board of higher education officially voted to remove it as well.

Business Implications *As society becomes more sensitive to diversity issues, businesses can expect that their trademarks will be subject to increased scrutiny. When choosing a trademark, logo, or motto, a business must consider the diverse groups in our society.*

a. 15 U.S.C. Section 1052(a).

b. *Pro-Football Inc. v. Harjo*, 565 F.3d 880 (2009; *cert.* denied, *Harjo v. Pro-Football, Inc.*, 130 S. Ct. 631 (2009).

Quiksilver had used on its clothing the stylized "X" mark that ESPN uses in connection with the "X Games" (competitions in extreme action sports). Quiksilver filed counterclaims for trademark infringement and dilution, arguing that it had a long history of using the stylized X on its products. ESPN created the X Games in the mid-1990s, and Quiksilver has used the X mark since 1994. ESPN asked the court to dismiss Quiksilver's counterclaims, but the court refused, holding that the X on Quiksilver's clothing was clearly an arbitrary mark. The court found that the two Xs were "similar enough that a consumer might well confuse them."[5] ●

Suggestive Trademarks Suggestive trademarks bring to mind something about a product without describing the product directly. For instance, "Dairy Queen" suggests an association between its products and milk, but it does not directly describe ice cream. "Blu-ray" is a suggestive mark that is associated with the high-quality, high-definition video contained on a particular optical data storage disc. Although blue-violet lasers are used to read blu-ray discs, the term *blu-ray* does not directly describe the disc.

5. *ESPN, Inc. v. Quiksilver, Inc.*, 586 F.Supp.2d 219 (S.D.N.Y. 2008).

Secondary Meaning   Descriptive terms, geographic terms, and personal names are not inherently distinctive and do not receive protection under the law *until* they acquire a secondary meaning.   **CASE EXAMPLE 5.3**   Frosty Treats, Inc., sells frozen desserts out of ice cream trucks. The video game series Twisted Metal depicted an ice cream truck with a clown character on it that was similar to the clowns on Frosty Treats' trucks. In the last game of the series, the truck bears the label "Frosty Treats." Frosty Treats sued for trademark infringement, but the court held that "Frosty Treats" is a descriptive term that is not protected by trademark law unless it has acquired a secondary meaning. To establish secondary meaning, Frosty Treats would have to show that the public recognizes its trademark and associates it with a single source. Because Frosty Treats failed to do so, the court entered a judgment in favor of the video game producer.[6] ●

A secondary meaning arises when customers begin to associate a specific term or phrase, such as "London Fog," with specific trademarked items (coats with "London Fog" labels) made by a particular company. Whether a secondary meaning becomes attached to a term or name usually depends on how extensively the product is advertised, the market for the product, the number of sales, and other factors. Once a secondary meaning is attached to a term or name, a trademark is considered distinctive and is protected. Even a color can qualify for trademark protection, such as the color schemes used by four state university sports teams, including Ohio State University and Louisiana State University.[7]

Generic Terms   Generic terms are terms that refer to an entire class of products, such as *bicycle* and *computer*. Generic terms receive no protection, even if they acquire secondary meanings. A particularly thorny problem for a business arises when its trademark acquires generic use. For instance, *aspirin* and *thermos* were originally trademarked products, but today the words are used generically. Other trademarks that have acquired generic use include *escalator, trampoline, raisin bran, dry ice, lanolin, linoleum, nylon,* and *cornflakes*.[8]

Service, Certification, and Collective Marks

A **service mark** is essentially a trademark that is used to distinguish the *services* (rather than the products) of one person or company from those of another. For instance, each airline has a particular mark or symbol associated with its name. Titles and character names used in radio and television are frequently registered as service marks.

Other marks protected by law include certification marks and collective marks. A **certification mark** is used by one or more persons, other than the owner, to certify the region, materials, mode of manufacture, quality, or other characteristic of specific goods or services. Certification marks include such marks as "Good Housekeeping Seal of Approval" and "UL Tested."

When used by members of a cooperative, association, labor union, or other organization, a certification mark is referred to as a **collective mark**.   **EXAMPLE 5.4**   Collective marks appear at the end of a movie's credits to indicate the various associations and organizations that participated in making the movie. The labor union marks found on the tags of certain products are also collective marks. ●

Trade Dress

The term **trade dress** refers to the image and overall appearance of a product. Trade dress is a broad concept that can include all or part of the total image or overall impression created by a product or its packaging.   **EXAMPLE 5.5**   The distinctive decor, menu, and style of

Service Mark A trademark that is used to distinguish the services (rather than the products) of one person or company from those of another.

Certification Mark A mark used by one or more persons, other than the owner, to certify the region, materials, mode of manufacture, quality, or other characteristic of specific goods or services.

Collective Mark A mark used by members of a cooperative, association, union, or other organization to certify the region, materials, mode of manufacture, quality, or other characteristic of specific goods or services.

Trade Dress The image and overall appearance ("look and feel") of a product that is protected by trademark law.

---

6. *Frosty Treats, Inc. v. Sony Computer Entertainment America, Inc.,* 426 F.3d 1001 (8th Cir. 2005).
7. *Board of Supervisors of LA State University v. Smack Apparel Co.,* 438 F.Supp.2d 653 (2006). See also *Qualitex Co. v. Jacobson Products Co.,* 514 U.S. 159, 115 S.Ct. 1300, 131 L.Ed.2d 248 (1995).
8. See, for example, *Boston Duck Tours, LP v. Super Duck Tours, LLC,* 531 F.3d 1 (1st Cir. 2008).

service of a particular restaurant may be regarded as the restaurant's trade dress. Similarly, trade dress can include the layout and appearance of a mail-order catalogue, the use of a lighthouse as part of a golf hole, the fish shape of a cracker, or the G-shaped design of a Gucci watch. •

Basically, trade dress is subject to the same protection as trademarks. In cases involving trade dress infringement, as in trademark infringement cases, a major consideration is whether consumers are likely to be confused by the allegedly infringing use.

Counterfeit Goods

Counterfeit goods copy or otherwise imitate trademarked goods but are not genuine. The importation of goods bearing counterfeit (fake) trademarks poses a growing problem for U.S. businesses, consumers, and law enforcement. It is estimated that nearly 7 percent of the goods imported into the United States are counterfeit. In addition to having negative financial effects on legitimate businesses, sales of certain counterfeit goods, such as pharmaceuticals and nutritional supplements, can present serious public health risks.

Although Congress has enacted statutes against counterfeit goods (discussed next), the United States cannot prosecute foreign counterfeiters because our national laws do not apply to them. Instead, one effective tool that U.S. officials are using to combat online sales of counterfeit goods is to obtain a court order to close down the domain names of Web sites that sell such goods. **EXAMPLE 5.6** In 2011, U.S. agents shut down 150 domain names on the Monday after Thanksgiving ("Cyber Monday," the online version of "Black Friday," the day after Thanksgiving when the holiday shopping season begins). Although the criminal enterprises may continue selling counterfeit versions of brand-name products under different domain names, shutting down the Web sites, particularly on key shopping days, prevents some counterfeit goods from entering the United States. •

Stop Counterfeiting in Manufactured Goods Act
In 2006, Congress enacted the Stop Counterfeiting in Manufactured Goods Act[9] (SCMGA) to combat counterfeit goods. The act made it a crime to intentionally traffic in, or attempt to traffic in,

---

9. Pub. L. No. 109-181 (2006), which amended 18 U.S.C. Sections 2318–2320.

A federal customs officer displays about $4 million of counterfeit goods that were seized in the Los Angeles area. Is it possible to control the foreign sources of such merchandise?

(AP Photo/Nick Ut)

counterfeit goods or services, or to knowingly use a counterfeit mark on or in connection with goods or services. Before this act, the law did not prohibit the creation or shipment of counterfeit labels that were not attached to products.[10] Therefore, counterfeiters would make labels and packaging bearing a fake trademark, ship the labels to another location, and then affix them to inferior products to deceive buyers. The SCMGA closed this loophole by making it a crime to traffic in counterfeit labels, stickers, packaging, and the like, whether or not they are attached to goods.

Penalties for Counterfeiting   Persons found guilty of violating the SCMGA may be fined up to $2 million or imprisoned for up to ten years (or more if they are repeat offenders). If a court finds that the statute was violated, it must order the defendant to forfeit the counterfeit products (which are then destroyed), as well as any property used in the commission of the crime. The defendant must also pay restitution to the trademark holder or victim in an amount equal to the victim's actual loss.

CASE EXAMPLE 5.7   Wajdi Beydoun pleaded guilty to conspiring to import cigarette-rolling papers from Mexico that were falsely marked as "Zig-Zags" and sell them in the United States. The defendant was sentenced to prison and ordered to pay $566,267 in restitution. On appeal, the court affirmed the prison sentence but ordered the trial court to reduce the amount of restitution because it exceeded the actual loss suffered by the legitimate sellers of Zig-Zag rolling papers.[11] ●

Trade Names

Trade Name A name that a business uses to identify itself and its brand. A trade name is directly related to a business's reputation and goodwill and is protected under trademark law.

Trademarks apply to *products*. The term **trade name** is used to indicate part or all of a *business's name,* whether the business is a sole proprietorship, a partnership, or a corporation. Generally, a trade name is directly related to a business and its goodwill. Trade names may be protected as trademarks if the trade name is the same as the company's trademarked product—for example, Coca-Cola. Unless it is also used as a trademark or service mark, a trade name cannot be registered with the federal government.

Trade names are protected under the common law, however. As with trademarks, words must be unusual or fancifully used if they are to be protected as trade names. For instance, the courts held that the word *Safeway* was sufficiently fanciful to obtain protection as a trade name for a grocery chain.

Licensing

License An agreement by the owner of intellectual property to permit another to use a trademark, copyright, patent, or trade secret for certain limited purposes.

One way to make use of another's trademark or other form of intellectual property, while avoiding litigation, is to obtain a license to do so. A **license** in this context is an agreement permitting the use of a trademark, copyright, patent, or trade secret for certain limited purposes. The party that owns the intellectual property rights and issues the license is the *licensor,* and the party obtaining the license is the *licensee.*

A license grants only the rights expressly described in the license agreement. A licensor might, for example, allow the licensee to use the trademark as part of its company name, or as part of its domain name, but not otherwise use the mark on any products or services. Disputes frequently arise over licensing agreements, particularly when the license involves Internet uses.

Typically, license agreements are very detailed and should be carefully drafted. **CASE EXAMPLE 5.8**   George V Restauration S.A. and others owned and operated the Buddha Bar Paris, a restaurant with an Asian theme in Paris, France. In 2005, one of the owners

---

10. See, for example, *Commonwealth v. Crespo*, 884 A.2d 960 (Pa. 2005).
11. *United States v. Beydoun*, 469 F.3d 102 (5th Cir. 2006).

allowed Little Rest Twelve, Inc., to use the Buddha Bar trademark and its associated concept in New York City under the name *Buddha Bar NYC*. Little Rest paid royalties for its use of the Buddha Bar mark and advertised Buddha Bar NYC's affiliation with Buddha Bar Paris, a connection also noted on its Web site and in the media. When a dispute arose, the owners of Buddha Bar Paris withdrew their permission for Buddha Bar NYC's use of their mark, but Little Rest continued to use it. The owners of the mark filed a suit in a New York state court against Little Rest, and ultimately a state appellate court granted an injunction preventing Little Rest from using the mark.[12] ●

PREVENTING LEGAL DISPUTES

Consult with an attorney before signing any licensing contract to make sure that the wording of the contract is very clear as to what rights are or are not being conveyed. This can help to avoid litigation. Moreover, to prevent misunderstandings over the scope of the rights being acquired, determine whether any other parties hold licenses to use that particular intellectual property and the extent of those rights.

Cyber Marks

Cyber Mark A trademark in cyberspace.

In cyberspace, trademarks are sometimes referred to as **cyber marks.** We turn now to a discussion of how new laws and the courts are addressing trademark-related issues in cyberspace.

Domain Names

Domain Name Part of an Internet address, such as "cengage.com." The part to the right of the period is the top level domain and indicates the type of entity that operates the site, and the part to the left of the period, called the second level domain, is chosen by the entity.

As e-commerce expanded worldwide, one issue that emerged involved the rights of a trademark owner to use the mark as part of a domain name. A **domain name** is part of an Internet address, such as "cengage.com." Every domain name ends with a top level domain (TLD), which is the part to the right of the period that indicates the type of entity that operates the site (for example, "com" is an abbreviation for "commercial").

The second level domain (SLD)—the part of the name to the left of the period—is chosen by the business entity or individual registering the domain name. Competition for SLDs among firms with similar names and products has led to numerous disputes. By using the same, or a similar, domain name, parties have attempted to profit from a competitor's goodwill, sell pornography, offer for sale another party's domain name, or otherwise infringe on others' trademarks.

The Internet Corporation for Assigned Names and Numbers (ICANN), a nonprofit corporation, oversees the distribution of domain names and operates an online arbitration system. Due to numerous complaints, ICANN completely overhauled the domain name distribution system. In 2012, ICANN started selling new generic top level domain names (gTLDs) for an initial price of $185,000 plus an annual fee of $25,000. Whereas TLDs were limited to only a few terms (such as "com," "net," and "org"), gTLDs can take any form. ICANN anticipates that many companies and corporations will want gTLDs based on their brands. For example, Apple, Inc., might want to use "ipad or "imac" as a gTLD, and Coca-Cola might want "coke."

Cybersquatting The act of registering a domain name that is the same as, or confusingly similar to, the trademark of another and then offering to sell that domain name back to the trademark owner.

One of the goals of the new system is to alleviate the problem of *cybersquatting*. **Cybersquatting** occurs when a person registers a domain name that is the same as, or confusingly similar to, the trademark of another and then offers to sell the domain name back to the trademark owner.

---

12. *George V Restoration S.A. v. Little Rest Twelve, Inc.*, 58 A.D.3d 428, 871 N.Y.S.2d 65 (2009).

Anti-cybersquatting Legislation

During the 1990s, cybersquatting led to so much litigation that Congress passed the Anticybersquatting Consumer Protection Act (ACPA), which amended the Lanham Act—the federal law protecting trademarks discussed earlier. The ACPA makes it illegal to "register, traffic in, or use" a domain name (1) if the name is identical or confusingly similar to the trademark of another and (2) if the person registering, trafficking in, or using the domain name has a "bad faith intent" to profit from that trademark.

The Ongoing Problem of Cybersquatting
Despite the ACPA, cybersquatting continues to present a problem for businesses, largely because more TLDs are now available and many more companies are registering domain names. Indeed, domain name registrars have proliferated. Registrar companies charge a fee to businesses and individuals to register new names and to renew annual registrations (often through automated software). Many of these companies also buy and sell expired domain names.

Although all registrars are supposed to relay information about these transactions to ICANN and the other companies that keep a master list of domain names, this does not always occur. The speed at which domain names change hands and the difficulty in tracking mass automated registrations have created an environment in which cybersquatting can flourish.

Cybersquatters have also developed new tactics, such as *typosquatting* (registering a name that is a misspelling of a popular brand, for example, hotmial.com). Because many Internet users are not perfect typists, Web pages using these misspelled names can generate significant traffic. More traffic generally means increased profits (advertisers often pay Web sites based on the number of unique visits, or hits), which in turn provides incentive for more cybersquatters. Also, if the misspelling is significant, the trademark owner may have difficulty proving that the name is identical or confusingly similar to the owner's mark, as required by the ACPA.

Cybersquatting is costly for businesses, which must attempt to register all variations of a name to protect their domain name rights from would-be cybersquatters. Large corporations may have to register thousands of domain names across the globe just to protect their basic brands and trademarks.

Applicability of the ACPA and Sanctions under the Act
The ACPA applies to all domain name registrations of trademarks. Successful plaintiffs in suits brought under the act can collect actual damages and lost profits or elect to receive statutory damages that range from $1,000 to $100,000.

Although some companies have been successful suing under the ACPA, there are roadblocks to pursuing such lawsuits. Some domain name registrars offer privacy services that hide the true owners of Web sites, making it difficult for trademark owners to identify cybersquatters. Thus, before bringing a suit, a trademark owner has to ask the court for a subpoena to discover the identity of the owner of the infringing Web site. Because of the high costs of court proceedings, discovery, and even arbitration, many disputes over cybersquatting are settled out of court.

Meta Tags

Search engines compile their results by looking through a Web site's key-word field. *Meta tags,* or key words (see Chapter 2 on page 46), may be inserted into this field to increase the likelihood that a site will be included in search engine results, even though the site may have nothing to do with the inserted words. Using this same technique, one site may appropriate the key words of other sites with more frequent hits so that the appropriating site appears in the same search engine results as the more popular sites. Using another's trademark in a meta tag without the owner's permission, however, normally constitutes trademark infringement.

Some uses of another's trademark as a meta tag may be permissible if the use is reasonably necessary and does not suggest that the owner authorized or sponsored the use. **CASE EXAMPLE 5.9**   Terri Welles, a former model who had been "Playmate of the Year" in *Playboy* magazine, established a Web site that used the terms *Playboy* and *Playmate* as meta tags. Playboy Enterprises, Inc., which publishes *Playboy,* filed a suit seeking to prevent Welles from using these meta tags. The court determined that Welles's use of Playboy's meta tags to direct users to her Web site was permissible because it did not suggest sponsorship and there were no descriptive substitutes for the terms *Playboy* and *Playmate*.[13] ●

Dilution in the Online World

As discussed earlier, trademark *dilution* occurs when a trademark is used, without authorization, in a way that diminishes the distinctive quality of the mark. Unlike trademark infringement, a claim of dilution does not require proof that consumers are likely to be confused by a connection between the unauthorized use and the mark. For this reason, the products involved do not have to be similar, as the following *Spotlight Case* illustrates.

---

13. *Playboy Enterprises, Inc. v. Welles,* 279 F.3d 796 (9th Cir. 2002). See also *Canfield v. Health Communications, Inc.,* 2008 WL 961318 (C.D.Cal. 2008).

Spotlight on Internet Porn

Case 5.2
Hasbro, Inc. v. Internet Entertainment Group, Ltd.
United States District Court, Western District of Washington, 1996 WL 84853 (1996).

(Reuters/Hasbro/Ray Stubblebine/Landov)

Candy Land is a children's board game. Why did its parent company, Hasbro, Inc., sue a Web site?

FACTS Hasbro, Inc., the maker of Candyland, a children's board game, owns the Candyland trademark. The defendants, Brian Cartmell and the Internet Entertainment Group, Ltd., used *candyland.com* as a domain name for a sexually explicit Internet site. Any person who performed an online search for "candyland" was directed to this adult Web site. Hasbro filed a trademark dilution claim in a federal court, seeking a permanent injunction to prevent the defendants from using the Candyland trademark.

ISSUE Did the defendants' use of the word *candyland* in connection with a sexually explicit Web site violate Hasbro's trademark rights?

DECISION Yes. The district court granted Hasbro a permanent injunction and ordered the defendants to remove all content from the *candyland.com* Web site and to stop using the Candyland mark.

REASON The court reasoned that Hasbro had shown that the defendants' use of the Candyland mark and the domain name candyland.com in connection with their Internet site was causing irreparable injury to Hasbro. As required to obtain an injunction, Hasbro had demonstrated a likelihood of prevailing on its claims that the defendants' conduct violated both the federal and the Washington State statutes against trademark dilution. "The probable harm to Hasbro from defendants' conduct outweighs any inconvenience that defendants will experience if they are required to stop using the CANDYLAND name."

WHY IS THIS CASE IMPORTANT? *This was the first case alleging dilution on the Web. The court precluded the use of* candyland.com *as a URL for an adult site, even though consumers were not likely to confuse an adult Web site with a children's board game.*

Patents

A **patent** is a grant from the government that gives an inventor the exclusive right to make, use, and sell an invention for a period of twenty years. Patents for designs, as opposed to inventions, are given for a fourteen-year period.

Until recently, patent law in the United States differed from the laws of many other countries because the first person to invent a product or process obtained the patent rights rather than the first person to file for a patent. It was often difficult to prove who invented an item first, however, which prompted Congress to change the system in 2011 by passing the America Invents Act.[14] Now the first person to file an application for a patent on a product or process will receive patent protection. In addition, the new law established a nine-month limit for challenging a patent on any ground.

The period of patent protection begins on the date when the patent application is filed, rather than when the patent is issued, which can sometimes be years later. After the patent period ends (either fourteen or twenty years later), the product or process enters the public domain, and anyone can make, sell, or use the invention without paying the patent holder.

Searchable Patent Databases

A significant development relating to patents is the availability online of the world's patent databases. The Web site of the U.S. Patent and Trademark Office (www.uspto.gov) provides searchable databases covering U.S. patents granted since 1976. The Web site of the European Patent Office (www.epo.org) provides online access to 50 million patent documents in more than seventy nations through a searchable network of databases. Businesses use these searchable databases in many ways. Because patents are valuable assets, businesses may need to perform patent searches to list or inventory their assets.

(www.uspto.gov)

This is the home page of the U.S. Patent and Trademark Office. Is its database searchable?

What Is Patentable?

Under federal law, "[w]hoever invents or discovers any new and useful process, machine, manufacture, or composition of matter, or any new and useful improvement thereof, may obtain a patent therefor, subject to the conditions and requirements of this title."[15] Thus, to be patentable, an invention must be *novel, useful,* and *not obvious* in light of current technology.

Almost anything is patentable, except the laws of nature,[16] natural phenomena, and abstract ideas (including algorithms[17]). Even artistic methods and works of art, certain business processes, and the structures of storylines are patentable, provided that they are novel and not obvious.[18]

Plants that are reproduced asexually (by means other than from seed), such as hybrid or genetically engineered plants, are patentable in the United States, as are genetically engineered (or cloned) microorganisms and animals. **CASE EXAMPLE 5.10**   Monsanto, Inc., has been selling its patented genetically modified (GM) seeds to farmers as a way to achieve higher yields from crops using fewer pesticides. Monsanto requires farmers who buy GM seeds to sign licensing agreements promising to plant the seeds for only one crop and to

---

14. The full title of this law is the Leahy-Smith America Invents Act, Pub. L. No. 112-29 (2011), which amended 35 U.S.C. Sections 1, 41, and 321.

15. 35 U.S.C. 101.

16. *Laboratory Corporation of America Holdings v. Metabolite Laboratories, Inc.*, 548 U.S. 124, 126 S.Ct. 2921, 165 L.Ed.2d 399 (2006).

17. An *algorithm* is a step-by-step procedure, formula, or set of instructions for accomplishing a specific task—such as the set of rules used by a search engine to rank the listings contained within its index in response to a particular query.

18. For a United States Supreme Court case discussing the obviousness requirement, see *KSR International Co. v. Teleflex, Inc.*, 550 U.S. 398, 127 S.Ct. 1727, 167 L.Ed.2d 705 (2007). For a discussion of business process patents, see *In re Bilski*, 535 F.3d 943 (Fed.Cir. 2008).

pay a technology fee for each acre planted. To ensure compliance, Monsanto has assigned seventy-five employees whose job is to investigate and prosecute farmers who use the GM seeds illegally. Monsanto has filed more than ninety lawsuits against nearly 150 farmers in the United States and has been awarded more than $15 million in damages (not including out-of-court settlement amounts).[19] ●

> "To invent, you need a good imagination and a pile of junk."
>
> Thomas Edison, 1847–1931
> (American inventor)

Patent Infringement

If a firm makes, uses, or sells another's patented design, product, or process without the patent owner's permission, it commits the tort of patent infringement. Patent infringement may occur even though the patent owner has not put the patented product in commerce. Patent infringement may also occur even though not all features or parts of an invention are copied. (To infringe the patent on a process, however, all steps or their equivalent must be copied.)

Patent Infringement Suits and High-Tech Companies
Obviously, companies that specialize in developing new technology stand to lose significant profits if someone "makes, uses, or sells" devices that incorporate their patented inventions. Because these firms are the holders of numerous patents, they are frequently involved in patent infringement lawsuits (as well as other types of intellectual property disputes). Many companies that make and sell electronics and computer software and hardware are based in foreign nations (for example, Samsung Electronics Company is a Korean firm). Foreign firms can apply for and obtain U.S. patent protection on items that they sell within the United States, just as U.S. firms can obtain protection in foreign nations where they sell goods.

Nevertheless, as a general rule, no patent infringement occurs under U.S. law when a patented product is made and sold in another country. The United States Supreme Court has narrowly construed patent infringement as it applies to exported software. **CASE EXAMPLE 5.11** AT&T Corporation holds a patent on a device used to digitally encode, compress, and process recorded speech. AT&T brought an infringement case against Microsoft Corporation, which admitted that its Windows operating system incorporated software code that infringed on AT&T's patent. The case reached the United States Supreme Court on the question of whether Microsoft's liability extended to computers made in another country. The Court held that it did not. Microsoft was liable only for infringement in the United States and not for the Windows-based computers produced in foreign locations. The Court reasoned that Microsoft had not "supplied" the software for the computers but had only electronically transmitted a master copy, which the foreign manufacturers then copied and loaded onto the computers.[20] ●

Galaxy Tab 10.1 tablet computer at the company's Galaxy Zone showroom in Seoul, Korea.

(Seongjoon Cho/Bloomberg via Getty Images)

Apple, Inc. v. Samsung Electronics Company
As mentioned in the chapter introduction, Apple sued Samsung in federal court alleging that Samsung's Galaxy mobile phones and tablets infringe on Apple's patents. The complaint also included allegations of trade dress violations (that Samsung copied the "look and feel" of iPhones and iPads) and trademark infringement (that the icons used for many of the apps on Samsung's products are nearly identical to Apple's apps).

Apple claimed that its design patents cover the graphical user interface (the display of icons on the home screen), the device's shell, and the screen and button design. It also claimed that its patents cover the way information is displayed on iPhones and other

---

19. See, for example, *Monsanto Co. v. Scruggs*, 459 F.3d 1328 (2006); *Monsanto Co. v. McFarling*, 2005 WL 1490051 (E.D.Mo. 2005); and *Sample v. Monsanto Co.*, 283 F.Supp.2d 1088 (2003).
20. *Microsoft Corp. v. AT&T Corp.*, 550 U.S. 437, 127 S.Ct. 1746, 167 L.Ed.2d 737 (2007).

devices, the way windows pop open, and the way information is scaled and rotated, among other things. Apple argued that Samsung's phones and tablets that use Google's HTC Android operating system violate all of these patents.

In 2012, a jury issued a verdict in favor of Apple and awarded more than $1 billion in damages.[21] The jury found that Samsung had willfully infringed five of Apple's patents and had "diluted" Apple's registered iPhone trade dress. The jury's award was one of the largest ever in a patent case. The case also provides an important precedent for Apple in its legal attacks against Android devices made by other companies because for every iPhone sold worldwide, more than three Android-based smartphones are sold.

Remedies for Patent Infringement

If a patent is infringed, the patent holder may sue for relief in federal court. The patent holder can seek an injunction against the infringer and can also request damages for royalties and lost profits. In some cases, the court may grant the winning party reimbursement for attorneys' fees and costs. If the court determines that the infringement was willful, the court can triple the amount of damages awarded (treble damages).

In the past, permanent injunctions were routinely granted to prevent future infringement. In 2006, however, the United States Supreme Court ruled that patent holders are not automatically entitled to a permanent injunction against future infringing activities. According to the Supreme Court, a patent holder must prove that it has suffered irreparable injury and that the public interest would not be *disserved* by a permanent injunction.[22] This decision gives courts discretion to decide what is equitable in the circumstances and allows them to consider the public interest rather than just the interests of the parties.

CASE EXAMPLE 5.12   In the first case applying this rule, a court found that although Microsoft had infringed on the patent of a small software company, the latter was not entitled to an injunction. According to the court, the small company was not irreparably harmed and could be adequately compensated by monetary damages. Also, the public might suffer negative effects from an injunction because the infringement involved part of Microsoft's widely used Office suite software.[23] ●

Copyright The exclusive right of an author or originator of a literary or artistic production to publish, print, sell, or otherwise use that production for a statutory period of time.

Copyrights

A **copyright** is an intangible property right granted by federal statute to the author or originator of certain literary or artistic productions. The Copyright Act of 1976,[24] as amended, governs copyrights. Works created after January 1, 1978, are automatically given statutory copyright protection for the life of the author plus 70 years. For copyrights owned by publishing companies, the copyright expires 95 years from the date of publication or 120 years from the date of creation, whichever is first. For works by more than one author, the copyright expires 70 years after the death of the last surviving author.

Copyrights can be registered with the U.S. Copyright Office (www.copyright.gov) in Washington, D.C. A copyright owner no longer needs to place a © or *Copr.* or *Copyright* on the work, however, to have the work protected against infringement. Chances are that if somebody created it, somebody owns it.

---

21. *Apple, Inc. v. Samsung Electronics Co.*, Case Nos. CV 11-1846 and CV 12-0630 (N.D. Cal. August 24, 2012).
22. *eBay, Inc. v. MercExchange, LLC*, 547 U.S. 388, 126 S.Ct. 1837, 164 L.Ed.2d 641 (2006).
23. See *Z4 Technologies, Inc. v. Microsoft Corp.*, 434 F.Supp.2d 437 (2006).
24. 17 U.S.C. Sections 101 *et seq.*

What Is Protected Expression?

Works that are copyrightable include books, records, films, artworks, architectural plans, menus, music videos, product packaging, and computer software. To be protected, a work must be "fixed in a durable medium" from which it can be perceived, reproduced, or communicated. Protection is automatic. Registration is not required.

To obtain protection under the Copyright Act, a work must be original and fall into one of the following categories:

1. Literary works (including newspaper and magazine articles, computer and training manuals, catalogues, brochures, and print advertisements).
2. Musical works and accompanying words (including advertising jingles).
3. Dramatic works and accompanying music.
4. Pantomimes and choreographic works (including ballets and other forms of dance).
5. Pictorial, graphic, and sculptural works (including cartoons, maps, posters, statues, and even stuffed animals).
6. Motion pictures and other audiovisual works (including multimedia works).
7. Sound recordings.
8. Architectural works.

(Jewel Samad/AFP/Getty Images)

Artist Shepard Fairey created a poster portrait of Barack Obama. It was clearly based on an Associated Press file photo taken by Manny Garcia. Did Fairey violate copyright law?

Section 102 Exclusions   It is not possible to copyright an idea. Section 102 of the Copyright Act specifically excludes copyright protection for any "idea, procedure, process, system, method of operation, concept, principle, or discovery, regardless of the form in which it is described, explained, illustrated, or embodied." Thus, others can freely use the underlying ideas or principles embodied in a work.

What is copyrightable is the particular way in which an idea is *expressed*. Whenever an idea and an expression are inseparable, the expression cannot be copyrighted. Generally, anything that is not an original expression will not qualify for copyright protection. Facts widely known to the public are not copyrightable. Page numbers are not copyrightable because they follow a sequence known to everyone. Mathematical calculations are not copyrightable.

ETHICAL ISSUE

Should the federal Copyright Act preempt plaintiffs from bringing "idea-submission" claims under state law? In the past, federal courts generally held that the Copyright Act preempted (or superseded—see Chapter 2) claims in state courts alleging the theft of ideas. In 2011, however, a federal appellate court's decision in the case, *Montz v. Pilgrim Films*,[25] opened the door to such claims. The plaintiff, Larry Montz, had presented representatives from NBC Universal with a concept for a reality-style television program that would follow two paranormal investigators who search for evidence of ghosts. A number of meetings and discussions took place during which Montz provided scripts, videos, and other materials for the proposed show. Ultimately, the studio decided that it was not interested. Three years later, however, NBC partnered with Pilgrim Films to produce *Ghost Hunters*, a series on the Syfy channel that depicts a team of investigators who travel around the country looking for paranormal activity. Montz sued the producers for copyright infringement, breach of contract, and breach of confidence. He claimed that he had expressly conditioned the disclosure of his idea on an expectation that he would be a partner with NBC on the production and would receive a share of any profits.

The lower court dismissed his case, but the appellate court reversed, finding that the Copyright Act did not preempt Montz's two state law claims (breach of an implied contract and breach of confidence). The court reasoned that the state claims asserted rights that are qualitatively different from the rights protected by copyright. The contract claim survived preemption because it required proof of an extra element—the implied agreement of payment for use of a concept—which is

---

25. 649 F.3d 975 (9th Cir. 2011). See also *Gross v. Miramax Film Corp.*, 383 F.3d 965 (9th Cir. 2004), *cert.* denied, 546 U.S. 824, 126 S.Ct. 361, 163 L.Ed.2d 68 (2005).

a personal right that is different from copyright law. Similarly, the breach of confidence claim required the extra element of a confidential relationship between the parties.

Compilations of Facts   Unlike ideas, *compilations* of facts are copyrightable. Under Section 103 of the Copyright Act, a compilation is a work formed by the collection and assembling of preexisting materials or of data that are selected, coordinated, or arranged in such a way that the resulting work as a whole constitutes an original work of authorship.

The key requirement for the copyrightability of a compilation is originality. The White Pages of a telephone directory do not qualify for copyright protection because they simply list alphabetically names and telephone numbers. The Yellow Pages of a directory can be copyrightable, provided that the information is selected, coordinated, or arranged in an original way. Similarly, a court held that a compilation of information about yachts listed for sale may qualify for copyright protection.[26]

Copyright Infringement

Whenever the form or expression of an idea is copied, an infringement of copyright occurs. The reproduction does not have to be exactly the same as the original, nor does it have to reproduce the original in its entirety. If a substantial part of the original is reproduced, copyright infringement has occurred.

Remedies for Copyright Infringement   Those who infringe copyrights may be liable for damages or criminal penalties. These range from actual damages or statutory damages, imposed at the court's discretion, to criminal proceedings for willful violations. Actual damages are based on the harm caused to the copyright holder by the infringement, while statutory damages, not to exceed $150,000, are provided for under the Copyright Act. In addition, criminal proceedings may result in fines and/or imprisonment. In some instances, a court may grant an injunction against the infringer.

CASE EXAMPLE 5.13   Rusty Carroll operated an online term paper business, R2C2, Inc., that offered up to 300,000 research papers for sale on nine different Web sites. Individuals whose work was posted on these Web sites without their permission filed a lawsuit against Carroll for copyright infringement. A federal district court in Illinois ruled that an injunction was proper because the plaintiffs had shown that they had suffered irreparable harm and that monetary damages were inadequate to compensate them. Because Carroll had repeatedly failed to comply with court orders regarding discovery, the court found that the copyright infringement was likely to continue unless an injunction was issued. The court therefore issued a permanent injunction prohibiting Carroll and R2C2 from selling any term paper without sworn documentary evidence that the paper's author had given permission.[27] •

The "Fair Use" Exception   An exception to liability for copyright infringement is made under the "fair use" doctrine. In certain circumstances, a person or organization can reproduce copyrighted material without paying royalties (fees paid to the copyright holder for the privilege of reproducing the copyrighted material). Section 107 of the Copyright Act provides as follows:

> [T]he fair use of a copyrighted work, including such use by reproduction in copies or phonorecords or by any other means specified by [Section 106 of the Copyright Act], for purposes such as criticism, comment, news reporting, teaching (including multiple copies for classroom use), scholarship, or research, is not an infringement of copyright. In determining whether the use

"Don't worry about people stealing an idea. If it's original and it's any good, you'll have to ram it down their throats."

Howard Aiken, 1900–1973
(Engineer and pioneer in computing)

---

26. *BUC International Corp. v. International Yacht Council, Ltd.,* 489 F.3d 1129 (11th Cir. 2007).
27. *Weidner v. Carroll,* No. 06-782-DRH, U.S. District Court for the Southern District of Illinois, January 21, 2010.

made of a work in any particular case is a fair use the factors to be considered shall include—

(1) the purpose and character of the use, including whether such use is of a commercial nature or is for nonprofit educational purposes;

(2) the nature of the copyrighted work;

(3) the amount and substantiality of the portion used in relation to the copyrighted work as a whole; and

(4) the effect of the use upon the potential market for or value of the copyrighted work.

What Is Fair Use?

Because these guidelines are very broad, the courts determine whether a particular use is fair on a case-by-case basis. Thus, anyone reproducing copyrighted material may be committing a violation. In determining whether a use is fair, courts have often considered the fourth factor to be the most important.

CASE EXAMPLE 5.14 The owner of copyrighted music, BMG Music Publishing, granted a license to Leadsinger, Inc., a manufacturer of karaoke devices. The license gave Leadsinger permission to reproduce the sound recordings, but not to reprint the song lyrics, which appeared at the bottom of a TV screen when the karaoke device was used. BMG demanded that Leadsinger pay a "lyric reprint" fee and a "synchronization" fee. Leadsinger refused to pay, claiming that its use of the lyrics was educational and thus did not constitute copyright infringement under the fair use exception. A federal appellate court disagreed. The court held that Leadsinger's display of the lyrics was not a fair use because it would have a negative effect on the value of the copyrighted work.[28] ●

The First Sale Doctrine

Section 109(a) of the Copyright Act—also known as the first sale doctrine—provides that "the owner of a particular copy or phonorecord lawfully made under [the Copyright Act], or any person authorized by such owner, is entitled, without the authority of the copyright owner, to sell or otherwise dispose of the possession of that copy or phonorecord." In other words, once a copyright owner sells or gives away a particular copy of a work, the copyright owner no longer has the right to control the distribution of that copy. Thus, for example, a person who buys a copyrighted book can sell it to another person.

Until 2011, it was unclear whether the first sale doctrine applied to the promotional CDs that music companies often send to individuals in the music industry, such as music critics and radio programmers. **CASE EXAMPLE 5.15** Universal Music Group (UMG) regularly ships promotional CDs to people in the music industry. The labels state that the CDs are "the property of the record company," "licensed to the intended recipient," and for "Promotional Use Only—Not for Sale." Troy Augusto obtained some of these promotional CDs from various sources and sold them through online auction sites. When UMG filed a copyright infringement lawsuit, Augusto argued that the music company had given up its right to control further distribution of the CDs under the first sale doctrine.

Ultimately, a federal appellate court held that UMG had conveyed title of the copyrighted promotional CDs to the recipients, rather than simply creating licenses. The court reasoned that the promotional CDs were dispatched to the recipients without any prior arrangement as to those particular copies. Furthermore, because the recipients had not agreed to a license, the written restriction placed on the CD labels was insufficient to create one. ●

Copyright Protection for Software

In 1980, Congress passed the Computer Software Copyright Act, which amended the Copyright Act of 1976 to include computer programs in the list of creative works protected by federal copyright law.

---

28. *Leadsinger, Inc. v. BMG Music Publishing,* 512 F.3d 522 (9th Cir. 2008).

Generally, the courts have extended copyright protection not only to those parts of a computer program that can be read by humans, such as the high-level language of a source code, but also to the binary-language object code of a computer program, which is readable only by the computer. Additionally, such elements as the overall structure, sequence, and organization of a program have been deemed copyrightable. Not all aspects of software are protected, however. For the most part, though, courts have not extended copyright protection to the "look and feel"—the general appearance, command structure, video images, menus, windows, and other screen displays—of computer programs. (Note that copying the "look and feel" of another's product may be a violation of trade dress or trademark laws, as Apple, Inc., alleged in its iPhone lawsuit discussed on page 139.)

Copyrights in Digital Information

Copyright law is probably the most important form of intellectual property protection on the Internet, largely because much of the material on the Web (software, for example) is copyrighted and, in order to be transferred online, it must be "copied." Technology has vastly increased the potential for copyright infringement. Generally, anytime a party downloads software or music into a device's random access memory, or RAM, without authorization, a copyright is infringed.

CASE EXAMPLE 5.16   In one case, a rap song that was included in the sound track of a movie had used only a few seconds from the guitar solo of another's copyrighted sound recording without permission. Nevertheless, a federal appellate court held that digitally sampling a copyrighted sound recording of any length constitutes copyright infringement.[29] ●

In 1998, Congress passed additional legislation to protect copyright holders—the Digital Millennium Copyright Act (DMCA). Because of its significance in protecting against the piracy of copyrighted materials in the online environment, this act is presented as this chapter's *Landmark in the Law* feature on the facing page.

Despite the DMCA and other efforts to combat online piracy, it has continued unabated and even grown, as downloading e-books and movies has become more popular. As media industries complained that counterfeit products were costing both profits and American jobs, two measures to curb piracy were introduced in Congress—the Stop Online Piracy Act (SOPA) in the House and the Protect IP Act (PIPA) in the Senate. Both versions were highly controversial, however.

MP3 and File-Sharing Technology

Soon after the Internet became popular, a few enterprising programmers created software to compress large data files, particularly those associated with music, so that they could be more easily transmitted online. The best-known compression and decompression system is MP3, which enables music fans to download songs or entire CDs onto their computers or onto a portable listening device, such as an iPod. The MP3 system also made it possible for music fans to access other fans' files by engaging in file-sharing via the Internet.

Peer-to-Peer (P2P) Networking The sharing of resources (such as files, hard drives, and processing styles) among multiple computers.

Distributed Network A network used by persons located (distributed) in different places to share computer files.

File-Sharing   File-sharing is accomplished through **peer-to-peer (P2P) networking.** The concept is simple. Rather than going through a central Web server, P2P involves numerous personal computers (PCs) that are connected to the Internet. Individuals on the same network can access files stored on a single PC through a **distributed network,** which has parts dispersed in many locations. Persons scattered throughout the country or the world can work together on the same project by using file-sharing programs. A popular method

---

29. *Bridgeport Music, Inc. v. Dimension Films,* 410 F.3d 792 (6th Cir. 2005).

LANDMARK IN THE LAW
The Digital Millennium Copyright Act of 1998

The United States leads the world in the production of creative products, including books, films, videos, recordings, and software. Exports of U.S. creative products surpass those of every other U.S. industry in value.

Given the importance of intellectual property to the U.S. economy, the United States has actively supported international efforts to protect ownership rights in intellectual property, including copyrights. In 1996, to curb unauthorized copying of copyrighted materials, the member nations of the World Intellectual Property Organization (WIPO) adopted a treaty to upgrade global standards of copyright protection, particularly for the Internet.

Implementing the WIPO Treaty Congress implemented the provisions of the WIPO treaty by enacting a new statute to update U.S. copyright law. The law—the Digital Millennium Copyright Act of 1998 (DCMA)—is a landmark step in the protection of copyright owners and, because of the leading position of the United States in the creative industries, serves as a model for other nations. Among other things, the DCMA established civil and criminal penalties for anyone who circumvents (bypasses) encryption software or other technological antipiracy protection. Also prohibited are the manufacture, import, sale, and distribution of devices or services for circumvention.

The act provides for exceptions to fit the needs of libraries, scientists, universities, and others. In general, the law does not restrict the "fair use" of circumvention methods for educational and other noncommercial purposes. For example, circumvention is allowed to test computer security, conduct encryption research, protect personal privacy, and enable parents to monitor their children's use of the Internet. The exceptions are to be reconsidered every three years.

Limiting the Liability of Internet Service Providers The DCMA also limited the liability of Internet service providers (ISPs). Under the act, an ISP is not liable for any copyright infringement by its customer *unless* the ISP is aware of the subscriber's violation. An ISP may be held liable only if it fails to take action to shut the subscriber down after learning of the violation. A copyright holder has to act promptly, however, by pursuing a claim in court, or the subscriber has the right to be restored to online access.

Application to Today's World *Without the DCMA, copyright owners would have a more difficult time obtaining legal redress against those who, without authorization, decrypt and/or copy copyrighted materials. Nevertheless, problems remain, particularly because of the global nature of the Internet.*

Cloud Computing A Web-based service that extends a computer's software or storage capabilities by allowing users to remotely access excess storage and computing capacity as needed.

of sharing very large files over the Internet uses torrenting programs such as the technology first developed by BitTorrent.

A newer method of sharing files via the Internet is **cloud computing**, which is essentially a subscription-based or pay-per-use service that extends a computer's software or storage capabilities. Cloud computing can deliver a single application through a browser to multiple users, or it may be a utility program to pool resources and provide data storage and virtual servers that can be accessed on demand. Amazon, Apple, Facebook, Google, IBM, and Sun Microsystems are using and developing additional cloud computing services.

Sharing Stored Music Files When file-sharing is used to download others' stored music files, copyright issues arise. Recording artists and their labels are losing large amounts of royalties and revenues because few CDs are purchased and then made available on distributed networks, from which everyone can download them for free. **CASE EXAMPLE 5.17** The issue of file-sharing infringement has been the subject of an ongoing debate since highly publicized cases against two companies (Napster, Inc. and Grokster, Ltd.) that created software used for copyright infringement. In the first case, Napster operated a Web site with free software that enabled users to copy and transfer MP3 files via the Internet. Firms in the recording industry sued Napster. Ultimately, the court held that Napster was liable for contributory and vicarious[30] (indirect) copyright infringement. As technology evolved, Grokster, Ltd., and several other companies created and distributed new types of file-sharing software that did not maintain a central index of content, but allowed P2P network users to share stored music files. The court held that because the companies distributed file-sharing software "with the object of promoting its use to infringe the copyright," they were liable for the resulting acts of infringement by third-party users.[31] ●

Trade Secrets

The law of trade secrets protects some business processes and information that are not or cannot be protected under patent, copyright, or trademark law against appropriation by a competitor. A **trade secret** is basically information of commercial value. Trade secrets may include customer lists, plans, research and development, pricing information, marketing techniques, and production methods—anything that makes an individual company unique and that would have value to a competitor.

Unlike copyright and trademark protection, protection of trade secrets extends both to ideas and to their expression. (For this reason, and because there are no registration or filing requirements for trade secrets, trade secret protection may be well suited for software.) Of course, the secret formula, method, or other information must be disclosed to some persons, particularly to key employees. Businesses generally attempt to protect their trade secrets by having all employees who use the process or information agree in their contracts, or in confidentiality agreements, never to divulge it.[32]

State and Federal Law on Trade Secrets

Under Section 757 of the *Restatement of Torts*, those who disclose or use another's trade secret, without authorization, are liable to that other party if (1) they discovered the secret by improper means or (2) their disclosure or use constitutes a breach of a duty owed to the other party. The theft of confidential business data by industrial espionage, as when a business taps into a competitor's computer, is a theft of trade secrets without any contractual violation and is actionable in itself.

Although trade secrets have long been protected under the common law, today most states' laws are based on the Uniform Trade Secrets Act, which has been adopted in forty-seven states. Additionally, in 1996 Congress passed the Economic Espionage Act, which made the theft of trade secrets a federal crime. We will examine the provisions and significance of this act in Chapter 6, in the context of crimes related to business.

Trade Secrets in Cyberspace

Today's computer technology undercuts a business firm's ability to protect its confidential information, including trade secrets. For instance, a dishonest employee could e-mail trade secrets in a company's computer to a competitor or a future employer. If e-mail is not an option, the employee might walk out with the information on a flash pen drive.

---

30. *Vicarious (indirect) liability* exists when one person is subject to liability for another's actions. A common example occurs in the employment context, when an employer is held vicariously liable by third parties for torts committed by employees in the course of their employment.

31. *A&M Records, Inc. v. Napster, Inc.,* 239 F.3d 1004 (9th Cir. 2001); and *Metro-Goldwyn-Mayer Studios, Inc. v. Grokster, Ltd.,* 545 U.S. 913, 125 S.Ct. 2764, 162 L.Ed.2d 781 (2005). Grokster, Ltd., later settled this dispute out of court and stopped distributing its software.

32. See, for example, *Verigy US, Inc. v. Mayder,* 2008 WL 5063873 (N.D.Cal. 2008); and *Gleeson v. Preferred Sourcing, LLC,* 883 N.E.2d 164 (Ind.App. 2008).

A former employee's continued use of a Twitter account after leaving the company may be the grounds for a suit alleging misappropriation of trade secrets. **CASE EXAMPLE 5.18** Noah Kravitz worked for a company called PhoneDog for four years as a product reviewer and video blogger. PhoneDog provided him with the Twitter account "@PhoneDog_Noah." Kravitz's popularity grew, and he had approximately 17,000 followers by the time he quit in 2010. PhoneDog requested that Kravitz stop using the Twitter account. Although Kravitz changed his handle to "@noahkravitz," he continued to use the account. PhoneDog subsequently sued Kravitz for misappropriation of trade secrets, among other things. Kravitz moved for a dismissal, but the court found that the complaint adequately stated a cause of action for misappropriation of trade secrets and allowed the suit to continue.[33] ●

For a summary of trade secrets and other forms of intellectual property, see Exhibit 5.1 below.

International Protection for Intellectual Property

For many years, the United States has been a party to various international agreements relating to intellectual property rights. For example, the Paris Convention of 1883, to which about 173 countries are signatory, allows parties in one country to file for patent and trademark protection in any of the other member countries. Other international agreements

---

33. *PhoneDog v. Kravitz*, 2011 WL 5415612 (N.D.Cal. 2011).

Exhibit 5.1 Forms of Intellectual Property

	DEFINITION	HOW ACQUIRED	DURATION	REMEDY FOR INFRINGEMENT
Patent	A grant from the government that gives an inventor exclusive rights to an invention.	By filing a patent application with the U.S. Patent and Trademark Office and receiving its approval.	Twenty years from the date of the application; for design patents, fourteen years.	Monetary damages, including royalties and lost profits, *plus* attorneys' fees. Damages may be tripled for intentional infringements.
Copyright	The right of an author or originator of a literary or artistic work, or other production that falls within a specified category, to have the exclusive use of that work for a given period of time.	Automatic (once the work or creation is put in tangible form). Only the *expression* of an idea (and not the idea itself) can be protected by copyright.	For authors: the life of the author, plus 70 years. For publishers: 95 years after the date of publication or 120 years after creation.	Actual damages plus profits received by the party who infringed *or* statutory damages under the Copyright Act, *plus* costs and attorneys' fees in either situation.
Trademark (service mark and trade dress)	Any distinctive word, name, symbol, or device (image or appearance), or combination thereof, that an entity uses to distinguish its goods or services from those of others. The owner has the exclusive right to use that mark or trade dress.	1. At common law, ownership created by use of the mark. 2. Registration with the appropriate federal or state office gives notice and is permitted if the mark is currently in use or will be within the next six months.	Unlimited, as long as it is in use. To continue notice by registration, the owner must renew by filing between the fifth and sixth years, and thereafter, every ten years.	1. Injunction prohibiting the future use of the mark. 2. Actual damages plus profits received by the party who infringed (can be increased under the Lanham Act). 3. Destruction of articles that infringed. 4. *Plus* costs and attorneys' fees.
Trade Secret	Any information that a business possesses and that gives the business an advantage over competitors (including formulas, lists, patterns, plans, processes, and programs).	Through the originality and development of the information and processes that constitute the business secret and are unknown to others.	Unlimited, so long as not revealed to others. Once revealed to others, it is no longer a trade secret.	Monetary damages for misappropriation (the Uniform Trade Secrets Act also permits punitive damages if willful), *plus* costs and attorneys' fees.

include the Berne Convention, the Trade-Related Aspects of Intellectual Property Rights (known as the TRIPS agreement), and the Madrid Protocol.

To learn about a new international treaty that will affect international property rights, see this chapter's *Beyond Our Borders* feature below.

The Berne Convention

Under the Berne Convention of 1886, an international copyright agreement, if a U.S. citizen writes a book, every country that has signed the convention must recognize her or his copyright in the book. Also, if a citizen of a country that has not signed the convention first publishes a book in one of the 163 countries that have signed, all other countries that have signed the convention must recognize that author's copyright. Copyright notice is not needed to gain protection under the Berne Convention for works published after March 1, 1989.

This convention and other international agreements have given some protection to intellectual property on a worldwide level. None of them, however, has been as significant and far reaching in scope as the TRIPS agreement, discussed in the next subsection.

In 2011, the European Union agreed to extend the period of royalty protection for musicians from fifty years to seventy years. This decision aids major record labels as well as performers and musicians who previously faced losing royalties from sales of their older recordings. The profits of musicians and record companies have been shrinking in recent years because of the sharp decline in sales of compact discs and the rise in digital downloads (both legal and illegal).

In the following case, the United States Supreme Court had to decide if Congress had exceeded its authority under the U.S. Constitution when it enacted a law that restored copyright protection to many foreign works that were already in the public domain.

 BEYOND OUR BORDERS   **The Anti-Counterfeiting Trade Agreement**

After several years of negotiations, in 2011 Australia, Canada, Japan, Korea, Morocco, New Zealand, Singapore, and the United States signed a new international treaty to combat global counterfeiting and piracy. The European Union, Mexico, Switzerland, and other nations that support the treaty are still developing domestic procedures to comply with its provisions. Once a nation has adopted appropriate procedures, it can ratify the treaty.

Provisions and Goals
The treaty, called the Anti-Counterfeiting Trade Agreement (ACTA), will have its own governing body. The goal of ACTA is to increase international cooperation, facilitate the best law enforcement practices,

and provide a legal framework to combat counterfeiting.

The treaty applies not only to counterfeit physical goods, such as medications, but also to pirated copyrighted works being distributed via the Internet. The idea is to create a new standard of enforcement for intellectual property rights that goes beyond the TRIPS agreement and encourages international cooperation and information sharing among signatory countries.

Border Searches
Under ACTA, member nations are required to establish border measures that allow officials, on their own initiative, to search commercial shipments of imports and exports for counterfeit goods. The treaty

neither requires nor prohibits random border searches of electronic devices, such as laptops and iPads, for infringing content. If border authorities reasonably believe that any goods in transit are counterfeit, the treaty allows them to keep the suspect goods unless the owner proves that the items are authentic and noninfringing.

The treaty allows member nations, in accordance with their own laws, to order online service providers to furnish information about (including the identity of) suspected trademark and copyright infringers.

Critical Thinking
Why will product counterfeiting always exist?

Case 5.3

Golan v. Holder

Supreme Court of the United States,
___ U.S. ___, 132 S.Ct. 873, 181 L.Ed.2d 835 (2012).

(cribben/Shutterstock.com)

Why do U.S. entertainers now have to pay royalties on older European compositions?

FACTS The United States joined the Berne Convention in 1989, but it failed to give foreign copyright holders the same protections enjoyed by U.S. authors. Contrary to the Berne Convention, the United States did not protect any foreign work that had already entered the public domain. In 1994, Congress enacted the Uruguay Round Agreements Act (URAA), which "restored" copyright protection for many foreign works that were already in the public domain. The URAA put foreign and domestic works on the same footing, allowing their copyrights to extend for the same terms. Lawrence Golan, along with a group of musicians, conductors, and publishers, filed a suit against Eric Holder, in his capacity as the U.S. Attorney General, challenging the URAA and claiming that it violated the copyright clause of the U.S. Constitution. These individuals had enjoyed free access to foreign works in the public domain before the URAA's enactment and argued that Congress had exceeded its constitutional authority in passing the URAA. A federal appellate court held that Congress did not violate the copyright clause by passing the URAA. The petitioners appealed. The United States Supreme Court granted *certiorari* to resolve the matter.

ISSUE Does the URAA violate the copyright clause in the U.S. Constitution by restoring copyright protection for foreign works in the public domain?

DECISION No. The United States Supreme Court affirmed the judgment of the federal appellate court. Thus, Golan and the others could no longer use, without permission, any of the previous public domain foreign works, which are indeed protected by the URAA. By passing the URAA in the United States, Congress, in effect, took the foreign works that Golan and others had been using out of the public domain. Henceforth, U.S. copyright and patent laws cover all such foreign intellectual property.

REASON The copyright clause empowers Congress "to promote the Progress of Science . . . by securing for limited Times to Authors . . . the exclusive Right to their Writings." The Court concluded that Congress is not barred from protecting works in the public domain simply because a copyright must exist for only a "limited time." The Court relied heavily on the precedent set by its decision in an earlier case in which it held that Congress did not violate the copyright clause by extending existing copyrights by twenty years.[a] In that case, the Court declined to interpret the text of the copyright clause as requiring that a "time prescription, once set, becomes forever 'fixed' or 'inalterable.'" In passing the URAA, Congress did not create perpetual copyrights. Therefore, the URAA does not violate the copyright clause.

CRITICAL THINKING—Global Consideration *What does the Court's decision in this case mean for copyright holders in the United States who want copyright protection in other countries? Will other nations be more or less inclined to protect U.S. authors? Explain.*

a. See *Eldred v. Ashcroft*, 537 U.S. 186, 123 S.Ct. 769, 154 L.Ed.2d 683 (2003).

The TRIPS Agreement

Representatives from more than one hundred nations signed the TRIPS agreement in 1994. The agreement established, for the first time, standards for the international protection of intellectual property rights, including patents, trademarks, and copyrights for movies, computer programs, books, and music. The TRIPS agreement provides that each member country must include in its domestic laws broad intellectual property rights and effective remedies (including civil and criminal penalties) for violations of those rights.

Generally, the TRIPS agreement forbids member nations from discriminating against foreign owners of intellectual property rights (in the administration, regulation, or adjudication of such rights). In other words, a member nation cannot give its own nationals (citizens) favorable treatment without offering the same treatment to nationals of all member countries. **EXAMPLE 5.19** A U.S. software manufacturer brings a suit for the infringement of intellectual property rights under Germany's national laws. Because Germany is a member of the TRIPS agreement, the U.S. manufacturer is entitled to receive the same treatment as a German manufacturer. ● Each member nation must also ensure that legal procedures are available for parties who wish to bring actions for infringement of intellectual property rights. Additionally, a related document established a mechanism for settling disputes among member nations.

The Madrid Protocol

In the past, one of the difficulties in protecting U.S. trademarks internationally was that it was time consuming and expensive to apply for trademark registration in foreign countries. The filing fees and procedures for trademark registration vary significantly among individual countries. The Madrid Protocol, however, which was signed into law in 2003, may help to resolve these problems. The Madrid Protocol is an international treaty that has been signed by seventy-three countries. Under its provisions, a U.S. company wishing to register its trademark abroad can submit a single application and designate other member countries in which it would like to register the mark. The treaty was designed to reduce the costs of obtaining international trademark protection by more than 60 percent.

Although the Madrid Protocol may simplify and reduce the cost of trademark registration in foreign nations, it remains to be seen whether it will provide significant benefits to trademark owners. Even with an easier registration process, the question of whether member countries will enforce the law and protect the mark still remains.

Reviewing . . . Intellectual Property and Internet Law

Two computer science majors, Trent and Xavier, have an idea for a new video game, which they propose to call "Hallowed." They form a business and begin developing their idea. Several months later, Trent and Xavier run into a problem with their design and consult with a friend, Brad, who is an expert in creating computer source codes. After the software is completed but before Hallowed is marketed, a video game called Halo 2 is released for both the Xbox and Playstation 3 systems. Halo 2 uses source codes similar to those of Hallowed and imitates Hallowed's overall look and feel, although not all the features are alike. Using the information presented in the chapter, answer the following questions.

1. Would the name *Hallowed* receive protection as a trademark or as trade dress?
2. If Trent and Xavier had obtained a business process patent on Hallowed, would the release of Halo 2 infringe on their patent? Why or why not?
3. Based only on the facts presented above, could Trent and Xavier sue the makers of Halo 2 for copyright infringement? Why or why not?
4. Suppose that Trent and Xavier discover that Brad took the idea of Hallowed and sold it to the company that produced Halo 2. Which type of intellectual property issue does this raise?

DEBATE THIS Congress has amended the Copyright Act several times. Copyright holders now have protection for many decades. Was Congress justified in extending the copyright time periods? Why or why not?

LINKING BUSINESS LAW to Marketing

Trademarks and Service Marks

In your marketing courses, you have learned or will learn about the importance of trademarks. If you become a marketing manager, you will be involved in creating trademarks or service marks for your firm, protecting the firm's existing marks, and ensuring that you do not infringe on anyone else's marks.

The Broad Range of Trademarks and Service Marks

The courts have held that trademarks and service marks consist of much more than well-known brand names, such as Apple or Amazon. As a marketing manager, you will need to be aware that parts of a brand or other product identification often qualify for trademark protection.

- **Catchy Phrases**—Certain brands have established phrases that are associated with them, such as Nike's "Just Do It!" As a marketing manager for a competing product, you will have to avoid such catchy phrases in your own marketing program. Note, though, that not all phrases can become part of a trademark or service mark. When a phrase is extremely common, the courts normally will not grant trademark or service mark protection to it.

- **Abbreviations**—The public sometimes abbreviates a well-known trademark. For example Budweiser beer is known as Bud and Coca-Cola as Coke. As a marketing manager, you should avoid using any name for a product or service that closely resembles a well-known abbreviation, such as Koke for a cola drink.

- **Shapes**—The shape of a brand name, a service mark, or a container can take on exclusivity if the shape clearly aids in product or service identification. For example, just about everyone throughout the world recognizes the shape of a Coca-Cola bottle. As a marketing manager, you would do well to avoid using a similar shape for a new carbonated drink.

- **Ornamental Colors**—Sometimes color combinations can become part of a service mark or trademark. For example,

FedEx established its unique identity with the use of bright orange and purple. The courts have protected this color combination. The same holds for the black-and-copper color combination of Duracell batteries.

- **Ornamental Designs**—Symbols and designs associated with a particular mark are normally protected. Marketing managers should not attempt to copy them. Levi's places a small tag on the left side of the rear pocket of its jeans. Cross uses a cutoff black cone on the top of its pens.

- **Sounds**—Sounds can also be protected. For example, the familiar roar of the Metro-Goldwyn-Mayer (MGM) lion is protected.

When to Protect Your Trademarks and Service Marks

Every business should register its logo as a trademark, and perhaps also its business name and Web site address, to provide the company with the highest level of protection. A trademark will discourage counterfeiting and will give your firm the advantage in the event of future infringement.

Once your company has established a trademark or a service mark, as a manager, you will have to decide how aggressively you wish to protect those marks. If you fail to protect them, your company faces the possibility that they will become generic. Remember that *aspirin, cellophane, thermos, dry ice, shredded wheat,* and many other familiar terms were once legally protected trademarks. Protecting exclusive rights to a mark can be expensive, however, so you will have to determine how much it is worth to your company to protect your rights. If you work in a small company, making major expenditures to protect your trademarks and service marks might not be cost-effective.

Critical Thinking

The U.S. Patent and Trademark Office requires that a registered trademark or service mark be put into commercial use within three years after the application has been approved. Why do you think the federal government established this requirement?

Key Terms

Chapter Summary: Intellectual Property and Internet Law

Trademarks and Related Property (See pages 127–135.)	1. A *trademark* is a distinctive word, symbol, or design that identifies the manufacturer as the source of the goods and distinguishes its products from those made or sold by others. 2. The major federal statutes protecting trademarks and related property are the Lanham Act of 1946 and the Federal Trademark Dilution Act of 1995. Generally, to be protected, a trademark must be sufficiently distinctive from all competing trademarks. 3. *Trademark infringement* occurs when one uses a mark that is the same as, or confusingly similar to, the protected trademark, service mark, trade name, or trade dress of another without permission when marketing goods or services.
Cyber Marks (See pages 135–137.)	A *cyber mark* is a trademark in cyberspace. Trademark infringement in cyberspace occurs when one person uses, in a domain name or in meta tags, a name that is the same as, or confusingly similar to, the protected mark of another.
Patents (See pages 138–140.)	1. A *patent* is a grant from the government that gives an inventor the exclusive right to make, use, and sell an invention for a period of twenty years (fourteen years for a design patent) from the date when the application for a patent is filed. To be patentable, an invention (or a discovery, process, or design) must be genuine, novel, useful, and not obvious in light of current technology. Computer software may be patented. 2. Almost anything is patentable, except the laws of nature, natural phenomena, and abstract ideas (including algorithms). Even business processes or methods are patentable if they relate to a machine or transformation. 3. *Patent infringement* occurs when one uses or sells another's patented design, product, or process without the patent owner's permission. The patent holder can sue the infringer in federal court and request an injunction, but must prove irreparable injury to obtain a permanent injunction against the infringer. The patent holder can also request damages and attorneys' fees. If the infringement was willful, the court can grant treble damages.
Copyrights (See pages 140–146.)	1. A *copyright* is an intangible property right granted by federal statute to the author or originator of certain literary or artistic productions. The Copyright Act of 1976, as amended, governs copyrights. Computer software may be copyrighted. 2. *Copyright infringement* occurs whenever the form or expression of an idea is copied without the permission of the copyright holder. An exception applies if the copying is deemed a "fair use." 3. To protect copyrights in digital information, Congress passed the Digital Millennium Copyright Act of 1998. 4. Technology that allows users to share files via the Internet on distributed networks often raises copyright infringement issues. 5. The courts have ruled that companies that provide file-sharing software to users can be held liable for contributory and vicarious copyright liability.
Trade Secrets (See pages 146–147.)	*Trade secrets* include customer lists, plans, research and development, and pricing information. Trade secrets are protected under the common law and, in some states, under statutory law against misappropriation by competitors. The Economic Espionage Act of 1996 made the theft of trade secrets a federal crime (see Chapter 6).
International Protection for Intellectual Property (See pages 147–150.)	Various international agreements provide international protection for intellectual property. A landmark agreement is the 1994 agreement on Trade-Related Aspects of Intellectual Property Rights (TRIPS), which provides for enforcement procedures in all countries signatory to the agreement.

ExamPrep

ISSUE SPOTTERS

1. Global Products develops, patents, and markets software. World Copies, Inc., sells Global's software without the maker's permission. Is this patent infringement? If so, how might Global save the cost of suing World for infringement and at the same time profit from World's sales? (**See pages 135 and 139.**)
2. Eagle Corporation began marketing software in 2001 under the mark "Eagle." In 2012, Eagle.com, Inc., a different company selling different products, begins to use *eagle* as part of its URL and registers it as a domain name. Can Eagle Corporation stop this use of *eagle*? If so, what must the company show? (**See page 137.**)

— **Check your answers to the Issue Spotters against the answers provided in Appendix E at the end of this text.**

BEFORE THE TEST
Go to www.cengagebrain.com, enter the ISBN 9781133273561 and click on "Find" to locate this textbook's Web site. Then, click on "Access Now" under "Study Tools," and select Chapter 5 at the top. There, you will find a Practice Quiz that you can take to assess your mastery of the concepts in this chapter, as well as Flashcards, a Glossary of important terms, and Video Questions (when assigned).

For Review

Answers to the even-numbered questions in this For Review section can be found in Appendix F at the end of this text.

1. What is intellectual property?
2. Why is the protection of trademarks important?
3. How does the law protect patents?
4. What laws protect authors' rights in the works they create?
5. What are trade secrets, and what laws offer protection for this form of intellectual property?

Business Scenarios and Case Problems

5–1 Patent Infringement. John and Andrew Doney invented a hard-bearing device for balancing rotors. Although they obtained a patent for their invention from the U.S. Patent and Trademark Office, it was never used as an automobile wheel balancer. Some time later, Exetron Corp. produced an automobile wheel balancer that used a hard-bearing device with a support plate similar to that of the Doneys' device. Given that the Doneys had not used their device for automobile wheel balancing, does Exetron's use of a similar device infringe on the Doneys' patent? **(See page 139.)**

5–2 ❓ **Question with Sample Answer—Copyright Infringement.** In which of the following situations would a court likely hold Maruta liable for copyright infringement? Why? **(See page 142.)**

  1. At the library, Maruta photocopies ten pages from a scholarly journal relating to a topic on which she is writing a term paper.
  2. Maruta makes leather handbags and sells them in her small shop. She advertises her handbags as "Vutton handbags," hoping that customers will mistakenly assume that they were made by Vuitton, the well-known maker of high-quality luggage and handbags.
  3. Maruta teaches Latin American history at a small university. She has a digital video recorder and frequently records television programs relating to Latin America and puts them on DVDs. She then takes the DVDs to her classroom so that her students can watch them.

—**For a sample answer to Question 5–2, go to Appendix G at the end of this text.**

5–3 Trade Secrets. Briefing.com offers Internet-based analyses of investment opportunities to investors. Richard Green is the company's president. One of Briefing.com's competitors is StreetAccount, LLC (limited liability company), whose owners include Gregory Jones and Cynthia Dietzmann. Jones worked for Briefing.com for six years until he quit in March 2003, and he was a member of its board of directors until April 2003. Dietzmann worked for Briefing.com for seven years until she quit in March 2003. As Briefing.com employees, Jones and Dietzmann had access to confidential business data. For instance, Dietzmann developed a list of contacts through which Briefing.com obtained market information to display online. When Dietzmann quit, however, she did not return all of the contact information to the company. Briefing.com and Green filed a suit in a federal district court against Jones, Dietzmann, and StreetAccount, alleging that they appropriated these data and other "trade secrets" to form a competing business. What are trade secrets? Why are they protected? Under what circumstances is a party liable at common law for their appropriation? How should these principles apply in this case? [*Briefing.com v. Jones,* 2006 WY 16, 126 P.3d 928 (2006)] **(See pages 146–147.)**

5–4 Licensing. Redwin Wilchcombe composed, performed, and recorded a song called *Tha Weedman* at the request of Lil Jon, a member of Lil Jon & the East Side Boyz (LJESB), for LJESB's album *Kings of Crunk.* Wilchcombe was not paid, but was given credit on the album as a producer. After the album had sold two million copies, Wilchcombe filed a suit against LJESB, alleging copyright infringement. The defendants claimed that they had a license to use the song. Do the facts support this claim? Explain. [*Wilchcombe v. TeeVee Toons, Inc.,* 555 F.3d 949 (11th Cir. 2009)] **(See page 134.)**

5–5 ⚖ **Case Problem with Sample Answer—Trade Secrets.** Jesse Edwards, an employee of Carbon Processing and Reclamation, LLC (CPR), put unmarked boxes of company records in his car. Edwards's wife, Channon, who suspected him of hiding financial information from her, gained access to the documents. William Jones, the owner of CPR, filed a suit, contending that Channon's unauthorized access to the files was a theft of trade secrets. Could the information in the documents be trade secrets? Should liability be imposed?

Why or why not? [*Jones v. Hamilton,* 59 So.3d 134 (Ala.Civ. App. 2010)] **(See page 146.)**

—For a sample answer to Problem 5–5, go to Appendix H at the end of this text.

5–6   **Spotlight on Macy's—Copyright Infringement.** United Fabrics International, Inc., bought a fabric design from an Italian designer and registered a copyright to it with the U.S. Copyright Office. When Macy's, Inc., began selling garments with a similar design, United filed a copyright infringement suit against Macy's. Macy's argued that United did not own a valid copyright to the design and so could not claim infringement. Does United have to prove that the copyright is valid to establish infringement? Explain. [*United Fabrics International, Inc. v. C & J Wear, Inc.,* 630 F.3d 1255 (9th Cir. 2011)] **(See page 142.)**

5–7   **Theft of Trade Secrets.** Hanjuan Jin, a citizen of the People's Republic of China, began working at Motorola in 1998. He worked as a software engineer in a division that created proprietary standards for cellular communications. In 2004 and 2005, in contradiction to Motorola's policies, Jin also began working as a consultant for Lemko Corp. Lemko introduced Jin to Sun Kaisens, a Chinese software company. During 2005, Jin returned to Beijing on several occasions and began working with Sun Kaisens and with the Chinese military. The following year, she started corresponding with Sun Kaisens's management about a possible full-time job in China. During this period, she took several medical leaves of absence from Motorola. In February 2007, after one of these medical leaves, she returned to Motorola. During the next several days at Motorola, she accessed and downloaded thousands of documents on her personal laptop as well as on pen drives. On the following day, she attempted to board a flight to China but was randomly searched by U.S. Customs and Border Protection officials at Chicago's O'Hare International Airport. Ultimately, U.S. officials discovered the thousands of downloaded Motorola documents. Are there any circumstances under which Jin could avoid being prosecuted for theft of trade secrets? If so, what are these circumstances? Discuss fully. [*United States v. Hanjuan Jin,* 833 F.Supp.2d 977 (N.D.Ill. 2012)] **(See pages 146–147.)**

5–8   **A Question of Ethics—Copyright Infringement.** Custom Copies, Inc., prepares and sells coursepacks, which contain compilations of readings for college courses. A teacher selects the readings and delivers a syllabus to the copy shop, which obtains the materials from a library, copies them, and binds the copies. Blackwell Publishing, Inc., which owns the copyright to some of the materials, filed a suit, alleging copyright infringement. [*Blackwell Publishing, Inc. v. Custom Copies, Inc.,* 2006 WL 152950 (N.D.Fla. 2006)] **(See pages 142–144.)**

1. Custom Copies argued, in part, that it did not "distribute" the coursepacks. Does a copy shop violate copyright law if it only copies materials for coursepacks? Does the fair use doctrine apply in these circumstances? Discuss.

2. What is the potential impact if copies of a book or journal are created and sold without the permission of, and the payment of royalties or a fee to, the copyright owner? Explain.

Critical Thinking and Writing Assignments

5–9   **Business Law Writing.** Sync Computers, Inc., makes computer-related products under the brand name "Sync," which the company registers as a trademark. Without Sync's permission, E-Product Corp. embeds the Sync mark in E-Product's Web site, in black type on a blue background. This tag causes the E-Product site to be returned at the top of the list of results on a search engine query for "Sync." Write three paragraphs explaining why E-Product's use of the Sync mark as a meta tag without Sync's permission constitutes trademark infringement. **(See pages 136–137.)**

5–10   **Business Law Critical Thinking Group Assignment.** After years of research, your company develops a product that might revolutionize the green (environmentally conscious) building industry. The product is made from relatively inexpensive and widely available materials combined in a unique way that can substantially lower the heating and cooling costs of residential and commercial buildings. The company has registered the trademark it intends to use on the product, and has filed a patent application with the U.S. Patent and Trademark Office.

1. One group should provide three reasons why this product does or does not qualify for patent protection.

2. Another group should develop a four-step procedure for how your company can best protect its intellectual property rights (trademark, trade secret, and patent) and prevent domestic and foreign competitors from producing counterfeit goods or cheap knockoffs.

3. Another group should list and explain three ways your company can utilize licensing.

Criminal Law and Cyber Crime

(AlexKosev/iStockphoto.com)

CHAPTER OUTLINE

- Civil Law and Criminal Law
- Criminal Liability
- Types of Crimes
- Defenses to Criminal Liability
- Constitutional Safeguards and Criminal Procedures
- Criminal Process
- Cyber Crime

LEARNING OBJECTIVES

The five learning objectives below are designed to help improve your understanding of the chapter. After reading this chapter, you should be able to answer the following questions:

1 What two elements normally must exist before a person can be held liable for a crime?

2 What are five broad categories of crimes? What is white-collar crime?

3 What defenses can be raised to avoid liability for criminal acts?

4 What constitutional safeguards exist to protect persons accused of crimes?

5 How has the Internet expanded opportunities for identity theft?

"The crime problem is getting really serious.
The other day, the Statue of Liberty had both hands up."
—Jay Leno, 1950–present (American comedian and television host)

Criminal law is an important part of the legal environment of business. Various sanctions are used to bring about a society in which businesses can compete and flourish. These sanctions include damages for various types of tortious conduct (see Chapter 4), damages for breach of contract (see Chapter 14), and various equitable remedies (see Chapter 1). Additional sanctions are imposed under criminal law. Many statutes regulating business provide for criminal as well as civil sanctions.

In this chapter, after a brief summary of the major differences between criminal and civil law, we look at the elements that must be present for criminal liability to exist. We then examine various categories of crimes, the defenses that can be raised to avoid liability for criminal actions, and the rules of criminal procedure. Advances in technology allow authorities to trace phone calls and track vehicle movements with greater ease and precision. One such technique is attaching tracking devices to a suspect's vehicle. Is such an action a violation of the constitutional rights of those suspects who are being tracked? You will discover what the courts have to say on this question later in this chapter.

Civil Law and Criminal Law

Remember from Chapter 1 that *civil law* spells out the duties that exist between persons or between persons and their governments, excluding the duty not to commit crimes. Contract law, for example, is part of civil law. The whole body of tort law, which deals with the infringement by one person on the legally recognized rights of another, is also an area of civil law.

Crime A wrong against society proclaimed in a statute and, if committed, punishable by society through fines, imprisonment, or death.

    Criminal law, in contrast, has to do with crime. A **crime** can be defined as a wrong against society proclaimed in a statute and, if committed, punishable by society through fines and/or imprisonment—and, in some cases, death. As mentioned in Chapter 1, because crimes are *offenses against society as a whole,* criminals are prosecuted by a public official, such as a district attorney (D.A.), rather than by the crime victims. Victims often report the crime to the police, but ultimately it is the D.A.'s office that decides whether to file criminal charges and to what extent to pursue the prosecution or carry out additional investigation.

Key Differences between Civil Law and Criminal Law

Because the state has extensive resources at its disposal when prosecuting criminal cases, and because the sanctions can be so severe, there are numerous procedural safeguards to protect the rights of defendants. We look here at one of these safeguards—the higher burden of proof that applies in a criminal case—and at the sanctions imposed for criminal acts. Exhibit 6.1 below summarizes these and other key differences between civil law and criminal law.

Burden of Proof

Beyond a Reasonable Doubt The standard of proof used in criminal cases.

In a civil case, the plaintiff usually must prove his or her case by a *preponderance of the evidence.* Under this standard, the plaintiff must convince the court that, based on the evidence presented by both parties, it is more likely than not that the plaintiff's allegation is true.

    In a criminal case, in contrast, the state must prove its case **beyond a reasonable doubt.** If the jury views the evidence in the case as reasonably permitting either a guilty or a not guilty verdict, then the jury's verdict must be *not* guilty. In other words, the government (prosecutor) must prove beyond a reasonable doubt that the defendant has committed every essential element of the offense with which she or he is charged. If the jurors are not convinced of the defendant's guilt beyond a reasonable doubt, they must find the defendant not guilty.

    Note also that in a criminal case, the jury's verdict normally must be unanimous— agreed to by all members of the jury—to convict the defendant.[1] (In a civil trial by jury, in contrast, typically only three-fourths of the jurors need to agree.)

---

1. Note that there are exceptions—a few states allow jury verdicts that are not unanimous. Arizona, for example, allows six of eight jurors to reach a verdict in criminal cases. Louisiana and Oregon have also relaxed the requirement of unanimous jury verdicts.

Exhibit 6.1 Key Differences between Civil Law and Criminal Law

ISSUE	CIVIL LAW	CRIMINAL LAW
Party who brings suit	The person who suffered harm.	The state.
Wrongful act	Causing harm to a person or to a person's property.	Violating a statute that prohibits some type of activity.
Burden of proof	Preponderance of the evidence.	Beyond a reasonable doubt.
Verdict	Three-fourths majority (typically).	Unanimous (almost always).
Remedy	Damages to compensate for the harm or a decree to achieve an equitable result.	Punishment (fine, imprisonment, or death).

Criminal Sanctions   The sanctions imposed on criminal wrongdoers are also harsher than those applied in civil cases. Remember from Chapter 4 that the purpose of tort law is to allow persons harmed by the wrongful acts of others to obtain compensation from the wrongdoer rather than to punish the wrongdoer.

In contrast, criminal sanctions are designed to punish those who commit crimes and to deter others from committing similar acts in the future. Criminal sanctions include fines as well as the much harsher penalty of the loss of one's liberty by incarceration in a jail or prison. The harshest criminal sanction is, of course, the death penalty.

Civil Liability for Criminal Acts

Some torts, such as assault and battery, provide a basis for a criminal prosecution as well as a tort action. **EXAMPLE 6.1**   Carlos is walking down the street, minding his own business, when suddenly a person attacks him. In the ensuing struggle, the attacker (assailant) stabs Carlos several times, seriously injuring him. A police officer restrains and arrests the wrongdoer. In this situation, the attacker may be subject both to criminal prosecution by the state and to a tort lawsuit brought by Carlos. •

Exhibit 6.2 below illustrates how the same act can result in both a tort action and a criminal action against the wrongdoer.

Exhibit 6.2 Tort Lawsuit and Criminal Prosecution for the Same Act

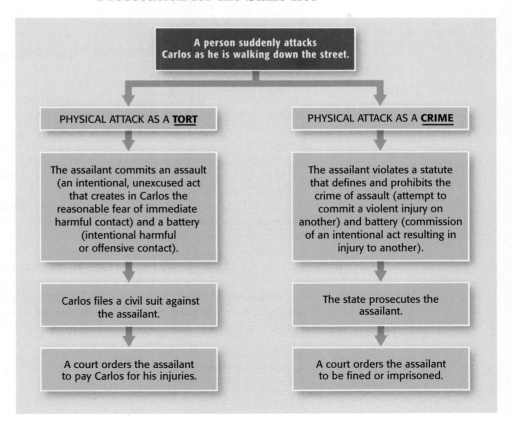

Criminal Liability

LEARNING OBJECTIVE 1
What two elements normally must exist before a person can be held liable for a crime?

Two elements normally must exist simultaneously for a person to be convicted of a crime: (1) the performance of a prohibited act and (2) a specified state of mind or intent on the part of the actor. Note that to establish criminal liability, there must be a *concurrence* between the act and the intent. In other words, these two elements must occur together.

The Criminal Act

Every criminal statute prohibits certain behavior. Most crimes require an act of *commission*. That is, a person must *do* something in order to be accused of a crime. In criminal law, a prohibited act is referred to as the **actus reus**,[2] or guilty act. In some situations, an act of *omission* can be a crime, but only when a person has a legal duty to perform the omitted act, such as failing to file a tax return.

Actus reus A guilty (prohibited) act. The commission of a prohibited act is one of the two essential elements required for criminal liability, the other element being the intent to commit a crime.

The *guilty act* requirement is based on one of the premises of criminal law—that a person is punished for harm done to society. For a crime to exist, the guilty act must cause some harm to a person or to property. Thinking about killing someone or about stealing a car may be wrong, but the thoughts do no harm until they are translated into action. Of course, a person can be punished for attempting murder or robbery, but normally only if he or she took substantial steps toward the criminal objective.

State of Mind

Mens rea The wrongful mental state ("guilty mind"), or intent, that is one of the key requirements to establish criminal liability for an act.

A wrongful mental state **(mens rea)**[3] is generally required to establish criminal liability. What constitutes such a mental state varies according to the wrongful action. For murder, the act is the taking of a life, and the mental state is the intent to take life. For theft, the guilty act is the taking of another person's property, and the mental state involves both the knowledge that the property belongs to another and the intent to deprive the owner of it.

Recklessness and Criminal Negligence   A court can also find that the required mental state is present when a defendant's acts are reckless or criminally negligent. A defendant is *criminally reckless* if he or she consciously disregards a substantial and unjustifiable risk. **EXAMPLE 6.2** A fourteen-year-old New Jersey girl posted a Facebook message saying that she was going to launch a terrorist attack on her high school and asking if anyone wanted to help. The police arrested the girl for the crime of making a terrorist threat, which requires the intent to commit an act of violence with "the intent to terrorize" or "in reckless disregard of the risk of causing" terror or inconvenience. Although the girl claimed that she did not intend to cause harm, she was prosecuted under the "reckless disregard" part of the statute. •

Criminal negligence occurs when the defendant takes an unjustified, substantial, and foreseeable risk that results in harm. A defendant can be negligent even if she or he was not actually aware of the risk but *should have been aware* of it.[4] A homicide is classified as *involuntary manslaughter* when it results from an act of criminal negligence and there is no intent to kill. **EXAMPLE 6.3** Dr. Conrad Murray, the personal physician of pop star Michael Jackson, was convicted of involuntary manslaughter in 2011 for prescribing the drug that led to Jackson's sudden death in 2009. Murray had given Jackson propofol, a powerful anesthetic normally used in surgery, as a sleep aid on the night of his death, even though Murray knew that Jackson had already taken other sedatives. •

---

2. Pronounced *ak-tuhs ray-uhs*.
3. Pronounced *mehns ray-uh*.
4. Model Penal Code Section 2.02(2)(d).

(Frederick M. Brown/Getty Images)

Why was Dr. Conrad Murray convicted of involuntary manslaughter in the death of pop star Michael Jackson?

Strict Liability and Overcriminalization   In recent years, an increasing number of laws and regulations have imposed criminal sanctions for strict liability crimes—that is, offenses that do not require a wrongful mental state, or malice, to establish criminal liability.

Federal Crimes   The federal criminal code now lists more than four thousand criminal offenses, many of which do not require a specific mental state. There are also at least ten thousand federal rules that can be enforced through criminal sanctions, and many of these rules do not require intent. **EXAMPLE 6.4** Eddie Leroy Anderson, a retired logger and former science teacher, and his son went digging for arrowheads near a campground in Idaho. They did not realize that they were on federal land and that it is a crime to take artifacts off federal land without a permit. Although the penalty could be as much as two years in prison, father and son pleaded guilty and were sentenced to probation and a $1,500 fine each. ●

Strict liability crimes are particularly common in environmental laws, laws aimed at combating illegal drugs, and other laws related to public health, safety, and welfare. Under federal law, for instance, tenants can be evicted from public housing if one of their relatives or guests used illegal drugs—regardless of whether the tenant knew or should have known about the drug activity.

State Crimes   Many states have also enacted laws that punish behavior as criminal without the need to show criminal intent. **EXAMPLE 6.5** Under Arizona law, a hunter who shoots an elk outside the area specified by his or her permit has committed a crime. Criminal liability is imposed regardless of the hunter's intent or knowledge of the law.[5] ●

Overcriminalization   Proponents of laws that establish strict liability crimes argue that they are necessary to protect the public and the environment. Critics say that the laws have led to *overcriminalization,* or the use of criminal law to attempt to solve social problems, such as illegal drug use. They argue that when the requirement of intent is removed from criminal offenses, people are more likely to commit crimes unknowingly—and perhaps even innocently. When an honest mistake can lead to a criminal conviction, the role of criminal law as a deterrent to future wrongful conduct is undermined.

Corporate Criminal Liability

As will be discussed in Chapter 29, a *corporation* is a legal entity created under the laws of a state. At one time, it was thought that a corporation could not incur criminal liability because, although a corporation is a legal person, it can act only through its agents (corporate directors, officers, and employees). Therefore, the corporate entity itself could not "intend" to commit a crime. Over time, this view has changed. Obviously, corporations cannot be imprisoned, but they can be fined or denied certain legal privileges (such as necessary licenses).

Liability of the Corporate Entity   Today, corporations are normally liable for the crimes committed by their agents and employees within the course and scope

---

5. See, for example, *State v. Slayton,* 214 Ariz. 511, 154 P.3d 1057 (2007).

of their employment.[6] For such criminal liability to be imposed, the prosecutor typically must show that the corporation could have prevented the act or that a supervisor within the corporation authorized or had knowledge of the act. In addition, corporations can be criminally liable for failing to perform specific duties imposed by law (such as duties under environmental laws or securities laws).

CASE EXAMPLE 6.6   A prostitution ring, the Gold Club, was operating out of motels in West Virginia. A motel manager, who was also an officer in the corporation that owned the motels, gave discounted rates to Gold Club prostitutes, and they paid him in cash. The corporation received a portion of the funds generated by the Gold Club's illegal operations. At trial, the jury found that the corporation was criminally liable because a supervisor within the corporation—the motel manager—had knowledge of the prostitution and the corporation had allowed it to continue.[7] •

Liability of Corporate Officers and Directors

Corporate directors and officers are personally liable for the crimes they commit, regardless of whether the crimes were committed for their personal benefit or on the corporation's behalf. Additionally, corporate directors and officers may be held liable for the actions of employees under their supervision. Under the *responsible corporate officer doctrine,* a court may impose criminal liability on a corporate officer regardless of whether she or he participated in, directed, or even knew about a given criminal violation.[8]

CASE EXAMPLE 6.7   The Roscoe family owned the Customer Company, which operated an underground storage tank that leaked gasoline. After the leak occurred, an employee, John Johnson, notified the state environmental agency, and the Roscoes hired an environmental services firm to clean up the spill. The clean-up did not occur immediately, however, and the state sent many notices to John Roscoe, a corporate officer, warning him that the company was violating federal and state environmental laws. Roscoe gave the letters to Johnson, who passed them on to the environmental services firm, but the spill was not cleaned up. The state eventually filed criminal charges against the corporation and the Roscoes individually, and they were convicted. On appeal, the court affirmed the Roscoes' convictions under the responsible corporate officer doctrine. The Roscoes were in positions of responsibility, they had influence over the corporation's actions, and their failure to act constituted a violation of environmental laws.[9] •

(AP Photo/Seth Wenig)

Gary Foster, formerly a Citigroup vice president, embezzled $22 million from his employer. Are corporate officers liable for their crimes?

PREVENTING LEGAL DISPUTES

If you become a corporate officer or director at some point in your career, you need to be aware that you can be held liable for the crimes of your subordinates. You should always be familiar with any criminal statutes relevant to the corporation's particular industry or trade. Also, make sure that corporate employees are trained in how to comply with the multitude of applicable laws, particularly environmental laws and health and safety regulations, which frequently involve criminal sanctions.

---

6. See Model Penal Code Section 2.07.

7. As a result of the convictions, the motel manager was sentenced to fifteen months in prison, and the corporation was ordered to forfeit the motel property. *United States v. Singh,* 518 F.3d 236 (4th Cir. 2008).

8. For a landmark case in this area, see *United States v. Park,* 421 U.S. 658, 95 S.Ct. 1903, 44 L.Ed.2d 489 (1975).

9. The Roscoes and the corporation were sentenced to pay penalties of $2,493,250. *People v. Roscoe,* 169 Cal.App.4th 829, 87 Cal.Rptr.3d 187 (3 Dist. 2008).

Types of Crimes

Federal, state, and local laws provide for the classification and punishment of hundreds of thousands of different criminal acts. Traditionally, though, crimes have been grouped into five broad categories: violent crime (crimes against persons), property crime, public order crime, white-collar crime, and organized crime. Within each of these categories, crimes may also be separated into more than one classification. Note also that many crimes may be committed in cyberspace, as well as the physical world. When they occur in the virtual world, we refer to them as cyber crimes, as discussed later in the chapter.

Violent Crime

Crimes against persons, because they cause others to suffer harm or death, are referred to as *violent crimes*. Murder is a violent crime. So, too, is sexual assault, or rape. **Robbery**—defined as the taking of cash, personal property, or any other article of value from a person by means of force or fear—is another violent crime. Typically, states have more severe penalties for *aggravated robbery*—robbery with the use of a deadly weapon.

Assault and battery, which were discussed in Chapter 4 in the context of tort law, are also classified as violent crimes. Recall that assault can involve an object or force put into motion by a person. **EXAMPLE 6.8** On the anniversary of a landmark abortion rights decision, Paul drives his sport utility vehicle into a local abortion clinic. The police arrest him for aggravated assault even though no one is injured by his act. ●

Each of these violent crimes is further classified by degree, depending on the circumstances surrounding the criminal act. These circumstances include the intent of the person committing the crime, whether a weapon was used, and (in cases other than murder) the level of pain and suffering experienced by the victim. (For a discussion of why some violent crimes committed on Indian reservations are not being prosecuted, see this chapter's *Law, Diversity, and Business: Managerial Implications* feature on the following page.)

Property Crime

The most common type of criminal activity is property crime—crimes in which the goal of the offender is some form of economic gain or the damaging of property. Robbery is a form of property crime, as well as a violent crime, because the offender seeks to gain the property of another. We look here at a number of other crimes that fall within the general category of property crime. (Note also that many types of cyber crime, discussed later in this chapter, are forms of property crime as well.)

Burglary Traditionally, **burglary** was defined under the common law as breaking and entering the dwelling of another at night with the intent to commit a felony. Originally, the definition was aimed at protecting an individual's home and its occupants. Most state statutes have eliminated some of the requirements found in the common law definition. The time of day at which the breaking and entering occurs, for example, is usually immaterial. State statutes frequently omit the element of breaking, and some states do not require that the building be a dwelling. When a deadly weapon is used in a burglary, the person can be charged with *aggravated burglary* and punished more severely.

Larceny Under the common law, the crime of **larceny** involved the unlawful taking and carrying away of someone else's personal property with the intent to permanently deprive the owner of possession. Put simply, larceny is stealing, or theft. Whereas robbery involves force or fear, larceny does not. Therefore, picking pockets is larceny, not robbery.

LEARNING OBJECTIVE 2
What are five broad categories of crimes? What is white-collar crime?

Robbery The act of forcefully and unlawfully taking personal property of any value from another.

Burglary The unlawful entry or breaking into a building with the intent to commit a felony.

Larceny The wrongful taking and carrying away of another person's personal property with the intent to permanently deprive the owner of the property.

LAW, DIVERSITY, AND BUSINESS: MANAGERIAL IMPLICATIONS

NATIVE AMERICANS AND CRIMINAL JUSTICE

Thanks to freedom from state antigambling laws and "sin" taxes on alcohol and cigarettes, Native American reservations are often considered to be somewhat outside the law. Indeed, Vernon Roanhorse, a Navajo tribal official, calls his reservation a "lawless land." The problems, however, go much deeper than casinos and cheap cigarettes.

In its earliest days, the U.S. government treated the various Native American tribes as individual sovereign nations. Ever since, the government has allowed Native Americans a considerable amount of self-rule. Nevertheless, tribal leaders do not have complete jurisdiction over all events that occur on tribal lands, including crimes.

Problems with Criminal Jurisdiction   As far as criminal law is concerned, the 275 tribes operate in a jurisdictional void. They run their own court systems, but federal law denies tribal courts criminal jurisdiction over defendants who are not Indians or are Indians from a different tribe.

Furthermore, Native American courts *cannot prosecute felonies* (the most serious crimes) under any circumstances. For these crimes, they must rely on the Federal Bureau of Investigation (FBI) to act as their police force and U.S. attorneys to act as their prosecutors.

Lack of Federal Enforcement   The federal government's record in this area is dismal. About 200 criminal charges

involving Native Americans are dismissed each year because FBI agents fail to file arrest reports. For their part, U.S. attorneys decline to prosecute about two-thirds of all Indian Country cases.

According to a 2011 report by the National Organization for Women, Native American women experience the highest rate of violence of any group in the United States. Domestic violence, sexual abuse, and stalking crimes are common. More than 80 percent of Native American rape victims identify their assailant as non-Indian, which means that these suspects are out of the reach of Native American jurisdiction and can be apprehended only by the often unresponsive federal criminal justice system.

Business Implications   *In today's legal environment, many crimes do not involve violence, but rather are violations of corporate, consumer, environmental, or intellectual property laws. Those who do business with Native Americans should be aware of the jurisdictional problems that affect criminal prosecutions, particularly with felony offenses. In contracts with Native Americans, businesspersons should consider using arbitration or forum-selection clauses that specify how and where any disputes will be resolved.*

Similarly, an employee who takes company products and supplies home for personal use without authorization commits larceny. (Note that a person who commits larceny generally can also be sued under tort law because the act of taking possession of another's property involves a trespass to personal property.)

Most states have expanded the definition of property that is subject to larceny statutes. Stealing computer programs may constitute larceny even though the "property" is not physical (see the discussion of computer crime later in this chapter). So, too, can the theft of natural gas or Internet and television cable service.

Obtaining Goods by False Pretenses   Obtaining goods by means of false pretenses is a form of theft that involves trickery or fraud, such as paying for an iPad with a stolen credit-card number. Statutes dealing with such illegal activities vary widely from state to state. They often apply not only to acquiring property, but also to obtaining services or funds by false pretenses—for example, selling an iPad that you claim is yours when you actually do not own it.

Receiving Stolen Goods   It is a crime to receive goods that a person knows or should have known were stolen or illegally obtained. To be convicted, the recipient of such goods need not know the true identity of the owner or the thief, and need not have paid for

the goods. All that is necessary is that the recipient knows or should have known that the goods were stolen, and intended to deprive the true owner of those goods.

Arson

Arson The intentional burning of a building.

The willful and malicious burning of a building (and, in some states, vehicles and other items of personal property) is the crime of **arson.** At common law, arson traditionally applied only to burning down another person's house. The law was designed to protect human life. Today, arson statutes have been extended to cover the destruction of any building, regardless of ownership, by fire or explosion.

Every state has a special statute that covers the act of burning a building for the purpose of collecting insurance. **EXAMPLE 6.9** Benton owns an insured apartment building that is falling apart. If he sets fire to it or pays someone else to do so, he is guilty not only of arson but also of defrauding the insurer, which is attempted larceny. • Of course, the insurer need not pay the claim when insurance fraud is proved.

Forgery

Forgery The fraudulent making or altering of any writing in a way that changes the legal rights and liabilities of another.

The fraudulent making or altering of any writing (including electronic records) in a way that changes the legal rights and liabilities of another is **forgery.** **EXAMPLE 6.10** Without authorization, Severson signs Bennett's name to the back of a check made out to Bennett and attempts to cash it. Severson has committed the crime of forgery. • Forgery also includes changing trademarks, falsifying public records, counterfeiting, and altering a legal document.

Public Order Crime

Historically, societies have always outlawed activities that are considered to be contrary to public values and morals. Today, the most common public order crimes include public drunkenness, prostitution, gambling, and illegal drug use. These crimes are sometimes referred to as victimless crimes because they normally harm only the offender. From a broader perspective, however, they are deemed detrimental to society as a whole because

This West Hollywood, California, carport fire was one of twelve such fires that were set by an individual during a short time period. What type of crime was that person guilty of committing?

(Gene Blevins/Reuters/Landov)

Bernard Madoff (right) perpetuated the largest fraudulent investment scheme in modern history.

White-Collar Crime Nonviolent crime committed by individuals or corporations to obtain a personal or business advantage.

Embezzlement The fraudulent appropriation of funds or other property by a person who was entrusted with the funds or property.

they may create an environment that gives rise to property and violent crimes.

EXAMPLE 6.11   A man flying from Texas to California on a commercial airliner becomes angry and yells obscenities at a flight attendant when a beverage cart strikes his knee. After the pilot diverts the plane and makes an unscheduled landing at a nearby airport, police remove the passenger and arrest him. If the man is later found guilty of the public order crime of interfering with a flight crew, he may be sentenced to more than two years in prison. •

White-Collar Crime

Crimes that typically occur only in the business context are popularly referred to as **white-collar crimes.** Although there is no official definition of white-collar crime, the term is commonly used to mean an illegal act or series of acts committed by an individual or business entity using some nonviolent means. Usually, this kind of crime is committed in the course of a legitimate occupation. Corporate crimes fall into this category. In addition, certain property crimes, such as larceny and forgery, may also be white-collar crimes if they occur within the business context.

Embezzlement   When a person who is entrusted with another person's funds or property fraudulently appropriates it, **embezzlement** occurs. Typically, embezzlement is carried out by an employee who steals funds. Banks are particularly prone to this problem, but embezzlement can occur in any firm. In a number of businesses, corporate officers or accountants have fraudulently converted funds for their own benefit and then "fixed" the books to cover up their crime. Embezzlement is not larceny, because the wrongdoer does not physically take the property from another's possession, and it is not robbery, because force or fear is not used.

Embezzlement occurs whether the embezzler takes the funds directly from the victim or from a third person. If the financial officer of a corporation pockets checks from third parties that were given to her to deposit into the corporate account, she is embezzling. Frequently, an embezzler takes a relatively small amount at one time but does so repeatedly over a long period. The embezzler might underreport income or deposits and keep the remaining amount, for example, or create fictitious persons or accounts and write checks to them from the corporate account. An employer's failure to remit state withholding taxes that were collected from employee wages can also constitute embezzlement.

The intent to return embezzled property—or its actual return—is not a defense to the crime of embezzlement, as the following *Spotlight Case* illustrates.

Spotlight on White-Collar Crime

Case 6.1
People v. Sisuphan
Court of Appeal of California, First District,
181 Cal.App.4th 800, 104 Cal.Rptr.3d 654 (2010).

A Toyota dealership employee committed embezzlement but returned the funds. Is this a defense?

FACTS   Lou Sisuphan was the director of finance at a Toyota dealership. Sisuphan complained repeatedly to management about another employee, Ian McClelland. The general manager, Michael Christian, would not terminate McClelland "because he brought a lot of money into the dealership." To jeopardize McClelland's employment, Sisuphan took and kept an envelope containing a payment of nearly $30,000 from one of McClelland's customers that McClelland had tried to deposit in the company's safe. Later, Sisuphan told the dealership what he had done, adding that he had "no intention of stealing the money"

Spotlight Case 6.1—Continued

and returned it. Christian fired Sisuphan the next day, and the district attorney later charged Sisuphan with embezzlement. After a jury trial, Sisuphan was found guilty. Sisuphan appealed.

ISSUE Did Sisuphan take the funds with the intent to defraud his employer?

DECISION Yes. The appellate court affirmed Sisphan's conviction for embezzlement. Sisuphan had the required intent at the time he took the funds, and the evidence that he repaid the dealership was properly excluded.

REASON The court reasoned that evidence of repayment is admissible only if it shows that a defendant's intent at the

time of the taking was not fraudulent. In determining whether Sisuphan's intent was fraudulent at the time of the taking, the main issue was not whether he intended to spend the funds that he had taken, but whether he intended to use the payment "for a purpose other than that for which the dealership entrusted it to him." Sisuphan's stated purpose was to get McClelland fired. Because this purpose was beyond the scope of his responsibility, it was "outside the trust afforded him by the dealership" and indicated that he had fraudulent intent.

CRITICAL THINKING—Legal Consideration *Why was Sisuphan convicted of embezzlement instead of larceny? What is the difference between these two crimes?*

Mail and Wire Fraud

One of the most potent weapons against white-collar criminals are the federal laws that prohibit mail fraud[10] and wire fraud.[11] These laws make it a federal crime to devise any scheme that uses the U.S. mail, commercial carriers—such as FedEx or UPS—or wire, including telegraph, telephone, television, e-mail, or online social media, with the intent to defraud the public. These laws are often applied when persons send out advertisements or e-mails with the intent to obtain cash or property by false pretenses.

CASE EXAMPLE 6.12 Cisco Systems, Inc., offers a warranty program to authorized resellers of Cisco parts. Iheanyi Frank Chinasa and Robert Kendrick Chambliss formulated a scheme to use this program to defraud Cisco by obtaining replacement parts to which they were not entitled. The two men sent numerous e-mails and Internet service requests to Cisco to convince the company to ship them new parts via commercial carriers. Ultimately, Chinasa and Chambliss were convicted of mail and wire fraud, and conspiracy to commit mail and wire fraud.[12] ●

"It was beautiful and simple as all truly great swindles are."

O. Henry, 1862–1910
(American writer)

The maximum penalty under these statutes is substantial. Persons convicted of mail, wire, and Internet fraud may be imprisoned for up to twenty years and/or fined. If the violation affects a financial institution or involves fraud in connection with emergency disaster-relief funds, the violator may be fined up to $1 million, imprisoned for up to thirty years, or both.

Bribery

The crime of bribery involves offering something of value to someone in an attempt to influence that person, who is usually, but not always, a public official, to act in a way that serves a private interest. Three types of bribery are considered crimes: bribery of public officials, commercial bribery, and bribery of foreign officials. As an element of the crime of bribery, intent must be present and proved. The bribe itself can be anything the recipient considers to be valuable. Realize that the *crime of bribery occurs when the bribe is offered*—it is not required that the bribe be accepted. *Accepting a bribe* is a separate crime.

Commercial bribery involves corrupt dealings between private persons or businesses. Typically, people make commercial bribes to obtain proprietary information, cover up an

---

10. The Mail Fraud Act of 1990, 18 U.S.C. Sections 1341–1342.
11. 18 U.S.C. Section 1343.
12. *United States v. Chinasa*, 789 F.Supp.2d 691 (E.D.Va. 2011).

inferior product, or secure new business. Industrial espionage sometimes involves commercial bribes.   **EXAMPLE 6.13**   Kent works at the firm of Jacoby & Meyers. He offers to pay Laurel, an employee in a competing firm, if she will give him her firm's trade secrets and pricing schedules. Kent has committed commercial bribery. ● So-called kickbacks, or payoffs for special favors or services, are a form of commercial bribery in some situations.

Bankruptcy Fraud

Federal bankruptcy law (see Chapter 21) allows individuals and businesses to be relieved of oppressive debt through bankruptcy proceedings. Numerous white-collar crimes may be committed during the many phases of a bankruptcy proceeding. A creditor may file a false claim against the debtor. Also, a debtor may attempt to protect assets from creditors by fraudulently transferring property to favored parties. For instance, a company-owned automobile may be "sold" at a bargain price to a trusted friend or relative. Closely related to the crime of fraudulent transfer of property is the crime of fraudulent concealment of property, such as hiding gold coins.

Theft of Trade Secrets

As discussed in Chapter 5 on page 146, trade secrets constitute a form of intellectual property that can be extremely valuable for many businesses. The Economic Espionage Act of 1996[13] made the theft of trade secrets a federal crime. The act also made it a federal crime to buy or possess trade secrets of another person, knowing that the trade secrets were stolen or otherwise acquired without the owner's authorization.

Violations of the act can result in steep penalties. An individual who violates the act can be imprisoned for up to ten years and fined up to $500,000. If a corporation or other organization violates the act, it can be fined up to $5 million. Additionally, the law provides that any property acquired as a result of the violation, such as airplanes and automobiles, and any property used in the commission of the violation, such as servers and other electronic devices, are subject to criminal *forfeiture*—meaning that the government can take the property. A theft of trade secrets conducted via the Internet, for example, could result in the forfeiture of every computer or other device used to commit or facilitate the crime.

Insider Trading

An individual who obtains "inside information" about the plans of a publicly listed corporation can often make stock-trading profits by purchasing or selling corporate securities based on the information. **Insider trading** is a violation of securities law and will be considered more fully in Chapter 31. Generally, the rule is that a person who possesses inside information and has a duty not to disclose it to outsiders may not profit from the purchase or sale of securities based on that information until the information is made available to the public.

Insider Trading The purchase or sale of securities on the basis of *inside information* (information that has not been made available to the public).

Organized Crime

As mentioned, white-collar crime takes place within the confines of the legitimate business world. *Organized crime,* in contrast, operates *illegitimately* by, among other things, providing illegal goods and services. For organized crime, the traditional preferred markets are gambling, prostitution, illegal narcotics, and loan sharking (lending at higher than legal interest rates), along with counterfeiting and credit-card scams.

Money Laundering

Organized crime and other illegal activities generate many billions of dollars in profits each year from illegal drug transactions and, to a lesser extent, from racketeering, prostitution, and gambling. Under federal law, banks and other financial institutions are required to report currency transactions involving more than $10,000. Consequently, those who engage in illegal activities face difficulties when they try to deposit their cash profits from illegal transactions.

---

13. 18 U.S.C. Sections 1831–1839.

Money Laundering Engaging in financial transactions to conceal the identity, source, or destination of illegally gained funds.

As an alternative to simply storing cash from illegal transactions in a safe-deposit box, wrongdoers and racketeers launder their "dirty" money to make it "clean" by passing it through a legitimate business. **Money laundering** is engaging in financial transactions to conceal the identity, source, or destination of illegally gained funds.

EXAMPLE 6.14 Harris, a successful drug dealer, becomes a partner with a restaurateur. Little by little, the restaurant shows increasing profits. As a partner in the restaurant, Harris is able to report the "profits" of the restaurant as legitimate income on which he pays federal and state taxes. He can then spend those funds without worrying that his lifestyle may exceed the level possible with his reported income. •

The Racketeer Influenced and Corrupt Organizations Act   To curb the entry of organized crime into the legitimate business world, Congress enacted the Racketeer Influenced and Corrupt Organizations Act (RICO).[14] The statute, which was enacted as part of the Organized Crime Control Act, makes it a federal crime to (1) use income obtained from racketeering activity to purchase any interest in an enterprise, (2) acquire or maintain an interest in an enterprise through racketeering activity, (3) conduct or participate in the affairs of an enterprise through racketeering activity, or (4) conspire to do any of the preceding activities.

Vincent Gotti (center) is one of sixty alleged mobsters—members of organized crime—in New York and Sicily, Italy. What types of crimes are the most commonly committed by such individuals?

Broad Application of RICO   The broad language of RICO has allowed it to be applied in cases that have little or nothing to do with organized crime. RICO incorporates by reference twenty-six separate types of federal crimes and nine types of state felonies[15] and declares that if a person commits two of these offenses, he or she is guilty of "racketeering activity." Under the criminal provisions of RICO, any individual found guilty is subject to a fine of up to $25,000 per violation, imprisonment for up to twenty years, or both. Additionally, the statute provides that those who violate RICO may be required to forfeit (give up) any assets, in the form of property or cash, that were acquired as a result of the illegal activity or that were "involved in" or an "instrumentality of" the activity.

Penalties   In the event of a RICO violation, the government can seek civil penalties, such as the divestiture of a defendant's interest in a business (called forfeiture) or the dissolution of the business. Moreover, in some cases, the statute allows private individuals to sue violators and potentially to recover three times their actual losses (treble damages), plus attorneys' fees, for business injuries caused by a violation of the statute. This is perhaps the most controversial aspect of RICO and one that continues to cause debate in the nation's federal courts. The prospect of receiving treble damages in civil RICO lawsuits has given plaintiffs a financial incentive to pursue businesses and employers for violations.

Classification of Crimes

Felony A crime—such as arson, murder, rape, or robbery—that carries the most severe sanctions, ranging from more than one year in a state or federal prison to the death penalty.

In addition to being grouped into the five categories just discussed, crimes are also classified as felonies or misdemeanors depending on their degree of seriousness. **Felonies** are serious crimes punishable by death or by imprisonment for more than a year. Many states

14. 18 U.S.C. Sections 1961–1968.
15. See 18 U.S.C. Section 1961(1)(A).

Misdemeanor A lesser crime than a felony, punishable by a fine or incarceration in jail for up to one year.

Petty Offense The least serious kind of criminal offense, such as a traffic or building-code violation.

LEARNING OBJECTIVE 3
What defenses can be raised to avoid liability for criminal acts?

Self-Defense The legally recognized privilege to do what is reasonably necessary to protect oneself, one's property, or someone else against injury by another.

also define different degrees of felony offenses and vary the punishment according to the degree. **Misdemeanors** are less serious crimes, punishable by a fine or by confinement for up to a year. In most jurisdictions, **petty offenses** are considered to be a subset of misdemeanors. Petty offenses are minor violations, such as jaywalking or violations of building codes. Even for petty offenses, however, a guilty party can be put in jail for a few days, fined, or both, depending on state or local law.

Defenses to Criminal Liability

Persons charged with crimes may be relieved of criminal liability if they can show that their criminal actions were justified under the circumstances. In certain circumstances, the law may also allow a person to be excused from criminal liability because she or he lacks the required mental state. We look at several of the defenses to criminal liability here.

Note that procedural violations, such as obtaining evidence without a valid search warrant, may also operate as defenses. As you will read later in this chapter, evidence obtained in violation of a defendant's constitutional rights normally may not be admitted in court. If the evidence is suppressed, then there may be no basis for prosecuting the defendant.

Justifiable Use of Force

Probably the best-known defense to criminal liability is **self-defense.** Other situations, however, also justify the use of force: the defense of one's dwelling, the defense of other property, and the prevention of a crime. In all of these situations, it is important to distinguish between deadly and nondeadly force. *Deadly force* is likely to result in death or serious bodily harm. *Nondeadly force* is force that reasonably appears necessary to prevent the imminent use of criminal force.

Generally speaking, people can use the amount of nondeadly force that seems necessary to protect themselves, their dwellings, or other property or to prevent the commission of a crime. Deadly force can be used in self-defense if the defender *reasonably believes* that imminent death or grievous bodily harm will otherwise result. In addition, normally the attacker must be using unlawful force, and the defender must not have initiated or provoked the attack.

Traditionally, deadly force could be used to defend a dwelling only when the unlawful entry was violent and the person believed deadly force was necessary to prevent imminent death or great bodily harm. Today, however, in some jurisdictions, deadly force can also be used if the person believes it is necessary to prevent the commission of a felony in the dwelling. Many states are expanding the situations in which the use of deadly force can be justified. Florida, for example, allows the use of deadly force to prevent the commission of a "forcible felony," including robbery, carjacking, and sexual battery. Similar laws have been passed in at least seventeen other states.

Necessity

Sometimes, criminal defendants are relieved of liability if they can show that a criminal act was necessary to prevent an even greater harm. **EXAMPLE 6.15** Trevor is a convicted felon and, as such, is legally prohibited from possessing a firearm. While he and his wife are in a convenience store, a man draws a gun, points it at the cashier, and demands all the cash. Afraid that the man will start shooting, Trevor grabs the gun and holds on to it until police arrive. In this situation, if Trevor is charged with possession of a firearm, he can assert the defense of necessity. •

Insanity

A person who suffers from a mental illness may be incapable of the state of mind required to commit a crime. Thus, insanity can be a defense to a criminal charge. Note that an insanity defense does not allow a person to avoid prison. It simply means that if the defendant successfully proves insanity, she or he will be placed in a mental institution.

The courts have had difficulty deciding what the test for legal insanity should be, however, and psychiatrists as well as lawyers are critical of the tests used. Almost all federal courts and some states use the relatively liberal substantial-capacity test set forth in the Model Penal Code:

> A person is not responsible for criminal conduct if at the time of such conduct as a result of mental disease or defect he [or she] lacks substantial capacity either to appreciate the wrongfulness of his [or her] conduct or to conform his [or her] conduct to the requirements of the law.

Some states use the *M'Naghten* test,[16] under which a criminal defendant is not responsible if, at the time of the offense, he or she did not know the nature and quality of the act or did not know that the act was wrong. Other states use the irresistible-impulse test. A person operating under an irresistible impulse may know an act is wrong but cannot refrain from doing it. Under any of these tests, proving insanity is extremely difficult. For this reason, the insanity defense is rarely used and usually is not successful.

Amy Bishop, shown with her attorney, killed three of her fellow college professors and wounded three more. She pleaded not guilty by reason of insanity. What does she have to prove to prevail at trial?

Mistake

Everyone has heard the saying "Ignorance of the law is no excuse." Ordinarily, ignorance of the law or a mistaken idea about what the law requires is not a valid defense. A *mistake of fact*, as opposed to a *mistake of law*, can excuse criminal responsibility if it negates the mental state necessary to commit a crime.

EXAMPLE 6.16   If Oliver Wheaton mistakenly walks off with Julie Tyson's briefcase because he thinks it is his, there is no crime. Theft requires knowledge that the property belongs to another. (If Wheaton's act causes Tyson to incur damages, however, she may sue him in a civil action for trespass to personal property or conversion—torts that were discussed in Chapter 4.) ●

> **◄ KNOW THIS ►**
>
> "Ignorance" is a lack of information. "Mistake" is a confusion of information, which can sometimes negate criminal intent.

Duress

Duress exists when the *wrongful threat* of one person induces another person to perform an act that she or he would not otherwise perform. In such a situation, duress is said to negate the mental state necessary to commit a crime because the defendant was forced or compelled to commit the act.

Duress can be used as a defense to most crimes except murder. The states vary in how duress is defined and what types of crimes it can excuse, however. Generally, to successfully assert duress as a defense, the defendant must reasonably believe in the immediate danger, and the jury (or judge) must conclude that the defendant's belief was reasonable.

Duress Unlawful pressure brought to bear on a person, causing the person to perform an act that she or he would not otherwise perform.

---

16. A rule derived from *M'Naghten's* Case, 8 Eng.Rep. 718 (1843).

Entrapment

Entrapment   A defense in which a defendant claims that he or she was induced by a public official to commit a crime that he or she would otherwise not have committed.

Entrapment is a defense designed to prevent police officers or other government agents from enticing persons to commit crimes so that they can later be prosecuted for criminal acts. In the typical entrapment case, an undercover agent *suggests* that a crime be committed and pressures or induces an individual to commit it. The agent then arrests the individual for the crime.

For entrapment to succeed as a defense, both the suggestion and the inducement must take place. The defense is not intended to prevent law enforcement agents from ever setting a trap for an unwary criminal. Rather, its purpose is to prevent them from pushing the individual into a criminal act. The crucial issue is whether the person who committed a crime was predisposed to commit the illegal act or did so only because the agent induced it.

Statute of Limitations

With some exceptions, such as for the crime of murder, statutes of limitations apply to crimes just as they do to civil wrongs. In other words, the state must initiate criminal prosecution within a certain number of years. If a criminal action is brought after the statutory time period has expired, the accused person can raise the statute of limitations as a defense.

Immunity

Self-Incrimination   Giving testimony in a trial or other legal proceeding that could expose the person testifying to criminal prosecution.

Accused persons are understandably reluctant to give information if it will be used to prosecute them, and they cannot be forced to do so. The privilege against **self-incrimination** is granted by the Fifth Amendment to the U.S. Constitution, which reads, in part, "nor shall [any person] be compelled in any criminal case to be a witness against himself." When the state wishes to obtain information from a person accused of a crime, the state can grant *immunity* from prosecution or agree to prosecute for a less serious offense in exchange for the information. Once immunity is given, the person can no longer refuse to testify on Fifth Amendment grounds because he or she now has an absolute privilege against self-incrimination.

Plea Bargaining   The process by which a criminal defendant and the prosecutor work out an agreement to dispose of the criminal case, subject to court approval.

Often, a grant of immunity from prosecution for a serious crime is part of the **plea bargaining** between the defendant and the prosecuting attorney. The defendant may be convicted of a lesser offense, while the state uses the defendant's testimony to prosecute accomplices for serious crimes carrying heavy penalties.

Constitutional Safeguards and Criminal Procedures

LEARNING OBJECTIVE 4
What constitutional safeguards exist to protect persons accused of crimes?

Criminal law brings the power of the state, with all its resources, to bear against the individual. Criminal procedures are designed to protect the constitutional rights of individuals and to prevent the arbitrary use of power by the government.

The U.S. Constitution provides specific safeguards for those accused of crimes, as mentioned in Chapter 2. Most of these safeguards protect individuals against state government actions, as well as federal government actions, by virtue of the due process clause of the Fourteenth Amendment. These protections are set forth in the Fourth, Fifth, Sixth, and Eighth Amendments.

Fourth Amendment Protections

Search Warrant An order granted by a public authority, such as a judge, that authorizes law enforcement personnel to search particular premises or property.

The Fourth Amendment protects the "right of the people to be secure in their persons, houses, papers, and effects." Before searching or seizing private property, law enforcement officers must obtain a **search warrant**—an order from a judge or other public official authorizing the search or seizure.

ETHICAL ISSUE

Should the police be able to use high-tech tracking devices without a search warrant? Police increasingly are using new technologies for surveillance. In particular, a Global Positioning System (GPS) tracker can easily be attached to a suspect's car while it is parked on a public street. If police do this without obtaining a search warrant, have they conducted an unreasonable search in violation of the Fourth Amendment? According to the United States Supreme Court, they have. In *United States v. Jones*,[17] a unanimous Court said that the government "physically occupied private property [the car] for the purpose of obtaining information. We have no doubt that such physical intrusion would have been considered a 'search' within the meaning of the Fourth Amendment when it was adopted." In other words, attaching a GPS tracker to a car is analogous to entering a person's home to make a search. Both require search warrants.

Undoubtedly, there will be continued debate about how technology can legally be used to track people's movements. How much surveillance should society accept? Should the Supreme Court's decision be extended to cell phones and other digital devices? For instance, federal and local law enforcement agents routinely engage in secret cell phone tracking by using devices called Stingrays. Does such tracking violate the Fourth Amendment? It may, given that the Supreme Court expressed concern about the invasion of privacy represented by the GPS tracker in the *Jones* case.

17. ___ U.S. ___, 132 S.Ct. 945, 181 L.Ed.2d 911 (2012). This case was presented in Exhibit 1A.3 on page 31.

Federal Bureau of Investigation (FBI) agents remove numerous boxes of documents from Solyndra, a bankrupt solar energy company in Fremont, California. U.S. taxpayers lost $535 million in loan guarantees because of the bankruptcy. Because of the Fourth Amendment, did the FBI have to first obtain a search warrant to enter the company's offices?

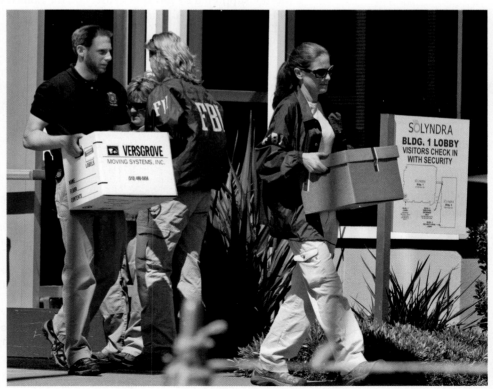

(AP Photo/Paul Sakuma)

Probable Cause Reasonable grounds for believing that a search should be conducted or that a person should be arrested.

Search Warrants and Probable Cause

To obtain a search warrant, law enforcement officers must convince a judge that they have reasonable grounds, or **probable cause,** to believe a search will reveal a specific illegality. Probable cause requires the officers to have trustworthy evidence that would convince a reasonable person that the proposed search or seizure is more likely justified than not.

Furthermore, the Fourth Amendment prohibits general warrants. It requires a particular description of what is to be searched or seized. General searches through a person's belongings are impermissible. The search cannot extend beyond what is described in the warrant. Although search warrants require specificity, if a search warrant is issued for a person's residence, items in that residence may be searched even if they do not belong to that individual.

CASE EXAMPLE 6.17   Paycom Billing Services, Inc., an online payment service, stores vast amounts of customer credit-card information in its computers. Christopher Adjani, a former employee, threatened to sell Paycom's confidential client information if the company did not pay him $3 million. The FBI obtained a search warrant to search Adjani's person, automobile, and residence, including computer equipment. When the FBI agents served the warrant, they discovered evidence of the criminal scheme on a computer in Adjani's residence. The computer belonged to Adjani's live-in girlfriend. Adjani filed a motion to suppress this evidence, claiming that because he did not own the computer, it was beyond the scope of the warrant. A federal appellate court disagreed, however, and held that the search of the computer was proper, given the alleged involvement of computers in the crime.[18] ●

In the following case, police officers obtained a search warrant and conducted a search of a gang member's foster mother's home for weapons. A judge later ruled that the warrant was not supported by probable cause, and the homeowners sued individual police officers for executing an illegal search warrant.

---

18. *United States v. Adjani,* 452 F.3d 1140 (9th Cir. 2006).

Case 6.2

Messerschmidt v. Millender

Supreme Court of the United States,
___ U.S. ___, 132 S.Ct. 1235,
182 L.Ed.2d 47 (2012).

FACTS   The Los Angeles County Sheriff's Department was protecting a woman from Jerry Ray Bowen when he tried to kill her with a sawed-off shotgun. The woman told the police that she and Bowen used to date, that Bowen was a gang member, and that she thought Bowen was staying at the home of Augusta Millender, his foster mother. After investigating the incident further, the police prepared a warrant to search the foster mother's home for all guns and gang-related material, and a judge approved it. When police officers, including Curt Messerschmidt, served the search warrant, they discovered that Bowen was not at the home but searched it anyway. Millender sued individual police officers in federal court for subjecting her to an illegal search. A federal appellate court held that the police lacked probable cause for such a broad search and that the police officers could be held personally liable. The police officers appealed.

Police officers conduct a search.

The United States Supreme Court granted *certiorari* to determine whether the police officers were immune from personal liability.

ISSUE   Assuming that the search violated the Fourth Amendment to the U.S. Constitution, are the police officers immune from liability?

DECISION   Yes. The United States Supreme Court reversed the decision of the federal appellate court, granting the officers immunity from liability.

REASON   The doctrine of qualified immunity "gives government officials breathing room to make reasonable but

Case 6.2—Continued

mistaken judgments." The Court explained that immunity depends on whether an official "acted in an objectively reasonable manner." Here, the police officers acted reasonably, in part, because a neutral judge approved the search warrant. Moreover, a reasonable police officer could have believed that the warrant was proper. For example, even if the warrant was too broad because it authorized a search for all guns rather than just the one Bowen fired, a reasonable police officer could conclude that Bowen had other guns. After all, the Court reasoned, he owned a sawed-off shotgun, he was a known gang member, and he had just tried to kill a woman

for calling the police. Similarly, one could reasonably conclude that there was probable cause to search for gang-related material because it would be helpful in prosecuting Bowen for attacking his ex-girlfriend. Finally, the officers conducted a detailed investigation and had the warrant application reviewed three times before submitting it to the judge.

CRITICAL THINKING—Legal Consideration *How would police officers behave if they could always be held personally liable for executing unconstitutional warrants? Would they be more or less inclined to apply for and execute search warrants? Explain.*

Searches and Seizures in the Business Context Because of the strong governmental interest in protecting the public, a warrant normally is not required for seizures of spoiled or contaminated food. Nor are warrants required for searches of businesses in such highly regulated industries as liquor, guns, and strip mining.

Generally, however, government inspectors do not have the right to search business premises without a warrant, although the standard of probable cause is not the same as in nonbusiness contexts. The existence of a general and neutral plan of enforcement will justify the issuance of a warrant. Lawyers and accountants frequently possess the business records of their clients, and inspecting these documents while they are out of the hands of their true owners also requires a warrant. Inspecting a physician's medical records also generally requires a warrant, although an exception may be made if the physician agrees to allow the search.[19]

Fifth Amendment Protections

The Fifth Amendment offers significant protections for accused persons. One is the guarantee that no one can be deprived of "life, liberty, or property without due process of law." Two other important Fifth Amendment provisions protect persons against double jeopardy and self-incrimination.

Due Process of Law Remember from Chapter 2 on page 49 that *due process of law* has both procedural and substantive aspects. Procedural due process requirements underlie criminal procedures. The law must be carried out in a fair and orderly way. In criminal cases, due process means that defendants should have an opportunity to object to the charges against them before a fair, neutral decision maker, such as a judge. Defendants must also be given the opportunity to confront and cross-examine witnesses and accusers and to present their own witnesses.

Double Jeopardy The Fifth Amendment requirement that prohibits a person from being tried twice for the same criminal offense.

Double Jeopardy The Fifth Amendment also protects persons from **double jeopardy** (being tried twice for the same criminal offense). The prohibition against double jeopardy means that once a criminal defendant is acquitted (found "not guilty") of a particular crime, the government may not retry him or her for the same crime.

---

19. See, for example, *United States v. Moon,* 513 F.3d 527 (2008).

The prohibition against double jeopardy does not preclude the crime victim from bringing a civil suit against that same defendant to recover damages, however. In other words, a person found "not guilty" of assault and battery in a state criminal case can be sued for damages by the victim in a civil tort case.

Additionally, a state's prosecution of a crime will not prevent a separate federal prosecution relating to the same activity (and vice versa), provided the activity can be classified as a different crime.   **CASE EXAMPLE 6.18**   Professional football player Michael Vick was convicted in federal court for operating a dogfighting ring and sentenced to serve twenty-three months in federal prison. A year later, the state where the crime took place, Virginia, filed its own charges against Vick for dogfighting. He pleaded guilty to those charges and received a *suspended sentence* (meaning that the judge reserved the option of imposing a sentence later if circumstances, such as future violations, warranted it).[20] •

Self-Incrimination   As explained earlier, the Fifth Amendment grants a privilege against self-incrimination. Thus, in any criminal proceeding, an accused person cannot be compelled to give testimony that might subject her or him to any criminal prosecution.

The Fifth Amendment's guarantee against self-incrimination extends only to natural persons. Because a corporation is a legal entity and not a natural person, the privilege against self-incrimination does not apply to it. Similarly, the business records of a partnership do not receive Fifth Amendment protection. When a partnership is required to produce these records, it must do so even if the information incriminates the persons who constitute the business entity. Sole proprietors and sole practitioners (those who fully own their businesses) who have not incorporated normally cannot be compelled to produce their business records. These individuals have full protection against self-incrimination because they function in only one capacity—there is no separate business entity (see Chapter 26).

Protections under the Sixth and Eighth Amendments

The Sixth Amendment guarantees several important rights for criminal defendants: the right to a speedy trial, the right to a jury trial, the right to a public trial, the right to confront witnesses, and the right to counsel. The Sixth Amendment right to counsel is one of the rights of which a suspect must be advised when he or she is arrested. In many cases, a statement that a criminal suspect makes in the absence of counsel is not admissible at trial unless the suspect has knowingly and voluntarily waived this right.

The Eighth Amendment prohibits excessive bail and fines, as well as cruel and unusual punishment. Under this amendment, prison officials are required to provide humane conditions of confinement, including adequate food, clothing, shelter, and medical care. If a prisoner has a serious medical problem, for instance, and a correctional officer is deliberately indifferent to it, a court could find that the prisoner's Eighth Amendment rights were violated. Critics of the death penalty claim that it constitutes cruel and unusual punishment.[21]

The Exclusionary Rule and the *Miranda* Rule

Two other procedural protections for criminal defendants are the exclusionary rule and the *Miranda* rule.

The Exclusionary Rule   Under what is known as the **exclusionary rule,** all evidence obtained in violation of the constitutional rights spelled out in the Fourth, Fifth,

> ► **KNOW THIS** ◄
>
> The Fifth Amendment protection against self-incrimination does not cover partnerships or corporations.

Exclusionary Rule A rule that prevents evidence that is obtained illegally or without a proper search warrant—and any evidence derived from illegally obtained evidence—from being admissible in court.

---

20. See *United States v. Kizeart,* 2010 WL 3768023 (S.D.Ill. 2010), for a discussion of the Michael Vick dogfighting case.

21. For an example of a case challenging the constitutionality of the death penalty, see *Baze v. Rees,* 552 U.S. 597, 128 S.Ct. 1520, 170 L.Ed.2d 420 (2008).

and Sixth Amendments, as well as all evidence derived from illegally obtained evidence, normally must be excluded from the trial. Evidence derived from illegally obtained evidence is known as the "fruit of the poisonous tree." For example, if a confession is obtained after an illegal arrest, the arrest is "the poisonous tree," and the confession, if "tainted" by the arrest, is the "fruit."

The purpose of the exclusionary rule is to deter police from conducting warrantless searches and engaging in other misconduct. The rule is sometimes criticized because it can lead to injustice. Many a defendant has "gotten off on a technicality" because law enforcement personnel failed to observe procedural requirements. Even though a defendant may be obviously guilty, if the evidence of that guilt was obtained improperly (without a valid search warrant, for example), it normally cannot be used against the defendant in court.

The *Miranda* Rule   In *Miranda v. Arizona,* a case decided in 1966, the United States Supreme Court established the rule that individuals who are arrested must be informed of certain constitutional rights, including their Fifth Amendment right to remain silent and their Sixth Amendment right to counsel. If the arresting officers fail to inform a criminal suspect of these constitutional rights, any statements the suspect makes normally will not be admissible in court. Although the Supreme Court's *Miranda* ruling was controversial, the decision has survived attempts by Congress to overrule it.[22] Because of its importance in criminal procedure, the *Miranda* case is presented as this chapter's *Landmark in the Law* feature on the following page.

Exceptions to the *Miranda* Rule   Over time, as part of a continuing attempt to balance the rights of accused persons against the rights of society, the United States Supreme Court has carved out numerous exceptions to the *Miranda* rule. For example, the Court has recognized a "public safety" exception, holding that certain statements—such as statements concerning the location of a weapon—are admissible even if the defendant was not given *Miranda* warnings. Additionally, to stop police questioning, a suspect must unequivocally and assertively request to exercise his or her right to counsel. Saying "Maybe I should talk to a lawyer" during an interrogation after being taken into custody is not enough. Police officers are not required to decipher the suspect's intentions in such situations.

Criminal Process

As mentioned, as a result of the effort to safeguard the rights of the individual against the state, a criminal prosecution differs from a civil case in several respects. Exhibit 6.3 on page 177 summarizes the major procedural steps in processing a criminal case. Here, we discuss three phases of the criminal process—arrest, indictment or information, and trial—in more detail.

Arrest

Before a warrant for arrest can be issued, there must be probable cause to believe that the individual in question has committed a crime. As discussed earlier, *probable cause* can be defined as a substantial likelihood that the person has committed or is about to commit a crime. Note that probable cause involves a likelihood, not just a possibility. An arrest can be made without a warrant if there is no time to get one, but the action of the arresting officer is still judged by the standard of probable cause.

---

22. *Dickerson v. United States,* 530 U.S. 428, 120 S.Ct. 2326, 147 L.Ed.2d 405 (2000).

LANDMARK IN THE LAW
Miranda v. Arizona (1966)

The United States Supreme Court's decision in *Miranda v. Arizona*[a] has been cited in more court decisions than any other case in the history of U.S law. Through television shows and other media, the case has also become familiar to most of the adult population in the United States.

The case arose after Ernesto Miranda was arrested in his home on March 13, 1963, for the kidnapping and rape of an eighteen-year-old woman. Miranda was taken to a police station in Phoenix, Arizona, and questioned by two police officers. Two hours later, the officers emerged from the interrogation room with a written confession signed by Miranda.

Rulings by the Lower Courts   The confession was admitted into evidence at the trial, and Miranda was convicted and sentenced to prison for twenty to thirty years. Miranda appealed his conviction, claiming that he had not been informed of his constitutional rights. He did not assert that he was innocent of the crime or that his confession was false or made under duress. He claimed only that he would not have confessed if he had been advised of his right to remain silent and to have an attorney. The Supreme Court of Arizona held that Miranda's constitutional rights had not been violated and affirmed his conviction. In its decision, the court emphasized that Miranda had not specifically requested an attorney.

a. 384 U.S. 436, 86 S.Ct. 1602, 16 L.Ed.2d 694 (1966).

The Supreme Court's Decision   The *Miranda* case was subsequently consolidated with three other cases involving similar issues and reviewed by the United States Supreme Court. In its decision, the Court stated that whenever an individual is taken into custody, "the following measures are required: He must be warned prior to any questioning that he has the right to remain silent, that anything he says can be used against him in a court of law, that he has the right to the presence of an attorney, and that if he cannot afford an attorney one will be appointed for him prior to any questioning if he so desires." If the accused waives his or her rights to remain silent and to have counsel present, the government must be able to demonstrate that the waiver was made knowingly, intelligently, and voluntarily.

Application to Today's World   *Today, both on television and in the real world, police officers routinely advise suspects of their "Miranda rights" on arrest. When Ernesto Miranda himself was later murdered, the suspected murderer was "read his Miranda rights." Interestingly, this decision has also had ramifications for criminal procedure in Great Britain. British police officers are required, when making arrests, to inform suspects, "You do not have to say anything. But if you do not mention now something which you later use in your defense, the court may decide that your failure to mention it now strengthens the case against you. A record will be made of everything you say, and it may be given in evidence if you are brought to trial."*

Indictment A formal charge by a grand jury that there is probable cause to believe that a named person has committed a crime.

Grand Jury A group of citizens who decide, after hearing the state's evidence, whether a reasonable basis (probable cause) exists for believing that a crime has been committed and that a trial ought to be held.

Information A formal accusation or complaint (without an indictment) issued in certain types of actions (usually criminal actions involving lesser crimes) by a government prosecutor.

Indictment or Information

Individuals must be formally charged with having committed specific crimes before they can be brought to trial. If issued by a grand jury, this charge is called an **indictment**.[23] A **grand jury** usually consists of more jurors than the ordinary trial jury. A grand jury does not determine the guilt or innocence of an accused party. Rather, its function is to hear the state's evidence and to determine whether a reasonable basis (probable cause) exists for believing that a crime has been committed and that a trial ought to be held.

Usually, grand juries are used in cases involving serious crimes, such as murder. For lesser crimes, an individual may be formally charged with a crime by what is called an **information,** or criminal complaint. An information will be issued by a government prosecutor if the prosecutor determines that there is sufficient evidence to justify bringing the individual to trial.

23. Pronounced in-*dyte*-ment.

Exhibit 6.3 Major Procedural Steps in a Criminal Case

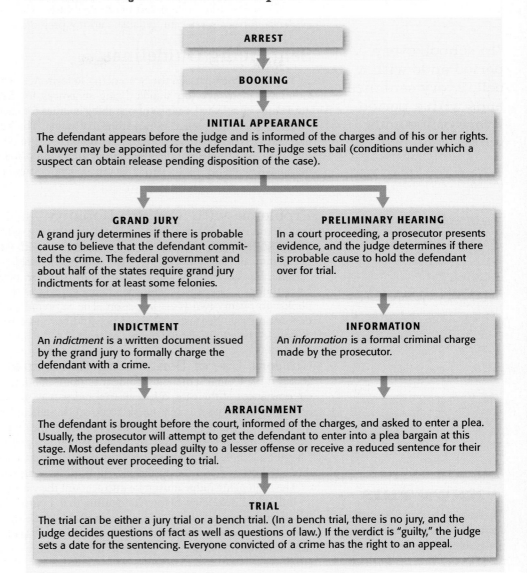

ARREST

BOOKING

INITIAL APPEARANCE
The defendant appears before the judge and is informed of the charges and of his or her rights. A lawyer may be appointed for the defendant. The judge sets bail (conditions under which a suspect can obtain release pending disposition of the case).

GRAND JURY
A grand jury determines if there is probable cause to believe that the defendant committed the crime. The federal government and about half of the states require grand jury indictments for at least some felonies.

PRELIMINARY HEARING
In a court proceeding, a prosecutor presents evidence, and the judge determines if there is probable cause to hold the defendant over for trial.

INDICTMENT
An *indictment* is a written document issued by the grand jury to formally charge the defendant with a crime.

INFORMATION
An *information* is a formal criminal charge made by the prosecutor.

ARRAIGNMENT
The defendant is brought before the court, informed of the charges, and asked to enter a plea. Usually, the prosecutor will attempt to get the defendant to enter into a plea bargain at this stage. Most defendants plead guilty to a lesser offense or receive a reduced sentence for their crime without ever proceeding to trial.

TRIAL
The trial can be either a jury trial or a bench trial. (In a bench trial, there is no jury, and the judge decides questions of fact as well as questions of law.) If the verdict is "guilty," the judge sets a date for the sentencing. Everyone convicted of a crime has the right to an appeal.

Trial

At a criminal trial, the accused person does not have to prove anything—the entire burden of proof is on the prosecutor (the state). As mentioned earlier, the prosecution must show that, based on all the evidence presented, the defendant's guilt is established *beyond a reasonable doubt*. If there is a reasonable doubt as to whether a criminal defendant committed the crime with which she or he has been charged, then the verdict must be "not guilty." Note that giving a verdict of "not guilty" is not the same as stating that the defendant is innocent. It merely means that not enough evidence was properly presented to the court to prove guilt beyond a reasonable doubt.

Courts have complex rules about what types of evidence may be presented and how the evidence may be brought out in criminal cases. These rules are designed to ensure that evidence in trials is relevant, reliable, and not prejudicial toward the defendant.

Sentencing Guidelines

> "In school, every period ends with a bell. Every sentence ends with a period. Every crime ends with a sentence."
>
> Steven Wright, 1955–present
> (American comedian)

In 1984, Congress passed the Sentencing Reform Act, which created the U.S. Sentencing Commission to develop standardizing sentences for federal crimes. The commission's guidelines established a range of possible penalties for each federal crime and required the judge to select a sentence from within that range. The guidelines originally established a mandatory system because judges were not allowed to deviate from the specified sentencing range. Some federal judges felt uneasy about imposing long prison sentences on certain criminal defendants, particularly first-time offenders, and in illegal substances cases involving small quantities of drugs.[24]

Problems with Constitutionality   In 2005, the Supreme Court held that certain provisions of the federal sentencing guidelines were unconstitutional. **CASE EXAMPLE 6.19**   Freddie Booker was arrested with 92.5 grams of crack cocaine in his possession. Booker admitted to police that he had sold an additional 566 grams of crack cocaine, but he was never charged with, or tried for, possessing this additional quantity. Nevertheless, under the federal sentencing guidelines the judge was required to sentence Booker to twenty-two years in prison. The Supreme Court ruled that this sentence was unconstitutional because a jury did not find beyond a reasonable doubt that Booker had possessed the additional 566 grams of crack.[25] ●

Current Use of Sentencing Guidelines   Essentially, the Court's ruling changed the federal sentencing guidelines from mandatory to advisory. Depending on the circumstances of the case, a federal trial judge may now depart from the guidelines if he or she believes that it is reasonable to do so. Sentencing guidelines still exist and provide for enhanced punishment for certain types of crimes, including white-collar crimes, violations of the Sarbanes-Oxley Act (see Chapter 7), and violations of securities laws (see Chapter 31).[26] The Supreme Court has also held that a sentencing judge cannot presume that a sentence within the applicable guidelines is reasonable.[27]

The sentencing judge must take into account the various sentencing factors that apply to an individual defendant before concluding that a particular sentence is reasonable. When the defendant is a business firm, these factors include the company's history of past violations, management's cooperation with federal investigators, and the extent to which the firm has undertaken specific programs and procedures to prevent criminal activities by its employees.

➤ **KNOW THIS** ◄

When determining the appropriate sentence for a business firm, courts focus on three things: previous violations, cooperation with authorities, and good faith efforts to avoid violations.

Cyber Crime

Computer Crime The unlawful use of a computer or network to take or alter data, or to gain the use of computers or services without authorization.

The U.S. Department of Justice broadly defines **computer crime** as any violation of criminal law that involves knowledge of computer technology for its perpetration, investigation, or prosecution. A number of the white-collar crimes discussed earlier in this chapter, such as fraud, embezzlement, and the theft of intellectual property, are now often committed with the aid of computers and are thus considered computer crimes.

---

24. See, for example, *United States v. Angelos*, 345 F.Supp.2d 1227 (D. Utah 2004).
25. *United States v. Booker*, 543 U.S. 220, 125 S.Ct. 738, 160 L.Ed.2d 621 (2005).
26. The sentencing guidelines were amended in 2003, as required under the Sarbanes-Oxley Act, to impose stiffer penalties for corporate securities fraud—see Chapter 31.
27. *Nelson v. United States*, 555 U.S. 350, 129 S.Ct. 890, 172 L.Ed.2d 719 (2009).

Cyber Crime A crime that occurs in the online environment rather than in the physical world.

Many computer crimes fall under the broad label of **cyber crime,** which describes any criminal activity occurring via a computer in the virtual community of the Internet. Most cyber crimes are not "new" crimes. Rather, they are existing crimes in which the Internet is the instrument of wrongdoing. Here, we look at several types of activity that constitute cyber crimes against persons or property. Other cyber crimes will be discussed in later chapters as they relate to particular topics, such as consumer law or investor protection.

Cyber Fraud

Cyber Fraud Any misrepresentation knowingly made over the Internet with the intention of deceiving another for the purpose of obtaining property or funds.

As mentioned in Chapter 4, fraud is any misrepresentation knowingly made with the intention of deceiving another and on which a reasonable person would and does rely to her or his detriment. **Cyber fraud** is fraud committed over the Internet. Frauds that were once conducted solely by mail or phone can now be found online, and new technology has led to increasingly creative ways to commit fraud.

EXAMPLE 6.20 The "Nigerian letter fraud scam" is perhaps the longest-running Internet fraud. Swindlers send e-mails asking recipients if they will send funds to help fictitious officials from Nigeria transfer millions of nonexistent dollars to Western banks. The e-mails promise that the recipients will be reimbursed and will also receive compensation (a fee or percentage) for transferring the funds. Variations of the scam reflect current events. For instance, the e-mails may ask for financial help in retrieving the fortune of a loved one or an associate who perished in the conflict in Iraq or Afghanistan or during the earthquake and tsunami in Japan. •

Online Auction Fraud   Online auction fraud, in its most basic form, is a simple process. A person puts up an expensive item for auction, on either a legitimate or a fake auction site, and then refuses to send the product after receiving payment. Or, as a variation, the wrongdoer may send the purchaser an item that is worth less than the one offered in the auction.

The larger online auction sites, such as eBay, try to protect consumers against such schemes by providing warnings about deceptive sellers or offering various forms of insurance. The nature of the Internet, however, makes it nearly impossible to completely block fraudulent auction activity. Because users can assume multiple identities, it is very difficult to pinpoint fraudulent sellers—they will simply change their screen names with each auction.

A state government official examines counterfeit jewelry, much of which would have been sold online.

(AP Photo/Paul Sakuma)

Online Retail Fraud   Somewhat similar to online auction fraud is online retail fraud, in which consumers pay directly (without bidding) for items that are never delivered. As with other forms of online fraud, it is difficult to determine the actual extent of online sales fraud, but anecdotal evidence suggests that it is a substantial problem. **CASE EXAMPLE 6.21** Jeremy Jaynes grossed more than $750,000 per week selling nonexistent or worthless products such as "penny stock pickers" and "Internet history erasers." By the time he was arrested, he had amassed an estimated $24 million from his various fraudulent schemes.[28] •

Cyber Theft

In cyberspace, thieves are not subject to the physical limitations of the "real" world. A thief can steal data stored in a networked computer with Internet access from anywhere on the globe. Only the speed of the connection and the thief's computer equipment limit the quantity of data that can be stolen.

---

28. *Jaynes v. Commonwealth of Virginia,* 276 Va.App. 443, 666 S.E.2d 303 (2008).

Identity Theft The illegal use of someone else's personal information to access the victim's financial resources.

LEARNING OBJECTIVE 5
How has the Internet expanded opportunities for identity theft?

Identity Theft　　Not surprisingly, there has been a marked increase in identity theft in recent years. **Identity theft** occurs when the wrongdoer steals a form of identification—such as a name, date of birth, or Social Security number—and uses the information to access the victim's financial resources. This crime existed to a certain extent before the widespread use of the Internet. Thieves would rifle through garbage to find credit-card or bank account numbers and then use those numbers to purchase goods or to withdraw funds from the victims' accounts.

The Internet has provided even easier access to private data. Frequent Web surfers surrender a wealth of information about themselves without knowing it. Many Web sites use "cookies" to collect data on those who visit their sites. The data may include the areas of the site the user visits and the links on which the user clicks.

Furthermore, Web browsers often store information such as the consumer's name and e-mail address. Finally, every time a purchase is made online, the item is linked to the purchaser's name, allowing Web retailers to amass a database of who is buying what. Of course, the database also includes purchasers' credit-card numbers. Cyber criminals who steal people's identities normally do not use the identifying information themselves. Instead, they sell the credit-card numbers and other information on the Internet.

In the following case, the court had to decide whether to suppress evidence of an identity theft crime that officers found at a defendant's girlfriend's house.

Case 6.3

United States v. Oliver

United States Court of Appeals, Fifth Circuit, 630 F.3d 397 (2011).

(pixinity/Shutterstock.com)

Identity theft often leads to various types of fraud.

FACTS　Lonnie Oliver, Jr., was arrested by officers investigating a scheme to file fraudulent claims for unemployment benefits. Oliver and others were suspected of gaining access to people's names and Social Security numbers and using this information to receive unemployment benefits. After he was read his *Miranda* rights, Oliver confessed to his role in the scheme. Oliver also consented to a search of his car, but he refused to consent to a search of his home. Oliver's co-defendant then told the police that Oliver had stored a laptop computer and a cardboard box containing items related to the scheme at the apartment of Erica Armstrong, Oliver's girlfriend. Acting on this information, agents went to Armstrong's apartment, and she gave them the box and the laptop computer. Inside the box, officers found hundreds of personal identifiers of victims, along with credit and debit cards. They also found a notebook labeled "business ideas" with Oliver's notes for the scheme.

After the laptop was seized, officers obtained a warrant to search its contents and found evidence that Oliver had used it to submit fraudulent unemployment claims. Oliver filed a motion to suppress the evidence in the cardboard box on the ground that it had been obtained unconstitutionally because he had not consented to the search. Further, he claimed that the evidence found on the laptop should also be excluded as "fruit of the poisonous tree" (see page 175) because the warrant to search the laptop was issued on the basis of an affidavit that relied, in part, on the evidence in the box. The district court denied the motion. Oliver appealed.

ISSUE　Were the searches of Oliver's laptop and box lawful under the Fourth Amendment?

DECISION　Yes. A federal appellate court affirmed the lower court's decision that the search was legal and that the evidence in the box and on the laptop computer was admissible.

REASON　The court explained that the private search doctrine legitimized the search of the box and that the independent source doctrine applied to the computer. Under the private search doctrine, when a private individual examines the contents of a closed container, a subsequent search of the container by government officials does not constitute an unlawful search for purposes of the Fourth Amendment. In this case, Armstrong

Case 6.3—Continued

testified that she had looked through the contents of the box before the police came to her apartment. Even though the officers were unaware of her actions at that time, the private search doctrine applied to and legitimized the officers' search.

As for the laptop, under the independent source doctrine, evidence obtained through a legal, independent source need not be suppressed. Both Oliver and his co-defendant had admitted to using a laptop computer to submit fraudulent

unemployment claims. Therefore, police had an independent source for obtaining a warrant to search the laptop, whether or not its original seizure was legal.

WHAT IF THE FACTS WERE DIFFERENT? *Suppose that Armstrong had not looked through the cardboard box before the police searched it. Would the box's contents have been admissible? Why or why not?*

Phishing An e-mail fraud scam in which the messages purport to be from legitimate businesses to induce individuals into revealing their personal financial data, passwords, or other information.

Phishing

A distinct form of identity theft known as **phishing** has added a different wrinkle to the practice. In a phishing attack, the perpetrators "fish" for financial data and passwords from consumers by posing as a legitimate business such as a bank or credit-card company. The "phisher" sends an e-mail asking the recipient to "update" or "confirm" vital information, often with the threat that an account or some other service will be discontinued if the information is not provided. Once the unsuspecting individual enters the information, the phisher can use it to masquerade as that person or to drain his or her bank or credit account.

EXAMPLE 6.22 Customers of Wells Fargo Bank receive official-looking e-mails telling them to input personal information on an online form to complete a mandatory installation of a new Internet security certificate. But the Web site is bogus. When the customers complete the forms, their computers are infected and funnel their data to a computer server. The cyber criminals then sell the data. •

Employment Fraud

Cyber criminals also look for victims at online job-posting sites. Claiming to be an employment officer in a well-known company, the criminal sends bogus e-mails to job seekers. The message asks the unsuspecting job seeker to reveal enough information to allow for identity theft. **EXAMPLE 6.23** The job site Monster.com had to ask all of its users to change their passwords after cyber thieves broke into its databases and stole user identities, passwords, and other data. The theft of 4.5 million users' personal information from Monster.com was one of Britain's largest cyber theft cases. •

Credit-Card Theft

As mentioned, identity theft often includes credit-card theft. An important point to note, however, is that stolen credit-card numbers are much more likely to hurt merchants and credit-card issuers (such as banks) than consumers. In most situations, the legitimate holders of credit cards are not held responsible for the costs of purchases made with a stolen number (see Chapter 33). That means the financial burden must be borne either by the merchant or by the credit-card company. Most credit-card issuers require merchants to cover the costs—especially if the address to which the goods are sent does not match the billing address of the credit card.

Additionally, companies take risks by storing their online customers' credit-card numbers. By doing so, companies can provide quicker service because a consumer can make a purchase by providing a code or clicking on a particular icon without entering a lengthy card number. These electronic warehouses are quite tempting to cyber thieves, however. **EXAMPLE 6.24** A cyber thief was able to gain access to computerized records at CardSystems Solutions, a company in Tucson, Arizona, that processes credit-card transactions for small Internet businesses. The breach exposed 40 million credit-card numbers. •

Hacking

Hacker A person who uses computers to gain unauthorized access to data.

Botnet A network of compromised computers connected to the Internet that can be used to generate spam, relay viruses, or cause servers to fail.

A **hacker** is someone who uses one computer to break into another. (Smartphones can be hacked, too.) The danger posed by hackers has increased significantly because of **botnets**, or networks of computers that have been appropriated by hackers without the knowledge of their owners. A hacker will secretly install a program on thousands, if not millions, of personal computer "robots," or "bots," that allows him or her to forward transmissions to an even larger number of systems. To read about a group of well-known hackers in Russia, see this chapter's *Beyond Our Borders* feature below.

EXAMPLE 6.25 In 2011, a hacker broke into Sony Corporation's PlayStation 3 video gaming and entertainment networks. The incident forced the company to temporarily shut down its online gaming services and affected more than 100 million online accounts that provide gaming, chat, and music streaming services. •

Malware Malicious software programs, such as viruses and worms, that are designed to cause harm to a computer, network, or other device.

Worm A software program that automatically replicates itself over a network but does not alter files and is usually invisible to the user until it has consumed system resources.

Virus A software program that can replicate itself over a network and spread from one device to another, altering files and interfering with normal operations.

Malware   Botnets are one of the latest forms of **malware**, a term that refers to any program that is harmful to a computer or, by extension, its user. A **worm,** for example, is a software program that is capable of reproducing itself as it spreads from one computer to the next. **EXAMPLE 6.26** Within three weeks, the computer worm called "Conflicker" spread to more than 1 million personal computers around the world in 2009. It was transmitted to some computers through the use of Facebook and Twitter. This worm also infected servers and devices plugged into infected computers via USB ports, such as iPods, iPhones, iPads, and USB flash drives. •

A **virus,** another form of malware, is also able to reproduce itself, but must be attached to an "infested" host file to travel from one computer network to another. For example, hackers are now capable of corrupting banner ads that use Adobe's Flash Player. When an Internet user clicks on the banner ad, a virus is installed. Worms and viruses can be programmed to perform a number of functions, such as prompting host computers to continually "crash" and reboot, or otherwise infect the system.

Service-Based Hacking   A recent trend in business computer applications is the use of "software as a service." Instead of buying software to install on a computer, the user connects to Web-based software. The user can write e-mails, edit spreadsheets, and

BEYOND OUR BORDERS   Hackers Hide in Plain Sight in Russia

According to the security software maker Symantec, few Internet users and businesses have completely avoided computer crime. Consumers alone lose about $120 billion a year worldwide because of hackers and e-fraudsters.

The KoobFace Gang
A group of at least five men who live comfortably in St. Petersburg, Russia, started hacking four years ago—and they are still at it. Calling themselves KoobFace, they created a system of illegal botnets that includes

800,000 infected personal computers. Via this system, they have succeeded in using the KoobFace worm to infiltrate Facebook accounts. The KoobFace gang continues to make $2 million to $5 million a year from this venture. KoobFace is considered a pioneer in the criminal exploitation of social networks.

Knowing the Perpetuators Does Not Lead to Convictions
Authorities worldwide know the identities of the members of KoobFace, yet so far none

of them has been charged with a crime. No law enforcement agencies have even confirmed that the group is under investigation. Because Western law officials do not have the resources to tackle even well-known hackers, the Russians hackers are free to continue their activities. It is not surprising that Russia has gained a reputation as a "hacker haven."

Critical Thinking
Why might it be difficult for U.S. authorities to ever investigate the KoobFace gang?

the like using his or her Web browser. Cyber criminals have adapted this method and now offer "crimeware as a service."

A would-be thief no longer has to be a computer hacker to create a botnet or steal banking information and credit-card numbers. He or she can rent the online services of cyber criminals to do the work on such sites as NeoSploit. The thief can even target individual groups, such as U.S. physicians or British attorneys. The cost of renting a Web site to do the work is only a few cents per target computer. (For some tips on protecting a company against hackers, see the *Business Application* on page 185.)

Cyberterrorism

Cyberterrorists, as well as hackers, may target businesses. Whereas the goals of a hacker might include theft of data, such as a merchant's customer files, or monitoring a server to discover a business firm's plans and transactions, a cyberterrorist would aim to do more immediate damage. For instance, by inserting false codes or data, a cyberterrorist might change the processing control system of a food manufacturer to alter the levels of ingredients so that consumers of the food would become ill.

A cyberterrorist attack on a major financial institution, such as the New York Stock Exchange or a large bank, could leave securities or money markets in flux and seriously affect the daily lives of millions of citizens. Similarly, any prolonged disruption of computer, cable, satellite, or telecommunications systems due to the actions of expert hackers would have serious repercussions on business operations—and national security—on a global level.

Prosecution of Cyber Crime

Cyber crime has raised new issues in the investigation of crimes and the prosecution of offenders. Determining the "location" of a cyber crime and identifying a criminal in cyberspace are two significant challenges for law enforcement.

Jurisdiction and Identification Challenges
A threshold issue is, of course, jurisdiction. Jurisdiction is normally based on physical geography, as discussed in Chapter 3 on page 61, and each state and nation has jurisdiction over crimes committed within its boundaries. But geographic boundaries simply do not apply in cyberspace. A person who commits an act against a business in California, where the act is a cyber crime, might never have set foot in California but might instead reside in New York, or even in Canada, where the act may not be a crime.

Identifying the wrongdoer can also be difficult. Cyber criminals do not leave physical traces, such as fingerprints or DNA samples, as evidence of their crimes. Even electronic "footprints" (digital evidence) can be hard to find and follow. For example, e-mail may be sent through a remailer, an online service that guarantees that a message cannot be traced to its source.

For these reasons, laws written to protect physical property are often difficult to apply in cyberspace. Nonetheless, governments at both the state and the federal level have taken significant steps toward controlling cyber crime, both by applying existing criminal statutes and by enacting new laws that specifically address wrongs committed in cyberspace. California, for instance, which has the highest identity theft rate in the nation, established a new eCrime unit in 2011 to investigate and prosecute cyber crimes. Other states, including

"THE PRISONS ARE FILLED WITH CYBER-CRIMINALS, SO I'M SENTENCING YOU TO FOUR YEARS OF WAITING FOR INTERNET ACCESS."

Florida, Louisiana, and Texas, also have special law enforcement units that focus solely on Internet crimes.

The Computer Fraud and Abuse Act

Perhaps the most significant federal statute specifically addressing cyber crime is the Counterfeit Access Device and Computer Fraud and Abuse Act of 1984.[29] This act is commonly known as the Computer Fraud and Abuse Act, or CFAA.

Among other things, the CFAA provides that a person who accesses a computer online, without authority, to obtain classified, restricted, or protected data (or attempts to do so) is subject to criminal prosecution. Such data could include financial and credit records, medical records, legal files, military and national security files, and other confidential information in government or private computers. The crime has two elements: accessing a computer without authority and taking the data.

This theft is a felony if it is committed for a commercial purpose or for private financial gain, or if the value of the stolen information exceeds $5,000. Penalties include fines and imprisonment for up to twenty years. For a discussion of whether it should be a violation of the CFAA to post fake pictures on the Internet's social media sites, see this chapter's *Adapting the Law to the Online Environment* feature below.

---

29. 18 U.S.C. Section 1030.

ADAPTING THE LAW TO THE ONLINE ENVIRONMENT

PROSECUTING THOSE WHO POST FALSE INFORMATION ON THE INTERNET

As discussed in the text, the Computer Fraud and Abuse Act (CFAA) was enacted nearly thirty years ago. At that time, the new law was aimed at computer hacking. Since then, Congress has greatly expanded the act's reach. Today, the CFAA criminalizes any computer use that "exceeds authorized access" to any computer.

Posting Fake Photos Can Be a Crime

Just a few years ago, the Justice Department prosecuted a woman for supposedly violating the "terms of service" of MySpace.com. The woman had set up a MySpace account pretending to be a sixteen-year-old boy and had used the account to harass a thirteen-year-old girl (who subsequently committed suicide). Because the woman's profile did not use her actual photo, she was charged with conspiracy to violate the CFAA because MySpace's terms of service require that all profile information be truthful.[a] Another defendant was prosecuted for posing as someone else and posting sexually inappropriate messages on Facebook that purported to be from her.[b] In both instances, many suggested that the prosecutors were attempting to criminalize actions that, however blameworthy they may have been, were hardly crimes under the law.

a. *United States v. Drew*, 259 F.R.D. 449 (C.D.Cal. 2009).
b. *In re Rolando S.*, 197 Cal.App.4th 936, 129 Cal.Rptr.3d 49 (2011).

Civil Suits Filed by Private Parties

In addition to potential criminal penalties, the CFAA also allows private parties to bring civil suits against other private parties. An employer can sue a former employee for excessive Internet usage while at work. In other words, if the employer can prove (through keystroke monitoring, for example) that the employee visited Facebook and sent too many personal e-mails from work, the employer has grounds to sue. In one case, the terms of service on a company's Web site stated that no competitors could visit it. When one of them did, the company sued that competitor.

Have We Gone Too Far?

Agreements are breached every day. Employees routinely ignore their bosses' instructions. If such actions involve a computer or the Internet, however, they become federal crimes. In other words, the law today gives computer owners the power to criminalize any computer use with which they disagree.

Critical Thinking

Is the expansion of the 1984 Computer Fraud and Abuse Act part of the overcriminalization trend in this country? Why or why not?

Reviewing . . . Criminal Law and Cyber Crime

Edward Hanousek worked for Pacific & Arctic Railway and Navigation Company (P&A) as a roadmaster of the White Pass & Yukon Railroad in Alaska. As an officer of the corporation, Hanousek was responsible "for every detail of the safe and efficient maintenance and construction of track, structures, and marine facilities of the entire railroad," including special projects. One project was a rock quarry, known as "6-mile," above the Skagway River. Next to the quarry, and just beneath the surface, ran a high-pressure oil pipeline owned by Pacific & Arctic Pipeline, Inc., P&A's sister company. When the quarry's backhoe operator punctured the pipeline, an estimated 1,000 to 5,000 gallons of oil were discharged into the river. Hanousek was charged with negligently discharging a harmful quantity of oil into a navigable water of the United States in violation of the criminal provisions of the Clean Water Act (CWA). Using the information presented in the chapter, answer the following questions.

1. Did Hanousek have the required mental state (*mens rea*) to be convicted of a crime? Why or why not?
2. Which theory discussed in the chapter would enable a court to hold Hanousek criminally liable for violating the statute regardless of whether he participated in, directed, or even knew about the specific violation?
3. Could the quarry's backhoe operator who punctured the pipeline also be charged with a crime in this situation? Explain.
4. Suppose that, at trial, Hanousek argued that he could not be convicted because he was not aware of the requirements of the CWA. Would this defense be successful? Why or why not?

DEBATE THIS Because of overcriminalization, particularly by the federal government, Americans may be breaking the law regularly without knowing it. Should Congress rescind many of the more than four thousand federal crimes now on the books?

BUSINESS APPLICATION

Protecting Your Company against Hacking of Your Bank Accounts*

Each year, conventional, old-fashioned crooks rob banks to the tune of about $50 million. In contrast, every year cybercrooks steal billions of dollars from the bank accounts of small and mid-size companies in Europe and the United States. Why? The reason is that small businesses tend to be lax in protecting themselves from hackers. They keep their accounts in community or regional banks, have only rudimentary security measures, and usually fail to hire an on-site cyber security expert.

You May Not Receive Compensation for Your Losses

Many small-business owners believe that if their bank accounts are hacked and disappear, their banks will reimburse them. That is not always the case, however. Just ask Mark Patterson, the owner of Patco Construction in Stanford, Maryland. He lost more than $350,000 to cyberthieves. When People's United Bank would not agree to a settlement, Patterson sued, claiming that the bank should have monitored his account. So far, federal judges have agreed with the bank—that its protections were "commercially reasonable," which is the only standard that banks have to follow.

Insurance May Not Be the Answer

Similarly, small-business owners often think that their regular insurance policy will cover cyber losses at their local banks. In reality, unless there is a specific "rider" to a business's insurance policy, its bank accounts are not covered. So, just because your business will be reimbursed if thieves break in and steal your machines and network servers, that does not mean you will be covered if cybercrooks break into your bank account.

Checklist for Preventing Cyberthefts of Your Bank Accounts

1. Meet with your bank managers and discuss what you can do to protect your company's bank accounts.
2. Have your company sign up for identity-theft services. Many large banks provide these.
3. Change your company's passwords frequently. Always use long, complicated passwords.
4. Instruct your employees never to reply to unknown e-mail requests, particularly if they ask for any information about the company.
5. Have a computer expert test the firewalls safeguarding your internal computer network.

*This *Business Application* is not meant to substitute for the services of an attorney who is licensed to practice law in your state.

Key Terms

actus reus 158
arson 163
beyond a reasonable doubt 156
botnet 182
burglary 161
computer crime 178
crime 156
cyber crime 179
cyber fraud 179
double jeopardy 173

duress 169
embezzlement 164
entrapment 170
exclusionary rule 174
felony 167
forgery 163
grand jury 176
hacker 182
identity theft 180
indictment 176

information 176
insider trading 166
larceny 161
malware 182
mens rea 158
misdemeanor 168
money laundering 167
petty offense 168
phishing 181
plea bargaining 170

probable cause 172
robbery 161
search warrant 171
self-defense 168
self-incrimination 170
virus 182
white-collar crime 164
worm 182

Chapter Summary: Criminal Law and Cyber Crime

Civil Law and Criminal Law (See pages 156–157.)	1. *Civil law*—Spells out the duties that exist between persons or between persons and their governments, excluding the duty not to commit crimes. 2. *Criminal law*—Has to do with crimes, which are wrongs against society proclaimed in statutes and, if committed, punishable by society through fines and/or imprisonment—and, in some cases, death. Because crimes are *offenses against society as a whole*, they are prosecuted by a public official, not by the victims. 3. *Key differences*—An important difference between civil and criminal law is that the standard of proof is higher in criminal cases (see Exhibit 6.1 on page 156 for other differences between civil and criminal law). 4. *Civil liability for criminal acts*—A criminal act may give rise to both criminal liability and tort liability (see Exhibit 6.2 on page 157 for an example of criminal and tort liability for the same act).
Criminal Liability (See pages 158–160.)	1. *Guilty act*—In general, some form of harmful act must be committed for a crime to exist. 2. *Intent*—An intent to commit a crime, or a wrongful mental state, is generally required for a crime to exist.

Types of Crimes (See pages 161–168.)	1. Crimes fall into five general categories: violent crime, property crime, public order crime, white-collar crime, and organized crime.
	    a. Violent crimes are those that cause others to suffer harm or death, including murder, assault and battery, sexual assault (rape), and robbery.
	    b. Property crimes are the most common form of crime. The offender's goal is to obtain some economic gain or to damage property. This category includes burglary, larceny, obtaining goods by false pretenses, receiving stolen property, arson, and forgery.
	    c. Public order crimes are acts, such as public drunkenness, prostitution, gambling, and illegal drug use, that a statute has established are contrary to public values and morals.
	    d. White-collar crimes are illegal acts committed by a person or business using nonviolent means to obtain a personal or business advantage. Usually, such crimes are committed in the course of a legitimate occupation. Examples include embezzlement, mail and wire fraud, bribery, bankruptcy fraud, theft of trade secrets, and insider trading.
	    e. Organized crime is a form of crime conducted by groups operating illegitimately to satisfy the public's demand for illegal goods and services (such as gambling or illegal narcotics). This category of crime also includes money laundering and racketeering (RICO) violations.
	 2. Crimes may also be classified according to their degree of seriousness. Felonies are serious crimes punishable by death or by imprisonment for more than one year. Misdemeanors are less serious crimes punishable by fines or by confinement for up to one year.

Defenses to Criminal Liability (See pages 168–170.)	Defenses to criminal liability include justifiable use of force, necessity, insanity, mistake, duress, entrapment, and the statute of limitations. Also, in some cases defendants may be relieved of criminal liability, at least in part, if they are given immunity.
Constitutional Safeguards and Criminal Procedures (See pages 170–175.)	1. *Fourth Amendment*—Provides protection against unreasonable searches and seizures and requires that probable cause exist before a warrant for a search or an arrest can be issued. 2. *Fifth Amendment*—Requires due process of law, prohibits double jeopardy, and protects against self-incrimination. 3. *Sixth Amendment*—Guarantees a speedy trial, a trial by jury, a public trial, the right to confront witnesses, and the right to counsel.

Chapter Summary: Criminal Law and Cyber Crime—Continued

Constitutional Safeguards and Criminal Procedures—Continued	4. *Eighth Amendment*—Prohibits excessive bail and fines, and cruel and unusual punishment. 5. *Exclusionary rule*—A criminal procedural rule that prohibits the introduction at trial of all evidence obtained in violation of constitutional rights, as well as any evidence derived from the illegally obtained evidence. 6. *Miranda rule*—A rule set forth by the Supreme Court in *Miranda v. Arizona* holding that individuals who are arrested must be informed of certain constitutional rights, including their right to counsel.
Criminal Process (See pages 175–178.)	1. *Arrest, indictment, and trial*—Procedures governing arrest, indictment, and trial for a crime are designed to safeguard the rights of the individual against the state. See Exhibit 6.3 on page 177 for a summary of the procedural steps involved in prosecuting a criminal case. 2. *Sentencing guidelines*—The federal government has established sentencing laws or guidelines, which are no longer mandatory but provide a range of penalties for each federal crime.
Cyber Crime (See pages 178–184.)	1. *Cyber fraud*—Occurs when misrepresentations are knowingly made over the Internet to deceive another. Two widely reported forms are online auction fraud and online retail fraud. 2. *Cyber theft*—In cyberspace, thieves can steal data from anywhere in the world. Identity theft is made easier by the fact that many e-businesses store information such as the consumer's name, e-mail address, and credit-card numbers. Phishing and employment fraud are variations of identity theft. The financial burden of stolen credit-card numbers falls more on merchants and credit-card issuers than on consumers. 3. *Hacking*—A hacker is a person who uses one computer to break into another. Malware is any program that is harmful to a computer or, by extension, a computer user. Worms, viruses, and botnets are examples. 4. *Cyberterrorism*—Cyberterrrorists aim to cause serious problems for computer systems. A cyberterrorist attack on a major U.S. financial institution or telecommunications system could have serious repercussions, including jeopardizing national security. 5. *Prosecution of cyber crime*—Prosecuting cyber crime is more difficult than prosecuting traditional crime. Identifying the wrongdoer through electronic footprints left on the Internet is complicated, and jurisdictional issues may arise when the suspect lives in another jurisdiction or nation. A significant federal statute addressing cyber crime is the Computer Fraud and Abuse Act of 1984.

ExamPrep

ISSUE SPOTTERS

1. Daisy takes her roommate's credit card, intending to charge expenses that she incurs on a vacation. Her first stop is a gas station, where she uses the card to pay for gas. With respect to the gas station, has she committed a crime? If so, what is it? **(See pages 160–163.)**
2. Without permission, Ben downloads consumer credit files from a computer belonging to Consumer Credit Agency. He then sells the data to Dawn. Has Ben committed a crime? If so, what is it? **(See page 184.)**

—**Check your answers to the Issue Spotters against the answers provided in Appendix E at the end of this text.**

BEFORE THE TEST

Go to www.cengagebrain.com, enter the ISBN 9781133273561, and click on "Find" to locate this textbook's Web site. Then, click on "Access Now" under "Study Tools," and select Chapter 6 at the top. There, you will find a Practice Quiz that you can take to assess your mastery of the concepts in this chapter, as well as Flashcards, a Glossary of important terms, and Video Questions (when assigned).

For Review

Answers to the even-numbered questions in this *For Review* section can be found in Appendix F at the end of this text.

1. What two elements normally must exist before a person can be held liable for a crime?
2. What are five broad categories of crimes? What is white-collar crime?
3. What defenses can be raised to avoid liability for criminal acts?
4. What constitutional safeguards exist to protect persons accused of crimes?
5. How has the Internet expanded opportunities for identity theft?

Business Scenarios and Case Problems

6–1 Double Jeopardy. Armington, while robbing a drugstore, shot and seriously injured Jennings, a drugstore clerk. Armington was subsequently convicted of armed robbery and assault and battery in a criminal trial. Jennings later brought a civil tort suit against Armington for damages. Armington contended that he could not be tried again for the same crime, as that would constitute double jeopardy, which is prohibited by the Fifth Amendment to the U.S. Constitution. Is Armington correct? Explain. (See pages 173–174.)

6–2 ❓ Question with Sample Answer—Cyber Fraud. Kayla, a student at Learnwell University, owes $20,000 in unpaid tuition. If Kayla does not pay the tuition, Learnwell will not allow her to graduate. To obtain the funds to pay the debt, she sends e-mails to people that she does not know asking them for financial help to send her child, who has a disability, to a special school. In reality, Kayla has no children. Is this a crime? If so, which one? (See pages 165 and 179.)

—**For a sample answer to Question 6–2, go to Appendix G at the end of this text.**

6–3 White-Collar Crime. Helm Instruction Co. hired Patrick Walsh to work as its comptroller. Walsh convinced Helm's president, Richard Wilhelm, to hire Shari Price as Walsh's assistant. Wilhelm was not aware that Walsh and Price were engaged in an extramarital affair. Over the next five years, Walsh and Price spent more than $200,000 of Helm's funds on themselves. Among other things, Walsh drew unauthorized checks on Helm's accounts to pay his personal credit-card bills. Walsh also issued unauthorized salary increases, overtime payments, and tuition reimbursement payments to Price and himself, altering Helm's records to hide the payments. After an investigation, Helm officials confronted Walsh. He denied the affair with Price and argued that his unauthorized use of Helm's funds was an "interest-free loan." Walsh claimed that it was less of a burden on the company to pay his credit-card bills than to give him the salary increases to which he felt he was entitled. Did Walsh commit a crime? If so, what crime did he commit? Discuss. [*State v. Walsh,* 113 Ohio St.3d 1515, 866 N.E.2d 513 (6 Dist. 2007)] (See pages 164–165.)

6–4 Cyber Crime. Jiri Klimecek was a member of a group that overrode copyright protection in movies and music to make them available for download online. Klimecek bought and installed a server and paid to connect it to the Internet. He knew that users could access the server to upload and download copyrighted works. He obtained access to movies and music to make them available. When charged with copyright infringement, he claimed that he had not understood the full scope of the operation. Did Klimecek commit a crime? Explain. [*United States v. Klimecek,* __ F.3d __ (7th Cir. 2009)] (See pages 158–159.)

6–5 ⚖ Case Problem with Sample Answer—Search and Seizure. Three police officers, including Maria Trevizo, pulled over a car with suspended registration. One of the occupants, Lemon Johnson, wore clothing consistent with membership in the Crips gang. Trevizo searched him "for officer safety" and found a gun. Johnson was charged with illegal possession of a weapon. What standard should apply to an officer's search of a passenger during a traffic stop? Should a warrant be required? Could a search proceed solely on the basis of probable cause? Would a reasonable suspicion short of probable cause be enough? Discuss. [*Arizona v. Johnson,* 555 U.S. 323, 129 S.Ct. 781, 172 L.Ed.2d 694 (2009)] (See page 172.)

—**For a sample answer to Problem 6–5, go to Appendix H at the end of this text.**

6–6 Search. Charles Byrd was in a minimum-security county jail awaiting trial. A team of sheriff's deputies wearing T-shirts and jeans took Byrd and several other inmates into a room for a strip search without any apparent justification. Byrd was ordered to remove all his clothing except his boxer shorts. A female deputy searched Byrd while several male deputies watched. One of the male deputies videotaped the search. Byrd filed a suit against the sheriff's department. Did the search violate Byrd's rights? Discuss. [*Byrd v. Maricopa County Sheriff's Department,* 629 F.3d. 1135 (9th Cir. 2011)] (See page 172.)

6–7 Credit- and Debit-Card Theft. Jacqueline Barden was shopping for school clothes with her children when her purse and automobile were taken. In Barden's purse were her car keys, credit and debit cards for herself and her children, as well as the children's Social Security cards and birth certificates needed for enrollment at school. Immediately after the purse and car were stolen, Rebecca Mary Turner attempted to use Barden's credit card at a local Exxon gas station, but the card was declined. The gas station attendant recognized Turner because she had previously written bad checks and used credit cards that did not belong to her. Turner was later arrested while attempting to use one of Barden's checks to pay for merchandise at a Walmart—where the clerk also recognized Turner from prior criminal activity. Turner claimed that she had not stolen Barden's purse or car, and that a friend had told her he had some checks and credit cards and asked her to try using them at Walmart. Turner was convicted at trial. She appealed, claiming that there was insufficient evidence that she committed credit- and debit-card theft. Was the evidence sufficient to uphold her conviction? Why or why not? [*Turner v. State of Arkansas,* 2012 Ark.App. 150 (2012)] (See page 162.)

6–8 ↔ A Question of Ethics—Identity Theft. Twenty-year-old Davis Omole had earned good grades in high school and played on the football and chess team. He then went on to college. Omole worked at a cell phone store where he stole customers' personal information. He used the stolen identities to create a hundred different accounts on eBay and held more than three hundred auctions listing for sale items that he did not own (including cell phones, plasma televisions, and stereos). From these auctions, he collected $90,000. To avoid getting caught, he continuously closed and opened the eBay accounts, activated and deactivated cell phone and e-mail accounts, and changed mailing addresses and post office boxes. Omole, who had previously been convicted in a state court for Internet fraud, was convicted in a federal district court of identity theft and wire fraud. [*United States v. Omole,* 523 F.3d 691 (7th Cir. 2008)] **(See page 180.)**

1. Omole displayed contempt for the court and ridiculed his victims, calling them stupid for having been cheated. What does this behavior suggest about Omole's ethics?
2. Under federal sentencing guidelines, Omole could have been imprisoned for more than eight years, but he received only three years, two of which were the mandatory sentence for identity theft. Was this sentence too lenient? Explain.

Critical Thinking and Writing Assignments

6–9 **Critical Legal Thinking.** Ray steals a purse from an unattended car at a gas station. Because the purse contains money and a handgun, Ray is convicted of grand theft of property (cash) and grand theft of a firearm. On appeal, Ray claims that he is not guilty of grand theft of a firearm because he did not know that the purse contained a gun. Can Ray be convicted of grand theft of a firearm even though he did not know that the gun was in the purse? Explain. **(See page 161.)**

6–10 **Business Law Critical Thinking Group Assignment.** Cyber crime costs consumers millions of dollars every year, and it costs businesses, including banks and other credit-card issuers, even more. Nonetheless, when cyber criminals are caught and convicted, they are rarely ordered to pay restitution or sentenced to long prison terms.

1. One group should argue that stiffer sentences would reduce the amount of cyber crime.
2. A second group should determine how businesspersons can best protect themselves from cyber crime and avoid the associated costs.

7 CHAPTER

Ethics and Business Decision Making

CHAPTER OUTLINE

- Business Ethics
- Ethical Transgressions by Financial Institutions
- Approaches to Ethical Reasoning
- Making Ethical Business Decisions
- Practical Solutions to Corporate Ethics Questions
- Business Ethics on a Global Level

LEARNING OBJECTIVES

The five learning objectives below are designed to help improve your understanding of the chapter. After reading this chapter, you should be able to answer the following questions:

1 What is business ethics, and why is it important?

2 How can business leaders encourage their companies to act ethically?

3 How do duty-based ethical standards differ from outcome-based ethical standards?

4 What are six guidelines that an employee can use to evaluate whether his or her actions are ethical?

5 What types of ethical issues might arise in the context of international business transactions?

(pixdeluxe/iStockphoto.com)

"New occasions teach new duties."
—James Russell Lowell, 1819–1891 (American editor, poet, and diplomat)

Ethics scandals erupted throughout corporate America during the first decade of the 2000s. Heads of major corporations were tried for fraud, conspiracy, grand larceny, and obstruction of justice. For example, Jeffrey Skilling, the head of Enron Corporation (a multibillion-dollar enterprise that ended in one of the largest bankruptcies in U.S. history), was convicted of securities fraud and insider trading for deceiving investors and covering up losses.

Ethical problems plagued many U.S. financial institutions and Wall Street firms as well. These ethical scandals contributed to the onset of the deepest recession since the Great Depression of the 1930s. In the economic crisis that began in 2008, not only did some $9 trillion in investment capital evaporate, but millions of workers lost their jobs. Many people lost their life savings in a Ponzi scheme (an illegal pyramid operation) perpetrated for decades by Bernard Madoff, who pleaded guilty in 2009 to bilking investors out of more than $65 billion.

In short, the scope and scale of corporate unethical behavior, especially in the financial sector, skyrocketed (with enormous repercussions worldwide). As the chapter-opening quotation states, "New occasions teach new duties." The ethics scandals of the last several years have taught everyone that business ethics cannot be taken lightly. How businesspersons should act and whose interests they should consider—the firm, its executives, its employees, its shareholders, and more—are the focus of this chapter on business ethics.

Business Ethics

Ethics Moral principles and values applied to social behavior.

As you might imagine, business ethics is derived from the concept of ethics. **Ethics** can be defined as the study of what constitutes right or wrong behavior. It is the branch of philosophy that focuses on morality and the way in which moral principles are derived and applied to one's conduct in daily life. Ethics has to do with questions relating to the fairness, justness, rightness, or wrongness of an action.

Business Ethics What constitutes right or wrong behavior and the application of moral principles in a business context.

Business ethics focuses on what constitutes right or wrong behavior in the business world and on how businesspersons apply moral and ethical principles to situations that arise in the workplace. Because business decision makers often address more complex ethical dilemmas than they face in their personal lives, business ethics is more complicated than personal ethics.

Why Is Business Ethics Important?

LEARNING OBJECTIVE 1
What is business ethics, and why is it important?

To see why business ethics is so important, think about the corporate executives who were sentenced to prison for the crimes that you read about in the first paragraphs of this chapter. They could have avoided this outcome had they engaged in ethical decision making during their careers. As a result of their crimes, all of their companies suffered losses, and some were forced to enter bankruptcy, causing thousands of workers to lose their jobs.

If the executives had acted ethically, the corporations, shareholders, and employees of those companies would not have paid such a high price. Thus, an in-depth understanding of business ethics is important to the long-run viability of a corporation. It is also important to the well-being of individual officers and directors and to the firm's employees. Finally, unethical corporate decision making can negatively affect suppliers, consumers, the community, and society as a whole.

Moral Minimum The minimum degree of ethical behavior expected of a business firm, which is usually defined as compliance with the law.

The Moral Minimum

The minimum acceptable standard for ethical business behavior—known as the **moral minimum**—normally is considered to be compliance with the law. In many corporate scandals, had most of the businesspersons involved simply followed the law, they would not have gotten into trouble. Note, though, that in the interest of preserving personal freedom, as well as for practical reasons, the law does not—and cannot—codify all ethical requirements.

As they make business decisions, businesspersons must remember that just because an action is legal does not necessarily make it ethical. For instance, no law specifies the salaries that public corporations can pay their officers. Nevertheless, if a corporation pays its officers an excessive amount relative to other employees, or to what officers at other corporations are paid, the executives' compensation might be challenged by some as unethical. (Executive bonuses can also present ethical problems—see the discussion later in this chapter.)

"Have you noticed ethics creeping into some of these deals lately?"

In the following case, the court had to determine if a repair shop was entitled to receive full payment of an invoice or some lesser amount given its conduct in the matter.

Case 7.1

Johnson Construction Co. v. Shaffer

Court of Appeal of Louisiana, Second Circuit,
87 So.3d 203 (2012).

(AlexKZ/Shutterstock.com)

Can an auto repair shop hold a truck "hostage" during a payment dispute with its owner?

FACTS A truck owned by Johnson Construction Company needed repairs. So John Robert Johnson, Jr., took the truck with its attached fifteen-ton trailer to Bubba Shaffer, doing business as Shaffer's Auto and Diesel Repair, LLC. The truck was supposedly fixed, and Johnson paid the bill. Thereafter, though, the truck continued to leak oil and water. Johnson returned the truck to Shaffer who again claimed to have fixed the problem. Johnson paid the second bill. The problems with the truck continued, however, so Johnson returned the truck and trailer to Shaffer a third time. Johnson was given a verbal estimate of $1,000 for the repairs, but Shaffer ultimately sent an invoice for $5,863. Johnson offered to settle for $2,480, the amount of the initial estimate ($1,000), plus the costs of parts and shipping. Shaffer refused the offer and would not return Johnson's truck or trailer until full payment was made. Shaffer retained possession for almost four years and also charged Johnson a storage fee of $50 a day and 18 percent interest on the $5,863.

Johnson Construction filed a suit against Shaffer alleging unfair trade practices. The trial court determined that Shaffer had acted deceptively and wrongfully in maintaining possession of Johnson Construction's trailer, on which it had performed no work. The trial court awarded Johnson $3,500 in general damages plus $750 in attorneys' fees. Shaffer was also awarded the initial estimate of $1,000. Shaffer appealed.

ISSUE Was Shaffer entitled to receive the full amount of his invoice ($5,863) and reasonable storage fees for the truck and trailer?

DECISION No. The reviewing court affirmed the trial court's decision and also assessed Shaffer all costs of the appeal.

REASON The reviewing court examined the testimony with respect to the verbal estimate of $1,000 for the repairs of the truck. In Louisiana, to enforce an oral agreement pertaining to something priced in excess of $500, the contract must be authenticated by at least one additional witness or other corroborating circumstances. Johnson testified that he had agreed to the initial $1,000 estimate but he had not authorized Shaffer to perform additional repairs or tear down the engine. A mechanic employed by Shaffer testified that Johnson had not authorized additional repairs to the truck. Thus, those repairs were not part of any agreement because they involved tearing down the engine. The trial court had not been in error when it viewed Shaffer's testimony on the issue as "disingenuous." The court noted, "As for the amount that Shaffer contends is due for storage, had it invoiced Mr. Johnson the amount of the original estimate in the first place, there would have been no need to store the truck or trailer." Therefore, the reviewing court rejected the request for storage fees.

Finally, that Shaffer kept the trailer for nearly four years even though no work had been done on it was viewed by the court as holding the trailer "hostage in an effort to force payment for unauthorized repairs." The award of $3,500 in general damages to Johnson Construction seemed appropriate for such lengthy unlawful conversion of the trailer.

WHAT IF THE FACTS WERE DIFFERENT? *Suppose that Shaffer had invoiced Johnson for only $1,500. Would the outcome have been different? Explain your answer.*

Short-Run Profit Maximization

Some people argue that a corporation's only goal should be profit maximization, which will be reflected in a higher market valuation. When all firms strictly adhere to the goal of profit maximization, resources tend to flow to where they are most highly valued by society. Thus, in theory, profit maximization ultimately leads to the most efficient allocation of scarce resources.

Corporate executives and employees have to distinguish, however, between *short-run* and *long-run* profit maximization. In the short run, a company may increase its profits by continuing to sell a product, even though it knows that the product is defective. In the long run, though, because of lawsuits, large settlements, and bad publicity, such unethical conduct will cause profits to suffer. Thus, business ethics is consistent only with long-run profit maximization. An overemphasis on short-term profit maximization is the most common reason that ethical problems occur in business.

CASE EXAMPLE 7.1 When the powerful narcotic painkiller OxyContin was first marketed, its manufacturer, Purdue Pharma, claimed that it was unlikely to lead to drug addiction or abuse. Internal company documents later showed, however, that the company's executives knew that OxyContin could be addictive, but they kept this risk a secret to boost sales and maximize short-term profits. Purdue Pharma and three former executives pleaded guilty to criminal charges that they misled regulators, patients, and physicians about OxyContin's risks. Purdue Pharma agreed to pay $600 million in fines and other payments. The three former executives agreed to pay $34.5 million in fines and were barred from federal health programs for a period of fifteen years. Thus, the company's focus on maximizing profits in the short run led to unethical conduct that hurt profits in the long run.[1] ●

"Gray Areas" in the Law

In many situations, business firms can predict with a fair amount of certainty whether a given action would be legal. For instance, firing an employee solely because of that person's race or gender would clearly violate federal laws prohibiting employment discrimination. In some situations, though, the legality of a particular action may be less clear. In part, this is because there are so many laws regulating business that it is increasingly possible to violate one of them without realizing it. The law also contains numerous "gray areas," making it difficult to predict with certainty how a court will apply a given law to a particular action.

In addition, many rules of law require a court to determine what is "foreseeable" or "reasonable" in a particular situation. Because a business has no way of predicting how a specific court will decide these issues, decision makers need to proceed with caution and evaluate an action and its consequences from an ethical perspective. The same problem often occurs in cases involving the Internet because it is often unclear how a court will apply existing laws in the context of cyberspace. Generally, if a company can demonstrate that it acted in good faith and responsibly in the circumstances, it has a better chance of successfully defending its action in court or before an administrative law judge.

The Importance of Ethical Leadership

Talking about ethical business decision making is meaningless if management does not set standards. Furthermore, managers must apply the same standards to themselves as they do to the employees of the company.

If a company discovers that a manager has behaved unethically or engaged in misconduct, the company should take prompt remedial action. The following case illustrates what can happen when a manager fails to follow the standards that apply to other employees.

"It's easy to make a buck. It's a lot tougher to make a difference."

Tom Brokaw, 1940–present
(American television journalist)

LEARNING OBJECTIVE 2
How can business leaders encourage their companies to act ethically?

---

1. *United States v. Purdue Frederick Co.*, 495 F. Supp.2d 569 (W.D.Va. 2007).

Case 7.2

Mathews v. B and K Foods, Inc.

Missouri Court of Appeals,
332 S.W.3d 275 (2011).

Many employees fill out timesheets for payroll purposes.

(Robyn Mackenzie/Shutterstock.com)

FACTS Dianne Mathews was employed by B and K Foods, Inc., as a floral manager. In 2010, she was terminated for submitting falsified timesheets. She filed for unemployment compensation (see Chapter 24), but B and K objected, arguing that Mathews was not entitled to unemployment benefits because she had been discharged for misconduct in connection with work. At an employment commission hearing, the chief executive officer of B and K testified that it was company policy to pay employees who worked through their lunch breaks. To be paid, a person turned in a "no-lunch sheet." Mathews, however, turned in "no-lunch sheets" when she ran personal errands.

She admitted to knowing about the policy, but she contended that her conduct was warranted. She claimed that a former employee who was a higher-level manager at B and K had told her that it was unnecessary to adjust her timesheet when she spent a few minutes on a personal errand. The employment commission ruled that Mathews could not receive unemployment compensation benefits. Mathews appealed.

ISSUE Was it misconduct for Mathews to be paid for time spent running personal errands when this was against company policy?

DECISION Yes. A state intermediate appellate court affirmed the employment commission's decision that Mathews should not receive unemployment benefits.

REASON According to the court, " 'work-related misconduct' must involve a willful violation of the rules or standards of the employer." The employer met its burden of proving such misconduct. B and K presented substantial evidence that Mathews had falsified time cards by turning in "no-lunch" sheets for time she had spent running personal errands. Mathews admitted that she was familiar with the company's no-lunch policy. Furthermore, she was responsible for seeing that her subordinate employees followed the policy. The court accepted the B and K executive's statement that "they had no choice but to terminate [Mathews] because she was in a higher position and had a responsibility to enforce the lunch policy."

WHAT IF THE FACTS WERE DIFFERENT? *Suppose that Mathews had not admitted to knowing about the "no-lunch sheet" policy. Would the result in this case have been different? Why or why not?*

Attitude of Top Management

One of the most important ways to create and maintain an ethical workplace is for top management to demonstrate its commitment to ethical decision making. A manager who is not totally committed to an ethical workplace rarely succeeds in creating one. Management's behavior, more than anything else, sets the ethical tone of a firm. Employees take their cues from management. **EXAMPLE 7.2** Devon, a BioTek employee, observes his manager cheating on her expense account. Later, when Devon is promoted to a managerial position, he "pads" his expense account as well, knowing that he is unlikely to face sanctions for doing so. ●

Managers who set unrealistic production or sales goals increase the probability that employees will act unethically. If a sales quota can be met only through high-pressure, unethical sales tactics, employees will try to act "in the best interest of the company" and will continue to behave unethically.

A manager who looks the other way when she or he knows about an employee's unethical behavior also sets an example—one indicating that ethical transgressions will be accepted. Managers have found that discharging even one employee for ethical reasons has a tremendous impact as a deterrent to unethical behavior in the workplace.

Behavior of Owners and Managers

Business owners and managers sometimes take more active roles in fostering unethical and illegal conduct. This may indicate to their co-owners, co-managers, employees, and others that unethical business behavior will be tolerated. **EXAMPLE 7.3** Lawyer Samir Zia Chowhan posted a help-wanted ad on Craigslist seeking an "energetic woman" for the position of legal secretary. The ad stated that the position included secretarial and paralegal work, as well as "additional duties" for two lawyers in the firm. Applicants were asked to send pictures and describe their physical features. When a woman applied for the job, Chowhan sent her an e-mail saying that "in addition to the legal work, you would be required to have sexual interaction with me and my partner, sometimes together sometimes separate." He also explained that she would need to perform sexual acts on them at the job interview so that he and his partner could determine whether she would be able to handle these duties. The woman filed a complaint with the Illinois Bar Association, which suspended Chowhan's law license for a year for making false statements about the ad. Because the bar association's ethics rules prohibited attorneys from having sex with their clients, but not with potential employees, Chowhan could only be disciplined for lying. •

Creating Ethical Codes of Conduct

One of the most effective ways of setting a tone of ethical behavior within an organization is to create an ethical code of conduct. A well-written code of ethics explicitly states a company's ethical priorities and demonstrates the company's commitment to ethical behavior.

This chapter concludes with a foldout exhibit showing the code of ethics of Costco Wholesale Corporation as an example. This code of conduct indicates Costco's commitment to legal compliance, as well as to the welfare of its members (those who purchase its goods), employees, and suppliers. The code also details some specific ways in which the interests and welfare of these different groups will be protected. You will also see that Costco acknowledges that by protecting these groups' interests, it will realize its "ultimate goal"—rewarding its shareholders with maximum shareholder value.

Providing Ethics Training to Employees

For an ethical code to be effective, its provisions must be clearly communicated to employees. Most large companies have implemented ethics training programs, in which managers discuss with employees on a face-to-face basis the firm's policies and the importance of ethical conduct. Smaller firms should also offer some form of ethics training to employees because if a firm is accused of an ethics violation, the court will consider the presence or absence of such training in evaluating the firm's conduct.

Some firms hold periodic ethics seminars during which employees can openly discuss any ethical problems that they may be experiencing and learn how the firm's ethical policies apply to those specific problems. Other companies require their managers to meet individually with employees and grade them on their ethical (or unethical) behavior.

Global companies are finding that they need to communicate their ethics policies to their foreign suppliers as well as their domestic employees. **EXAMPLE 7.4** Like other high-tech companies, Apple, Inc., relies heavily on foreign suppliers for components and assembly of many of its products. Following a number of high-profile labor problems with its foreign suppliers and manufacturers, Apple started to evaluate practices at companies in its supply chain and to communicate its ethics policies to them. After its audits revealed numerous violations, in 2012 Apple released a list of its suppliers for the first time. Apple's five-hundred-page "Supplier Responsibility Report" showed that sixty-seven facilities had docked worker pay as a disciplinary measure. Some had falsified pay records and forced workers to use machines without safeguards. Others had engaged in unsafe environmental practices, such as dumping wastewater on neighboring farms. Apple terminated its relationship with one supplier and turned over its findings to the Fair Labor Association for further inquiry. •

"What you do speaks so loudly that I cannot hear what you say."

Ralph Waldo Emerson,
1803–1882
(American essayist and poet)

To avoid disputes over ethical violations, you should first create a written ethical code that is expressed in clear and understandable language. The code should establish specific procedures that employees can follow if they have questions or complaints. It should assure employees that their jobs will be secure and that they will not face reprisals if they do file a complaint. A well-written code might also include examples to clarify what the company considers to be acceptable and unacceptable conduct. You should also hold periodic training meetings so that you can explain to employees face to face why ethics is important to the company. If your company does business internationally, you might also communicate the code to firms in your supply chain and make sure they follow your ethics policies.

The Sarbanes-Oxley Act and Web-Based Reporting Systems

Congress enacted the Sarbanes-Oxley Act[2] to help reduce corporate fraud and unethical management decisions. The act requires companies to set up confidential systems so that employees and others can "raise red flags" about suspected illegal or unethical auditing and accounting practices. (The Sarbanes-Oxley Act will be discussed in more detail in Chapters 31 and 34, and excerpts and explanatory comments on this important law appear in Appendix D of this text.)

Some companies have implemented online reporting systems to accomplish this goal. In one system, employees can click on an icon on their computers that anonymously links them with EthicsPoint, an organization based in Portland, Oregon. Through EthicsPoint, employees can report suspicious accounting practices, sexual harassment, and other possibly unethical behavior. EthicsPoint, in turn, alerts management personnel or the audit committee at the designated company to the possible problem. Those who have used the system say that it is less inhibiting than calling a company's toll-free number.

Ethical Transgressions by Financial Institutions

> "Never let your sense of morals prevent you from doing what is right."
>
> Isaac Asimov, 1920–1992
> (Russian-born writer and scientist)

One of the best ways to learn the ethical responsibilities inherent in operating a business is to look at the mistakes made by other companies. In the following subsections, we describe some of the most egregious ethical failures of financial institutions during the last decade. Many of these ethical wrongdoings received wide publicity and raised public awareness of the need for ethical leadership throughout all businesses.

Corporate Stock Buybacks

During the economic crisis that started in 2008, many of the greatest financial companies in the United States either went bankrupt, were taken over by the federal government, or had to be bailed out by U.S. taxpayers. What many people do not know is that those same corporations were using their own cash funds to prop up the value of their stock in the years just before the economic crisis.

Stock Buyback The purchase of shares of a company's own stock by that company on the open market.

The theory behind a **stock buyback** is simple—the management of a corporation believes that the market price of its shares is "below their fair value." Therefore, instead of issuing dividends to shareholders or reinvesting profits, management uses the company's funds to buy its shares in the open market, thereby boosting the price of the stock. From 2005 to 2007, stock buybacks for the top five hundred U.S. corporations added up to $1.4 *trillion*.

---

2. 15 U.S.C. Sections 7201 *et seq.*

Stock Option An agreement that grants the owner the option to buy a given number of shares of stock at a set price, usually within a specific time period.

Who benefits from stock buybacks? The main individual beneficiaries are corporate executives who have been given **stock options**, which enable them to buy shares of the corporation's stock at a set price. When the market price rises above that level, the executives can profit by selling their shares. Although stock buybacks are legal and can serve legitimate purposes, they can easily be abused if managers use them just to increase the stock price in the short term so that they can profit from their options without considering the long-term needs of the company.

In the investment banking business, which almost disappeared in the latter half of 2008, stock buybacks were particularly egregious. **EXAMPLE 7.5** Goldman Sachs, an investment bank, bought back $15 billion of its stock in 2007. Yet by 2009, U.S. taxpayers had provided $10 billion in bailout funds to that same company. Lehman Brothers Holdings had also bought back large amounts of stock before it filed for bankruptcy in 2008. •

Startling Executive Decisions at American International Group

American International Group (AIG) was once a respected, conservative worldwide insurance company based in New York. Then it decided to enter an area in which it had little expertise—the issuance of insurance contracts guaranteeing certain types of complicated financial contracts. When many of those insured contracts failed, AIG experienced multibillion-dollar losses. Finally, the company sought a federal bailout that eventually amounted to almost $200 billion of U.S. taxpayers' funds.

While some company executives were testifying before Congress after receiving the funds, other AIG executives spent almost $400,000 on a retreat at a resort in California. In essence, U.S. taxpayers were footing the bill.

Executive Bonuses

Until the economic crisis began in 2008, the bonuses paid in the financial industry did not make headlines. After all, times were good, and why shouldn't those responsible for record company earnings be rewarded? When investment banks and commercial banks began to fail, however, or had to be bailed out or taken over by the federal government, executive bonuses became an important issue.

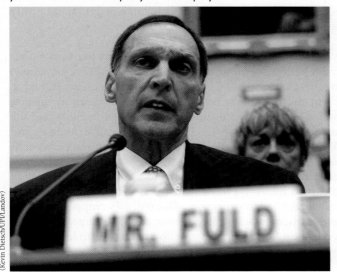

Richard Fuld, a former head of investment bank Lehman Brothers, earned $500 million in bonuses during the seven years before the company's bankruptcy.

(Kevin Dietsch/UPI/Landov)

The industry had been profiting from the sale of risky assets to investors. Executives and others in the industry who had created and sold those risky assets suffered no liability—and even received bonuses. Of course, some of those firms that had enjoyed high short-run returns from their risky investments—and paid bonuses based on those profits—found themselves facing bankruptcy. **EXAMPLE 7.6** Lehman Brothers' chief executive officer earned almost $500 million between 2000 and the firm's demise in 2008. Even after Lehman Brothers entered bankruptcy, its new owners, Barclays and Nomura, legally owed $3.5 billion in bonuses to employees still on the payroll. In 2006, Goldman Sachs awarded its employees a total of $16.5 billion in bonuses, or an average of almost $750,000 for each employee. •

Public outrage at the bonuses paid by firms receiving taxpayer funds subsequently caused Congress to include a provision in the American Recovery and Reinvestment Tax Act of

2009 to change the compensation system in the financial industry. The provision did not cap executive salaries but did severely restrict the bonuses that could be paid by firms that had received bailout funds under the Troubled Asset Relief Program (TARP).[3] Although cash bonuses to Wall Street executives fell, the total compensation for financial service firms increased in 2010 to nearly $150 billion.

Approaches to Ethical Reasoning

Ethical Reasoning A reasoning process in which an individual links his or her moral convictions or ethical standards to the particular situation at hand.

Each individual, when faced with a particular ethical dilemma, engages in **ethical reasoning**—that is, a reasoning process in which the individual examines the situation at hand in light of his or her moral convictions or ethical standards. Businesspersons do likewise when making decisions with ethical implications.

How do business decision makers decide whether a given action is the "right" one for their firms? What ethical standards should be applied? Broadly speaking, ethical reasoning relating to business traditionally has been characterized by two fundamental approaches. One approach defines ethical behavior in terms of duty, which also implies certain rights. The other approach determines what is ethical in terms of the consequences, or outcome, of any given action. We examine each of these approaches here.

In addition to the two basic ethical approaches, several theories have been developed that specifically address the social responsibility of corporations. Because these theories also influence today's business decision makers, we conclude this section with a short discussion of the different views of corporate social responsibility.

LEARNING OBJECTIVE 3
How do duty-based ethical standards differ from outcome-based ethical standards?

Duty-Based Ethics

Duty-based ethical standards often are derived from revealed truths, such as religious precepts. They can also be derived through philosophical reasoning.

Religious Ethical Standards   In the Judeo-Christian tradition, the Ten Commandments of the Old Testament establish fundamental rules for moral action. Other religions have their own sources of revealed truth. Religious rules generally are absolute with respect to the behavior of their adherents. The commandment "Thou shalt not steal" is an absolute mandate for a person who believes that the Ten Commandments reflect revealed truth. Even a benevolent motive for stealing (such as Robin Hood's) cannot justify the act because the act itself is inherently immoral and thus wrong.

"When I do good, I feel good. When I do bad, I feel bad. And that's my religion."

Abraham Lincoln, 1809–1865
(Sixteenth president of the United States, 1861–1865)

Kantian Ethics   Duty-based ethical standards may also be derived solely from philosophical reasoning. The German philosopher Immanuel Kant (1724–1804), for example, identified some general guiding principles for moral behavior based on what he believed to be the fundamental nature of human beings. Kant believed that human beings are qualitatively different from other physical objects and are endowed with moral integrity and the capacity to reason and conduct their affairs rationally. Therefore, a person's thoughts and actions should be respected. When human beings are treated merely as a means to an end, they are being treated as the equivalent of objects and are being denied their basic humanity.

Categorical Imperative An ethical guideline developed by Immanuel Kant under which an action is evaluated in terms of what would happen if everybody else in the same situation, or category, acted the same way.

A central theme in Kantian ethics is that individuals should evaluate their actions in light of the consequences that would follow if *everyone* in society acted in the same way. This **categorical imperative** can be applied to any action. **EXAMPLE 7.7**   Suppose that you are deciding whether to cheat on an examination. If you have adopted Kant's categorical imperative, you will decide *not* to cheat because if everyone cheated, the examination (and the entire education system) would be meaningless. ●

---

3. 12 U.S.C. Section 5211.

The Principle of Rights   Because a duty cannot exist without a corresponding right, duty-based ethical standards imply that human beings have basic rights. The principle that human beings have certain fundamental rights (to life, liberty, and the pursuit of happiness, for example) is deeply embedded in Western culture. As discussed in Chapter 1, the natural law tradition embraces the concept that certain actions (such as killing another person) are morally wrong because they are contrary to nature (the natural desire to continue living).

Principle of Rights The belief that human beings have certain fundamental rights. Whether an action or decision is ethical depends on how it affects the rights of various groups, such as owners, employees, consumers, suppliers, the community, and society.

Those who adhere to this **principle of rights,** or "rights theory," believe that a key factor in determining whether a business decision is ethical is how that decision affects the rights of others. These others include the firm's owners, its employees, the consumers of its products or services, its suppliers, the community in which it does business, and society as a whole.

Conflicting Rights   A potential dilemma for those who support rights theory, however, is that there are often conflicting rights and people may disagree on which rights are most important. When considering all those affected by a business decision to downsize a firm, for example, how much weight should be given to employees relative to shareholders? Which employees should be laid off first, those with the highest salaries or those who have worked there for less time (and have less seniority)? How should the firm weigh the rights of customers relative to the community, or employees relative to society as a whole?

Resolving Conflicts   In general, rights theorists believe that whichever right is stronger in a particular circumstance takes precedence. **EXAMPLE 7.8**   A firm can either keep a manufacturing plant open, saving the jobs of twelve workers, or shut the plant down and avoid contaminating a river with pollutants that would endanger the health of tens of thousands of people. In this situation, a rights theorist can easily choose which group to favor. (Not all choices are so clear-cut, however.) •

Outcome-Based Ethics: Utilitarianism

Utilitarianism An approach to ethical reasoning in which an action is evaluated in terms of its consequences for those whom it will affect. A "good" action is one that results in the greatest good for the greatest number of people.

"The greatest good for the greatest number" is a paraphrase of the major premise of the utilitarian approach to ethics. **Utilitarianism** is a philosophical theory developed by Jeremy Bentham (1748–1832) and modified by John Stuart Mill (1806–1873)—both British philosophers. In contrast to duty-based ethics, utilitarianism is outcome oriented. It focuses on the consequences of an action, not on the nature of the action itself or on any set of preestablished moral values or religious beliefs.

Under a utilitarian model of ethics, an action is morally correct, or "right," when, among the people it affects, it produces the greatest amount of good for the greatest number. When an action affects the majority adversely, it is morally wrong. Applying the utilitarian theory thus requires (1) a determination of which individuals will be affected by the action in question; (2) a **cost-benefit analysis,** which involves an assessment of the negative and positive effects of alternative actions on these individuals; and (3) a choice among alternative actions that will produce maximum societal utility (the greatest positive net benefits for the greatest number of individuals).

Cost-Benefit Analysis A decision-making technique that involves weighing the costs of a given action against the benefits of that action.

Corporate Social Responsibility

Corporate Social Responsibility The idea that corporations can and should act ethically and be accountable to society for their actions.

For many years, groups concerned with civil rights, employee safety and welfare, consumer protection, environmental preservation, and other causes have pressured U.S. corporations to behave in a responsible manner with respect to these causes. Thus was born the concept of **corporate social responsibility**—the idea that those who run corporations can and should act ethically and be accountable to society for their actions. Just what constitutes corporate social responsibility has been debated for some time, however, and there are a number of different theories today.

Stakeholder Approach   One view of corporate social responsibility stresses that corporations have a duty not just to shareholders, but also to other groups affected by corporate decisions ("stakeholders"). Under this approach, a corporation would consider the impact of its decision on the firm's employees, customers, creditors, suppliers, and the community in which the corporation operates. The reasoning behind this "stakeholder view" is that in some circumstances, one or more of these other groups may have a greater stake in company decisions than the shareholders do. Although this may be true, as mentioned earlier, it is often difficult to decide which group's interests should receive greater weight if the interests conflict.

During the last few years, layoffs numbered in the millions. Nonetheless, some corporations succeeded in reducing labor costs without layoffs. To avoid slashing their workforces, these employers turned to alternatives such as (1) four-day workweeks, (2) unpaid vacations and voluntary furloughs, (3) wage freezes, (4) pension cuts, and (5) flexible work schedules. Some companies asked their workers to accept wage cuts to prevent layoffs, and the workers agreed. Companies finding alternatives to layoffs included Dell (extended unpaid holidays), Cisco Systems (four-day end-of-year shutdowns), Motorola (salary cuts), and Honda (voluntary unpaid vacation time).

Corporate Citizenship   Another theory of social responsibility argues that corporations should be good citizens by promoting goals that society deems worthwhile and taking positive steps toward solving social problems. The idea is that because business controls so much of the wealth and power of this country, business, in turn, has a responsibility to society to use that wealth and power in socially beneficial ways.

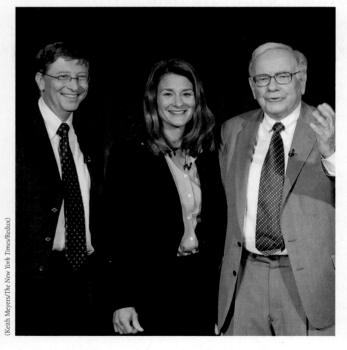

Microsoft founder Bill Gates and his wife, Melinda, are shown below with financier Warren Buffett (right) after Buffett gave $40 billion to the Bill and Melinda Gates Foundation.

(Keith Meyers/The New York Times/Redux)

Under a corporate citizenship view, companies are judged on how much they donate to social causes, as well as how they conduct their operations with respect to employment discrimination, human rights, environmental concerns, and similar issues.   **EXAMPLE 7.9**   Google has teamed up with investment firm Kohlberg Kravis Roberts to develop four solar energy farms that will serve the Sacramento Municipal Utility District in California. The four solar farms reportedly cost $95 million and will provide enough power for more than 13,000 average U.S. homes. •

A Way of Doing Business   A survey of U.S. executives undertaken by the Boston College Center for Corporate Citizenship found that more than 70 percent of those polled agreed that corporate citizenship must be treated as a priority. More than 60 percent said that good corporate citizenship added to their companies' profits. Strategist Michelle Bernhart has argued that corporate social responsibility cannot attain its maximum effectiveness unless it is treated as a way of doing business rather than as a special program.

Not all socially responsible activities can benefit a corporation, however. Corporate responsibility is most successful when a company undertakes activities that are relevant and significant to its stakeholders and related to its business operations.   **EXAMPLE 7.10**   A Brazilian mining firm invested more than $150 million in social projects, including health care, infrastructure, and education. At the same time, it invested more than $300 million in environmental protection. One of its projects involves the rehabilitation of native species in the Amazon Valley. To that end, it is planting almost 200 million trees in an attempt to restore 1,150 square miles of land where cattle breeding and farming have caused deforestation. ● (See the *Linking Business Law to Accounting and Finance* feature at the end of this chapter for more examples of corporate responsibility.)

Making Ethical Business Decisions

The George S. May International Company has provided six basic guidelines to help corporate employees judge their actions. Each employee—no matter what her or his level in the organization—should evaluate her or his actions using the following six guidelines:

1. *The law.* Is the action you are considering legal? If you do not know the laws governing the action, then find out. Ignorance of the law is no excuse.
2. *Rules and procedures.* Are you following the internal rules and procedures that have already been laid out by your company? They have been developed to avoid problems. Is what you are planning to do consistent with your company's policies and procedures? If not, stop.
3. *Values.* Laws and internal company policies reinforce society's values. You might wish to ask yourself whether you are attempting to find a loophole in the law or in your company's policies. Next, you have to ask yourself whether you are following the "spirit" of the law as well as the letter of the law or the internal policy.
4. *Conscience.* If you feel any guilt, let your conscience be your guide. Alternatively, ask yourself whether you would be happy to be interviewed by the national news media about the actions you are going to take.
5. *Promises.* Every business organization is based on trust. Your customers believe that your company will do what it is supposed to do. The same is true for your suppliers and employees. Will your actions live up to the commitments you have made to others, both inside the business and outside?
6. *Heroes.* We all have heroes who are role models for us. Is what you are planning on doing an action that your "hero" would take? If not, how would your hero act? That is how you should be acting.

"Next to doing the right thing, the most important thing is to let people know you are doing the right thing."

John D. Rockefeller, 1839–1897 (American industrialist and philanthropist)

LEARNING OBJECTIVE 4
What are six guidelines that an employee can use to evaluate whether his or her actions are ethical?

ETHICAL ISSUE

Should you do the right thing even when it puts your job at risk? Dean Krehmeyer, executive director of the Business Roundtable's Institute for Corporate Ethics, once said, "Evidence strongly suggests being ethical—doing the right thing—pays." Sometimes, however, being ethical in the business world costs an employee his or her job. For instance, Michael Woodford was chief executive officer for Olympus Corporation, a Tokyo-based camera maker. He had worked thirty years for Olympus when he discovered that the company had been engaging in questionable accounting practices. After confronting management in 2011 about excessive spending on certain acquisitions, Woodford was fired from the board of directors.

He then resigned as chair and called for the other board members to resign and for a shareholders' meeting to be held to select a new board. Olympus initially denied any wrongdoing but later acknowledged a $687 million payment for financial advice and expensive acquisitions to cover up investment losses. Many speculate that the company falsified a large amount of information in its financial reports over the years. Olympus's bookkeeping is now under investigation in Japan, the United States, and Great Britain. But Woodford, who did the right thing by encouraging the company to come clean about the cover-up, no longer works for the company. He plans to sue Olympus, but because it is a Japanese company, he may never be compensated for losing his job.

Practical Solutions to Corporate Ethics Questions

Corporate ethics officers and ethics committees require a practical method to investigate and solve specific ethics problems. Ethics consultant Leonard H. Bucklin of Corporate-Ethics.US has devised a procedure that he calls Business Process Pragmatism.[4] It involves the following five steps:

1. *Inquiry.* Of course, an understanding of the facts must be the initial action. The parties involved might include the mass media, the public, employees, or customers. At this stage of the process, the ethical problem or problems are specified. A list of relevant ethical principles is created.
2. *Discussion.* Here, a list of action options is developed. Each option carries with it certain ethical principles. Finally, resolution goals should also be listed.
3. *Decision.* Working together, those participating in the process craft a consensus decision, or a consensus plan of action for the corporation.
4. *Justification.* Does the consensus solution withstand moral scrutiny? At this point in the process, reasons should be attached to each proposed action or series of actions. Will the stakeholders involved accept these reasons?
5. *Evaluation.* Do the solutions to the corporate ethics issue satisfy corporate values, community values, and individual values? Ultimately, can the consensus resolution to the corporate ethics problem withstand the moral scrutiny of the decisions taken and the process used to reach those decisions?

Business Ethics on a Global Level

Given the various cultures and religions throughout the world, it is not surprising that conflicts in ethics frequently arise between foreign and U.S. businesspersons. For instance, in certain countries, the consumption of alcohol and specific foods is forbidden for religious reasons. Under such circumstances, it would be thoughtless and imprudent for a U.S. businessperson to invite a local business contact out for a drink.

The role played by women in other countries may also present some difficult ethical problems for firms doing business internationally. Equal employment opportunity is a fundamental public policy in the United States, and Title VII of the Civil Rights Act of 1964 prohibits discrimination against women in the employment context (see Chapter 25). Some other countries, however, offer little protection for women against gender discrimination in the workplace, including sexual harassment. (See this chapter's *Law, Diversity, and Business: Managerial Implications* feature on the facing page for a discussion of the impact of cultural differences on global marketing strategies.)

We look here at how laws governing workers in other countries, particularly developing countries, have created some especially difficult ethical problems for U.S. sellers of goods manufactured in foreign countries. We also examine some of the ethical ramifications of laws prohibiting U.S. businesspersons from bribing foreign officials to obtain favorable business contracts.

Monitoring the Employment Practices of Foreign Suppliers

Many U.S. businesses now contract with companies in developing nations to produce goods, such as shoes and clothing, because the wage rates in those nations are significantly lower than wages in the United States. Yet what if a foreign company exploits its

---

4. Corporate-Ethics and Business Process Pragmatism are registered trademarks.

"If you are uncertain about an issue, it's useful to ask yourself, 'Would I be absolutely comfortable for my actions to be disclosed on the front page of my hometown newspaper?'"

Warren E. Buffett, 1930–present
(American businessperson and philanthropist)

LEARNING OBJECTIVE 5
What types of ethical issues might arise in the context of international business transactions?

LAW, DIVERSITY, AND BUSINESS: MANAGERIAL IMPLICATIONS

RESPECTING CULTURAL DIFFERENCES IN FOREIGN MARKETS

Today, more businesses engage in global activities than ever before. Certainly, anyone developing marketing strategies for a foreign market needs to be aware of all aspects of culture, including religion, language, values, and customs.

Global Marketing and the Need to Consider Each Culture Separately No matter how "small" the world has become, countries still have different sets of shared values that affect their citizens' preferences. Samsonite, for example, made a major cultural blunder when it used an advertisement showing its luggage being carried on a "magic" flying carpet. Most Middle Eastern consumers thought that Samsonite was selling carpets. As another example, Green Giant learned to its dismay that it could not use its logo with a man in a green hat in certain parts of Asia. Why not? The reason was that in those areas a green hat signifies a man who has an unfaithful wife.

The Translation of Names and Slogans Can Be a Problem, Too In the same vein, the translation of slogans and names into other languages is fraught with pitfalls. Toyota had to drop the "2" from its model MR2 in France because the combination of sounds was very close to a French swear word. Mitsubishi Motors had to rename one of its models in Spanish-speaking countries because the original name described a sexual activity.

Can Global Marketing Standardization Work in a Diverse World? Many multinationals have adopted global marketing standardization, meaning that they try to adapt product features, advertising, and packaging so that they are usable throughout the world. Those in favor of such standardization—a global vision, as it were—contend that advances in communications and technology have created a small, interconnected world. Consumers everywhere want the same items that they see in popular movies. Coca-Cola, Colgate-Palmolive, and McDonald's, for example, tend toward global marketing standardization.

Business Implications *Managers in any company wishing to do business abroad have to be aware that their marketing campaigns may offend potential consumers (and even governments). Given that almost 15 percent of U.S. production is sold abroad, this issue is an important one and will become more important as standards of living increase in poorer parts of the globe. Higher standards of living usually lead to more imports. Many of those imports will come from the United States and will have to be marketed carefully.*

workers—by hiring women and children at below-minimum-wage rates, for example, or by requiring its employees to work long hours in a workplace full of health hazards? What if the company's supervisors routinely engage in workplace conduct that is offensive to women? What if plants that are operated abroad routinely violate labor and environmental standards?

EXAMPLE 7.11 Apple, Inc., owns Pegatron Corporation, a subsidiary company based in China, that supplies parts for iPads and other Apple products. In December 2011, dozens of employees at the Pegatron factory in Shanghai were injured when aluminum dust created from polishing cases for iPads caught fire and exploded. Apple did not respond to allegations that conditions at the factory violated labor and environmental standards. •

Given today's global communications network, few companies can assume that their actions in other nations will go unnoticed by "corporate watch" groups that discover and publicize unethical corporate behavior. (For a discussion of how the Internet has increased the ability of critics to publicize a corporation's misdeeds, see this chapter's *Adapting the Law to the Online Environment* feature on the following page.) As a result, U.S. businesses today usually take steps to avoid such adverse publicity—either by refusing to deal with certain suppliers or by arranging to monitor their suppliers' workplaces to make sure that the employees are not being mistreated.

ADAPTING THE LAW TO THE ONLINE ENVIRONMENT

CORPORATE REPUTATIONS UNDER ATTACK

In the pre-Internet days, disgruntled employees and customers wrote letters of complaint to corporate management or to the editors of local newspapers. Occasionally, an investigative reporter would write an exposé of alleged corporate misdeeds. Today, those unhappy employees and customers have gone online. To locate them, just type in the name of any major corporation. You will find electronic links to blogs, wikis, message boards, and online communities—many of which post harsh criticisms of corporate giants. Some disgruntled employees and consumers have even created rogue Web sites that mimic the look of the target corporation's official Web site—except that the rogue sites feature chat rooms and postings of "horror stories" about the corporation.

Damage to Corporate Reputations

Clearly, by providing a forum for complaints, the Internet has increased the potential for damage to the reputation of any major (or minor) corporation. Now a relatively small number of unhappy employees, for example, may make the entire world aware of a single incident that is not at all representative of how the corporation ordinarily operates.

Special Interest Groups Go on the Attack

Special interest groups are also using the Internet to attack corporations they do not like. Rather than writing letters or giving speeches to a limited audience, a special interest group can now go online and mercilessly "expose" what it considers to be a corporation's "bad practices." Wal-Mart and Nike in particular have been frequent targets for advocacy groups that believe that those corporations exploit their workers.

Online Attacks: Often Inaccurate, but Probably Legal

Corporations often point out that many of the complaints and charges leveled against them are unfounded or exaggerated. Sometimes, management has tried to argue that the online attacks are libelous. The courts, however, disagree. To date, most courts have regarded online attacks as simply the expression of opinion and therefore a form of speech protected by the First Amendment.

In contrast, if employees breach company rules against the disclosure of internal financial information or trade secrets, the courts have been willing to side with the employers. Note, also, that companies that succeed in lawsuits against inappropriate employee online disclosures always have a clear set of written guidelines about what employees can do when they blog or generate other online content.

Critical Thinking

How might online attacks actually help corporations in the long run? (Hint: Some online criticisms might be accurate.)

The Foreign Corrupt Practices Act

> "Never doubt that a small group of committed citizens can change the world; indeed, it is the only thing that ever has."
>
> Margaret Mead, 1901–1978
> (American anthropologist)

Another ethical problem in international business dealings has to do with the legitimacy of certain "side" payments to government officials. In the United States, most contracts are formed within the private sector. In many countries, however, government regulation and control over trade and industry are much more extensive than in the United States, so government officials make the decisions on most major construction and manufacturing contracts. Side payments to government officials in exchange for favorable business contracts are not unusual in such countries, where they are not considered to be unethical. In the past, U.S. corporations doing business in these countries largely followed the dictum "When in Rome, do as the Romans do."

In the 1970s, however, large side payments by U.S. corporations to foreign representatives for the purpose of securing advantageous international trade contracts led to a number of scandals. In response, in 1977 Congress passed the Foreign Corrupt Practices Act[5] (FCPA), which prohibits U.S. businesspersons from bribing foreign officials to secure advantageous contracts.

---

5. 15 US.C. Sections 78 dd-1 *et seq.*

Prohibition against the Bribery of Foreign Officials The first part of the FCPA applies to all U.S. companies and their directors, officers, shareholders, employees, and agents. This part prohibits the bribery of officials of foreign governments if the purpose of the payment is to induce the officials to act in their official capacity to provide business opportunities.

The FCPA does not prohibit payment of substantial sums to minor officials whose duties are ministerial. These payments are often referred to as "grease," or facilitating payments. They are meant to accelerate the performance of administrative services that might otherwise be carried out at a slow pace. Thus, for example, if a firm makes a payment to a minor official to speed up an import licensing process, the firm has not violated the FCPA. Generally, the act, as amended, permits payments to foreign officials if such payments are lawful within the foreign country. The act also does not prohibit payments to private foreign companies or other third parties unless the U.S. firm knows that the payments will be passed on to a foreign government in violation of the FCPA. Business firms that violate the FCPA may be fined up to $2 million. Individual officers or directors who violate the act may be fined up to $100,000 (the fine cannot be paid by the company) and may be imprisoned for up to five years.

Accounting Requirements In the past, bribes were often concealed in corporate financial records. Thus, the second part of the FCPA is directed toward accountants. All companies must keep detailed records that "accurately and fairly" reflect the company's financial activities. In addition, all companies must have an accounting system that provides "reasonable assurance" that all transactions entered into by the company are accounted for and legal. These requirements assist in detecting illegal bribes. The FCPA further prohibits any person from making false statements to accountants or false entries in any record or account.

Reviewing . . . Ethics and Business Decision Making

Isabel Arnett was promoted to be chief executive officer of Tamik, Inc., a pharmaceutical company that manufactures a vaccine called Kafluk, which supposedly provides some defense against bird flu. The company began marketing Kafluk throughout Asia. After numerous media reports that bird flu might soon become a worldwide epidemic, the demand for Kafluk increased, sales soared, and Tamik earned record profits. Arnett then began receiving disturbing reports from Southeast Asia that in some patients, Kafluk had caused psychiatric disturbances, including severe hallucinations, and heart and lung problems. She was also informed that six children in Japan had committed suicide by jumping out of windows after receiving the vaccine. To cover up the story and prevent negative publicity, Arnett instructed Tamik's partners in Asia to offer cash to the Japanese families whose children had died in exchange for their silence. Arnett also refused to authorize additional research within the company to study the potential side effects of Kafluk. Using the information presented in the chapter, answer the following questions.

1. This scenario illustrates one of the main reasons why ethical problems occur in business. What is that reason?
2. Would a person who adheres to the principle of rights consider it ethical for Arnett not to disclose potential safety concerns and to refuse to perform additional research on Kafluk? Why or why not?
3. If Kafluk prevented fifty Asian people who were exposed to bird flu from dying, would Arnett's conduct in this situation be ethical under a utilitarian cost-benefit analysis? Why or why not?
4. Did Tamik or Arnett violate the Foreign Corrupt Practices Act in this scenario? Why or why not?

DEBATE THIS Executives in large corporations are ultimately rewarded if their companies do well, particularly as evidenced by rising stock prices. Consequently, shouldn't we just let those who run corporations decide what level of negative side effects of their goods or services is "acceptable"?

LINKING BUSINESS LAW to Accounting and Finance

Managing a Company's Reputation

While in business school, all of you must take basic accounting courses. Accounting generally is associated with developing balance sheets and profit-and-loss statements, but it can also be used as a support system to provide information that can help managers do their jobs correctly. Enter managerial accounting, which involves the provision of accounting information for a company's internal use. Managerial accounting is used within a company for planning, controlling, and decision making.

Increasingly, managerial accounting is also being used to *manage corporate reputations*. To this end, more than 2,500 multinationals now release to the public large quantities of managerial accounting information.

Internal Reports Designed for External Scrutiny

Some large companies refer to the managerial accounting information that they release to the public as their corporate sustainability reports. Dow Chemical Company, for example, issues its Global Reporting Initiative Sustainability Report annually. So does Waste Management, Inc., which calls its report "The Color of Our World."

Other corporations call their published documents social responsibility reports. The antivirus software company Symantec Corporation issued its first corporate responsibility report in 2008. The report demonstrated the company's focus on critical environmental, social, and governance issues. Among other things, Symantec pointed out that it had adopted the Calvert Women's Principles, the first global code of corporate conduct designed to empower, advance, and invest in women worldwide.

A smaller number of multinationals provide what they call citizenship reports. For example, in 2011 General Electric (GE) released its Seventh Annual Citizenship Report, which it calls "Sustainable Growth." GE's emphasis is on energy and climate change, demographics, growth markets, and financial markets. It even has a Web site that provides detailed performance metrics (www.ge.com/citizenship).

The Hitachi Group releases an Annual Corporate Social Responsibility Report, which outlines its environmental strategy, including its attempts to reduce carbon dioxide emissions (so-called greenhouse gases). It typically discusses human rights policy and its commitment to human rights awareness.

Why Use Managerial Accounting to Manage Reputations?

We live in an age of information. Any news, whether positive or negative, about a corporation will be known throughout the world almost immediately given the 24/7 cable and online news networks, social media, Internet bloggers, and smartphones. Consequently, corporations want to manage their reputations by preparing and releasing the news that the public, their shareholders, and government officials will receive. In a world in which corporations are often blamed for anything bad that happens, corporations are finding that managerial accounting information can provide a useful counterweight. To this end, some corporations have combined their social responsibility reports with their traditional financial accounting information. When a corporation's reputation is on the line, the future is at stake.

Critical Thinking

Valuable company resources are used to create and publish corporate social responsibility reports. Under what circumstances can a corporation justify such expenditures?

Key Terms

business ethics 191	cost-benefit analysis 199	moral minimum 191	stock option 197
categorical imperative 198	ethical reasoning 198	principle of rights 199	utilitarianism 199
corporate social responsibility 199	ethics 191	stock buyback 196	

Chapter Summary: Ethics and Business Decision Making

Business Ethics (See pages 191–196.)	1. *Ethics*—Business ethics focuses on how moral and ethical principles are applied in the business context. 2. *The moral minimum*—Lawful behavior is the moral minimum. The law has its limits, though, and some actions may be legal but not ethical. 3. *Short-term profit maximization*—One of the most pervasive reasons why ethical breaches occur is the focus on short-term profit maximization. Executives should distinguish between short-run and long-run profit goals and focus on maximizing profits over the long run because only long-run profit maximization is consistent with business ethics. 4. *Legal uncertainties*—It may be difficult to predict with certainty whether particular actions are legal, given the numerous and frequent changes in the laws regulating business and the "gray areas" in the law. 5. *The importance of ethical leadership*—Management's commitment and behavior are essential in creating an ethical workplace. Management's behavior, more than anything else, sets the ethical tone of a firm and influences the behavior of employees. 6. *Ethical codes*—Most large firms have ethical codes or policies and training programs to help employees determine whether specific actions are ethical. In addition, the Sarbanes-Oxley Act requires firms to set up confidential systems so that employees and others can report suspected illegal or unethical auditing or accounting practices.
Ethical Transgressions by Financial Institutions (See pages 196–198.)	During the first decade of the 2000s, corporate wrongdoing among U.S. financial institutions escalated. A number of investment banking firms, such as Goldman Sachs, were nearly bankrupted by their risky investments, and others, such as Lehman Brothers, were forced into bankruptcy. Earlier these same firms had engaged in the abusive use of stock buybacks and stock options. AIG, an insurance giant, was also on the brink of bankruptcy when the government stepped in with federal bailout funds. Exorbitant bonuses paid to Wall Street executives added to the financial industry's problems and fueled public outrage. U.S. taxpayers paid the price through the federal bailouts and a deepening nationwide recession.
Approaches to Ethical Reasoning (See pages 198–201.)	1. *Duty-based ethics*—Ethics based on religious beliefs; philosophical reasoning, such as that of Immanuel Kant; and the basic rights of human beings (the principle of rights). A potential problem for those who support this approach is deciding which rights are more important in a given situation. Management constantly faces ethical conflicts and trade-offs when considering all those affected by a business decision. 2. *Outcome-based ethics (utilitarianism)*—Ethics based on philosophical reasoning, such as that of Jeremy Bentham and John Stuart Mill. Applying this theory requires a cost-benefit analysis, weighing the negative effects against the positive and deciding which course of action produces the better outcome. 3. *Corporate social responsibility*—A number of theories based on the idea that corporations can and should act ethically and be accountable to society for their actions. These include the stakeholder approach and corporate citizenship.
Making Ethical Business Decisions (See page 201.)	Making ethical business decisions is crucial in today's legal environment. Doing the right thing pays off in the long run, both by increasing profits and by avoiding negative publicity and the potential for bankruptcy. We provide six guidelines for making ethical business decisions on page 201.
Practical Solutions to Corporate Ethics Questions (See page 202.)	Corporate ethics officers and ethics committees require a practical method to investigate and solve specific ethics problems. For a five-step pragmatic procedure to solve ethical problems recommended by one expert, see page 202.
Business Ethics on a Global Level (See pages 202–205.)	Businesses must take account of the many cultural, religious, and legal differences among nations. Notable differences relate to the role of women in society, employment laws governing workplace conditions, and the practice of giving side payments to foreign officials to secure favorable contracts.

ExamPrep

ISSUE SPOTTERS

1. Delta Tools, Inc., markets a product that under some circumstances is capable of seriously injuring consumers. Does Delta have an ethical duty to remove this product from the market, even if the injuries result only from misuse? Why or why not? **(See pages 192–193.)**
2. Acme Corporation decides to respond to what it sees as a moral obligation to correct for past discrimination by adjusting pay differences among its employees. Does this raise an ethical conflict between Acme and its employees? Between Acme and its shareholders? Explain your answers. **(See page 201.)**

—Check your answers to the Issue Spotters against the answers provided in Appendix E at the end of this text.

For Review

Answers to the even-numbered questions in this For Review *section can be found in Appendix F at the end of this text.*

1. What is business ethics, and why is it important?
2. How can business leaders encourage their companies to act ethically?
3. How do duty-based ethical standards differ from outcome-based ethical standards?
4. What are six guidelines that an employee can use to evaluate whether his or her actions are ethical?
5. What types of ethical issues might arise in the context of international business transactions?

Business Scenarios and Case Problems

7–1 Business Ethics. Jason Trevor owns a commercial bakery in Blakely, Georgia, that produces a variety of goods sold in grocery stores. Trevor is required by law to perform internal tests on food produced at his plant to check for contamination. Three times in 2011, the tests of food products that contained peanut butter were positive for salmonella contamination. Trevor was not required to report the results to U.S. Food and Drug Administration officials, however, so he did not. Instead, Trevor instructed his employees to simply repeat the tests until the outcome was negative. Therefore, the products that had originally tested positive for salmonella were eventually shipped out to retailers. Five people who ate Trevor's baked goods in 2011 became seriously ill, and one person died from salmonella. Even though Trevor's conduct was legal, was it unethical for him to sell goods that had once tested positive for salmonella? If Trevor had followed the six basic guidelines for making ethical business decisions, would he still have sold the contaminated goods? Why or why not? **(See page 201.)**

7–2 ❓ **Question with Sample Answer—Ethical Duties.** Shokun Steel Co. owns many steel plants. One of its plants is much older than the others. Equipment at that plant is outdated and inefficient, and the costs of production at that plant are now twice as high as at any of Shokun's other plants. The company cannot raise the price of steel because of competition, both domestic and international. The plant employs more than a thousand workers and is located in Twin Firs, Pennsylvania, which has a population of about 45,000. Shokun is contemplating whether to close the plant. What factors should the firm consider in making its decision? Will the firm violate any ethical duties if it closes the plant? Analyze these questions from the two basic perspectives on ethical reasoning discussed in this chapter. **(See page 198.)**

—For a sample answer to Question 7–2, go to Appendix G at the end of this text.

7–3 📱 **Spotlight on Pfizer—Corporate Social Responsibility.** Methamphetamine (meth) is an addictive drug made chiefly in small toxic labs (STLs) in homes, tents, barns, or hotel rooms. The manufacturing process is dangerous, often resulting in explosions, burns, and toxic fumes. Government entities spend time and resources to find and destroy STLs, imprison meth dealers and users, treat addicts, and provide services for affected families. Meth cannot be made without ingredients that are also used in cold and allergy medications. Arkansas has one of the highest numbers of STLs in the United States. To recoup the costs of fighting the meth epidemic, twenty counties in Arkansas filed a suit against Pfizer, Inc., which makes cold and allergy medications. What is Pfizer's ethical responsibility here, and to whom is it owed? Why? [*Ashley County, Arkansas v. Pfizer, Inc.,* 552 F.3d 659 (8th Cir. 2009)] **(See page 200.)**

7–4 ⚖️ **Case Problem with Sample Answer—Ethics and the Law.** Prudential Insurance Co. of America has a company guideline not to change the amount of a salesperson's commission once a client has been quoted a price for insurance. Despite this principle, in order to reduce the quoted price for insurance offered to York International Corp., Prudential cut the fee that it paid to a broker. A competing broker, Havensure, LLC, filed a suit, arguing that the reduced quote caused it to lose York as a potential customer. Is a company's violation of its own policy unethical? Is it a basis for legal liability? Explain. [*Havensure, LLC v. Prudential Insurance Co. of America,* 595 F.3d 312 (6th Cir. 2010)] **(See page 195.)**

—For a sample answer to Problem 7–4, go to Appendix H at the end of this text.

7–5 Ethical Leadership. David Krasner, who worked for HSH Nordbank AG, complained that his supervisor, Roland Kiser, fostered an atmosphere of sexism that was demeaning to women. Among other things, Krasner claimed that career advancement was based on "sexual favoritism." He objected to Kiser's relationship with a female employee, Melissa Campfield, who was promoted before more qualified employees, including Krasner. How do a manager's attitudes and actions affect the workplace? [*Krasner v. HSH Nordbank AG,* 680 F.Supp.2d 502 (S.D.N.Y. 2010)] **(See pages 194–195.)**

7–6   Ethical Misconduct. Frank Pasquale used his father's Social Security number to obtain a credit card. Later, pretending to act on behalf of his father's firm, Pasquale borrowed $350,000. When he defaulted on the loan and his father confronted him, he produced forged documents that showed the loan had been paid. Adams Associates, LLC, which held the unpaid loan, filed a suit against both Pasquales. Should the court issue a judgment against the father and the son? Discuss. [*Adams Associates, LLC v. Frank Pasquale Limited Partnership,* __ A.3d __ (N.J.Super. A.D. 2011)] **(See pages 196–197.)**

7–7   ⬌ A Question of Ethics—Copyrights. Steven Soderbergh is the Academy Award–winning director of *Erin Brockovich, Traffic,* and many other films. CleanFlicks, LLC, filed a suit in a federal district court against Soderbergh, fifteen other directors, and the Directors Guild of America. The plaintiff asked the court to rule that it had the right to sell DVDs of the defendants' films altered without the defendants' consent to delete scenes of "sex, nudity, profanity and gory violence." CleanFlicks sold or rented the edited DVDs under the slogan "It's About Choice" to consumers, sometimes indirectly through retailers. It would not sell to retailers that made unauthorized copies of the edited films. The defendants, with DreamWorks LLC and seven other movie studios that own the copyrights to the films, filed a counterclaim against CleanFlicks and others engaged in the same business, alleging copyright infringement. Those filing the counterclaim asked the court to enjoin (prevent) CleanFlicks and the others from making and marketing altered versions of the films. [*CleanFlicks of Colorado, LLC v. Soderbergh,* 433 F.Supp.2d 1236 (D.Colo. 2006)] **(See page 201.)**

1. Movie studios often edit their films to conform to content and other standards and sell the edited versions to network television and other commercial buyers. In this case, however, the studios objected when CleanFlicks edited the films and sold the altered versions directly to consumers. Similarly, CleanFlicks made unauthorized copies of the studios' DVDs to edit the films, but objected when others made unauthorized copies of the altered versions. Is there anything unethical about these apparently contradictory positions? Why or why not?

2. CleanFlicks and its competitors asserted, in part, that they were making "fair use" of the studios' copyrighted works. They argued that by their actions "they are criticizing the objectionable content commonly found in current movies and that they are providing more socially acceptable alternatives to enable families to view the films together, without exposing children to the presumed harmful effects emanating from the objectionable content." If you were the judge, how would you view this argument? Is a court the appropriate forum for making determinations of public or social policy? Explain.

Critical Thinking and Writing Assignments

7–8   Critical Legal Thinking. Human rights groups, environmental activists, and other interest groups concerned with unethical business practices have often conducted publicity campaigns against various corporations that those groups feel have engaged in unethical practices. Can a small group of well-organized activists dictate how a major corporation conducts its affairs? Should a small group be able to do so? Discuss fully. **(See page 202.)**

7–9   Business Law Writing. Assume that you are a high-level manager for a shoe manufacturer. You know that your firm could increase its profit margin by producing shoes in Indonesia, where you could hire women for $100 a month to assemble them. You also know that human rights advocates recently accused a competing shoe manufacturer of engaging in exploitative labor practices because the manufacturer sold shoes made by Indonesian women for similarly low wages. You personally do not believe that paying $100 a month to Indonesian women is unethical because you know that in their country, $100 a month is a better-than-average wage rate. Write one page explaining whether you would have the shoes manufactured in Indonesia and make higher profits for the company or avoid the risk of negative publicity and its potential adverse consequences for the firm's reputation. Are there other alternatives? Discuss fully. **(See page 202.)**

7–10   Business Law Critical Thinking Group Assignment. In the 1990s, Pfizer, Inc., developed a new antibiotic called Trovan (trovafloxacin mesylate). Tests showed that in animals Trovan had life-threatening side effects, including joint disease, abnormal cartilage growth, liver damage, and a degenerative bone condition. In 1996, an epidemic of bacterial meningitis swept across Nigeria. Pfizer sent three U.S. physicians to test Trovan on children who were patients in Nigeria's Infectious Disease Hospital. Pfizer did not obtain the patients' consent, alert them to the risks, or tell them that Médecins Sans Frontières (Doctors without Borders) was providing an effective conventional treatment at the same site. Eleven children died in the experiment, and others were left blind, deaf, paralyzed, or brain damaged. Rabi Abdullahi and other Nigerian children filed a suit in a U.S. federal court against Pfizer, alleging a violation of a customary international law norm prohibiting involuntary medical experimentation on humans. [*Abdullahi v. Pfizer, Inc.,* 562 F.3d 163 (2d Cir. 2009)]

1. One group should use the principles of ethical reasoning discussed in this chapter to develop three arguments on how Pfizer's conduct was a violation of ethical standards.

2. A second group should take a pro-Pfizer position and argue that the company did not violate any ethical standards (and counter the first group).

3. A third group should come up with proposals for what Pfizer might have done differently to avert the consequences.

UNIT 1 The Legal Environment of Business

Business Case Study with Dissenting Opinion
Paduano v. American Honda Motor Co.

The effect and importance of the U.S. Constitution's supremacy clause were discussed in Chapter 2. When there is a direct conflict between a federal law and a state law, the state law is rendered invalid. If Congress has chosen to act exclusively in an area, the federal statute will take precedence over a conflicting state law on the same subject under the doctrine of preemption.

There is a strong presumption against preemption, however, because the states are independent "sovereigns" in our federal system. In areas in which the states have traditionally exercised their police power, such as consumer protection, for example, this presumption applies with particular force.

In this *Business Case Study with Dissenting Opinion,* we review *Paduano v. American Honda Motor Co.,*[1] a case in which the buyer of a new car complained about the vehicle's inability to achieve the fuel economy advertised in the automaker's brochure. The defendant contended that federal law preempted the plaintiff's claims, which were founded on state law.

Case Background

Gaetano Paduano bought a new Honda Civic Hybrid in California in June 2004. The Environmental Protection Agency's (EPA's) fuel economy estimate stated on the federally mandated new car label was forty-seven miles per gallon (mpg) for city driving and forty-eight mpg for highway driving. Honda's sales brochure repeated the fuel economy estimate and added, "Just drive the Hybrid like you would a conventional car and save on fuel bills."

Paduano drove the vehicle for about a year but was frustrated with its fuel economy performance,

which was less than half of the EPA estimate. A service employee at a Honda dealership told him that to achieve the estimate he would have to drive differently. The employee said, "It is very difficult to get MPG on [the] highway and to drive with traffic in a safe manner." The required "special" manner "would create a driving hazard." Paduano asked American Honda Motor Company to repurchase the vehicle. Honda refused.

Paduano filed a suit in a California state court against the automaker, alleging, among other things,

deceptive advertising in violation of the state's Consumer Legal Remedies Act and Unfair Competition Law. Honda argued that the federal Energy Policy and Conservation Act, which prescribed the EPA fuel economy estimate, preempted Paduano's claims. The court issued a summary judgment in Honda's favor. Paduano appealed to a state intermediate appellate court.

Majority Opinion

AARON, J. [Judge]
    * * * *

The basic rules of preemption are not in dispute: *Under the supremacy clause of the United States Constitution, Congress has the power to preempt state law concerning matters that lie within the authority of Congress.* In determining whether federal law preempts state law, a court's task is to discern congressional intent. Congress's express intent in this regard will be found when Congress explicitly states that it is preempting state authority. [Emphasis added.]

----
1. 169 Cal.App.4th 1453, 88 Cal.Rptr.3d 90 (4 Dist. 2009).

* * * *

Honda * * * argues that [the EPCA] prevents Paduano from pursuing his * * * claims. That provision states in pertinent part,

> When a requirement under [the EPCA] is in effect, a State or a political subdivision of a State may adopt or enforce a law or regulation on disclosure of fuel economy or fuel operating costs for an automobile covered by [the EPCA] only if the law or regulation is identical to that requirement.

Business Case Study with Dissenting Opinion—Continues next page ➡

Business Case Study with Dissenting Opinion—Continued

* * * Honda goes on to assert that "Paduano's deceptive advertising and misrepresentation claims would impose *non* identical disclosure requirements."

Contrary to Honda's characterization * * *, Paduano's claims are based on statements Honda made in its advertising brochure to the effect that one may drive a Civic Hybrid in the same manner as one would a conventional car, and need not do anything "special," in order to achieve the beneficial fuel economy of the EPA estimates. * * * Paduano is challenging * * * Honda's * * * commentary in which it alludes to those estimates in a manner that may give consumers the misimpression that they will be able to achieve mileage close to the EPA estimates while driving a Honda hybrid in the same manner as they would a conventional vehicle. Paduano does not seek to require Honda to provide "additional alleged facts" regarding the Civic Hybrid's fuel economy, as Honda suggests, but rather, seeks to prevent Honda from making misleading claims about how easy it is to achieve better fuel economy. Contrary to Honda's assertions, if Paduano were to prevail on his claims, Honda would not have to do anything differently with regard to its disclosure of the EPA mileage estimates.

* * * *

* * * [The EPCA's] express preemption provisions do not purport to take away states' power to regulate the advertising of new vehicles, even when that advertising includes the EPA mileage estimates. *As long as a state's regulation does not require a manufacturer to provide a fuel estimate different from the EPA fuel economy estimate, or to make claims that go beyond, or are contrary to, what the federal scheme requires, the EPCA does not preempt such regulation.* * * * Allowing states to regulate false advertising and unfair business practices may further the goals of the EPCA, and we reject Honda's claim. [Emphasis added.]

* * * *

* * * We * * * conclude that federal law does not preempt Paduano's claims concerning Honda's advertising.

* * * *

The summary judgment is reversed. * * * The matter is remanded to the trial court for further proceedings.

Dissenting Opinion

O'ROURKE, J., [Judge] * * * DISSENTING * * * .

* * * In my view, Paduano's false advertising claims under the Consumer Legal Remedies Act (CLRA) and Unfair Competition Law (UCL) are * * * preempted by the Energy Policy and Conservation Act of 1975 (EPCA) because those claims are necessarily predicated on Honda's representations about fuel economy and the Honda Civic Hybrid's asserted failure to meet the federal Environmental Protection Agency's (EPA) estimates as to fuel economy. * * * Paduano seeks to impose a legal duty on Honda to change its disclosures concerning fuel economy to something different from the EPA estimate. In such a case, the EPCA expressly preempts enforcement of his UCL and CLRA causes of action. * * * Accordingly, I respectfully dissent from * * * the majority opinion.

* * * *

Because Paduano's sought-after relief would require that Honda change its advertising to either eliminate or reduce the EPA mileage estimate, or include additional disclosures relating to the EPA mileage estimate and his car's fuel economy, his state law false advertising claims fail under express preemption principles as imposing a legal obligation related to fuel economy standards or they fail because they would impose disclosure requirements concerning fuel economy that are not identical to the EPCA.

This conclusion as to preemption is not impacted by the fact that Paduano's claims are made under consumer protection laws. A presumption against preemption is characteristically applied where the field is one that the states have traditionally occupied and regulated, but such a presumption is not triggered when the state regulates in an area where there has been a history of significant federal presence. In my view, the EPCA and its corresponding federal regulations reflect a significant federal presence with respect to the measurement and disclosure of automobile fuel economy estimates and standards, as well as the advertising concerning a new vehicle's fuel economy.

Business Case Study with Dissenting Opinion—Continued

Questions for Analysis

1. **Law** What was the majority's decision on the principal issue before the court in this case? What were the reasons for this decision?
2. **Law** How would the dissent apply the law to the facts differently than the majority did? What were the dissent's reasons?
3. **Ethics** Suppose that the defendant automaker opposed this action solely to avoid paying for a car that had

proved to be a "lemon." Would this have been unethical? Explain.
4. **Economic Dimensions** Is the majority's ruling or the dissent's position more favorable for the auto market? Why?
5. **Implications for the Businessperson** What does the interpretation of the law in this case suggest to businesspersons who sell products labeled with statements mandated by federal or state law?

UNIT 1 The Legal Environment of Business

Business Scenario

CompTac, Inc., which is headquartered in San Francisco, California, is one of the leading software manufacturers in the United States. The company invests millions of dollars to research and develop new software applications and computer games that are sold worldwide. It also has a large service department and takes great pains to offer its customers excellent support services.

1. **Jurisdiction.** CompTac routinely purchases some of the materials necessary to produce its computer games from a New York firm, Electrotex, Inc. A dispute arises between the two firms, and CompTac wants to sue Electrotex for breach of contract. Can CompTac bring the suit in a California state court? Can CompTac bring the suit in a federal court? Explain. **(See pages 62–65.)**
2. **Negligence.** A customer at one of CompTac's retail stores stumbles over a crate in the parking lot and breaks her leg. Just moments earlier, the crate had fallen off a CompTac truck that was delivering goods from a CompTac warehouse to the store. The customer

sues CompTac, alleging negligence. Will she succeed in her suit? Why or why not? **(See page 111.)**
3. **Wrongful Interference.** Roban Electronics, a software manufacturer and one of CompTac's major competitors, has been trying to convince one of CompTac's key employees, Jim Baxter, to come to work for Roban. Roban knows that Baxter has a written employment contract with CompTac, which Baxter would breach if he left CompTac before the contract expired. Baxter goes to work for Roban, and the departure of its key employee causes CompTac to suffer substantial losses due to delays in completing new software. Can CompTac sue Roban to recoup some of these losses? If so, on what ground? **(See page 107.)**
4. **Cyber Crime.** One of CompTac's employees in its accounting division, Alan Green, has a gambling problem. To repay a gambling debt of $10,000, Green decides to "borrow" from CompTac to cover the debt. Using his knowledge of CompTac account numbers, Green electronically transfers $10,000 from a CompTac account into his personal checking account.

Business Scenario—Continues next page

Business Scenario—Continued

A week later, he is luckier at gambling and uses the same electronic procedures to transfer funds from his personal checking account back to the CompTac account. Has Green committed any crimes? If so, what are they? **(See pages 178–180.)**

5. **Ethical Decision Making.** One of CompTac's best-selling products is a computer game that includes some extremely violent actions. Groups of parents, educators, and consumer activists have bombarded CompTac with letters and e-mail messages calling on the company to stop selling the product. CompTac executives are concerned about the public outcry, but at the same time, they realize that the game is CompTac's major source of profits. If it ceased

marketing the game, the company could go bankrupt. If you were a CompTac decision maker, what would your decision be in this situation? How would you justify your decision from an ethical perspective? **(See page 201.)**

6. **Intellectual Property.** CompTac wants to sell one of its best-selling software programs to An Phat Company, a firm located in Ho Chi Minh City, Vietnam. CompTac is concerned, however, that after an initial purchase, An Phat will duplicate the software without permission (in violation of U.S. copyright laws) and sell the illegal bootleg software to other firms in Vietnam. How can CompTac protect its software from being pirated by An Phat Company? **(See page 148.)**

UNIT 1 The Legal Environment of Business

Group Project

Drawing on your knowledge of *Paduano v. American Honda Motor Co.,* assume that your group makes decisions for an automaker that sells cars in every state and that each state has slightly different consumer protection statutes.

1. One group will list two underlying reasons why there is a strong presumption against preemption.
2. One group will evaluate the truth or falsity of the majority's conclusion that "as long as a state's regulation does

not require a manufacturer to provide a fuel estimate different from the EPA fuel economy estimate," there is no preemption.

3. Another group will develop the dissent's argument that a presumption against preemption is not triggered when the state regulates in an area where there has been a "history of significant federal presence."

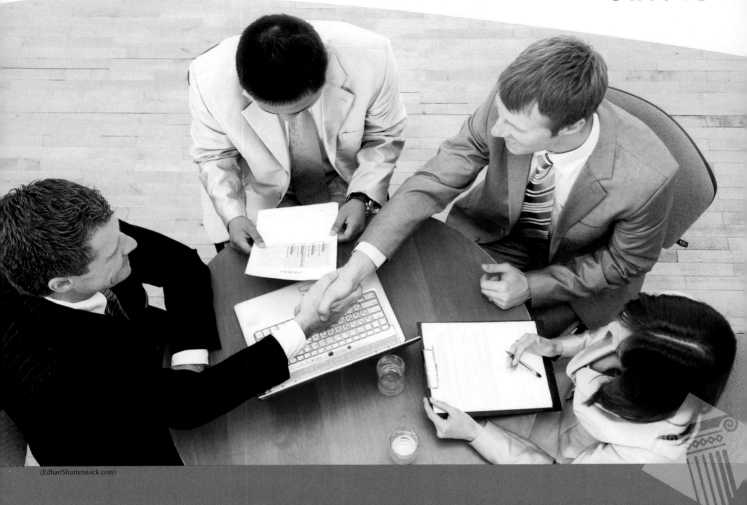

(Edhar/Shutterstock.com)

Contracts

UNIT CONTENTS

(nuno/iStockphoto.com)

Nature and Classification

CHAPTER OUTLINE

- An Overview of Contract Law
- Elements of a Contract
- Types of Contracts
- Quasi Contracts
- Interpretation of Contracts

LEARNING OBJECTIVES

The five learning objectives below are designed to help improve your understanding of the chapter. After reading this chapter, you should be able to answer the following questions:

1 What is a contract? What is the objective theory of contracts?

2 What are the four basic elements necessary to the formation of a valid contract?

3 What is the difference between express and implied contracts?

4 How does a void contract differ from a voidable contract? What is an unenforceable contract?

5 What rules guide the courts in interpreting contracts?

"All sensible people are selfish,
and nature is tugging at every contract to make the terms of it fair."
—Ralph Waldo Emerson, 1803–1882 (American poet)

Promise A declaration that binds a person who makes it (the promisor) to do or not to do a certain act.

As Ralph Waldo Emerson observed in the chapter-opening quotation, people tend to act in their own self-interest, and this influences the terms they seek in their contracts. Contract law must therefore provide rules to determine which contract terms will be enforced and which promises must be kept. A **promise** is a declaration by a person (the *promisor*) to do or not to do a certain act. As a result, the person to whom the promise is made (the *promisee*) has a right to expect or demand that something either will or will not happen in the future.

Like other types of law, contract law reflects our social values, interests, and expectations at a given point in time. It shows, for example, what kinds of promises our society thinks should be legally binding. It distinguishes between promises that create only *moral* obligations (such as a promise to take a friend to lunch) and promises that are legally binding (such as a promise to pay for merchandise purchased).

Increasingly, contracts are formed online. While some believe that we need a new body of law to cover e-contracts, others point out that we can apply existing contract law quite easily.

Through the following chapters you will see how in fact contract law can be used to resolve online disputes. For instance, in this chapter you will read about the validity of the *disclaimers* that you often see on e-mails that you receive from professionals (or even nonprofessionals!).

An Overview of Contract Law

Before we look at the numerous rules that courts use to determine whether a particular promise will be enforced, it is necessary to understand some fundamental concepts of contract law. In this section, we describe the sources and general function of contract law and introduce the objective theory of contracts.

Sources of Contract Law

The common law governs all contracts except when it has been modified or replaced by statutory law, such as the Uniform Commercial Code (UCC),[1] or by administrative agency regulations. Contracts relating to services, real estate, employment, and insurance, for example, generally are governed by the common law of contracts. (See the appendix at the end of Chapter 14 for an example of a common law contract used in employment.)

Contracts for the sale and lease of goods, however, are governed by the UCC—to the extent that the UCC has modified general contract law. The relationship between general contract law and the law governing sales and leases of goods will be explored in detail in Chapter 15. In this unit covering the common law of contracts (Chapters 9 through 14), we indicate briefly in footnotes the areas in which the UCC has significantly altered common law contract principles.

The Function of Contracts

No aspect of modern life is entirely free of contractual relationships. You acquire rights and obligations, for example, when you borrow funds, buy or lease a house, obtain insurance, form a business, and purchase goods or services. Contract law is designed to provide stability and predictability for both buyers and sellers in the marketplace.

Contract law assures the parties to private agreements that the promises they make will be enforceable. Clearly, many promises are kept because the parties involved feel a moral obligation to do so or because keeping a promise is in their mutual self-interest. The **promisor** (the person making the promise) and the **promisee** (the person to whom the promise is made) may decide to honor their agreement for other reasons. Nevertheless, the rules of contract law are often followed in business agreements to avoid potential problems.

By supplying procedures for enforcing private agreements, contract law provides an essential condition for the existence of a market economy. Without a legal framework of reasonably assured expectations within which to plan and venture, businesspersons would be able to rely only on the good faith of others. Duty and good faith are usually sufficient, but when dramatic price changes or adverse economic conditions make it costly to comply with a promise, these elements may not be enough. Contract law is necessary to ensure compliance with a promise or to entitle the innocent party to some form of relief.

Definition of a Contract

A **contract** is an agreement that can be enforced in court. It is formed by two or more parties who agree to perform or to refrain from performing some act now or in the future. Generally, contract disputes arise when there is a promise of future performance. If the

Promisor A person who makes a promise.

Promisee A person to whom a promise is made.

Contract A set of promises constituting an agreement between parties, giving each a legal duty to the other and also the right to seek a remedy for the breach of the promises or duties.

---

1. See Chapter 1 on page 8 and Chapter 15 for further discussions of the significance and coverage of the Uniform Commercial Code. Excerpts from the UCC are presented in Appendix C at the end of this book.

LEARNING OBJECTIVE 1
What is a contract?
What is the objective theory of contracts?

contractual promise is not fulfilled, the party who made it is subject to the sanctions of a court (see Chapter 14). That party may be required to pay monetary damages for failing to perform the contractual promise and, in certain limited instances, may be required to perform the promised act.

The Objective Theory of Contracts

Objective Theory of Contracts The view that contracting parties shall only be bound by terms that can objectively be inferred from promises made.

In determining whether a contract has been formed, the element of intent is of prime importance. In contract law, intent is determined by what is referred to as the **objective theory of contracts,** not by the personal or subjective intent, or belief, of a party. The theory is that a party's intention to enter into a contract is judged by outward, objective facts as interpreted by a *reasonable person,* rather than by the party's secret, subjective intentions.

Objective facts include (1) what the party said when entering into the contract, (2) how the party acted or appeared, and (3) the circumstances surrounding the transaction. As will be discussed later in this chapter, in the section on express versus implied contracts, intent to form a contract may be manifested by conduct, as well as by words, oral or written.

Freedom of Contract and Freedom from Contract

As a general rule, the law recognizes everyone's ability to enter freely into contractual arrangements. This recognition is called *freedom of contract,* a freedom protected in Article I, Section 10, of the U.S. Constitution. Because freedom of contract is a fundamental public policy of the United States, courts rarely interfere with contracts that have been voluntarily made.

Of course, as in other areas of the law, there are many exceptions to the general rule that contracts voluntarily negotiated will be enforced. For example, illegal bargains, agreements that unreasonably restrain trade, and certain unfair contracts made between one party with a great amount of bargaining power and another with little power are generally not enforced. In addition, as you will read in Chapter 11, certain contracts and clauses may not be enforceable if they are contrary to public policy, fairness, and justice. These exceptions provide *freedom from contract* for persons who may have been pressured into making contracts unfavorable to their interests.

Elements of a Contract

The many topics that will be discussed in the following chapters on contract law require an understanding of the basic elements of a valid contract and the way in which a contract is created. You will also need an understanding of the types of circumstances in which even legally valid contracts will not be enforced. (See the sample contract on pages 372–375.)

Requirements of a Valid Contract

The following list briefly describes the four requirements that must be met for a valid contract to exist. If any of these elements is lacking, no contract will have been formed. (Each item will be explained more fully in subsequent chapters.)

LEARNING OBJECTIVE 2
What are the four basic elements necessary to the formation of a valid contract?

1. *Agreement.* An agreement to form a contract includes an *offer* and an *acceptance.* One party must offer to enter into a legal agreement, and another party must accept the terms of the offer (see Chapter 10).
2. *Consideration.* Any promises made by the parties must be supported by legally sufficient and bargained-for consideration (something of value received or promised to convince a person to make a deal) (see Chapter 11).

3. *Contractual capacity.* Both parties entering into the contract must have the contractual capacity to do so, meaning that the law must recognize them as possessing characteristics that qualify them as competent parties (see Chapter 11).
4. *Legality.* The contract's purpose must be to accomplish some goal that is legal and not against public policy (see Chapter 11).

Defenses to the Enforceability of a Contract

Even if all of the elements of a valid contract are present, a contract may be unenforceable if the following requirements are not met.

1. *Voluntary consent.* The apparent consent of both parties must be voluntary. For instance, if a contract was formed as a result of fraud, mistake, or duress (coercion), the contract may not be enforceable.
2. *Form.* The contract must be in whatever form the law requires. Some contracts must be in writing to be enforceable.

The failure to fulfill either requirement may be raised as a defense to the enforceability of an otherwise valid contract. Both requirements will be explained in more detail in Chapter 12.

Types of Contracts

There are numerous types of contracts. They are categorized based on legal distinctions as to their *formation, performance,* and *enforceability.*

Contract Formation

Contracts are classified based on how and when a contract is formed. Exhibit 9.1 below illustrates three classifications of contracts based on their mode of formation. The best way to explain each type of contract is to compare one type with another, as we do in the following pages.

Bilateral versus Unilateral Contracts
Every contract involves at least two parties. The **offeror** is the party making the offer. The **offeree** is the party to whom the offer is made. The offeror always promises to do or not to do something and thus is also a

Offeror A person who makes an offer.

Offeree A person to whom an offer is made.

Exhibit 9.1 Classifications Based on Contract Formation

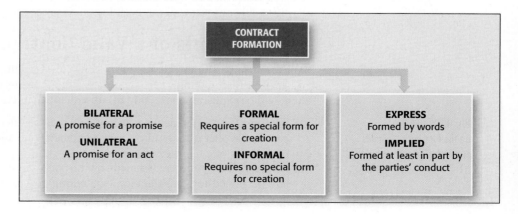

CONTRACT FORMATION

| BILATERAL
A promise for a promise
UNILATERAL
A promise for an act | FORMAL
Requires a special form for creation
INFORMAL
Requires no special form for creation | EXPRESS
Formed by words
IMPLIED
Formed at least in part by the parties' conduct |

promisor. Whether the contract is classified as *bilateral* or *unilateral* depends on what the offeree must do to accept the offer and bind the offeror to a contract.

Bilateral Contract A type of contract that arises when a promise is given in exchange for a return promise.

Bilateral Contracts   If the offeree can accept simply by promising to perform, the contract is a **bilateral contract.** Hence, a bilateral contract is a "promise for a promise." An example of a bilateral contract is a contract in which one person agrees to buy another person's automobile for a specified price. No performance, such as the payment of funds or delivery of goods, need take place for a bilateral contract to be formed. The contract comes into existence at the moment the promises are exchanged. (The appendix to Chapter 14 includes an example of a bilateral contract.)

EXAMPLE 9.1   Javier offers to buy Ann's Android-based smartphone for $200. Javier tells Ann that he will give her the cash for the phone on the following Friday, when he gets paid. Ann accepts Javier's offer and promises to give him the phone when he pays her on Friday. Javier and Ann have formed a bilateral contract. ●

Unilateral Contract A contract that results when an offer can be accepted only by the offeree's performance.

Unilateral Contracts   If the offer is phrased so that the offeree can accept only by completing the contract performance, the contract is a **unilateral contract.** Hence, a unilateral contract is a "promise for an act." In other words, the contract is formed not at the moment when promises are exchanged but rather when the contract is *performed*.

EXAMPLE 9.2   Reese says to Kata, "If you drive my car from New York to Los Angeles, I'll give you $1,000." Only on Kata's completion of the act—bringing the car to Los Angeles—does she fully accept Reese's offer to pay $1,000. If she chooses not to accept the offer to drive the car to Los Angeles, there are no legal consequences. ●

Contests, lotteries, and other competitions offering prizes are also examples of offers for unilateral contracts. If a person complies with the rules of the contest—such as by submitting the right lottery number at the right place and time—a unilateral contract is formed, binding the organization offering the prize to a contract to perform as promised in the offer.

ETHICAL ISSUE

Can a company that sponsors a contest change the prize from what it originally advertised? Courts have historically treated contests as unilateral contracts, which typically cannot be modified by the offeror after the offeree has begun to perform. But this principle may not always apply to contest terms or advertisements. For instance, John Rogalski entered a poker tournament conducted by Little Poker League, LLC (LPL). The tournament lasted several months as players competed for spots in a winner-take-all final event. During the final event, Rogalski and the other contestants signed a "World Series of Poker (WSOP) Agreement," which stated that LPL would pay the $10,000 WSOP entry fee on the winner's behalf and provide $2,500 for travel-related expenses. The agreement also stated that if the winner did not attend the WSOP, he or she would relinquish the WSOP seat and return the expense money to LPL.

Rogalski won the poker tournament and took the $2,500 for travel expenses, but he did not attend the WSOP tournament. He then filed a suit for $10,000 against LPL, arguing that it had advertised that the winner could choose to receive the cash value of the prizes ($12,500) instead of attending the WSOP tournament. Rogalski claimed that by participating in LPL's tournament, he had accepted the advertised offer to take the cash in lieu of entering the WSOP tournament, and that the later agreement was an invalid contract modification. LPL filed a counterclaim to recover the $2,500 in expenses. The court ruled in favor of LPL, finding that the contract was formed when Rogalski signed the WSOP agreement, and not when he began participating in the contest. Under the contest rules as stated in the WSOP agreement, Rogalski had to return the $2,500 to LPL.[2]

In the following case, the court was asked to resolve a dispute that arose from an employer's refusal to pay a bonus to a former employee. The court's decision depended, in part, on whether the parties' employment contract was bilateral or unilateral.

---

2. *Rogalski v. Little Poker League, LLC,* 2011 WL 589636 (Minn.App. 2011).

Case 9.1

Schwarzrock v. Remote Technologies, Inc.

Court of Appeals of Minnesota,
2011 WL 68262 (2011).

(Brian A Jackson/Shutterstock.com)

Is an employment agreement a unilateral contract?

FACTS Nick Schwarzrock applied for a job at Remote Technologies, Inc., a Minnesota-based manufacturer of home-theater and home-automation controls. Remote wrote a letter to Schwarzrock offering him a job for an annual salary of $60,000, plus a bonus. The day after he started work, Schwarzrock signed an employment agreement (EA) that expressly "superseded all previous correspondence." The EA stated that "any bonus to Employee shall rest in the sole discretion of the employer." When Remote fired Schwarzrock, he filed a lawsuit to recover the bonus that he believed he was owed under a bilateral contract. Remote argued that the bonus was discretionary and that when Schwarzrock accepted the EA, he created a binding unilateral contract.

ISSUE Was Schwarzrock's EA an enforceable unilateral contract?

DECISION Yes. The state appellate court affirmed the lower court's judgment that the EA was a unilateral contract, not a bilateral contract.

REASON An employer's offer of a position on certain terms for an indefinite period becomes a unilateral contract on the employee's acceptance. The court reasoned that the EA was a unilateral offer of employment by Remote that specifically made any bonus subject to the employer's discretion. Schwarzrock accepted this offer when he signed the EA and continued working. Both the letter and Remote's EA expressed the employer's intent to offer a salary and a potential bonus to Schwarzrock. The letter may have implied that the bonus was not discretionary, but the EA clarified or modified the offer by clearly stating that it was.

WHAT IF THE FACTS WERE DIFFERENT? *Suppose that the court had ruled that Schwarzrock was employed under a bilateral contract, as he alleged. Would the result have been different? Explain.*

Revocation of Offers for Unilateral Contracts   A problem arises in unilateral contracts when the promisor attempts to *revoke* (cancel) the offer after the promisee has begun performance but before the act has been completed.   **EXAMPLE 9.3**   Seiko offers to buy Jin's sailboat, moored in San Francisco, on delivery of the boat to Seiko's dock in Newport Beach, three hundred miles south of San Francisco. Jin rigs the boat and sets sail. Shortly before his arrival at Newport Beach, Jin receives a message from Seiko withdrawing her offer. Seiko's offer is to form a unilateral contract, and only Jin's delivery of the sailboat at her dock is an acceptance. ●

In contract law, offers are normally *revocable* (capable of being taken back, or canceled) until accepted. Under the traditional view of unilateral contracts, Seiko's revocation would terminate the offer. Because of the harsh effect on the offeree of the revocation of an offer to form a unilateral contract, the modern-day view is that once performance has been *substantially* undertaken, the offeror cannot revoke the offer. Thus, in our example, even though Jin has not yet accepted the offer by complete performance, Seiko is prohibited from revoking it. Jin can deliver the boat and bind Seiko to the contract.

Formal Contract An agreement that by law requires a specific form for its validity.

Formal versus Informal Contracts   Another classification system divides contracts into formal contracts and informal contracts. **Formal contracts** are contracts that require a special form or method of creation (formation) to be enforceable.[3] For example, *negotiable instruments,* which include checks, drafts, promissory notes, and certificates of deposit (as will be discussed in Chapter 18), are formal contracts because, under the Uniform Commercial Code, a special form and language are required to create them.

---

3. See *Restatement (Second) of Contracts*, Section 6, which explains that formal contracts include (1) contracts under seal, (2) recognizances, (3) negotiable instruments, and (4) letters of credit. As mentioned in Chapter 1, *Restatements of the Law* are books that summarize court decisions on a particular topic and that courts often refer to for guidance.

Letters of credit, which are frequently used in international sales contracts (as discussed in Chapter 8), are another type of formal contract.

Informal contracts (also called *simple contracts*) include all other contracts. No special form is required (except for certain types of contracts that must be in writing), as the contracts are usually based on their substance rather than their form. Typically, businesspersons put their contracts in writing to ensure that there is some proof of a contract's existence should problems arise.

Informal Contract A contract that does not require a specific form or method of creation to be valid.

Express versus Implied Contracts

Contracts may also be categorized as express or implied by the conduct of the parties. In an **express contract,** the terms of the agreement are fully and explicitly stated in words, oral or written. A signed lease for an apartment or a house is an express written contract. If a classmate accepts your offer to sell your textbooks from last semester for $75, an express oral contract has been made.

A contract that is implied from the conduct of the parties is called an **implied contract.** This type of contract differs from an express contract in that the *conduct* of the parties, rather than their words, creates and defines at least some of the terms of the contract. For an implied contract to arise, certain requirements must be met.

Express Contract A contract in which the terms of the agreement are stated in words, oral or written.

Implied Contract A contract formed in whole or in part from the conduct of the parties.

Requirements for Implied Contracts

Normally, if the following conditions exist, a court will hold that an implied contract was formed:

1. The plaintiff furnished some service or property.
2. The plaintiff expected to be paid for that service or property, and the defendant knew or should have known that payment was expected (based on the objective theory of contracts discussed on page 241).
3. The defendant had a chance to reject the services or property and did not.

EXAMPLE 9.4   Oleg, a small-business owner, needs an accountant to complete his tax return. He drops by a local accountant's office, explains his situation to the accountant, and learns what fees she charges. The next day, he returns and gives the receptionist all of the necessary documents to complete his return. Then he walks out without saying anything further to the accountant. In this situation, Oleg has entered into an implied contract to pay the accountant the usual fees for her services. The contract is implied because of Oleg's conduct and hers. She expects to be paid for completing the tax return, and by bringing in the records she will need to do the job, Oleg has implied an intent to pay her. •

LEARNING OBJECTIVE 3
What is the difference between express and implied contracts?

Mixed Contracts with Express and Implied Terms

Note that a contract can be a mixture of an express contract and an implied contract. In other words, a contract may contain some express terms, while others are implied. During the construction of a home, for instance, the homeowner often asks the builder to make changes in the original specifications.

CASE EXAMPLE 9.5   Lamar Hopkins hired Uhrhahn Construction & Design, Inc., for several projects during the construction of his home. Each project was based on a cost estimate and specifications, and had a signed contract that required modifications to be in writing. When work was in progress, however, Hopkins made several requests for changes. There was no written record of these changes, but Uhrhahn performed the work and Hopkins paid for it. A dispute arose after Hopkins requested that Uhrhahn use Durisol blocks rather than cinder blocks. Uhrhahn orally agreed to the modification, but then demanded extra payment because the Durisol blocks were more complicated and costly to install. Hopkins refused to pay. Uhrhahn sued and won. The court found that that there was an implied contract for the Durisol blocks. The builder did the work, and the buyer accepted the work. Such oral modification of the original contract creates an enforceable contract, and payment is due for the extra work.[4] •

Danica Patrick signs a contract to drive full-time in the NASCAR Nationwide Series circuit and select Sprint Cup.

(AP Photo/Paul Connors)

---

4. *Uhrhahn Construction & Design, Inc. v. Hopkins,* 179 P.3d 808 (Utah App. 2008).

Contract Performance

Executed Contract A contract that has been fully performed by both parties.

Executory Contract A contract that has not yet been fully performed.

Contracts are also classified according to their state of performance. A contract that has been fully performed on both sides is called an **executed contract.** A contract that has not been fully performed on either side is called an **executory contract.** If one party has fully performed but the other has not, the contract is said to be executed on the one side and executory on the other, but the contract is still classified as executory.

EXAMPLE 9.6 You agreed to buy ten tons of coal from Western Coal Company. Western has delivered the coal to your steel mill, where it is now being burned. At this point, the contract is an executory contract—it is executed on the part of Western and executory on your part. After you pay Western for the coal, the contract will be executed on both sides. ●

Contract Enforceability

Valid Contract A contract that results when the elements necessary for contract formation (agreement, consideration, legal purpose, and contractual capacity) are present.

A **valid contract** has the four elements necessary for contract formation: (1) an agreement (offer and acceptance) (2) supported by legally sufficient consideration (3) for a legal purpose and (4) made by parties who have the legal capacity to enter into the contract. As mentioned, we will discuss each of these elements in the following chapters. (See this chapter's *Adapting Law to the Online Environment* feature on the facing page for a discussion of how businesses today frequently include disclaimers on their e-mail messages to avoid the potential of enforceable obligations.)

LEARNING OBJECTIVE 4
How does a void contract differ from a voidable contract? What is an unenforceable contract?

As you can see in Exhibit 9.2 below, valid contracts may be enforceable, voidable, or unenforceable. Additionally, a contract may be referred to as a *void contract.* We look next at the meaning of the terms *voidable, unenforceable,* and *void* in relation to contract enforceability.

Voidable Contract A contract that may be legally avoided at the option of one or both of the parties.

Voidable Contracts   A **voidable contract** is a *valid* contract but one that can be avoided at the option of one or both of the parties. The party having the option can elect either to avoid any duty to perform or to *ratify* (make valid) the contract. If the contract is avoided, both parties are released from it. If it is ratified, both parties must fully perform their respective legal obligations.

As a general rule, for example, contracts made by minors are voidable at the option of the minor (as will be discussed in Chapter 11). Additionally, contracts entered into under

Exhibit 9.2 Enforceable, Voidable, Unenforceable, and Void Contracts

ADAPTING THE LAW TO THE ONLINE ENVIRONMENT

CAN A DISCLAIMER PREVENT AN E-MAIL FROM FORMING AN AGREEMENT?

When you receive an e-mail from a business, the e-mail will usually include a list of disclaimers, which may be longer than the message itself. Indeed, disclaimers have grown longer over the years, but does that make them more enforceable?

Simple in the Beginning but Longer and More Complex Today

About twenty years ago, when e-mail first began to be used in business, disclaimers simply stated that the information contained in the e-mail was privileged, confidential, or proprietary. The typical disclaimer further said (and continues to say) that any use, distribution, copying, or disclosure to another person of the e-mail was strictly prohibited. Finally, the disclaimer generally told the recipient to destroy the message if it was not intended for him or her and to notify the sender by reply e-mail.

Today, disclaimers may also include automatic digital signatures with the sender's contact information and perhaps a reminder to be "green" and protect the environment by not printing the e-mail. In addition, disclaimers are likely to include a number of warnings, such as the e-mail could contain viruses and the recipient is responsible for guarding against them, the recipient should not rely on any professional advice contained in the e-mail, and the e-mail does not constitute a contractual offer or acceptance.

Are All E-Mail Disclaimers Enforceable?

Relatively few cases have dealt with the issue of whether e-mail disclaimers are enforceable, and the court decisions have not yet answered the question of enforceability. Another issue is whether e-mails with no disclaimers are less protected than ones without them.

One issue that can easily arise is whether a series of e-mails creates a contract. Although e-mails may seem to impose a contractual obligation between the sender and the recipient, the courts generally deem unilateral contracts unenforceable. Thus, a disclaimer stating that an e-mail is not intended as an offer or an acceptance might be useful. The disclaimer should be carefully worded, however.

A court in Scotland, for example, held that an e-mail disclaimer did not extend to a detailed proposal attached to the e-mail. Therefore, the attached proposal was deemed a valid offer.[a]

As disclaimers are added to more and more e-mails, the less likely it is that a judge will be convinced that e-mails with disclaimers are more privileged or confidential than others. In addition, making the disclaimers longer does not guarantee that the e-mails to which the disclaimers are attached will be considered more privileged and confidential than others.

In 2012, for instance, the investment bank Nomura Group attached a nearly three-thousand-word disclaimer to a Federal Reserve report that it had e-mailed to its clients. One phrase in the disclaimer stated that the opinions expressed in the e-mail were subject to change without notice.

Critical Thinking

One commentator likened e-mail disclaimers to the tags on new mattresses that forbid removal of the tags under penalty of law or to twenty-page booklets on safety that accompany new products. No one reads the tags or the booklets, and no one cares. Why do e-mail disclaimers continue to proliferate nonetheless and become ever longer?

---

a. *Baillie Estates Limited v. Du Pont (UK) Limited* (June 30, 2009).

---

fraudulent conditions are voidable at the option of the defrauded party. Contracts entered into under legally defined duress or undue influence are also voidable (see Chapter 12).

Unenforceable Contract A valid contract rendered unenforceable by some statute or law.

Unenforceable Contracts An **unenforceable contract** is one that cannot be enforced because of certain legal defenses against it. It is not unenforceable because a party failed to satisfy a legal requirement of the contract. Rather, it is a valid contract rendered unenforceable by some statute or law. For example, some contracts must be in writing (see Chapter 12), and if they are not, they will not be enforceable except in certain exceptional circumstances.

Void Contract A contract having no legal force or binding effect.

Void Contracts A **void contract** is no contract at all. The terms *void* and *contract* are contradictory. None of the parties has any legal obligations if a contract is void. A contract can be void because, for example, one of the parties was previously determined by a court to be legally insane and thus lacked the legal capacity to enter into a contract. Or, a contract can be void because the purpose of the contract was illegal, such as contracting to rob a bank or burn down a building (arson).

Quasi Contracts

Quasi Contract An obligation or contract imposed by law (a court), in the absence of an agreement, to prevent the unjust enrichment of one party.

Quasi contracts, or contracts *implied in law,* are wholly different from actual contracts. Express contracts and implied contracts are actual or true contracts formed by the words or actions of the parties. The word *quasi* is Latin for "as if." Quasi contracts are not true contracts because they do not arise from any agreement, express or implied, between the parties themselves. Rather, quasi contracts are fictional contracts that courts can impose on the parties "as if" the parties had entered into an actual contract. They are equitable rather than legal contracts.

When the court imposes a quasi contract, a plaintiff may recover in *quantum meruit,*[5] a Latin phrase meaning "as much as he or she deserves." *Quantum meruit* essentially describes the extent of compensation owed under a quasi contract.

Usually, quasi contracts are imposed to avoid the *unjust enrichment* of one party at the expense of another. The doctrine of unjust enrichment is based on the theory that individuals should not be allowed to profit or enrich themselves inequitably at the expense of others.

In the following case, the parties did not have an express contract, but one party enjoyed the benefits of the other party's services. The court had to decide if the parties had a quasi contract.

---

5. Pronounced *kwahn*-tuhm *mehr*-oo-wit.

Case 9.2

Seawest Services Association v. Copenhaver

Court of Appeals of Washington,
2012 WL 255857 (2012).
www.courts.wa.gov[a]

(LordRunar/iStockphoto.com)

FACTS Seawest Services Association owned and operated a water-distribution system that served homes both inside and outside a housing development. Seawest had two classes of members. Full members owned property in the housing development, and limited members received water services for homes outside the development. Both full and limited members paid water bills and, as necessary, assessments for work performed on the water system. In 2001, the Copenhavers purchased a home outside the housing development. They did not have an express contract with Seawest, but they paid water bills for eight years and paid one $3,950 assessment for water system upgrades. In 2009, a dispute arose between the parties, and the Copenhavers began refusing to pay their water bills and assessments. Seawest sued the Copenhavers in a Washington state court. The trial court found that the Copenhavers were limited members of Seawest and thus were liable for the unpaid water bills and assessments. The Copenhavers appealed.

ISSUE Did the Copenhavers have a quasi contract with Seawest?

DECISION Yes. The Washington appellate court affirmed the decision of the trial court, holding that the Copenhavers were liable to Seawest for breach of a quasi contract.

What purpose does a water meter serve?

REASON The court explained that a quasi contract exists when a person knowingly receives a benefit from another party and it would be "inequitable for the [person] to retain the benefit without the payment of its value." The Copenhavers enjoyed the benefits of Seawest's water services and even paid for them before their dispute arose. The court found that "the Copenhavers would be unjustly enriched if they could retain benefits provided by Seawest without paying for them." After all, the court reasoned, they purchased a home that received water services, and they knew that they could not receive water without being a limited member of Seawest.

CRITICAL THINKING—Ethical Consideration *In recognizing quasi contracts, does the law try to correct for unethical behavior? Discuss.*

---

a. In the left-hand column, click on "Court Opinions." In the page that opens, type "Seawest Services" in the "Search Opinions" box and click on "Search." In the result, click on the link to access the case. The Administrative Office of the Washington Courts administers this Web site.

Limitations on Quasi-Contractual Recovery

Although quasi contracts exist to prevent unjust enrichment, in some situations, the party who obtains a benefit is not liable for its fair value. Basically, a party who has conferred a benefit on someone else unnecessarily or as a result of misconduct or negligence cannot invoke the doctrine of quasi contract. The enrichment in those situations will not be considered "unjust."

CASE EXAMPLE 9.7 Qwest Wireless, LLC, provides wireless phone services in Arizona and thirteen other states. Qwest marketed and sold handset insurance to its wireless customers, although it did not have a license to sell insurance in Arizona or in any other state. Patrick and Vicki Van Zanen sued Qwest in a federal court for unjust enrichment based on its receipt of sales commissions for the insurance. The court agreed that Qwest had violated the insurance-licensing statute, but found that the sales commissions did not constitute unjust enrichment because the customers had, in fact, received the handset insurance. Also, Qwest had not retained a benefit (the commissions) without paying for it (providing insurance). Therefore, the Van Zanens and other customers did not suffer unfair detriment.[6] ●

When an Actual Contract Exists

The doctrine of quasi contract generally cannot be used when an actual contract covers the area in controversy. In this situation, a remedy already exists if a party is unjustly enriched because the other fails to perform—the nonbreaching party can sue the breaching party for breach of contract.

EXAMPLE 9.8 Fung contracts with Cameron to deliver a furnace to a building owned by Bateman. Fung delivers the furnace, but Cameron never pays Fung. Bateman has been unjustly enriched in this situation, to be sure. Nevertheless, Fung cannot recover from Bateman in quasi contract because Fung had an actual contract with Cameron. Fung already has a remedy—he can sue for breach of contract to recover the price of the furnace from Cameron. In this situation, the court does not need to impose a quasi contract to achieve justice. ●

Interpretation of Contracts

Sometimes, parties agree that a contract has been formed but disagree on its meaning or legal effect. One reason that this may happen is that one of the parties is not familiar with the legal terminology used in the contract. To an extent, *plain language laws* have helped to avoid this difficulty. Sometimes, though, a dispute may still arise over the meaning of a contract simply because the rights or obligations under the contract are not expressed clearly—no matter how "plain" the language used.

In this section, we look at some common law rules of contract interpretation. These rules, including the *plain meaning rule* and various other rules that have evolved over time, provide the courts with guidelines for deciding disputes over how contract terms or provisions should be interpreted. Exhibit 9.3 on the following page provides a brief graphic summary of how these rules are applied.

PREVENTING LEGAL DISPUTES

To avoid disputes over contract interpretation, make sure your intentions are clearly expressed in your contracts. Careful drafting of contracts not only helps prevent potential disputes over the meaning of certain terms but may also be crucial if the firm brings a lawsuit or needs to defend against a lawsuit for breach of contract. By using simple, clear language and avoiding legalese, you can take a major step toward avoiding contract disputes.

---

6. *Van Zanen v. Qwest Wireless, LLC,* 522 F.3d 1127 (10th Cir. 2008).

Exhibit 9.3 Rules of Contract Interpretation

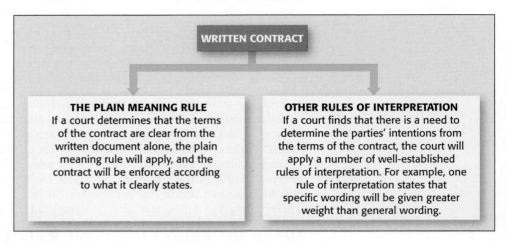

WRITTEN CONTRACT

THE PLAIN MEANING RULE
If a court determines that the terms of the contract are clear from the written document alone, the plain meaning rule will apply, and the contract will be enforced according to what it clearly states.

OTHER RULES OF INTERPRETATION
If a court finds that there is a need to determine the parties' intentions from the terms of the contract, the court will apply a number of well-established rules of interpretation. For example, one rule of interpretation states that specific wording will be given greater weight than general wording.

Plain Language Laws

The federal government and a majority of the states have enacted plain language laws to regulate legal writing and eliminate "legalese." All federal agencies are required to use plain language in most of their forms and written communications. Plain language requirements have been extended to agency rulemaking as well. States frequently have plain language laws that apply to consumer contracts, which are those made primarily for personal, family, or household purposes. The legal profession has also moved toward plain English, and court rules in many jurisdictions require attorneys to use plain language in court documents.

The Plain Meaning Rule

When a contract's language is clear and unequivocal, a court will enforce the contract according to its obvious terms. The meaning of the terms must be determined from *the face of the instrument*—from the written document alone. This is sometimes referred to as the *plain meaning rule*.

The words—and their plain, ordinary meaning—determine the intent of the parties at the time that they entered into the contract. A court is bound to give effect to the contract according to this intent. The importance of each word or phrase in a contract will also be discussed in the Appendix to Chapter 14: An Annotated Employment Contract.

Ambiguity
A court will consider a contract to be ambiguous in the following situations:

1. When the intent of the parties cannot be determined from its language.
2. When it lacks a provision on a disputed issue.
3. When a term is susceptible to more than one interpretation.
4. When there is uncertainty about a provision.

Extrinsic Evidence
If a contract term is ambiguous, a court may consider *extrinsic evidence* (outside evidence), or it may interpret the ambiguity against the party who drafted the contract term. Extrinsic evidence is any evidence not contained in the document itself, and may include the testimony of the parties, additional agreements or communications, or other information relevant to determining the parties' intent.

Whether extrinsic evidence is considered can significantly affect how a court interprets ambiguous contractual provisions and thus can affect the outcome of litigation. When the contract is clear and unambiguous, a court cannot consider evidence outside the contract. The following *Spotlight Case* illustrates these points.

Spotlight on Columbia Pictures

Case 9.3
Wagner v. Columbia Pictures Industries, Inc.
California Court of Appeal, Second District, 146 Cal.App.4th 586, 52 Cal.Rptr.3d 898 (2007).

Actor Robert Wagner had the rights to the TV series, *Charlie's Angels.*

(Photo by John M. Heller/Getty Images)

FACTS   Actor Robert Wagner entered into an agreement with Spelling-Goldberg Productions (SGP) "relating to *Charlie's Angels* (herein called the 'series')." The contract entitled Wagner to 50 percent of the net profits that SGP received from broadcasting the series and from all ancillary, music, and subsidiary rights in connection with the series. SGP hired Ivan Goff and Ben Roberts to write the series, under a contract subject to the Writers Guild of America Minimum Basic Agreement (MBA).**ᵃ** The MBA stipulated that the writer of a television show retains the right to make and market films based on the material, subject to the producer's right to buy this right if the writer decides to sell it within five years.

The first *Charlie's Angels* episode aired in 1976. In 1982, SGP sold its rights to the series to Columbia Pictures Industries, Inc. Thirteen years later, Columbia bought the movie rights to the material from Goff's and Roberts's heirs. In 2000 and 2003, Columbia produced and distributed two *Charlie's Angels* movies. Wagner filed a suit in a California state court against Columbia, claiming a share of the profits from the films. The court granted Columbia's motion for summary judgment. Wagner appealed to a state intermediate appellate court.

ISSUE   Did the language of Wagner's contract with SGP entitle Columbia to all of the profits from the two *Charlie's Angels* movies?

DECISION   Yes. The state intermediate appellate court affirmed the lower court's judgment.

REASON   Wagner offered evidence to show that a previous contract with SGP involving a property titled *Love Song* had been intended to give him half of the net profits that SGP received from the property from all sources without limitation as to source or time. Wagner argued that because the profits provision in the *Charlie's Angels* agreement used identical language, the provision should be interpreted to give him the same share. The court stated that an "agreement is the writing itself." Extrinsic evidence is not admissible "to show intention independent of an unambiguous written instrument." The court reasoned that even if the parties intended Wagner to share in the profits from all sources, "they did not say so in their contract." Under the language of the contract, Wagner was not entitled to share in the profits from the exercise of the movie rights to *Charlie's Angels* if those rights were acquired separately. SGP did not acquire the movie rights to *Charlie's Angels* by exercising this right within the five-year period. Columbia obtained those rights separately more than five years later.

CRITICAL THINKING—Legal Consideration   *How might the result in this case have been different if the court had allowed Wagner's extrinsic evidence of the prior contract regarding* Love Song *to be used as evidence in this dispute?*

a. The Writers Guild of America is an association of screen and television writers that negotiates industry-wide agreements with motion picture and television producers to cover the rights of its members.

Other Rules of Interpretation

LEARNING OBJECTIVE 5
What rules guide the courts in interpreting contracts?

Generally, a court will interpret the language to give effect to the parties' intent *as expressed in their contract.* This is the primary purpose of the rules of interpretation—to determine the parties' intent from the language used in their agreement and to give effect to that intent. A court normally will not make or remake a contract, nor will it normally interpret the language according to what the parties *claim* their intent was when they made the contract.[7]

7. Nevertheless, if a court finds that, even after applying the rules of interpretation, the terms are susceptible to more than one meaning, the court may admit extrinsic evidence to prove what the parties intended. See, for example, *Langdon v. United Restaurants, Inc.,* 105 S.W.3d 882 (Mo.Ct.App. 2003).

Rules the Courts Use

The courts use the following rules in interpreting contractual terms:

1. Insofar as possible, a reasonable, lawful, and effective meaning will be given to all of a contract's terms.
2. A contract will be interpreted as a whole. Individual, specific clauses will be considered subordinate to the contract's general intent. All writings that are a part of the same transaction will be interpreted together.
3. Terms that were the subject of separate negotiation will be given greater consideration than standardized terms and terms that were not negotiated separately.
4. A word will be given its ordinary, commonly accepted meaning, and a technical word or term will be given its technical meaning, unless the parties clearly intended something else.
5. Specific and exact wording will be given greater consideration than general language.
6. Written or typewritten terms prevail over preprinted terms.
7. Because a contract should be drafted in clear and unambiguous language, a party that uses ambiguous expressions is held to be responsible for the ambiguities. Thus, when the language has more than one meaning, it will be interpreted *against* the party that drafted the contract.
8. Evidence of *trade usage, prior dealing,* and *course of performance* may be admitted to clarify the meaning of an ambiguously worded contract. (We will define and discuss these terms in Chapter 15.) What each of the parties does pursuant to the contract will be interpreted as consistent with what the other does and with any relevant usage of trade and course of dealing or performance.

Express Terms Usually Given Most Weight

Express terms (terms expressly stated in the contract) are given the greatest weight, followed by course of performance, course of dealing, and custom and usage of trade—in that order. When considering custom and usage, a court will look at the trade customs and usage common to the particular business or industry and to the locale in which the contract was made or is to be performed.

CASE EXAMPLE 9.9 Jessica Robbins bought a house in Tennessee. U.S. Bank financed the purchase, and Tennessee Farmers Mutual Insurance Company issued the homeowner's insurance policy. The policy included a standard mortgage clause that promised payment to the bank unless the house was lost due to an "increase in hazard" that the bank knew about but did not tell the insurer. When Robbins fell behind on her mortgage payments, the bank started foreclosure proceedings (see Chapter 22). No one told the insurer. Robbins filed for bankruptcy, which postponed foreclosure. Meanwhile, the house was destroyed in a fire. The bank filed a claim under the policy, but the insurer refused to pay on the ground that it had not been told by the bank of an "increase in hazard"—the foreclosure. The bank then filed a lawsuit. The court found that the plain meaning of the words "increase in hazard" in the policy referred to physical conditions on the property that posed a risk, not to events such as foreclosure. Thus, the bank was not required to notify the insurer under the terms of the policy, and the lack of notice did not invalidate the coverage.[8] ●

"The difference between the right word and the almost right word is the difference between lightning and a lightning bug."

Mark Twain, 1835–1910
(American author and humorist)

---

8. *U.S. Bank, N.A. v. Tennessee Farmers Mutual Insurance Co.,* 277 S.W.3d 381 (Tenn.Sup.Ct. 2009).

Reviewing . . . Nature and Classification

Mitsui Bank hired Ross Duncan as a branch manager in one of its Southern California locations. At that time, Duncan received an employee handbook informing him that Mitsui would review his performance and salary level annually. In 2010, Mitsui decided to create a new lending program to help financially troubled businesses stay afloat. It hired Duncan as the credit development officer (CDO) and gave him a written compensation plan. Duncan's compensation was to be based on the new program's success and involved a bonus and commissions based on new loans and sales volume. The written plan also stated, "This compensation plan will be reviewed and potentially amended after one year and will be subject to such review and amendment annually thereafter." Duncan's efforts as CDO were successful, and the business-lending program he developed grew to represent 25 percent of Mitsui's business in 2011 and 40 percent by 2012. Nevertheless, Mitsui not only refused to give Duncan a raise in 2011 but also amended his compensation plan to significantly reduce his compensation and to change his performance evaluation schedule to every six months. When he had still not received a raise by 2012, Duncan retired as CDO and filed a lawsuit claiming breach of contract. Using the information presented in the chapter, answer the following questions.

1. What are the four requirements of a valid contract?
2. Did Duncan have a valid contract with Mitsui for employment as credit development officer? If so, was it a bilateral or a unilateral contract?
3. What are the requirements of an implied contract?
4. Can Duncan establish an implied contract based on the employment manual or the written compensation plan? Why or why not?

DEBATE THIS Companies should be able to make or break employment contracts whenever and however they wish.

Key Terms

bilateral contract 243
contract 240
executed contract 246
executory contract 246
express contract 245

formal contract 244
implied contract 245
informal contract 245
objective theory of contracts 241
offeree 242

offeror 242
promise 239
promisee 240
promisor 240
quasi contract 248

unenforceable contract 247
unilateral contract 243
valid contract 246
void contract 247
voidable contract 246

Chapter Summary: Nature and Classification

An Overview of Contract Law (See pages 240–241.)	1. *Sources of contract law*—The common law governs all contracts except when it has been modified or replaced by statutory law, such as the Uniform Commercial Code (UCC), or by administrative agency regulations. The UCC governs contracts for the sale or lease of goods (see Chapter 15).
	2. *The function of contracts*—Contract law establishes what kinds of promises will be legally binding and supplies procedures for enforcing legally binding promises, or agreements.
	3. *Definition of a contract*—A contract is an agreement that can be enforced in court. It is formed by two or more competent parties who agree to perform or to refrain from performing some act now or in the future.
	4. *Objective theory of contracts*—In contract law, intent is determined by objective facts, not by the personal or subjective intent, or belief, of a party.

Continued

Chapter Summary: Nature and Classification—Continued

Elements of a Contract (See pages 241–242.)	1. *Requirements of a valid contract*—The four requirements of a valid contract are agreement, consideration, contractual capacity, and legality. 2. *Defenses to the enforceability of a contract*—Even if the four requirements of a valid contract are met, a contract may be unenforceable if it lacks voluntary consent or is not in the required form.
Types of Contracts (See pages 242–247.)	1. *Bilateral*—A promise for a promise. 2. *Unilateral*—A promise for an act (acceptance is the completed—or substantial—performance of the contract by the offeree). 3. *Formal*—Requires a special form for contract formation. 4. *Informal*—Requires no special form for contract formation. 5. *Express*—Formed by words (oral, written, or a combination). 6. *Implied*—Formed at least in part by the conduct of the parties. 7. *Executed*—A fully performed contract. 8. *Executory*—A contract not yet fully performed. 9. *Valid*—A contract that has the four necessary contractual elements of agreement, consideration, capacity, and legality. 10. *Voidable*—A contract in which a party has the option of avoiding or enforcing the contractual obligation. 11. *Unenforceable*—A valid contract that cannot be enforced because of a legal defense. 12. *Void*—No contract exists, or there is a contract without legal obligations.
Quasi Contracts (See pages 248–249.)	A quasi contract, or a contract implied in law, is a contract that is imposed by law to prevent unjust enrichment.
Interpretation of Contracts (See pages 249–252.)	Increasingly, plain language laws require contracts to be written in plain language so that the terms are clear and understandable to the parties. Under the plain meaning rule, a court will enforce the contract according to its plain terms, the meaning of which must be determined from the written document alone. Other rules applied by the courts when interpreting are set out on page 252.

ExamPrep

ISSUE SPOTTERS

1. Joli signs and returns a letter from Kerin, in which he said that he had a book at a certain price. When Kerin delivers the book, Joli sends it back, claiming that they do not have a contract. Kerin claims they do. What standard determines whether these parties have a contract? (**See page 241.**)
2. Dyna tells Ed that she will pay him $1,000 to set fire to her store so that she can collect under a fire insurance policy. Ed sets fire to the store, but Dyna refuses to pay. Can Ed recover? Why or why not? (**See page 247.**)

—**Check your answers to the Issue Spotters against the answers provided in Appendix E at the end of this text.**

BEFORE THE TEST

Go to www.cengagebrain.com, enter the ISBN 9781133273561, and click on "Find" to locate this textbook's Web site. Then, click on "Access Now" under "Study Tools," and select Chapter 9 at the top. There, you will find a Practice Quiz that you can take to assess your mastery of the concepts in this chapter, as well as Flashcards, a Glossary of important terms, and Video Questions (when assigned).

For Review

Answers to the even-numbered questions in this For Review section can be found in Appendix F at the end of this text.

1. What is a contract? What is the objective theory of contracts?
2. What are the four basic elements necessary to the formation of a valid contract?
3. What is the difference between express and implied contracts?

4. How does a void contract differ from a voidable contract? What is an unenforceable contract?
5. What rules guide the courts in interpreting contracts?

Business Scenarios and Case Problems

9–1 Unilateral Contract. Rocky Mountain Races, Inc., sponsors the "Pioneer Trail Ultramarathon" with an advertised first prize of $10,000. The rules require the competitors to run 100 miles from the floor of Blackwater Canyon to the top of Pinnacle Mountain. The rules also provide that Rocky reserves the right to change the terms of the race at any time. Monica enters the race and is declared the winner. Rocky offers her a prize of $1,000 instead of $10,000. Did Rocky and Monica have a contract? Explain. **(See page 243.)**

9–2 ? Question with Sample Answer—Implied Contract. Janine was hospitalized with severe abdominal pain and placed in an intensive care unit. Her doctor told the hospital personnel to order around-the-clock nursing care for Janine. At the hospital's request, a nursing services firm, Nursing Services Unlimited, provided two weeks of in-hospital care and, after Janine was sent home, an additional two weeks of at-home care. During the at-home period of care, Janine was fully aware that she was receiving the benefit of the nursing services. Nursing Services later billed Janine $4,000 for the nursing care, but Janine refused to pay on the ground that she had never contracted for the services, either orally or in writing. In view of the fact that no express contract was ever formed, can Nursing Services recover the $4,000 from Janine? If so, under what legal theory? Discuss. **(See page 245.)**

—For a sample answer to Question 9–2, go to Appendix G at the end of this text.

9–3 Contract Classification. For employment with the Firestorm Smokejumpers—a crew of elite paratroopers who parachute into dangerous situations to fight fires—applicants must complete a series of tests. The crew chief sends the most qualified applicants a letter stating that they will be admitted to Firestorm's training sessions if they pass a medical exam. Jake Kurzyniec receives the letter and passes the exam, but a new crew chief changes the selection process and rejects him. Is there a contract between Kurzyniec and Firestorm? If there is a contract, what type of contract is it? **(See pages 242–243.)**

9–4 Spotlight on Taco Bell—Implied Contract. Thomas Rinks and Joseph Shields developed Psycho Chihuahua, a caricature of a Chihuahua dog with a "do-not-back-down" attitude. They promoted and marketed the character through their company, Wrench, LLC. Ed Alfaro and Rudy Pollak, representatives of Taco Bell Corp., learned of Psycho Chihuahua and met with Rinks and Shields to talk about using the character as a Taco Bell "icon." Wrench sent artwork, merchandise, and marketing ideas to Alfaro, who promoted the character within Taco Bell. Alfaro asked Wrench to propose terms for Taco Bell's use of Psycho Chihuahua. Taco Bell did not accept Wrench's terms, but Alfaro continued to promote the character within the company. Meanwhile, Taco Bell hired a new advertising agency, which proposed an advertising campaign involving a Chihuahua. When Alfaro learned of this proposal, he sent the Psycho Chihuahua materials to the agency. Taco Bell made a Chihuahua the focus of its marketing but paid nothing to Wrench. Wrench filed a suit against Taco Bell in a federal court claiming that it had an implied contract with Taco Bell and that Taco Bell breached that contract. Do these facts satisfy the requirements for an implied contract? Why or why not? [*Wrench, LLC. v. Taco Bell Corp.*, 256 F.3d 446 (6th Cir. 2001), *cert.* denied, 534 U.S. 1114, 122 S.Ct. 921, 151 L.Ed.2d 805 (2002)] **(See page 245.)**

9–5 Quasi Contract. Kim Panenka asked to borrow $4,750 from her sister, Kris, to make a mortgage payment. Kris deposited a check for that amount into Kim's bank account. Hours later, Kim asked to borrow another $1,100. Kris took a cash advance on her credit card and deposited this amount into Kim's account. When Kim did not repay Kris, the sister filed a suit, arguing that she had "loaned" Kim the money. Can the court impose a contract between the sisters? Explain. [*Panenka v. Panenka,* 331 Wis.2d 731, 795 N.W.2d 493 (2011)] **(See pages 248–249.)**

9–6 Interpretation of Contracts. Lisa and Darrell Miller had a son, Landon. When the Millers divorced, they entered into a "Joint Plan" (JP). Under the JP, Darrell agreed to "begin setting funds aside for Landon to attend college." After Landon's eighteenth birthday, Lisa asked a court to order Darrell to pay the boy's college expenses based on the JP. Darrell contended that the JP was not clear on this point. Do the rules of contract interpretation support Lisa's request or Darrell's contention? Explain. [*Miller v. Miller,* 1 So.3d 815 (La.App. 2009)] **(See pages 249–252.)**

9–7 Case Problem with Sample Answer—Quasi Contract. Robert Gutkowski, a sports marketing expert, met with George Steinbrenner, the owner of the New York Yankees, many times to discuss the Yankees Entertainment and Sports Network (YES). Gutkowski was paid as a consultant. Later, he filed a suit, seeking an ownership share in YES. There was no written contract for the share, but he claimed that there were discussions about him being a part owner. Does Gutkowski have a valid claim for payment? Discuss. [*Gutkowski v. Steinbrenner,* 680 F.Supp.2d 602 (S.D.N.Y. 2010)] **(See pages 248–249.)**

—For a sample answer to Problem 9–7, go to Appendix H at the end of this text.

9–8 ◆▶ **A Question of Ethics—Unilateral Contracts.** International Business Machines Corp. (IBM) hired Niels Jensen as a software sales representative. According to the brochure on IBM's "Sales Incentive Plan" (SIP), "the more you sell, the more earnings for you." But "the SIP program does not constitute a promise by IBM. IBM reserves the right to modify the program at any time." Jensen was given a "quota letter" that said he would be paid $75,000 as a base salary and, if he attained his quota, an additional $75,000 as incentive pay. Jensen closed a deal worth more than $24 million to IBM. When IBM paid him less than $500,000 as a commission, Jensen filed a suit. He argued that the SIP was a unilateral offer that became a binding contract when he closed the sale. [*Jensen v. International Business Machines Corp.*, 454 F.3d 382 (4th Cir. 2006)] **(See pages 243–244.)**

1. Would it be fair to the employer for the court to hold that the SIP brochure and the quota letter created a unilateral contract if IBM did not *intend* to create such a contract? Would it be fair to the employee to hold that *no* contract was created? Explain.

2. The "Sales Incentives" section of IBM's brochure included a clause providing that "management will decide if an adjustment to the payment is appropriate" when an employee closes a large transaction. Does this affect your answers to the above questions? From an ethical perspective, would it be fair to hold that a contract exists despite this statement? Explain.

Critical Thinking and Writing Assignments

9–9 💡 **Business Law Critical Thinking Group Assignment.** Review the basic requirements for a valid contract listed at the beginning of this chapter. Now consider the relationship entered into when a student enrolls in a college or university.

1. One group should analyze and discuss whether a contract has been formed between the student and the college or university.

2. A second group should assume that there is a contract and explain whether it is bilateral or unilateral.

Agreement in Traditional and E-Contracts

(Khafizov Ivan Harisovich/Shutterstock.com)

LEARNING OBJECTIVES

The five learning objectives below are designed to help improve your understanding of the chapter. After reading this chapter, you should be able to answer the following questions:

1 What elements are necessary for an effective offer? What are some examples of nonoffers?

2 In what circumstances will an offer be irrevocable?

3 What are the elements that are necessary for an effective acceptance?

4 How do shrink-wrap and click-on agreements differ from other contracts? How have traditional laws been applied to these agreements?

5 What is the Uniform Electronic Transactions Act? What are some of the major provisions of this act?

"It is necessity that makes laws."
—Voltaire, 1649–1778 (French intellectual and writer)

Voltaire's statement that it is "necessity that makes laws" is certainly true in regard to contracts. In Chapter 9, we pointed out that promises and agreements, and the knowledge that some of those promises and agreements will be legally enforced, are essential to civilized society. The homes we live in, the food we eat, the clothes we wear, and the cars we drive—all of these have been purchased through implicit or explicit contractual agreements. Contract law developed over time, through the common law tradition, to meet society's need to know with certainty what kinds of promises, or contracts, will be enforced and the point at which a valid and binding contract is formed.

For a contract to be valid and enforceable, the requirements listed in Chapter 9 must be met. In this chapter, we look closely at the first of these requirements, *agreement.* Agreement is required to form a contract, regardless of whether it is formed in the traditional way by exchanging paper documents or created online by exchanging electronic messages or documents, as many contracts are formed today. We discuss online offers and acceptances and examine some laws that have been created to apply to electronic contracts, or *e-contracts,* in the latter part of the chapter. Can a series of e-mails bind Amazon.com to a contract? You will see what the court had to say when you read the *Spotlight Case* on page 262.

Agreement

Agreement A mutual understanding or meeting of the minds between two or more individuals regarding the terms of a contract.

An essential element for contract formation is **agreement**—the parties must agree on the terms of the contract. Ordinarily, agreement is evidenced by two events: an *offer* and an *acceptance.* One party offers a certain bargain to another party, who then accepts that bargain.

Because words often fail to convey the precise meaning intended, the law of contracts generally adheres to the *objective theory of contracts,* as discussed in Chapter 9 on page 241. Under this theory, a party's words and conduct are held to mean whatever a reasonable person in the offeree's position would think they meant.

Requirements of the Offer

Offer A promise or commitment to perform or refrain from performing some specified act in the future.

An **offer** is a promise or commitment to perform or refrain from performing some specified act in the future. As discussed in Chapter 9, the party making an offer is called the *offeror,* and the party to whom the offer is made is called the *offeree.*

Three elements are necessary for an offer to be effective:

LEARNING OBJECTIVE 1
What elements are necessary for an effective offer? What are some examples of nonoffers?

1. There must be a serious, objective intention by the offeror.
2. The terms of the offer must be reasonably certain, or definite, so that the parties and the court can ascertain the terms of the contract.
3. The offer must be communicated to the offeree.

Once an effective offer has been made, the offeree's acceptance of that offer creates a legally binding contract (providing the other essential elements for a valid and enforceable contract are present).

Intention   The first requirement for an effective offer is a serious, objective intention on the part of the offeror. Intent is not determined by the *subjective* intentions, beliefs, or assumptions of the offeror. Rather, it is determined by what a reasonable person in the offeree's position would conclude the offeror's words and actions meant. Offers made in obvious anger, jest, or undue excitement do not meet the requirement of a serious, objective intent. Because these offers are not effective, an offeree's acceptance does not create an agreement.

EXAMPLE 10.1   You ride to school each day with Julio in his new automobile, which has a market value of $20,000. One cold morning, the car will not start. Julio yells in anger, "I'll sell this car to anyone for $500!" You drop $500 in his lap. A reasonable person, taking into consideration Julio's frustration and the obvious difference in value between the car's market price and the purchase price, would declare that Julio's offer was not made with serious and objective intent and that you do not have an agreement. •

The concept of intention can be further clarified through an examination of the types of statements that are *not* offers. We look at these expressions and statements in the subsections that follow.

In the *Classic Case* presented next, the court considered whether an offer made "after a few drinks" met the serious-intent requirement.

Classic Case 10.1

Lucy v. Zehmer

Supreme Court of Appeals of Virginia,
196 Va. 493, 84 S.E.2d 516 (1954).

A farm that might be for sale.

FACTS   W. O. Lucy and A. H. Zehmer had known each other for fifteen to twenty years. For some time, Lucy had been wanting to buy Zehmer's farm, but Zehmer had always said that he was not interested in selling. One night, Lucy stopped in to visit with the Zehmers at a restaurant they operated. Lucy said to Zehmer, "I bet you wouldn't take $50,000 for that place." Zehmer replied, "Yes, I would, too; you wouldn't give fifty." Throughout the evening, the conversation returned to the sale of the farm. All the while, the parties were drinking whiskey.

Eventually, Zehmer wrote up an agreement, on the back of a restaurant check, for the sale of the farm, and he asked his wife, Ida, to sign it—which she did. When Lucy brought an action in a Virginia state court to enforce the agreement, Zehmer argued that he had been "high as a Georgia pine" at the time and that the offer had been made in jest: "two doggoned drunks bluffing to see who could talk the biggest and say the most." Lucy claimed that he had not been intoxicated and did not think Zehmer had been, either, given the way Zehmer handled the transaction. The trial court ruled in favor of the Zehmers, and Lucy appealed.

ISSUE   Did the agreement meet the serious-intent requirement despite the claim of intoxication?

DECISION   Yes. The agreement to sell the farm was binding.

REASON   The court held that the evidence given about the nature of the conversation, the appearance and completeness of the agreement, and the signing all tended to show that a serious business transaction, not a casual jest, was intended. The court had to look into the objective meaning of the Zehmers' words and acts: "An agreement or mutual assent is of course essential to a valid contract, but the law imputes to a person an intention corresponding to the reasonable meaning of his words and acts. If his words and acts, judged by a reasonable standard, manifest an intention to agree, it is immaterial what may be the real but unexpressed state of mind."

WHAT IF THE FACTS WERE DIFFERENT?   *Suppose that the day after Lucy signed the agreement, he decided that he did not want the farm after all, and Zehmer sued Lucy to perform the contract. Would this change in the facts alter the court's decision that Lucy and Zehmer had created an enforceable contract? Why or why not?*

IMPACT OF THIS CASE ON TODAY'S LAW   *This is a classic case in contract law because it so clearly illustrates the objective theory of contracts (see page 241) with respect to determining whether an offer was intended. Today, the courts continue to apply the objective theory of contracts and routinely cite the* Lucy v. Zehmer *decision as a significant precedent in this area.*

Expressions of Opinion   An expression of opinion is not an offer. It does not demonstrate an intention to enter into a binding agreement. **CASE EXAMPLE 10.2**   Hawkins took his son to McGee, a physician, and asked McGee to operate on the son's hand. McGee said that the boy would be in the hospital three or four days and that the hand would *probably* heal a few days later. The son's hand did not heal for a month, but nonetheless the father did not win a suit for breach of contract. The court held that McGee did not make an offer to heal the son's hand in three or four days. He merely expressed an opinion as to when the hand would heal.[1] ●

Statements of Future Intent   A statement of an *intention* to do something in the future is not an offer. **EXAMPLE 10.3**   If Samir says, "I *plan* to sell my stock in Novation, Inc., for $150 per share," no contract is created if John "accepts" and gives Samir $150 per share for the

---

1. *Hawkins v. McGee,* 84 N.H. 114, 146 A. 641 (1929).

stock. Samir has merely expressed his intention to enter into a future contract for the sale of the stock. If John accepts and hands over the $150 per share, no contract is formed, because a reasonable person would conclude that Samir was only *thinking about* selling his stock, not *promising* to sell it. ●

When a contractor submits a bid proposal, is that proposal binding on the entity to whom the bid was addressed?

Preliminary Negotiations   A request or invitation to negotiate is not an offer. It only expresses a willingness to discuss the possibility of entering into a contract. Examples are statements such as "Will you sell Forest Acres?" and "I wouldn't sell my car for less than $8,000." A reasonable person in the offeree's position would not conclude that such statements indicated an intention to enter into binding obligations.

Likewise, when the government and private firms need to have construction work done, they invite contractors to submit bids. The *invitation* to submit bids is not an offer, and a contractor does not bind the government or private firm by submitting a bid. (The bids that the contractors submit are offers, however, and the government or private firm can bind the contractor by accepting the bid.) For a discussion of some problems with programs designed to promote equal opportunity in government contracting, see this chapter's *Law, Diversity, and Business: Managerial Implications* feature on the facing page.

Advertisements, Catalogues, and Circulars   In general, advertisements, catalogues, price lists, and circular letters (meant for the general public) are treated as invitations to negotiate, not as offers to form a contract.[2] This applies whether the ads and the like are in traditional media or online. **CASE EXAMPLE 10.4**   An ad on *Science*NOW's Web site asked for "news tips." Erik Trell, a professor and physician, submitted a manuscript in which he claimed to have solved a famous mathematical problem. When *Science*NOW did not publish his solution, Trell filed a lawsuit for breach of contract. He claimed that *Science*NOW's ad was an offer, which he had accepted by submitting his manuscript. The court dismissed Trell's suit, holding that an ad is only an invitation for offers, and not an offer itself. Hence, responses to an ad are not acceptances—instead, the responses are the offers. Thus, Trell's submission of the manuscript for publication was the offer, which *Science*NOW did not accept.[3] ●

Price lists are another form of invitation to negotiate or trade. A seller's price list is not an offer to sell at that price. It merely invites the buyer to offer to buy at that price. In fact, the seller usually puts "prices subject to change" on the price list. Only in rare circumstances will a price quotation be construed as an offer.

Although most advertisements and the like are treated as invitations to negotiate, this does not mean that an advertisement can never be an offer. On some occasions, courts have construed advertisements to be offers because the ads contained definite terms that invited acceptance (such as an ad offering a reward for the return of a lost dog).

Agreements to Agree   In the past, agreements to agree—that is, agreements to agree to the material terms of a contract at some future date—were not considered to be binding contracts. The modern view, however, is that agreements to agree may be enforceable agreements (contracts) if it is clear that the parties intended to be bound by the agreements. In other words, today the emphasis is on the parties' intent rather than on form.

CASE EXAMPLE 10.5   After a customer nearly drowned on a water ride at one of its amusement parks, Six Flags, Inc., filed a lawsuit against the manufacturer that had designed the ride. The manufacturer claimed that the parties did not have a binding contract but had only engaged in preliminary negotiations that were never formalized into a contract to

---

2. *Restatement (Second) of Contracts*, Section 26, Comment b.
3. *Trell v. American Association for the Advancement of Science*, 2007 WL 1500497 (W.D.N.Y. 2007).

LAW, DIVERSITY, AND BUSINESS: MANAGERIAL IMPLICATIONS

EQUAL OPPORTUNITY IN PUBLIC CONTRACTING

Cities and states put projects out for bids. Undoubtedly, there has been discrimination against minorities and female contractors in such bidding processes in the past. The city of San Francisco, California, along with other cities, such as Seattle, Washington, and Madison, Wisconsin, created a system to "make up" for such past discrimination.

San Francisco's Public Contracting Policy San Francisco has allowed its city government officials to treat bids from businesses owned by women or members of minority groups as though the bids were as much as 10 percent lower than bids from other businesses. Hence, if a bid from a minority-owned construction company was, say, $1 million, city officials could consider it to be only $900,000 when comparing it with bids from nonminority-owned businesses.

Proposition 209 Changes the Policy In 1996, the voters of California approved Proposition 209, known as the California Civil Rights Initiative. The proposition amended the state constitution to prohibit state government institutions from considering ethnicity, race, and gender in the areas of public contracting, public employment, and public education. Thus, San Francisco's preferential treatment of minority- and female-owned companies in public contracting was viewed as a violation of Proposition 209. When the California Supreme Court reviewed San Francisco's preferential bidding procedure, it ruled that the process was indeed a violation of the state constitution, as amended.[a]

Seattle, perhaps not wishing to be challenged in court, changed its preferential bidding system by replacing race and gender preferences with geographic preferences for "small" and "disadvantaged" businesses.

Business Implications *Without using preferential bidding, how might managers ensure that their bidding procedure is fair to all businesses, including those that may be suffering the effects of past discrimination?*

---

a. *Coral Construction, Inc. v. San Francisco,* 50 Cal.4th 315, 235 P.3d 947 (2010).

---

construct the ride. The court, however, held that a faxed document specifying the details of the ride, along with the parties' subsequent actions (beginning construction and handwriting notes on the fax), was sufficient to show an intent to be bound. Because of the court's finding, the manufacturer was required to provide insurance for the water ride at Six Flags, and its insurer was required to defend Six Flags in the personal-injury lawsuit that arose out of the incident.[4] ●

Preliminary Agreements Increasingly, the courts are holding that a preliminary agreement constitutes a binding contract if the parties have agreed on all essential terms and no disputed issues remain to be resolved.[5] In contrast, if the parties agree on certain major terms but leave other terms open for further negotiation, a preliminary agreement is binding only in the sense that the parties have committed themselves to negotiate the undecided terms in good faith in an effort to reach a final agreement.

In the following *Spotlight Case,* one party claimed that the agreement formed via e-mail was binding, and the other party claimed that it was merely an agreement to agree or to work out the terms of a settlement in the future.

---

4. *Six Flags, Inc. v. Steadfast Insurance Co.,* 474 F.Supp.2d 201 (D.Mass. 2007).
5. See, for example, *Tractebel Energy Marketing, Inc. v. AEP Power Marketing, Inc.,* 487 F.3d 89 (2d Cir. 2007); and *Barrand v. Whataburger, Inc.,* 214 S.W.3d 122 (Tex.App.—Corpus Christi 2006).

Spotlight on Amazon.com

Case 10.2
Basis Technology Corp. v. Amazon.com, Inc.
Appeals Court of Massachusetts, 71 Mass.App.Ct. 29, 878 N.E.2d 952 (2008).

Jeff Bezos, the founder and CEO of Amazon.com, with a Japanese manager.

FACTS Basis Technology Corporation created software and provided technical services for a Japanese-language Web site operated by Amazon.com, Inc. The agreement between the two companies allowed for separately negotiated contracts for additional services that Basis might provide to Amazon. At the end of 1999, Basis and Amazon entered into stock-purchase agreements. Later, Amazon objected to certain actions related to the securities that Basis sold. Basis sued Amazon for various claims involving these securities and for failing to pay for services performed by Basis that were not included in the original agreement. During the trial, the two parties appeared to reach an agreement to settle out of court via a series of e-mail exchanges outlining the settlement. When Amazon reneged, Basis served a motion to enforce the proposed settlement. The trial judge entered a judgment against Amazon, which appealed.

ISSUE Did the agreement that Amazon entered into with Basis via e-mail constitute a binding settlement contract?

DECISION Yes. The Appeals Court of Massachusetts affirmed the trial court's finding that Amazon intended to be bound by the terms of the e-mail exchanges.

REASON The court examined the evidence consisting of e-mails between the two parties. It pointed out that in open court and on the record, counsel "reported the result of the settlement without specification of the terms." Amazon claimed that the e-mail terms were incomplete and were not definite enough to form an agreement. The court noted, however, that "provisions are not ambiguous simply because the parties have developed different interpretations of them." In the exchange of e-mails, the essential business terms were indeed resolved. Afterward, the parties were simply proceeding to record the settlement terms, not to create them. The e-mails constituted a complete and unambiguous statement of the parties' desire to be bound by the settlement terms.

WHAT IF THE FACTS WERE DIFFERENT? Assume that, instead of exchanging e-mails, the attorneys for both sides had a phone conversation that included all of the terms to which they actually agreed in their e-mail exchanges. Would the court have ruled differently? Why or why not?

PREVENTING LEGAL DISPUTES

To avoid potential legal disputes, be cautious when drafting a memorandum that outlines a preliminary agreement or understanding with another party. If all the major terms are included, a court might hold that the agreement is binding even though you intended it to be only a tentative agreement. One way to avoid being bound is to include in the writing the points of disagreement, as well as those points on which you and the other party agree. Alternatively, you could add a disclaimer to the memorandum stating that, although you anticipate entering a contract in the future, neither party intends to be legally bound to the terms that were discussed. That way, the other party cannot claim that you have already reached an agreement on all essential terms.

Definiteness The second requirement for an effective offer involves the definiteness of its terms. An offer must have reasonably definite terms so that a court can determine if a breach has occurred and give an appropriate remedy.[6] The specific terms required depend, of course, on the type of contract. Generally, a contract must include the following terms, either expressed in the contract or capable of being reasonably inferred from it:

---

6. *Restatement (Second) of Contracts*, Section 33. The UCC has relaxed the requirements regarding the definiteness of terms in contracts for the sale of goods. See UCC 2–204(3).

1. The identification of the parties.
2. The identification of the object or subject matter of the contract (also the quantity, when appropriate), including the work to be performed, with specific identification of such items as goods, services, and land.
3. The consideration to be paid.
4. The time of payment, delivery, or performance.

An offer may invite an acceptance to be worded in such specific terms that the contract is made definite. **EXAMPLE 10.6** Nintendo of America, Inc., contacts your Play 2 Win Games store and offers to sell "from one to twenty-five Nintendo 3DS gaming systems for $75 each. State number desired in acceptance." You agree to buy twenty systems. Because the quantity is specified in the acceptance, the terms are definite, and the contract is enforceable. •

Communication   A third requirement for an effective offer is communication—the offer must be communicated to the offeree. **EXAMPLE 10.7** Tolson advertises a reward for the return of her lost cat. Dirk, not knowing of the reward, finds the cat and returns it to Tolson. Ordinarily, Dirk cannot recover the reward because an essential element of a reward contract is that the one who claims the reward must have known it was offered. A few states would allow recovery of the reward, but not on contract principles—Dirk would be allowed to recover on the basis that it would be unfair to deny him the reward just because he did not know about it. •

Termination of the Offer

The communication of an effective offer to an offeree gives the offeree the power to transform the offer into a binding, legal obligation (a contract) by an acceptance. This power of acceptance does not continue forever, though. It can be terminated by either the *action of the parties* or by *operation of law*. Termination by the action of the parties can involve a revocation by the offeror or a rejection or counteroffer by the offeree.

Revocation The withdrawal of a contract offer by the offeror. Unless an offer is irrevocable, it can be revoked at any time prior to acceptance without liability.

Termination by Action of the Offeror   The offeror's act of withdrawing an offer is referred to as **revocation.** Unless an offer is irrevocable, the offeror usually can revoke the offer (even if he or she has promised to keep it open), as long as the revocation is communicated to the offeree before the offeree accepts. Revocation may be accomplished by an express repudiation of the offer (such as "I withdraw my previous offer of October 17") or by the performance of acts that are inconsistent with the existence of the offer and that are made known to the offeree.

EXAMPLE 10.8 Misha offers to sell some land to Gary. A month passes, and Gary, who has not accepted the offer, learns that Misha has sold the property to Liam. Because Misha's sale of the land to Liam is inconsistent with the continued existence of the offer to Gary, the offer to Gary is effectively revoked. •

The general rule followed by most states is that a revocation becomes effective when the offeree or the offeree's *agent* (a person who acts on behalf of another—see Chapter 23) actually receives it. Therefore, a statement of revocation sent via FedEx on April 1 and delivered at the offeree's residence or place of business on April 2 becomes effective on April 2.

Termination by Action of the Offeree   If the offeree rejects the offer—by words or by conduct—the offer is terminated. Any subsequent attempt by the offeree to accept will be construed as a new offer, giving the original offeror (now the offeree) the power of acceptance.

Like a revocation, a rejection of an offer is effective only when it is actually received by the offeror or the offeror's agent. **EXAMPLE 10.9** Goldfinch Farms offers to sell specialty

Maitake mushrooms to a Japanese buyer, Kinoko Foods. If Kinoko rejects the offer by sending a letter via U.S. mail, the rejection will not be effective (and the offer will not be terminated) until Goldfinch receives the letter. •

Inquiries about an Offer   Merely inquiring about an offer does not constitute rejection. **EXAMPLE 10.10**   Your friend offers to buy your Inkling digital pen—which automatically remembers whatever is drawn with it on any kind of paper—for $100. You respond, "Is that your best offer?" A reasonable person would conclude that you have not rejected the offer but have merely made an inquiry. You could still accept and bind your friend to the $100 price. •

Counteroffers   A **counteroffer** is a rejection of the original offer and the simultaneous making of a new offer. **EXAMPLE 10.11**   Burke offers to sell his home to Lang for $270,000. Lang responds, "Your price is too high. I'll offer to purchase your house for $250,000." Lang's response is called a counteroffer because it rejects Burke's offer to sell at $270,000 and creates a new offer by Lang to purchase the home at a price of $250,000. •

At common law, the **mirror image rule** requires that the offeree's acceptance match the offeror's offer exactly. In other words, the terms of the acceptance must "mirror" those of the offer. If the acceptance materially changes or adds to the terms of the original offer, it will be considered not an acceptance but a counteroffer— which, of course, need not be accepted. The original offeror can, however, accept the terms of the counteroffer and create a valid contract.[7]

Termination by Operation of Law
The power of the offeree to transform the offer into a binding, legal obligation can be terminated by operation of law through the occurrence of any of the following events:

1. Lapse of time.
2. Destruction of the specific subject matter of the offer.
3. Death or incompetence of the offeror or the offeree.
4. Supervening illegality of the proposed contract. (A statute or court decision that makes an offer illegal automatically terminates the offer.)

Lapse of Time   An offer terminates automatically by law when the period of time *specified in the offer* has passed. If the offer states that it will be left open until a particular date, then the offer will terminate at midnight on that day. If the offer states that it will be left open for a number of days, this time period normally begins to run when the offer is actually *received* by the offeree, not when it is formed or sent.

If the offer does not specify a time for acceptance, the offer terminates at the end of a *reasonable* period of time. A reasonable period of time is determined by the subject matter of the contract, business and market conditions, and other relevant circumstances. An offer to sell farm produce, for instance, will terminate sooner than an offer to sell farm equipment because produce is perishable and subject to greater fluctuations in market value.

Destruction or Death   An offer is automatically terminated if the specific subject matter of the offer (such as an iPad or a house) is destroyed before the offer is accepted. An offeree's power of acceptance is also terminated when the offeror or offeree dies or becomes legally incapacitated (capacity will be discussed in Chapter 11), *unless the offer is irrevocable.*

Counteroffer An offeree's response to an offer in which the offeree rejects the original offer and at the same time makes a new offer.

Mirror Image Rule A common law rule that requires that the terms of the offeree's acceptance adhere exactly to the terms of the offeror's offer for a valid contract to be formed.

---

7. The mirror image rule has been greatly modified in regard to sales contracts. Section 2–207 of the UCC provides that a contract is formed if the offeree makes a definite expression of acceptance (such as signing the form in the appropriate location), even though the terms of the acceptance modify or add to the terms of the original offer (see Chapter 15).

LEARNING OBJECTIVE 2
In what circumstances will an offer be irrevocable?

Option Contract A contract under which the offeror cannot revoke the offer for a stipulated time period (because the offeree has given consideration for the offer to remain open).

Irrevocable Offers Although most offers are revocable, some can be made irrevocable. Increasingly, courts refuse to allow an offeror to revoke an offer when the offeree has changed position because of justifiable reliance on the offer (under the doctrine of *promissory estoppel*—see Chapter 11). In some circumstances, "firm offers" made by merchants may also be considered irrevocable. We will discuss these offers in Chapter 15.

Another form of irrevocable offer is an option contract. An **option contract** is created when an offeror promises to hold an offer open for a specified period of time in return for a payment (consideration) given by the offeree. An option contract takes away the offeror's power to revoke an offer for the period of time specified in the option. If no time is specified, then a reasonable period of time is implied.

Option contracts are frequently used in conjunction with the sale of real estate. **EXAMPLE 10.12** Tyrell agrees to lease a house from Jackson, the property owner. The lease contract includes a clause stating that Tyrell is paying an additional $15,000 for an option to purchase the property within a specified period of time. If Tyrell decides not to purchase the house after the specified period has lapsed, he loses the $15,000, and Jackson is free to sell the property to another buyer. ●

Acceptance

Acceptance The act of voluntarily agreeing, through words or conduct, to the terms of an offer, thereby creating a contract.

An **acceptance** is a voluntary act by the offeree that shows assent, or agreement, to the terms of an offer. The offeree's act may consist of words or conduct. The acceptance must be unequivocal and must be communicated to the offeror. Generally, only the person to whom the offer is made or that person's agent can accept the offer and create a binding contract.

LEARNING OBJECTIVE 3
What are the elements that are necessary for an effective acceptance?

Unequivocal Acceptance To exercise the power of acceptance effectively, the offeree must accept unequivocally. This is the *mirror image rule* previously discussed. If the acceptance is subject to new conditions or if the terms of the acceptance materially change the original offer, the acceptance may be deemed a counteroffer that implicitly rejects the original offer.

Certain terms included in an acceptance will not change the offer sufficiently to constitute rejection. **EXAMPLE 10.13** In response to an art dealer's offer to sell a painting, the offeree, Ashton Gibbs, replies, "I accept. Please send a written contract." Gibbs is requesting a written contract but is not making it a condition for acceptance. Therefore, the acceptance is effective without the written contract. In contrast, if Gibbs replies, "I accept *if* you send a written contract," the acceptance is expressly conditioned on the request for a writing, and the statement is not an acceptance but a counteroffer. (Notice how important each word is!)[8] ●

> ► **KNOW THIS** ◄
> When an offer is rejected, it is terminated.

Silence as Acceptance Ordinarily, silence cannot constitute acceptance, even if the offeror states, "By your silence and inaction, you will be deemed to have accepted this offer." This general rule applies because an offeree should not be put under a burden of liability to act affirmatively in order to reject an offer. No consideration—that is, nothing of value (see Chapter 11)—has passed to the offeree to impose such a liability.

In some instances, however, the offeree does have a duty to speak. If so, his or her silence or inaction will operate as an acceptance. Silence may be an acceptance when an offeree takes the benefit of offered services even though he or she had an opportunity to reject them and knew that they were offered with the expectation of compensation.

---

8. As noted in footnote 7, in regard to sales contracts, the UCC provides that an acceptance may still be effective even if some terms are added. The new terms are simply treated as proposals for additions to the contract, unless both parties are merchants. If the parties are merchants, the additional terms (with some exceptions) become part of the contract [UCC 2–207(2)].

EXAMPLE 10.14 Juan earns extra income by washing store windows. Juan taps on the window of a store, catches the attention of the store's manager, and points to the window and raises his cleaner, signaling that he will be washing the window. The manager does nothing to stop him. Here, the store manager's silence constitutes an acceptance, and an implied contract is created. The store is bound to pay a reasonable value for Juan's work. ●

Silence can also operate as an acceptance when the offeree has had prior dealings with the offeror. If a merchant, for instance, routinely receives shipments from a supplier and in the past has always notified the supplier when defective goods are rejected, then silence constitutes acceptance. Also, if a buyer solicits an offer specifying that certain terms and conditions are acceptable, and the seller makes the offer in response to the solicitation, the buyer has a duty to reject—that is, a duty to tell the seller that the offer is not acceptable. Failure to reject (silence) will operate as an acceptance.

Communication of Acceptance

In a bilateral contract, communication of acceptance is necessary because acceptance is in the form of a promise (not performance), and the contract is formed when the promise is made (rather than when the act is performed). Communication of acceptance is not necessary if the offer dispenses with the requirement, however, or if the offer can be accepted by silence.[9]

Because a unilateral contract calls for the full performance of some act, acceptance is usually evident, and notification is unnecessary. Nevertheless, exceptions do exist, such as when the offeror requests notice of acceptance or has no way of determining whether the requested act has been performed.

In the following case, the court had to decide whether a party's failure to respond to a settlement offer constituted acceptance.

---

9. Under UCC 2–206(1)(b), an order or other offer to buy goods that are to be promptly shipped may be treated as either a bilateral or a unilateral offer and can be accepted by a promise to ship or by actual shipment.

Case 10.3

Powerhouse Custom Homes, Inc. v. 84 Lumber Co.

Court of Appeals of Georgia, 307 Ga.App. 605, 705 S.E.2d 704 (2011).

(gmnicholas/iStockphoto.com)

A custom home being built.

FACTS Powerhouse Custom Homes, Inc., entered into a credit agreement with 84 Lumber Company under which Powerhouse owed $95,260.42. When Powerhouse failed to pay, 84 Lumber filed a suit to collect. During mediation, the parties agreed to a deadline for objections to whatever agreement they might reach. If there was no objection, the agreement would be binding. Powerhouse then offered to pay less than the amount owed, and 84 Lumber did not respond. Powerhouse argued that 84 Lumber accepted the offer by not objecting to it within the deadline.

ISSUE Did 84 Lumber, by its failure to object to Powerhouse's proposal to settle the debt for less than was owed, unequivocally accept the offer?

DECISION No. The court held that for a contract to be formed, an offer must be accepted unequivocally. Without such an acceptance, there is no enforceable contract.

REASON Powerhouse made an offer of a proposed settlement, but 84 Lumber did not communicate its acceptance. Thus, the court reasoned that the parties did not reach an agreement. Because 84 Lumber had not agreed to Powerhouse's proposal, the ten-day deadline did not apply. Powerhouse was liable for the entire debt, plus interest, attorneys' fees, and costs.

CRITICAL THINKING—Economic Consideration *Why do judgments often include awards of interest, attorneys' fees, and costs?*

Mode and Timeliness of Acceptance

Acceptance in bilateral contracts must be timely. The general rule is that acceptance in a bilateral contract is timely if it is made before the offer is terminated. Problems may arise, though, when the parties involved are not dealing face to face. In such situations, the offeree should use an authorized mode of communication.

Mailbox Rule A common law rule that acceptance takes effect, and thus completes formation of the contract, at the time the offeree sends or delivers the acceptance via the communication mode expressly or impliedly authorized by the offeror.

The Mailbox Rule

Acceptance takes effect, and thus completes formation of the contract, at the time the offeree sends or delivers the acceptance via the mode of communication expressly or impliedly authorized by the offeror. This is the so-called **mailbox rule,** also called the *deposited acceptance rule,* which the majority of courts follow. Under this rule, if the authorized mode of communication is the mail, then an acceptance becomes valid when it is dispatched (placed in the control of the U.S. Postal Service)—not when it is received by the offeror.

The mailbox rule does not apply to instantaneous forms of communication, such as when the parties are dealing face to face, by phone, by fax, and usually by e-mail. Under the Uniform Electronic Transactions Act (UETA—see page 273 later in this chapter), e-mail is considered sent when it either leaves the sender's control or is received by the recipient. This rule, which takes the place of the mailbox rule if the parties have agreed to conduct transactions electronically, allows an e-mail acceptance to become effective when sent.

Authorized Means of Communication

A means of communicating acceptance can be expressly authorized by the offeror or impliedly authorized by the facts and circumstances of the situation. An acceptance sent by means not expressly or impliedly authorized normally is not effective until it is received by the offeror.

When an offeror specifies how acceptance should be made, such as by overnight delivery, the contract is not formed unless the offeree uses that mode of acceptance. Both the offeror and the offeree are bound in contract the moment the specified means of acceptance is employed. **EXAMPLE 10.15** Motorola Mobility, Inc., offers to sell 144 Atrix 4G smartphones and 72 Lapdocks to Call Me Plus phone stores. The offer states that Call Me Plus must accept the offer via FedEx overnight delivery. The acceptance is effective (and a binding contract is formed) the moment that Call Me Plus gives the overnight envelope containing the acceptance to the FedEx driver. •

If the offeror does not expressly authorize a certain mode of acceptance, then acceptance can be made by *any reasonable means.*[10] Courts look at the prevailing business usages and the surrounding circumstances to determine whether the mode of acceptance used was reasonable. Usually, the offeror's choice of a particular means in making the offer implies that the offeree can use the *same or a faster* means for acceptance. **EXAMPLE 10.16** If the offer is made via Priority U.S. mail, it would be reasonable to accept the offer via Priority mail or by a faster method, such as e-mail, fax, or overnight delivery. •

Substitute Method of Acceptance

If the offeror authorizes a particular method of acceptance, but the offeree accepts by a different means, the acceptance may still be effective if the substituted method serves the same purpose as the authorized means. The use of a substitute method of acceptance is not effective on dispatch, though, and no contract will be formed until the acceptance is received by the offeror. Thus, if an offer specifies FedEx overnight delivery but the offeree accepts by overnight delivery from another carrier, such as UPS, the acceptance will still be effective, but not until the offeror receives it.

---

10. Note that UCC 2–206(1)(a) states specifically that an acceptance of an offer for the sale of goods can be made by any medium that is *reasonable* under the circumstances.

E-Contracts

Numerous contracts are formed online. Electronic contracts, or **e-contracts,** must meet the same basic requirements (agreement, consideration, contractual capacity, and legality) as paper contracts. Disputes concerning e-contracts, however, tend to center on contract terms and whether the parties voluntarily agreed to those terms.

Online contracts may be formed not only for the sale of goods and services but also for *licensing.* The "sale" of software generally involves a license, or a right to use the software, rather than the passage of title (ownership rights) from the seller to the buyer. **EXAMPLE 10.17** Galynn wants to obtain software that will allow her to work on spreadsheets on her BlackBerry. She goes online and purchases GridMagic. During the transaction, she has to click on several on-screen "I agree" boxes to indicate that she understands that she is purchasing only the right to use the software and will not obtain any ownership rights. After she agrees to these terms (the licensing agreement), she can download the software. ●

As you read through the following subsections, keep in mind that although we typically refer to the offeror and the offeree as a *seller* and a *buyer,* in many online transactions these parties would be more accurately described as a *licensor* and a *licensee.*

Online Offers

Sellers doing business via the Internet can protect themselves against contract disputes and legal liability by creating offers that clearly spell out the terms that will govern their transactions if the offers are accepted. All important terms should be conspicuous and easy to view.

Displaying the Offer
The seller's Web site should include a hypertext link to a page containing the full contract so that potential buyers are made aware of the terms to which they are assenting. The contract generally must be displayed online in a readable format such as in a twelve-point typeface.

All provisions should be reasonably clear. **EXAMPLE 10.18** Netquip sells a variety of heavy equipment, such as trucks and trailers, online at its Web site. Because Netquip's pricing schedule is very complex, the schedule must be fully provided and explained on the Web site. In addition, the terms of the sale (such as any warranties and the refund policy) must be fully disclosed. ●

Provisions to Include
An important rule to keep in mind is that the offeror (seller) controls the offer and thus the resulting contract. The seller should therefore anticipate the terms she or he wants to include in a contract and provide for them in the offer. In some instances, a standardized contract form may suffice. At a minimum, an online offer should include the following provisions:

1. *Acceptance of terms.* A clause that clearly indicates what constitutes the buyer's agreement to the terms of the offer, such as a box containing the words "I accept" that the buyer can click on to indicate acceptance. (Mechanisms for accepting online offers will be discussed in detail later in this chapter.)
2. *Payment.* A provision specifying how payment for the goods (including any applicable taxes) must be made.
3. *Return policy.* A statement of the seller's refund and return policies.
4. *Disclaimer.* Disclaimers of liability for certain uses of the goods. For example, an online seller of business forms may add a disclaimer that the seller does not accept responsibility for the buyer's reliance on the forms rather than on an attorney's advice.

5. *Limitation on remedies.* A provision specifying the remedies available to the buyer if the goods are found to be defective or if the contract is otherwise breached. Any limitation of remedies should be clearly spelled out.

6. *Privacy policy.* A statement indicating how the seller will use the information gathered about the buyer. (See the *Linking Business Law to Marketing* feature on page 276 for a discussion of how the information may be used.)

7. *Dispute resolution.* Provisions relating to dispute settlement, such as an arbitration clause.

Dispute-Settlement Provisions   Online offers frequently include provisions relating to dispute settlement. For example, the offer might include an arbitration clause specifying that any dispute arising under the contract will be arbitrated in a designated forum. (For a discussion of how students enrolling in online education courses may agree to arbitration of any future disputes, see this chapter's *Adapting the Law to the Online Environment* below.)

ADAPTING THE LAW TO THE ONLINE ENVIRONMENT

THE VALIDITY OF E-SIGNATURES ON AGREEMENTS WITH ONLINE COLLEGES AND UNIVERSITIES

The number of online institutions offering bachelor's, master's, and even doctorate degrees has grown dramatically over the past decade. The enrollment procedures for these online colleges and universities are conducted online. Most, if not all, of these schools ask enrolling students to agree that any disputes will be solved by arbitration. How valid are these enrollment agreements when the students simply indicate their assent via what the online universities call e-signatures?

At Least Two Online Students Claimed That Their E-Signatures Were Invalid

Scott Rosendahl alleged that online Ashford University's enrollment adviser misleadingly claimed that Ashford offered one of the cheapest undergraduate degree programs in the country. In fact, it did not. Veronica Clarke enrolled in the doctor of psychology program at the online University of the Rockies. She alleged that its enrollment adviser told her that the doctor of psychology program would qualify her to become a clinical psychologist in the U.S. military, but that statement was false.

Rosendahl and Clarke sued their respective universities for violation of unfair competition laws and false advertising laws, fraud, and negligent misrepresentation.

The Online Universities Argued for Arbitration

The universities pointed out that each student electronically agreed to the enrollment agreement that clearly contained a requirement that all disputes be arbitrated. Each agreement stated, "Such arbitration shall be the sole remedy for the resolution of any dispute or controversies between the parties to this agreement."

One issue was whether the e-signatures on the agreement were valid. Each application form had an "acknowledgment and signature" paragraph that stated, "My signature on this application certifies that I have read, understood, and agreed to my rights and responsibilities as set forth in this application."

Both students had to click on an electronic box acknowledging that they had read the agreement and consented to it. When they clicked on the box, the phrase "Signed by E-Signature" appeared on the signature line.

The Court Ruled in Favor of the Online Universities

The universities submitted copies of Rosendahl's and Clarke's online application forms to the court. Both forms contained the arbitration agreement and were signed with e-signatures. Rosendahl and Clarke provided no proof that they did not consent to the enrollment agreements. Thus, the court held that the online universities had proved the existence of valid arbitration agreements.[a]

Critical Thinking

Did the fact that the arbitration agreements were valid prevent Rosendahl and Clarke from pursuing their claims for negligent misrepresentation and fraud? Why or why not?

a. *Rosendahl v. Bridgepoint Education, Inc.,* 2012 WL 667049 (S.D.Cal. 2012).

Many online contracts also contain a *forum-selection clause* (see page 221 in Chapter 8) indicating the forum, or location (such as a court or jurisdiction), for the resolution of any dispute arising under the contract. As discussed in Chapter 3 on page 68, significant jurisdictional issues may occur when parties are at a great distance, as they often are when they form contracts via the Internet. A forum-selection clause will help to avert future jurisdictional problems and also help to ensure that the seller will not be required to appear in court in a distant state.

Some online contracts may also include a *choice-of-law clause* specifying that any dispute arising out of the contract will be settled in accordance with the law of a particular jurisdiction, such as a state or country. Choice-of-law clauses are particularly common in international contracts, but they may also appear in e-contracts to specify which state's laws will govern in the United States.

Online Acceptances

The *Restatement (Second) of Contracts*—a compilation of common law contract principles—states that parties may agree to a contract "by written or spoken words or by other action or by failure to act."[11] The Uniform Commercial Code (UCC), which governs sales contracts, has a similar provision. Section 2–204 of the UCC states that any contract for the sale of goods "may be made in any manner sufficient to show agreement, including conduct by both parties which recognizes the existence of such a contract."

Click-On Agreement An agreement that arises when an online buyer clicks on "I agree," or otherwise indicates her or his assent to be bound by the terms of an offer.

Click-On Agreements
The courts have used these provisions to conclude that a binding contract can be created by conduct, including the act of clicking on a box indicating "I accept" or "I agree" to accept an online offer. The agreement resulting from such an acceptance is often called a **click-on agreement** (sometimes, *click-on license* or *click-wrap agreement*). Exhibit 10.1 on the facing page shows a portion of a click-on agreement that accompanies a software package.

Generally, the law does not require that the parties have read all of the terms in a contract for it to be effective. Therefore, clicking on a box that states "I agree" to certain terms can be enough. The terms may be contained on a Web site through which the buyer is obtaining goods or services, or they may appear on a computer screen when software is loaded from a CD-ROM or DVD or downloaded from the Internet.

LEARNING OBJECTIVE 4
How do shrink-wrap and click-on agreements differ from other contracts? How have traditional laws been applied to these agreements?

CASE EXAMPLE 10.19 Facebook, Inc., is headquartered in California. The "Terms of Use" that govern Facebook users' accounts include a forum-selection clause that provides for the resolution of all disputes in a court in Santa Clara County. Potential Facebook users cannot become actual users unless they click on an acknowledgment that they have agreed to this term. Mustafa Fteja was an active user of facebook.com when his account was disabled. He sued Facebook in a federal court in New York, claiming that it had disabled his Facebook page without justification and for discriminatory reasons. Facebook filed a motion to transfer the case to California under the forum-selection clause. The court found that the forum-selection clause in Facebook's online contract was binding and transferred the case. Fteja had been informed of the consequences of his click—he would be bound to the forum-selection clause. When he clicked on the button and became a Facebook user, he agreed to resolve all disputes with Facebook in Santa Clara County, California.[12] ●

Shrink-Wrap Agreement An agreement whose terms are expressed in a document located inside a box in which goods (usually software) are packaged.

Shrink-Wrap Agreements
A **shrink-wrap agreement** (or *shrink-wrap license*) is an agreement whose terms are expressed inside a box in which the goods are packaged. (The term *shrink-wrap* refers to the plastic that covers the box.) Usually, the party who opens the box is told that she or he agrees to the terms by keeping whatever is in the box. Similarly, when the purchaser opens a software package, he or she agrees to abide by the terms of the limited license agreement.

11. *Restatement (Second) of Contracts*, Section 19.
12. *Fteja v. Facebook, Inc.*, 841 F.Supp.2d 829 (S.D.N.Y. 2012).

Exhibit 10.1 A Click-On Agreement

This exhibit illustrates an online offer to form a contract. To accept the offer, the user simply scrolls down the page and clicks on the "I Accept" button.

EXAMPLE 10.20 Arial orders a new iMac from Big Dog Electronics, which ships it to her. Along with the iMac, the box contains an agreement setting forth the terms of the sale, including what remedies are available. The document also states that Arial's retention of the iMac for longer than thirty days will be construed as an acceptance of the terms. •

In most instances, a shrink-wrap agreement is not between a retailer and a buyer, but between the manufacturer of the hardware or software and the ultimate buyer-user of the product. The terms generally concern warranties, remedies, and other issues associated with the use of the product.

Shrink-Wrap Agreements and Enforceable Contract Terms In some cases, the courts have enforced the terms of shrink-wrap agreements in the same way as the terms of other contracts. These courts have reasoned that by including the terms with the product, the seller proposed a contract that the buyer could accept by using the product after having an opportunity to read the terms. Thus, a buyer's failure to object to terms contained within a shrink-wrapped software package may constitute an acceptance of the terms by conduct.

Shrink-Wrap Terms That May Not Be Enforced Sometimes, however, courts have refused to enforce certain terms included in shrink-wrap agreements because the buyer did not expressly consent to them. An important factor is when the parties form their contract.

Suppose that a buyer orders a product over the telephone. If the contract is formed at that time and the seller does not mention terms such as an arbitration clause or forum-selection clause, clearly the buyer has not expressly agreed to these terms. If the clauses are then included in the shrink-wrap agreement, a court may conclude that those terms were only proposals for additional terms, and not part of the original contract. After all, the buyer did not discover them until *after* the contract was formed.

ETHICAL ISSUE

Is it fair to enforce shrink-wrap and click-wrap terms that buyers were not aware of at the time they agreed to a purchase? Most people realize that if they sign a written contract without reading it, they can be held to its terms. But are most people aware that they can be legally bound by a whole host of conditions included in the packaging of electronics or software, not to mention the music, movies, and software they download from the Web? Simply by buying and keeping the latest electronic gadgets, we enter into binding contracts with the manufacturers that include rather one-sided terms. The terms may be unfair, but the law says we are bound. For instance, just by installing or downloading certain software today, users routinely agree to allow the companies to install tracking software on their computers.

Moreover, many software programs—including some that are designed to combat *malware* (see Chapter 6 on page 182)—automatically delete files from the users' hard drives. Consumers and businesspersons are often unaware of these consequences, and yet by buying and installing the software, they have agreed that they will not hold the manufacturer liable.

Browse-Wrap Term A term or condition of use that is presented when an online buyer downloads a product but the buyer does not have to agree to before installing or using the product.

Browse-Wrap Terms Like the terms of a click-on agreement, **browse-wrap terms** can occur in a transaction conducted over the Internet. Unlike a click-on agreement, however, browse-wrap terms do not require the buyer or user to assent to the terms before, say, downloading or using certain software. In other words, a person can install the software without clicking "I agree" to the terms of a license. Browse-wrap terms are often unenforceable because they do not satisfy the agreement requirement of contract formation.[13]

E-Signature Technologies

E-Signature An electronic sound, symbol, or process attached to or logically associated with a record and adopted by a person with the intent to sign the record.

Today, numerous technologies allow electronic documents to be signed. An **e-signature** has been defined as "an electronic sound, symbol, or process attached to or logically associated with a record and executed or adopted by a person with the intent to sign the record."[14] Thus, e-signatures include encrypted digital signatures, names (intended as signatures) at the ends of e-mail messages, and "clicks" on a Web page if the click includes the identification of the person.

Federal Law on E-Signatures and E-Documents

In 2000, Congress enacted the Electronic Signatures in Global and National Commerce Act (E-SIGN Act),[15] which provides that no contract, record, or signature may be "denied legal effect" solely because it is in electronic form. In other words, under this law, an electronic signature is as valid as a signature on paper, and an e-document can be as enforceable as a paper one.

For an e-signature to be enforceable, the contracting parties must have agreed to use electronic signatures. For an electronic document to be valid, it must be in a form that can be retained and accurately reproduced.

The E-SIGN Act does not apply to all types of documents, however. Contracts and documents that are exempt include court papers, divorce decrees, evictions, foreclosures, health-insurance terminations, prenuptial agreements, and wills. Also, the only agreements governed by the UCC that fall under this law are those covered by Articles 2 and 2A and UCC 1–107 and 1–206. Despite these limitations, the E-SIGN Act significantly expanded the possibilities for contracting online.

Many e-signatures are legally binding today.

Partnering Agreements

Partnering Agreement An agreement between a seller and a buyer who frequently do business with each other concerning the terms and conditions that will apply to all subsequently formed electronic contracts.

One way that online sellers and buyers can prevent disputes over signatures in their e-contracts, as well as disputes over the terms and conditions of those contracts, is to form partnering agreements. In a **partnering agreement,** a seller and a buyer who frequently do business with each other agree in advance on the terms and conditions that will apply to all transactions subsequently conducted electronically. The partnering agreement can also establish special access and identification codes to be used by the parties when transacting business electronically.

A partnering agreement reduces the likelihood that disputes will arise under the contract because the buyer and the seller have agreed in advance to the terms and conditions that will accompany each sale. Furthermore, if a dispute does arise, a court or arbitration forum will be able to refer to the partnering agreement when determining the parties' intent.

The Uniform Electronic Transactions Act

Although most states have laws governing e-signatures and other aspects of electronic transactions, these laws are far from uniform. In an attempt to create more uniformity among the states, in 1999 the National Conference of Commissioners on Uniform State

---

13. See, for example, *Jesmer v. Retail Magic, Inc.,* 863 N.Y.S.2d 737 (2008).
14. This definition is from the Uniform Electronic Transactions Act on page 273.
15. 15 U.S.C. Sections 7001 *et seq.*

Laws and the American Law Institute promulgated the Uniform Electronic Transactions Act (UETA). The UETA has been adopted, at least in part, by forty-eight states.

The primary purpose of the UETA is to remove barriers to e-commerce by giving the same legal effect to electronic records and signatures as is given to paper documents and signatures. As mentioned earlier, the UETA broadly defines an *e-signature* as "an electronic sound, symbol, or process attached to or logically associated with a record and executed or adopted by a person with the intent to sign the record."[16] A **record** is "information that is inscribed on a tangible medium or that is stored in an electronic or other medium and is retrievable in perceivable [visual] form."[17]

Record Information that is either inscribed on a tangible medium or stored in an electronic or other medium and is retrievable.

The Scope and Applicability of the UETA

LEARNING OBJECTIVE 5
What is the Uniform Electronic Transactions Act? What are some of the major provisions of this act?

The UETA does not create new rules for electronic contracts but rather establishes that records, signatures, and contracts may not be denied enforceability solely due to their electronic form. The UETA does not apply to all writings and signatures. It covers only electronic records and electronic signatures *relating to a transaction*. A *transaction* is defined as an interaction between two or more parties relating to business, commercial, or governmental activities.[18]

The act specifically does not apply to wills or testamentary trusts or to transactions governed by the UCC (other than those covered by Articles 2 and 2A).[19] In addition, the provisions of the UETA allow the states to exclude its application to other areas of law.

The Federal E-SIGN Act and the UETA

When Congress passed the E-SIGN Act in 2000, a year after the UETA was presented to the states for adoption, a significant issue was to what extent the federal E-SIGN Act preempted the UETA as adopted by the states. The E-SIGN Act[20] refers explicitly to the UETA and provides that if a state has enacted the uniform version of the UETA, it is not preempted by the E-SIGN Act. In other words, if the state has enacted the UETA without modification, state law will govern.

The problem is that many states have enacted nonuniform (modified) versions of the UETA, largely for the purpose of excluding other areas of state law from the UETA's terms. The E-SIGN Act specifies that those exclusions will be preempted to the extent that they are inconsistent with the E-SIGN Act's provisions.

The E-SIGN Act, however, explicitly allows the states to enact alternative requirements for the use of electronic records or electronic signatures. Generally, however, the requirements must be consistent with the provisions of the E-SIGN Act, and the state must not give greater legal status or effect to one specific type of technology. Additionally, if a state enacts alternative requirements *after* the E-SIGN Act was adopted, the state law must specifically refer to the E-SIGN Act.

The relationship between the E-SIGN Act and the UETA is illustrated in Exhibit 10.2 on the following page.

Highlights of the UETA

The UETA will not apply to a transaction unless each of the parties has previously agreed to conduct transactions by electronic means. The agreement need not be explicit, however, and it may be implied by the conduct of the parties and the surrounding circumstances.[21]

---

16. UETA 102(8).
17. UETA 102(15).
18. UETA 2(12) and 3.
19. UETA 3(b).
20. 15 U.S.C. Section 7002(2)(A)(i).
21. UETA 5(b).

Exhibit 10.2 The E-SIGN Act and the UETA

THE UNIFORM ELECTRONIC TRANSACTIONS ACT (UETA)

The UETA is enacted **WITHOUT MODIFICATIONS**

The UETA is enacted **WITH MODIFICATIONS**

State law governs

State law governs if—
- The state's procedures or requirements are consistent with the E-SIGN Act.
- The state does not give priority to one type of technology.
- The state law was enacted after the E-SIGN Act and refers to it.

The E-SIGN Act governs if—
- The modifications are inconsistent with the E-SIGN Act.

It may be reasonable to infer that a person who gives out a business card with an e-mail address on it has consented to transact business electronically.[22] The party's agreement may also be inferred from a letter or other writing, as well as from some verbal communication. A person who has previously agreed to an electronic transaction can also withdraw his or her consent and refuse to conduct further business electronically.

Attribution Under the UETA, if an electronic record or signature is the act of a particular person, the record or signature may be attributed to that person. If a person types her or his name at the bottom of an e-mail purchase order, that name will qualify as a "signature" and be attributed to the person whose name appears. In some contexts, a record may have legal effect even if no one has signed it. **EXAMPLE 10.21** J. P. Darby sends a fax to Corina Scott. The fax contains a letterhead identifying Darby as the sender, but Darby's signature does not appear on the faxed document. Depending on the circumstances, the fax may be attributed to Darby. •

Authorized Signatures The UETA does not contain any express provisions about what constitutes fraud or whether an agent is authorized to enter a contract. Under the UETA, other state laws control if any issues relating to agency, authority, forgery, or contract formation arise. If existing state law requires a document to be notarized, the UETA provides that this requirement is satisfied by the electronic signature of a notary public or other person authorized to verify signatures.

The Effect of Errors The UETA encourages, but does not require, the use of security procedures (such as encryption) to verify changes to electronic documents and to

---

22. UETA 5, Comment 4B.

correct errors. If the parties have agreed to a security procedure and one party does not detect an error because he or she did not follow the procedure, the conforming party can legally avoid the effect of the change or error. To avoid the effect of errors, a party must promptly notify the other party of the error and of her or his intent not to be bound by the error. In addition, the party must take reasonable steps to return any benefit received. Parties cannot avoid a transaction if they have benefited.

Timing   An electronic record is considered *sent* when it is properly directed to the intended recipient in a form readable by the recipient's computer system. Once the electronic record leaves the control of the sender or comes under the control of the recipient, the UETA deems it to have been sent. An electronic record is considered *received* when it enters the recipient's processing system in a readable form—*even if no individual is aware of its receipt.*

Reviewing . . . Agreement in Traditional and E-Contracts

Ted and Betty Hyatt live in California, a state that has extensive statutory protection for consumers. The Hyatts decided to buy a computer so that they could use e-mail to stay in touch with their grandchildren, who live in another state. Over the phone, they ordered a computer from CompuEdge, Inc. When the box arrived, it was sealed with a brightly colored sticker warning that the terms enclosed within the box would govern the sale unless the customer returned the computer within thirty days. Among those terms was a clause that required any disputes to be resolved in Tennessee state courts. The Hyatts then signed up for Internet service through CyberTool, an Internet service provider. They downloaded CyberTool's software and clicked on the "quick install" box that allowed them to bypass CyberTool's "Terms of Service" page. It was possible to read this page by scrolling to the next screen, but the Hyatts did not realize this. The terms included a clause stating that all disputes were to be submitted to a Virginia state court. As soon as the Hyatts attempted to e-mail their grandchildren, they experienced problems using CyberTool's e-mail service, which continually stated that the network was busy. They also were unable to receive the photos sent by their grandchildren. Using the information presented in the chapter, answer the following questions.

1. Did the Hyatts accept the list of contract terms included in the computer box? Why or why not? What is this type of e-contract called?
2. What type of agreement did the Hyatts form with CyberTool?
3. Suppose that the Hyatts experienced trouble with the computer's components after they had used the computer for two months. What factors will a court consider in deciding whether to enforce the forum-selection clause? Would a court be likely to enforce the clause in this contract? Why or why not?
4. Are the Hyatts bound by the contract terms specified on CyberTool's "Terms of Service" page that they did not read? Which of the required elements for contract formation might the Hyatts claim were lacking? How might a court rule on this issue?

DEBATE THIS   The terms and conditions in click-on agreements are so long and detailed that no one ever reads the agreement. Therefore, the act of clicking on "Yes, I agree" is not really an acceptance.

LINKING BUSINESS LAW to Marketing

Customer Relationship Management

As you learned in this chapter, increasingly the contracting process is moving online. Large and small e-commerce Web sites offer to sell millions of goods and services. The vast amount of data collected from online shoppers has pushed *customer relationship management* (CRM) to the fore. CRM is a marketing strategy that allows companies to acquire information about customers' wants, needs, and behaviors. The companies can then use that information to build customer relationships and loyalty. The focus of CRM is understanding customers as individuals rather than simply as a group of consumers. As Exhibit 10.3 shows, CRM is a closed system that uses feedback from customers to build relationships with those customers.

Two Examples—Netflix and Amazon

If you are a customer of Netflix.com, you choose Blu-ray discs and DVDs that are sent to you by mail or streamed online based on your individual tastes and preferences. Netflix asks you to rate movies you have rented (or even seen in theaters) on a scale of one to five stars. Using a computer algorithm, Netflix then creates an individualized rating system that predicts how you will rate thousands of different movies. As you rate more movies, the predictive reliability becomes more accurate. By applying your individual rating system to movies you have not seen, Netflix is able to suggest movies that you might like.

Amazon.com uses similar technology to recommend books and music that you might wish to buy. Amazon sends out numerous "personalized" e-mails to its customers with suggestions based on those customers' individual buying habits.

Thus, CRM allows both Netflix and Amazon to use a focused marketing effort, rather than the typical shotgun approach used by spam advertising on the Internet.

CRM in Online versus Traditional Companies

For online companies such as Amazon and Netflix, all customer information has some value because the cost of obtaining it, analyzing it, and utilizing it is so small. In contrast, traditional companies often must use a different process that is much more costly to obtain data to be used for CRM. An automobile company, for

Exhibit 10.3 A Customer Relationship Management Cycle

example, obtains customer information from a variety of sources, including dealers, customer surveys, online inquiries, and the like. Integrating, storing, and managing such information generally makes CRM much more expensive for traditional companies than for online companies.

Critical Thinking

Online companies such as Amazon not only target individual customers but also utilize each customer's buying habits to create generalized marketing campaigns. Might any privacy issues arise as an online company creates a database to be used for generalized marketing campaigns?

Key Terms

acceptance 265	counteroffer 264	mirror image rule 264	record 273
agreement 258	e-contract 268	offer 258	revocation 263
browse-wrap term 271	e-signature 272	option contract 265	shrink-wrap agreement 270
click-on agreement 270	mailbox rule 267	partnering agreement 272	

Chapter Summary: Agreement in Traditional and E-Contracts

Requirements of the Offer (See pages 258–263.)	1. *Intent*—There must be a serious, objective intention by the offeror to become bound by the offer. Nonoffer situations include (a) expressions of opinion; (b) statements of future intent; (c) preliminary negotiations; (d) generally, advertisements, catalogues, price lists, and circulars; and (e) traditionally, agreements to agree in the future. 2. *Definiteness*—The terms of the offer must be sufficiently definite to be ascertainable by the parties or by a court. 3. *Communication*—The offer must be communicated to the offeree.

Termination of the Offer
(See pages 263–265.)
	1. *By action of the parties*—
	  a. Revocation—Unless the offer is irrevocable, it can be revoked at any time before acceptance without liability. Revocation is not effective until received by the offeree or the offeree's agent. Some offers, such as a merchant's firm offer and option contracts, are irrevocable.
	  b. Rejection—Accomplished by words or actions that demonstrate a clear intent not to accept the offer. A rejection is not effective until it is received by the offeror or the offeror's agent.
	  c. Counteroffer—A rejection of the original offer and the making of a new offer.
	2. *By operation of law*—
	  a. Lapse of time—The offer terminates (1) at the end of the time period specified in the offer or (2) if no time period is stated in the offer, at the end of a reasonable time period.
	  b. Destruction of the specific subject matter of the offer—Automatically terminates the offer.
	  c. Death or incompetence of the offeror or offeree—Terminates the offer unless the offer is irrevocable.
	  d. Illegality—Supervening illegality terminates the offer.

Acceptance (See pages 265–267.)	1. Can be made only by the offeree or the offeree's agent. 2. Must be unequivocal. Under the common law (mirror image rule), if new terms or conditions are added to the acceptance, it will be considered a counteroffer. 3. Acceptance of a unilateral offer is effective on full performance of the requested act. Generally, no communication is necessary. 4. Except in a few situations, an offeree's silence does not constitute an acceptance. 5. Acceptance of a bilateral offer can be communicated by the offeree by any authorized mode of communication and is effective on dispatch. If the offeror does not specify the mode of communication, acceptance can be made by any reasonable means. Usually, the same means used by the offeror or a faster means can be used.
Online Offers (See pages 268–270.)	The terms of contract offers presented via the Internet should be as inclusive as the terms in an offer made in a written (paper) document. The offer should be displayed in an easily readable format and should include some mechanism, such as an "I agree" or "I accept" box, by which the customer may accept the offer. Because jurisdictional issues frequently arise with online transactions, the offer should include dispute-settlement provisions, as well as a forum-selection clause.

Online Acceptances
(See pages 270–272.)
	1. *Click-on agreement*—
	  a. Definition—An agreement created when a buyer, completing a transaction on a computer, is required to indicate her or his assent to be bound by the terms of an offer by clicking on a box that says, for example, "I agree." The terms of the agreement may appear on the Web site through which the buyer is obtaining goods or services, or they may appear on a computer screen when software is downloaded.
	  b. Enforceability—The courts have enforced click-on agreements, holding that by clicking on "I agree," the offeree has indicated acceptance by conduct. Browse-wrap terms (terms in a license that an Internet user does not have to read prior to downloading the product, such as software), however, may not be enforced on the ground that the user is not made aware that he or she is entering into a contract.
	2. *Shrink-wrap agreement*—
	  a. Definition—An agreement whose terms are expressed inside a box in which the goods are packaged. The party who opens the box is informed that, by keeping the goods that are in the box, he or she agrees to the terms of the shrink-wrap agreement.
	  b. Enforceability—The courts have often enforced shrink-wrap agreements, even if the purchaser-user of the goods did not read the terms of the agreement. A court may deem a shrink-wrap agreement unenforceable, however, if the buyer learns of the shrink-wrap terms after the parties entered into the agreement.

E-Signatures (See page 272.)	The Uniform Electronic Transactions Act (UETA) defines an e-signature as "an electronic sound, symbol, or process attached to or logically associated with a record and executed or adopted by a person with the intent to sign the record." 1. *E-signatures*—E-signatures may include encrypted digital signatures, names at the ends of e-mail messages, and clicks on a Web page.

Continued

Chapter Summary: Agreement in Traditional and E-Contracts— Continued

E-Signatures — Continued	2. *Federal law on e-signatures and e-documents*—The Electronic Signatures in Global and National Commerce Act (E-SIGN Act) of 2000 gave validity to e-signatures by providing that no contract, record, or signature may be "denied legal effect" solely because it is in an electronic form.
The Uniform Electronic Transactions Act (UETA) (See pages 272–275.)	This uniform act has been adopted, at least in part, by most states, to create rules to support the enforcement of e-contracts. 1. *Scope and applicability*—Under the UETA, contracts entered into online, as well as other documents, are presumed to be valid. The UETA does not apply to certain transactions governed by the UCC or to wills or testamentary trusts. 2. *State laws governing e-signatures*—Although most states have laws governing e-signatures, these laws are not uniform. The UETA provides for the validity of e-signatures and may ultimately create more uniformity among the states in this respect.

ExamPrep

ISSUE SPOTTERS

1. Fidelity Corporation offers to hire Ron to replace Monica, who has given Fidelity a month's notice of intent to quit. Fidelity gives Ron a week to decide whether to accept. Two days later, Monica decides not to quit and signs an employment contract with Fidelity for another year. The next day, Monica tells Ron of the new contract. Ron immediately faxes a formal letter of acceptance to Fidelity. Do Fidelity and Ron have a contract? Why or why not? **(See page 263.)**

2. Applied Products, Inc., does business with Beltway Distributors, Inc., online. Under the Uniform Electronic Transactions Act, what determines the effect of the electronic documents evidencing the parties' deal? Is a party's "signature" necessary? Explain. **(See pages 272–275.)**

—Check your answers to the Issue Spotters against the answers provided in Appendix E at the end of this text.

BEFORE THE TEST

Go to www.cengagebrain.com, enter the ISBN 9781133273561 and click on "Find" to locate this textbook's Web site. Then, click on "Access Now" under "Study Tools," and select Chapter 10 at the top. There, you will find a Practice Quiz that you can take to assess your mastery of the concepts in this chapter, as well as Flashcards, a Glossary of important terms, and Video Questions (when assigned).

For Review

Answers to the even-numbered questions in this For Review section can be found in Appendix F at the end of this text.

1. What elements are necessary for an effective offer? What are some examples of nonoffers?
2. In what circumstances will an offer be irrevocable?
3. What are the elements that are necessary for an effective acceptance?
4. How do shrink-wrap and click-on agreements differ from other contracts? How have traditional laws been applied to these agreements?
5. What is the Uniform Electronic Transactions Act? What are some of the major provisions of this act?

Business Scenarios and Case Problems

10–1 Agreement. Ball writes to Sullivan and inquires how much Sullivan is asking for a specific forty-acre tract of land Sullivan owns. Ball then receives a letter from Sullivan stating, "I will not take less than $60,000 for the forty-acre tract as specified." Ball immediately sends Sullivan a fax stating, "I accept your offer for $60,000 for the forty-acre tract as specified." Discuss whether Ball can hold Sullivan to a contract for sale of the land. **(See page 258.)**

10–2 Online Acceptance. Anne is a reporter for *Daily Business Journal,* a print publication consulted by investors and other businesspersons. She often uses the Internet to perform research for the articles that she writes for the publication. While visiting the Web site of Cyberspace Investments Corp., Anne reads a pop-up window that states, "Our business newsletter, *E-Commerce Weekly,* is available at a one-year subscription rate of $5 per issue. To subscribe, enter your e-mail address below and click 'SUBSCRIBE.' By subscribing, you agree to the terms of the subscriber's agreement. To read this agreement, click 'AGREEMENT.' " Anne enters her e-mail address but does not click on "AGREEMENT" to read the terms. Has Anne entered into an enforceable contract to pay for *E-Commerce Weekly*? Explain. **(See page 270.)**

10–3 🔮 **Question with Sample Answer—Acceptances.** Chernek, the sole owner of a small business, has a large piece of used farm equipment for sale. He offers to sell the equipment to Bollow for $10,000. Discuss the legal effects of the following events on the offer. **(See page 264.)**
1. Chernek dies prior to Bollow's acceptance, and at the time she accepts, Bollow is unaware of Chernek's death.
2. The night before Bollow accepts, a fire destroys the equipment.
3. Bollow pays $100 for a thirty-day option to purchase the equipment. During this period, Chernek dies, and Bollow accepts the offer, knowing of Chernek's death.
4. Bollow pays $100 for a thirty-day option to purchase the equipment. During this period, Bollow dies, and Bollow's estate accepts Chernek's offer within the stipulated time period.

—For a sample answer to Question 10–3, go to Appendix G at the end of this text.

10–4 Shrink-Wrap Agreements. TracFone Wireless, Inc., sells phones and wireless service. The phones are sold for less than their cost, which TracFone recoups by selling prepaid airtime for their use on its network. Software in the phones prohibits their use on other networks. The phones are sold subject to the condition that the buyer agrees "not to tamper with or alter the software." This is printed on the packaging. Bequator Corp. bought at least 18,616 of the phones, disabled the software so that they could be used on other networks, and resold them. Is Bequator liable for breach of contract? Explain. [*TracFone Wireless, Inc. v. Bequator Corp.,* __ F.Supp.2d __ (S.D.Fla. 2011)] **(See pages 270–271.)**

10–5 🗣 **Spotlight on Crime Stoppers—Communication.** The Baton Rouge Crime Stoppers (BCS) offered a reward for information about the "South Louisiana Serial Killer." The information was to be provided via a hot line. Dianne Alexander had survived an attack by a person suspected of being the killer. She identified a suspect in a police photo lineup and later sought to collect the reward. BCS refused to pay because she did not provide information to them via the hot line. Did Alexander comply with the terms of the offer? Explain. [*Alexander v. Lafayette Crime Stoppers, Inc.,* 38 So.3d 282 (La.App. 3 Dist. 2010) **(See pages 266–267.)**

10–6 ⚖ **Case Problem with Sample Answer— Acceptance.** Troy Blackford smashed a slot machine while he was gambling at Prairie Meadows Casino. He was banned from the premises. Despite the ban, he later gambled at the casino and won $9,387. When he tried to collect his winnings, the casino refused to pay. He filed a suit for breach of contract, arguing that he and the casino had a contract because he had accepted its offer to gamble. Is there a contract between the casino and Blackford? Discuss. [*Blackford v. Prairie Meadows Racetrack and Casino,* 778 N.W.2d 184 (Iowa 2010)] **(See page 265.)**

—For a sample answer to Problem 10–6, go to Appendix H at the end of this text.

10–7 Online Acceptances. Heather Reasonover opted to try Internet service from Clearwire Corp. Clearwire sent her a confirmation e-mail that included a link to its Web site. Clearwire also sent her a modem. In the enclosed written materials, at the bottom of a page, in small type was the Web site URL. When Reasonover plugged in the modem, an "I accept terms" box appeared. Without clicking on the box, Reasonover quit the page. A clause in Clearwire's "Terms of Service," accessible only through its Web site, required its subscribers to submit any dispute to arbitration. Is Reasonover bound to this clause? Why or why not? [*Kwan v. Clearwire Corp.,* 2012 WL 32380 (W.D.Wash. 2012)] **(See page 270.)**

10–8 ⬌ **A Question of Ethics—Dispute-Settlement Provisions.** Dewayne Hubbert, Elden Craft, Chris Grout, and Rhonda Byington bought computers from Dell Corp. through its Web site. Before buying, Hubbert and the others configured their own computers. To make a purchase, each buyer completed forms on five Web pages. On each page, Dell's "Terms and Conditions of Sale" were accessible by clicking on a blue hyperlink. A statement on three of the pages read, "All sales are subject to Dell's Term[s] and Conditions of Sale," but a buyer was not required to click an assent to the terms to complete a purchase. The terms were also printed on the backs of the invoices and on separate documents contained in the shipping boxes with the computers. Among those terms was a "Binding Arbitration" clause.

The computers contained Pentium 4 microprocessors, which Dell advertised as the fastest, most powerful Intel Pentium processor available at that time. Hubbert and the others filed a suit in an Illinois state court against Dell, alleging that this marketing was false, misleading, and deceptive. The plaintiffs claimed that the Pentium 4 microprocessor was slower and less powerful, and provided less performance, than either a Pentium III or an AMD Athlon, and at a greater cost. Dell asked the court to compel arbitration. [*Hubbert v. Dell Corp.,* 359 Ill.App.3d 976, 835 N.E.2d 113, 296 Ill.Dec. 258 (5 Dist. 2005)] **(See pages 269–272.)**

1. Should the court enforce the arbitration clause in this case? If you were the judge, how would you rule on this issue?

2. In your opinion, do shrink-wrap, click-on, and browse-wrap terms impose too great a burden on purchasers? Why or why not?

3. An ongoing complaint about shrink-wrap, click-on, and browse-wrap terms is that sellers (often large corporations) draft them and buyers (typically individual consumers) do not read them. Should purchasers be bound in contract by terms that they have not even read? Why or why not?

Critical Thinking and Writing Assignments

10–9 **Case Analysis Question.** Go to Appendix I at the end of this text and examine the excerpt of Case No. 2, *Feldman v. Google, Inc.* Review and then brief the case, making sure that your brief answers the following questions.

1. **Issue:** The dispute between the parties to this case centered on what agreement and asked which question?

2. **Rule of Law:** What rule concerning the existence of a contract did the court apply in this case?

3. **Applying the Rule of Law:** How did the language in the parties' agreement and its context affect the application of the rule of law?

4. **Conclusion:** In whose favor did the court rule? Why?

10–10 **Business Law Critical Thinking Group Assignment.** To download a specific app to your smartphone or tablet device, you usually have to check a box indicating that you agree to the company's terms and conditions. Most individuals do so without ever reading those terms and conditions. Print out a specific set of terms and conditions from the same downloaded app to use in this assignment.

1. One group will determine which of these terms and conditions are favorable to the company.

2. Another group will determine which of these terms and conditions conceivably will be favorable to the individual.

3. A third group will determine which terms and conditions, on net, favor the company too much.

Consideration, Capacity, and Legality

(pixdeluxe/iStockphoto.com)

CHAPTER OUTLINE

- Consideration
- Promissory Estoppel
- Contractual Capacity
- Legality
- The Effect of Illegality

LEARNING OBJECTIVES

The five learning objectives below are designed to help improve your understanding of the chapter. After reading this chapter, you should be able to answer the following questions:

1 What is consideration? What is required for consideration to be legally sufficient?

2 In what circumstances might a promise be enforced despite a lack of consideration?

3 Does a minor have the capacity to enter into an enforceable contract? What does it mean to disaffirm a contract?

4 Under what circumstances will a covenant not to compete be enforced? When will such covenants not be enforced?

5 What is an exculpatory clause? In what circumstances might exculpatory clauses be enforced? When will they not be enforced?

"Liberty of contract is not an absolute concept.
It is relative to many conditions of time and place and circumstance."
—Benjamin Cardozo, 1870–1938 (Associate justice of the United States Supreme Court, 1932–1938)

Courts generally want contracts to be enforceable, and much of the law is devoted to aiding the enforceability of contracts. Before a court will enforce a contractual promise, however, it must be convinced that there was some exchange of consideration underlying the bargain.

Furthermore, as indicated in the chapter-opening quotation, "liberty of contract" is not absolute. In other words, not all people can make legally binding contracts at all times. Contracts entered into by persons lacking the capacity to do so may be voidable. Similarly, contracts calling for the performance of an illegal act are illegal and thus void—they are not contracts at all. In this chapter, we first examine the requirement of consideration and then look at contractual capacity and legality.

As more commerce is done online, the issues of consideration, capacity, and legality have become the subject of many disputes. Should people be able to exchange organs for transplants on Craigslist? Should online gambling be allowed? These are some current topics you will learn about in this chapter.

Consideration

Consideration The value given in return for a promise or performance in a contractual agreement.

In every legal system, some promises will be enforced, and other promises will not be enforced. The simple fact that a party has made a promise does not necessarily mean that the promise is enforceable. Under the common law, a primary basis for the enforcement of promises is consideration. **Consideration** usually is defined as the value given in return for a promise.

Often, consideration is broken down into two parts: (1) something of *legally sufficient value* must be given in exchange for the promise, and (2) there must be a *bargained-for exchange*.

Legally Sufficient Value

LEARNING OBJECTIVE 1
What is consideration? What is required for consideration to be legally sufficient?

To be legally sufficient, consideration must be something of value in the eyes of the law. The "something of legally sufficient value" may consist of any of the following:

1. A promise to do something that one has no prior legal duty to do (to pay on receipt of certain goods, for example).
2. The performance of an action that one is otherwise not obligated to undertake (such as providing accounting services).
3. The refraining from an action that one has a legal right to undertake (called a **forbearance**).

Forbearance The act of refraining from an action that one has a legal right to undertake.

Consideration in bilateral contracts normally consists of a promise in return for a promise, as explained in Chapter 9. In a contract for the sale of goods, for instance, the seller promises to ship specific goods to the buyer, and the buyer promises to pay for those goods when they are received. Each of these promises constitutes consideration for the contract.

In contrast, unilateral contracts involve a promise in return for a performance. **EXAMPLE 11.1** Anita says to her neighbor, "If you paint my garage, I will pay you $800." Anita's neighbor paints the garage. The act of painting the garage is the consideration that creates Anita's contractual obligation to pay her neighbor $800. •

What if, in return for a promise to pay, a person refrains from pursuing harmful habits, such as the use of tobacco and alcohol? Does such forbearance create consideration for the contract? This was the issue in the 1891 case *Hamer v. Sidway* that we present as this chapter's *Landmark in the Law* feature on the facing page.

Bargained-for Exchange

"Understanding does not necessarily mean agreement."

Howard Vernon, 1918–1992
(American author)

The second element of consideration is that it must provide the basis for the bargain struck between the contracting parties. The item of value must be given or promised by the promisor (offeror) in return for the promisee's promise, performance, or promise of performance.

This element of bargained-for exchange distinguishes contracts from gifts. **EXAMPLE 11.2** Sheng-Li says to his son, "In consideration of the fact that you are not as wealthy as your brothers, I will pay you $5,000." The fact that the word *consideration* is used does not, by itself, mean that consideration has been given. Indeed, Sheng-Li's promise is not enforceable because the son need not do anything to receive the $5,000 promised. Because the son does not need to give Sheng-Li something of legal value in return for his promise, there is no bargained-for exchange. Rather, Sheng-Li has simply stated his motive for giving his son a gift. •

LANDMARK IN THE LAW
Hamer v. Sidway (1891)

In *Hamer v. Sidway*,[a] the issue before the court arose from a contract created in 1869 between William Story, Sr., and his nephew, William Story II. The uncle promised his nephew that if the nephew refrained from drinking alcohol, using tobacco, and playing billiards and cards for money until he reached the age of twenty-one, the uncle would pay him $5,000 (about $75,000 in today's dollars). The nephew, who indulged occasionally in all of these "vices," agreed to refrain from them and did so for the next six years. Following his twenty-first birthday in 1875, the nephew wrote to his uncle that he had performed his part of the bargain and was thus entitled to the promised $5,000 (plus interest). A few days later, the uncle wrote the nephew a letter stating, "[Y]ou shall have the five thousand dollars, as I promised you." The uncle said that the money was in the bank and that the nephew could "consider this money on interest."

The Issue of Consideration The nephew left the money in the care of his uncle, who held it for the next twelve years. When the uncle died in 1887, however, the executor of the uncle's estate refused to pay the $5,000 (plus interest) claim brought by Hamer, a third party to whom the promise had been *assigned*. (The law allows parties to assign, or transfer, rights in contracts

_____
a. 124 N.Y. 538, 27 N.E. 256 (1891).

to third parties—see Chapter 13.) The executor, Sidway, contended that the contract was invalid because there was insufficient consideration to support it. The uncle had received nothing, and the nephew had actually benefited by fulfilling the uncle's wishes. Therefore, no contract existed.

The Court's Conclusion Although a lower court upheld Sidway's position, the New York Court of Appeals reversed and ruled in favor of the plaintiff, Hamer. "The promisee used tobacco, occasionally drank liquor, and he had a legal right to do so," the court stated. "That right he abandoned for a period of years upon the strength of the promise of the testator [one who makes a will] that for such forbearance he would give him $5,000. We need not speculate on the effort which may have been required to give up the use of those stimulants. It is sufficient that he restricted his lawful freedom of action within certain prescribed limits upon the faith of his uncle's agreement."

Application to Today's World *Although this case was decided more than a century ago, the principles enunciated by the court remain applicable to contracts formed today, including online contracts. For a contract to be valid and binding, consideration must be given, and that consideration must be something of legally sufficient value.*

Adequacy of Consideration

Adequacy of consideration involves "how much" consideration is given. Essentially, adequacy of consideration concerns the fairness of the bargain. On the surface, fairness would appear to be an issue when the items exchanged are of unequal value. In general, however, a court will not question the adequacy of consideration if the consideration is legally sufficient.

Under the doctrine of freedom of contract (see Chapter 9 on page 241), parties are usually free to bargain as they wish. The determination of whether consideration exists does not depend on the comparative value of the things exchanged. If people could sue merely because they had entered into an unwise contract, the courts would be overloaded with frivolous suits.

Nevertheless, a large disparity in the amount or value of the consideration exchanged may raise a red flag, causing a court to look more closely at the bargain. Shockingly inadequate consideration can indicate that fraud, duress, or undue influence was involved. (Defenses to enforceability will be discussed in Chapter 12.) Judges are uneasy about enforcing unequal bargains, and it is their task to make certain that there was not some defect in the contract's formation that negated voluntary consent.

> ➤ **KNOW THIS** ➤
>
> A consumer's signature on a contract does not always guarantee that the contract will be enforced. The contract must also comply with state and federal consumer protection laws.

Agreements That Lack Consideration

Sometimes, one or both of the parties to a contract may think that they have exchanged consideration when in fact they have not. Here, we look at some situations in which the parties' promises or actions do not qualify as contractual consideration.

Preexisting Duty   Under most circumstances, a promise to do what one already has a legal duty to do does not constitute legally sufficient consideration. A sheriff, for example, cannot collect a reward for information leading to the capture of a criminal if the sheriff already has a legal duty to capture the criminal.

Likewise, if a party is already bound by contract to perform a certain duty, that duty cannot serve as consideration for a second contract. **EXAMPLE 11.3**   Bauman-Bache, Inc., begins construction on a seven-story office building and after three months demands an extra $75,000 on its contract. If the extra $75,000 is not paid, the firm will stop working. The owner of the land, having no one else to complete construction, agrees to pay the extra $75,000. The agreement is not enforceable because it is not supported by legally sufficient consideration—Bauman-Bache had a preexisting contractual duty to complete the building. ●

Unforeseen Difficulties   The preexisting duty rule is intended to prevent extortion and the so-called holdup game. Nonetheless, if, during performance of a contract, extraordinary difficulties arise that were totally unforeseen at the time the contract was formed, a court may allow an exception to the rule.

Suppose that in *Example 11.3* above, Bauman-Bache had asked for the extra $75,000 because it encountered a rock formation that no one knew existed, and the landowner had agreed to pay the extra amount to excavate the rock. In this situation, the court may refrain from applying the preexisting duty rule and enforce the agreement to pay the extra $75,000.

Note, however, that for the rule to be waived, the difficulties must be truly unforeseen and not be the types of risks ordinarily assumed in business. In *Example 11.3*, if the construction was taking place in an area where rock formations were common, a court would likely enforce the preexisting duty rule on the basis that Bauman-Bache had assumed the risk that it would encounter rock.

Rescission and New Contract   The law recognizes that two parties can mutually agree to rescind, or cancel, their contract, at least to the extent that it is *executory*—that is, not yet performed by both parties. **Rescission**[1] is the unmaking of a contract so as to return the parties to the positions they occupied before the contract was made.

Sometimes, parties rescind a contract and make a new contract at the same time. When this occurs, it is often difficult to determine whether there was consideration for the new contract or whether the parties had a preexisting duty under the previous contract. If a court finds there was a preexisting duty, then the new contract will be invalid because there was no consideration.

Past Consideration   Promises made in return for actions or events that have already taken place are unenforceable. These promises lack consideration in that the element of bargained-for exchange is missing. In short, you can bargain for something to take place now or in the future but not for something that has already taken place. Therefore, **past consideration** is no consideration.

CASE EXAMPLE 11.4   Jamil Blackmon became friends with Allen Iverson when Iverson was a high school student who showed tremendous promise as an athlete. Blackmon

Are there circumstances under which a contractor, who has performed cement work, can legally demand a payment amount that is greater than what was stated in the contract?

Rescission A remedy whereby a contract is canceled and the parties are returned to the positions they occupied before the contract was made.

Past Consideration An act that takes place before the contract is made and that ordinarily, by itself, cannot be consideration for a later promise to pay for the act.

---

1. Pronounced reh-*sih*-zhen.

suggested that Iverson use "The Answer" as a nickname in the league tournaments, and said that Iverson would be "The Answer" to the National Basketball Association's declining attendance. Later, Iverson said that he would give Blackmon 25 percent of any proceeds from the merchandising of products that used "The Answer" as a logo or a slogan. Because Iverson's promise was made in return for past consideration (Blackmon's earlier suggestion), it was unenforceable. In effect, Iverson stated his intention to give Blackmon a gift.[2] ●

Illusory Promises   If the terms of the contract express such uncertainty of performance that the promisor has not definitely promised to do anything, the promise is said to be *illusory*—without consideration and unenforceable.   **EXAMPLE 11.5**   The president of Tuscan Corporation says to his employees, "All of you have worked hard, and if profits remain high, a 10 percent bonus at the end of the year will be given—if management thinks it is warranted." This is an *illusory promise,* or no promise at all, because performance depends solely on the discretion of the president (the management). There is no bargained-for consideration. The statement declares merely that management may or may not do something in the future. ●

Option-to-cancel clauses in contracts for specified time periods sometimes present problems in regard to consideration.   **EXAMPLE 11.6**   Abe contracts to hire Chris for one year at $5,000 per month, reserving the right to cancel the contract at any time. On close examination of these words, you can see that Abe has not actually agreed to hire Chris, as Abe can cancel without liability before Chris starts performance. Abe has not given up the opportunity of hiring someone else. This contract is therefore illusory. ●

If worded correctly, option-to-cancel contracts can also create enforceable obligations. **EXAMPLE 11.7**   Now suppose that Abe contracts to hire Chris for a one-year period at $5,000 per month, reserving the right to cancel the contract at any time after Chris has begun performance by giving Chris thirty days' notice. Abe, by saying that he will give Chris thirty days' notice, is relinquishing the opportunity (legal right) to hire someone else instead of Chris for a thirty-day period. If Chris works for one month, and Abe then gives him thirty days' notice, Chris has a valid and enforceable contractual claim for $10,000 for two months' salary. ●

Settlement of Claims

Businesspersons and others often enter into contracts to settle legal claims. It is important to understand the nature of the consideration given in these settlement agreements, or contracts. Claims are commonly settled through an *accord and satisfaction,* in which a debtor offers to pay a lesser amount than the creditor says is owed. Claims may also be settled by the signing of a *release* or a *covenant not to sue.*

Accord and Satisfaction   In an **accord and satisfaction,** a debtor offers to pay, and a creditor accepts, a lesser amount than the creditor originally claimed was owed. The *accord* is the agreement under which one of the parties promises to give or perform, and the other to accept, in satisfaction of a claim, something other than that on which the parties originally agreed. *Satisfaction* is the performance (usually payment), which takes place after the accord is executed. A basic rule is that there can be no satisfaction unless there is first an accord. For accord and satisfaction to occur, the amount of the debt *must be in dispute.*

If a debt is *liquidated,* accord and satisfaction cannot take place. A **liquidated debt** is one whose amount has been ascertained, fixed, agreed on, settled, or exactly determined. **EXAMPLE 11.8**   Barbara Kwan signs an installment loan contract with her banker. In the

Accord and Satisfaction A common means of settling a disputed claim, whereby a debtor offers to pay a lesser amount than the creditor purports to be owed.

Liquidated Debt A debt whose amount has been ascertained, fixed, agreed on, settled, or exactly determined.

---

2. *Blackmon v. Iverson,* 324 F.Supp.2d 602 (E.D.Pa. 2003).

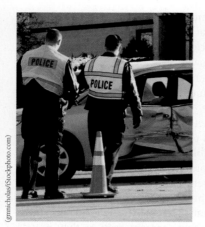

Is it possible to limit one's liability after a car accident?

Release An agreement in which one party gives up the right to pursue a legal claim against another party.

Covenant Not to Sue An agreement to substitute a contractual obligation for some other type of legal action based on a valid claim.

Promissory Estoppel A doctrine that can be used to enforce a promise when the promisee has justifiably relied on it and when justice will be better served by enforcing the promise.

contract, Kwan agrees to pay a specified rate of interest on a specified amount of borrowed funds at monthly intervals for two years. Because both parties know the precise amount of the total obligation, it is a liquidated debt. •

In the majority of states, acceptance of (an accord for) a lesser sum than the entire amount of a liquidated debt is not satisfaction, and the balance of the debt is still legally owed. The reason for this rule is that the debtor has given no consideration to satisfy the obligation of paying the balance to the creditor—because the debtor has a preexisting legal obligation to pay the entire debt.

Unliquidated Debts   An *unliquidated debt* is the opposite of a liquidated debt. The amount of the debt is *not* settled, fixed, agreed on, ascertained, or determined, and reasonable persons may differ over the amount owed. In these circumstances, acceptance of payment of the lesser sum operates as a satisfaction, or discharge, of the debt because there is valid consideration—the parties give up a legal right to contest the amount in dispute.

Release   A **release** is a contract in which one party forfeits the right to pursue a legal claim against the other party. It bars any further recovery beyond the terms stated in the release. Releases will generally be binding if they are (1) given in good faith, (2) stated in a signed writing (required by many states), and (3) accompanied by consideration.[3] Clearly, parties are better off if they know the extent of their injuries or damages before signing releases.

> **EXAMPLE 11.9**   Kara's car is damaged in an accident caused by Raoul's negligence. Raoul offers to give Kara $3,000 if she will release him from further liability resulting from the accident. Kara believes that this amount will cover her repairs, so she agrees and signs the release. Later, Kara discovers that the repairs will cost $4,200. Can she collect the balance from Raoul? Normally, the answer is no— Kara is limited to the $3,000 in the release. Why? The reason is that a valid contract existed. Kara and Raoul both voluntarily consented to the terms (hence, agreement existed), and sufficient consideration was present. The consideration was the legal detriment Kara suffered (she forfeited her right to sue to recover damages, should they be more than $3,000) in exchange for Raoul's promise to give her $3,000. •

Covenant Not to Sue   Unlike a release, a **covenant not to sue** does not always prevent further recovery. The parties simply substitute a contractual obligation for some other type of legal action based on a valid claim. Suppose (in the preceding example) that Kara agrees with Raoul not to sue for damages in a tort action if he will pay for the damage to her car. If Raoul fails to pay, Kara can bring an action for breach of contract.

Promissory Estoppel

Sometimes, individuals rely on promises, and their reliance may form a basis for a court to infer contract rights and duties. Under the doctrine of **promissory estoppel** (also called *detrimental reliance*), a person who has reasonably and substantially relied on the promise of another can obtain some measure of recovery. Promissory estoppel is applied in a variety of contexts and allows a party to recover on a promise even though it was made *without consideration*. Under this doctrine, a court may enforce an otherwise unenforceable promise to avoid an injustice that would otherwise result.

---

3. Under the Uniform Commercial Code (UCC), a written, signed waiver or renunciation by an aggrieved party discharges any further liability for a breach, even without consideration [UCC 1–107].

LEARNING OBJECTIVE 2
In what circumstances might a promise be enforced despite a lack of consideration?

Requirements to Establish Promissory Estoppel

For the doctrine of promissory estoppel to be applied, the following elements are required:

1. There must be a clear and definite promise.
2. The promisor should have expected that the promisee would rely on the promise.
3. The promisee reasonably relied on the promise by acting or refraining from some act.
4. The promisee's reliance was definite and resulted in substantial detriment.
5. Enforcement of the promise is necessary to avoid injustice.

Estopped Barred, impeded, or precluded.

If these requirements are met, a promise may be enforced even though it is not supported by consideration. In essence, the promisor (the offeror) will be **estopped** (barred or prevented) from asserting lack of consideration as a defense.

Promissory estoppel is similar in some ways to the doctrine of quasi contract that was discussed in Chapter 9 on pages 248–249. In both situations, a court is acting in the interests of equity and imposes contract obligations on the parties to prevent unfairness even though no actual contract exists. In quasi contracts, however, no promise at all was made, whereas with promissory estoppel, a promise was made and relied on, but it was unenforceable.

Application of Promissory Estoppel

Promissory estoppel was originally applied to situations involving gifts (I promise to pay you $1,000 a week so that you will not have to work) and donations to charities (I promise to contribute $50,000 a year to the All Saints orphanage). Later, courts began to apply the doctrine to avoid inequity or hardship in other situations, including business transactions. **EXAMPLE 11.10**   An employer, Jay Bailey, orally promises to pay each of his five employees $2,000 a month for the remainder of their lives after they retire. When Sal Hernandez retires, he receives the monthly amount for two years, but then Bailey stops paying. Under the doctrine of promissory estoppel, Hernandez can sue Bailey in an attempt to enforce his promise. •

In the following case, a daughter built a house on her parents' land with their help and permission. When the parents refused to deed the land on which the house was built to her, she filed a lawsuit against them on a claim of promissory estoppel.

Case 11.1

Harvey v. Dow

Supreme Judicial Court of Maine,
2011 ME 4, 11 A.3d 303 (2011).

FACTS Jeffrey and Kathryn Dow owned 125 acres of land in Corinth, Maine. The Dows regarded the land as their children's heritage, and the subject of the children's living on the land was often discussed within the family. With the Dows' permission, their daughter, Teresa, installed a mobile home and built a garage on the land. After Teresa married Jarrod Harvey, the Dows agreed to finance the construction of a house on the land for the couple.

When Jarrod died in a motorcycle accident, however, Teresa financed the house with life insurance proceeds. The construction cost about $200,000. Jeffrey performed a substantial amount of work on the house, doing general carpentry and much of the foundation work, and helping to install the underground electrical lines. Teresa then asked her parents for a

(George Muresan/Shutterstock.com)

When must a property owner transfer a deed to his or her child?

Case 11.1—Continues next page ➡

Case 11.1—Continued

deed to the property so that she could obtain a mortgage. They refused. Teresa filed a suit in a Maine state court against her parents. The court rejected the claim that she was entitled to a judgment on a theory of promissory estoppel. Teresa appealed.

ISSUE Did Teresa Harvey detrimentally rely on her parents' promise to convey the land to her when she and her husband built a house on it?

DECISION Yes. The Supreme Judicial Court of Maine vacated the lower court's judgment and remanded the case for the entry of a judgment in Teresa's favor. The state's highest court held that the Dows showed a present commitment to transfer land to their daughter or to forgo a challenge to her ownership of it.

REASON The court reasoned that the Dows' support and encouragement of their daughter's construction of a house on the land "conclusively demonstrated" their intent. For years, they had made general promises to convey the land to their children, including Teresa. In addition, Jeffrey had approved the site for the house, obtained the building permit, and built much of the house himself. The court explained, "Statements or conduct representing a present commitment to do or refrain from doing something in the future reasonably can be expected to induce reliance and the promisee's reliance on such statements is reasonable."

CRITICAL THINKING—Legal Consideration *On remand, the lower court was ordered to determine the appropriate remedy. Should Teresa be awarded specific performance to compel a transfer of the land? Or should she obtain damages? Discuss.*

Contractual Capacity

Contractual Capacity The capacity required by the law for a party who enters into a contract to be bound by that contract.

Contractual capacity is the legal ability to enter into a contractual relationship. Courts generally presume the existence of contractual capacity, but in some situations, capacity is lacking or may be questionable. A person who has been determined by a court to be mentally incompetent, for example, cannot form a legally binding contract with another party. In other situations, a party may have the capacity to enter into a valid contract but may also have the right to avoid liability under it. For example, minors—or *infants,* as they are commonly referred to in the law—usually are not legally bound by contracts.

In this section, we look at the effect of youth, intoxication, and mental incompetence on contractual capacity.

Minors

Emancipation In regard to minors, the act of being freed from parental control.

Today, in almost all states, the *age of majority* (when a person is no longer a minor) for contractual purposes is eighteen years—the so-called coming of age.[4] In addition, some states provide for the termination of minority on marriage.

Minority status may also be terminated by a minor's **emancipation,** which occurs when a child's parent or legal guardian relinquishes the legal right to exercise control over the child. Normally, minors who leave home to support themselves are considered emancipated. Several jurisdictions permit minors to petition a court for emancipation. For business purposes, a minor may petition a court to be treated as an adult.

LEARNING OBJECTIVE 3
Does a minor have the capacity to enter into an enforceable contract? What does it mean to disaffirm a contract?

The general rule is that a minor can enter into any contract an adult can, provided that the contract is not one prohibited by law for minors (for example, the sale of alcoholic beverages or tobacco products). A contract entered into by a minor, however, is voidable at the option of that minor, subject to certain exceptions (to be discussed shortly). To exercise the option to avoid a contract, a minor need only manifest (clearly show) an intention not to be bound by it. The minor "avoids" the contract by disaffirming it.

---

4. The age of majority may still be twenty-one for other purposes, such as the purchase and consumption of alcohol.

Disaffirmance The legal avoidance, or setting aside, of a contractual obligation.

Disaffirmance

The legal avoidance, or setting aside, of a contractual obligation is referred to as **disaffirmance.** To disaffirm, a minor must express, through words or conduct, his or her intent not to be bound to the contract. The minor must disaffirm the entire contract, not merely a portion of it. For instance, a minor cannot decide to keep part of the goods purchased under a contract and return the remaining goods. When a minor disaffirms a contract, the minor can recover any property that she or he transferred to the adult as consideration for the contract, even if it is then in the possession of a third party.[5]

A contract can ordinarily be disaffirmed at any time during minority[6] or for a reasonable time after the minor comes of age. What constitutes a "reasonable" time may vary. If an individual fails to disaffirm an executed contract within a reasonable time after reaching the age of majority, a court will likely hold that the contract has been ratified (*ratification* will be discussed shortly).

Note that an adult who enters into a contract with a minor cannot avoid his or her contractual duties on the ground that the minor can do so. Unless the minor exercises the option to disaffirm the contract, the adult party normally is bound by it.

A Minor's Obligations on Disaffirmance

Although all states' laws permit minors to disaffirm contracts (with certain exceptions), including executed contracts, state laws differ on the extent of a minor's obligations on disaffirmance. Courts in most states hold that the minor need only return the goods (or other consideration) subject to the contract, provided the goods are in the minor's possession or control. Even if the minor returns damaged goods, the minor often is entitled to disaffirm the contract and obtain a refund of the purchase price.

A growing number of states place an additional duty on the minor to restore the adult party to the position she or he held before the contract was made. These courts may hold a minor responsible for damage, ordinary wear and tear, and depreciation of goods that the minor used prior to disaffirmance.

CASE EXAMPLE 11.11 Sixteen-year-old Joseph Dodson bought a truck for $4,900 from a used-car dealer. Although the truck developed mechanical problems nine months later, Dodson continued to drive it until the engine blew up and the truck stopped running. Dodson then disaffirmed the contract and attempted to return the truck to the dealer for a refund of the full purchase price. The dealer refused to accept the truck or to provide a refund. Dodson filed a suit. Ultimately, the Tennessee Supreme Court allowed Dodson to disaffirm the contract but required him to compensate the seller for the depreciated value—not the purchase price—of the truck.[7] ●

Exceptions to a Minor's Right to Disaffirm

State courts and legislatures have carved out several exceptions to the minor's right to disaffirm. Some contracts, such as marriage contracts and contracts to enlist in the armed services, cannot be avoided on the ground of public policy. Other contracts may not be disaffirmed for different reasons.

Although ordinarily minors can disaffirm contracts even when they have misrepresented their age, a growing number of states have enacted laws to prohibit disaffirmance in such situations. Some state laws also prohibit minors from disaffirming contracts entered into by a minor who is engaged in business as an adult.

---

5. Section 2–403(1) of the UCC allows an exception if the third party is a "good faith purchaser for value." See Chapter 16.

6. In some states, however, a minor who enters into a contract for the sale of land cannot disaffirm the contract until she or he reaches the age of majority.

7. *Dodson by Dodson v. Shrader,* 824 S.W.2d 545 (Tenn. 1992).

Necessaries Necessities required for life, such as food, shelter, clothing, and medical attention.

Ratification The acceptance or confirmation of an act or agreement that gives legal force to an obligation that previously was not enforceable.

In addition, a minor who enters into a contract for necessaries may disaffirm the contract but remains liable for the reasonable value of the goods. **Necessaries** are basic needs, such as food, clothing, shelter, and medical services, at a level of value required to maintain the minor's standard of living or financial and social status. Thus, what will be considered a necessary for one person may be a luxury for another.

Ratification   In contract law, **ratification** is the acceptance or confirmation of an act or agreement that gives legal force to an obligation that previously was not enforceable. A minor who has reached the age of majority can ratify a contract expressly or impliedly. *Express* ratification occurs when the individual, on reaching the age of majority, states orally or in writing that she or he intends to be bound by the contract. *Implied* ratification takes place when the minor, on reaching the age of majority, behaves in a manner inconsistent with disaffirmance.

EXAMPLE 11.12   Lin enters into a contract to sell her laptop to Andrew, a minor. Andrew does not disaffirm the contract. If, on reaching the age of majority, he writes a letter to Lin stating that he still agrees to buy the laptop, he has expressly ratified the contract. If, instead, Andrew takes possession of the laptop as a minor and continues to use it well after reaching the age of majority, he has impliedly ratified the contract. ●

If a minor fails to disaffirm a contract within a reasonable time after reaching the age of majority, then a court must determine whether the conduct constitutes implied ratification or disaffirmance. Generally, courts presume that a contract that is *executed* (fully performed by both parties) was ratified. A contract that is still executory is normally considered to be disaffirmed.

Parents' Liability   As a general rule, parents are not liable for the contracts made by minor children acting on their own, except contracts for necessaries, which the parents are legally required to provide. This is why businesses ordinarily require parents to cosign any contract made with a minor. The parents then become personally obligated to perform the conditions of the contract, even if their child avoids liability. (See the *Business Application* feature on page 300 for additional tips on dealing with minors.)

Intoxicated Persons

Intoxication is a condition in which a person's normal capacity to act or think is inhibited by alcohol or some other drug. A contract entered into by an intoxicated person can be either voidable or valid (and thus enforceable).

If the person was sufficiently intoxicated to lack mental capacity, then the transaction may be voidable at the option of the intoxicated person even if the intoxication was purely voluntary. If, despite intoxication, the person understood the legal consequences of the agreement, the contract is enforceable. Courts look at objective indications of the situation to determine if the intoxicated person possessed or lacked the required capacity.

For the contract to be voidable, the person must prove that the intoxication impaired her or his reason and judgment so severely that she or he did not comprehend the legal consequences of entering into the contract. In addition, the person claiming intoxication must be able to return all consideration received.

Mentally Incompetent Persons

Contracts made by mentally incompetent persons can be void, voidable, or valid. If a court has previously determined that a person is mentally incompetent and has appointed a guardian to represent the person, any contract made by that mentally incompetent person is *void*—no contract exists. Only the guardian can enter into a binding contract on behalf of the mentally incompetent person.

If a court has not previously judged a person to be mentally incompetent, the contract may be *voidable*. A contract is voidable if the person did not know that he or she was entering into the contract or lacked the mental capacity to comprehend its nature, purpose, and consequences. In such situations, the contract is voidable (or can be ratified) at the option of the mentally incompetent person but not at the option of the other party.

A contract entered into by a mentally incompetent person (whom a court has not previously declared incompetent) may also be *valid* if the person had capacity *at the time the contract was formed*. Some people who are incompetent due to age or illness have *lucid intervals*—temporary periods of sufficient intelligence, judgment, and will—during which they will be considered to have legal capacity to enter into contracts.

Legality

For a contract to be valid and enforceable, it must be formed for a legal purpose. Legality is the fourth requirement for a valid contract to exist. A contract to do something that is prohibited by federal or state statutory law is illegal and, as such, is void from the outset and thus unenforceable. Additionally, a contract to commit a tortious act (see Chapter 4 on page 96) or to commit an action that is contrary to public policy is illegal and unenforceable.

ETHICAL ISSUE

Should advertisements to buy or sell human organs be made legal on Web sites such as Craigslist? According to the United Network for Organ Sharing, between 4,500 and 5,000 people die each year in the United States while waiting on organ transplant lists. Increasingly, though, patients who need an organ transplant are sidestepping these traditional lists and advertising for organs on Web sites, such as Craigslist.com. The organ most requested is a kidney because most individuals have two but can survive with just one.

For example, Salina Hodge posted a plea for help on Craigslist asking for someone to donate a kidney. She received more than eight hundred responses from all over the world. One came from a young woman who lived just a few miles away. The transplant was successful, and both donor and donee are leading normal lives.

Federal law prohibits the sale or purchase of any organ for a payment that exceeds the donor's travel and hospital expenses. Nonetheless, individuals facing death will often try desperate means, and some ads posted on Craigslist clearly violate the law—for example, an offer to buy a kidney in exchange for $250,000 worth of paintings. Because the purchase or sale of an organ is illegal, such a contract would not be enforceable.

Some commentators argue that the law should be changed to allow an open market in human organs. They point out that dying patients and their families and friends will continue to offer side payments to obtain organs, even though the payments are technically illegal. Furthermore, some poor individuals will always be willing to provide a kidney for, say, $100,000. Proponents of a legal market in organs claim that such a market would be preferable to a black market where there is nothing to prevent those living in poverty from being exploited.

Contracts Contrary to Statute

Statutes often set forth rules specifying which terms and clauses may be included in contracts and which are prohibited. Thus, a contract to sell illegal drugs in violation of criminal laws is unenforceable, as is a contract to hide a corporation's violation of the Sarbanes-Oxley Act (see Chapter 31). Similarly, a contract to smuggle undocumented workers from another country into the United States for an employer is illegal (see Chapter 24), as is a contract to dump hazardous waste in violation of environmental laws (see Chapter 33).

If the object or performance of a contract is rendered illegal by statute *after* the contract has been formed, the contract is considered to be discharged by law. (See the discussion in Chapter 13.)

Usury Charging an illegal rate of interest.

Usury   Almost every state has a statute that sets the maximum rate of interest that can be charged for different types of transactions, including ordinary loans. A lender who makes a loan at an interest rate above the lawful maximum commits **usury.** Although usurious contracts are illegal, most states simply limit the interest that the lender may collect on the contract to the lawful maximum interest rate in that state. In a few states, the lender can recover the principal amount of the loan but no interest.

Although usury statutes place a ceiling on allowable rates of interest, exceptions are made to facilitate business transactions. For example, many states exempt corporate loans from the usury laws. In addition, almost all states have special statutes allowing much higher interest rates on small loans to help those borrowers who need funds and could not otherwise obtain loans.

Note, though, that in 2009 the federal government placed some restrictions on the interest rates and fees that banks and credit-card companies can legally charge consumers, particularly for late payments (discussed in Chapter 33).

Gambling   Gambling is the creation of risk for the purpose of assuming it. Any scheme that involves the distribution of property by chance among persons who have paid valuable consideration for the opportunity (chance) to receive the property is gambling. Traditionally, the states have deemed gambling contracts illegal and thus void. It is sometimes difficult, however, to distinguish a gambling contract from the risk sharing inherent in almost all contracts. (For a discussion of how the federal government has changed its interpretation of the laws pertaining to online gambling, see the *Adapting the Law to the Online Environment* feature on page 294.)

All states have statutes that regulate gambling, and many states allow certain forms of gambling, such as horse racing, video poker machines, and charity-sponsored bingo. In addition, nearly all states allow state-operated lotteries and gambling on Native American reservations. Nevertheless, even in states that permit certain types of gambling, courts often find that gambling contracts are illegal.

CASE EXAMPLE 11.13   Video poker machines are legal in Louisiana, but their use requires the approval of the state video gaming commission. Gaming Venture, Inc., did not obtain this approval before agreeing with Tastee Restaurant Corporation to install poker machines in some of its restaurants. For this reason, when Tastee allegedly reneged on the deal by refusing to install poker machines, a state court held that their agreement was an illegal gambling contract and therefore void.[8] ●

Licensing Statutes   All states require members of certain professions—including physicians, lawyers, real estate brokers, accountants, architects, electricians, and stockbrokers—to have licenses. Some licenses are obtained only after extensive schooling and examinations, which indicate to the public that a special skill has been acquired. Others require only that the particular person be of good moral character and pay a fee.

Whether a contract with an unlicensed person is legal and enforceable depends on the purpose of the licensing statute. If the statute's purpose is to protect the public from unauthorized practitioners, then a contract involving an unlicensed practitioner generally is illegal and unenforceable. If the purpose is merely to raise government revenues, however, a contract with an unlicensed person may be enforced (and the unlicensed practitioner fined).

EXAMPLE 11.14   A state requires a stockbroker to be licensed and to file a bond with the state to protect the public from fraudulent transactions in stocks. Because the purpose of the statute is to protect the public, a court will deem a contract with an unlicensed stockbroker in that state to be illegal and unenforceable. ●

---

8. *Gaming Venture, Inc. v. Tastee Restaurant Corp.,* 996 So.2d 515 (La.App. 5 Cir. 2008).

Can a member of a profession licensed in one jurisdiction recover on a contract to perform professional services in another jurisdiction? What if the contract was the result of a winning entry in an international competition? The court in the following case was asked these questions.

Case 11.2

Sturdza v. United Arab Emirates

District of Columbia Court of Appeals,
11 A.3d 251 (2011).

A team of architects checking its plans.

FACTS The United Arab Emirates (UAE) held a competition for the design of a new embassy in Washington, D.C. Elena Sturdza—an architect licensed in Maryland but not in the District of Columbia—won. Sturdza and the UAE exchanged proposals, but the UAE stopped communicating with her before the parties had signed a contract. Two years later, Sturdza learned that the UAE had contracted with a District of Columbia architect to use another design. Sturdza filed a suit against the UAE, alleging breach of contract.

ISSUE Can an architect who is not licensed in the District of Columbia sue to enforce a contract under which she was to perform architectural services in the District of Columbia?

DECISION No. According to the licensing statute, an architect cannot recover on a contract to perform architectural services in the District of Columbia if she or he lacks a District of Columbia license.

REASON Sturdza argued that the licensing statute should not apply to architects who submit plans in international architectural design competitions. The court held, however, that licensing requirements are necessary to ensure the safety of those who work in and visit buildings in the District of Columbia, as well as the safety of neighboring buildings. Besides, the statute contains no exception for international design competitions or any other type of client or service. "We must apply the statute as it is written and not create *ad hoc* [impromptu] exceptions by judicial decree based on nebulous [unclear] policy considerations."

CRITICAL THINKING—Global Consideration *The architectural services at the center of this case were to be performed for a foreign embassy. Should the court have made an exception for such a circumstance? Why or why not?*

Contracts Contrary to Public Policy

Although contracts involve private parties, some are not enforceable because of the negative impact they would have on society. These contracts are said to be *contrary to public policy*. Examples include a contract to commit an immoral act, such as selling a child, and a contract that prohibits marriage. **EXAMPLE 11.15** Everett offers a young man $10,000 if he will refrain from marrying Everett's daughter. If the young man accepts, no contract is formed (the contract is void) because it is contrary to public policy. Thus, if the man marries Everett's daughter, Everett cannot sue him for breach of contract. • Business contracts that may be contrary to public policy include contracts in restraint of trade and unconscionable contracts or clauses.

LEARNING OBJECTIVE 4
Under what circumstances will a covenant not to compete be enforced? When will such covenants not be enforced?

Contracts in Restraint of Trade The United States has a strong public policy favoring competition in the economy. Thus, contracts in restraint of trade (anticompetitive agreements) generally are unenforceable because they are contrary to public policy. Typically, such contracts also violate one or more federal or state antitrust laws (these laws will be discussed in Chapter 32). An exception is recognized when the restraint is reasonable and is an ancillary (secondary, or subordinate) part of the contract. Such restraints often are included in contracts for the sale of an ongoing business and employment contracts.

ADAPTING THE LAW TO THE ONLINE ENVIRONMENT

AN INCREASING AMOUNT OF ONLINE GAMBLING IS IN OUR FUTURE

Until very recently, the federal government interpreted the Wire Act of 1961[a] as prohibiting all forms of interstate transmission of gambling-related communications. Presumably, that law meant that all online gambling was effectively illegal when it became a reality more than three decades later. In 2006, Congress passed the Unlawful Internet Gambling Enforcement Act[b] to further reduce the amount of online gambling. That act essentially prohibited credit-card companies from collecting online bets for online gambling companies.

The Justice Department Releases a Game Changer

In 2011, Illinois and New York asked the Office of Legal Counsel of the U.S. Justice Department to clarify the interpretation of the Wire Act of 1961. In response, the department declared that the Wire Act applies only to bets or wagers on sporting events or contests and that it does not cover purely *intra*state communications. In short, under the Obama administration's interpretation of the Wire Act, almost all federal antigambling legislation no longer applies to gaming that is legal under state laws. The decision will pave the way for all states to legalize Internet poker and certain other types of online betting.

a. 18 U.S.C. Section 1084.
b. 31 U.S.C. Section 5361–5367.

The District of Columbia and Nevada Are Just Starting Points

As of 2012, only two jurisdictions had legalized online gambling—the District of Columbia and Nevada. Therefore, start-up online gambling businesses can be expected to increase dramatically in the next few years in those jurisdictions.

Other jurisdictions are also seeking additional revenues to reduce their budget deficits. Several states, including California, are already considering changing their laws to allow legal in-state Internet gambling. The lure of taxing billions of online gambling profits each year is very tempting.

Expect More Mobile Gambling Apps

For the last two years, the residents of Nevada have been able to utilize a mobile gambling app. Even bettors who do not live in Nevada can use an app that allows them to place sports bets via their phones. The first mobile app was created by America Wagering, Inc., for BlackBerry mobile phone devices.

Today, a number of casinos in Nevada offer mobile gambling apps that work on iPhones and Android-based smartphones. More apps will follow as more states legalize online gaming.

Critical Thinking

Why do you think that the Justice Department still believes that the Wire Act of 1961 applies to betting on sporting events or contests?

Covenant Not to Compete A contractual promise of one party to refrain from conducting business similar to that of another party for a certain period of time and within a specified geographical area.

Covenants Not to Compete and the Sale of an Ongoing Business   Many contracts involve a type of restraint called a **covenant not to compete,** or a restrictive covenant (promise). A covenant not to compete may be created when a seller agrees not to open a new store in a certain geographic area surrounding the old store. Such an agreement enables the seller to sell, and the purchaser to buy, the goodwill and reputation of an ongoing business without having to worry that the seller will open a competing business a block away. Provided the restrictive covenant is reasonable and is an ancillary part of the sale of an ongoing business, it is enforceable.

Employment Contract A contract between an employer and an employee in which the terms and conditions of employment are stated.

Covenants Not to Compete in Employment Contracts   Agreements not to compete can also be included in **employment contracts.** (See the annotated contract at the end of Chapter 14 for an example of an employment contract containing a noncompete clause.) People in middle-level and upper-level management positions commonly agree not to work for competitors or not to start a competing business for a specified period of time after terminating employment. Such agreements are generally legal in most states so long as the specified period of time (of restraint) is not excessive in duration and the geographic restriction is reasonable. What constitutes a reasonable time period may be shorter in the online environment than in conventional employment contracts because the restrictions would apply worldwide.

To be reasonable, a restriction on competition must protect a legitimate business interest and must not be any greater than necessary to protect that interest.[9] **CASE EXAMPLE 11.16** Safety and Compliance Management, Inc. (SCMI), provides drug-testing services. When SCMI hired Angela to pick up test specimens, she signed a covenant not to compete "in any area of SCMI business." Angela later quit SCMI's employ to work in a hospital where she sometimes collected patient specimens. SCMI claimed this was a breach of their noncompete agreement. A court ruled that the covenant was unreasonable because it imposed a greater restriction on Angela than was necessary to protect SCMI.[10] ●

The contract in the following *Spotlight Case* provided an exclusive license to open and operate comedy clubs under a certain famous trademark. It also included a covenant not to compete. The question was whether the restraint was reasonable.

---

9. See, for example, *Gould & Lamb LLC v. D'Alusio,* 949 So.2d 1212 (Fla.App. 2007), and *Freeman v. Brown Hiller, Inc.,* 102 Ark.App. 76, 281 S.W.3d 749 (2008).
10. *Stultz v. Safety and Compliance Management, Inc.,* 285 Ga.App. 799, 648 S.E.2d 129 (2007).

Spotlight on the Improv

Case 11.3
Comedy Club, Inc. v. Improv West Associates
United States Court of Appeals, Ninth Circuit, 553 F.3d 1277 (2009).
www.ca9.uscourts.gov[a]

(Ralph Notaro/Getty Images)

How much control over the name Improv Comedy Club does its owner have?

FACTS Improv West Associates is the founder of the Improv Comedy Club and owner of the "Improv" trademark. Comedy Club, Inc. (CCI), owns and operates restaurants and comedy clubs. Improv West granted CCI an exclusive license to open four Improv clubs per year in 2001, 2002, and 2003. Their agreement prohibited CCI from opening any non-Improv comedy clubs "in the contiguous United States" until 2019. When CCI failed to open eight clubs by the end of 2002, Improv West commenced arbitration. The arbitrator's award in 2005 stated that CCI had forfeited its right to open Improv clubs, but that the parties' agreement had not terminated and the covenant not to compete was enforceable—CCI could not open any new comedy clubs for its duration. A federal district court confirmed the award, and CCI appealed.

ISSUE Is a covenant not to compete in the comedy club business for fourteen years in forty-eight states too broad to be enforced?

DECISION Yes. The U.S. Court of Appeals for the Ninth Circuit reversed part of the lower court's confirmation of the award and remanded the case.

REASON The court said that terminating CCI's exclusive right to open Improv clubs due to its inadequate performance of the parties' contract "makes sense" and that Improv West should be protected from "improper" competition. But the covenant not to compete in this case has "dramatic geographic and temporal [relating to time] scope. . . . For more than fourteen years the entire contiguous United States comedy club market, except for CCI's current Improv clubs, is off limits to CCI." The effect would be to foreclose competition in a substantial share of the comedy club business. This restraint is "too broad to be countenanced." The covenant should be tailored to cover only the areas in which CCI is operating Improv clubs under the parties' agreement. It should allow CCI to open non-Improv clubs in "all those counties" where it does not operate an Improv club.

WHY IS THIS CASE IMPORTANT? *Competition is a paramount principle of our capitalist economic system. But business competitiveness requires the support of our laws if it is to be a reality. This case shows the multifaceted role that the law can play to encourage competition by removing unfair restraints and by enforcing proper limits to prevent its abuse.*

---

a. In the left-hand column, in the "Opinions" pull-down menu, click on "Published." On that page, click on "Advanced Search." Then, in the "by Case No.:" box, type "05-55739" and click on "Search." In the result, click on the "01/29/2009" link to access the opinion.

Enforcement Problems   The laws governing the enforceability of covenants not to compete vary significantly from state to state. California prohibits the enforcement of all covenants not to compete. In some states, such as Texas, such a covenant will not be enforced unless the employee has received some benefit in return for signing the noncompete agreement. This is true even if the covenant is reasonable as to time and area. If the employee receives no benefit, the covenant will be deemed void.

Occasionally, depending on the jurisdiction, courts will *reform* covenants not to compete. If a covenant is found to be unreasonable in time or geographic area, the court may convert the terms into reasonable ones and then enforce the reformed covenant. This presents a problem, however, in that the judge has implicitly become a party to the contract. Consequently, courts usually resort to contract **reformation** only when necessary to prevent undue burdens or hardships.

Reformation A court-ordered correction of a written contract so that it reflects the true intentions of the parties.

PREVENTING LEGAL DISPUTES

A business clearly has a legitimate interest in having employees sign covenants not to compete and in preventing them from using the valuable skills and training provided by the business for the benefit of a competitor. The problem is that these covenants frequently lead to litigation. Moreover, it is difficult to predict what a court will consider reasonable in a given situation. Therefore, you need to be aware of the difficulties in enforcing noncompete agreements. Seek the advice of counsel in the relevant jurisdiction when drafting covenants not to compete. Avoid overreaching in terms of time and geographic restrictions, particularly if you are the manager of a high-tech or Web-based company. Consider using noncompete clauses only for key employees and, if necessary, offer some compensation (consideration) for signing the agreement. If an employee signed a noncompete clause when he or she was hired, be sure to discuss the meaning of that clause and your expectations with the employee at the time of termination.

Unconscionable Contracts or Clauses

Ordinarily, a court does not look at the fairness or equity of a contract, or, as discussed earlier, inquire into the adequacy of consideration. Persons are assumed to be reasonably intelligent, and the courts will not come to their aid just because they have made unwise or foolish bargains. In certain circumstances, however, bargains are so oppressive that the courts relieve innocent parties of part or all of their duties. Such bargains are deemed **unconscionable**[11] because they are so unscrupulous or grossly unfair as to be "void of conscience."

The Uniform Commercial Code (UCC) incorporates the concept of unconscionability in its provisions with regard to the sale and lease of goods.[12] A contract can be unconscionable on either procedural or substantive grounds, as discussed in the following subsections and illustrated graphically in Exhibit 11.1 on the facing page.

Unconscionable (Contract or Clause) A contract or clause that is void on the basis of public policy because one party was forced to accept terms that are unfairly burdensome and that unfairly benefit the stronger party.

"Better a friendly refusal than an unwilling consent."

Spanish Proverb

Adhesion Contract A standard-form contract in which the stronger party dictates the terms.

Procedural Unconscionability   Procedural unconscionability often involves inconspicuous print, unintelligible language ("legalese"), or the lack of an opportunity to read the contract or ask questions about its meaning. This type of unconscionability typically arises when a party's lack of knowledge or understanding of the contract terms deprived him or her of any meaningful choice.

Procedural unconscionability can also occur when there is such a disparity in bargaining power between the two parties that the weaker party's consent is not voluntary. This type of situation often involves an **adhesion contract,** which is a standard-form contract written exclusively by one party (the dominant party, usually the seller or creditor) and presented to the other (the adhering party, usually the buyer or borrower) on a take-it-or-leave-it basis. In

---

11. Pronounced un-*kon*-shun-uh-bul.
12. See UCC 2–302 and 2–719.

Exhibit 11.1 Unconscionability

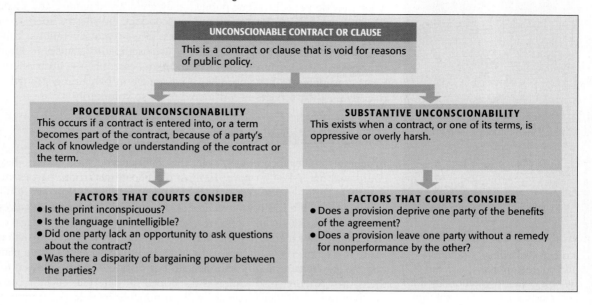

other words, the adhering party has no opportunity to negotiate the terms of the contract. Not all adhesion contracts are unconscionable, only those that unreasonably favor the drafter.[13]

Substantive Unconscionability   Substantive unconscionability occurs when contracts, or portions of contracts, are oppressive or overly harsh. Courts generally focus on provisions that deprive one party of the benefits of the agreement or leave that party without remedy for nonperformance by the other.   **CASE EXAMPLE 11.17**   A person with little income and only a fourth-grade education agrees to purchase a refrigerator for $4,500 and signs a two-year installment contract. The same type of refrigerator usually sells for $900 on the market. Despite the general rule that the courts will not inquire into the adequacy of the consideration, some courts have held that this type of contract is unconscionable because the contract terms are so oppressive as to "shock the conscience" of the court.[14] •

Substantive unconscionability can arise in a wide variety of business contexts. For example, a contract clause that gives the business entity unrestricted access to the courts but requires the other party to arbitrate any dispute with the firm may be unconscionable. Similarly, contracts drafted by cell phone providers and insurance companies have been struck down as substantively unconscionable when they included provisions that were overly harsh or one sided.[15]

Exculpatory Clauses
Often closely related to the concept of unconscionability are **exculpatory clauses,** which release a party from liability in the event of monetary or physical injury, *no matter who is at fault.* Indeed, courts sometimes refuse to enforce such clauses because they deem them to be unconscionable. Exculpatory clauses found in rental agreements for commercial property are frequently held to be contrary to public policy, and such clauses are almost always unenforceable in residential property leases. Exculpatory clauses in the employment context may be deemed unconscionable when they attempt to remove the employer's potential liability for injuries to employees.

LEARNING OBJECTIVE 5
What is an exculpatory clause? In what circumstances might exculpatory clauses be enforced? When will they not be enforced?

Exculpatory Clause A clause that releases a contractual party from liability in the event of monetary or physical injury, no matter who is at fault.

---

13. See, for example, *Thibodeau v. Comcast Corp.,* 2006 PA Super. 346, 912 A.2d 874 (2006).
14. See, for example, *Jones v. Star Credit Corp.,* 59 Misc.2d 189, 298 N.Y.S.2d 264 (1969). This classic case will be presented in Chapter 15 as Case 15.2 on pages 398–399.
15. See, for example, *Gatton v. T-Mobile USA, Inc.,* 152 Cal.App.4th 571, 61 Cal.Rptr.3d 344 (2007); and *Aul v. Golden Rule Insurance Co.,* 2007 WL 1695243 (Wis.App. 2007).

If a carnival swing is defective and causes an injury, can the swing's owner avoid liability if it had made each participant sign an exculpatory clause?

Although courts view exculpatory clauses with disfavor, they do enforce such clauses when they do not contravene public policy, are not ambiguous, and do not claim to protect parties from liability for intentional misconduct. Businesses such as health clubs, race-tracks, amusement parks, skiing facilities, horse-rental operations, golf-cart concessions, and skydiving organizations frequently use exculpatory clauses to limit their liability for patrons' injuries. Because these services are not essential, the firms offering them are some-times considered to have no relative advantage in bargaining strength, and anyone con-tracting for their services is considered to do so voluntarily.

The Effect of Illegality

In general, an illegal contract is void: the contract is deemed never to have existed, and the courts will not aid either party. In most illegal contracts, both parties are considered to be equally at fault—*in pari delicto*. If the contract is executory (not yet fulfilled), neither party can enforce it. If it has been executed, neither party can recover damages.

The courts usually are not concerned if one wrongdoer in an illegal contract is unjustly enriched at the expense of the other—except under certain circumstances (to be discussed shortly). The main reason for this hands-off attitude is a belief that a plaintiff who has bro-ken the law by entering into an illegal bargain should not be allowed to obtain help from the courts. Another justification is the hoped-for deterrent effect: a plaintiff who suffers a loss because of an illegal bargain will presumably be deterred from entering into similar illegal bargains in the future.

There are exceptions to the general rule that neither party to an illegal bargain can sue for breach and neither party can recover for performance rendered. We look at these excep-tions here.

Justifiable Ignorance of the Facts

When one of the parties to a contract is relatively innocent (has no reason to know that the contract is illegal), that party can often recover any benefits conferred in a partially executed contract. In this situation, the courts will not enforce the contract but will allow the parties to return to their original positions.

A court may sometimes permit an innocent party who has fully performed under a con-tract to enforce the contract against the guilty party. **EXAMPLE 11.18** A trucking company contracts with Gillespie to carry crated goods to a specific destination for a normal fee of $5,000. The trucker delivers the crates and later finds out that they contained illegal goods. Although the shipment, use, and sale of the goods are illegal under the law, the trucker, being an innocent party, can normally still legally collect the $5,000 from Gillespie. •

Members of Protected Classes

When a statute protects a certain class of people, a member of that class can enforce an illegal contract even though the other party cannot. **EXAMPLE 11.19** Statutes prohibit cer-tain employees (such as flight attendants or pilots) from working more than a specified number of hours per month. These employees thus constitute a class protected by statute. An employee who is required to work more than the maximum can recover for those extra hours of service. •

Other examples of statutes designed to protect a particular class of people are **blue sky laws**—state laws that regulate the offering and sale of securities for the protection of the public (see Chapter 31)—and state statutes regulating the sale of insurance. If an insurance company violates a statute when selling insurance, the purchaser can nevertheless enforce the policy and recover from the insurer.

Blue Sky Laws State laws that regulate the offering and sale of securities for the protection of the public.

Withdrawal from an Illegal Agreement

If the illegal part of a bargain has not yet been performed, the party rendering performance can withdraw from the contract and recover the performance or its value. **EXAMPLE 11.20** Marta and Ande decide to wager (illegally) on the outcome of a boxing match. Each deposits $1,000 with a stakeholder, who agrees to pay the winner of the bet. At this point, each party has performed part of the agreement, but the illegal part of the agreement will not occur until the winner is paid. Before such payment occurs, either party is entitled to withdraw from the agreement by giving notice to the stakeholder of his or her withdrawal. •

Severable, or Divisible, Contracts

A contract that is *severable,* or divisible, consists of distinct parts that can be performed separately, with separate consideration provided for each part. With an *indivisible* contract, in contrast, the parties intended that complete performance by each party would be essential, even if the contract contains a number of seemingly separate provisions.

If a contract is divisible into legal and illegal portions, a court may enforce the legal portion but not the illegal one, so long as the illegal portion does not affect the essence of the bargain. This approach is consistent with the basic policy of enforcing the legal intentions of the contracting parties whenever possible. **EXAMPLE 11.21** Cole signs an employment contract that includes an overly broad and thus illegal covenant not to compete. In this situation, a court might allow the employment contract to be enforceable but reform the unreasonably broad covenant by converting its terms into reasonable ones. Alternatively, the court could declare the covenant illegal (and thus void) and enforce the remaining employment terms. • (See the appendix to Chapter 14 that starts on page 374 for an example of how some contracts include a clause indicating that the parties intend the contract terms to be enforced to the "fullest extent possible.")

Fraud, Duress, or Undue Influence

Often, one party to an illegal contract is more at fault than the other. When a party has been induced to enter into an illegal bargain through fraud, duress, or undue influence on the part of the other party to the agreement, the first party will be allowed to recover for the performance or its value.

Reviewing . . . Consideration, Capacity, and Legality

Renee Beaver started racing go-karts competitively in 2009, when she was fourteen. Many of the races required her to sign an exculpatory clause to participate, which she or her parents regularly signed. In 2012, right before her birthday, she participated in the annual Elkhart Grand Prix, a series of races in Elkhart, Indiana. During the event in which she drove, a piece of foam padding used as a course barrier was torn from its base and ended up on the track. A portion of the padding struck Beaver in the head, and another portion was thrown into oncoming traffic, causing a multikart collision during which she sustained severe injuries. Beaver filed an action against the race organizers for negligence. The organizers could not locate the exculpatory clause that Beaver was supposed to have signed. Race organizers argued that she must have signed one to enter the race, but even if she had not signed one, her actions showed her intent to be bound by its terms. Using the information presented in the chapter, answer the following questions.

1. Did Beaver have the contractual capacity to enter a contract with an exculpatory clause? Why or why not?
2. Assuming that Beaver did, in fact, sign the exculpatory clause, did she later disaffirm or ratify the contract? Explain.
3. Now assume that Beaver had stated that she was eighteen years old at the time that she signed the exculpatory clause. How might this affect Beaver's ability to disaffirm or ratify the contract?

Continued

4. Now suppose that Beaver can prove that she did not actually sign an exculpatory clause and this convinces race organizers to pursue a settlement. They offer to pay Beaver one-half of the amount that she is claiming in damages if she now signs a release of all claims. Because Beaver is young and the full effects of her injuries may not be clear at this time, what other type of settlement agreement might she prefer? What is the consideration to support any settlement agreement that Beaver enters into with the race organizers?

DEBATE THIS After agreeing to an exculpatory clause or purchasing some item, such as an iPad, minors often seek to avoid the contracts. Today's minors are far from naïve and should not be allowed to avoid their contractual obligations.

BUSINESS APPLICATION

Should Retailers Enter into Contracts with Minors and Intoxicated Persons?*

Sales personnel, particularly those who are paid on a commission basis, are often eager to make contracts. Sometimes, however, these salespersons must deal with minors and intoxicated persons, both of whom have limited contractual capacity. Therefore, if you are a retailer, you should make sure that your employees are acquainted with the law governing contracts with minors and intoxicated persons.

Contracts with Minors

If your business involves selling consumer durables, such as cell phones, electronics, gaming equipment, appliances, furniture, or automobiles, your sales personnel must be careful in forming contracts with minors and should heed the adage, "When in doubt, check." Remember that a contract signed by a minor (unless it is for necessaries) normally is voidable, and the minor may exercise the option to disaffirm the contract. Employees should demand proof of legal age when they have any doubt about whether a customer is a minor. If the customer is a minor, the employees should insist that an adult (such as a parent) be the purchaser or at least cosign any sales contract.

In addition, because the law governing minors' rights varies substantially from state to state, you should check with your attorney concerning the laws governing disaffirmance in your state. You and

those you hire to sell your products should know, for example, what the consequences will be if a minor disaffirms the sale or has misrepresented his or her age when forming a sales contract. Similarly, you need to find out whether and in what circumstances a minor, on disaffirming a contract, can be required to pay for damage to goods sold under the contract.

Dealing with Intoxicated Persons

Little need be said about a salesperson's dealings with obviously intoxicated persons. If the customer, despite intoxication, understands the legal consequences of the contract being signed, the contract is enforceable. Nonetheless, it may be extremely difficult to establish that the intoxicated customer understood the consequences of entering into the contract if the customer claims that she or he did not understand. Therefore, the best advice is, "When in doubt, don't." In other words, if you suspect a customer may be intoxicated, do not sign a contract with that customer.

Checklist for the Retailer

1. *When in doubt about the age of a customer to whom you are about to sell major consumer durable goods or anything other than necessaries, require proof of legal age.*
2. *If such proof is not forthcoming, require that a parent or guardian sign the contract.*

*This *Business Application* is not meant to substitute for the services of an attorney who is licensed to practice law in your state.

Key Terms

Chapter Summary: Consideration, Capacity, and Legality

Consideration
(See pages 282–286.)
	1. *Elements of consideration* —
	   a. Something of *legally sufficient value* must be given in exchange for a promise.
	   b. There must be a bargained-for exchange.
	2. *Legal sufficiency and adequacy of consideration* —Legal sufficiency means that something of legal value must be given in exchange for a promise. Adequacy relates to "how much" consideration is given and whether a fair bargain was reached. Courts will inquire into the adequacy of consideration only when fraud, undue influence, duress, or unconscionability may be involved.
	3. *Contracts that lack consideration* —Consideration is lacking in the following situations:
	   a. Preexisting duty —A promise to do what one already has a legal duty to do is not legally sufficient consideration for a new contract.
	   b. Past consideration —Actions or events that have already taken place do not constitute legally sufficient consideration.
	   c. Illusory promises —When the nature or extent of performance is too uncertain, the promise is rendered illusory (without consideration and unenforceable).
	4. *Settlement of claims* —Disputes may be settled by the following, which are enforceable provided there is consideration:
	   a. Accord and satisfaction —An *accord* is an agreement in which a debtor offers to pay a lesser amount than the creditor claims is owed. *Satisfaction* takes place when the accord is executed.
	   b. Release —An agreement in which, for consideration, a party forfeits the right to seek further recovery beyond the terms specified in the release.
	   c. Covenant not to sue —An agreement not to sue on a present, valid claim.

Promissory Estoppel (See pages 286–288.)	The equitable doctrine of promissory estoppel applies when a promisor should have expected a promise to induce definite and substantial action or forbearance by the promisee, and the promisee does act in reliance on the promise. Such a promise is binding, even though there is no consideration, if injustice can be avoided only by enforcement of the promise. Also known as the doctrine of *detrimental reliance*.
CONTRACTUAL CAPACITY	

Minors
(See pages 288–290.)
	1. *General rule* —Contracts with minors are voidable at the option of the minor.
	2. *Disaffirmance* —The legal avoidance of a contractual obligation.
	   a. Disaffirmance can take place (in most states) at any time during minority and within a reasonable time after the minor has reached the age of majority.
	   b. The minor must disaffirm the entire contract, not just part of it.
	   c. When disaffirming executed contracts, the minor has a duty to return the received goods if they are still in the minor's control or (in some states) to pay their reasonable value.
	   d. A minor who has committed an act of fraud (such as misrepresenting her or his age) will be denied the right to disaffirm by some courts.
	   e. A minor may disaffirm a contract for necessaries but remains liable for the reasonable value of the goods.
	3. *Ratification* —The acceptance, or affirmation, of a legal obligation.
	   a. Express ratification —Occurs when the minor, in writing or orally, explicitly assumes the obligations imposed by the contract.
	   b. Implied ratification —Occurs when the conduct of the minor is inconsistent with disaffirmance or when the minor fails to disaffirm an executed contract within a reasonable time after reaching the age of majority.
	4. *Parents' liability* —Generally, except for contracts for necessaries, parents are not liable for the contracts made by minor children acting on their own. Parents may be liable for minors' torts in certain circumstances, however.
	5. *Emancipation* —Occurs when a child's parent or legal guardian relinquishes the legal right to exercise control over the child. Normally, minors who leave home to support themselves are considered emancipated. In some jurisdictions, minors are permitted to petition a court for emancipation for limited purposes.

Continued

Chapter Summary: Consideration, Capacity, and Legality—Continued

Intoxicated Persons (See page 290.)	1. A contract entered into by an intoxicated person is voidable at the option of the intoxicated person if the person was sufficiently intoxicated to lack mental capacity, even if the intoxication was voluntary. 2. A contract with an intoxicated person is enforceable if, despite being intoxicated, the person understood the legal consequences of entering into the contract.
Mentally Incompetent Persons (See pages 290–291.)	1. A contract made by a person previously judged by a court to be mentally incompetent is void. 2. A contract made by a person who is mentally incompetent, but has not been previously declared incompetent by a court, is voidable at the option of that person.
LEGALITY	
Contracts Contrary to Statute (See pages 291–294.)	1. *Usury*—Usury occurs when a lender makes a loan at an interest rate above the lawful maximum, which varies from state to state. 2. *Gambling*—Gambling contracts that contravene (go against) state statutes are deemed illegal and thus void. 3. *Licensing statutes*—Contracts entered into by persons who do not have a license, when one is required by statute, will not be enforceable unless the underlying purpose of the statute is to raise government revenues (and not to protect the public from unauthorized practitioners).
Contracts Contrary to Public Policy (See pages 294–298.)	1. *Contracts in restraint of trade*—Contracts to reduce or restrain free competition are illegal and prohibited by statutes. An exception is a *covenant not to compete.* Such covenants usually are enforced by the courts if the terms are secondary to a contract (such as a contract for the sale of a business or an employment contract) and are reasonable as to time and area of restraint. Courts tend to scrutinize covenants not to compete closely and, at times, may reform them if they are overbroad rather than declaring the entire covenant unenforceable. 2. *Unconscionable contracts and clauses*—When a contract or contract clause is so unfair that it is oppressive to one party, it may be deemed unconscionable. As such, it is illegal and cannot be enforced. 3. *Exculpatory clauses*—An exculpatory clause is a clause that releases a party from liability in the event of monetary or physical injury, no matter who is at fault. In certain situations, exculpatory clauses may be contrary to public policy and thus unenforceable.
EFFECT OF ILLEGALITY	
General Rule (See page 298.)	In general, an illegal contract is void, and the courts will not aid either party when both parties are considered to be equally at fault (*in pari delicto*). If the contract is executory, neither party can enforce it. If the contract is executed, neither party can recover damages.
Exceptions (See pages 298–299.)	Several exceptions exist to the general rule that neither party to an illegal bargain will be able to recover. In the following situations, the court may grant recovery: 1. *Justifiable ignorance of the facts*—When one party to the contract is relatively innocent. 2. *Members of protected classes*—When one party to the contract is a member of a group of persons protected by statute, such as employees. 3. *Withdrawal from an illegal agreement*—When either party seeks to recover consideration given for an illegal contract before the illegal act is performed. 4. *Severable, or divisible, contracts*—When the court can divide the contract into illegal and legal portions and the illegal portion is not essential to the bargain. 5. *Fraud, duress, or undue influence*—When one party was induced to enter into an illegal bargain through fraud, duress, or undue influence.

ExamPrep

ISSUE SPOTTERS

1. In September, Sharyn agrees to work for Totem Productions, Inc., at $500 a week for a year beginning January 1. In October, Sharyn is offered $600 a week for the same work by Umber Shows, Ltd. When Sharyn tells Totem about the other offer, they tear up their contract and agree that Sharyn will be paid $575. Is the new contract binding? Explain. **(See page 284.)**

2. Sun Airlines, Inc., prints on its tickets that it is not liable for any injury to a passenger caused by the airline's negligence. If the cause of an accident is found to be the airline's negligence, can it use the clause as a defense to liability? Why or why not? (**See pages 297–298.**)

—**Check your answers to the Issue Spotters against the answers provided in Appendix E at the end of this text.**

BEFORE THE TEST

Go to www.cengagebrain.com, enter the ISBN 9781133273561 and click on "Find" to locate this textbook's Web site. Then, click on "Access Now" under "Study Tools," and select Chapter 11 at the top. There, you will find a Practice Quiz that you can take to assess your mastery of the concepts in this chapter, as well as Flashcards, a Glossary of important terms, and Video Questions (when assigned).

For Review

Answers to the even-numbered questions in this For Review section can be found in Appendix F at the end of this text.

1. What is consideration? What is required for consideration to be legally sufficient?
2. In what circumstances might a promise be enforced despite a lack of consideration?
3. Does a minor have the capacity to enter into an enforceable contract? What does it mean to disaffirm a contract?
4. Under what circumstances will a covenant not to compete be enforced? When will such covenants not be enforced?
5. What is an exculpatory clause? In what circumstances might exculpatory clauses be enforced? When will they not be enforced?

Business Scenarios and Case Problems

11–1 **Contracts by Minors.** Kalen is a seventeen-year-old minor who has just graduated from high school. He is attending a university two hundred miles from home and has contracted to rent an apartment near the university for one year at $500 per month. He is working at a convenience store to earn enough income to be self-supporting. After living in the apartment and paying monthly rent for four months, he becomes involved in a dispute with his landlord. Kalen, still a minor, moves out and returns the key to the landlord. The landlord wants to hold Kalen liable for the balance of the payments due under the lease. Discuss fully Kalen's liability in this situation. (**See pages 288–290.**)

11–2 **Question with Sample Answer—Past Consideration.** Daniel, a recent college graduate, is on his way home for the Christmas holidays from his new job. He gets caught in a snowstorm and is taken in by an elderly couple who provide him with food and shelter. After the snowplows have cleared the road, Daniel proceeds home. Daniel's father, Fred, is most appreciative of the elderly couple's action and in a letter promises to pay them $500. The elderly couple, in need of funds, accept Fred's offer. Then, because of a dispute with Daniel, Fred refuses to pay the elderly couple the $500. Discuss whether the couple can hold Fred liable in contract for the services rendered to Daniel. (**See page 284.**)

—**For a sample answer to Question 11–2, go to Appendix G at the end of this text.**

11–3 **Past Consideration.** Access Organics, Inc., hired Andy Hernandez to sell organic produce. Later, Hernandez signed an agreement not to compete with Access for two years following the termination of his employment. He did not receive a pay increase or any other new benefits in return for signing the agreement. When Access encountered financial trouble, Hernandez left and began to compete with his former employer. Access filed a lawsuit against Hernandez. Is the noncompete agreement enforceable? Discuss. [*Access Organics, Inc. v. Hernandez,* 341 Mont. 73, 175 P.3d 899 (2008)] (**See page 284.**)

11–4 **Spotlight on Arbitration Clauses—Unconscionable Contracts or Clauses.** Roberto Basulto and Raquel Gonzalez, who did not speak English, responded to an ad on Spanish-language television sponsored by Hialeah Automotive, LLC, which does business as Potamkin Dodge. Potamkin's staff understood that Basulto and Gonzalez did not speak or read English and conducted the entire transaction in Spanish. They explained the English-language contract, but did not explain an accompanying arbitration agreement. This agreement limited the amount of damages that the buyers could seek in court to less than $5,000, but did not limit Potamkin's right to pursue greater damages. Basulto and Gonzalez bought a Dodge Caravan and signed the contract in blank—that is, leaving some terms to be filled in later. Potamkin later filled in a lower trade-in allowance than agreed and refused to change it. The buyers returned the van—having driven it a total of seven miles—and asked for a return of their trade-in vehicle, but it had been sold. The buyers filed a suit in a Florida state court against Potamkin. The dealer sought arbitration. Was the arbitration agreement unconscionable? Why or why not? [*Hialeah Automotive, LLC v. Basulto,* 22 So.3d 586 (Fla.App. 3 Dist. 2009)] **(See page 296.)**

11–5   Disaffirmance. J.T., a minor, is a motocross competitor. At Monster Mountain MX Park, he signed a waiver of liability to "hold harmless the park for any loss due to negligence." Riding around the Monster Mountain track, J.T. rode over a blind jump, became airborne, and crashed into a tractor that he had not seen until he was in the air. To recover for his injuries, J.T. filed a suit against Monster Mountain, alleging negligence for its failure to remove the tractor from the track. Does the liability waiver bar this claim? Explain. [*J.T. v. Monster Mountain, LLC,* 754 F.Supp.2d 1323 (M.D.Ala. 2010)] **(See page 289.)**

11–6   Case Problem with Sample Answer—Unconscionable Contracts or Clauses. Geographic Expeditions, Inc. (GeoEx), which guided climbs up Mount Kilimanjaro, required climbers to sign a release to participate in an expedition. The form required any disputes to be submitted to arbitration in San Francisco and limited damages to the cost of the trip. GeoEx told climbers that the terms were nonnegotiable and that other travel firms imposed the same terms. Jason Lhotka died on a GeoEx climb. His mother filed a suit against GeoEx. GeoEx sought arbitration. Was the arbitration clause unconscionable? Why or why not? [*Lhotka v. Geographic Expeditions, Inc.,* 181 Cal.App.4th 816, 104 Cal. Rptr.3d 844 (1 Dist. 2010)] **(See page 297.)**

—For a sample answer to Problem 11–6, go to Appendix H at the end of this text.

11–7   Mental Incompetence. Dorothy Drury suffered from dementia and chronic confusion. When she became unable to manage her own affairs, including decisions about medical and financial matters, her son Eddie arranged for her to move to an assisted living facility. During admission, she signed a residency agreement, which included an arbitration clause. After she sustained injuries in a fall at the facility, a suit was filed to recover damages. The facility asked the court to compel arbitration. Was Dorothy bound to the residency agreement? Discuss. [*Drury v. Assisted Living Concepts, Inc.,* 245 Or.App. 217, 262 P.3d 1162 (2011)] **(See page 290.)**

11–8   Licensing Statutes. PEMS Co. International, Inc., agreed to find a buyer for Rupp Industries, Inc., for a commission of 2 percent of the purchase price, which was to be paid by the buyer. Using PEMS's services, an investment group bought Rupp for $20 million and changed its name to Temp-Air, Inc. PEMS asked Temp-Air to pay a commission on the sale. Temp-Air refused, arguing that PEMS had acted as a broker in the deal without a license. The applicable statute defines a broker as any person who deals with the sale of a business. If this statute was intended to protect the public, can PEMS collect its commission? Explain. [*PEMS Co. International, Inc. v. Temp-Air, Inc.,* __ N.W.2d __ (Minn.App. 2011)] **(See page 292.)**

11–9   ⬌ A Question of Ethics—Promissory Estoppel. Claudia Aceves borrowed $845,000 from U.S. Bank to buy a home. Less than two years into the loan, she could no longer afford the monthly payments. The bank notified her that it planned to foreclose on her home. (Foreclosure is a process that allows a lender to repossess and sell the property that secures a loan—see Chapter 22.) The bank offered to modify Aceves's mortgage if she would forgo bankruptcy. In reliance on the bank's promise, she agreed. Once she withdrew the filing, however, the bank foreclosed and began eviction proceedings. Aceves filed a suit against the bank for promissory estoppel. [*Aceves v. U.S. Bank, N.A.,* 192 Cal.App.4th 218, 120 Cal.Rptr.3d 507 (2 Dist. 2011)] **(See page 286.)**

1. Could Aceves succeed in her claim of promissory estoppel? Why or why not?
2. Did Aceves or U.S. Bank behave unethically? Discuss.

Critical Thinking and Writing Assignments

11–10   Critical Legal Thinking. Are legalized forms of gambling, such as state-operated lotteries, consistent with a continuing public policy against the enforcement of gambling contracts? Why or why not? **(See page 292.)**

11–11   Business Law Critical Thinking Group Assignment. Assume that you are a group of executives at a large software corporation. The company is considering whether to add covenants not to compete to its employment contracts. You know that there are some issues with the enforceability of these covenants and want to make an informed decision.

1. One group should make a list of interests that are served by enforcing covenants not to compete.
2. A second group should create a list of interests that are served by refusing to enforce covenants not to compete.
3. A third group should discuss whether a court that determines that a covenant not to compete is illegal should reform (and then enforce) the covenant. The group should present arguments for and against reformation.

Defenses to Contract Enforceability

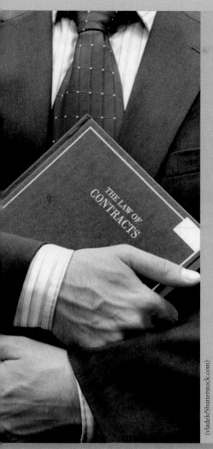

(vladek/Shutterstock.com)

CHAPTER OUTLINE

- Voluntary Consent
- The Statute of Frauds — Writing Requirement
- The Statute of Frauds — Sufficiency of the Writing
- The Parol Evidence Rule

LEARNING OBJECTIVES

The five learning objectives below are designed to help improve your understanding of the chapter. After reading this chapter, you should be able to answer the following questions:

1 In what types of situations might voluntary consent to a contract's terms be lacking?

2 What is the difference between a mistake of value or quality and a mistake of fact?

3 What are the elements of fraudulent misrepresentation?

4 What contracts must be in writing to be enforceable?

5 What is parol evidence? When is it admissible to clarify the terms of a written contract?

"Understanding is a two-way street."
—Eleanor Roosevelt, 1884–1962 (First Lady of the United States, 1933–1945)

An otherwise valid contract may still be unenforceable if the parties have not genuinely agreed to its terms. As mentioned in Chapter 9, a lack of voluntary consent is a *defense* to the enforcement of a contract. As Eleanor Roosevelt stated in the chapter-opening quotation, "Understanding is a two-way street." If one party does not voluntarily consent to the terms of a contract, then there is no genuine "meeting of the minds," and the law will not normally enforce the contract, as we discuss in the first part of this chapter.

A contract that is otherwise valid may also be unenforceable if it is not in the proper form. For example, if a contract is required by law to be in writing and there is no written evidence of the contract, it may not be enforceable. In the second part of this chapter, we examine the kinds of contracts that require a writing under what is called the *Statute of Frauds*. This chapter concludes with a discussion of the parol evidence rule, under which courts determine the admissibility at trial of evidence extraneous (external) to written contracts.

Voluntary Consent

LEARNING OBJECTIVE 1
In what types of situations might voluntary
consent to a contract's terms be lacking?

Voluntary consent (assent) may be lacking because of mistake, fraudulent misrepresentation, undue influence, or duress. Generally, a party who demonstrates that he or she did not genuinely agree to the terms of a contract can choose either to carry out the contract or to rescind (cancel) it and thus avoid the entire transaction.

This is one reason why many contracts include definitions of important terms (see the *Appendix to Chapter 14: An Annotated Employment Contract* for an example).

Mistakes

We all make mistakes, so it is not surprising that mistakes are made when contracts are created. In certain circumstances, contract law allows a contract to be avoided on the basis of mistake. It is important to distinguish between *mistakes of fact* and *mistakes of value or quality*. Only a mistake of fact may allow a contract to be avoided.

LEARNING OBJECTIVE 2
What is the difference between a mistake
of value or quality and a mistake of fact?

EXAMPLE 12.1   Paco buys a violin from Beverly for $250. Although the violin is very old, neither party believes that it is valuable. Later, however, an antiques dealer informs the parties that the violin is rare and worth thousands of dollars. Here, both parties were mistaken, but the mistake is a mistake of *value* rather than a mistake of *fact* that warrants contract rescission. Therefore, Beverly cannot rescind the contract. ●

Mistakes of fact occur in two forms—*unilateral* and *bilateral (mutual)*. A unilateral mistake is made by only one of the contracting parties, whereas a mutual mistake is made by both. We look next at these two types of mistakes and illustrate them graphically in Exhibit 12.1 on the facing page.

Unilateral Mistakes
A unilateral mistake occurs when only one party is mistaken as to a *material fact*—that is, a fact important to the subject matter of the contract. Generally, a unilateral mistake does not give the mistaken party any right to relief from the contract. In other words, the contract normally is enforceable against the mistaken party.

EXAMPLE 12.2   Elena intends to sell her motor home for $17,500. When she learns that Chin is interested in buying a used motor home, she sends him an e-mail offering to sell the vehicle to him. When typing the e-mail, however, she mistakenly keys in the price of $15,700. Chin immediately sends an e-mail to Elena, accepting her offer. Even though Elena intended to sell her motor home for $17,500, she has made a unilateral mistake and is bound by the contract to sell the vehicle to Chin for $15,700. ●

This rule has at least two exceptions, however.[1]

➤ KNOW THIS ➤
What a party to a contract knows or should
know can determine whether the contract is
enforceable.

When the Other Party Has Reason to Know That a Mistake Was Made   If the *other* party to the contract knows or should have known that a mistake of fact was made, the contract may not be enforceable. **EXAMPLE 12.3**   In *Example 12.2*, if Chin knew that Elena intended to sell her motor home for $17,500, then Elena's unilateral mistake (stating $15,700 in her offer) may render the resulting contract unenforceable. ●

Mathematical Mistakes   The second exception arises when a unilateral mistake of fact was due to a mathematical mistake in addition, subtraction, division, or multiplication and was made inadvertently and without gross (extreme) negligence. If a contractor's bid was significantly low because he or she made a mistake in addition when totaling the estimated costs, any contract resulting from the bid normally may be rescinded. Of course, in both situations, the mistake must still involve some *material fact* (one that is important and central to the contract).

Bilateral (Mutual) Mistakes
A bilateral mistake is a "mutual misunderstanding concerning a basic assumption on which the contract was made."[2] When both parties

---

1. The *Restatement (Second) of Contracts*, Section 153, liberalizes the general rule to take into account the modern trend of allowing avoidance in some circumstances even though only one party has been mistaken.

2. *Restatement (Second) of Contracts*, Section 152.

Exhibit 12.1 Mistakes of Fact

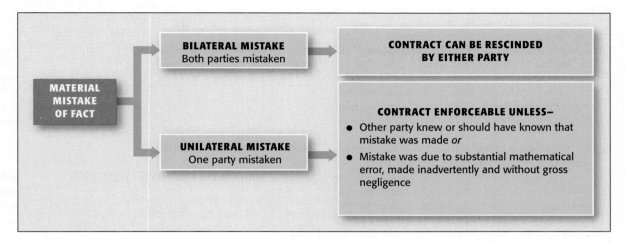

are mistaken about the same material fact, the contract can be rescinded by either party. Note that, as with unilateral mistakes, the mistake must be about a material fact. When a bilateral mistake occurs, normally the contract is voidable by the adversely affected party and can be rescinded, or canceled.

A word or term in a contract may be subject to more than one reasonable interpretation. If the parties to the contract attach materially different meanings to the term, their mutual misunderstanding may allow the contract to be rescinded.

CASE EXAMPLE 12.4   In a classic case, Wichelhaus purchased a shipment of cotton from Raffles to arrive on a ship called the *Peerless* sailing from Bombay, India. Wichelhaus meant a ship called *Peerless* leaving Bombay in October, but Raffles meant a different ship also named *Peerless* leaving Bombay in December. When the goods arrived on the December *Peerless* and Raffles tried to deliver them, Wichelhaus refused to accept them. The British court held for Wichelhaus, concluding that a mutual mistake had been made because the parties had attached materially different meanings to an essential term of the contract (which ship *Peerless* was to transport the goods).[3] ●

In the following case, the court had to grapple with the question of whether a mutual mistake of fact had occurred.

> "Mistakes are the inevitable lot of mankind."
>
> Sir George Jessel, 1824–1883 (English jurist)

---

3. *Raffles v. Wichelhaus,* 159 Eng.Rep. 375 (1864).

Case 12.1

L&H Construction Co. v. Circle Redmont, Inc.

District Court of Appeal of Florida, Fifth District, 55 So.3d 630 (2011).
www.5dca.org/opinions.shtml[a]

The Thomas Edison historic site in West Orange, New Jersey.

FACTS L&H Construction Company was a general contractor involved in the renovation of the Thomas Edison historic site in West Orange, New Jersey, for the National Park Service. L&H contracted with Circle Redmont, Inc. (Redmont), which is based in Melbourne, Florida, to make a cast-iron staircase and a glass flooring system. Redmont's original proposal was to "engineer, fabricate, and install" the staircase and flooring

---

a. In the "Search Opinions" section, in the "Search for this:" box, type "5D09-2609" and click on "Submit." In the result, click on the appropriate link to view the opinion. The Florida Fifth District Court of Appeal maintains this Web site.

Case 12.1—Continues next page ➡

Case 12.1—Continued

system. During negotiations, however, installation and its costs were cut from the deal. In the final agreement, payment was due on "Supervision of Installation" instead of "Completion of Installation." Nevertheless, the final agreement stated that Redmont would "engineer, fabricate, and install." Later, Redmont claimed that this was a mistake. L&H insisted that installation was included. L&H filed a suit in a Florida state court against Redmont. The court found that the word *install* in the phrase "engineer, fabricate, and install" was the result of a mutual mistake. L&H appealed.

ISSUE   Was the use of the word *install* in the phrase "engineer, fabricate, and install" a mutual mistake of fact?

DECISION   Yes. A state intermediate appellate court upheld the lower court's decision on the question of whether the use of the word *install* in the parties' agreement was a mutual mistake. The appellate court reversed the lower court's final judgment in Redmont's favor on other grounds, however.

REASON   The appellate court explained that the contract between these parties was ambiguous. The proposal indicated that Redmont would "engineer, fabricate, and install" the staircase and flooring system, but the agreement stated that L&H's final payment was due on "Supervision" of the installation. According to the testimony of Redmont's witnesses, the final agreement stated the parties' understanding that Redmont would only supervise the installation, not perform it. Installation was cut from the contract as a cost-saving measure at the request of L&H's president. The trial court determined that these witnesses were credible.

WHAT IF THE FACTS WERE DIFFERENT?   *Suppose that Redmont had intentionally misled L&H to believe that installation was included in the price. Would the court's decision on the mutual mistake issue have been different? Discuss.*

Fraudulent Misrepresentation

Although fraud is a tort (see Chapter 4), the presence of fraud also affects the authenticity of the innocent party's consent to a contract. When an innocent party is fraudulently induced to enter into a contract, the contract usually can be avoided because she or he has not *voluntarily* consented to the terms.[4] Normally, the innocent party can either rescind (cancel) the contract and be restored to her or his original position or enforce the contract and seek damages for any harms resulting from the fraud.

Generally, fraudulent misrepresentation refers only to misrepresentation that is consciously false and is intended to mislead another. Typically, fraud involves three elements:

1. A misrepresentation of a material fact must occur.
2. There must be an intent to deceive.
3. The innocent party must justifiably rely on the misrepresentation.

Additionally, to collect damages, a party must have been harmed as a result of the misrepresentation.

Fraudulent misrepresentation can occur in the online as well as the offline environment. For a case involving allegations that Yahoo fraudulently posted online personal ads, see this chapter's *Adapting the Law to the Online Environment* feature on the facing page. Because curbing Internet fraud is a major challenge in today's world, we will explore the topic further in Chapter 33 in the context of consumer law.

Misrepresentation Has Occurred   The first element of proving fraud is to show that misrepresentation of a material fact has occurred. This misrepresentation can occur by words or actions. For instance, an art gallery owner's statement "This painting is a Picasso" is a misrepresentation of fact if the painting was done by another artist. Similarly, if a customer asks to see only Jasper Johns paintings and the owner immediately leads the customer over to paintings that were not done by Johns, the owner's actions can be a misrepresentation.

LEARNING OBJECTIVE 3
What are the elements of fraudulent misrepresentation?

KNOW THIS

To collect damages in almost any lawsuit, there must be some sort of injury.

---

4. *Restatement (Second) of Contracts,* Sections 163 and 164.

ADAPTING THE LAW TO THE ONLINE ENVIRONMENT

MISREPRESENTATION IN ONLINE PERSONALS

If you type "online personals" into any search engine, you will get more than 15 million hits. In the past, a major player in the online personals matching business was Yahoo! Personals. Indeed, for a time, it called itself the "top online dating site." It offered two options—one for casual dates and another for people who wanted serious relationships. The latter was called Yahoo! Personals Primer. Users had to take a relationship test and then used Yahoo's matching system software to "zero in on marriage material."

Misrepresentation Reared Its Ugly Head

Everyone who uses online dating services is aware that people tend to exaggerate their positive features and downplay their negatives when they create their profiles. But users generally assume that the profiles are not completely made up. A few years ago, however, a disgruntled user of Yahoo! Personals Primer brought a lawsuit claiming that Yahoo had done exactly that. The suit alleged fraud and negligent misrepresentation, among other things.

Robert Anthony claimed that Yahoo deliberately and intentionally originated, created, and perpetuated false and/or nonexistent profiles. Not only did many profiles use the exact same phrases to describe people, but the same photo appeared for different profiles. Anthony also claimed that when a subscription term neared its end, Yahoo would send the subscriber a fake profile, heralding it as a "potential new match."

The Court Disagreed with Yahoo

Yahoo asked the court to dismiss the complaint on the ground that it was barred by the Communications Decency Act (CDA) of 1996,[a] which protects Internet service providers from liability for material supplied by their users. The court rejected that argument and held that Yahoo had become an information content provider itself when it created bogus user profiles. The case was allowed to continue.[b]

---

a. 47 U.S.C. Section 230.
b. *Anthony v. Yahoo!, Inc.*, 421 F.Supp.2d 1257 (N.D.Cal. 2006). See also *Doe v. SexSearch.com*, 502 F.Supp.2d 719 (N.D. Ohio 2007); and *Fair Housing Council of San Fernando Valley v. Roommate.com, LLC*, 521 F.3d 1157 (9th Cir. 2008).

When is misrepresentation actionable on online dating Web sites?

Match.com Faced Similar Charges

Earlier, Match.com, another large online dating service, faced a similar lawsuit. Matthew Evans claimed that he had obtained a date through Match.com with a woman who later confessed that she was actually an employee. The lawsuit claimed that Match.com "secretly employs people as 'date bait' to send bogus e-mails and to go on as many as 300 dates a month in order to keep customers paying for the use of the site." That suit was dismissed, however.

A class-action suit brought in 2009 accused Match.com of matching customers with individuals who were nonpaying customers or who were not customers at all. This suit has not yet been resolved.

As of 2010, Match.com became the exclusive online dating service provider for Yahoo!, Inc. The co-branded site is called Match.com on Yahoo!

Critical Thinking

Assume that a user of Match.com on Yahoo! discovered that each profile exaggerated the person's physical appearance, intelligence, and occupation. Would that user prevail if she or he brought a lawsuit for fraudulent misrepresentation? Why or why not?

Misrepresentation by Conduct Misrepresentation also occurs when a party takes specific action to conceal a fact that is material to the contract.[5] For instance, if a seller, by her or his actions, prevents a buyer from learning of some fact that is material to the contract, the seller's behavior constitutes misrepresentation by conduct.

---

5. *Restatement (Second) of Contracts*, Section 160.

CASE EXAMPLE 12.5   Actor Tom Selleck contracted to purchase a horse named Zorro for his daughter from Dolores Cuenca. Cuenca acted as though Zorro was fit to ride in competitions, when in reality the horse suffered from a medical condition. Selleck filed a lawsuit against Cuenca for wrongfully concealing the horse's condition, and a jury awarded Selleck more than $187,000 for Cuenca's misrepresentation by conduct.[6] ●

Another example of misrepresentation by conduct is the untruthful denial of knowledge or information concerning facts that are material to the contract when such knowledge or information is requested.

Statements of Opinion

Statements of opinion and representations of future facts (predictions) are generally not subject to claims of fraud. Every person is expected to exercise care and judgment when entering into contracts, and the law will not come to the aid of one who simply makes an unwise bargain. Statements such as "This land will be worth twice as much next year" and "This car will last for years and years" are statements of opinion, not fact. Contracting parties should recognize them as opinions and not rely on them. A fact is objective and verifiable, whereas an opinion is usually subject to debate. Therefore, a seller is allowed to use *puffery* to sell her or his goods without being liable for fraud.

Nevertheless, in certain situations, such as when a naïve purchaser relies on an opinion from an expert, the innocent party may be entitled to rescission or reformation. (Reformation is an equitable remedy by which a court alters the terms of a contract to reflect the true intentions of the parties.)

CASE EXAMPLE 12.6   In a classic case, an instructor at an Arthur Murray dance school told Audrey Vokes, a widow without family, that she had the potential to become an accomplished dancer. The instructor sold her 2,302 hours of dancing lessons for a total amount of $31,090.45 (equivalent to $142,000 in 2013). When it became clear to Vokes that she did not, in fact, have the potential to be an excellent dancer, she sued the school for fraudulent misrepresentation. The court held that because the dance school had superior knowledge about a person's dance potential, the instructor's statements could be considered statements of fact rather than opinion.[7] ●

Misrepresentation of Law

Misrepresentation of law *ordinarily* does not entitle a party to be relieved of a contract. **EXAMPLE 12.7**   Tanya has a parcel of property that she is trying to sell to Lev. Tanya knows that a local ordinance prohibits building anything higher than three stories on the property. Nonetheless, she tells Lev, "You can build a condominium one hundred stories high if you want to." Lev buys the land and later discovers that Tanya's statement is false. Lev generally cannot avoid the contract because under the common law, people are assumed to know state and local laws. ●

Exceptions to this rule occur, however, when the misrepresenting party is in a profession known to require greater knowledge of the law than the average citizen possesses, such as real estate brokers or lawyers.

Misrepresentation by Silence

Ordinarily, neither party to a contract has a duty to come forward and disclose facts, and a contract normally will not be set aside because certain pertinent information has not been volunteered. **EXAMPLE 12.8**   Jude is selling a car that has been in an accident and has been repaired. He does not need to volunteer this information to a potential buyer. If, however, the buyer asks him if the car has had extensive bodywork and he lies, Jude has committed fraudulent misrepresentation. ●

In general, if the seller knows of a serious defect or a serious potential problem that the buyer cannot reasonably be expected to discover, the seller may have a duty to speak.

---

6. *Selleck v. Cuenca*, Case No. GIN056909, North County of San Diego, California, decided September 9, 2009.
7. *Vokes v. Arthur Murray, Inc.*, 212 So.2d 906 (Fla.App. 1968).

"If a man smiles all the time, he's probably selling something that doesn't work."

George Carlin, 1937–2008 (American comedian)

Should an architect have greater knowledge about building codes than the person paying for the project?

(shutbydave/iStockphoto.com)

Normally, the seller must disclose only *latent defects*—that is, defects that could not readily be ascertained. Because a buyer of a house could easily discover the presence of termites through an inspection, for instance, termites may not qualify as a latent defect. Also, when the parties are in a *fiduciary relationship*—one of trust, such as partners, physician and patient, or attorney and client—there is a duty to disclose material facts. Failure to do so may constitute fraud.

In the following case, the issue of misrepresentation by silence was at the heart of the dispute. A real estate investor sued for fraud after a seller failed to disclose material facts about the property's value.

Case 12.2

Fazio v. Cypress/GR Houston I, LP

Court of Appeals of Texas, First District, 2012 WL 5324842 (2012).

(matkin/iStockphoto.com)

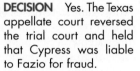
What does a rent-reduction request from a shopping mall's main tenant indicate?

FACTS Peter Fazio began talks with Cypress/GR Houston I, LP, to buy retail property whose main tenant was a Garden Ridge store. In performing a background investigation, Fazio and his agents became concerned about Garden Ridge's financial health. Nevertheless, after being assured that Garden Ridge had a positive financial outlook, Fazio sent Cypress a letter of intent to buy the property for $7.67 million "[b]ased on the currently reported absolute net income of $805,040.00." Cypress then agreed to provide all information in its possession, but it failed to disclose that (1) a consultant for Garden Ridge had recently requested a $240,000 reduction in the annual rent as part of a restructuring of the company's real estate leases and (2) Cypress's bank was so concerned about Garden Ridge's financial health that it had required a personal guaranty of the property's loan. The parties entered into a purchase agreement, but Garden Ridge went into bankruptcy shortly after the deal closed. Fazio sued Cypress for fraud after he was forced to sell the property for only $3.75 million. A jury found in Fazio's favor, but the trial court awarded a *judgment notwithstanding the verdict* (see page 80) to Cypress. Fazio appealed.

ISSUE Was Fazio fraudulently induced to enter into the purchase agreement?

DECISION Yes. The Texas appellate court reversed the trial court and held that Cypress was liable to Fazio for fraud.

REASON The court found that Cypress had engaged in fraud as a matter of law. Before the parties entered into the purchase agreement, Cypress had agreed to provide all information in its possession. Cypress knew that Fazio had been concerned about Garden Ridge's financial health and that he had based the purchase price on the anticipated income from the property. Moreover, a reasonable person in Fazio's position would have attached significance to Garden Ridge's recent request for a $240,000 rent reduction and to the fact that Cypress had been required to provide a personal guaranty of the property's loan. Finally, in the purchase agreement, Fazio did not disclaim his reliance on Cypress's misrepresentations or waive possible claims for fraud.

CRITICAL THINKING—Ethical Consideration *Was Cypress's conduct unethical? Why or why not?*

Scienter Knowledge by a misrepresenting party that material facts have been falsely represented or omitted with an intent to deceive.

Intent to Deceive The second element of fraud is knowledge on the part of the misrepresenting party that facts have been misrepresented. This element, usually called **scienter,**[8] or "guilty knowledge," generally signifies that there was an intent to deceive. *Scienter* clearly exists if a party knows that a fact is not as stated. *Scienter* also exists if a party

8. Pronounced *sy-en-*ter.

makes a statement that he or she believes not to be true or makes a statement recklessly, without regard to whether it is true or false. Finally, this element is met if a party says or implies that a statement is made on some basis, such as personal knowledge or personal investigation, when it is not.

CASE EXAMPLE 12.9   Robert Sarvis applied for a position as a business law professor two weeks after his release from prison. On his résumé, he said that he had been a corporate president for fourteen years and had taught business law at another college. After he was hired, his probation officer alerted the school to Sarvis's criminal history. The school immediately fired him, and Sarvis sued for breach of his employment contract. The court concluded that by not disclosing his history, Sarvis clearly exhibited an intent to deceive and that the school had justifiably relied on his misrepresentations. Therefore, the school could rescind Sarvis's employment contract.[9] ●

Justifiable Reliance on the Misrepresentation

The third element of fraud is *justifiable reliance* on the misrepresentation of fact. The deceived party must have a justifiable reason for relying on the misrepresentation, and the misrepresentation must be an important factor (but not necessarily the sole factor) in inducing the party to enter into the contract.

Reliance is not justified if the innocent party knows the true facts or relies on obviously extravagant statements.   **EXAMPLE 12.10**   If a used-car dealer tells you, "This old Cadillac will get over sixty miles to the gallon," you normally would not be justified in relying on this statement. Suppose, however, that Merkel, a bank director, induces O'Connell, a co-director, to sign a statement that the bank has sufficient assets to meet its liabilities by telling O'Connell, "We have plenty of assets to satisfy our creditors." This statement is false. If O'Connell knows the true facts or, as a bank director, should know the true facts, he is not justified in relying on Merkel's statement. If O'Connell does not know the true facts, however, *and has no way of finding them out,* he may be justified in relying on the statement. ●

Injury to the Innocent Party

Most courts do not require a showing of harm when the action is to rescind (cancel) the contract. These courts hold that because rescission returns the parties to the positions they held before the contract was made, a showing of injury to the innocent party is unnecessary.

To recover damages caused by fraud, however, proof of an injury is universally required. The measure of damages is ordinarily equal to the property's value had it been delivered as represented, less the actual price paid for the property. Courts may also award *punitive,* or *exemplary, damages,* which compensate a plaintiff over and above the amount of the actual loss. As discussed on pages 96 and 97 of Chapter 4, the public-policy consideration underlying punitive damages is to punish the defendant and thereby set an example that will deter similar wrongdoing by others.

PREVENTING LEGAL DISPUTES

If you are selling products or services, assume that all clients and customers are naïve and that they rely on your representations. Instruct employees to phrase their comments so that customers understand that any statements that are not factual are the employee's opinion. If someone asks a question that is beyond the employee's knowledge, it is better to say that he or she does not know than to guess and have the customer rely on a representation that turns out to be false. This can be particularly important when the questions concern topics such as compatibility or speed of electronic and digital goods, software, or related services.

---

9. *Sarvis v. Vermont State Colleges,* 172 Vt. 76, 772 A.2d 494 (2001).

Undue Influence

Undue influence arises from relationships in which one party can greatly influence another party, thus overcoming that party's free will. A contract entered into under excessive or undue influence lacks voluntary consent and is therefore voidable.[10]

In various types of relationships, one party may have an opportunity to dominate and unfairly influence another party. Minors and elderly people, for instance, are often under the influence of guardians (persons who are legally responsible for others). If a guardian induces a young or elderly ward (a person whom the guardian looks after) to enter into a contract that benefits the guardian, the guardian may have exerted undue influence. Undue influence can arise from a number of confidential or fiduciary relationships, including attorney-client, physician-patient, guardian-ward, parent-child, husband-wife, and trustee-beneficiary.

The essential feature of undue influence is that the party being taken advantage of does not, in reality, exercise free will in entering into a contract. It is not enough that a person is elderly or suffers from some mental or physical impairment. There must be clear and convincing evidence that the person did not act out of her or his free will.

Duress

Agreement to the terms of a contract is not voluntary if one of the parties is forced into the agreement. The use of threats to force a party to enter into a contract constitutes *duress*,[11] as does blackmail or extortion to induce consent to a contract. Duress is both a defense to the enforcement of a contract and a ground for rescission of a contract.

To establish duress, there must be proof of a threat. The threatened act must be wrongful or illegal and must render the person incapable of exercising free will. A threat to exercise a legal right, such as the right to sue someone, ordinarily does not constitute duress.

The Statute of Frauds— Writing Requirement

LEARNING OBJECTIVE 4
What contracts must be in writing to be enforceable?

Another defense to the enforceability of a contract is *form*—that is, some contracts must be in writing. Every state has a statute that stipulates that certain types of contracts must be in writing or be evidenced by a written memorandum or electronic record that is signed by the party against whom enforcement is sought, unless certain exceptions apply. Although the statutes vary slightly from state to state, their primary purpose is to ensure that, for certain types of contracts, there is reliable evidence of the contracts and their terms. In this text, we refer to these statutes collectively as the **Statute of Frauds**.

Statute of Frauds A state statute that requires certain types of contracts to be in writing to be enforceable.

The following types of contracts are said to fall "within" or "under" the Statute of Frauds and therefore require a writing:

1. Contracts involving interests in land.
2. Contracts that cannot by their terms be performed within one year from the day after the date of formation.
3. Collateral contracts, such as promises to answer for the debt or duty of another.
4. Promises made in consideration of marriage.
5. Under the Uniform Commercial Code (UCC—see Chapter 15), contracts for the sale of goods priced at $500 or more.

---

10. *Restatement (Second) of Contracts*, Section 177.
11. *Restatement (Second) of Contracts*, Sections 174 and 175.

The actual name of the Statute of Frauds is misleading because it does not apply to fraud. Rather, in an effort to prevent fraud, the statute denies *enforceability* to certain contracts that do not comply with its requirements. The name derives from an English act passed in 1677 that was titled "An Act for the Prevention of Frauds and Perjuries."

Contracts Involving Interests in Land

Under the Statute of Frauds, a contract involving an interest in land must be evidenced by a writing to be enforceable.[12] **EXAMPLE 12.11**   If Carol contracts orally to sell Seaside Shelter to Axel but later decides not to sell, Axel cannot enforce the contract. Similarly, if Axel refuses to close the deal, Carol cannot force Axel to pay for the land by bringing a lawsuit. The Statute of Frauds is a defense to the enforcement of this type of oral contract. ●

A contract for the sale of land ordinarily involves the entire interest in the real property (discussed in Chapter 36), including buildings, growing crops, vegetation, minerals, timber, and anything else permanently attached to the land. Therefore, a *fixture* (personal property so affixed or so used as to become a part of the realty) is treated as real property.

The Statute of Frauds requires written contracts not just for the sale of land but also for the transfer of other interests in land, such as mortgages, easements, and leases. We describe these other interests in Chapters 22 and 36.

The One-Year Rule

Contracts that cannot, *by their own terms,* be performed within one year *from the day after* the contract is formed must be in writing to be enforceable. Because disputes over such contracts are unlikely to occur until some time after the contracts are made, resolution of these disputes is difficult unless the contract terms have been put in writing.

Time Period Starts the Day after the Contract Is Formed
The one-year period begins to run *the day after the contract is made.* **EXAMPLE 12.12**   Superior University forms a contract with Kimi San stating that San will teach three courses in history during the coming academic year (September 15 through June 15). If the contract is formed in March, it must be in writing to be enforceable—because it cannot be performed within one year. If the contract is not formed until July, however, it will not have to be in writing to be enforceable—because it can be performed within one year. ●

Exhibit 12.2 on the facing page graphically illustrates the one-year rule.

Is Performance within One Year Possible?
Normally, the test for determining whether an oral contract is enforceable under the one-year rule of the Statute of Frauds is whether performance is *possible* within one year from the day after the date of contract formation—not whether the agreement is *likely* to be performed within one year. When performance of a contract is objectively impossible during the one-year period, the oral contract will be unenforceable.

 EXAMPLE 12.13   Bankers Life orally contracts to lend $40,000 to Janet Lawrence "as long as Lawrence & Associates operates its financial consulting firm in Omaha, Nebraska." The contract does not fall within the Statute of Frauds—no writing is required—because Lawrence & Associates could go out of business in one year or less. In this event, the contract would be fully performed within one year. Similarly, an oral contract for lifetime employment does not fall within the Statute of Frauds. Because an employee who is hired

"A verbal contract isn't worth the paper it's written on."

Samuel Goldwyn, 1879–1974
(Hollywood motion picture producer)

---

12. In some states, the contract will be enforced if each party admits to the existence of the oral contract in court or admits to its existence during discovery before trial (see Chapter 3).

Exhibit 12.2 The One-Year Rule

Under the Statute of Frauds, contracts that by their terms are impossible to perform within one year from the day after the date of contract formation must be in writing to be enforceable. Put another way, if it is at all possible to perform an oral contract within one year from the day after the contract is made, the contract will fall outside the Statute of Frauds and be enforceable.

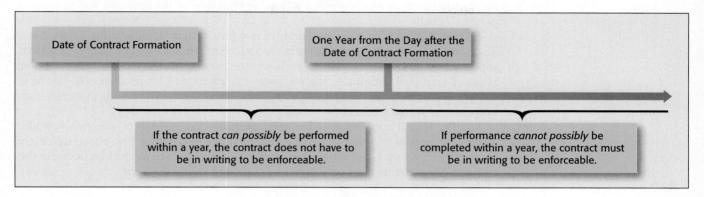

"for life" can die within a year, the courts reason that the contract can be performed within one year. ●

Collateral Promises

Collateral Promise A secondary promise to a primary transaction, such as a promise made by one person to pay the debts of another if the latter fails to perform. A collateral promise normally must be in writing to be enforceable.

A **collateral promise,** or secondary promise, is one that is ancillary (subsidiary) to a principal transaction or primary contractual relationship. In other words, a collateral promise is one made by a third party to assume the debts or obligations of a primary party to a contract if that party does not perform. Any collateral promise of this nature falls under the Statute of Frauds and therefore must be in writing to be enforceable. To understand this concept, it is important to distinguish between primary and secondary promises and obligations.

Primary versus Secondary Obligations   A contract in which a party assumes a primary obligation normally does not need to be in writing to be enforceable. **EXAMPLE 12.14**   Kareem orally contracts with Joanne's Floral Boutique to send his mother a dozen roses for Mother's Day. He agrees to pay when he receives the bill from Joanne's. Because Kareem is a direct party to this contract and has incurred a *primary* obligation to Joanne's, this contract does not have to be in writing under the Statute of Frauds. If Kareem fails to pay and the florist sues him for payment, Kareem cannot raise the Statute of Frauds as a defense. He cannot claim that the contract is unenforceable because it was not in writing. ●

In contrast, a contract in which a party assumes a secondary obligation does have to be in writing to be enforceable. **EXAMPLE 12.15**   Kareem's mother borrows $10,000 from the Medford Trust Company on a promissory note payable in six months. Kareem promises the bank officer handling the loan that he will pay the $10,000 *if his mother does not pay the loan on time.* Kareem, in this situation, becomes what is known as a *guarantor* on the loan. He is guaranteeing to the bank (the creditor) that he will pay the loan if his mother fails to do so. This kind of collateral promise, in which the guarantor states that he or she will become responsible only if the primary party does not perform, must be in writing to be enforceable. ●   We will return to the concept of guaranty and the distinction between primary and secondary obligations in Chapter 21 in the context of creditors' rights.

An Exception—The "Main Purpose" Rule

An oral promise to answer for the debt of another is covered by the Statute of Frauds *unless* the guarantor's purpose in accepting secondary liability is to secure a personal benefit. Under the "main purpose" rule, this type of contract need not be in writing.[13] The assumption is that a court can infer from the circumstances of a case whether a "leading objective" of the promisor was to secure a personal benefit.

EXAMPLE 12.16   Carrie Braswell contracts with Custom Manufacturing Company to have some machines custom made for her factory. She promises Newform Supply, Custom's supplier, that if Newform continues to deliver the materials to Custom for the production of the custom-made machines, she will guarantee payment. This promise need not be in writing, even though the effect may be to pay the debt of another, because Braswell's main purpose is to secure a benefit for herself. ●

Another typical application of the main purpose doctrine occurs when one creditor guarantees the debtor's debt to another creditor to forestall litigation. This allows the debtor to remain in business long enough to generate profits sufficient to pay *both* creditors. In this situation, the guaranty does not need to be in writing to be enforceable.

Promises Made in Consideration of Marriage

A unilateral promise to make a monetary payment or to give property in consideration of marriage must be in writing.   **EXAMPLE 12.17**   Baumann promises to pay Joe Villard $10,000 if Villard marries Baumann's daughter. Because the promise is in consideration of marriage, it must be in writing to be enforceable. ●

The same rule applies to **prenuptial agreements**—agreements made before marriage (also called *antenuptial agreements*) that define each partner's ownership rights in the other partner's property. A prospective wife or husband may wish to limit the amount the prospective spouse can obtain if the marriage ends in divorce. Prenuptial agreements must be in writing to be enforceable. Generally, courts tend to give more credence to prenuptial agreements that are accompanied by consideration.

EXAMPLE 12.18   After a divorce from actor Tom Cruise, actress Nicole Kidman entered into a prenuptial agreement with her second husband, country singer Keith Urban. Kidman agreed that in the event of a divorce, she would pay Urban $640,000 for every year they were married, unless Urban relapsed and used drugs again (then he would receive nothing). ●

Prenuptial Agreement An agreement made before marriage that defines each partner's ownership rights in the other partner's property. Prenuptial agreements must be in writing to be enforceable.

Contracts for the Sale of Goods

The Uniform Commercial Code (UCC—see Chapter 15) includes Statute of Frauds provisions that require written evidence or an electronic record of a contract. Section 2–201 requires a writing or memorandum for the sale of goods priced at $500 or more under the UCC (this low threshold amount may be increased in the future). To satisfy the UCC requirement, a writing need only state the quantity term. Other terms agreed on do not have to be stated "accurately" in the writing, as long as they adequately reflect both parties' intentions.

The contract will not be enforceable, however, for any quantity greater than that set forth in the writing. In addition, the writing must have been signed by the person to be charged—that is, by the person who refuses to perform or the one being sued. Beyond

"*Wallace, have you forgotten our prenuptial contract? No whistling!*"

---

13. *Restatement (Second) of Contracts*, Section 116.

these two requirements, the writing need not designate the buyer or the seller, the terms of payment, or the price. (See this chapter's *Beyond Our Borders* feature below to learn whether other countries have requirements similar to those in the Statute of Frauds.)

Exceptions to the Statute of Frauds

Exceptions to the applicability of the Statute of Frauds are made in certain situations. We describe those situations here.

Partial Performance   When a contract has been partially performed and the parties cannot be returned to their positions prior to the contract, a court may grant *specific performance* (an equitable remedy that requires a contract to be performed according to its precise terms—see Chapter 14).

In cases involving oral contracts for the transfer of interests in land, courts usually look at whether justice is better served by enforcing the oral contract when partial performance has taken place. For instance, if the purchaser has paid part of the price, taken possession, and made valuable improvements to the property, a court may grant specific performance. The parties still have to prove that an oral contract existed, however.

In some states, mere reliance on certain types of oral contracts is enough to remove them from the Statute of Frauds. Under the UCC, an oral contract for goods priced at $500 or more is enforceable to the extent that a seller accepts payment or a buyer accepts delivery of the goods.[14]

Admissions   In some states, if a party against whom enforcement of an oral contract is sought admits in pleadings, testimony, or otherwise in court proceedings that a contract for sale was made, the contract will be enforceable.[15] A contract subject to the UCC will be enforceable, but only to the extent of the quantity admitted.[16]

EXAMPLE 12.19   The president of Ashley Corporation admits under oath that an oral agreement was made with Com Best to pay $10,000 for certain business equipment. In this situation, a court will enforce the agreement only to the extent admitted (the $10,000), even if Com Best claims that the agreement involved $20,000 of equipment. •

---

14. UCC 2–201(3)(c). See Chapter 15.
15. *Restatement (Second) of Contracts*, Section 133.
16. UCC 2–201(3)(b). See Chapter 15.

BEYOND OUR BORDERS

The Statute of Frauds and International Sales Contracts

As you will read in Chapter 15, the Convention on Contracts for the International Sale of Goods (CISG) provides rules that govern international sales contracts between citizens of countries that have ratified the convention (agreement). Article 11 of the CISG does not incorporate any Statute of Frauds provisions. Rather, it states that a "contract for sale need not be concluded in or evidenced by writing and is not subject to any other requirements as to form."

Article 11 accords with the legal customs of most nations, which no longer require contracts to meet certain formal or writing requirements to be enforceable. Ironically, even England, the nation that enacted the original Statute of Frauds in 1677, has repealed all of it except the provisions relating to collateral promises and to transfers of interests in land. Many other countries that once had such statutes have also repealed all or parts of them.

Civil law countries, such as France, have never required certain types of contracts to be in writing. Obviously, without a writing requirement, contracts can take on any form.

Critical Thinking

If a country does not have a Statute of Frauds and a dispute arises over an oral agreement, how can the parties substantiate their positions?

Promissory Estoppel   In some states, an oral contract that would otherwise be unenforceable under the Statute of Frauds may be enforced under the doctrine of promissory estoppel (see page 286 in Chapter 11). Section 139 of the *Restatement (Second) of Contracts* provides that an oral promise can be enforceable, notwithstanding the Statute of Frauds, if the promisee has justifiably relied on it to her or his detriment. For the contract to be enforceable, the reliance must have been foreseeable to the person making the promise, and enforcing the promise must be the only way to avoid injustice.

Special Exceptions under the UCC   Special exceptions to the applicability of the Statute of Frauds exist for sales contracts. Oral contracts for customized goods may be enforced in certain circumstances. Another exception has to do with oral contracts *between merchants* that have been confirmed in writing. We will examine these exceptions in Chapter 15.

Exhibit 12.3 below graphically summarizes the types of contracts that fall under the Statute of Frauds and the various exceptions that apply.

The Statute of Frauds— Sufficiency of the Writing

A written contract will satisfy the writing requirement of the Statute of Frauds. (See the Appendix to Chapter 14 for an example of a written contract and descriptions of the meaning of its terms.) A *written memorandum* (written or electronic evidence of the oral contract) signed by the party against whom enforcement is sought will also satisfy the writing requirement.

The signature need not be placed at the end of the document but can be anywhere in the writing. It can even be initials rather than the full name. As mentioned in Chapter 10, in today's business world, there are many ways to create signatures electronically, and electronic signatures generally satisfy the Statute of Frauds.

What Constitutes a Writing?

A writing can consist of any confirmation, invoice, sales slip, check, fax, or e-mail—or such items in combination. The written contract need not consist of a single document to constitute an enforceable contract. One document may incorporate another document by expressly referring to it. Several documents may form a single contract if they are physically

Exhibit 12.3 **Contracts Subject to the Statute of Frauds**

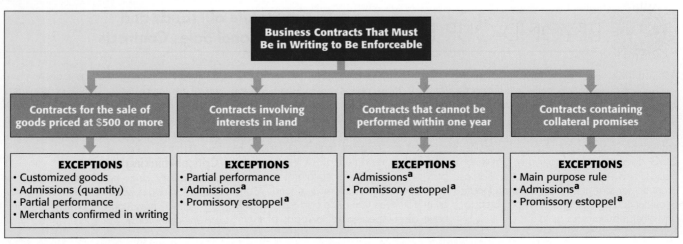

Business Contracts That Must Be in Writing to Be Enforceable

Contracts for the sale of goods priced at $500 or more	Contracts involving interests in land	Contracts that cannot be performed within one year	Contracts containing collateral promises
EXCEPTIONS • Customized goods • Admissions (quantity) • Partial performance • Merchants confirmed in writing	**EXCEPTIONS** • Partial performance • Admissions[a] • Promissory estoppel[a]	**EXCEPTIONS** • Admissions[a] • Promissory estoppel[a]	**EXCEPTIONS** • Main purpose rule • Admissions[a] • Promissory estoppel[a]

a. Some states follow Section 133 (on admissions) and Section 139 (on promissory estoppel) of the *Restatement (Second) of Contracts*.

attached—such as by staple, paper clip, or glue—or even if they are only placed in the same envelope. (See the *Business Application* feature on page 323.)

EXAMPLE 12.20 Simpson orally agrees to sell some land next to a shopping mall to Terro Properties. Simpson gives Terro an unsigned memo that contains a legal description of the property, and Terro gives Simpson an unsigned first draft of their contract. Simpson sends Terro a signed letter that refers to the memo and to the first and final drafts of the contract. Terro sends Simpson an unsigned copy of the final draft of the contract with a signed check stapled to it. Together, the documents can constitute a writing sufficient to satisfy the Statute of Frauds and bind both parties to the terms of the contract as evidenced by the writings. •

> "The pen is mightier than the sword, and considerably easier to write with."
>
> Marty Feldman, 1934–1982
> (English actor and comedian)

What Must Be Contained in the Writing?

A memorandum or note evidencing the oral contract need only contain the essential terms of the contract, not every term. There must, of course, also be some indication that the parties voluntarily agreed to the terms. A faxed or e-mailed memo of the terms of an agreement could be sufficient if it showed that there was a meeting of the minds and that the terms were not just part of the preliminary negotiations.[17] Under the UCC, in regard to the sale of goods, the writing need only state the quantity and be signed by the party against whom enforcement is sought.

Because only the party against whom enforcement is sought must have signed the writing, a contract may be enforceable by one of its parties but not by the other. **EXAMPLE 12.21** Rock orally agrees to buy Betty Devlin's lake house and lot for $350,000. Devlin writes Rock a letter confirming the sale by identifying the parties and the essential terms of the sales contract—price, method of payment, and legal address—and signs the letter. Devlin has made a written memorandum of the oral land contract. Because she signed the letter, she normally can be held to the oral contract by Rock. Devlin cannot enforce the agreement against Rock, however. Because he has not signed or entered into a written contract or memorandum, Rock can plead the Statute of Frauds as a defense. •

In the following case, the court was presented with a written document that the plaintiff sought to enforce. The writing, however, was missing at least one element needed to satisfy the Statute of Frauds—the signatures of the parties against whom the enforcement was being sought.

---

17. See, for example, *Coca-Cola Co. v. Babyback's International, Inc.*, 841 N.E.2d 557 (Ind.App. 2006).

Case 12.3

Beneficial Homeowner Service Corp. v. Steele

Supreme Court of New York, Suffolk County, 2011 WL 61728 (2011).

(Feverpitched/iStockphoto.com)

Lenders foreclose on many houses and then sell them.

FACTS Beneficial Homeowner Service Corporation filed a suit against Stephen and Susan Steele to foreclose on a mortgage. (A mortgage is a written instrument that gives a creditor an interest in the property that the debtor provides as security for the payment of the loan, and foreclosure is a process that allows the lender to repossess and sell that property—see Chapter 22.) Beneficial sought $91,614.34 in unpaid principal, plus interest, and claimed that the loan was secured by real property in East Hampton, New York. Beneficial's copy of the loan agreement identified Stephen Steele as the sole obligor (the party owing the debt); however, it had not been signed.

Case 12.3—Continues next page ➡

Case 12.3—Continued

ISSUE Does the Statute of Frauds require the borrowers' signatures on a contract that gives the lender an interest in real property (a mortgage loan)?

DECISION Yes. The court concluded that the agreement was unenforceable.

REASON Because a mortgage involves the transfer of an interest in real property, the mortgage agreement and its underlying obligation must be in writing to satisfy the Statute of Frauds. To be enforceable, the writing must be signed by the parties to be charged. Beneficial was seeking to foreclose on a mortgage that purportedly constituted security for a certain loan agreement.

Beneficial sought to enforce the agreement against two parties—Stephen and Susan Steele—who had not signed it. In fact, Susan was not even mentioned in the agreement as a party to it. The lender's assertions about the document were "painfully obvious misstatements of facts" and meant that the agreement was most likely unenforceable. The court ordered a hearing to determine whether Beneficial had acted in good faith.

WHAT IF THE FACTS WERE DIFFERENT? *Suppose that at the hearing, the Steeles admitted they had an obligation to pay the outstanding loan amount. Would the result have been different? Explain.*

The Parol Evidence Rule

Parol Evidence Rule A rule of contracts under which a court will not receive into evidence prior or contemporaneous oral statements and agreements that contradict the terms of the parties' written contract.

LEARNING OBJECTIVE 5
What is parol evidence? When is it admissible to clarify the terms of a written contract?

Sometimes, a written contract does not include—or contradicts—an oral understanding reached by the parties before or at the time of contracting. For instance, a landlord might tell a person who agrees to rent an apartment that she or he can have a cat, whereas the lease contract clearly states that no pets are allowed. In determining the outcome of such disputes, the courts look to a common law rule governing the admissibility in court of oral evidence, or *parol evidence*.

Under the **parol evidence rule,** if a court finds that a written contract represents the complete and final statement of the parties' agreement, then it will not allow either party to present parol evidence (testimony or other evidence of communications between the parties that is not contained in the contract itself). In other words, a party normally cannot introduce in court evidence of the parties' prior negotiations, prior agreements, or contemporaneous oral agreements if that evidence contradicts or varies the terms of the parties' written contract.[18]

Exceptions to the Parol Evidence Rule

Because of the rigidity of the parol evidence rule, courts make several exceptions. These exceptions include the following:

1. *Contracts subsequently modified.* Evidence of a *subsequent modification* of a written contract can be introduced in court. Keep in mind that the oral modifications may not be enforceable if they come under the Statute of Frauds—for example, if they increase the price of the goods for sale to $500 or more or extend the term for performance to more than one year. Also, oral modifications will not be enforceable if the original contract provides that any modification must be in writing.[19]
2. *Voidable or void contracts.* Oral evidence can be introduced in all cases to show that the contract was voidable or void (for example, induced by mistake, fraud, or misrepresentation). In this situation, if deception led one of the parties to agree to the terms of a written contract, oral evidence indicating fraud should not be excluded. Courts frown on bad faith and are quick to allow the introduction at trial of parol evidence when it establishes fraud.
3. *Contracts containing ambiguous terms.* When the terms of a written contract are ambiguous, evidence is admissible to show the meaning of the terms.
4. *Incomplete contracts.* Evidence is admissible when the written contract is incomplete in that it lacks one or more of the essential terms. The courts allow evidence to "fill in the gaps" in the contract.

---

18. *Restatement (Second) of Contracts,* Section 213.
19. UCC 2–209(2), (3). See Chapter 15.

5. *Prior dealing, course of performance, or usage of trade.* Under the UCC, evidence can be introduced to explain or supplement a written contract by showing a prior dealing, course of performance, or usage of trade.[20] When buyers and sellers deal with each other over extended periods of time, certain customary practices develop. These practices are often overlooked in the writing of the contract, so courts allow the introduction of evidence to show how the parties have acted in the past. Usage of trade—practices and customs generally followed in a particular industry—can also shed light on the meaning of certain contract provisions, and thus evidence of trade usage may be admissible. We will discuss these terms in further detail in Chapter 15, in the context of sales contracts.

6. *Contracts subject to an orally agreed-on condition precedent.* As you will read in Chapter 13, sometimes the parties agree that a condition must be fulfilled before a party is required to perform the contract. This is called a *condition precedent.* If the parties have orally agreed on a condition precedent and the condition does not conflict with the terms of a written agreement, then a court may allow parol evidence to prove the oral condition. The parol evidence rule does not apply here because the existence of the entire written contract is subject to an orally agreed-on condition. Proof of the condition does not alter or modify the written terms but affects the *enforceability* of the written contract.
   EXAMPLE 12.22 A city leases property for an airport from a well-established helicopter business. The lease is renewable every five years. During the second five-year lease, a dispute arises, and the parties go to mediation (see Chapter 3 on page 84). They enter into a settlement memorandum under which they agree to amend the lease agreement subject to the approval of the city council. The city amends the lease, but the helicopter business refuses to sign it, contending that the council has not given its approval. In this situation, the council's approval is a condition precedent to the formation of the settlement memorandum contract. Therefore, the parol evidence rule does not apply, and oral evidence is admissible to show that no agreement exists as to the terms of the settlement. •

7. *Contracts with an obvious or gross clerical (or typographic) error.* When an *obvious* or *gross* clerical (or typographic) error exists that clearly would not represent the agreement of the parties, parol evidence is admissible to correct the error. **EXAMPLE 12.23** Davis agrees to lease 1,000 square feet of office space from Stone Enterprises at the current monthly rate of $3 per square foot. The signed written lease provides for a monthly lease payment of $300 rather than the $3,000 agreed to by the parties. Because the error is obvious, Stone Enterprises would be allowed to admit parol evidence to correct the mistake. •

Integrated Contracts

The determination of whether evidence will be allowed basically depends on whether the written contract is intended to be a complete and final statement of the terms of the agreement. If it is so intended, it is referred to as an **integrated contract,** and extraneous evidence (evidence from outside the contract) is excluded. For an example of an integration clause within a contract, see Paragraph 19 on page 374 in the Appendix to Chapter 14.
   CASE EXAMPLE 12.24 The Pittsburgh Steelers sent Ronald Yocca a brochure offering to sell the right to buy season tickets to Steelers games at their new football stadium. Prices and locations of seats were indicated in diagrams. Yocca responded, listing his seating preferences. The Steelers sent him the tickets with a diagram that showed different seating sections than were shown in the brochure. Also enclosed was a document that read, "This agreement contains the entire agreement of the parties." Yocca was asked to sign and return the document. Later, when Yocca went to the first game, he discovered that his seat was not where he expected it to be based on the brochure. He sued for breach of contract. The court, however, concluded that the brochure was not part of the parties' contract and dismissed the suit. Under the parol evidence rule, the signed document could not be supplemented by evidence of previous negotiations or agreements.[21] •

Integrated Contract A written contract that constitutes the final expression of the parties' agreement. Evidence extraneous to the contract that contradicts or alters the meaning of the contract in any way is inadmissible.

---

20. UCC 1–205, 2–202. See Chapter 15.
21. *Yocca v. Pittsburgh Steelers Sports, Inc.,* 578 Pa. 479, 854 A.2d 425 (2004).

Exhibit 12.4 The Parol Evidence Rule

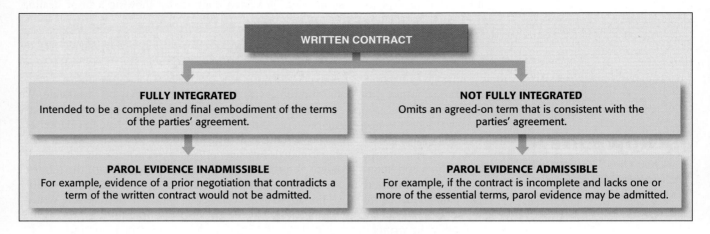

An integrated contract can be either completely or partially integrated. If it contains all of the terms of the parties' agreement, then it is completely integrated. If it contains only some of the terms that the parties agreed on and not others, it is partially integrated. If the contract is only partially integrated, evidence of consistent additional terms is admissible to supplement the written agreement.[22] Note that for both completely and partially integrated contracts, courts exclude any evidence that *contradicts* the writing and allow parol evidence only to add to the terms of a partially integrated contract.

Exhibit 12.4 above illustrates the relationship between integrated contracts and the parol evidence rule.

_____

22. *Restatement (Second) of Contracts*, Section 216.

Reviewing . . . Defenses to Contract Enforceability

Charter Golf, Inc., manufactures and sells golf apparel and supplies. Ken Odin had worked as a Charter sales representative for six months when he was offered a position with a competing firm. Charter's president, Jerry Montieth, offered Odin a 10 percent commission "for the rest of his life" if Ken would turn down the offer and stay on with Charter. He also promised that Odin would not be fired unless he was dishonest. Odin turned down the competitor's offer and stayed with Charter. Three years later, Charter fired Odin for no reason. Odin sued, alleging breach of contract. Using the information presented in the chapter, answer the following questions.

1. Would a court likely decide that Montieth's employment contract with Odin falls within the Statute of Frauds? Why or why not?
2. Assume that the court does find that the contract falls within the Statute of Frauds and that the state in which the court sits recognizes every exception to the Statute of Frauds discussed in the chapter. What exception provides Odin with the best chance of enforcing the oral contract in this situation?
3. Now suppose that Montieth had taken out a pencil, written "10 percent for life" on the back of a register receipt, and handed it to Odin. Would this satisfy the Statute of Frauds? Why or why not?
4. Assume that Odin had signed a written employment contract at the time he was hired by Charter, but it was not completely integrated. Would a court allow Odin to present parol evidence of Montieth's subsequent promises? Why or why not?

DEBATE THIS Many countries have eliminated the Statute of Frauds except for sales of real estate. The United States should do the same.

BUSINESS APPLICATION

When E-Mails Become Enforceable Contracts*

Most business students must take a course in business communication. These courses cover the planning and preparation of oral and written communications, including electronic messages. Indeed, e-mails have become so pervasive that an increasing number of contracts are created via e-mail.

Voluntary Consent and Mistakes

One possible defense to contract enforceability is a lack of voluntary consent, sometimes due to mistakes. Often, when a mistake is unilateral, the courts will still enforce the contract. Consequently, the e-mail communications that you create can result in an enforceable contract even if you make a typographic error in, say, a dollar amount.

If you are making an offer or an acceptance via e-mail, you should treat that communication as carefully as if you were writing or typing it on a sheet of paper. Unfortunately, many individuals in the business world treat e-mails somewhat casually. When you realize that you are creating an enforceable contract if you make an offer or an acceptance via e-mail, then you know that you have to reread your e-mails several times before you hit the send button.

The Sufficiency of the Writing

In this chapter, you learned about the Statute of Frauds. The legal definitions of written memoranda and signatures have changed in our electronic age. Today, an e-mail definitely constitutes a writing.

A writing can also be a series of e-mail exchanges between two parties. In other words, five e-mail exchanges taken together may form a single contract. (In the past, before e-mails and faxes, this rule applied to written communications on pieces of paper that were stapled or clipped together.) If one or more e-mails name the parties, identify the subject matter, and lay out the consideration,

a court normally will accept those e-mails as constituting a writing sufficient to satisfy the Statute of Frauds.

The Importance of Clear, Precise E-Mail Language

In addition to typographic errors, casually written e-mails may contain ambiguities and miscommunications. Nevertheless, those e-mails may create an enforceable contract, whether you intended to create one or not. Therefore, all of your business e-mails should be carefully written.

Checklist for the Businessperson

1. **Create a precise and informative subject line.** *Rather than saying "we should discuss" or "important information," be specific in the subject line of the e-mail, such as "change delivery date for line portable generators."*
2. **Repeat the subject matter within the body of the e-mail message.** *In the actual e-mail message, avoid phrases with indefinite antecedents such as "This is . . . ." Good business e-mail communication involves a repetition of most of the subject line. That way, if your recipient skips the subject line, the message will still be clear.*
3. **Focus on a limited number of subjects, usually one.** *Do not ramble and discuss a variety of topics in your e-mail. If necessary, send several e-mails on several different topics.*
4. **Create e-mails that are just as attractive as communications written on letterhead.** *Obviously, e-mails that have no particular format, no paragraphs, bad grammar, misspellings, and incorrect punctuation create a negative impression. More important, if your language is not precise, you may find that you have created an enforceable contract when you did not intend to do so. At a minimum, use the spelling and grammar checkers in your word-processing program.*
5. **Proof your work.** *This aspect of e-mail communication is so important that it is worth repeating. Proofreading your e-mails before you hit the send button is the most important step that you can take to avoid contract misinterpretations.*

---

*This *Business Application* is not meant to substitute for the services of an attorney who is licensed to practice law in your state.

Key Terms

collateral promise 315	parol evidence rule 320	*scienter* 311	Statute of Frauds 313
integrated contract 321	prenuptial agreement 316		

Chapter Summary: Defenses to Contract Enforceability

VOLUNTARY CONSENT	
Mistakes (See pages 306–308.)	1. *Unilateral*—Generally, the mistaken party is bound by the contract *unless* (a) the other party knows or should have known of the mistake or (b) the mistake is an inadvertent mathematical error—such as an error in addition or subtraction—committed without gross negligence. 2. *Bilateral (mutual)*—When both parties are mistaken about the same material fact, such as identity, either party can avoid the contract.
Fraudulent Misrepresentation (See pages 308–312.)	When fraud occurs, usually the innocent party can enforce or avoid the contract. The following elements are necessary to establish fraud: 1. A misrepresentation of a material fact must occur. 2. There must be an intent to deceive. 3. The innocent party must justifiably rely on the misrepresentation.
Undue Influence (See page 313.)	Undue influence arises from special relationships, such as fiduciary or confidential relationships, in which one party's free will has been overcome by the undue influence exerted by the other party. Usually, the contract is voidable.
Duress (See page 313.)	Duress is the tactic of forcing a party to enter a contract under the fear of a threat—for example, the threat of violence or serious economic loss. The party forced to enter the contract can rescind the contract.
FORM	

The Statute of Frauds— Writing Requirement (See pages 313–318.)	1. *Applicability*—The following types of contracts fall under the Statute of Frauds and must be in writing to be enforceable:
	  a. Contracts involving interests in land, such as sales, leases, or mortgages.
	  b. Contracts that cannot by their terms be fully performed within one year from (the day after) the contract's formation.
	  c. Collateral promises, such as contracts made between a guarantor and a creditor whose terms make the guarantor secondarily liable. *Exception:* the "main purpose" rule.
	  d. Promises made in consideration of marriage, including promises to make a monetary payment or give property in consideration of a promise to marry and prenuptial agreements made in consideration of marriage.
	  e. Contracts for the sale of goods priced at $500 or more under the Statute of Frauds provision in Section 2–201 of the Uniform Commercial Code.
	2. *Exceptions*—Partial performance, admissions, and promissory estoppel.

The Statute of Frauds— Sufficiency of the Writing (See pages 318–320.)	To constitute an enforceable contract under the Statute of Frauds, a writing must be signed by the party against whom enforcement is sought, name the parties, identify the subject matter, and state with reasonable certainty the essential terms of the contract. Under the UCC, a contract for a sale of goods is not enforceable beyond the quantity of goods shown in the contract.
The Parol Evidence Rule (See pages 320–322.)	The parol evidence rule prohibits the introduction at trial of evidence of the parties' prior negotiations, prior agreements, or contemporaneous oral agreements that contradicts or varies the terms of the parties' written contract. The written contract is assumed to be the complete embodiment of the parties' agreement. Exceptions are made in the circumstances listed on pages 320–321.

ExamPrep

ISSUE SPOTTERS

1. Elle, an accountant, certifies several audit reports for Flite Corporation, her client, knowing that Flite intends to use the reports to obtain loans from Good Credit Company (GCC). Elle believes that the reports are true and does not intend to deceive GCC, but she does not check the reports before certifying them. Can Elle be held liable to GCC? Why or why not? **(See pages 309 and 310.)**
2. My-T Quality Goods, Inc., and Nu! Sales Corporation orally agree to a deal. My-T's president has the essential terms written up on company letterhead stationery, and the memo is filed in My-T's office. If Nu! Sales later refuses to complete the transaction, is this memo a sufficient writing to enforce the contract against it? Explain your answer. **(See page 318.)**

—**Check your answers to the Issue Spotters against the answers provided in Appendix E at the end of this text.**

BEFORE THE TEST

Go to www.cengagebrain.com, enter the ISBN 9781133273561 and click on "Find" to locate this textbook's Web site. Then, click on "Access Now" under "Study Tools," and select Chapter 12 at the top. There, you will find a Practice Quiz that you can take to assess your mastery of the concepts in this chapter, as well as Flashcards, a Glossary of important terms, and Video Questions (when assigned).

For Review

Answers to the even-numbered questions in this For Review section can be found in Appendix F at the end of this text.

1. In what types of situations might voluntary consent to a contract's terms be lacking?
2. What is the difference between a mistake of value or quality and a mistake of fact?
3. What are the elements of fraudulent misrepresentation?
4. What contracts must be in writing to be enforceable?
5. What is parol evidence? When is it admissible to clarify the terms of a written contract?

Business Scenarios and Case Problems

12–1 Voluntary Consent. Jerome is an elderly man who lives with his nephew, Philip. Jerome is totally dependent on Philip's support. Philip tells Jerome that unless Jerome transfers a tract of land he owns to Philip for a price 30 percent below market value, Philip will no longer support and take care of him. Jerome enters into the contract. Discuss fully whether Jerome can set aside this contract. **(See page 313.)**

12–2 Question with Sample Answer—Statute of Frauds. Gemma promises a local hardware store that she will pay for a lawn mower that her brother is purchasing on credit if the brother fails to pay the debt. Must this promise be in writing to be enforceable? Why or why not? **(See pages 313–316.)**

—For a sample answer to Question 12–2, go to Appendix G at the end of this text.

12–3 The Parol Evidence Rule. Evangel Temple Assembly of God leased a facility from Wood Care Centers, Inc., to house evacuees who had lost their homes in a hurricane. The lease stated that Evangel could end it at any time by giving notice and paying 10 percent of the rent that would otherwise be paid over the rest of the term. The lease also stated that if the facility did not retain its tax exemption—which was granted to it on Evangel's behalf as a church—Evangel could end the lease without making the 10 percent payment. Is parol evidence admissible to interpret this lease? Why or why not? [*Wood Care Centers, Inc. v. Evangel Temple Assembly of God of Wichita Falls,* 307 S.W.3d 816 (Tex.App.—Fort Worth 2010)] **(See page 320.)**

12–4 Case Problem with Sample Answer—Contract Involving Interests in Land. Mohammad Salim offered to sell a convenience store and gas station to Talat Solaiman and Sabina Chowdhury. The prospective buyers drafted a "Purchase Agreement" that described its object as "the property and business known as BP Food Mart" at a specific address. The parties signed the agreement. Later, the buyers wanted out of the deal. Is the property description sufficient for the seller to enforce the agreement? Explain. [*Salim v. Solaiman,* 302 Ga.App. 607, 691 S.E.2d 389 (2010)] **(See page 314.)**

—For a sample answer to Problem 12–4, go to Appendix H at the end of this text.

12–5 Mutual Mistake. When Steven Simkin divorced Laura Blank, they agreed to split their assets equally. They owned an account with Bernard L. Madoff Investment Securities estimated to be worth $5.4 million. Simkin kept the account and paid Blank more than $6.5 million—including $2.7 million to offset the amount of the funds that they believed were in the account. Later, they learned that the account actually contained no funds due to its manager's fraud. Could their agreement be rescinded on the basis of a mistake? Discuss. [*Simkin v. Blank,* 80 A.D.3d 401, 915 N.Y.S.2d 47 (1 Dept. 2011)] **(See pages 306–307.)**

12–6 Misrepresentation. Charter One Bank owned a fifteen-story commercial building. A fire inspector told Charter that the building's drinking-water and fire-suppression systems were linked. Without disclosing this information, Charter sold the building to Northpoint Properties, Inc. Northpoint spent $280,000 to repair the water and fire-suppression systems and filed a suit against Charter One. Is the seller liable for not disclosing the building's defects? Discuss. [*Northpoint Properties, Inc. v. Charter One Bank,* 2011-Ohio-2512 (Ohio App. 8 Dist. 2011)] **(See pages 308–312.)**

12–7 Statute of Frauds. Newmark & Co. Real Estate, Inc., contacted 2615 East 17 Street Realty, LLC, to lease certain real property on behalf of a client. Newmark e-mailed the landlord a separate agreement for the payment of Newmark's commission. The landlord e-mailed it back with a separate demand to pay the commission in installments. Newmark revised the agreement and e-mailed a final copy to the landlord. Do the parties have an agreement that qualifies as a writing under the Statute of Frauds? Explain. [*Newmark & Co. Real Estate, Inc. v. 2615 East 17 Street Realty,* LLC, 80 A.D.3d 476, 914 N.Y.S.2d 162 (1 Dept. 2011)] (**See page 318.**)

12–8 The Parol Evidence Rule. Rimma Vaks and her husband, Steven Mangano, executed a written contract with Denise Ryan and Ryan Auction Co. to auction their furnishings. The six-page contract provided a detailed summary of the parties' agreement. It addressed the items to be auctioned, how reserve prices would be determined, and the amount of Ryan's commission. When a dispute arose between the parties, Vaks and Mangano sued Ryan for breach of contract. Vaks and Mangano asserted that, before they executed the contract, Ryan had made various oral representations that were inconsistent with the terms of their written agreement. Assuming that their written contract was valid, can Vaks and Mangano recover for breach of an oral contract? Why or why not? [*Vaks v. Ryan,* 2012 WL 194398 (Mass.App. 2012)] (**See pages 320–322.**)

12–9 ◆➤ **A Question of Ethics—Bilateral Mistake.** On behalf of BRJM, LLC, Nicolas Kepple offered Howard Engelsen $210,000 for a parcel of land known as lot five on the north side of Barnes Road in Stonington, Connecticut. Engelsen's company, Output Systems, Inc., owned the land. Engelsen had the lot surveyed and obtained an appraisal. The appraiser valued the property at $277,000, after determining that it was three acres and thus could not be subdivided because it did not meet the town's minimum legal requirement of 3.7 acres for subdivision. Engelsen responded to Kepple's offer with a counteroffer of $230,000, which Kepple accepted. The parties signed a contract. When Engelsen refused to go through with the deal, BRJM filed a suit against Output, seeking specific performance and other relief. Output asserted the defense of mutual mistake on at least two grounds. [*BRJM, LLC v. Output Systems, Inc.,* 100 Conn.App. 143, 917 A.2d 605 (2007)] (**See pages 306–307.**)

1. In the counteroffer, Engelsen asked Kepple to remove from their contract a clause requiring written confirmation of the availability of a "free split," which meant that the property could be subdivided without the town's prior approval. Kepple agreed. After signing the contract, Kepple learned that the property was *not* entitled to a free split. Would this circumstance qualify as a mistake on which the *defendant* could avoid the contract? Why or why not?

2. After signing the contract, Engelsen obtained a second appraisal that established the size of lot five as 3.71 acres, which meant that it could be subdivided, and valued the property at $490,000. Can the defendant avoid the contract on the basis of a mistake in the first appraisal? Explain.

Critical Thinking and Writing Assignments

12–10 Critical Legal Thinking. Describe the types of individuals who might be capable of exerting undue influence on others. (**See page 313.**)

12–11 💡 **Business Law Critical Thinking Group Assignment.** Jason Novell, doing business as Novell Associates, hired Barbara Meade as an independent contractor. The parties orally agreed on the terms of employment, including payment of a share of the company's income to Meade, but they did not put anything in writing. Two years later, Meade quit. Novell then told Meade that she was entitled to $9,602—25 percent of the difference between the accounts receivable and the accounts payable as of Meade's last day of work. Meade disagreed and demanded more than $63,500— 25 percent of the revenue from all invoices, less the cost of materials and outside processing, for each of the years that she had worked for Novell. Meade filed a lawsuit against Novell for breach of contract.

1. The first group will evaluate whether the parties had an enforceable contract.

2. The second group will decide whether the parties' oral agreement falls within any exception to the Statute of Frauds.

3. The third group will discuss how the lawsuit would be affected if Novell admitted that the parties had an oral contract under which Meade was entitled to 25 percent of the difference between the accounts receivable and payable as of the day Meade quit.

Third Party Rights and Discharge

(Muellek Josef/Shutterstock.com)

CHAPTER OUTLINE

- Assignments
- Delegations
- Third Party Beneficiaries
- Contract Discharge

LEARNING OBJECTIVES

The five learning objectives below are designed to help improve your understanding of the chapter. After reading this chapter, you should be able to answer the following questions:

1 What is an assignment? What is the difference between an assignment and a delegation?

2 In what situations is the delegation of duties prohibited?

3 What factors indicate that a third party beneficiary is an intended beneficiary?

4 How are most contracts discharged?

5 What is a contractual condition, and how might a condition affect contractual obligations?

"The laws of a state change with the changing times."
—Aeschylus, 525–456 B.C.E. (Greek dramatist)

Privity of Contract The relationship that exists between the promisor and the promisee of a contract.

Because a contract is a private agreement between the parties who have entered into that contract, it is fitting that these parties alone should have rights and liabilities under the contract. This concept is referred to as **privity of contract,** and it establishes the basic principle that third parties have no rights in contracts to which they are not parties.

You may be convinced by now that for every rule of contract law, there is an exception. As times change, so must the laws, as indicated in the chapter-opening quotation. When justice cannot be served by adherence to a rule of law, exceptions to the rule must be made.

In this chapter, we look at some exceptions to the rule of privity of contract. These exceptions include *assignments, delegations,* and *third party beneficiary contracts.* We also examine how contractual obligations can be *discharged.* Normally, contract discharge is accomplished by both parties performing the acts promised in the contract. In the latter part of the chapter, we look at the degree of performance required to discharge a contractual obligation, as well as at some other ways that contract discharge can occur.

Assignments

LEARNING OBJECTIVE 1
What is an assignment? What is the difference between an assignment and a delegation?

Assignment The transfer to another of all or part of one's rights arising under a contract.

In a bilateral contract, the two parties have corresponding rights and duties. One party has a *right* to require the other to perform some task, and the other has a *duty* to perform it. Sometimes, though, a party will transfer her or his rights under the contract to someone else. The transfer of contract *rights* to a third person is known as an **assignment.** (The transfer of contract duties is a *delegation,* as will be discussed later in this chapter.)

Assignments are important because they are often used in business financing. Lending institutions, such as banks, frequently assign the rights to receive payments under their loan contracts to other firms, which pay for those rights. If you obtain a loan from your local bank to purchase a car, you may later receive a notice stating that your bank has transferred (assigned) its rights to receive payments on the loan to another firm and that you should make your payments to that other firm.

Lenders that make *mortgage loans* (loans to allow prospective home buyers to purchase real estate—see Chapter 22) often assign their rights to collect the mortgage payments to a third party, such as Chase Home Mortgage Company. Following an assignment, the home buyer is notified that future payments must be made to the third party, rather than to the original lender. Billions of dollars change hands daily in the business world in the form of assignments of rights in contracts.

Effect of an Assignment

Assignor A party who transfers (assigns) his or her rights under a contract to another party (called the *assignee*).

Assignee A party to whom the rights under a contract are transferred, or assigned.

Obligee One to whom an obligation is owed.

Obligor One who owes an obligation to another.

In an assignment, the party assigning the rights to a third party is known as the **assignor,**[1] and the party receiving the rights is the **assignee.**[2] Other terms traditionally used to describe the parties in assignment relationships are the **obligee** (the person to whom a duty, or obligation, is owed) and the **obligor** (the person who is obligated to perform the duty). Exhibit 13.1 on the facing page illustrates assignment relationships.

Extinguishes the Rights of the Assignor   When rights under a contract are assigned unconditionally, the rights of the *assignor* (the party making the assignment) are extinguished.[3] The third party (the *assignee,* or the party receiving the assignment) has a right to demand performance from the other original party to the contract (the *obligor,* the person who is obligated to perform).

EXAMPLE 13.1   Brent (the obligor) owes Alex $1,000, and Alex, the obligee, assigns to Carmen the right to receive the $1,000 (thus, Alex is now the assignor). Here, a valid assignment of a debt exists. Carmen, the assignee, can enforce the contract against Brent, the obligor, if Brent fails to perform (pay the $1,000). •

In the following case, a lender assigned its rights to loan payments from a borrower. The court had to decide whether the borrower owed the payments to the assignee.

---

1. Pronounced uh-*sye*-nore.
2. Pronounced uh-*sye*-nee.
3. *Restatement (Second) of Contracts,* Section 317.

Case 13.1

Hosch v. Colonial Pacific Leasing Corp.

Court of Appeals of Georgia,
313 Ga.App. 873, 722 S.E.2d 778 (2012).
www.findlaw.com/casecode/index.html[a]

Can a loan for equipment be assigned without notice?

FACTS Edward Hosch entered into four loan agreements with Citicapital Commercial Corporation to finance the purchase of heavy construction equipment. A few months later, Citicapital merged into Citicorp Leasing, Inc., which was then renamed GE Capital Commercial, Inc. One year later, GE Capital assigned the loans to Colonial Pacific Leasing Corporation. When Hosch defaulted on the loans, Colonial Pacific served him with a notice of default and demanded payment. Hosch failed to repay the loans, so Colonial Pacific sued to collect. The trial court granted summary judgment to Colonial Pacific and entered final judgment against Hosch. On appeal, Hosch argued that there was insufficient evidence that the loans were assigned to Colonial Pacific.

ISSUE Is Hosch liable to Colonial Pacific?

DECISION Yes. The Georgia appellate court affirmed the trial court's judgment in favor of the assignee, Colonial Pacific.

REASON The court stated that "a party may assign a contractual right to collect payment, including the right to sue to enforce the right." To be enforceable, the assignment must be in writing. In this case, there was sufficient evidence that GE Capital assigned Hosch's loans to Colonial Pacific. Significantly, the record included a written assignment, other documents showing that the loans had been assigned, and affidavits of a GE litigation specialist.

Against that evidence, Hosch merely asserted that he had not been notified of the assignment. Under the loan agreements, however, GE Capital could assign its rights without Hosch's knowledge or consent.

CRITICAL THINKING—Legal Consideration *Do borrowers benefit when lenders may freely assign their rights under loan agreements? If so, how?*

---

a. Under "State Resources," click on "Georgia." On the next page, under "State Court Opinions," click on "Georgia Court of Appeals Opinions." In the "Party name:" box, enter "Hosch" and click on "Search." In the result, click on the case name to access the opinion.

Exhibit 13.1 Assignment Relationships

In the assignment relationship illustrated here, Alex assigns his *rights* under a contract that he made with Brent to a third party, Carmen. Alex thus becomes the *assignor* and Carmen the *assignee* of the contractual rights. Brent, the *obligor*, now owes performance to Carmen instead of to Alex. Alex's original contract rights are extinguished after the assignment.

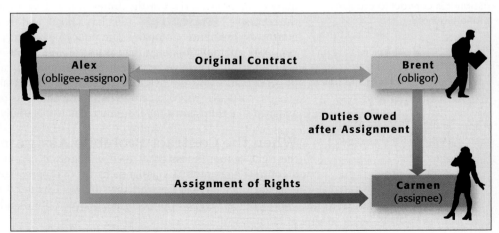

Assignee Takes Rights Subject to Defenses   The assignee obtains only those rights that the assignor originally had. Also, the assignee's rights are subject to the defenses that the obligor has against the assignor.

EXAMPLE 13.2   Brent owes Alex $1,000 under a contract in which Brent agreed to buy Alex's MacBook Pro laptop. Alex assigns his right to receive the $1,000 to Carmen. Brent, in deciding to purchase the laptop, relied on Alex's fraudulent misrepresentation that the computer had 8 megabytes of memory. When Brent discovers that the computer has only 4 megabytes of memory, he tells Alex that he is going to return the laptop and cancel the contract. Even though Alex has assigned his "right" to receive the $1,000 to Carmen, Brent need not pay Carmen the $1,000—Brent can raise the defense of Alex's fraudulent misrepresentation to avoid payment. •

Rights That Cannot Be Assigned

As a general rule, all rights can be assigned. Exceptions are made, however, in the following special circumstances.

When a Statute Expressly Prohibits Assignment   If a statute expressly prohibits assignment, the particular right in question cannot be assigned. **EXAMPLE 13.3** Marn is a new employee of CompuFuture, Inc. CompuFuture is an employer governed by workers' compensation statutes (see Chapter 24) in this state, so Marn is a covered employee. Marn has a rather high-risk job. In need of a loan, she borrows from Stark, assigning to Stark all workers' compensation benefits due her should she be injured on the job. A state statute prohibits the assignment of *future* workers' compensation benefits, and thus such rights cannot be assigned. •

This piano teacher has signed a contract to give weekly piano lessons. Can the teacher then assign this contract to another piano teacher?

"Man, an animal that makes bargains."

Adam Smith, 1723–1790
(Scottish economist and author)

When a Contract Is Personal in Nature   When a contract is for personal services, the rights under the contract normally cannot be assigned unless all that remains is a monetary payment.[4] **EXAMPLE 13.4**   Brent signs a contract to be a tutor for Alex's children. Alex then attempts to assign to Carmen his right to Brent's services. Carmen cannot enforce the contract against Brent. Brent may not like Carmen's children or for some other reason may not want to tutor them. Because personal services are unique to the person rendering them, rights to receive personal services cannot be assigned. •

When an Assignment Will Significantly Change the Risk or Duties of the Obligor   A right cannot be assigned if assignment will significantly increase or alter the risks or the duties of the obligor (the party owing performance under the contract).[5] **EXAMPLE 13.5**   Alex has a hotel, and to insure it, he takes out a policy with Northwest Insurance Company. The policy insures against fire, theft, floods, and vandalism. Alex attempts to assign the insurance policy to Carmen who also owns a hotel. The assignment is ineffective because it may substantially alter the insurance company's duty of performance and the risk that the company undertakes. An insurance company evaluates the particular risk of a certain party and tailors its policy to fit that risk. If the policy is assigned to a third party, the insurance risk is materially altered. •

When the Contract Prohibits Assignment   If a contract stipulates that the right cannot be assigned, then *ordinarily* it cannot be assigned. (For an example of a contract that prohibits assignment by one party, see page 374, Paragraph 12, of the *Annotated Employment Contract* that follows Chapter 14.) **EXAMPLE 13.6**   Brent agrees to build a house for Alex. The contract between Brent and Alex states, "This contract cannot

---

4. *Restatement (Second) of Contracts*, Sections 317 and 318.
5. See Section 2–210(2) of the Uniform Commercial Code (UCC).

be assigned by Alex without Brent's consent. Any assignment without such consent renders this contract void, and all rights hereunder will thereupon terminate." Alex then assigns his rights to Carmen without first obtaining Brent's consent. Carmen cannot enforce the contract against Brent. ●   This rule has several exceptions:

1. A contract cannot prevent an assignment of the right to receive funds. This exception exists to encourage the free flow of funds and credit in modern business settings.
2. The assignment of ownership rights in real estate often cannot be prohibited because such a prohibition is contrary to public policy in most states. Prohibitions of this kind are called restraints against **alienation** (the voluntary transfer of land ownership).
3. The assignment of negotiable instruments (see Chapter 18) cannot be prohibited.
4. In a contract for the sale of goods, the right to receive damages for breach of contract or for payment of an account owed may be assigned even though the sales contract prohibits such an assignment.[6]

Alienation The of transfer of land out of one's possession (thus "alienating" the land from oneself).

Notice of Assignment

Once a valid assignment of rights has been made to a third party, the third party should notify the obligor of the assignment (for example, in Exhibit 13.1 on page 329, Carmen should notify Brent). Giving notice is not legally necessary to establish the validity of the assignment because an assignment is effective immediately, whether or not notice is given. Two major problems arise, however, when notice of the assignment is *not* given to the obligor.

Priority Issues   If the assignor assigns the same right to two different persons, the question arises as to which one has priority—that is, which one has the right to the performance by the obligor. The rule most often observed in the United States is that the first assignment in time is the first in right.

Nevertheless, some states follow the English rule, which basically gives priority to the first assignee who gives notice. **EXAMPLE 13.7**   Brent owes Alex $5,000 on a contractual obligation. On May 1, Alex assigns this monetary claim to Carmen, but she does not give notice of the assignment to Brent. On June 1, for services Dorman has rendered to Alex, Alex assigns the same monetary claim (to collect $5,000 from Brent) to Dorman. Dorman immediately notifies Brent of the assignment. In the majority of states, Carmen would have priority because the assignment to her was first in time. In some states, however, Dorman would have priority because he gave first notice. ●

Potential for Discharge by Performance to the Wrong Party

Until the obligor has notice of an assignment, the obligor can discharge his or her obligation by performance to the assignor, and this performance constitutes a discharge to the assignee. Once the obligor receives proper notice, only performance to the assignee can discharge the obligor's obligations.

EXAMPLE 13.8   Suppose that Alex, in the above example, assigns to Carmen his right to collect $5,000 from Brent, and Carmen does not give notice to Brent. Brent subsequently pays Alex the $5,000. Although the assignment was valid, Brent's payment to Alex is a discharge of the debt, and Carmen's failure to notify Brent of the assignment causes her to lose the right to collect the $5,000 from Brent. (Note that Carmen still has a claim against Alex for the $5,000.) If Carmen had given Brent notice of the assignment, however, Brent's payment to Alex would not have discharged the debt. ●

In the following *Spotlight Case*, the parties disputed whether the right to buy advertising space in publications at a steep discount was validly assigned from the original owner to companies that he later formed.

---

6. UCC 2–210(2).

Spotlight on PC Magazine

Case 13.2
Gold v. Ziff Communications Co.
Appellate Court of Illinois, First District,
322 Ill.App.3d 32, 748 N.E.2d 198, 254 Ill. Dec. 752 (2001).

Ziff bought *PC Magazine* from its founder, Anthony Gold.

(Dusan Jankovic/Shutterstock.com)

FACTS Ziff Communications Company publishes specialty magazines. In 1982, Ziff bought *PC Magazine* from its founder, Anthony Gold, for more than $10 million. As part of the deal, Ziff gave Gold, or a company that he "controlled," "ad/list rights"—rights to advertise at an 80 percent discount on a limited number of pages in Ziff publications and free use of Ziff's subscriber lists. Gold then formed Software Communications, Inc. (SCI), a mail-order software business that he wholly owned, to use the ad/list rights. In 1987 and 1988, Gold formed two new mail-order companies, Hanson & Connors, Inc., and PC Brand, Inc. Gold told Ziff that he was allocating his ad/list rights to Hanson & Connors, which took over most of SCI's business, and to PC Brand, of which Gold owned 90 percent. Ziff's other advertisers complained about this "allocation."

Ziff refused to run large ads for Hanson & Connors or to release its subscriber lists to the company. Ziff also declared PC Brand ineligible for the ad discount because it "was not controlled by Gold." Gold and his companies filed a suit in an Illinois state court against Ziff, alleging breach of contract. The court ordered Ziff to pay more than $88 million in damages and interest. Ziff appealed, arguing in part that Gold had not properly assigned the ad/list rights to Hanson & Connors and PC Brand.

ISSUE Was there a valid assignment of rights from Gold and SCI to Hanson & Connors and PC Brand?

DECISION Yes. The state intermediate appellate court affirmed the lower court's decision on this issue. The appellate court remanded the case, however, for a new trial on the amount of the damages, reasoning that some parts of the award "were not within the reasonable contemplation of the parties."

REASON The court explained, "We agree with plaintiffs that assignments can be implied from circumstances. No particular mode or form . . . is necessary to effect a valid assignment, and any acts or words are sufficient which show an intention of transferring or appropriating the owner's interest. In the instant case, it is undisputed that Gold owned 100 [percent] of SCE. In a letter dated May 13, 1988, Gold, as president of SCI, instructed Ziff that he was allocating the ad/list rights to Hanson and PC Brand. Additionally, SCI stopped using the ad/list rights when PC Brand and Hanson were formed. . . . Gold's behavior toward his companies and his conduct toward the obligor, Ziff, implied that the ad/list rights were assigned to PC Brand and Hanson."

FOR CRITICAL ANALYSIS—Social Consideration *Would the assignments in this case have been valid if Gold had not notified Ziff? Explain.*

PREVENTING LEGAL DISPUTES

Providing notice of assignment, though not legally required, is one of the best ways to avoid potential legal disputes over assignments. Whether you are the assignee or the assignor, you should inform the obligor of the assignment. An assignee who does not give notice may lose the right to performance, but failure to notify the obligor may have repercussions for the assignor as well. If no notice is given and the obligor performs the duty for the assignor, the assignee, to whom the right to receive performance was assigned, can sue the assignor for breach of contract. Litigation may also ensue if the assignor has assigned a right to two different parties, as may happen when rights that overlap (such as rights to receive various profits from a given enterprise) are assigned.

Delegation of Duties The transfer to another of all or part of one's duties arising under a contract.

Delegator A party who transfers (delegates) her or his obligations under a contract to another party (called the *delegatee*).

Delegations

Just as a party can transfer rights to a third party through an assignment, a party can also transfer duties. Duties are not assigned, however. They are *delegated*. Normally, a **delegation of duties** does not relieve the party making the delegation (the **delegator**) of the obligation

Delegatee A party to whom contractual obligations are transferred, or delegated.

to perform in the event that the party to whom the duty has been delegated (the **delegatee**) fails to perform. No special form is required to create a valid delegation of duties. As long as the delegator expresses an intention to make the delegation, it is effective. The delegator need not even use the word *delegate*. Exhibit 13.2 below graphically illustrates delegation relationships.

Duties That Cannot Be Delegated

LEARNING OBJECTIVE 2
In what situations is the delegation of duties prohibited?

As a general rule, any duty can be delegated. This rule has some exceptions, however. Delegation is prohibited in the following circumstances:

1. When performance depends on the personal skill or talents of the obligor.
2. When special trust has been placed in the obligor.
3. When performance by a third party will vary materially from that expected by the obligee (the one to whom performance is owed) under the contract.
4. When the contract expressly prohibits delegation.

When the Duties are Personal in Nature When special trust has been placed in the obligor or when performance depends on the obligor's personal skill or talents, contractual duties cannot be delegated. **EXAMPLE 13.9** Horton, who is impressed with Brower's ability to perform veterinary surgery, contracts with Brower to have her perform surgery on Horton's prize-winning stallion in July. Brower later decides that she would rather spend the summer at the beach, so she delegates her duties under the contract to Kuhn, who is also a competent veterinary surgeon. The delegation is not effective without Horton's consent, no matter how competent Kuhn is, because the contract is for *personal* performance. ●

In contrast, nonpersonal duties may be delegated. Assume that Brower contracts with Horton to pick up and deliver heavy construction machinery to Horton's property. Brower delegates this duty to Kuhn, who is in the business of delivering heavy machinery. This delegation is effective because the performance required is of a *routine* and *nonpersonal* nature.

Exhibit 13.2 Delegation Relationships

In the delegation relationship illustrated here, Brent delegates his *duties* under a contract that he made with Alex to a third party, Carmen. Brent thus becomes the *delegator* and Carmen the *delegatee* of the contractual duties. Carmen now owes performance of the contractual duties to Alex. Note that a delegation of duties normally does not relieve the delegator (Brent) of liability if the delegatee (Carmen) fails to perform the contractual duties.

When Performance by a Third Party Will Vary Materially from That Expected by the Obligee
When performance by a third party will vary materially from that expected by the obligee under the contract, contractual duties cannot be delegated. **EXAMPLE 13.10** Jared, a wealthy investor, established the company Heaven Sent to provide grants of capital to struggling but potentially successful businesses. Jared contracted with Merilyn, whose judgment Jared trusted, to select the recipients of the grants. Later, Merilyn delegated this duty to Donald. Jared did not trust Donald's ability to select worthy recipients. This delegation is not effective because it materially alters Jared's expectations under the contract with Merilyn. •

When the Contract Prohibits Delegation
When the contract expressly prohibits delegation by including an *antidelegation clause,* the duties cannot be delegated. **EXAMPLE 13.11** Dakota Company contracted with Belisario, a certified public accountant, to perform its audits. Because the contract prohibited delegation, Belisario could not delegate the duty to perform the audits to another accountant—not even an accountant at the same firm. •

Effect of a Delegation

If a delegation of duties is enforceable, the *obligee* (the one to whom performance is owed) must accept performance from the delegatee (the one to whom the duties are delegated). **EXAMPLE 13.12** Brent has a duty to pick up and deliver heavy construction machinery to Alex's property. Brent delegates his duty to Carmen. In this situation, Alex (the obligee) must accept performance from Carmen (the delegatee) because the delegation is effective. The obligee can legally refuse performance from the delegatee only if the duty is one that cannot be delegated. •

A valid delegation of duties does not relieve the delegator of obligations under the contract.[7] Although there are many exceptions, the general rule today is that the obligee can sue both the delegatee and the delegator.

EXAMPLE 13.13 In the situation in *Example 13.12,* if Carmen (the delegatee) fails to perform, Brent (the delegator) is still liable to Alex (the one to whom performance is owed). The obligee can also hold the delegatee liable if the delegatee made a promise of performance that will directly benefit the obligee. In this situation, there is an "assumption of duty" on the part of the delegatee, and breach of this duty makes the delegatee liable to the obligee. For instance, if Carmen (the delegatee) promised Brent (the delegator), in a contract, to pick up and deliver the construction equipment to Alex's property but fails to do so, Alex (the obligee) can sue Brent, Carmen, or both. •

Exhibit 13.3 on the facing page summarizes the basic principles of the laws governing assignments and delegations.

"Assignment of All Rights"

Sometimes, a contract provides for an "assignment of all rights." The traditional view was that under this type of assignment, the assignee did not assume any duties. This view was based on the theory that the assignee's agreement to accept the benefits of the contract was not sufficient to imply a promise to assume the duties of the contract.

Modern courts, however, take the view that the probable intent in using such general words is to create both an assignment of rights and an assumption of duties.[8] Therefore,

> **KNOW THIS**
>
> In an assignment, the assignor's original contract rights are extinguished after the assignment. In a delegation, the delegator remains liable for performance under the contract if the delegatee fails to perform.

---

7. For a classic case on this issue, see *Crane Ice Cream Co. v. Terminal Freezing & Heating Co.,* 147 Md. 588, 128 A. 280 (1925).

8. See UCC 2–210(1), (4); and *Restatement (Second) of Contracts,* Section 328.

Exhibit 13.3 Assignments and Delegations

Which rights can be assigned, and which duties can be delegated?	All rights can be assigned *unless:* 1. A statute expressly prohibits assignment. 2. The contract is for personal services. 3. The assignment will materially alter the obligor's risk or duties. 4. The contract prohibits assignment.	All duties can be delegated *unless:* 1. Performance depends on the obligor's personal skills or talents, or special trust has been placed in the obligor. 2. Performance by a third party will vary materially from that expected by the obligee. 3. The contract prohibits delegation.
What if the contract prohibits assignment or delegation?	No rights can be assigned *except:* 1. Rights to receive funds. 2. Ownership rights in real estate. 3. Rights to negotiable instruments. 4. Rights to payments under a sales contract or to damages for breach of a sales contract.	No duties can be delegated.
What is the effect on the original party's rights?	On a valid assignment, effective immediately, the original party (assignor) no longer has any rights under the contract.	On a valid delegation, if the delegatee fails to perform, the original party (delegator) is liable to the obligee (who may also hold the delegatee liable).

when general words are used (for example, "I assign the contract" or "all my rights under the contract"), the contract is construed as implying both an assignment of rights and an assumption of duties.

Third Party Beneficiaries

Third Party Beneficiary One for whose benefit a promise is made in a contract but who is not a party to the contract.

Intended Beneficiary A third party for whose benefit a contract is formed. An intended beneficiary can sue the promisor if the contract is breached.

As mentioned earlier in this chapter, to have contractual rights, a person normally must be a party to the contract. In other words, privity of contract must exist. An exception to the doctrine of privity exists when the original parties to the contract intend, *at the time of contracting,* that the contract performance directly benefit a third person. In this situation, the third person becomes a **third party beneficiary** of the contract. As an **intended beneficiary** of the contract, the third party has legal rights and can sue the promisor directly for breach of the contract.

Who Is the Promisor?

Who, though, is the promisor? In bilateral contracts, both parties to the contract are promisors because they both make promises that can be enforced. In third party beneficiary contracts, courts determine the identity of the promisor by asking which party made the promise that benefits the third party—that person is the promisor. In effect, allowing the third party to sue the promisor directly circumvents the "middle person" (the promisee) and thus reduces the burden on the courts. Otherwise, the third party would sue the promisee, who would then sue the promisor.

Indeed, at one time, this circuitous route was the rule. The reason was that the third party beneficiary was not a party to the contract and thus, under the doctrine of privity of contract, had no legal rights under the contract.

CASE EXAMPLE 13.14 In the classic case of *Lawrence v. Fox*[9]—decided in 1859—a court for the first time departed from the doctrine of privity of contract and allowed a third party to sue the promisor directly. The case involved three parties—Holly, Lawrence, and Fox. Holly had borrowed $300 from Lawrence. Shortly thereafter, Holly loaned $300 to Fox. In return, Fox promised Holly that he would pay Holly's debt to Lawrence on the following day. But Fox did not pay Lawrence, so Lawrence filed a suit against Fox to recover the

---

9. 20 N.Y. 268 (1859).

amount of the debt. The issue before the court was whether Lawrence, who was not a party to the Holly-Fox contract, could sue Fox directly to recover the $300. The court held that Lawrence could do so, thereby establishing the modern rule that an intended beneficiary can sue the promisor directly. •

Types of Intended Beneficiaries

Two of the most common types of intended beneficiaries are creditor beneficiaries and donee beneficiaries. We discuss both types of beneficiaries next.

Creditor Beneficiary   One type of intended beneficiary is a *creditor beneficiary*. Like the plaintiff in *Lawerence v. Fox,* a creditor beneficiary benefits from a contract in which one party (the promisor) promises another party (the promisee) to pay a debt that the promisee owes to a third party (the creditor beneficiary). As an intended beneficiary, the creditor beneficiary can sue the promisor directly to enforce the contract.

CASE EXAMPLE 13.15   Autumn Allan owned a condominium unit in a Texas complex located directly beneath a condo unit owned by Aslan Koraev. Over the course of two years, Allan's unit suffered eight incidents of water and sewage incursion as a result of plumbing problems and misuse of appliances in Koraev's unit. Allan sued Koraev for breach of contract and won. Koraev appealed, arguing that he had no contractual duty to Allan. The court found that Allan was an intended third party beneficiary of the contract between Koraev and the condominium owner's association. Because the governing documents stated that each owner had to comply strictly with their provisions, failure to comply created grounds for an action by the condominium association or an aggrieved (wronged) owner. Here, Allan was clearly an aggrieved owner and could sue Koraev directly for his failure to perform his contract duties to the condominium association.[10] •

Donee Beneficiary   Another type of intended beneficiary is a *donee beneficiary*. When a contract is made for the express purpose of giving a *gift* to a third party, the third party (the donee beneficiary) can sue the promisor directly to enforce the promise.[11]

The most common donee beneficiary contract is a life insurance contract. **EXAMPLE 13.16** Ang (the promisee) pays premiums to Standard Life, a life insurance company, and Standard Life (the promisor) promises to pay a certain amount on Ang's death to anyone Ang designates as a beneficiary. The designated beneficiary is a donee beneficiary under the life insurance policy and can enforce the promise made by the insurance company to pay her or him on Ang's death. •

When the Rights of an Intended Beneficiary Vest

An intended third party beneficiary cannot enforce a contract against the original parties until the third party's rights have *vested,* meaning that the rights have taken effect and cannot be taken away. Until these rights have vested, the original parties to the contract—the promisor and the promisee—can modify or rescind the contract without the consent of the third party.

When do the rights of third parties vest? Generally, the rights vest when one of the following occurs:

1. When the third party demonstrates express consent to the agreement, such as by sending a letter or note acknowledging awareness of, and consent to, a contract formed for her or his benefit.

---

10. *Allan v. Nersesova,* 307 S.W.3d 564 (Tx.App—Dallas 2010).
11. This principle was first enunciated in *Seaver v. Ransom,* 224 N.Y. 233, 120 N.E. 639 (1918).

2. When the third party materially alters his or her position in detrimental reliance on the contract, such as when a donee beneficiary contracts to have a home built in reliance on the receipt of funds promised to him or her in a donee beneficiary contract.
3. When the conditions for vesting are satisfied. For instance, the rights of a beneficiary under a life insurance policy vest when the insured person dies.

Incidental Beneficiaries

Incidental Beneficiary A third party who benefits from a contract even though the contract was not formed for that purpose. An incidental beneficiary has no rights in the contract and cannot sue to have it enforced.

Sometimes, a third person receives a benefit from a contract even though that person's benefit is not the reason the contract was made. Such a person is known as an **incidental beneficiary.** Because the benefit is unintentional, an incidental beneficiary cannot sue to enforce the contract.

CASE EXAMPLE 13.17 Spectators at the infamous boxing match in which Mike Tyson was disqualified for biting his opponent's ear sued Tyson and the fight's promoters for a refund on the basis of breach of contract. The spectators claimed that they were third party beneficiaries of the contract between Tyson and the fight's promoters. The court, however, held that the spectators could not sue because they were not in contractual privity with the defendants. Any benefits they received from the contract were incidental to the contract, and according to the court, the spectators got what they paid for: "the right to view whatever event transpired."[12] ●

LEARNING OBJECTIVE 3
What factors indicate that a third party beneficiary is an intended beneficiary?

Intended versus Incidental Beneficiaries

In determining whether a party is an intended or an incidental beneficiary, the courts focus on the parties' intent, as expressed in the contract language and implied by the surrounding circumstances. Any beneficiary who is not deemed an intended beneficiary is considered incidental.

Exhibit 13.4 below graphically illustrates the distinction between intended and incidental beneficiaries.

---

12. *Castillo v. Tyson,* 268 A.D.2d 336, 701 N.Y.S.2d 423 (Sup.Ct.App.Div. 2000).

Exhibit 13.4 Third Party Beneficiaries

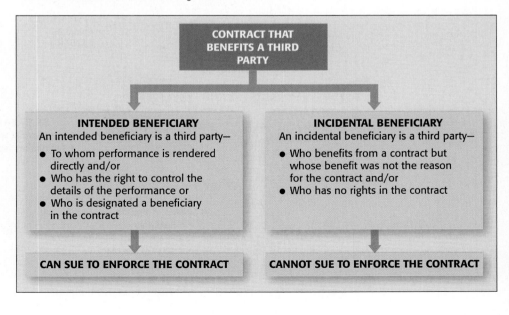

Reasonable Person Test　Although no single test can embrace all possible situations, courts often apply the *reasonable person* test: Would a reasonable person in the position of the beneficiary believe that the promisee intended to confer on the beneficiary the right to enforce the contract?

Other Factors Indicating an Intended Beneficiary　In addition, the presence of one or more of the following factors strongly indicates that the third party is an intended beneficiary of the contract:

1. Performance is rendered directly to the third party.
2. The third party has the right to control the details of performance.
3. The third party is expressly designated as a beneficiary in the contract.

LEARNING OBJECTIVE 4
How are most contracts discharged?

Discharge　The termination of an obligation, such as occurs when the parties to a contract have fully performed their contractual obligations.

Performance　The fulfillment of one's duties under a contract — the normal way of discharging one's contractual obligations.

Contract Discharge

The most common way to **discharge,** or terminate, one's contractual duties is by the **performance** of those duties. The duty to perform under a contract may be *conditioned* on the occurrence or nonoccurrence of a certain event, or the duty may be *absolute.* As shown in Exhibit 13.5 below, in addition to performance, a contract can be discharged in numerous other ways, including discharge by agreement of the parties and discharge by operation of law.

Conditions of Performance

In most contracts, promises of performance are not expressly conditioned or qualified. Instead, they are *absolute promises.* They must be performed, or the party promising the act will be in breach of contract.　**EXAMPLE 13.18**　JoAnne contracts to sell Alfonso a painting for $10,000. The parties' promises are unconditional: JoAnne will transfer the painting to

Exhibit 13.5 Contract Discharge

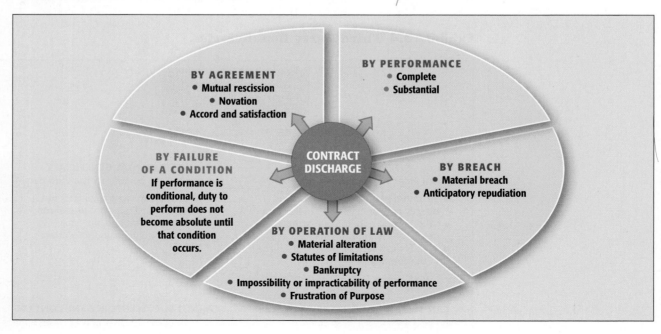

Condition A qualification, provision, or clause in a contractual agreement, the occurrence or nonoccurrence of which creates, suspends, or terminates the obligations of the contracting parties.

Alfonso, and Alfonso will pay $10,000 to JoAnne. The payment does not have to be made if the painting is not transferred. •

In some situations, however, contractual promises are conditioned. A **condition** is a qualification in a contract based on a possible future event, the occurrence or nonoccurrence of which will trigger the performance of a legal obligation or terminate an existing obligation under a contract. If the condition is not satisfied, the obligations of the parties are discharged.

EXAMPLE 13.19 Alfonso, in *Example 13.18*, offers to purchase JoAnne's painting only if an independent appraisal indicates that it is worth at least $10,000. JoAnne accepts Alfonso's offer. Their obligations (promises) are conditioned on the outcome of the appraisal. Should this condition not be satisfied (for example, if the appraiser deems the value of the painting to be only $5,000), their obligations to each other are discharged and cannot be enforced. •

We look next at three types of conditions that can be present in any given contract: *conditions precedent, conditions subsequent,* and *concurrent conditions.*

LEARNING OBJECTIVE 5
What is a contractual condition, and how might a condition affect contractual obligations?

Conditions Precedent

A condition that must be fulfilled before a party's promise becomes absolute is called a **condition precedent.** The condition precedes the absolute duty to perform, as in the JoAnne-Alfonso example just given. For instance, insurance contracts frequently specify that certain conditions, such as passing a physical examination, must be met before the insurance company will be obligated to perform under the contract.

Sometimes, a lease of real property (see Chapter 36) includes an option to buy that property. The lease in the following case required timely rent payments as a condition of exercising such an option, but the lessee often failed to make the payments on time. The court had to decide whether the lessee could still exercise the option even though it had not strictly complied with the condition precedent.

Condition Precedent A condition in a contract that must be met before a party's promise becomes absolute.

Case 13.3

Pack 2000, Inc. v. Cushman

Appellate Court of Connecticut,
126 Conn.App. 339, 11 A.3d 181 (2011).
www.jud.ct.gov/index.asp[a]

An employee works at a Midas muffler shop.

(leezsnow/iStockphoto.com)

FACTS Eugene Cushman agreed to transfer two Midas muffler shops to Pack 2000, Inc. The deal included leases for the real estate on which the shops were located. Each lease provided Pack with an option to buy the leased real estate subject to certain conditions. Pack was to pay rent by the first day of each month, make payments on the notes by the eighth day of each month, and pay utilities and other accounts on time. Pack, however, was often late in making these payments. The utility and phone companies threatened to cut off services, an insurance company canceled Pack's liability coverage, and other delinquencies prompted collection calls and letters. When Pack sought to exercise the options to buy the real estate, Cushman responded that Pack had not complied with the conditions.

Pack filed a suit in a Connecticut state court against Cushman, seeking specific performance of the options. The court rendered a judgment in Pack's favor. Cushman appealed.

ISSUE Can Pack exercise its option to buy the leased real estate even though it did not strictly comply with the condition precedent that required it to make payments on time?

DECISION No. A state intermediate appellate court reversed the lower court's judgment and remanded the case for the entry

---

a. In the left column, in the "Opinions" pull-out menu, click on "Appellate Court." On that page, in the "Search the Archives:" section, click on "Appellate Court Archive." In the result, click on "2011." Scroll to the "Published in Connecticut Law Journal—2/1/11" section, and click on the docket number next to the title of the case to view the opinion. The Connecticut judicial branch maintains this Web site.

Case 13.3—Continues next page ➡

Case 13.3—Continued

of a judgment for Cushman. A party retains its right to exercise an option to buy real estate only by complying strictly with any conditions precedent to its exercise of the option.

REASON   The leases provided Pack with the option to buy the leased real estate. But to take advantage of the options, Pack had to comply with the condition precedent of making periodic payments to Cushman and to certain third parties by specific

dates. Pack was often late in making these payments and thus did not strictly comply with the condition. The court reasoned that because of this failure of strict compliance, Pack lost the right to exercise the options to buy the real estate.

WHAT IF THE FACTS WERE DIFFERENT?   *Suppose that Pack had not made any late payments. Would the result have been different? Explain.*

Condition Subsequent A condition in a contract that, if it occurs, operates to terminate a party's absolute promise to perform.

Conditions Subsequent   When a condition operates to terminate a party's absolute promise to perform, it is called a **condition subsequent.** The condition follows, or is subsequent to, the absolute duty to perform. If the condition occurs, the party need not perform any further. **EXAMPLE 13.20**   A law firm hires Julia Darby, a recent law school graduate and a newly licensed attorney. Their contract provides that the firm's obligation to continue employing Darby is discharged if she fails to maintain her license to practice law. This is a condition subsequent because a failure to maintain the license will discharge a duty that has already arisen. ●

Generally, conditions precedent are common, and conditions subsequent are rare. The *Restatement (Second) of Contracts* omits the terms *condition subsequent* and *condition precedent* and refers to both simply as "conditions."[13]

Concurrent Conditions Conditions that must occur or be performed at the same time—they are mutually dependent. No obligations arise until these conditions are simultaneously performed.

Concurrent Conditions   When each party's absolute duty to perform is conditioned on the other party's absolute duty to perform, **concurrent conditions** are present. These conditions exist only when the parties expressly or impliedly are to perform their respective duties *simultaneously.*

EXAMPLE 13.21   If a buyer promises to pay for goods when they are delivered by the seller, each party's absolute duty to perform is conditioned on the other party's absolute duty to perform. The buyer's duty to pay for the goods does not become absolute until the seller either delivers or attempts to deliver the goods. Likewise, the seller's duty to deliver the goods does not become absolute until the buyer pays or attempts to pay for the goods. Therefore, neither can recover from the other for breach without first tendering performance. ●

Discharge by Performance

Tender An unconditional offer to perform an obligation by a person who is ready, willing, and able to do so.

The contract comes to an end when both parties fulfill their respective duties by performing the acts they have promised. Performance can also be accomplished by tender. **Tender** is an unconditional offer to perform by a person who is ready, willing, and able to do so. Therefore, a seller who places goods at the disposal of a buyer has tendered delivery and can demand payment according to the terms of the agreement. A buyer who offers to pay for goods has tendered payment and can demand delivery of the goods.

Once performance has been tendered, the party making the tender has done everything possible to carry out the terms of the contract. If the other party then refuses to perform, the party making the tender can consider the duty discharged and sue for breach of contract.

13. *Restatement (Second) of Contracts,* Section 224. Note that the difference between conditions precedent and conditions subsequent can be important procedurally, because a plaintiff must prove a condition precedent whereas the defendant normally proves a condition subsequent.

When is a deal to sell a new car completed?

Complete Performance   When a party performs exactly as agreed, there is no question as to whether the contract has been performed. When a party's performance is perfect, it is said to be complete.

Normally, conditions expressly stated in the contract must fully occur in all aspects for complete performance (strict performance) of the contract to take place. Any deviation breaches the contract and discharges the other party's obligations to perform.

For instance, most construction contracts require the builder to meet certain specifications. If the specifications are conditions, complete performance is required to avoid material breach. (*Material breach* will be discussed shortly.) If the conditions are met, the other party to the contract must then fulfill her or his obligation to pay the builder.

For some construction contracts, specifications are not explicitly stated as conditions. In such situations, sometimes the builder fails to meet the specifications and that means the performance is not complete. What effect does that failure have on the other party's obligation to pay? The answer is part of the doctrine of *substantial performance*.

Substantial Performance   A party who in good faith performs substantially all of the terms of a contract can enforce the contract against the other party under the doctrine of substantial performance. Note that good faith is required. Intentionally failing to comply with the terms is a breach of the contract.

To qualify as *substantial performance,* the performance must not vary greatly from the performance promised in the contract, and it must create substantially the same benefits as those promised in the contract. If the omission, variance, or defect in performance is unimportant and can easily be compensated by awarding damages, a court is likely to hold that the contract has been substantially performed. Courts decide whether the performance was substantial on a case-by-case basis, examining all of the facts of the particular situation. If performance is substantial, the other party's duty to perform remains absolute (except that the party can sue for damages due to the minor deviations).

CASE EXAMPLE 13.22   Wisconsin Electric Power Company (WEPCO) contracted with Union Pacific Railroad to transport coal to WEPCO from mines in Colorado. The contract required WEPCO to notify Union Pacific monthly of how many tons of coal (below a certain maximum) it wanted to have shipped the next month. Union Pacific was to make "good faith reasonable efforts" to meet the schedule. The contract also required WEPCO to supply the railcars. When WEPCO did not supply the railcars, Union Pacific used its own railcars and delivered 84 percent of the requested coal. In this situation, a federal court held that the delivery of 84 percent of the contracted amount constituted substantial performance.[14] ●

Performance to the Satisfaction of Another   Contracts often state that completed work must personally satisfy one of the parties or a third person. The question is whether this satisfaction becomes a condition precedent, requiring actual personal satisfaction or approval for discharge, or whether the test of satisfaction is performance that would satisfy a *reasonable person* (substantial performance).

When the subject matter of the contract is *personal*, a contract to be performed to the satisfaction of one of the parties is conditioned, and performance must actually satisfy that party. For instance, contracts for portraits and works of art are considered personal. Therefore, only the personal satisfaction of the party fulfills the condition—unless a court

---

14. *Wisconsin Electric Power Co. v. Union Pacific Railroad Co., 557 F.3d 504 (7th Cir. 2009).*

finds that the party is expressing dissatisfaction to avoid payment or otherwise is not acting in good faith.

Most other contracts need to be performed only to the satisfaction of a reasonable person unless they *expressly state otherwise*. When such contracts require performance to the satisfaction of a third party (such as, "to the satisfaction of Robert Ames, the supervising engineer"), the courts are divided. A majority of courts require the work to be satisfactory to a reasonable person, but some courts hold that the personal satisfaction of the third party designated in the contract (here, Robert Ames) must be met. Again, the personal judgment must be made honestly, or the condition will be excused.

Breach of Contract The failure, without legal excuse, of a promisor to perform the obligations of a contract.

(AP Photo/Chris Pizzello)

If Paris Hilton agrees to attend a large party in exchange for $3,000, is she in breach of contract if she leaves after ten minutes?

ETHICAL ISSUE

Material Breach of Contract

A **breach of contract** is the nonperformance of a contractual duty. A breach is *material* when performance is not at least substantial.[15] If there is a material breach, the nonbreaching party is excused from the performance of contractual duties and can sue for damages caused by the breach. If the breach is *minor* (not material), the nonbreaching party's duty to perform may sometimes be suspended until the breach is remedied, but the duty is not entirely excused. Once the minor breach is cured (corrected), the nonbreaching party must resume performance of the contractual obligations.

Any breach entitles the nonbreaching party to sue for damages, but only a material breach discharges the nonbreaching party from the contract. The policy underlying these rules is that contracts should go forward when only minor problems occur, but that contracts should be terminated if major problems arise.[16]

CASE EXAMPLE 13.23   Su Yong Kim sold an apartment building in Portland, Oregon. At the time of the sale, the building's plumbing violated the city's housing code. The contract therefore provided that Kim would correct the violations within eight months after signing the contract. A year later, Kim still had not made the necessary repairs, and the buyers were being fined by the city for the code violations. The buyers stopped making payments under the contract, and the dispute ended up in court. The court found that Kim's failure to make the repairs was a material breach of the contract because it defeated the purpose of the contract. The buyers had purchased the building to lease it out to tenants, but instead they were losing tenants and paying fines to the city due to the substandard plumbing. Because Kim's breach was material, the buyers were not obligated to continue to perform their obligation to make payments under the contract.[17] ●

Is it a material breach for a hospital to accept a country singer's donation but then refuse to honor its commitment to name a new women's health center after the singer's mother? Country singer Garth Brooks was born in Yukon, Oklahoma. Since he has become famous, he has made generous contributions to charities in that town. When his mother, Colleen Brooks, died, he donated $500,000 to Integris Rural Health, Inc., in Yukon with the intention that the funds would be used to build a new women's health center named after his mother. Several years passed after Brooks's donation, but the health center was not built. Integris claimed that it intended to do something to honor Colleen Brooks but insisted that it had never promised to build a new health center. When Integris refused to return the $500,000, Garth Brooks sued for breach of contract.

Was the hospital's failure to build a women's health center and name it after Brooks's mother a material breach of the contract? A jury thought so. In January 2012, a jury in Rogers County, Oklahoma, awarded Brooks $500,000 in actual damages for breach of contract. The jury also awarded Brooks another $500,000 because it found the hospital guilty of reckless disregard and intentionally acting with malice toward others.

---

15. *Restatement (Second) of Contracts,* Section 241.
16. See UCC 2–612, which deals with installment contracts for the sale of goods.
17. *Kim v. Park,* 192 Or.App. 365, 86 P.3d 63 (2004).

Anticipatory Repudiation An assertion or action by a party indicating that he or she will not perform a contractual obligation.

Anticipatory Repudiation of a Contract
Before either party to a contract has a duty to perform, one of the parties may refuse to perform her or his contractual obligations. This is called **anticipatory repudiation**.[18]

Repudiation Is a Material Breach   When anticipatory repudiation occurs, it is treated as a material breach of the contract, and the nonbreaching party is permitted to bring an action for damages immediately, even though the scheduled time for performance under the contract may still be in the future.[19] Until the nonbreaching party treats this early repudiation as a breach, however, the breaching party can retract the anticipatory repudiation by proper notice and restore the parties to their original obligations.

An anticipatory repudiation is treated as a present, material breach for two reasons. First, the nonbreaching party should not be required to remain ready and willing to perform when the other party has already repudiated the contract. Second, the nonbreaching party should have the opportunity to seek a similar contract elsewhere and may have the duty to do so to minimize his or her loss.

May Occur When Market Prices Fluctuate   Quite often, an anticipatory repudiation occurs when a sharp fluctuation in market prices creates a situation in which performance of the contract would be extremely unfavorable to one of the parties.

EXAMPLE 13.24   Shasta Corporation contracts to manufacture and sell 100,000 laptop computers to New Age, Inc., a retailer of computer equipment. Delivery is to be made two months from the date of the contract. One month later, three suppliers of computer parts raise their prices to Shasta. Because of these higher prices, Shasta stands to lose $500,000 if it sells the computers to New Age at the contract price. Shasta writes to New Age, stating that it cannot deliver the 100,000 computers at the contract price. Even though some may sympathize with Shasta, its letter is an anticipatory repudiation of the contract. New Age can treat the repudiation as a material breach and immediately pursue remedies, even though the contract delivery date is still a month away. •

Discharge by Agreement

Any contract can be discharged by agreement of the parties. The agreement can be contained in the original contract, or the parties can form a new contract for the express purpose of discharging the original contract.

Discharge by Mutual Rescission
As mentioned in previous chapters, rescission occurs when the parties cancel the contract and are returned to the positions they occupied prior to the contract's formation. For *mutual rescission* to take place, the parties must make another agreement that also satisfies the legal requirements for a contract—there must be an *offer,* an *acceptance,* and *consideration.* Ordinarily, if the parties agree to rescind the original contract, their promises not to perform those acts promised in the original contract will be legal consideration for the second contract.

Oral agreements to rescind executory contracts (that neither party has performed) are enforceable even if the original agreement was in writing. Under the Uniform Commercial Code, however, an agreement rescinding a contract for the sale of goods, regardless of price, must be in writing when the contract requires a written rescission. Also, agreements to rescind contracts involving transfers of realty must be evidenced by a writing.

KNOW THIS
The risks that prices will fluctuate and values will change are ordinary business risks for which the law does not provide relief.

---

18. *Restatement (Second) of Contracts,* Section 253; and UCC 2–610.
19. The doctrine of anticipatory repudiation first arose in the landmark case of *Hochster v. De La Tour,* 2 Ellis and Blackburn Reports 678 (1853), when an English court recognized the delay and expense inherent in a rule requiring a nonbreaching party to wait until the time of performance before suing for an anticipatory repudiation.

When one party has fully performed, an agreement to rescind the original contract usually is not enforceable unless additional consideration or restitution is made. Because the performing party has received no consideration for the promise to call off the original bargain, additional consideration is necessary.

Novation The substitution, by agreement, of a new contract for an old one, with the rights under the old one being terminated.

Discharge by Novation

The process of **novation** substitutes a third party for one of the original parties. Essentially, the parties to the original contract and one or more new parties get together and agree to the substitution. The requirements of a novation are as follows:

1. The existence of a previous, valid obligation.
2. Agreement by all of the parties to a new contract.
3. The extinguishing of the old obligation (discharge of the prior party).
4. A new, valid contract.

   EXAMPLE 13.25 Union Corporation contracts to sell its pharmaceutical division to British Pharmaceuticals, Ltd. Before the transfer is completed, Union, British Pharmaceuticals, and a third company, Otis Chemicals, execute a new agreement to transfer all of British Pharmaceuticals' rights and duties in the transaction to Otis Chemicals. As long as the new contract is supported by consideration, the novation will discharge the original contract (between Union and British Pharmaceuticals) and replace it with the new contract (between Union and Otis Chemicals). •

   A novation expressly or impliedly revokes and discharges a prior contract. The parties involved may expressly state in the new contract that the old contract is now discharged. If the parties do not expressly discharge the old contract, it will be impliedly discharged if the new contract's terms are inconsistent with the old contract's terms.

Discharge by Accord and Satisfaction

As Chapter 11 explained, in an *accord and satisfaction*, the parties agree to accept performance different from the performance originally promised. An *accord* is an executory contract (one that has not yet been performed) to perform some act to satisfy an existing contractual duty that is not yet discharged.[20] A *satisfaction* is the performance of the accord agreement. An *accord* and its *satisfaction* discharge the original contractual obligation.

Once the accord has been made, the original obligation is merely suspended until the accord agreement is fully performed. If it is not performed, the party to whom performance is owed can bring an action on the original obligation or for breach of the accord. **EXAMPLE 13.26** Shea obtains a judgment of $8,000 against Marla. Later, both parties agree that the judgment can be satisfied by Marla's transfer of her automobile to Shea. This agreement to accept the auto in lieu of $8,000 in cash is the accord. If Marla transfers her automobile to Shea, the accord agreement is fully performed, and the $8,000 debt is discharged. If Marla refuses to transfer her car, the accord is breached. Because the original obligation is merely suspended, Shea can sue to enforce the judgment for $8,000 in cash or bring an action for breach of the accord. •

"Law is a practical matter."

Roscoe Pound, 1870–1964 (American jurist)

Discharge by Operation of Law

Under some circumstances, contractual duties may be discharged by operation of law. These circumstances include material alteration of the contract, the running of the relevant statute of limitations, bankruptcy, and impossibility of performance.

Material Alteration

To discourage parties from altering written contracts, the law allows an innocent party to be discharged when one party has materially altered a

---

20. *Restatement (Second) of Contracts,* Section 281.

written contract without the knowledge or consent of the other party. If a party alters a material term of the contract—such as the quantity term or the price term—without the knowledge or consent of the other party, the party who was unaware of the alteration can treat the contract as discharged or terminated.

Statutes of Limitations

As mentioned earlier in this text (see Chapter 1 on page 15), statutes of limitations limit the period during which a party can sue on a particular cause of action. After the applicable limitations period has passed, a suit can no longer be brought. The period for bringing lawsuits for breach of oral contracts is usually two to three years, and for written contracts, four to five years. Lawsuits for breach of a contract for the sale of goods must be brought within four years after the cause of action has accrued. In their original contract, the parties can agree to reduce this four-year period to not less than one year. They cannot, however, agree to extend it beyond four years.

Bankruptcy

A proceeding in bankruptcy attempts to allocate the debtor's assets to the creditors in a fair and equitable fashion. Once the assets have been allocated, the debtor receives a *discharge in bankruptcy* (see Chapter 21). A discharge in bankruptcy ordinarily bars the creditors from enforcing most of the debtor's contracts.

Impossibility of Performance

After a contract has been made, performance may become impossible in an objective sense. This is known as **impossibility of performance** and may discharge the contract.[21] The doctrine of impossibility of performance is applied only when the parties could not have reasonably foreseen, at the time the contract was formed, the event or events that rendered performance impossible. Performance may also become so difficult or costly due to some unforeseen event that a court will consider it commercially unfeasible, or impracticable, as will be discussed later in the chapter.

Objective impossibility ("It cannot be done") must be distinguished from subjective impossibility ("I'm sorry, I cannot do it"). An example of subjective impossibility occurs when a party cannot deliver goods on time because of railcar shortages or cannot make payment on time because the bank is closed. In effect, the nonperforming party is saying, "It is impossible for *me* to perform," rather than "It is impossible for *anyone* to perform." Accordingly, such excuses do not discharge a contract, and the nonperforming party is normally held in breach of contract.

When Performance Is Impossible   Three basic types of situations will generally qualify as grounds for the discharge of contractual obligations based on impossibility of performance:[22]

1. *When a party whose personal performance is essential to the completion of the contract dies or becomes incapacitated prior to performance.*   **EXAMPLE 13.27**   Fred, a famous dancer, contracts with Ethereal Dancing Guild to play a leading role in its new ballet. Before the ballet can be performed, Fred becomes ill and dies. His personal performance was essential to the completion of the contract. Thus, his death discharges the contract and his estate's liability for his nonperformance. •
2. *When the specific subject matter of the contract is destroyed.*   **EXAMPLE 13.28**   A-1 Farm Equipment agrees to sell Gudgel the green tractor on its lot and promises to have the tractor ready for Gudgel to pick up on Saturday. On Friday night, however, a truck veers off the nearby highway and smashes into the tractor, destroying it beyond repair. Because the contract was for this specific tractor, A-1's performance is rendered impossible owing to the accident. •

Impossibility of Performance A doctrine under which a party to a contract is relieved of his or her duty to perform when performance becomes objectively impossible or totally impracticable.

The star dancer below has a contract to appear in five ballets during the winter season. If he breaks his leg before the season, is he still bound by the contract?

(Yuri Arcurs/Shutterstock.com)

---

21. *Restatement (Second) of Contracts,* Section 261.
22. *Restatement (Second) of Contracts,* Sections 262–266; and UCC 2–615.

3. *When a change in the law renders performance illegal.* **EXAMPLE 13.29** Russo contracts with Playlist, Inc., to create a Web site through which users can post and share movies, music, and other forms of digital entertainment. Russo goes to work. Before the site is operational, however, Congress passes the No Online Piracy in Entertainment (NOPE) Act. The NOPE Act makes it illegal to operate a Web site on which copyrighted works are posted without the copyright owners' consent. In this situation, the contract is discharged by operation of law. The purpose of the contract has been rendered illegal, and contract performance is objectively impossible. •

Temporary Impossibility   An occurrence or event that makes performance temporarily impossible operates to suspend performance until the impossibility ceases. Ordinarily, the parties must then perform the contract as originally planned. Only if the lapse of time and the change in circumstances surrounding the contract make it substantially more burdensome for the parties to perform the promised acts will the contract be discharged.

CASE EXAMPLE 13.30   On August 22, Keefe Hurwitz contracted to sell his home in Louisiana to Wesley and Gwendolyn Payne for a price of $241,500. On August 26—just four days after the parties signed the contract—Hurricane Katrina made landfall and caused extensive damage to the house. The cost of repairs was estimated at $60,000, and Hurwitz would have to make the repairs before the closing date (see Chapter 36). Hurwitz refused to pay $60,000 for the repairs only to sell the property to the Paynes for the previously agreed-on price of $241,500. The Paynes sued to enforce the contract. Hurwitz claimed that Hurricane Katrina had made it impossible for him to perform and had discharged his duties under the contract. The court ruled that Hurricane Katrina had caused only a temporary impossibility. Therefore, Hurwitz had to pay for the necessary repairs and to perform the contract as written. He could not obtain a higher purchase price to offset the cost of the repairs.[23] •

Commercial Impracticability

Courts may excuse parties from their performance obligations when the performance becomes much more difficult or expensive than the parties originally contemplated at the time the contract was formed. For someone to invoke the doctrine of **commercial impracticability** successfully, however, the anticipated performance must become *extremely* difficult or costly.[24]

The added burden of performing not only must be extreme but also *must not have been known by the parties when the contract was made.* For instance, in one classic case, a court held that a contract could be discharged because a party would have to pay ten times more than the original estimate to excavate a certain amount of gravel.[25] In another case, a power failure during a wedding reception relieved the owner of a banquet hall from the duty to perform a contract.[26] (See this chapter's *Beyond Our Borders* feature on the facing page for a discussion of Germany's approach to impracticability and impossibility of performance.)

Commercial Impracticability A doctrine that may excuse the duty to perform a contract when performance becomes much more difficult or costly due to forces that neither party could control or contemplate at the time the contract was formed.

Frustration of Purpose A court-created doctrine under which a party to a contract will be relieved of her or his duty to perform when the objective purpose for performance no longer exists (due to reasons beyond that party's control).

Frustration of Purpose

Closely allied with the doctrine of commercial impracticability is the doctrine of **frustration of purpose.** In principle, a contract will be discharged if supervening circumstances make it impossible to attain the purpose both parties had in mind when making the contract. As with commercial impracticability, the supervening event must not have been foreseeable at the time of the contracting.[27]

---

23. *Payne v. Hurwitz*, 978 So.2d 1000 (La.App. 1st Cir. 2008).
24. *Restatement (Second) of Contracts*, Section 264.
25. *Mineral Park Land Co. v. Howard*, 172 Cal. 289, 156 P. 458 (1916).
26. *Facto v. Panagis*, 390 N.J.Super. 227, 915 A.2d 59 (2007).
27. See, for example, *East Capitol View Community Development Corp. v. Robinson*, 941 A.2d 1036 (D.C.App. 2008).

BEYOND OUR BORDERS

Impossibility or Impracticability of Performance in Germany

In the United States, when a party alleges that contract performance is impossible or impracticable because of circumstances unforeseen at the time the contract was formed, a court will either discharge the party's contractual obligations or hold the party to the contract. In other words, if a court agrees that the contract is impossible or impracticable to perform, the remedy is to rescind (cancel) the contract. Under German law, however, a court may adjust the terms of (reform) a contract in light of economic developments. If an unforeseen event affects the foundation of the agreement, the court can alter the contract's terms to align with the parties' original expectations, thus making the contract fair to the parties.

Critical Thinking

When a contract becomes impossible or impracticable to perform, which remedy would a businessperson prefer—rescission or reformation? Why? Explain your answer.

Reviewing . . . Third Party Rights and Discharge

Val's Foods signs a contract to buy 1,500 pounds of basil from Sun Farms, a small organic herb grower, as long as an independent organization inspects the crop and certifies that it contains no pesticide or herbicide residue. Val's has a contract with several restaurant chains to supply pesto and intends to use Sun Farms' basil in the pesto to fulfill these contracts. When Sun Farms is preparing to harvest the basil, an unexpected hailstorm destroys half the crop. Sun Farms attempts to purchase additional basil from other farms, but it is late in the season and the price is twice the normal market price. Sun Farms is too small to absorb this cost and immediately notifies Val's that it will not fulfill the contract. Using the information presented in the chapter, answer the following questions.

1. Suppose that Sun Farms supplies the basil that survived the storm but the basil does not pass the chemical-residue inspection. Which concept discussed in the chapter might allow Val's to refuse to perform the contract in this situation?
2. Under which legal theory or theories might Sun Farms claim that its obligation under the contract has been discharged by operation of law? Discuss fully.
3. Suppose that Sun Farms contacts every basil grower in the country and buys the last remaining chemical-free basil anywhere. Nevertheless, Sun Farms is able to ship only 1,475 pounds to Val's. Would this fulfill Sun Farms' obligations to Val's? Why or why not?
4. Now suppose that Sun Farms sells its operations to Happy Valley Farms. As part of the sale, all three parties agree that Happy Valley will provide the basil as stated under the original contract. What is this type of agreement called?

DEBATE THIS The doctrine of commercial impracticability should be abolished.

BUSINESS APPLICATION

Dealing with Third Party Rights*

Assignments of contractual rights and delegations of duties are common in the business world. As you discovered in this chapter, third party rights and duties stem from the law on assignments, delegations, and third party beneficiaries. A third party may not even be aware that he or she has rights in a contract, as can happen when a person is the beneficiary of a life insurance policy. In certain situations, businesses may wish to attempt to prohibit a third party from acquiring such rights.

The general rule, though, is that any contractual right or duty can be assigned or delegated unless the assignment or delegation is prohibited by (1) the contract, (2) a statute, or (3) other limitations.

For example, a tenant under a long-term lease contract may assign the lease to another party. To avoid such assignments, property owners often prohibit the assignment of the balance of a lease term unless the property owner's consent is obtained. (See Chapter 36).

*This *Business Application* is not meant to substitute for the services of an attorney who is licensed to practice law in your state.

When a contract calls for the manufacture and sale of goods, the manufacturer may assign or delegate the production of such goods to a third party unless prohibited by the contract. Consequently, most purchase orders (contracts) have a clause that prohibits such assignments or delegations without the buyer's consent.

Checklist for the Businessperson

1. Determine whether you can assign or delegate your rights or duties under a contract to a third party.
2. If you can assign or delegate your contract rights or performance, attempt to determine your benefits and obligations, such as notice to customers, if you do make the assignment or delegation.
3. If you do not want your contract rights or duties to be assigned or delegated, insert a contract clause that prohibits assignment or delegation without your consent.
4. Whenever you might be a third party beneficiary to a contract, such as a creditor beneficiary, take steps to determine your rights.

Key Terms

alienation 331
anticipatory repudiation 343
assignee 328
assignment 328
assignor 328
breach of contract 342
commercial impracticability 346

concurrent conditions 340
condition 339
condition precedent 339
condition subsequent 340
delegatee 333
delegation of duties 332
delegator 332

discharge 338
frustration of purpose 346
impossibility of performance 345
incidental beneficiary 337
intended beneficiary 335
novation 344
obligee 328

obligor 328
performance 338
privity of contract 327
tender 340
third party beneficiary 335

Chapter Summary: Third Party Rights and Discharge

THIRD PARTY RIGHTS
Assignments (See pages 328–332.) 1. An assignment is the transfer of rights under a contract to a third party. The person assigning the rights is the *assignor,* and the party to whom the rights are assigned is the *assignee.* The assignee has a right to demand performance from the other original party to the contract. 2. Generally, all rights can be assigned. For exceptions, see Exhibit 13.3 on page 335. 3. The assignee should notify the obligor of the assignment. Although not legally required, notification avoids two potential problems: a. If the assignor assigns the same right to two different persons, generally the first assignment in time is the first in right, but in some states the first assignee to give notice takes priority. b. Until the obligor is notified of the assignment, the obligor can tender performance to the assignor. If the assignor accepts the performance, the obligor's duties under the contract are discharged without benefit to the assignee.

Continued

Chapter Summary: Third Party Rights and Discharge—Continued

Delegations (See pages 332–335.)	1. A delegation is the transfer of duties under a contract to a third party (the *delegatee*), who then assumes the obligation of performing the contractual duties previously held by the one making the delegation (the *delegator*). 2. As a general rule, any duty can be delegated, except in the circumstances listed in Exhibit 13.3 on page 335. 3. A valid delegation of duties does not relieve the delegator of obligations under the contract. If the delegatee fails to perform, the delegator is still liable to the obligee. 4. An "assignment of all rights" or an "assignment of the contract" is often construed to mean that both the rights and the duties arising under the contract are transferred to a third party.
Third Party Beneficiaries (See pages 335–338.)	A third party beneficiary contract is one made for the purpose of benefiting a third party. 1. *Intended beneficiary*—One for whose benefit a contract is created. When the promisor (the one making the contractual promise that benefits a third party) fails to perform as promised, the third party can sue the promisor directly. Examples of third party beneficiaries are creditor and donee beneficiaries. 2. *Incidental beneficiary*—A third party who indirectly (incidentally) benefits from a contract but for whose benefit the contract was not specifically intended. Incidental beneficiaries have no rights to the benefits received and cannot sue to have the contract enforced.
	CONTRACT DISCHARGE
Conditions of Performance (See pages 338–340.)	Contract obligations may be subject to the following types of conditions: 1. *Condition precedent*—A condition that must be fulfilled before a party's promise becomes absolute. 2. *Condition subsequent*—A condition that, if it occurs, operates to terminate a party's absolute promise to perform. 3. *Concurrent conditions*—Conditions that must be performed simultaneously. Each party's absolute duty to perform is conditioned on the other party's absolute duty to perform.
Discharge by Performance (See pages 340–343.)	A contract may be discharged by complete (strict) performance or by substantial performance. In some instances, performance must be to the satisfaction of another. Totally inadequate performance constitutes a material breach of the contract. An anticipatory repudiation of a contract allows the other party to sue immediately for breach of contract.
Discharge by Agreement (See pages 343–344.)	Parties may agree to discharge their contractual obligations in several ways: 1. *By rescission*—The parties mutually agree to rescind (cancel) the contract. 2. *By novation*—A new party is substituted for one of the primary parties to a contract. 3. *By accord and satisfaction*—The parties agree to render and accept performance different from that on which they originally agreed.
Discharge by Operation of Law (See pages 344–346.)	Parties' obligations under contracts may be discharged by operation of law owing to one of the following: 1. Contract alteration. 2. Statutes of limitations. 3. Bankruptcy. 4. Impossibility of performance. 5. Impracticability of performance. 6. Frustration of purpose.

ExamPrep

ISSUE SPOTTERS

1. Eagle Company contracts to build a house for Frank. The contract states that "any assignment of this contract renders the contract void." After Eagle builds the house, but before Frank pays, Eagle assigns its right to payment to Good Credit Company. Can Good Credit enforce the contract against Frank? Why or why not? **(See page 330.)**
2. Ready Foods contracts to buy two hundred carloads of frozen pizzas from Speedy Distributors. Before Ready or Speedy starts performing, can the parties call off the deal? What if Speedy has already shipped the pizzas? Explain your answers. (See pages 343–344.)

—Check your answers to the Issue Spotters against the answers provided in Appendix E at the end of this text.

For Review

Answers to the even-numbered questions in this For Review section can be found in Appendix F at the end of this text.

1. What is an assignment? What is the difference between an assignment and a delegation?
2. In what situations is the delegation of duties prohibited?
3. What factors indicate that a third party beneficiary is an intended beneficiary?
4. How are most contracts discharged?
5. What is a contractual condition, and how might a condition affect contractual obligations?

Business Scenarios and Case Problems

13–1 Third Party Beneficiaries. Wilken owes Rivera $2,000. Howie promises Wilken that he will pay Rivera the $2,000 in return for Wilken's promise to give Howie's children guitar lessons. Is Rivera an intended beneficiary of the Howie-Wilken contract? Explain. **(See pages 336–338.)**

13–2 **Question with Sample Answer—Assignment.** Aron, a college student, signs a one-year lease agreement that runs from September 1 to August 31. The lease agreement specifies that the lease cannot be assigned without the landlord's consent. In late May, Aron decides not to go to summer school and assigns the balance of the lease (three months) to a close friend, Erica. The landlord objects to the assignment and denies Erica access to the apartment. Aron claims that Erica is financially sound and should be allowed the full rights and privileges of an assignee. Discuss fully whether the landlord or Aron is correct. **(See page 330.)**

—For a sample answer to Question 13–2, go to Appendix G at the end of this text.

13–3 **Spotlight on Drug Testing—Third Party Beneficiaries.** Bath Iron Works (BIW) offered a job to Thomas Devine, contingent on Devine's passing a drug test. The testing was conducted by NorDx, a subcontractor of Roche Biomendical Laboratories. When NorDx found that Devine's urinalysis showed the presence of opiates, a result confirmed by Roche, BIW refused to offer Devine permanent employment. Devine sued Roche, claiming that the ingestion of poppy seeds can lead to a positive result and that he tested positive for opiates only because of his daily consumption of poppy seed muffins. Devine argued that he was a third party beneficiary of the contract between his employer (BIW) and NorDx (Roche). Is Devine an intended third party beneficiary of the BIW—NorDx contract? Why or why not? Do drug-testing labs have a duty to the employees to exercise reasonable care in conducting the

tests? Explain. [*Devine v. Roche Biomedical Laboratories*, 659 A.2d 868 (Me. 1995)] **(See pages 335–336.)**

13–4 Assignments. Senna Hills, Ltd., granted Southern Union Co. the right to distribute propane in a residential subdivision developed by Senna in exchange for a fee. Under their agreement, Senna's "right to receive a Fee shall continue for so long as the Propane System is owned by Southern Union." The agreement also allowed Southern Union to assign the distribution right. Later, Sonterra Energy Corp. bought the distribution system and was assigned the distribution right, but did not pay the fee to Senna. Did Sonterra breach the propane service agreement? Why or why not? [*Senna Hills, Ltd. v. Sonterra Energy Corp.*, __ S.W.3d __ (Tex.App.—Austin 2010)] **(See pages 328–332.)**

13–5 Duties That Cannot Be Delegated. Bruce Albea Contracting, Inc., the contractor on a highway project, subcontracted the asphalt work to APAC-Southeast, Inc. Their contract prohibited any delegation without Albea's consent. In midproject, APAC delegated its duties to Matthews Contracting Co. Although Albea allowed Matthews to finish the work, Albea did not pay APAC for its work on the project. Albea argued that APAC had violated the antidelegation clause, rendering their contact void. Is Albea correct? Explain. [*Western Surety Co. v. APAC-Southeast, Inc.*, 302 Ga.App. 654, 691 S.E.2d 234 (2010)] **(See page 333.)**

13–6 **Case Problem with Sample Answer—Conditions of Performance.** James Maciel leased an apartment in Regent Village, a university-owned housing facility for Regent University (RU) students in Virginia Beach, Virginia. The lease ran until the end of the fall semester. Maciel had an option to renew the lease semester by semester as long as he maintained his status as an RU student. When Maciel completed his coursework for the spring semester, he told RU that he intended to withdraw. The university told him that he could stay in the apartment until May 31, the final day of the spring semester. Maciel asked for two additional weeks, but the university denied the request. On June 1, RU changed the locks on the apartment. Maciel entered through a window and e-mailed the university that he planned to stay "for another one or two weeks." When he was charged with trespassing, Maciel argued that he had "legal authority" to occupy the apartment. Was Maciel correct? Explain. [*Maciel v. Commonwealth,* __ S.E.2d __ (Va.App. 2011)] **(See pages 338–340, 342.)**

—For a sample answer to Problem 13–6, go to Appendix H at the end of this text.

13–7 Notice of Assignment. Arnold Kazery was the owner of a hotel leased to George Wilkinson. The lease included renewal options of ten years each. When Arnold transferred his interest in the property to his son Sam, no one notified Wilkinson. For the next twenty years, Wilkinson paid the rent to Arnold and renewed the lease by notice to Arnold. When Wilkinson wrote to Arnold that he was exercising another option to renew, Sam filed a suit against him, claiming that the lease was void. Did Wilkinson give proper notice to renew? Discuss. [*Kazery v. Wilkinson,* 52 So.3d 1270 (Miss.App. 2011)] **(See page 331.)**

13–8 ⬌ **A Question of Ethics—Assignment and Delegation.** Premier Building & Development, Inc., entered a listing agreement giving Sunset Gold Realty, LLC, the exclusive right to find a tenant for some commercial property. The terms of the listing agreement stated that it was binding on both parties and "their * * * assigns." Premier Building did not own the property at the time, but had the option to purchase it. To secure financing for the project, Premier Building established a new company called Cobblestone Associates. Premier Building then bought the property and conveyed it to Cobblestone the same day. Meanwhile, Sunset Gold found a tenant for the property, and Cobblestone became the landlord. Cobblestone acknowledged its obligation to pay Sunset Gold for finding a tenant, but it later refused to pay Sunset Gold's commission. Sunset Gold then sued Premier Building and Cobblestone for breach of the listing agreement. [*Sunset Gold Realty, LLC v. Premier Building & Development, Inc.,* 133 Conn.App. 445, 36 A.3d 243 (2012)] **(See pages 328–335.)**

1. Is Premier Building relieved of its contractual duties if it assigned the contract to Cobblestone? Why or why not?
2. Given that Sunset Gold performed its obligations under the listing agreement, did Cobblestone behave unethically in refusing to pay Sunset Gold's commission? Why or why not?

Critical Thinking and Writing Assignments

13–9 Critical Legal Thinking. The concept of substantial performance permits a party to be discharged from a contract even though the party has not fully performed her or his obligations according to the contract's terms. Is this fair? Why or why not? What policy interests are at issue here? **(See page 341.)**

13–10 💡 **Business Law Critical Thinking Group Assignment.** ABC Clothiers, Inc., has a contract with John Taylor, owner of Taylor & Sons, a retailer, to deliver one thousand summer suits to Taylor's place of business on or before May 1. On April 1, John receives a letter from ABC informing him that ABC will not be able to make the delivery as scheduled. John is very upset, as he had planned a big ad campaign.

1. The first group will discuss whether John Taylor can immediately sue ABC for breach of contract (on April 2).
2. Now suppose that John Taylor's son, Tom, tells his father that they cannot file a lawsuit until ABC actually fails to deliver the suits on May 1. The second group will decide who is correct, John or Tom.
3. Assume that Taylor & Sons can either file immediately or wait until ABC fails to deliver the goods. The third group will evaluate which course of action is better, given the circumstances.

14 CHAPTER

Breach and Remedies

(Philip Hunton/Shutterstock)

CHAPTER OUTLINE

- Damages
- Equitable Remedies
- Recovery Based on Quasi Contract
- Contract Provisions Limiting Remedies

LEARNING OBJECTIVES

The five learning objectives below are designed to help improve your understanding of the chapter. After reading this chapter, you should be able to answer the following questions:

1 What is the standard measure of compensatory damages when a contract is breached? How are damages computed differently in construction contracts?

2 What is the difference between compensatory damages and consequential damages? What are nominal damages, and when do courts award nominal damages?

3 Under what circumstances is the remedy of rescission and restitution available?

4 When do courts grant specific performance as a remedy?

5 What is a limitation-of-liability clause, and when will courts enforce it?

"There's a remedy for everything except death."
—Miguel de Cervantes, 1547–1616 (Spanish author)

Normally, people enter into contracts to secure some advantage. When it is no longer advantageous for a party to fulfill her or his contractual obligations, that party may *breach,* or fail to perform, the contract.[1] Once one party breaches the contract, the other party—the nonbreaching party—can choose one or more of several remedies. A *remedy* is the relief provided to an innocent party when the other party has breached the contract. It is the means employed to enforce a right or to redress an injury. Although it may be an exaggeration to say there is a remedy for "everything" in life, as in the chapter-opening quotation, there is a remedy available for nearly every contract breach.

The most common remedies available to a nonbreaching party under contract law include damages, rescission and restitution, specific performance, and reformation. As discussed in Chapter 1 on pages 13–14, courts distinguish between *remedies at law* and *remedies in equity.* Today, the remedy at law is normally monetary damages. We discuss this

---

1. A *breach of contract* occurs when one party fails to perform part or all of the required duties under a contract. *Restatement (Second) of Contracts,* Section 235(2).

remedy in the first part of this chapter. Equitable remedies include rescission and restitution, specific performance, and reformation, all of which we examine later in the chapter. Usually, a court will not award an equitable remedy unless the remedy at law is inadequate. In the final pages of this chapter, we look at some special legal doctrines and concepts relating to remedies.

Damages

KNOW THIS
The terms of a contract must be sufficiently definite for a court to determine the amount of damages to award.

A breach of contract entitles the nonbreaching party to sue for monetary damages. As you read in Chapter 4, tort law damages are designed to compensate a party for harm suffered as a result of another's wrongful act. In the context of contract law, damages are designed to compensate the nonbreaching party for the loss of the bargain. Often, courts say that innocent parties are to be placed in the position they would have occupied had the contract been fully performed.[2]

Types of Damages

There are basically four broad categories of damages:

1. Compensatory (to cover direct losses and costs).
2. Consequential (to cover indirect and foreseeable losses).
3. Punitive (to punish and deter wrongdoing).
4. Nominal (to recognize wrongdoing when no monetary loss is shown).

Compensatory and punitive damages were discussed in Chapter 4 in the context of tort law. Here, we look at these types of damages, as well as consequential and nominal damages, in the context of contract law. (See this chapter's *Adapting the Law to the Online Environment* feature on the following page for a discussion of the effect of breaching the terms of use in an online service contract.)

LEARNING OBJECTIVE 1
What is the standard measure of compensatory damages when a contract is breached? How are damages computed differently in construction contracts?

Compensatory Damages   Damages that compensate the nonbreaching party for the *loss of the bargain* are known as *compensatory damages*. These damages compensate the injured party only for damages actually sustained and proved to have arisen directly from the loss of the bargain caused by the breach of contract. They simply replace what was lost because of the wrong or damage.

In general, the standard measure of compensatory damages is the difference between the value of the breaching party's promised performance under the contract and the value of her or his actual performance. This amount is reduced by any loss that the injured party has avoided.

EXAMPLE 14.1   You contract with Marinot Industries to perform certain personal services exclusively for Marinot during August for a payment of $4,000. Marinot cancels the contract and is in breach. You are able to find another job during August but can earn only $3,000. You normally can sue Marinot for breach and recover $1,000 as compensatory damages. You may also recover from Marinot the amount that you spent to find the other job. ● Expenses that are directly incurred because of a breach of contract—such as those incurred to obtain performance from another source—are called **incidental damages.**

Incidental Damages Damages that compensate for expenses directly incurred because of a breach of contract, such as those incurred to obtain performance from another source.

The measurement of compensatory damages varies by type of contract. Certain types of contracts deserve special mention—contracts for the sale of goods, contracts for the sale of land, and construction contracts.

---

2. *Restatement (Second) of Contracts,* Section 347.

ADAPTING THE LAW TO THE ONLINE ENVIRONMENT

THE EFFECT OF BREACHING AN ONLINE TESTING SERVICE'S TERMS OF USE

Increasingly, online testing services are available for almost any subject. Employers, for example, use online behavioral testing to evaluate the employability of applicants. Schools and counseling services can administer an online test to assess the probability that an adolescent is chemically dependent.

California uses an online test to establish a driver impairment index for those who have been arrested for drunk driving.

Typical Terms and Conditions of Use

The majority of online testing services have a relatively short list of terms and conditions for using their tests. For example, most testing services require that fees be paid for each test and for its scoring.

Also, the school, employer, or other entity that is using the online test usually must agree that the persons who administer the test are qualified. In addition, the test user must agree that no decision or diagnosis can be made solely on the basis of the online test results.

Violation of the Online Terms

If the test user violates any of the terms and conditions, the implied contract with the testing service has been breached. The following is a typical provision from an online testing service:

> When You Breach This Agreement: Each time you administer a test, the agreement granted herein will automatically terminate once the scoring has been provided to you. The Company has the right to terminate the authorization granted to you if you breach the terms and conditions of use for any test or if you violate the terms and conditions and obligations under this agreement. Once you breach your duties under this agreement, the Company will suffer immediate and irreparable damages. You therefore acknowledge that injunctive relief will be appropriate.

Critical Thinking

What possible "immediate and irreparable" damages might an online testing service experience if the test user breaches the contract?

Under what circumstances will a court award monetary damages for a breached sale-of-land contract?

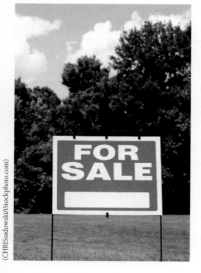

(CHRISsadowski/iStockphoto.com)

Sale of Goods   In a contract for the sale of goods, the usual measure of compensatory damages is the difference between the contract price and the market price.[3] **EXAMPLE 14.2** Medik Laboratories contracts to buy ten model UTS 400 network servers from Cal Industries for $4,000 each, but Cal Industries fails to deliver the servers. The market price of the servers at the time Medik learns of the breach is $4,500. Therefore, Medik's measure of damages is $5,000 (10 × $500), plus any incidental damages (expenses) caused by the breach. ● When the buyer breaches and the seller has not yet produced the goods, compensatory damages normally equal the seller's lost profits on the sale, rather than the difference between the contract price and the market price.

Sale of Land   Ordinarily, because each parcel of land is unique, the remedy for a seller's breach of a contract for a sale of real estate is specific performance—that is, the buyer is awarded the parcel of property for which he or she bargained (*specific performance* will be discussed more fully later in the chapter). When this remedy is unavailable (because the property has been sold, for example) or when the buyer is the party in breach, the measure of damages is typically the difference between the contract price and the market price of the land. The majority of states follow this rule.

---

3. This is the difference between the contract price and the market price at the time and place at which the goods were to be delivered or tendered. See Sections 2–708, 2–713, and 2–715(1) of the Uniform Commercial Code (UCC).

Construction Contracts The measure of damages in a building or construction contract depends on which party breaches and when the breach occurs. If the owner breaches *before performance has begun*, the contractor can recover only the profits that would have been made on the contract—that is, the total contract price less the cost of materials and labor. If the owner breaches *during performance*, the contractor can recover the profits plus the costs incurred in partially constructing the building. If the owner breaches *after the construction has been completed*, the contractor can recover the entire contract price plus interest.

When the contractor breaches the construction contract—either by failing to begin construction or by stopping work partway through the project—the measure of damages is the cost of completion, which includes reasonable compensation for any delay in performance. If the contractor finishes late, the measure of damages is the loss of use. Exhibit 14.1 on the next page summarizes the rules for the measure of damages in breached construction contracts. (The *Business Application* feature on page 366 offers some suggestions on what to do if you cannot perform.)

How should a court rule when the performance of both parties—the construction contractor and the owner—falls short of what their contract required? That was the issue in the following case.

> "A long dispute means that both parties are wrong."
>
> Voltaire, 1694–1778
> (French author)

Case 14.1

Jamison Well Drilling, Inc. v. Pfeifer

Court of Appeals of Ohio, Third District,
2011 Ohio 521 (2011).

FACTS Jamison Well Drilling, Inc., contracted to drill a water well for Ed Pfeifer in Crawford County, Ohio, for $4,130 in labor and supplies. Jamison drilled the well and installed a storage tank. The Ohio Department of Health requires that a well be lined with a minimum of twenty-five vertical feet of casing, but Jamison installed only eleven feet of casing in the drilled well. The county health department later tested the water in the well for bacteria and repeatedly found that the levels were too high. The state health department investigated and discovered that the well's casing did not comply with its requirements. The department ordered that the well be abandoned and sealed. Pfeifer used the storage tank but paid Jamison nothing. Jamison filed a suit in an Ohio state court against Pfeifer to recover the contract price and other costs. The court entered a judgment for Jamison for $970 for the storage tank. Jamison appealed.

ISSUE Does the owner have to pay the full contract price to the contractor that drilled a well and installed a storage tank when the well cannot be used because it does not meet health department standards?

DECISION No. A state appellate court affirmed the lower court's decision. The judgment had struck a balance that took into consideration that the completed construction project had value and the storage tank was functional, but the well was not usable.

A water well-drilling system.

REASON The court reasoned that the parties entered into a contract for the drilling of a well for a certain price. The work included the installation of a storage tank. The drilled well was not in compliance with state law and consequently had to be sealed and abandoned. Pfeifer may have assumed the risk that the well could not be used due to inadequate water production, but he did not assume the risk that it would have to be sealed for noncompliance with state law. Thus, Jamison was not entitled to the full contract price of $4,130. Yet the storage tank was usable, and Pfeifer had kept it. Because it would not be fair to allow Pfeifer to keep the tank without paying for it, Jamison should recover the cost of the tank.

WHAT IF THE FACTS WERE DIFFERENT? *Suppose that Pfeifer had paid Jamison for the work before the well was ordered to be sealed and had later filed a suit to recover for breach of contract. What would have been the measure of damages?*

Exhibit 14.1 Measurement of Damages—Breach of Construction Contracts

PARTY IN BREACH	TIME OF BREACH	MEASUREMENT OF DAMAGES
Owner	Before construction has begun.	Profits (contract price less cost of materials and labor).
Owner	During construction.	Profits plus costs incurred up to time of breach.
Owner	After construction is completed.	Full contract price, plus interest.
Contractor	Before construction has begun.	Cost in excess of contract price to complete work.
Contractor	Before construction is completed.	Generally, all costs incurred by owner to complete.

LEARNING OBJECTIVE 2
What is the difference between compensatory damages and consequential damages? What are nominal damages, and when do courts award nominal damages?

Consequential Damages Foreseeable damages that result from a party's breach of contract but are caused by special circumstances beyond the contract itself.

KNOW THIS

To avoid the risk of consequential damages, a seller can limit the buyer's remedies via contract.

Nominal Damages A small monetary award (often one dollar) granted to a plaintiff when no actual damage was suffered.

Consequential Damages
Foreseeable damages that result from a party's breach of contract are called **consequential damages,** or *special damages.* They differ from compensatory damages in that they are caused by special circumstances beyond the contract itself and flow from the consequences, or results, of a breach.

When a seller fails to deliver goods, knowing that the buyer is planning to use or resell those goods immediately, a court may award consequential damages (in addition to compensatory damages) for the loss of profits from the planned use or resale. **EXAMPLE 14.3** Gilmore contracts to have a specific machine part shipped to her—one that she desperately needs to repair her printing press. In her contract with the shipper, Gilmore states that she must receive the part by Monday, or she will not be able to print her paper and will lose $3,000. If the shipper is late, Gilmore normally can recover the consequential damages caused by the delay (that is, the $3,000 in losses). •

For the nonbreaching party to recover consequential damages, the breaching party must know (or have reason to know) that special circumstances will cause the nonbreaching party to suffer an additional loss.[4] See this chapter's *Landmark in the Law* feature on the facing page for a discussion of the nineteenth-century English case that established this rule on consequential damages.

Punitive Damages
Punitive, or exemplary, damages, generally are not awarded in an action for breach of contract. Such damages have no legitimate place in contract law because they are, in essence, penalties, and a breach of contract is not unlawful in a criminal sense. A contract is simply a civil relationship between the parties. The law may compensate one party for the loss of the bargain—no more and no less.

In a few situations, when a person's actions cause both a breach of contract and a tort, punitive damages may be available. Overall, though, punitive damages are almost never available in contract disputes.

Nominal Damages
When no actual damage or financial loss results from a breach of contract and only a technical injury is involved, the court may award **nominal damages** to the innocent party. Nominal damages awards are often small, such as one dollar, but they do establish that the defendant acted wrongfully. Most lawsuits for nominal damages are brought as a matter of principle under the theory that a breach has occurred and some damages must be imposed regardless of actual loss. **EXAMPLE 14.4** Hernandez contracts to buy potatoes at fifty cents a pound from Stanley. Stanley breaches the contract and does not deliver the potatoes. Meanwhile, the price of

---

4. UCC 2–715(2). See Chapter 16.

LANDMARK IN THE LAW
Hadley v. Baxendale (1854)

The rule that requires a breaching party to have notice of special ("consequential") circumstances that will result in additional loss to the nonbreaching party before consequential damages can be awarded was first enunciated in *Hadley v. Baxendale,*[a] a landmark case decided in 1854.

Case Background   This case involved a broken crankshaft used in a flour mill run by the Hadley family in Gloucester, England. The crankshaft attached to the steam engine in the mill broke, and the shaft had to be sent to a foundry in Greenwich so that a new shaft could be made to fit the engine.

The Hadleys hired Baxendale, a common carrier, to transport the shaft from Gloucester to Greenwich. Baxendale received payment in advance and promised to deliver the shaft the following day. It was not delivered for several days, however. The Hadleys had no extra crankshaft on hand to use, so they had to close the mill during those days. The Hadleys sued Baxendale to recover the profits they lost during that time. Baxendale contended that the loss of profits was "too remote."

In the mid-1800s, it was common knowledge that large mills, such as that run by the Hadleys, normally had more than one crankshaft in case the main one broke and had to be repaired. It is against this background that the parties presented their arguments on whether the damages resulting from the loss of profits while the crankshaft was out for repair were "too remote" to be recoverable.

a. 9 Exch. 341, 156 Eng.Rep. 145 (1854).

The Issue before the Court and the Court's Ruling   The crucial issue for the court was whether the Hadleys had informed the carrier, Baxendale, of the special circumstances surrounding the crankshaft's repair. Specifically, did Baxendale know at the time of the contract that the mill would have to shut down while the crankshaft was being repaired?

In the court's opinion, the only circumstances communicated by the Hadleys to Baxendale at the time the contract was made were that the item to be transported was a broken crankshaft of a mill and that the Hadleys were the owners and operators of that mill. The court concluded that these circumstances did not reasonably indicate that the mill would have to stop operations if the delivery of the crankshaft was delayed.

Application to Today's World   *Today, the rule enunciated by the court in this case still applies. When damages are awarded, compensation is given only for those injuries that the defendant could reasonably have foreseen as a probable result of the usual course of events following a breach. If the alleged injury is outside the usual and foreseeable course of events, the plaintiff must show specifically that the defendant had reason to know the facts and foresee the injury. This rule applies to contracts in the online environment as well. For example, suppose that a Web merchant loses business (and profits) due to a computer system's failure. If the failure was caused by malfunctioning software, the merchant normally may recover the lost profits from the software maker if these consequential damages were foreseeable.*

potatoes falls. Hernandez is able to buy them in the open market at half the price he agreed to pay Stanley. Hernandez is clearly better off because of Stanley's breach. Thus, because Hernandez sustained only a technical injury and suffered no monetary loss, if he sues for breach of contract and wins, the court will likely award only nominal damages. ●

Mitigation of Damages

Mitigation of Damages The requirement that a plaintiff do whatever is reasonable to minimize the damages caused by the defendant.

In most situations, when a breach of contract occurs, the injured party is held to a duty to mitigate, or reduce, the damages that he or she suffers. Under this doctrine of **mitigation of damages,** the required action depends on the nature of the situation.

Employment Contracts

In the majority of states, a person whose employment has been wrongfully terminated has a duty to mitigate damages incurred because of the employer's breach of the employment contract. In other words, a wrongfully terminated employee has a duty to take a similar job if one is available. If the person fails to do this, the damages received will be equivalent to the person's former salary less the income he or she would have received in a similar job obtained by reasonable means. Normally, a terminated employee is under no duty to take a job that is not of the same type and rank.

CASE EXAMPLE 14.5   Harry De La Concha was employed by Fordham University. He claimed that he was injured in an fight with Fordham's director of human resources and filed for workers' compensation benefits (which are available for on-the-job injuries regardless of fault—see Chapter 24). Fordham then fired De La Concha, who argued that he had been terminated in retaliation for filing a workers' compensation claim. The New York state workers' compensation board held that De La Concha had failed to mitigate his damages because he had not even looked for another job, and a state court affirmed the decision. Because De La Concha had failed to mitigate his damages, any compensation he received for wrongful termination would be reduced by the amount he *could have obtained* from other employment.[5] ●

Rental Agreements   Some states require a landlord to use reasonable means to find a new tenant if a tenant abandons the premises and fails to pay rent. If an acceptable tenant becomes available, the landlord is required to lease the premises to this tenant to mitigate the damages recoverable from the former tenant. The former tenant is still liable for the difference between the amount of the rent under the original lease and the rent received from the new tenant. If the landlord has not taken reasonable steps to find a new tenant, a court will likely reduce any award by the amount of rent the landlord could have received had he or she done so.

Liquidated Damages versus Penalties

Liquidated Damages An amount, stipulated in a contract, that the parties to the contract believe to be a reasonable estimation of the damages that will occur in the event of a breach.

Penalty A contract clause that specifies a certain amount to be paid in the event of a default or breach of contract but is unenforceable because it is designed to punish the breaching party rather than to provide a reasonable estimate of damages.

A **liquidated damages** provision in a contract specifies that a certain dollar amount is to be paid in the event of a future default or breach of contract. (*Liquidated* means determined, settled, or fixed.)

Liquidated damages differ from penalties. A **penalty** specifies a certain amount to be paid in the event of a default or breach of contract and is designed to penalize the breaching party. Liquidated damages provisions normally are enforceable. In contrast, if a court finds that a provision calls for a penalty, the agreement as to the amount will not be enforced, and recovery will be limited to actual damages.[6]

Determining Enforceability   To determine whether a particular provision is for liquidated damages or a penalty, the court must answer two questions:

1. At the time the contract was formed, was it apparent that damages would be difficult to estimate in the event of a breach?
2. Was the amount set as damages a reasonable estimate and not excessive?[7]

If the answers to both questions are yes, the provision normally will be enforced. If either answer is no, the provision usually will not be enforced.

In the following *Spotlight Case,* the court had to decide whether a clause in a contract was an enforceable liquidated damages provision or an unenforceable penalty.

---

5. *De La Concha v. Fordham University,* 814 N.Y.S.2d 320, 28 A.3d 963 (2006).
6. This is also the rule under the UCC. See UCC 2–718(1).
7. *Restatement (Second) of Contracts,* Section 356(1).

Spotlight on Liquidated Damages

Case 14.2
B-Sharp Musical Productions, Inc. v. Haber
New York Supreme Court, 27 Misc.3d 41, 899 N.Y.S.2d 792 (2010).

Bands contract their performance dates months in advance.

FACTS B-Sharp Musical Productions, Inc., and James Haber entered into a contract under which B-Sharp was to provide a band on a specified date to perform at Haber's son's bar mitzvah. Haber was to pay approximately $30,000 for the band's services. The contract contained a liquidated damages clause stating, "If [the contract] is terminated in writing by [Haber] for any reason within ninety (90) days prior to the engagement, the remaining balance of the contract will be immediately due and payable. If [the contract] is terminated in writing by [Haber] for any reason before the ninety (90) days period, 50% of the balance will be immediately due and payable."

Within ninety days before the date of the bar mitzvah, Haber sent a letter to B-Sharp stating that he was canceling the contract. When Haber refused to pay the remaining amount due under the contract—approximately $25,000—B-Sharp sued Haber and his wife in a New York state court to recover the damages. The court granted B-Sharp's motion for summary judgment, enforcing the liquidated damages clause, and the defendants appealed.

ISSUE Was the liquidated damages clause, which specified the amount to be paid in the event that the performance was canceled, enforceable?

DECISION Yes. The appellate court upheld the trial court's judgment. The clause in question was "not an unenforceable penalty." It was a reasonable estimate of damages, given that B-Sharp would be unlikely to book another engagement that close to the performance.

REASON The clause used an estimate of B-Sharp's probable loss in the event of a cancellation as the measure of loss. This estimate reflected an understanding that "although the expense and possibility of rebooking a cancelled [performance] could not be ascertained with certainty, as a practical matter, the expense would become greater, and the possibility would be less, the closer to the [performance] the cancellation was made, until a point was reached, [ninety] days before the [performance], that any effort to rebook could not be reasonably expected."

CRITICAL THINKING—Ethical Consideration *Were there ethical reasons for the court to enforce the liquidated damages clause in this case? Explain.*

Liquidated Damages in Construction Contracts Liquidated damages provisions are frequently used in construction contracts because it is difficult to estimate the amount of damages that would be caused by a delay in completing the work.

EXAMPLE 14.6 Ray Curl, a builder, enters into a contract with a developer to build a home in a new subdivision. The contract includes a clause that requires Curl to pay $300 for every day he is late in completing the project. This is a liquidated damages provision that is enforceable because it specifies a reasonable amount that Curl must pay to the developer if his performance is late. •

Equitable Remedies

Sometimes, damages are an inadequate remedy for a breach of contract. In these situations, the nonbreaching party may ask the court for an equitable remedy. Equitable remedies include rescission and restitution, specific performance, and reformation.

Restitution An equitable remedy under which a person is restored to his or her original position prior to loss or injury, or placed in the position he or she would have been in had the breach not occurred.

► KNOW THIS ◄

Restitution offers several advantages over traditional damages. First, restitution may be available in situations when damages cannot be proved or are difficult to prove. Second, restitution can be used to recover specific property. Third, restitution sometimes results in a greater overall award.

Specific Performance An equitable remedy in which a court orders the parties to perform as promised in the contract. This remedy normally is granted only when the legal remedy (monetary damages) is inadequate.

Former Detroit mayor Kwame Kilpatrick (below) at his restitution hearing.

(AP Photo/Paul Sancya, File)

Rescission and Restitution

As discussed in Chapter 13, *rescission* is essentially an action to undo, or cancel, a contract—to return nonbreaching parties to the positions that they occupied prior to the transaction.[8] When fraud, mistake, duress, undue influence, lack of capacity, or failure of consideration is present, rescission is available. Rescission may also be available by statute.[9] The failure of one party to perform under a contract entitles the other party to rescind the contract. The rescinding party must give prompt notice to the breaching party.

Restitution
To rescind a contract, both parties generally must make **restitution** to each other by returning goods, property, or funds previously conveyed.[10] If the property or goods can be returned, they must be. If the property or goods have been consumed, restitution must be made in an equivalent dollar amount.

Essentially, restitution involves the recapture of a benefit conferred on the defendant that has unjustly enriched her or him. **EXAMPLE 14.7** Andrea pays $32,000 to Miles in return for his promise to design a house for her. The next day, Miles calls Andrea and tells her that he has taken a position with a large architectural firm in another state and cannot design the house. Andrea decides to hire another architect that afternoon. Andrea can require restitution of $32,000 because Miles has received an unjust benefit of $32,000. •

Restitution Is Not Limited to Rescission Cases
Restitution may be required when a contract is rescinded, but the right to restitution is not limited to rescission cases. Because an award of restitution basically gives back, or returns, something to its rightful owner, a party can seek restitution in actions for breach of contract, tort actions, and other types of actions. For instance, restitution can be obtained when funds or property has been transferred by mistake or because of fraud or incapacity. Similarly, restitution might be available when there has been misconduct by a party with a special relationship with the other party. Even in criminal cases, a court can order restitution of funds or property obtained through embezzlement, conversion, theft, or copyright infringement.

Specific Performance

The equitable remedy of **specific performance** calls for the performance of the act promised in the contract. This remedy is attractive to a nonbreaching party because it provides the exact bargain promised in the contract. It also avoids some of the problems inherent in a suit for monetary damages, such as collecting a judgment and arranging another contract. Moreover, the actual performance may be more valuable (to the promisee) than the monetary damages.

Normally, however, specific performance will not be granted unless the party's legal remedy (monetary damages) is inadequate.[11] For this reason, contracts for the sale of goods rarely qualify for specific performance. Monetary damages ordinarily are adequate in sales contracts because substantially identical goods can be bought or sold in the market. Only if the goods are unique will a court grant specific performance. For instance, paintings, sculptures, and rare books and coins are often unique, and monetary damages will not enable a buyer to obtain substantially identical substitutes in the market.

---

8. The rescission discussed here refers to *unilateral* rescission, in which only one party wants to undo the contract. In *mutual* rescission, which we discussed in Chapter 13, both parties agree to undo the contract. Mutual rescission discharges the contract, whereas unilateral rescission is generally available as a remedy for breach of contract.
9. Many states have laws that allow individuals who enter into "home solicitation contracts" to rescind these contracts within three business days for any reason. See, for example, California Civil Code Section 1689.5.
10. *Restatement (Second) of Contracts*, Section 370.
11. *Restatement (Second) of Contracts*, Section 359.

(dimdimich/iStockphoto.com)

Why would specific performance be preferred when antiques are the item in dispute?

Sale of Land A court may grant specific performance to a buyer in an action for a breach of contract involving the sale of land. In this situation, the legal remedy of monetary damages will not compensate the buyer adequately because every parcel of land is unique, as was discussed on page 354. The same land in the same location obviously cannot be obtained elsewhere. Only when specific performance is unavailable (for example, when the seller has sold the property to someone else) will damages be awarded instead.

CASE EXAMPLE 14.8 Howard Stainbrook entered into a contract to sell Trent Low forty acres of mostly timbered land for $45,000. Low agreed to pay for a survey of the property and other costs in addition to the price. He gave Stainbrook a check for $1,000 to show his intent to fulfill the contract. One month later, Stainbrook died. His son David became the executor of the estate. After he discovered that the timber on the property was worth more than $100,000, David asked Low to withdraw his offer to buy the forty acres. Low refused and filed a suit against David seeking specific performance of the contract. The court found that because Low had substantially performed his obligations under the contract and offered to perform the rest, he was entitled to specific performance.[12] ●

Contracts for Personal Services Personal-service contracts require one party to work personally for another party. Courts normally refuse to grant specific performance of contracts for personal services. This is because ordering a party to perform personal services against his or her will amounts to a type of involuntary servitude, which is contrary to the public policy expressed in the Thirteenth Amendment to the U.S. Constitution (see Appendix B). Moreover, the courts do not want to monitor contracts for personal services, which usually require the exercise of personal judgment or talent.

EXAMPLE 14.9 If Mikhail contracts with a surgeon to perform brain surgery and she later refuses to perform, the court will not compel (nor would Mikhail want) the surgeon to perform under these circumstances. There is no possible procedure that the court can assure meaningful performance in such a situation.[13] ●

If a contract is not deemed personal, the remedy at law of monetary damages may be adequate if substantially identical service (for instance, lawn mowing) is available from other persons.

"Controversy equalizes fools and wise men—and the fools know it."

Oliver Wendell Holmes, 1809–1894 (American author)

Reformation

Reformation is an equitable remedy used when the parties have *imperfectly* expressed their agreement in writing. Reformation allows a court to rewrite the contract to reflect the parties' true intentions.

Fraud or Mutual Mistake Courts order reformation most often when fraud or mutual mistake is present. **EXAMPLE 14.10** If Carson contracts to buy a forklift from Yoshie but the written contract refers to a crane, a mutual mistake has occurred. Accordingly, a court could reform the contract so that the writing conforms to the parties' original intention as to which piece of equipment is being sold. ● Exhibit 14.2 on page 362 graphically presents the remedies, including reformation, that are available to the nonbreaching party.

Written Contract Incorrectly States the Parties' Oral Agreement

A court will also reform a contract when two parties enter into a binding oral contract but

---

12. *Stainbrook v. Low,* 842 N.E.2d 386 (Ind.App. 2006).

13. Similarly, courts often refuse to order specific performance of construction contracts because courts are not set up to operate as construction supervisors or engineers.

Exhibit 14.2 Remedies for Breach of Contract

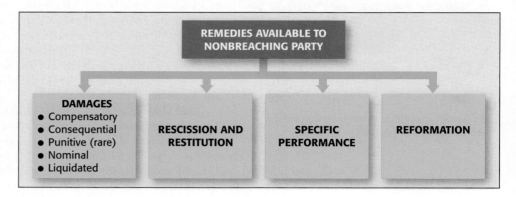

REMEDIES AVAILABLE TO
NONBREACHING PARTY

DAMAGES
- Compensatory
- Consequential
- Punitive (rare)
- Nominal
- Liquidated

**RESCISSION AND
RESTITUTION**

**SPECIFIC
PERFORMANCE**

REFORMATION

later make an error when they attempt to put the terms into writing. Usually, the court will allow into evidence the correct terms of the oral contract, thereby reforming the written contract.

Covenants Not to Compete   Courts also may reform contracts when the parties have executed a written covenant not to compete (see page 294 of Chapter 11). If the covenant not to compete is for a valid and legitimate purpose (such as the sale of a business) but the area or time restraints are unreasonable, some courts will reform the restraints by making them reasonable and will enforce the entire contract as reformed. Other courts, however, will throw out the entire restrictive covenant as illegal.

In the following case, a physician claimed that the covenant not to compete he signed was unreasonable and should therefore be declared illegal.

Case 14.3

Emerick v. Cardiac Study Center, Inc.

Court of Appeals of Washington, Division 2,
166 Wash.App. 1039 (2012).

Can a covenant not to compete apply to physician-shareholders in a medical group?

FACTS   Cardiac Study Center, Inc., is a medical practice group of approximately fifteen cardiologists. In 2002, Cardiac hired Dr. Robert Emerick as an employee. In 2004, Emerick became a shareholder of Cardiac. He signed a shareholder employment agreement, which included a covenant not to compete. The covenant stated that a physician who left the group promised not to practice competitively in the surrounding area for a period of five years. In 2005, patients and other medical providers began to complain to Cardiac about Emerick's conduct. Some physicians stopped referring patients to Cardiac as a result. Finally, Cardiac terminated Emerick's employment in 2009. Emerick sued Cardiac seeking a declaration that the covenant not to compete was unenforceable. He prevailed at trial, and Cardiac appealed.

ISSUE   Was the Cardiac Study Center's covenant not to compete unenforceable as against public policy?

DECISION   No. The state appellate court held that the covenant not to compete was reasonable.

REASON   The reviewing court examined the reasonableness of the covenant not to compete in terms of how it protected the employer's business or goodwill. The court pointed out that "an employee who joins an established business gains access to his employer's customers and acquires valuable information as to the nature and character of the business." Further, an employer has a "legitimate interest in protecting its existing client base and prohibiting the employee from taking its clients." Cardiac had provided Emerick with an immediate client base and established referral sources when he moved to the area. Emerick had access to Cardiac's

Case 14.3—Continued

business model and goodwill. Finally, the reviewing court explained that many Washington courts have held that restrictive covenants among physicians are enforceable. Indeed, "restrictive covenants are common among professionals because they allow a new professional to step in to an already established practice while protecting the employer from future competition."

WHY IS THIS CASE IMPORTANT? *Many covenants not to compete are found to be unenforceable. Nonetheless, if businesspersons create restrictive covenants that are reasonable, do not extend to a very large geographic area, and do not last for decades, courts will often hold that they are enforceable. The ability to use enforceable covenants encourages businesses to hire employees who will have access to client lists and unique business models.*

Recovery Based on Quasi Contract

In some situations, when no actual contract exists, a court may step in to prevent one party from being unjustly enriched at the expense of another party. As discussed in Chapter 9, *quasi contract* is a legal theory under which an obligation is imposed in the absence of an agreement. A quasi contract is not a true contract but rather a fictional contract that is imposed on the parties to prevent unjust enrichment.

When Quasi Contract Is Used

Quasi contract allows a court to act as if a contract exists when there is no actual contract or agreement between the parties. Therefore, if the parties have entered into a contract concerning the matter in controversy, a court normally will not impose a quasi contract. A court can also use the doctrine when the parties entered into a contract, but it is unenforceable for some reason.

> **KNOW THIS**
>
> The function of a quasi contract is to impose a legal obligation on a party who made no actual promise.

Quasi-contractual recovery is often granted when one party has partially performed under a contract that is unenforceable. Quasi contracts provide an alternative to suing for damages and allow the party to recover the reasonable value of the partial performance. **EXAMPLE 14.11** Ericson contracts to build two oil derricks for Petro Industries. The derricks are to be built over a period of three years, but the parties do not create a written contract. Therefore, the Statute of Frauds will bar the enforcement of the contract.[14] After Ericson completes one derrick, Petro Industries informs him that it will not pay for the derrick. Ericson can sue Petro Industries under the theory of quasi contract. •

The Requirements of Quasi Contract

To recover on a quasi contract theory, the party seeking recovery must show the following:

1. The party conferred a benefit on the other party.
2. The party conferred the benefit with the reasonable expectation of being paid.
3. The party did not act as a volunteer in conferring the benefit.
4. The party receiving the benefit would be unjustly enriched if allowed to retain the benefit without paying for it.

Applying these requirements to *Example 14.11* above, Ericson can sue in quasi contract because all of the conditions for quasi-contractual recovery have been fulfilled. Ericson

---

14. Contracts that by their terms cannot be performed within one year from the day after the date of contract formation must be in writing to be enforceable (see Chapter 12).

conferred a benefit on Petro Industries by building the oil derrick. Ericson build the derrick with the reasonable expectation of being paid. He did not intend to act as a volunteer. Petro Industries would be unjustly enriched if it was allowed to keep the derrick without paying Ericson for the work. Therefore, Ericson should be able to recover the reasonable value of the oil derrick that was built (under the theory of *quantum meruit*[15]—"as much as he or she deserves"). The reasonable value is ordinarily equal to the fair market value.

> **KNOW THIS**
>
> Exculpatory clauses may be held unconscionable, depending on the relative bargaining positions of the parties and the importance to the public interest of the business seeking to enforce the clause.

Contract Provisions Limiting Remedies

A contract may include provisions stating that no damages can be recovered for certain types of breaches or that damages will be limited to a maximum amount. The contract may also provide that the only remedy for breach is replacement, repair, or refund of the purchase price. The contract can also provide that one party can seek injunctive relief if the other party breaches the contract (see Paragraph 11 on page 374 in the *Annotated Employment Contract* that follows this chapter). Provisions stating that no damages can be recovered are called *exculpatory clauses* (see Chapter 11). Provisions that affect the availability of certain remedies are called *limitation-of-liability clauses*.

The UCC Allows Sales Contracts to Limit Remedies

The Uniform Commercial Code (UCC) provides that remedies can be limited in a contract for the sale of goods. We will examine the UCC provisions on limitation-of-liability clauses in Chapter 16, in the context of the remedies available on the breach of a contract for the sale or lease of goods.[16]

Enforceability of Limitation-of-Liability Clauses

LEARNING OBJECTIVE 5
What is a limitation-of-liability clause, and when will courts enforce it?

Whether a limitation-of-liability clause in a contract will be enforced depends on the type of breach that is excused by the provision. Normally, a provision excluding liability for fraudulent or intentional injury will not be enforced. Likewise, a clause excluding liability for illegal acts or violations of law will not be enforced.

A clause excluding liability for negligence may be enforced in certain situations, however. When an exculpatory clause for negligence is contained in a contract made between parties who have roughly equal bargaining positions, the clause usually will be enforced.

CASE EXAMPLE 14.12   Engineering Consulting Services, Ltd. (ECS), contracted with RSN Properties, Inc., a real estate developer, to perform soil studies for $2,200 and render an opinion on the use of septic systems in a residential subdivision being developed. A clause in the contract limited ECS's liability to RSN to the value of the engineering services or the sum of $50,000, whichever was greater. ECS concluded that most of the lots were suitable for septic systems, so RSN proceeded with development. RSN completed roads and waterline construction in reliance on ECS's conclusions, which turned out to be incorrect. The county refused to approve further development of the lots because they were unsuitable for septic systems. RSN sued ECS for breach of contract and argued that the limitation-of-liability clause was against public policy and unenforceable. The court, however, held that the "contract represented a reasonable allocation of risks in an arm's-length business transaction, and did not violate public policy for professional engineering practice." The court therefore enforced the limitation-of-liability clause.[17] ●

---

15. Pronounced *kwahn*-tuhm *mehr*-oo-wuht.
16. UCC 2–719.
17. *RSN Properties, Inc. v. Engineering Consulting Services, Ltd.*, 301 Ga.App. 52, 686 S.E.2d 853 (2009).

Should courts enforce a limitation-of-liability clause in a contract that cruise ship passengers are required to sign? In 2012, a cruise ship carrying 4,200 passengers and crew capsized off the coast of Italy, killing more than thirty people. Captain Francesco Schettino, the captain of the ship *Costa Concordia*, was blamed for causing the accident because he brought the ship too close to shore where it struck a rock that punctured its hull. Passengers have attempted to sue the corporate owner of the ship, Carnival Cruise Lines, over the incident. But Carnival included a carefully drafted limitation-of-liability clause in its contract, which each passenger is required to sign when purchasing a ticket. The clause limits the kind of suits that can be brought, where they can be filed, and how much passengers can ultimately recover from Carnival.

U.S. courts have upheld similar limitations of liability in other cruise ship cases. Because no U.S. port was involved with the Italian cruise ship's accident, however, the contract specifies that litigation must take place in Italy. Thus, no U.S. court will be involved. Under international law, limitations on liability can be set aside only if the ship's owner engaged in egregious (highly unacceptable) acts. The captain's acts were arguably egregious. For instance, he increased the *Costa Concordia*'s speed in shallow waters, in the dark, despite the proximity of obstacles, to make up for time he had spent having dinner with a woman. Then he abandoned the ship while passengers were stranded aboard. Nevertheless, the ship's owner, Carnival Cruise Lines, claims that it was unaware of the captain's reckless conduct until after the accident. Unless the passengers can persuade a court that Carnival is responsible for the acts of its captain, their recovery from the cruise line is likely to be limited.

Reviewing . . . Breach and Remedies

Kyle Bruno enters into a contract with X Entertainment to be a stuntman in a movie being produced. Bruno is widely known as the best motorcycle stuntman in the business, and the movie to be produced, *Xtreme Riders*, has numerous scenes involving high-speed freestyle street-bike stunts. Filming is set to begin August 1 and end by December 1 so that the film can be released the following summer. Both parties to the contract have stipulated that the filming must end on time in order to capture the profits from the summer movie market. The contract states that Bruno will be paid 10 percent of the net proceeds from the movie for his stunts. The contract also includes a liquidated damages provision, which specifies that if Bruno breaches the contract, he will owe X Entertainment $1 million. In addition, the contract includes a limitation-of-liability clause stating that if Bruno is injured during filming, X Entertainment's liability is limited to nominal damages. Using the information presented in the chapter, answer the following questions.

1. One day, while Bruno is preparing for a difficult stunt, he gets into an argument with the director and refuses to perform any stunts. Can X Entertainment seek specific performance of the contract? Why or why not?
2. Suppose that while performing a high-speed wheelie on a motorcycle, Bruno is injured by an intentionally reckless act of an X Entertainment employee. Will a court be likely to enforce the limitation-of-liability clause? Why or why not?
3. What factors would a court consider to determine if the $1 million liquidated damages clause is valid or is a penalty?
4. Suppose that there was no liquidated damages clause (or the court refused to enforce it) and X Entertainment breached the contract. The breach caused the release of the film to be delayed until after summer. Could Bruno seek consequential (special) damages for lost profits from the summer movie market in that situation? Explain.

DEBATE THIS Courts should always uphold limitation-of-liability clauses, whether or not the two parties to the contract had equal bargaining power.

BUSINESS APPLICATION

What Do You Do When You Cannot Perform?*

Not every contract can be performed. If you are a contractor, you may take on a job that, for one reason or another, you cannot or do not wish to perform. Simply walking away from the job and hoping for the best normally is not the most effective way to avoid litigation—which can be costly, time consuming, and emotionally draining. Instead, you should consider various options that may reduce the likelihood of litigation.

For example, suppose that you are a building contractor and you sign a contract to build a home for the Andersons according to a set of plans that they provided. Performance is to begin on June 15. On June 1, Central Enterprises offers you a position that will pay you two and a half times as much net income as you could earn as an independent builder. To take the job, you have to start on June 15. You cannot be in two places at the same time, so to accept the new position, you must breach the contract with the Andersons.

Consider Your Options

What can you do in this situation? One option is to subcontract the work to another builder and oversee the work yourself to make sure it conforms to the contract. Another option is to negotiate with the Andersons for a release. You can offer to find another qualified builder who will build a house of the same quality at the same

price. Alternatively, you can offer to pay any additional costs if another builder takes the job and is more expensive. In any event, this additional cost would be one measure of damages that a court would impose on you if the Andersons prevailed in a suit for breach of contract (in addition to any costs the Andersons suffer as a result of the breach, such as costs due to the delay in construction). Thus, by making the offer, you might be able to avoid the expense of litigation—if the Andersons accept your offer.

Settlement Offers

Often, parties are reluctant to propose compromise settlements because they fear that what they say will be used against them in court if litigation ensues. Generally, however, offers for settlement will not be admitted in court to prove that you are liable for a breach of contract (though they are at times admissible to prove a party breached the duty of good faith).

Checklist for When You Cannot Perform
1. *Consider a compromise.*
2. *Subcontract out the work and oversee it.*
3. *Offer to find an alternative contractor to fulfill your obligation.*
4. *Make a cash offer to "buy" a release from your contract. Work with an attorney in making the offer unless the amount involved is insignificant.*

*This *Business Application* is not meant to substitute for the services of an attorney who is licensed to practice law in your state.

Key Terms

Chapter Summary: Breach and Remedies

COMMON REMEDIES AVAILABLE TO NONBREACHING PARTY	
Damages **(See pages 353–359.)**	The legal remedy designed to compensate the nonbreaching party for the loss of the bargain. By awarding monetary damages, the court tries to place the parties in the positions that they would have occupied had the contract been fully performed. The nonbreaching party frequently has a duty to *mitigate* (lessen or reduce) the damages incurred as a result of the contract's breach. There are four broad categories of damages. In addition, a contract may contain a provision for liquidated damages. 1. *Compensatory damages*—Damages that compensate the nonbreaching party for injuries actually sustained and proved to have arisen directly from the loss of the bargain resulting from the breach of contract.

Chapter Summary: Breach and Remedies—Continued

Damages—Continued	a. In breached contracts for the sale of goods, the usual measure of compensatory damages is the difference between the contract price and the market price. b. In breached contracts for the sale of land, the measure of damages is ordinarily the same as in contracts for the sale of goods. c. In breached construction contracts, the measure of damages depends on which party breaches and at what stage of construction the breach occurs. 2. *Consequential damages*—Damages that result from special circumstances beyond the contract itself. The damages flow only from the consequences of a breach. For a party to recover consequential damages, the damages must be the foreseeable result of a breach of contract, and the breaching party must have known at the time the contract was formed that special circumstances existed that would cause the nonbreaching party to incur additional loss on breach of the contract. Also called *special damages*. 3. *Punitive damages*—Damages awarded to punish the breaching party. Usually not awarded in an action for breach of contract unless a tort is involved. 4. *Nominal damages*—Damages small in amount (such as one dollar) that are awarded when a breach has occurred but no actual injury has been suffered. Awarded only to establish that the defendant acted wrongfully. 5. *Liquidated damages*—Damages that may be specified in a contract as the amount to be paid to the nonbreaching party in the event the contract is breached. Clauses providing for liquidated damages are enforced if the damages were difficult to estimate at the time the contract was formed and if the amount stipulated is reasonable. If the amount is construed to be a penalty, the clause will not be enforced.
Rescission and Restitution (See page 360.)	1. *Rescission*—A remedy whereby a contract is canceled and the parties are restored to the original positions that they occupied prior to the transaction. Available when fraud, a mistake, duress, or failure of consideration is present. The rescinding party must give prompt notice of the rescission to the breaching party. 2. *Restitution*—When a contract is rescinded, both parties must make restitution to each other by returning the goods, property, or funds previously conveyed. Restitution prevents the unjust enrichment of the parties.
Specific Performance (See pages 360–361.)	An equitable remedy calling for the performance of the act promised in the contract. This remedy is available only in special situations—such as those involving contracts for the sale of unique goods or land—when monetary damages would be an inadequate remedy. Specific performance is not available as a remedy for breached contracts for personal services.
Reformation (See pages 361–362.)	An equitable remedy allowing a contract to be "reformed," or rewritten, to reflect the parties' true intentions. Available when an agreement is imperfectly expressed in writing.
Recovery Based on Quasi Contract (See pages 363–364.)	An equitable theory imposed by the courts to obtain justice and prevent unjust enrichment in a situation in which no enforceable contract exists. The party seeking recovery must show the following: 1. A benefit was conferred on the other party. 2. The party conferring the benefit did so with the expectation of being paid. 3. The benefit was not volunteered. 4. The party receiving the benefit would be unjustly enriched if allowed to retain the benefit without paying for it.
CONTRACT DOCTRINES RELATING TO REMEDIES	
Contract Provisions Limiting Remedies (See pages 364–365.)	A contract may provide that no damages (or only a limited amount of damages) can be recovered in the event the contract is breached. Under the Uniform Commercial Code, remedies may be limited in contracts for the sale of goods. Clauses excluding liability for fraudulent or intentional injury or for illegal acts cannot be enforced. Clauses excluding liability for negligence may be enforced if both parties hold roughly equal bargaining power.

ExamPrep

ISSUE SPOTTERS

1. Greg contracts to build a storage shed for Haney, who pays Greg in advance, but Greg completes only half the work. Haney pays Ipswich $500 to finish the shed. If Haney sues Greg, what would be the measure of recovery? **(See page 355.)**
2. Lyle contracts to sell his ranch to Marley, who is to take possession on June 1. Lyle delays the transfer until August 1. Marley incurs expenses in providing for cattle that he bought for the ranch. When they made the contract, Lyle had no reason to know of the cattle. Is Lyle liable for Marley's expenses in providing for the cattle? Why or why not? **(See page 356.)**

—Check your answers to the Issue Spotters against the answers provided in Appendix E at the end of this text.

BEFORE THE TEST

Go to www.cengagebrain.com, enter the ISBN 9781133273561, and click on "Find" to locate this textbook's Web site. Then, click on "Access Now" under "Study Tools," and select Chapter 14 at the top. There, you will find a Practice Quiz that you can take to assess your mastery of the concepts in this chapter, as well as Flashcards, a Glossary of important terms, and Video Questions (when assigned).

For Review

Answers to the even-numbered questions in this For Review section can be found in Appendix F at the end of this text.

1. What is the standard measure of compensatory damages when a contract is breached? How are damages computed differently in construction contracts?
2. What is the difference between compensatory damages and consequential damages? What are nominal damages, and when do courts award nominal damages?
3. Under what circumstances is the remedy of rescission and restitution available?
4. When do courts grant specific performance as a remedy?
5. What is a limitation-of-liability clause and when will courts enforce it?

Business Scenarios and Case Problems

14–1 Liquidated Damages. Carnack contracts to sell his house and lot to Willard for $100,000. The terms of the contract call for Willard to make a deposit of 10 percent of the purchase price as a down payment. The terms further stipulate that if the buyer breaches the contract, Carnack will retain the deposit as liquidated damages. Willard makes the deposit, but because her expected financing of the $90,000 balance falls through, she breaches the contract. Two weeks later, Carnack sells the house and lot to Balkova for $105,000. Willard demands her $10,000 back, but Carnack refuses, claiming that Willard's breach and the contract terms entitle him to keep the deposit. Discuss who is correct. **(See pages 358–359.)**

14–2 ❓ Question with Sample Answer—Mitigation of Damages. Lauren Barton, a single mother with three children, lived in Portland, Oregon. Cynthia VanHorn also lived in Oregon until she moved to New York City to open and operate an art gallery. VanHorn asked Barton to manage the gallery under a one-year contract for an annual salary of $72,000. To begin work, Barton relocated to New York. As part of the move, Barton transferred custody of her children to her husband, who lived in London, England. In accepting the job, Barton also forfeited her husband's alimony and child-support payments, including unpaid amounts of nearly $30,000. Before Barton started work, VanHorn repudiated the contract. Unable to find employment for more than an annual salary of $25,000, Barton moved to London to be near her children. Barton filed a suit in an Oregon state court against VanHorn, seeking damages for breach of contract. Should the court hold, as VanHorn argued, that Barton did not take reasonable steps to mitigate her damages? Why or why not? **(See pages 357–358.)**

—**For a sample answer to Question 14–2, go to Appendix G at the end of this text.**

14–3 🖥 Spotlight on Types of Damages—Compensatory Damages. Tyna Ek met Russell Peterson in Seattle, Washington. Peterson persuaded Ek to buy a boat that he had once owned, the *O'Hana Kai*, which was in Juneau, Alaska, for $43,000. Ek and Peterson then entered into a contract under which Peterson was to make the boat seaworthy so that it could be transported to Seattle within a month, where he would pay its moorage costs and renovate the boat at his own expense. In return, Peterson would receive a portion of the profit on its resale the following year. On the sale, Ek would recover her costs, and then Peterson would be reimbursed for his. Ek loaned Peterson her cell phone so that they could communicate while he prepared the vessel for the trip to Seattle. In March, Peterson, who was still in Alaska, borrowed $4,000 from Ek. Two months later, Ek began to receive unanticipated, unauthorized bills for vessel parts and moorage, the use of her phone, and charges on her credit card. She went to Juneau to take possession of the boat. Peterson moved it to Petersburg, Alaska, where he registered it under a false name, and then to Taku Harbor, where the police seized it. Ek filed a suit in an Alaska state court against Peterson, alleging breach of contract and seeking damages. If the court finds in Ek's favor, what should her damages include? Discuss. [*Peterson v. Ek*, 93 P.3d 458 (Alaska 2004)] **(See page 353.)**

14–4 Quasi Contract. Middleton Motors, Inc., a struggling Ford dealership in Wisconsin, sought managerial and financial assistance from Lindquist Ford, Inc., a successful Ford dealership in Iowa. While the two dealerships negotiated the terms for the services and a cash infusion, Lindquist sent Craig Miller, its general manager, to assume control of Middleton. After a year, the parties had not agreed on the terms, Lindquist had not invested any funds, Middleton had not made a profit, and

Miller was fired without being paid. Can Miller recover pay for his time on a quasi-contract theory? Why or why not? Which of the quasi-contract requirements is most likely to be disputed in this case? Why? [*Lindquist Ford, Inc. v. Middleton Motors, Inc.,* 557 F.3d 469 (7th Cir. 2009)] **(See pages 363–364.)**

14–5 Liquidated Damages. Planned Pethood Plus, Inc. (PPP), a veterinary clinic, borrowed $389,000 from KeyBank. The term of the loan was ten years. A "prepayment penalty" clause provided a formula to add an amount to the balance due if PPP offered to repay its loan early. The additional amount depended on the time of the prepayment. Such clauses are common in loan agreements. After one year, PPP offered to pay its loan. KeyBank applied the formula to add $40,525.92 to the balance due. Is this a penalty or liquidated damages? Explain. [*Planned Pethood Plus, Inc. v. KeyCorp, Inc.,* 228 P.3d 262 (Colo.App. 2010)] **(See page 358.)**

14–6 Damages. Before buying a house, Dean and Donna Testa hired Ground Systems, Inc. (GSI), to inspect the sewage and water disposal system. GSI reported a split system with a watertight septic tank, a wastewater tank, a distribution box, and a leach field. The Testas bought the house. Later, Dean saw that the system was not as GSI described—there was no distribution box or leach field, and there was only one tank, which was not watertight. The Testas arranged for the installation of a new system and sold the house. Assuming that GSI is liable for breach of contract, what is the measure of damages? [*Testa v. Ground Systems, Inc.,* 206 N.J. 330, 20 A.3d 435 (App.Div. 2011)] **(See pages 353–354.)**

14–7 ⚖ **Case Problem with Sample Answer—Consequential Damages.** After submitting the high bid at a foreclosure sale, David Simard entered into a contract to purchase real property in Maryland for $192,000. Simard defaulted (failed to pay) on the contract, so a state court ordered the property to be resold at Simard's expense, as required by state law. The property was then resold for $163,000, but the second purchaser also defaulted on his contract. The court then ordered a second resale, resulting in a final price of $130,000. Assuming that Simard is liable for consequential damages, what is the extent of his liability? Is he liable for losses and expenses related to the first resale? If so, is he also liable for losses and expenses related to the second resale? Why or why not? [*Burson v. Simard,* 35 A.3d 1154 (Md. 2012)] **(See page 356.)**

—**For a sample answer to Problem 14–7, go to Appendix H at the end of this text.**

14–8 ⬌ **A Question of Ethics—Performance and Damages.** On a weekday, Tamara Cohen, a real estate broker, showed a townhouse owned by Ray and Harriet Mayer to Jessica Seinfeld, the wife of comedian Jerry Seinfeld. On the weekend, when Cohen was unavailable because her religious beliefs prevented her from working, the Seinfelds revisited the townhouse on their own and agreed to buy it. The contract stated that the "buyers will pay buyer's real estate broker's fees." [*Cohen v. Seinfeld,* 15 Misc.3d 1118(A), 839 N.Y.S.2d 432 (Sup. 2007)] **(See page 353.)**

1. Is Cohen entitled to payment even though she was not available to show the townhouse to the Seinfelds on the weekend? Explain.

2. What obligation do parties involved in business deals owe to each other with respect to their religious beliefs? How might the situation in this case have been avoided?

Critical Thinking and Writing Assignments

14–9 Critical Legal Thinking. Review the discussion of the doctrine of mitigation of damages in this chapter. What are some of the advantages and disadvantages of this doctrine? **(See pages 357–358.)**

14–10 💡 **Business Law Critical Thinking Group Assignment.** Frances Morelli agreed to sell Judith Bucklin a house in Rhode Island for $177,000. The sale was supposed to be closed by September 1, when the parties were to exchange the deed for the price. The contract included a provision that "if Seller is unable to convey good, clear, insurable, and marketable title, Buyer shall have the option to: (a) accept such title as Seller is able to convey without reduction of the Purchase Price, or (b) cancel this Agreement and receive a return of all Deposits."

An examination of the public records revealed that the house did not have marketable title. Bucklin offered Morelli additional time to resolve the problem, and the closing did not occur as scheduled. Morelli decided "the deal is over" and offered to return the deposit. Bucklin refused and, in mid-October, decided to exercise her option to accept the house without marketable title. She notified Morelli, who did not respond. She then filed a lawsuit against Morelli in a state court.

1. One group will discuss whether Morelli has breached the contract, and will decide in whose favor the court should rule.

2. A second group will assume that Morelli did breach the contract and will determine what the appropriate remedy is in this situation.

Appendix to Chapter 14

An Annotated Employment Contract

As the text and cases in this unit have indicated, businesses use contracts to make their transactions more predictable. Contracts allow parties to clarify their obligations in great detail. Businesses also use contracts to resolve anticipated problems or conflicts and to clarify responsibility in the event of a breach. An understanding of what is in a typical contract is crucial to using contracts effectively.

Being able to read and understand a contract takes some practice, however. Contract terms often are highly technical and complex, and sometimes the vocabulary and phrasing can be unfamiliar. Nevertheless, businesspersons need to be able to understand the meaning of various contract provisions so that they will know what their business's obligations and rights are under the contract.

Reading a Contract

A contract is generally intended to serve two purposes:

1. To achieve some commercial purpose—such as, a sale of goods, a lease of property, or an employment agreement.
2. To prevent future conflict by clarifying the obligations and rights of the parties.

Parties should address the details of the business agreement and also should think strategically about how a conflict should be resolved if something goes awry.

Different types of contracts will have different provisions. Sales contracts should contain information on the products being sold, the quantity, the price, and delivery terms. Employment contracts may contain information on the term of employment, employment duties, confidentiality and nondisclosure of the employer's documents and information, and restrictions on competing with the employer after leaving the position.

Although standard forms exist for many types of contracts, the parties to a particular contract may have specific requirements and thus may need to tailor the contract to fit their transaction. A larger transaction or more specialized goods or real estate will require a more specific and probably a longer contract. For example, a sales contract between Airbus and American Airlines for the sale of an Airbus S.A.S. plane was more than 109 pages, not counting the eleven exhibits that followed the main contract.[1]

Regardless of the specificity of the contract provisions, it is important for a businessperson to read and evaluate the responsibilities or commitments of both parties to the contract. Sometimes, a single word or phrase can make an enormous difference. For example, a rental contract for a house may state that the owner is responsible for any plumbing issues, or it may specify that the renter is the responsible party. If a plumber has to be called to deal with clogged pipes on a holiday, that single phrase in the contract will determine who has to pay the plumber's very high holiday rates.

---

1. "Sample Business Contracts." *Onecle.com*. 14 July 2012. Web.

Usually, someone signs a contract after having reviewed it in detail (or after one's attorney has reviewed it).

(Denis Opolja/Shutterstock.com)

Contract Analysis Exercise

The sample contract on pages 372–375 is based on an actual employment-related contract between a company called Boulder Dry and its chief financial officer (CFO). As you read the contract, think about the following questions:

1. Which party seems to have had the stronger bargaining position, and why?
2. Which specific provisions favor the employer?
3. Which specific provisions favor the employee?
4. The parties' main intentions in signing this contract were to protect the firm's confidential information and to explain how the CFO could use that information. Which provisions are related to those two purposes?
5. Which provisions seem entirely unrelated to the main purposes? Why are these other provisions included in the contract? What do they do for the parties?
6. What terms in the contract do you find difficult to understand?
7. As a potential employee being asked to sign this agreement, what concerns might you have?
8. If after one year the employee resigns from Boulder Dry, what provisions of this contract should the employee have reviewed before resigning because they would affect his or her future? When leaving the company, what actions would the employee take to ensure that he or she was in compliance with all obligations?

SEE SAMPLE CONTRACT ON THE FOLLOWING PAGES.

EMPLOYEE NONCOMPETITION
AND NONDISCLOSURE AGREEMENT

In consideration of my employment or continued employment, with Boulder Dry (the "Company"), and the compensation received from the Company, I hereby agree as follows:

1. *Proprietary Information and Inventions:* I understand and acknowledge that:

   A. The Company is engaged in research, development, production, marketing, and servicing. I am expected to make new contributions and inventions of value to the Company as part of my employment.

   B. My employment creates a relationship of trust between the Company and me with respect to information that may be made known to me or learned by me during my employment.

   C. The Company possesses information that has been discovered or developed by the Company that has commercial value to the Company and is treated by the Company as confidential. All such information is hereinafter called "Proprietary Information," which term shall include, but shall not be limited to, systems, processes, data, computer programs, discoveries, marketing plans, strategies, forecasts, new products, unpublished financial statements, licenses, and customer and supplier lists. The term "Proprietary Information" shall not include any of the foregoing that is in the public domain.

   D. All existing confidential lists of customers of the Company, and all confidential lists of customers developed during my employment, are the sole and exclusive property of the Company and I shall not have any right, title, or interest therein.

2. *Ownership of Proprietary Information:* All Proprietary Information shall be the sole property of the Company, including patents, copyrights, and trademarks. I hereby assign to the Company any rights I may have or acquire in such Proprietary Information. Both during and after my employment, I will keep in strictest confidence and trust all Proprietary Information. I will not use or disclose any Proprietary Information without the written consent of the Company, except as may be necessary in performing my duties as a Company employee.

3. *Commitment to Company and Other Employment:* During my employment, I will devote substantially all of my time to the Company, and I will not, without the Company's prior written consent, engage in any employment or business other than for the Company.

4. *Documentation:* Upon the termination of my employment, I will deliver to the Company all documents, computer programs, data, and other materials of any nature pertaining to my work with the Company. I will not take any originals or reproductions of the foregoing that are embodied in a tangible medium of expression.

5. *Disclosure of Inventions:* I will promptly disclose to the Company all discoveries, designs, inventions, blueprints, computer programs, and data ("Inventions") made by me, either alone or jointly with others, during my employment. Inventions include by definition those things that are related to the business of the Company or that result from the use of property owned, leased, or contracted for by the Company.

6. *Ownership of Inventions:* All Inventions shall be the sole property of the Company, and the Company shall be the sole owner of all patents, copyrights, trademarks, and other rights. I assign to the Company any rights I may have or acquire in such Inventions. I shall assist the Company to obtain and enforce patents, copyrights, trademarks, and other rights and protections relating to Inventions. This obligation shall continue beyond the termination of my employment, but the Company shall compensate me at a reasonable rate after my termination.

7. *Other Agreements:* I represent and warrant that this Agreement and the performance of it do not breach any other agreement to which I am a party. I have not entered into and shall not enter into any agreement in conflict with this Agreement.

8. *Use of Confidential Information of Other Persons:* I have not brought and will not bring with me to the Company any materials or documents of an employer or a former employer that are not generally available to the public. If I desire or need to use any materials from a prior employer, I will obtain express written authorization from such employer.

9. *Restrictive Covenant:* I hereby acknowledge my possession of Proprietary Information and the highly competitive nature of the business of the Company. I will not, during my employment and for three (3) years following my termination, directly or indirectly engage in any competitive business or assist others in engaging in any competitive business. I understand that this Section is not meant to prevent me from earning a living. It does intend to prevent any competitive business from gaining any unfair advantage from my knowledge of Proprietary Information. I understand that by making my new employer aware of the provisions of this Section 9, that employer can take such action as to avoid my breaching the provisions hereof and to indemnify me in the event of a breach.

COMMENTS TO CONTRACT PARAGRAPHS

Paragraph 1A. This is essentially a broad description of the employee's role at the company and explains why this agreement is necessary. Often, a clause like this precedes a statement indicating that the employer gets to keep any value that the employee adds to the firm.

Paragraph 1B. This paragraph establishes that a relationship of trust and confidence exists between employer and employee. Through this clause, both parties are agreeing they owe duties to each other related to information that benefits the company. The clause implies that that there will be negative consequences for the employee if he or she breaks that relationship.

Paragraph 1C. This paragraph establishes what the term "Proprietary Information" means. In contracts, terms that are capitalized and placed in quotation marks (sometimes in parentheses as well) are called "defined terms." Whenever the term "Proprietary Information" appears throughout the rest of the contract, it will have the definition set out in this paragraph. The definition is extremely broad and captures almost any intellectual property, data, and similar items. The contract asserts that this information is important to the business and gives the company some strategic advantage.

Paragraph 1D. This clause clarifies that customer lists belong to the employer even if the employee develops or expands the lists in some way. This may become important if the employee leaves the company because the clause clarifies that the employee may not recruit or "steal" customers.

Paragraph 2. Here, we see the defined term "Proprietary Information" again. This paragraph documents that the employer owns all Proprietary Information, as defined, even if it was created by the employee. Further, the employee agrees to give the employer any legal rights that the employee may obtain to any Proprietary Information.

Paragraph 3. In this clause, the employee promises that he or she will work full-time for the employer and will not take any additional employment without the employer's permission.

Paragraph 4. This clause further asserts that the company takes the confidential nature of the Proprietary Information seriously. Here, the employee promises that if he or she leaves the company's employment, he or she will turn over any work-related material to the company.

Paragraph 5. If the employee creates something of any kind at work, he or she must tell the employer about it, and the employer will receive any disclosures confidentially. The contract goes out of its way to ensure that almost anything the employee invents at work or that is related to work fits under this paragraph. Such items are given a new term called "Inventions." Note that the definition of inventions includes the same items that are in the definition of Proprietary Information as well as some additional ones. The paragraphs discussing Proprietary Information deal with information that the company already possesses and will continue to possess and that the employee will access or need. This paragraph expands the obligations of the employee to what could be called new proprietary information, defined as "Inventions."

Paragraph 6. Just as the employee agreed to give any right in already existing information (such as a modified customer list) to the employer, here the employee promises to give all legal rights to inventions to the employer. In addition, because the rights may originally belong to the employee, the employee promises to help the employer secure any rights or protections necessary to increase the value of the invention. This obligation to help the employer continues to exist after the employee leaves the firm, and the employer agrees to pay for the work required in that situation. The employer is making sure that it can keep anything the employee invents during work time or with company resources.

Paragraph 7. The employer wants to ensure that this contract does not conflict with any others the employee may have already signed. Here, the employee affirms that he or she has made no conflicting agreements. The clause implies that the employee will be responsible for any consequences that arise from such conflicts.

Paragraph 8. The employer does not want to become involved in a dispute with another company by hiring this employee. In this clause, the employee states that he or she is not bringing the employer any confidential information belonging to someone else.

Paragraph 9. This paragraph is a covenant not to compete, one of the most important provisions from the perspective of the employee. Employers worry that former employees will join a rival company and take their information and expertise with them. A covenant not to compete helps prevent that from happening. In short, a covenant not to compete prohibits an employee from working for a competing business for a specified time. This covenant applies regardless of whether the employee leaves the company or is terminated. Covenants not to compete have to be carefully drafted. A court will not enforce a covenant that is too broad in its coverage or that lasts for too long. Three years, the length of this covenant not to compete, is not unduly long. If the covenant is challenged, however, the employer will have to show that this length of time was necessary to protect its business interests. Employees do not appreciate covenants not to compete, but find that they are an inevitable part of employment in information-sensitive industries.

10. *Agreement Not to Solicit Customers:* During the course of my employment and for a period of three (3) years following my termination, I will not attempt to solicit any person, firm, or corporation that has been a customer account of the Company.

11. *Remedies:* I acknowledge that a remedy at law for any breach or threatened breach of the provisions of this Agreement would be inadequate. I therefore agree that the Company shall be entitled to injunctive relief in addition to any other available rights and remedies in case of any such breach or threatened breach. Nothing contained herein shall be construed as prohibiting the Company from pursuing any other remedies available for any such breach or threatened breach.

12. *Assignment:* This Agreement and the rights and obligations of the parties hereto shall bind and inure to the benefit of any successor(s) of the Company, whether by reorganization, merger, consolidation, sale of assets, or otherwise. Neither this Agreement nor any rights or benefits hereunder may be assigned by me.

13. *Interpretation:* It is the desire and intent of the parties hereto that the provisions of this Agreement shall be enforced to the fullest extent permissible. Accordingly, if any provision of this Agreement shall be adjudicated to be invalid or unenforceable, such provision shall be deemed deleted. Such deletion will apply only to the deleted provision in the particular jurisdiction in which such adjudication is made. If any provision contained herein shall be held to be excessively broad as to duration, geographical scope, activity, or subject, it shall be construed by limiting and reducing it so as to be enforceable.

14. *Notices:* All notices pursuant to this Agreement shall be given by personal delivery or by certified mail, return receipt requested. Notices to the Employee shall be addressed to the Employee at the address of record with the Company. Notices to the Company shall be addressed to its principal office. The date of personal delivery or the date of mailing any such notice shall be deemed to be the date of delivery thereof.

15. *Waivers:* Any waiver of breach of any provision of this Agreement shall not thereby be deemed a waiver of any preceding or succeeding breach of the same or any other provision of this Agreement.

16. *Headings:* The headings of the sections hereof are inserted for convenience only and shall not be deemed to constitute a part hereof nor to affect the meaning hereof.

17. *Governing Law:* This Agreement shall be governed by and construed and enforced in accordance with the laws of the State of New Hampshire.

18. *No Employment Agreement:* I acknowledge that this Agreement does not constitute an employment agreement. This Agreement shall be binding upon me regardless of whether my employment shall continue for any length of time and whether my employment is terminated for any reason whatsoever. This is true whether my employment is terminated by the Company or by me.

19. *Complete Agreement, Amendments, and Prior Agreements:* The foregoing is the entire agreement of the parties with respect to the subject matter hereof and may not be amended, supplemented, canceled, or discharged except by written instrument executed by both parties hereto. This Agreement supersedes any and all prior agreements between the parties hereto with respect to the matters covered hereby.

Date: _____   Employee: _____

Accepted and agreed to as of this date by Company:

Date: _____   By: _____

Name: _____

Title: _____

Paragraph 10.   Similar to a covenant not to compete, this clause prohibits an employee from soliciting the company's customers during his or her employment or for up to three years afterward. Without such protection, an employer would be vulnerable to any former employee taking customer lists and using them to solicit customers at a new employer or at his or her own business.

Paragraph 11.   This paragraph allows the employer to seek injunctive relief against the employee, should it be necessary. Here, the employee agrees that the employer not only may seek monetary damages from the employee in the event that this agreement is breached but may also prohibit him or her from engaging in whatever behavior violates the contract. Recall that typically the first line of remedies is damages to compensate for injury. Here the parties are acknowledging in advance (for the benefit of any court that later is involved) that the harm caused by a breach of the contract cannot be compensated or corrected with monetary damages.

Paragraph 12.   Companies change, and so do their owners. This paragraph states that the contract will survive even if ownership of the company changes due to a merger, reorganization, or other reason. The employee cannot avoid this contract simply because the owner that signed the agreement later sells the company to someone else. This paragraph and many of the subsequent paragraphs are often referred to as "boilerplate language," meaning provisions that appear in some form in many contracts. They are included because conflicts have arisen over these points in the past and courts have interpreted contracts without this language in a way that the parties want to avoid. Boilerplate language can be very dangerous because parties may see the headings and not read further because the language is similar from contract to contract. But boilerplate language can make a difference in which party later wins a dispute (because the language spells out the law that will be used to interpret the contract, where a case must be brought, the proper way to give notice of changes, and the like).

Paragraph 13.   Employers know that even the most carefully drafted agreements can sometimes be rendered unenforceable by a reviewing court. Laws change over time, and so do attitudes toward contract terms. This paragraph states that if part of this contract is rendered unenforceable for some reason, the rest of the contract will survive intact (that is, the unenforceable part of the contract is severable). The paragraph specifically references the covenant not to compete and the prohibition against solicitation. If a court rejects those terms as too broad in scope or too lengthy, the parties agree that the court should adjust the clause in order to make it enforceable under the law.

Paragraph 14.   This paragraph deals with notices. If the employer or the employee wants to communicate about the contract, the communication must be sent by personal delivery or registered/certified mail. Note that this means that an e-mail is not sufficient notice under this agreeeement.

Paragraph 15.   This paragraph says "any party," but it is really meant to protect the employer. Sometimes, through generosity or neglect, employers fail to enforce every clause of a contract. For example, an employer may allow a former employee to start a competing business earlier than the contract states or permit an employee to take a second job. This paragraph ensures that if the employer allows some action that is prohibited in the contract, that does not mean that the contract term is waived forever. Just because the employer does not fully enforce the contract every time does not necessarily mean the employer is barred from doing so in the future.

Paragraph 16.   This clause is meant to clarify that the headings are just headings and do not change the interpretation of the language in the paragraphs or the overall meaning of the contract.

Paragraph 17.   This contract will be interpreted using the law of the state of New Hampshire. It is likely that the employer selected New Hampshire for some particular reason. Typically, an employer chooses a state where the law provides the most benefits for the employer. For example, employers typically choose the law of a particular state because it is their geographic home state and the employer's lawyers are familiar with its law. Employers may also choose a legal jurisdiction because its laws create a climate that is more favorable to the employer than the employee.

Paragraph 18.   In this paragraph, the employee acknowledges that this contract is about nondisclosure of information and does not constitute an employment agreement that promises any length of service or any promise of continued employment.

Paragraph 19.   This paragraph states that this contract is the complete agreement between the employer and the employee. Any other side agreements, e-mails, conversations, or other communications are irrelevant. The employee cannot rely on a manager's promise of a particular salary or terms of a covenant not to compete. This agreement is the final statement of the relationship between the employer and the employee.

UNIT 2 Contracts

Business Case Study with Dissenting Opinion
Braddock v. Braddock

Fraudulent misrepresentation (discussed in Chapter 12) is one of the events that may cause a contract to lack voluntary consent. For a misrepresentation to be fraudulent, it must misrepresent a present, material fact. A representation, or prediction, of a future fact does not qualify. The misrepresentation must be consciously false and intended to mislead an innocent party, who must justifiably rely on it. When an innocent party is fraudulently induced to enter into a contract, the party can rescind the contract and be restored to her or his original position or enforce the contract and seek damages for injuries resulting from the fraud.

In this *Business Case Study with Dissenting Opinion,* we set out *Braddock v. Braddock,*[1] a case involving an individual who gave up his career and relocated his home and family based on his cousin's representations about a newly formed entrepreneurial venture. The individual's position in the new enterprise, however, was not what the cousin had told him it would be. Were the cousin's statements fraudulent? Or were they simply expressions of expectation—predictions of future possibilities—subject to contingencies that neither party could control?

Case Background

David Braddock wanted to form Broad Oak Energy, Inc. (BOE), to tap oil and gas reserves in Louisiana and Texas. He asked his cousin John, an investment banker in New York, to find an investor to provide BOE with $75 to $150 million and also asked John to come to work for BOE. David assured John that he would be BOE's chief financial officer (CFO) and land manager and that he would receive half as much stock in the company as would be issued to David, who would serve as the company's chief executive officer. John quit his job, agreed to accept a significantly reduced fee to find an investor for BOE, and moved his family to Texas. As a result of John's efforts, Warburg Pincus, LLC, agreed to provide $150 million in start-up capital.

Two weeks later, David told John that Warburg Pincus insisted that John not be made CFO or land manager. Instead, David offered him the position of landman, a substantially reduced position with lesser salary, benefits, and terms. Surprised, John nevertheless cooperated. He signed "engagement agreements" to accept the lesser position as an "employee at will," subject to discharge for any reason at any time. Stress soon began to take a toll on his health, and he was granted a conditional medical leave of absence. The next month, BOE terminated his employment.

John filed a suit in a New York state court against David, asserting that these circumstances constituted fraud. The court dismissed the complaint. John appealed to a state intermediate appellate court.

Majority Opinion

SAXE, J. [Judge]
* * * *

To plead a claim for [fraud], a plaintiff must assert the misrepresentation of a material fact, which was known by the defendant to be false and intended to be relied on when made, and that there was justifiable reliance and resulting injury. The complaint here sufficiently sets forth these elements. [Emphasis added.]
* * * *

[John's] allegations satisfy the particularity requirement for a fraud claim.
* * * *

* * * Since David and John are cousins, John's reliance on David's good faith may be found to be reasonable even where it might not be reasonable in the context of an arm's length transaction with a stranger. Family members stand in a fiduciary relationship [one of trust] toward one another in a co-owned business venture. * * * Under the

---

1. 60 A.D.3d 84, 871 N.Y.S.2d 68 (1 Dept. 2009).

circumstances alleged here, John had reason to believe that David would treat him, in their interaction, with good faith and integrity.

* * * *

The situation presented here should be distinguished from cases in which a plaintiff who was involved in a business deal claims that, in the original discussions of the deal, misrepresentations were made as to its terms but the falsity of those representations was revealed by the time the deal was executed. In such cases, the ultimate terms of the deal, if agreed upon, are all that the plaintiff is entitled to, and he will not be permitted to seek damages based upon the original misrepresentations, because he did not rely on them in electing to go through with the deal. Here, in contrast, John's subsequent execution of documents that fundamentally altered the originally promised terms of his position with the company was not merely an election to enter into the deal anyway. First of all, even before he executed * * * the agreements * * * , the deal was essentially under way, at least on his part, in that he had already sacrificed his former life and undertaken tasks to forward the venture, and he was no longer in a position to reject the offered terms or even to negotiate effectively. Indeed, when the allegations are understood in the context of an ongoing

attempt by John to salvage something from his dashed expectations, the fact that he subsequently acceded to new and lesser terms should not justify holding * * * that he did not reasonably rely on his cousin's alleged misrepresentations and false assurances, to his own severe detriment.

If all these interactions had been between strangers conducting an arm's length business transaction, strict reliance on the signed written documents, to the exclusion of the parties' words and conduct, would be appropriate. But the expectation of the good faith of a family member in circumstances such as these may justify some reliance on assurances that are not incorporated into written documents drafted and executed later.

* * * *

Here, * * * the issues of material misrepresentation and reasonable reliance are not subject to summary disposition [settlement], and the fiduciary relationship between the parties, with its concomitant [associated] mutual obligation to act in good faith, makes John's reliance on David's assurances all the more reasonable.

* * * *

* * * Defendants' motion to dismiss the complaint for failure to state a cause of action * * * [is] denied * * * so as to reinstate the [plaintiff's fraud] cause of action.

Dissenting Opinion

LIPPMAN, P.J. [Presiding Judge], (DISSENTING).

* * * *

* * * It is, in essence, alleged that John's entire course of conduct in providing investment banking services for a discounted fee, giving up his lucrative New York employment as an investment banker and advisor, moving to Texas and agreeing to take the non-executive position with BOE from which he was eventually dismissed * * * was induced by David's * * * assurances.

* * * *

* * * At the time of David's nominal assurances, BOE was but an unfunded shell requiring for its viability an enormous infusion of capital. And, while John was confident of procuring financing for the venture, there had been, at the time, neither a commitment of funds nor even the emergence of a leading candidate to provide such a commitment. Moreover, John, in addition to being an experienced investment banker and financial consultant,

was, by reason of his own prior professional involvement in oil and gas ventures and his extensive familial connections to the industry, particularly well aware of the risks such ventures entailed. * * * In these circumstances, * * * no promise of high executive-level employment in the company * * * could reasonably have been viewed as an "assurance" or a "guarantee." * * * What he now terms "assurances" and "guarantees" could have been reasonably understood as only expressions of expectation or intent, the realization of which would depend upon contingencies not within the power of the parties to foreseeably accommodate to their stated objectives.

* * * While he may have had a moral claim to rely upon his cousin even when objective circumstances counseled otherwise, there is no legal right to recovery in fraud that may be vindicated upon such a predicate.

Accordingly, I would affirm the dismissal of plaintiffs' fraud cause of action.

Business Case Study with Dissenting Opinion—Continues next page

Business Case Study with Dissenting Opinion—Continued

Questions for Analysis

1. **Law** What did the majority conclude on the issue before the court in this case? What reasoning supported this conclusion?
2. **Law** On what important point did the dissent disagree with the majority, and why?
3. **Ethics** How do you view David's statements and John's actions? Did David take unethical advantage of his cousin, luring him in bad faith? Was John too willing to rely on assurances of events that he should have known from experience might not occur? Discuss.
4. **Economic Dimensions** What does this case indicate about employment and employment contracts?
5. **Implications for the Investor** Why would an investor like Warburg Pincus not want someone like John in an executive role in an enterprise for which the investor was providing significant capital?

UNIT 2 Contracts

Business Scenario

Alberto Corelli offers to pay $2,500 to purchase a painting titled *Moonrise* from Tara Shelley, an artist whose works have been causing a stir in the art world. Shelley accepts Corelli's offer. Assuming that the contract has met all of the requirements for a valid contract, answer the following questions.

1. **Minors.** Corelli was a minor when he purchased the painting. Is the contract void? Is it voidable? What is the difference between these two concepts? A month after his eighteenth birthday, Corelli decides that he would rather have the $2,500 than the painting. He informs Shelley that he is disaffirming the contract and requests that Shelley return the $2,500 to him. When she refuses to do so, Corelli brings a court action to recover the $2,500. What will the court likely decide in this situation? Why? **(See page 288.)**
2. **Statute of Frauds.** Both parties are adults, the contract is oral, and the painting is still in progress. Corelli pays Shelley the $2,500 in return for her promise to deliver the painting to his home when it is finished. A week later, after Shelley finishes the painting, a visitor to her gallery offers her $3,500 for it. Shelley sells the painting to the visitor and sends Corelli a signed letter explaining that she is "canceling" their contract for the *Moonrise* painting. Corelli sues Shelley to enforce the contract. Is the contract enforceable? Explain. **(See page 313.)**
3. **Capacity.** Both parties are adults, and the contract, which is in writing, states that Corelli will pay Shelley the $2,500 the following day. In the meantime, Shelley allows Corelli to take the painting home with him. The next day, Corelli's son returns the painting to Shelley, stating that he is canceling the contract. He explains that his father has been behaving strangely lately, that he seems to be mentally incompetent at times, and that he clearly was not acting rationally when he bought the painting, which he could not afford. Is the contract enforceable? Discuss fully. **(See pages 290–291.)**
4. **Impossibility of Performance.** Both parties are adults, and the contract is in writing. The contract calls for Shelley to deliver the painting to Corelli's gallery in two weeks. Corelli has already arranged to sell the painting to a third party for $4,000, for a $1,500 profit, but it must be available for the third party in two weeks or the sale will not go through. Shelley knows this but does not deliver the painting at the time promised. Corelli sues Shelley for $1,500 in

Business Scenario—Continued

damages. Shelley claims that performance was impossible because her mother fell seriously ill and required Shelley's care. Who will win this lawsuit, and why? **(See page 345.)**

5. **Agreement in E-Contracts.** Both parties are adults, and Shelley, on her Web site, offers to sell the painting for $2,500. Corelli accepts the offer by clicking on an "I accept" box on the computer screen displaying the offer. Among other terms, the online offer includes a forum-selection clause stating that any disputes under the contract are to be resolved by a court in California, the state in which Shelley lives. After Corelli receives the painting, he notices a smear of paint across the lower corner of the painting that was not visible in the digitized image that appeared on Shelley's Web site. Corelli calls Shelley, tells her about the smear, and says that he wants to cancel the contract and return the painting. When Shelley refuses to cooperate, Corelli sues her in a Texas state court, seeking to rescind the contract. Shelley claims that any suit against her must be filed in a California court in accordance with the forum-selection clause. Corelli maintains that the forum-selection clause is unconscionable and should not be enforced. What factors will the court consider in deciding this case? What will the court likely decide? Would it matter whether Corelli read the terms of the online offer before clicking on "I accept"? **(See page 268.)**

UNIT 2 Contracts

Group Project

RiotGear, LLC, contracts with Standard Transit, Inc., to distribute RiotGear's "Occupy Earth/Global Movement" line of apparel to retail outlets for a certain price. RiotGear promises to donate a share of the proceeds from the sale of the "Occupy Earth/Global Movement" line to The Cause, a charitable organization dedicated to supporting those who seek social and economic change through protest. In reliance on the expected donation, The Cause contracts for medical and other supplies. When Standard increases the distribution cost, RiotGear tells The Cause that there will be no donation.

1. While the goods are in transit, RiotGear receives this tweet from Standard: "Price increase of 99 percent or no delivery." RiotGear agrees and pays, but later sues Standard for the increase over the original price. The first group will identify the rule that a court would apply in this situation and decide whether RiotGear is entitled to the difference in price.

2. The second group will determine whether The Cause can enforce RiotGear's original promise despite the lack of consideration. What doctrine might a court apply in this situation, and what are the requirements to enforce a promise?

The Formation of Sales and Lease Contracts

(Matthew Staver/Landov)

CHAPTER OUTLINE

- The Scope of the UCC and Articles 2 (Sales) and 2A (Leases)
- The Formation of Sales and Lease Contracts
- Title and Risk of Loss
- Contracts for the International Sale of Goods

LEARNING OBJECTIVES

The five learning objectives below are designed to help improve your understanding of the chapter. After reading this chapter, you should be able to answer the following questions:

1 How do Article 2 and Article 2A of the UCC differ? What types of transactions does each article cover?

2 In a sales contract, if an offeree includes additional or different terms in an acceptance, will a contract result? If so, what happens to these terms?

3 What exceptions to the writing requirements of the Statute of Frauds are provided in Article 2 and Article 2A of the UCC?

4 Risk of loss does not necessarily pass with title. If the parties to a contract do not expressly agree when risk passes and the goods are to be delivered without movement by the seller, when does risk pass?

5 What law governs contracts for the international sale of goods?

"I am for free commerce with all nations."
—George Washington, 1732–1799 (First president of the United States, 1789–1797)

The chapter-opening quotation echoes a sentiment that most Americans believe—free commerce will benefit our nation. This is particularly true with respect to the Uniform Commercial Code (UCC). The UCC facilitates commercial transactions by making the laws governing sales and lease contracts uniform and, as far as possible, clear, simple, and readily applicable to the numerous difficulties that can arise during such transactions.

Recall from Chapter 1 that the UCC is one of many uniform (model) acts drafted by the National Conference of Commissioners on Uniform State Laws and submitted to the states for adoption. Once a state legislature has adopted a uniform act, the act becomes statutory law in that state. Thus, when we turn to sales and lease contracts, we move away from common law principles and into the area of statutory law.

The Scope of the UCC and Articles 2 (Sales) and 2A (Leases)

The UCC attempts to provide a consistent, integrated framework of rules to deal with all phases ordinarily arising in a commercial sales or lease transaction. For example, consider the following events, all of which may occur during a single transaction:

1. *A contract for the sale or lease of goods is formed and executed.* Article 2 and Article 2A of the UCC provide rules governing all aspects of this transaction.
2. *The transaction may involve a payment—by check, electronic fund transfer, or other means.* Article 3 (on negotiable instruments), Article 4 (on bank deposits and collections), Article 4A (on fund transfers), and Article 5 (on letters of credit) cover this part of the transaction.
3. *The transaction may involve a bill of lading or a warehouse receipt that covers goods when they are shipped or stored.* Article 7 (on documents of title) deals with this subject.
4. *The transaction may involve a demand by the seller or lender for some form of security for the remaining balance owed.* Article 9 (on secured transactions) covers this part of the transaction.

The UCC has been adopted in whole or in part by all of the states.[1] Because of its importance in the area of commercial transactions, we present the UCC as this chapter's *Landmark in the Law* feature on the facing page.

Article 2—Sales

Sales Contract A contract for the sale of goods.

Article 2 of the UCC governs **sales contracts,** or contracts for the sale of goods. To facilitate commercial transactions, Article 2 modifies some of the common law contract requirements that were discussed in Chapters 9 through 14. To the extent that it has not been modified by the UCC, however, the common law of contracts also applies to sales contracts.

In general, the rule is that when a UCC provision addresses a certain issue, the UCC governs, but when the UCC is silent, the common law governs. The relationship between general contract law and the law governing sales of goods is illustrated in Exhibit 15.1 on the facing page. (For a discussion of an issue involving state taxation of sales that take place over the Internet, see this chapter's *Adapting the Law to the Online Environment* feature on page 386.)

Keep in mind that Article 2 deals with the sale of *goods*—it does not deal with real property (real estate), services, or intangible property such as stocks and bonds. Thus, if a dispute involves real estate or services, the common law applies. Also note that in some situations, the rules under the UCC can vary quite a bit depending on whether the buyer or the seller is a merchant. We look now at how the UCC defines a *sale, goods,* and *merchant status.*

Sale The passing of title to property from the seller to the buyer for a price.

What Is a Sale?   The UCC defines a **sale** as "the passing of title [evidence of ownership] from the seller to the buyer for a price" [UCC 2–106(1)]. The price may be payable in cash (or its equivalent) or in other goods or services.

Tangible Property Property that has physical existence and can be distinguished by the senses of touch and sight.

What Are Goods?   To be characterized as a *good,* the item of property must be *tangible,* and it must be *movable.*

Intangible Property Property that cannot be seen or touched but exists only conceptually, such as corporate stocks. Such property is not governed by Article 2 of the UCC.

Tangible and Movable Property   **Tangible property** has physical existence—it can be touched or seen. **Intangible property**—such as corporate stocks and bonds, patents and

---

1. Louisiana has not adopted Articles 2 and 2A, however.

LANDMARK IN THE LAW
The Uniform Commercial Code

Of all the attempts to produce a uniform body of laws relating to commercial transactions in the United States, none has been as comprehensive or successful as the Uniform Commercial Code (UCC).

The Origins of the UCC   The UCC was the brainchild of William A. Schnader, president of the National Conference of Commissioners on Uniform State Laws (NCCUSL). The drafting of the UCC began in 1945. The most significant individual involved in the project was its chief editor, Karl N. Llewellyn of the Columbia University Law School. Llewellyn's intellect, continuous efforts, and ability to compromise made the first version of the UCC—completed in 1949—a legal landmark. Over the next several years, the UCC was substantially accepted by almost every state in the nation.

Periodic Changes and Updates   Various articles and sections of the UCC are periodically changed or supplemented to clarify certain rules or to establish new rules when changes in business

customs render the existing UCC provisions inapplicable. For example, because of the increasing importance of leases of goods in the commercial context, Article 2A governing leases was added to the UCC. To clarify the rights of parties to commercial fund transfers, particularly electronic fund transfers, Article 4A was issued. Articles 3 and 4, on negotiable instruments and banking relationships, underwent significant revision in the 1990s. Because of other changes in business and in the law, the NCCUSL has recommended the repeal of Article 6 (on bulk transfers) and has offered a revised Article 6 to those states that prefer not to repeal it. The NCCUSL has also revised Article 9, covering secured transactions. The revised Article 9, which has been adopted by all of the states, will be discussed at length in Chapter 20.

Application to Today's World   *By periodically revising the UCC's articles, the NCCUSL has been able to adapt its provisions to changing business customs and practices. UCC provisions governing sales and lease contracts have also been extended to contracts formed in the online environment.*

Exhibit 15.1 The Law Governing Contracts

This exhibit graphically illustrates the relationship between general contract law and statutory law (UCC Articles 2 and 2A) governing contracts for the sale and lease of goods. Sales contracts are not governed exclusively by Article 2 of the UCC but are also governed by general contract law whenever it is relevant and has not been modified by the UCC.

ADAPTING THE LAW TO THE ONLINE ENVIRONMENT

LOCAL GOVERNMENTS ATTEMPT TO TAX ONLINE TRAVEL COMPANIES

A battle is raging across the United States between state and local governments and online retailers. The online retailers claim that because they do not have a physical presence in a state, they should not have to collect state and local taxes for the goods and services they sell. Although most states have laws that require their residents to report online purchases and pay taxes on them (so-called use taxes), few U.S. consumers comply with these laws.

Local Governments Sue Online Travel Companies

Travelocity, Priceline.com, Hotels.com, and Orbitz.com are online travel companies (OTCs) that offer, among other things, hotel booking services. By 2013, more than twenty cities, including Atlanta, Charleston, Philadelphia, and San Antonio, had filed suits claiming that the OTCs owed taxes on hotel reservations that they had booked. All of the cities involved in the suits impose a hotel occupancy tax, which is essentially a sales tax.

The issue is not whether the OTCs should pay the tax but rather how it should be assessed and collected. OTCs typically purchase blocks of hotel rooms at a wholesale rate and then resell the rooms to customers at a marked-up resale rate, keeping the difference as profit. The OTCs forward to the hotels an amount intended to cover the hotel occupancy tax (sales tax) based on the wholesale prices of the rooms sold. The hotels then remit to the city taxing authority the tax on the rooms sold by the OTCs.

The cities claim, however, that the OTCs should assess the occupancy tax rates on the retail prices that they charge, rather than on the wholesale prices of the rooms. Of course, the retail prices are higher, so the cities would collect more tax if the retail price is used as the base. The cities also want the OTCs to register with the local jurisdictions and to collect and remit the required taxes directly.

The Cities Are Losing in Court

When these lawsuits were first brought a few years ago, city governments generally obtained favorable rulings, both in federal district courts[a] and in state courts.[b] In contrast, when some of these suits were retried or reviewed by higher courts, the OTCs prevailed. In 2012, for example, the city of Goodlettsville, Tennessee, lost its continuing case against Priceline.com and nine other OTCs. In siding with the OTCs, the court said, "If the Tennessee legislature intends to permit its political subdivisions to tax the retail rate paid by the consumers to the OTCs for hotel bookings, the legislature may do so through appropriate statutory language."[c]

In contrast, when the South Carolina Department of Revenue sued Travelscape, LLC, the Supreme Court of South Carolina held that the OTC had to remit taxes based on the retail price of the hotel rooms sold.[d] The South Carolina decision reflected a minority opinion, however. As of early 2012, the OTCs had prevailed in fifteen of nineteen cases nationwide.

Critical Thinking

What are possible benefits if cities and states do not impose a sales tax on the difference between the wholesale price of rooms and the retail price of rooms sold by OTCs?

---

a. See, for example, *City of Goodlettsville v. Priceline.com, Inc.*, 605 F.Supp.2d 982 (M.D.Tenn. 2009).

b. See *City of Atlanta v. Hotels.com, L.P.*, 285 Ga. 231, 674 S.E.2d 898 (2009).

c. *City of Goodlettsville v. Priceline.com, Inc.*, 2012 WL 573681 (M.D.Tenn. 2012).

d. *Travelscape, LLC v. South Carolina Department of Revenue*, 391 S.C. 89, 705 S.E.2d 28 (2011).

---

copyrights, and ordinary contract rights—has only conceptual existence and thus does not come under Article 2. A movable item can be carried from place to place (real estate is therefore excluded from Article 2).

Goods *associated* with real estate often fall within the scope of Article 2, however [UCC 2–107]. For instance, a contract for the sale of minerals, oil, or natural gas is a contract for the sale of goods if *severance, or separation, is to be made by the seller*. Similarly, a contract for the sale of growing crops or timber to be cut is a contract for the sale of goods *regardless of who severs them from the land*.

Predominant-Factor Test A test courts use to determine whether a contract is primarily for the sale of goods or for the sale of services.

Goods and Services Combined   In cases involving contracts in which goods and services are combined, courts generally use the **predominant-factor test** to determine whether a

If a couple buys a concessions business that includes a truck, trailer, and tables and chairs, would this purchase be a sale of goods or of services?

contract is primarily for the sale of goods or for the sale of services.[2] This determination is important because the UCC will apply to services provided under a mixed contract that is predominantly for goods, even though the majority of courts treat services as being excluded by the UCC.

If Contract Is Primarily for Goods, UCC Applies to All Disputes

If a court decides that a mixed contract is primarily a goods contract, *any* dispute, even a dispute over the services portion, will be decided under the UCC. **CASE EXAMPLE 15.1** Gene and Martha Jannusch agreed to sell Festival Foods, a concessions business, to Lindsey and Louann Naffziger for a price of $150,000. The deal included a truck, a trailer, freezers, roasters, chairs, tables, a fountain service, signs, and lighting. The Naffzigers paid $10,000 down with the balance to come from a bank loan. They took possession of the equipment and began to use it immediately in Festival Foods operations at various events.

After six events, the Naffzigers returned the truck and all the equipment and wanted out of the deal because the business did not generate as much income as they expected. The Jannusches sued the Naffzigers for the balance due on the purchase price, claiming that the Naffzigers could no longer reject the goods under the UCC. The Naffzigers claimed that the UCC did not apply because the deal primarily involved the sale of a business rather than the sale of goods. The court found that the UCC governed under the predominant-factor test. The primary value of the contract was in the goods, not the value of the business. The parties had agreed on the essential terms of the contract (such as the price). Thus, a contract had been formed, and the Naffzigers had breached it. The Naffzigers took possession of the business and had no right to return it.[3] ●

Who Is a Merchant?

Article 2 governs the sale of goods in general. It applies to sales transactions between all buyers and sellers. In a limited number of instances, however, the UCC presumes that certain special business standards ought to be imposed on merchants because they possess a relatively high degree of commercial expertise.[4] Such standards do not apply to the casual or inexperienced seller or buyer (a "consumer"). Section 2–104 sets out three ways in which merchant status can arise:

1. A merchant is a person who *deals in goods of the kind* involved in the sales contract. Thus, a retailer, a wholesaler, or a manufacturer is a merchant of those goods sold in the business. A merchant for one type of goods is not necessarily a merchant for another type. For instance, a sporting equipment retailer is a merchant when selling tennis rackets but not when selling a used iPad.
2. A merchant is a person who, by occupation, *holds himself or herself out as having special knowledge and skill* related to the practices or goods involved in the transaction. Note that this broad definition may include banks or universities as merchants.
3. A person who *employs a merchant as a broker, agent, or other intermediary* has the status of merchant in that transaction. Hence, if an art collector hires a broker to purchase or sell art for her, the collector is considered a merchant in the transaction.

In summary, a person is a **merchant** when she or he, acting in a mercantile (commercial) capacity, possesses or uses an expertise specifically related to the goods being sold. This basic distinction is not always clear-cut. For instance, state courts appear to be split on whether farmers should be considered merchants.

Merchant Under the UCC, a person who deals in goods of the kind involved in the sales contract or who holds herself or himself out as having skill or knowledge peculiar to the practices or goods being purchased or sold.

---

2. UCC 2–314(1) does stipulate that serving food or drinks is a "sale of goods" for purposes of the implied warranty of merchantability, as will be discussed in Chapter 17. The UCC also specifies that selling unborn animals and rare coins qualifies as a "sale of goods."
3. *Jannusch v. Naffziger,* 379 Ill.App.3d 381, 883 N.E.2d 711 (2008).
4. The provisions that apply only to merchants deal principally with the Statute of Frauds, firm offers, confirmatory memorandums, warranties, and contract modifications. These special rules reflect expedient business practices commonly known to merchants in the commercial setting. They will be discussed later in this chapter.

ETHICAL ISSUE

Should merchants be allowed to use buying patterns to learn personal information about their customers, such as whether they are pregnant? Whether you shop on the Internet or in stores, most major retailers compile information about you based on what, when, and how you buy. Sometimes, based on your purchases, you will instantly be given printed coupons at the cash register. These customized coupons reflect your preferences based on past behavior. If you regularly use Amazon.com, for instance, you receive customized offers every time you visit that site.

Target Brands, Inc., uses a very sophisticated data collection process that assigns each shopper a unique guest identification code. Over time, a shopper's habits become the source of predictions for future consumer behavior. For example, Target can accurately predict which female shoppers are pregnant based on their recent purchases of vitamin and mineral supplements. When Target's system detects a buying pattern suggesting that a customer is pregnant, it starts offering coupons for baby-related products and services.

A father in Minneapolis, Minnesota, complained to a Target manager that his daughter was receiving such coupons for no reason. In reality, Target's system had accurately discovered his daughter's pregnancy. The father was even more furious that his daughter had lied to him. Was Target's action legal? Probably, it was. Target had complied with the relevant federal and state privacy laws. Current laws even allow retailers to share their customer data with affiliate companies.

The Scope of Article 2A—Leases

Leases of personal property (goods) have become increasingly common. In this context, a **lease** is a transfer of the right to possess and use goods for a period of time in exchange for payment. Article 2A of the UCC was created to fill the need for uniform guidelines in this area.

Article 2A covers any transaction that creates a lease of goods, as well as subleases of goods [UCC 2A–102, 2A–103(1)(k)]. Except that it applies to leases, rather than sales, of goods, Article 2A is essentially a repetition of Article 2 and varies only to reflect differences between sales and lease transactions. (Note that Article 2A is not concerned with leases of real property, such as land or buildings. The laws governing leases of real property will be discussed in Chapter 36.)

Definition of a Lease Agreement
Article 2A defines a **lease agreement** as the bargain between a lessor and a lessee with respect to the lease of goods, as found in their language and as implied by other circumstances, including course of dealing and usage of trade or course of performance [UCC 2A–103(1)(k)]. A **lessor** is one who transfers the right to the possession and use of goods under a lease [UCC 2A–103(1)(p)]. A **lessee** is one who acquires the right to the temporary possession and use of goods under a lease [UCC 2A–103(1)(o)].

In other words, the lessee is the party who is leasing the goods from the lessor. Article 2A applies to all types of leases of goods, including commercial leases and consumer leases. Special rules apply to certain types of leases, however, including consumer leases.

Consumer Leases
Under UCC 2A–103(1)(e), a *consumer lease* involves three elements:

1. A lessor who regularly engages in the business of leasing or selling.
2. A lessee (except an organization) who leases the goods "primarily for a personal, family, or household purpose."
3. Total lease payments that are less than a dollar amount set by state statute.

To ensure special protection for consumers, certain provisions of Article 2A apply only to consumer leases. For instance, one provision states that a consumer may recover attorneys' fees if a court finds that a term in a consumer lease contract is unconscionable [UCC 2A–108(4)(a)].

LEARNING OBJECTIVE 1
How do Article 2 and Article 2A of the UCC differ? What types of transactions does each article cover?

Lease Under Article 2A of the UCC, a transfer of the right to possess and use goods for a period of time in exchange for payment.

Lease Agreement An agreement in which one person (the lessor) agrees to transfer the right to the possession and use of property to another person (the lessee) in exchange for rental payments.

Lessor A person who transfers the right to the possession and use of goods to another in exchange for rental payments.

Lessee A person who acquires the right to the possession and use of another's goods in exchange for rental payments.

The Formation of Sales and Lease Contracts

In regard to the formation of sales and lease contracts, Article 2 and Article 2A of the UCC modify common law contract rules in several ways. Remember, though, that parties to sales contracts are normally free to establish whatever terms they wish.

The UCC comes into play only when the parties have failed to provide in their contract for a contingency that later gives rise to a dispute. The UCC makes this clear time and again by using such phrases as "unless the parties otherwise agree" or "absent a contrary agreement by the parties."

Offer

In general contract law, the moment a definite offer is met by an unqualified acceptance, a binding contract is formed. In commercial sales transactions, the verbal exchanges, correspondence, and actions of the parties may not reveal exactly when a binding contractual obligation arises. The UCC states that an agreement sufficient to constitute a contract can exist even if the moment of its making is undetermined [UCC 2–204(2), 2A–204(2)].

Open Terms   Remember from pages 262 and 263 of Chapter 10 that under the common law of contracts, an offer must be definite enough for the parties (and the courts) to ascertain its essential terms when it is accepted. In contrast, the UCC states that a sales or lease contract will not fail for indefiniteness even if one or more terms are left open as long as (1) the parties intended to make a contract and (2) there is a reasonably certain basis for the court to grant an appropriate remedy [UCC 2–204(3), 2A–204(3)].

The UCC provides numerous *open-term* provisions (discussed next) that can be used to fill the gaps in a contract. Thus, if a dispute occurs, all that is necessary to prove the existence of a contract is an indication (such as a purchase order) that there is a contract. Missing terms can be proved by evidence, or a court can presume that the parties intended whatever is reasonable under the circumstances.

The *quantity* of goods involved must be expressly stated in the contract, however. If the quantity term is left open, the courts will have no basis for determining a remedy.

Open Price Term   If the parties have not agreed on a price, the court will determine a "reasonable price at the time for delivery" [UCC 2–305(1)]. If either the buyer or the seller is to determine the price, the price is to be fixed (set) in good faith [UCC 2–305(2)]. Under the UCC, *good faith* means honesty in fact and the observance of reasonable commercial standards of fair dealing in the trade [UCC 2–103(1)(b)]. The concepts of *good faith* and *commercial reasonableness* permeate the UCC.

Sometimes, the price fails to be fixed (specified) through the fault of one of the parties. In that situation, the other party can treat the contract as canceled or specify a reasonable price. **EXAMPLE 15.2**   Perez and Merrick enter into a contract for the sale of unfinished doors and agree that Perez will determine the price. Perez refuses to specify the price. Merrick can either treat the contract as canceled or set a reasonable price [UCC 2–305(3)]. ●

Open Payment Term   When parties do not specify payment terms, payment is due at the time and place at which the buyer is to receive the goods [UCC 2–310(a)]. The buyer can tender payment using any commercially normal or acceptable means, such as a check or credit card. If the seller demands payment in cash, however, the buyer must be given a reasonable time to obtain it [UCC 2–511(2)].

CASE EXAMPLE 15.3   Max Alexander agreed to purchase hay from Wagner's farm. Alexander left his truck and trailer at the farm for the seller to load the hay. Nothing was said about when payment was due, and the parties were unaware of the UCC's rules. When Alexander came back to get the hay, a dispute broke out. Alexander claimed that he had been given less hay than he had ordered and argued that he did not have to pay at that time. Wagner refused to release the hay (or the vehicles on which the hay was loaded) until Alexander paid for it. Eventually, Alexander jumped into his truck and drove off without paying for the hay—for which he was later prosecuted for the crime of theft (see Chapter 6). Because the parties had failed to specify when payment was due, UCC 2–310(a) controlled, and payment was due at the time Alexander picked up the hay.[5] ●

Open Delivery Term   When no delivery terms are specified, the buyer normally takes delivery at the seller's place of business [UCC 2–308(a)]. If the seller has no place of business, the seller's residence is used. When goods are located in some other place and both parties know it, delivery is made there. If the time for shipment or delivery is not clearly specified in the sales contract, the court will infer a "reasonable" time for performance [UCC 2–309(1)].

Duration of an Ongoing Contract   A single contract might specify successive performances but not indicate how long the parties are required to deal with each other. In this situation, either party may terminate the ongoing contractual relationship. Principles of good faith and sound commercial practice call for reasonable notification before termination, however, to give the other party time to make substitute arrangements [UCC 2–309(2), (3)].

Options and Cooperation Regarding Performance   When the contract contemplates shipment of the goods but does not specify the shipping arrangements, the *seller* has the right to make these arrangements in good faith, using commercial reasonableness in the situation [UCC 2–311].

When a sales contract omits terms relating to the assortment of goods, the *buyer* can specify the assortment.   **EXAMPLE 15.4**   Petry Drugs, Inc., agrees to purchase one thousand toothbrushes from Marconi's Dental Supply. The toothbrushes come in a variety of colors, but the contract does not specify color. Petry, the buyer, has the right to take six hundred blue toothbrushes and four hundred green ones if it wishes. Petry, however, must exercise good faith and commercial reasonableness in making its selection [UCC 2–311]. ●

Requirements and Output Contracts

Normally, if the parties do not specify a quantity, a court will have no basis for determining a remedy. No contract is formed because there is almost no way to determine objectively what is a reasonable quantity of goods for someone to buy (whereas a court can objectively determine a reasonable price for particular goods by looking at the market). Nevertheless, the UCC recognizes two exceptions involving requirements and output contracts [UCC 2–306(1)].

Requirements Contracts   In a **requirements contract**, the buyer agrees to purchase and the seller agrees to sell all or up to a stated amount of what the buyer *needs* or *requires*. **EXAMPLE 15.5**   Umpqua Cannery forms a contract with Al Garcia. The cannery agrees to purchase from Garcia, and Garcia agrees to sell to the cannery, all of the green beans that the cannery needs or requires during the following summer. ●

There is implicit consideration in a requirements contract because the buyer (the cannery, in this situation) gives up the right to buy goods (green beans, in this example) from any other seller, and this forfeited right creates a legal detriment (that is, consideration).

Requirements contracts are common in the business world and normally are enforceable. In contrast, if the buyer promises to purchase only if the buyer *wishes* to do so, or

---

5. *State v. Alexander*, 186 Or.App. 600, 64 P.3d 1148 (2003).

if the buyer reserves the right to buy the goods from someone other than the seller, the promise is illusory (without consideration) and unenforceable by either party.

Output Contract An agreement in which a seller agrees to sell and a buyer agrees to buy all or up to a stated amount of what the seller produces.

Output Contracts In an **output contract,** the seller agrees to sell and the buyer agrees to buy all or up to a stated amount of what the seller *produces.* **EXAMPLE 15.6** Al Garcia forms a contract with Umpqua Cannery. Garcia agrees to sell to the cannery, and the cannery agrees to purchase from Garcia, all of the beans that Garcia produces on his farm during the following summer. ● Again, because the seller essentially forfeits the right to sell goods to another buyer, there is implicit consideration in an output contract.

The UCC imposes a *good faith limitation* on requirements and output contracts. The quantity under such contracts is the amount of requirements or the amount of output that occurs during a *normal* production year. The actual quantity purchased or sold cannot be unreasonably disproportionate to normal or comparable prior requirements or output [UCC 2–306(1)].

PREVENTING LEGAL DISPUTES

If a business owner leaves certain terms of a sales or lease contract open, the UCC allows a court to supply the missing terms. Although this rule can sometimes be advantageous (to establish that a contract existed, for instance), it can also be a major disadvantage. If a party fails to state a price in the contract offer, for example, a court will impose a reasonable price by looking at the market price of similar goods *at the time of delivery.* Thus, instead of receiving the usual price for the goods, a business will receive what a court considers a reasonable price when the goods are delivered. Therefore, when drafting contracts for the sale or lease of goods, make sure that the contract clearly states any terms that are essential to the bargain, particularly the price. It is generally better to establish the terms of a contract than to leave it up to a court to determine what terms are reasonable after a dispute has arisen.

Merchant's Firm Offer Under regular contract principles, an offer can be revoked at any time before acceptance. The major common law exception is an *option contract* (discussed in Chapter 10), in which the offeree pays consideration for the offeror's irrevocable promise to keep the offer open for a stated period. The UCC creates a second exception for firm offers made by a merchant to sell, buy, or lease goods.

Firm Offer An offer (by a merchant) that is irrevocable without the necessity of consideration for a stated period of time or, if no definite period is stated, for a reasonable time (neither period to exceed three months).

A **firm offer** arises when a merchant-offeror gives *assurances* in a *signed writing* that the offer will remain open. The offer must be both *written* and *signed* by the offeror.[6] When a firm offer is contained in a form contract prepared by the offeree, the offeror must also sign a separate assurance of the firm offer. A merchant's firm offer is irrevocable without the necessity of consideration[7] for the stated period or, if no definite period is stated, a reasonable period (neither period to exceed three months) [UCC 2–205, 2A–205].

EXAMPLE 15.7 Osaka, a used-car dealer, e-mails Saucedo on January 1 stating, "I have a 2013 Kia Sportage on the lot that I'll sell you for $18,000 any time between now and January 31." This e-mail creates a firm offer, and Osaka will be liable for breach if he sells that Kia Sportage to someone other than Saucedo before January 31. ●

Acceptance

Acceptance of an offer to buy, sell, or lease goods generally may be made in any reasonable manner and by any reasonable means. The UCC permits acceptance of an offer to buy goods "either by a prompt *promise* to ship or by the prompt or current shipment of

KNOW THIS
The UCC provides that acceptance can be made by any means that is reasonable under the circumstances—including prompt shipment of the goods.

---

6. *Signed* includes any symbol executed or adopted by a party with a present intention to authenticate a writing [UCC 1–201(39)]. A complete signature is not required. Therefore, initials, a thumbprint, a trade name, or any mark used in lieu of a written signature will suffice, regardless of its location on the document.

7. If the offeree pays consideration, then an option contract (not a merchant's firm offer) is formed.

Seasonably Within a specified time period or, if no period is specified, within a reasonable time.

conforming or nonconforming goods" [UCC 2–206(1)(b)]. *Conforming goods* accord with the contract's terms, whereas *nonconforming goods* do not.

The prompt shipment of nonconforming goods constitutes both an acceptance, which creates a contract, and a breach of that contract. This rule does not apply if the seller **seasonably** (within a reasonable amount of time) notifies the buyer that the nonconforming shipment is offered only as an *accommodation,* or a favor. The notice of accommodation must clearly indicate to the buyer that the shipment does not constitute an acceptance and that, therefore, no contract has been formed.

EXAMPLE 15.8 McFarrell Pharmacy orders five cases of Johnson & Johnson 3-by-5-inch gauze pads from H.T. Medical Supply, Inc. If H.T. ships five cases of Xeroform 3-by-5-inch gauze pads instead, the shipment acts as both an acceptance of McFarrell's offer and a *breach* of the resulting contract. McFarrell may sue H.T. for any appropriate damages. If, however, H.T. notifies McFarrell that the Xeroform gauze pads are being shipped *as an accommodation*—because H.T. has only Xeroform pads in stock—the shipment will constitute a counteroffer, not an acceptance. A contract will be formed only if McFarrell accepts the Xeroform gauze pads. •

Notice of Acceptance Required   Under the common law, because a unilateral offer invites acceptance by a performance, the offeree need not notify the offeror of performance unless the offeror would not otherwise know about it. In other words, a unilateral offer can be accepted by beginning performance.

The UCC is more stringent than the common law in this regard because it requires notification. Under the UCC, if the offeror is not notified within a reasonable time that the offeree has accepted the contract by beginning performance, then the offeror can treat the offer as having lapsed before acceptance [UCC 2–206(2), 2A–206(2)].

LEARNING OBJECTIVE 2
In a sales contract, if an offeree includes additional or different terms in an acceptance, will a contract result? If so, what happens to these terms?

Additional Terms   Recall from page 264 of Chapter 10 that under the common law, the *mirror image rule* requires that the terms of the acceptance exactly match those of the offer. Thus, if Alderman makes an offer to Beale, and Beale accepts but in the acceptance makes some slight modification to the terms of the offer, there is no contract.

To avoid these problems, the UCC dispenses with the mirror image rule. Generally, the UCC takes the position that if the offeree's response indicates a *definite* acceptance of the offer, a contract is formed even if the acceptance includes additional or different terms from those contained in the offer [UCC 2–207(1)]. Whether the additional terms become part of the contract depends, in part, on whether the parties are nonmerchants or merchants.

In the following case, a party conditioned its acceptance of an offer on the other parties' agreement to additional terms by a specific date. When the parties agreed to the most important terms after the deadline, the court had to decide if there was an enforceable contract.

Case 15.1

WPS, Inc. v. Expro Americas, LLC

Court of Appeals of Texas, First District, 2012 WL 310937 (2012).
www.findlaw.com/casecode[a]

FACTS In April 2006, WPS, Inc., submitted a formal proposal to manufacture equipment for Expro Americas, LLC, and Surface Production Systems, Inc. (SPS). Expro and SPS then submitted two purchase orders. WPS accepted the first purchase order in part and the second order conditionally. Among other things, WPS required that, by April 28, 2006, Expro and SPS give their "full release to proceed" and agree "to pay all valid costs associated with any order cancellation." The parties' negotiations continued, and Expro and SPS eventually submitted a third purchase order on May 9,

---

a. Under "Popular State Resources," click on "Texas Caselaw." Under "Browse Texas Courts," click on "Court of Appeals of Texas." In the result, enter "WPS, Inc." in the "Party name:" box and click on "Search." When that page opens, click on the case name to access the opinion.

Case 15.1—Continued

2006. The third purchase order did not comply with all of WPS's requirements, but it did give WPS full permission to proceed and agreed that Expro and SPS would pay all cancellation costs. With Expro and SPS's knowledge, WPS then began work under the third purchase order. Expro and SPS soon canceled the order, however, so WPS sent them an invoice for the cancellation costs. At trial, the jury and court concluded that there was a contract and found in WPS's favor. Expro and SPS appealed.

ISSUE Did the parties have a contract even though Expro and SPS did not comply with all the requirements of WPS's conditional acceptance?

DECISION Yes. The Texas appellate court affirmed the judgment for WPS.

REASON The court found that the parties had a contract based on WPS's conditional acceptance and Expro and SPS's

third purchase order. It did not matter that Expro and SPS submitted the third purchase order after WPS's deadline of April 28, 2006. Regardless of what WPS originally required, the parties continued their negotiations and "operated as if they had additional time to resolve the outstanding differences." Moreover, Expro and SPS agreed to nearly everything that WPS requested. Most important, they gave WPS "full release to proceed" and agreed "to pay all valid costs associated with any order cancellation." Those terms had been holding up the contract, and SPS's vice president conceded that the "release to proceed" "basically means that one party is in agreement." A jury could have reasonably concluded that, since the parties were in agreement, WPS was contractually obligated to move forward with its work.

CRITICAL THINKING—Legal Consideration *By allowing a party to condition its acceptance on additional terms, does contract law make negotiations more or less efficient? Explain.*

Rules When One Party or Both Parties Are Nonmerchants

If one (or both) of the parties is a *nonmerchant,* the contract is formed according to the terms of the original offer submitted by the original offeror and not according to the additional terms of the acceptance [UCC 2–207(2)].

   EXAMPLE 15.9 Tolsen offers in writing to sell his laptop and printer to Valdez for $1,500. Valdez replies to Tolsen stating, "I accept your offer to purchase your laptop and printer for $1,500. I *would like* a box of laser printer paper and two extra toner cartridges to be included in the purchase price." Valdez has given Tolsen a definite expression of acceptance (creating a contract), even though the acceptance also *suggests* an added term for the offer. Because Tolsen is not a merchant, the additional term is merely a proposal (suggestion), and Tolsen is not legally obligated to comply with that term. •

Rules When Both Parties Are Merchants

The drafters of the UCC created a special rule for merchants to avoid the "battle of the forms," which occurs when two merchants exchange separate standard forms containing different contract terms.

   Under UCC 2–207(2), in contracts *between merchants,* the additional terms *automatically* become part of the contract unless one of the following conditions exists:

1. The original offer expressly limited acceptance to its terms.
2. The new or changed terms materially alter the contract.
3. The offeror objects to the new or changed terms within a reasonable period of time.

Generally, if the modification does not involve any unreasonable element of surprise or hardship for the offeror, the court will hold that the modification did not materially alter the contract. Courts also consider the parties' prior dealings and course of performance when determining whether the alteration is material.

Conditioned on Offeror's Assent

Regardless of merchant status, the UCC provides that the offeree's expression cannot be construed as an acceptance if it contains additional or different terms that are explicitly conditioned on the offeror's assent to those terms

[UCC 2–207(1)].   **EXAMPLE 15.10**   Philips offers to sell Hundert 650 pounds of turkey thighs at a specified price and with specified delivery terms. Hundert responds, "I accept your offer for 650 pounds of turkey thighs *on the condition that you give me ninety days to pay for them.*" Hundert's response will be construed not as an acceptance but as a counteroffer, which Philips may or may not accept. •

Additional Terms May Be Stricken   The UCC provides yet another option for dealing with conflicting terms in the parties' writings. Section 2–207(3) states that conduct by both parties that recognizes the existence of a contract is sufficient to establish a contract for the sale of goods even though the writings of the parties do not otherwise establish a contract. In this situation, "the terms of the particular contract will consist of those terms on which the writings of the parties agree, together with any supplementary terms incorporated under any other provisions of this Act."

In a dispute over contract terms, this provision allows a court simply to strike from the contract those terms on which the parties do not agree.   **EXAMPLE 15.11**   SMT Marketing orders goods over the phone from Brigg Sales, Inc., which ships the goods with an acknowledgment form (confirming the order) to SMT. SMT accepts and pays for the goods. The parties' writings do not establish a contract, but there is no question that a contract exists. If a dispute arises over the terms, such as the extent of any warranties, UCC 2–207(3) provides the governing rule. •

Consideration

The common law rule that a contract requires consideration also applies to sales and lease contracts. Unlike the common law, however, the UCC does not require a contract modification to be supported by new consideration. An agreement modifying a contract for the sale or lease of goods "needs no consideration to be binding" [UCC 2–209(1), 2A–208(1)]. Of course, a contract modification must be sought in good faith [UCC 1–304].

In some situations, an agreement to modify a sales or lease contract without consideration must be in writing to be enforceable. If the contract itself prohibits any changes to the contract unless they are in a signed writing, for instance, then only those changes agreed to in a signed writing are enforceable.

If a consumer (nonmerchant buyer) is dealing with a merchant and the merchant supplies the form that contains a prohibition against oral modification, the consumer must sign a separate acknowledgment of such a clause [UCC 2–209(2), 2A–208(2)]. Also, any modification that brings a sales contract under Article 2's Statute of Frauds provision (discussed next) usually must be in writing to be enforceable.

The Statute of Frauds

The UCC contains Statute of Frauds provisions covering sales and lease contracts. Under these provisions, sales contracts for goods priced at $500 or more and lease contracts requiring payments of $1,000 or more must be in writing to be enforceable [UCC 2–201(1), 2A–201(1)]. (These low threshold amounts may eventually be raised.)

Sufficiency of the Writing   The UCC has greatly relaxed the requirements for the sufficiency of a writing to satisfy the Statute of Frauds. A writing or a memorandum will be sufficient as long as it indicates that the parties intended to form a contract and as long as it is signed by the party (or agent of the party—see Chapter 23) against whom enforcement is sought. The contract normally will not be enforceable beyond the quantity of goods shown in the writing, however. All other terms can be proved in court by oral testimony. For leases, the writing must reasonably identify and describe the goods leased and the lease term.

Special Rules for Contracts between Merchants   Once again, the UCC provides a special rule for merchants in sales transactions (there is no corresponding rule that applies to leases under Article 2A). Merchants can satisfy the Statute of Frauds if, after the parties have agreed orally, one of the merchants sends a signed written confirmation to the other merchant within a reasonable time. The communication must indicate the terms of the agreement, and the merchant receiving the confirmation must have reason to know of its contents. Unless the merchant who receives the confirmation gives written notice of objection to its contents within ten days after receipt, the writing is sufficient against the receiving merchant, even though she or he has not signed anything [UCC 2–201(2)]. Generally, courts even hold that it is sufficient if a merchant sends an e-mail confirmation of the agreement.[8]

(Csaba Vanyi/Shutterstock.com)

The buyer and the seller of aircraft parts are both merchants.

EXAMPLE 15.12   Alfonso is a merchant-buyer in Cleveland. He contracts over the telephone to purchase $4,000 worth of spare aircraft parts from Goldstein, a merchant-seller in New York City. Two days later, Goldstein sends a written and signed confirmation detailing the terms of the oral contract, and Alfonso subsequently receives it. If Alfonso does not notify Goldstein in writing of his objection to the contents of the confirmation within ten days of receipt, Alfonso cannot raise the Statute of Frauds as a defense against the enforcement of the oral contract. •

Exceptions   In addition to the special rules for merchants, the UCC defines three exceptions to the writing requirements of the Statute of Frauds. An oral contract for the sale of goods priced at $500 or more or the lease of goods involving total payments of $1,000 or more will be enforceable despite the absence of a writing in the circumstances discussed in the following subsections [UCC 2–201(3), 2A–201(4)].

These exceptions and other ways in which sales law differs from general contract law are summarized in Exhibit 15.2 on the next page.

LEARNING OBJECTIVE 3
What exceptions to the writing requirements of the Statute of Frauds are provided in Article 2 and Article 2A of the UCC?

Specially Manufactured Goods   An oral contract is enforceable if (1) it is for goods that are specially manufactured for a particular buyer or specially manufactured or obtained for a particular lessee, (2) these goods are not suitable for resale or lease to others in the ordinary course of the seller's or lessor's business, and (3) the seller or lessor has substantially started to manufacture the goods or has made commitments for their manufacture or procurement. In this situation, once the seller or lessor has taken action, the buyer or lessee cannot repudiate the agreement claiming the Statute of Frauds as a defense.

EXAMPLE 15.13   Womach orders custom-made draperies for her new boutique. The price is $6,000, and the contract is oral. When the merchant-seller manufactures the draperies and tenders delivery to Womach, she refuses to pay for them even though the job has been completed on time. Womach claims that she is not liable because the contract was oral. Clearly, if the unique style and color of the draperies make it improbable that the seller can find another buyer, Womach is liable to the seller. Note that the seller must have made a substantial beginning in manufacturing the specialized item prior to the buyer's repudiation. (Here, the manufacture was completed.) Of course, the court must still be convinced by evidence of the terms of the oral contract. •

Admissions   An oral contract for the sale or lease of goods is enforceable if the party against whom enforcement of the contract is sought admits in pleadings, testimony, or

---

8. See, for example, *Bazak International Corp. v. Tarrant Apparel Group*, 378 F.Supp.2d 377 (S.D.N.Y. 2005); and *Great White Bear, LLC v. Mervyns, LLC*, 2007 WL 1295747 (S.D.N.Y. 2007).

other court proceedings that a contract for sale or lease was made. In this situation, the contract will be enforceable even though it was oral, but enforceability will be limited to the quantity of goods admitted.

    CASE EXAMPLE 15.14   Gerald Lindgren, a farmer, agreed by phone to sell his crops to Glacial Plains Cooperative. The parties reached four oral agreements: two for the delivery of soybeans and two for the delivery of corn. Lindgren made the soybean deliveries and part of the first corn delivery, but he sold the rest of his corn to another dealer. Glacial Plains bought corn elsewhere, paying a higher price, and then sued Lindgren for breach of contract. In papers filed with the court, Lindgren acknowledged his oral agreements with Glacial Plains and admitted that he did not fully perform. The court applied the admissions exception and held that the four agreements were enforceable.[9] ●

Partial Performance   An oral contract for the sale or lease of goods is enforceable if payment has been made and accepted or goods have been received and accepted. This is the "partial performance" exception. The oral contract will be enforced at least to the extent that performance *actually* took place.

    EXAMPLE 15.15   Jamal orally contracts to lease to Opus Enterprises a thousand chairs at $2 each to be used during a one-day concert. Before delivery, Opus sends Jamal a check for $1,000, which Jamal cashes. Later, when Jamal attempts to deliver the chairs, Opus refuses delivery, claiming the Statute of Frauds as a defense, and demands the return of its $1,000. Under the UCC's partial performance rule, Jamal can enforce the oral contract by tender of delivery of five hundred chairs for the $1,000 accepted. Similarly, if Opus had made no payment but had accepted the delivery of five hundred chairs from Jamal, the oral contract would have been enforceable against Opus for $1,000, the lease payment due for the five hundred chairs delivered. ●

Parol Evidence

Recall from page 320 in Chapter 12 that *parol evidence* is testimony or other evidence of the parties' prior negotiations, prior agreements, or contemporaneous oral agreements. When the parties to a sales contract set forth its terms in a confirmatory memorandum

---

9. *Glacial Plains Cooperative v. Lindgren,* 759 N.W.2d 661 (Minn.App. 2009).

Exhibit 15.2 **Major Differences between Contract Law and Sales Law**

TOPIC	CONTRACT LAW	SALES LAW
Contract Terms	Contract must contain all material terms.	Open terms are acceptable, if parties intended to form a contract, but the contract is not enforceable beyond quantity term.
Acceptance	Mirror image rule applies. If additional terms are added in acceptance, counteroffer is created.	Additional terms will not negate acceptance unless acceptance is made expressly conditional on assent to the additional terms.
Contract Modification	Modification requires consideration.	Modification does not require consideration.
Irrevocable Offers	Option contracts (with consideration).	Merchants' firm offers (without consideration).
Statute of Frauds Requirements	All material terms must be included in the writing.	Writing is required only for the sale of goods of $500 or more, but contract is not enforceable beyond quantity specified. Merchants can satisfy the requirement by a confirmatory memorandum evidencing their agreement. *Exceptions:* 1. Specially manufactured goods. 2. Admissions by party against whom enforcement is sought. 3. Partial performance.

or in other writing that is intended as a complete and final statement of their agreement, the contract is considered *fully integrated,* and the *parol evidence rule* applies. The terms of a fully integrated contract cannot be contradicted by evidence of any prior agreements or contemporaneous oral agreements.

If, however, the writing contains some of the terms the parties agreed on but not others, the contract is not fully integrated. When a court finds that the terms of a sales contract are *not fully integrated* or are ambiguous, the court may allow evidence of *consistent additional terms* to explain or supplement the terms stated in the contract. The court may also allow the parties to submit evidence of *course of dealing, usage of trade,* or *course of performance* [UCC 2–202, 2A–202]. A court will not under any circumstances allow the parties to submit evidence that contradicts the stated terms (this is also the rule under the common law).

Course of Dealing and Usage of Trade

Under the UCC, the meaning of any agreement, evidenced by the language of the parties and by their actions, must be interpreted in light of commercial practices and other surrounding circumstances. In interpreting a commercial agreement, the court will assume that the course of prior dealing between the parties and the usage of trade were taken into account when the agreement was phrased.

Course of Dealing Prior conduct between the parties to a contract that establishes a common basis for their understanding.

Course of Dealing A **course of dealing** is a sequence of previous actions and communications between the parties to a particular transaction that establishes a common basis for their understanding [UCC 1–303(b)]. A course of dealing is restricted to that previous sequence of actions and communications. Under the UCC, a course of dealing between the parties is relevant in ascertaining the meaning of the parties' agreement. It may give particular meaning to specific terms of the agreement, and may supplement or qualify the terms of its agreement [UCC 1–303(d)]. (Usage of trade and course of performance may be relevant for the same purposes, as will be discussed next.)

Usage of Trade Any practice or method of dealing that is so regularly observed in a place, vocation, or trade that parties justifiably expect it will be observed in their transaction.

Usage of Trade Any practice or method of dealing that is so regularly observed in a place, vocation, or trade that the parties justifiably expect (or should expect) it to be observed in their transaction is a **usage of trade** [UCC 1–303(c)].

EXAMPLE 15.16 Phat Khat Loans, Inc., hires Title Review, LLC, to search the public records for prior claims on potential borrrowers' assets. Title's invoice states, "Liability limited to amount of fee." In the search industry, liability limits are common. After conducting many searches for Phat Khat, Title reports that there are no claims with respect to Main St. Autos. Phat Khat loans $100,000 to Main, with payment guaranteed by Main's assets. When Main defaults on the loan, Phat Khat learns that another lender has priority to Main's assets under a previous claim. In Phat Khat's suit against Title for breach of contract, Title's liability is limited to the amount of its fee. The statement in the invoice was part of the contract between Phat Khat and Title, according to the usage of trade in the industry and the parties' course of dealing. ●

Course of Performance The conduct that occurs under the terms of a particular agreement, which indicates what the parties to that agreement intended it to mean.

Course of Performance

A **course of performance** is the conduct that occurs under the terms of a particular agreement [UCC 1–303(a)]. Presumably, the parties themselves know best what they meant by their words, and the course of performance actually undertaken under their agreement is the best indication of what they meant [UCC 2–208(1), 2A–207(1)].

EXAMPLE 15.17 Janson's Lumber Company contracts with Barrymore to sell Barrymore a specified number of "two-by-fours." The lumber does not in fact measure 2 inches by 4 inches but rather 1⅞ inches by 3¾ inches. Janson's agrees to deliver the lumber in five deliveries, and Barrymore, without objection, accepts the lumber in the first three deliveries.

On the fourth delivery, however, Barrymore objects that the two-by-fours do not measure 2 inches by 4 inches.

The course of performance in this transaction—that is, Barrymore's acceptance of three deliveries without objection under the agreement—is relevant in determining that here the term *two-by-four* actually means "1⅞ by 3¾." Janson's can also prove that two-by-fours need not be exactly 2 inches by 4 inches by applying course of prior dealing, usage of trade, or both. Janson's can, for example, show that in previous transactions, Barrymore took 1⅞-by-3¾-inch lumber without objection. In addition, Janson's can show that in the lumber trade, two-by-fours are commonly 1⅞ inches by 3¾ inches. ●

Rules of Construction   The UCC provides *rules of construction* for interpreting contracts. Express terms, course of performance, course of dealing, and usage of trade are to be construed together when they do not contradict one another. When such a construction is unreasonable, however, the following order of priority controls: (1) express terms, (2) course of performance, (3) course of dealing, and (4) usage of trade [UCC 1–303(e), 2–208(2), 2A–207(2)].

Unconscionability

As discussed on page 296 in Chapter 11, an unconscionable contract is one that is so unfair and one sided that it would be unreasonable to enforce it. The UCC allows the court to evaluate a contract or any clause in a contract, and if the court deems it to have been unconscionable at the time it was made, the court can (1) refuse to enforce the contract, (2) enforce the remainder of the contract without the unconscionable clause, or (3) limit the application of any unconscionable clauses to avoid an unconscionable result [UCC 2–302, 2A–108].

The following *Classic Case* illustrates an early application of the UCC's unconscionability provisions.

 Classic Case 15.2

Jones v. Star Credit Corp.

Supreme Court of New York, Nassau County, 59 Misc.2d 189, 298 N.Y.S.2d 264 (1969).

HISTORICAL AND ECONOMIC SETTING   *In the sixth century, Roman civil law allowed the courts to rescind a contract if the goods that were the subject of the contract had a market value that was less than half the contract price. This same ratio has appeared over the last decade in many cases in which courts have found contract clauses to be unconscionable under UCC 2–302 on the ground that the price was excessive. Most of the litigants who have used UCC 2–302 successfully have been consumers who were poor or otherwise at a disadvantage. In a Connecticut case, for example, the court held that a contract requiring a person who was poor to make payments totaling $1,248 for a television set that ordinarily sold for $499 was unconscionable.[a] The seller had not told the buyer the full purchase price. In a New York case, the court held that a contract* requiring a Spanish-speaking consumer to make payments totaling nearly $1,150 for a freezer that had a wholesale price of less than $350 was unconscionable.[b] *The contract was in English, and the salesperson did not translate or explain it.*

Can a retailer sell a freezer at four times its wholesale price?

FACTS   The Joneses, the plaintiffs, agreed to purchase a freezer for $900 as the result of a salesperson's visit to their home. Tax and financing charges raised the total price to $1,234.80. At trial, the freezer was found to have a maximum retail value of approximately $300. The plaintiffs, who had made payments totaling $619.88, brought a suit in a New York state court

---

a. *Murphy v. McNamara*, 36 Conn.Supp. 183, 416 A.2d 170 (1979).
b. *Frostifresh Corp. v. Reynoso*, 52 Misc.2d 26, 274 N.Y.S.2d 757 (1966), reversed on issue of damages, 54 Misc.2d 119, 281 N.Y.S.2d 946 (1967).

Classic Case 15.2—Continued

to have the purchase contract declared unconscionable under the UCC.

ISSUE Could this contract be denied enforcement on the ground of unconscionability?

DECISION Yes. The court held that the contract was not enforceable as it stood, and the contract was reformed so that no further payments were required.

REASON The court relied on UCC 2–302(1), which states that if "the court as a matter of law finds the contract or any clause of the contract to have been unconscionable at the time it was made, the court may . . . so limit the application of any

unconscionable clause as to avoid any unconscionable result." The court then considered the disparity between the $900 purchase price and the $300 retail value, as well as the fact that the credit charges alone exceeded the retail value. These excessive charges were exacted despite the seller's knowledge of the plaintiffs' limited resources. The court reformed the contract so that the plaintiffs' payments, amounting to more than $600, were regarded as payment in full.

IMPACT OF THIS CASE ON TODAY'S LAW *This early case illustrates the approach that many courts today take when deciding whether a sales contract is unconscionable—an approach that focuses on "excessive" price and unequal bargaining power.*

Title and Risk of Loss

"To win, you have to risk loss."

Jean-Claude Killy, 1943–present (French Alpine skier)

Before the creation of the UCC, *title*—the right of ownership—was the central concept in sales law and controlled all issues of rights and remedies of the parties to a sales contract. In some situations, title is still relevant under the UCC, and the UCC has special rules for determining who has title. (These rules do not apply to leased goods, obviously, because title remains with the lessor, or owner, of the goods.) In most situations, however, the UCC has replaced the concept of title with three other concepts: (1) identification, (2) risk of loss, and (3) insurable interest.

Identification

Identification In a sale of goods, the express designation of the goods provided for in the contract.

Before any interest in specific goods can pass from the seller or lessor to the buyer or lessee, the goods must exist and be identified as the specific goods designated in the contract. **Identification** takes place when specific goods are designated as the subject matter of a sales or lease contract.

Title and risk of loss cannot pass from seller to buyer unless the goods are identified to the contract. (Remember that title to leased goods does not pass to the lessee.) Identification is important because it gives the buyer or lessee the right to insure the goods and the right to recover from third parties who damage the goods.

The parties can agree in their contract on when identification will take place (although it will not effectively pass title and risk of loss to the buyer on future goods, such as unborn cattle). If the parties do not so specify, however, the UCC provisions discussed here determine when identification takes place [UCC 2–501(1), 2A–217].

Existing Goods If the contract calls for the sale or lease of specific goods that are already in existence, identification takes place at the time the contract is made. **EXAMPLE 15.18** You contract to purchase or lease a fleet of five cars designated by their vehicle identification numbers (VINs). Because the cars are identified by their VINs, identification has taken place, and you acquire an insurable interest in them at the time of contracting. •

Future Goods Goods that are not both existing and identified to the contract are called *future goods*. For instance, if a sale involves unborn animals to be born within twelve months after contracting, identification takes place when the animals are conceived. If a lease involves any unborn animals, identification also occurs when the animals are conceived. If a sale involves crops that are to be harvested within twelve months (or the next harvest season occurring after contracting, whichever is longer), identification takes place when the crops are planted. Otherwise, identification takes place when the crops begin to grow.

In a sale or lease of any other future goods, identification occurs when the goods are shipped, marked, or otherwise designated by the seller or lessor as the goods to which the contract refers.

Goods That Are Part of a Larger Mass

As a general rule, goods that are part of a larger mass are identified when the goods are marked, shipped, or somehow designated by the seller or lessor as the particular goods that are the subject of the contract. **EXAMPLE 15.19** A buyer orders 1,000 cases of beans from a 10,000-case lot. Until the seller separates the 1,000 cases of beans from the 10,000-case lot, title and risk of loss remain with the seller. ●

Fungible Goods Goods that are alike by physical nature, agreement, or trade usage.

A common exception to this rule involves fungible goods. **Fungible goods** are goods that are alike by physical nature, by agreement, or by trade usage. They are usually stored in large containers—for example, specific grades or types of wheat, oil, and inexpensive wine. If two or more persons own an interest in fungible goods as *tenants in common* (see Chapter 36), one of those persons can pass title and risk of loss to a buyer without an actual separation of the goods. The buyer replaces the seller as an owner in common [UCC 2–105(4)].

Passage of Title

Once goods exist and are identified, the provisions of UCC 2–401 apply to the passage of title. In nearly all subsections of UCC 2–401, the words "unless otherwise explicitly agreed" appear, meaning that any explicit understanding between the buyer and the seller determines when title passes. Without an explicit agreement to the contrary, *title passes to the buyer at the time and the place the seller performs by delivering the goods* [UCC 2–401(2)]. For instance, if a person buys cattle at a livestock auction, title will pass to the buyer when the cattle are physically delivered to him or her (unless, of course, the parties agree otherwise).

If a seller gives up possession or control of goods, but keeps a "Certificate of Origin" supposedly showing ownership, has there been a delivery sufficient to pass title? That was the question in the following case.

Case 15.3

United States v. 2007 Custom Motorcycle

United States District Court, District of Arizona, __ F.Supp.2d __ (2011).

(Margo Harrison/Shutterstock.com)

When does passage of title occur?

FACTS Timothy Allen commissioned a custom motorcycle from Indy Route 66 Cycles, Inc. Indy built the motorcycle and issued a "Certificate of Origin." Two years later, federal law enforcement officers arrested Allen on drug charges and seized his home and other property. The officers also seized the Indy-made motorcycle from the garage of the home of Allen's sister, Tena. The government alleged that the motorcycle was subject to forfeiture as the proceeds of drug trafficking. Indy filed a claim against the government, arguing that it owned the motorcycle, as evidenced by the "Certificate of Origin," which the company still possessed. Indy claimed that it had been keeping the motorcycle in storage. The government filed a motion to strike the claim, asserting that title to the motorcycle had passed when it was delivered to Allen.

ISSUE Did ownership to the motorcycle pass at the time that Indy gave Allen possession and control over it?

Case 15.3—Continued

DECISION Yes. The district court issued a ruling in the government's favor and granted the motion to strike Indy's claim.

REASON Under UCC 2–401(2), "unless otherwise explicitly agreed, title passes to the buyer at the time and place at which the seller completes his performance with reference to the physical delivery of the goods." In the sales transaction in this case, the parties did not "otherwise explicitly agree" to different terms. Thus, the critical question was whether Indy had delivered the cycle to Allen. Testimony by Indy's former vice president, Vince Ballard, was "inconclusive" but implied that Indy had delivered the motorcycle to Allen. The cycle was found in Tena's garage, which also indicated that Indy had delivered it to Allen. Thus, Indy had given up possession of the cycle to Allen. This was sufficient to pass title even though Indy had kept a "Certificate of Origin." As a consequence, the motorcycle was subject to forfeiture as the proceeds of drug trafficking.

WHAT IF THE FACTS WERE DIFFERENT? *Suppose that Indy had given the "Certificate of Origin" to Allen and had kept the motorcycle. Would the result have been different? Explain.*

Shipment Contract A contract for the sale of goods in which the seller is required or authorized to ship the goods by carrier. The seller assumes liability for any losses or damage to the goods until they are delivered to the carrier.

Destination Contract A contract for the sale of goods in which the seller is required or authorized to ship the goods by carrier and tender delivery of the goods at a particular destination. The seller assumes liability for any losses or damage to the goods until they are tendered at the destination specified in the contract.

Document of Title A paper exchanged in the regular course of business that evidences the right to possession of goods (for example, a bill of lading or a warehouse receipt).

LEARNING OBJECTIVE 4
Risk of loss does not necessarily pass with title. If the parties to a contract do not expressly agree when risk passes and the goods are to be delivered without movement by the seller, when does risk pass?

Shipment and Destination Contracts Unless otherwise agreed, delivery arrangements can determine when title passes from the seller to the buyer. In a **shipment contract,** the seller is required or authorized to ship goods by carrier, such as a trucking company. Under a shipment contract, the seller is required only to deliver conforming goods into the hands of a carrier, and title passes to the buyer at the time and place of shipment [UCC 2–401(2)(a)]. Generally, *all contracts are assumed to be shipment contracts if nothing to the contrary is stated in the contract.*

In a **destination contract,** the seller is required to deliver the goods to a particular destination, usually directly to the buyer, but sometimes to another party designated by the buyer. Title passes to the buyer when the goods are *tendered* at that destination [UCC 2–401(2)(b)]. As you will read in Chapter 16, *tender of delivery* occurs when the seller places or holds conforming goods at the buyer's disposal (with any necessary notice), enabling the buyer to take possession [UCC 2–503(1)].

Delivery without Movement of the Goods When the sales contract does not call for the seller to ship or deliver the goods (when the buyer is to pick up the goods), the passage of title depends on whether the seller must deliver a **document of title,** such as a bill of lading or a warehouse receipt, to the buyer. A *bill of lading* is a receipt for goods that is signed by a carrier and serves as a contract for the transport of the goods. A *warehouse receipt* is a receipt issued by a warehouser for goods stored in a warehouse.

When a document of title is required, title passes to the buyer *when and where the document is delivered.* Thus, if the goods are stored in a warehouse, title passes to the buyer when the appropriate documents are delivered to the buyer. The goods never move. In fact, the buyer can choose to leave the goods at the same warehouse for a period of time, and the buyer's title to those goods will be unaffected.

When no documents of title are required and delivery is made without moving the goods, title passes at the time and place the sales contract is made, if the goods have already been identified. If the goods have not been identified, title does not pass until identification occurs [UCC 2–401(3)]. **EXAMPLE 15.20** Juarez sells lumber to Bodan. They agree that Bodan will pick up the lumber at the lumberyard. If the lumber has been identified (segregated, marked, or in any other way distinguished from all other lumber), title passes to Bodan when the contract is signed. If the lumber is still in large storage bins at the lumberyard, title does not pass to Bodan until the particular pieces of lumber to be sold under this contract are identified. •

Sales or Leases by Nonowners

Problems occur when a person who acquires goods with *imperfect* title attempts to sell or lease them. Sections 2–402 and 2–403 of the UCC deal with the rights of two parties who lay claim to the same goods, sold with imperfect title. Generally, a buyer acquires at least whatever title the seller has to the goods sold.

Void Title   A buyer may unknowingly purchase goods from a seller who is not the owner of the goods. If the seller is a thief, the seller's title is *void*—legally, no title exists. Thus, the buyer acquires no title, and the real owner can reclaim the goods from the buyer. If the goods were leased, the same result would occur because the lessor has no leasehold interest to transfer.

EXAMPLE 15.21   If Saki steals diamonds owned by Maren, Saki has a *void title* to those diamonds. If Saki sells the diamonds to Shannon, Maren can reclaim them from Shannon even though Shannon acted in good faith and honestly was not aware that the goods were stolen. ● (Article 2A contains similar provisions for leases.)

Voidable Title   A seller has *voidable title* if the goods that she or he is selling were obtained by fraud, paid for with a check that is later *dishonored*—that is, returned for insufficient funds—purchased from a minor, or purchased on credit when the seller was insolvent. Under the UCC, a person is **insolvent** when that person ceases to pay his or her debts in the ordinary course of business, cannot pay his or her debts as they come due, or is insolvent within the meaning of federal bankruptcy law [UCC 1–201(23)].

In contrast to a seller with *void title,* a seller with *voidable title* has the power to transfer good title to a good faith purchaser for value. A **good faith purchaser** is one who buys without knowledge of circumstances that would make a person of ordinary prudence inquire about the validity of the seller's title to the goods. One who purchases *for value* gives legally sufficient consideration (value) for the goods purchased. The real, or original, owner cannot recover goods from a good faith purchaser for value [UCC 2–403(1)].[10] If the buyer of the goods is not a good faith purchaser for value, then the actual owner of the goods can reclaim them from the buyer (or from the seller, if the goods are still in the seller's possession). Exhibit 15.3 on the facing page illustrates these concepts.

The Entrustment Rule

According to Section 2–403(2), when goods are entrusted to a merchant *who deals in goods of that kind,* the merchant has the power to transfer all rights to *a buyer in the ordinary course of business.* This is known as the **entrustment rule.** Entrusted goods include both goods that are turned over to the merchant and purchased goods left with the merchant for later delivery or pickup [UCC 2–403(3)]. Article 2A provides a similar rule for leased goods [UCC 2A–305(2)].

A buyer in the ordinary course of business is a person who, in good faith and without knowledge that the sale violates the ownership rights or security interest of a third party, buys in ordinary course from a person (other than a pawnbroker) in the business of selling goods of that kind [UCC 1–201(9)]. (A *security interest* is any interest in personal property that secures the payment of or the performance of an obligation—see Chapter 20.)

EXAMPLE 15.22   Jan leaves her watch with a jeweler to be repaired. The jeweler sells new and used watches. The jeweler sells Jan's watch to Kim, a customer, who is unaware that the jeweler has no right to sell it. Kim, as a good faith buyer, gets good title against Jan's claim of ownership.[11] Kim, however, obtains only those rights held by the person entrusting the goods (here, Jan). Suppose that Jan had stolen the watch from Greg and then left it with the jeweler to be repaired. The jeweler then sells it to Kim. In this situation, Kim gets good title against Jan, who entrusted the watch to the jeweler, but not against Greg (the real owner), who neither entrusted the watch to Jan nor authorized Jan to entrust it. ●

Insolvent A condition in which a person cannot pay his or her debts as they become due or ceases to pay debts in the ordinary course of business.

Good Faith Purchaser A purchaser who buys without notice of any circumstance that would cause a person of ordinary prudence to inquire as to whether the seller has valid title to the goods being sold.

Entrustment Rule The rule that entrusting goods to a merchant who deals in goods of that kind gives that merchant the power to transfer those goods and all rights to them to a buyer in the ordinary course of business.

➡ KNOW THIS ⬅

The purpose of holding most goods in inventory is to turn those goods into revenues by selling them. That is one of the reasons for the entrustment rule.

---

10. The real owner could, of course, sue the person who initially obtained voidable title to the goods.

11. Jan, of course, can sue the jeweler for the tort of trespass to personalty or conversion (see Chapter 4) for the equivalent cash value of the watch.

Exhibit 15.3 Void and Voidable Titles

If goods are transferred from their owner to another by theft, the thief acquires no ownership rights. Because the thief's title is *void*, a later buyer can acquire no title, and the owner can recover the goods. If the transfer occurs by fraud, the transferee acquires a *voidable* title. A later good faith purchaser for value can acquire good title, and the original owner cannot recover the goods.

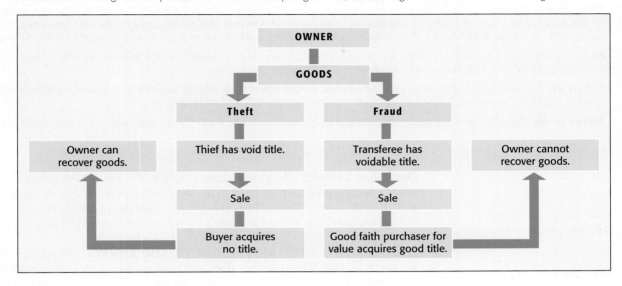

Risk of Loss

Under the UCC, risk of loss does not necessarily pass with title. When risk of loss passes from a seller or lessor to a buyer or lessee is generally determined by the contract between the parties. Sometimes, the contract states expressly when the risk of loss passes. At other times, it does not, and a court must interpret the performance and delivery terms of the contract to determine whether the risk has passed.

Delivery with Movement of the Goods—Carrier Cases
When the contract involves movement of the goods through a common carrier but does not specify when risk of loss passes, the courts first look for specific delivery terms in the contract.

The terms that have traditionally been used in contracts within the United States are listed and defined in Exhibit 15.4 on the following page. These terms determine which party will pay the costs of delivering the goods and who bears the risk of loss. If the contract does not include these terms, then the courts must decide whether the contract is a shipment or a destination contract.

Shipment Contracts In a shipment contract, the seller or lessor is required or authorized to ship goods by carrier, but is not required to deliver them to a particular final destination. The risk of loss in a shipment contract passes to the buyer or lessee when the goods are delivered to the carrier [UCC 2–319(1)(a), 2–509(1)(a), 2A–219(2)(a)].

EXAMPLE 15.23 A seller in Texas sells five hundred cases of grapefruit to a buyer in New York, F.O.B. Houston (free on board in Houston—that is, the buyer pays the transportation charges from Houston). The contract authorizes shipment by carrier. It does not require that the seller tender the grapefruit in New York. Risk passes to the buyer when conforming goods are properly placed in the possession of the carrier. If the goods are damaged in transit, the loss is the buyer's. (Actually, buyers have recourse against carriers, subject to certain limitations, and buyers usually insure the goods from the time the goods leave the seller.) ●

Exhibit 15.4 Contract Terms—Definitions

The contract terms listed and defined in this exhibit help to determine which party will bear the costs of delivery and when risk of loss will pass from the seller to the buyer.

F.O.B. (free on board) — Indicates that the selling price of goods includes transportation costs to the specific F.O.B. place named in the contract. The seller pays the expenses and carries the risk of loss to the F.O.B. place named [UCC 2–319(1)]. If the named place is the place from which the goods are shipped (for example, the seller's city or place of business), the contract is a shipment contract. If the named place is the place to which the goods are to be shipped (for example, the buyer's city or place of business), the contract is a destination contract.

F.A.S. (free alongside ship) — Requires that the seller, at his or her own expense and risk, deliver the goods alongside the vessel in the manner usual in that port or on a dock designated and provided by the buyer [UCC 2–319(2)]. An F.A.S. contract is essentially an F.O.B. contract for ships.

C.I.F. or **C.&F.** (cost, insurance, and freight or just cost and freight) — Requires, among other things, that the seller "put the goods in the possession of a carrier" before risk passes to the buyer [UCC 2–320(2)]. (These are basically pricing terms, and the contracts remain shipment contracts, not destination contracts.)

Delivery ex-ship (delivery from the carrying vessel) — Means that risk of loss does not pass to the buyer until the goods are properly unloaded from the ship or other carrier [UCC 2–322].

Destination Contracts   In a destination contract, the risk of loss passes to the buyer or lessee when the goods are tendered to the buyer or lessee at the specified destination [UCC 2–319(1)(b), 2–509(1)(b), 2A–219(2)(b)]. In *Example 15.23,* if the contract had been F.O.B. New York, the risk of loss during transit to New York would have been the seller's.

Delivery without Movement of the Goods

The UCC also addresses situations in which the contract does not require the goods to be shipped or moved. Frequently, the buyer or lessee is to pick up the goods from the seller or lessor, or the goods are held by a bailee.

Under the UCC, a **bailee** is a party who, by a bill of lading, warehouse receipt, or other document of title, acknowledges possession of goods and/or contracts to deliver them. A warehousing company, for example, or a trucking company that normally issues documents of title for the goods it receives is a bailee.[12]

Bailee Under the UCC, a party who, by a bill of lading, warehouse receipt, or other document of title, acknowledges possession of goods and/or contracts to deliver them.

Goods Held by the Seller   When the seller keeps the goods for pickup, a document of title usually is not used. If the seller is a merchant, risk of loss to goods held by the seller passes to the buyer when the buyer *actually takes physical possession of the goods* [UCC 2–509(3)]. In other words, the merchant bears the risk of loss between the time the contract is formed and the time the buyer picks up the goods.

If the seller is not a merchant, the risk of loss to goods held by the seller passes to the buyer on *tender of delivery* [UCC 2–509(3)]. This means that the seller bears the risk of loss until he or she makes the goods available to the buyer and notifies the buyer that the goods are ready to be picked up. With respect to leases, the risk of loss passes to the lessee on the lessee's receipt of the goods if the lessor is a merchant. Otherwise, the risk passes to the lessee on tender of delivery [UCC 2A–219(2)(c)].

Goods Held by a Bailee   When a bailee is holding goods for a person who has contracted to sell them and the goods are to be delivered without being moved, the goods are usually represented by a document of title, such as a bill of lading or a warehouse receipt.

Risk of loss passes to the buyer when (1) the buyer receives a negotiable document of title for the goods, (2) the bailee acknowledges the buyer's right to possess the goods, or (3) the buyer receives a nonnegotiable document of title or a writing (record) directing the bailee to deliver the goods *and* has had a *reasonable time* to present the document to the bailee and demand the goods. Obviously, if the bailee refuses to honor the document, the risk of loss remains with the seller [UCC 2–503(4)(b), 2–509(2)].

---

12. Bailments will be discussed in Chapter 35.

With respect to leases, if goods held by a bailee are to be delivered without being moved, the risk of loss passes to the lessee on acknowledgment by the bailee of the lessee's right to possession of the goods [UCC 2A–219(2)(b)].

Risk of Loss When the Contract Is Breached
When a sales or lease contract is breached, the transfer of risk operates differently depending on which party breaches. Generally, the party in breach bears the risk of loss.

When the Seller or Lessor Breaches   If the goods are so nonconforming that the buyer has the right to reject them, the risk of loss does not pass to the buyer until (1) the defects are **cured**—that is, until the goods are repaired, replaced, or discounted in price by the seller or (2) the buyer accepts the goods in spite of their defects (thus waiving the right to reject).

Cure The rights of a party who tenders nonconforming performance to correct his or her performance within the contract period.

EXAMPLE 15.24   A buyer orders ten stainless steel refrigerators from a seller, F.O.B. the seller's plant. The seller ships white refrigerators instead. The white refrigerators (nonconforming goods) are damaged in transit. The risk of loss falls on the seller. Had the seller shipped stainless steel refrigerators (conforming goods) instead, the risk would have fallen on the buyer [UCC 2–510(1)]. •

If a buyer accepts a shipment of goods and later discovers a defect, acceptance can be revoked. Revocation allows the buyer to pass the risk of loss back to the seller, at least to the extent that the buyer's insurance does not cover the loss [UCC 2–510(2)].

When the Buyer or Lessee Breaches   The general rule is that when a buyer or lessee breaches a contract, the risk of loss immediately shifts to the buyer or lessee. This rule has three important limitations:

1. The seller or lessor must already have identified the contract goods.
2. The buyer or lessee bears the risk for only a commercially reasonable time after the seller or lessor has learned of the breach.
3. The buyer or lessee is liable only to the extent of any deficiency in the seller's insurance coverage [UCC 2–510(3), 2A–220(2)].

Insurable Interest

Parties to sales and lease contracts often obtain insurance coverage to protect against damage, loss, or destruction of goods. Any party purchasing insurance, however, must have a sufficient interest in the insured item to obtain a valid policy. Insurance laws—not the UCC—determine sufficiency (see Chapter 37). The UCC is helpful, however, because it contains certain rules regarding insurable interests in goods.

Insurable Interest of the Buyer or Lessee
A buyer or lessee has an **insurable interest** in identified goods. The moment the contract goods are identified by the seller or lessor, the buyer or lessee has a special property interest that allows the buyer or lessee to obtain necessary insurance coverage for those goods even before the risk of loss has passed [UCC 2–501(1), 2A–218(1)]. Buyers obtain an insurable interest in crops at the time of identification. **EXAMPLE 15.25**   In March, a farmer sells a cotton crop that he hopes to harvest in October. When the crop is planted, the buyer acquires an insurable interest in it because those goods (the cotton crop) are identified to the sales contract between the seller and the buyer. •

Insurable Interest A property interest in goods being sold or leased that is sufficiently substantial to permit a party to insure against damage to the goods.

Insurable Interest of the Seller or Lessor
A seller has an insurable interest in goods if she or he retains title to the goods. Even after title passes to the buyer, a seller who has a security interest in the goods (a right to secure payment—see Chapter 20) still has an insurable interest and can insure the goods [UCC 2–501(2)]. Hence, both a buyer and a

seller can have an insurable interest in the same goods at the same time. Of course, the buyer or seller must sustain an actual loss to have the right to recover from an insurance company. In regard to leases, the lessor retains an insurable interest in leased goods until the lessee exercises an option to buy and the risk of loss has passed to the lessee [UCC 2A–218(3)]. (See the *Business Application* feature on page 408 for a discussion of insurance coverage and other measures that buyers and sellers can take to protect against losses.)

Contracts for the International Sale of Goods

LEARNING OBJECTIVE 5
What law governs contracts for the international sale of goods?

International sales contracts between firms or individuals located in different countries are governed by the 1980 United Nations Convention on Contracts for the International Sale of Goods (CISG). The CISG governs international contracts only if the countries of the parties to the contract have ratified the CISG and if the parties have not agreed that some other law will govern their contract. As of 2012, the CISG had been adopted by seventy-eight countries, including the United States, Canada, Mexico, some Central and South American countries, and most European nations.

Applicability of the CISG

Essentially, the CISG is to international sales contracts what Article 2 of the UCC is to domestic sales contracts. As discussed earlier, in domestic transactions the UCC applies when the parties to a contract for a sale of goods have failed to specify in writing some important term concerning price, delivery, or the like. Similarly, whenever the parties subject to the CISG have failed to specify in writing the precise terms of a contract for the international sale of goods, the CISG will be applied.

Unlike the UCC, *the CISG does not apply to consumer sales.* Neither the UCC nor the CISG applies to contracts for services.

Businesspersons must take special care when drafting international sales contracts to avoid problems caused by distance, including language differences and varying national laws. The fold-out exhibit for this chapter, which shows an actual international sales contract used by Starbucks Coffee Company, illustrates many of the special terms and clauses that are typically contained in international contracts for the sale of goods. Annotations in the exhibit explain the meaning and significance of specific clauses in the contract. (Other laws that frame global business transactions were discussed in Chapter 8.)

A Comparison of CISG and UCC Provisions

The provisions of the CISG, although similar for the most part to those of the UCC, differ from them in certain respects. We have already mentioned some of these differences. In the *Beyond Our Borders* feature in Chapter 12 on page 317, for example, we pointed out that the CISG does not include any Statute of Frauds provisions. Under Article 11 of the CISG, an international sales contract does not need to be evidenced by a writing or to be in any particular form. We look here at some differences between the UCC and the CISG with respect to contract formation.

Offers   Some differences between the UCC and the CISG have to do with offers. For instance, the UCC provides that a merchant's firm offer is irrevocable, even without consideration, if the merchant gives assurances in a signed writing.

In contrast, under the CISG, an offer can become irrevocable without a signed writing. Article 16(2) of the CISG provides that an offer will be irrevocable if the merchant-offeror simply states orally that the offer is irrevocable or if the offeree reasonably relies on the offer as being irrevocable. In both of these situations, the offer will be irrevocable even without a writing and without consideration.

Another difference is that, under the UCC, if the price term is left open, the court will determine "a reasonable price at the time for delivery" [UCC 2–305(1)]. Under the CISG, however, the price term must be specified, or at least provisions for its specification must be included in the agreement. Otherwise, normally no contract will exist.

Acceptances   Like UCC 2–207, the CISG provides that a contract can be formed even though the acceptance contains additional terms, unless the additional terms materially alter the contract. Under the CISG, however, the definition of a "material alteration" includes virtually any change in the terms. If an additional term relates to payment, quality, quantity, price, time and place of delivery, extent of one party's liability to the other, or the settlement of disputes, the CISG considers the added term a "material alteration." In effect, then, the CISG requires that the terms of the acceptance mirror those of the offer.

Additionally, under the UCC, an acceptance is effective on dispatch. Under the CISG, however, a contract is not created until the offeror receives the acceptance. (The offer becomes irrevocable, however, when the acceptance is sent.) Also, in contrast to the UCC, the CISG provides that acceptance by performance does not require that the offeror be notified of the performance.

Reviewing . . . The Formation of Sales and Lease Contracts

Guy Holcomb owns and operates Oasis Goodtime Emporium, an adult entertainment establishment. Holcomb wanted to create an adult Internet system for Oasis that would offer customers adult theme videos and "live" chat room programs using performers at the club. On May 10, Holcomb signed a work order authorizing Crossroads Consulting Group (CCG) "to deliver a working prototype of a customer chat system, demonstrating the integration of live video and chatting in a Web browser." In exchange for creating the prototype, Holcomb agreed to pay CCG $64,697. On May 20, Holcomb signed an additional work order in the amount of $12,943 for CCG to install a customized firewall system. The work orders stated that Holcomb would make monthly installment payments to CCG, and both parties expected the work would be finished by September. Due to unforeseen problems largely attributable to system configuration and software incompatibility, the project required more time than anticipated. By the end of the summer, the Web site was still not ready, and Holcomb had fallen behind in the payments to CCG. CCG was threatening to cease work and file suit for breach of contract unless the bill was paid. Rather than make further payments, Holcomb wanted to abandon the Web site project. Using the information presented in the chapter, answer the following questions.

1. Would a court be likely to decide that the transaction between Holcomb and CCG was covered by the Uniform Commercial Code (UCC)? Why or why not?
2. Would a court be likely to consider Holcomb a merchant under the UCC? Why or why not?
3. Did the parties have a valid contract under the UCC? Explain.
4. Suppose that Holcomb and CCG meet in October in an attempt to resolve their problems. At that time, the parties reach an oral agreement that CCG will continue to work without demanding full payment of the past-due amounts and Holcomb will pay CCG $5,000 per week. Assuming that the contract falls under the UCC, is the oral agreement enforceable? Why or why not?

DEBATE THIS The UCC should require the same degree of definiteness of terms, especially with respect to price and quantity, as general contract law does.

BUSINESS APPLICATION

Who Bears the Risk of Loss—the Seller or the Buyer?*

The shipment of goods is a major aspect of commercial transactions. Many issues arise when an unforeseen event, such as fire or theft, causes damage to goods in transit. At the time of contract negotiation, both the seller and the buyer should determine the importance of the risk of loss. In some circumstances, risk is relatively unimportant (such as when ten boxes of copier paper are being sold), and the delivery terms should simply reflect costs and price. In other circumstances, risk is extremely important (such as when a fragile piece of pharmaceutical testing equipment is being sold), and the parties will need an express agreement as to the moment risk is to pass so that they can insure the goods accordingly. Risk should always be considered before a loss occurs, not after.

A major consideration relating to risk is when to insure goods against possible losses. Buyers and sellers should determine the point at which risk passes so that they can obtain insurance coverage to protect themselves against loss when they have an insurable interest in the goods.

Checklist to Determine Risk of Loss

The UCC uses a three-part checklist to determine risk of loss:

1. If the contract includes terms allocating the risk of loss, those terms are binding and must be applied.
2. If the contract is silent as to risk and either party breaches the contract, the breaching party is liable for the risk of loss.
3. If the contract makes no reference to risk and the goods are to be shipped or delivered, the risk of loss is borne by the party having control over the goods (delivery terms) if neither party breaches.

---

*This *Business Application* is not meant to substitute for the services of an attorney who is licensed to practice law in your state.

If You Are the Seller

If you are a seller of goods to be shipped, realize that as long as you have control over the goods, you are liable for any loss unless the buyer is in breach or the contract contains an explicit agreement to the contrary. When there is no explicit agreement, the delivery terms in your contract can serve as a basis for determining control. Thus, if goods are shipped "F.O.B. buyer's business," risk of loss does not pass to the buyer until there is a tender of delivery at the destination—the buyer's business. Any loss or damage in transit falls on the seller because the seller has control until proper tender has been made.

If You Are the Buyer

If you are a buyer of goods, it is important to remember that most sellers prefer "F.O.B. seller's business" as a delivery term. Under this term, once the goods are delivered to the carrier, the buyer bears the risk of loss. Thus, if conforming goods are completely destroyed or lost in transit, the buyer not only suffers the loss but is obligated to pay the seller the contract price.

Checklist for the Seller or the Buyer

1. Before entering into a contract, determine the importance of the risk of loss for a given sale.
2. If risk is extremely important, the contract should expressly state the moment the risk of loss will pass from the seller to the buyer. This clause could even provide that risk will not pass until the goods are "delivered, installed, inspected, and tested (or in running order for a period of time)."
3. If an express clause is not included, delivery terms determine the passage of risk of loss.
4. When appropriate, either party or both parties should consider procuring insurance.

Key Terms

bailee 404	firm offer 391	lease 388	requirements contract 390
course of dealing 397	fungible goods 400	lease agreement 388	sale 384
course of performance 397	good faith purchaser 402	lessee 388	sales contract 384
cure 405	identification 399	lessor 388	seasonably 392
destination contract 401	insolvent 402	merchant 387	shipment contract 401
document of title 401	insurable interest 405	output contract 391	tangible property 384
entrustment rule 402	intangible property 384	predominant-factor test 386	usage of trade 397

Chapter Summary: The Formation of Sales and Lease Contracts

The Scope of the UCC and Articles 2 (Sales) and 2A (Leases) (See pages 384–388.)	1. *The UCC*—The UCC attempts to provide a consistent, uniform, and integrated framework of rules to deal with all phases *ordinarily arising* in a commercial sales or lease transaction, including contract formation, passage of title and risk of loss, performance, remedies, payment for goods, warehoused goods, and secured transactions. 2. *Article 2 (sales)*—Article 2 governs contracts for the sale of goods (tangible, movable personal property). The common law of contracts also applies to sales contracts to the extent that the common law has not been modified by the UCC. If there is a conflict between a common law rule and the UCC, the UCC controls. 3. *Article 2A (leases)*—Article 2A governs contracts for the lease of goods. Except that it applies to leases, instead of sales, of goods, Article 2A is essentially a repetition of Article 2 and varies only to reflect differences between sales and lease transactions.

The Formation of Sales and Lease Contracts (See pages 389–398.)	1. *Offer*—
	  a. Not all terms have to be included for a contract to be formed (only the subject matter and quantity term must be specified).
	  b. The price does not have to be included for a contract to be formed.
	  c. Particulars of performance can be left open.
	  d. A written and signed offer by a *merchant,* covering a period of three months or less, is irrevocable without payment of consideration.
	2. *Acceptance*—
	  a. Acceptance may be made by any reasonable means of communication. It is effective when dispatched.
	  b. An offer can be accepted by a promise to ship or by prompt shipment of conforming goods, or by prompt shipment of nonconforming goods if not accompanied by a notice of accommodation.
	  c. Acceptance by performance requires notice within a reasonable time. Otherwise, the offer can be treated as lapsed.
	  d. A definite expression of acceptance creates a contract even if the terms of the acceptance differ from those of the offer, unless the additional or different terms in the acceptance are expressly conditioned on the offeror's assent to those terms.
	3. *Consideration*—A modification of a contract for the sale of goods does not require consideration.
	4. *The Statute of Frauds*—
	  a. All contracts for the sale of goods priced at $500 or more must be in writing. A writing is sufficient as long as it indicates a contract between the parties and is signed by the party against whom enforcement is sought. A contract is not enforceable beyond the quantity shown in the writing.
	  b. When written confirmation of an oral contract *between merchants* is not objected to in writing by the receiver within ten days, the contract is enforceable.
	  c. For exceptions to the Statute of Frauds, see Exhibit 15.2 on page 396.
	5. *Parol evidence rule*—
	  a. The terms of a clear and complete written contract cannot be contradicted by evidence of prior agreements or contemporaneous oral agreements.
	  b. Evidence is admissible to clarify the terms of a writing if the contract terms are ambiguous or if evidence of course of dealing, usage of trade, or course of performance is necessary to learn or to clarify the parties' intentions.
	6. *Unconscionability*—An unconscionable contract is one that is so unfair and one sided that it would be unreasonable to enforce it. If the court deems a sales contract to have been unconscionable at the time it was made, the court can (a) refuse to enforce the contract, (b) refuse to enforce the unconscionable clause, or (c) limit the application of any unconscionable clauses to avoid an unconscionable result.

Title and Risk of Loss (See pages 399–406.)	1. *Shipment contract*—In the absence of an agreement, title and risk pass on the seller's or lessor's delivery of conforming goods to the carrier [UCC 2–319(1)(a), 2–401(2)(a), 2–509(1)(a), 2A–219(2)(a)].
	2. *Destination contract*—In the absence of an agreement, title and risk pass on the seller's or lessor's *tender* of delivery of conforming goods to the buyer or lessee at the point of destination [UCC 2–319(1)(b), 2–401(2)(b), 2–509(1)(b), 2A–219(2)(b)].
	3. *Delivery without movement of the goods*—In the absence of an agreement, if the goods are not represented by a document of title, title passes on the formation of the contract, and risk passes on the buyer's or lessee's receipt of the goods if the seller or lessor is a merchant or on the tender of delivery if the seller or lessor is a nonmerchant.
	4. *Sales and leases by nonowners*—Between the owner and a good faith purchaser or between the lessee and a sublessee:
	  a. Void title—Owner prevails [UCC 2–403(1)].
	  b. Voidable title—Buyer prevails [UCC 2–403(1)].
	  c. Entrusted to a merchant—Buyer or sublessee prevails [UCC 2–403(2), (3); 2A–305(2)].

Continued

Chapter Summary: The Formation of Sales and Lease Contracts— Continued

Title and Risk of Loss — Continued	5. *Risk of loss when the contract is breached—*
	a. If the seller or lessor breaches by tendering nonconforming goods that are rejected by the buyer or lessee, the risk of loss does not pass to the buyer or lessee until the defects are cured (unless the buyer or lessee accepts the goods in spite of their defects, thus waiving the right to reject) [UCC 2–510(1), 2A–220(1)].
	b. If the buyer or lessee breaches the contract, the risk of loss immediately shifts to the buyer or lessee for goods that are identified to the contract. The buyer or lessee bears the risk for only a commercially reasonable time after the seller or lessor has learned of the breach [UCC 2–510(3), 2A–220(2)].
Contracts for the International Sale of Goods (See pages 406–407.)	International sales contracts are governed by the United Nations Convention on Contracts for the International Sale of Goods (CISG) — if the countries of the parties to the contract have ratified the CISG (and if the parties have not agreed that some other law will govern their contract). Essentially, the CISG is to international sales contracts what Article 2 of the UCC is to domestic sales contracts. Whenever parties who are subject to the CISG have failed to specify in writing the precise terms of a contract for the international sale of goods, the CISG will be applied.

ExamPrep

ISSUE SPOTTERS

1. E-Design, Inc., orders 150 computer desks. Fav-O-Rite Supplies, Inc., ships 150 printer stands. Is this an acceptance of the offer or a counteroffer? If it is an acceptance, is it a breach of the contract? What if Fav-O-Rite told E-Design it was sending the printer stands as "an accommodation"? **(See pages 391–394.)**
2. Truck Parts, Inc. (TPI), often sells supplies to United Fix-It Company (UFC), which services trucks. Over the phone, they negotiate for the sale of eighty-four sets of tires. TPI sends a letter to UFC detailing the terms and two weeks later ships the tires. Is there an enforceable contract between them? Why or why not? **(See pages 389–391.)**

—**Check your answers to the Issue Spotters against the answers provided in Appendix E at the end of this text.**

BEFORE THE TEST

Go to www.cengagebrain.com, enter the ISBN 9781133273561, and click on "Find" to locate this textbook's Web site. Then, click on "Access Now" under "Study Tools," and select Chapter 15 at the top. There, you will find a Practice Quiz that you can take to assess your mastery of the concepts in this chapter, as well as Flashcards, a Glossary of important terms, and Video Questions (when assigned).

For Review

Answers to the even-numbered questions in this For Review section can be found in Appendix F at the end of this text.

1. How do Article 2 and Article 2A of the UCC differ? What types of transactions does each article cover?
2. In a sales contract, if an offeree includes additional or different terms in an acceptance, will a contract result? If so, what happens to these terms?
3. What exceptions to the writing requirements of the Statute of Frauds are provided in Article 2 and Article 2A of the UCC?
4. Risk of loss does not necessarily pass with title. If the parties to a contract do not expressly agree when risk passes and the goods are to be delivered without movement by the seller, when does risk pass?
5. What law governs contracts for the international sale of goods?

Business Scenarios and Case Problems

15–1 Statute of Frauds. Fresher Foods, Inc., orally agreed to purchase one thousand bushels of corn for $1.25 per bushel from Dale Vernon, a farmer. Fresher Foods paid $125 down and agreed to pay the remainder of the purchase price on delivery, which was scheduled for one week later. When Fresher Foods tendered the balance of $1,125 on the scheduled day of delivery and requested the corn, Vernon refused to deliver it. Fresher Foods sued Vernon for damages, claiming that Vernon had breached their oral contract. Can Fresher Foods recover? If so, to what extent? **(See pages 394–396.)**

15–2 ❓ **Question with Sample Answer—Merchant's Firm Offer.** On September 1, Jennings, a used-car dealer, wrote a letter to Wheeler, stating, "I have a 1955 Thunderbird convertible in mint condition that I will sell you for $13,500 at any time before October 9. [signed] Peter Jennings." By September 15, having heard nothing from Wheeler, Jennings sold the Thunderbird to another party. On September 29, Wheeler accepted Jennings's offer and tendered the $13,500. When Jennings told Wheeler he had sold the car to another party, Wheeler claimed Jennings had breached their contract. Is Jennings in breach? Explain. **(See page 391.)**

—**For a sample answer to Question 15–2, go to Appendix G at the end of this text.**

15–3 🔨 **Spotlight on Goods and Services—The Statute of Frauds.** Fallsview Glatt Kosher Caterers ran a business that provided travel packages, including food, entertainment, and lectures on religious subjects, to customers during the Passover holiday at a New York resort. Willie Rosenfeld verbally agreed to pay Fallsview $24,050 for the Passover package for himself and his family. Rosenfeld did not appear at the resort and never paid the money owed. Fallsview sued Rosenfeld for breach of contract. Rosenfeld claimed that the contract was unenforceable because it was not in writing and violated the UCC's Statute of Frauds. Is the contract valid? Explain. [*Fallsview Glatt Kosher Caterers, Inc. v. Rosenfeld,* 794 N.Y.S.2d 790 (N.Y. Super. 2005)] **(See pages 394–396.)**

15–4 ⚖️ **Case Problem with Sample Answer—Passage of Title.** Kenzie Godfrey was a passenger in a taxi when it collided with a car driven by Dawn Altieri. Altieri had originally leased the car from G.E. Capital Auto Lease, Inc. By the time of the accident, she had bought it, but she had not fully paid for it or completed the transfer-of-title paperwork. Godfrey suffered a brain injury and sought to recover damages from the owner of the car that Altieri was driving. Who had title to the car at the time of the accident? Explain. [*Godfrey v. G.E. Capital Auto Lease, Inc.,* 89 A.D.3d 471, 933 N.Y.S.2d 208 (1 Dept. 2011)] **(See page 400.)**

—**For a sample answer to Problem 15–4, go to Appendix H at the end of this text.**

15–5 **Additional Terms.** B.S. International, Ltd. (BSI), makes costume jewelry. JMAM, LLC, is a wholesaler of costume jewelry. JMAM sent BSI a letter with the terms for orders, including the necessary procedure for obtaining credit for items that customers rejected. The letter stated, "By signing below, you agree to the terms." Steven Baracsi, BSI's owner, signed the letter and returned it. For six years, BSI made jewelry for JMAM, which resold it. Items rejected by customers were sent back to JMAM, but were never returned to BSI. BSI filed

a suit against JMAM, claiming $41,294.21 for the unreturned items. BSI showed the court a copy of JMAM's terms. Across the bottom had been typed a "PS" requiring the return of rejected merchandise. Was this "PS" part of the contract? Discuss. [*B.S. International, Ltd. v. JMAM, LLC,* 13 A.3d 1057 (R.I. 2011)] **(See page 392.)**

15–6 **Delivery without Movement of the Goods.** Aleris International, Inc., signed a contract to buy a John Deere loader from Holt Equipment Co. The agreement provided that "despite physical delivery of the equipment, title shall remain in the seller until" Aleris paid the full price. The next month, Aleris filed for bankruptcy. Holt asserted that it was the owner of the loader and filed a claim with the court to repossess it. Who is entitled to the loader, and why? [*In re Aleris International, Ltd.,* __ Bankr. __ (D.Del. 2011)] **(See page 401.)**

15–7 **Goods Held by the Seller or Lessor.** Douglas Singletary bought a manufactured home from Andy's Mobile Home and Land Sales. The contract stated that the buyer accepted the home "as is where is." Singletary paid the full price, and his crew began to ready the home to relocate it to his property. The night before the home was to be moved, however, it was destroyed by fire. Who suffered the loss? Explain. [*Singletary, III v. P&A Investments, Inc.,* 712 S.E.2d 681 (N.C.App. 2011)] **(See page 404.)**

15–8 **Partial Performance and the Statute of Frauds.** After a series of e-mails, Jorge Bonilla, the sole proprietor of a printing company in Uruguay, agreed to buy a used printer from Crystal Graphics Equipment, Inc., in New York. Crystal Graphics, through its agent, told Bonilla that the printing press was fully operational, contained all of its parts, and was in excellent condition except for some damage to one of the printing towers. Bonilla paid $95,000. Crystal Graphics sent him a signed, stamped invoice reflecting this payment. The invoice was dated six days after Bonilla's conversation with the agent. When the printing press arrived, Bonilla discovered that it was missing parts and was damaged. Crystal Graphics sent replacement parts, but they did not work. Ultimately, Crystal Graphics was never able to make the printer operational. Bonilla sued, alleging breach of contract, breach of the implied covenant of good faith and fair dealing, breach of express warranty, and breach of implied warranty. Crystal Graphics claimed that the contract was not enforceable because it did not satisfy the Statute of Frauds. Can Crystal Graphics prevail on this basis? Why or why not? [*Bonilla v. Crystal Graphics Equipment, Inc.,* 2012 WL 360145 (S.D.Fla. 2012)] **(See page 396.)**

15–9 ↔️ **A Question of Ethics—Statute of Frauds.** Daniel Fox owned Fox & Lamberth Enterprises, Inc., a kitchen remodeling business. Fox leased a building from Carl Hussong. When Fox planned to close his business, Craftsmen Home Improvement, Inc., expressed an interest in buying his assets. Fox set a price of $50,000. Craftsmen's owners agreed and gave Fox a list of the desired items and a "Bill of Sale" that set the terms for payment. Craftsmen expected to negotiate a new lease with Hussong and modified the premises, including removal of some of the displays. When Hussong and Craftsmen could not agree on new terms, Craftsmen told Fox that the deal was off. [*Fox & Lamberth Enterprises, Inc. v. Craftsmen Home Improvement, Inc.,* __ N.E.2d __ (2 Dist. 2006)]

1. In Fox's suit for breach of contract, Craftsmen raised the Statute of Frauds as a defense. What are the requirements of the Statute of Frauds? Did the deal between Fox and Craftsmen meet these requirements? Did it fall under one of the exceptions? Explain. (**See pages 394–396.**)

2. Craftsmen also claimed that the "predominant factor" of its agreement with Fox was a lease for Hussong's building. What is the predominant-factor test? Does it apply here? In any event, is it fair to hold a party to a contract to buy a business's assets when the buyer is unable to negotiate a favorable lease of the premises on which the assets are located? Discuss. (**See pages 386–387.**)

Critical Thinking and Writing Assignments

15–10 **Case Analysis Question.** Go to Appendix I at the end of this text and examine the excerpt of Case No. 3, *Spray-Tek, Inc. v. Robbins Motor Transportation, Inc.* Review and then brief the case, making sure that your brief answers the following questions.

1. **Issue:** What contract provision was at the heart of the dispute between the parties to this case, and why?

2. **Rule of Law:** What rule of law did the court apply to interpret this provision?

3. **Applying the Rule of Law:** How did the court apply this rule to interpret the provision at the center of this case?

4. **Conclusion:** Did the court resolve the dispute between the parties with respect to determining who suffered the loss and how much that loss was? Explain.

15–11 **Business Law Critical Thinking Group Assignment.** Mountain Stream Trout Co. agreed to buy "market size" trout from trout grower Lake Farms, LLC. Their five-year contract did not define *market size*. At the time, in the trade, *market size* referred to fish of one-pound live weight. After three years, Mountain Stream began taking fewer, smaller deliveries of larger fish, claiming that *market size* varied according to whatever its customers demanded and that its customers now demanded larger fish. Lake Farms filed a suit for breach of contract.

1. The first group will decide whether parol (outside) evidence is admissible to explain the terms of this contract. Are there any exceptions that could apply?

2. A second group will determine the impact of course of dealing and usage of trade on the interpretation of contract terms.

3. A third group will discuss how parties to a commercial contract can avoid the possibility that a court will interpret the contract terms in accordance with trade usage.

Warranties and Product Liability

(Lisa/Shutterstock.com)

CHAPTER OUTLINE

- Warranties
- Lemon Laws
- Product Liability
- Strict Product Liability
- Defenses to Product Liability

LEARNING OBJECTIVES

The five learning objectives below are designed to help improve your understanding of the chapter. After reading this chapter, you should be able to answer the following questions:

1 What factors determine whether a seller's or lessor's statement constitutes an express warranty or is mere puffery?

2 What implied warranties arise under the UCC?

3 Can a manufacturer be held liable to any person who suffers an injury proximately caused by the manufacturer's negligently made product?

4 What are the elements of a cause of action in strict product liability?

5 What defenses to liability can be raised in a product liability lawsuit?

"I'll warrant him heart-whole."
—William Shakespeare, 1564–1616 (English dramatist and poet)

Warranty is an age-old concept. In sales and lease law, a warranty is an assurance by the seller or lessor of certain facts concerning the goods being sold or leased. In the chapter-opening quotation, a character in William Shakespeare's play *As You Like It* warranted his friend "heart-whole." Likewise, in commercial law, sellers and lessors warrant to those who purchase or lease their goods that the goods are as represented or will be as promised.

The Uniform Commercial Code (UCC) has numerous rules governing product warranties as they occur in sales and lease contracts. Those rules are the subject matter of the first part of this chapter. A natural addition to the discussion is *product liability:* Who is liable to consumers, users, and bystanders for physical harm and property damage caused by a particular good or its use? In today's social environment of consumerism, businesspersons need to be keenly aware of how the sale or lease of defective products can lead to substantial liability.

Product liability encompasses not only the contract theory of warranty but also the tort theories of negligence and strict liability (discussed in Chapter 4). Warranty law is also part of the broad body of consumer protection law that will be discussed in Chapter 33.

Warranties

Most goods are covered by some type of warranty designed to protect consumers. Article 2 (on sales) and Article 2A (on leases) of the UCC designate several types of warranties that can arise in a sales or lease contract, including warranties of title, express warranties, and implied warranties.

Warranties of Title

Under the UCC, three types of title warranties—*good title, no liens,* and *no infringements*—can automatically arise in sales and lease contracts.

Good Title
In most sales, sellers warrant that they have good and valid title to the goods sold and that transfer of the title is rightful [UCC 2–312(1)(a)]. If the buyer subsequently learns that the seller did not have good title to goods that were purchased, the buyer can sue the seller for breach of this warranty.

EXAMPLE 17.1   Alexis steals a diamond ring from Calvin and sells it to Emma, who does not know that the ring is stolen. If Calvin discovers that Emma has the ring, then he has the right to reclaim it from Emma. When Alexis sold Emma the ring, Alexis automatically warranted to Emma that the title conveyed was valid and that its transfer was rightful. Because a thief has no title to stolen goods, Alexis breached the warranty of title imposed by the UCC and became liable to Emma for appropriate damages. ● (There is no warranty of good title in lease contracts because title to the goods does not pass to the lessee, as discussed on page 399 of Chapter 15.)

No Liens
A second warranty of title shields buyers and lessees who are *unaware* of any encumbrances, or **liens** (claims, charges, or liabilities—see Chapter 21), against goods at the time the contract is made [UCC 2–312(1)(b), 2A–211(1)]. This warranty protects buyers who, for example, unknowingly purchase goods that are subject to a creditor's *security interest* (an interest in the goods that secures payment or performance—see Chapter 20). If a creditor legally repossesses the goods from a buyer *who had no actual knowledge of the security interest,* the buyer can recover from the seller for breach of warranty.

No Infringements
A third type of title warranty is a warranty against infringement of any patent, trademark, or copyright. When the seller or lessor is a merchant, he or she automatically warrants that the buyer or lessee takes the goods *free of infringements.* In other words, a merchant promises that the goods delivered are free from any copyright, trademark, or patent claims of a third person [UCC 2–312(3), 2A–211(2)].

Express Warranties

A seller or lessor can create an **express warranty** by making representations concerning the quality, condition, description, or performance potential of the goods. Under UCC 2–313 and 2A–210, express warranties arise when a seller or lessor indicates any of the following:

1. That the goods conform to any *affirmation* (declaration that something is true) or *promise* of fact that the seller or lessor makes to the buyer or lessee about the goods. Such affirmations or promises are usually made during the bargaining process. Statements such as "these drill bits will penetrate stainless steel—and without dulling" are express warranties.
2. That the goods conform to any *description* of them. For example, a label that reads "Crate contains one 150-horsepower diesel engine" or a contract that calls for the delivery of a "camel's hair coat" creates an express warranty.
3. That the goods conform to any *sample* or *model* of the goods shown to the buyer or lessee.

Lien An encumbrance on a property to satisfy a debt or protect a claim for payment of a debt.

Express Warranty A promise that is included in a contract concerning the quality, condition, description, or performance of the goods being sold or leased.

Is this logo an express warranty?

(Arcady/Shutterstock.com)

Basis of the Bargain   To create an express warranty, a seller or lessor does not have to use words such as *warrant* or *guarantee* [UCC 2–313(2), 2A–210(2)]. It is only necessary that a reasonable buyer or lessee would regard the representation of fact as part of the basis of the bargain [UCC 2–313(1), 2A–210(1)]. The UCC does not define the "basis of the bargain," however, and it is a question of fact in each case whether a representation was made at such a time and in such a way that it induced the buyer or lessee to enter into the contract.

LEARNING OBJECTIVE 1
What factors determine whether a seller's or lessor's statement constitutes an express warranty or is mere puffery?

Statements of Opinion and Value   Only statements of fact create express warranties. If the seller or lessor makes a statement about the supposed value or worth of the goods, or offers an opinion or recommendation about the goods, the seller or lessor is not creating an express warranty [UCC 2–313(2), 2A–210(2)].

   EXAMPLE 17.2   A car salesperson claims that "this is the best used car to come along in years. It has four new tires and a 250-horsepower engine just rebuilt this year." The seller has made several *affirmations of fact* that can create a warranty: the automobile has an engine, the engine has 250 horsepower and was rebuilt this year, and there are four new tires on the automobile. The seller's *opinion* that the vehicle is "the best used car to come along in years," however, is known as "puffery" and creates no warranty. (*Puffery* is an expression of opinion by a seller or lessor that is not made as a representation of fact.) •

   A statement about the value of the goods, such as "this is worth a fortune" or "anywhere else you'd pay $10,000 for it," usually does not create a warranty. If the seller or lessor is an expert and gives an opinion as an expert to a layperson, though, then a warranty may be created.

   It is not always easy to determine whether a statement constitutes an express warranty or puffery. Often, the reasonableness of the buyer's or lessee's reliance is the controlling criterion. For instance, a salesperson's statements that a ladder "will never break" and will "last a lifetime" are so clearly improbable that no reasonable buyer should rely on them. Courts also look at the context in which a statement is made to determine the reasonableness of the buyer's or lessee's reliance. For instance, a reasonable person is more likely to rely on a written statement made in an advertisement than on a statement made orally by a salesperson.

PREVENTING LEGAL DISPUTES

If you are in the business of selling or leasing goods, be careful about the words you use with customers, in writing and orally. If you do not intend to make an express warranty, do not make a promise or an affirmation of fact concerning the performance or quality of a product that you sell. Examine your firm's advertisements, brochures, and promotional materials, as well as any standard order forms and contracts, for statements that could be considered express warranties. To avoid unintended warranties, instruct all employees on how the promises they make to buyers during a sale can create warranties.

Implied Warranties

Implied Warranty   A warranty that arises by law because of the circumstances of a sale rather than by the seller's express promise.

An **implied warranty** is one that *the law derives* by implication or inference because of the circumstances of a sale, rather than by the seller's express promise. In an action based on breach of implied warranty, it is necessary to show that an implied warranty existed and that the breach of the warranty proximately caused[1] the damage sustained. We look here at some of the implied warranties that arise under the UCC.

Implied Warranty of Merchantability   A warranty that goods being sold or leased are reasonably fit for the general purpose for which they are sold or leased, are properly packaged and labeled, and are of proper quality.

Implied Warranty of Merchantability   Every sale or lease of goods made *by a merchant who deals in goods of the kind sold or leased* automatically gives rise to an **implied warranty of merchantability** [UCC 2–314, 2A–212].   **EXAMPLE 17.3**   A

---

1. Proximate, or legal, cause exists when the connection between an act and an injury is strong enough to justify imposing liability—see Chapter 4 on page 114.

merchant who is in the business of selling ski equipment makes an implied warranty of merchantability every time she sells a pair of skis. A neighbor selling his skis at a garage sale does not (because he is not in the business of selling goods of this type). •

Merchantable Goods   Goods that are *merchantable* are "reasonably fit for the ordinary purposes for which such goods are used." They must be of at least average, fair, or medium-grade quality. The quality must be comparable to a level that will pass without objection in the trade or market for goods of the same description. To be merchantable, the goods must also be adequately packaged and labeled, and they must conform to the promises or affirmations of fact made on the container or label, if any.

The warranty of merchantability may be breached even though the merchant did not know or could not have discovered that a product was defective (not merchantable). Of course, merchants are not absolute insurers against all accidents occurring in connection with their goods. For instance, a bar of soap is not unmerchantable merely because stepping on it could cause a user to slip and fall.

CASE EXAMPLE 17.4   Darrell Shoop bought a Dodge Dakota truck that had been manufactured by DaimlerChrysler Corporation. Almost immediately, he had problems with the truck. During the first eighteen months, the truck's engine, suspension, steering, transmission, and other components required repairs twelve times, including at least five times for the same defect, which remained uncorrected. Shoop eventually traded in the truck and filed a lawsuit against DaimlerChrysler for breach of the implied warranty of merchantability. The court held that Shoop could maintain an action against DaimlerChrysler and use the fact that the truck had required a significant number of repairs as evidence that it was unmerchantable.[2] •

Merchantable Food   The UCC recognizes the serving of food or drink to be consumed on or off the premises as a sale of goods subject to the implied warranty of merchantability [UCC 2–314(1)]. "Merchantable" food means food that is fit to eat.

Courts generally determine whether food is fit to eat on the basis of consumer expectations. The courts assume that consumers should reasonably expect on occasion to find bones in fish fillets, cherry pits in cherry pie, or a nutshell in a package of shelled nuts, for example—because such substances are natural incidents of the food. In contrast, consumers would not reasonably expect to find moth larvae in a can of peas or a piece of glass in a soft drink—because these substances are not natural to the food product.[3]

In the following *Classic Case,* the court had to determine whether a diner should reasonably expect to find a fish bone in fish chowder.

LEARNING OBJECTIVE 2
What implied warranties arise under the UCC?

---

2. *Shoop v. DaimlerChrysler Corp.,* 371 Ill.App.3d 1058, 864 N.E.2d 785 (2007).
3. See, for example, *Ruvolo v. Homovich,* 149 Ohio App.3d 701, 778 N.E.2d 661 (2002).

✳ Classic Case 17.1

Webster v. Blue Ship Tea Room, Inc.

Supreme Judicial Court of Massachusetts,
347 Mass. 421, 198 N.E.2d 309 (1964).

Who is liable for fish bones in seafood chowder?

HISTORICAL AND CULTURAL SETTING   *Chowder, a soup or stew made with fresh fish, possibly originated in the fishing villages of Brittany (a French province to the west of Paris) and was probably carried to Canada and New England by Breton immigrants. In the nineteenth century* *and earlier, recipes for chowder did not call for the removal of the fish bones. Chowder recipes in the first half of the twentieth century were the same as in previous centuries, sometimes*

Classic Case 17.1—Continued

specifying that the fish head, tail, and backbone were to be broken in pieces and boiled, with the "liquor thus produced . . . added to the balance of the chowder."[a] By the middle of the twentieth century, there was a considerable body of case law concerning implied warranties and foreign and natural substances in food. It was perhaps inevitable that sooner or later, a consumer injured by a fish bone in chowder would challenge the merchantability of chowder containing fish bones.

FACTS Blue Ship Tea Room, Inc., was located in Boston in an old building overlooking the ocean. Priscilla Webster, who had been born and raised in New England, went to the restaurant and ordered fish chowder. The chowder was milky in color. After three or four spoonfuls, she felt something lodged in her throat. As a result, she underwent two esophagoscopies; in the second esophagoscopy, a fish bone was found and removed. Webster filed a lawsuit against the restaurant in a Massachusetts state court for breach of the implied warranty of merchantability. The jury rendered a verdict for Webster, and the restaurant appealed to the state's highest court.

ISSUE Does serving fish chowder that contains a bone constitute a breach of an implied warranty of merchantability by the restaurant?

DECISION No. The Supreme Judicial Court of Massachusetts held that Webster could not recover against Blue Ship Tea Room because no breach of warranty had occurred.

REASON The court, citing UCC Section 2–314, stated that "a warranty that goods shall be merchantable is implied in a contract for their sale if the seller is a merchant with respect to goods of that kind. Under this section the serving for value of food or drink to be consumed either on the premises or elsewhere is a sale. . . . Goods to be merchantable must at least be . . . fit for the ordinary purposes for which such goods are used." The question here was whether a fish bone made the chowder unfit for eating. In the judge's opinion, "the joys of life in New England include the ready availability of fresh fish chowder. We should be prepared to cope with the hazards of fish bones, the occasional presence of which in chowders is, it seems to us, to be anticipated, and which, in the light of a hallowed tradition, do not impair their fitness or merchantability."

IMPACT OF THIS CASE ON TODAY'S LAW *This classic case, phrased in memorable language, was an early application of the UCC's implied warranty of merchantability to food products. The case established the rule that consumers should expect to occasionally find elements of food products that are natural to the product (such as fish bones in fish chowder). Courts today still apply this rule.*

a. Fannie Farmer, *The Boston Cooking School Cook Book* (Boston: Little, Brown, 1937), p. 166.

Implied Warranty of Fitness for a Particular Purpose A warranty that goods sold or leased are fit for the particular purpose for which the buyer or lessee will use the goods.

Implied Warranty of Fitness for a Particular Purpose

The **implied warranty of fitness for a particular purpose** arises when any seller or lessor (merchant or nonmerchant) knows the particular purpose for which a buyer or lessee will use the goods *and* knows that the buyer or lessee is relying on the skill and judgment of the seller or lessor to select suitable goods [UCC 2–315, 2A–213].

A "particular purpose" of the buyer or lessee differs from the "ordinary purpose for which goods are used" (merchantability). Goods can be merchantable but unfit for a particular purpose. **EXAMPLE 17.5** Cheryl needs a gallon of paint to match the color of her living room walls—a light shade between coral and peach. She takes a sample to the local hardware store and requests a gallon of paint of that color. Instead, she is given a gallon of bright blue paint. Here, the salesperson has not breached any warranty of implied merchantability—the bright blue paint is of high quality and suitable for interior walls—but he has breached an implied warranty of fitness for a particular purpose. •

A seller or lessor is not required to have actual knowledge of the buyer's or lessee's particular purpose, so long as the seller or lessor "has reason to know" the purpose. For an implied warranty to be created, however, the buyer or lessee must have *relied* on the skill or judgment of the seller or lessor in selecting or furnishing suitable goods.

Warranties Implied from Prior Dealings or Trade Custom

Implied warranties can also arise (or be excluded or modified) as a result of course of dealing or usage of trade [UCC 2–314(3), 2A–212(3)]. In the absence of evidence to the contrary, when both parties to a sales or lease contract have knowledge of a well-recognized trade custom, the courts will infer that both parties intended for that trade custom to apply to their contract.

EXAMPLE 17.6   Suppose that it is an industry-wide custom to lubricate new cars before they are delivered to buyers. Latoya buys a new car from Bender Chevrolet. After the purchase, Latoya discovers that Bender failed to lubricate the car before delivering it to her. In this situation, Latoya can hold the dealer liable for damages resulting from the breach of an implied warranty. (This, of course, would also be negligence on the part of the dealer.) •

Overlapping Warranties

Sometimes, two or more warranties are made in a single transaction. An implied warranty of merchantability, an implied warranty of fitness for a particular purpose, or both can exist in addition to an express warranty. For instance, when a sales contract for a new car states that "this car engine is warranted to be free from defects for 36,000 miles or thirty-six months, whichever occurs first," the seller has made an express warranty against all defects and an implied warranty that the car will be fit for normal use.

The rule under the UCC is that express and implied warranties are construed as *cumulative* if they are consistent with one another [UCC 2–317, 2A–215]. In other words, courts interpret two or more warranties as being in agreement with each other unless this construction is unreasonable. If it is unreasonable, then a court will hold that the warranties are inconsistent and apply the following rules to interpret which warranty is most important:

1. *Express* warranties displace inconsistent *implied* warranties, except for implied warranties of fitness for a particular purpose.
2. Samples take precedence over inconsistent general descriptions.
3. Exact or technical specifications displace inconsistent samples or general descriptions.

Warranty Disclaimers

The UCC generally permits warranties to be disclaimed or limited by specific and unambiguous language, provided that the buyer or lessee is protected from surprise. The manner in which a seller or lessor can disclaim warranties varies depending on the type of warranty.

Express Warranties   A seller or lessor can disclaim all oral express warranties by including in the contract a written (or an electronically recorded) disclaimer that is expressed in clear language, is conspicuous, and calls the buyer's or lessee's attention to the disclaimer [UCC 2–316(1), 2A–214(1)]. This allows the seller or lessor to avoid false allegations that oral warranties were made, and it ensures that only representations made by properly authorized individuals are included in the bargain.

Note, however, that a buyer or lessee must be made aware of any warranty disclaimers or modifications *at the time the contract is formed*. In other words, any oral or written warranties—or disclaimers—made during the bargaining process as part of a contract's formation cannot be modified at a later time by the seller or lessor.

Implied Warranties   Generally, unless circumstances indicate otherwise, the implied warranties of merchantability and fitness are disclaimed by the expressions "as is" or "with all faults," or other similar phrases. The phrase must be one that, in common understanding for both parties, calls the buyer's or lessee's attention to the fact that there are no implied warranties [UCC 2–316(3)(a), 2A–214(3)(a)]. (Note, however, that some states have laws that forbid "as is" sales. Other states do not allow disclaimers of warranties of merchantability for consumer goods.)

CASE EXAMPLE 17.7   Mandy Morningstar advertised a "lovely, eleven-year-old mare" with extensive jumping ability for sale. After examining the mare twice, Sue Hallett contracted to buy the horse. The contract she signed described the horse as an eleven-year-old mare, but indicated that the horse was being sold "as is." Shortly after the purchase, a veterinarian determined that the horse was actually sixteen years old and in no condition for jumping. Hallett stopped payment and tried to return the horse and cancel the contract. Morningstar sued for breach of contract. The court held that the statement in the contract describing the horse as eleven years old constituted an express warranty, which Morningstar had breached. Although the "as is" clause effectively disclaimed any implied warranties (of merchantability and fitness for a particular purpose, such as jumping), the court ruled that it did not disclaim the express warranty concerning the horse's age.[4] ●

Disclaimer of the Implied Warranty of Merchantability To specifically disclaim an implied warranty of merchantability, a seller or lessor must mention the word *merchantability* [UCC 2–316(2), 2A–214(2)]. The disclaimer need not be written, but if it is, the writing (or record) must be conspicuous [UCC 2–316(2), 2A–214(4)].

Under the UCC, a term or clause is conspicuous when it is written or displayed in such a way that a reasonable person would notice it. Words are conspicuous when they are in capital letters, in a larger font size, or in a different color than the surrounding text.

Disclaimer of the Implied Warranty of Fitness To specifically disclaim an implied warranty of fitness for a particular purpose, the disclaimer *must* be in a writing (or record) and must be conspicuous. The word *fitness* does not have to be mentioned. It is sufficient if, for example, the disclaimer states, "THERE ARE NO WARRANTIES THAT EXTEND BEYOND THE DESCRIPTION ON THE FACE HEREOF."

◄ KNOW THIS ◄

Courts generally view warranty disclaimers unfavorably, especially when consumers are involved.

Buyer's or Lessee's Examination or Refusal to Inspect

If a buyer or lessee actually examines the goods (or a sample or model) as fully as desired before entering into a contract, or if the buyer or lessee refuses to examine the goods on the seller's or lessor's request, *there is no implied warranty with respect to defects that a reasonable examination would reveal or defects that are actually found* [UCC 2–316(3)(b), 2A–214(2)(b)].

EXAMPLE 17.8 Azumi buys a lamp at Gershwin's Store. No express warranties are made. Gershwin asks Azumi to inspect the lamp before buying it, but she refuses. Had Azumi inspected the lamp, she would have noticed that the base was obviously cracked and the electrical cord was loose. If the lamp later cracks or starts a fire in Azumi's home and she is injured, she normally will not be able to hold Gershwin's liable for breach of the warranty of merchantability. Because Azumi refused to examine the lamp when asked by Gershwin, Azumi will be deemed to have assumed the risk that it was defective. ●

Warranty Disclaimers and Unconscionability

The UCC sections dealing with warranty disclaimers do not refer specifically to unconscionability as a factor. Ultimately, however, the courts will test warranty disclaimers with reference to the UCC's unconscionability standards [UCC 2–302, 2A–108]. Such factors as lack of bargaining position, take-it-or-leave-it choices, and a buyer's or lessee's failure to understand or know of a warranty disclaimer will be relevant to the issue of unconscionability.

Magnuson-Moss Warranty Act

The Magnuson-Moss Warranty Act of 1975[5] was designed to prevent deception in warranties by making them easier to understand. The act modifies UCC warranty rules to some extent when *consumer* transactions are involved. The UCC, however, remains the primary codification of warranty rules for commercial transactions.

---

4. *Morningstar v. Hallett*, 858 A.2d 125 (Pa.Super.Ct. 2004).
5. 15 U.S.C. Sections 2301–2312.

Under the Magnuson-Moss Act, a seller is not required to give an express written warranty for consumer goods sold. If a seller chooses to make an express written warranty, however, and the goods are priced at more than $25, the warranty must be labeled as "full" or "limited."

A *full warranty* requires free repair or replacement of any defective part. If the product cannot be repaired within a reasonable time, the consumer has the choice of a refund or a replacement without charge. A full warranty can be for an unlimited or limited time period, such as a "full twelve-month warranty." With a *limited warranty,* the buyer's recourse is limited in some fashion, such as to replacement of the item. The fact that only a limited warranty is being given must be conspicuously stated.

The Magnuson-Moss Act further requires the warrantor to make certain disclosures fully and conspicuously in a single document in "readily understood language." The document must state the names and addresses of all warrantors, indicate specifically what is warranted, and explain the procedures for enforcing the warranty. It must also clarify that the buyer has legal rights and explain any limitations on warranty relief.

► KNOW THIS ◄

When a buyer or lessee is a consumer, a limitation on consequential damages for personal injuries resulting from nonconforming goods is *prima facie* unconscionable.

Lemon Laws

Some purchasers of defective automobiles—called "lemons"—found that the remedies provided by the UCC were inadequate due to limitations imposed by the seller. In response to the frustrations of these buyers, all of the states have enacted *lemon laws*.

Coverage of Lemon Laws

Basically, state lemon laws provide remedies to consumers who buy automobiles that repeatedly fail to meet standards of quality and performance because they are "lemons." Although lemon laws vary by state, typically they apply to automobiles under warranty that are defective in a way that significantly affects the vehicle's value or use. Lemon laws do not necessarily cover used-car purchases (unless the car is covered by a manufacturer's extended warranty) or vehicles that are leased.[6]

Generally, the seller or manufacturer is given a number of opportunities to remedy the defect (usually four). If the seller fails to cure the problem despite a reasonable number of attempts (as specified by state law), the buyer is entitled to a new car, replacement of defective parts, or return of all consideration paid. Buyers who prevail in a lemon-law dispute may also be entitled to reimbursement of their attorneys' fees.

Arbitration Is Typical Procedure

When do lemon laws apply?

(Monkey Business Images/Shutterstock)

In most states, lemon laws require an aggrieved new-car owner to give the dealer or manufacturer an opportunity to solve the problem. If the problem persists, the owner must then submit complaints to the arbitration program specified in the manufacturer's warranty before taking the case to court. Decisions by arbitration panels are binding on the manufacturer—that is, cannot be appealed by the manufacturer to the courts—but usually are not binding on the purchaser.

Most major automobile companies operate their own arbitration panels, but some use independent arbitration services, such as those provided by the Better Business Bureau. Because industry-sponsored arbitration boards have been criticized for not being truly impartial,

---

6. Note that in some states, such as California, these laws may extend beyond automobile purchases and apply to other consumer goods.

some states have established mandatory, state government-sponsored arbitration programs for lemon-law disputes.

Product Liability

Product Liability The legal liability of manufacturers, sellers, and lessors of goods for injuries or damage caused by the goods to consumers, users, or bystanders.

Those who make, sell, or lease goods can be held liable for physical harm or property damage caused by those goods to a consumer, user, or bystander. This is called **product liability.** Product liability claims may be based on the warranty theories just discussed, as well as on the theories of negligence, misrepresentation, and strict liability. We look here at product liability based on negligence and misrepresentation.

Negligence

Chapter 4 defined *negligence* as the failure to exercise the degree of care that a reasonable, prudent person would have exercised under the circumstances. If a manufacturer fails to exercise "due care" to make a product safe, a person who is injured by the product may sue the manufacturer for negligence.

Due Care Must Be Exercised   The manufacturer must exercise due care in designing the product, selecting the materials, using the appropriate production process, assembling the product, and placing adequate warnings on the label informing the user of dangers of which an ordinary person might not be aware. The duty of care also extends to the inspection and testing of any purchased products that are used in the final product sold by the manufacturer.

LEARNING OBJECTIVE 3
Can a manufacturer be held liable to any person who suffers an injury proximately caused by the manufacturer's negligently made product?

Privity of Contract Not Required   A product liability action based on negligence does not require *privity of contract* between the injured plaintiff and the defendant manufacturer. As discussed in Chapter 13, *privity of contract* refers to the relationship that exists between the promisor and the promisee of a contract. Privity is the reason that normally only the parties to a contract can enforce that contract.

In the context of product liability law, privity is not required. A person who is injured by a defective product can bring a negligence suit against the product's manufacturer or seller, even though that person is not the one who actually purchased the product—and thus is not in privity. A manufacturer is liable for its failure to exercise due care to *any person* who sustains an injury proximately caused by a negligently made (defective) product.

Relative to the long history of the common law, this exception to the privity requirement is a fairly recent development, dating to the early part of the twentieth century. A leading case in this respect is *MacPherson v. Buick Motor Co.,* which is presented as this chapter's *Landmark in the Law* feature on the following page.

Misrepresentation

When a user or consumer is injured as a result of a manufacturer's or seller's fraudulent misrepresentation, the basis of liability may be the tort of fraud. The intentional mislabeling of packaged cosmetics, for instance, or the intentional concealment of a product's defects constitutes fraudulent misrepresentation.

The misrepresentation must be of a material fact, and the seller must have intended to induce the buyer's reliance on the misrepresentation. Misrepresentation on a label or advertisement is enough to show an intent to induce reliance. Of course, to bring a lawsuit on this ground, the buyer must have relied on the misrepresentation.

LANDMARK IN THE LAW

MacPherson v. Buick Motor Co. (1916)

In the landmark case of *MacPherson v. Buick Motor Co.*,[a] the New York Court of Appeals—New York's highest court—considered the liability of a manufacturer that failed to exercise reasonable care in manufacturing a finished product.

Case Background   Donald MacPherson suffered injuries while riding in a Buick automobile that suddenly collapsed because one of the wheels was made of defective wood. The spokes crumbled into fragments, throwing MacPherson out of the vehicle and injuring him.

MacPherson had purchased the car from a Buick dealer, but he brought a lawsuit against the manufacturer, Buick Motor Company. Buick itself had not made the wheel but had bought it from another manufacturer. There was evidence, though, that the defects could have been discovered by a reasonable inspection by Buick and that no such inspection had taken place. MacPherson charged Buick with negligence for putting a human life in imminent danger.

The Issue before the Court and the Court's Ruling   The primary issue was whether Buick owed a duty of care to anyone except the immediate purchaser of the car—that is, the Buick

a. 217 N.Y. 382, 111 N.E. 1050 (1916).

dealer. In deciding the issue, Justice Benjamin Cardozo stated that "if the nature of a thing is such that it is reasonably certain to place life and limb in peril when negligently made, it is then a thing of danger. . . . If to the element of danger there is added knowledge that the thing will be used by persons other than the purchaser, and used without new tests, then, irrespective of contract, the manufacturer of this thing of danger is under a duty to make it carefully."

The court concluded that "beyond all question, the nature of an automobile gives warning of probable danger if its construction is defective. This automobile was designed to go 50 miles an hour. Unless its wheels were sound and strong, injury was almost certain." Although Buick itself had not manufactured the wheel, the court held that Buick had a duty to inspect the wheels and that Buick "was responsible for the finished product." Therefore, Buick was liable to MacPherson for the injuries he sustained when he was thrown from the car.

Application to Today's World   *This landmark decision was a significant step in creating the legal environment of the modern world. As often happens, technological developments necessitated changes in the law. Today, automobile manufacturers are commonly held liable when their negligence causes automobile users to be injured.*

Strict Product Liability

Under the doctrine of strict liability (discussed in Chapter 4), people may be liable for the results of their acts regardless of their intentions or their exercise of reasonable care. In addition, liability does not depend on privity of contract. The injured party does not have to be the buyer or a *third party beneficiary* (see page 335 in Chapter 13), as required under contract warranty theory. In the 1960s, courts applied the doctrine of strict liability in several landmark cases involving manufactured goods, and this doctrine has since become a common method of holding manufacturers liable.

Strict Product Liability and Public Policy

The law imposes strict product liability as a matter of public policy. This public policy rests on the threefold assumption that:

1. Consumers should be protected against unsafe products.
2. Manufacturers and distributors should not escape liability for faulty products simply because they are not in privity of contract with the ultimate user of those products.
3. Manufacturers, sellers, and lessors of products are generally in a better position than consumers to bear the costs associated with injuries caused by their products—costs that they can ultimately pass on to all consumers in the form of higher prices.

California was the first state to impose strict product liability in tort on manufacturers. In a landmark decision, *Greenman v. Yuba Power Products, Inc.,*[7] the California Supreme Court set out the reason for applying tort law rather than contract law in cases involving consumers injured by defective products. According to the court, the "purpose of such liability is to [e]nsure that the costs of injuries resulting from defective products are borne by the manufacturers . . . rather than by the injured persons who are powerless to protect themselves."

Public policy may be expressed in a statute or in the common law. Sometimes, public policy may be revealed in a court's interpretation of a statute, as in the following *Spotlight Case.*

---

7. *59 Cal.2d 57, 377 P.2d 897, 27 Cal.Rptr. 697 (1963).*

Spotlight on Injuries from Vaccinations

Case 17.2
Bruesewitz v. Wyeth, LLC
Supreme Court of the United States, __ U.S. __, 131 S.Ct. 1068, 179 L.Ed.2d 1 (2011).
www.supremecourt.gov [a]

What happens when a vaccine causes adverse side effects?

FACTS When Hannah Bruesewitz was six months old, her pediatrician administered a dose of the diphtheria, tetanus, and pertussis (DTP) vaccine according to the Centers for Disease Control and Prevention's recommended childhood immunization schedule. Within twenty-four hours, Hannah began to experience seizures. She suffered more than one hundred seizures during the next month. Her doctors diagnosed her with "residual seizure disorder" and "developmental delay." Hannah's parents, Russell and Robalee Bruesewitz, filed a claim for relief in the U.S. Court of Federal Claims under the National Childhood Vaccine Injury Act (NCVIA) of 1986. The NCVIA set up a no-fault compensation program for persons injured by vaccines. The claim was denied. The Bruesewitzes then filed a suit in a Pennsylvania state court against Wyeth, LLC, the maker of the vaccine, alleging strict product liability. The suit was moved to a federal district court. The court held that the claim was preempted by the NCVIA, which includes provisions protecting manufacturers from liability for "a vaccine's unavoidable, adverse side effects." A federal appellate court affirmed the district court's judgment. The Bruesewitzes appealed to the United States Supreme Court.

ISSUE Was the Bruesewitzes' strict product liability claim against Wyeth for the injuries that their child suffered from vaccination preempted by the National Childhood Vaccine Injury Act?

DECISION Yes. The United States Supreme Court affirmed the lower court's judgment. The NCVIA preempted the Bruesewitzes' claim against Wyeth for injury to their daughter caused by the DTP vaccine's side effects.

REASON The Court reasoned that Congress enacted the NCVIA as a matter of public policy to stabilize the vaccine market and facilitate compensation. In the no-fault compensation program set up by the NCVIA, a person with a vaccine-related claim files a petition with the U.S. Court of Federal Claims. The court may award compensation for legal, medical, rehabilitation, counseling, special education, and vocational training expenses, as well as for diminished earning capacity, pain and suffering, and death. The awards are funded by a tax on the vaccine. In exchange for the "informal, efficient" compensation program, vaccine manufacturers that comply with the regulatory requirements are "immunized" from liability. The statute thus strikes a balance between paying victims harmed by vaccines and protecting the vaccine industry from collapsing under the costs of tort liability.

CRITICAL THINKING—Political Consideration *If the public wants to change the policy outlined in this case, which branch of the government—and at what level—should be lobbied to make the change? Explain.*

---

a. In the "Supreme Court Documents" column, in the "Opinions" pull-down menu, select "Bound Volumes." On the next page, in the "For Search Term:" box, type "Bruesewitz" and click on "Search." In the result, click on the name of the case to access the opinion. The United States Supreme Court maintains this Web site.

Requirements for Strict Liability

After the *Restatement (Second) of Torts* was issued in 1964, Section 402A became a widely accepted statement of how the doctrine of strict liability should be applied to sellers of goods (including manufacturers, processors, assemblers, packagers, bottlers, wholesalers, distributors, retailers, and lessors).

The bases for an action in strict liability that are set forth in Section 402A of the *Restatement* can be summarized as the following six requirements. Depending on the jurisdiction, if these requirements are met, a manufacturer's liability to an injured party can be almost unlimited.

1. The product must have been in a *defective condition* when the defendant sold it.
2. The defendant must normally be engaged in the *business of selling* (or otherwise distributing) that product.
3. The product must be *unreasonably dangerous* to the user or consumer because of its defective condition (in most states).
4. The plaintiff must incur *physical harm* to self or property by use or consumption of the product.
5. The defective condition must be the *proximate cause* of the injury or damage.
6. The *goods must not have been substantially changed* from the time the product was sold to the time the injury was sustained.

LEARNING OBJECTIVE 4
What are the elements of a cause of action in strict product liability?

(Michael Temchine/AFP/Getty Images)

Under what circumstances can a consumer prove that tires were sold in a defective condition?

Unreasonably Dangerous Product
A product that is so defective that it is dangerous beyond the expectation of an ordinary consumer or a product for which a less dangerous alternative was feasible but the manufacturer failed to produce it.

Proving a Defective Condition   Under these requirements, in any action against a manufacturer, seller, or lessor, the plaintiff does not have to show why or how the product became defective. The plaintiff does, however, have to prove that the product was defective at the time it left the seller or lessor and that this defective condition made it "unreasonably dangerous" to the user or consumer. (See this chapter's *Beyond Our Borders* feature on the facing page for a discussion of how foreign suppliers were held liable for defective goods sold in the United States.)

Unless evidence can be presented that will support the conclusion that the product was defective when it was sold or leased, the plaintiff normally will not succeed. If the product was delivered in a safe condition and subsequent mishandling made it harmful to the user, the seller or lessor usually is not strictly liable.

Unreasonably Dangerous Products   The *Restatement* recognizes that many products cannot possibly be made entirely safe for all uses. Thus, sellers or lessors are held liable only for products that are *unreasonably* dangerous. A court may consider a product so defective as to be an **unreasonably dangerous product** in either of the following situations.

1. The product is dangerous beyond the expectation of the ordinary consumer.
2. A less dangerous alternative was economically feasible for the manufacturer, but the manufacturer failed to produce it.

As will be discussed next, a product may be unreasonably dangerous due to a flaw in the manufacturing process or in the design, or due to an inadequate warning.

Product Defects—*Restatement (Third) of Torts*

The *Restatement (Third) of Torts: Products Liability* defines the three types of product defects that have traditionally been recognized in product liability law—manufacturing defects, design defects, and inadequate warnings.

Manufacturing Defects   According to Section 2(a) of the *Restatement (Third) of Torts: Products Liability,* a product "contains a manufacturing defect when the product

BEYOND OUR BORDERS

Imposing Product Liability as Far Away as China

Chinese drywall started being used in the construction of houses in the United States in 2003. By 2007, thousands of homes had been constructed with this product in Alabama, Florida, Louisiana, Mississippi, and a few other states. There was a problem, though—use of the Chinese drywall caused blackening and pitting of electrical wires. Homeowners began to notice an odor similar to rotten eggs. Air-conditioning units started failing, as did ceiling fans, alarm systems, refrigerators, and other appliances.

Numerous lawsuits were filed against the Chinese drywall manufacturers, which initially fought the claims. When the number of lawsuits ran into the thousands, however, the Chinese companies decided to settle.

The estimated value of the settlement is between $800 million and $1 billion.

It includes an uncapped fund to pay for repairs for about 4,500 homes and a separate fund capped at $30 million that will be used to pay for health problems stemming from the defective Chinese drywall.

Critical Thinking
Could U.S. companies that sold Chinese drywall to consumers also be held liable for damages? Why or why not?

---

departs from its intended design even though all possible care was exercised in the preparation and marketing of the product." Basically, a manufacturing defect is a departure from a product unit's design specifications that results in products that are physically flawed, damaged, or incorrectly assembled. A glass bottle that is made too thin, causing it to explode in a consumer's face, is an example of a product with a manufacturing defect.

Usually, such defects occur when a manufacturer fails to assemble, test, or adequately check the quality of a product. Liability is imposed on the manufacturer (and on the wholesaler and retailer) regardless of whether the manufacturer's quality control efforts were "reasonable." The idea behind holding defendants strictly liable for manufacturing defects is to encourage greater investment in product safety and stringent quality control standards. (For more information on how effective quality control procedures can help businesses reduce their potential legal liability for breached warranties and defective products, see the *Linking Business Law to Corporate Management* feature on page 457.)

CASE EXAMPLE 17.9   Kevin Schmude purchased an eight-foot stepladder and used it to install radio-frequency shielding in a hospital room. While Schmude was standing on the ladder, it collapsed, and he was seriously injured. He filed a lawsuit against the ladder's maker, Tricam Industries, Inc., based on a manufacturing defect. Experts testified that when the ladder was assembled, the preexisting holes in the top cap did not properly line up with the holes in the rear right rail and backing plate. As a result of the misalignment, the rivet at the rear legs of the ladder was more likely to fail. A jury concluded that this manufacturing defect made the ladder unreasonably dangerous and awarded Schmude more than $677,000 in damages.[8]

Design Defects   Unlike a product with a manufacturing defect, a product with a design defect is made in conformity with the manufacturer's design specifications, but it nevertheless results in injury to the user because the design itself is flawed. The product's design creates an unreasonable risk to the user. A product "is defective in design when the foreseeable risks of harm posed by the product could have been reduced or avoided by the adoption of a reasonable alternative design by the seller or other distributor, or a predecessor in the commercial chain of distribution, and the omission of the alternative design renders the product not reasonably safe."[9]

---

8. *Schmude v. Tricam Industries, Inc.*, 550 F.Supp.2d 846 (E.D.Wis. 2008).
9. *Restatement (Third) of Torts: Products Liability*, Section 2(b).

If this ladder collapses and the worker is injured, who could be held liable?

Test for Design Defects   To successfully assert a design defect, a plaintiff has to show that a reasonable alternative design was available and that the defendant's failure to adopt the alternative design rendered the product unreasonably dangerous. In other words, a manufacturer or other defendant is liable only when the harm was reasonably preventable.   **CASE EXAMPLE 17.10**   After Gillespie cut off several of his fingers while operating a table saw, he filed a lawsuit against the maker of the saw. Gillespie alleged that the blade guards on the saw were defectively designed. At trial, however, an expert testified that the alternative design for blade guards used for table saws could not have been used for the particular cut that Gillespie was performing at the time he was injured. The court found that Gillespie's claim about defective blade guards must fail because there was no proof that the "better" design of guard would have prevented his injury.[10] ●

Factors to Be Considered   According to the Official Comments accompanying the *Restatement (Third) of Torts,* a court can consider a broad range of factors in deciding claims of design defects. These factors include the magnitude and probability of the foreseeable risks, as well as the relative advantages and disadvantages of the product as designed and as it alternatively could have been designed. Basically, most courts engage in a risk-utility analysis, determining whether the risk of harm from the product as designed outweighs its utility to the user and to the public   **CASE EXAMPLE 17.11**   Jodie Bullock smoked cigarettes manufactured by Philip Morris for forty-five years. When she was diagnosed with lung cancer, Bullock brought a product liability suit against Philip Morris. She presented evidence that by the late 1950s, scientists had proved that smoking caused lung cancer. Nonetheless, Philip Morris had issued full-page announcements stating that there was no proof that smoking caused cancer and that "numerous scientists" questioned "the validity of the statistics." At trial, the judge instructed the jury to consider the gravity of the danger posed by the design, as well as the likelihood that the danger would cause injury.

The jury found that there was a defect in the design of the cigarettes and that they had been negligently designed. It awarded Bullock $850,000 in compensatory damages and $28 million in punitive damages. Philip Morris appealed, claiming that no evidence had been offered to show that there was a safer design for cigarettes. The reviewing court affirmed the jury's verdict but remanded the case for a reconsideration of the proper amount of punitive damages.[11] ●

Inadequate Warnings
A product may also be deemed defective because of inadequate instructions or warnings. A product will be considered defective "when the foreseeable risks of harm posed by the product could have been reduced or avoided by the provision of reasonable instructions or warnings by the seller or other distributor, or a predecessor in the commercial chain of distribution, and the omission of the instructions or warnings renders the product not reasonably safe."[12] Generally, a seller must also warn consumers of the harm that can result from the *foreseeable misuse* of its product.

Content of Warnings   Important factors for a court to consider include the risks of a product, the "content and comprehensibility" and "intensity of expression" of warnings and instructions, and the "characteristics of expected user groups."[13] Courts apply a "reasonableness" test to determine if the warnings adequately alert consumers to the

10. *Gillespie v. Sears, Roebuck & Co.,* 386 F.3d 21 (1st Cir. 2004).
11. *Bullock v. Philip Morris USA, Inc.,* 159 Cal.App.4th 655, 71 Cal.Rptr.3d 775 (2008). The California Court of Appeal subsequently upheld a punitive damages award of $13.8 million. See *Bullock v. Philip Morris USA, Inc.,* 198 Cal.App.4th 543, 131 Cal.Rptr.3d 382 (2011).
12. *Restatement (Third) of Torts: Products Liability,* Section 2(c).
13. *Restatement (Third) of Torts: Products Liability,* Section 2, Comment h.

product's risks. For example, children will likely respond more readily to bright, bold, simple warning labels, while educated adults might need more detailed information.

In the following case, a patient filed a product liability suit alleging that a product had a design defect and that the manufacturer had provided inadequate warnings. The court had to decide whether the plaintiff could pursue either theory of recovery.

Case 17.3

Johnson v. Medtronic, Inc.

Missouri Court of Appeals, 365 S.W.3d 226 (2012). www.courts.mo.gov[a]

(Munshi Ahmed/Bloomberg via Getty Images)

Medtronic manufactures medical devices, including defibrillators.

FACTS In 2005, Jeffrey Johnson was taken to the emergency room for an episode of atrial fibrillation, a heart rhythm disorder. Dr. David Hahn used a defibrillator manufactured by Medtronic, Inc., to deliver electric shocks to Johnson's heart. The defibrillator had synchronous and asynchronous modes, and it reverted to the asynchronous mode after each use. Hahn intended to deliver synchronized shocks, which required him to select the synchronous mode for each shock. Hahn did not read the device's instructions, which Medtronic had provided in both a manual and on the device itself. As a result, he delivered a synchronized shock, followed by twelve asynchronous shocks that endangered Johnson's life. Johnson and his wife filed a product liability suit against Medtronic asserting that Medtronic had provided inadequate warnings about the defibrillator and that the device had a design defect. The trial court found for Medtronic under both product liability theories, and the Johnsons appealed.

ISSUE Could the Johnsons pursue a product liability claim alleging either that Medtronic's warnings were inadequate or that the device had a design defect?

DECISION No and yes, respectively. The Missouri appellate court held that the Johnsons could not pursue a claim based on the inadequacy of Medtronic's warnings, but that they could pursue a claim alleging a design defect. Thus, the trial court's

decision was affirmed in part and reversed in part.

REASON The court first held that the Johnsons could not pursue a claim alleging that Medtronic provided inadequate warnings. Johnson offered no evidence that he was harmed because the defibrillator was sold without an adequate warning. Instead, the record showed that Medtronic's instructions would have prevented Johnson's injuries, but Hahn had failed to follow or even read them. Nevertheless, the court held that the Johnsons could pursue their design defect claim. The Johnsons had provided evidence that Hahn's misuse was reasonably foreseeable. Importantly, Medtronic had known that other users had inadvertently delivered asynchronous shocks after failing to reset the device. The court concluded that the Johnsons were not precluded from bringing a claim for design defect simply because they could not pursue a claim of inadequate warnings. In some cases, "a manufacturer may be held liable where it chooses to warn of the danger . . . rather than preclude the danger by design."

CRITICAL THINKING—Legal Consideration *What could Medtronic do to avoid possible liability to plaintiffs like the Johnsons? Was there a reasonable alternative design for the defibrillator?*

a. In the right-hand column, click on "Opinions & Minutes." In the middle of the next page, after "Missouri Court of Appeals, Western District," click on "opinions." In the "Search Opinions . . ." box, type "Johnson v. Medtronic," and click on "Search." In the result, click on the case name to access the opinion.

ETHICAL ISSUE

Should tobacco companies be required to use graphic warnings to discourage smoking? Scientists long ago established that smoking is injurious to one's health and that nicotine is highly addictive. For decades, cigarette manufacturers have been required to put explicit warning labels on packages of cigarettes sold in the United States to discourage people from smoking. Although the number of smokers has declined over time, the Centers for Disease Control and Prevention estimates that more than 45 million adults still smoke and that 443,000 deaths each year can be attributed to smoking. Smoking also contributes substantially to the nation's health-care costs.

Continued

In an attempt to reduce smoking further, the U.S. Food and Drug Administration (FDA) issued a new rule requiring U.S. tobacco companies to include large graphic images on cigarette packages that show how smoking can kill. The images include pictures of diseased lungs and a cadaver on an autopsy table. In 2012, the U.S. District Court for the District of Columbia ruled against the FDA. The judge stated that the required labels did not convey facts to inform, but rather would force cigarette makers to display the government's antismoking message more prominently than the tobacco companies' own branding. In other words, the FDA requirement was "the impermissible expropriation of a company's advertising space for government advocacy." Though cigarette smoking may be harmful, it is not illegal. Therefore, tobacco companies have free speech rights.[14]

Of course, antismoking advocacy groups are unhappy with the district court's ruling. Matthew L. Meyers, president of the Campaign for Tobacco-Free Kids, said the decision was "wrong on the science and the law. The warnings unequivocally tell the truth about cigarette smoking."

Obvious Risks   There is no duty to warn about risks that are obvious or commonly known. Warnings about such risks do not add to the safety of a product and could even detract from it by making other warnings seem less significant. The obviousness of a risk and a user's decision to proceed in the face of that risk may be a defense in a product liability suit based on a warning defect. (This defense and other defenses in product liability suits will be discussed later in this chapter.)

An action alleging that a product is defective due to an inadequate label can be based on state law. (For a discussion of a case involving a state law that required warning labels on violent video games, see this chapter's *Adapting the Law to the Online Environment* feature on the facing page.)

Market-Share Liability

Generally, in cases involving product liability, a plaintiff must prove that the defective product that caused her or his injury was made by a specific defendant. In a few situations, however, courts have dropped this requirement when a plaintiff cannot prove which of many distributors of a harmful product supplied the particular product that caused the injury. Under a theory of **market-share liability,** all firms that manufactured and distributed the product during the period in question are held liable for the plaintiff's injury in proportion to the firms' respective shares of the market for that product during that period.

Market-Share Liability A theory under which liability is shared among all firms that manufactured and distributed a particular product during a certain period of time. This form of liability sharing is used only when the true source of the harmful product is unidentifiable.

CASE EXAMPLE 17.12   John Smith suffered from hemophilia (a blood-clotting disorder). Because of his condition, he received injections of a blood protein known as antihemophiliac factor (AHF) concentrate. When he later tested positive for the AIDS (acquired immune deficiency syndrome) virus, he sued. Because it was not known which manufacturer was responsible for the particular AHF received by the plaintiff, the court held that all of the manufacturers of AHF could be held liable under a market-share theory of liability.[15] •

Courts in many jurisdictions do not recognize this theory of liability, believing that it deviates too significantly from traditional legal principles.[16] In jurisdictions that do recognize market-share liability, it is usually applied in cases involving drugs or

---

14. *R.J. Reynolds Tobacco Co. v. U.S. Food and Drug Administration,* 2012 WL 653828 (D.D.C. 2012).

15. *Smith v. Cutter Biological, Inc.,* 72 Haw. 416, 823 P.2d 717 (1991). See also *Sutowski v. Eli Lilly & Co.,* 92 Ohio St.3d 347, 696 N.E.2d 187 (1998); and *In re Methyl Tertiary Butyl Ether (MTBE) Products Liability Litigation,* 447 F.Supp.2d 289 (S.D.N.Y. 2006).

16. For the Illinois Supreme Court's position on market-share liability, see *Smith v. Eli Lilly Co.,* 137 Ill.2d 252, 560 N.E.2d 324, 148 Ill.Dec. 22 (1990). Pennsylvania law also does not recognize market-share liability. See *Bortell v. Eli Lilly & Co.,* 406 F.Supp.2d 1 (D.D.C. 2005).

ADAPTING THE LAW TO THE ONLINE ENVIRONMENT

THE SUPREME COURT TAKES A STAND ON WARNING LABELS FOR VIDEO GAMES

Almost every product that you purchase in the physical world has one or more warning labels. Indeed, some critics argue that these labels have become so long and ubiquitous that consumers ignore them. In other words, putting warnings on just about everything defeats their original purpose. In the online environment, warning labels are not so extensive—at least not yet.

Until now, video games have largely escaped mandated warning labels, although the video game industry has instituted a voluntary rating system to provide information about a video game's content. Each video game is assigned one of six age-specific ratings, ranging from "Early Childhood" to "Adults Only."

Should video games, whether downloaded or bought on a CD-ROM or DVD, have additional warnings to advise potential users (or their parents) that the games might be overly violent? When the California legislature enacted a law imposing restrictions and a labeling requirement on the sale or rental of "violent video games" to minors, this issue became paramount.[a]

Video Software Dealers Sue the State

The Video Software Dealers Association, along with the Entertainment Software Association, immediately brought a suit in federal district court seeking to invalidate the law. The court granted summary judgment in favor of the plaintiffs.

The act defined a violent video game as one in which "the range of options available to a player includes killing, maiming, dismembering, or sexually assaulting an image of a human being." While agreeing that some video games are unquestionably violent by everyday standards, the trial court pointed out that many video games are based on popular novels or motion pictures and have extensive plot lines.

Accordingly, the court found that the definition of a violent video game was unconstitutionally vague and thus violated the First Amendment's guarantee of freedom of speech. The court also noted the existence of the voluntary rating system. The U.S. Court of Appeals for the Ninth Circuit affirmed the district court's decision.[b]

The United States Supreme Court's Decision

The state of California appealed to the United States Supreme Court, but in 2011 the Court affirmed the decision in favor of the video game and software industries. The Court noted that video games are entitled to First Amendment protection. Because California had failed to show that the statute was justified by a compelling government interest and that the law was narrowly tailored to serve that interest, the Court ruled that the statute was unconstitutional.[c]

Critical Thinking

Why do you think that some legislators believe that the six-part, age-specific voluntary labeling system for video games is not sufficient to protect minors?

---

a. California Civil Code Sections 1746–1746.5.

b. *Video Software Dealers Association v. Schwarzenegger,* 556 F.3d 950 (9th Cir. 2009).

c. *Brown v. Entertainment Merchants Association,* ___ U.S. ___, 131 S.Ct. 2729, 180 L.Ed.2d 708 (2011).

---

chemicals, when it is difficult or impossible to determine which company made a particular product.

Other Applications of Strict Liability

Almost all courts extend the strict liability of manufacturers and other sellers to injured bystanders. **EXAMPLE 17.13** A forklift that Trent is operating will not go into reverse, and as a result, it runs into a bystander. In this situation, the bystander can sue the manufacturer of the defective forklift under strict liability (and possibly bring a negligence action against the forklift operator as well). •

Strict liability also applies to suppliers of component parts. **EXAMPLE 17.14** Toyota buys brake pads from a subcontractor and puts them in Corollas without changing their composition. If those pads are defective, both the supplier of the brake pads and Toyota will be held strictly liable for the injuries caused by the defects. •

Defenses to Product Liability

LEARNING OBJECTIVE 5
What defenses to liability can be raised in a product liability lawsuit?

Defendants in product liability suits can raise a number of defenses. One defense, of course, is to show that there is no basis for the plaintiff's claim. For instance, in a product liability case based on negligence, if a defendant can show that the plaintiff has *not* met the requirements (such as causation) for an action in negligence, generally the defendant will not be liable.

Similarly, in a case involving strict product liability, a defendant can claim that the plaintiff failed to meet one of the requirements. If the defendant establishes that the goods were altered after they were sold, for instance, the defendant normally will not be held liable.[17] A defendant may also assert that the *statute of limitations* (see page 15 in Chapter 1) for a product liability claim has lapsed.[18] Several other defenses may also be available to defendants, as discussed next.

Preemption

Today, some defendants are raising the defense of preemption—that government regulations preempt claims for product liability (see *Spotlight Case 17.2* on page 447, for example). The federal government has instituted numerous regulations that attempt to ensure the safety of products distributed to the public (consumer law is discussed in Chapter 33). In the past, a person who was injured by a product could assert a product liability claim regardless of whether the product was subject to government regulations. But that changed in 2008 when the United States Supreme Court held that an injured party may not be able to sue the manufacturer of defective products that are subject to federal regulatory schemes.

CASE EXAMPLE 17.15   In *Riegel v. Medtronic, Inc.,*[19] the United States Supreme Court held that a man who was injured by an approved medical device (in this case, a balloon catheter) could not sue its maker for negligence or strict product liability, or claim that the device was defectively designed. The Court observed that the Medical Device Amendments of 1976 (MDA) created a comprehensive scheme of federal safety oversight for medical devices. The MDA requires the U.S. Food and Drug Administration to review the design, labeling, and manufacturing of these devices before they are marketed to make sure that they are safe and effective. The Court reasoned that because premarket approval is a "rigorous process," it preempts all common law claims challenging the safety or effectiveness of a medical device that has been approved. ●

Since the *Medtronic* decision, some courts have extended the preemption defense to other product liability actions. Other courts have been unwilling to deny an injured party relief simply because the federal government was supposed to ensure the product's safety.[20] Even the United States Supreme Court refused to extend the preemption defense to preclude a drug maker's liability in one subsequent case.[21]

Assumption of Risk

Assumption of risk can sometimes be used as a defense in a product liability action. To establish such a defense, the defendant must show that (1) the plaintiff knew and appreciated the risk created by the product defect and (2) the plaintiff voluntarily assumed the

---

17. See, for example, *Edmondson v. Macclesfield L-P Gas Co.,* 642 S.E.2d 265 (N.C.App. 2007); and *Pichardo v. C. S. Brown Co.,* 35 A.D.3d 303, 827 N.Y.S.2d 131 (N.Y.App. 2006).

18. Similar state statutes, called *statutes of repose,* place outer time limits on product liability actions.

19. 552 U.S. 312, 128 S.Ct. 999, 169 L.Ed.2d 892 (2008).

20. See, for example, *Paduano v. American Honda Motor Co.,* 169 Cal.App.4th 1453, 88 Cal.Rptr.3d 90 (2009), which was presented as the *Business Case Study with Dissenting Opinion* for Unit 1 on page 233; and *McDarby v. Merck & Co.,* 402 N.J.Super. 10, 949 A.2d 223 (2008).

21. *Wyeth v. Levine,* 555 U.S. 555, 129 S.Ct. 1187, 173 L.Ed.2d 51 (2009).

risk, even though it was unreasonable to do so. (See Chapter 4 for a more detailed discussion of assumption of risk.)

Although assumption of the risk is a defense in product liability actions, some courts do not allow it to be used as a defense to strict product liability claims. **CASE EXAMPLE 17.16** Executive Tans operated an upright tanning booth that had been manufactured by Sun Ergoline, Inc. Before using the booth, Savannah Boles signed a release form that contained an *exculpatory clause* (see page 297 in Chapter 11). The clause stated that she was using the booth at her own risk and that she released the manufacturer, among others, from any liability for injuries. After Boles entered the booth, several of her fingers came in contact with an exhaust fan located at the top of the booth, partially amputating them. Boles sued Sun Ergoline alleging strict product liability. Sun Ergoline argued that Boles's claims were barred by the release that she had signed. The lower courts agreed that Boles's claims were barred. The Supreme Court of Colorado reversed, however, because it concluded that, as a matter of public policy, assumption of risk (via the exculpatory clause) was not appropriate in a strict liability context. Therefore, Boles could sue Sun Ergoline to recover for her injuries.[22] ●

Product Misuse

Similar to the defense of voluntary assumption of risk is that of product misuse, which occurs when a product is used for a purpose for which it was not intended. The courts have severely limited this defense, however, and it is now recognized as a defense only when the particular use was not reasonably foreseeable. If the misuse is foreseeable, the seller must take measures to guard against it.

Comparative Negligence (Fault)

Developments in the area of comparative negligence, or fault (discussed in Chapter 4), have also affected the doctrine of strict liability. In the past, the plaintiff's conduct was not a defense to liability for a defective product. Today, courts in many jurisdictions consider the negligent or intentional actions of both the plaintiff and the defendant when apportioning liability and awarding damages.[23] A defendant may be able to limit at least some of its liability for injuries caused by its defective product if it can show that the plaintiff's misuse of the product contributed to the injuries.

When proved, comparative negligence differs from other defenses in that it does not completely absolve the defendant of liability, but it can reduce the amount of damages that will be awarded to the plaintiff.

CASE EXAMPLE 17.17 Dan Smith, a mechanic in Alaska, was not wearing a hard hat at work when he was asked to start a diesel engine of an air compressor. Because the compressor was an older model, he had to prop open a door to start it. When Smith got the engine started, the door fell from its position and hit his head. The injury caused him to suffer from seizures and epilepsy. Smith sued the manufacturer, claiming that the engine was defectively designed. The manufacturer argued that Smith had been negligent by failing to wear his hard hat and by propping the door open in an unsafe manner. Smith's attorney claimed that the plaintiff's ordinary negligence could not be used as a defense in product liability cases, but the Alaska Supreme Court disagreed. Alaska, like many other states, allows comparative negligence to be raised as a defense in product liability lawsuits.[24] ●

22. *Boles v. Sun Ergoline, Inc.*, 222 P.3d 724 (Co.Sup.Ct. 2010).

23. See, for example, *State Farm Insurance Companies v. Premier Manufactured Systems, Inc.*, 213 Ariz. 419, 142 P.3d 1232 (2006); and *Industrial Risk Insurers v. American Engineering Testing, Inc.*, 318 Wis.2d 148, 769 N.W.2d 82 (Wis.App. 2009).

24. *Smith v. Ingersoll-Rand Co.*, 14 P.3d 990 (Alaska 2000). See also *Winschel v. Brown*, 171 P.3d 142 (Alaska 2007).

Commonly Known Dangers

The dangers associated with certain products (such as sharp knives and guns) are so commonly known that manufacturers need not warn users of those dangers. If a defendant succeeds in convincing the court that a plaintiff's injury resulted from a *commonly known danger,* the defendant normally will not be liable.

CASE EXAMPLE 17.18   A classic case on this issue involved a plaintiff who was injured when an elastic exercise rope that she had purchased slipped off her foot and struck her in the eye, causing a detachment of the retina. The plaintiff claimed that the manufacturer should be liable because it had failed to warn users that the exercise rope might slip off a foot in this manner. The court stated that to hold the manufacturer liable in these circumstances "would go beyond the reasonable dictates of justice in fixing the liabilities of manufacturers." After all, stated the court, "[a]lmost every physical object can be inherently dangerous or potentially dangerous in a sense. . . . A manufacturer cannot manufacture a knife that will not cut or a hammer that will not mash a thumb or a stove that will not burn a finger. The law does not require [manufacturers] to warn of such common dangers."[25] ●

Knowledgeable User

A related defense is the *knowledgeable user* defense. If a particular danger (such as electrical shock) is or should be commonly known by particular users of the product (such as electricians), the manufacturer of electrical equipment need not warn these users of the danger.

CASE EXAMPLE 17.19   The parents of a group of teenagers who had become overweight and developed health problems filed a product liability lawsuit against McDonald's. The teenagers claimed that the well-known fast-food chain should be held liable for failing to warn customers of the adverse health effects of eating its food products. The court rejected this claim, however, based on the *knowledgeable user defense.* The court found that it is well known that the food at McDonald's contains high levels of cholesterol, fat, salt, and sugar and is therefore unhealthful. The court's opinion, which thwarted numerous future lawsuits against fast-food restaurants, stated: "If consumers know (or reasonably should know) the potential ill health effects of eating at McDonald's, they cannot blame McDonald's if they, nonetheless, choose to satiate [satisfy] their appetite with a surfeit [excess] of super-sized McDonald's products."[26] ●

---

25. *Jamieson v. Woodward & Lothrop,* 247 F.2d 23, 101 D.C.App. 32 (1957).
26. *Pelman v. McDonald's Corp.,* 237 F.Supp.2d 512 (S.D.N.Y. 2003).

Reviewing . . . Warranties and Product Liability

Shalene Kolchek bought a Great Lakes Spa from Val Porter, a dealer who was selling spas at the state fair. Porter told Kolchek that Great Lakes spas are "top of the line" and "the Cadillac of spas" and indicated that the spa she was buying was "fully warranted for three years." After Kolchek signed an installment sale contract, Porter gave her the manufacturer's paperwork and arranged for the spa to be delivered and installed for her. Three months later, Kolchek noticed that one corner of the spa was leaking onto her new deck and causing damage. She complained to Porter, but he did nothing about the problem. Kolchek's family continued to use the spa. Using the information presented in the chapter, answer the following questions.

1. Did Porter's statement that the spa was "top of the line" and "the Cadillac of spas" create any type of warranty? Why or why not?
2. Did Porter breach the implied warranty of merchantability? Why or why not?

3. One night, Kolchek's six-year-old daughter, Litisha, was in the spa with her mother. Litisha's hair became entangled in the spa's drain, and she was sucked down and held under water for a prolonged period, causing her to suffer brain damage. Under which theory or theories of product liability can Kolchek sue Porter to recover for Litisha's injuries?

4. If Kolchek had negligently left Litisha alone in the spa before the incident described in the previous question, what defense to liability might Porter assert?

DEBATE THIS No express warranties should be created by the oral statements made by salespersons about a product.

LINKING BUSINESS LAW to Corporate Management

Quality Control

In this chapter, you learned that breaches of warranties and manufacturing and design defects can give rise to liability. Although it is possible to minimize liability through warranty disclaimers and various defenses to product liability claims, all businesspersons know that such disclaimers and defenses do not necessarily fend off expensive lawsuits.

The legal issues surrounding product liability and warranties relate directly to quality control. As all of your management courses will emphasize, quality control is a major issue facing every manager in all organizations. Companies that have cost-effective quality control systems produce products with fewer manufacturing and design defects. As a result, these companies incur fewer potential and actual warranty and product liability lawsuits.

Three Types of Quality Control

Most management systems involve three types of quality control—preventive, concurrent, and feedback. They apply at different stages of the manufacturing process: preventive quality control occurs before the process begins, concurrent control takes place during the process, and feedback control occurs after it is finished.

In a typical manufacturing process, for example, preventive quality control might involve inspecting raw materials before they are put into the production process. Once the process begins, measuring and monitoring devices constantly assess quality standards as part of a concurrent quality control system. When the standards are not being met, employees correct the problem.

Once the manufacturing is completed, the products undergo a final quality inspection as part of the feedback quality control system. Of course, there are economic limits to how complete the final inspection will be. A refrigerator can be tested for an hour, a day, or a year. Management faces a trade-off. The less the refrigerator is tested, the sooner it gets to market and the faster the company receives its payment. The shorter the testing period, however, the higher the probability of a defect that will cost the manufacturer because of its expressed or implied warranties.

Total Quality Management (TQM)

Some managers attempt to reduce warranty and product liability costs by relying on a concurrent quality control system known as total quality management (TQM). This is an organization-wide effort to infuse quality into every activity in a company through continuous improvement.

Quality circles are a popular TQM technique. These are groups of six to twelve employees who volunteer to meet regularly to discuss problems and how to solve them. In a continuous stream manufacturing process, for example, a quality circle might consist of workers from different phases in the production process. Quality circles force changes in the production process that affect workers who are actually on the production line.

Benchmarking is another technique used in TQM. In benchmarking, a company continuously measures its products against those of its toughest competitors or the industry leaders in order to identify areas for improvement. In the automobile industry, benchmarking enabled several Japanese firms to overtake U.S. automakers in terms of quality. Some argue that Toyota gained worldwide market share by effectively using this type of quality control management system.

Another TQM system is called *Six Sigma*. Motorola introduced the quality principles in this system in the late 1980s, but Six Sigma has now become a generic term for a quality control approach that takes nothing for granted. It is based on

Continued

a five-step methodology: define, measure, analyze, improve, and control. Six Sigma controls emphasize discipline and a relentless attempt to achieve higher quality (and lower costs). A possible impediment to the institution of a Six Sigma program is that it requires a major commitment from top management because it may involve widespread changes throughout the entire organization.

Critical Thinking

Quality control leads to fewer defective products and fewer lawsuits. Consequently, managers know that quality control is important to their company's long-term financial health. At the same time, the more quality control managers impose on their organization, the higher the average cost per unit of whatever is produced and sold. How does a manager decide how much quality control to undertake?

Key Terms

express warranty 438
implied warranty 439
implied warranty of fitness for a particular purpose 441

implied warranty of merchantability 439
lien 438

market-share liability 452
product liability 445

unreasonably dangerous product 448

Chapter Summary: Warranties and Product Liability

WARRANTIES	
Warranties of Title (See page 438.)	In most sales, sellers warrant that they have good and valid title to the goods sold and that transfer of the title is rightful [UCC 2–312(1)(a)]. A second warranty of title shields buyers and lessees who are *unaware* of any encumbrances, or liens, against goods at the time the contract is made [UCC 2–312(1)(b), 2A–211(1)]. Third, when the seller or lessor is a merchant, he or she automatically warrants that the buyer or lessee takes the goods *free of infringements* [UCC 2–312(3), 2A–211(2)].

Express Warranties (See pages 438–439.)	1. *Under the UCC*—An express warranty arises under the UCC when a seller or lessor indicates, as part of the basis of the bargain, any of the following [UCC 2–313, 2A–210]:
	   a. An affirmation or promise of fact.
	   b. A description of the goods.
	   c. A sample shown as conforming to the contract goods.
	2. *Under the Magnuson-Moss Warranty Act*—Express written warranties covering consumer goods priced at more than $25, *if made,* must be labeled as one of the following:
	   a. Full warranty—Free repair or replacement of defective parts. Or, if the goods cannot be repaired in a reasonable time, refund or replacement is available.
	   b. Limited warranty—When less than a full warranty is being offered.

Implied Warranty of Merchantability (See pages 439–440.)	When a seller or lessor is a merchant who deals in goods of the kind sold or leased, the seller or lessor warrants that the goods sold or leased are properly packaged and labeled, are of proper quality, and are reasonably fit for the ordinary purposes for which such goods are used [UCC 2–314, 2A–212].
Implied Warranty of Fitness for a Particular Purpose (See page 441.)	Arises when the buyer's or lessee's purpose or use is expressly or impliedly known by the seller or lessor, and the buyer or lessee purchases or leases the goods in reliance on the seller's or lessor's selection [UCC 2–315, 2A–213]. Other implied warranties can arise as a result of course of dealing or usage of trade [UCC 2–314(3), 2A–212(3)].
Overlapping Warranties (See page 442.)	The UCC construes warranties as cumulative if they are consistent with each other. If warranties are inconsistent, then express warranties take precedence over implied warranties, except for the implied warranty of fitness for a particular purpose. Also, samples take precedence over general descriptions, and exact or technical specifications displace inconsistent samples or general descriptions.
Warranty Disclaimers (See pages 442–443.)	Express warranties can be disclaimed if the disclaimer is written in clear language, conspicuous, and called to the buyer's or lessee's attention at the time the contract is formed. A disclaimer of the implied warranty of merchantability must specifically mention the word *merchantability*. The disclaimer need not be in writing, but if it is written, it must be conspicuous. A disclaimer of the implied warranty of fitness *must* be in writing and be conspicuous, though it need not mention the word *fitness*.

Chapter Summary: Warranties and Product Liability—Continued

PRODUCT LIABILITY	
Liability Based on Negligence (See page 445.)	1. The manufacturer must use due care in designing the product, selecting materials, using the appropriate production process, assembling and testing the product, and placing adequate warnings on the label or product. 2. Privity of contract is not required. A manufacturer is liable for failure to exercise due care to any person who sustains an injury proximately caused by a negligently made (defective) product. 3. Fraudulent misrepresentation of a product may result in product liability based on the tort of fraud.
Strict Liability—Requirements (See pages 446–448.)	1. The defendant must have sold the product in a defective condition. 2. The defendant must normally be engaged in the business of selling that product. 3. The product must be unreasonably dangerous to the user or consumer because of its defective condition (in most states). 4. The plaintiff must incur physical harm to self or property by use or consumption of the product. 5. The defective condition must be the proximate cause of the injury or damage. 6. The goods must not have been substantially changed from the time the product was sold to the time the injury was sustained.
Strict Liability—Product Defects (See pages 448–452.)	A product may be defective in three basic ways: 1. In its manufacture. 2. In its design. 3. In the instructions or warnings that come with it.
Market-Share Liability (See pages 452–453.)	When plaintiffs cannot prove which of many distributors of a defective product supplied the particular product that caused the plaintiffs' injuries, some courts apply market-share liability. All firms that manufactured and distributed the harmful product during the period in question are then held liable for the plaintiffs' injuries in proportion to the firms' respective shares of the market, as directed by the court.
Other Applications of Strict Liability (See page 453.)	1. Manufacturers and other sellers are liable for harms suffered by bystanders as a result of defective products. 2. Suppliers of component parts are strictly liable for defective parts that, when incorporated into a product, cause injuries to users.
Defenses to Product Liability (See pages 454–456.)	1. *Preemption*—An injured party may not be able to sue the manufacturer of a product that is subject to comprehensive federal safety regulations, such as medical devices. 2. *Assumption of risk*—The user or consumer knew of the risk of harm and voluntarily assumed it. 3. *Product misuse*—The user or consumer misused the product in a way unforeseeable by the manufacturer. 4. *Comparative negligence*—Liability may be distributed between the plaintiff and the defendant under the doctrine of comparative negligence if the plaintiff's misuse of the product contributed to the risk of injury. 5. *Commonly known dangers*—If a defendant succeeds in convincing the court that a plaintiff's injury resulted from a commonly known danger, such as the danger associated with using a sharp knife, the defendant will not be liable. 6. *Knowledgeable user*—If a particular danger is or should be commonly known by particular users of the product, the manufacturer of the product need not warn these users of the danger.

ExamPrep

ISSUE SPOTTERS

1. Rim Corporation makes tire rims that it sells to Superior Vehicles, Inc., which installs them on cars. One set of rims is defective, which an inspection would reveal. Superior does not inspect the rims. The car with the defective rims is sold to Town Auto Sales, which sells the car to Uri. Soon, the car is in an accident caused by the defective rims, and Uri is injured. Is Superior Vehicles liable? Explain your answer. **(See page 445.)**
2. Real Chocolate Company makes a box of candy, which it sells to Sweet Things, Inc., a distributor. Sweet sells the box to a Tasty Candy store, where Jill buys it. Jill gives it to Ken, who breaks a tooth on a stone the same size and color as a piece of the candy. If Real, Sweet, and Tasty were not negligent, can they be liable for the injury? Why or why not? **(See page 445.)**

—Check your answers to the Issue Spotters against the answers provided in Appendix E at the end of this text.

BEFORE THE TEST

Go to www.cengagebrain.com, enter the ISBN 9781133273561, and click on "Find" to locate this textbook's Web site. Then, click on "Access Now" under "Study Tools," and select Chapter 17 at the top. There, you will find a Practice Quiz that you can take to assess your mastery of the concepts in this chapter, as well as Flashcards, a Glossary of important terms, and Video Questions (when assigned).

For Review

Answers to the even-numbered questions in this For Review section can be found in Appendix F at the end of this text.

1. What factors determine whether a seller's or lessor's statement constitutes an express warranty or is mere puffery?
2. What implied warranties arise under the UCC?
3. Can a manufacturer be held liable to any person who suffers an injury proximately caused by the manufacturer's negligently made product?
4. What are the elements of a cause of action in strict product liability?
5. What defenses to liability can be raised in a product liability lawsuit?

Business Scenarios and Case Problems

17–1 Product Liability. Carmen buys a television set manufactured by AKI Electronics. She is going on vacation, so she takes the set to her mother's house for her mother to use. Because the set is defective, it explodes, causing considerable damage to her mother's house. Carmen's mother sues AKI for the damage to her house. Discuss the theories under which Carmen's mother can recover from AKI. **(See page 445.)**

17–2 Question with Sample Answer—Implied Warranties. Tandy purchased a washing machine from Marshall Appliances. The sales contract included a provision explicitly disclaiming all express and implied warranties, including the implied warranty of merchantability. The disclaimer was printed in the same size and color as the rest of the contract. The machine turned out to be a "lemon" and never functioned properly. Tandy sought a refund of the purchase price, claiming that Marshall had breached the implied warranty of merchantability. Can Tandy recover her payment, notwithstanding the warranty disclaimer in the contract? Explain. **(See page 441.)**

—**For a sample answer to Question 17–2, go to Appendix G at the end of this text.**

17–3 Product Liability. Jason Clark, an experienced hunter, bought a paintball gun. Clark practiced with the gun and knew how to screw in the carbon dioxide cartridge, pump the gun, and use its safety and trigger. Although Clark was aware that he could purchase protective eyewear, he chose not to buy it. Clark had taken gun safety courses and understood that it was "common sense" not to shoot anyone in the face. Clark's friend, Chris Wright, also owned a paintball gun and was similarly familiar with the gun's use and its risks. Clark, Wright, and their friends played a game that involved shooting paintballs at cars whose occupants also had the guns. One night, while Clark and Wright were cruising with their guns, Wright shot at Clark's car, but hit Clark in the eye. Clark filed a product liability lawsuit against the manufacturer of Wright's

paintball gun to recover for the injury. Clark claimed that the gun was defectively designed. During the trial, Wright testified that his gun "never malfunctioned." In whose favor should the court rule? Why? **(See pages 455–456.)**

17–4 Defenses to Product Liability. Brandon Stroud was driving a golf car made by Textron, Inc. The golf car did not have lights, but Textron did not warn against using it on public roads at night. When Stroud attempted to cross a road at 8:30 P.M., his golf car was struck by a vehicle driven by Joseph Thornley. Stroud was killed. His estate filed a suit against Textron, alleging strict product liability and product liability based on negligence. The charge was that the golf car was defective and unreasonably dangerous. What defense might Textron assert? Explain. [*Moore v. Barony House Restaurant, LLC,* 382 S.C. 35, 674 S.E.2d 500 (S.C.App. 2009)] **(See pages 454–456.)**

17–5 Product Misuse. Five-year-old Cheyenne Stark was riding in the backseat of her parents' Ford Taurus. Cheyenne was not sitting in a booster seat. Instead, she was using a seatbelt designed by Ford, but was wearing the shoulder belt behind her back. The car was involved in a collision. As a result, Cheyenne suffered a spinal cord injury and was paralyzed from the waist down. The family filed a suit against Ford Motor Co., alleging that the seatbelt was defectively designed. Could Ford successfully claim that Cheyenne had misused the seatbelt? Why or why not? [*Stark v. Ford Motor Co.,* 693 S.E.2d 253 (N.C.App. 2010)] **(See page 455.)**

17–6 Product Liability. Yun Tung Chow tried to unclog a floor drain in the kitchen of the restaurant where he worked. He used a drain cleaner called Lewis Red Devil Lye that contained crystalline sodium hydroxide. The product label said to wear eye protection, to put one tablespoon of lye directly into the drain, and to keep your face away from the drain because there could be dangerous backsplash. Not wearing eye protection, Chow mixed three spoonfuls of lye in a can and poured that mixture down the drain while bending over it. Liquid splashed back into his face, causing injury. He sued for product liability based on inadequate warnings and a design defect. The trial court granted summary judgment to the manufacturer. Chow appealed. An expert for Chow stated that the product was defective because it had a tendency to backsplash. Is that a convincing argument? Why or why not? [*Yun Tung Chow v. Reckitt & Coleman, Inc.,* 69 A.D.3d 413, 891 N.Y.S.2d 402 (N.Y.A.D. 1 Dept. 2010)] **(See pages 449–452.)**

17–7 **Case Problem with Sample Answer—Product Liability.** David Dobrovolny bought a new Ford F-350 pickup truck. A year later, the truck spontaneously caught fire in Dobrovolny's driveway. The truck was destroyed, but no other property was damaged, and no one was injured. Dobrovolny filed a suit in a Nebraska state court against Ford Motor Co. on a theory of strict product liability to recover the cost of the truck. Nebraska limits the application of strict product liability to situations involving personal injuries. Is Dobrovolny's claim likely to succeed? Why or why not? Is there another basis for liability on which he might recover? Explain. [*Dobrovolny v. Ford Motor Co.,* 281 Neb. 86, 793 N.W.2d 445 (2011)] **(See pages 446–453.)**

—For a sample answer to Problem 17–7, go to Appendix H at the end of this text.

17–8 **Spotlight on Apple—Implied Warranties.** Alan Vitt purchased an iBook G4 laptop computer from Apple, Inc. Shortly after the one-year warranty expired, the laptop failed to work due to a weakness in the product manufacture. Vitt sued Apple, arguing that the laptop should have lasted "at least a couple of years," which Vitt believed was a reasonable consumer expectation for a laptop. Vitt claimed that Apple's descriptions of the laptop as "durable," "rugged," "reliable," and "high performance" were affirmative statements concerning the quality and performance of the laptop, which Apple did not meet. How should the court rule? Why? [*Vitt v. Apple Computer, Inc.,* 2012 WL 627702 (9th Cir. 2011)] **(See pages 439–442.)**

17–9 **A Question of Ethics—Strict Product Liability.** Susan Calles lived with her four daughters, Amanda, age 11, Victoria, age 5, and Jenna and Jillian, age 3. In March 1998, Calles bought an Aim N Flame utility lighter, which she stored on the top shelf of her kitchen cabinet. A trigger can ignite the Aim N Flame after an "ON/OFF" switch is slid to the "on" position. On the night of March 31, Calles and Victoria left to get videos. Jenna and Jillian were in bed, and Amanda was watching television. Calles returned to find fire trucks and emergency vehicles around her home. Robert Finn, a fire investigator, determined that Jenna had started a fire using the lighter. Jillian suffered smoke inhalation, was hospitalized, and died on April 21. Calles filed a suit in an Illinois state court against Scripto-Tokai Corp., which distributed the Aim N Flame, and others. In her suit, which was grounded, in part, in strict liability claims, Calles alleged that the lighter was an "unreasonably dangerous product." Scripto filed a motion for summary judgment. [*Calles v. Scripto-Tokai Corp.,* 224 Ill.2d 247, 864 N.E.2d 249, 309 Ill.Dec. 383 (2007)] **(See pages 448–452.)**

1. A product is "unreasonably dangerous" when it is dangerous beyond the expectation of the ordinary consumer. Whose expectation—Calles's or Jenna's—applies here? Why? Does the lighter pass this test? Explain.

2. A product is also "unreasonably dangerous" when a less dangerous alternative was economically feasible for its maker, which failed to produce it. Scripto contended that because its product was "simple" and the danger was "obvious," it should not be liable under this test. Do you agree? Why or why not?

3. Calles presented evidence as to the likelihood and seriousness of injury from lighters that do not have child-safety devices. Scripto argued that the Aim N Flame is a useful, inexpensive, alternative source of fire and is safer than a match. Calles admitted that she was aware of the dangers presented by lighters in the hands of children. Scripto admitted that it had been a defendant in at least twenty-five suits for injuries that occurred under similar circumstances. With these factors in mind, how should the court rule? Why?

Critical Thinking and Writing Assignments

17–10 **Business Law Critical Thinking Group Assignment.** Bret D'Auguste was an experienced skier when he rented equipment to ski at Hunter Mountain Ski Bowl in New York. When D'Auguste entered an extremely difficult trail, he noticed immediately that the surface consisted of ice with almost no snow. He tried to exit the steeply declining trail by making a sharp right turn, but in the attempt, his left ski snapped off. D'Auguste lost his balance, fell, and slid down the mountain, striking his face and head against a fence along the trail. According to a report by a rental shop employee, one of the bindings on D'Auguste's skis had a "cracked heel housing." D'Auguste filed a lawsuit against the bindings' manufacturer on a theory of strict product liability. The manufacturer filed a motion for summary judgment.

1. The first group will take the position of the manufacturer and develop an argument why the court should *grant* the summary judgment motion and dismiss the strict product liability claim.

2. The second group will take the position of D'Auguste and formulate a basis for why the court should *deny* the motion and allow the strict product liability claim.

Employment Discrimination and Diversity

(Andres/Shutterstock.com)

CHAPTER OUTLINE

- Title VII of the Civil Rights Act of 1964
- Discrimination Based on Age
- Discrimination Based on Disability
- Defenses to Employment Discrimination
- Affirmative Action

LEARNING OBJECTIVES

The five learning objectives below are designed to help improve your understanding of the chapter. After reading this chapter, you should be able to answer the following questions:

1 Generally, what kind of conduct is prohibited by Title VII of the Civil Rights Act of 1964, as amended?

2 What is the difference between disparate-treatment discrimination and disparate-impact discrimination?

3 What remedies are available under Title VII of the 1964 Civil Rights Act, as amended?

4 What federal act prohibits discrimination based on age?

5 What are three defenses to claims of employment discrimination?

"Equal rights for all, special privileges for none."
—Thomas Jefferson, 1743–1826 (Third president of the United States, 1801–1809)

Out of the civil rights movement of the 1960s grew a body of law protecting employees against discrimination in the workplace. Legislation, judicial decisions, and administrative agency actions restrict employers from discriminating against workers on the basis of race, color, religion, national origin, gender, age, or disability. A class of persons defined by one or more of these criteria is known as a **protected class.** The laws designed to protect these individuals embody the sentiment expressed by Thomas Jefferson in the chapter-opening quotation above.

A person does not have to be a member of a minority group to be in a protected class. Women form a protected class although they outnumber men in the United States and thus are not statistically a minority. Conversely, not every minority group is protected. In 2012, the U.S. Census Bureau announced that for the first time the majority of babies born in the United States were not white. Instead, they were members of various other racial or ethnic groups. Although whites still make up the majority of the population—and will to do so for several

Protected Class A group of persons protected by specific laws because of the group's defining characteristics, including race, color, religion, national origin, gender, age, and disability.

President Lyndon B. Johnson signs the 1964 Civil Rights Act. This legislation represented the most far-reaching set of antidiscrimination laws in modern times. Which groups in our country benefited most from this act?

Employment Discrimination Treating employees or job applicants unequally on the basis of race, color, national origin, religion, gender, age, or disability.

LEARNING OBJECTIVE 1
Generally, what kind of conduct is prohibited by Title VII of the Civil Rights Act of 1964, as amended?

decades to come—at some point, whites will simply form the largest minority group among many other minority groups. Thus, protected classes are based not on rigid statistical definitions of minority versus majority but on whether a group is subject to discrimination.

The federal statutes discussed in this chapter prohibit **employment discrimination** against members of protected classes. Although this chapter focuses on federal statutes, many states have their own laws that protect employees against discrimination, and some provide more protection to employees than federal laws do.

Title VII of the Civil Rights Act of 1964

The most important statute covering employment discrimination is Title VII of the Civil Rights Act of 1964.[1] Title VII prohibits discrimination against employees, applicants, and union members on the basis of race, color, national origin, religion, or gender at any stage of employment. (Although federal law prohibits job discrimination only if it is based on these specific categories, some jurisdictions are expanding their laws to include other types of discrimination. See this chapter's *Law, Diversity, and Business: Managerial Implications* feature on the following page for a discussion on this issue.)

Title VII applies to employers with fifteen or more employees and labor unions with fifteen or more members. Title VII also applies to labor unions that operate hiring halls (to which members go regularly to be rationed jobs as they become available), employment agencies, and state and local governing units or agencies A special section of the act prohibits discrimination in most federal government employment.

The Equal Employment Opportunity Commission

Compliance with Title VII is monitored by the Equal Employment Opportunity Commission (EEOC). A victim of alleged discrimination must file a claim with the EEOC before bringing a suit against the employer. The EEOC may investigate the dispute and attempt to arrange an out-of-court settlement. If a voluntary agreement cannot be reached, the EEOC may file a suit against the employer on the employee's behalf. If the EEOC decides not to investigate the claim, the victim may bring her or his own lawsuit against the employer.

The EEOC does not investigate every claim of employment discrimination, regardless of the merits of the claim. Generally, it investigates only "priority cases," such as cases involving retaliatory discharge (firing an employee in retaliation for submitting a claim to the EEOC) and cases involving types of discrimination that are of particular concern to the EEOC.

Note that in 2011, the United States Supreme Court issued an important decision that limits the rights of employees—as a group, or class— to bring discrimination claims against their employer. **CASE EXAMPLE 25.1**   A group of female employees sued Wal-Mart, the nation's largest private employer, alleging that store managers who had discretion over pay and promotions were biased against women and disproportionately favored men. The United States Supreme Court ruled in favor of Wal-Mart, effectively blocking the class

---

1. 42 U.S.C. Sections 2000e–2000e-17.

LAW, DIVERSITY, AND BUSINESS: MANAGERIAL IMPLICATIONS

COMBATING APPEARANCE-BASED DISCRIMINATION

Research has shown that short men make less income than tall men. Statistical research has also shown that compared with attractive individuals, less attractive people generally receive poorer performance reviews, lower salaries, and smaller damages awards if they win lawsuits. Should something be done about this?

Can "Lookism" Be Prohibited?

Although there is certainly evidence that appearance-based discrimination exists in the workplace and elsewhere, it is not so clear that it can be prohibited. In the 1970s, Michigan decided to do something about "lookism" and passed a law barring various kinds of appearance-based discrimination.[a] Whether because of the cost or the difficulty of proving this type of discrimination, however, only a few lawsuits based on the law have been filed each year. At least six cities have similar laws, but these laws also have not given rise to many lawsuits.

Federal and state laws prohibit discrimination against people who are clinically obese, but discrimination against those who are merely overweight is usually not illegal. Given that one study found that more than 40 percent of overweight women felt stigmatized by their employers, this remains a serious problem.

A Double Standard for Grooming

Women sometimes complain that they are held to different grooming standards in the workplace than their male counterparts. A female bartender at a casino in Nevada brought a lawsuit after she was fired for not complying with rules that required her to wear makeup and teased hair while male bartenders were just told to "look neat." The court ruled, however, that these allegations were not enough to outweigh an at-will employment contract.[b]

At the same time, women in senior management positions find that they can look "too sexy." A few years ago, a Citibank employee made headlines when she claimed that she was fired for her excessive sexiness, which supposedly distracted her male co-workers.

Business Implications

The United States has fought racism, sexism, and homophobia, and it seems likely that businesses will see an effort to combat "lookism." Managers should make sure that the jurisdiction in which their business operates does not already have laws against appearance-based discrimination. Moreover, even without such laws, female employees who suffer appearance-based discrimination may be able to assert a valid claim of gender discrimination instead.

a. Michigan Compiled Laws Section 37.2202.

b. *Jespersen v. Harrah's Operating Co.*, 444 F.3d 1104 (9th Cir. 2006).

---

action (a lawsuit in which a small number of plaintiffs sue on behalf of a larger group). The Court held that the women could not maintain a class action because they had failed to prove a company-wide policy of discrimination that had a common effect on all women covered by the class action.[2] • This decision did not affect the rights of individual employees to sue under Title VII, however.

Intentional and Unintentional Discrimination

Title VII prohibits both intentional and unintentional discrimination.

Disparate-Treatment Discrimination
A form of employment discrimination that results when an employer intentionally discriminates against employees who are members of protected classes.

Intentional Discrimination Intentional discrimination by an employer against an employee is known as **disparate-treatment discrimination.** Because intent can be difficult to prove, courts have established certain procedures for resolving disparate-treatment cases. **EXAMPLE 25.2** Barbara applies for employment with a construction firm and is rejected. If she sues on the basis of disparate-treatment discrimination in hiring, she

2. *Wal-Mart Stores, Inc. v. Dukes*, ___ U.S. ___, 131 S.Ct. 2541, 180 L.Ed.2d 374 (2011).

must show that (1) she is a member of a protected class, (2) she applied and was qualified for the job in question, (3) she was rejected by the employer, and (4) the employer continued to seek applicants for the position or filled the position with a person not in a protected class. ●

If the woman can meet these relatively easy requirements, she has made out a *prima facie* **case** of illegal discrimination. *Prima facie* is Latin for "at first sight." Legally, it refers to a fact that is presumed to be true unless contradicted by evidence. Making out a *prima facie* case of discrimination means that the plaintiff has met her initial burden of proof and will win in the absence of a legally acceptable employer defense. (Defenses will be discussed later in this chapter.)

The burden then shifts to the employer-defendant, who must articulate a legal reason for not hiring the plaintiff. To prevail, the plaintiff must then show that the employer's reason is a *pretext* (not the true reason) and that the employer's decision was actually motivated by discriminatory intent.

Unintentional Discrimination

Employers often use interviews and tests to choose from among a large number of applicants for job openings. Minimum educational requirements are also common. These practices and procedures may have an unintended discriminatory impact on a protected class. (For tips on how human resources managers can prevent these types of discrimination claims, see the *Linking Business Law to Corporate Management* feature on page 674.)

Disparate-impact discrimination occurs when a protected group of people is adversely affected by an employer's practices, procedures, or tests, even though they do not appear to be discriminatory. In a disparate-impact discrimination case, the complaining party must first show statistically that the employer's practices, procedures, or tests are discriminatory in effect. Once the plaintiff has made out a *prima facie* case, the burden of proof shifts to the employer to show that the practices or procedures in question were justified. There are two ways of proving that disparate-impact discrimination exists, as discussed next.

Pool of Applicants A plaintiff can prove a disparate impact by comparing the employer's workforce to the pool of qualified individuals available in the local labor market. The plaintiff must show that (1) as a result of educational or other job requirements or hiring procedures, (2) the percentage of nonwhites, women, or members of other protected classes in the employer's workforce (3) does not reflect the percentage of that group in the pool of qualified applicants. If the plaintiff can show a connection between the practice and the disparity, he or she has made out a *prima facie* case and need not provide evidence of discriminatory intent.

Rate of Hiring A plaintiff can also prove disparate-impact discrimination by comparing the selection rates of whites and nonwhites (or members of another protected class). When a job requirement or hiring procedure excludes members of a protected class from an employer's workforce at a substantially higher rate than nonmembers, discrimination occurs, regardless of the racial balance in the employer's workforce.

The EEOC has devised a test, called the "four-fifths rule," to determine whether an employment selection procedure is discriminatory on its face. Under this rule, a selection rate for protected classes that is less than four-fifths, or 80 percent, of the rate for the group with the highest rate will generally be regarded as evidence of disparate impact. **EXAMPLE 25.3** One hundred white applicants take an employment test, and fifty pass the test and are hired. One hundred minority applicants take the test, and twenty pass the test and are hired. Because twenty is less than four-fifths (80 percent) of fifty, the test would be considered discriminatory under the EEOC guidelines. ●

Prima Facie Case A case in which the plaintiff has produced sufficient evidence of his or her claim that the case will be decided for the plaintiff unless the defendant produces no evidence to rebut it.

Disparate-Impact Discrimination
Discrimination that results from certain employer practices or procedures that, although not discriminatory on their face, have a discriminatory effect.

LEARNING OBJECTIVE 2
What is the difference between disparate-treatment discrimination and disparate-impact discrimination?

ETHICAL ISSUE

Is there an implicit bias against job applicants who have been unemployed long term? Even though the recession that started in December 2007 has officially ended, the national unemployment rate has remained around 8 percent. As a result, many individuals have been unable to find work for several years. Now, the long-term unemployed are facing apparent discrimination when they apply for jobs. Some employers have indicated that they will not consider an applicant who has been unemployed longer than six months, especially if he or she has not pursued additional training or education during the period of unemployment.

Because the long-term unemployed do not form a protected class, they cannot sue for discrimination under federal law. They may soon get help from the states, however. At least thirteen states are considering legislation to prohibit discrimination against the unemployed in help-wanted ads. The New York–based National Employment Law Project is urging legislation that would explicitly prohibit employers and employment agencies from eliminating long-term unemployed applicants from consideration for jobs.

Discrimination Based on Race, Color, and National Origin

Title VII prohibits employers from discriminating against employees or job applicants on the basis of race, color, or national origin. If an employer's standards for selecting or promoting employees have a discriminatory effect on job applicants or employees in these protected classes, then a presumption of illegal discrimination arises. To avoid liability, the employer must then show that its standards have a substantial, demonstrable relationship to realistic qualifications for the job in question.
CASE EXAMPLE 25.4   Jiann Min Chang was an instructor at Alabama Agricultural and Mechanical University (AAMU). When AAMU terminated his employment, Chang filed a lawsuit claiming discrimination based on national origin. Chang established a *prima facie* case because he (1) was a member of a protected class, (2) was qualified for the job, (3) suffered an adverse employment action, and (4) was replaced by someone outside his protected class (a non-Asian instructor). AAMU, however, showed that Chang had argued with a university vice president and refused to comply with her instructions. The court ruled that the university had not renewed Chang's contract for a legitimate reason— insubordination—and therefore was not liable for unlawful discrimination.[3] ●

Reverse Discrimination   Note that discrimination based on race can also take the form of *reverse discrimination,* or discrimination against "majority" individuals, such as white males. **CASE EXAMPLE 25.5**   An African American woman fired four white men from their management positions at a school district. The men filed a lawsuit for racial discrimination, alleging that the woman was trying to eliminate white males from the department. The woman claimed that the terminations were part of a reorganization plan to cut costs. The jury sided with the men and awarded them nearly $3 million in damages. The verdict was upheld on appeal (though the damages award was reduced slightly).[4] ●

In 2009, the United States Supreme Court issued a decision that has had a significant impact on disparate-impact and reverse discrimination litigation. **CASE EXAMPLE 25.6**   The fire department in New Haven, Connecticut, administered a test to identify firefighters eligible for promotions. No African Americans and only two Hispanic firefighters passed the test. Fearing that it would be sued for discrimination if it based promotions on the test results, the city refused to use the results. The white firefighters (and one Hispanic) who had passed the test then sued the city, claiming reverse discrimination.

The United States Supreme Court held that an employer can engage in intentional discrimination to remedy an unintentional disparate impact only if the employer has "a strong

---

3. *Jiann Min Chang v. Alabama Agricultural and Mechanical University,* 2009 WL 3403180 (11th Cir. 2009).
4. *Johnston v. School District of Philadelphia,* 2006 WL 999966 (E.D.Pa. 2006).

basis in evidence" to believe that it will be successfully sued for disparate-impact discrimination "if it fails to take the race-conscious, discriminatory action." Mere fear of litigation was not sufficient reason for the city to discard its test results.[5] Subsequently, the city certified the test results and promoted the firefighters. •

Potential "Section 1981" Claims   Victims of racial or ethnic discrimination may also have a cause of action under 42 U.S.C. Section 1981. This section, which was enacted as part of the Civil Rights Act of 1866 to protect the rights of freed slaves, prohibits discrimination on the basis of race or ethnicity in the formation or enforcement of contracts. Because employment is often a contractual relationship, Section 1981 can provide an alternative basis for a plaintiff's action and is potentially advantageous because it does not place a cap on damages.

Discrimination Based on Religion

Title VII also prohibits government employers, private employers, and unions from discriminating against persons because of their religion. Employers cannot treat their employees more or less favorably based on their religious beliefs or practices and cannot require employees to participate in any religious activity (or forbid them from participating in one). **EXAMPLE 25.7**   Jason Sewell claimed that his employer, a car dealership, fired him for not attending the weekly prayer meetings of dealership employees. If the dealership did require its employees to attend prayer gatherings and fired Sewell for not attending, he has a valid claim of religious discrimination. •

(Juanmonino/iStockphoto.com)

Under Title VII, can employers prohibit employees from participating in religious activities such as reciting prayers? Why or why not?

Reasonable Accommodation   An employer must "reasonably accommodate" the religious practices of its employees, unless to do so would cause undue hardship to the employer's business. Employers must reasonably accommodate an employee's religious belief even if the belief is not based on the doctrines of a traditionally recognized religion, such as Christianity or Judaism, or a denomination, such as Baptist. The only requirement is that the belief be sincerely held by the employee.

Undue Hardship   If an employee's religion prohibits him or her from working on a certain day of the week or at a certain type of job, for instance, the employer must make a reasonable attempt to accommodate these religious requirements. A reasonable attempt to accommodate does not necessarily require the employer to permanently give an employee the requested day off, if to do so would cause the employer undue hardship. **CASE EXAMPLE 25.8**   Miguel Sánchez–Rodríguez sold cell phones in shopping malls for AT&T in Puerto Rico. After six years, Sánchez informed his supervisors that he had become a Seventh Day Adventist and could no longer work on Saturdays for religious reasons. AT&T responded that his inability to work on Saturdays would cause it hardship.

As a reasonable accommodation, the company suggested that Sánchez swap schedules with others and offered him two other positions that did not require work on Saturdays. Sánchez could not find workers to swap shifts with him, however, and he declined the other jobs because they would result in less income. He began missing work on Saturdays. After a time, AT&T indicated that it would discipline him for any additional Saturdays that he missed. Eventually, he was placed on active disciplinary status. Sánchez resigned and filed a religious discrimination lawsuit against AT&T. The court found in favor of AT&T, and a federal appellate court affirmed. The company had made adequate efforts at accommodation by allowing Sánchez to swap shifts and offering him other positions that did not require work on Saturdays.[6] •

---

5. *Ricci v. DeStefano,* 557 U.S. 557, 129 S.Ct. 2658, 174 L.Ed.2d 490 (2009).
6. *Sánchez-Rodríquez v. AT&T Mobility Puerto Rico, Inc.,* 673 F.3d 1 (1st Cir. 2012).

Discrimination Based on Gender

Under Title VII, as well as other federal acts (including the Equal Pay Act of 1963, which we also discuss here), employers are forbidden from discriminating against employees on the basis of gender. Employers are prohibited from classifying jobs as male or female and from advertising positions as male or female unless the employer can prove that the gender of the applicant is essential to the job. Employers also cannot have separate male and female seniority lists or refuse to promote employees based on gender.

Gender Must Be a Determining Factor   Generally, to succeed in a suit for gender discrimination, a plaintiff must demonstrate that gender was a determining factor in the employer's decision to fire or refuse to hire or promote her or him. Typically, this involves looking at all of the surrounding circumstances.

   CASE EXAMPLE 25.9   Wanda Collier worked for Turner Industries Group, LLC, in the maintenance department. She complained to her supervisor that Jack Daniell, the head of the department, treated her unfairly. Her supervisor told her that Daniell had a problem with her gender and was harder on women. The supervisor talked to Daniell but did not take any disciplinary action.

   A month later, Daniell confronted Collier, pushing her up against a wall and berating her. After this incident, Collier filed a formal complaint and kept a male co-worker with her at all times. A month later, she was fired. She subsequently filed a lawsuit alleging gender discrimination. The court concluded that there was enough evidence that gender was a determining factor in Daniell's conduct to allow Collier's claims to go to a jury.[7] •

Pregnancy Discrimination   The Pregnancy Discrimination Act of 1978,[8] which amended Title VII, expanded the definition of gender discrimination to include discrimination based on pregnancy. Women affected by pregnancy, childbirth, or related medical conditions must be treated—for all employment-related purposes, including the receipt of benefits under employee benefit programs—the same as other persons not so affected but similar in ability to work.

Wage Discrimination   Several laws prohibit employers from gender-based wage discrimination. The Equal Pay Act of 1963 requires equal pay for male and female employees doing similar work at the same establishment (a barber and a hair stylist, for example). To determine whether the Equal Pay Act has been violated, a court will look to the primary duties of the two jobs—the job content rather than the job description controls. If the wage differential is due to "any factor other than gender," such as a seniority or merit system, then it does not violate the Equal Pay Act.

   The continuing disparity between the wages of men and women prompted Congress to pass the Paycheck Fairness Act of 2009, which closed some of the loopholes in the Equal Pay Act. The Paycheck Fairness Act clarified employers' defenses and prohibited the use of gender-based differentials in assessing an employee's education, training, or experience. It also provided additional remedies for wage discrimination similar to those available for discrimination based on race and national origin.

   Congress also enacted the Lilly Ledbetter Fair Pay Act of 2009, which made discriminatory wages actionable under federal law regardless of when the discrimination began.[9] This act overturned a previous decision by the United States Supreme Court that had

---

> "A sign that says 'men only' looks very different on a bathroom door than a courthouse door."
>
> Thurgood Marshall, 1908–1993 (Associate justice of the United States Supreme Court, 1967–1991)

President Obama signed the Lilly Ledbetter Fair Act in 2009. How does this act differ from the Paycheck Fairness Act?

(AP Photo/Pablo Martinez Monsivais)

---

7. *Collier v. Turner Industries Group, LLC,* 797 F.Supp.2d 1029 (D. Idaho 2011).
8. 42 U.S.C. Section 2000e(k).
9. Pub. L. No. 111-2, 123 Stat. 5 (January 5, 2009), amending 42 U.S.C. Section 2000e-5[e].

limited plaintiffs' time period to file a wage discrimination complaint to 180 days after the employer's decision.[10] Today, if a plaintiff continues to work for the employer while receiving discriminatory wages, the time period for filing a complaint is basically unlimited.

Constructive Discharge

Constructive Discharge A termination of employment brought about by making the employee's working conditions so intolerable that the employee reasonably feels compelled to leave.

The majority of Title VII complaints involve unlawful discrimination in decisions to hire or fire employees. In some situations, however, employees who leave their jobs voluntarily can claim that they were "constructively discharged" by the employer. **Constructive discharge** occurs when the employer causes the employee's working conditions to be so intolerable that a reasonable person in the employee's position would feel compelled to quit.

Proving Constructive Discharge   The plaintiff must present objective proof of intolerable working conditions, which the employer knew or had reason to know about yet failed to correct within a reasonable time period. Courts generally also require the employee to show causation—that the employer's unlawful discrimination caused the working conditions to be intolerable. Put a different way, the employee's resignation must be a foreseeable result of the employer's discriminatory action.

Although courts weigh the facts on a case-by-case basis, employee demotion is one of the most frequently cited reasons for a finding of constructive discharge, particularly when the employee was subjected to humiliation. **EXAMPLE 25.10**   Khalil's employer humiliates him in front of his co-workers by informing him that he is being demoted to an inferior position. Khalil's co-workers then continually insult and harass him about his national origin (he is from Iran). The employer is aware of this discriminatory treatment but does nothing to remedy the situation, despite repeated complaints from Khalil. After several months, Khalil quits his job and files a Title VII claim. In this situation, Khalil would likely have sufficient evidence to maintain an action for constructive discharge in violation of Title VII. ●

Applies to All Title VII Discrimination   Note that constructive discharge is a theory that plaintiffs can use to establish any type of discrimination claims under Title VII, including race, color, national origin, religion, gender, pregnancy, and sexual harassment. Constructive discharge has also been successfully used in situations involving discrimination based on age or disability (both of which will be discussed later in this chapter). Constructive discharge is most commonly asserted in cases involving sexual harassment, however.

When constructive discharge is claimed, the employee can pursue damages for loss of income, including back pay. These damages ordinarily are not available to an employee who left a job voluntarily.

Sexual Harassment

Sexual Harassment The demanding of sexual favors in return for job promotions or other benefits, or language or conduct that is so sexually offensive that it creates a hostile working environment.

Title VII also protects employees against **sexual harassment** in the workplace. Sexual harassment can take two forms: *quid pro quo* harassment and hostile-environment harassment. *Quid pro quo* is a Latin phrase that is often translated to mean "something in exchange for something else." *Quid pro quo* harassment occurs when sexual favors are demanded in return for job opportunities, promotions, salary increases, and the like. According to the United States Supreme Court, hostile-environment harassment occurs when "the workplace is permeated with discriminatory intimidation, ridicule, and insult, that is sufficiently severe or pervasive to alter the conditions of the victim's employment and create an abusive working environment." [11]

---

10. *Ledbetter v. Goodyear Tire Co.*, 550 U.S. 618, 127 S.Ct. 2162, 167 L.Ed.2d 982 (2007).

11. *Harris v. Forklift Systems*, 510 U.S. 17, 114 S.Ct. 367, 126 L.Ed.2d 295 (1993). See also *Billings v. Town of Grafton*, 515 F.3d 39 (1st Cir. 2008).

The courts determine whether the sexually offensive conduct was sufficiently severe or pervasive to create a hostile environment on a case-by-case basis. Typically, a single incident of sexually offensive conduct is not enough to create a hostile environment (although there have been exceptions when the conduct was particularly objectionable). Note also that if the employee who is alleging sexual harassment has signed an employment contract with an arbitration clause (see Chapter 3), she or he will most likely be required to arbitrate the claim.[12]

······························

PREVENTING LEGAL DISPUTES

To avoid sexual-harassment complaints, you should be proactive in preventing sexual harassment in the workplace. Establish written policies, distribute them to employees, and review them annually. Make it clear that the policies prohibiting harassment and discrimination apply to everyone at all levels of your organization. Provide training. Assure employees that no one will be punished for making a complaint. If you receive complaints, always take them seriously and investigate—no matter how trivial they might seem.

Prompt remedial action is key, but it must not include any adverse action against the complainant (such as immediate termination). Also, never discourage employees from seeking the assistance of government agencies (such as the EEOC) or threaten or punish them for doing so. It is generally best to obtain the advice of counsel when you receive a sexual-harassment complaint.

Harassment by Supervisors

For an employer to be held liable for a supervisor's sexual harassment, the supervisor normally must have taken a *tangible employment action* against the employee. A **tangible employment action** is a significant change in employment status or benefits, such as when an employee is fired, refused a promotion, demoted, or reassigned to a position with significantly different responsibilities. Only a supervisor, or another person acting with the authority of the employer, can cause this sort of injury. A constructive discharge also qualifies as a tangible employment action.[13]

Tangible Employment Action A significant change in employment status or benefits, such as occurs when an employee is fired, refused a promotion, or reassigned to a lesser position.

The *Ellerth/Faragher* Affirmative Defense

In 1998, the United States Supreme Court issued several important rulings that have had a lasting impact on cases alleging sexual harassment by supervisors.[14] The Court held that an employer (a city) was liable for a supervisor's harassment of employees even though the employer was unaware of the behavior. Although the city had a written policy against sexual harassment, it had not distributed the policy to its employees and had not established any complaint procedures for employees who felt that they had been sexually harassed. In another case, the Court held that an employer can be liable for a supervisor's sexual harassment even though the employee does not suffer adverse job consequences.

The Court's decisions in these cases established what has become known as the "*Ellerth/Faragher* affirmative defense" to charges of sexual harassment. The defense has two elements:

A presumed victim of sexual harassment (on the right) attends a press conference with her attorney. What hurdles will she face in such litigation?

(AP Photo/Bay Area News Group, Oakland Tribune, Laura A. Oda)

1. That the employer has taken reasonable care to prevent and promptly correct any sexually harassing behavior (by establishing effective antiharassment policies and complaint procedures, for example).

---

12. See, for example, *EEOC v. Cheesecake Factory, Inc.,* 2009 WL 1259359 (D.Ariz. 2009).
13. See, for example, *Pennsylvania State Police v. Suders,* 542 U.S. 129, 124 S.Ct. 2342, 159 L.Ed.2d 204 (2004).
14. *Burlington Industries, Inc. v. Ellerth,* 524 U.S. 742, 118 S.Ct. 2257, 141 L.Ed.2d 633 (1998); and *Faragher v. City of Boca Raton,* 524 U.S. 775, 118 S.Ct. 2275, 141 L.Ed.2d 662 (1998).

2. That the plaintiff-employee unreasonably failed to take advantage of any preventive or corrective opportunities provided by the employer to avoid harm.

An employer that can prove both elements will not be liable for a supervisor's harassment.

Retaliation by Employers   Employers sometimes retaliate against employees who complain about sexual harassment or other Title VII violations. Retaliation can take many forms. An employer might demote or fire the person, or otherwise change the terms, conditions, and benefits of employment. Title VII prohibits retaliation, and employees can sue their employers. In a *retaliation claim*, an individual asserts that she or he has suffered a harm as a result of making a charge, testifying, or participating in a Title VII investigation or proceeding.

Plaintiffs do not have to prove that the challenged action adversely affected their workplace or employment.[15] Instead, to prove retaliation, plaintiffs must show that the challenged action was one that would likely have dissuaded a reasonable worker from making or supporting a charge of discrimination. Title VII's retaliation protection extends to an employee who speaks out about discrimination against another employee during an employer's internal investigation.[16] A court also held that it protected an employee who was fired after his fiancée filed a gender discrimination claim against their employer.[17]

In the following case, a female law professor lost her job after she complained about comments made by her dean and colleagues. The court had to decide whether she had been retaliated against for engaging in protected conduct.

15. *Burlington Northern and Santa Fe Railroad Co. v. White*, 548 U.S. 53, 126 S.Ct. 2405, 165 L.Ed.2d 345 (2006). (See the *Case Analysis Question* on page 677).
16. See *Crawford v. Metropolitan Government of Nashville and Davidson County, Tennessee*, 555 U.S. 271, 129 S.Ct. 846, 172 L.Ed.2d 650 (2009).
17. See *Thompson v. North American Stainless, LP*, ___ U.S. ___, 131 S.Ct. 863, 178 L.Ed.2d 694 (2011).

Case 25.1

Morales-Cruz v. University of Puerto Rico

United States Court of Appeals, First Circuit,
676 F.3d 220 (2012).
www.ca1.uscourts.gov[a]

(Diego Cervo/Shutterstock.com)

FACTS In 2003, Myrta Morales-Cruz began a tenure-track teaching position at the University of Puerto Rico School of Law. During her probationary period, one of her colleagues in a law school clinic had an affair with one of their students that resulted in a pregnancy. In 2008, Morales-Cruz asked the university's administrative committee to approve a one-year extension for her tenure review. The law school's dean criticized Morales-Cruz for failing to report her colleague's affair. He later recommended granting the extension but called Morales-Cruz "insecure," "immature," and "fragile." Similarly, a law school committee recommended granting the extension, but a dissenting professor commented that Morales-Cruz had shown poor judgment, had "personality flaws," and had trouble with "complex and sensitive" situations.

Morales-Cruz soon learned about the negative comments and complained in writing to the university's chancellor. The dean then recommended denying the one-year extension, and the administrative committee ultimately did so. When her employment was terminated, Morales-Cruz sued the university under Title VII. Among other things, she asserted that the dean had retaliated against her for complaining to the chancellor. A federal district court found that Morales-Cruz had not stated a proper retaliation claim under Title VII, and she appealed.

ISSUE Can Morales-Cruz bring a retaliation claim under Title VII because the law school's dean retaliated against her for complaining to the university's chancellor?

a. In the right-hand column, click on "Opinions." On the next page, in the "Short Title *contains*" box, type "Morales-Cruz," and click on "Submit Search." In the result, click on the link to access the opinion.

Case 25.1—Continues next page ➡

Case 25.1—Continued

DECISION   No. The appellate court affirmed the district court's judgment for the University of Puerto Rico.

REASON   Under Title VII, an employer may not retaliate against an employee because he or she has opposed a practice prohibited by Title VII. In this case, Morales-Cruz argued that the dean recommended against the one-year extension because she had complained about "discriminatory" comments. The court found that Morales-Cruz did not allege any facts that could be construed as gender-based discrimination. While the comments were hardly flattering, they were entirely gender-neutral. After all, the dean and dissenting professor said only that Morales-Cruz had shown poor judgment, had personality flaws, and was fragile, insecure, and immature. Thus, even if the dean retaliated against Morales-Cruz, it was not for engaging in conduct protected by Title VII.

CRITICAL THINKING—Ethical Consideration   *Could the dean have had legitimate reasons for changing his mind about the one-year extension? If so, what were they?*

Harassment by Co-Workers and Nonemployees   When the harassment of co-workers, rather than supervisors, creates a hostile working environment, an employee may still have a cause of action against the employer. Normally, though, the employer will be held liable only if the employer knew, or should have known, about the harassment and failed to take immediate remedial action.

Occasionally, a court may also hold an employer liable for harassment by *nonemployees* if the employer knew about the harassment and failed to take corrective action. **EXAMPLE 25.11**   Gordon, who owns and manages a Great Bites restaurant, knows that one of his regular customers, Dean, repeatedly harasses Sharon, a waitress. If Gordon does nothing and permits the harassment to continue, he may be liable under Title VII even though Dean is not an employee of the restaurant. •

Same-Gender Harassment   In *Oncale v. Sundowner Offshore Services, Inc.,*[18] the United States Supreme Court held that Title VII protection extends to individuals who are sexually harassed by members of the same gender. Proving that the harassment in same-gender cases is "based on sex" can be difficult, though. It is usually easier to establish a case of same-gender harassment when the harasser is homosexual.

Sexual Orientation Harassment   Although federal law (Title VII) does not prohibit discrimination or harassment based on a person's sexual orientation, a growing number of states have enacted laws that prohibit sexual orientation discrimination in private employment. Some states, such as Michigan, explicitly prohibit discrimination based on a person's gender identity or expression. Also, many companies have voluntarily established nondiscrimination policies that include sexual orientation. (Workers in the United States often have more protection against sexual harassment in the workplace than workers in other countries, as this chapter's *Beyond Our Borders* feature on the facing page explains.)

Online Harassment

Employees' online activities can create a hostile working environment in many ways. Racial jokes, ethnic slurs, or other comments contained in e-mail, text or instant messages, and social media or blog posts can become the basis for a claim of hostile-environment harassment or other forms of discrimination. A worker who regularly sees sexually explicit and

---

18. 523 U.S. 75, 118 S.Ct. 998, 140 L.Ed.2d 207 (1998).

BEYOND OUR BORDERS   Sexual Harassment in Other Nations

The problem of sexual harassment in the workplace is not confined to the United States. Indeed, it is a worldwide problem for female workers. In Argentina, Brazil, Egypt, Turkey, and many other countries, there is no legal protection against any form of employment discrimination.

Even in those countries that do have laws prohibiting discriminatory employment practices, including gender-based discrimination, those laws often do not specifically include sexual harassment as a discriminatory practice.

Several countries have attempted to remedy this omission by passing new laws or amending others to specifically prohibit sexual harassment in the workplace. Japan, for example, has amended its Equal Employment Opportunity Law to include a provision making sexual harassment illegal. Thailand has also passed its first sexual-harassment law. The European Union has adopted a directive that specifically identifies sexual harassment as a form of discrimination.

Nevertheless, women's groups throughout Europe contend that corporations in European countries tend to view sexual harassment with "quiet tolerance." They contrast this attitude with that of most U.S. corporations, which have implemented specific procedures to deal with harassment claims.

Critical Thinking
Why do you think U.S. corporations are more aggressive than European companies in taking steps to prevent sexual harassment in the workplace?

---

offensive images on a co-worker's computer screen or tablet device may claim that they create a hostile working environment.[19]

Nevertheless, employers may be able to avoid liability for online harassment if they take prompt remedial action. **EXAMPLE 25.12** While working at TriCom, Shonda Dean receives racially harassing e-mailed jokes from another employee. Shortly afterward, the company issues a warning to the offending employee about the proper use of the e-mail system and holds two meetings to discuss company policy on the use of the system. If Dean sues TriCom for racial discrimination, a court may find that because the employer took prompt remedial action, TriCom should not be held liable for its employee's racially harassing e-mails. •

Remedies under Title VII

LEARNING OBJECTIVE 3
What remedies are available under Title VII of the 1964 Civil Rights Act, as amended?

Employer liability under Title VII may be extensive. If the plaintiff successfully proves that unlawful discrimination occurred, he or she may be awarded reinstatement, back pay, retroactive promotions, and damages. Compensatory damages are available only in cases of intentional discrimination. Punitive damages may be recovered against a private employer only if the employer acted with malice or reckless indifference to an individual's rights.

The statute limits the total amount of compensatory and punitive damages that the plaintiff can recover from specific employers, depending on the size of the employer. The cap ranges from $50,000 for employers with one hundred or fewer employees to $300,000 for employers with more than five hundred employees.

Discrimination Based on Age

Age discrimination is potentially the most widespread form of discrimination, because anyone—regardless of race, color, national origin, or gender—could eventually be a victim. The Age Discrimination in Employment Act (ADEA) of 1967[20] prohibits employment

---

19. See, for example, *Doe v. XYC Corp.*, 382 N.J.Super. 122 (App.Div. 2005).
20. 29 U.S.C. Sections 621–634.

LEARNING OBJECTIVE 4
What federal act prohibits discrimination based on age?

discrimination on the basis of age against individuals forty years of age or older. The act also prohibits mandatory retirement for nonmanagerial workers.

For the act to apply, an employer must have twenty or more employees, and the employer's business activities must affect interstate commerce. The EEOC administers the ADEA, but the act also permits private causes of action against employers for age discrimination.

The ADEA includes a provision that extends protections against age discrimination to federal government employees.[21] This provision encompasses not only claims of age discrimination, but also claims of retaliation for complaining about age discrimination, which are not specifically mentioned in the statute.[22] Thus, the ADEA protects federal and private-sector employees from retaliation based on age-related complaints.

Procedures under the ADEA

The burden-shifting procedure under the ADEA differs from the procedure under Title VII as a result of a United States Supreme Court decision in 2009, which dramatically changed the burden of proof in age discrimination cases.[23] As explained earlier, if the plaintiff in a Title VII case can show that the employer was motivated, at least in part, by unlawful discrimination, the burden of proof shifts to the employer to articulate a legitimate non-discriminatory reason. Thus, in cases in which the employer has a "mixed motive" for discharging an employee, the employer has the burden of proving its reason was legitimate.

Under the ADEA, in contrast, a plaintiff must show that the unlawful discrimination was not just a reason but *the* reason for the adverse employment action. In other words, the employee has the burden of establishing "but for" causation—that is, but for the plaintiff's age, the adverse action would not have happened.

Thus, to establish a *prima facie* case, the plaintiff must show that he or she (1) was a member of the protected age group, (2) was qualified for the position from which he or she was discharged, and (3) was discharged because of age discrimination. Then the burden shifts to the employer. If the employer offers a legitimate reason for its action, then the plaintiff must show that the stated reason is only a pretext and that the plaintiff's age was the real reason for the employer's decision. The following case illustrates this procedure.

---

21. See 29 U.S.C. Section 632(a) (2000 ed., Supp. V).
22. *Gomez-Perez v. Potter,* 553 U.S. 474, 128 S.Ct. 1931, 170 L.Ed.2d 887 (2008).
23. *Gross v. FBL Financial Services,* 557 U.S. 167, 129 S.Ct. 2343, 174 L.Ed.2d 119 (2009).

Case 25.2

Mora v. Jackson Memorial Foundation, Inc.

United States Court of Appeals, Eleventh Circuit,
597 F.3d 1201 (2010).
www.ca11.uscourts.gov/opinions/search.php[a]

When is firing an older worker considered age discrimination?

FACTS Josephine Mora, a fund-raiser for Jackson Memorial Foundation, Inc., was sixty-two years old when the foundation's chief executive officer (CEO) fired her, citing errors and issues with professionalism. Mora filed a suit against the foundation, alleging age discrimination. She asserted that when she was fired, the CEO told her, "I need someone younger I can pay less." She had a witness who had heard that statement as well as another in which the CEO said that Mora was "too old to be working

---

a. In the "Search by Keyword:" box, type "Jackson Memorial," and click on "Search." When that page opens, click on the link to access the opinion.

Case 25.2—Continued

here anyway." The foundation moved for summary judgment, arguing that Mora was fired chiefly because she was incompetent. The district court granted the motion, and Mora appealed.

ISSUE Did Mora present sufficient evidence that the employer's stated reason for firing her was only a pretext?

DECISION Yes. The U.S. Court of Appeals for the Eleventh Circuit vacated (set aside) the decision of the trial court and remanded the case for a trial.

REASON Because there was a "disputed question of material fact" as to whether the plaintiff had been fired because of her

age, the defendant was not entitled to summary judgment. The district court should *not* have examined the question of whether Mora would have been fired no matter what her age was simply because she had become incompetent. "The resolution of this case depends on whose account of the pertinent conversations a jury would credit. A reasonable juror could accept that [the CEO] made the discriminatory-sounding remarks and that the remarks are sufficient evidence of a discriminatory motive." A reasonable juror could conclude that that the CEO fired Mora because of her age.

CRITICAL THINKING—Ethical Consideration *Is the court's decision fair to employers? Why or why not?*

State Employees Not Covered by the ADEA

Generally, the states are immune from lawsuits brought by private individuals in federal court—unless a state consents to the suit. This immunity stems from the United States Supreme Court's interpretation of the Eleventh Amendment (the text of this amendment is included in Appendix B of this text). **CASE EXAMPLE 25.13** In two Florida cases, professors and librarians contended that their employers—two Florida state universities—denied them salary increases and other benefits because they were getting old and their successors could be hired at lower cost. The universities claimed that as agencies of a sovereign state, they could not be sued in federal court without the state's consent. The cases ultimately reached the United States Supreme Court, which held that the Eleventh Amendment bars private parties from suing state employers for violations of the ADEA.[24] ●

State immunity under the Eleventh Amendment is not absolute, however. In some situations, such as when fundamental rights are at stake, Congress has the power to abrogate (abolish) state immunity to private suits through legislation that unequivocally shows Congress's intent to subject states to private suits.[25]

As a general rule, though, the Court has found that state employers are immune from private suits brought by employees under the ADEA (for age discrimination, as noted above), the Americans with Disabilities Act[26] (for disability discrimination), and the Fair Labor Standards Act[27] (which relates to wages and hours—see Chapter 24). In contrast, states are not immune from the requirements of the Family and Medical Leave Act[28] (see Chapter 24).

> "Growing old is like being increasingly penalized for a crime you have not committed."
>
> Anthony Powell, 1905–2000 (English novelist)

Discrimination Based on Disability

The Americans with Disabilities Act (ADA) of 1990[29] prohibits disability-based discrimination in workplaces with fifteen or more workers (with the exception of state government employers, who are generally immune under the Eleventh Amendment, as just discussed).

---

24. *Kimel v. Florida Board of Regents,* 528 U.S. 62, 120 S.Ct. 631, 145 L.Ed.2d 522 (2000).
25. *Tennessee v. Lane,* 541 U.S. 509, 124 S.Ct. 1978, 158 L.Ed.2d 820 (2004).
26. *Board of Trustees of the University of Alabama v. Garrett,* 531 U.S. 356, 121 S.Ct. 955, 148 L.Ed.2d 866 (2001).
27. *Alden v. Maine,* 527 U.S. 706, 119 S.Ct. 2240, 144 L.Ed.2d 636 (1999).
28. *Nevada Department of Human Resources v. Hibbs,* 538 U.S. 721, 123 S.Ct. 1972, 155 L.Ed.2d 953 (2003).
29. 42 U.S.C. Sections 12102–12118.

Basically, the ADA requires that employers reasonably accommodate the needs of persons with disabilities unless to do so would cause the employer to suffer an undue hardship. In 2008, Congress broadened the coverage of the ADA's protections in the ADA Amendments Act,[30] which will be discussed shortly.

Procedures under the ADA

To prevail on a claim under the ADA, a plaintiff must show that he or she (1) has a disability, (2) is otherwise qualified for the employment in question, and (3) was excluded from the employment solely because of the disability. As in Title VII cases, a plaintiff must pursue her or his claim through the EEOC before filing an action in court for a violation of the ADA.

The EEOC may decide to investigate and perhaps even sue the employer on behalf of the employee. If the EEOC decides not to sue, then the employee is entitled to sue in court. According to the United States Supreme Court, the EEOC can bring a suit against an employer for disability-based discrimination even though the employee previously agreed to submit any job-related disputes to arbitration (see Chapter 3).[31]

Plaintiffs in lawsuits brought under the ADA may obtain many of the same remedies available under Title VII. These include reinstatement, back pay, a limited amount of compensatory and punitive damages (for intentional discrimination), and certain other forms of relief. Repeat violators may be ordered to pay fines of up to $100,000.

What Is a Disability?

The ADA is broadly drafted to cover persons with a wide range of disabilities. Specifically, the ADA defines *disability* to include any of the following:

1. A physical or mental impairment that substantially limits one or more of an individual's major life activities.
2. A record of such impairment.
3. Being regarded as having such an impairment.

Health conditions that have been considered disabilities under the federal law include blindness, alcoholism, heart disease, cancer, muscular dystrophy, cerebral palsy, paraplegia, diabetes, acquired immune deficiency syndrome (AIDS), testing positive for the human immunodeficiency virus (HIV), and morbid obesity (defined as existing when an individual's weight is two times the normal weight for his or her height).

A separate provision in the ADA prevents employers from taking adverse employment actions based on stereotypes or assumptions about individuals who associate with people who have disabilities.[32] At one time, the courts focused on whether a person was disabled *after* the use of corrective devices or medication. With this approach, a person with severe myopia, or nearsightedness, which can be corrected with lenses, for instance, would not qualify as disabled because that individual's major life activities were not substantially impaired. In 2008, Congress amended the ADA to strengthen its protections and prohibit employers from considering mitigating measures or medications when determining if an individual has a disability. Disability is now determined on a case-by-case basis.

"Jobs are physically easier, but the worker now takes home worries instead of an aching back."

Homer Bigart, 1907–1991
(American journalist)

---

30. 42 U.S.C. Sections 12103 and 12205a.

31. *EEOC v. Waffle House, Inc.*, 534 U.S. 279, 122 S.Ct. 754, 151 L.Ed.2d 755 (2002).

32. 42 U.S.C. Section 12112(b)(4). Under this provision, an employer cannot, for instance, refuse to hire the parent of a child with a disability based on the assumption that the parent will miss work too often or be unreliable.

A condition may fit the definition of disability in one set of circumstances, but not in another. What makes the difference in a particular situation? The court in the following case answered that question.

Case 25.3

Rohr v. Salt River Project Agricultural Improvement and Power District

United States Court of Appeals, Ninth Circuit,
555 F.3d 850 (2009).
www.ca9.uscourts.gov[a]

(Lightpoet/Shutterstock.com)

Can this man's diabetes be considered a disability?

HISTORICAL AND SOCIAL SETTING *Diabetes is a chronic and incurable disease associated with an increased risk of heart disease, stroke, high blood pressure, blindness, kidney disease, and many other disorders. Type 1 diabetes, or juvenile diabetes, results from the body's failure to produce insulin—a hormone that is needed to convert food into energy. Type 2 results from the body's failure to properly use insulin. If left untreated, type 2 can cause seizures and a coma. In the United States, approximately 23.6 million children and adults, or 7.8 percent of the population, have diabetes.*

FACTS Larry Rohr has type 2 diabetes. If he fails to follow a complex regimen of daily insulin injections, blood tests, and a strict diet, his blood sugar rises to a level that aggravates his disease. At the time of his diagnosis, he was a welding metallurgy specialist for the Salt River Project Agricultural Improvement and Power District, which provides utility services to homes in Arizona. Due to the effort required to manage his diabetes, particularly his strict diet, Rohr's physician forbade his assignment to tasks involving overnight, out-of-town travel. Salt River told Rohr that this would prevent him from performing the essential functions of his job, such as responding to power outages. Rohr was asked to transfer, apply for disability benefits, or take early retirement. He filed a suit against Salt River, alleging discrimination. The court issued a summary judgment in the employer's favor. Rohr appealed.

ISSUE Is diabetes a disability under the ADA if it significantly restricts an individual's eating?

DECISION Yes. The U.S. Court of Appeals for the Ninth Circuit vacated the lower court's judgment and remanded the case for trial.

REASON The ADA's definition of disability includes physical impairments that substantially limit a major life activity. Diabetes is a physical impairment because it affects the digestive, hemic (blood), and endocrine systems. Major life activities include eating patterns. Thus, if the symptoms of diabetes and the efforts to manage the disease significantly restrict an individual's eating, the definition of disability is met. In many instances, failure to take insulin can result in severe health problems and even death. Determining how much insulin to take can require frequent, self-administered blood tests and adjustments in activity and food levels. Rohr must follow these steps. Because insulin alone does not stabilize his blood sugar levels, he must strictly monitor what, and when, he eats every day. Failure to do so would endanger his health. "Straying from a diet for more than one or two meals is not a cause for medical concern for most people, and skipping a meal, or eating a large one, does not expose them to the risk of fainting." But for Rohr the effort to control his diet is substantially limiting.

CRITICAL THINKING—Technological Consideration *If Rohr could have monitored his condition and regimen through a cell phone or other portable Internet connection, would the result in this case likely have been affected? Explain.*

---

a. In the left-hand column, in the "Opinions" pull-out menu, click on "Published." On that page, click on "Advanced Search." In the "by Case No.:" box, type "06-16527" and click on "Search." In the result, click on the case title to access the opinion.

Reasonable Accommodation

The ADA does not require that employers accommodate the needs of job applicants or employees with disabilities who are not otherwise qualified for the work. If a job applicant or an employee with a disability can perform essential job functions with a reasonable accommodation, however, the employer must make the accommodation.

Required modifications may include installing ramps for a wheelchair, establishing more flexible working hours, creating or modifying job assignments, and creating or improving training materials and procedures. Generally, employers should give primary consideration to employees' preferences in deciding what accommodations should be made.

Undue Hardship

Employers who do not accommodate the needs of persons with disabilities must demonstrate that the accommodations will cause "undue hardship" in terms of being significantly difficult or expensive for the employer. Usually, the courts decide whether an accommodation constitutes an undue hardship on a case-by-case basis by looking at the employer's resources in relation to the specific accommodation.

EXAMPLE 25.14   Bryan Lockhart, who uses a wheelchair, works for a cell phone company that provides parking for its employees. Lockhart informs the company supervisors that the parking spaces are so narrow that he is unable to extend the ramp on his van that allows him to get in and out of the vehicle. Lockhart therefore requests that the company reasonably accommodate his needs by paying a monthly fee for him to use a larger parking space in an adjacent lot. In this situation, a court would likely find that it would not be an undue hardship for the employer to pay for additional parking for Lockhart. •

Job Applications and Preemployment Physical Exams

Employers must modify their job-application process so that those with disabilities can compete for jobs with those who do not have disabilities. For instance, a job announcement might be modified to allow job applicants to respond by e-mail or letter, as well as by telephone, so that it does not discriminate against potential applicants with hearing impairments.

Employers are restricted in the kinds of questions they may ask on job-application forms and during preemployment interviews. Furthermore, they cannot require persons with disabilities to submit to preemployment physicals unless such exams are required of all other applicants. Employers can condition an offer of employment on the applicant's successfully passing a medical examination, but can disqualify the applicant only if the medical problems they discover would render the applicant unable to perform the job.

CASE EXAMPLE 25.15   When filling the position of delivery truck driver, a company cannot automatically screen out all applicants who are unable to meet the U.S. Department of Transportation's hearing standard. The company would first have to prove that drivers who are deaf are not qualified to perform the essential job function of driving safely and pose a higher risk of accidents than drivers who are not deaf.[33] •

Substance Abusers

Drug addiction is a disability under the ADA because drug addiction is a substantially limiting impairment. Those who are actually using illegal drugs are not protected by the act, however. The ADA protects only persons with *former* drug addictions—those who have completed or are now in a supervised drug-rehabilitation program. Individuals who have used drugs casually in the past are not protected under the act. They are not considered addicts and therefore do not have a disability (addiction).

People suffering from alcoholism are protected by the ADA. Employers cannot legally discriminate against employees simply because they are suffering from alcoholism. Of course, employers have the right to prohibit the use of alcohol in the workplace and can require that employees not be under the influence of alcohol while working. Employers can also fire or refuse to hire a person who is an alcoholic if he or she poses a substantial risk of harm either to himself or herself or to others and the risk cannot be reduced by reasonable accommodation.

---

33. *Bates v. United Parcel Service, Inc.*, 465 F.3d 1069 (9th Cir. 2006).

Health-Insurance Plans   Workers with disabilities must be given equal access to any health insurance provided to other employees. Under 2010 health-care reforms, employers cannot exclude preexisting health conditions from coverage. An employer can also put a limit, or cap, on health-care payments under its group health policy—as long as such caps are "applied equally to all insured employees" and do not "discriminate on the basis of disability." Whenever a group health-care plan makes a disability-based distinction in its benefits, the plan violates the ADA (unless the employer can justify its actions under the business necessity defense, which will be discussed shortly).

Defenses to Employment Discrimination

LEARNING OBJECTIVE 5
What are three defenses to claims of employment discrimination?

The first line of defense for an employer charged with employment discrimination is, of course, to assert that the plaintiff has failed to meet his or her initial burden of proving that discrimination occurred. Once a plaintiff succeeds in proving discrimination, the burden shifts to the employer to justify the discriminatory practice.

Possible justifications include that the discrimination was the result of a business necessity, a bona fide occupational qualification, or a seniority system. In some situations, as noted earlier, an effective antiharassment policy and prompt remedial action when harassment occurs may shield employers from liability for sexual harassment under Title VII.

Business Necessity

Business Necessity A defense to an allegation of employment discrimination in which the employer demonstrates that an employment practice that discriminates against members of a protected class is related to job performance.

An employer may defend against a claim of disparate-impact (unintentional) discrimination by asserting that a practice that has a discriminatory effect is a **business necessity.** EXAMPLE 25.16 If requiring a high school diploma is shown to have a discriminatory effect, an employer might argue that a high school education is necessary for workers to perform the job at a required level of competence. If the employer can demonstrate a definite connection between a high school education and job performance, the employer normally will succeed in this business necessity defense. •

Bona Fide Occupational Qualification

Bona Fide Occupational Qualification (BFOQ) Identifiable characteristics reasonably necessary to the normal operation of a particular business. These characteristics can include gender, national origin, and religion, but not race.

Another defense applies when discrimination against a protected class is essential to a job—that is, when a particular trait is a **bona fide occupational qualification (BFOQ).** Race, however, can never be a BFOQ.

Generally, courts have restricted the BFOQ defense to instances in which the employee's gender is essential to the job. EXAMPLE 25.17 A women's clothing store might legitimately hire only female sales attendants if part of an attendant's job involves assisting clients in the store's dressing rooms. Similarly, the Federal Aviation Administration can legitimately impose age limits for airline pilots—but an airline cannot impose weight limits only on female flight attendants. •

Seniority Systems

Seniority System A system in which those who have worked longest for an employer are first in line for promotions, salary increases, and other benefits, and are last to be laid off if the workforce must be reduced.

An employer with a history of discrimination might have no members of protected classes in upper-level positions. Even if the employer now seeks to be unbiased, some employees may bring a lawsuit asking a court to order that minorities be promoted ahead of schedule to compensate for past discrimination. If no present intent to discriminate is shown, however, and if promotions or other job benefits are distributed according to a fair **seniority system** (in which workers with more years of service are promoted first or laid off last), the employer normally has a good defense against the suit.

CASE EXAMPLE 25.18   According to the United States Supreme Court, this defense may also apply to alleged discrimination under the ADA. The case involved a baggage handler who had injured his back and asked to be reassigned to a mailroom at U.S. Airways, Inc. The airline refused to give the employee the position because another employee had seniority. The Court sided with U.S. Airways. If an employee with a disability requests an accommodation that conflicts with an employer's seniority system, the accommodation generally will not be considered "reasonable" under the act.[34] •

After-Acquired Evidence of Employee Misconduct

In some situations, employers have attempted to avoid liability for employment discrimination on the basis of "after-acquired evidence"—that is, evidence that the employer discovers after a lawsuit is filed—of an employee's misconduct.   **EXAMPLE 25.19**   An employer fires a worker who then sues the employer for employment discrimination. During pretrial investigation, the employer learns that the employee made material misrepresentations on his employment application—misrepresentations that, had the employer known about them, would have served as grounds to fire the individual. •

According to the United States Supreme Court, after-acquired evidence of wrongdoing cannot shield an employer entirely from liability for employment discrimination. It may, however, be used to limit the amount of damages for which the employer is liable.[35]

Affirmative Action

Affirmative Action Job-hiring policies that give special consideration to members of protected classes in an effort to overcome present effects of past discrimination.

Federal statutes and regulations providing for equal opportunity in the workplace were designed to reduce or eliminate discriminatory practices with respect to hiring, retaining, and promoting employees. **Affirmative action** programs go further and attempt to "make up" for past patterns of discrimination by giving members of protected classes preferential treatment in hiring or promotion. During the 1960s, all federal and state government agencies, private companies that contracted to do business with the federal government, and institutions that received federal funding were required to implement affirmative action policies.

Title VII of the Civil Rights Act of 1964 neither requires nor prohibits affirmative action. Thus, most private firms have not been required to implement affirmative action policies, though many have voluntarily done so. Affirmative action programs have been controversial, however, particularly when they have resulted in reverse discrimination (discussed on page 658).

Constitutionality of Affirmative Action Programs

Because of their inherently discriminatory nature, affirmative action programs may violate the equal protection clause of the Fourteenth Amendment to the U.S. Constitution. The United States Supreme Court has held that any federal, state, or local affirmative action program that uses racial or ethnic classifications as the basis for making decisions is subject to strict scrutiny by the courts.[36] Recall from Chapter 2 that strict scrutiny is the highest standard, which means that most affirmative action programs do not survive a court's analysis under this test.

Today, an affirmative action program normally is constitutional only if it attempts to remedy past discrimination and does not make use of quotas or preferences. Furthermore, once such a program has succeeded in the goal of remedying past discrimination, it must be changed or dropped.

---

34. *U.S. Airways, Inc. v. Barnett,* 535 U.S. 391, 122 S.Ct. 1516, 152 L.Ed.2d 589 (2002).
35. *McKennon v. Nashville Banner Publishing Co.,* 513 U.S. 352, 115 S.Ct. 879, 130 L.Ed.2d 852 (1995).
36. See the landmark decision in *Adarand Constructors, Inc. v. Peña,* 515 U.S. 200, 115 S.Ct. 2097, 132 L.Ed.2d 158 (1995).

Affirmative Action in Schools

Most of the affirmative action cases that have reached the United States Supreme Court in the last twenty years have involved university admissions programs and schools, rather than employment. Generally, the Court has found that a school admissions policy that *automatically* awards minority applicants a specified number of points needed to guarantee admission violates the equal protection clause.[37]

A school can, however, "consider race or ethnicity more flexibly as a 'plus' factor in the context of individualized consideration of each and every applicant."[38] In other words, it is unconstitutional for schools to apply a mechanical formula that gives "diversity bonuses" based on race or ethnicity.

CASE EXAMPLE 25.20   School districts in Seattle, Washington, and Jefferson County, Kentucky, adopted plans that relied on race to assign certain children to schools. The Seattle plan classified children as "white" or "nonwhite" and used the racial classifications as a "tiebreaker" to determine which high school students would attend. The school district in Jefferson County classified students as "black" or "other" to assign children to elementary schools. Parent groups filed lawsuits claiming that the racial preferences violated the equal protection clause.

The United States Supreme Court held that the school districts had failed to show that the use of racial classifications in their student assignment plans was necessary to achieve their stated goal of racial diversity. Hence, the affirmative action programs of both school districts were unconstitutional.[39] ●

---

37. *Gratz v. Bollinger,* 539 U.S. 244, 123 S.Ct. 2411, 156 L.Ed.2d 257 (2003).
38. *Grutter v. Bollinger,* 539 U.S. 306, 123 S.Ct. 2325, 156 L.Ed.2d 304 (2003).
39. The Court consolidated the two cases and issued one opinion for both. See *Parents Involved in Community Schools v. Seattle School District No. 1,* 551 U.S. 701, 127 S.Ct. 2738, 168 L.Ed.2d 508 (2007).

Reviewing . . . Employment Discrimination and Diversity

Amaani Lyle, an African American woman, took a job as a scriptwriters' assistant at Warner Brothers Television Productions. She worked for the writers of *Friends,* a popular, adult-oriented television series. One of her essential job duties was to type detailed notes for the scriptwriters during brainstorming sessions in which they discussed jokes, dialogue, and story lines. The writers then combed through Lyle's notes after the meetings for script material. During these meetings, the three male scriptwriters told lewd and vulgar jokes and made sexually explicit comments and gestures. They often talked about their personal sexual experiences and fantasies, and some of these conversations were then used in episodes of *Friends.*

During the meetings, Lyle never complained that she found the writers' conduct offensive. After four months, she was fired because she could not type fast enough to keep up with the writers' conversations during the meetings. She filed a suit against Warner Brothers alleging sexual harassment and claiming that her termination was based on racial discrimination. Using the information presented in the chapter, answer the following questions.

1. Would Lyle's claim of racial discrimination be for intentional (disparate-treatment) or unintentional (disparate-impact) discrimination? Explain.
2. Can Lyle establish a *prima facie* case of racial discrimination? Why or why not?
3. When she was hired, Lyle was told that typing speed was extremely important to her position. At the time, she maintained that she could type eighty words per minute, so she was not given a typing test. It later turned out that Lyle could type only fifty words per minute. What impact might typing speed have on Lyle's lawsuit?

Continued

4. Lyle's sexual-harassment claim is based on the hostile work environment created by the writers' sexually offensive conduct at meetings that she was required to attend. The writers, however, argue that their behavior was essential to the "creative process" of writing *Friends*, a show that routinely contained sexual innuendos and adult humor. Which defense discussed in the chapter might Warner Brothers assert using this argument?

DEBATE THIS: Members of minority groups and women have made enough economic progress in the last several decades that they no longer need special legislation to protect them.

LINKING BUSINESS LAW to Corporate Management

Human Resource Management

Your career may lead to running a small business, managing a small part of a larger business, or making decisions for the operations of a big business. In any context, you may be responsible for employment decisions. As this chapter has suggested, an ill-conceived hiring or firing process can lead to a lawsuit. As a manager, you must also ensure that employees do not practice discrimination on the job. Enter the human resource management specialist.

What Is Human Resource Management?

Human resource management (HRM) is the acquisition, maintenance, and development of an organization's employees. HRM involves the design and application of formal systems in an organization to ensure the effective and efficient use of human talent to accomplish organizational goals.

All managers need to be skilled in HRM. Some firms require managers to play an active role in recruiting and selecting personnel, as well as in developing training programs. Those who work in a human resources department should be especially aware of the issues outlined in this chapter (and in Chapters 23 and 24).

The Acquisition Phase of HRM

Acquiring talented employees is the first step in an HRM system. All recruitment must be done without violating any of the laws and regulations outlined in this chapter. Obviously, recruitment must be colorblind, as well as indifferent to gender, religion, national origin, and age. Devise recruitment methods that do not have even the slightest hint of discriminatory basis. Recruitment methods must also give an equal chance to people with disabilities.

Only the applicant's qualifications can be considered, not his or her disability. If a candidate with a disability is rejected, make sure to document that the rejection is based solely on the applicant's lack of training or ability.

On-the-Job HRM Issues

In addition, the HRM professional must also monitor the working environment. Sexual harassment is a major concern. You may need to work closely with an employment law specialist to develop antiharassment rules and policies. You also need to publish them and provide training to ensure that all employees are familiar with the firm's policy. In addition, you should create and supervise a grievance system so that any harassment can be stopped before it becomes actionable.

HRM Issues concerning Employee Termination

Even in employment-at-will jurisdictions, lawsuits can arise for improper termination. Develop a system to protect your company from lawsuits, such as procedures for documenting an employee's misconduct and the employer's warnings or other disciplinary actions. The company should also have an established policy for dealing with improper or incompetent behavior, and should be clear about the amount of severance pay that terminated employees will receive. Sometimes, it is better to err on the side of generosity to maintain the goodwill of terminated employees.

Critical Thinking

What are some types of actions that an HRM professional can take to reduce the probability of harassment lawsuits against her or his company?

Key Terms

affirmative action 672
bona fide occupational
   qualification (BFOQ) 671
business necessity 671

constructive discharge 661
disparate-impact discrimination 657
disparate-treatment discrimination 656

employment discrimination 655
prima facie case 657
protected class 654

seniority system 671
sexual harassment 661
tangible employment action 662

Chapter Summary: Employment Discrimination and Diversity

Title VII of the Civil Rights Act of 1964 (See pages 655–658.)	Title VII prohibits employment discrimination based on race, color, national origin, religion, or gender. 1. *Procedures*—Employees must file a claim with the Equal Employment Opportunity Commission (EEOC). The EEOC may sue the employer on the employee's behalf. If not, the employee may sue the employer directly. 2. *Types of discrimination*—Title VII prohibits both intentional (disparate-treatment) and unintentional (disparate-impact) discrimination. Disparate-impact discrimination occurs when an employer's practice, such as requiring a certain level of education, has the effect of discriminating against a protected class. Title VII also extends to discriminatory practices, such as various forms of harassment, in the online environment. 3. *Remedies for discrimination under Title VII*—Remedies include reinstatement, back pay, and retroactive promotions. Damages (both compensatory and punitive) may be awarded for intentional discrimination.
Discrimination Based on Age (See pages 665–667.)	The Age Discrimination in Employment Act (ADEA) of 1967 prohibits employment discrimination on the basis of age against individuals forty years of age or older. Procedures for bringing a case under the ADEA are similar to those for bringing a case under Title VII.
Discrimination Based on Disability (See pages 667–671.)	The Americans with Disabilities Act (ADA) of 1990 prohibits employment discrimination against persons with disabilities who are otherwise qualified to perform the essential functions of the jobs for which they apply. 1. *Procedures and remedies*—To prevail on a claim, the plaintiff must show that she or he has a disability, is otherwise qualified for the employment in question, and was excluded from it solely because of the disability. Procedures and remedies under the ADA are similar to those in Title VII cases. 2. *Definition of disability*—The ADA defines the term *disability* as a physical or mental impairment that substantially limits one or more major life activities, a record of such impairment, or being regarded as having such an impairment. 3. *Reasonable accommodation*—Employers are required to reasonably accommodate the needs of persons with disabilities through such measures as modifying the physical work environment and permitting more flexible work schedules. Employers are not required to accommodate the needs of all workers with disabilities, such as who pose a definite threat to health and safety in the workplace or who are not otherwise qualified for their jobs.
Defenses to Employment Discrimination (See pages 671–672.)	As defenses to claims of employment discrimination, employers may assert that the discrimination was required for reasons of business necessity, to meet a bona fide occupational qualification, or to maintain a legitimate seniority system. Evidence of prior employee misconduct acquired after the employee has been fired is not a defense to discrimination.
Affirmative Action (See pages 672–673.)	Affirmative action programs attempt to "make up" for past patterns of discrimination by giving members of protected classes preferential treatment in hiring or promotion. Such programs are subject to strict scrutiny by the courts and are often struck down for violating the Fourteenth Amendment.

ExamPrep

ISSUE SPOTTERS

1. Ruth is a supervisor for a Subs & Suds restaurant. Tim is a Subs & Suds employee. The owner announces that some employees will be discharged. Ruth tells Tim that if he has sex with her, he can keep his job. Is this sexual harassment? Why or why not? (**See pages 661–665.**)
2. Koko, a person with a disability, applies for a job at Lively Sales Corporation for which she is well qualified, but she is rejected. Lively continues to seek applicants and eventually fills the position with a person who does not have a disability. Could Koko succeed in a suit against Lively for discrimination? Explain. (**See page 668.**)

— **Check your answers to the Issue Spotters against the answers provided in Appendix E at the end of this text.**

For Review

Answers to the even-numbered questions in this For Review section can be found in Appendix F at the end of this text.

1. Generally, what kind of conduct is prohibited by Title VII of the Civil Rights Act of 1964, as amended?
2. What is the difference between disparate-treatment discrimination and disparate-impact discrimination?
3. What remedies are available under Title VII of the 1964 Civil Rights Act, as amended?
4. What federal act prohibits discrimination based on age?
5. What are three defenses to claims of employment discrimination?

Business Scenarios and Case Problems

25–1 Title VII Violations. Discuss fully whether either of the following actions would constitute a violation of Title VII of the 1964 Civil Rights Act, as amended.
 1. Tennington, Inc., is a consulting firm and has ten employees. These employees travel on consulting jobs in seven states. Tennington has an employment record of hiring only white males. **(See page 657.)**
 2. Novo Films, Inc., is making a film about Africa and needs to employ approximately one hundred extras for this picture. To hire these extras, Novo advertises in all major newspapers in Southern California. The ad states that only African Americans need apply. **(See page 671.)**

25–2 ❓ **Question with Sample Answer—Disparate-Impact Discrimination.** Chinawa, a major processor of cheese sold throughout the United States, employs one hundred workers at its principal processing plant. The plant is located in Heartland Corners, which has a population that is 50 percent white and 25 percent African American, with the balance Hispanic American, Asian American, and others. Chinawa requires a high school diploma as a condition of employment for its cleaning crew. Three-fourths of the white population complete high school, compared with only one-fourth of those in the minority groups. Chinawa has an all-white cleaning crew. Has Chinawa violated Title VII of the Civil Rights Act of 1964? Explain. **(See pages 657 and 671.)**

—**For a sample answer to Question 25–2, go to Appendix G at the end of this text.**

25–3 Religious Discrimination. Gina Gomez, a devout Roman Catholic, worked for Sam's Department Stores, Inc., in Phoenix, Arizona. Sam's considered Gomez a productive employee because her sales exceeded $200,000 per year. At the time, the store gave its managers the discretion to grant unpaid leave to employees but prohibited vacations or leave during the holiday season—October through December. Gomez felt that she had a "calling" to go on a "pilgrimage" in October to Bosnia where some persons claimed to have had visions of the Virgin Mary. The Catholic Church had not designated the site an official pilgrimage site, the visions were not expected to be stronger in October, and tours were available at other times. The store managers denied Gomez's request for leave, but she had a nonrefundable ticket and left anyway. Sam's terminated her employment, and she could not find another job. Can Gomez establish a *prima facie* case of religious discrimination? Explain. **(See page 659.)**

25–4 🧳 **Spotlight on the Civil Rights Act—Discrimination Based on Gender.** Burlington Coat Factory Warehouse, Inc., had a dress code that required male salesclerks to wear business attire consisting of slacks, shirt, and a necktie. Female salesclerks, by contrast, were required to wear a smock so that customers could readily identify them. Karen O'Donnell and other female employees refused to wear the smock. Instead they reported to work in business attire and were suspended. After numerous suspensions, the female employees were fired for violating Burlington's dress code policy. All other conditions of employment, including salary, hours, and benefits, were the same for female and male employees. Was the dress code policy discriminatory? Why or why not? [*O'Donnell v. Burlington Coat Factory Warehouse, Inc.*, 656 F.Supp. 263 (S.D. Ohio 1987)] **(See page 660.)**

25–5 ⚖️ **Case Problem with Sample Answer—Retaliation by Employers.** Entek International hired Shane Dawson, a male homosexual. Some of Dawson's co-workers, including his supervisor, made derogatory comments about his sexual orientation. Dawson's work deteriorated. He filed a complaint with Entek's human resources department. Two days later, he was fired. State law

hostile
work
environment
illegal
CHAPTER 25 Employment Discrimination and Diversity
677

made it unlawful for an employer to discriminate against an individual based on sexual orientation. Could Dawson establish a claim for retaliation? Explain. [*Dawson v. Entek International*, 630 F.3d 928 (9th Cir. 2011)] **(See page 663.)**

—For a sample answer to Problem 25–5, go to Appendix H at the end of this text.

25–6 **Sexual Harassment by Co-Worker.** Billie Bradford worked for the Kentucky Department of Community Based Services (DCBS). One of Bradford's co-workers, Lisa Stander, routinely engaged in extreme sexual behavior (such as touching herself and making crude comments) in Bradford's presence. Bradford and others regularly complained about Stander's conduct to their supervisor, Angie Taylor. Rather than resolve the problem, Taylor nonchalantly told Stander to stop, encouraged Bradford to talk to Stander, and suggested that Stander was just having fun. Assuming that Bradford was subjected to a hostile-work environment, could DCBS be liable? Why or why not? [*Bradford v. Department of Community Based Services*, 2012 WL 360032 (E.D.Ky. 2012)] **(See page 664.)**

25–7 ⟷ **A Question of Ethics—Discrimination Based on Disability.** Titan Distribution, Inc., employed Quintak, Inc., to run its tire mounting and distribution operation in Des Moines, Iowa. Robert Chalfant worked for Quintak as a second-shift supervisor at Titan. He suffered a heart attack in 1992 and underwent heart bypass surgery in 1997. He also

had arthritis. In July 2002, Titan decided to terminate Quintak. Chalfant applied to work at Titan. On his application, he described himself as having a disibility. After a physical exam, Titan's doctor concluded that Chalfant could work in his current capacity, and he was notified that he would be hired. Despite the notice, Nadis Barucic, a Titan employee, wrote "not pass px" at the top of Chalfant's application, and he was not hired. He took a job with AMPCO Systems, a parking ramp management company. This work involved walking up to five miles a day and lifting more weight than he had at Titan. In September, Titan eliminated its second shift. Chalfant filed a suit in a federal district court against Titan, in part, under the Americans with Disabilities Act (ADA). Titan argued that the reason it had not hired Chalfant was not that he did not pass the physical, but no one—including Barucic—could explain why she had written "not pass px" on his application. Later, Titan claimed that Chalfant was not hired because the entire second shift was going to be eliminated. [*Chalfant v. Titan Distribution, Inc.*, 475 F.3d 982 (8th Cir. 2007)] **(See pages 667–671.)**

1. What must Chalfant establish to make his case under the ADA? Can he meet these requirements? Explain.

2. In employment-discrimination cases, punitive damages can be appropriate when an employer acts with malice or reckless indifference to an employee's protected rights. Would an award of punitive damages to Chalfant be appropriate in this case? Discuss.

Critical Thinking and Writing Assignments

25–8 **Critical Legal Thinking.** Why has the federal government limited the application of the statutes discussed in this chapter to firms with a specified number of employees, such as fifteen or twenty? Should these laws apply to all employers, regardless of size? Why or why not?

25–9 **Case Analysis Question.** Go to Appendix I at the end of this text and examine the excerpt of Case No. 5, *Burlington Northern and Santa Fe Railway Co. v. White*. Review and then brief the case, making sure that your brief answers the following questions.

1. **Issue:** What was the plaintiff's complaint, the defendant's response, and the chief legal dispute between them?

2. **Rule of Law:** Which provisions of Title VII did the Supreme Court consider here, and which rule of statutory interpretation governed the Court's consideration?

3. **Applying the Rule of Law:** How did the Court interpret these provisions, and how did that interpretation apply to the circumstances in this case?

4. **Conclusion:** Based on its application of the principles in this case, what did the Court conclude?

25–10 💡 **Business Law Critical Thinking Group Assignment.** Two African American plaintiffs sued the producers

of the reality television series *The Bachelor* and *The Bachelorette* for racial discrimination. The plaintiffs claimed that the shows have never featured a person of color in the lead role. Plaintiffs also alleged that the producers failed to provide people of color who auditioned for lead roles with the same opportunities to compete as white people who auditioned.

1. The first group will assess whether the plaintiffs can establish a *prima facie* case of disparate-treatment (intentional) discrimination.

2. The second group will consider whether the plaintiffs can establish disparate-impact discrimination.

3. The third group will assume that the plaintiffs established a *prima facie* case and that the burden has shifted to the employer to articulate a legal reason for not hiring the plaintiffs. What legitimate reasons might the employer assert for not hiring the plaintiffs in this situation? Should the law require television producers to hire persons of color for lead roles in reality television shows? Explain your answer.

UNIT 4 Agency and Employment Law

Business Case Study with Dissenting Opinion
EEOC v. Greater Baltimore Medical Center, Inc.

As discussed in Chapter 25, the Americans with Disabilities Act (ADA) prohibits employment discrimination based on a disability. Although an employer is often required to reasonably accommodate the needs of an employee with a disability, the ADA does not protect an employee who cannot perform the essential functions of a job even when given a reasonable accommodation.

In this *Business Case Study with Dissenting Opinion,* we review *EEOC v. Greater Baltimore Medical Center, Inc.*[1] In this case, the Equal Employment Opportunity Commission (EEOC) filed an enforcement action on behalf of a disabled employee who was receiving Social Security Disability Income benefits. To receive the benefits, the employee had to state that he was incapable of working. The issue for the court was whether, despite the employee's representations, the EEOC could still show that he was capable of performing the job's essential functions.

Case Background

Michael Turner worked as a secretary for Greater Baltimore Medical Center (GBMC). Beginning in January 2005, Turner was hospitalized for five months because of a life-threatening condition called necrotizing fasciitis. Turner returned to work in November 2005 with his doctor's permission, but he soon suffered a stroke and was hospitalized again until late December.

On December 29, 2005, with his mother's help, Turner applied to the Social Security Administration (SSA) for Social Security Disability Income (SSDI) benefits. The application stated, "I became unable to work because of my disabling condition on January 15, 2005. I am still disabled." The application also said that Turner would tell the SSA if his condition improved to the point that he could work. A few days later, Turner's mother also submitted a report stating that Turner could not work because of his disabilities. Turner began receiving SSDI benefits in January 2006.

That same month, Turner told GBMC that he wanted to return to work as a part-time secretary. Turner submitted a form from his physician, but GBMC concluded that his conditions prevented him from performing his old job. As a result, GBMC said that it was not obligated to give Turner a position. By May 2006, Turner's condition had improved, and his doctor found that he could work full-time without any restrictions.

But GBMC disagreed, and it terminated Turner in June 2006, when his leave expired. Afterward, Turner did more than 1,100 hours of volunteer work for GBMC. All the while, he continued to receive SSDI benefits. In February 2007, Turner filed a discrimination charge with the EEOC. In September 2009, the EEOC filed an enforcement action in federal court on Turner's behalf. The district court granted summary judgment for GBMC because it found that, given Turner's SSDI benefits, the EEOC could not show that Turner could perform his old job's essential functions. The EEOC appealed.

Majority Opinion

O'GRADY, District Judge:

* * * *

The ADA prohibits a covered employer from discriminating "against a qualified individual with a disability because of the disability of such individual." *Among other things, EEOC must show that Mr. Turner is a "qualified individual with a disability," that is, "an individual with a disability who, with or without reasonable accommodation, can perform the essential functions of the employment position * * * ."* [Emphasis added.]

Many persons who experience disabling medical problems become eligible for programs like SSDI, at least temporarily, during medical leave. If such a person seeks SSDI benefits and attempts to bring a claim under the ADA, he may assert disability in an application for SSDI benefits while simultaneously asserting that he is a "qualified individual" under the ADA, that is, he is able to work with or without reasonable accommodation. A conflict of this sort may appear to bar the claimant from receiving both disability benefits and ADA coverage.

---

1. 2012 WL 1302604 (4th Cir. 2012).

Business Case Study with Dissenting Opinion—Continued

* * * *

* * * There can be little doubt that the conflict between Mr. Turner's SSDI application and his ability to work with or without reasonable accommodation is genuine. Mr. Turner's SSDI application, submitted on December 29, 2005, states, "I became unable to work because of my disabling condition on January 15, 2005," and, "I am still disabled." Moreover, "I [Mr. Turner] agree to notify the Social Security Administration * * * [i]f my medical condition improves so that I would be able to work, even though I have not yet returned to work." The record indicates without contradiction that Mr. Turner was unable to work after he left the hospital on December 27, 2005. Mrs. Turner later submitted a form called a "Function Report" * * * in which she described Mr. Turner's symptoms and impairment. She noted severe disability in his left arm or hand, use of a bedside commode with hand rails, left-sided weakness requiring assistance, leg bracing, inability to drive, inability to lift more than 2–3 pounds, severely limited ability to stand, bend over and back, and walking. * * * Taken together, the SSDI application and documentation reasonably communicated that Mr. Turner was and would continue to be [unable to work].

Consistent with the application, the SSA awarded benefits to Mr. Turner on January 22, 2006. Mr. Turner continued to receive SSDI benefits at the time of the district court's decision. Mr. Turner did not revise his statements to SSDI, and apparently never notified the SSA about a change in his condition.

These reported disabilities conflict with the multiple work releases provided by [Turner's doctor] * * * . * * * They all indicated that Mr. Turner could have returned to work, directly contradicting the assertion in his SSDI application that he was and continued to be unable to work. * * * If Mr. Turner told GBMC in good faith that he could return to work, then he had no reason to believe that his earlier representations of disability were still accurate.

* * * *

* * * We in no way condone GBMC's refusal to reinstate Mr. Turner. Quite the contrary. We are deeply concerned about GBMC's attempts to prevent a partially disabled former employee from returning to work after he was cleared to return without restriction. Our result is nonetheless mandated by the plain language of the ADA and the relevant case law. The district court's judgment is therefore affirmed.

Dissenting Opinion

GREGORY, Circuit Judge, dissenting:

* * * *

This case * * * involves two different parties' context-related legal representations—*Turner's* assertion in the proceedings before the SSA and the *EEOC's* assertion in this action. While it is true that the EEOC is seeking relief on Turner's behalf, it cannot be said that the EEOC made a prior inconsistent statement in Turner's SSDI application. Its action should not be barred through the happenstance of an unemployed victim having applied for and received SSDI benefits. Moreover, the Supreme Court has repeatedly recognized that "the EEOC is not merely a proxy" for the individuals for whom it seeks relief. Rather, the Court has observed, "[w]hen the EEOC acts, albeit at

the behest of and for the benefit of specific individuals, it acts also to vindicate the public interest in preventing employment discrimination." [Emphasis in original.]

Barring EEOC enforcement actions based on a charging party's legal assertions of disability in SSA proceedings * * * is also contrary to public policy. The EEOC's enforcement actions typically seek not only victim-specific relief but also injunctive relief such as training, posting of notices, and reporting requirements. As discussed above, these enforcement actions not only benefit the individuals on whose behalf the agency sues, but also benefit the public, which has an interest in the eradication of employment discrimination.

* * * *

Business Case Study with Dissenting Opinion—Continues next page

Business Case Study with Dissenting Opinion—Continued

Questions for Analysis

1. **Law** What was the majority's decision in this case? What were the reasons for its decision?
2. **Law** Why did the dissent disagree with the majority? If the court had adopted the dissent's position, how would this have affected the result?
3. **Ethics** Does the majority express any ethical reservations about its decision? If so, what are they? Do you have any ethical concerns about the majority's decision?

4. **Economic Dimensions** Based on this case, what do you think is the purpose of SSDI benefits? Did Turner need them?
5. **Implications for the Businessperson** What does the majority's ruling mean for employers who have disabled employees? Are the repercussions of disability discrimination more or less serious? Explain your answer.

UNIT 4 Agency and Employment Law

Business Scenario

Two brothers, Ray and Paul Ashford, start a business—Ashford Brothers, Inc.—manufacturing a new type of battery system for hybrid automobiles. The batteries hit the market at the perfect time and are in great demand.

1. **Agency.** Loren, one of Ashford's salespersons, anxious to make a sale, intentionally quotes a price to a customer that is $500 lower than Ashford had authorized for that particular product. The customer purchases the product at the quoted price. When Ashford learns of the deal, it claims that it is not legally bound to the sales contract because it did not authorize Loren to sell the product at that price. Is Ashford bound to the contract? Discuss fully. **(See pages 610–612.)**
2. **Workers' Compensation.** One day Gina, an Ashford employee, suffered a serious burn when she accidentally spilled some acid on her hand. The accident occurred because another employee, who was suspected of using illegal drugs, carelessly bumped into her. Gina's hand required a series of skin grafts before it healed sufficiently to allow her to return to work. Gina wants to obtain compensation for her lost wages

and medical expenses. Can she do that? If so, how? **(See pages 631–632.)**
3. **Drug Testing.** After Gina's injury, Ashford decides to conduct random drug tests on all of its employees. Several employees claim that the testing violates their privacy rights and bring a lawsuit. What factors will the court consider in deciding whether the random drug testing is legally permissible? **(See page 637.)**
4. **COBRA.** Ashford provides health insurance for its two hundred employees, including Dan. For personal medical reasons, Dan takes twelve weeks' leave. During this period, can Dan continue his coverage under Ashford's health-insurance plan? After Dan returns to work, Ashford closes Dan's division and terminates the employees, including Dan. Can Dan continue his coverage under Ashford's health-insurance plan? Explain. **(See page 634.)**
5. **Sexual Harassment.** Aretha, another employee at Ashford, is disgusted by the sexually offensive behavior of several male employees. She has complained to her supervisor on several occasions about the behavior, but the supervisor merely laughs at

Business Scenario—Continued

her concerns. Aretha decides to bring a legal action against the company for sexual harassment. Does Aretha's complaint concern *quid pro quo* harassment or hostile-environment harassment? What federal statute protects employees from sexual harassment? What remedies are available under that statute? What procedures must Aretha follow in pursuing her legal action? **(See pages 661–665.)**

UNIT 4 Agency and Employment Law

Group Project

Hasna Azad, an Iranian, worked at Gold Standard, Inc., and was issued a smartphone for her business use.

1. One group will assume that Azad received harassing e-mails from another employee that disparaged her Iranian origin. Decide whether Gold Standard can be held liable for these e-mails.
2. A second group will assume that Gold Standard issued a warning to the offending employee immediately after the incident was reported and held two meetings about the proper use of the company's e-mail system. This group will determine how this might affect Gold Standard's liability.
3. A third group will assume that when Azad exceeded the company's limit on text messages, Gold Standard read her stored messages without her knowledge to determine whether they were work related or personal. This group will determine whether Azad can sue Gold Standard for violating her privacy rights.

33 CHAPTER

Consumer and Environmental Law

(VTC/iStockphoto.com)

CHAPTER OUTLINE

- Consumer Law
- Environmental Law

LEARNING OBJECTIVES

The five learning objectives below are designed to help improve your understanding of the chapter. After reading this chapter, you should be able to answer the following questions:

1 When will advertising be deemed deceptive?

2 What are the major federal statutes providing for consumer protection in credit transactions?

3 Under what common law theories can polluters be held liable?

4 What is contained in an environmental impact statement, and who must file one?

5 What major federal statutes regulate air and water pollution?

"The good of the people is the greatest law."
—Marcus Tullius Cicero, 106–43 B.C.E. (Roman politician and orator)

During the heyday of the consumer movement in the 1960s and 1970s, Congress enacted a substantial amount of legislation to protect "the good of the people," to borrow a phrase from Marcus Tullius Cicero (see the chapter-opening quotation above). All statutes, agency rules, and common law judicial decisions that attempt to protect the interests of consumers are classified as *consumer law.*

Since the financial crisis that started in 2008, there has been a renewed interest in protecting consumers from credit-card companies, financial institutions, and insurance companies. Congress enacted new credit-card regulations, as well as certain financial reforms to regulate the nation's largest banks. Congress also enacted health-care reforms, including a law that requires chain restaurants to post the caloric content of foods on their menus.

In the first part of this chapter, we examine some of the major laws and regulations protecting consumers. We then turn to a discussion of environmental law, which consists of all of the laws and regulations designed to protect and preserve the environment.

Consumer Law

Sources of consumer protection exist at all levels of government. At the federal level, a number of laws have been passed to define the duties of sellers and the rights of consumers. Exhibit 33.1 below indicates many of the areas of consumer law that are regulated by statutes. Federal administrative agencies, such as the Federal Trade Commission (FTC), also provide an important source of consumer protection. Nearly every agency and department of the federal government has an office of consumer affairs, and most states have one or more such offices, including the offices of state attorneys general, to assist consumers.

Deceptive Advertising

One of the earliest—and still one of the most important—federal consumer protection laws is the Federal Trade Commission Act (mentioned in Chapter 32). The act created the FTC to carry out the broadly stated goal of preventing unfair and deceptive trade practices, including deceptive advertising.

Generally, **deceptive advertising** occurs if a reasonable consumer would be misled by the advertising claim. Vague generalities and obvious exaggerations (that a reasonable person would not believe to be true) are permissible. These claims are known as *puffery* (see page 439 in Chapter 17). When a claim has the appearance of authenticity, however, it may create problems. Advertising that *appears* to be based on factual evidence but that in fact cannot be scientifically supported will be deemed deceptive. A classic example occurred in a 1944 case in which the claim that a skin cream would restore youthful qualities to aged skin was deemed deceptive.[1]

Half-Truths   Some advertisements contain "half-truths," meaning that the information is true but incomplete and, therefore, leads consumers to a false conclusion. **EXAMPLE 33.1** The maker of Campbell's soups advertised that "most" Campbell's soups were low in fat and cholesterol and thus were helpful in fighting heart disease. What the ad did not say was that Campbell's soups were also high in sodium and that high-sodium diets may increase the risk of heart disease. Hence, the FTC ruled that the company's claims were deceptive. • Advertising featuring an endorsement by a celebrity may be deemed deceptive if the celebrity does not actually use the product.

Bait-and-Switch Advertising   The FTC has issued rules that govern specific advertising techniques. One of the more important rules is contained in the

---

Were Campbell's claims truthful?

LEARNING OBJECTIVE 1
When will advertising be deemed deceptive?

Deceptive Advertising Advertising that misleads consumers, either by making unjustified claims about a product's performance or by omitting a material fact concerning the product's composition or performance.

Exhibit 33.1 Selected Areas of Consumer Law Regulated by Statutes

Advertising
Example—The Federal Trade Commission Act

Labeling and Packaging
Example—The Fair Packaging and Labeling Act

Sales
Example—The FTC Mail-Order Rule

CONSUMER LAW

Food and Drugs
Example—The Federal Food, Drug, and Cosmetic Act

Product Safety
Example—The Consumer Product Safety Act

Credit Protection
Example—The Consumer Credit Protection Act

---

1. *Charles of the Ritz Distributors Corp. v. FTC*, 143 F.2d 676 (2d Cir. 1944).

Bait-and-Switch Advertising Advertising a product at an attractive price and then telling the consumer that the advertised product is not available or is of poor quality and encouraging her or him to purchase a more expensive item.

FTC's "Guides Against Bait Advertising."[2] The rule is designed to prevent **bait-and-switch advertising**—that is, advertising a very low price for a particular item that will likely be unavailable to the consumer and then encouraging him or her to purchase a more expensive item.

The low price is the "bait" to lure the consumer into the store. The salesperson is instructed to "switch" the consumer to a different, more expensive item. According to the FTC guidelines, bait-and-switch advertising occurs if the seller refuses to show the advertised item, fails to have reasonable quantities of it available, fails to promise to deliver the advertised item within a reasonable time, or discourages employees from selling the item.

Online Deceptive Advertising

Deceptive advertising can occur in the online environment as well. The FTC actively monitors online advertising and has identified numerous Web sites that have made false or deceptive claims for products ranging from medical treatments for various diseases to exercise equipment and weight-loss aids.

The FTC has issued guidelines to help online businesses comply with the laws prohibiting deceptive advertising.[3] These guidelines include the following three basic requirements:

1. All ads—both online and offline—must be truthful and not misleading.
2. The claims made in an ad must be substantiated—that is, advertisers must have evidence to back up their claims.
3. Ads cannot be unfair, which the FTC defines as "likely to cause substantial consumer injury that consumers could not reasonably avoid and that is not outweighed by the benefit to consumers or competition."

> "Ads are the cave art of the twentieth century."
>
> Marshall McLuhan, 1911–1980 (Canadian academic and commentator)

Clear and Conspicuous Disclosure   The guidelines also call for "clear and conspicuous" disclosure of any qualifying or limiting information. Because consumers may not read an entire Web page, the disclosure should be placed as close as possible to the claim being qualified. The next-best location is on a section of the page to which a consumer can easily scroll. Generally, hyperlinks to a disclosure are recommended only for lengthy disclosures.

Spam   As discussed on page 120 in Chapter 4, Congress passed the federal CAN-SPAM Act to combat the problems associated with unsolicited commercial e-mails, commonly referred to as spam. Many states have also passed consumer protection laws that regulate deceptive online advertising.

In the following case, an e-mail service provider claimed that an online marketing company had violated a California statute that prohibited deceptive content in e-mail advertising. The court had to decide whether the CAN-SPAM Act preempted the state statute (preemption was discussed on page 39 in Chapter 2).

---

2. 16 C.F.R. Section 288.
3. "Advertising and Marketing on the Internet: Rules of the Road," Federal Trade Commission, Sept. 2000, Web.

Case 33.1

Hypertouch, Inc. v. ValueClick, Inc.

California Court of Appeal, Second District,
192 Cal.App.4th 805, 123 Cal.Rptr.3d 8 (2011).

(pressureUA/Shutterstock.com)

FACTS Hypertouch, Inc., provides e-mail service to customers located inside and outside California. ValueClick, Inc., and its subsidiaries provide online marketing services to third party advertisers that promote retail products. ValueClick

contracts with these advertisers to place offers on its Web sites. ValueClick also contracts with affiliates that send out commercial e-mail advertisements. The advertisements include links redirecting consumers to promotions on ValueClick's

Case 33.1—Continued

Web sites. If a consumer clicks through an e-mail advertisement and participates in a promotional offer, the affiliate that sent the initial e-mail is compensated for generating a customer "lead." The affiliate, rather than ValueClick, controls the content and headers of the e-mails. Hypertouch filed a complaint against ValueClick, its subsidiaries, and others for violating a California state statute that prohibits e-mail advertising that contains deceptive content and headings. The trial court held that the federal CAN-SPAM Act preempts the California statute and granted a summary judgment in favor of ValueClick. Hypertouch appealed.

ISSUE Does the federal CAN-SPAM Act preempt California's statute on deceptive e-mail advertising (spam)?

DECISION No. The California Court of Appeal held that California's anti-spam statute is not preempted by the federal CAN-SPAM Act.

REASON The CAN-SPAM Act expressly exempts from preemption state laws that prohibit "falsity or deception" in commercial e-mail. The trial court had interpreted this exemption to apply only to state statutes that require a plaintiff to establish the elements of common law fraud. But the appellate court disagreed, finding that "sections of the CAN-SPAM Act indicate that the phrase 'falsity and deception' was not intended to apply only to common law fraud." According to the court, the states are "free to regulate the use of deceptive practices in commercial e-mails in whatever manner they [choose]." The California statute imposes strict liability on anyone who advertises in a commercial e-mail that contains false, deceptive, or misleading information, whether or not the advertiser has knowledge of the violation. Evidence showed that ValueClick had advertised in more than 45,000 e-mails received by Hypertouch customers that contained deceptive "header information" in violation of the statute. Therefore, the court reversed the lower court's decision and remanded the case for trial.

CRITICAL THINKING—Social Consideration *How might the heading of an e-mail advertisement be deceptive? Describe several ways.*

Federal Trade Commission Actions If the FTC concludes that a given advertisement is unfair or deceptive, it sends a formal complaint to the alleged offender. The company may agree to settle the complaint without further proceedings. If not, the FTC can conduct a hearing before an *administrative law judge* (see page 10 in Chapter 1) in which the company can present its defense.

FTC Orders and Remedies If the FTC succeeds in proving that an advertisement is unfair or deceptive, it usually issues a **cease-and-desist order** requiring the company to stop the challenged advertising. In some circumstances, the FTC may also require **counteradvertising** in which the company advertises anew—in print, on the Internet, on radio, and on television—to inform the public about the earlier misinformation. The FTC sometimes institutes a **multiple product order,** which requires a firm to cease and desist from false advertising in regard to all of its products, not just the product that was the subject of the action.

Cease-and-Desist Order An administrative or judicial order prohibiting a person or business firm from conducting activities that an agency or court has deemed illegal.

Counteradvertising New advertising that is undertaken to correct earlier false claims that were made about a product.

Multiple Product Order An order requiring a firm that has engaged in deceptive advertising to cease and desist from false advertising in regard to all the firm's products.

Damages When Consumers Are Injured When a company's deceptive ad involves wrongful charges to consumers, the FTC may seek other remedies, including restitution. **CASE EXAMPLE 33.2** Verity International, Ltd., billed phone-line subscribers who accessed certain online pornography sites at the rate for international calls to Madagascar. When consumers complained about the charges, Verity employees told them that the charges were valid and had to be paid, or the consumers would face further collection action. A federal appellate court held that this representation of "uncontestability" was deceptive and a violation of the FTC Act and ordered Verity to pay nearly $18 million in restitution to consumers.[4] •

---

4. *FTC v. Verity International, Ltd.,* 443 F.3d 48 (2d Cir. 2006).

The Telemarketing Sales Rule

The FTC's Telemarketing Sales Rule (TSR)[5] requires a telemarketer to identify the seller, describe the product being sold, and disclose all material facts related to the sale. Material facts include the total cost of the goods being sold, any restrictions on obtaining or using the goods, and whether a sale will be considered final and nonrefundable. The act makes it illegal for telemarketers to misrepresent information (including facts about their goods or services and earnings potential, for example).

A telemarketer must also remove a consumer's name from its list of potential contacts if the consumer so requests. An amendment to the Telemarketing Sales Rule established the national Do Not Call Registry. Telemarketers may not call consumers who have placed their names on the list.

Labeling and Packaging

In general, labels must be accurate, and they must use words that are understood by the ordinary consumer. In some instances, labels must specify the raw materials used in the product, such as the percentage of cotton, nylon, or other fibers used in a garment. In other instances, the product must carry a warning, such as those required on cigarette packages and advertising.[6]

(AP Photo/Reed Saxon)

Does federal law preempt state deceptive advertising laws with respect to published fuel economy estimates?

Fuel Economy Labels on Automobiles   The Energy Policy and Conservation Act (EPCA)[7] requires automakers to attach an information label to every new car. This label must include the Environmental Protection Agency's fuel economy estimate for the vehicle. **CASE EXAMPLE 33.3**   Gaetano Paduano bought a new Honda Civic Hybrid in California. The information label on the car included the fuel economy estimate from the Environmental Protection Agency (EPA). Honda's sales brochure added, "Just drive the Hybrid like you would a conventional car and save on fuel bills."

When Paduano discovered that the car's fuel economy was less than half of the EPA's estimate, he sued Honda for deceptive advertising. The automaker claimed that the federal law (the EPCA) preempted the state's deceptive advertising law, but the court held in Paduano's favor, finding that the federal statute did not preempt a claim for deceptive advertising made under state law.[8] ●

Food Labeling   Several statutes deal specifically with food labeling. The Fair Packaging and Labeling Act requires that food product labels identify (1) the product, (2) the net quantity of the contents, (3) the manufacturer, and (4) the packager or distributor.[9] The Nutrition Labeling and Education Act requires food labels to provide standard nutrition facts and regulates the use of such terms as *fresh* and *low fat*. The U.S. Food and Drug Administration (FDA) and the U.S. Department of Agriculture (USDA) are the primary agencies that issue regulations on food labeling. These rules are updated annually and require the labels on fresh meats, vegetables, and fruits to indicate where the food originated.

---

5. 16 C.F.R. Sections 310.1–310.8.

6. 15 U.S.C. Sections 1331 *et seq.*

7. 49 U.S.C. Section 32908(b)(1).

8. *Paduano v. American Honda Motor Co.*, 169 Cal.App. 4th 1453, 88 Cal.Rptr.3d 90 (2009). This case is also featured in Unit 1's *Business Case Study with Dissenting Opinion* on pages 233–235.

9. 15 U.S.C. Sections 4401–4408.

Menu Labeling Regulations The health-care reform bill enacted in 2010 (see page 864) included a provision aimed at combating the problem of obesity in the United States. The provision requires all restaurant chains with twenty or more locations to post the caloric content of the foods on their menus so that customers will know how many calories they are eating.[10] In addition, restaurants are required to post guidelines on the number of calories that an average person requires daily. Customers can use this information to determine what portion of a day's calories a particular food choice will provide. The new federal law supersedes all state and local laws already in existence.

Any restaurant to which the law applies must post the caloric content of the foods listed on its standard menu, menu boards, or menu lists for drive-thru windows. Signs also have to be posted near salad bars and buffets, providing information on the foods offered there. Exempt from the rules are condiments, daily specials, and foods offered for only a limited period (less than sixty days). The FDA is developing specific regulations supporting the standards for menu labeling.

Sales

A number of statutes protect consumers by requiring the disclosure of certain terms in sales transactions and providing rules governing specific types of sales and unsolicited merchandise. Many states and the FTC, for example, have **"cooling-off" laws** that permit the buyers of goods sold door to door to cancel their contracts within three business days. The FTC rule further requires that consumers be notified in Spanish of this right if the oral negotiations for the sale were in that language.

"Cooling-Off" Laws Laws that allow buyers to cancel door-to-door sales contracts within a certain period of time, such as three business days.

Telephone and Mail-Order Sales The FTC's Mail or Telephone Order Merchandise Rule[11] protects consumers who purchase goods over the phone, through the mail or fax machine, or via the Internet. Merchants are required to ship orders within the time promised in their advertisements and to notify consumers when orders cannot be shipped on time. Merchants must also issue a refund within a specified period of time when a consumer cancels an order.

Online Sales The FTC and other federal agencies have brought numerous enforcement actions against perpetrators of online fraud. Nonetheless, protecting consumers from fraudulent and deceptive sales practices conducted via the Internet has proved to be a challenging task. Faced with economic recession, job losses, mounting debt, and dwindling savings, consumers have increasingly fallen prey to Internet fraud in recent years. Complaints to the FTC about sales of business opportunities, such as work-at-home offers, have grown dramatically in the last ten years.

"A consumer is a shopper who is sore about something."

Harold Coffin, 1905–1981 (American humorist)

Many consumers also complain that companies are tracking their online purchases. You can read about a new bill of rights for consumer privacy in this chapter's *Adapting the Law to the Online Environment* feature on the following page.

Protection of Health and Safety

Although labeling and packaging laws (discussed earlier) promote consumer health and safety, there is a significant distinction between regulating the information dispensed about a product and regulating the actual content of the product. The classic example is tobacco products. Producers of tobacco products are required to warn consumers about the hazards associated with the use of their products, but the sale of tobacco products has not

---

10. See Section 4205 of the Patient Protection and Affordable Care Act, Pub. L. No.111-148, March 23, 2010, 124 Stat. 119.
11. 16 C.F.R. Sections 435.1–435.2.

ADAPTING THE LAW TO THE ONLINE ENVIRONMENT

A CONSUMER PRIVACY BILL OF RIGHTS

Whenever consumers purchase items from an online retailer, such as Amazon.com, or a retailer that sells both offline and online, such as Target Brands, Inc., the retailer collects information about the consumer. Over time, the retailer can amass considerable data about a person's shopping habits. Does collecting this information violate a consumer's right to privacy? Should the retailers be able to pass on the data they have collected to their affiliates? Should they be able to use the information to predict what a consumer might want and then create online "coupons" customized to fit the person's buying history?

The President Proposes a Consumer Privacy Bill of Rights

To protect consumers' personal information, the Obama administration drafted a consumer privacy bill of rights that would apply both online and offline. In introducing the bill of rights and asking Congress to enact it into law, President Obama said that "American consumers can't wait any longer for clear rules of the road that ensure their personal information is safe online."

The following is the bill of rights proposed by the president:

1. **Individual Control**—Consumers have a right to exercise control over what personal data organizations collect from them and how they use it.
2. **Transparency**—Consumers have the right to easily understandable information about privacy and security practices.
3. **Respect for Context**—Consumers have a right to expect that organizations will collect, use, and disclose personal data in ways that are consistent with the context in which consumers provide the data.

4. **Security**—Consumers have the right to secure and responsible handling of personal data.
5. **Access and Accuracy**—Consumers have a right to access and correct personal data in usable formats, in a manner that is appropriate to the sensitivity of the data and the risk of adverse consequences to consumers if the data are inaccurate.
6. **Focus Collection**—Consumers have a right to reasonable limits on the personal data that companies collect and retain.
7. **Accountability**—Consumers have a right to have personal data handled by companies with appropriate measures in place to assure that they adhere to the Consumer Privacy Bill of Rights.

The Implications of the Consumer Privacy Bill of Rights

If this proposed privacy bill of rights becomes law, retailers will have to change some of their procedures:

1. Retailers will have to give customers better choices about what data are collected and how the data are used for marketing.
2. Retailers will have to take into account consumers' expectations about how their information will be used once it is collected.
3. Retailers will have to allow consumers to set reasonable limits on the personal information that is collected about them.

Critical Thinking

Some argue that restricting retailers' tracking ability will actually make consumers worse off. How would this be possible?

---

been subjected to significant restrictions or banned outright despite the obvious dangers to health. (See this chapter's *Law, Diversity, and Business: Managerial Implications* feature on the facing page for a discussion of a safety issue facing airlines.) We now examine various laws that regulate the actual products made available to consumers.

Food and Drugs   The most important legislation regulating food and drugs is the Federal Food, Drug, and Cosmetic Act (FDCA).[12] To protect consumers against adulterated (contaminated) and misbranded foods and drugs, the FDCA establishes food standards, specifies safe levels of potentially hazardous food additives, and sets classifications of food and food advertising. Most of these statutory requirements are enforced by the U.S. Food and Drug Administration (FDA).

> **➤ KNOW THIS ◀**
>
> The U.S. Food and Drug Administration is authorized to obtain, among other things, orders for the recall and seizure of certain products.

---

12. 21 U.S.C. Section 301.

(AP Photo/Office of Public Affairs, FDA.)

Can the FDA prevent fake drugs from being sold to consumers?

Under the FDCA, the FDA is also responsible for ensuring that drugs are safe, as well as effective, before they are marketed to the public. The FDA has established extensive procedures that drug manufacturers must follow to show that their drugs are safe.

CASE EXAMPLE 33.4 A group of terminally ill patients claimed that they were entitled, under the U.S. Constitution, to better access to experimental drugs before the FDA completed its clinical tests. The court, however, found that the FDA's policy of limiting access to drugs that were undergoing tests was rationally related to protecting patients from potentially unsafe drugs. Therefore, the court held that terminally ill patients do not have a fundamental constitutional right of access to experimental drugs.[13] ●

The FDA also has the authority to regulate medical devices, such as pacemakers, and to withdraw from the market any such device that is mislabeled.[14]

Consumer Product Safety In 1972, the Consumer Product Safety Act[15] created the first comprehensive scheme of regulation over matters concerning consumer safety. The act also established the Consumer Product Safety Commission (CPSC).

---

13. *Abigail Alliance for Better Access to Developmental Drugs v. von Eschenbach*, 495 F.3d 695 (D.C.Cir. 2007).
14. 21 U.S.C. Sections 352(o), 360(j), 360(k), and 360c–360k.
15. 15 U.S.C. Section 2051.

LAW, DIVERSITY, AND BUSINESS: MANAGERIAL IMPLICATIONS

HOW SHOULD AIRLINES DEAL WITH "CUSTOMERS OF SIZE"?

Anyone who travels on commercial airlines is aware that planes are crowded and seats are narrow. For some, they are too narrow. Airlines face a particular problem with "customers of size" because they may impinge on the comfort of those seated next to them. The issue involves more than comfort, however—it can also be a matter of safety.

Challenging Southwest Airlines Southwest Airlines has a policy for "customers of size." When an agent believes that a passenger will reduce the comfort of anyone seated next to her or him, the agent can ask that a second seat be purchased. Kenlie Tiggeman, an overweight passenger, however, was allowed to proceed to the gate. A gate attendant looked at her and told her, in the presence of other passengers, that she would have to purchase a second seat because of her size. Tiggeman refused and filed a lawsuit against Southwest, asserting that the airline's employees "did not follow their company policy and chose to discriminate, humiliate, and harass."

Further, she argued that Southwest takes "discriminatory action . . . toward obese customers." Tiggeman did not ask for damages. Rather, she wanted a court to order Southwest to clarify its policy with respect to larger passengers.

The Airlines Also Face a Safety Issue In 2010, to adjust for Americans' increasing weight, the Federal Aviation Administration (FAA) revised the passenger weights that it uses to calculate a flight's total weight and balance. The FAA now requires the airlines to use an average weight of 200 pounds for men and 179 pounds for women.

Yet the government's regulations for the strength of airline seats and seatbelts have not been revised since they were written about seventy years ago. They are based on a passenger weight of 170 pounds, even though today the average U.S. man weighs 194 pounds. Engineers and scientists claim that airline seats are unsafe for today's heavier passengers.

The safety implications are obvious. Airlines have a unique challenge of protecting larger passengers. Dr. Dietrich Jehle, a professor of emergency medicine at the State University of New York at Buffalo, says, "Since a third of the population is obese, we need to be doing some of our crash testing with obese dummies."

Business Implications *Government experts predict that by the year 2030, 44 percent of adult Americans will be obese—a development that businesses will have to take into consideration. Persons of size represent a significant segment of Americans, and businesses must adapt.*

The CPSC's Authority   The CPSC conducts research on the safety of individual products and maintains a clearinghouse on the risks associated with various products. The Consumer Product Safety Act authorizes the CPSC to do the following:

1. Set safety standards for consumer products.
2. Ban the manufacture and sale of any product that the commission believes poses an "unreasonable risk" to consumers. (Products banned by the CPSC have included various types of fireworks, cribs, and toys, as well as many products containing asbestos or vinyl chloride.)
3. Remove from the market any products it believes to be imminently hazardous. The CPSC frequently works with manufacturers to voluntarily recall defective products from stores. **EXAMPLE 33.5**   In cooperation with the CPSC, Kolcraft Enterprises, Inc., recalled one million infant play yards because of a defective latch that could cause a rail to fall, posing a risk to children. •
4. Require manufacturers to report any products already sold or intended for sale that have proved to be hazardous.
5. Administer other product-safety legislation, including the Child Protection and Toy Safety Act[16] and the Federal Hazardous Substances Act.[17]

Notification Requirements   The Consumer Product Safety Act imposes notification requirements on distributors of consumer products. Distributors must immediately notify the CPSC when they receive information that a product "contains a defect which . . . creates a substantial risk to the public" or "an unreasonable risk of serious injury or death."

Health-Care Reforms

In 2010, the health-care reforms enacted by Congress went into effect and gave Americans new rights and benefits with regard to health care.[18] By 2014, these laws will prohibit certain insurance company practices, such as denying coverage for preexisting conditions.

Expanded Coverage for Children and Seniors   The reforms expanded access to health care by enabling more children to obtain health-insurance coverage and allowing young adults (under age twenty-six) to stay on their parents' health-insurance policies. The act also ended lifetime and most annual limits on care and gave patients access to recommended preventive services (such as cancer screening, vaccinations, and well-baby checks) without cost. Medicare recipients now receive a 50 percent discount on name-brand drugs, and the gap in Medicare's prescription drug coverage will be eliminated by 2020.

Controlling Costs of Health Insurance   In an attempt to control the rising costs of health insurance, the law requires insurance companies to spend at least 85 percent of all premium dollars collected from large employers—and 80 percent of the premiums collected from individuals and small employers—on benefits and quality improvement. If insurance companies do not meet these goals, they must provide rebates to consumers. Additionally, states can require insurance companies to justify their premium increases to be eligible to participate in the new health-insurance exchanges.

---

16. 15 U.S.C. Section 1262(e).
17. 15 U.S.C. Sections 1261–1273.
18. Patient Protection and Affordable Health Care Act of 2010, Pub. L. No.111-148, March 23, 2010, 124 Stat. 119; and the Health Care and Education Reconciliation Act of 2010, Pub. L. No. 111-152, March 30, 2010, 124 Stat. 1029.

Credit Protection

Credit protection is one of the most important aspects of consumer protection legislation. Nearly 80 percent of U.S. consumers have credit cards, and most carry a balance on these cards, which amounts to about $2.5 trillion of debt nationwide. In 2010, Congress established a new agency, the Consumer Financial Protection Bureau, to oversee the practices of banks, mortgage lenders, and credit-card companies.

LEARNING OBJECTIVE 2
What are the major federal statutes providing for consumer protection in credit transactions?

Truth-in-Lending Act A key statute regulating the credit and credit-card industries is the Truth-in-Lending Act (TILA), the name commonly given to Title 1 of the Consumer Credit Protection Act (CCPA), as amended.[19] The TILA is basically a *disclosure law.* It is administered by the Federal Reserve Board and requires sellers and lenders to disclose credit terms or loan terms (such as the annual percentage rate, or APR, and any finance charges) so that individuals can shop around for the best financing arrangements.

Application TILA requirements apply only to persons who, in the ordinary course of business, lend funds, sell on credit, or arrange for the extension of credit. Thus, sales or loans made between two consumers do not come under the act. Additionally, this law protects only debtors who are *natural* persons (as opposed to the artificial "person" of a corporation) and does not extend to other legal entities.

Regulation Z A set of rules issued by the Federal Reserve Board of Governors to implement the provisions of the Truth-in-Lending Act.

Disclosure The disclosure requirements are found in **Regulation Z,** issued by the Federal Reserve Board of Governors. If the contracting parties are subject to the TILA, the requirements of Regulation Z apply to any transaction involving an installment sales contract that calls for payment to be made in more than four installments. Transactions subject to Regulation Z typically include installment loans, retail and installment sales, car loans, home-improvement loans, and certain real estate loans if the amount of financing is less than $25,000.

➤ **KNOW THIS** ➤
The Federal Reserve Board is part of the Federal Reserve System, which influences the lending and investing activities of commercial banks and the cost and availability of credit.

Equal Credit Opportunity The Equal Credit Opportunity Act (ECOA) amended the TILA in 1974. The ECOA prohibits the denial of credit solely on the basis of race, religion, national origin, color, gender, marital status, or age. The act also prohibits credit discrimination on the basis of whether an individual receives certain forms of income, such as public-assistance benefits.

Under the ECOA, a creditor may not require the signature of an applicant's spouse, or a cosigner, on a credit instrument if the applicant qualifies under the creditor's standards of creditworthiness for the amount requested. **CASE EXAMPLE 33.6** Tonja, an African American, applied for financing with a used-car dealer. The dealer reviewed Tonja's credit report and, without submitting the application to the lender, decided that she would not qualify. Instead of informing Tonja that she did not qualify, the dealer told her that she needed a cosigner on the loan to purchase the car. According to a federal appellate court, the dealership qualified as a creditor in this situation because it unilaterally denied credit. Thus, the dealer could be held liable under the ECOA.[20] ●

Which federal law prohibits discrimination for credit-card applications?

Credit-Card Rules The TILA also contains provisions regarding credit cards. One provision limits the liability of a cardholder to $50 per card for unauthorized charges made before the creditor is notified that the card has

---

19. 15 U.S.C. Sections 1601–1693r. The TILA was amended in 1980 by the Truth-in-Lending Simplification and Reform Act and again in 2009 by the Credit Card Accountability Responsibility and Disclosure Act of 2009.
20. *Treadway v. Gateway Chevrolet Oldsmobile, Inc.,* 362 F.3d 971 (7th Cir. 2004).

been lost. If a consumer received an *unsolicited* credit card in the mail that is later stolen, the company that issued the card cannot charge the consumer for any unauthorized charges.

Another provision requires credit-card companies to disclose the balance computation method that is used to determine the outstanding balance, and to state when finance charges begin to accrue. Other provisions set forth procedures for resolving billing disputes with the credit-card company. These procedures may be used if, for instance, a cardholder wishes to withhold payment for a faulty product purchased with a credit card.

Amendments to Credit-Card Rules   Amendments to TILA's credit-card rules that became effective in 2010 added the following protections:

1. Protect consumers from retroactive increases in interest rates on existing card balances unless the account is sixty days delinquent.
2. Require companies to provide forty-five days' advance notice to consumers before changing credit-card terms, such as the annual percentage rate.
3. Require companies to send out monthly bills to cardholders twenty-one days before the due date.
4. Prevent companies from increasing the interest rate charged on a customer's credit-card balance except in specific situations, such as when a promotional rate ends.
5. Prevent companies from charging overlimit fees except in specified situations.
6. Require companies to apply payments in excess of the minimum amount due to the customer's higher-interest balances first when the borrower has balances with different rates (such as the higher interest rates commonly charged for cash advances).
7. Prevent companies from computing finance charges based on the previous billing cycle (known as double-cycle billing, which hurts consumers because they are charged interest for the previous cycle even though they have paid the bill in full).

Fair Credit Reporting Act

The Fair Credit Reporting Act (FCRA)[21] protects consumers against inaccurate credit reporting and requires that lenders and other creditors report correct, relevant, and up-to-date information. The act provides that consumer credit reporting agencies may issue credit reports to users only for specified purposes, including the extension of credit, the issuance of insurance policies, and compliance with a court order, or in response to a consumer's request for a copy of her or his own credit report. (See the *Business Application* feature on page 877 for tips on how businesspersons can use credit reporting services.)

How does the Fair Credit Reporting Act protect consumers?

(teekid/iStockphoto.com)

Consumer Notification and Inaccurate Information   Any time a consumer is denied credit or insurance on the basis of his or her credit report, the consumer must be notified of that fact and of the name and address of the credit reporting agency that issued the report. The same notice must be sent to consumers who are charged more than others ordinarily would be for credit or insurance because of their credit reports.

Under the FCRA, consumers can request the source of any information used by the credit agency, as well as the identity of anyone who has received an agency's report. Consumers are also permitted to have access to the information contained about them in a credit reporting agency's files. If a consumer discovers that the agency's files contain inaccurate information, the agency, on the consumer's written request, must investigate the disputed information. Any unverifiable or erroneous information must be deleted within a reasonable period of time.

---

21. 15 U.S.C. Sections 1681 *et seq.*

Remedies for Violations An agency that fails to comply with the act is liable for actual damages, plus additional damages not to exceed $1,000 and attorneys' fees.[22] Creditors and other companies that use information from credit reporting agencies may also be liable for violations of the FCRA. The United States Supreme Court has held that an insurance company's failure to notify new customers that they were paying higher insurance rates as a result of their credit scores was a *willful* violation of the FCRA.[23]

CASE EXAMPLE 33.7 Branch Banking & Trust Company of Virginia (BB&T) gave Rex Saunders an auto loan but failed to give him a payment coupon book and rebuffed his attempts to make payments on the loan. Eventually, BB&T discovered its mistake and demanded full payment, plus interest and penalties. When payment was not immediately forthcoming, BB&T declared that Saunders was in default. It then repossessed the car and forwarded adverse credit information about Saunders to credit reporting agencies without noting that Saunders disputed the information. Saunders filed a lawsuit alleging violations of the FCRA and was awarded $80,000 in punitive damages. An appellate court found that the damages award was reasonable, given BB&T's willful violation.[24] •

Fair and Accurate Credit Transactions Act

Congress passed the Fair and Accurate Credit Transactions (FACT) Act to combat identity theft.[25] The act established a national fraud alert system so that consumers who suspect that they have been or may be victimized by identity theft can place an alert in their credit files. The act also requires the major credit reporting agencies to provide consumers with a free copy of their credit reports every twelve months.

Another provision requires account numbers on credit-card receipts to be truncated (shortened) so that merchants, employees, and others who have access to the receipts cannot obtain a consumer's name and full credit-card number. The act also mandates that financial institutions work with the FTC to identify "red flag" indicators of identity theft and to develop rules for disposing of sensitive credit information.

Fair Debt-Collection Practices

The Fair Debt Collection Practices Act (FDCPA)[26] attempts to curb abuses by collection agencies. The act applies only to specialized debt-collection agencies and attorneys who regularly attempt to collect debts on behalf of someone else, usually for a percentage of the amount owed. Creditors attempting to collect debts are not covered by the act unless, by misrepresenting themselves, they cause the debtors to believe that they are collection agencies. A debt collector who fails to comply with the act is liable for actual damages, plus additional damages not to exceed $1,000[27] and attorneys' fees.

Under the FDCPA, a collection agency may not do any of the following:

1. Contact the debtor at the debtor's place of employment if the debtor's employer objects.
2. Contact the debtor at inconvenient or unusual times (such as three o'clock in the morning), or at any time if the debtor is being represented by an attorney.
3. Contact third parties other than the debtor's parents, spouse, or financial adviser about payment of a debt unless a court authorizes such action.
4. Harass or intimidate the debtor (by using abusive language or threatening violence, for instance) or make false or misleading statements (such as posing as a police officer).

> "Credit is a system whereby a person who can't pay gets another person who can't pay to guarantee that he can pay."
>
> Charles Dickens, 1812–1870
> (English novelist)

---

22. 15 U.S.C. Section 1681n.
23. *Safeco Insurance Co. of America v. Burr,* 551 U.S. 47, 127 S.Ct. 2201, 167 L.Ed.2d 1045 (2007).
24. *Saunders v. Branch Banking & Trust Co. of Virginia,* 526 F.3d 142 (4th Cir. 2008).
25. Pub. L. No. 108-159, 117 Stat. 1952 (December 4, 2003).
26. 15 U.S.C. Section 1692.
27. According to the U.S. Court of Appeals for the Sixth Circuit, the $1,000 limit on damages applies to each lawsuit, not to each violation. See *Wright v. Finance Service of Norwalk, Inc.,* 22 F.3d 647 (6th Cir. 1994).

5. Communicate with the debtor at any time after receiving notice that the debtor is refusing to pay the debt, except to advise the debtor of further action to be taken by the collection agency.

The FDCPA also requires a collection agency to include a *validation notice* whenever it initially contacts a debtor for payment of a debt or within five days of that initial contact. The notice must state that the debtor has thirty days in which to dispute the debt and to request a written verification of the debt from the collection agency. The debtor's request for debt validation must be in writing.

Does leaving voice mail messages for a debtor violate the Fair Debt Collection Practices Act? Debt-collection practices have often raised privacy concerns. There have been many lawsuits against collection agencies over voice messages or voice mails left by debt collectors. The FDCPA prohibits disclosures about a debt to third parties. Does leaving a voice message regarding a debt collection on an answering machine constitute such a disclosure? That depends on the jurisdiction and the situation. In one example, a Florida court ruled in favor of the debtor. It stated that if a collection agency leaves a voice message for a consumer on an answering machine—even at home—other people (third parties) could hear the message.[28]

In contrast, a federal court in Minnesota held that leaving voice messages on a debtor's cell phone did not violate the FDCPA, even though the debtor's children listened to them. Because the messages did not identify the debtor or the debt, the court reasoned that "they conveyed no more information than would have been obvious in caller ID." The suit against the debt collector was dismissed.[29]

Environmental Law

We now turn to a discussion of the various ways in which businesses are regulated by the government in the interest of attempting to protect the environment. Environmental protection is not without a price, however. For many businesses, the costs of complying with environmental regulations are high, and for some, they may seem too high.

Common Law Actions

Common law remedies against environmental pollution originated centuries ago in England. Those responsible for operations that created dirt, smoke, noxious odors, noise, or toxic substances were sometimes held liable under common law theories of nuisance or negligence. Today, injured individuals continue to rely on the common law to obtain damages and injunctions against business polluters.

Nuisance   Under the common law doctrine of **nuisance**, persons may be held liable if they use their property in a manner that unreasonably interferes with others' rights to use or enjoy their own property. In these situations, the courts commonly balance the harm caused by the pollution against the costs of stopping it.

Courts have often denied injunctive relief on the ground that the hardships that would be imposed on the polluter and on the community are relatively greater than the hardships suffered by the plaintiff. **EXAMPLE 33.8**   Hewitt's Factory causes neighboring landowners to suffer from smoke, soot, and vibrations. The factory, however, may be left in operation if it is the core of the local economy. The injured parties may be awarded only monetary damages, which may include compensation for the decrease in the value of their property caused by Hewitt's operation. •

To obtain relief from pollution under the nuisance doctrine, a property owner may have to identify a distinct harm separate from that affecting the general public. This harm is referred to as a "private" nuisance. Under the common law, individuals were denied

---

28. *Berg v. Merchants Association Collection Division, Inc.,* 586 F.Supp.2d 1336 (S.D.Fla. 2008).
29. *Zortman v. J.C. Christensen & Associates, Inc.,* 2012 WL 1563918 (D.Minn. 2012).

standing (access to the courts—see Chapter 3) unless they suffered a harm distinct from the harm suffered by the public at large. Some states still require this. A public authority (such as a state's attorney general), though, can sue to abate a "public" nuisance.

Negligence and Strict Liability
An injured party may sue a business polluter in tort under the negligence and strict liability theories discussed in Chapter 4. The basis for a negligence action is the business's failure to use reasonable care toward the party whose injury was foreseeable and caused by the lack of reasonable care. For instance, employees might sue an employer whose failure to use proper pollution controls contaminated the air and caused the employees to suffer respiratory illnesses. Lawsuits for personal injuries caused by exposure to a toxic substance, such as asbestos, radiation, or hazardous waste, have given rise to a growing body of tort law known as **toxic torts.**

Businesses that engage in ultrahazardous activities—such as the transportation of radioactive materials—are strictly liable for any injuries the activities cause. In a strict liability action, the injured party does not need to prove that the business failed to exercise reasonable care.

Toxic Tort A civil wrong arising from exposure to a toxic substance, such as asbestos, radiation, or hazardous waste.

Federal Regulation

All levels of government in the United States regulate some aspect of the environment. Congress has enacted a number of statutes to control the impact of human activities on the environment. Some of these laws have been passed in an attempt to improve the quality of air and water. Other laws specifically regulate toxic chemicals, including pesticides, herbicides, and hazardous wastes.

Environmental Regulatory Agencies
The primary agency regulating environmental law is the Environmental Protection Agency (EPA). Other federal agencies with authority to regulate specific environmental matters include the Department of the Interior, the Department of Defense, the Department of Labor, the Food and Drug Administration, and the Nuclear Regulatory Commission. All agencies of the federal government must take environmental factors into consideration when making significant decisions. In addition, state and local agencies also play an important role in enforcing federal environmental legislation.

Most federal environmental laws provide that private parties can sue to enforce environmental regulations if government agencies fail to do so. Typically, a threshold hurdle in such suits is meeting the requirements for standing to sue.

LEARNING OBJECTIVE 4
What is contained in an environmental impact statement, and who must file one?

Environmental Impact Statement (EIS)
A formal analysis required for any major federal action that will significantly affect the quality of the environment to determine the action's impact and explore alternatives.

Environmental Impact Statements
The National Environmental Policy Act (NEPA) of 1969[30] requires that an **environmental impact statement (EIS)** be prepared for every major federal action that significantly affects the quality of the environment. An EIS must analyze the following:

1. The impact on the environment that the action will have.
2. Any adverse effects on the environment and alternative actions that might be taken.
3. Irreversible effects the action might generate.

An action qualifies as "major" if it involves a substantial commitment of resources (monetary or otherwise). An action is "federal" if a federal agency has the power to control it. Construction by a private developer of a ski resort on federal land, for example, may require an EIS. Building or operating a nuclear plant, which requires a federal permit, requires an EIS. If an agency decides that an EIS is unnecessary, it must issue a statement supporting this conclusion. Private individuals, consumer interest groups, businesses, and others who believe that a federal agency's actions threaten the environment often use EISs as a means of challenging those actions.

---

30. 42 U.S.C. Sections 4321–4370d.

Why are stationary sources of pollution regulated differently than mobile sources?

LEARNING OBJECTIVE 5
What major federal statutes regulate air and water pollution?

"There's so much pollution in the air now that if it weren't for our lungs, there'd be no place to put it all."

Robert Orben, 1927–present
(American comedian)

Air Pollution

Congress first authorized funds for air-pollution research and enacted the Clean Air Act to address multistate air pollution in the 1950s and 1960s.[31] The Clean Air Act provides the basis for issuing regulations to control pollution coming from mobile sources (such as automobiles and other vehicles) and stationary sources (such as electric utilities and industrial plants).

Mobile Sources of Air Pollution
Regulations governing air pollution from automobiles and other mobile sources specify pollution standards and establish time schedules for meeting the standards. The EPA periodically updates the pollution standards to reduce the amount of emissions allowed in light of new developments and data.

Reducing Emissions over the Long Term   The Obama administration announced a long-term goal of reducing emissions of nitrogen oxide and other pollutants, including those from automobiles, by 80 percent by 2050. In 2010, the administration ordered the EPA to develop national standards regulating fuel economy and emissions for medium- and heavy-duty trucks, starting with 2014 models.

Greenhouse Gases   A growing concern is that greenhouse gases, such as carbon dioxide (CO_2), may contribute to global warming. The Clean Air Act, as amended, however, does not specifically mention CO_2 emissions. Therefore, until 2009, the EPA did not regulate CO_2 emissions from motor vehicles. **CASE EXAMPLE 33.9**   Environmental groups and several states sued the EPA in an effort to force the agency to regulate CO_2 emissions. When the case reached the United States Supreme Court, the EPA argued that the plaintiffs lacked standing (see page 69 of Chapter 3). The agency claimed that because global warming has widespread effects, an individual plaintiff could not show the particularized harm required for standing. The agency also maintained that it did not have authority under the Clean Air Act to address global climate change and regulate CO_2.

The Court, however, ruled that Massachusetts had standing because its coastline, including state-owned lands, faced a threat from rising sea levels potentially caused by global warming. The Court also held that the Clean Air Act's broad definition of air pollutant gives the EPA authority to regulate CO_2 and requires the EPA to regulate any air pollutants that might "endanger public health or welfare." Accordingly, the Court ordered the EPA to determine whether CO_2 was a pollutant that endangered the public health.[32] ● The EPA later concluded that greenhouse gases, including CO_2 emissions, do constitute a public danger.

Stationary Sources of Air Pollution
The Clean Air Act authorizes the EPA to establish air-quality standards for stationary sources (such as manufacturing plants) but recognizes that the primary responsibility for preventing and controlling air pollution rests with state and local governments.

The EPA sets primary and secondary levels of ambient standards— that is, the maximum permissible levels of certain pollutants—and the states formulate plans to achieve those standards. Different standards apply depending on whether the sources of pollution are located in clean areas or polluted areas and whether they are existing sources or major new sources.

---

31. 42 U.S.C. Sections 7401 *et seq.*
32. *Massachusetts v. EPA*, 549 U.S. 497, 127 S.Ct. 1438, 167 L.Ed.2d 248 (2007).

Hazardous Air Pollutants The EPA standards are aimed at controlling hazardous air pollutants—those likely to cause death or serious irreversible or incapacitating illness such as cancer or neurological and reproductive damage. The Clean Air Act requires the EPA to list all regulated hazardous air pollutants on a prioritized schedule. In all, nearly two hundred substances, including asbestos, benzene, beryllium, cadmium, and vinyl chloride, have been classified as hazardous. They are emitted from stationary sources by a variety of business activities, including smelting (melting ore to produce metal), dry cleaning, house painting, and commercial baking.

Maximum Achievable Control Technology Instead of establishing specific emissions standards for each hazardous air pollutant, the Clean Air Act requires major sources of pollutants to use pollution-control equipment that represents the *maximum achievable control technology,* or MACT, to reduce emissions. The EPA issues guidelines as to what equipment meets this standard.[33]

Violations of the Clean Air Act

For violations of emission limits under the Clean Air Act, the EPA can assess civil penalties of up to $25,000 per day. Additional fines of up to $5,000 per day can be assessed for other violations, such as failing to maintain the required records. To penalize those who find it more cost-effective to violate the act than to comply with it, the EPA is authorized to obtain a penalty equal to the violator's economic benefits from noncompliance. Persons who provide information about violators may be paid up to $10,000. Private individuals can also sue violators.

Those who knowingly violate the act may be subject to criminal penalties, including fines of up to $1 million and imprisonment for up to two years (for false statements or failures to report violations). Corporate officers are among those who may be subject to these penalties.

Water Pollution

Water pollution stems mostly from industrial, municipal, and agricultural sources. Pollutants entering streams, lakes, and oceans include organic wastes, heated water, sediments from soil runoff, nutrients (including fertilizers and human and animal wastes), and toxic chemicals and other hazardous substances. We look here at laws and regulations governing water pollution.

Federal regulations governing the pollution of water can be traced back to the Rivers and Harbors Appropriations Act of 1899.[34] These regulations prohibited ships and manufacturers from discharging or depositing refuse in navigable waterways without a permit. In 1948, Congress passed the Federal Water Pollution Control Act (FWPCA),[35] but its regulatory system and enforcement powers proved to be inadequate.

The Clean Water Act

In 1972, amendments to the FWPCA—known as the Clean Water Act (CWA)—established the following goals: (1) make waters safe for swimming, (2) protect fish and wildlife, and (3) eliminate the discharge of pollutants into the water. The amendments set specific time schedules, which were extended by amendment and by the Water Quality Act.[36] Under these schedules, the EPA limits the discharge of various types of pollutants based on the technology available for controlling them.

Permit System for Point Source Emissions The CWA established a permit system, called the *National Pollutant Discharge Elimination System (NPDES),* for regulating discharges

"Among the treasures of our land is water— fast becoming our most valuable, most prized, most critical resource."

Dwight D. Eisenhower, 1890–1969 (Thirty-fourth president of the United States, 1953–1961)

---

33. The EPA has also issued rules to regulate hazardous air pollutants emitted by landfills. See 40 C.F.R. Sections 60.750–60.759.
34. 33 U.S.C. Sections 401–418.
35. 33 U.S.C. Sections 1251–1387.
36. This act amended 33 U.S.C. Section 1251.

from "point sources" of pollution. Point sources include industrial, municipal (such as sewer pipes and sewage treatment plants), and agricultural facilities.[37] Under this system, industrial, municipal, and agricultural polluters must apply for permits before discharging wastes into surface waters.

NPDES permits can be issued by the EPA and authorized state agencies and Indian tribes, but only if the discharge will not violate water-quality standards (both federal and state standards). Special requirements must be met to discharge toxic chemicals and residue from oil spills. NPDES permits must be renewed every five years. Although initially the NPDES system focused mainly on industrial wastewater, it was later expanded to cover storm water discharges.

When water from rainstorms flows over streets, parking lots, commercial sites, and other developed areas, the water collects sediments, trash, used motor oil, raw sewage, pesticides, and other toxic contaminants. This polluted runoff flows into urban storm sewers, which often empty into rivers or oceans. In the following case, the plaintiffs claimed that Los Angeles County, California, was responsible for heavily polluted storm water runoff flowing into navigable rivers in the surrounding area.

---

37. 33 U.S.C. Section 1342.

Case 33.2

Natural Resources Defense Council, Inc. v. County of Los Angeles

United States Court of Appeals, Ninth Circuit, 673 F.3d 880 (2011).

Which entities can be sued for discharge of urban storm water into navigable waters?

FACTS   Two environmental organizations—the Natural Resources Defense Council (NRDC) and the Santa Monica Baykeeper—brought a lawsuit against the county of Los Angeles and the Los Angeles County Flood Control District, which included eighty-four cities and some unincorporated areas. The NRDC and Santa Monica alleged that the county and the district were discharging urban storm water runoff into navigable waters in violation of the Clean Water Act. The levels of pollutants detected in four rivers—the Santa Clara River, the Los Angeles River, the San Gabriel River, and Malibu Creek—exceeded the limits allowed in the National Pollutant Discharge Elimination System (NPDES) permit that governs municipal storm water discharges in Los Angeles County.

All parties agreed that the rivers did not meet water-quality standards. The issue was whether the NRDC and Santa Monica had proved that the county and the district were responsible. The defendants claimed that there was no evidence establishing their responsibility for discharging storm water carrying pollutants into the rivers. The federal district court held in favor of the defendants (the county and district agencies), and the NRDC and Santa Monica appealed.

ISSUE   Were Los Angeles County and its Flood Control District responsible for discharging pollutants into navigable rivers?

DECISION   Yes. The federal appellate court held that the agencies were liable for discharging polluted storm water into two of the four waterways. The court reversed the district court's decision regarding the Los Angeles River and the San Gabriel River

and affirmed it with regard to the other two waterways.

REASON   The court noted that in Los Angeles County, storm water runoff is collected by thousands of storm drains and channeled to a main storm-sewer system, or MS4. The Los Angeles River and San Gabriel River Monitoring Stations are located in a channelized portion of the MS4 that is owned and operated by the district. Storm water known to contain standards-exceeding pollutants passes through these monitoring stations and is discharged into the two rivers. Because the monitoring makes the district aware of the pollution levels in the water, the court found that there was sufficient evidence to establish liability. The district (along with the county) was responsible for exceeding the amount of pollutants it was permitted to discharge from the storm-sewer systems into the Los Angeles River and the San Gabriel River. Evidence did not establish that the district was responsible for excess pollution in the Santa Clara River and Malibu Creek, because those monitoring stations were not located within the channelized portion of the MS4, and thus they were not under the district's control.

WHAT IF THE FACTS WERE DIFFERENT?   *Suppose that Los Angeles County had moved all of its monitoring stations outside the "channelized portion of the MS4." If none of the stations that monitored pollution in the four waterways was located within the district's MS4 system, how might the outcome have been changed?*

Standards for Equipment   Regulations generally specify that the *best available control technology*, or BACT, be installed. The EPA issues guidelines as to what equipment meets this standard. Essentially, the guidelines require the most effective pollution-control equipment available.

New sources must install BACT equipment before beginning operations. Existing sources are subject to timetables for the installation of BACT equipment and must immediately install equipment that utilizes the *best practical control technology*, or BPCT. The EPA also issues guidelines as to what equipment meets this standard.

Wetlands Water-saturated, protected areas of land that support wildlife and cannot be filled in or dredged without a permit.

Wetlands

The CWA prohibits the filling or dredging of **wetlands** unless a permit is obtained from the Army Corps of Engineers. The EPA defines *wetlands* as "those areas that are inundated or saturated by surface or ground water at a frequency and duration sufficient to support . . . vegetation typically adapted for life in saturated soil conditions."

Wetlands are thought to be vital to the ecosystem because they filter streams and rivers and provide habitat for wildlife. In the past, the EPA's broad interpretation of what constitutes a wetland generated substantial controversy, but the courts have considerably scaled back the CWA's protection of wetlands in recent years.[38]

Violations of the Clean Water Act

Under the CWA, violators are subject to a variety of civil and criminal penalties. Depending on the violation, civil penalties range from $10,000 per day to $25,000 per day, but not more than $25,000 per violation. Criminal penalties, which apply only if a violation was intentional, range from a fine of $2,500 per day and imprisonment for up to one year to a fine of $1 million and fifteen years' imprisonment. Injunctive relief and damages can also be imposed. The polluting party can be required to clean up the pollution or pay for the cost of doing so.

In the following case, landowners filed a lawsuit challenging an EPA order finding that they had violated the CWA. The United States Supreme Court had to decide whether the federal courts could review the EPA's decision.

---

38. See, for example, *Rapanos v. United States*, 547 U.S. 715, 126 S.Ct. 2208, 165 L.Ed.2d 159 (2006).

Case 33.3

Sackett v. Environmental Protection Agency

Supreme Court of the United States,
___ U.S. ___, 132 S.Ct. 1367, 182 L.Ed.2d 367 (2012).
www.supremecourt.gov/opinions[a]

FACTS To build a home in Idaho, Michael and Chantell Sackett filled in part of their residential lot with dirt and rock. A few months later, they received a compliance order from the Environmental Protection Agency (EPA). The order stated that, because their property was near a major lake, the Sacketts had polluted wetlands in violation of the Clean Water Act. The order required the Sacketts to restore their property immediately and told them that they faced fines of $75,000 a day until they complied. The Sacketts requested a hearing with the EPA. When a hearing was denied, they sued the EPA in federal district court, asserting, among other things, that the compliance order was "arbitrary and capricious" under the Administrative Procedure Act. The district court found that it could not review the EPA's compliance order. On appeal, a federal appellate court affirmed, concluding that the Sacketts had to wait for the EPA to bring an enforcement action against them. The Sacketts appealed to the United States Supreme Court.

ISSUE Under the Administrative Procedure Act, could the Sacketts challenge the EPA's compliance order in federal court?

---

a. Under "Current Term," click on "Latest Slip Opinions." In the resulting list, scroll down to "35" in the first column, and click on the case name to access the opinion. The United States Supreme Court maintains this Web site.

Case 33.3—Continues next page ➡

Case 33.3—Continued

DECISION Yes. The United States Supreme Court held that the Sacketts could challenge the EPA's compliance order in federal court. The Court reversed the judgment of the federal appellate court.

REASON The Administrative Procedure Act (APA) allows courts to review any "final agency action for which there is no other adequate remedy in court." The Court concluded that the EPA's compliance order was a "final" agency action because it determined the Sacketts' rights and obligations. The compliance order required the Sacketts to restore their property to its previous condition, and they could not seek further review with the EPA. In fact, the EPA denied them that opportunity when it rejected their request for a hearing. Second, the Court found that the Sacketts had "no other adequate remedy in court." Given that they faced such heavy daily fines, the Sacketts could not realistically wait for the EPA to bring an enforcement action. Finally, the Clean Water Act itself did not preclude judicial review under the APA. The courts are not prevented from reviewing compliance orders simply because the EPA also has the option of bringing enforcement actions.

CRITICAL THINKING—Legal Consideration *What does the Court's decision in this case mean for people and businesses that face compliance orders? Are they more or less likely to acquiesce to orders they find objectionable?*

Drinking Water   The Safe Drinking Water Act[39] requires the EPA to set maximum levels for pollutants in public water systems. Public water system operators must come as close as possible to meeting the EPA's standards by using the best available technology that is economically and technologically feasible.

Under the act, each supplier of drinking water is required to send every household that it supplies with water an annual statement describing the source of its water. Suppliers must also disclose the level of any contaminants contained in the water and any possible health concerns associated with the contaminants.

The EPA is particularly concerned about contamination from underground sources, such as pesticides and wastes leaked from landfills or disposed of in underground injection wells. Many of these substances are associated with cancer and may cause damage to the central nervous system, liver, and kidneys. Although some evidence suggests that trace amounts of pharmaceuticals may be entering the nation's drinking water, the law does not yet require suppliers to test for or report these substances. The drugs come from prescription medications taken by humans and antibiotics and other medications given to livestock.

Oil Pollution   When more than 10 million gallons of oil leaked into Alaska's Prince William Sound from the *Exxon Valdez* supertanker in 1989, Congress responded by passing the Oil Pollution Act.[40] (At that time, the *Exxon Valdez* disaster was the worst oil spill in U.S. history, but the British Petroleum oil spill in the Gulf of Mexico in 2010 surpassed it.) Under this act, any onshore or offshore oil facility, oil shipper, vessel owner, or vessel operator that discharges oil into navigable waters or onto an adjoining shore can be liable for clean-up costs and damages.

Toxic Chemicals

Today, the control of toxic chemicals used in agriculture and in industry has become increasingly important.

Pesticides and Herbicides   Under the Federal Insecticide, Fungicide, and Rodenticide Act (FIFRA),[41] pesticides and herbicides must be (1) registered before they can

---

39. 42 U.S.C. Sections 300f to 300j-25.
40. 33 U.S.C. Sections 2701–2761.
41. 7 U.S.C. Sections 135–136y.

be sold, (2) certified and used only for approved applications, and (3) used in limited quantities when applied to food crops. The EPA can cancel or suspend registration of substances that are identified as harmful and may also inspect factories where the chemicals are made. There must be no more than a one-in-a-million risk to people of developing cancer from any kind of exposure to the substance, including eating food that contains pesticide residues.[42]

It is a violation of FIFRA to sell a pesticide or herbicide that is unregistered or has had its registration canceled or suspended. It is also a violation to sell a pesticide or herbicide with a false or misleading label or to destroy or deface any labeling required under the act. Penalties for commercial dealers include imprisonment for up to one year and a fine of up to $25,000. Farmers and other private users of pesticides or herbicides who violate the act are subject to a $1,000 fine and incarceration for up to thirty days.

Note that a state can also regulate the sale and use of federally registered pesticides. **CASE EXAMPLE 33.10** The EPA conditionally registered Strongarm, a weed-killing pesticide, in 2000. Dow Agrosciences, LLC, immediately sold Strongarm to Texas peanut farmers. When the farmers applied it, however, Strongarm damaged their crops while failing to control the growth of weeds. The farmers sued Dow, but the lower courts ruled that FIFRA preempted their claims. The farmers appealed to the United States Supreme Court. The Supreme Court held that under a specific provision of FIFRA, a state can regulate the sale and use of federally registered pesticides so long as the regulation does not permit anything that FIFRA prohibits.[43] ●

Toxic Substances   The Toxic Substances Control Act[44] was passed to regulate chemicals and chemical compounds that are known to be toxic and to institute investigation of any possible harmful effects from new chemical compounds. The act applies to compounds such as asbestos and polychlorinated biphenyls, popularly known as PCBs.

The regulations authorize the EPA to require that manufacturers, processors, and other organizations planning to use chemicals first determine their effects on human health and the environment. The EPA can regulate substances that potentially pose an imminent hazard or an unreasonable risk of injury to health or the environment. The EPA may require special labeling, limit the use of a substance, set production quotas, or prohibit the use of a substance altogether.

Hazardous Waste Disposal

Some industrial, agricultural, and household wastes pose more serious threats than others. If not properly disposed of, these toxic chemicals may present a substantial danger to human health and the environment. If released into the environment, they may contaminate public drinking water resources.

Resource Conservation and Recovery Act   In 1976, Congress passed the Resource Conservation and Recovery Act (RCRA)[45] in reaction to concern over the effects of hazardous waste materials on the environment. The RCRA required the EPA to determine which forms of solid waste should be considered hazardous and to establish regulations to monitor and control hazardous waste disposal.

The act also requires all producers of hazardous waste materials to label and package properly any hazardous waste to be transported. Amendments to the RCRA decrease the use of land containment in the disposal of hazardous waste and require smaller generators of hazardous waste to comply with the act.

---

42. 21 U.S.C. Section 346a.
43. *Bates v. Dow Agrosciences, LLC,* 544 U.S. 431, 125 S.Ct. 1788, 161 L.Ed.2d 687 (2005).
44. 15 U.S.C. Sections 2601–2692.
45. 42 U.S.C. Sections 6901 *et seq.*

Under the RCRA, a company may be assessed a civil penalty of up to $25,000 for each violation.[46] Penalties are based on the seriousness of the violation, the probability of harm, and the extent to which the violation deviates from RCRA requirements. Criminal penalties include fines of up to $50,000 for each day of violation, imprisonment for up to two years (in most instances), or both.[47] Criminal fines and the period of imprisonment can be doubled for certain repeat offenders.

Superfund

In 1980, Congress passed the Comprehensive Environmental Response, Compensation, and Liability Act (CERCLA),[48] commonly known as Superfund, to regulate the clean-up of leaking hazardous waste–disposal sites. A special federal fund was created for that purpose.

CERCLA, as amended, has four primary elements:

1. It established an information-gathering and analysis system that enables the government to identify chemical dump sites and determine the appropriate action.
2. It authorized the EPA to respond to hazardous substance emergencies and to arrange for the clean-up of a leaking site directly if the persons responsible for the problem fail to clean up the site.
3. It created a Hazardous Substance Response Trust Fund (also called Superfund) to pay for the clean-up of hazardous sites using funds obtained through taxes on certain businesses.
4. It allowed the government to recover the cost of clean-up from the persons who were (even remotely) responsible for hazardous substance releases.

Potentially Responsible Parties under Superfund   Superfund provides that when a release or a threatened release of hazardous chemicals from a site occurs, the EPA can clean up the site and recover the cost of the clean-up from the following persons: (1) the person who generated the wastes disposed of at the site, (2) the person who transported the wastes to the site, (3) the person who owned or operated the site at the time of the disposal, or (4) the current owner or operator.

A person falling within one of these categories is referred to as a **potentially responsible party (PRP)**. If the PRPs do not clean up the site, the EPA can clean up the site and recover the clean-up costs from the PRPs.

Potentially Responsible Party (PRP)
A party liable for the costs of cleaning up a hazardous waste–disposal site under the Comprehensive Environmental Response, Compensation, and Liability Act.

Joint and Several Liability under Superfund   Liability under Superfund is usually joint and several—that is, a person who generated *only a fraction of the hazardous waste* disposed of at the site may nevertheless be liable for *all* of the clean-up costs. CERCLA authorizes a party who has incurred clean-up costs to bring a "contribution action" against any other person who is liable or potentially liable for a percentage of the costs.

---

46. 42 U.S.C. Section 6928(a).
47. 42 U.S.C. Section 6928(d).
48. 42 U.S.C. Sections 9601–9675.

Reviewing . . . Consumer and Environmental Law

Residents of Lake Caliopa, Minnesota, began noticing an unusually high number of lung ailments among their population. Several concerned local citizens pooled their resources and commissioned a study of the frequency of these health conditions per capita in Lake Caliopa as compared with national averages. The study concluded that residents of Lake Caliopa experienced four to seven times the rate of frequency of asthma, bronchitis, and emphysema as the population nationwide. During the study period, citizens began expressing concerns about the large volumes of smog emitted by the Cotton Design apparel manufacturing plant on the outskirts of town. The plant had opened its production facility two miles east of town beside the Tawakoni River and employed seventy workers.

Just downstream on the Tawakoni River, the city of Lake Caliopa operated a public waterworks facility, which supplied all city residents with water. The Minnesota Pollution Control Agency required Cotton Design to install new equipment to control air and water pollution. Later, citizens brought a lawsuit in a Minnesota state court against Cotton Design for various respiratory ailments allegedly caused or compounded by smog from Cotton Design's factory. Using the information presented in the chapter, answer the following questions.

1. Under the common law, what would each plaintiff be required to identify in order to be given relief by the court?
2. What standard for limiting emissions into the air does Cotton Design's pollution-control equipment have to meet?
3. If Cotton Design's emissions violated the Clean Air Act, how much can the EPA assess in fines per day?
4. What information must the city send to every household that it supplies with water?

DEBATE THIS Laws against bait-and-switch advertising should be abolished because no consumer is ever forced to buy anything.

BUSINESS APPLICATION

The Proper Way to Use Credit Reporting Services*

As explained in the chapter, the Fair Credit Reporting Act (FCRA) protects consumers against inaccurate credit reporting. Many credit reporting agencies provide much more than just credit reports, however. Increasingly, they are providing employers with employment history, information on educational attainment, and criminal records for current employees and job applicants.

Disclosure Issues When Making Background Checks

If a company uses credit reporting agencies, it must disclose this to current employees and to applicants. If a company does not conform to the requirements of advance notice, disclosure, and consent, it can become involved in litigation.

For example, Vitran Express used credit reporting agencies to determine whether prospective employees had criminal records without disclosing this practice to applicants as required by the FCRA. One applicant lost a job offer because the credit reporting agency forwarded inaccurate information indicating that he had a criminal history when he did not. When he and other job applicants brought a class-action lawsuit against Vitran Express, the company ultimately agreed to pay millions of dollars to settle the case.

Steps That Employers Should Take to Avoid Litigation

All companies must make sure that they comply with federal law when they do background checks. Employers must give advance notice and disclosure, and obtain each employee's or applicant's consent to any background check that exceeds a simple credit check.

To ensure that there are no legal problems, an employer should certify in writing to each credit reporting agency that it will follow federal rules concerning notice, authorization, disclosure, and adverse action notices (letters rejecting applicants).

Each prospective employee should be given a clear disclosure—in a separate document—stating that a background report may be requested from a consumer reporting service. At that time, the company should obtain the person's written consent.

Whenever a consumer report influences the company's decision not to hire someone, to avoid a lawsuit, the company should provide the following documents to the individual *before* rejecting him or her:

• The Federal Trade Commission document called "A Summary of Your Rights under the Fair Credit Reporting Act."
• A copy of the consumer report on which the company based its negative decision.

Checklist for the Businessperson

1. *Your in-house counsel or you should carefully review federal law in this matter.*
2. *Always let prospective employees know that you're going to use a consumer reporting service's report as part of the process of evaluating their application.*
3. *Create a separate document that indicates that you are going to use a consumer reporting service.*

*This *Business Application* is not meant to substitute for the services of an attorney who is licensed to practice law in your state.

Key Terms

Chapter Summary: Consumer and Environmental Law

CONSUMER LAW	

Deceptive Advertising
(See pages 857–860.)
	1. *Definition of deceptive advertising*—Generally, an advertising claim will be deemed deceptive if it would mislead a reasonable consumer.
	2. *Bait-and-switch advertising*—Advertising a lower-priced product (the bait) to lure consumers into the store and then telling them the product is unavailable and urging them to buy a higher-priced product (the switch) is prohibited by the FTC.
	3. *Online deceptive advertising*—The FTC has issued guidelines to help online businesses comply with the laws prohibiting deceptive advertising.
	4. *FTC actions against deceptive advertising*—
	   a. Cease-and-desist orders—Requiring the advertiser to stop the challenged advertising.
	   b. Counteradvertising—Requiring the advertiser to advertise to correct the earlier misinformation.

Labeling and Packaging (See pages 860–861.)	Manufacturers must comply with the labeling or packaging requirements for their specific products. In general, all labels must be accurate and not misleading.
Sales (See page 861.)	Federal and state statutes and regulations govern certain practices of sellers who solicit over the telephone or through the mails and protect consumers to some extent against fraudulent and deceptive online sales practices.
Protection of Health and Safety (See pages 861–864.)	1. *Food and drugs*—The Federal Food, Drug, and Cosmetic Act protects consumers against adulterated and misbranded foods and drugs. The act establishes food standards, specifies safe levels of potentially hazardous food additives, and sets classifications of food and food advertising. 2. *Consumer product safety*—The Consumer Product Safety Act seeks to protect consumers from injury from hazardous products. The Consumer Product Safety Commission has the power to remove products that are deemed imminently hazardous from the market and to ban the manufacture and sale of hazardous products.

Credit Protection
(See pages 865–868.)
	1. *Consumer Credit Protection Act, Title I (Truth-in-Lending Act, or TILA)*—A disclosure law that requires sellers and lenders to disclose credit terms or loan terms in certain transactions, including retail and installment sales and loans, car loans, home-improvement loans, and certain real estate loans. Additionally, the TILA provides for the following:
	   a. Equal credit opportunity—Creditors are prohibited from discriminating on the basis of race, religion, marital status, gender, national origin, color, or age.
	   b. Credit-card protection—Liability of cardholders for unauthorized charges is limited to $50, providing notice requirements are met. Consumers are not liable for unauthorized charges made on unsolicited credit cards. The act also sets out procedures to be used in settling disputes between credit-card companies and their cardholders.
	2. *Fair Credit Reporting Act*—Entitles consumers to request verification of the accuracy of a credit report and to have unverified or false information removed from their files.
	3. *Fair and Accurate Credit Transaction Act*—Combats identity theft by establishing a national fraud alert system. Requires account numbers to be truncated and credit reporting agencies to provide one free credit report per year to consumers.
	4. *Fair Debt Collection Practices Act*—Prohibits debt collectors from using unfair debt-collection practices, such as contacting the debtor at his or her place of employment if the employer objects or at unreasonable times, contacting third parties about the debt, and harassing the debtor.

ENVIRONMENTAL LAW	
Common Law Actions (See pages 868–869.)	1. *Nuisance*—A common law doctrine under which persons may be held liable if their use of their property unreasonably interferes with others' rights to use their own property. 2. *Negligence and strict liability*—Parties may recover damages for injuries sustained as a result of a firm's pollution-causing activities if they can demonstrate that the harm was a foreseeable result of the firm's failure to exercise reasonable care (negligence). Businesses engaging in ultrahazardous activities are liable for whatever injuries the activities cause, regardless of whether the firms exercise reasonable care.

Chapter Summary: Consumer and Environmental Law—Continued

Federal Regulation **(See pages 869–876.)**	1. *Environmental protection agencies*—The primary agency regulating environmental law is the federal Environmental Protection Agency (EPA), which administers most federal environmental policies and statutes. 2. *Assessing environmental impact*—The National Environmental Policy Act requires the preparation of an environmental impact statement (EIS) for every major federal action. An EIS must analyze the action's impact on the environment, its adverse effects and possible alternatives, and its irreversible effects on environmental quality. 3. *Important areas regulated by the federal government*—These include the following: a. Air pollution—Regulated under the authority of the Clean Air Act and its amendments. b. Water pollution—Regulated under the authority of the Rivers and Harbors Appropriations Act and the Federal Water Pollution Control Act, as amended by the Clean Water Act. c. Toxic chemicals and hazardous waste—Pesticides and herbicides, toxic substances, and hazardous waste are regulated under the authority of the Federal Insecticide, Fungicide, and Rodenticide Act, the Toxic Substances Control Act, and the Resource Conservation and Recovery Act, respectively. The Comprehensive Environmental Response, Compensation, and Liability Act (CERCLA), as amended, regulates the clean-up of hazardous waste–disposal sites.

ExamPrep

ISSUE SPOTTERS

1. Gert buys a notebook computer from EZ Electronics. She pays for it with her credit card. When the computer proves defective, she asks EZ to repair or replace it, but EZ refuses. What can Gert do? **(See page 866.)**
2. Resource Refining Company's plant emits smoke and fumes. Resource's operation includes a short railway system, and trucks enter and exit the grounds continuously. Constant vibrations from the trains and trucks rattle nearby residential neighborhoods. The residents sue Resource. Are there any reasons that the court might refuse to enjoin Resource's operation? Explain. **(See page 868.)**

—**Check your answers to the Issue Spotters against the answers provided in Appendix E at the end of this text.**

BEFORE THE TEST

Go to www.cengagebrain.com, enter the ISBN 9781133273561, and click on "Find" to locate this textbook's Web site. Then, click on "Access Now" under "Study Tools," and select Chapter 33 at the top. There, you will find a Practice Quiz that you can take to assess your mastery of the concepts in this chapter, as well as Flashcards, a Glossary of important terms, and Video Questions (when assigned).

For Review

Answers to the even-numbered questions in this For Review section can be found in Appendix F at the end of this text.

1. When will advertising be deemed deceptive?
2. What are the major federal statutes providing for consumer protection in credit transactions?
3. Under what common law theories can polluters be held liable?
4. What is contained in an environmental impact statement, and who must file one?
5. What major federal statutes regulate air and water pollution?

Business Scenarios and Case Problems

33–1 Environmental Laws. Fruitade, Inc., is a processor of a soft drink called Freshen Up. Fruitade uses returnable bottles, which it cleans with a special acid to allow for further beverage processing. The acid is diluted with water and then allowed to pass into a navigable stream. Fruitade crushes its broken bottles and throws the crushed glass into the stream. Discuss fully any environmental laws that Fruitade has violated. **(See pages 871–874.)**

33–2   **Question with Sample Answer—Credit Protection.** Maria Ochoa receives two new credit cards on May 1. She had solicited one of them from Midtown Department Store, and the other arrived unsolicited from High-Flying Airlines. During the month of May, Ochoa makes numerous credit-card purchases from Midtown Department Store, but she does not use the High-Flying Airlines card. On May 31, a burglar breaks into Ochoa's home and steals both credit cards, along with other items. Ochoa notifies Midtown Department Store of the theft on June 2, but she fails to notify High-Flying Airlines. Using the Midtown credit card, the burglar makes a $500 purchase on June 1 and a $200 purchase on June 3. The burglar then charges a vacation flight on the High-Flying Airlines card for $1,000 on June 5. Ochoa receives the bills for these charges and refuses to pay them. Discuss Ochoa's liability in these situations. **(See page 866.)**

—For a sample answer to Question 33–2, go to Appendix G at the end of this text.

33–3   **Case Problem with Sample Answer—Food Labeling.** The Nutrition Labeling and Education Act (NLEA) requires packaged food to have a "Nutrition Facts" panel that sets out "nutrition information," including "the total number of calories" per serving. Restaurants are exempt from this requirement. Before the 2010 health-care reforms provisions on menu labeling (see page 861), the NLEA also regulated nutrition-content claims, such as "low sodium," that a purveyor might choose to add to a label. The NLEA permitted a state or local law to require restaurants to disclose nutrition information about the food they serve, but expressly preempted state or local attempts to regulate nutrition-content claims. New York City Health Code Section 81.50 required 10 percent of the restaurants in the city, including McDonald's, Burger King, and Kentucky Fried Chicken, to post calorie-content information on their menus. The New York State Restaurant Association (NYSRA) filed a suit in a federal district court, contending that the NLEA preempted Section 81.50. (Under the U.S. Constitution, state or local laws that conflict with federal laws are preempted.) Was the NYSRA correct? Explain. [*New York State Restaurant Association v. New York City Board of Health*, 556 F.3d 114 (2d Cir. 2009)] **(See pages 860–861.)**

—For a sample answer to Problem 33–3, go to Appendix H at the end of this text.

33–4   **Deceptive Advertising.** Brian Cleary and Rita Burke filed a suit against cigarette maker Philip Morris USA, Inc., seeking class-action status for a claim of deceptive advertising. They claimed that "light" cigarettes, such as Marlboro Lights, were advertised as safer than regular cigarettes, even though the health effects are the same. They contended that the tobacco companies concealed the true nature of light cigarettes. Philip

Morris correctly claimed that it was authorized by the government to advertise cigarettes, including light cigarettes. Assuming that is true, should Cleary and Burke still be able to bring a deceptive advertising claim against the tobacco company? Why or why not? [*Cleary v. Philip Morris USA, Inc.*, 683 F.Supp.2d 730 (N.D.Ill. 2010)] **(See pages 857–860.)**

33–5   **Environmental Impact Statement.** The U.S. National Park Service (NPS) manages the Grand Canyon National Park in Arizona under a management plan that is subject to periodic review. In 2006, after nine years of background work and the completion of a comprehensive environmental impact statement, the NPS issued a new management plan for the park. One part of the plan allowed for the continued use of rafts on the Colorado River, which runs through the Grand Canyon. The number of the rafts was limited, however. Several environmental groups criticized the plan because they felt that it still allowed too many rafts on the river. The groups asked a federal appellate court to overturn the plan, claiming that it violated the wilderness status of the national park. When can a federal court overturn a determination by an agency such as the NPS? Explain. [*River Runners for Wilderness v. Martin*, 593 F.3d 1064 (9th Cir. 2010)] **(See page 869.)**

33–6   **Fair Debt-Collection Practices.** Bank of America hired Atlantic Resource Management, LLC, to collect a debt from Michael Engler. Atlantic called Engler's employer and asked his supervisor about the company's policy concerning the execution of warrants. It then told the supervisor that, to stop the process, Engler needed to call Atlantic about "Case Number 37291 NY0969" during the first three hours of his next shift. When Engler's supervisor told him about the call, Engler feared that he might be arrested, and he experienced discomfort, embarrassment, and emotional distress at work. Can Engler recover under the Fair Debt Collection Practices Act? Why or why not? [*Engler v. Atlantic Resource Management, LLC*, 2012 WL 464728 (W.D.N.Y. 2012)] **(See pages 867–868.)**

33–7   **A Question of Ethics—Clean Air Act.** In the Clean Air Act, Congress allowed California, which has particular problems with clean air, to adopt its own standard for emissions from cars and trucks, subject to the approval of the Environmental Protection Agency (EPA) according to certain criteria. Congress also allowed other states to adopt California's standard after the EPA's approval. In 2004, in an effort to address global warming, the California Air Resources Board amended the state's standard to attain "the maximum feasible and cost-effective reduction of GHG [greenhouse gas] emissions from motor vehicles." The regulation, which applies to new passenger vehicles and light-duty trucks for 2009 and later, imposes decreasing limits on emissions of carbon dioxide through 2016. While EPA approval was pending, Vermont and other states adopted similar standards. Green Mountain Chrysler Plymouth Dodge Jeep and other auto dealers, automakers, and associations of automakers filed a suit in a federal district court against George Crombie (secretary of the Vermont Agency of Natural Resources) and others, seeking relief from the state regulations. [*Green Mountain Chrysler Plymouth Dodge Jeep v. Crombie,* 508 F.Supp.2d 295 (D.Vt. 2007)] **(See pages 870–871.)**

1. Under the Environmental Policy and Conservation Act (EPCA), the National Highway Traffic Safety Administration sets fuel economy standards for new cars. The plaintiffs argued, among other things, that the EPCA, which prohibits states from adopting fuel economy standards, preempts

Vermont's GHG regulation. Do the GHG rules equate to the fuel economy standards? Discuss.

2. Do Vermont's rules tread on the efforts of the federal government to address global warming internationally? Who should regulate GHG emissions? The federal government? The state governments? Both? Neither? Why?

3. The plaintiffs claimed that they would go bankrupt if they were forced to adhere to the state's GHG standards. Should they be granted relief on this basis? Does history support their claim? Explain.

Critical Thinking and Writing Assignments

33–8   💡 **Business Law Critical Thinking Group Assignment.** Many states have enacted laws that go even further than federal laws to protect consumers. These laws vary tremendously from state to state.

1. The first group will decide whether having different laws is fair to sellers who may be prohibited from engaging in a practice in one state that is legal in another.

2. The second group will consider how these different laws might affect a business.

3. A third group will determine whether it is fair that residents of one state have more protection than residents of another.

APPENDIX C

The Uniform Commercial Code (Excerpts)

(Adopted in fifty-two jurisdictions; all fifty States, although Louisiana has adopted only Articles 1, 3, 4, 7, 8, and 9; the District of Columbia; and the Virgin Islands.)

The Uniform Commercial Code consists of the following articles:

Articles:

1. **General Provisions**
2. **Sales**
2A. **Leases**
3. **Negotiable Instruments**
4. **Bank Deposits and Collections**
4A. **Fund Transfers**
5. **Letters of Credit**
6. **Repealer of Article 6—Bulk Transfers and [Revised] Article 6—Bulk Sales**
7. **Warehouse Receipts, Bills of Lading and Other Documents of Title**
8. **Investment Securities**
9. **Secured Transactions**
10. **Effective Date and Repealer**
11. **Effective Date and Transition Provisions**

Article 1
GENERAL PROVISIONS

Part 1   General Provisions

§ 1–101.   Short Titles.

(a) This [Act] may be cited as Uniform Commercial Code.

(b) This article may be cited as Uniform Commercial Code—Uniform Provisions.

§ 1–102.   Scope of Article.

This article applies to a transaction to the extent that it is governed by another article of [the Uniform Commercial Code].

§ 1–103.   Construction of [Uniform Commercial Code] to Promote Its Purpose and Policies; Applicability of Supplemental Principles of Law.

(a) [The Uniform Commercial Code] must be liberally construed and applied to promote its underlying purposes and policies, which are:

(1) to simplify, clarify, and modernize the law governing commercial transactions;

(2) to permit the continued expansion of commercial practices through custom, usage, and agreement of the parties; and

(3) to make uniform the law among the various jurisdictions.

(b) Unless displaced by the particular provisions of [the Uniform Commercial Code], the principles of law and equity, including the law merchant and the law relative to capacity to contract, principal and agent, estoppel, fraud, misrepresentation, duress, coercion, mistake, bankruptcy, and other validating or invalidating cause, supplement its provisions.

§ 1–104.   Construction Against Implicit Repeal.

This Act being a general act intended as a unified coverage of its subject matter, no part of it shall be deemed to be impliedly repealed by subsequent legislation if such construction can reasonably be avoided.

§ 1–105.   Severability.

If any provision or clause of [the Uniform Commercial Code] or its application to any person or circumstance is held invalid, the invalidity does not affect other provisions or applications of [the Uniform Commercial Code] which can be given effect without the invalid provision or application, and to this end the provisions of [the Uniform Commercial Code] are severable.

§ 1–106.   Use of Singular and Plural; Gender.

In [the Uniform Commercial Code], unless the statutory context otherwise requires:

(1) words in the singular number include the plural, and those in the plural include the singular; and

(2) words of any gender also refer to any other gender.

§ 1–107.   Section Captions.

Section captions are part of [the Uniform Commercial Code].

§ 1–108.   Relation to Electronic Signatures in Global and National Commerce Act.

This article modifies, limits, and supersedes the Federal Electronic Signatures in Global and National Commerce Act, 15 U.S.C. Sections 7001 *et seq.*, except that nothing in this article modifies, limits, or supersedes section 7001(c) of that act or authorizes electronic delivery of any of the notices described in section 7003(b) of that Act.

Part 2   General Definitions and Principles of Interpretation

§ 1–201.   General Definitions.

Subject to additional definitions contained in the subsequent Articles of this Act which are applicable to specific Articles or Parts thereof, and unless the context otherwise requires, in this Act:

(1) "Action", in the sense of a judicial proceeding, includes recoupment, counterclaim, set-off, suit in equity, and any other proceedings in which rights are determined.

(2) "Aggrieved party" means a party entitled to resort to a remedy.

(3) "Agreement", as distinguished from "contract", means the bargain of the parties in fact, as found in their language or by implication from other circumstances, including course of performance, course of dealing, or usage of trade as provided in Section 1–303.

(4) "Bank" means a person engaged in the business of banking and includes a savings bank, savings and loan association, credit union, and trust company.

(5) "Bearer" means a person in control of a negotiable electronic document of title or a person in possession of a negotiable instrument, negotiable tangible document of title, or certificated security that is payable to bearer or indorsed in blank.

(6) "Bill of lading" means a document of title evidencing the receipt of goods for shipment issued by a person engaged in the business of directly or indirectly transporting or forwarding goods. The term does not include a warehouse receipt.

(7) "Branch" includes a separately incorporated foreign branch of a bank.

(8) "Burden of establishing" a fact means the burden of persuading the trier of fact that the existence of the fact is more probable than its nonexistence.

(9) "Buyer in ordinary course of business" means a person that buys goods in good faith, without knowledge that the sale violates the rights of another person in the goods, and in the ordinary course from a person, other than a pawnbroker, in the business of selling goods of that kind. A person buys goods in the ordinary course if the sale to the person comports with the usual or customary practices in the kind of business in which the seller is engaged or with the seller's own usual or customary practices. A person that sells oil, gas, or other minerals at the wellhead or minehead is a person in the business of selling goods of that kind. A buyer in ordinary course of business may buy for cash, by exchange of other property, or on secured or unsecured credit, and may acquire goods or documents of title under a pre-existing contract for sale. Only a buyer that takes possession of the goods or has a right to recover the goods from the seller under Article 2 may be a buyer in ordinary course of business. A person that acquires goods in a transfer in bulk or as security for or in total or partial satisfaction of a money debt is not a buyer in ordinary course of business.

(10) "Conspicuous", with reference to a term, means so written, displayed, or presented that a reasonable person against which it is to operate ought to have noticed it. Whether a term is "conspicuous" or not is a decision for the court. Conspicuous terms include the following:

(A) a heading in capitals equal to or greater in size than the surrounding text, or in contrasting type, font, or color to the surrounding text of the same or lesser size; and

(B) language in the body of a record or display in larger type than the surrounding text, or in contrasting type, font, or color to the surrounding text of the same size, or set off from surrounding text of the same size by symbols or other marks that call attention to the language.

(11) "Consumer" means an individual who enters into a transaction primarily for personal, family, or household purposes.

(12) "Contract", as distinguished from "agreement", means the total legal obligation that results from the parties' agreement as determined by [the Uniform Commercial Code] as supplemented by any other laws.

(13) "Creditor" includes a general creditor, a secured creditor, a lien creditor and any representative of creditors, including an assignee for the benefit of creditors, a trustee in bankruptcy, a receiver in equity and an executor or administrator of an insolvent debtor's or assignor's estate.

(14) "Defendant" includes a person in the position of defendant in a counterclaim, cross-action, or third-party claim.

(15) "Delivery" with respect to an electronic document of title means voluntary transfer of control and with respect to an instrument, a tangible document of title, or chattel paper means voluntary transfer of possession.

(16) "Document of title" means a record (i) that in regular course of business or financing is treated as adequately evidencing that the person in possession or control of the record is entitled to receive, control, hold, and dispose of the record and the goods the record covers and (ii) that purports to be issued by or addressed to a bailee and to cover goods in the bailee's possession which are either identified or are fungible portions of an identified mass. The term includes a bill of lading, transport document, dock warrant, dock receipt, warehouse receipt, and order for delivery of goods. An electronic document of title means a document of title evidenced by a record consisting of information stored in an electronic medium. A tangible document of title means a document of title evidenced by a record consisting of information that is inscribed on a tangible medium.

(17) "Fault" means a default, breach, or wrongful act or omission.

(18) "Fungible goods" means:

(A) goods of which any unit, by nature or usage of trade, is the equivalent of any other like unit; or

(B) goods that by agreement are treated as equivalent.

(19) "Genuine" means free of forgery or counterfeiting.

(20) "Good faith," except as otherwise provided in Article 5, means honesty in fact and the observance of reasonable commercial standards of fair dealing.

(21) "Holder" means:

(A) the person in possession of a negotiable instrument that is payable either to bearer or to an identified person that is the person in possession;

(B) the person in possession of a negotiable tangible document of title if the goods are deliverable either to bearer or to the order of the person in possession; or

(C) the person in control of a negotiable electronic document of title.

(22) "Insolvency proceeding" includes an assignment for the benefit of creditors or other proceeding intended to liquidate or rehabilitate the estate of the person involved.

(23) "Insolvent" means:

(A) having generally ceased to pay debts in the ordinary course of business other than as a result of bona fide dispute;

(B) being unable to pay debts as they become due; or

(C) being insolvent within the meaning of federal bankruptcy law.

(24) "Money" means a medium of exchange currently authorized or adopted by a domestic or foreign government. The term includes a monetary unit of account established by an intergovernmental organization or by agreement between two or more countries.

(25) "Organization" means a person other than an individual.

(26) "Party", as distinguished from "third party", means a person that has engaged in a transaction or made an agreement subject to [the Uniform Commercial Code].

(27) "Person" means an individual, corporation, business trust, estate, trust, partnership, limited liability company, association, joint venture, government, governmental subdivision, agency, or instrumentality, public corporation, or any other legal or commercial entity.

(28) "Present value" means the amount as of a date certain of one or more sums payable in the future, discounted to the date certain by use of either an interest rate specified by the parties if that rate is not manifestly unreasonable at the time the transaction is entered into or, if an interest rate is not so specified, a commercially reasonable rate that takes into account the facts and circumstances at the time the transaction is entered into.

(29) "Purchase" means taking by sale, lease, discount, negotiation, mortgage, pledge, lien, security interest, issue or reissue, gift, or any other voluntary transaction creating an interest in property.

(30) "Purchaser" means a person that takes by purchase.

(31) "Record" means information that is inscribed on a tangible medium or that is stored in an electronic or other medium and is retrievable in perceivable form.

(32) "Remedy" means any remedial right to which an aggrieved party is entitled with or without resort to a tribunal.

(33) "Representative" means a person empowered to act for another, including an agent, an officer of a corporation or association, and a trustee, executor, or administrator of an estate.

(34) "Right" includes remedy.

(35) "Security interest" means an interest in personal property or fixtures which secures payment or performance of an obligation. "Security interest" includes any interest of a consignor and a buyer of accounts, chattel paper, a payment intangible, or a promissory note in a transaction that is subject to Article 9. "Security interest" does not include the special property interest of a buyer of goods on identification of those goods to a contract for sale under Section 2–401, but a buyer may also acquire a "security interest" by complying with Article 9. Except as otherwise provided in Section

2–505, the right of a seller or lessor of goods under Article 2 or 2A to retain or acquire possession of the goods is not a "security interest", but a seller or lessor may also acquire a "security interest" by complying with Article 9. The retention or reservation of title by a seller of goods notwithstanding shipment or delivery to the buyer under Section 2–401 is limited in effect to a reservation of a "security interest." Whether a transaction in the form of a lease creates a "security interest" is determined pursuant to Section 1–203.

(36) "Send" in connection with a writing, record, or notice means:

(A) to deposit in the mail or deliver for transmission by any other usual means of communication with postage or cost of transmission provided for and properly addressed and, in the case of an instrument, to an address specified thereon or otherwise agreed, or if there be none to any address reasonable under the circumstances; or

(B) in any other way to cause to be received any record or notice within the time it would have arrived if properly sent.

(37) "Signed" includes using any symbol executed or adopted with present intention to adopt or accept a writing.

(38) "State" means a State of the United States, the District of Columbia, Puerto Rico, the United States Virgin Islands, or any territory or insular possession subject to the jurisdiction of the United States.

(39) "Surety" includes a guarantor or other secondary obligor.

(40) "Term" means a portion of an agreement that relates to a particular matter.

(41) "Unauthorized signature" means a signature made without actual, implied, or apparent authority. The term includes a forgery.

(42) "Warehouse receipt" means a document of title issued by a person engaged in the business of storing goods for hire.

(43) "Writing" includes printing, typewriting, or any other intentional reduction to tangible form. "Written" has a corresponding meaning.

As amended in 2003.

* * * *

§ 1–205. Reasonable Time; Seasonableness.

(a) Whether a time for taking an action required by [the Uniform Commercial Code] is reasonable depends on the nature, purpose, and circumstances of the action.

(b) An action is taken seasonably if it is taken at or within the time agreed or, if no time is agreed, at or within a reasonable time.

* * * *

Part 3   Territorial Applicability and General Rules

* * * *

§ 1–303. Course of Performance, Course of Dealing, and Usage of Trade.

(a) A "course of performance" is a sequence of conduct between the parties to a particular transaction that exists if:

(1) the agreement of the parties with respect to the transaction involves repeated occasions for performance by a party; and

(2) the other party, with knowledge of the nature of the performance and opportunity for objection to it, accepts the performance or acquiesces in it without objection.

(b) A "course of dealing" is a sequence of conduct concerning previous transactions between the parties to a particular transaction that is fairly to be regarded as establishing a common basis of understanding for interpreting their expressions and other conduct.

(c) A "usage of trade" is any practice or method of dealing having such regularity of observance in a place, vocation, or trade as to justify an expectation that it will be observed with respect to the transaction in question. The existence and scope of such a usage must be proved as facts. If it is established that such a usage is embodied in a trade code or similar record, the interpretation of the record is a question of law.

(d) A course of performance or course of dealing between the parties or usage of trade in the vocation or trade in which they are engaged or of which they are or should be aware is relevant in ascertaining the meaning of the parties' agreement, may give particular meaning to specific terms of the agreement, and may supplement or qualify the terms of the agreement. A usage of trade applicable in the place in which part of the performance under the agreement is to occur may be so utilized as to that part of the performance.

(e) Except as otherwise provided in subsection (f), the express terms of an agreement and any applicable course of performance, course of dealing, or usage of trade must be construed whenever reasonable as consistent with each other. If such a construction is unreasonable:

  (1) express terms prevail over course of performance, course of dealing, and usage of trade;

  (2) course of performance prevails over course of dealing and usage of trade; and

  (3) course of dealing prevails over usage of trade.

(f) Subject to Section 2–209 and Section 2A–208, a course of performance is relevant to show a waiver or modification of any term inconsistent with the course of performance.

(g) Evidence of a relevant usage of trade offered by one party is not admissible unless that party has given the other party notice that the court finds sufficient to prevent unfair surprise to the other party.

§ 1–304. Obligation of Good Faith.

Every contract or duty within [the Uniform Commercial Code] imposes an obligation of good faith in its performance and enforcement.

* * * *

§ 1–309. Option to Accelerate at Will.

A term providing that one party or that party's successor in interest may accelerate payment or performance or require collateral or additional collateral "at will" or when the party "deems itself insecure," or words of similar import, means that the party has power to do so only if that party in good faith believes that the prospect of payment or performance is impaired. The burden of establishing lack of good faith is on the party against which the power has been exercised.

§ 1–310. Subordinated Obligations.

An obligation may be issued as subordinated to performance of another obligation of the person obligated, or a creditor may subordinate its right to performance of an obligation by agreement with either the person obligated or another creditor of the person obligated. Subordination does not create a security interest as against either the common debtor or a subordinated creditor.

Article 2
SALES

Part 1 Short Title, General Construction and Subject Matter

§ 2–101. Short Title.

This Article shall be known and may be cited as Uniform Commercial Code—Sales.

§ 2–102. Scope; Certain Security and Other Transactions Excluded From This Article.

Unless the context otherwise requires, this Article applies to transactions in goods; it does not apply to any transaction which although in the form of an unconditional contract to sell or present sale is intended to operate only as a security transaction nor does this Article impair or repeal any statute regulating sales to consumers, farmers or other specified classes of buyers.

§ 2–103. Definitions and Index of Definitions.

(1) In this Article unless the context otherwise requires

  (a) "Buyer" means a person who buys or contracts to buy goods.

  (b) "Good faith" in the case of a merchant means honesty in fact and the observance of reasonable commercial standards of fair dealing in the trade.

  (c) "Receipt" of goods means taking physical possession of them.

  (d) "Seller" means a person who sells or contracts to sell goods.

(2) Other definitions applying to this Article or to specified Parts thereof, and the sections in which they appear are:

"Acceptance". Section 2–606.
"Banker's credit". Section 2–325.
"Between merchants". Section 2–104.
"Cancellation". Section 2–106(4).
"Commercial unit". Section 2–105.
"Confirmed credit". Section 2–325.
"Conforming to contract". Section 2–106.
"Contract for sale". Section 2–106.
"Cover". Section 2–712.
"Entrusting". Section 2–403.
"Financing agency". Section 2–104.
"Future goods". Section 2–105.
"Goods". Section 2–105.
"Identification". Section 2–501.
"Installment contract". Section 2–612.
"Letter of Credit". Section 2–325.

"Lot". Section 2–105.

"Merchant". Section 2–104.

"Overseas". Section 2–323.

"Person in position of seller". Section 2–707.

"Present sale". Section 2–106.

"Sale". Section 2–106.

"Sale on approval". Section 2–326.

"Sale or return". Section 2–326.

"Termination". Section 2–106.

(3) The following definitions in other Articles apply to this Article:

"Check". Section 3–104.

"Consignee". Section 7–102.

"Consignor". Section 7–102.

"Consumer goods". Section 9–109.

"Dishonor". Section 3–507.

"Draft". Section 3–104.

(4) In addition Article 1 contains general definitions and principles of construction and interpretation applicable throughout this Article. As amended in 1994 and 1999.

§ 2–104.   Definitions: "Merchant"; "Between Merchants"; "Financing Agency".

(1) "Merchant" means a person who deals in goods of the kind or otherwise by his occupation holds himself out as having knowledge or skill peculiar to the practices or goods involved in the transaction or to whom such knowledge or skill may be attributed by his employment of an agent or broker or other intermediary who by his occupation holds himself out as having such knowledge or skill.

(2) "Financing agency" means a bank, finance company or other person who in the ordinary course of business makes advances against goods or documents of title or who by arrangement with either the seller or the buyer intervenes in ordinary course to make or collect payment due or claimed under the contract for sale, as by purchasing or paying the seller's draft or making advances against it or by merely taking it for collection whether or not documents of title accompany the draft. "Financing agency" includes also a bank or other person who similarly intervenes between persons who are in the position of seller and buyer in respect to the goods (Section 2–707).

(3) "Between merchants" means in any transaction with respect to which both parties are chargeable with the knowledge or skill of merchants.

§ 2–105.   Definitions: Transferability; "Goods"; "Future" Goods; "Lot"; "Commercial Unit".

(1) "Goods" means all things (including specially manufactured goods) which are movable at the time of identification to the contract for sale other than the money in which the price is to be paid, investment securities (Article 8) and things in action. "Goods" also includes the unborn young of animals and growing crops and other identified things attached to realty as described in the section on goods to be severed from realty (Section 2–107).

(2) Goods must be both existing and identified before any interest in them can pass. Goods which are not both existing and identi-

fied are "future" goods. A purported present sale of future goods or of any interest therein operates as a contract to sell.

(3) There may be a sale of a part interest in existing identified goods.

(4) An undivided share in an identified bulk of fungible goods is sufficiently identified to be sold although the quantity of the bulk is not determined. Any agreed proportion of such a bulk or any quantity thereof agreed upon by number, weight or other measure may to the extent of the seller's interest in the bulk be sold to the buyer who then becomes an owner in common.

(5) "Lot" means a parcel or a single article which is the subject matter of a separate sale or delivery, whether or not it is sufficient to perform the contract.

(6) "Commercial unit" means such a unit of goods as by commercial usage is a single whole for purposes of sale and division of which materially impairs its character or value on the market or in use. A commercial unit may be a single article (as a machine) or a set of articles (as a suite of furniture or an assortment of sizes) or a quantity (as a bale, gross, or carload) or any other unit treated in use or in the relevant market as a single whole.

§ 2–106.   Definitions: "Contract"; "Agreement"; "Contract for Sale"; "Sale"; "Present Sale"; "Conforming" to Contract; "Termination"; "Cancellation".

(1) In this Article unless the context otherwise requires "contract" and "agreement" are limited to those relating to the present or future sale of goods. "Contract for sale" includes both a present sale of goods and a contract to sell goods at a future time. A "sale" consists in the passing of title from the seller to the buyer for a price (Section 2–401). A "present sale" means a sale which is accomplished by the making of the contract.

(2) Goods or conduct including any part of a performance are "conforming" or conform to the contract when they are in accordance with the obligations under the contract.

(3) "Termination" occurs when either party pursuant to a power created by agreement or law puts an end to the contract otherwise than for its breach. On "termination" all obligations which are still executory on both sides are discharged but any right based on prior breach or performance survives.

(4) "Cancellation" occurs when either party puts an end to the contract for breach by the other and its effect is the same as that of "termination" except that the cancelling party also retains any remedy for breach of the whole contract or any unperformed balance.

§ 2–107.   Goods to Be Severed From Realty: Recording.

(1) A contract for the sale of minerals or the like (including oil and gas) or a structure or its materials to be removed from realty is a contract for the sale of goods within this Article if they are to be severed by the seller but until severance a purported present sale thereof which is not effective as a transfer of an interest in land is effective only as a contract to sell.

(2) A contract for the sale apart from the land of growing crops or other things attached to realty and capable of severance without material harm thereto but not described in subsection (1) or of timber to be cut is a contract for the sale of goods within this

Article whether the subject matter is to be severed by the buyer or by the seller even though it forms part of the realty at the time of contracting, and the parties can by identification effect a present sale before severance.

(3) The provisions of this section are subject to any third party rights provided by the law relating to realty records, and the contract for sale may be executed and recorded as a document transferring an interest in land and shall then constitute notice to third parties of the buyer's rights under the contract for sale.

As amended in 1972.

Part 2   Form, Formation and Readjustment of Contract

§ 2–201.   Formal Requirements; Statute of Frauds.

(1) Except as otherwise provided in this section a contract for the sale of goods for the price of $500 or more is not enforceable by way of action or defense unless there is some writing sufficient to indicate that a contract for sale has been made between the parties and signed by the party against whom enforcement is sought or by his authorized agent or broker. A writing is not insufficient because it omits or incorrectly states a term agreed upon but the contract is not enforceable under this paragraph beyond the quantity of goods shown in such writing.

(2) Between merchants if within a reasonable time a writing in confirmation of the contract and sufficient against the sender is received and the party receiving it has reason to know its contents, its satisfies the requirements of subsection (1) against such party unless written notice of objection to its contents is given within ten days after it is received.

(3) A contract which does not satisfy the requirements of subsection (1) but which is valid in other respects is enforceable

(a) if the goods are to be specially manufactured for the buyer and are not suitable for sale to others in the ordinary course of the seller's business and the seller, before notice of repudiation is received and under circumstances which reasonably indicate that the goods are for the buyer, has made either a substantial beginning of their manufacture or commitments for their procurement; or

(b) if the party against whom enforcement is sought admits in his pleading, testimony or otherwise in court that a contract for sale was made, but the contract is not enforceable under this provision beyond the quantity of goods admitted; or

(c) with respect to goods for which payment has been made and accepted or which have been received and accepted (Sec. 2–606).

§ 2–202.   Final Written Expression: Parol or Extrinsic Evidence.

Terms with respect to which the confirmatory memoranda of the parties agree or which are otherwise set forth in a writing intended by the parties as a final expression of their agreement with respect to such terms as are included therein may not be contradicted by evidence of any prior agreement or of a contemporaneous oral agreement but may be explained or supplemented

(a) by course of dealing or usage of trade (Section 1–205) or by course of performance (Section 2–208); and

(b) by evidence of consistent additional terms unless the court finds the writing to have been intended also as a complete and exclusive statement of the terms of the agreement.

§ 2–203.   Seals Inoperative.

The affixing of a seal to a writing evidencing a contract for sale or an offer to buy or sell goods does not constitute the writing a sealed instrument and the law with respect to sealed instruments does not apply to such a contract or offer.

§ 2–204.   Formation in General.

(1) A contract for sale of goods may be made in any manner sufficient to show agreement, including conduct by both parties which recognizes the existence of such a contract.

(2) An agreement sufficient to constitute a contract for sale may be found even though the moment of its making is undetermined.

(3) Even though one or more terms are left open a contract for sale does not fail for indefiniteness if the parties have intended to make a contract and there is a reasonably certain basis for giving an appropriate remedy.

§ 2–205.   Firm Offers.

An offer by a merchant to buy or sell goods in a signed writing which by its terms gives assurance that it will be held open is not revocable, for lack of consideration, during the time stated or if no time is stated for a reasonable time, but in no event may such period of irrevocability exceed three months; but any such term of assurance on a form supplied by the offeree must be separately signed by the offeror.

§ 2–206.   Offer and Acceptance in Formation of Contract.

(1) Unless other unambiguously indicated by the language or circumstances

(a) an offer to make a contract shall be construed as inviting acceptance in any manner and by any medium reasonable in the circumstances;

(b) an order or other offer to buy goods for prompt or current shipment shall be construed as inviting acceptance either by a prompt promise to ship or by the prompt or current shipment of conforming or nonconforming goods, but such a shipment of non-conforming goods does not constitute an acceptance if the seller seasonably notifies the buyer that the shipment is offered only as an accommodation to the buyer.

(2) Where the beginning of a requested performance is a reasonable mode of acceptance an offeror who is not notified of acceptance within a reasonable time may treat the offer as having lapsed before acceptance.

§ 2–207.   Additional Terms in Acceptance or Confirmation.

(1) A definite and seasonable expression of acceptance or a written confirmation which is sent within a reasonable time operates as an acceptance even though it states terms additional to or different from those offered or agreed upon, unless acceptance is expressly made conditional on assent to the additional or different terms.

(2) The additional terms are to be construed as proposals for addition to the contract. Between merchants such terms become part of the contract unless:

(a) the offer expressly limits acceptance to the terms of the offer;

(b) they materially alter it; or

(c) notification of objection to them has already been given or is given within a reasonable time after notice of them is received.

(3) Conduct by both parties which recognizes the existence of a contract is sufficient to establish a contract for sale although the writings of the parties do not otherwise establish a contract. In such case the terms of the particular contract consist of those terms on which the writings of the parties agree, together with any supplementary terms incorporated under any other provisions of this Act.

§ 2–208.   Course of Performance or Practical Construction.

(1) Where the contract for sale involves repeated occasions for performance by either party with knowledge of the nature of the performance and opportunity for objection to it by the other, any course of performance accepted or acquiesced in without objection shall be relevant to determine the meaning of the agreement.

(2) The express terms of the agreement and any such course of performance, as well as any course of dealing and usage of trade, shall be construed whenever reasonable as consistent with each other; but when such construction is unreasonable, express terms shall control course of performance and course of performance shall control both course of dealing and usage of trade (Section 1–205).

(3) Subject to the provisions of the next section on modification and waiver, such course of performance shall be relevant to show a waiver or modification of any term inconsistent with such course of performance.

§ 2–209.   Modification, Rescission and Waiver.

(1) An agreement modifying a contract within this Article needs no consideration to be binding.

(2) A signed agreement which excludes modification or rescission except by a signed writing cannot be otherwise modified or rescinded, but except as between merchants such a requirement on a form supplied by the merchant must be separately signed by the other party.

(3) The requirements of the statute of frauds section of this Article (Section 2–201) must be satisfied if the contract as modified is within its provisions.

(4) Although an attempt at modification or rescission does not satisfy the requirements of subsection (2) or (3) it can operate as a waiver.

(5) A party who has made a waiver affecting an executory portion of the contract may retract the waiver by reasonable notification received by the other party that strict performance will be required of any term waived, unless the retraction would be unjust in view of a material change of position in reliance on the waiver.

§ 2–210.   Delegation of Performance; Assignment of Rights.

(1) A party may perform his duty through a delegate unless otherwise agreed or unless the other party has a substantial interest in having his original promisor perform or control the acts required by the contract. No delegation of performance relieves the party delegating of any duty to perform or any liability for breach.

(2) Except as otherwise provided in Section 9–406, unless otherwise agreed, all rights of either seller or buyer can be assigned except where the assignment would materially change the duty of the other party, or increase materially the burden or risk imposed on him by his contract, or impair materially his chance of obtaining return performance. A right to damages for breach of the whole contract or a right arising out of the assignor's due performance of his entire obligation can be assigned despite agreement otherwise.

(3) The creation, attachment, perfection, or enforcement of a security interest in the seller's interest under a contract is not a transfer that materially changes the duty of or increases materially the burden or risk imposed on the buyer or impairs materially the buyer's chance of obtaining return performance within the purview of subsection (2) unless, and then only to the extent that, enforcement actually results in a delegation of material performance of the seller. Even in that event, the creation, attachment, perfection, and enforcement of the security interest remain effective, but (i) the seller is liable to the buyer for damages caused by the delegation to the extent that the damages could not reasonably by prevented by the buyer, and (ii) a court having jurisdiction may grant other appropriate relief, including cancellation of the contract for sale or an injunction against enforcement of the security interest or consummation of the enforcement.

(4) Unless the circumstances indicate the contrary a prohibition of assignment of "the contract" is to be construed as barring only the delegation to the assignee of the assignor's performance.

(5) An assignment of "the contract" or of "all my rights under the contract" or an assignment in similar general terms is an assignment of rights and unless the language or the circumstances (as in an assignment for security) indicate the contrary, it is a delegation of performance of the duties of the assignor and its acceptance by the assignee constitutes a promise by him to perform those duties. This promise is enforceable by either the assignor or the other party to the original contract.

(6) The other party may treat any assignment which delegates performance as creating reasonable grounds for insecurity and may without prejudice to his rights against the assignor demand assurances from the assignee (Section 2–609).

As amended in 1999.

Part 3   General Obligation and Construction of Contract
§ 2–301.   General Obligations of Parties.

The obligation of the seller is to transfer and deliver and that of the buyer is to accept and pay in accordance with the contract.

§ 2–302.   Unconscionable Contract or Clause.

(1) If the court as a matter of law finds the contract or any clause of the contract to have been unconscionable at the time it was made

the court may refuse to enforce the contract, or it may enforce the remainder of the contract without the unconscionable clause, or it may so limit the application of any unconscionable clause as to avoid any unconscionable result.

(2) When it is claimed or appears to the court that the contract or any clause thereof may be unconscionable the parties shall be afforded a reasonable opportunity to present evidence as to its commercial setting, purpose and effect to aid the court in making the determination.

§ 2–303.   Allocations or Division of Risks.

Where this Article allocates a risk or a burden as between the parties "unless otherwise agreed", the agreement may not only shift the allocation but may also divide the risk or burden.

§ 2–304.   Price Payable in Money, Goods, Realty, or Otherwise.

(1) The price can be made payable in money or otherwise. If it is payable in whole or in part in goods each party is a seller of the goods which he is to transfer.

(2) Even though all or part of the price is payable in an interest in realty the transfer of the goods and the seller's obligations with reference to them are subject to this Article, but not the transfer of the interest in realty or the transferor's obligations in connection therewith.

§ 2–305.   Open Price Term.

(1) The parties if they so intend can conclude a contract for sale even though the price is not settled. In such a case the price is a reasonable price at the time for delivery if

(a) nothing is said as to price; or

(b) the price is left to be agreed by the parties and they fail to agree; or

(c) the price is to be fixed in terms of some agreed market or other standard as set or recorded by a third person or agency and it is not so set or recorded.

(2) A price to be fixed by the seller or by the buyer means a price for him to fix in good faith.

(3) When a price left to be fixed otherwise than by agreement of the parties fails to be fixed through fault of one party the other may at his option treat the contract as cancelled or himself fix a reasonable price.

(4) Where, however, the parties intend not to be bound unless the price be fixed or agreed and it is not fixed or agreed there is no contract. In such a case the buyer must return any goods already received or if unable so to do must pay their reasonable value at the time of delivery and the seller must return any portion of the price paid on account.

§ 2–306.   Output, Requirements and Exclusive Dealings.

(1) A term which measures the quantity by the output of the seller or the requirements of the buyer means such actual output or requirements as may occur in good faith, except that no quantity unreasonably disproportionate to any stated estimate or in the absence of a stated estimate to any normal or otherwise comparable prior output or requirements may be tendered or demanded.

(2) A lawful agreement by either the seller or the buyer for exclusive dealing in the kind of goods concerned imposes unless otherwise agreed an obligation by the seller to use best efforts to supply the goods and by the buyer to use best efforts to promote their sale.

§ 2–307.   Delivery in Single Lot or Several Lots.

Unless otherwise agreed all goods called for by a contract for sale must be tendered in a single delivery and payment is due only on such tender but where the circumstances give either party the right to make or demand delivery in lots the price if it can be apportioned may be demanded for each lot.

§ 2–308.   Absence of Specified Place for Delivery.

Unless otherwise agreed

(a) the place for delivery of goods is the seller's place of business or if he has none his residence; but

(b) in a contract for sale of identified goods which to the knowledge of the parties at the time of contracting are in some other place, that place is the place for their delivery; and

(c) documents of title may be delivered through customary banking channels.

§ 2–309.   Absence of Specific Time Provisions; Notice of Termination.

(1) The time for shipment or delivery or any other action under a contract if not provided in this Article or agreed upon shall be a reasonable time.

(2) Where the contract provides for successive performances but is indefinite in duration it is valid for a reasonable time but unless otherwise agreed may be terminated at any time by either party.

(3) Termination of a contract by one party except on the happening of an agreed event requires that reasonable notification be received by the other party and an agreement dispensing with notification is invalid if its operation would be unconscionable.

§ 2–310.   Open Time for Payment or Running of Credit; Authority to Ship Under Reservation.

Unless otherwise agreed

(a) payment is due at the time and place at which the buyer is to receive the goods even though the place of shipment is the place of delivery; and

(b) if the seller is authorized to send the goods he may ship them under reservation, and may tender the documents of title, but the buyer may inspect the goods after their arrival before payment is due unless such inspection is inconsistent with the terms of the contract (Section 2–513); and

(c) if delivery is authorized and made by way of documents of title otherwise than by subsection (b) then payment is due at the time and place at which the buyer is to receive the documents regardless of where the goods are to be received; and

(d) where the seller is required or authorized to ship the goods on credit the credit period runs from the time of shipment but post-dating the invoice or delaying its dispatch will correspondingly delay the starting of the credit period.

§ 2–311.   Options and Cooperation Respecting Performance.

(1) An agreement for sale which is otherwise sufficiently definite (subsection (3) of Section 2–204) to be a contract is not made invalid by the fact that it leaves particulars of performance to be specified

by one of the parties. Any such specification must be made in good faith and within limits set by commercial reasonableness.

(2) Unless otherwise agreed specifications relating to assortment of the goods are at the buyer's option and except as otherwise provided in subsections (1)(c) and (3) of Section 2–319 specifications or arrangements relating to shipment are at the seller's option.

(3) Where such specification would materially affect the other party's performance but is not seasonally made or where one party's cooperation is necessary to the agreed performance of the other but is not seasonably forthcoming, the other party in addition to all other remedies

(a) is excused for any resulting delay in his own performance; and

(b) may also either proceed to perform in any reasonable manner or after the time for a material part of his own performance treat the failure to specify or to cooperate as a breach by failure to deliver or accept the goods.

§ 2–312. Warranty of Title and Against Infringement; Buyer's Obligation Against Infringement.

(1) Subject to subsection (2) there is in a contract for sale a warranty by the seller that

(a) the title conveyed shall be good, and its transfer rightful; and

(b) the goods shall be delivered free from any security interest or other lien or encumbrance of which the buyer at the time of contracting has no knowledge.

(2) A warranty under subsection (1) will be excluded or modified only by specific language or by circumstances which give the buyer reason to know that the person selling does not claim title in himself or that he is purporting to sell only such right or title as he or a third person may have.

(3) Unless otherwise agreed a seller who is a merchant regularly dealing in goods of the kind warrants that the goods shall be delivered free of the rightful claim of any third person by way of infringement or the like but a buyer who furnishes specifications to the seller must hold the seller harmless against any such claim which arises out of compliance with the specifications.

§ 2–313. Express Warranties by Affirmation, Promise, Description, Sample.

(1) Express warranties by the seller are created as follows:

(a) Any affirmation of fact or promise made by the seller to the buyer which relates to the goods and becomes part of the basis of the bargain creates an express warranty that the goods shall conform to the affirmation or promise.

(b) Any description of the goods which is made part of the basis of the bargain creates an express warranty that the goods shall conform to the description.

(c) Any sample or model which is made part of the basis of the bargain creates an express warranty that the whole of the goods shall conform to the sample or model.

(2) It is not necessary to the creation of an express warranty that the seller use formal words such as "warrant" or "guarantee" or that he have a specific intention to make a warranty, but an affir-

mation merely of the value of the goods or a statement purporting to be merely the seller's opinion or commendation of the goods does not create a warranty.

§ 2–314. Implied Warranty: Merchantability; Usage of Trade.

(1) Unless excluded or modified (Section 2–316), a warranty that the goods shall be merchantable is implied in a contract for their sale if the seller is a merchant with respect to goods of that kind. Under this section the serving for value of food or drink to be consumed either on the premises or elsewhere is a sale.

(2) Goods to be merchantable must be at least such as

(a) pass without objection in the trade under the contract description; and

(b) in the case of fungible goods, are of fair average quality within the description; and

(c) are fit for the ordinary purposes for which such goods are used; and

(d) run, within the variations permitted by the agreement, of even kind, quality and quantity within each unit and among all units involved; and

(e) are adequately contained, packaged, and labeled as the agreement may require; and

(f) conform to the promises or affirmations of fact made on the container or label if any.

(3) Unless excluded or modified (Section 2–316) other implied warranties may arise from course of dealing or usage of trade.

§ 2–315. Implied Warranty: Fitness for Particular Purpose.

Where the seller at the time of contracting has reason to know any particular purpose for which the goods are required and that the buyer is relying on the seller's skill or judgment to select or furnish suitable goods, there is unless excluded or modified under the next section an implied warranty that the goods shall be fit for such purpose.

§ 2–316. Exclusion or Modification of Warranties.

(1) Words or conduct relevant to the creation of an express warranty and words or conduct tending to negate or limit warranty shall be construed wherever reasonable as consistent with each other; but subject to the provisions of this Article on parol or extrinsic evidence (Section 2–202) negation or limitation is inoperative to the extent that such construction is unreasonable.

(2) Subject to subsection (3), to exclude or modify the implied warranty of merchantability or any part of it the language must mention merchantability and in case of a writing must be conspicuous, and to exclude or modify any implied warranty of fitness the exclusion must be by a writing and conspicuous. Language to exclude all implied warranties of fitness is sufficient if it states, for example, that "There are no warranties which extend beyond the description on the face hereof."

(3) Notwithstanding subsection (2)

(a) unless the circumstances indicate otherwise, all implied warranties are excluded by expressions like "as is", "with all faults" or other language which in common understanding calls the buyer's attention to the exclusion of warranties and makes plain that there is no implied warranty; and

(b) when the buyer before entering into the contract has examined the goods or the sample or model as fully as he desired or has refused to examine the goods there is no implied warranty with regard to defects which an examination ought in the circumstances to have revealed to him; and

(c) an implied warranty can also be excluded or modified by course of dealing or course of performance or usage of trade.

(4) Remedies for breach of warranty can be limited in accordance with the provisions of this Article on liquidation or limitation of damages and on contractual modification of remedy (Sections 2–718 and 2–719).

§ 2–317.   Cumulation and Conflict of Warranties Express or Implied.

Warranties whether express or implied shall be construed as consistent with each other and as cumulative, but if such construction is unreasonable the intention of the parties shall determine which warranty is dominant. In ascertaining that intention the following rules apply:

(a) Exact or technical specifications displace an inconsistent sample or model or general language of description.

(b) A sample from an existing bulk displaces inconsistent general language of description.

(c) Express warranties displace inconsistent implied warranties other than an implied warranty of fitness for a particular purpose.

§ 2–318.   Third Party Beneficiaries of Warranties Express or Implied.

Note: If this Act is introduced in the Congress of the United States this section should be omitted. (States to select one alternative.)

Alternative A

A seller's warranty whether express or implied extends to any natural person who is in the family or household of his buyer or who is a guest in his home if it is reasonable to expect that such person may use, consume or be affected by the goods and who is injured in person by breach of the warranty. A seller may not exclude or limit the operation of this section.

Alternative B

A seller's warranty whether express or implied extends to any natural person who may reasonably be expected to use, consume or be affected by the goods and who is injured in person by breach of the warranty. A seller may not exclude or limit the operation of this section.

Alternative C

A seller's warranty whether express or implied extends to any person who may reasonably be expected to use, consume or be affected by the goods and who is injured by breach of the warranty. A seller may not exclude or limit the operation of this section with respect to injury to the person of an individual to whom the warranty extends.

As amended 1966.

§ 2–319.   F.O.B. and F.A.S. Terms.

(1) Unless otherwise agreed the term F.O.B. (which means "free on board") at a named place, even though used only in connection with the stated price, is a delivery term under which

(a) when the term is F.O.B. the place of shipment, the seller must at that place ship the goods in the manner provided in this Article (Section 2–504) and bear the expense and risk of putting them into the possession of the carrier; or

(b) when the term is F.O.B. the place of destination, the seller must at his own expense and risk transport the goods to that place and there tender delivery of them in the manner provided in this Article (Section 2–503);

(c) when under either (a) or (b) the term is also F.O.B. vessel, car or other vehicle, the seller must in addition at his own expense and risk load the goods on board. If the term is F.O.B. vessel the buyer must name the vessel and in an appropriate case the seller must comply with the provisions of this Article on the form of bill of lading (Section 2–323).

(2) Unless otherwise agreed the term F.A.S. vessel (which means "free alongside") at a named port, even though used only in connection with the stated price, is a delivery term under which the seller must

(a) at his own expense and risk deliver the goods alongside the vessel in the manner usual in that port or on a dock designated and provided by the buyer; and

(b) obtain and tender a receipt for the goods in exchange for which the carrier is under a duty to issue a bill of lading.

(3) Unless otherwise agreed in any case falling within subsection (1)(a) or (c) or subsection (2) the buyer must seasonably give any needed instructions for making delivery, including when the term is F.A.S. or F.O.B. the loading berth of the vessel and in an appropriate case its name and sailing date. The seller may treat the failure of needed instructions as a failure of cooperation under this Article (Section 2–311). He may also at his option move the goods in any reasonable manner preparatory to delivery or shipment.

(4) Under the term F.O.B. vessel or F.A.S. unless otherwise agreed the buyer must make payment against tender of the required documents and the seller may not tender nor the buyer demand delivery of the goods in substitution for the documents.

§ 2–320.   C.I.F. and C. & F. Terms.

(1) The term C.I.F. means that the price includes in a lump sum the cost of the goods and the insurance and freight to the named destination. The term C. & F. or C.F. means that the price so includes cost and freight to the named destination.

(2) Unless otherwise agreed and even though used only in connection with the stated price and destination, the term C.I.F. destination or its equivalent requires the seller at his own expense and risk to

(a) put the goods into the possession of a carrier at the port for shipment and obtain a negotiable bill or bills of lading covering the entire transportation to the named destination; and

(b) load the goods and obtain a receipt from the carrier (which may be contained in the bill of lading) showing that the freight has been paid or provided for; and

(c) obtain a policy or certificate of insurance, including any war risk insurance, of a kind and on terms then current at the port of shipment in the usual amount, in the currency of the contract, shown to cover the same goods covered by the bill of lading and providing for payment of loss to the order of the buyer or for the account of whom it may concern; but the seller may add to the price the amount of the premium for any such war risk insurance; and

(d) prepare an invoice of the goods and procure any other documents required to effect shipment or to comply with the contract; and

(e) forward and tender with commercial promptness all the documents in due form and with any indorsement necessary to perfect the buyer's rights.

(3) Unless otherwise agreed the term C. & F. or its equivalent has the same effect and imposes upon the seller the same obligations and risks as a C.I.F. term except the obligation as to insurance.

(4) Under the term C.I.F. or C. & F. unless otherwise agreed the buyer must make payment against tender of the required documents and the seller may not tender nor the buyer demand delivery of the goods in substitution for the documents.

§ 2–321.   C.I.F. or C. & F.: "Net Landed Weights"; "Payment on Arrival"; Warranty of Condition on Arrival.

Under a contract containing a term C.I.F. or C. & F.

(1) Where the price is based on or is to be adjusted according to "net landed weights", "delivered weights", "out turn" quantity or quality or the like, unless otherwise agreed the seller must reasonably estimate the price. The payment due on tender of the documents called for by the contract is the amount so estimated, but after final adjustment of the price a settlement must be made with commercial promptness.

(2) An agreement described in subsection (1) or any warranty of quality or condition of the goods on arrival places upon the seller the risk of ordinary deterioration, shrinkage and the like in transportation but has no effect on the place or time of identification to the contract for sale or delivery or on the passing of the risk of loss.

(3) Unless otherwise agreed where the contract provides for payment on or after arrival of the goods the seller must before payment allow such preliminary inspection as is feasible; but if the goods are lost delivery of the documents and payment are due when the goods should have arrived.

§ 2–322.   Delivery "Ex-Ship".

(1) Unless otherwise agreed a term for delivery of goods "ex-ship" (which means from the carrying vessel) or in equivalent language is not restricted to a particular ship and requires delivery from a ship which has reached a place at the named port of destination where goods of the kind are usually discharged.

(2) Under such a term unless otherwise agreed

(a) the seller must discharge all liens arising out of the carriage and furnish the buyer with a direction which puts the carrier under a duty to deliver the goods; and

(b) the risk of loss does not pass to the buyer until the goods leave the ship's tackle or are otherwise properly unloaded.

§ 2–323.   Form of Bill of Lading Required in Overseas Shipment; "Overseas".

(1) Where the contract contemplates overseas shipment and contains a term C.I.F. or C. & F. or F.O.B. vessel, the seller unless otherwise agreed must obtain a negotiable bill of lading stating that the goods have been loaded on board or, in the case of a term C.I.F. or C. & F., received for shipment.

(2) Where in a case within subsection (1) a bill of lading has been issued in a set of parts, unless otherwise agreed if the documents are not to be sent from abroad the buyer may demand tender of the full set; otherwise only one part of the bill of lading need be tendered. Even if the agreement expressly requires a full set

(a) due tender of a single part is acceptable within the provisions of this Article on cure of improper delivery (subsection (1) of Section 2–508); and

(b) even though the full set is demanded, if the documents are sent from abroad the person tendering an incomplete set may nevertheless require payment upon furnishing an indemnity which the buyer in good faith deems adequate.

(3) A shipment by water or by air or a contract contemplating such shipment is "overseas" insofar as by usage of trade or agreement it is subject to the commercial, financing or shipping practices characteristic of international deep water commerce.

§ 2–324.   "No Arrival, No Sale" Term.

Under a term "no arrival, no sale" or terms of like meaning, unless otherwise agreed,

(a) the seller must properly ship conforming goods and if they arrive by any means he must tender them on arrival but he assumes no obligation that the goods will arrive unless he has caused the non-arrival; and

(b) where without fault of the seller the goods are in part lost or have so deteriorated as no longer to conform to the contract or arrive after the contract time, the buyer may proceed as if there had been casualty to identified goods (Section 2–613).

§ 2–325.   "Letter of Credit" Term; "Confirmed Credit".

(1) Failure of the buyer seasonably to furnish an agreed letter of credit is a breach of the contract for sale.

(2) The delivery to seller of a proper letter of credit suspends the buyer's obligation to pay. If the letter of credit is dishonored, the seller may on seasonable notification to the buyer require payment directly from him.

(3) Unless otherwise agreed the term "letter of credit" or "banker's credit" in a contract for sale means an irrevocable credit issued by a financing agency of good repute and, where the shipment is overseas, of good international repute. The term "confirmed credit"

means that the credit must also carry the direct obligation of such an agency which does business in the seller's financial market.

§ 2–326.   Sale on Approval and Sale or Return; Rights of Creditors.

(1) Unless otherwise agreed, if delivered goods may be returned by the buyer even though they conform to the contract, the transaction is

(a) a "sale on approval" if the goods are delivered primarily for use, and

(b) a "sale or return" if the goods are delivered primarily for resale.

(2) Goods held on approval are not subject to the claims of the buyer's creditors until acceptance; goods held on sale or return are subject to such claims while in the buyer's possession.

(3) Any "or return" term of a contract for sale is to be treated as a separate contract for sale within the statute of frauds section of this Article (Section 2–201) and as contradicting the sale aspect of the contract within the provisions of this Article or on parol or extrinsic evidence (Section 2–202).

As amended in 1999.

§ 2–327.   Special Incidents of Sale on Approval and Sale or Return.

(1) Under a sale on approval unless otherwise agreed

(a) although the goods are identified to the contract the risk of loss and the title do not pass to the buyer until acceptance; and

(b) use of the goods consistent with the purpose of trial is not acceptance but failure seasonably to notify the seller of election to return the goods is acceptance, and if the goods conform to the contract acceptance of any part is acceptance of the whole; and

(c) after due notification of election to return, the return is at the seller's risk and expense but a merchant buyer must follow any reasonable instructions.

(2) Under a sale or return unless otherwise agreed

(a) the option to return extends to the whole or any commercial unit of the goods while in substantially their original condition, but must be exercised seasonably; and

(b) the return is at the buyer's risk and expense.

§ 2–328.   Sale by Auction.

(1) In a sale by auction if goods are put up in lots each lot is the subject of a separate sale.

(2) A sale by auction is complete when the auctioneer so announces by the fall of the hammer or in other customary manner. Where a bid is made while the hammer is falling in acceptance of a prior bid the auctioneer may in his discretion reopen the bidding or declare the goods sold under the bid on which the hammer was falling.

(3) Such a sale is with reserve unless the goods are in explicit terms put up without reserve. In an auction with reserve the auctioneer may withdraw the goods at any time until he announces completion of the sale. In an auction without reserve, after the auctioneer calls for bids on an article or lot, that article or lot cannot be withdrawn unless no bid is made within a reasonable time. In either case a bidder may retract his bid until the auctioneer's announcement of completion of the sale, but a bidder's retraction does not revive any previous bid.

(4) If the auctioneer knowingly receives a bid on the seller's behalf or the seller makes or procures such as bid, and notice has not been given that liberty for such bidding is reserved, the buyer may at his option avoid the sale or take the goods at the price of the last good faith bid prior to the completion of the sale. This subsection shall not apply to any bid at a forced sale.

Part 4   Title, Creditors and Good Faith Purchasers

§ 2–401.   Passing of Title; Reservation for Security; Limited Application of This Section.

Each provision of this Article with regard to the rights, obligations and remedies of the seller, the buyer, purchasers or other third parties applies irrespective of title to the goods except where the provision refers to such title. Insofar as situations are not covered by the other provisions of this Article and matters concerning title became material the following rules apply:

(1) Title to goods cannot pass under a contract for sale prior to their identification to the contract (Section 2–501), and unless otherwise explicitly agreed the buyer acquires by their identification a special property as limited by this Act. Any retention or reservation by the seller of the title (property) in goods shipped or delivered to the buyer is limited in effect to a reservation of a security interest. Subject to these provisions and to the provisions of the Article on Secured Transactions (Article 9), title to goods passes from the seller to the buyer in any manner and on any conditions explicitly agreed on by the parties.

(2) Unless otherwise explicitly agreed title passes to the buyer at the time and place at which the seller completes his performance with reference to the physical delivery of the goods, despite any reservation of a security interest and even though a document of title is to be delivered at a different time or place; and in particular and despite any reservation of a security interest by the bill of lading

(a) if the contract requires or authorizes the seller to send the goods to the buyer but does not require him to deliver them at destination, title passes to the buyer at the time and place of shipment; but

(b) if the contract requires delivery at destination, title passes on tender there.

(3) Unless otherwise explicitly agreed where delivery is to be made without moving the goods,

(a) if the seller is to deliver a document of title, title passes at the time when and the place where he delivers such documents; or

(b) if the goods are at the time of contracting already identified and no documents are to be delivered, title passes at the time and place of contracting.

(4) A rejection or other refusal by the buyer to receive or retain the goods, whether or not justified, or a justified revocation of acceptance revests title to the goods in the seller. Such revesting occurs by operation of law and is not a "sale".

§ 2–402. Rights of Seller's Creditors Against Sold Goods.

(1) Except as provided in subsections (2) and (3), rights of unsecured creditors of the seller with respect to goods which have been identified to a contract for sale are subject to the buyer's rights to recover the goods under this Article (Sections 2–502 and 2–716).

(2) A creditor of the seller may treat a sale or an identification of goods to a contract for sale as void if as against him a retention of possession by the seller is fraudulent under any rule of law of the state where the goods are situated, except that retention of possession in good faith and current course of trade by a merchant-seller for a commercially reasonable time after a sale or identification is not fraudulent.

(3) Nothing in this Article shall be deemed to impair the rights of creditors of the seller

(a) under the provisions of the Article on Secured Transactions (Article 9); or

(b) where identification to the contract or delivery is made not in current course of trade but in satisfaction of or as security for a pre-existing claim for money, security or the like and is made under circumstances which under any rule of law of the state where the goods are situated would apart from this Article constitute the transaction a fraudulent transfer or voidable preference.

§ 2–403. Power to Transfer; Good Faith Purchase of Goods; "Entrusting".

(1) A purchaser of goods acquires all title which his transferor had or had power to transfer except that a purchaser of a limited interest acquires rights only to the extent of the interest purchased. A person with voidable title has power to transfer a good title to a good faith purchaser for value. When goods have been delivered under a transaction of purchase the purchaser has such power even though

(a) the transferor was deceived as to the identity of the purchaser, or

(b) the delivery was in exchange for a check which is later dishonored, or

(c) it was agreed that the transaction was to be a "cash sale", or

(d) the delivery was procured through fraud punishable as larcenous under the criminal law.

(2) Any entrusting of possession of goods to a merchant who deals in goods of that kind gives him power to transfer all rights of the entruster to a buyer in ordinary course of business.

(3) "Entrusting" includes any delivery and any acquiescence in retention of possession regardless of any condition expressed between the parties to the delivery or acquiescence and regardless of whether the procurement of the entrusting or the possess- or's disposition of the goods have been such as to be larcenous under the criminal law.

(4) The rights of other purchasers of goods and of lien creditors are governed by the Articles on Secured Transactions (Article 9), Bulk Transfers (Article 6) and Documents of Title (Article 7).

As amended in 1988.

Part 5 Performance

§ 2–501. Insurable Interest in Goods; Manner of Identification of Goods.

(1) The buyer obtains a special property and an insurable interest in goods by identification of existing goods as goods to which the contract refers even though the goods so identified are nonconforming and he has an option to return or reject them. Such identification can be made at any time and in any manner explicitly agreed to by the parties. In the absence of explicit agreement identification occurs

(a) when the contract is made if it is for the sale of goods already existing and identified;

(b) if the contract is for the sale of future goods other than those described in paragraph (c), when goods are shipped, marked or otherwise designated by the seller as goods to which the contract refers;

(c) when the crops are planted or otherwise become growing crops or the young are conceived if the contract is for the sale of unborn young to be born within twelve months after contracting or for the sale of crops to be harvested within twelve months or the next normal harvest season after contracting whichever is longer.

(2) The seller retains an insurable interest in goods so long as title to or any security interest in the goods remains in him and where the identification is by the seller alone he may until default or insolvency or notification to the buyer that the identification is final substitute other goods for those identified.

(3) Nothing in this section impairs any insurable interest recognized under any other statute or rule of law.

§ 2–502. Buyer's Right to Goods on Seller's Insolvency.

(1) Subject to subsections (2) and (3) and even though the goods have not been shipped a buyer who has paid a part or all of the price of goods in which he has a special property under the provisions of the immediately preceding section may on making and keeping good a tender of any unpaid portion of their price recover them from the seller if:

(a) in the case of goods bought for personal, family, or household purposes, the seller repudiates or fails to deliver as required by the contract; or

(b) in all cases, the seller becomes insolvent within ten days after receipt of the first installment on their price.

(2) The buyer's right to recover the goods under subsection (1)(a) vests upon acquisition of a special property, even if the seller had not then repudiated or failed to deliver.

(3) If the identification creating his special property has been made by the buyer he acquires the right to recover the goods only if they conform to the contract for sale.

As amended in 1999.

§ 2–503.   Manner of Seller's Tender of Delivery.

(1) Tender of delivery requires that the seller put and hold conforming goods at the buyer's disposition and give the buyer any notification reasonably necessary to enable him to take delivery. The manner, time and place for tender are determined by the agreement and this Article, and in particular

(a) tender must be at a reasonable hour, and if it is of goods they must be kept available for the period reasonably necessary to enable the buyer to take possession; but

(b) unless otherwise agreed the buyer must furnish facilities reasonably suited to the receipt of the goods.

(2) Where the case is within the next section respecting shipment tender requires that the seller comply with its provisions.

(3) Where the seller is required to deliver at a particular destination tender requires that he comply with subsection (1) and also in any appropriate case tender documents as described in subsections (4) and (5) of this section.

(4) Where goods are in the possession of a bailee and are to be delivered without being moved

(a) tender requires that the seller either tender a negotiable document of title covering such goods or procure acknowledgment by the bailee of the buyer's right to possession of the goods; but

(b) tender to the buyer of a non-negotiable document of title or of a written direction to the bailee to deliver is sufficient tender unless the buyer seasonably objects, and receipt by the bailee of notification of the buyer's rights fixes those rights as against the bailee and all third persons; but risk of loss of the goods and of any failure by the bailee to honor the non-negotiable document of title or to obey the direction remains on the seller until the buyer has had a reasonable time to present the document or direction, and a refusal by the bailee to honor the document or to obey the direction defeats the tender.

(5) Where the contract requires the seller to deliver documents

(a) he must tender all such documents in correct form, except as provided in this Article with respect to bills of lading in a set (subsection (2) of Section 2–323); and

(b) tender through customary banking channels is sufficient and dishonor of a draft accompanying the documents constitutes non-acceptance or rejection.

§ 2–504.   Shipment by Seller.

Where the seller is required or authorized to send the goods to the buyer and the contract does not require him to deliver them at a particular destination, then unless otherwise agreed he must

(a) put the goods in the possession of such a carrier and make such a contract for their transportation as may be reasonable having regard to the nature of the goods and other circumstances of the case; and

(b) obtain and promptly deliver or tender in due form any document necessary to enable the buyer to obtain possession of the goods or otherwise required by the agreement or by usage of trade; and

(c) promptly notify the buyer of the shipment.

Failure to notify the buyer under paragraph (c) or to make a proper contract under paragraph (a) is a ground for rejection only if material delay or loss ensues.

§ 2–505.   Seller's Shipment under Reservation.

(1) Where the seller has identified goods to the contract by or before shipment:

(a) his procurement of a negotiable bill of lading to his own order or otherwise reserves in him a security interest in the goods. His procurement of the bill to the order of a financing agency or of the buyer indicates in addition only the seller's expectation of transferring that interest to the person named.

(b) a non-negotiable bill of lading to himself or his nominee reserves possession of the goods as security but except in a case of conditional delivery (subsection (2) of Section 2–507) a non-negotiable bill of lading naming the buyer as consignee reserves no security interest even though the seller retains possession of the bill of lading.

(2) When shipment by the seller with reservation of a security interest is in violation of the contract for sale it constitutes an improper contract for transportation within the preceding section but impairs neither the rights given to the buyer by shipment and identification of the goods to the contract nor the seller's powers as a holder of a negotiable document.

§ 2–506.   Rights of Financing Agency.

(1) A financing agency by paying or purchasing for value a draft which relates to a shipment of goods acquires to the extent of the payment or purchase and in addition to its own rights under the draft and any document of title securing it any rights of the shipper in the goods including the right to stop delivery and the shipper's right to have the draft honored by the buyer.

(2) The right to reimbursement of a financing agency which has in good faith honored or purchased the draft under commitment to or authority from the buyer is not impaired by subsequent discovery of defects with reference to any relevant document which was apparently regular on its face.

§ 2–507.   Effect of Seller's Tender; Delivery on Condition.

(1) Tender of delivery is a condition to the buyer's duty to accept the goods and, unless otherwise agreed, to his duty to pay for them. Tender entitles the seller to acceptance of the goods and to payment according to the contract.

(2) Where payment is due and demanded on the delivery to the buyer of goods or documents of title, his right as against the seller to retain or dispose of them is conditional upon his making the payment due.

§ 2–508.   Cure by Seller of Improper Tender or Delivery; Replacement.

(1) Where any tender or delivery by the seller is rejected because non-conforming and the time for performance has not yet expired,

the seller may seasonably notify the buyer of his intention to cure and may then within the contract time make a conforming delivery.

(2) Where the buyer rejects a non-conforming tender which the seller had reasonable grounds to believe would be acceptable with or without money allowance the seller may if he seasonably notifies the buyer have a further reasonable time to substitute a conforming tender.

§ 2–509.   Risk of Loss in the Absence of Breach.

(1) Where the contract requires or authorizes the seller to ship the goods by carrier

> (a) if it does not require him to deliver them at a particular destination, the risk of loss passes to the buyer when the goods are duly delivered to the carrier even though the shipment is under reservation (Section 2–505); but

> (b) if it does require him to deliver them at a particular destination and the goods are there duly tendered while in the possession of the carrier, the risk of loss passes to the buyer when the goods are there duly so tendered as to enable the buyer to take delivery.

(2) Where the goods are held by a bailee to be delivered without being moved, the risk of loss passes to the buyer

> (a) on his receipt of a negotiable document of title covering the goods; or

> (b) on acknowledgment by the bailee of the buyer's right to possession of the goods; or

> (c) after his receipt of a non-negotiable document of title or other written direction to deliver, as provided in subsection (4)(b) of Section 2–503.

(3) In any case not within subsection (1) or (2), the risk of loss passes to the buyer on his receipt of the goods if the seller is a merchant; otherwise the risk passes to the buyer on tender of delivery.

(4) The provisions of this section are subject to contrary agreement of the parties and to the provisions of this Article on sale on approval (Section 2–327) and on effect of breach on risk of loss (Section 2–510).

§ 2–510.   Effect of Breach on Risk of Loss.

(1) Where a tender or delivery of goods so fails to conform to the contract as to give a right of rejection the risk of their loss remains on the seller until cure or acceptance.

(2) Where the buyer rightfully revokes acceptance he may to the extent of any deficiency in his effective insurance coverage treat the risk of loss as having rested on the seller from the beginning.

(3) Where the buyer as to conforming goods already identified to the contract for sale repudiates or is otherwise in breach before risk of their loss has passed to him, the seller may to the extent of any deficiency in his effective insurance coverage treat the risk of loss as resting on the buyer for a commercially reasonable time.

§ 2–511.   Tender of Payment by Buyer; Payment by Check.

(1) Unless otherwise agreed tender of payment is a condition to the seller's duty to tender and complete any delivery.

(2) Tender of payment is sufficient when made by any means or in any manner current in the ordinary course of business unless the seller demands payment in legal tender and gives any extension of time reasonably necessary to procure it.

(3) Subject to the provisions of this Act on the effect of an instrument on an obligation (Section 3–310), payment by check is conditional and is defeated as between the parties by dishonor of the check on due presentment.

As amended in 1994.

§ 2–512.   Payment by Buyer Before Inspection.

(1) Where the contract requires payment before inspection non-conformity of the goods does not excuse the buyer from so making payment unless

> (a) the non-conformity appears without inspection; or

> (b) despite tender of the required documents the circumstances would justify injunction against honor under this Act (Section 5–109(b)).

(2) Payment pursuant to subsection (1) does not constitute an acceptance of goods or impair the buyer's right to inspect or any of his remedies.

As amended in 1995.

§ 2–513.   Buyer's Right to Inspection of Goods.

(1) Unless otherwise agreed and subject to subsection (3), where goods are tendered or delivered or identified to the contract for sale, the buyer has a right before payment or acceptance to inspect them at any reasonable place and time and in any reasonable manner. When the seller is required or authorized to send the goods to the buyer, the inspection may be after their arrival.

(2) Expenses of inspection must be borne by the buyer but may be recovered from the seller if the goods do not conform and are rejected.

(3) Unless otherwise agreed and subject to the provisions of this Article on C.I.F. contracts (subsection (3) of Section 2–321), the buyer is not entitled to inspect the goods before payment of the price when the contract provides

> (a) for delivery "C.O.D." or on other like terms; or

> (b) for payment against documents of title, except where such payment is due only after the goods are to become available for inspection.

(4) A place or method of inspection fixed by the parties is presumed to be exclusive but unless otherwise expressly agreed it does not postpone identification or shift the place for delivery or for passing the risk of loss. If compliance becomes impossible, inspection shall be as provided in this section unless the place or method fixed was clearly intended as an indispensable condition failure of which avoids the contract.

§ 2–514.   When Documents Deliverable on Acceptance; When on Payment.

Unless otherwise agreed documents against which a draft is drawn are to be delivered to the drawee on acceptance of the draft if it is payable more than three days after presentment; otherwise, only on payment.

§ 2–515.   Preserving Evidence of Goods in Dispute.

In furtherance of the adjustment of any claim or dispute

(a) either party on reasonable notification to the other and for the purpose of ascertaining the facts and preserving evidence has the right to inspect, test and sample the goods including such of them as may be in the possession or control of the other; and

(b) the parties may agree to a third party inspection or survey to determine the conformity or condition of the goods and may agree that the findings shall be binding upon them in any subsequent litigation or adjustment.

Part 6   Breach, Repudiation and Excuse

§ 2–601.   Buyer's Rights on Improper Delivery.

Subject to the provisions of this Article on breach in installment contracts (Section 2–612) and unless otherwise agreed under the sections on contractual limitations of remedy (Sections 2–718 and 2–719), if the goods or the tender of delivery fail in any respect to conform to the contract, the buyer may

(a) reject the whole; or

(b) accept the whole; or

(c) accept any commercial unit or units and reject the rest.

§ 2–602.   Manner and Effect of Rightful Rejection.

(1) Rejection of goods must be within a reasonable time after their delivery or tender. It is ineffective unless the buyer seasonably notifies the seller.

(2) Subject to the provisions of the two following sections on rejected goods (Sections 2–603 and 2–604),

(a) after rejection any exercise of ownership by the buyer with respect to any commercial unit is wrongful as against the seller; and

(b) if the buyer has before rejection taken physical possession of goods in which he does not have a security interest under the provisions of this Article (subsection (3) of Section 2–711), he is under a duty after rejection to hold them with reasonable care at the seller's disposition for a time sufficient to permit the seller to remove them; but

(c) the buyer has no further obligations with regard to goods rightfully rejected.

(3) The seller's rights with respect to goods wrongfully rejected are governed by the provisions of this Article on Seller's remedies in general (Section 2–703).

§ 2–603.   Merchant Buyer's Duties as to Rightfully Rejected Goods.

(1) Subject to any security interest in the buyer (subsection (3) of Section 2–711), when the seller has no agent or place of business at the market of rejection a merchant buyer is under a duty after rejection of goods in his possession or control to follow any reasonable instructions received from the seller with respect to the goods and in the absence of such instructions to make reasonable

efforts to sell them for the seller's account if they are perishable or threaten to decline in value speedily. Instructions are not reasonable if on demand indemnity for expenses is not forthcoming.

(2) When the buyer sells goods under subsection (1), he is entitled to reimbursement from the seller or out of the proceeds for reasonable expenses of caring for and selling them, and if the expenses include no selling commission then to such commission as is usual in the trade or if there is none to a reasonable sum not exceeding ten per cent on the gross proceeds.

(3) In complying with this section the buyer is held only to good faith and good faith conduct hereunder is neither acceptance nor conversion nor the basis of an action for damages.

§ 2–604.   Buyer's Options as to Salvage of Rightfully Rejected Goods.

Subject to the provisions of the immediately preceding section on perishables if the seller gives no instructions within a reasonable time after notification of rejection the buyer may store the rejected goods for the seller's account or reship them to him or resell them for the seller's account with reimbursement as provided in the preceding section. Such action is not acceptance or conversion.

§ 2–605.   Waiver of Buyer's Objections by Failure to Particularize.

(1) The buyer's failure to state in connection with rejection a particular defect which is ascertainable by reasonable inspection precludes him from relying on the unstated defect to justify rejection or to establish breach

(a) where the seller could have cured it if stated seasonably; or

(b) between merchants when the seller has after rejection made a request in writing for a full and final written statement of all defects on which the buyer proposes to rely.

(2) Payment against documents made without reservation of rights precludes recovery of the payment for defects apparent on the face of the documents.

§ 2–606.   What Constitutes Acceptance of Goods.

(1) Acceptance of goods occurs when the buyer

(a) after a reasonable opportunity to inspect the goods signifies to the seller that the goods are conforming or that he will take or retain them in spite of their nonconformity; or

(b) fails to make an effective rejection (subsection (1) of Section 2–602), but such acceptance does not occur until the buyer has had a reasonable opportunity to inspect them; or

(c) does any act inconsistent with the seller's ownership; but if such act is wrongful as against the seller it is an acceptance only if ratified by him.

(2) Acceptance of a part of any commercial unit is acceptance of that entire unit.

§ 2–607.   Effect of Acceptance; Notice of Breach; Burden of Establishing Breach After Acceptance; Notice of Claim or Litigation to Person Answerable Over.

(1) The buyer must pay at the contract rate for any goods accepted.

(2) Acceptance of goods by the buyer precludes rejection of the goods accepted and if made with knowledge of a non-conformity cannot be revoked because of it unless the acceptance was on the reasonable assumption that the non-conformity would be seasonably cured but acceptance does not of itself impair any other remedy provided by this Article for non-conformity.

(3) Where a tender has been accepted

(a) the buyer must within a reasonable time after he discovers or should have discovered any breach notify the seller of breach or be barred from any remedy; and

(b) if the claim is one for infringement or the like (subsection (3) of Section 2–312) and the buyer is sued as a result of such a breach he must so notify the seller within a reasonable time after he receives notice of the litigation or be barred from any remedy over for liability established by the litigation.

(4) The burden is on the buyer to establish any breach with respect to the goods accepted.

(5) Where the buyer is sued for breach of a warranty or other obligation for which his seller is answerable over

(a) he may give his seller written notice of the litigation. If the notice states that the seller may come in and defend and that if the seller does not do so he will be bound in any action against him by his buyer by any determination of fact common to the two litigations, then unless the seller after seasonable receipt of the notice does come in and defend he is so bound.

(b) if the claim is one for infringement or the like (subsection (3) of Section 2–312) the original seller may demand in writing that his buyer turn over to him control of the litigation including settlement or else be barred from any remedy over and if he also agrees to bear all expense and to satisfy any adverse judgment, then unless the buyer after seasonable receipt of the demand does turn over control the buyer is so barred.

(6) The provisions of subsections (3), (4) and (5) apply to any obligation of a buyer to hold the seller harmless against infringement or the like (subsection (3) of Section 2–312).

§ 2–608. Revocation of Acceptance in Whole or in Part.

(1) The buyer may revoke his acceptance of a lot or commercial unit whose non-conformity substantially impairs its value to him if he has accepted it

(a) on the reasonable assumption that its nonconformity would be cured and it has not been seasonably cured; or

(b) without discovery of such non-conformity if his acceptance was reasonably induced either by the difficulty of discovery before acceptance or by the seller's assurances.

(2) Revocation of acceptance must occur within a reasonable time after the buyer discovers or should have discovered the ground for it and before any substantial change in condition of the goods which is not caused by their own defects. It is not effective until the buyer notifies the seller of it.

(3) A buyer who so revokes has the same rights and duties with regard to the goods involved as if he had rejected them.

§ 2–609. Right to Adequate Assurance of Performance.

(1) A contract for sale imposes an obligation on each party that the other's expectation of receiving due performance will not be impaired. When reasonable grounds for insecurity arise with respect to the performance of either party the other may in writing demand adequate assurance of due performance and until he receives such assurance may if commercially reasonable suspend any performance for which he has not already received the agreed return.

(2) Between merchants the reasonableness of grounds for insecurity and the adequacy of any assurance offered shall be determined according to commercial standards.

(3) Acceptance of any improper delivery or payment does not prejudice the party's right to demand adequate assurance of future performance.

(4) After receipt of a justified demand failure to provide within a reasonable time not exceeding thirty days such assurance of due performance as is adequate under the circumstances of the particular case is a repudiation of the contract.

§ 2–610. Anticipatory Repudiation.

When either party repudiates the contract with respect to a performance not yet due the loss of which will substantially impair the value of the contract to the other, the aggrieved party may

(a) for a commercially reasonable time await performance by the repudiating party; or

(b) resort to any remedy for breach (Section 2–703 or Section 2–711), even though he has notified the repudiating party that he would await the latter's performance and has urged retraction; and

(c) in either case suspend his own performance or proceed in accordance with the provisions of this Article on the seller's right to identify goods to the contract notwithstanding breach or to salvage unfinished goods (Section 2–704).

§ 2–611. Retraction of Anticipatory Repudiation.

(1) Until the repudiating party's next performance is due he can retract his repudiation unless the aggrieved party has since the repudiation cancelled or materially changed his position or otherwise indicated that he considers the repudiation final.

(2) Retraction may be by any method which clearly indicates to the aggrieved party that the repudiating party intends to perform, but must include any assurance justifiably demanded under the provisions of this Article (Section 2–609).

(3) Retraction reinstates the repudiating party's rights under the contract with due excuse and allowance to the aggrieved party for any delay occasioned by the repudiation.

§ 2–612. "Installment Contract"; Breach.

(1) An "installment contract" is one which requires or authorizes the delivery of goods in separate lots to be separately accepted, even though the contract contains a clause "each delivery is a separate contract" or its equivalent.

(2) The buyer may reject any installment which is non-conforming if the non-conformity substantially impairs the value of that installment

and cannot be cured or if the non-conformity is a defect in the required documents; but if the non-conformity does not fall within subsection (3) and the seller gives adequate assurance of its cure the buyer must accept that installment.

(3) Whenever non-conformity or default with respect to one or more installments substantially impairs the value of the whole contract there is a breach of the whole. But the aggrieved party reinstates the contract if he accepts a non-conforming installment without seasonably notifying of cancellation or if he brings an action with respect only to past installments or demands performance as to future installments.

§ 2–613.   Casualty to Identified Goods.

Where the contract requires for its performance goods identified when the contract is made, and the goods suffer casualty without fault of either party before the risk of loss passes to the buyer, or in a proper case under a "no arrival, no sale" term (Section 2–324) then

(a) if the loss is total the contract is avoided; and

(b) if the loss is partial or the goods have so deteriorated as no longer to conform to the contract the buyer may nevertheless demand inspection and at his option either treat the contract as voided or accept the goods with due allowance from the contract price for the deterioration or the deficiency in quantity but without further right against the seller.

§ 2–614.   Substituted Performance.

(1) Where without fault of either party the agreed berthing, loading, or unloading facilities fail or an agreed type of carrier becomes unavailable or the agreed manner of delivery otherwise becomes commercially impracticable but a commercially reasonable substitute is available, such substitute performance must be tendered and accepted.

(2) If the agreed means or manner of payment fails because of domestic or foreign governmental regulation, the seller may withhold or stop delivery unless the buyer provides a means or manner of payment which is commercially a substantial equivalent. If delivery has already been taken, payment by the means or in the manner provided by the regulation discharges the buyer's obligation unless the regulation is discriminatory, oppressive or predatory.

§ 2–615.   Excuse by Failure of Presupposed Conditions.

Except so far as a seller may have assumed a greater obligation and subject to the preceding section on substituted performance:

(a) Delay in delivery or non-delivery in whole or in part by a seller who complies with paragraphs (b) and (c) is not a breach of his duty under a contract for sale if performance as agreed has been made impracticable by the occurrence of a contingency the nonoccurrence of which was a basic assumption on which the contract was made or by compliance in good faith with any applicable foreign or domestic governmental regulation or order whether or not it later proves to be invalid.

(b) Where the causes mentioned in paragraph (a) affect only a part of the seller's capacity to perform, he must allocate production and deliveries among his customers but may at his option include regular customers not then under contract as well as his own requirements for further manufacture. He may so allocate in any manner which is fair and reasonable.

(c) The seller must notify the buyer seasonably that there will be delay or non-delivery and, when allocation is required under paragraph (b), of the estimated quota thus made available for the buyer.

§ 2–616.   Procedure on Notice Claiming Excuse.

(1) Where the buyer receives notification of a material or indefinite delay or an allocation justified under the preceding section he may by written notification to the seller as to any delivery concerned, and where the prospective deficiency substantially impairs the value of the whole contract under the provisions of this Article relating to breach of installment contracts (Section 2–612), then also as to the whole,

(a) terminate and thereby discharge any unexecuted portion of the contract; or

(b) modify the contract by agreeing to take his available quota in substitution.

(2) If after receipt of such notification from the seller the buyer fails so to modify the contract within a reasonable time not exceeding thirty days the contract lapses with respect to any deliveries affected.

(3) The provisions of this section may not be negated by agreement except in so far as the seller has assumed a greater obligation under the preceding section.

Part 7   Remedies

§ 2–701.   Remedies for Breach of Collateral Contracts Not Impaired.

Remedies for breach of any obligation or promise collateral or ancillary to a contract for sale are not impaired by the provisions of this Article.

§ 2–702.   Seller's Remedies on Discovery of Buyer's Insolvency.

(1) Where the seller discovers the buyer to be insolvent he may refuse delivery except for cash including payment for all goods theretofore delivered under the contract, and stop delivery under this Article (Section 2–705).

(2) Where the seller discovers that the buyer has received goods on credit while insolvent he may reclaim the goods upon demand made within ten days after the receipt, but if misrepresentation of solvency has been made to the particular seller in writing within three months before delivery the ten day limitation does not apply. Except as provided in this subsection the seller may not base a right to reclaim goods on the buyer's fraudulent or innocent misrepresentation of solvency or of intent to pay.

(3) The seller's right to reclaim under subsection (2) is subject to the rights of a buyer in ordinary course or other good faith purchaser under this Article (Section 2–403). Successful reclamation of goods excludes all other remedies with respect to them.

§ 2–703. Seller's Remedies in General.

Where the buyer wrongfully rejects or revokes acceptance of goods or fails to make a payment due on or before delivery or repudiates with respect to a part or the whole, then with respect to any goods directly affected and, if the breach is of the whole contract (Section 2–612), then also with respect to the whole undelivered balance, the aggrieved seller may

(a) withhold delivery of such goods;

(b) stop delivery by any bailee as hereafter provided (Section 2–705);

(c) proceed under the next section respecting goods still unidentified to the contract;

(d) resell and recover damages as hereafter provided (Section 2–706);

(e) recover damages for non-acceptance (Section 2–708) or in a proper case the price (Section 2–709);

(f) cancel.

§ 2–704. Seller's Right to Identify Goods to the Contract Notwithstanding Breach or to Salvage Unfinished Goods.

(1) An aggrieved seller under the preceding section may

(a) identify to the contract conforming goods not already identified if at the time he learned of the breach they are in his possession or control;

(b) treat as the subject of resale goods which have demonstrably been intended for the particular contract even though those goods are unfinished.

(2) Where the goods are unfinished an aggrieved seller may in the exercise of reasonable commercial judgment for the purposes of avoiding loss and of effective realization either complete the manufacture and wholly identify the goods to the contract or cease manufacture and resell for scrap or salvage value or proceed in any other reasonable manner.

§ 2–705. Seller's Stoppage of Delivery in Transit or Otherwise.

(1) The seller may stop delivery of goods in the possession of a carrier or other bailee when he discovers the buyer to be insolvent (Section 2–702) and may stop delivery of carload, truckload, planeload or larger shipments of express or freight when the buyer repudiates or fails to make a payment due before delivery or if for any other reason the seller has a right to withhold or reclaim the goods.

(2) As against such buyer the seller may stop delivery until

(a) receipt of the goods by the buyer; or

(b) acknowledgment to the buyer by any bailee of the goods except a carrier that the bailee holds the goods for the buyer; or

(c) such acknowledgment to the buyer by a carrier by reshipment or as warehouseman; or

(d) negotiation to the buyer of any negotiable document of title covering the goods.

(3) (a) To stop delivery the seller must so notify as to enable the bailee by reasonable diligence to prevent delivery of the goods.

(b) After such notification the bailee must hold and deliver the goods according to the directions of the seller but the seller is liable to the bailee for any ensuing charges or damages.

(c) If a negotiable document of title has been issued for goods the bailee is not obliged to obey a notification to stop until surrender of the document.

(d) A carrier who has issued a non-negotiable bill of lading is not obliged to obey a notification to stop received from a person other than the consignor.

§ 2–706. Seller's Resale Including Contract for Resale.

(1) Under the conditions stated in Section 2–703 on seller's remedies, the seller may resell the goods concerned or the undelivered balance thereof. Where the resale is made in good faith and in a commercially reasonable manner the seller may recover the difference between the resale price and the contract price together with any incidental damages allowed under the provisions of this Article (Section 2–710), but less expenses saved in consequence of the buyer's breach.

(2) Except as otherwise provided in subsection (3) or unless otherwise agreed resale may be at public or private sale including sale by way of one or more contracts to sell or of identification to an existing contract of the seller. Sale may be as a unit or in parcels and at any time and place and on any terms but every aspect of the sale including the method, manner, time, place and terms must be commercially reasonable. The resale must be reasonably identified as referring to the broken contract, but it is not necessary that the goods be in existence or that any or all of them have been identified to the contract before the breach.

(3) Where the resale is at private sale the seller must give the buyer reasonable notification of his intention to resell.

(4) Where the resale is at public sale

(a) only identified goods can be sold except where there is a recognized market for a public sale of futures in goods of the kind; and

(b) it must be made at a usual place or market for public sale if one is reasonably available and except in the case of goods which are perishable or threaten to decline in value speedily the seller must give the buyer reasonable notice of the time and place of the resale; and

(c) if the goods are not to be within the view of those attending the sale the notification of sale must state the place where the goods are located and provide for their reasonable inspection by prospective bidders; and

(d) the seller may buy.

(5) A purchaser who buys in good faith at a resale takes the goods free of any rights of the original buyer even though the seller fails to comply with one or more of the requirements of this section.

(6) The seller is not accountable to the buyer for any profit made on any resale. A person in the position of a seller (Section 2–707)

or a buyer who has rightfully rejected or justifiably revoked acceptance must account for any excess over the amount of his security interest, as hereinafter defined (subsection (3) of Section 2–711).

§ 2–707. "Person in the Position of a Seller".

(1) A "person in the position of a seller" includes as against a principal an agent who has paid or become responsible for the price of goods on behalf of his principal or anyone who otherwise holds a security interest or other right in goods similar to that of a seller.

(2) A person in the position of a seller may as provided in this Article withhold or stop delivery (Section 2–705) and resell (Section 2–706) and recover incidental damages (Section 2–710).

§ 2–708. Seller's Damages for Non-Acceptance or Repudiation.

(1) Subject to subsection (2) and to the provisions of this Article with respect to proof of market price (Section 2–723), the measure of damages for non-acceptance or repudiation by the buyer is the difference between the market price at the time and place for tender and the unpaid contract price together with any incidental damages provided in this Article (Section 2–710), but less expenses saved in consequence of the buyer's breach.

(2) If the measure of damages provided in subsection (1) is inadequate to put the seller in as good a position as performance would have done then the measure of damages is the profit (including reasonable overhead) which the seller would have made from full performance by the buyer, together with any incidental damages provided in this Article (Section 2–710), due allowance for costs reasonably incurred and due credit for payments or proceeds of resale.

§ 2–709. Action for the Price.

(1) When the buyer fails to pay the price as it becomes due the seller may recover, together with any incidental damages under the next section, the price

(a) of goods accepted or of conforming goods lost or damaged within a commercially reasonable time after risk of their loss has passed to the buyer; and

(b) of goods identified to the contract if the seller is unable after reasonable effort to resell them at a reasonable price or the circumstances reasonably indicate that such effort will be unavailing.

(2) Where the seller sues for the price he must hold for the buyer any goods which have been identified to the contract and are still in his control except that if resale becomes possible he may resell them at any time prior to the collection of the judgment. The net proceeds of any such resale must be credited to the buyer and payment of the judgment entitles him to any goods not resold.

(3) After the buyer has wrongfully rejected or revoked acceptance of the goods or has failed to make a payment due or has repudiated (Section 2–610), a seller who is held not entitled to the price under this section shall nevertheless be awarded damages for non-acceptance under the preceding section.

§ 2–710. Seller's Incidental Damages.

Incidental damages to an aggrieved seller include any commercially reasonable charges, expenses or commissions incurred in stopping delivery, in the transportation, care and custody of goods after the buyer's breach, in connection with return or resale of the goods or otherwise resulting from the breach.

§ 2–711. Buyer's Remedies in General; Buyer's Security Interest in Rejected Goods.

(1) Where the seller fails to make delivery or repudiates or the buyer rightfully rejects or justifiably revokes acceptance then with respect to any goods involved, and with respect to the whole if the breach goes to the whole contract (Section 2–612), the buyer may cancel and whether or not he has done so may in addition to recovering so much of the price as has been paid

(a) "cover" and have damages under the next section as to all the goods affected whether or not they have been identified to the contract; or

(b) recover damages for non-delivery as provided in this Article (Section 2–713).

(2) Where the seller fails to deliver or repudiates the buyer may also

(a) if the goods have been identified recover them as provided in this Article (Section 2–502); or

(b) in a proper case obtain specific performance or replevy the goods as provided in this Article (Section 2–716).

(3) On rightful rejection or justifiable revocation of acceptance a buyer has a security interest in goods in his possession or control for any payments made on their price and any expenses reasonably incurred in their inspection, receipt, transportation, care and custody and may hold such goods and resell them in like manner as an aggrieved seller (Section 2–706).

§ 2–712. "Cover"; Buyer's Procurement of Substitute Goods.

(1) After a breach within the preceding section the buyer may "cover" by making in good faith and without unreasonable delay any reasonable purchase of or contract to purchase goods in substitution for those due from the seller.

(2) The buyer may recover from the seller as damages the difference between the cost of cover and the contract price together with any incidental or consequential damages as hereinafter defined (Section 2–715), but less expenses saved in consequence of the seller's breach.

(3) Failure of the buyer to effect cover within this section does not bar him from any other remedy.

§ 2–713. Buyer's Damages for Non-Delivery or Repudiation.

(1) Subject to the provisions of this Article with respect to proof of market price (Section 2–723), the measure of damages for non-delivery or repudiation by the seller is the difference between the market price at the time when the buyer learned of the breach and the contract price together with any incidental and consequential damages provided in this Article (Section 2–715), but less expenses saved in consequence of the seller's breach.

(2) Market price is to be determined as of the place for tender or, in cases of rejection after arrival or revocation of acceptance, as of the place of arrival.

§ 2–714.   Buyer's Damages for Breach in Regard to Accepted Goods.

(1) Where the buyer has accepted goods and given notification (subsection (3) of Section 2–607) he may recover as damages for any non-conformity of tender the loss resulting in the ordinary course of events from the seller's breach as determined in any manner which is reasonable.

(2) The measure of damages for breach of warranty is the difference at the time and place of acceptance between the value of the goods accepted and the value they would have had if they had been as warranted, unless special circumstances show proximate damages of a different amount.

(3) In a proper case any incidental and consequential damages under the next section may also be recovered.

§ 2–715.   Buyer's Incidental and Consequential Damages.

(1) Incidental damages resulting from the seller's breach include expenses reasonably incurred in inspection, receipt, transportation and care and custody of goods rightfully rejected, any commercially reasonable charges, expenses or commissions in connection with effecting cover and any other reasonable expense incident to the delay or other breach.

(2) Consequential damages resulting from the seller's breach include

(a) any loss resulting from general or particular requirements and needs of which the seller at the time of contracting had reason to know and which could not reasonably be prevented by cover or otherwise; and

(b) injury to person or property proximately resulting from any breach of warranty.

§ 2–716.   Buyer's Right to Specific Performance or Replevin.

(1) Specific performance may be decreed where the goods are unique or in other proper circumstances.

(2) The decree for specific performance may include such terms and conditions as to payment of the price, damages, or other relief as the court may deem just.

(3) The buyer has a right of replevin for goods identified to the contract if after reasonable effort he is unable to effect cover for such goods or the circumstances reasonably indicate that such effort will be unavailing or if the goods have been shipped under reservation and satisfaction of the security interest in them has been made or tendered. In the case of goods bought for personal, family, or household purposes, the buyer's right of replevin vests upon acquisition of a special property, even if the seller had not then repudiated or failed to deliver.
As amended in 1999.

§ 2–717.   Deduction of Damages From the Price.

The buyer on notifying the seller of his intention to do so may deduct all or any part of the damages resulting from any breach of the contract from any part of the price still due under the same contract.

§ 2–718.   Liquidation or Limitation of Damages; Deposits.

(1) Damages for breach by either party may be liquidated in the agreement but only at an amount which is reasonable in the light of the anticipated or actual harm caused by the breach, the difficulties of proof of loss, and the inconvenience or nonfeasibility of otherwise obtaining an adequate remedy. A term fixing unreasonably large liquidated damages is void as a penalty.

(2) Where the seller justifiably withholds delivery of goods because of the buyer's breach, the buyer is entitled to restitution of any amount by which the sum of his payments exceeds

(a) the amount to which the seller is entitled by virtue of terms liquidating the seller's damages in accordance with subsection (1), or

(b) in the absence of such terms, twenty per cent of the value of the total performance for which the buyer is obligated under the contract or $500, whichever is smaller.

(3) The buyer's right to restitution under subsection (2) is subject to offset to the extent that the seller establishes

(a) a right to recover damages under the provisions of this Article other than subsection (1), and

(b) the amount or value of any benefits received by the buyer directly or indirectly by reason of the contract.

(4) Where a seller has received payment in goods their reasonable value or the proceeds of their resale shall be treated as payments for the purposes of subsection (2); but if the seller has notice of the buyer's breach before reselling goods received in part performance, his resale is subject to the conditions laid down in this Article on resale by an aggrieved seller (Section 2–706).

§ 2–719.   Contractual Modification or Limitation of Remedy.

(1) Subject to the provisions of subsections (2) and (3) of this section and of the preceding section on liquidation and limitation of damages,

(a) the agreement may provide for remedies in addition to or in substitution for those provided in this Article and may limit or alter the measure of damages recoverable under this Article, as by limiting the buyer's remedies to return of the goods and repayment of the price or to repair and replacement of nonconforming goods or parts; and

(b) resort to a remedy as provided is optional unless the remedy is expressly agreed to be exclusive, in which case it is the sole remedy.

(2) Where circumstances cause an exclusive or limited remedy to fail of its essential purpose, remedy may be had as provided in this Act.

(3) Consequential damages may be limited or excluded unless the limitation or exclusion is unconscionable. Limitation of consequential damages for injury to the person in the case of consumer goods is prima facie unconscionable but limitation of damages where the loss is commercial is not.

§ 2–720.   Effect of "Cancellation" or "Rescission" on Claims for Antecedent Breach.

Unless the contrary intention clearly appears, expressions of "cancellation" or "rescission" of the contract or the like shall not be construed as a renunciation or discharge of any claim in damages for an antecedent breach.

§ 2-721.   Remedies for Fraud.

Remedies for material misrepresentation or fraud include all remedies available under this Article for non-fraudulent breach. Neither rescission or a claim for rescission of the contract for sale nor rejection or return of the goods shall bar or be deemed inconsistent with a claim for damages or other remedy.

§ 2-722.   Who Can Sue Third Parties for Injury to Goods.

Where a third party so deals with goods which have been identified to a contract for sale as to cause actionable injury to a party to that contract

(a) a right of action against the third party is in either party to the contract for sale who has title to or a security interest or a special property or an insurable interest in the goods; and if the goods have been destroyed or converted a right of action is also in the party who either bore the risk of loss under the contract for sale or has since the injury assumed that risk as against the other;

(b) if at the time of the injury the party plaintiff did not bear the risk of loss as against the other party to the contract for sale and there is no arrangement between them for disposition of the recovery, his suit or settlement is, subject to his own interest, as a fiduciary for the other party to the contract;

(c) either party may with the consent of the other sue for the benefit of whom it may concern.

§ 2-723.   Proof of Market Price: Time and Place.

(1) If an action based on anticipatory repudiation comes to trial before the time for performance with respect to some or all of the goods, any damages based on market price (Section 2-708 or Section 2-713) shall be determined according to the price of such goods prevailing at the time when the aggrieved party learned of the repudiation.

(2) If evidence of a price prevailing at the times or places described in this Article is not readily available the price prevailing within any reasonable time before or after the time described or at any other place which in commercial judgment or under usage of trade would serve as a reasonable substitute for the one described may be used, making any proper allowance for the cost of transporting the goods to or from such other place.

(3) Evidence of a relevant price prevailing at a time or place other than the one described in this Article offered by one party is not admissible unless and until he has given the other party such notice as the court finds sufficient to prevent unfair surprise.

§ 2-724.   Admissibility of Market Quotations.

Whenever the prevailing price or value of any goods regularly bought and sold in any established commodity market is in issue, reports in official publications or trade journals or in newspapers or periodicals of general circulation published as the reports of such market shall be admissible in evidence. The circumstances of the preparation of such a report may be shown to affect its weight but not its admissibility.

§ 2-725.   Statute of Limitations in Contracts for Sale.

(1) An action for breach of any contract for sale must be commenced within four years after the cause of action has accrued. By the original agreement the parties may reduce the period of limitation to not less than one year but may not extend it.

(2) A cause of action accrues when the breach occurs, regardless of the aggrieved party's lack of knowledge of the breach. A breach of warranty occurs when tender of delivery is made, except that where a warranty explicitly extends to future performance of the goods and discovery of the breach must await the time of such performance the cause of action accrues when the breach is or should have been discovered.

(3) Where an action commenced within the time limited by subsection (1) is so terminated as to leave available a remedy by another action for the same breach such other action may be commenced after the expiration of the time limited and within six months after the termination of the first action unless the termination resulted from voluntary discontinuance or from dismissal for failure or neglect to prosecute.

(4) This section does not alter the law on tolling of the statute of limitations nor does it apply to causes of action which have accrued before this Act becomes effective.

Article 2A
LEASES

Part 1   General Provisions

§ 2A-101.   Short Title.

This Article shall be known and may be cited as the Uniform Commercial Code—Leases.

§ 2A-102.   Scope.

This Article applies to any transaction, regardless of form, that creates a lease.

§ 2A-103.   Definitions and Index of Definitions.

(1) In this Article unless the context otherwise requires:

(a) "Buyer in ordinary course of business" means a person who in good faith and without knowledge that the sale to him [or her] is in violation of the ownership rights or security interest or leasehold interest of a third party in the goods buys in ordinary course from a person in the business of selling goods of that kind but does not include a pawnbroker. "Buying" may be for cash or by exchange of other property or on secured or unsecured credit and includes receiving goods or documents of title under a pre-existing contract for sale but does not include a transfer in bulk or as security for or in total or partial satisfaction of a money debt.

(b) "Cancellation" occurs when either party puts an end to the lease contract for default by the other party.

(c) "Commercial unit" means such a unit of goods as by commercial usage is a single whole for purposes of lease and division of which materially impairs its character or value on the market or in use. A commercial unit may be a single article, as a machine, or a set of articles, as a suite of furniture or a line of machinery, or a quantity, as a gross or carload, or any other unit treated in use or in the relevant market as a single whole.

Answers to *Issue Spotters*

Chapter 1

1A: No. The U.S. Constitution is the supreme law of the land and applies to all jurisdictions. A law in violation of the Constitution (in this question, the First Amendment to the Constitution) will be declared unconstitutional.

2A: Yes. Administrative rulemaking starts with the publication of a notice of the rulemaking in the *Federal Register*. Among other details, this notice states where and when the proceedings, such as a public hearing, will be held. Proponents and opponents can offer their comments and concerns regarding the pending rule. After reviewing all the comments from the proceedings, the agency's decision makers consider what was presented and draft the final rule.

Chapter 2

1A: No. Even if commercial speech is not related to illegal activities or misleading, it may be restricted if a state has a substantial government interest that cannot be achieved by less restrictive means. In this case, the interest in energy conservation is substantial, but it could be achieved by less restrictive means. That would be the utilities' defense against the enforcement of this state law.

2A: Yes. The tax would limit the liberty of some persons, such as out-of-state businesses, so it is subject to a review under the equal protection clause. Protecting local businesses from out-of-state competition is not a legitimate government objective. Thus, such a tax would violate the equal protection clause.

Chapter 3

1A: Yes. Submission of the dispute to mediation or nonbinding arbitration is mandatory, but compliance with the decision of the mediator or arbitrator is voluntary.

2A: Tom could file a motion for a directed verdict. This motion asks the judge to direct a verdict for Tom on the ground that Sue presented no evidence that would justify granting her relief. The judge grants the motion if there is insufficient evidence to raise an issue of fact.

Chapter 4

1A: Probably. To recover on the basis of negligence, the injured party as a plaintiff must show that the truck's owner owed the plaintiff a duty of care, that the owner breached that duty, that the plaintiff was injured, and that the breach caused the injury. In

this problem, the owner's actions breached the duty of reasonable care. The billboard falling on the plaintiff was the direct cause of the injury, not the plaintiff's own negligence. Thus, liability turns on whether the plaintiff can connect the breach of duty to the injury. This involves the test of proximate cause—the question of foreseeability. The consequences to the injured party must have been a foreseeable result of the owner's carelessness.

2A: The company might defend against this electrician's claim by asserting that the electrician should have known of the risk and, therefore, the company had no duty to warn. According to the problem, the danger is common knowledge in the electrician's field and should have been apparent to this electrician, given his years of training and experience. In other words, the company most likely had no need to warn the electrician of the risk.

The firm could also raise comparative negligence. Both parties' negligence, if any, could be weighed and the liability distributed proportionately. The defendant could furthermore assert assumption of risk, claiming that the electrician voluntarily entered into a dangerous situation, knowing the risk involved.

Chapter 5

1A: This is patent infringement. A software maker in this situation might best protect its product, save litigation costs, and profit from its patent by the use of a license. In the context of this problem, a license would grant permission to sell a patented item. (A license can be limited to certain purposes and to the licensee only.)

2A: Yes. This may be an instance of trademark dilution. Dilution occurs when a trademark is used, without permission, in a way that diminishes the distinctive quality of the mark. Dilution does not require proof that consumers are likely to be confused by the use of the unauthorized mark. The products involved do not have to be similar. Dilution does require, however, that a mark be famous when the dilution occurs.

Chapter 6

1A: Yes. With respect to the gas station, Daisy has obtained goods by false pretenses. She might also be charged with the crimes of larceny and forgery, and most states have special statutes covering illegal use of credit cards.

2A: Yes. The Counterfeit Access Device and Computer Fraud and Abuse Act of 1984 provides that a person who accesses a computer online, without permission, to obtain classified data—such as consumer credit files in a credit agency's database—is subject to criminal prosecution. The crime has two elements: accessing the computer without permission and taking data. It is a felony if done for private financial gain. Penalties include fines and imprisonment for up to twenty years. The victim of the theft can also bring a civil suit against the criminal to obtain damages and other relief.

Chapter 7

1A: Maybe. On the one hand, it is not the company's "fault" when a product is misused. Also, keeping the product on the market is not a violation of the law, and stopping sales would hurt profits. On the other hand, suspending sales could reduce suffering and could prevent negative publicity that might occur if sales continued.

2A: When a corporation decides to respond to what it sees as a moral obligation to correct for past discrimination by adjusting pay differences among its employees, an ethical conflict is raised between the firm and its employees and between the firm and its shareholders. This dilemma arises directly out of the effect such a decision has on the firm's profits. If satisfying this obligation increases profitability, then the dilemma is easily resolved in favor of "doing the right thing."

Chapter 8

1A: Under the principle of comity, a U.S court would defer and give effect to foreign laws and judicial decrees that are consistent with U.S. law and public policy.

2A: The practice described in this problem is known as dumping, which is regarded as an unfair international trade practice. Dumping is the sale of imported goods at "less than fair value." Based on the price of those goods in the exporting country, an extra tariff—known as an antidumping duty—can be imposed on the imports.

Chapter 9

1A: Under the objective theory of contracts, if a reasonable person would have thought that Joli had accepted Keerin's offer when she signed and returned the letter, then a contract was made, and Joli is obligated to buy the book. This depends, in part, on what was said in the letter and what was said in response. For instance, did the letter contain a valid offer, and did the response constitute a valid acceptance? Under any circumstances, the issue is not whether either party subjectively believed that they did, or did not, have a contract.

2A: No. This contract, although not fully executed, is for an illegal purpose and therefore is void. A void contract gives rise to no legal obligation on the part of any party. A contract that is void is no contract. There is nothing to enforce.

Chapter 10

1A: No. Revocation of an offer may be implied by conduct inconsistent with the offer. When Fidelity Corporation rehired Monica, and Ron learned of the hiring, the offer was revoked. His acceptance was too late.

2A: First, it might be noted that the Uniform Electronic Transactions Act (UETA) does not apply unless the parties to a contract agree to use e-commerce in their transaction. In this deal, of course, the parties used e-commerce. The UETA removes barriers to e-commerce by giving the same legal effect to e-records and e-signatures as to paper documents and signatures. The UETA itself does not include rules for e-commerce transactions, however.

Chapter 11

1A: Yes. The original contract was executory—that is, not yet performed by both parties. The parties rescinded the original contract and agreed to a new contract.

2A: No. Generally, an exculpatory clause (a clause attempting to absolve a party of negligence or other wrongs) is not enforced if the party seeking its enforcement is involved in a business that is important to the public as a matter of practical necessity, such as an airline. Because of the essential nature of such services, the party would have an advantage in bargaining strength and could insist that anyone contracting for its services agree not to hold it liable.

Chapter 12

1A: Yes. Elle may be liable on the ground of negligent misrepresentation. A misrepresentation is negligent if a person fails to exercise reasonable care in disclosing material facts or does not use the skill and competence required by his or her business or profession.

2A: No. The memo would be a sufficient writing to enforce the contract against My-T if that party chose not to complete the deal, however. Letterhead stationery can constitute a signature. If the memo names the parties, the subject matter, the consideration, and the quantity involved in the transaction, it may be sufficient to be enforced against the party whose letterhead appears on it.

Chapter 13

1A: Yes. Generally, if a contract clearly states that a right is not assignable, no assignment will be effective, but there are exceptions. Assignment of the right to receive monetary payment cannot be prohibited.

2A: Contracts that are executory on both sides—contracts on which neither party has performed—can be rescinded solely by agreement. Contracts that are executed on one side—contracts on which one party has performed—can be rescinded only if the party who has performed receives consideration for the promise to call off the deal.

Chapter 14

1A: A nonbreaching party is entitled to her or his benefit of the bargain under the contract. Here, the innocent party is entitled to be put in the position she would have been in if the contract had been fully performed. The measure of the benefit is the cost to complete the work ($500). These are compensatory damages.

2A: No. To recover damages that flow from the consequences of a breach but that are caused by circumstances beyond the contract (consequential damages), the breaching party must know, or have reason to know, that special circumstances will cause the nonbreaching party to suffer the additional loss. That was not the circumstance in this problem.

Chapter 15

1A: A shipment of nonconforming goods constitutes an acceptance and a breach, unless the seller seasonably notifies the buyer that the nonconforming shipment does not constitute an acceptance and is offered only as an accommodation. Thus, since there was no notification in this problem, the shipment was both an acceptance and a breach.

2A: Yes. In a transaction between merchants, the requirement of a writing is satisfied if one of them sends to the other a signed written confirmation that indicates the terms of the agreement, and the merchant receiving it has reason to know of its contents. If the merchant who receives the confirmation does not object in writing within ten days after receipt, the writing will be enforceable against him or her even though he or she has not signed anything.

Chapter 16

1A: Yes. A seller is obligated to deliver goods in conformity with a contract in every detail. This is the perfect tender rule. The exception of the seller's right to cure does not apply here because the seller delivered too little too late to take advantage of this exception.

2A: Yes. When anticipatory repudiation occurs, a buyer (or lessee) can resort to any remedy for breach even if the buyer tells the seller (the repudiating party in this problem) that the buyer will wait for the seller's performance.

Chapter 17

1A: Yes. The manufacturer is liable for the injuries to the user of the product. A manufacturer is liable for its failure to exercise due care to any person who sustains an injury proximately caused by a negligently made (defective) product. In this problem, the failure to inspect is a failure to use due care. Of course, the maker of the component part may also be liable.

2A: Yes. Under the doctrine of strict liability, persons may be liable for the results of their acts regardless of their intentions or their exercise of reasonable care (that is, regardless of fault).

Chapter 18

1A: A statement that "I.O.U." money (or anything else) or an instruction to a bank stating, "I wish you would pay," would render any instrument nonnegotiable. To be negotiable, an instrument must contain an express promise to pay. An I.O.U. is only an acknowledgment of indebtedness. An order stating, "I wish you would pay," is not sufficiently precise.

2A: No. When a drawer's employee provides the drawer with the name of a fictitious payee (a payee whom the drawer does not actually intend to have any interest in an instrument), a forgery of the payee's name is effective to pass good title to subsequent transferees.

Chapter 19

1A: Yes, to both questions. In a civil suit, a drawer (Lyn) is liable to a payee (Nan) or to a holder of a check that is not honored. If intent to defraud can be proved, the drawer (Lyn) can also be subject to criminal prosecution for writing a bad check.

2A: The drawer is entitled to $6,300—the amount to which the check was altered ($7,000) less the amount that the drawer ordered the bank to pay ($700). The bank may recover this amount from the party who presented the altered check for payment.

Chapter 20

1A: A creditor can put other creditors on notice by perfecting her or his interest: by filing a financing statement in the appropriate public office, or by taking possession of the collateral until the debtor repays the loan.

2A: When collateral consists of consumer goods, and the debtor has paid less than 60 percent of the debt or the purchase price, the creditor has the option of disposing of the collateral in a commercially reasonable manner. This generally requires notice to the debtor of the place, time, and manner of sale. A debtor can waive the right to notice, but only after default. Before the disposal, a debtor can redeem the collateral by tendering performance of all of the obligations secured by the collateral and by paying the creditor's reasonable expenses in retaking and maintaining the collateral.

Chapter 21

1A: Each of the parties can place a mechanic's lien on the debtor's property. If the debtor does not pay what is owed, the property can be sold to satisfy the debt. The only requirements are that the lien be filed within a specific time from the time of the work, depending on the state statute, and that notice of the foreclosure and sale be given to the debtor in advance.

2A: Yes. A debtor's payment to a creditor made for a preexisting debt, within ninety days (one year in the case of an insider or fraud) of a bankruptcy filing, can be recovered if it gives the creditor more than he or she would have received in the bankruptcy proceedings. A trustee can recover this preference using her or his specific avoidance powers.

Chapter 22

1A: The major terms that must be disclosed under the Truth-in-Lending Act include the loan principal, the interest rate at which the loan is made, the annual percentage rate or APR (the actual cost of the loan on a yearly basis), and all fees and costs associated with the loan. These disclosures must be made on standardized forms and based on uniform formulas of calculation. Certain types of loans have special disclosure requirements.

2A: Foreclosure is the process that allows a lender to repossess and auction off property that is securing a loan. The two most common types of foreclosure are judicial foreclosure and power of sale foreclosure. In the former—available in all states—a court supervises the process. This is the more common method of foreclosure. In the latter—available in only a few states—a lender forecloses on and sells the property without court supervision.

If the sale proceeds cover the mortgage debt and foreclosure costs, the debtor receives any surplus. If the proceeds do not cover the debt and costs, the mortgagee can seek to recover the difference through a deficiency judgment, which is obtained in a separate action. A deficiency judgment entitles the creditor to recover this difference from a sale of the debtor's other nonexempt property. Before a foreclosure sale, a mortgagor can redeem the property by paying the debt, plus any interest and costs. This is called the equitable right of redemption.

Chapter 23

1A: When a person enters into a contract on another's behalf without the authority to do so, the other may be liable on the contract if he or she approves or affirms that contract. In other words, the employer-principal would be liable for the note in this problem on ratifying it. Whether the employer-principal ratifies the note or not, the unauthorized agent is most likely also liable for it.

2A: Yes. A principal has a duty to indemnify (reimburse) an agent for liabilities incurred because of authorized and lawful acts and transactions and for losses suffered because of the principal's failure to perform his or her duties.

Chapter 24

1A: Workers' compensation laws establish a procedure for compensating workers who are injured on the job. Instead of suing to collect benefits, an injured worker notifies the employer of the injury and files a claim with the appropriate state agency. The right to recover is normally determined without regard to negligence or fault, but intentionally inflicted injuries are not covered. Unlike the potential for recovery in a lawsuit based on negligence or fault, recovery under a workers' compensation statute is limited to the specific amount designated in the statute for the employee's injury.

2A: No. A closed shop (a company that requires union membership as a condition of employment) is illegal. A union shop (a company that does not require union membership as a condition of employment but requires workers to join the union after a certain time on the job) is illegal in a state with a right-to-work law, which makes it illegal to require union membership for continued employment.

Chapter 25

1A: Yes. One type of sexual harassment occurs when a request for sexual favors is a condition of employment, and the person making the request is a supervisor or acts with the authority of the employer. A tangible employment action, such as continued employment, may also lead to the employer's liability for the supervisor's conduct. That the injured employee is a male and the supervisor a female, instead of the other way around, would not affect the outcome. Same-gender harassment is also actionable.

2A: Yes, Koko could succeed in a discrimination suit if she can show that she was not hired solely because of her disability. The other elements for a discrimination suit based on a disability are that the plaintiff (1) has a disability and (2) is otherwise qualified for the job. Both of these elements appear to be satisfied in this scenario.

Chapter 26

1A: When a business is relatively small and is not diversified, employs relatively few people, has modest profits, and is not likely to expand significantly or require extensive financing in the immediate future, the most appropriate form for doing business may be a sole proprietorship.

2A: Yes. Failing to meet a specified sales quota can constitute a breach of a franchise agreement. If the franchisor is acting in good faith, "cause" may also include the death or disability of the franchisee, the insolvency of the franchisee, and a breach of another term of the franchise agreement.

Chapter 27

1A: No. A widow (or widower) has no right to take a dead partner's place. A partner's death causes dissociation after which the partnership must purchase the dissociated partner's partnership interest. Therefore, the surviving partners must pay the decedent's estate (for his widow) the value of the deceased partner's interest in the partnership.

2A: No. Under the partners' fiduciary duty, a partner must account to the partnership for any personal profits or benefits derived without the consent of all the partners in connection with the use of any partnership property. Here, the leasing partner may not keep the funds.

Chapter 28

1A: The members of a limited liability company (LLC) may designate a group to run their firm. In that situation, the firm would be a manager-managed LLC. The group may include only members, only nonmembers, or members and nonmembers. If, instead, all members participate in management, the firm would be a member-managed LLC. In fact, unless the members agree otherwise, all members are considered to participate in the management of the firm.

2A: Although there are differences, all of these forms of business organizations resemble corporations. A joint stock company, for example, features ownership by shares of stock, it is managed by directors and officers, and it has perpetual existence. A business trust, like a corporation, distributes profits to persons who are not personally responsible for the debts of the organization, and management of the business is in the hands of trustees, just as the management of a corporation is in the hands of directors and officers. An incorporated cooperative, which is subject to state laws covering nonprofit corporations, distributes profits to its owners.

Chapter 29

1A: Yes. Small businesses that meet certain requirements can qualify as S corporations, created specifically to permit small businesses to avoid double taxation. The six requirements of an S corporation are (1) the firm must be a domestic corporation; (2) the firm must not be a member of an affiliated group of corporations; (3) the firm must have fewer than a certain number of shareholders; (4) the shareholders must be individuals, estates, or qualified trusts (or corporations in some cases); (5) there can be only one class of stock; and (6) no shareholder can be a nonresident alien.

2A: The first combination is a merger. One of the previously existing corporations absorbed the other. The second combination is a consolidation. Neither of the combining corporations continue after the combination, and a new firm continues in their place.

Chapter 30

1A: Yes. A shareholder can bring a derivative suit on behalf of a corporation, if some wrong is done to the corporation. Normally, any damages recovered go into the corporate treasury.

2A: Yes. A single shareholder—or a few shareholders acting together—who owns enough stock to exercise *de facto* control over a corporation owes the corporation and the minority shareholders a fiduciary duty when transferring those shares.

Chapter 31

1A: The average investor is not concerned with minor inaccuracies but with facts that if disclosed would tend to deter him or her from buying the securities. These would include material facts that have an important bearing on the condition of the issuer and its business—such as liabilities, loans to officers and directors, customer delinquencies, and pending lawsuits.

2A: No. The Securities Exchange Act of 1934 extends liability to officers and directors in their personal transactions for taking advantage of inside information when they know it is unavailable to the persons with whom they are dealing.

Chapter 32

1A: Size alone does not determine whether a firm is a monopoly—size in relation to the market is what matters. A small store in a small, isolated town is a monopolist if it is the only store serving that market. Monopoly involves the power to affect prices and output. If a firm has sufficient market power to control prices and exclude competition, that firm has monopoly power. Monopoly power in itself is not a violation of Section 2 of the Sherman Act. The offense also requires an intent to acquire or maintain that power through anticompetitive means.

2A: This agreement is a tying arrangement. The legality of a tying arrangement depends on the purpose of the agreement, the agreement's likely effect on competition in the relevant markets (the market for the tying product and the market for the tied product), and other factors. Tying arrangements for commodities are subject to Section 3 of the Clayton Act. Tying arrangements for services can be agreements in restraint of trade in violation of Section 1 of the Sherman Act.

Chapter 33

1A: Under the Truth-in-Lending Act, a buyer who wishes to withhold payment for a faulty product purchased with a credit card must follow specific procedures to settle the dispute. The credit-card issuer then must intervene and attempt to settle the dispute.

2A: Yes. On the ground that the hardships to be imposed on the polluter and on the community are greater than the hardships suffered by the residents, the court might deny an injunction—if the plant is the core of the local economy, for instance, the residents may only be awarded damages.

Chapter 34

1A: Yes. In these circumstances, when the accountant knows that the bank will use the statement, the bank is a foreseeable user. A foreseeable user is a third party within the class of parties to whom an accountant may be liable for negligence.

2A: No. In the circumstances described, the accountant will not be held liable to a purchaser of the securities. Although an accountant may be liable under securities laws for including untrue statements or omitting material facts from financial statements, due diligence is a defense to liability. Due diligence requires an accountant to conduct a reasonable investigation and have reason to believe that the financial statements were true at the time. The facts say that the misstatement of material fact in Omega's financial statement was not attributable to any fraud or negligence on Nora's part. Therefore, Nora can show that she used due diligence and will not be held liable to Pat.

Chapter 35

1A: Yes. A bailee's right of possession, even though temporary, permits the bailee to recover damages from any third persons for damage or loss to the property.

2A: Rosa de la Mar Corporation, the shipper, suffers the loss. A common carrier is liable for damage caused by the willful acts of third persons or by an accident. Other losses must be borne by the shipper (or the recipient, depending on the terms of their contract). In this situation, this shipment was lost due to an act of God.

Chapter 36

1A: This is a breach of the warranty deed's covenant of quiet enjoyment. Consuela can sue Bernie and recover the purchase price of the house, plus any damages.

2A: Yes. An owner of a fee simple has the most rights possible—he or she can give the property away, sell it, transfer it by will, use it for almost any purpose, possess it to the exclusion of all the world, or, as in this case, transfer possession for any period of time. The party to whom possession is transferred can also transfer her or his interest (usually only with the owner's permission) for any lesser period of time.

Chapter 37

1A: No. To have testamentary capacity, a testator must be of legal age and sound mind *at the time the will is made*. Generally, the testator must (1) know the nature of the act, (2) comprehend and remember the "natural objects of his or her bounty," (3) know the nature and extent of her or his property, and (4) understand the distribution of assets called for by the will. In this situation, Sheila had testamentary capacity at the time she made the will. The fact that she was ruled mentally incompetent two years after making the will does not provide sufficient grounds to revoke it.

2A: The estate will pass according to the state's intestacy laws. Intestacy laws set out how property is distributed when a person dies without a will. Their purpose is to carry out the likely intent of the decedent. The laws determine which of the deceased's natural heirs (including, in this order, the surviving spouse, lineal descendants, parents, and collateral heirs) inherit his or her property.

APPENDIX F

Answers to Even-Numbered *For Review* Questions

Chapter 1

2. What is the common law tradition?

Because of our colonial heritage, much of American law is based on the English legal system. After the Norman Conquest of England in 1066, the king's courts sought to establish a uniform set of rules for the entire country. What evolved in these courts was the common law—a body of general legal principles that applied throughout the entire English realm. Courts developed the common law rules from the principles underlying judges' decisions in actual legal controversies.

4. What is the difference between remedies at law and remedies in equity?

An award of compensation in either money or property, including land, is a remedy at law. Remedies in equity include the following:

1. A decree for specific performance—that is, an order to perform what was promised.
2. An injunction, which is an order directing a party to do or refrain from doing a particular act.
3. A rescission, or cancellation, of a contract and a return of the parties to the positions that they held before the contract's formation.

As a rule, courts will grant an equitable remedy only when the remedy at law (monetary damages) is inadequate. Remedies in equity on the whole are more flexible than remedies at law.

Chapter 2

2. What constitutional clause gives the federal government the power to regulate commercial activities among the various states?

To prevent states from establishing laws and regulations that would interfere with trade and commerce among the states, the Constitution expressly delegated to the national government the power to regulate interstate commerce. The commerce clause—Article I, Section 8, of the U.S. Constitution—expressly permits Congress "to regulate Commerce with foreign Nations, and among the several States, and with the Indian Tribes."

4. What is the Bill of Rights? What freedoms does the First Amendment guarantee?

The Bill of Rights consists of the first ten amendments to the U.S. Constitution. Adopted in 1791, the Bill of Rights embodies protections for individuals against interference by the federal government. Some of the protections also apply to business entities. The First Amendment guarantees the freedoms of religion, speech,

and the press, and the rights to assemble peaceably and to petition the government.

Chapter 3

2. Before a court can hear a case, it must have jurisdiction. Over what must it have jurisdiction? How are the courts applying traditional jurisdictional concepts to cases involving Internet transactions?

To hear a case, a court must have jurisdiction over the person against whom the suit is brought or over the property involved in the suit. The court must also have jurisdiction over the subject matter. Generally, courts apply a "sliding-scale" standard to determine when it is proper to exercise jurisdiction over a defendant whose only connection with the jurisdiction is the Internet.

4. What is discovery, and how does electronic discovery differ from traditional discovery?

Discovery is the process of obtaining information and evidence about a case from the other party or third parties. Discovery entails gaining access to witnesses, documents, records, and other types of evidence. Electronic discovery differs in its subject—that is, e-media, such as e-mail or text messages, rather than traditional sources of information, such as paper documents.

Chapter 4

2. What are two basic categories of torts?

Generally, the purpose of tort law is to provide remedies for the invasion of legally recognized and protected interests, such as personal safety, freedom of movement, property, and some intangibles, including privacy and reputation. The two broad categories of torts are intentional and unintentional.

4. Identify the four elements of negligence.

The four elements of negligence are as follows:

1. A duty of care owed by the defendant to the plaintiff.
2. The defendant's breach of that duty.
3. The plaintiff's suffering a legally recognizable injury.
4. The in-fact and proximate cause of that injury by the defendant's breach.

Chapter 5

2. Why is the protection of trademarks important?

Article I, Section 8, of the U.S. Constitution authorizes Congress "to promote the Progress of Science and useful Arts, by securing for limited Times to Authors and Inventors the exclusive Right to their respective Writings and Discoveries." Laws protecting trademarks—and patents and copyrights as well—are designed to protect and reward inventive and artistic creativity.

4. What laws protect authors' rights in the works they create?

Copyright law protects the rights of the authors of certain literary or artistic productions. The Copyright Act of 1976, as amended, covers these rights.

Chapter 6

2. What are five broad categories of crimes? What is white-collar crime?

Traditionally, crimes have been grouped into the following categories: violent crime (crimes against persons), property crime, public order crime, white-collar crime, and organized crime.

White-collar crime is an illegal act or series of acts committed by an individual or business entity using some nonviolent means, usually in the course of a legitimate occupation.

4. What constitutional safeguards exist to protect persons accused of crimes?

Under the Fourth Amendment, before searching or seizing private property, law enforcement officers must obtain a search warrant, which requires probable cause.

Under the Fifth Amendment, no one can be deprived of "life, liberty, or property without due process of law." The Fifth Amendment also protects persons against double jeopardy and self-incrimination.

The Sixth Amendment guarantees the right to a speedy trial, the right to a jury trial, the right to a public trial, the right to confront witnesses, and the right to counsel. Individuals who are arrested must be informed of certain constitutional rights, including their Fifth Amendment right to remain silent and their Sixth Amendment right to counsel. All evidence obtained in violation of the Fourth, Fifth, and Sixth Amendments, as well as all evidence derived from the illegally obtained evidence, must be excluded from the trial.

The Eighth Amendment prohibits excessive bail and fines, and cruel and unusual punishment.

Chapter 7

2. How can business leaders encourage their companies to act ethically?

Ethical leadership is important to create and maintain an ethical workplace. Managers can set standards and then apply those standards to themselves and their firm's employees.

4. What are six guidelines that an employee can use to evaluate whether his or her actions are ethical?

Guidelines for evaluating whether behavior is ethical can be found (1) in the law, (2) business rules and procedures, (3) social values, (4) an individual's conscience, (5) an individual's promises and obligations to others, and (6) personal or societal heroes.

An action is most likely ethical if it is consistent with the law, or at least the "spirit" of the law, as well as company policies, and if it can survive the scrutiny of one's conscience and the regard of one's heroes without betraying commitments to others.

Chapter 8

2. What is the act of state doctrine? In what circumstances is this doctrine applied?

The act of state doctrine is a judicially created doctrine that provides that the judicial branch of one country will not examine the validity of public acts committed by a recognized foreign government within its own territory. This doctrine is often employed in cases involving expropriation or confiscation.

4. What are three clauses commonly included in international business contracts?

Choice-of-language, forum-selection, and choice-of-law clauses are commonly used in international business contracts.

Chapter 9

2. What are the four basic elements necessary to the formation of a valid contract?

The basic elements for the formation of a valid contract are an agreement, consideration, contractual capacity, and legality.

4. How does a void contract differ from a voidable contract? What is an unenforceable contract?

A void contract is not a valid contract—it is not a contract at all. A voidable contract is a valid contract, but one that can be avoided at the option of one or both of the parties.

An unenforceable contract is one that cannot be enforced because of certain legal defenses against it.

Chapter 10

2. In what circumstances will an offer be irrevocable?

An offeror may not effectively revoke an offer if the offeree has changed position in justifiable reliance on the offer. Also, an option contract takes away the offeror's power to revoke an offer for the period of time specified in the option (or, if unspecified, for a reasonable time).

4. How do shrink-wrap and click-on agreements differ from other contracts? How have traditional laws been applied to these agreements?

With a shrink-wrap agreement, the terms are expressed inside the box in which the goods are packaged. A click-on agreement arises when a buyer, completing a transaction on a computer, is required to indicate assent to the terms by clicking on a button that says, for example, "I agree."

Generally, courts have enforced the terms of these agreements the same as the terms of other contracts, applying the traditional common law of contracts. Article 2 of the Uniform Commercial Code provides that acceptance can be made by conduct. The *Restatement (Second) of Contracts* has a similar provision. Under these provisions, a binding contract can be created by conduct, including conduct accepting the terms in a shrink-wrap or click-on agreement.

Chapter 11

2. In what circumstances might a promise be enforced despite a lack of consideration?

Under the doctrine of promissory estoppel (or detrimental reliance), a promisor (the offeror) is estopped, or prevented, from revoking a promise even in the absence of consideration. There are three required elements:

1. A clear and definite promise.
2. The promisee's justifiable reliance on the promise.
3. Reliance of a substantial and definite character.

4. Under what circumstances will a covenant not to compete be enforced? When will such covenants not be enforced?

A covenant not to compete can be enforced:

1. If it is ancillary (secondary) to an agreement to sell an ongoing business, thus enabling the seller to sell, and the purchaser to buy, the goodwill and reputation of the business.
2. If it is contained in an employment contract and is reasonable in terms of time and geographic area.

A covenant not to compete will be unenforceable if it does not protect a legitimate business interest or is broader than necessary to protect a legitimate interest. This is because such a covenant would unreasonably restrain trade and be contrary to public policy.

Chapter 12

2. What is the difference between a mistake of value or quality and a mistake of fact?

A mistake as to the value of a deal is an ordinary risk of business for which a court normally will not provide relief. A mistake concerning a fact important to the subject matter of a contract, however, may provide a basis for relief.

4. What contracts must be in writing to be enforceable?

Contracts that are normally required to be in writing or evidenced by a written memorandum include:

- Contracts involving interests in land.
- Contracts that cannot by their terms be performed within one year from the day after the date of formation.
- Collateral contracts, such as promises to answer for the debt or duty of another.
- Promises made in consideration of marriage.
- Contracts for the sale of goods priced at $500 or more.

Chapter 13

2. In what situations is the delegation of duties prohibited?

Delegation of duties is prohibited in the following situations:

1. When the performance depends on the personal skill or talents of the obligor.
2. When special trust has been placed in the obligor.
3. When performance by a third party will vary materially from that expected by the obligee under the contract.
4. When the contract expressly prohibits delegation.

4. How are most contracts discharged?

The most common way to discharge, or terminate, a contract is by the performance of contractual duties.

Chapter 14

2. What is the difference between compensatory damages and consequential damages? What are nominal damages, and when do courts award nominal damages?

Compensatory damages compensate an injured party for injuries or damages. Foreseeable damages that result from a party's breach of contract are consequential damages. Consequential damages differ from compensatory damages in that they are caused by special circumstances beyond the contract.

Nominal damages are awarded to an innocent party when no actual damage has been suffered. Nominal damages might be awarded as a matter of principle to establish fault or wrongful behavior.

4. When do courts grant specific performance as a remedy?

Specific performance might be granted as a remedy when damages offer an inadequate remedy and the subject matter of the contract is unique.

Chapter 15

2. In a sales contract, if an offeree includes additional or different terms in an acceptance, will a contract result? If so, what happens to these terms?

Under the Uniform Commercial Code, a contract can be formed, even if the offeree's acceptance includes additional or different terms. If one of the parties is a nonmerchant, the contract does not include the additional terms. If both parties are merchants, the additional terms automatically become part of the contract unless one of the following occurs:

1. The original offer expressly limits acceptance to the terms of the offer.
2. The new or changed terms materially alter the contract.
3. The offeror objects to the new or changed terms within a reasonable period of time.

(If the additional terms expressly require the offeror's assent, the offeree's response is not an acceptance, but a counteroffer.) Under some circumstances, a court might strike the additional terms.

4. Risk of loss does not necessarily pass with title. If the parties to a contract do not expressly agree when risk passes and the goods are to be delivered without movement by the seller, when does risk pass?

If the seller holds the goods and is a merchant, the risk of loss passes to the buyer when the buyer takes physical possession of the goods. If the seller holds the goods and is not a merchant, the risk of loss passes to the buyer on tender of delivery. When a bailee is holding the goods, the risk of loss passes to the buyer when (1) the buyer receives a negotiable document of title for the goods, (2) the bailee acknowledges the buyer's right to possess the goods, or (3) the buyer receives a nonnegotiable document of title and has had a reasonable time to present the document to the bailee and demand the goods.

Chapter 16

2. What is the perfect tender rule? What are some important exceptions to this rule that apply to sales and lease contracts?

Under the perfect tender rule, the seller or lessor has an obligation to ship or tender conforming goods. If the goods or tender of delivery fails in any respect, the buyer or lessee has the right to accept the goods, reject the entire shipment, or accept part and reject part. Exceptions to the rule may be established by agreement.

When goods are rejected because they are nonconforming and the time for performance has not expired, the seller or lessor can notify the buyer or lessee promptly of the intention to cure and then do so within the contract time for performance. If the time for performance has expired, the seller or lessor can still cure within a reasonable time if, at the time of delivery, he or she had reasonable grounds to believe that the nonconforming tender would be acceptable. When an agreed-on manner of delivery becomes impracticable or unavailable through no fault of either party, a seller may choose a commercially reasonable substitute.

4. What remedies are available to a seller or lessor when the buyer or lessee breaches the contract? What remedies are available to a buyer or lessee if the seller or lessor breaches the contract?

Depending on the circumstances at the time of a buyer's or lessee's breach, a seller or lessor may have the right to cancel the contract, withhold delivery, resell or dispose of the goods subject to the contract, recover the purchase price (or lease payments), recover damages, stop delivery in transit, or reclaim the goods.

Similarly, on a seller's or lessor's breach, a buyer or lessee may have the right to cancel the contract, recover the goods, obtain specific performance, obtain cover, replevy the goods, recover damages, reject the goods, withhold delivery, resell or dispose of the goods, stop delivery, or revoke acceptance.

Chapter 17

2. What implied warranties arise under the UCC?

Implied warranties that arise under the UCC include the implied warranty of merchantability, the implied warranty of fitness for a particular purpose, and implied warranties that may arise from, or be excluded or modified by, course of dealing, course of performance, or usage of trade.

4. What are the elements of a cause of action in strict product liability?

Under Section 402A of the *Restatement (Second) of Torts*, the elements of an action for strict product liability are as follows:

1. The product must be in a defective condition when the defendant sells it.
2. The defendant must normally be engaged in the business of selling (or distributing) that product.
3. The product must be unreasonably dangerous to the user or consumer because of its defective condition (in most states).
4. The plaintiff must incur physical harm to self or property by use or consumption of the product.
5. The defective condition must be the proximate cause of the injury or damage.
6. The goods must not have been substantially changed from the time the product was sold to the time the injury was sustained.

Chapter 18

2. What are the requirements for attaining the status of a holder in due course (HDC)?

A holder of a negotiable instrument becomes an HDC if he or she takes the instrument (1) for value; (2) in good faith; and (3) without notice that the instrument is overdue, that it has been dishonored, that any person has a defense against it or a claim to it, or that it contains unauthorized signatures or alterations, or is so irregular or incomplete as to call into question its authenticity.

4. Certain defenses are valid against all holders, including HDCs. What are these defenses called? Name four defenses that fall within this category.

Universal, or real, defenses are good against the claims of all holders, including HDCs. These defenses include forgery of a maker's or drawer's signature, fraud in the execution of an instrument, material alteration of an instrument, discharge in bankruptcy, minority to the extent recognized by state law, illegality to the extent that state law makes a transaction void, mental incapacity if a person has been so adjudged in a state proceeding, and extreme duress.

Chapter 19

2. When may a bank properly dishonor a customer's check without being liable to the customer?

A bank may dishonor a customer's check without liability to the customer when the customer's account contains insufficient funds to pay the check, providing the bank did not agree to cover overdrafts. A bank may also properly dishonor a stale check, a timely check subject to a valid stop-payment order, a check drawn after the customer's death, and forged or altered checks.

4. What is electronic check presentment, and how does it differ from the traditional check-clearing process?

With electronic check presentment, items are encoded with information (such as the amount of the check) that is read and processed by other banks' computers. A check may sometimes be retained at its place of deposit, and then only its image or description is presented for payment. A bank that encodes information on an item warrants to any subsequent bank or payor that the encoded information is correct.

This differs from the traditional check-clearing process because employees of each bank in the collection chain no longer have to physically handle each check that passes through the bank for collection or payment. Therefore, obtaining payment is much quicker. Whereas manual check processing can take days, electronic check presentment can be done on the day of deposit.

Chapter 20

2. What three requirements must be met to create an enforceable security interest?

The three requirements that must be met to create an enforceable security interest are as follows:

1. Either the collateral must be in the possession of the secured party in accordance with an agreement, or there must be a written or authenticated security agreement that describes the collateral subject to the security interest and is signed or authenticated by the debtor.
2. The secured party must give to the debtor something of value.
3. The debtor must have "rights" in the collateral.

4. If two secured parties have perfected security interests in the collateral of the debtor, which party has priority to the collateral on the debtor's default?

When two or more secured parties have perfected security interests in the same collateral, the first to perfect has priority, unless an applicable state statute provides otherwise.

Chapter 21

2. What is garnishment? When might a creditor undertake a garnishment proceeding?

Garnishment occurs when a creditor is permitted to collect a debt by seizing property of the debtor that is being held by a third party (such as a paycheck held by an employer or a checking account held by a bank). A creditor might use garnishment in a situation in which a debt has not been paid, but the process is closely regulated.

4. What is the difference between an exception to discharge and an objection to discharge?

An exception to discharge is a claim that is not dischargeable in bankruptcy, such as a government claim for unpaid taxes. An objection to discharge is a circumstance that causes a discharge to be denied, such as concealing assets.

Chapter 22

2. When is private mortgage insurance required? Which party does it protect?

A creditor may require private mortgage insurance if a mortgagor does not make a down payment of at least 20 percent of the purchase price for residential real property.

The creditor is protected if the borrower defaults because in that event the insurer reimburses the creditor for a portion of the loan.

4. What is a short sale? What advantages over mortgage foreclosure might it offer borrowers? Does the lender receive the full balance due on the mortgage loan in a short sale?

A short sale is a sale of real property for an amount that is less than the balance owed on the mortgage loan. Unlike a mortgage foreclosure, both the lender and the borrower must consent to a short sale. A short sale can be advantageous for a borrower because it has a less negative effect on the homeowner's credit than a foreclosure does and because the homeowner is not evicted from her or his home.

Following a short sale, and after the sale proceeds are applied, the borrower still owes the balance of the mortgage debt to the lender unless the lender agrees to forgive the remaining debt.

Chapter 23

2. How do agency relationships arise?

Agency relationships normally are consensual—that is, they arise by voluntary consent and agreement between the parties.

4. When is a principal liable for the agent's actions with respect to third parties? When is the agent liable?

A disclosed or partially disclosed principal is liable to a third party for a contract made by an agent who was acting within the scope of her or his authority. If the agent exceeds the scope of authority and the principal fails to ratify the contract, the agent may be liable (and the principal may not).

When neither the fact of agency nor the identity of the principal is disclosed, the agent is liable, and if the agent has acted within the scope of his or her authority, the undisclosed principal is also liable. Each party is liable for his or her own torts and crimes. A principal may also be liable for an agent's torts committed within the course or scope of employment. A principal is liable for an agent's crime if the principal participated by conspiracy or other action.

Chapter 24

2. What federal statute governs working hours and wages?

The Fair Labor Standards Act is the most significant federal statute governing working hours and wages.

4. What are the two most important federal statutes governing immigration and employment today?

The most important federal statutes governing immigration and the employment of noncitizens are the Immigration Reform and Control Act (IRCA) of 1986 and the Immigration Act of 1990.

Chapter 25

2. What is the difference between disparate-treatment discrimination and disparate-impact discrimination?

Intentional discrimination by an employer against an employee is known as disparate-treatment discrimination.

Disparate-impact discrimination occurs when, as a result of educational or other job requirements or hiring procedures, an employer's workforce does not reflect the percentage of nonwhites, women, or members of other protected classes that characterizes qualified individuals in the local labor market. Disparate-impact discrimination does not require evidence of intent.

4. What federal act prohibits discrimination based on age?

The Age Discrimination in Employment Act of 1967 prohibits discrimination on the basis of age.

Chapter 26

2. What are the most common types of franchises?

The majority of franchises are distributorships, chain-style business operations, or manufacturing or processing-plant arrangements.

4. What terms and conditions are typically included in a franchise contract?

A franchise contract typically covers such issues as the franchisee's payment for the franchise, any lease or purchase of the business premises, any lease or purchase of equipment, the location of the franchise, the territory to be served, the business organization of the franchisee, quality standards to be met, the degree of supervision and control by the franchisor, pricing arrangements, and termination of the franchise.

Chapter 27

2. What are the rights and duties of partners in an ordinary partnership?

The rights and duties of partners may be whatever the partners declare them to be. In the absence of partners' agreements to the contrary, the law imposes certain rights and duties. These include:

- A sharing of profits and losses in equal measure.
- The ability to assign a partnership interest.
- Equal rights in managing the firm (subject to majority rule).
- Access to all of the firm's books and records.
- An accounting of assets and profits.
- A sharing of the firm's property.

The duties include fiduciary duties, being bound to third parties through contracts entered into with other partners, and liability for the firm's debts and liabilities.

4. What advantages do limited liability partnerships offer to businesspersons that are not offered by general partnerships?

An advantage of a limited liability partnership over a general partnership is that, depending on the applicable state statute, the liability of the partners for partnership and partners' debts and torts can be limited to the amount of the partners' investments. Another advantage is that partners in a limited liability partnership generally are not liable for other partners' malpractice.

Chapter 28

2. What advantages do limited liability companies offer to businesspersons that are not offered by sole proprietorships or partnerships?

An important advantage of limited liability companies (LLCs) is that the liability of the members is limited to the amount of their investments. Another advantage of LLCs is the flexibility they offer in regard to taxation and management.

4. What is a joint venture? How is it similar to a partnership? How is it different?

A joint venture is an enterprise in which two or more persons or business entities combine their efforts or their property for a single transaction or project, or a related series of transactions or projects.

Generally, partnership law applies to joint ventures, although joint venturers have less implied and apparent authority than partners because they have less power to bind the members of their organization.

Chapter 29

2. What steps are involved in bringing a corporation into existence?

The steps to bring a corporation into existence are (1) preliminary organizational and promotional undertakings and (2) the legal process of incorporation. A promoter (one who takes the preliminary steps in organizing a corporation) is liable on preincorporation contracts unless the other contracting party agrees not to hold the promoter liable or the corporation assumes the contract by novation.

4. What are the basic differences between a merger, a consolidation, and a share exchange?

A merger involves the legal combination of two or more corporations so that only one of the original corporations remains after the merger is completed. The remaining company continues as the surviving corporation and possesses all the assets and liabilities of the disappearing corporation.

In a consolidation, two or more corporations combine to form an entirely new corporation. The original corporations cease to exist when the new corporation is formed. The new corporation also assumes any assets and liabilities previously possessed by the original corporations.

In a share exchange, some or all of the stock of a company is exchanged for some or all of the stock of another company, and both firms continue to exist.

Chapter 30

2. Directors are expected to use their best judgment in managing the corporation. What must directors do to avoid liability for honest mistakes of judgment and poor business decisions?

Directors and officers must exercise due care in performing their duties. They are expected to:

- Be informed on corporate matters.
- Act in accordance with their own knowledge and training.
- Exercise a reasonable amount of supervision when they delegate work to others.
- Attend board of directors' meetings.

In general, directors and officers must act in good faith, in what they consider to be the best interests of the corporation, and with the care that an ordinarily prudent person in a similar position would exercise in similar circumstances. This requires an informed decision, with a rational basis, and with no conflict between the decision maker's personal interest and the interest of the corporation.

4. From what sources may dividends be paid legally? In what circumstances is a dividend illegal? What happens if a dividend is illegally paid?

Depending on state law, dividends may be paid from retained earnings, current net profits, and any surplus. A dividend paid while the corporation is insolvent is an illegal dividend. Dividends improperly paid from an unauthorized account are illegal.

Shareholders must return illegal dividends if they knew that the dividends were illegal when they received them. Whenever dividends are illegal or improper, the board of directors can be held personally liable for the amount of the payment.

Chapter 31

2. What are the two major statutes regulating the securities industry?

The major statutes regulating the securities industry are the Securities Act of 1933 and the Securities Exchange Act of 1934, which created the Securities and Exchange Commission.

4. What are some of the features of state securities laws?

Typically, state laws have disclosure requirements and antifraud provisions patterned after Section 10(b) of the Securities Exchange Act of 1934 and SEC Rule 10b-5. State laws provide for the registration or qualification of securities offered or issued for sale within the state with the appropriate state official. Also, most state securities laws regulate securities brokers and dealers.

Chapter 32

2. What anticompetitive activities are prohibited by Section 1 of the Sherman Act?

Section 1 prohibits agreements that are anticompetitively restrictive—that is, agreements that have the wrongful purpose of restraining competition, such as price fixing.

4. What agencies of the federal government enforce the federal antitrust laws?

The federal agencies that enforce the antitrust laws are the U.S. Department of Justice and the Federal Trade Commission.

Chapter 33

2. What are the major federal statutes providing for consumer protection in credit transactions?

Federal statutes that protect consumers in credit transactions include the various titles of the Consumer Credit Protection Act—the Truth-in-Lending Act, of which the Equal Credit Opportunity Act and the Consumer Leasing Act are a part—as well as the Fair Credit Reporting Act and the Fair Debt Collection Practices Act.

4. What is contained in an environmental impact statement, and who must file one?

An environmental impact statement (EIS) analyzes the following:

- The impact on the environment that an action will have.
- Any adverse effects on the environment and alternative actions that might be taken.
- Irreversible effects the action might generate.

An EIS must be prepared for every major federal action that significantly affects the quality of the environment. An action is "major" if it involves a substantial commitment of resources (monetary or otherwise). An action is "federal" if a federal agency has the power to control it.

Chapter 34

2. What are the rules concerning an auditor's liability to third parties?

An auditor may be liable to a third party on the ground of negligence, when the auditor knew or should have known that the third party would benefit from the auditor's work. Depending on the jurisdiction, liability may be imposed only if one of the following occurs:

1. The auditor is in privity, or near privity, with the third party.
2. The third party's reliance on the auditor's work was foreseen, or the third party was within a class of known or foreseeable users.
3. The third party's use of the auditor's work was reasonably foreseeable.

4. What crimes might an accountant commit under the Internal Revenue Code?

Crimes under the Internal Revenue Code include the following:

1. Aiding or assisting in the preparation of a false tax return.
2. Aiding or abetting an individual's understatement of tax liability.
3. Negligently or willfully understating a client's tax liability, or recklessly or intentionally disregarding Internal Revenue Code rules or regulations.
4. Failing to provide a taxpayer with a copy of a tax return, failing to sign the return, or failing to furnish the appropriate tax identification numbers.

Chapter 35

2. What is the difference between a joint tenancy and a tenancy in common?

A tenancy in common is a form of co-ownership in which each of two or more persons owns an undivided interest in the whole property. On the death of a tenant in common, that tenant's interest passes to his or her heirs. In a joint tenancy, each of two or more persons owns an undivided interest in the property, and a deceased joint tenant's interest passes to the surviving joint tenant or tenants. This right distinguishes the joint tenancy from the tenancy in common.

4. What are the three elements of a bailment?

A bailment is formed (1) by the delivery of personal property without transfer of title, (2) by a bailor to a bailee, under an agreement, often for (3) a particular purpose.

Chapter 36

2. What is an easement? Describe three ways that easements are created.

An easement is the right of a person to make limited use of another person's real property without taking anything from the property, such as a right-of-way to cross another's property. Most easements are created by express grant in a contract.

An easement may also be created by the following:

1. *Implication* when surrounding circumstances imply its existence.
2. *Necessity* when an easement is required to access one's own property.
3. *Prescription* when authorized by a statute. Prescription occurs when someone utilizes an easement on property without the owner's permission and the use is apparent and continues for the length of time required by the applicable statute of limitations.

4. What is a leasehold estate? What types of leasehold estates, or tenancies, can be created when real property is leased?

A leasehold estate is property in the possession of a tenant. A leasehold estate can include a fixed-term tenancy, periodic tenancy, tenancy at will, and tenancy at sufferance.

Chapter 37

2. What is an insurable interest? When must an insurable interest exist—at the time the insurance policy is obtained, at the time the loss occurs, or both?

For real and personal property, an insurable interest exists when the insured derives a pecuniary (monetary) benefit from the existence of the property and would sustain a pecuniary loss from its destruction.

For a life, an insurable interest exists when a person has a reasonable expectation of benefit from the continued life of another. The benefit may be monetary, or it may be founded on the relationship between the parties (by blood or affinity).

For property insurance, the interest must exist at the time the loss occurs but need not exist when the policy is purchased. For life insurance, the interest must exist at the time the policy is obtained.

4. What is the difference between a *per stirpes* distribution and a *per capita* distribution of an estate to the grandchildren of the deceased?

Per stirpes distribution dictates that grandchildren share the part of the estate that their deceased parent (and descendant of the deceased grandparent) would have been entitled to inherit.

Per capita distribution dictates that each grandchild takes an equal share of the estate.

Sample Answers for *Questions with Sample Answer*

1–3A. Question with Sample Answer

The U.S. Constitution is the supreme law of the land. A law in violation of the Constitution, no matter what its source, will be declared unconstitutional and will not be enforced. In this problem, the court determined that a Massachusetts state statute was in conflict with the U.S. Constitution. The Constitution takes priority, so the statute will not be enforced.

In the actual case on which this problem is based, the trial court held that the statute violated the Constitution, and the U.S. Court of Appeals for the First Circuit affirmed this holding. Under the statute's definitions of large and small wineries, most of the small wineries were in state, and all of the large wineries were out of state. The court found that the purpose of the statute was to "ensure that Massachusetts' wineries obtained an advantage over their out-of-state counterparts."

2–2A. Question with Sample Answer

Thomas has a constitutionally protected right to the free exercise of his religion. In denying his claim for unemployment benefits, the state violated this right. Employers are obligated to make reasonable accommodations for their employees' beliefs that are openly and sincerely held, as were Thomas's beliefs. By moving him to a department that made military goods, his employer effectively forced him to choose between his job and his religious principles. This unilateral decision on the part of the employer was the reason Thomas left his job and why the company was required to compensate Thomas for his resulting unemployment.

3–2A. Question with Sample Answer

Marya can bring suit in all three courts. The trucking firm did business in Florida, and the accident occurred there. Thus, the state of Florida would have jurisdiction over the defendant. Because the firm was headquartered in Georgia and had its principal place of business in that state, Marya could also sue in a Georgia court. Finally, because the amount in controversy exceeds $75,000, the suit could be brought in federal court on the basis of diversity of citizenship.

4–2A. Question with Sample Answer

Yes. The *Restatement (Second) of Torts* defines *negligence* as "conduct that falls below the standard established by law for the protection of others against unreasonable risk of harm." The standard established by law is that of a reasonable person acting with due care in the circumstances. Shannon was well aware that the medication she took would make her drowsy, and her failure to observe due care—that is, refrain from driving—under the circumstances was negligent.

5–2A. Question with Sample Answer

1. Making a photocopy of an article in a scholarly journal "for purposes such as . . . scholarship, or research, is not an infringement of copyright" under Section 107 of the Copyright Act.
2. This is an example of trademark infringement. When a trademark is copied to a substantial degree or used in its entirety by one who is not entitled to use it, the trademark has been infringed.
3. This is the most likely example of copyright infringement. Generally, the determination of whether the reproduction of copyrighted material constitutes copyright infringement is made on a case-by-case basis under the "fair use" doctrine, as expressed in Section 107 of the Copyright Act. Courts consider such factors as the "purpose and character" of the use, such as whether it is "of a commercial nature"; "the amount and substantiality of the portion used in relation to the copyrighted work as a whole"; and "the effect of the use on the potential market" for the copied work. Here, the DVD storeowner is copying copyrighted works in their entirety for commercial purposes, thereby affecting the market for the works.

6–2A. Question with Sample Answer

Kayla has committed fraud in her e-mail. The elements of the tort of fraud are as follows:

1. The misrepresentation of material facts or conditions was made with knowledge that they were false or with reckless disregard for the truth.
2. There was an intent to induce another to rely on the misrepresentation.
3. There was justifiable reliance on the misrepresentation by the deceived party.
4. Damages were suffered as a result of the reliance.
5. There was a causal connection between the misrepresentation and the injury.

If any of Kayla's recipients reply to her false plea with cash, it is likely that all of these requirements for fraud will have been met.

7–2A. Question with Sample Answer

Factors for the firm to consider in making its decision include the appropriate ethical standard. Under the utilitarian standard, an action is correct, or "right," when, among the people it affects, it produces the greatest amount of good for the greatest number of people. When an action affects the majority adversely, it is morally wrong.

Applying the utilitarian standard requires three steps: (1) determine which individuals will be affected by the action in question; (2) perform an assessment, or cost-benefit analysis, of the negative and positive effects of alternative actions on these individuals; and (3) choose the alternative that will produce the maximum societal utility.

Ethical standards may also be based on a concept of duty, which suggests that the end can never justify the means and that human beings should not be treated as mere means to an end. But ethical decision making in a business context is not always simple. It is particularly difficult when an action will have different effects on different groups of people—shareholders, employees, society, and other stakeholders, such as the local community. Thus, another factor to consider is to whom the firm believes it owes a duty.

8–2A. Question with Sample Answer

Yes, it is reasonable to rely on the producers' financial records, which are reasonably reflective of their costs because their normal allocation methods were used for a number of years. These records are historically relied on to present important financial information to shareholders, lenders, tax authorities, auditors, and other third parties. Provided that the producers' records and books comply with generally accepted accounting principles and were verified by independent auditors, it is reasonable to use them to determine the production costs and fair market value of canned pineapple in the United States.

9–2A. Question with Sample Answer

Janine was unconscious or otherwise unable to agree to a contract for the nursing services she received while she was in the hospital. Under the doctrine of quasi contract, however, the law will sometimes create a fictional contract in order to prevent one party from unjustly receiving a benefit at the expense of another. Quasi contract provides a basis for Nursing Services to recover the value of the services it provided while Janine was in the hospital.

Nursing Services can recover for the at-home services under an implied contract because Janine was aware that the services were being provided for her. Under this type of contract, the conduct of the parties creates and defines the terms. Janine's acceptance of the services constitutes her agreement to form a contract, and she will probably be required to pay Nursing Services in full.

10–3A. Question with Sample Answer

1. Death of either the offeror or the offeree prior to acceptance automatically terminates a revocable offer. The basic legal reason is that the offer is personal to the parties and cannot be passed on to others, not even to the estate of the deceased. This rule applies even if the other party is unaware of the death. Thus, Cherneck's offer terminates on Cherneck's death, and Bollow's later acceptance does not constitute a contract.

2. An offer is automatically terminated by the destruction of the specific subject matter of the offer prior to acceptance. Thus, Bollow's acceptance after the fire does not constitute a contract.

3. When the offer is irrevocable, under an option contract, death of the offeror does not terminate the option contract, and the offeree can accept the offer to sell the equipment, binding the offeror's estate to performance. Performance is not personal to Cherneck, as the estate can transfer title to the equipment. Knowledge of the death is immaterial to the offeree's right of acceptance. Thus, Bollow can hold Cherneck's estate to a contract for the purchase of the equipment.

4. When the offer is irrevocable, under an option contract, death of the offeree also does not terminate the offer. Because the option is a separate contract, the contract survives and passes to the offeree's estate, which can exercise the option by acceptance within the option period. Thus, acceptance by Bollow's estate binds Cherneck to a contract for the sale of the equipment.

11–2A. Question with Sample Answer

Past consideration is no consideration. Therefore, a promise to pay for an event that has already taken place is not enforceable. There is nothing to bargain for in this situation. Also, there is no consideration if the promise is based on a moral duty (obligation) to pay. Because Daniel is presumed to be an adult responsible for his own care, Fred has no legal duty of care to Daniel. Because Fred had at best only a moral obligation to reimburse the elderly couple for the care rendered, and because the promise to pay was for an event already performed, Fred's promise cannot be enforced.

Because of the harshness of this rule, a few states have passed statutes enforcing such agreements (usually only up to the value of care received), or a court will enforce such a promise if the promisor received a substantial benefit (such as being saved from physical harm or financial disaster). In this situation, though, it is unlikely that the court would hold for the elderly couple, as the recipient of the benefit was Daniel, and not the promisor, Fred.

12–2A. Question with Sample Answer

In this situation, Gemma becomes a guarantor on the loan. That is, she guarantees the hardware store that she will pay for the mower if her brother fails to do so. This kind of collateral promise, in which the guarantor states that he or she will become responsible only if the primary party does not perform, must be in writing to be enforceable.

There is an exception, however. If the main purpose in accepting secondary liability is to secure a personal benefit—for example, if Gemma's brother bought the mower for her—the contract need not be in writing. The court will determine from the circumstances of the case whether the main purpose was to secure a personal benefit and thus, in effect, to answer for the guarantor's own debt.

13–2A. Question with Sample Answer

As a general rule, any rights flowing from a contract can be assigned. There are, however, exceptions, such as when the contract expressly prohibits or limits assignment. Under the principle of freedom of contract, such prohibitions are enforced—unless they are deemed contrary to public policy. For example, courts have held that a clause prohibiting assignment that restrains the alienation of property is invalid by virtue of being against public policy.

Authorities differ on how a case like Aron's should be decided. Some courts would enforce the prohibition and hold that Aron's assignment to Erica is ineffective without the landlord's consent. Others would permit the assignment to be effective and would limit the landlord's remedies to the normal contract remedies ensuing from Aron's breach.

14-2A. Question with Sample Answer

The question of whether a party has properly mitigated damages is a question of fact. Here, there is evidence to support a finding that Barton attempted to mitigate her damages—she apparently made reasonable efforts to find, and did find, employment. Because the position paid a significantly lower salary, it was not unreasonable for her to refuse it. Thus, under the circumstances, it was not unreasonable for her to choose to move to London.

A court should therefore award Barton $72,000 for the one year's salary she would have been paid if VanHorn had not repudiated their contract and the costs to move to London.

15-2A. Question with Sample Answer

Yes. Under UCC 2–205, a merchant offeror, who in a signed writing gives assurance that an offer will remain open, creates an irrevocable offer (without payment of consideration) for the time period stated in the assurance up to a period of three months. As a merchant, Jennings was obliged to hold the offer (which had been made in a signed writing—the letter) open until October 9. Wheeler's acceptance of the offer before October 9 created a valid contract, which Jennings breached when he sold the Thunderbird to a third party.

16-2A. Question with Sample Answer

Hammer is correct. Moore's refusal to deliver the car to Hammer on Friday, when Hammer tendered the $8,500 to Moore, constituted a breach of their contract. Moore could have canceled the contract on Hammer's anticipatory repudiation but did not do so and did not change her position in any way as a result of Hammer's anticipatory breach. Hammer could retract his repudiation of the contract at any time prior to the time performance was due.

Because Hammer did retract his repudiation and decided to buy the car at the time performance was due (and not later), Moore was obligated to abide by the terms of the contract

17-2A. Question with Sample Answer

Yes. To disclaim the implied warranty of fitness for a particular purpose, the disclaimer must be in writing and be conspicuous. Although the implied warranty of merchantability can be disclaimed orally, if the disclaimer is in writing, it must be conspicuously written. This means that through different color or size of type or some other technique, the disclaimer must stand out from the context in which it is printed so as to alert the reader of the document to the disclaimer.

In this case, the disclaimer was printed in the same size and color of type as the rest of the contract and was not conspicuous. If this was the only warranty disclaimer, it is not effective and Tandy can recover.

18-2A. Question with Sample Answer

For an instrument to be negotiable, it must meet the following requirements:

1. Be in writing.
2. Be signed by the maker or the drawer.
3. Be an unconditional promise or order to pay.
4. State a fixed amount of money.
5. Be payable on demand or at a definite time.
6. Be payable to order or to bearer, unless it is a check.

The instrument in this case meets the writing requirement because it is handwritten on something with a degree of permanence that is transferable. The instrument meets the requirement of being signed by the maker, as Muriel Evans's signature (her name in her handwriting) appears in the body of the instrument. The instrument's payment is not conditional and contains Muriel Evans's definite promise to pay.

In addition, the sum of $100 is both a fixed amount and payable in money (U.S. currency). Because the instrument is payable on demand and to bearer (Karen Marvin or any holder), the instrument is negotiable.

19-2A. Question with Sample Answer

Gary goes grocery shopping and carelessly leaves his checkbook in his shopping cart. His checkbook, with two blank checks remaining, is stolen by Dolores. On May 5, Dolores forges Gary's name on a check for $100 and cashes the check at Gary's bank, Citizens Bank of Middletown. Gary has not reported the loss of his blank checks to his bank.

On June 1, Gary receives his monthly bank statement from Citizens Bank that includes the forged check, but he does not notice the item nor does he examine his bank statement.

On June 20, Dolores forges Gary's last check. This check is for $1,000 and is cashed at Eastern City Bank, a bank with which Dolores has previously done business. Eastern City Bank puts the check through the collection process, and Citizens Bank honors it.

On July 1, on receipt of his bank statement and canceled checks covering June transactions, Gary discovers both forgeries and immediately notifies Citizens Bank. Dolores cannot be found. Gary claims that Citizens Bank must recredit his account for both checks, as his signature was forged. Discuss fully Gary's claim.

20-2A. Question with Sample Answer

Yes. Mendez has both a security interest in Arabian Knight and is a perfected secured party. He has met all the necessary criteria listed under UCC 9–203 to be a secured creditor. Mendez has given value of $5,000 and has taken possession of the collateral, Arabian Knight, owned by Marsh (who has rights in the collateral). Thus, Mendez has a security interest even though Marsh did not sign a security agreement. Once a security interest attaches, a transfer of possession of the collateral to the secured party can perfect the party's security interest without a filing [UCC 9–310(b)(6), 9–313]. Thus, a security interest was created and perfected at the time Marsh transferred Arabian Knight to Mendez as security for the loan.

21–2A. Question with Sample Answer

1. Any person, including a rancher or farmer, can voluntarily petition himself or herself into bankruptcy. The person has only to be a debtor. This includes partnerships and corporations that are liable on a claim held by a creditor, as well as individuals. The debtor does not have to be insolvent to file a petition. Under the Code, a debtor is presumed to be insolvent when his or her debts exceed the fair market value of nonexempt assets. Thus, even though Burke owns a $500,000 ranch and has debts of only $70,000, she can voluntarily petition herself into bankruptcy.

2. Neither Oman nor Sneed—nor any combination of Burke's creditors—can involuntarily petition Burke into bankruptcy. The Code provides that involuntary bankruptcy proceedings cannot be commenced against a farmer. The definition of a *farmer* includes a person who receives 50 percent of her or his gross income from farming operations, such as tilling the soil, ranching, or the production or raising of crops or livestock. Because Burke obviously fits the definition of a farmer, no creditor can force her into bankruptcy.

22–2A. Question with Sample Answer

The answer is likely no. If the loan was split without the consumer's consent, prior court cases have found that such practices violate the requirement of the Truth-in-Lending Act (TILA) that all disclosures for a single transaction must be grouped into a single writing.

Even if the plaintiff acquiesced to splitting the loan, the practice appears to circumvent the purpose of the Home Ownership and Equity Protection Act through an artificial restructuring of the loan transaction. If consumer protections could be circumvented by splitting loans, lenders would have a strong incentive to divide loans as necessary to keep individual loan costs as low as possible.

23–3A. Question with Sample Answer

Agency is usually a consensual relationship in that the principal and agent agree that the agent will have the authority to act for the principal, binding the principal to any contract with a third party. If no agency in fact exists, the purported agent's contracts with third parties are not binding on the principal. In this case, no agency by agreement was created.

Brown may claim that an agency by estoppel was created, but this argument will fail. Agency by estoppel is applicable only when a principal causes a third person to believe that another person is the principal's agent. In that situation, the principal's words or actions lead the third party to reasonably believe that the agent has authority. Hence, the principal is estopped (prevented) from claiming that no agency actually existed. Acts and declarations of the agent, however, do not in and of themselves create an agency by estoppel, because such actions should not reasonably lead a third person to believe that the purported agent has authority.

In this case, Wade's declarations and allegations alone led Brown to believe that Wade was an agent. Gett's actions were not involved. It is not reasonable to believe that someone is an agent solely because he or she is a friend of the principal. Therefore, Brown cannot hold Gett liable unless Gett ratifies Wade's contract—which is unlikely, as Wade has disappeared with the rare coin.

24–2A. Question with Sample Answer

The Occupational Safety and Health Act requires employers to provide safe working conditions for employees. The act prohibits employers from discharging or discriminating against any employee who refuses to work when the employee believes in good faith that he or she will risk death or great bodily harm by undertaking the employment activity. Denton and Carlo had sufficient reason to believe that the maintenance job required of them by their employer involved great risk.

Therefore, under the act, their discharge was wrongful. Denton and Carlo can turn to the Occupational Safety and Health Administration, which is part of the U.S. Department of Labor, for assistance.

25–2A. Question with Sample Answer

Educational requirements can be legally imposed as long as the requirement is directly related to, and necessary for, performance of the job. The requirement of a high school diploma is not a direct, job-related requirement in this case. Chinawa obviously comes under the 1964 Civil Rights Act, Title VII, as amended, and the educational requirement under the circumstances is definitely discriminatory against minorities.

26–2A. Question with Sample Answer

The court would likely conclude that National Foods was responsible for the acts of harassment by the manager at the franchised restaurant because the employees were the agents of National Foods. An agency relationship can be implied from the circumstances and conduct of the parties. The important question is the degree of control that a franchisor has over its franchisees. Whether the franchisor actually exercises that control is beside the point. Here, National Foods retained considerable control over new hires and the franchisee's policies, as well as the right to terminate the franchise for violations. That its supervisors routinely approved the policies would not undercut National Foods' liability.

27–2A. Question with Sample Answer

1. A limited partner's interest is assignable. In fact, assignment allows the assignee to become a substituted limited partner

with the consent of the remaining partners. The assignment does not dissolve the limited partnership.

2. Bankruptcy of the limited partnership itself causes dissolution, but bankruptcy of one of the limited partners does not dissolve the partnership unless it causes the bankruptcy of the firm.

3. The retirement, death, or insanity of a general partner dissolves the partnership unless the business can be continued by the remaining general partners. Because Dorinda was the only general partner, her death dissolves the limited partnership.

28–2A. Question with Sample Answer

Although a joint stock company has characteristics of a corporation, it is usually treated as a partnership. Therefore, although the joint stock company issues transferable shares of stock and is managed by directors and officers, the shareholders have personal liability. Unless the shareholders transfer their stock and ownership to a third party, not only are the joint stock company's assets available for damages caused by a breach, but the individual shareholders' assets are also subject to such liability.

A business trust resembles and is treated like a corporation in many respects. One is the limited liability of the beneficiaries. Unless state law treats the beneficiaries as partners, making them liable to the business trust's creditors, Faraway Corp. can look to only the business trust's assets in the event of a breach.

29–2A. Question with Sample Answer

It could be argued that Kora exceeded his authority when he cosigned the note on behalf of the corporation. The board of directors of a corporation delegates the authority to transact all ordinary business of the corporation to the president. If cosigning a note for a personal loan is not "ordinary business of the corporation," then the board, as principal, must ratify the act. There is no indication that the board did so in this instance.

30–2A. Question with Sample Answer

Directors are personally answerable to the corporation and the shareholders for breach of their duty to exercise reasonable care in conducting the affairs of the corporation. Reasonable care is the degree of care that a reasonably prudent person would use in the conduct of personal business affairs. When directors delegate the running of the corporate affairs to officers, the directors are expected to use reasonable care in selecting and supervising the officers. Failure to do so will make the directors liable for negligence or mismanagement. A director who dissents to an action by the board is not personally liable for losses resulting from that action. Unless the dissent is entered into the board meeting minutes, however, the director is presumed to have assented.

Therefore, the first issue in the case of Starboard, Inc., is whether the board members failed to use reasonable care in selecting the president, Tyson. If so, and particularly if the board failed to provide a reasonable amount of supervision (as openly embezzled funds would indicate), the directors will be personally liable. This liability will include Ellsworth unless she can prove that

she dissented and that she tried to reasonably supervise Tyson. Considering the facts in this case, it is questionable that Ellsworth could prove this.

31–2A. Question with Sample Answer

No. Under federal securities law, a stock split is exempt from registration requirements because no stock is being sold. The existing shares are merely being split, and the corporation does not receive any consideration for the additional shares created.

32–2A. Question with Sample Answer

Yes. The major antitrust law being violated is the Sherman Act, Section 1. Allitron and Donovan are engaged in interstate commerce, and the agreement to divide marketing territories between them is a contract in restraint of trade. The U.S. Department of Justice could seek fines of up to $1 million from each corporation, and the officers or directors responsible could be imprisoned for up to three years.

33–2A. Question with Sample Answer

The Truth-in-Lending Act (TILA) deals specifically with lost or stolen credit cards and the unauthorized use of credit cards. For credit cards solicited by the cardholder and then lost or stolen, the act limits the liability of the cardholder to $50 for unauthorized charges made before the card issuer is notified. There is no liability for any unauthorized charges made after the date of notice.

Therefore, for the Midtown Department Store credit card stolen on May 31, Ochoa is liable for $50 of the $500 charge made on June 1, which occurred before Ochoa notified the card issuer. Ochoa has no liability for the $200 charge on June 3 because it was made after the issuer was notified.

TILA prohibits the issuance of unsolicited credit cards. Unless an individual accepts an unsolicited card (such as by using it), she or he is not liable for any unauthorized charges if the card is lost or stolen. The person does not have to notify the issuer of an unsolicited, unaccepted card to be relieved of all liability for unauthorized charges. Therefore, Ochoa owes $50 to Midtown Department Store and nothing to High-Flying Airlines.

34–2A. Question with Sample Answer

Assuming that the circuit court has abandoned the *Ultramares* rule, it is likely that the accounting firm of Goldman, Walters, Johnson & Co. will be held liable to Happydays State Bank for negligent preparation of financial statements.

As a side note, this hypothetical question is partially derived from the case, *Citizens State Bank v. Timm, Schmidt & Co.* In that case, the Supreme Court of Wisconsin enunciated various policy reasons for holding accountants liable to third parties even in the absence of privity. The court suggested that this potential liability would make accountants more careful in preparing financial statements.

Moreover, in some situations the accountants may be the only solvent defendants. Hence, unless liability is imposed on the accountants, third parties who reasonably rely on financial statements may go unprotected. The court also observed that if third parties, such as banks, have to absorb the costs of bad loans made as a result of negligently prepared financial statements, then the cost of credit to the public in general will increase. The court suggested that accountants are in a better position to absorb the risk by purchasing liability insurance.

35–3A. Question with Sample Answer

For Curtis to recover against the hotel, he must first prove that a bailment relationship was created between himself and the hotel as to the car or the fur coat, or both. For a bailment to exist, there must be a delivery of personal property that gives the bailee exclusive possession of the property, and the bailee must knowingly accept the bailed property. If either element is lacking, there is no bailment relationship and no liability on the part of the bailee hotel.

The facts clearly indicate that the bailee hotel took exclusive possession and control of Curtis's car. The hotel knowingly accepted the car when the attendant took the car from Curtis and parked it in the underground garage, retaining the keys. Thus, a bailment was created as to the car. Since this was a mutual-benefit bailment, the hotel owed Curtis the duty to exercise reasonable care over the car and to return it at the end of the bailment.

Failure to return the car creates a presumption of negligence (lack of reasonable care). Unless the hotel can rebut this presumption, the hotel is liable to Curtis for the loss of the car. As to the fur coat, the hotel neither knew nor expected that the trunk contained an expensive fur coat. Thus, although the hotel knowingly took exclusive possession of the car, the hotel did not do so with the fur coat. (But for a regular coat and other items likely to be in a car, the hotel would be liable.) Because no bailment of the expensive fur coat was created, the hotel has no liability for its loss.

36–2A. Question with Sample Answer

Wiley understandably wants a general warranty deed, as this type of deed will give him the most extensive protection against any defects of title claimed against the property transferred. The general warranty deed would have Gemma warranting the following:

1. That she has the title to, and the power to convey, the property.
2. A covenant of quiet enjoyment (a warranty that the buyer will not be disturbed in his possession of the land).
3. That transfer of the property is made without knowledge of adverse claims of third parties.

Gemma, however, is conveying only ten feet along a property line that may not even be accurately surveyed. Therefore, she does not wish to make these warranties.

Consequently, Gemma is offering a quitclaim deed, which does not convey any warranties but conveys only whatever interest, if any, the grantor owns. Although title is passed by a quitclaim deed, the quality of the title is not warranted. Because Wiley really needs the property, it appears that he has three choices. He can accept the quitclaim deed, he can increase his offer price to obtain the general warranty deed he wants, or he can offer to have a title search made, which should satisfy both parties.

37–2A. Question with Sample Answer

1. In most states, for a will to be valid, it must be in writing, signed by the testator, and witnessed (attested to) according to the statutes of the state. In this instance, Benjamin's will was unquestionably written (typewritten) and signed by the testator. The only problem is with the witnesses. Some states require three witnesses, and some states invalidate a will if a named beneficiary is also a witness. The Uniform Probate Code provides that a will is valid even if attested to by an interested witness. Therefore, whether the will is valid depends on the state laws dealing with witness qualifications.

2. If the will is declared invalid, Benjamin's estate will pass in accordance with the state's intestacy laws. These statutes provide for distribution of an estate when there is no valid will. The intent of the statutes is to distribute the estate in the way that the deceased person would have wished. Generally, the estate is divided between a surviving spouse and all surviving children. Because Benjamin is a widower, if his only surviving child is Edward, the entire estate will go to Edward, and Benjamin's grandchildren, Perry and Paul, will receive nothing from the estate.

3. If the will is valid, the estate will be divided between Benjamin's two children, Patricia and Edward. Should either or both predecease Benjamin, leaving children (Benjamin's grandchildren), the grandchildren take *per stirpes* the share that would have gone to their parent. In this situation, Edward, as a surviving child of Benjamin, would receive one-half of the estate, and Perry and Paul, as grandchildren, would each receive *per stirpes* one-fourth of the estate (one-half of the share that would have gone to their deceased mother, Patricia).

Sample Answers for *Case Problems with Sample Answer*

1–6A. Case Problem with Sample Answer

The common law system spread throughout medieval England after the Norman Conquest in 1066. Courts developed the common law rules from the principles behind the decisions in actual legal controversies. Judges attempted to be consistent. When possible, they based their decisions on the principles suggested by earlier cases. They sought to decide similar cases in a similar way and considered new cases with care because they knew that their decisions would make new law. Each interpretation became part of the law on the subject and served as a legal precedent. Later cases that involved similar legal principles or facts could be decided with reference to that precedent.

The practice of deciding new cases with reference to former decisions, or precedents, eventually became a cornerstone of the English and American judicial systems. It forms a doctrine called *stare decisis*. Under this doctrine, judges are obligated to follow the precedents established within their jurisdictions. Generally, those countries that were once colonies of Great Britain retained their English common law heritage after they achieved their independence. Today, common law systems exist in Australia, Canada, India, Ireland, and New Zealand, as well as the United States.

Most of the other European nations base their legal systems on Roman civil law. Civil law is codified law—an ordered grouping of legal principles enacted into law by a legislature or governing body. In a civil law system, the primary source of law is a statutory code, and case precedents are not judicially binding as they are in a common law system. Nonetheless, judges in such systems commonly refer to previous decisions as sources of legal guidance. The difference is that judges in a civil law system are not bound by precedent—in other words, the doctrine of *stare decisis* does not apply.

2–6A. Case Problem with Sample Answer

The establishment clause prohibits the government from passing laws or taking actions that promote religion or show a preference for one religion over another. In assessing a government action, the courts look at the predominant purpose for the action and ask whether the action has the effect of endorsing religion.

Although DeWeese claimed to have a nonreligious purpose for displaying the poster of the Ten Commandments in a courtroom, his own statements showed a religious purpose. These statements reflected his views about "warring" legal philosophies and his belief that "our legal system is based on moral absolutes from divine law handed down by God through the Ten Commandments." This plainly constitutes a religious purpose that violates the establishment clause because it has the effect of endorsing Judaism or Christianity over other religions. In the case on which this problem is based, the court ruled in favor of the American Civil Liberties Union.

3–4A. Case Problem with Sample Answer

Based on a recent holding by the Washington state supreme court, the federal appeals court held that the arbitration provision was *unconscionable* (see page 296 in Chapter 11) and therefore invalid. Because it was invalid, the restriction on class-action suits was also invalid. The state court reasoned that by offering a contract that restricted class actions and required arbitration, the company had improperly stripped consumers of rights they would normally have to attack certain industry practices.

Class-action suits are often brought in cases of deceptive or unfair industry practices when the losses suffered by an individual consumer are too small to warrant a consumer suing.

In this case, the alleged added cell phone fees are so small that no one consumer would be likely to litigate or arbitrate the matter due to the expenses involved. Because the arbitration agreement eliminates the possibility of class actions, it violates public policy and is void and unenforceable.

4–4A. Case Problem with Sample Answer

Defamation involves wrongfully hurting a person's good reputation. Doing so in writing is the tort of libel. The basis of the tort of defamation is the publication of a statement that holds an individual up to contempt, ridicule, or hatred. Publication means that the statement is communicated to someone other than the defamed party. A person who republishes defamatory statements is liable. The publication of information that places a person in a false light, such as a story that she did something she did not actually do, could also constitute an invasion of privacy. Truth normally is an absolute defense to a charge of defamation.

In this problem, the police communicated to the *Herald* that Eubanks was charged with a crime, and the paper published the information. Its publication might hold Eubanks up to contempt, ridicule, or hatred. The information was not correct, placing Eubanks in a false light. Yet the *Herald*'s publication of the information was an accurate, truthful summary of a police report. No information was changed. There is no indication that the paper was aware of the second e-mail before it published its summary of the first. Thus, truth is most likely an absolute defense to Eubanks's charges. In the actual case on which this problem is based, the court issued a judgment in favor of the newspaper.

5–5A. Case Problem with Sample Answer

Some business information that cannot be protected by trademark, patent, or copyright law is protected against appropriation by competitors as trade secrets. Trade secrets consist of anything that makes a company unique and that would have value to a competitor—customer lists, plans, research and development, pricing information, marketing techniques, and production techniques, for example. Theft of trade secrets is a federal crime.

In this problem, the documents in the boxes in the car could constitute trade secrets. But a number of factors suggest that a finding of theft and imposition of liability would not be appropriate. The boxes were not marked in any way that would indicate they contained confidential information. The boxes were stored in an employee's car. The alleged thief was the employee's spouse, not a CPR competitor, and she apparently had no idea what was in the boxes. Leaving trade secrets so accessible does not show an effort to protect the information.

In the case on which this problem is based, the court dismissed Jones's claim, in part, on the reasoning stated above.

6–5A. Case Problem with Sample Answer

Under the Fourth Amendment, a police officer must obtain a search warrant to search private property. In a traffic stop, however, it seems unreasonable to require an officer to obtain a warrant to search one of the vehicle's occupants. But it seems reasonable to apply some standard to prevent police misconduct. An officer might be held to a standard of probable cause, which consists of reasonable grounds to believe that a person should be searched.

In some situations, however, an officer may have a reasonable suspicion short of probable cause to believe that a person poses a risk of violence. In a traffic-stop setting, for example, the normal reaction of a person stopped for a driving infraction would not pose this risk, but it might arise if the person feared that evidence of a more serious crime might be discovered. A criminal's motivation to use violence to prevent the discovery could be great, and because the vehicle is already stopped, the additional intrusion is minimal. Under these circumstances, a limited search of the person for weapons would protect the officer, the individual, and the public. Thus, an officer who conducts a routine traffic stop could perform a pat-down search of a passenger on a reasonable suspicion that the person may be armed and dangerous.

7–4A. Case Problem with Sample Answer

The law does not codify all ethical requirements. A firm may have acted unethically but still not be legally accountable unless the party that was wronged can establish some basis for liability. Rules of law are designed to require plaintiffs to prove certain elements that establish a defendant's liability in order to recover for injuries or loss. Ethical codes and internal guidelines may have significance in evaluating a company's conduct, but they are not rules of law—a violation of a company policy is not a basis for liability.

In this case, Havensure had the burden of proving liability. Prudential's violation of its own company guideline was clearly wrongful—and might be a matter of concern for insurance regulators—but this misconduct did not create an obligation to Havensure. Havensure cannot establish a cause of action against Prudential for violating its own policy. In the actual case on which this problem is based, the court ruled in Prudential's favor.

8–3A. Case Problem with Sample Answer

The court ruled that it had jurisdiction over Voda's foreign patent infringement claims. Cordis appealed to a federal appellate court, which concluded that the lower court did not have jurisdiction. The appellate court found that "considerations of comity" "constitute compelling reasons to decline jurisdiction" in this case.

The court explained, "Comity, in the legal sense, is neither a matter of absolute obligation, on the one hand, nor of mere courtesy and good will, upon the other. But it is the recognition which one nation allows within its territory to the legislative, executive or judicial acts of another nation, having due regard both to international duty and convenience, and to the rights of its own citizens or of other persons who are under the protection of its laws.

Courts must also bear in mind that whatever laws are carried into execution, within the limits of any government, are considered as having the same effect everywhere, so far as they do not occasion a prejudice to the rights of the other governments, or their citizens."

Here, Voda did not identify any international duty that required the U.S. judicial system to adjudicate foreign patent infringement claims, and the court found none. Voda also did not show that it would be more convenient for U.S. courts to assume jurisdiction or that foreign courts would inadequately protect his foreign patent rights. Therefore, the court saw "no reason why American courts should supplant British, Canadian, French, or German courts in interpreting and enforcing British, Canadian, European, French, or German patents. . . . Because the purpose underlying comity is not furthered and potentially hindered in this case, adjudication of Voda's foreign patent infringement claims should be left to the sovereigns that create the property rights in the first instance."

9–7A. Case Problem with Sample Answer

Gutkowski does not have a valid claim for payment, nor should he recover on the basis of a quasi contract. Quasi contracts are imposed by courts on parties in the interest of fairness and justice. Usually, a quasi contract is imposed to avoid the unjust enrichment of one party at the expense of another. Gutkowski was compensated as a consultant. For him to establish a claim that he is due more compensation based on unjust enrichment, he must have proof. As it is, he has only his claim that there were discussions about him being a part owner of YES. Discussions and negotiations are not a basis for recovery on a quasi contract.

In the actual case on which this problem is based, the court dismissed Gutkowski's claim for payment.

10–6A. Case Problem with Sample Answer

An offer is a manifestation of willingness to enter into a bargain that is made in a way that justifies another person in understanding that his or her assent to that bargain is invited and will conclude it. The test for an offer is whether it induces a reasonable belief in the recipient that the recipient can, by accepting, bind the sender. In making an offer, the offeror may decide to whom to extend it.

In this situation, Prairie Meadows Casino is the offeror. It extends an offer to wager to its patrons, promising that if a patron accepts the offer by wagering an amount and wins, the casino will pay off the wager. Because the casino has the ability to determine the individuals to whom the offer is made, it may also exclude certain individuals. Blackford was banned from the casino. Under an objective test, unless the ban was lifted, Blackford could not reasonably believe that he was among the individuals invited to accept the offer. In addition, the ban against Blackford had not been lifted—the casino had not extended him an offer to wager. Because there was no offer to him, no contract could result.

In the actual case on which this problem is based, the court entered a judgment in the casino's favor on this reasoning.

11–6A. Case Problem with Sample Answer

In this case, the agreement that restricted the buyer's options for resolution of a dispute to arbitration and limited the amount of damages was both procedurally and substantively unconscionable. Procedural unconscionability concerns the manner in which the parties enter into a contract. Substantive unconscionability can occur when a contract leaves one party to the agreement without a remedy for the nonperformance of the other.

Here, GeoEx told customers that the arbitration terms in its release form were nonnegotiable and that climbers would encounter the same requirements with any other travel company. This amounted to procedural unconscionability, underscoring the customers' lack of bargaining power. The imbalance resulted in oppressive terms, with no real negotiation and an absence of meaningful choice. Furthermore, the restriction on forum (San Francisco) and the limitation on damages (the cost of the trip)—with no limitation on GeoEx's damages—amounted to substantive unconscionability.

In the actual case on which this problem is based, the court ruled that the agreement was unconscionable.

12–4A. Case Problem with Sample Answer

No. Generally, a contract for a sale of land must be in writing and state the essential terms (such as location and price) and describe the property with sufficient clarity to allow the terms to be determined from the writing, without reference to outside sources. In this problem, the parties' "Purchase Agreement" was void for lack of an adequate property description. The agreement merely provided the name of the business and a street address. Thus, the seller could not enforce it, and the prospective buyers could back out of the deal.

In the actual case on which this problem is based, the court ruled that the agreement was unenforceable because the description was not sufficient.

13–6A. Case Problem with Sample Answer

Maciel was not correct. In this problem, the performance of a legal obligation under the parties' contract was contingent on a condition—the occurrence of a certain event. If the condition was not satisfied, the obligations of the parties were discharged. Here, Regent University promised to provide an apartment in its housing facility to Maciel as long as he maintained his status as a Regent student. Maintaining student status was the condition for the university's provision of an apartment. On the termination of that status, Regent was entitled to require Maciel to vacate the apartment.

According to the facts in the problem, Maciel decided to withdraw from the university at the end of the spring semester. This rendered him ineligible to remain in the apartment. In other words, this decision resulted in noncompliance with the condition for the university's provision of an apartment, and the university was thus no longer bound to perform. Contrary to Maciel's argument, he did not have the "legal authority" to continue to occupy the apartment. In the actual case on which this problem is based, the court convicted Maciel of trespassing. In response to Maciel's argument, a state intermediate appellate court applied the reasoning set out above to affirm the conviction.

14–7A. Case Problem with Sample Answer

Simard is liable only for the losses and expenses related to the first resale. Simard could reasonably anticipate that his breach would require another sale and that the sales price might be less than what he agreed to pay. Therefore, he should be liable for the difference between his sales price and the first resale price ($29,000), plus any expenses arising from the first resale.

Simard is not liable, however, for any expenses and losses related to the second resale. After all, Simard did not cause the second purchaser's default, and he could not reasonably foresee that default as a probable result of his breach.

15–4A. Case Problem with Sample Answer

Altieri held title to the car that she was driving at the time of the accident in which Godfrey was injured. Once goods exist and are identified, title can be determined. Under the UCC, any explicit understanding between the buyer and the seller determines when title passes. If there is no such agreement, title passes to the buyer at the time and place that the seller physically delivers the goods.

In lease contracts, title to the goods is retained by the lessor-owner of the goods. The UCC's provisions relating to passage to title do not apply to leased goods. Here, Altieri originally leased the car from G.E. Capital Auto Lease, Inc., but by the time of the accident she had bought it. Even though she had not fully paid for the car or completed the transfer-of-title paperwork, she owned it. Title to the car passed to Altieri when she bought it and took delivery of it. Thus, Altieri, not G.E., was the owner of the car at the time of the accident.

In the actual case on which this problem is based, the court concluded that G.E. was not the owner of the vehicle when Godfrey was injured.

16–7A. Case Problem with Sample Answer

Padma notified Universal Exports about its breach, so Padma has two ways to recover even though it accepted the goods. Padma's first option is to argue that it revoked its acceptance, giving it the right to reject the goods. To revoke acceptance, Padma would have to show that:

1. The nonconformity substantially impaired the value of the shipment.
2. It predicated its acceptance on a reasonable assumption that Universal Exports would cure the nonconformity.
3. Universal Exports did not cure the nonconformity within a reasonable time.

Padma's second option is to keep the goods and recover for the damages caused by Universal Exports' breach. Under this option, Padma could recover at least the difference between the value of the goods as promised and their value as accepted.

17–7A. Case Problem with Sample Answer

No. Dobrovolny's claim is not likely to succeed. The majority of states recognize strict product liability. The purpose of strict product liability is to ensure that the costs of injuries resulting from defective products are borne by the manufacturers rather than by the injured persons. The law imposes this liability as a matter of public policy. Some state courts limit the application of the tort theory of strict product liability to situations involving personal injuries rather than property damage.

In this problem, Nebraska recognizes strict product liability, but the state's courts limit its application. The issue is whether these limits apply when a product self-destructs without causing damage to persons or other property. When a product injures only itself, the reasons for imposing liability in tort lose their significance. The consumer has not been injured, and the loss concerns the consumer's benefit of the bargain from the contract with the seller of the product.

Although a consumer with only a damaged product may not recover in tort, the consumer is not without other remedies. Recovery can be sought on a contract theory for breach of warranty. Product value and quality are the purposes of warranties. Thus, even though the court is likely to deny Dobrovolny's strict product liability claim, he might seek to recover for breach of warranty on contract principles for the loss of his truck. If there were no express warranties that the truck would not spontaneously combust, relief may be possible for breach of the implied warranty of merchantability or fitness for a particular purpose.

In the actual case on which this problem is based, the court issued a decision in Ford's favor.

18–6A. Case Problem with Sample Answer

No. Novel is not correct. The instrument is a note and Novel is bound to pay it. For an instrument to be negotiable under UCC 3–104, it must meet the following requirements: (1) be in writing, (2) be signed by the maker or the drawer, (3) be an unconditional promise or order to pay, (4) state a fixed amount of money, (5) be payable on demand or at a definite time, and (6) be payable to order or to bearer unless it is a check. When no time for payment is stated on an instrument, the instrument is payable on demand.

Applying these principles to the facts in this problem, all of the requirements to establish the instrument as negotiable are met:

1. The instrument is in writing.
2. It is signed by Novel.
3. There are no conditions or promises other than the unconditional promise to pay.
4. The instrument states a fixed amount—$10,000.
5. The instrument does not include a definite repayment date, which means that it is payable on demand.
6. The instrument is payable to Gallwitz.

In the actual case on which this problem is based, the court ruled in favor of Gallwitz for payment of the note.

19–6A. Case Problem with Sample Answer

Wells Fargo is liable to W Financial for the amount of the check. A bank that pays a customer's check bearing a forged indorsement must recredit the customer's account or be liable to the customer-drawer for breach of contract. The bank must recredit the account because it failed to carry out the drawer's order to pay to the order of the named party. Eventually, the loss falls on the first party to take the instrument bearing the forged indorsement because a forged indorsement does not transfer title. Thus, whoever takes an instrument with a forged indorsement cannot become a holder.

Under these rules, Wells Fargo is liable to W Financial for the amount of the check. The bank had an obligation to ensure that the check was properly indorsed. The bank did not pay the check to the order of Lateef, the named payee, but accepted the check for deposit into the account of CA Houston without Lateef's indorsement. The bank did not obtain title to the instrument and could not become a holder, nor was it entitled to enforce the instrument on behalf of any other party who was entitled to enforce it.

In the actual case on which this problem is based, the court held the bank liable to pay the amount of the check to W Financial.

20–4A. Case Problem with Sample Answer

A secured creditor can take various steps to satisfy a debt. Under the UCC, these remedies are cumulative and can be exercised simultaneously. A secured creditor can repossess and retain a debtor's collateral in full or partial satisfaction of the debt. The collateral does not have to be disposed of first unless the parties have agreed otherwise. If the collateral satisfies the debt only partially, the creditor can seek a judgment for the balance due. Of course, it would not be fair for a creditor to deprive the debtor of the possession of the collateral for an unreasonable length of time and not apply the property, or the proceeds from its sale, against the debt.

The creditor must act in a commercially reasonable manner and take steps to sell, lease, retain, or otherwise dispose of the collateral. In this problem, it does not appear that the bank failed to proceed in a commercially reasonable manner. The bank chose to retain the collateral and seek a judgment on the debt. The amount that OAI owes the bank might be at issue, but the facts state that the debtor did not dispute the amount due.

In the case on which this problem is based, the court issued a judgment in the bank's favor based on the principles stated here.

21–8A. Case Problem with Sample Answer

Gholston can recover damages because EZ Auto willfully violated the automatic stay. EZ Auto repossessed the car even though it received notice of the automatic stay from the bankruptcy court. Moreover, EZ Auto retained the car even after it was reminded of the stay by Gholston's attorney. Thus, EZ Auto knew about the automatic stay and violated it intentionally. Because Gholston suffered direct damages as a result, she can recover from EZ Auto.

22–8A. Case Problem with Sample Answer

Ordinarily, a deficiency judgment will be for the difference between the borrower's outstanding debt and the final sales price at the foreclosure sale. Courts will not apply the sales price, however, if the property sells for far less than its fair market value. That happened here, so Beach Community Bank is entitled to the difference between First Brownsville's outstanding debt and the property's fair market value at the time of the foreclosure sale. Based on the court's foreclosure judgment and the expert testimony at the deficiency judgment hearing, First Brownsville owes $454,475.

23–8A. Case Problem with Sample Answer

Hall may be held personally liable. Hall could not be an agent for House Medic because it was a fictitious name and not a real entity. Moreover, when the contract was formed, Hall did not disclose his true principal, which was Hall Hauling, Ltd. Thus, Hall may be held personally liable as a party to the contract.

24–6A. Case Problem with Sample Answer

No. Woody Woo's tip-pooling policy did not violate the minimum wage provisions of the Fair Labor Standards Act (FLSA). When tipping is a customary part of a business as it is in the restaurant industry, the tips—in the absence of an explicit agreement to the contrary—belong to the recipient. When another arrangement is made, however, it is likely valid unless there is a statutory limitation. The FLSA does not prevent employers, who are paying at least the minimum wage, from taking employee tips and making another arrangement for tip distributions.

Here, Woody Woo's tip-pool arrangement is fine so long as it does not reduce the servers' hourly wages to less than the state's minimum wage. That does not occur because Woody Woo pays its servers more than the state's minimum wage before tips.

25–5A. Case Problem with Sample Answer

Yes. Dawson could establish a claim for retaliation. Title VII prohibits retaliation. In a retaliation claim, an individual asserts that he or she suffered harm as a result of making a charge, testifying, or participating in a Title VII investigation or proceeding. To prove retaliation, a plaintiff must show that the challenged action was one that would likely have dissuaded a reasonable worker from making or supporting a charge of discrimination.

In this problem, under applicable state law, it was unlawful for an employer to discriminate against an individual based on sexual orientation. Dawson was subjected to derision on the part of co-workers, including his supervisor, based on his sexual orientation. He filed a complaint with his employer's human resources department. Two days later, he was fired. The proximity in time and the other circumstances, especially the supervisor's conduct, would support a retaliation claim. Also, the discharge would likely have dissuaded Dawson, or any reasonable worker, from making a claim of discrimination.

In the actual case on which this problem is based, the court held that Dawson offered enough evidence that "a reasonable trier of fact could find in favor of Dawson on his retaliation claim."

26–7A. Case Problem with Sample Answer

Oshana and GTO have stated a claim for wrongful termination of their franchise. A franchisor must act in good faith when terminating a franchise agreement. If the termination is arbitrary or unfair, a franchisee may have a claim for wrongful termination.

In this case, Oshana and GTO have alleged that Buchanan acted in bad faith. Their failure to pay rent would ordinarily be a valid basis for termination, but not if it was entirely precipitated by Buchanan. Thus, Oshana and GTO may recover if they can prove that their allegations are true.

27–7A. Case Problem with Sample Answer

Garcia and Lucero probably satisfied all three requirements for forming a partnership. They owned the two properties equally, agreed to share both profits and losses, and enjoyed equal management rights. Moreover, it is immaterial that they lacked a written partnership agreement. The Statute of Frauds does not apply to these facts, and a partnership agreement can be oral or implied by the parties' conduct.

28–7A. Case Problem with Sample Answer

No. One Bluewater member could not unilaterally "fire" another member without providing a reason. Part of the attractiveness of an LLC as a form of business enterprise is its flexibility. The members can decide how to operate the business through an operating agreement. For example, the agreement can set forth procedures for choosing or removing members or managers.

Here, the Bluewater operating agreement provided for a "super majority" vote to remove a member under circumstances that would jeopardize the firm's contractor status. Thus, one Bluewater member could not unilaterally "fire" another member without providing a reason. In fact, a majority of the members could not terminate the other's interest in the firm without providing a reason. Moreover, the only acceptable reason would be a circumstance that undercut the firm's status as a contractor.

The flexibility of the LLC business form relates to its framework, not to its members' capacity to violate its operating agreement. In the actual case on which this problem is based, Smith attempted to "fire" Williford without providing a reason. In Williford's suit, the court issued a judgment in his favor.

29-7A. Case Problem with Sample Answer

Yes. Most likely, Interline is liable for the unpaid amount on the GATT contract with Call Center. An acquiring corporation will be held to have assumed the liabilities of the selling corporation in the following situations:

1. The purchasing corporation expressly or impliedly assumes the seller's liabilities.
2. The sale transaction is in effect a merger or consolidation of the two companies.
3. The purchaser continues the seller's business and retains the same personnel (shareholders, directors, and officers).
4. The sale is entered into fraudulently for the purpose of escaping liability.

In this problem, Interline acquired GATT's assets at a public sale. There is no indication that Interline agreed to assume GATT's liabilities, there was no merger or other combination of the two companies, and it does not appear that the sale was fraudulently entered into to escape liability.

Thus, the focus is on the third item listed above—whether Interline was liable for GATT's debts because it continued GATT's business with the same personnel. Boyd was not a GATT employee, but he was a former GATT director. Other members of Interline's staff were former GATT employees. GATT and Interline operated out of the same office building. Both companies were in the business of providing travel services to many of the same customers. These factors indicate that Interline is responsible for GATT's liabilities, including its debt to Call Center.

In the actual case on which this problem is based, the court focused on the same principles discussed here to issue a judgment in Call Center's favor.

30-6A. Case Problem with Sample Answer

Yes. Woods has a right to inspect Biolustré's books and records. Every shareholder is entitled to examine corporate records. A shareholder can inspect the books in person or through an agent such as an attorney, accountant, or other authorized assistant.

The right of inspection is limited to the inspection and copying of corporate books and records for a proper purpose. This is because the power of inspection is fraught with potential for abuse—for example, it can involve the disclosure of trade secrets and other confidential information. Thus, a corporation is allowed to protect itself.

Here, Woods, through Hair Ventures, has the right to inspect Biolustré's books and records. She has a proper purpose for the inspection—to obtain information about Biolustré's financial situation. She, and other shareholders, had not received notice of shareholders' meetings or corporate financial reports for years, or notice of Biolustré's plan to issue additional stock. Hair Ventures had a substantial investment in the company.

In the actual case on which this problem is based, the court ordered Biolustré to produce its books and records for Hair Ventures' inspection.

31-5A. Case Problem with Sample Answer

An omission or misrepresentation of a material fact in connection with the purchase or sale of a security may violate Section 10(b) of the Securities Exchange Act of 1934 and SEC Rule 10b-5. The key question is whether the omitted or misrepresented information is material. A fact, by itself, is not automatically material. A fact will be regarded as material only if it is significant enough that it would likely affect an investor's decision as to whether to buy or sell the company's securities. For example, a company's potential liability in a product liability suit and the financial consequences to the firm are material facts that must be disclosed because they are significant enough to affect an investor's decision as to whether to buy stock in the company.

In this case, the plaintiffs' claim should not be dismissed. To prevail on their claim that the defendants made material omissions in violation of Section 10(b) and SEC Rule 10-5, the plaintiffs must prove that the omission was material. Their complaint alleged the omission of information linking Zicam and anosmia (a loss of the sense of smell) and plausibly suggested that reasonable investors would have viewed this information as material. Zicam products account for 70 percent of Matrixx's sales. Matrixx received reports of consumers who suffered anosia after using Zicam Cold Remedy.

In public statements discussing revenues and product safety, Matrixx did not disclose this information. But the information was significant enough to likely affect a consumer's decision to use the product, and this would affect revenue and ultimately the commercial viability of the product. The information was therefore significant enough to likely affect an investor's decision whether to buy or sell Matrixx's stock, and this would affect the stock price. Thus, the plaintiffs' allegations were sufficient. Contrary to the defendants' assertion, statistical sampling is not required to show materiality—reasonable investors could view reports of adverse events as material even if the reports did not provide statistically significant evidence.

32-4A. Case Problem with Sample Answer

No. DVRC's action does not represent an attempt to monopolize in violation of the Sherman Act. DVRC merely returned to a position that it had a right to have from the beginning. In their contract DVRC had expressly informed Christy that their relationship could change at any time. Thus, Christy knew from the beginning that its ski rental business could operate only with DVRC's permission, subject to DVRC's business judgment.

If DVRC had terminated a profitable relationship without any economic justification, it might have shown a willingness to forgo short-term profits to achieve an anticompetitive end. But there is no indication that DVRC terminated a profitable business relationship or that DVRC was motivated by anything other than a desire to increase profits. Rather than forgoing short-term profits, DVRC can expect to increase its short-term profits by operating its own ski rental facility.

The court in the case on which this problem is based dismissed Christy's suit, a decision that the U.S. Court of Appeals for the Tenth Circuit affirmed.

33–3A. Case Problem with Sample Answer

According to the facts set out in the problem, the Nutrition Labeling and Education Act (NLEA) does not regulate nutrition information labeling for restaurant food, and state and local governments can adopt their own rules. The NLEA does regulate nutrition content claims on restaurant food, however, and attempts by state and local governments to regulate those claims are expressly preempted.

The issue in this case is whether the calorie disclosures mandated for chain restaurants' menus and menu boards under New York City Health Code Section 81.50 are "information" or "claims." The types of information covered by the provision on "nutrition information" include "total number of calories." Thus, the calorie-content information required by Section 81.50 falls under this provision. Therefore, Section 81.50 is within the area that the NLEA leaves to state and local governments. In other words, the NLEA permits the information required by Section 81.50.

Therefore, federal law at the time of this dispute—before the new menu labeling requirements enacted in 2010 and discussed in the chapter—did not preempt this local regulation.

The court in the actual case on which this problem is based issued a summary judgment in the defendants' favor, and on the reasoning stated above, the U.S. Court of Appeals for the Second Circuit affirmed.

34–7A. Case Problem with Sample Answer

KPMG is potentially liable to the hedge funds' partners under the *Restatement (Third) of Torts*. Under Section 552 of the *Restatement,* an auditor owes a duty to "persons for whose benefit and guidance the accountant intends to supply . . . information."

In this case, KPMG prepared annual reports on the hedge funds and addressed them to the funds' "Partners." Additionally, KPMG knew who the partners were because it prepared individual tax forms for them each year. Thus, KPMG's annual reports were for the partners' benefit and guidance. The partners relied on the reports, including their representations that they complied with generally accepted accounting principles.

As a result, they lost millions of dollars, which exposes KPMG to possible liability under Section 552.

35–7A. Case Problem with Sample Answer

Moreland should be awarded damages, and Gray should take nothing. The bailee must exercise reasonable care in preserving the bailed property. What constitutes reasonable care in a bailment situation normally depends on the nature and specific circumstances of the bailment. If the bailed property has been lost or is returned damaged, a court will presume that the bailee was negligent.

In the circumstances of this problem, when the bailor (Moreland, the owner of the aircraft) entrusted the plane to the bailee's (Gray's)

repair shop for painting, the work was not properly performed. This violated the bailee's duty to exercise reasonable care and breached the bailment contract. Because the plane was returned damaged, this may also constitute negligence. In the event of a breach, the bailor may sue for damages. The measure of damages is the difference between the value of the bailed property in its present condition and what it would have been worth if the work had been properly performed.

Thus, Gray is liable to Moreland for failing to properly paint the plane. In the actual case on which this problem is based, the court upheld a jury award to Moreland of damages and attorneys' fees.

36–6A. Case Problem with Sample Answer

The McKeags satisfied the first three requirements for adverse possession:

1. Their possession was actual and exclusive because they used the beach and prevented others from doing so, including the Finleys.
2. Their possession was open, visible, and notorious because they made improvements to the beach and regularly kept their belongings there.
3. Their possession was continuous and peaceable for the required ten years. They possessed the property for more than four decades, and they even kept a large float there during the winter months.

Nevertheless, the McKeags' possession was *not* hostile and adverse, which is the fourth requirement. The Finleys had substantial evidence that they gave the McKeags permission to use the beach. Rather than reject the Finleys' permission as unnecessary, the McKeags sometimes said nothing and other times seemingly affirmed that the property belonged to the Finleys. Thus, because the McKeags did not satisfy all four requirements, they cannot establish adverse possession.

37–5A. Case Problem with Sample Answer

Arvin and Carolyn were not correct. An executed will is revocable by the testator at any time during his or her life. The physical acts by which a testator may revoke a will include intentionally canceling it. In some states, partial revocation by physical act is recognized. Thus, those portions of a will lined out can be dropped, and the remaining parts of the will can be given effect.

Here, Peterson clearly altered her will by crossing out Arvin's and Carolyn's names as the beneficiaries of the trust. Apparently, Peterson intended to cancel only this portion of the will, not the entire will—her alterations left the bequest to Lucas intact. There is no indication in the facts of undue influence or other improper circumstances. Thus, the part of the will that Peterson lined out can be dropped, and the rest of the will can be given effect.

In the actual case on which this problem is based, the court held that the will was valid as altered.

Case Excerpts for *Case Analysis Questions*

CASE NO. 1 FOR CHAPTER 4

Lott v. Levitt,
469 F.Supp.2d 575 (E.D.Ill. 2007)

In 2005, well-known economist Steven Levitt ("Levitt") and journalist Stephen J. Dubner ("Dubner") coauthored the best-selling book *Freakonomics*[.] * * * In the book, Levitt and Dubner [discuss] * * * the theory for which fellow economist, * * * John R. Lott, Jr. ("Lott"), is known[:] * * * that laws permitting individuals to carry concealed weapons result in a statistically significant and provable reduction in serious crime rates. Lott filed the instant lawsuit against Levitt and [others] * * * . Lott claims [in part] that an email written by Levitt to another economist * * * constitutes defamation * * * . [Levitt filed a motion to dismiss this claim.]
* * * *

Lott is discussed in the following single paragraph in Chapter 4 of *Freakonomics*, entitled "Where Have All the Criminals Gone?":

* * * There is an * * * argument—that we need more guns on the street, but in the hands of the right people * * * . The economist John R. Lott Jr. is the main champion of this idea. * * * [H]e argues that violent crime has decreased in areas where law abiding citizens are allowed to carry concealed weapons. His theory might be surprising, but it is sensible. If a criminal thinks his potential victim may be armed, he may be deterred from committing the crime. Handgun opponents call Lott a pro-gun ideologue * * * . There was the troubling allegation that Lott actually invented some of the survey data that support his more-guns/less-crime theory. Regardless of whether the data were faked, Lott's admittedly intriguing hypothesis doesn't seem to be true. When other scholars have tried to replicate his results, they found that right-to-carry laws simply don't bring down crime.

On May 24 or May 25, 2005, John McCall ("McCall"), described by Lott as an economist residing in Texas, sent Levitt an email regarding the above passage, stating:

I * * * found the following citations—have not read any of them yet, but it appears they all replicate Lott's research. [McCall referred to a "Special Issue" of *The Journal of Law and Economics* published in October 2001 that contained a collection of articles delivered at an academic conference co-sponsored by the Center for Law, Economics and Public Policy at Yale Law School and the American Enterprise Institute, where Lott had recently been a resident scholar.] *The Journal of Law and Economics* is not chopped liver.

That same day, Levitt responded:

It was not a peer refereed edition of the *Journal*. For $15,000 he was able to buy an issue and put in only work that supported him. My best friend was the editor and was outraged the press let Lott do this.
* * * *

A statement is considered defamatory if it tends to cause such harm to the reputation of another that it lowers that person in the eyes of the community or deters third persons from associating with that person. [Emphasis added.]
* * * *

* * * Lott contends that the statements about him in * * * the email * * * imply that his results were falsified or that his theories lack merit, and thus impute a lack of ability and integrity in his profession as an economist, academic, and researcher. Indeed, a claim that an academic or economist falsified his results and could only publish his theories by buying an issue of a journal and avoiding peer review would surely impute a lack of ability and prejudice that person in his profession.
* * * *

* * * *The First Amendment protects statements that cannot be reasonably interpreted as stating actual facts.* [Emphasis added.]

The test for whether a statement is a factual assertion is whether the statement is precise, readily understood, and susceptible of being verified as true or false. This test * * * is a reasonableness standard; whether a reasonable reader would understand the defendant to be informing him of a fact or opinion. Language that is loose, figurative, or hyperbolic negates the impression that a statement is asserting actual facts. Accordingly, *vague, unprovable statements and statements of opinion do not give rise to a defamation claim.* If it is plain that the speaker is expressing a subjective view, an interpretation, a theory, conjecture, or surmise, rather than claiming to be in possession of objectively verifiable facts, the statement is not actionable. [Emphasis added.]

In this case, however, Levitt's email sounds as if he was in possession of objectively verifiable facts. * * * First, it would be unreasonable to interpret Levitt's unqualified statement that the *Journal* edition was not "peer refereed" as Levitt [argues that he was] merely giving his opinion on the "peers" chosen to review, or referee, the Special Issue. Indeed, the editor of the *Journal* might be able to verify the truth or falsity of whether the Special Issue was reviewed by peers. * * * Second, a reasonable reader would not interpret Levitt's assertion that "For $15,000 [Lott] was able to buy an issue and put in only work that supported him" as simply a statement of Levitt's opinion. Levitt's email appears to state objectively verifiable facts: that Lott paid $15,000 to control the content of the Special Issue. The editor of the *Journal* again might be the source to verify the truth or falsity of this statement. Third, the same editor could verify whether he was "outraged" by the acts described in the foregoing statements. Therefore, the defamatory statements in Levitt's email to McCall are objectively verifiable * * *.

* * * *

* * * In his email to McCall, * * * Levitt made a string of defamatory assertions about Lott's involvement in the publication of the Special Issue of the *Journal* that—no matter how rash or short-sighted Levitt was when he made them—cannot be reasonably interpreted as innocent or mere opinion.

* * * Levitt's motion to dismiss [this part of Lott's] Complaint is denied.

CASE NO. 2 FOR CHAPTER 10

Feldman v. Google, Inc.,
513 F.Supp.2d 229 (E.D.Pa. 2007)

Before the court is Defendant Google, Inc.'s Motion to * * * Transfer [the case to Santa Clara County]. Also before the court is Plaintiff Lawrence E. Feldman's Cross-Motion for Summary Judgment. The ultimate issues raised by the motions and determined by the court are whether a forum selection clause in an Internet "clickwrap" agreement is enforceable * * *.

Defendant's motion seeks to enforce the forum selection clause in an online "clickwrap" agreement, which provides for venue in Santa Clara County * * *.

On or about January 2003, Plaintiff, a lawyer with his own law firm, Lawrence E. Feldman & Associates, purchased advertising from Defendant Google, Inc.'s "AdWords" Program, to attract potential clients who may have been harmed by drugs under scrutiny by the U.S. Food and Drug Administration.

In the AdWords program, whenever an internet user searched on the internet search engine, Google.com, for keywords or "Adwords" purchased by Plaintiff, such as "Vioxx," "Bextra," and "Celebrex," Plaintiff's ad would appear. If the searcher clicked on Plaintiff's ad, Defendant would charge Plaintiff for each click made on the ad.

This procedure is known as "pay per click" advertising. The price per keyword is determined by a bidding process, wherein the highest bidder for a keyword would have its ad placed at the top of the list of results from a Google.com search by an Internet user.

Plaintiff claims that he was the victim of "click fraud." Click fraud occurs when entities or persons, such as competitors or pranksters, without any interest in Plaintiff's services, click repeatedly on Plaintiff's ad, the result of which drives up his advertising cost and discourages him from advertising. * * * Plaintiff alleges that twenty to thirty percent of all clicks for which he was charged were fraudulent. He claims that Google required him to pay for all clicks on his ads, including those which were fraudulent.

* * * *

The type of contract at issue here is commonly referred to as a "clickwrap" agreement. A clickwrap agreement appears on an Internet web page and requires that a user consent to any terms or conditions by clicking on a dialog box on the screen in order to proceed with the Internet transaction. *Even though they are electronic, clickwrap agreements are considered to be writings because they are printable and storable.* [Emphasis added.]

To determine whether a clickwrap agreement is enforceable, courts * * * apply traditional principles of contract law and focus on whether the plaintiffs had reasonable notice of and manifested assent to the clickwrap agreement. *Absent a showing of fraud, failure to read an enforceable clickwrap agreement, as with any binding contract, will not excuse compliance with its terms.* [Emphasis added.]

* * * *

Plaintiff [Feldman] claims he did not have notice or knowledge of the forum selection clause, and therefore that there was no "meeting of the minds" required for contract formation.

* * * *

* * * In order to activate an AdWords account, the user had to visit a Web page which displayed the Agreement in a scrollable text box. * * * The user did not have to scroll down to a submerged screen or click on a series of hyperlinks to view the Agreement. Instead, text of the AdWords Agreement was immediately visible to the user, as was a prominent admonition in bold-face to read the terms and conditions carefully, and with instruction to indicate assent if the user agreed to the terms.

That the user would have to scroll through the text box of the Agreement to read it in its entirety does not defeat notice because there was sufficient notice of the Agreement itself and clicking "Yes" constituted assent to all of the terms. The preamble, which was immediately visible, also made clear that assent to the terms was binding. The Agreement was presented in readable 12-point font. It was only seven paragraphs long—not so long so as to render scrolling down to view all of the terms inconvenient or impossible. A printer-friendly, full-screen version was made readily available. The user had ample time to review the document.

* * * The user * * * had to take affirmative action and click the "Yes, I agree to the above terms and conditions" button in order to proceed to the next step. Clicking "Continue" without clicking the "Yes" button would have returned the user to the same Web page. If the user did not agree to all of the terms, he could not have activated his account, placed ads, or incurred charges.

* * * *

A reasonably prudent Internet user would have known of the existence of terms in the AdWords Agreement. Plaintiff had to have had reasonable notice of the terms. By clicking on "Yes, I agree to the above terms and conditions" button, Plaintiff indicated assent to the terms.

* * * *

For the foregoing reasons, * * * Defendant's motion to transfer is granted and Plaintiff's motion for summary judgment is denied.

CASE NO. 3 FOR CHAPTER 15

Spray-Tek, Inc. v. Robbins Motor Transportation, Inc., 426 F.Supp.2d 875 (W.D.Wis. 2006)

* * * *

Plaintiff Spray-Tek, Inc. is engaged in the business of commercial dehydration of food flavor, pharmaceutical and soft chemical products. In 2003 plaintiff entered into a contract with Niro, Inc. (hereinafter Niro) in which Niro was to design and manufacture a fourteen-foot diameter conebottom drying chamber * * * for plaintiff. Pursuant to the terms of the contract Niro was also responsible for shipping the drying chamber from its facility in Hudson, Wisconsin to plaintiff's facility in Bethlehem, Pennsylvania. The contract stated in relevant part:

* * * *

For one (1) Niro-Bowen * * * drying chamber, * * * F.O.B. points of manufacture in the U.S.A. * * * Price * * * $1,161,500.00.

* * * *

IX. RISKS OF LOSS. The Purchaser shall bear the risk of loss of or damage to the equipment and parts after delivery of the equipment and parts to the job site or to the shipping point if delivery F.O.B. shipping point is specified.

On October 14, 2004, Niro's representative Mr. David Thoen contacted defendant Robbins Motor Transportation, Inc. to obtain an estimate for transporting the drying chamber to plaintiff. * * * Mr. Robert Kauffman, Jr. who serves as defendant's Southwest Regional Terminal Manager * * * prepared and sent an estimate to Niro.

Mr. Thoen signed the estimate and faxed it back to defendant * * * .

On October 18, 2004, defendant arrived at Niro's facility in Hudson, Wisconsin and the drying chamber was loaded onto its trailer. Niro prepared a Bill of Lading * * * .

* * * *

On or about October 28, 2004 the drying chamber was damaged while it was in transit * * * when it struck an overpass and became dislodged from defendant's vehicle. It was inspected and declared a total loss. Accordingly, Niro manufactured a replacement drying chamber for plaintiff and invoiced it $233,100.00 in replacement costs.

* * * *

[Spray-Tek filed a suit in a federal district court against Robbins under a federal statute known as the Carmack Amendment to recover the replacement cost and other expenses.] The Carmack Amendment * * * states in relevant part:

A carrier providing transportation or service * * * shall issue a receipt or bill of lading for property it receives for transportation under this part. That carrier * * * [is] liable to the person entitled to recover under the receipt or bill of lading.

The purpose of the Carmack Amendment is to establish uniform federal guidelines designed in part to remove the uncertainty surrounding a carrier's liability when damage occurs to a shipper's interstate shipment.

Under the Carmack Amendment plaintiff bears the burden of establishing a *prima facie* [legally sufficient] case which requires it to demonstrate: (1) delivery to the carrier in good condition; (2) arrival in damaged condition; and (3) the amount of damages. * * * The excepted causes [relieving a carrier of liability] are: (1) acts of God; (2) the public enemy; (3) acts of the shipper himself; (4) public authority; or (5) the inherent vice or nature of the goods.

Defendant concedes that it received the drying chamber in good condition. Accordingly, plaintiff's first element of its *prima facie* case is established.

* * * *

It is undisputed that the drying chamber was damaged when it struck an overpass and became dislodged from defendant's vehicle. Additionally, it is undisputed that after the accident the drying chamber was inspected and declared a total loss.

An * * * argument defendant asserts concerning plaintiff's second element of its *prima facie* case is that plaintiff cannot demonstrate it owned the drying chamber during transport. However, the contract plaintiff entered into with Niro establishes that it was the owner of the drying chamber when it was damaged. The contract provided that the terms of sale were "F.O.B. points of manufacture in the U.S.A." According to * * * plaintiff's vice president and general manager "F.O.B. points of manufacture" means that the drying chamber became plaintiff's property once it was "placed on board the delivery truck at its point of manufacture in Hudson, Wisconsin."

[This] assertion * * * is reinforced by the provision in the contract concerning risks of loss. * * * [T]he "F.O.B. points of manufacture" language * * * demonstrates that plaintiff bore the risk of loss once the drying chamber departed from Niro's Hudson, Wisconsin facility. * * * Accordingly, plaintiff established the second element of its *prima facie* case.

Finally, defendant asserts plaintiff cannot meet its burden of establishing the third element of its *prima facie* case because it failed to demonstrate what "it is obligated to pay for the dryer." However, * * * Niro invoiced plaintiff $233,100.00 for the replacement dryer. Accordingly, plaintiff established the third element of its *prima facie* case because its amount of damages is $233,100.00.

Plaintiff met its burden of establishing a *prima facie* case under the Carmack Amendment. * * * Defendant concedes it failed to produce any evidence establishing that damage to the shipment was due to one of the excepted causes. Accordingly, plaintiff is entitled to summary judgment on the issue of defendant's liability under the Carmack Amendment.

* * * *

[The court allowed the case to go to trial on another issue, however.]

CASE NO. 4 FOR CHAPTER 19

NBT Bank, N.A. v. First National Community Bank,
393 F.3d 404 (3d Cir. 2004)

* * * *

* * * [A] small group of Pennsylvania business entities arranged to write checks on one account, drawing on non-existent funds, and then cover these overdrafts with checks drawn on another account that also lacked sufficient funds. * * * The scheme collapsed when three checks initially deposited at [NBT Bank, N.A.,] and subsequently presented for payment to [First National Community Bank (FNCB)] were discovered by FNCB to have been drawn on an FNCB account that lacked sufficient funds. There is no dispute between the parties that two of these three checks were properly returned by FNCB to the [Federal Reserve Bank of Philadelphia] prior to the applicable midnight deadline.

* * * *

[On March 8, 2001, the third check (the "Disputed Check"), which was drawn on an FNCB account in the amount of $706,000, was deposited at NBT by an entity called PA Health.] After the Disputed Check was presented for deposit at NBT, the bank gave provisional credit to the depositor, PA Health, for the amount of the Disputed Check. NBT also transmitted the Disputed Check to the Reserve Bank for presentment to FNCB. * * * The Reserve Bank then forwarded the Disputed Check to FNCB, and FNCB received it on March 12, 2001.

* * * *

On March 13, 2001, FNCB determined it would not pay the Disputed Check because of the absence of sufficient funds in the account on which the check was drawn. That same day, FNCB sought to return the Disputed Check to NBT through the Reserve Bank. * * * [T]he Disputed Check was physically delivered to the Reserve Bank prior to 11:59 P.M. on March 13.* * * FNCB also sent a notice of dishonor to NBT * * * in which FNCB indicated that it did not intend to pay the Disputed Check. NBT received this notice prior to the close of business on March 13.

* * * *

When FNCB sent the Disputed Check to the Reserve Bank on March 13, 2001, FNCB * * * erroneously encoded [it] with the routing number for PNC Bank instead of the routing number for NBT [Bank].

* * * Because the Disputed Check was improperly encoded, NBT did not receive it back * * * until March 16, 2001. * * * NBT suffered no damages or actual loss as a result of the encoding error * * *.

* * * *

NBT instituted this action [in a federal district court] against FNCB on May 25, 2001. * * * NBT claimed that FNCB's encoding error meant FNCB had failed to return the Disputed Check prior to the midnight deadline as required by the UCC, and that FNCB was therefore accountable to NBT for the full amount of the Disputed Check.

The District Court granted FNCB's motion [for summary judgment]. NBT appeals.

* * * *

* * * Federal law forms part of the legal framework within which check-processing activities take place. Of particular relevance to this appeal are the 1988 regulations adopted by the Federal Reserve implementing the Expedited Funds Availability Act. These regulations, referred to collectively as "Regulation CC," complement but do not necessarily replace the requirements of Article 4 of the UCC.

* * * *

* * * Regulation CC indisputably binds the parties, pursuant to both its own terms, as well as [13 Pennsylvania Consolidated Statutes Annotated Section 4103 (Pennsylvania's version of UCC 4–103)], which indicates that "Federal Reserve regulations" are to be treated as agreements that may vary the terms of the UCC.

Because Regulation CC * * * is binding on the parties, and because Regulation CC is the source of the encoding requirement invoked by NBT, the extent of FNCB's liability for its encoding error must be measured by the standards set forth in Regulation CC. *Regulation CC states that a bank that fails to exercise ordinary care in complying with the [encoding] provisions of * * * Regulation CC * * * "may be liable" to the depositary bank.* Then, in broad, unrestricted language, Regulation CC states: [Emphasis added.]

> The measure of damages for failure to exercise ordinary care is the amount of the loss incurred, up to the amount of the check, reduced by the amount of the loss that the [plaintiff bank] would have incurred even if the [defendant] bank had exercised ordinary care.

This provision does not provide an exception to this standard for measuring damages in instances where noncompliance with Regulation CC is alleged to have resulted in noncompliance with the UCC's midnight deadline rule. Here, the parties have stipulated that NBT suffered no loss as a result of FNCB's encoding error. Thus, under the plain language of Regulation CC, NBT may not recover from FNCB for the amount of the Disputed Check.

* * * *

Accordingly,* * * we affirm the order of the District Court * * *.

CASE NO. 5 FOR CHAPTER 25

Burlington Northern and Santa Fe Railway Co. v. White,
548 U.S. 53, 126 S.Ct. 2405, 165 L.Ed.2d 345 (2006)

* * * *

* * * Sheila White [was] the only woman working in the Maintenance of Way department at [Burlington Northern & Santa Fe Railway Company's] Tennessee Yard. In September 1997, White complained to Burlington officials that her * * * supervisor, Bill Joiner, had repeatedly told her that women should not be working in the Maintenance of Way department. [Joiner was disciplined. White was reassigned from forklift duty to "track laborer" tasks.]

* * * *

On October 10, White filed a complaint with the Equal Employment Opportunity Commission (EEOC * * *).

[In December, White's supervisor, Percy Sharkey, complained to Burlington officials that White had been insubordinate. She was suspended without pay but reinstated after an investigation and awarded back pay for the period of the suspension. White filed a second charge with the EEOC.]

* * * *

* * * [Later] White filed this Title VII action against Burlington in federal [district] court. * * * [S]he claimed that Burlington's actions—(1) changing her job responsibilities, and (2) suspending her * * * without pay—amounted to unlawful retaliation in violation of Title VII. A jury found in White's favor * * * [and] awarded her $43,500 in * * * damages * * * .

* * * [On appeal, the U.S. Court of Appeals for the Sixth Circuit held that Title VII's antiretaliation ban is limited to acts that adversely affect the terms, conditions, or benefits of employment, and] affirmed the District Court's judgment in White's favor on both retaliation claims. [Burlington appealed to the United States Supreme Court.]

* * * *

* * * The language of the [antidiscrimination] provision differs from that of the antiretaliation provision in important ways.

The * * * words in the [antidiscrimination] provision—"hire," "discharge," "compensation, terms, conditions, or privileges of employment," "employment opportunities," and "status as an employee"—explicitly limit the scope of that provision to actions that affect employment or alter the conditions of the workplace. No such limiting words appear in the antiretaliation provision.

* * * The two provisions differ not only in language but in purpose as well. The antidiscrimination provision seeks a workplace where individuals are not discriminated against because of their racial, ethnic, religious, or gender-based status. *The antiretaliation provision seeks to secure that primary objective by preventing an employer from interfering (through retaliation) with an employee's efforts to secure or advance enforcement of the Act's basic guarantees.* The [antidiscrimination] provision seeks to prevent injury to individuals based on who they are, i.e., their status. *The antiretaliation provision seeks to prevent harm to individuals based on what they do, i.e., their conduct.* [Emphasis added.]

To secure the first objective, Congress did not need to prohibit anything other than employment related discrimination.

But one cannot secure the second objective by focusing only upon employer actions and harm that concern employment and the workplace. * * * *An employer can effectively retaliate against an employee by taking actions not directly related to his employment or by causing him harm outside the workplace.* [Emphasis added.]

* * * *

* * * We conclude that * * * the anti-retaliation provision extends beyond workplace related or employment-related retaliatory acts * * * .

* * * *

* * * A plaintiff must show that a reasonable employee would have found the challenged action materially adverse, which in this context means it well might have dissuaded a reasonable worker from making or supporting a charge of discrimination.

* * * *

* * * [In this case] the track labor duties were by all accounts more arduous and dirtier; * * * the forklift operator position required more qualifications, which is an indication of prestige; and * * * the forklift operator position was objectively considered a better job and the male employees resented White for occupying it. Based on this record, a jury could reasonably conclude that the reassignment of responsibilities would have been materially adverse to a reasonable employee.

* * * *

For these reasons, the judgment of the Court of Appeals is affirmed.

CASE NO. 6 FOR CHAPTER 31

Merrill Lynch, Pierce, Fenner & Smith, Inc. v. Dabit,
547 U.S. 71, 126 S.Ct. 1503, 164 L.Ed.2d 179 (2006)

* * * *

Petitioner Merrill Lynch, Pierce, Fenner & Smith, Inc. (Merrill Lynch), * * * offers research and brokerage services to investors.

Respondent, Shadi Dabit, is a former Merrill Lynch broker. He filed this class action in the United States District Court for the Western District of Oklahoma on behalf of himself and all other former or current brokers who, while employed by Merrill Lynch, purchased (for themselves and for their clients) certain stocks between December 1, 1999, and December 31, 2000. * * * Dabit * * * advanced his claims under Oklahoma state law.

* * * [Dabit's theory was that Merrill Lynch] research analysts * * * issued overly optimistic appraisals of the stocks' value; the brokers * * * relied on the analysts' reports in advising their investor clients * * * ; and the clients and brokers both continued to hold their stocks long beyond the point when, had the truth been known, they would have sold. * * * [W]hen the truth was actually revealed * * * , the stocks' prices plummeted.

* * * *

* * * [The case was transferred] to the United States District Court for the Southern District of New York * * * [which granted Merrill Lynch's motion to dismiss. The U.S. Court of Appeals for the Second Circuit reversed this ruling. Merrill Lynch appealed to the United States Supreme Court.]

* * * *

The magnitude of the federal interest in protecting the integrity and efficient operation of the market for nationally traded securities cannot be overstated. In response to the sudden and disastrous collapse in prices of listed stocks in 1929, and the Great Depression that followed, Congress enacted the Securities Act of 1933, and the Securities Exchange Act of 1934. Since their enactment, these two statutes have anchored federal regulation of vital elements of our economy.

* * * *

Policy considerations * * * prompted Congress, in 1995, to adopt [the Private Securities Litigation Reform Act] targeted at perceived abuses of the class-action vehicle in litigation involving nationally traded securities.

* * * *

* * * [P]laintiffs and their representatives began bringing class actions under state law, often in state court. * * * To stem this shift from Federal to State courts * * * , Congress enacted SLUSA.

* * * *

The core provision of SLUSA reads as follows:

* * * No * * * class action based upon the * * * law of any State * * * may be maintained in any * * * court by any private party alleging—* * * a misrepresentation or omission of a material fact in connection with the purchase or sale of a * * * security * * * .

* * * *

* * * Under our precedents, it is enough that the fraud alleged "coincide" with a securities transaction—whether by the plaintiff or by someone else. *The requisite showing, in other words, is deception "in connection with the purchase or sale of any security," not deception of an identifiable purchaser or seller.* Notably, this broader interpretation of the statutory language comports [is consistent] with the longstanding views of the [Securities and Exchange Commission (SEC)]. [Emphasis added.]

Congress can hardly have been unaware of the broad construction adopted by both this Court and the SEC when it imported the key phrase—"in connection with the purchase or sale"—into SLUSA's core provision. *And when judicial interpretations have settled the meaning of an existing statutory provision, repetition of the same language in a new statute indicates * * * the intent to incorporate its * * * judicial interpretations as well.* [Emphasis added.]

* * * A narrow reading of the statute would undercut the effectiveness of the 1995 Reform Act and thus run contrary to SLUSA's stated purpose "to prevent certain State private securities class action lawsuits alleging fraud from being used to frustrate the objectives" of the 1995 Act.

* * * The prospect is raised, then, of parallel class actions proceeding in state and federal court, with different standards governing claims asserted on identical facts. That prospect * * * squarely conflicts with the congressional preference for national standards for securities class action lawsuits involving nationally traded securities.

* * * *

The judgment of the Court of Appeals for the Second Circuit is vacated, and the case is remanded * * * .

CASE NO. 7 FOR CHAPTER 36

Kelo v. City of New London, Connecticut,
545 U.S. 469, 125 S.Ct. 2655, 162 L.Ed.2d 439 (2005)

* * * *

The city of New London (hereinafter City) sits at the junction of the Thames River and the Long Island Sound in southeastern Connecticut. Decades of economic decline led a state agency in 1990 to designate the City a "distressed municipality." In 1996, the Federal Government closed the Naval Undersea Warfare Center, which had been located in the Fort Trumbull area of the City and had employed over 1,500 people. In 1998, the City's unemployment rate was nearly double that of the State, and its population of just under 24,000 residents was at its lowest since 1920.

These conditions prompted state and local officials to target New London * * * for economic revitalization. * * * In February [1998] the pharmaceutical company Pfizer Inc. announced that it would build a $300 million research facility on a site immediately adjacent to Fort Trumbull; local planners hoped that Pfizer would draw new business to the area * * * .

* * * *

The city council approved [a] plan in January 2000 [to redevelop the area that once housed the federal facility]. The [City] successfully negotiated the purchase of most of the real estate in the 90-acre area, but its negotiations with [some of the property owners] failed. As a consequence, in November 2000, the [City] initiated * * * condemnation proceedings * * * .

* * * *

* * * Susette Kelo has lived in the Fort Trumbull area since 1997. * * * [S]he prizes [her house] for its water view. * * *

In December 2000 [Kelo and others] brought this action in [a Connecticut state court against the City and others]. They claimed, among other things, that the taking of their properties would violate the "public use" restriction in the [U.S. Constitution's] Fifth Amendment. * * * [The court issued a ruling partly in favor of both sides].

* * * [B]oth sides took appeals to the Supreme Court of Connecticut [which] held * * * that all of the City's proposed takings were valid.

* * * *

We granted *certiorari* to determine whether a city's decision to take property for the purpose of economic development satisfies the "public use" requirement of the Fifth Amendment.

* * * *

* * * [T]his Court long ago rejected any literal requirement that condemned property be put into use for the general public. * * * Not only was the "use by the public" test difficult to administer (e.g., what proportion of the public need have access to the property? at what price?), but it proved to be impractical given the diverse and always evolving needs of society. Accordingly, * * * *this Court * * * embraced the broader and more natural interpretation of public use as "public purpose."* * * * [Emphasis added.]

The disposition of this case therefore turns on the question whether the City's development plan serves a "public purpose."

* * * *

Viewed as a whole, our jurisprudence has recognized that the needs of society have varied between different parts of the Nation, just as they have evolved over time in response to changed circumstances. * * * *For more than a century, our public use jurisprudence has wisely eschewed [avoided] rigid formulas and intrusive scrutiny in favor of affording legislatures broad latitude in* *determining what public needs justify the use of the takings power.* [Emphasis added.]

* * * *

Those who govern the City were not confronted with the need to remove blight in the Fort Trumbull area, but their determination that the area was sufficiently distressed to justify a program of economic rejuvenation is entitled to our deference. The City has carefully formulated an economic development plan that it believes will provide appreciable benefits to the community, including—but by no means limited to—new jobs and increased tax revenue. * * * To effectuate this plan, the City has invoked a state statute that specifically authorizes the use of eminent domain to promote economic development. Given the comprehensive character of the plan, the thorough deliberation that preceded its adoption, and the limited scope of our review, it is appropriate for us * * * to resolve the challenges of the individual owners, not on a piecemeal basis, but rather in light of the entire plan. *Because that plan unquestionably serves a public purpose, the takings challenged here satisfy the public use requirement of the Fifth Amendment.* [Emphasis added.]

* * * *

The judgment of the Supreme Court of Connecticut is affirmed.

Additional Cases

TABLE OF CASES

Case 4-1

In addition to showing that the tortfeasor engaged in negligent conduct (duty and breach), the victim of negligence must show that the breach was the proximate cause of harm to him. This case examines the issue of proximate cause.

Palsgraf v. Long Island Railroad Co.
Court of Appeals of New York, 1928
248 N.Y. 339; 162 N.E. 99

CARDOZO, C.J.

Plaintiff was standing on a platform of defendant's railroad after buying a ticket to go to Rockaway Beach. A train stopped at the station, bound for another place. Two men ran forward to catch it. One of the men reached the platform of the car without mishap, though the train was already moving. The other man, carrying a package, jumped aboard the car, but seemed unsteady as if about to fall. A guard on the car, who had held the door open, reached forward to help him in, and another guard on the platform pushed him from behind. In this act, the package was dislodged, and fell upon the rails. It was a package of small size, about fifteen inches long, and was covered by a newspaper. In fact it contained fireworks, but there was nothing in its appearance to give notice of its contents. The fireworks when they fell exploded. The shock of the explosion threw down some scales at the other end of the platform, many feet away. The scales struck the plaintiff, causing injuries for which she sues.

The conduct of the defendant's guard, if a wrong in its relation to the holder of the package, was not a wrong in its relation to the plaintiff, standing far away. Relatively to her it was not negligence at all. Nothing in the situation gave notice that the falling package had in it the potency of peril to persons thus removed. Negligence is not actionable unless it involves the invasion of a legally protected interest, the violation of a right. "Proof of negligence in the air, so to speak, will not do" [Citations] "Negligence is the absence of care, according to the circumstances." [Citations]

* * *

If no hazard was apparent to the eye of ordinary vigilance, an act innocent and harmless, at least to outward seeming, with reference to her, did not take to itself the quality of a tort because it happened to be a wrong, though apparently not one involving the risk of bodily insecurity, with reference to someone else. "In every instance, before negligence can be predicated of a given act, back of the act must be sought and found a duty to the individual complaining, the observance of which would have averted or avoided the injury." [Citation].

* * *

A different conclusion will involve us, and swiftly too, in a maze of contradictions. A guard stumbles over a package which has been left upon a platform. It seems to be a bundle of newspapers. It turns out to be a can of dynamite. To the eye of ordinary vigilance, the bundle is abandoned waste, which may be kicked or trod on with impunity. Is a passenger at the other end of the platform protected by the law against the unsuspected hazard concealed beneath the waste? If not, is the result to be any different, so far as the distant passenger is concerned, when the guard stumbles over a valise which a truckman or a porter has left upon the walk? The passenger far away, if the victim of a wrong at all, has a cause of action, not derivative, but original and primary. His claim to be protected against invasion of his bodily security is neither greater nor less because the act resulting in the invasion is a wrong to another far removed. In this case, the rights that are said to have been violated, the interests said to have been invaded, are not even of the same order. The man was not injured in his person nor even put in danger. The purpose of the act, as well as its effect, was to make his person safe. If there was a wrong to him at all, which may very well be doubted, it was a wrong to a property interest only, the safety of his package. Out of this wrong to property, which threatened injury to nothing else, there has passed, we are told, to the plaintiff by derivation or succession a right of action for the invasion of an interest of another order, the right to bodily security. The diversity of interests emphasizes the futility of the effort to build the plaintiff's right upon the basis of a wrong to someone else. . . . One who jostles one's neighbor in a crowd does not invade the rights of others standing at the outer fringe when the unintended contact casts a bomb upon the ground. The wrongdoer as to them is the man who carries the bomb, not the one who explodes it without suspicion of the danger. Life will have to be made over, and human nature transformed, before prevision so extravagant can be accepted as the norm of conduct, the customary standard to which behavior must conform.

The argument for the plaintiff is built upon the shifting meanings of such words as "wrong" and "wrongful," and shares their instability. What the plaintiff must show is "a wrong" to herself, *i. e.*, a violation of her own right, and not merely a wrong to someone else, nor conduct "wrongful" because unsocial, but not "a wrong" to anyone. We are told that one who drives at reckless speed through a crowded city street is guilty of a negligent act and, therefore, of a wrongful one irrespective of the consequences. Negligent the act is, and wrongful in the sense that it is unsocial, but wrongful and unsocial in relation to other travelers, only because the eye of vigilance perceives the risk of damage. If the same act were to be committed on a speedway or a race course, it would lose its wrongful quality. The risk reasonably to be perceived defines the duty to be obeyed, and risk imports relation; it is risk to another or to others within the range of apprehension. [Citations] This does not mean, of course, that one who launches a destructive force is always relieved of liability if the force, though known to be destructive, pursues an unexpected path. "It was not necessary that the defendant should have had notice of the particular method in which an accident would occur, if

the possibility of an accident was clear to the ordinarily prudent eye." [Citations] Some acts, such as shooting, are so imminently dangerous to anyone who may come within reach of the missile, however unexpectedly, as to impose a duty of prevision not far from that of an insurer. Even today, and much oftener in earlier stages of the law, one acts sometimes at one's peril. [Citation] Under this head, it may be, fall certain cases of what is known as transferred intent, an act willfully dangerous to A resulting by misadventure in injury to B. [Citation] These cases aside, wrong is defined in terms of the natural or probable, at least when unintentional. [Citation] The range of reasonable apprehension is at times a question for the court, and at times, if varying inferences are possible, a question for the jury. Here, by concession, there was nothing in the situation to suggest to the most cautious mind that the parcel wrapped in newspaper would spread wreckage through the station. If the guard had thrown it down knowingly and willfully, he would not have threatened the plaintiff's safety, so far as appearances could warn him. His conduct would not have involved, even then, an unreasonable probability of invasion of her bodily security. Liability can be no greater where the act is inadvertent.

* * *

The judgment of the Appellate Division and that of the Trial Term should be reversed, and the complaint dismissed, with costs in all courts.

CASE 9-1

An implied in fact contract may be formed by the conduct of the parties, rather than by their words. This case illustrates how a court determines whether such a contract was formed, and if so, what its terms are.

WATTS v. COLUMBIA ARTISTS MANAGEMENT INC.
Appellate Division, New York (3rd Dept.), 1992
188 A.D.2d 799, 591 N.Y.S.2d 234

CASEY, Justice. Appeal (transferred to this court by order of the Appellate Division, Second Department) from a judgment of the Supreme Court (Weiner, J.), entered May 17, 1991 in Rockland County, upon a decision of the court in favor of defendant.

Plaintiff, a concert pianist, commenced this declaratory judgment action seeking, *inter alia,* a determination of his liability to defendant, which provides managerial services to performing artists, for services performed by defendant prior to September 1,

1988. Defendant began to provide its services to plaintiff in 1983 when it entered into a contract with Andre Watts Performances Inc. (hereinafter the Corporation), which provided that defendant would act as plaintiff's exclusive agent and that defendant would be compensated for its services by receiving, *inter alia,* 15% of plaintiff's earnings for American concerts, but defendant would be entitled to no fee if plaintiff was not paid for an engagement. Although the Corporation dissolved in August 1985 and the term of the contract expired September 1, 1986, defendant continued to provide services to plaintiff and plaintiff continued to pay for those services in the manner provided for in the expired contract between defendant and the Corporation. Plaintiff notified defendant in writing on August 9, 1988 that he wished to terminate his relationship with defendant effective September 1, 1988.

When the parties' relationship was terminated, defendant had scheduled a total of 82 engagements for plaintiff for the next two concert seasons. Contracts had been executed as of September 1, 1988 for 48 of the 82 scheduled engagements, and plaintiff performed and was paid for 46 of those 48 engagements. Of the remaining 34 scheduled engagements, for which no contract had been executed as of September 1, 1988, plaintiff performed 33 of them and was paid for 32 of the performances. Defendant claims entitlement to its 15% commission for all 78 of the engagements performed by plaintiff for which he was paid. Plaintiff contends that defendant is entitled to no commission on the 32 engagements for which no contract had been executed prior to September 1, 1988. As to the remaining 46 engagements, plaintiff contends that defendant is entitled only to one half of its usual 15% commission because additional managerial services, including travel arrangements, rehearsal schedules, piano delivery and tuning, receptions, master classes and other details, were required after September 1, 1988. According to plaintiff, the additional services were performed by another manager retained by plaintiff after September 1, 1988.

At the nonjury trial, plaintiff, an officer of defendant and other witnesses testified. Much of the testimony concerned the managerial services provided to plaintiff in particular and the industry practice in general. Supreme Court found that a contract implied in fact existed between the parties with the same terms and conditions as the expired written contract between the Corporation and defendant, and that defendant was entitled to full commissions for all 78 engagements at issue. Plaintiff appeals from the judgment entered on Supreme Court's decision.

According to plaintiff, Supreme Court erred in "piercing the corporate veil" to bind plaintiff to the terms and conditions of a contract to which he was not a party. Although Supreme Court's decision is not entirely clear on the issue, we read it as finding a separate and distinct contractual relationship between plaintiff and defendant, implied in fact, which arose out of the parties' continued relationship after the Corporation was dissolved and the written contract expired. A contract implied in fact rests upon the conduct of the parties and not their verbal or written words [Citation] Thus, the theories of express contract and of contract implied in fact are mutually exclusive [Citation] Whether an implied-in-fact contract was formed and, if so, the extent of its terms involve factual issues regarding the intent of the parties and the surrounding circumstances [Citation]. We are of the view that the parties' conduct after the expiration of the written contract, including defendant's continued rendition of services, plaintiff's acceptance of those services and plaintiff's payment of commissions in accordance with the terms of the written contract, clearly establish a contract implied in fact with substantially the same terms and conditions as embodied in the expired written contract between defendant and the Corporation [Citations]. The mere fact that plaintiff was not a party to the written contract does not preclude the formation of a new contract, implied in fact, between plaintiff and defendant, with terms and conditions similar to those contained in the written contract.

The remaining question is whether defendant was entitled to full commissions on all 78 engagements booked by defendant prior to September 1, 1988 for which plaintiff was ultimately paid, as found by Supreme Court, or whether defendant was limited to the recovery of one half of its regular commission on only those 46 engagements for which a contract had been executed prior to September 1, 1988, as plaintiff contends. The evidence establishes that an engagement was booked by defendant when it arranged the date, time and fee for a performance, informed plaintiff of the engagement and was informed by plaintiff that he accepted the engagement. Plaintiff offered evidence that additional management services prior to the execution of a contract are necessary to assure a meeting of the minds between the presenter and plaintiff on the essential terms of the engagement. Defendant offered evidence that the essential terms of date, time and fee were arranged with the booking and that the execution of a contract was largely a formality, involving ministerial details. That plaintiff actually performed 33 of the 34 engagements booked by defendant for which no contract was executed prior to September 1, 1988 tends to support defendant's position. In any event, the terms of the written contract, which were continued by the parties in their new contract implied in fact formed after the expiration of the written contract, contains no reference to the execution of a formal contract with the presenter. Rather, defendant's commission is dependent upon the scheduling of the engagement during the term of the contract and plaintiff's receipt of payment for the engagement. We conclude, therefore, that Supreme Court correctly found plaintiff liable for commissions on all 78 bookings, regardless of whether a contract had been executed prior to September 1, 1988.

We also agree with Supreme Court that defendant is entitled to the full commission on each of the engagements. As previously noted, defendant earned its commission when the engagement was booked and plaintiff received payment for his performance, and it is undisputed that defendant remained ready, willing and able to provide the additional management services which plaintiff contends were necessary before he actually performed the engagements booked by defendant. That plaintiff elected to have those services performed by another manager does not, in the facts and circumstances revealed by the evidence in the record, preclude defendant from receiving the full amount of its commissions. Supreme Court's judgment should, therefore, be affirmed.

ORDERED that the judgment is affirmed, with costs.

CASE 9-2

Here a court applies the doctrine of promissory estoppel to an entertainer's promise to appear in a musical production although no contract had yet been agreed to.

ELVIN ASSOCIATES V. ARETHA FRANKLIN
United States District Court, S.D. New York, 1990
735 F. Supp. 1171

Whitman Knapp, District Judge.

* * *

In early 1984 Ashton Springer, the principal of plaintiff Elvin Associates, began efforts to mount a Broadway musical production about the life and music of Mahalia Jackson, and wrote to defendant Aretha Franklin seeking her agreement to appear in the title role. Franklin called Springer and expressed her strong interest in the production, and told Springer to contact her agents at the William Morris Agency. Springer spoke with Phil Citron and Katy Rothacker of that agency and in several conversations with the latter discussed the basic financial terms of Franklin's engagement to appear. Several proposals and counter-proposals were exchanged, in each instance relayed by Rothacker to Franklin and then back to Springer. Near the end of February 1984, Rothacker called Springer and informed him that his final proposal was acceptable.

In the interim, Springer had already set about making the necessary arrangements to get the production going. He was in frequent consultation with Franklin concerning artistic and production matters, although he negotiated the financial terms of the agreement strictly through her agents. During a conversation about rehearsal and performance dates, Franklin indicated to Springer that there were no other conflicting engagements on her schedule, stating: "This is what I am doing."

After consulting with Franklin, Springer hired George Faison as director-choreographer. In the second week of March, Springer and Faison flew to Detroit to meet with Franklin to discuss various aspects of the production, including rehearsal and performance dates. Franklin agreed on a tentative schedule that called for rehearsals to begin in April and performances to begin in May.

After returning to New York, Springer began negotiating limited partnership agreements with various investors to finance the "Mahalia" production. He also began calling promoters and theaters in various cities in an effort to reserve dates for performances. During discussions with several promoters he learned for the first time that Franklin had recently cancelled several performances, purportedly due to a newly acquired fear of flying. Springer spoke with Citron at William Morris regarding these incidents, and the latter stated that the cancellations resulted from commitments made by prior agents for Franklin without her approval, and reassured Springer that there was no such problem here. Springer also spoke with Franklin, who reassured him that she wanted to do the show and that she would fly as necessary. Springer offered to make alternative arrangements for transportation to the various performance sites, and to alter the performance schedule to accommodate slower forms of transportation. Franklin told Springer that she was uncomfortable traveling more than 200 miles per day by ground transportation, but strongly assured him that she would overcome her fear of flying.

Springer had also in the interim contacted Jay Kramer, his attorney, about the proposed production and the terms he had discussed with Franklin's representatives. Kramer set up a meeting for March 23, 1984 with Franklin's representatives for the purpose of finalizing the agreement.

* * *

A final draft of the contract was ready for signature as of June 7, the date that Franklin was scheduled to come to New York to begin rehearsals for the show.

Springer had in the intervening weeks made all of the arrangements necessary for rehearsals to begin. He had hired set, lighting and costume designers, stage and technical crew, and had reserved dance studios. Springer was in frequent communication with Franklin during this period, as were Faison and other members of the production staff, concerning such varied matters as the compositions to be performed, the costumes she would wear, and the hiring of her own regular backup singers to be in the chorus. At one point, Franklin sang one of the production songs to Springer over the telephone. At some point during this period, Faison made final determinations as to the compositions to be performed and as to the cast and chorus.

As planned, rehearsals actually began on June 4 without Franklin, and continued for several days. Franklin did not arrive in New York on June 7 and, indeed, never came to New York for the rehearsals. Kramer immediately sought an explanation from Franklin's representatives and was informed that she would not fly. Springer paid the cast through the end of that week, but then suspended the production. He attempted to secure some other well-known performer to fill the title role, but none of the performers whom he contacted would agree to step into the role at that juncture.

On July 18, after having positive discussions with Les Matthews, a Texas financier who purported to be interested in backing the production, Springer wrote to Franklin with a proposal to revive it, whereby rehearsals and opening performances would take place in Detroit, with Franklin covering the excess expense caused by such an arrangement. The terms of Franklin's profit-sharing would be altered to account for the losses and additional costs caused by the suspended production. In August Franklin agreed to sign a draft agreement (doing so only on behalf of Crown Productions) so that Springer could regain some of his lost credibility with potential investors. Franklin's attorney held the signed draft in escrow, release from which was expressly conditioned on Springer's finalization of a performance schedule.

A final performance schedule was never arranged. One of the difficulties Springer encountered was that, due to the collapse of the earlier production, theaters and concert halls were now requiring substantial deposits to reserve particular dates. Springer lacked the capital to make those deposits. Matthews failed to appear for the scheduled closing of the investment agreement in early September, and Springer was unable to obtain any other financing for the production. He ultimately abandoned this second attempt at mounting the "Mahalia" production.

This lawsuit ensued, with Springer (suing in the name of Elvin Associates) alleging breach of the original agreement to appear in "Mahalia," and Franklin counter-claiming for breach of the second agreement concerning the proposed Detroit-based production. In his pre-trial memorandum, Springer asserted an alternative right to recover on a theory of promissory estoppel.

DISCUSSION

The central issue pertaining to plaintiff's claim for breach of contract is whether or not the parties to that proposed contract, i.e. Springer, Crown Productions, Inc., and Franklin in her capacity as guarantor of Crown's performance, evinced an intent not to be formally bound before execution of a written, integrated contract. Language inserted in a draft of the agreement referring to its validity upon execution has generally been found to be strong (though not conclusive) evidence of intent *not* to be bound prior to execution. . . . Although we based our tentative findings largely on the fact that all of the incidental terms had been worked out by the final draft, and that the understanding was that Franklin would sign the agreement when she came to New York, there remains the obstacle of the preamble that Kramer drafted and that remained in every draft, namely: "This letter, when countersigned by you, shall constitute our understanding until a more formal agreement is prepared." After reviewing the above cited authorities and the post-trial submissions, we are constrained to find that such language indicates that Crown Productions, Inc. was not to be contractually bound to Springer until the draft agreement was executed. . . . The cause of action for breach of contract must therefore be dismissed as against both defendants . . .

That, however, does not end the case. As above noted, plaintiff has asserted, in the alternative, a right to recover on a theory of promissory estoppel. The elements of a claim for promissory estoppel are: "[A] clear and unambiguous promise; a reasonable and foreseeable reliance by the party to whom the promise is made; and an injury sustained by the party asserting the estoppel by reason of his reliance." The " 'circumstances [must be] such as to render it *unconscionable* to deny' the promise upon which plaintiff has relied." [Citations omitted.]

It is difficult to imagine a more fitting case for applying the above-described doctrine. Although for her own business purposes Franklin insisted that the formal contract be with the corporate entity through which her services were to be "furnished," in the real world the agreement was with her, and we find that she had unequivocally and intentionally committed herself to appear in the production long before day on which it was intended that the finalized agreement with her corporation would be signed.

First, it is clear from the testimony of all of the witnesses that Franklin was enthusiastic about appearing in the production and that at all times during the relevant period gave it the highest professional priority. She early on stated to Springer: "This is what I am doing." Combined with her oral agreement, through her agents, to the basic financial terms of her engagement, her continued expression of this enthusiasm to Springer more than amply afforded Springer a reasonable basis for beginning to make the various arrangements and expenditures necessary to bring the production to fruition.

Second, Franklin could not possibly have assumed that Springer could have performed his obligations to her-which, among other things, included arranging a complicated schedule of performances to commence shortly after her arrival in New York-without committing himself to and actually spending considerable sums prior to her affixing her signature to the contract on the date of such arrival. Throughout the time that he was making those commitments and advancing the necessary sums, she accepted his performance without any disclaimer of her prior promises to him. Indeed, she actively participated in many aspects of the necessary arrangements.

Third, Franklin's expression to Springer of her fear of flying did not, as she has contended, make her promise conditional or coat it with a patina of ambiguity that should have alerted Springer to suspend his efforts to mount the production. Although Franklin rejected Springer's offer to make alternative ground transportation arrangements, her primary reason for doing so was that she was determined to overcome her fear of flying, and it was reasonable for Springer to rely on her reassurances that she would be able to fly. Moreover, it was also entirely reasonable for him to assume that if she could not overcome her fear she would travel to New York by other means, even if it meant spreading the trip over several days. In short, Franklin's fear of flying provides no basis whatsoever for avoiding liability for failing to fulfill her promise, reiterated on several occasions, to appear in "Mahalia." If she could not bring herself to fly, she should have traveled by way of ground transportation. It has not been established that she was otherwise unable to come to New York to meet her obligations.

We conclude that under the circumstances as we have outlined them it would be unconscionable not to compensate Springer for the losses he incurred through his entirely justified reliance on Franklin's oral promises. A determination of the exact amount to be awarded has been reserved for a later trial on damages.

CASE 10-1

The following case involves the question of whether an advertisement constitutes an offer.

Lefkowitz v. Great Minneapolis Surplus Store Inc.
Minn. Sup. Ct. 1957
251 Minn. 188, 86 N.W.2d 689

Murphy, J.

This is an appeal from an order of the municipal court of Minneapolis denying the motion of the defendant for amended findings of fact, or, in the alternative, for a new trial. The order for judgment awarded the plaintiff the sum of $138.50 as damages for breach of contract.

This case grows out of the alleged refusal of the defendant to sell to the plaintiff a certain fur piece which it had offered for sale in a newspaper advertisement. It appears from the record that on April 6, 1956, the defendant published the following advertisement in a Minneapolis newspaper:

'Saturday 9 A.M. sharp 3 brand new fur coats worth to $100.00

First come first served $1 each'

On April 13, the defendant again published an advertisement in the same

Newspaper as follows: 'Saturday 9 A.M. 2 brand new pastel mink 3-skin scarfs selling for $89.50

Out they go Saturday. Each ... $1.00

1 black lapin stole beautiful, worth $139.50 ... $1.00

First come first served'

The record supports the findings of the court that on each of the Saturdays following the publication of the above-described ads the plaintiff was the first to present himself at the appropriate counter in the defendant's store and on each occasion demanded the coat and the stole so advertised and indicated his readiness to pay the sale price of $1. On both occasions, the defendant refused to sell the merchandise to the plaintiff, stating on the first occasion that by a 'house rule' the offer was intended for women only and sales would not be made to men, and on the second visit that plaintiff knew defendant's house rules.

* * *

The defendant contends that a newspaper advertisement offering items of merchandise for sale at a named price is a 'unilateral offer' which may be withdrawn without notice. He relies upon authorities which hold that, where an advertiser publishes in a newspaper that he has a certain quantity or quality of goods which he wants to dispose of at certain prices and on certain terms, such advertisements are not offers which become contracts as soon as any person to whose notice they may come signifies his acceptance by notifying the other that he will take a certain quantity of them. Such advertisements have been construed as an invitation for an offer of sale on the terms stated, which offer, when received, may be accepted or rejected and which therefore does not become a contract of sale until accepted by the seller; and until a contract has been so made, the seller [Citations]

* * *

. . . . On the facts before us we are concerned with whether the advertisement constituted an offer, and, if so, whether the plaintiff's conduct constituted an acceptance.

There are numerous authorities which hold that a particular advertisement in a newspaper or circular letter relating to a sale of articles may be construed by the court as constituting an offer, acceptance of which would complete a contract. [Citations]

The test of whether a binding obligation may originate in advertisements addressed to the general public is 'whether the facts show that some performance was promised in positive terms in return for something requested.' [Citation]

Whether in any individual instance a newspaper advertisement is an offer rather than an invitation to make an offer depends on the legal intention of the parties and the surrounding circumstances. [Citations]

We are of the view on the facts before us that the offer by the defendant of the sale of the lapin fur was clear, definite, and explicit, and left nothing open for negotiation. The plaintiff having successfully managed to be the first one to appear at the seller's place of business to be served, as requested by the advertisement, and having offered the stated purchase price of the article, he was entitled to performance on the part of the defendant. We think the trial court was correct in holding that there was in the conduct of the parties a sufficient mutuality of obligation to constitute a contract of sale.

* * *

Affirmed.

CASE 10-2

This case concerns the need for definiteness and certainty in the terms of a contract.

DOMBROWSKI v. SOMERS
Court of Appeals of New York, 1977
41 N.Y.2d 858, 393 N.Y.2d 706

MEMORANDUM. By this action plaintiff seeks compensation for housekeeping chores rendered pursuant to an alleged oral agreement between herself and the decedent, Edward Vogel, whose household she was sharing.

Three witnesses testified that they heard Vogel say he would "take care of" plaintiff. None recalled any reference to a specific date. The claim itself was not filed until 18 months after the decedent's death.

The words to "take care of", in the context of this record, are too vague to spell out a meaningful promise. Even if they were not, standing alone, they would be legally insufficient to support a finding that there was a contract to compensate plaintiff during her lifetime rather than one to do so by bequest. In the latter case, an enforceable agreement would be required to be in writing…. In short, plaintiff has not met her burden of proof as a matter of law….

Accordingly, the order of the Appellate Division is reversed and the complaint dismissed.

CASE 10-3

In the following case, the court applies the rules regarding definiteness and certainty of contractual terms to an interesting set of facts.

TRIMMER v. VAN BOMEL
Supreme Court of New York (N.Y. Co.), 1980
107 Misc.2d 201, 434 N.Y.S.2d 82

GREENFIELD, Judge. The complex and varied relationships between men and women, when they come to an end, oft leave a bitter residue and a smoldering irritation for which the salve, often the only soothing balm, is cash. It is a poor substitute for love, affection or attention, but for many its satisfactions are longer lasting. "Ordinarily, alimony is the end product of the fission of matrimony by acrimony." More recently, the termination of informal "live-in" relationships has given rise to claims for "palimony". Now, in this case, a man who claims to have been the constant companion of an elderly wealthy widow, who changed his life style from genteel poverty to luxury at her behest, sues at the breakup of their relationship for what may be called, for want of a better term, "companiomony".

Plaintiff is a 67-year-old gentleman, who was earning a modest but respectable living as a travel tour operator, when a person on one of his tours, the defendant, Mrs. Catherine Bryer Van Bomel, a wealthy widow with assets stated to be in excess of $40,000,000, began making demands on his time, and allegedly agreed to support him in luxurious fashion, if he would devote all his time and attention to her. He gave up his business career, in which he admits he was earning no more than $8,900 a year and became the ever-present companion of Mrs. Von Bomel. He moved to larger quarters and modified his wardrobe to suit her tastes. He accompanied her to lunch and dinner, escorted her to the theatre and parties, and traveled with her on her trips to Europe. All this was at the lady's expense, of course. He also acted as her confidante and her friends became his friends.

For five years his life was constantly dominated by the needs, whims and desires of Mrs. Van Bomel. She spent money lavishly on him. Apart from taking care of his rent and his travel expenses, she had his suits hand tailored in Italy and in London, presented him with two Pontiacs and a Jaguar and gave him a monthly stipend. All in all, she expended well over $300,000 for his personal needs. Then, suddenly, it all came to an end. Accustomed to a life of luxury, and now without the means to attain it, plaintiff sues his former benefactress for $1,500,000.

In the first cause of action, plaintiff seeks recovery on an alleged express oral agreement, pursuant to which he agreed to give up his business and render services to the defendant, in return for which defendant would pay and provide (a) all his costs and expenses incurred in connection with the performance of his services, (b) all his costs and expenses for sumptuous living during the time the services were rendered, and (c) to pay "within a reasonable time" an amount sufficient to pay for all his costs and expenses for sumptuous living for the rest of his life. The plaintiff further alleges that he fully performed the agreement on his part and that the defendant, in part performance, paid all his costs and expenses during the period of rendition of services, but has failed and refused to provide plaintiff with a sum sufficient to maintain him on a standard of "sumptuous living" for the remainder of his life, which sum plaintiff contends would be $1,500,000.

In his second cause of action, which sounds in quantum meruit, plaintiff alleges that he performed the various services for defendant for a five-year period and gave up pursuit of his separate business career. For the agreed and reasonable value of his services on the second cause of action, he seeks $1,500,000.

Defendant has moved for summary judgment...contending that the action is without merit and that the purported agreement is too vague and indefinite to be enforceable; that defendant's obligations under the alleged agreement are illusory; that the agreement is void for lack of consideration and that plaintiff has already been paid far in excess of the value of any purported services.

Defendant had previously moved for summary judgment...and a denial of the motion at that time was affirmed by the Appellate Division. Plaintiff misconstrues the nature of that prior order, since, in clarification, the Appellate Division specifically held that its affirmance of the denial of summary judgment was "without prejudice to renewal thereof after the conclusion of pretrial procedures herein." The Appellate Division specifically noted: "We do not pass upon the merits of plaintiff's claims or defendant's position with respect thereto at this time". Depositions having been concluded, defendant has moved again for summary judgment. That right to renew in these circumstances is predicated not upon the allegation of new or additional material, but upon the completion of discovery. There is now a complete record before the court containing the entire recollections of both plaintiff and defendant, the only parties to the alleged agreement.

While there have been a number of cases dealing with lawsuits by one partner in a nonmarital relationship seeking to recover against the other on the basis of an express or implied agreement the court in this case is not confronted with the public policy considerations which compel the judiciary to uphold the institution of marriage and to distinguish its consequences from less formal and less permanent living arrangements. No meretricious relationship appears to be here involved. At best, plaintiff may be regarded as a companion and paid escort, and not as a substitute mate. These cases are instructive, however, as to which type of agreements may be enforceable and whether recovery is to be permitted on a theory of implied contract or quantum meruit.

In this State, cases of unmarried persons living together who thereafter seek financial recovery frequently run afoul of the theory that a contract founded upon an agreement to live together as man and wife will not be enforced. While one may not claim compensation for having been a paramour, if there are services rendered which are nonsexual in nature and do not arise directly from such a relationship, then such services may be deemed separable, and form the basis for compensation....

The extramatrimonial case involving a claim for the value of services rendered which has received the most publicity to date is *Marvin v Marvin*. In that case the California Supreme Court had reversed the dismissal of Michelle Marvin's complaint as a de facto spouse, and remanded the matter for trial to determine whether or not she was entitled to recovery on an express or implied contract. It was not the holding of the California court that a mistress was entitled to "palimony". At Trial Term, the court found that the allegations that there had been an explicit contract to compensate the plaintiff were not borne out by the facts. Nevertheless, the court, exercising its equitable powers, decided to award the sum of $1,000 per week for a two-year period to enable the plaintiff, who had allegedly given up her budding career, to rehabilitate herself. Interestingly, on the same day that Michelle Marvin was awarded "severance pay" by the California trial court, in New York the female companion of rock star Peter Frampton was cut off without compensation....

The most recent case in this State dealing with extramarital contracts is *Morone v Morone*. In that case, as here, two causes of action were alleged -- the first based upon implied contract and the second alleging an explicit oral "partnership agreement". The concept of an implied contract to compensate for services was declared by the court "to be conceptually so amorphous as practically to defy equitable enforcement". Nevertheless, the court concluded that the allegations of an express contract that the woman would furnish domestic services and the man was to have full charge of business transactions and that the "net profits" from the partnership were to be shared equally, set forth an enforceable cause of action. Evidently, "housewifely" services are to be distinguished from such other services as may be rendered during the course of a living-together relationship. When the "tainted" consideration for such contracts is removed, the claim for recovery in extramarital cases stands in precisely the same posture as in this case.

In this case, the services for which plaintiff seeks compensation on a quantum meruit basis, like those in a quasimarital relationship, arise out of the nature of the relationship of the parties to one another. The services involved -- to devote time and attention to the defendant, to allow her wishes to prevail concerning his deportment, habits and associations and to act as companion, to accompany defendant to restaurants, to travel with her, to accept gifts and jewelry, clothing and motor cars from her are of a nature which would ordinarily be exchanged without expectation of pay. As Judge Meyer noted in *Morone v Morone*: "As a matter of human experience personal services will frequently be rendered by two people...because they value each other's company or because they find it a convenient or rewarding thing to do.... For courts to attempt through hindsight to sort out the intentions of the parties and affix jural significance to conduct carried out within an essentially private and generally noncontractual relationship runs too great a risk of error. Absent an express agreement, there is no frame of reference against which to compare the testimony presented and the character of the evidence that can be presented becomes more evanescent. There is,

therefore, substantially greater risk of emotion-laden afterthought, not to mention fraud, in attempting to ascertain by implication what services, if any, were rendered gratuitously and what compensation, if any, the parties intended to be paid."

As to personal services between unmarried persons living together or unmarried persons whose actions flow out of mutual friendship and reciprocal regard, there is very little difference. An implied contract to compensate for those things which are ordinarily done by one person for another as a matter of regard and affection should not, under these well-established principles, be recognized in this State. Plaintiff has already received $300,000 from the defendant during the course of their relationship. What further "obligation" can be implied?

The claims of friendship, like the claims of kinship, may be many and varied. To imply an obligation by a wealthy friend to compensate a less wealthy companion for being together, dining together, talking together and accepting tokens of regard stretches the bond of friendship to the breaking point. The implied obligation to compensate arises from those things which, in normal society, we expect to pay for. An obligation to pay for friendship is not ordinarily to be implied -- it is too crass. Friendship, like virtue, must be its own reward.

Accordingly, the second cause of action, founded in implied contract, must be dismissed.

The first cause of action, however, alleges an express agreement to pay the plaintiff. For the purposes of this motion for summary judgment, the court must accept as true plaintiff's allegation that defendant agreed to set up a fund which would permit plaintiff to live for the remainder of his life in the sumptuous style to which he had become accustomed. While defendant denies that there were specific conversations about setting up a fund, she does admit having discussions from time to time about making finances available to the plaintiff. She denies, however, and the plaintiff's testimony in his deposition confirms, that no specific dollar amounts were ever specified, no time for performance was ever set and no conditions as to the manner of payment were given, nor was anything ever said about what would happen if the relationship between the parties terminated. Thus, the principal issue presented is whether such an agreement as alleged in the complaint, and as expanded upon in plaintiff's deposition, can be regarded as enforceable. While there is no public policy bar to such an agreement, as an alleged express oral contract, its validity must be tested exactly the same as other contracts. Such a contract is not conceptually invalid....

All courts would agree with the doctrine, although not necessarily the application, that as a basic premise of contract law "'It is a necessary requirement in the nature of things that an agreement in order to be binding must be sufficiently definite to enable a court to give it an exact meaning' (1 Williston, Contracts [3d ed], § 37)." In *Dombrowski v Somers*, a unanimous Court of Appeals found that an alleged oral agreement, pursuant to which the decedent said that in return for plaintiff's services he would "take care of" the plaintiff, was too vague to spell out a meaningful promise.

The question in this case is whether an alleged agreement by defendant to pay an amount sufficient to take care of all of plaintiff's "costs and expenses for sumptuous living and maintenance for the remainder of his life" as amplified by plaintiff's testimony, will enable the court to award plaintiff a judgment in a specific sum of dollars. It is clear from the pretrial depositions of both parties, that no specific dollar amount, or approximate dollar amount, of any alleged fund was ever discussed. No facts are presented which would tend to establish a meeting of minds as to the definition of "sumptuous living". In his 237-page bill of particulars, plaintiff asserted that the defendant had agreed "to provide and set up for him a fund, either by giving him a block of stock or cash, or both, which would take care of all his living expenses in the same expensive style for the rest of his life." Plaintiff is alleging, in essence, a contract of employment, but as reference to his own testimony indicates, there was no specification as to the length of the term, the amount of the compensation, the terms of the payment, the nature of the duties, the manner in which the employment could be terminated and the method of computing "severance pay". Plaintiff's deposition indicates that there was no specific time at which the alleged agreement was worked out, but rather that it developed as part of numerous conversations over an extended period of time, and it is clear that he commenced his "employment" long before any such agreement to take care of him for the rest of his life was discussed.

With respect to the alleged promise of the defendant to set up a "fund" to take care of his needs for "sumptuous living", no specifics were ever discussed....

Nor, admittedly, was there ever any discussion about what was necessary for the plaintiff's living expenses either at that time or at some point off in the future....

What we are talking about, then, at best is "a fund" in some unspecified amount to be set up on some unspecified date in some unspecified manner, and that it was wholly in the discretion of the defendant. The agreement boils down to these words, "She would do it in some way."

Plaintiff has attempted to overcome the inherent vagueness of this "agreement" by trying to spell out, after the fact, what amounts he deems to be required for "sumptuous living". What is "sumptuous" to one person may be merely adequate to another, of course.

"Sumptuous" is defined as involving great expense; costly, lavish, magnificent (Webster's Dictionary, p 1825,...)

Moreover, sumptuous living "cannot be computed from anything that was said by the parties or by reference to any document, paper or other transaction" nor would it be provable by evidence of custom. Nor, for that matter, could defendant be required to account since no partnership agreement is alleged and additionally, defendant's vast holdings were accumulated before she had ever met plaintiff. Essentially, then the amount was left subject to the will of the defendant or for further negotiation. Courts cannot aid parties who have not specified the terms of their own agreements....

Plaintiff calculates that since he was given an average of $71,672 (tax free) by Mrs. Van Bomel during their five-year relationship, that this is the sum he should be given for the rest of his life. That is how he comes to the $1,500,000 set forth in the ad damnum. One million five hundred dollars in six-month certificates would give him $180,000 a year and that same sum in tax-free municipals would produce well over $100,000 per year, in which case the principal would be left intact. It appears clear that we are dealing with an alleged agreement which is too vague in any of its material terms to be deemed enforceable. No amount being specified, no time having been set forth, no mechanics for the payments having been spelled out and there being no specification as to what had to be done to qualify or disqualify the plaintiff for the payments, what we have, at best, is some vague but legally unenforceable reassurance that plaintiff "would be taken care of".

Since plaintiff alleges an express agreement which is to be governed by the law applicable to all contracts, it is instructive to compare the kind of agreement upon which plaintiff relies with other, more detailed contracts which the courts have nevertheless found to be unenforceable. Thus, in *Brause v Goldman*, where negotiations had progressed to a point of much greater detail than what was involved here, the court found that many of the essentials of an agreement were lacking. In that case, the court declared: "When the wording...exchanged between the parties reveal no present intent to form a binding contract, but rather to continue negotiations with the possible ultimate meeting of minds deferred until some future time, either party may withdraw with impunity prior to that time...."

Further, "The absence of any of the essential elements of an agreement is a bar to its enforcibility." The court found that even though there were memoranda of agreement prepared after oral negotiations, there was no indication as to the date on which the arrangement was to be commenced nor as to the method of payment, nor as to the rights of the parties in the event of various contingencies coming to pass. The Appellate Division declared, "It is not for the court to dictate such terms to the parties, for its function is to enforce agreements only if they exist, and not to create them by the imposition of such terms as it considers reasonable."

In essence, if the relationship between the plaintiff and defendant was that of employer and employee rather than that of friends or benefactress and protege, then clearly it was an employment relationship terminable at will. Plaintiff recognized that he would be rendering services at the pleasure of Mrs. Van Bomel, and that could be for months, for years or on into the indefinite future. Plaintiff testified, "The discussion was that I was to start doing this for her. There was no time limit put on it... I knew that if she decided that she would like to terminate my employment with her, she could do that. She had a perfect right to do that." Would a defendant be bound by a committment to put up a fund of $1,500,000 for someone who rendered "services" to her for a matter of months by accompanying her to restaurants such as Lutece and the Palm Court? Plaintiff would accompany the defendant to lunch two or three times weekly. He agreed that the defendant never imposed any restrictions upon his activities. For these companionable social activities, it cannot be said that defendant, or her estate, is to be bound for the rest of plaintiff's life.

In an agreement terminable at will, and with no clear bounds and parameters set forth, an alleged obligation which would continue and survive beyond the termination of employment must appear with specificity. What if the relationship had been terminated for "cause"? Suppose plaintiff had been disloyal or discourteous or had secretly embezzled some of defendant's funds, would the agreement to take care of him for life continue nevertheless? Since this relationship was terminable at will, and the relationship had come to an end, this court can see no legal basis upon which the defendant can be compelled to continue lavishing her favors and her bounty upon the plaintiff. There are no guarantees in life, and good fortune, to be enjoyed while it lasts, does not invariably bring with it a life-long annuity. It was defendant who decided to get plaintiff tickets for the Royal Enclosure at Ascot, to buy him fabrics in London to be tailored in Rome. It was defendant who took pleasure in seeing that plaintiff's shoes came from Gucci and his accessories from Saks. When the relationship is terminated, the law does not compel... the dead relationship to continue.

Accordingly, defendant is entitled to summary judgment on the first cause of action as well as the second. The complaint should be dismissed.

CASE 10-4

In the following case, the court determines whether the parties have reached agreement on all material terms and thus have an enforceable contract.

ANSORGE v. KANE
Court of Appeals of New York, 1927
244 N.Y. 395

POUND, Judge. The main point is simply stated. Defendant owned real property in Flushing, New York. Plaintiff desired to purchase it. Through her agent the parties came together March 25, 1925, and made a memorandum of purchase and sale which describes the property and acknowledges the receipt of $500 as binder thereon and then provides:

"The price is $32,625; payable $12,625 cash; balance of $20,000 to remain on 1st mortgage for five years. The sum to be paid on signing of contract on March 26th, 1925, to be agreed on. The balance of cash payment on passing of title on May 26th, 1925."

The parties never agreed on the sum to be paid on signing the contract. When the owner refused to sign a contract or execute a deed the court below ordered specific performance at the suit of the purchaser. That the parties had not agreed was held immaterial. It was said that the agreement in substance was that the balance of the cash payment would be payable when title passed unless the parties in the interim agreed otherwise....

Appellant contends that the scheme or plan of the parties was left incomplete by the failure to name the sum to be paid when the contract was signed; and that until the sum was named the contract was unenforceable…. The memorandum states the price to be paid but it does not state all the terms of payment…. The fundamental question here presented is whether there was any contract; any actual meeting of minds on all the material elements of the agreement.

If a material element of a contemplated contract is left for future negotiations, there is no enforceable contract…. The price is a material element of any contract of sale and an agreement to agree thereon in the future is too indefinite to be enforceable….

The terms of payment may be no less material. Is this memorandum in effect an agreement to convey the property described if the parties can agree upon the amount to be paid on the signing of the contract but for no sale if they do not agree? Or is the agreement on the sum to be paid on signing the contract a minor and non-essential detail of the transaction? That is the question before us…. The memorandum was on its face a mere binder. The formal contract was to be prepared and executed on the next day. As a part of the agreement was left to future negotiations, the contract was embryonic. It never reached full time. It was not for nothing that the parties provided that a sum should be agreed on to be paid on the signing of the contract; nor was it a minor matter for the owner whether nothing should be paid when the contract was signed and she should wait two months for her money, or whether she should receive a substantial sum, the stronger to bind the agreement, on which she also might receive interest, or even a greater increment, if she had her hands on it. In this connection we observe that the broker demanded that his full commission of ten per cent be paid on the signing of the contract which further suggests that the down payment had more than theoretical importance to the vendor.

The parties had decided to purchase and sell. They had agreed on the purchase price. They had not agreed on the terms of payment. The law implies nothing as to such terms as it does in cases where the rate of interest and date of maturity of a mortgage are not stated…or where it appears that an agreement is to take effect and be ·acted upon before the details reserved for future agreement, such as time of delivery, are settled, when an implication may arise that, in the event of a failure to agree, the terms shall be such as are reasonable or customary…. The amount to be paid on the signing of the contract was an important element of the complete contract. It was left open. The contract was never completed. The transaction was destitute of legal effect. Specific performance is, therefore, impossible. . . .

The judgment of the Appellate Division and that of the Special Term should be reversed and the complaint dismissed.

CASE 10-5

If the duration of an offer is not specified, it expires in a "reasonable time." The following case illustrates that a court will consider the particular circumstances in determining whether acceptance has been made in a reasonable time.

22 WEST MAIN STREET, INC. v. BOGUSZEWSKI
Appellate Division, New York (4ᵗʰ Dept.), 1970
34 A.D. 2d 358, 311 N.Y.S.2d 565

DEL VECCHIO, Justice. Plaintiff appeals from an order of Special Term denying its motion for summary judgment in an action to compel specific performance of a real estate contract.

There is no dispute about the events which preceded this action.

On February 21, 1968 defendant executed an offer to purchase approximately 4.9 acres of land in the Village of Fredonia for $7,000. The offer stated that the closing was to be held at the offices of the attorneys for the defendant 'on or before March 22, 1968 or as soon thereafter as abstracts can be brought to date'. There was no acceptance by plaintiff until March 26, 1968 (four days after the closing date specified in the offer), when the seller crossed out the closing date of March 22, 1968, inserted the date 'April 10, 1968' and signed the acceptance portion of the offer. On April 2, 1968 the seller's attorneys wrote to defendant's attorney enclosing the executed purchase offer, the abstract of title, a copy of a proposed deed and other papers relating to the premises. Receiving no reply, plaintiff's attorneys wrote on five subsequent occasions requesting that a closing date for the transfer be set. Defendant's counsel did not respond directly to any of these letters but did send plaintiff's attorneys a copy of a letter sent to defendant by his attorney on July 5 in which the latter advised that since the client was unwilling to close the transaction he was no longer representing him in the matter and enclosing a bill for his services. He also advised that the abstract of title and the proposed deed description were being returned to the seller's attorneys. By letter to defendant dated July 26 plaintiff tendered a deed and set August 5 as a date for closing. When the tender was not accepted plaintiff commenced this action for specific performance.

After service of the pleadings which put in issue the making of the contract plaintiff served on defendant a notice to admit the execution by him of the purchase offer, the genuineness of his signature thereon and the fact that the offer was not withdrawn prior to acceptance. When no response to the notice was served plaintiff moved for summary judgment on the basis of the notice and an affidavit and supporting papers setting forth the facts recited above.

It is plaintiff's contention that its execution of the acceptance of defendant's purchase offer on March 26, 1968 created a binding contract between the parties which it is now entitled to enforce. Defendant takes the position that the acceptance on March 26 was not an acceptance of a viable offer but was merely a counter offer which was never accepted by the buyer. . . .

Upon the undisputed facts there was never a contract entered into by the parties. The act of the plaintiff in signing the acceptance of the purchase offer on March 26 was too late to constitute an acceptance of defendant's offer to buy made one month and five days prior thereto.

The offer executed on February 21 did not contain any express time limit on its duration. In that circumstance the offer remained open for a reasonable time. 'Where an offer specifies the time of its duration, it must of course by accepted within the time limited; where, however, no time is specified for the offer's duration, it is the general rule that it must be accepted within a reasonable time.' . . . . The circumstances surrounding the offer, or usage or custom of trade, may also raise an implied limitation on the offer. (9 N.Y.Jur., Contracts §24.) Here, the original offer to buy contained a proposed closing date one month after the offer. The inclusion of the closing date of March 22 is compelling evidence that acceptance of the offer, if it were to occur, must happen before that date, else the closing date would be an impossibility. A similar case is *Hamilton v. Patrick*, . . . in which the court said:

'The proposal itself implies the necessity of acceptance on or before that day. It is therein proposed that the deed should be executed and delivered to the plaintiff 'on or before March 1, 1885, at which date said money shall be paid.' Acceptance must precede any obligation to perform, and of necessity must be made so as to admit of performance as proposed. Any subsequent acceptance would imply a contract different from the terms proposed.' . . .

The reasonable time for duration of the offer was not longer than the one month within which the offeror hoped to complete the transaction. An acceptance which occurred four days after the proposed closing date and one month and five days after the tender of the offer is clearly beyond a reasonable period of duration. The late acceptance was merely a counter offer which must in turn be accepted by the original offeror to create a contract. (1 Williston on Contracts, 3d ed. §§ 92, 93; Restatement, Law of Contracts, § 73; . . ..) Since there was never any acceptance by defendant of plaintiff's counter proposal, there was no contract between the parties to be enforced.

The order should be modified to grant summary judgment to defendant dismissing the complaint.

CASE 10-6

This case illustrates the operation of the three month limitation on the irrevocability of firm offers under UCC §2-205 and also how revocation may occur by conduct.

NORCA CORPORATION v. TOKHEIM CORPORATION
Appellate Division, New York (2d Dept.), 1996
227 A.D.2d 458, 643 N.Y.S.2d 139

MEMORANDUM BY THE COURT. In an action, *inter alia,* to recover damages for breach of contract, the plaintiff appeals from an order and judgment (one paper) of the Supreme Court, Nassau County (Alpert, J.), entered April 11, 1995, which, *inter alia,* granted the respective motions of the defendants for summary judgment dismissing the complaint.

ORDERED that the order and judgment is affirmed, with costs.

If a firm offer is made for a specified period which is in excess of three months, the offer is subject to revocation at the expiration of the three month period (*see,* Uniform Commercial Code § 2-205, Official Comment 3; [Citations]). An offer may be terminated by indirect revocation . . . . An offeror need not say "revoke" to effectuate a revocation . . . . Where an offeror takes "definite action inconsistent with an intention to enter into the proposed contract", such action is considered a valid revocation (Restatement [Second] of Contracts § 43; *see also,* 1 Farnsworth, Contracts § 3.17, at 250 [1990]).

In the instant case, the defendant Saint Switch, Inc.

(hereinafter Saint Switch), agreed to purchase the assets of the manufacturing pump division of the defendant Tokheim Corporation. On April 14, 1993, Saint Switch offered, on Tokheim Corporation letterhead, to sell fuel pumps to the appellant. The offer was firm until July 31, 1994. On August 18, 1993, more than three months after the original offer was made, Saint Switch forwarded to the appellant a new offer stating different price terms for the fuel pumps. On November 4, 1993, the appellant attempted to accept the original offer made on April 14, 1993.

We find that the offer made by Saint Switch on August 18, 1993, revoked its earlier offer made on April 14, 1993. The offer made on August 18, 1993, was inconsistent with the original offer in that it had a different price term . . . . In addition, it was made prior to any effective acceptance on the part of the appellant . . . . Accordingly, the Supreme Court properly granted the respective motions of the defendants for summary judgment.

The appellant's remaining contentions are without merit.

CASE 10-7

The following case deals with the reasonableness of the means of acceptance used by the offeror.

DEFEO v. AMFARMS ASSOCIATES

Appellate Division, New York (3rd Dept.), 1990
161 A.D.2d 904, 557 N.Y.S.2d 469

WEISS, Justice. Appeal from an order of the Supreme Court (Rose, J.), entered July 14, 1989 in Tioga County, which, *inter alia,* granted defendant's motion for summary judgment dismissing the complaint.

In 1986 defendant listed its farm located in the Town of Candor, Tioga County, for sale with W.D. Seeley Real Estate. On September 5, 1987 defendant received an offer from plaintiffs submitted through the broker. It rejected the offer on September 7, 1987 and submitted a counteroffer in which the sale price was increased and certain conditions which defendant found objectionable were deleted. This counteroffer was made through the broker with instructions that the sale would have to proceed promptly. A month later, on October 5, 1987, plaintiffs submitted another offer with an acceptable price, but again included the objectionable conditions. On October 9, 1987 defendant rejected this offer

and, using the same form, countered by deleting and initialing the objectionable conditions. In this final counteroffer, a new additional term appeared in handwriting: "13. Offer valid to Oct. 17, 1987 at 1700 hours." Peculiarly, the parties claim to be unaware who inserted the clause. This counteroffer was forwarded directly by defendant's attorney . . . to plaintiffs' attorney by Federal Express overnight delivery. Thereafter, plaintiffs' attorney contacted defendant's attorney by telephone on October 13, 1987 and another of defendant's partners on October 15, 1987. The parties dispute the contents of these communications. In the meantime, on October 13, 1987, defendant received a purchase offer with a higher price from third parties through a different real estate broker which it accepted on October 16, 1987. On that very same day, plaintiffs accepted the October 9, 1987 counteroffer and sent it to Seeley Real Estate by certified mail, which Seeley received on October 19, 1987. Defendant denied the effectiveness of acceptance. Supreme Court granted summary judgment dismissing the complaint seeking specific performance, holding that since the offer had been transmitted to plaintiffs' attorney by Federal Express, acceptance sent by mail to the listing real estate broker was unauthorized and ineffective to accept the offer. The court found that since plaintiffs failed to timely communicate acceptance before the offer expired, no binding contract was formed and plaintiffs were not entitled to specific performance. This appeal followed.

The reasonableness of the manner in which an offer is accepted must be viewed under the circumstances in which the offer had been made, with speed and reliability being relevant factors (Restatement [Second] of Contracts § 65; *see,* 1 Williston, Contracts § 83, at 273 [Jaeger 3d ed.]). Here, the transmission using Federal Express overnight delivery invited acceptance by similar dispatch . . . and plaintiffs' acceptance by mail, particularly to an agent who had been uninvolved in the negotiations of the moment and who had lost contact with the parties, was not invited especially in view of defendant's expressed concern with time. The receipt of the acceptance by the broker two days after the appointed day was not operative (Restatement [Second] of Contracts § 67).

Order affirmed, with costs.

CASE 10-8

The following case concerns whether an effective acceptance was made before revocation of the offer.

TENCZA v. HYLAND
Appellate Division, New York (4th *Dept.), 1991*
171 A.D.2d 1057, 569 N.Y.S.2d 242

MEMORANDUM: Supreme Court erred in finding that there was a binding contract between the parties and granting plaintiffs' request for specific performance. On or about April 15, 1987, plaintiffs submitted to defendants an offer to purchase a mobile home park in New Hartford, New York. Defendants responded by inserting four modifications to the purchase offer and advised plaintiffs' counsel that, if the changes were acceptable, plaintiffs should initial them and return the signed purchase offer. One of the modifications was that plaintiff corporation's three principal shareholders would be required to sign, individually, a $160,000 note to secure payment of the purchase price. Another modification made defendants responsible only for commencing eviction proceedings against all tenants in arrears more than 30 days, rather than for evicting those tenants before closing. Defendants' material alterations of plaintiffs' offer to purchase constituted a counteroffer that required plaintiffs' acceptance to form a binding contract . . . . Plaintiffs signed the counteroffer, but their agreement was never communicated by their counsel to defendants. Counsel instead attempted to negotiate changes in the contract that were beneficial to his clients. On May 12, 1987 defendants' counsel advised plaintiffs' counsel by letter that his clients were no longer interested in selling the property and returned plaintiffs' $5,000 deposit. Because the signed counteroffer was never delivered to defendants and defendants were never advised of plaintiffs' acceptance of the counteroffer prior to their revocation, no contract was entered into between the parties . . . .

Order and judgment unanimously reversed on the law with costs and complaint dismissed; motion for stay denied as moot.

CASE 11-1

The common law rule requires that consideration be given by each party to the other in order for the contract to be binding. This leading case addresses the question of whether consideration is given when a party incurs a legal detriment by giving up a legal right if the other party receives no benefit.

HAMER v. SIDWAY
Court of Appeals of New York, 1891
124 N.Y. 538

PARKER, Judge. The question which provoked the most discussion by counsel on this appeal, and which lies at the foundation of plaintiff's asserted right of recovery, is whether by virtue of a contract defendant's testator William E. Story became indebted to his nephew William E. Story, 2d, on his twenty-first birthday in the sum of five thousand dollars. The trial court found as a fact that "on the 20th day of March, 1869, William E. Story agreed to and with William E. Story, 2d, that if he would refrain from drinking liquor, using tobacco, swearing, and playing cards or billiards for money until he should become 21 years of age then he, the said William E. Story, would at that time pay him, the said William E. Story, 2d, the sum of $5,000 for such refraining, to which the said William E. Story, 2d, agreed," and that he "in all things fully performed his part of said agreement."

The defendant contends that the contract was without consideration to support it, and, therefore, invalid. He asserts that the promisee by refraining from the use of liquor and tobacco was not harmed but benefited; that that which he did was best for him to do independently of his uncle's promise, and insists that it follows that unless the promisor was benefited, the contract was without consideration. A contention, which if well founded, would seem to leave open for controversy in many cases whether that which the promisee did or omitted to do was, in fact, of such benefit to him as to leave no consideration to support the enforcement of the promisor's agreement. Such a rule could not be tolerated, and is without foundation in the law. The Exchequer Chamber, in 1875, defined consideration as follows: "A valuable consideration in the sense of the law may consist either in some right, interest, profit or benefit accruing to the one party, or some forbearance, detriment, loss or responsibility given, suffered or undertaken by the other." Courts "will not ask whether the thing which forms the consideration does in fact benefit the promisee or a third party, or is of any substantial value to anyone. It is enough that something is promised, done, forborne or suffered by the party to whom the promise is made as consideration for the promise made to him."

"In general a waiver of any legal right at the request of another party is a sufficient consideration for a promise."

"Any damage, or suspension, or forbearance of a right will be sufficient to sustain a promise."

Pollock, in his work on contracts, page 166, after citing the definition given by the Exchequer Chamber already quoted, says: "The second branch of this judicial description is really the most important one. Consideration means not so much that one party is profiting as that the other abandons some legal right in the present or limits his legal freedom of action in the future as an inducement for the promise of the first."

Now, applying this rule to the facts before us, the promisee used tobacco, occasionally drank liquor, and he had a legal right to do so. That right he abandoned for a period of years upon the strength of the promise of the testator that for such forbearance he would give him $5,000. We need not speculate on the effort which may have been required to give up the use of those stimulants. It is sufficient that he restricted his lawful freedom of action within certain prescribed limits upon the faith of his uncle's agreement, and now having fully performed the conditions imposed, it is of no moment whether such performance actually proved a benefit to the promisor, and the court will not inquire into it, but were it a proper subject of inquiry, we see nothing in this record that would permit a determination that the uncle was not benefited in a legal sense.

The cases cited by the defendant on this question are not in point.

CASE 11-2

Often good faith disputes arise between a creditor and debtor as to whether any money is owed or how much money is owed. In such cases, a debtor may tender a check to the creditor for a smaller amount and may write words such as "paid in full" on the check or indicate such facts in a letter. May the creditor cash the check and still sue to collect the balance he claims is due? The following case illustrates the common law rules as to whether a debt is unliquidated and whether an accord and satisfaction discharging the debt has occurred.

SCHNELL v. PERLMON
Court of Appeals of New York, 1924
238 N.Y. 362; 144 N.E. 641

CRANE, Judge. This action is brought to recover an alleged balance due for goods, wares and merchandise sold by the plaintiffs to the defendant. Defendant pleaded an accord and satisfaction. The trial court directed a verdict for the plaintiffs for the full amount claimed, and the judgment entered thereon has been unanimously affirmed by the Appellate Division. That court, however, granted leave to appeal to this court, certifying that in its opinion there is a question of law involved which ought to be reviewed by us.

The question of law referred to arises through the payment by the defendant of an amount less than the agreed price in full payment and satisfaction of the claimed debt. As in all like cases the result depends very much upon the facts of each case, it is, therefore, necessary at the outset to state fully the transaction between these parties. The plaintiffs, trading under the firm name of H. Schnell & Co., sold to Sol Perlmon, the defendant, trading under the firm name of Detroit Celery & Produce Co., ten cars of Spanish onions, pursuant to the terms of a written contract dated November 14, 1921. These ten carloads were to consist of 2,500 crates to be shipped by the Michigan Central Railroad from New York to Detroit; all goods sold F. O. B. New York, delivery to the common carrier being delivery to the purchaser. When the onions arrived in Detroit some of them were found to be in a defective condition due to decay consisting of fusarean rot, slimy soft rot, and a bacteria heart rot involving the greater portion of the onions. The defendant had the onions inspected by the Food Products Inspector of the United States Department of Agriculture, who gave five separate certificates certifying to this condition of the onions examined by him and stating that the decay amounted in some of the containers from ten per cent to thirty-five per cent, in others from fifteen to twenty-five per cent of the

contents. The percentage varied in these certificates, running as high, however, as fifty per cent and as low as three per cent. The defendant notified the plaintiffs by letter regarding this condition, and sent them copies of the government official's report. On December 13, 1921, the defendant sent to the plaintiffs five checks in payment of five of the cars shipped and deducted a total of $425 for a percentage of the decay as covered by the government reports. Accompanying these checks was a letter in which an explanation of the deduction was made in the following words: "These deductions are made to cover the percentage of decay on each car. We mailed you, some time ago, the inspection reports covering each of these cars in order that you might satisfy yourself that we are making only reasonable deductions." Each of the checks was marked in full payment of the car number for which payment was remitted.

On December 16th the plaintiffs acknowledged receipt of checks totaling $4,575, which they stated they had placed to the credit of the defendant, but insisted that there was still a balance due of $425 for which they demanded payment. In other words, they accepted the checks but rejected the proposed deduction.

On February 11, 1922, the defendant, who was still indebted to the plaintiffs for five cars, sent to them a check for $2,000 and a promissory note for $2,328.70 with interest payable in thirty days. On the back of this note there was this notation: "Payment in full of balance owing you on the following cars of Onions:" (giving numbers of cars). A letter also accompanied this note showing the reasons for the deductions mentioned therein, reading as follows: "We have already advised you the percentage of decay on cars NYC-138745 and NYC-138762 and have deducted off the first car Two Hundred and Eight Dollars ($208.00), representing twenty per cent of the invoice which the Government inspection shows as running from ten to thirty-five per cent decay and an average of fifteen to twenty-five per cent. You know that decay of this particular kind Slimy Soft Rot, hurts the sale of the entire shipment as the onions that are sound lose in value after being sorted over as they are never so bright and clean as when shipment is sound.

Car NYC-138762 also shows the same kind of decay and we have deducted fifteen per cent from the invoice and this in no way represents what we should have deducted as the bad onions affected the sale and condition of the others."

The plaintiffs replied to this letter crediting these amounts on the account of the defendant and demanding all the balance due, $801.29, the amount sued for in this action....

The facts, briefly stated, therefore, are: The plaintiffs sold to the defendant onions for an agreed price. The shipment in part was rotten and decayed. The defendant notified the plaintiffs of the fact sending to them the government reports made by the Food Products Inspector. The defendant paid for the goods which were in good condition, deducting $801.29 for those which he claimed to have been decayed. The payment was made by checks and notes and accompanying letters notifying the plaintiffs that if accepted by them they would be in full payment of the amount due, and the balance, $801.29, the amount of the deduction, would thus be paid by agreement or by accord and satisfaction (to use the legal terms). The claim put forth by the defendant for deduction was apparently made in good faith, and in view of the government reports seems to be reasonable and fair. The percentage of the deduction made by the defendant was not as large as the percentage of decay reported by the government reports sent to the plaintiffs and might be less than the amount which the defendant could have recovered if he had sued the plaintiffs for damages or upon their warranty. Under these circumstances, was the trial judge justified in holding as a matter of law that there had been no accord and satisfaction and that the plaintiffs were entitled to the balance claimed?

The general rule is that a liquidated claim, that is, a claim which is not disputed, but admitted to be due, cannot be discharged by any payment of a less amount. In *Jackson v. Volkening* we find the following language used: "The rule of law is well established, undoubtedly, that where a liquidated sum is due, the payment of part only, although accepted in satisfaction, is not, for want of consideration, a discharge of the entire indebtedness, but this rule is not looked upon with favor and is confined strictly to

cases falling within it." In *Fuller v. Kemp* it was said: "Where the demand is liquidated, and the liability of the debtor is not in good faith disputed, a different rule has been applied. In such cases the acceptance of a less sum than is the creditor's due, will not of itself discharge the debt, even if a receipt in full is given." And in *Simons v. Supreme Council American Legion of Honor* the point was stated in these words: "Now it is the settled law of this state that if a debt or claim be disputed or contingent at the time of payment, the payment, when accepted, of a part of the whole debt is a good satisfaction and it matters not that there was no solid foundation for the dispute." And in *Eames Vacuum Brake Co. v. Prosser* this court said: "It is only in cases where a dispute has arisen between the parties as to the amount due and a check is tendered on one side in full satisfaction of the matter in controversy that the other party will be deemed to have acquiesced in the amount offered by an acceptance and a retention of the check." The term "liquidated," therefore, when used in connection with the subject of accord and satisfaction has reference to a claim which the debtor does not dispute; a claim which he admits to be due but attempts to satisfy by the payment of a smaller amount. Thus in *Nassoiy v. Tomlinson* this court said: "A demand is not liquidated, even if it appears that something is due, unless it appears how much is due; and when it is admitted that one of two specific sums is due, but there is a genuine dispute as to which is the proper amount, the demand is regarded as unliquidated, within the meaning of that term as applied to the subject of accord and satisfaction."

In this case before us, the full amount claimed by the plaintiffs was not admittedly due. The fact that the contract called for a stated amount or an amount which could be easily figured according to deliveries did not make the claim liquidated within this meaning of the law as applied to accord and satisfaction. The term "liquidated" has an entirely different meaning in this connection than it has when used to determine whether or not interest is payable upon a recovery. The amount claimed by the plaintiffs and specified in the contract was repudiated by the defendant. He denied that he owed the money. He disputed the plaintiffs' demand. The contract had not been fulfilled and completed. Deliveries had not been made as called for. The goods were rotten and decayed, and not as warranted. For the purpose of this subject, to my mind, it makes no difference whether the defendant had a claim for breach of warranty or whether he had a right to reject or claimed a right to reject the imperfect goods. The fact still exists that he insisted with the plaintiffs that he should not be obliged to pay for articles he had not purchased. It is a statement inconsistent with the fact to say that the plaintiffs' claim was liquidated in the sense that it was admitted and acknowledged to be due by the defendant. He disputed it at every step, and sent to the plaintiffs written evidence to justify the honesty and good faith of his statements. Thus there was a difference between these parties over the amount due on this contract. If the plaintiffs had sued the defendant for the full amount, the latter could have defended. There was some evidence at least to indicate that the onions were rotten at the heart when delivered to the railroad. Thus, there never had been a complete delivery and the defendant might have defended, or if there had been acceptance and no rejection within a reasonable time, then the defendant

having given notice, could have counterclaimed on his warranty. However we look at it there was relief at law in some form for the defendant. He was not obliged to pay for rotten onions.

Thus within all the cases the claim of the plaintiffs was not liquidated within the meaning of that term as used in this connection. It was a disputed claim. The plaintiffs knew it was disputed. They knew also that the checks and notes which they received and cashed were received in full payment of their disputed claim. They could not under these circumstances keep the money and reject the conditions attached to payment. Having accepted payment the conditions attached and the balance of $801.29 has been satisfied.

Therefore, the judgments below must be reversed and judgment directed for the defendant dismissing the complaint....

CASE 11-3

The following case explains how and why the Uniform Commercial Code has changed common law rules regarding accord and satisfaction in New York. The changes allow a creditor who complies with UCC § 1-207 to cash a debtor's "full satisfaction" check but avoid an accord and satisfaction and reserve its rights against the debtor for the balance the creditor claims is due.

HORN WATERPROOFING CORP. v. BUSHWICK IRON & STEEL CO.
Court of Appeals of New York, 1985
66 N.Y.2d 321; 497 N.Y.S.2d 310

JASEN, Judge. This appeal presents an issue of first impression: whether the common-law doctrine of accord and satisfaction has been superseded by operation of Uniform Commercial Code § 1-207 in situations involving the tender of a negotiable instrument as full payment of a disputed claim.

The relevant facts are uncomplicated. The parties entered into an oral agreement whereby plaintiff was to repair the leaking roof on defendant's building. After two days work, plaintiff concluded that a new roof was needed and submitted a bill for work already done. Defendant disputed the amount charged and plaintiff revised the bill downward from $1,241 to $1,080. Defendant remained unsatisfied with the charges and sent plaintiff a check for only $500. The check bore the following notation affixed on the reverse side: "This check is accepted in full payment, settlement, satisfaction, release and discharge of any and all claims and/or demands of whatsoever kind and nature." Directly thereunder, plaintiff printed the words "Under Protest", indorsed the check with its stamp, and deposited the $500 into its account.

Plaintiff then commenced this action in Civil Court seeking $580 as the balance due on its revised bill. Defendant moved for summary judgment on the ground that plaintiff's acceptance and negotiation of the check constituted an accord and satisfaction. The motion was denied and the Appellate Term affirmed. The court held that the Uniform Commercial Code (the Code) was applicable to the type of commercial transaction in which the parties were involved and that, under the provisions of § 1-207, plaintiff was entitled to reserve its right to demand the balance due.

On appeal by leave of the Appellate Term, the Appellate Division reversed, granted defendant's motion, and dismissed the complaint. The majority of that court held that the parties' agreement, being a contract for the performance of services, fell outside the scope of the Code. It was, therefore, concluded that the common law applied and that the doctrine of accord and satisfaction precluded plaintiff's recovery. In dissent, Justice Weinstein argued that application of the common-law doctrine to the facts of this case is inequitable and needlessly constricts the modernizing effect of the Code. We now reverse and hold that, under § 1-207 of the Code, a creditor may preserve his right to the balance of a disputed claim, by explicit reservation in his indorsement of a check tendered by the debtor as full payment.

The effect of Code § 1-207 upon the common-law doctrine of accord and satisfaction has been much debated. Indeed, the courts that have addressed the issue in this State have rendered conflicting decisions, and our sister state courts are likewise divided. In our view, applying § 1-207 to a "full payment" check situation, to permit a creditor to reserve his rights and, thereby, preclude an accord and satisfaction, more nearly comports with the content and context of the statutory provision and with the legislative history and underlying purposes of the Code as well, and is a fairer policy in debtor-creditor transactions.

It has long been the general rule in this State that "if a debt or claim be disputed or contingent at the time of payment, the payment, when accepted, of a part of the whole debt is a good satisfaction and it matters not that there was no solid foundation for the dispute. The test in such cases is, Was the dispute honest or fraudulent? If honest, it affords the basis for an accord between the parties, which the law favors, the execution of which is the satisfaction."

The theory underlying this common-law rule of accord and satisfaction is that the parties have thus entered into a new contract displacing all or part of their original one. Although the creditor might have been confronted with an "embarrassing... choice" upon the debtor's presentment to him of partial payment, such as in the case of a "full payment" or "conditional" check, nevertheless, the rule of accord and satisfaction has generally been accepted as a legitimate and expeditious means of settling contract disputes. As this court stated more than 70 years ago: "The law wisely favors settlements, and where there is a real and genuine contest between the parties and a settlement is had without fraud or misrepresentation for an amount determined upon as a compromise between the conflicting claims such settlement should be upheld, although such amount is materially less than the amount claimed by the person to whom it is paid."

Still, where the creditor is presented with partial payment as satisfaction in full, but, nevertheless, wishes to preserve his claim to the balance left unpaid, it cannot be gainsaid that conflicting considerations of policy and fairness are implicated. This is particularly so in the case of a full payment check. On the one hand, the debtor, as the master of his offer, has reason to expect that his offer will either be accepted or his check returned. At the same time, however, the creditor has good cause to believe that he is fully entitled to retain the partial payment that is rightfully his and presently in his possession, without having to forfeit entitlement to whatever else is his due.

In dismissing these latter considerations with specific regard to the applicability of Code § 1-207 to a check tendered as "full payment", one commentary argued that: "Besides operating as an unnecessary destruction of a valuable common law doctrine, the expansive interpretation of U.C.C. § 1-207 conflicts with another basic principle of the Uniform Commercial Code, the duty of good faith imposed by § 1-203, certainly the more fundamental concept.... It is unfair to the party who writes the check thinking that he will be spending his money only if the whole dispute will be over, to allow the other party, knowing of that reasonable expectation, to weasel around the deal by putting his own markings on the other person's checks. There is no reason why § 1-207 should be interpreted as being an exception to the basic duty of good faith, when it is possible to interpret the two sections consistently. The academic writers who support this result offer no analysis, to the current knowledge of this treatise, which would justify licensing the recipient of the check to so deceive the drawer."

However, an entirely different conclusion is reached in another commentary which explains that:

"Offering a check for less than the contract amount, but 'in full settlement' inflicts an exquisite form of commercial torture on the payee. If the offer is reasonable it creates a marvelous anxiety in some recipients: 'Shall I risk the loss of $9,000 for the additional $1,000 that the bloke really owes me?' In general the law has authorized such drawer behavior by regarding such a check as an offer of accord and satisfaction which the payee accepts if he cashes the check. Traditionally the payee could write all manner of disclaimers over his indorsement without avail; by cashing the check he was held to have accepted the offer on the drawer's terms. Even if he scratched out the drawer's notation or indorsed it under protest he was deemed to have accepted subject to the conditions under which the drawer offered it.
* * * *

"However, we believe... that 1-207 authorizes the payee to indorse under protest and accept the amount of the check without entering an accord and satisfaction or otherwise forsaking his claim to any additional sum allegedly due him."

We concur with the latter view. Indeed, the common-law doctrine of accord and satisfaction creates a cruel dilemma for the good-faith creditor in possession of a full payment check. Under that rule, the creditor would have no other choice but to surrender the partial payment or forfeit his right to the remainder. We are persuaded, however, that the common law was changed with the adoption of § 1-207 pursuant to which a fairer rule now prevails.

§ 1-207 provides: "A party who with explicit reservation of rights performs or promises performance or assents to performance in a manner demanded or offered by the other party does not thereby prejudice the rights reserved. Such words as 'without prejudice', 'under protest' or the like are sufficient." The plain language of the provision, "without much stretching", would seem applicable to a full payment check. A fortiori, if liberally construed, as the Code's provisions are explicitly intended to be, it seems clear that the reach of § 1-207 is sufficiently extensive to alter the doctrine of accord and satisfaction by permitting a creditor to reserve his rights though accepting the debtor's check.

The Comment prepared by the National Conference of Commissioners on Uniform State Laws and the American Law Institute is fairly subject to a variety of interpretations as to the purpose of § 1-207. It simply does not, however, specifically address the law of accord and satisfaction and how it might have been altered. By contrast, the Report of the State of New York Commission on Uniform State Laws quite clearly took the position that the common-law doctrine would be changed. With specific reference to § 1-207, the report stated:

"This section permits a party involved in a Code-covered transaction to accept whatever he can get by way of payment, performance, etc., without losing his rights to demand the remainder of the goods, to set-off a failure of quality, or to sue for the balance of the payment, so long as he explicitly reserves his rights.

"In *Nassoiy v. Tomlinson*, the debtor paid no more than the exact amount he claimed was due. The court held that the conditional payment was payment of an unliquidated claim if any part was disputed, and that the acceptance of the payment discharged the entire debt. The Code rule would permit, in Code-covered transactions, the acceptance of a part performance or payment tendered in full settlement without requiring the acceptor to gamble with his legal right to demand the balance of the performance or payment." (Report of Comm. on Uniform State Laws to Legislature, at 19-20 [1961].)

This interpretive analysis, which was submitted to the Legislature together with the Commission's recommendation for enactment of the Code,

unmistakeably addresses the common-law doctrine and notes that the section permits a reservation of rights upon acceptance of partial payment where an accord and satisfaction might otherwise have resulted. Particularly significant is the reference to *Nassoiy v Tomlinson*, a seminal decision in this State applying the doctrine of accord and satisfaction under facts involving a full payment check. This commentary clearly apprised the Legislature that § 1-207 would change the rule upheld in that case. Moreover, it is notable that the analysis explicitly speaks of the acceptance of part "payment tendered in full settlement." The section was clearly not deemed restricted to situations involving the acceptance of goods or such other "performance" in part.

This view derives further support from the very context of § 1-207 within the Code. The provision is set forth in the introductory article 1, among the general provisions of the Code dealing with such matters as its title, underlying purposes, general definitions, and principles of interpretation. Presumably, § 1-207, as with other provisions in the introductory article, is to apply to any commercial transaction within the reach of one of the substantive articles -- i.e., to any "Code-covered" transaction, as denominated in the New York Annotations. There is simply no language in § 1-207 expressing or intimating a more restrictive intention to limit its application to specific kinds of transactions particular to one of the articles, or sections, of the Code such as the purchase and acceptance of goods (art 2), investment securities (art 8) or chattel paper (art 9). Rather, the nonlimiting language of § 1-207 and its placement in the Code with the other generally applicable provisions of article 1 is persuasive that the section is, indeed, applicable to all commercial transactions fairly considered to be "Code-covered".

Hence, the payment of a contract debt by check or other commercial paper and its acceptance by the creditor fall within the reach of § 1-207. Whether the underlying contract between the parties be for the purchase of goods, chattel paper or personal services, the use of a negotiable instrument for the purpose of payment or attempted satisfaction of a contract debt is explicitly and specifically regulated by the provisions of article 3 and, therefore, undeniably a Code-covered transaction. Consequently, a debtor's tender of a full payment check is an article 3 transaction which is governed by § 1-207, regardless of the nature of the contract underlying the parties' commercial relationship.

Indeed, Dean Rosenthal, who otherwise contended that § 1-207 was not originally intended by the drafters to alter the doctrine of accord and satisfaction by full payment checks, observed that:

"Article three ('Commercial Paper'), however, is a special case. Does the fact that a check is used as the device to effect a settlement in itself bring the transaction within the Code (and therefore make § 1-207 arguably applicable) even if the underlying transaction was one not otherwise covered by the Code? Article three contains no scope provision analogous to the "transactions in goods' language in [article 2].

* * * *

"[I]t seems fairly clear that if such a check is tendered in settlement, the transaction must be regarded as being within article three, and if § 1-207 is otherwise relevant its application cannot be avoided by showing either that article one was not meant to be applied to non-Code transactions or that the underlying obligation did not arise out of one of the other substantive articles of the Code." (Rosenthal, *Discord and Dissatisfaction: § 1-207 of the Uniform Commercial Code*, 78 Colum L Rev 48, 70.)

Finally, . . . such a reading of § 1-207 would seem to promote the underlying policies and purposes of the Code. . . . By construing the section to permit a reservation of rights whenever a negotiable instrument is used to make payment on an existing debt, regardless of the nature of the underlying obligation between the parties, the commercial law of negotiable instruments is rendered more simple, clear and uniform. Moreover, the policy embodied in § 1-207, to favor a preservation of rights despite acceptance of partial satisfaction of the underlying obligation, is thus extended to reach all commercial transactions in which the Code is implicated by reason of payment by an article 3 instrument. As a consequence, such a reading of § 1-207 serves to liberalize, or "de-technicalize", that important branch of commercial law governing the full payment check.

Application of the foregoing to the facts of this case is evident. Defendant presented a "full payment" check for $500 in satisfaction of a debt in the amount of $1,080. Plaintiff indorsed the check below its notation, "Under Protest", thereby indicating its intent to preserve all rights to the $580 balance. Such an explicit reservation of rights, falling squarely within § 1-207 as we construe that provision today, was an effective means of precluding an accord and satisfaction or any other prejudice to the rights thus reserved. Regardless of whether the underlying transaction between the parties was a contract for the performance of services rather than for the sale of goods, defendant's tender of a check to plaintiff brought the attempted full payment or satisfaction of the underlying obligation within the scope of article 3, thereby rendering it a "Code-covered" transaction to which the provisions of § 1-207 are applicable.

Accordingly, the order of the Appellate Division should be reversed, with costs, and defendant's motion to dismiss denied.

CASE 11-4

The following case interprets what is required under UCC § 1-207 for a creditor to make an "explicit reservation" of rights to avoid an accord and satisfaction when cashing a "full satisfaction" check.

SULLIVAN v. CONANT VALLEY ASSOCIATES

Supreme Court of New York, Westchester County, 1990
148 Misc. 2d 483; 560 N.Y.S.2d 617

DONOVAN, Judge. Plaintiff... has sued the two first-named defendants in contract for a balance of moneys allegedly due him for performing plumbing work and providing certain materials improving defendants' property.

By motion, the main defendants... seek summary judgment dismissing the complaint upon ground of payment or accord and satisfaction....

The central issue presented is whether plaintiff's scratching out of "complete and final payment" verbiage placed by defendants at the top of the endorsement blocks, followed by his depositing of the checks for collection, sufficiently reserved his rights so as to permit the subsequent suit here for the higher claimed amount. The court concedes that a close and novel question of law is presented.

The rule at common law is that acceptance and cashing of a final check even with explicit words of reservation of rights by the payee as to further claims constitute in all events an accord and satisfaction. This rule was, however, substantially changed upon the passage of Uniform Commercial Code § 1-207 which allows for such reservation by the payee. That section reads in full as follows: "A party who with explicit reservation of rights performs or promises performance or assents to performance in a manner demanded or offered by the other party does not thereby prejudice the rights reserved. Such words as 'without prejudice', 'under protest' or the like are sufficient."

While much case law has construed the section, it has primarily dealt with the types of transactions and situations covered by the provision. Research by the court has not disclosed any precedent examining what verbiage short of the type indicated in the statute would still be "explicit". The common thread, however, running between both the near cases examined and the statute itself is the necessity for "explicit" verbiage reserving further rights despite endorsement and cashing (see, "Horn Waterproofing Corp."). Here, in addition to the defendants' "full payment" conditions appearing over the endorsement blocks on the checks themselves, letters accompanying the checks from the defendants indicated the existence of the dispute and tender of the checks as a "complete amount and final payment" and "should you elect not to accept this final payment then all documents and backcharges are withdrawn".

On strength of general case authority, the statute itself which must be narrowly interpreted since in derogation of the common law and under the particular facts here, the court must conclude that standing alone, mere scratching out of final payment conditions on a check followed by endorsement and cashing is not the explicit and unambiguous reservation of rights required; further added words clearly bespeaking reservation are necessary.

CASE 11-5

The following case deals with a claim by a debtor that a creditor's acceptance of a "full satisfaction" check resulted in an accord and satisfaction that discharged the debtor's liquidated debt.

CENTURY 21 KAATERSKILL REALTY v. GRASSO
Appellate Division, New York (3rd Dept.), 1986
124 A.D.2d 316; 508 N.Y.S.2d 99

MIKOLL, Judge. Appeal from an order of the Supreme Court at Special Term (Williams, J.), entered August 8, 1985 in Sullivan County, which denied defendants' motion to dismiss the complaint.

Plaintiff sued defendants seeking judgment in the sum of $2,200 claimed to be the balance due and owing for a real estate broker's commission for the sale of real property belonging to defendant Michele Grasso (hereinafter Grasso). Defendants moved to dismiss the complaint on the grounds of discharge and failure to state a cause of action.

Plaintiff was retained to sell land owned by Grasso, who agreed pursuant to a written contract to pay brokerage fees of 10% of the purchase price. The property was sold for $82,000 and title was transferred on May 11, 1984. Plaintiff demanded payment of $8,200. Grasso's attorney sent plaintiff a check for $6,000 which bore the legend:

"In full accord and satisfaction for any real estate commission claimed by Centruy 21 against Michele Grasso."

The check was indorsed by Rubin J. Katz, an officer of plaintiff, and deposited in plaintiff's account. Defendants contend that the $2,200 sought in plaintiff's complaint was discharged by plaintiff's acceptance without protest of the check tendered on Grasso's behalf in full satisfaction of the debt owed. Special Term held that defendants were not entitled to a dismissal of the complaint based on an accord and satisfaction in that the submissions failed to evidence the existence of a dispute which would make viable the accord and satisfaction defense.

Defendants contend that plaintiff's failure to protest the partial payment as to conform to UCC 1-207 entitles defendants to a dismissal of the complaint. . . . We concur with Special Term's interpretation that UCC 1-207 is not implicated absent a pending dispute as to delivery, acceptance or payment. Defendants never disputed the amount owed before the check was sent to plaintiff. Accord and satisfaction pursuant to UCC 1-207 pertains only to a method of procedure where one party is claiming as of right something which the other feels is unwarranted.

Order affirmed, with costs.

CASE 11-6

This case considers whether endorsement of a full payment check constitutes a written signed promise to discharge a debt under GOL 5-1103.

KING METAL PRODUCTS, INC. v. WORKMEN'S COMPENSATION BD.
Appellate Division, New York (2d Dept.), 1963
20 A.D.2d 565, 245 N.Y.S.2d 882

Memorandum. In our opinion, respondent's retention and deposit of a check in the sum of $250, drawn by petitioner's attorney to its order and bearing legends on the face and back thereof indicating that it was in full satisfaction and settlement of the judgment, did not constitute an accord and satisfaction. On the record presented, the general rule applies that a liquidated and undisputed claim cannot be discharged by the payment of a lesser amount.

We are also of the opinion that the endorsement of the check did not constitute an agreement which was enforceable under section [5-1103 of the General Obligations Law].

CASE 11-7

Unless prohibited by statute, courts may enforce contracts in which parties agree to waive claims arising from another party's negligence. The following case illustrates how the courts view such exculpatory clauses in general and what tests must be met before a court will enforce an exculpatory clause and deny recovery to an injured party. Not surprisingly, these issues have arisen in the context of recreational parachute jumping.

GROSS v. SWEET
Court of Appeals of New York, 1979
49 N.Y.2d 102, 424 N.Y.S.2d 365

FUCHSBERG, Judge. We hold that, in the circumstances of this case, a release signed by the plaintiff as a precondition for his enrollment in defendant's parachute jumping course does not bar him from suing for personal injuries he allegedly incurred as a result of defendant's negligence.

Plaintiff Bruce Gross, wishing to learn how to parachute, enrolled in the Stormville Parachute Center Training School, a facility owned and operated by the defendant William Sweet for the purpose of offering instruction in the sport. The ensuing events are essentially undisputed. As a prerequisite for admission into the course, Gross had to pay a fee and sign a form entitled "Responsibility Release". He was then given the standard introductory lesson, which consisted of approximately one hour of on-land training, including oral instruction as well as several jumps off a two and a half foot table. Plaintiff then was equipped with a parachute and flown to an altitude of 2,800 feet for his first practice jump. Upon coming in contact with the ground on his descent, plaintiff suffered serious personal injuries.

The suit is grounded on negligence, breach of warranty and gross negligence. In the main, plaintiff claims that defendant failed to provide adequate training and safe equipment, violated certain rules and procedures promulgated by the Federal Aviation Administration governing the conduct of parachute jumping schools and failed to warn him sufficiently of the attendant dangers.

Defendant pleaded the release plaintiff had signed and moved for summary judgment, contending that the terms of the release exculpated the defendant from any liability. Plaintiff, in turn, cross-moved to strike this affirmative defense contending, primarily, that the terms of the release did not specifically bar a suit for personal injuries negligently caused by the defendant. He also urged that, as a matter of policy, the release should not be enforceable as between a student and his teacher, a relationship in which one of the parties holds himself out as qualified and responsible to provide training in a skill and the other party relies on this expertise, particularly in the context of an activity in which the degree of training necessary for safe participation is much greater than might be apparent to a novice. Alternatively, plaintiff argues that the release in any event does not excuse defendant's violation of the Federal Aviation Administration's regulations governing parachute jumping schools and student parachutists, one of which allegedly required that a medical certificate be furnished as a prerequisite to enrollment in a parachute jumping course. Defendant's failure to request one, plaintiff asserts, bore critically on his situation because, despite his having informed defendant that several years earlier an orthopedic pin had been inserted in his leg, he was accepted as a student though, as the school must have known, landing in a parachute puts special stress on one's legs.

However, Special Term granted defendant's motion, denied plaintiff's cross motion and dismissed the complaint. On plaintiff's appeal from that order, a divided Appellate Division reversed, reinstated the complaint and granted plaintiff's motion to dismiss the affirmative defense. The appeal is now before us on a certified question: "Was the order of this Court, which reinstated the complaint and granted plaintiff's motion to dismiss the affirmative defense of release, correct as a matter of law?" Our answer is that it was.

We begin with the proposition, too well settled to invoke any dispute, that the law frowns upon contracts intended to exculpate a party from the consequences of his own negligence and though, with certain exceptions, they are enforceable, such agreements are subject to close judicial scrutiny.... To the extent that agreements purport to grant exemption for liability for willful or grossly negligent acts they have been viewed as wholly void.... And so, here, so much of plaintiff's complaint as contains allegations that defendant was grossly negligent, may not be barred by the release in any event. But we need not explore further this possibility for we conclude the complaint in its entirety withstands the exculpatory agreement.

Nor need we consider plaintiff's request that we ignore the release on the grounds that the special relationship of the parties and the public interest involved forbids its enforcement. While we have, for example, had occasion to invalidate such provisions when they were contained in the contract between a passenger and a common carrier... or in a contract between a customer and a public utility under a duty to furnish telephone service... or when imposed by an employer as a condition of employment... the circumstances here do not fit within any of these relationships. And, though we note that a recent statute renders void agreements purporting to exempt from liability for negligence those engaged in a variety of businesses that serve the public (e.g., landlords (General Obligations Law, § 5-321); caterers (§ 5-322); building service or maintenance contractors (§ 5-323); those who maintain garages or parking garages (§ 5-325); or pools, gymnasiums or places of public amusement or recreation (§ 5-326)), defendant's occupation does not fall within any of these classes either. We also decline, at this point, plaintiff's invitation that we proceed further to consider what effect, if any, the alleged contravention of Federal regulations may have on the relationship of the parties or the public interest involved. Such questions need not be reached in view of our holding that the wording of the exculpatory agreement does not preclude plaintiff's suit for negligence.

As the cases make clear, the law's reluctance to enforce exculpatory provisions of this nature has resulted in the development of an exacting standard by which courts measure their validity. So, it has been repeatedly emphasized that unless the intention of the parties is expressed in unmistakable language, an exculpatory clause will not be deemed to insulate a party from liability for his own negligent acts.... Put another way, it must appear plainly and precisely that the "limitation of liability extends to negligence or other fault of the party attempting to shed his ordinary responsibility"....

Not only does this stringent standard require that the drafter of such an agreement make its terms unambiguous, but it mandates that the terms be understandable as well. Thus, a provision that would exempt its drafter from any liability occasioned by his fault should not compel resort to a magnifying glass and lexicon.... Of course, this does not imply that only simple or monosyllabic language can be used in such clauses. Rather, what the law demands is that such provisions be clear and coherent....

By and large, if such is the intention of the parties, the fairest course is to provide explicitly that claims based on negligence are included.... That does not mean that the word "negligence" must be employed for courts to give effect to an exculpatory agreement; however, words conveying a similar import must appear....

We are, of course, cognizant of the fact that the general rule of strict judicial construction has been somewhat liberalized in its application to exoneration clauses in indemnification agreements, which are usually "negotiated at arm's length between... sophisticated business entities" and which can be viewed as merely "allocating the risk of liability to third parties between themselves, essentially through the employment of insurance". In such cases, the law, reflecting the economic realities, will recognize an agreement to relieve one party from the consequences of his negligence on the strength of a broadly worded clause framed in less precise language than would normally be required, though even then it must evince the "unmistakable intent of the parties".

The case before us today obviously does not fit within this exception to the strict legal standard generally employed by the courts of this State under which exculpatory provisions drawn in broad and sweeping language have not been given effect. For example, agreements to release from "any and all responsibility or liability of any nature whatsoever for any loss of property or personal injury occurring on this trip"... or to "waive claim for any loss to personal property, or for any personal injury while a member of (a) club"... have not barred claims based on negligence.... Moreover, in *Boll v Sharp & Dohme...* we held not sufficiently unambiguous a release form in which a blood donor was required to agree that defendants were not "in any way responsible for any consequences... resulting from the giving of such blood or from any of the tests, examinations or procedures incident thereto", and further "release(d) and discharge(d) (defendants) from all claims and demands whatsoever against them or any of them by reason of any matter relative or incident to such donation of blood".... The donor was thus allowed to sue in negligence for injuries he sustained when, on the completion of the blood donation, he fainted and fell to the floor.

With all this as background, the language of the "Responsibility Release" in the case before us, must be viewed as no more explicit than that in *Boll*. In its entirety, it reads:

"I, the undersigned, hereby, and by these covenants, do waive any and all claims that I, my heirs, and/or assignees may have against Nathaniel Sweet, the Stormville Parachute Center, the Jumpmaster and the Pilot who shall operate the aircraft when used for the purpose of parachute jumping for any personal injuries or property damage that I may sustain or which may arise out of my learning, practicing or actually jumping from an aircraft. I also assume full responsibility for any damage that I may do or cause while participating in this sport".

Assuming that this language alerted the plaintiff to the dangers inherent in parachute jumping and that he entered into the sport with apprehension of the risks, it does not follow that he was aware of, much less intended to accept, any enhanced exposure to injury occasioned by the carelessness of the very persons on which he depended for his safety. Specifically, the release nowhere expresses any intention to exempt the defendant from liability for injury or property damages which may result from his failure to use due care either in his training methods or in his furnishing safe equipment. Thus, whether on a running reading or a careful analysis, the agreement could most reasonably be taken merely as driving home the fact that the defendant was not to bear any responsibility for injuries that ordinarily and inevitably would occur, without any fault of the defendant, to those who participate in such a physically demanding sport.

In short, instead of specifying to prospective students that they would have to abide any consequences attributable to the instructor's own carelessness, the defendant seems to have preferred the use of opaque terminology rather than suffer the possibility of lower enrollment. But, while, with exceptions not pertinent to this case, the law grudgingly accepts the proposition that men may contract away their liability for negligently caused injuries, they may do so only on the condition that their intention be expressed clearly and in "unequivocal terms".

Accordingly, the certified question is answered in the affirmative, and the order of the Appellate Division reversing the grant of summary judgment, reinstating the complaint and dismissing the defense based on the release should be affirmed.

CASE 11-8

Courts are reluctant to enforce contracts exculpating professionals from acts of negligence. In the following case, a New York court addressed the enforceability of a contract that attempted to release dentists from liability for malpractice.

DEVITO v. N.Y.U. COLLEGE OF DENTISTRY
Supreme Court of New York (N.Y. Co.), 1989
145 Misc. 2d 144, 544 N.Y.S.2d 109

PREMINGER, Judge. Defendants move for summary judgment dismissing this dental malpractice action on the ground that a release executed by plaintiff precludes the action.

Defendant New York University College of Dentistry (NYU) operates a dental clinic where, in exchange for reduced fees, patients agree to be treated by students working under faculty supervision. Plaintiff was treated at the clinic for approximately one year beginning in December 1982 by various students including defendants Wisun and Chiha.

Prior to any treatment plaintiff executed a release which reads, in relevant part: "In consideration of the reduced rates given to me by New York University, I hereby release and agree to save harmless New York University, its doctors, and students, from any and all liability arising out of, or in connection with, any injuries or damages which I may sustain while on its premises, or as a result of any treatment in its infirmaries."

Defendants contend that this release bars plaintiff's claims against them for malpractice. Plaintiff argues that the release was not intended to relieve defendants from responsibility for their negligent acts, and that to give the release such effect would be against public policy.

The very release involved here has been examined by several New York courts with disparate results.

* * * *

… [t]his court will reexamine the legal principles governing the validity and effect of contracts which attempt to release a doctor or hospital from liability to a patient.

In general, the law frowns upon contracts which seek to exculpate persons from their own negligence, and to the extent such contracts bar suits against willful or gross negligence, they are void. However,

where, as here, the claim sought to be foreclosed is one grounded in ordinary negligence, the contract may generally be enforced, but only after being subjected to intense judicial scrutiny on a variety of issues.

The threshold consideration is whether the parties have a special relationship which would make enforcement of an exculpatory clause between them against the public interest. This occurs where the party seeking exculpation is in a business or profession which is either publicly regulated or providing an essential service to members of the public. Examples include common carriers and their passengers; public utilities and their customers; employers who impose the clause as a condition of employment and a host of statutorily created prohibited persons, such as landlords, caterers, and those who maintain parking lots, gymnasiums, and other public places. (See, GOL § 5-321 et seq.)

In these relationships, the consumer's need for the service creates an inequality in bargaining strength which enables the purveyor to insist upon a release, generally on its own prepared form, as a condition to providing the service. As in any adhesion contract a true and voluntary meeting of the minds on the terms of the agreement is unlikely.
* * * *

The courts of this State have not conclusively determined whether it would be against the public interest to allow physicians to insulate themselves from liability for negligence. However, other jurisdictions have held that the physician-patient relationship precludes the enforcement of such exculpatory agreements.

Thus, in *Olson v Molzen* the Supreme Court of Tennessee declared that the "general rule [that] a party may contract against his or her own negligence… do[es] not afford a satisfactory solution in a case involving a professional person operating in an area of public interest and pursuing a profession subject to licensure by the state. The rules that govern tradesmen in the marketplace are of little relevancy in dealing with professional persons who hold themselves out as experts and whose practice is regulated by the state." To the same effect are *Meiman v Rehabilitation Center* (Kentucky), *Tunkl v Regents of Univ. of Cal.* and *Smith v Hospital Auth.* (Georgia).

Assuming that the status of the parties withstands scrutiny, it next becomes necessary to examine the actual wording of the agreement. One must determine whether its terms are so clear, explicit and unambiguous that it appears certain that the limitation of liability is intended to cover negligent, as well as ordinary, acts of the party seeking to shed responsibility....

Although the word "negligent" need not actually be used, the Court of Appeals has indicated that such would be the "fairest course." In those instances where releases from liability which do not contain the word "negligence" have been construed to include negligent behavior, the words used have referred to the concept of fault in specific and unambiguous terms.

All-encompassing or open-ended phrases such as "any and all claims" or "any and all responsibility or liability of any nature whatsoever" and "all claims and demands whatsoever" are considered insufficient to indicate an intention to waive injury occasioned by fault.

Even if a clause is found to be clear and unambiguous, it must be examined further to determine whether it would be understandable to a layman, which, while not requiring "only... monosyllabic language", does compel that the language used be "clear and coherent".

The NYU release cannot survive the close scrutiny mandated by the concepts discussed above. It fails, in all particulars, to meet the established standards. Even if the status of the parties is removed from consideration, the contract cannot be construed to include exemption from negligent acts. There is no reference, either explicitly or implicitly, by "words... [of] similar import" to the concept of negligence or fault. No layman perusing this release would find it immediately understandable that the signatory had contracted to accept not only injuries that might ordinarily and inevitably occur, but also any and all consequences of defendants' carelessness.

Although the law grudgingly accepts the proposition that men may contract away their liability for negligently caused injuries it may not do so here. The circumstances of this case and the wording of the release militate against such a result. The parties' status is, at the very least, suspect, the contract is ambiguous, and the language used is far from instantly coherent to a layman.

For all of the foregoing reasons, defendants' motion for summary judgment is denied. Although no cross motion was brought by plaintiff the court searches the record (CPLR 3212 [b]) and awards summary judgment dismissing defendants' affirmative defense based on the release.

CASE 11-9

The types of legitimate employer interests that might support enforcement of a restrictive covenant are noted in this case.

1 MODEL MANAGEMENT, LLC, v. KAVOUSSI
NY App. Div. 1st Dept., 2011
82 A.D. 3d 502, 918 N.Y.S. 2d 431

Plaintiff 1 Model Management (1MM), a model agency, seeks damages and injunctive relief against Ali Kavoussi, a former 1MM model agent employed pursuant to a May 2004 contract. In May 2008, Kavoussi terminated the contract, left 1MM, and began working for another model agency, Men Women N.Y. Model Management Inc. d/b/a Women Management (Men Women). During the next eight months, three models whom 1MM had been representing when Kavoussi terminated the contract also left 1MM for Men Women.

* * *

The contract also provided that, for the one-year period after his termination, which has now passed, Kavoussi could not "be employed by ... any entity which ... represents ... any model managed by 1MM at the time of Employee's termination or at any time during the 90–day period preceding such termination." Such a restrictive covenant is enforceable only to the extent, among other things, that it is reasonable and necessary to protect the employer's legitimate interest and does not impose undue hardship on the employee. [Citation]

An employer's legitimate interest can include preventing an employee from misappropriating trade secrets or confidential customer lists or keeping an employee with unique or extraordinary skills from joining a competitor to the employer's detriment. [Citations] Here, 1MM failed to establish that its customer lists and model contact information are confidential, since it has not shown that the information is not readily available to others in the modeling industry. [Citation] But 1MM has raised a viable issue of fact as to whether Kavoussi's services were "special, unique or extraordinary," given that he had cultivated personal relationships with 1MM's models while working for 1MM and using its resources. [Citation]

Kavoussi argues that enforcing the restrictive covenant as written would prevent him from working in the modeling industry, but a triable issue has been raised concerning whether the restriction against working for agencies representing former 1MM models was unreasonably burdensome.

[Breach of contract claim reinstated]

CASE 11-10

In this case the court considers whether the employer demonstrated a sufficient legitimate interest to justify restraining a former employee from working for a competitor.

NATURAL ORGANICS, INC. v. KIRKENDALL
N.Y. App. Div. 2d Dept., 2008
52 A.D. 2d 488, 860 N.Y.S.2d 142

The defendant James A. Kirkendall worked for the plaintiff for approximately nine years selling vitamins and dietary supplements to specialized health food stores under the plaintiff's national brand name. When he was hired for the position, Kirkendall signed a nondisclosure and noncompetition agreement for employees (hereinafter the noncompete agreement),

which prohibited employment with a competitor of the plaintiff for a period of 18 months from the date of termination of employment, and where the employee is a sales person, for an additional 18 months within 300 miles of the boundaries of his or her territory. Kirkendall resigned from his position with the plaintiff and began working for the defendant Reliance Vitamin Company, Inc. (hereinafter Reliance), which sold "private label" vitamins and dietary supplements to vitamin stores, health food stores, and others, who wanted to market the items to customers under their own name. The plaintiff commenced the instant action against Kirkendall and Reliance (hereinafter collectively the defendants) seeking, *inter alia*, injunctive relief and monetary damages for breach of the noncompete agreement.

In BDO Seidman v. Hirshberg, [Citation] the Court of Appeals set forth the "modern, prevailing common-law standard of reasonableness" for the enforceability of employee noncompete agreements [Citation]. "A restraint is reasonable only if it: (1) is no greater than is required for the protection of the legitimate interest of the employer, (2) does not impose undue hardship on the employee, and (3) is not injurious to the public" [Citation]. A noncompete agreement must also be reasonably limited temporally and geographically. [Citation]

Here, the defendants met their prima facie burden of establishing their entitlement to judgment as a matter of law by demonstrating that the noncompete agreement does not serve to protect a legitimate employer interest. The evidence demonstrated that

Kirkendall, after leaving the plaintiff's employ, did not physically appropriate, copy, or intentionally memorize any purported confidential business information. [Citations]

In opposition, the plaintiff failed to raise a triable issue of fact. Although the plaintiff submitted evidence that Kirkendall was privy to reports containing detailed sales information concerning the plaintiff's customers, "an employee's recollection of information pertaining to specific needs and business habits of particular customers is not confidential." [Citations] Furthermore, the plaintiff failed to show that enforcement of the noncompete agreement was necessary to protect the goodwill of its clients. . . [Citation] or that Kirkendall used or threatened to use any protected trade lists or confidential customer lists. [Citation]

Since there is no legitimate employer interest to protect, the noncompete agreement is unenforceable and the issue of partial enforcement does not arise. [Citations] Accordingly, the Supreme Court properly granted the defendants' motion for summary judgment dismissing the complaint.

Case 12-1

The following case deals with the question of whether a party has a claim for fraud based on an affirmative misrepresentation of a material fact, when the party has been put on notice of material facts that have not been documented, but nevertheless goes forward with the transaction.

RODAS v. MANITARAS
Appellate Division, New York (1st Dept.), 1990
159 A.D.2d 341; 552 N.Y.S.2d 618

MEMORANDUM.

Pursuant to a contract of sale dated November 6, 1987, plaintiffs purchased a restaurant business from defendant Oyster House, Inc. Plaintiffs later signed a lease agreement for the premises dated March 9, 1988 with defendant Manitaras. Plaintiffs brought this action seeking rescission of the sale and lease agreements on the ground that defendants' false representations that the income of the business was $20,000 a week fraudulently induced them to enter into said agreements.

Paragraph 20 of the contract of sale contains a general merger clause and specifically recites that the business, its equipment, fixtures, chattels and furnishings are purchased in the exercise of plaintiffs' business judgment "and not upon any representations

made by the seller, or by anyone acting in his behalf, as to the character, condition or quality of said chattels, fixtures, equipment and furnishings or as to the past, present or prospective income or profits of the said business, other than those contained in this agreement." While a general merger clause will not operate to bar parol evidence of fraud in the inducement where the parties expressly disclaim reliance on the representations alleged to be fraudulent, parol evidence as to those representations will not be admitted. Plaintiffs, however, allege that a specific disclaimer clause cannot bar the introduction of parol evidence of prior misrepresentations where the facts misrepresented were peculiarly within the knowledge of the defendant.

The defect in plaintiffs' reasoning lies not in the statement of the rule, but in their perception of its application. A classic example is provided by *Tahini Invs. v Bobrowsky*, in which the purchaser of land discovered 15 or more drums containing a hazardous material buried on the property. Although the contract contained specific language that the purchaser was not relying on representations as to the physical condition of the property, the court ruled that questions of fact were presented as to (1) whether the seller knew of the existence of the dumping site and (2) whether the purchaser, with reasonable diligence, could have ascertained the site's existence. The case illustrates that a party seeking to avoid a specific disclaimer clause must demonstrate that the facts alleged to have been fraudulently concealed could not be discovered through the exercise of reasonable diligence.

In the matter under review, by contrast, plaintiffs specifically requested examination of the records of the business and were refused. It is apparent that they were aware that the income of the business was a material fact in which they had received no documentation. In entering into the contract, with the assistance of counsel and without conducting an examination of the books and records, plaintiffs clearly assumed the risk that the documentation might not support the $20,000 weekly income that was represented to them.

Plaintiffs could have easily protected themselves by insisting on an examination of the books as a condition of closing. Alternatively, the contract could have included a condition subsequent that the sale would be rescinded if the actual sales experienced were significantly less than the represented figure. The standard which a party claiming fraud must meet in order to overcome a specific disclaimer clause is set forth in *Danann Realty Corp. v Harris*, relied upon by plaintiffs. It quotes *Schumaker v Mather*, which states that "if the facts represented are not matters peculiarly within the party's knowledge, and the other party has the means available to him of knowing, by the exercise of ordinary intelligence, the truth or the real quality of the subject of the representation, he must make use of those means, or he will not be heard to complain that he was induced to enter into the transaction by misrepresentations."

Where a party has no knowledge of a latent condition and no way of discovering the existence of that condition in the exercise of reasonable diligence then, as in *Tahini Invs. v Bobrowsky*, he may overcome a specific disclaimer clause and introduce parol evidence of fraudulent inducement. But where, as here, a party has been put on notice of the existence of material facts which have not been documented and he nevertheless proceeds with a transaction without securing the available documentation or inserting appropriate language in the agreement for his protection, he may truly be said to have willingly assumed the business risk that the facts may not be as represented. Succinctly put, a party will not be heard to complain that he has been defrauded when it is his own evident lack of due care which is responsible for his predicament.

CASE 12-2

A statement of opinion generally may not be the basis of a claim for fraud. This case discusses when a statement of opinion may be regarded and as statement of fact and thus may be actionable as fraud.

VOKES v. ARTHUR MURRAY, INC.
Fla. Dist. Ct. of Appeal of Florida, Sec. Dist., 1968
212 So.2d 906

PIERCE, J.

This is an appeal by Audrey E. Vokes, plaintiff below, from a final order dismissing with prejudice, for failure to state a cause of action, . . . plaintiff's complaint.

Defendant Arthur Murray, Inc., a corporation, authorizes the operation throughout the nation of dancing schools under the name of 'Arthur Murray School of Dancing' through local franchised operators,

one of whom was defendant J. P. Davenport whose dancing establishment was in Clearwater.

Plaintiff Mrs. Audrey E. Vokes, a widow of 51 years and without family, had a yen to be 'an accomplished dancer' with the hopes of finding 'new interest in life'. So, on February 10, 1961, a dubious fate, with the assist of a motivated acquaintance, procured her to attend a 'dance party' at Davenport's 'School of Dancing' where she whiled away the pleasant hours, sometimes in a private room, absorbing his accomplished sales technique, during which her grace and poise were elaborated upon and her rosy future as 'an excellent dancer' was painted for her in vivid and glowing colors. As an incident to this interlude, he sold her eight 1/2-hour dance lessons to be utilized within one calendar month therefrom, for the sum of $14.50 cash in hand paid, obviously a baited 'comeon'.

Thus she embarked upon an almost endless pursuit of the terpsichorean art during which, over a period of less than sixteen months, she was sold fourteen 'dance courses' totalling in the aggregate 2302 hours of dancing lessons for a total cash outlay of $31,090.45, all at Davenport's dance emporium. . . . .

These dance lesson contracts and the monetary consideration therefor of over $31,000 were procured from her by means and methods of Davenport and his associates which went beyond the unsavory, yet legally permissible, perimeter of 'sales puffing' and intruded well into the forbidden area of undue influence, the suggestion of falsehood, the suppression of truth, and the free exercise of rational judgment, if what plaintiff alleged in her complaint was true. From the time of her first contact with the dancing school in February, 1961, she was influenced unwittingly by a constant and continuous barrage of flattery, false praise, excessive compliments, and panegyric encomiums, to such extent that it would be not only inequitable, but unconscionable, for a Court exercising inherent chancery power to allow such contracts to stand.

She was incessantly subjected to overreaching blandishment and cajolery. She was assured she had 'grace and poise'; that she was 'rapidly improving and developing in her dancing skill'; that the additional lessons would 'make her a beautiful dancer, capable of dancing with the most accomplished dancers'; that she was 'rapidly progressing in the development of her dancing skill and gracefulness', etc., etc. She was given 'dance aptitude tests' for the ostensible purpose of 'determining' the number of remaining hours of instructions needed by her from time to time.

At one point she was sold 545 additional hours of dancing lessons to be entitled to award of the 'Bronze Medal' signifying that she had reached 'the Bronze Standard', a supposed designation of dance achievement by students of Arthur Murray, Inc. Later she was sold an additional 926 hours in order to gain the 'Silver Medal', indicating she had reached 'the Silver Standard', at a cost of $12,501.35. At one point, while she still had to her credit about 900 unused hours of instructions, she was induced to purchase an additional 24 hours of lessons to participate in a trip to Miami at her own expense, where she would be 'given the opportunity to dance with members of the Miami Studio'.

She was induced at another point to purchase an additional 123 hours of lessons in order to be not only eligible for the Miami trip but also to become 'a life member of the Arthur Murray Studio', carrying with it certain dubious emoluments, at a further cost of $1,752.30.

At another point, while she still had over 1,000 unused hours of instruction she was induced to buy 151 additional hours at a cost of $2,049.00 to be eligible for a 'Student Trip to Trinidad', at her own expense as she later learned.

Also, when she still had 1100 unused hours to her credit, she was prevailed upon to purchase an additional 347 hours at a cost of $4,235.74, to qualify her to receive a 'Gold Medal' for achievement, indicating she had advanced to 'the Gold Standard'. On another occasion, while she still had over 1200 unused hours, she was induced to buy an additional 175 hours of instruction at a cost of $2,472.75 to be eligible 'to take a trip to Mexico'.

Finally, sandwiched in between other lesser sales promotions, she was influenced to buy an additional 481 hours of instruction at a cost of $6,523.81 in order to 'be classified as a Gold Bar Member, the ultimate achievement of the dancing studio'.

All the foregoing sales promotions, illustrative of the entire fourteen separate contracts, were procured by defendant Davenport and Arthur Murray, Inc., by false representations to her that she was improving in her dancing ability, that she had excellent potential, that she was responding to instructions in dancing grace, and that they were developing her into a beautiful dancer, whereas in truth and in fact she did not develop in her dancing ability, she had no 'dance aptitude', and in fact had difficulty in 'hearing that musical beat'. The complaint alleged that such representations to her 'were in fact false and known by the defendant to be false and contrary to the plaintiff's true ability, the truth of plaintiff's ability being fully known to the defendants, but withheld from the plaintiff for the sole and specific intent to deceive and defraud the plaintiff and to induce her in the purchasing of additional hours of dance lessons'. It was averred that the lessons were sold to her 'in total disregard to the true physical, rhythm, and mental ability of the plaintiff'. In other words, while she first exulted that she was entering the 'spring of her life', she finally was awakened to the fact there was 'spring' neither in her life nor in her feet.

* * *

. . . . Defendants contend that contracts can only be rescinded for fraud or misrepresentation when the alleged misrepresentation is as to a material fact, rather than an opinion, prediction or expectation, and that the statements and representations set forth at length in the complaint were in the category of 'trade puffing', within its legal orbit.

It is true that 'generally a misrepresentation, to be actionable, must be one of fact rather than of opinion'. [Citations] But this rule has significant qualifications, applicable here. . . . As stated by Judge Allen of this Court in [Citation]:

'* * * A statement of a party having * * * superior knowledge may be regarded as a statement of fact although it would be considered as opinion if the parties were dealing on equal terms.'

It could be reasonably supposed here that defendants had 'superior knowledge' as to whether plaintiff had 'dance potential' and as to whether she was noticeably improving in the art of terpsichore. And it would be a reasonable inference from the undenied averments of the complaint that the flowery eulogiums heaped upon her by defendants as a prelude to her contracting for 1944 additional hours of instruction in order to attain the rank of the Bronze Standard, thence to the bracket of the Silver Standard, thence to the class of the Gold Bar Standard, and finally to the crowning plateau of a Life Member of the Studio, proceeded as much or more from the urge to 'ring the cash register' as from any honest or realistic appraisal of her dancing prowess or a factual representation of her progress.

Even in contractual situations where a party to a transaction owes no duty to disclose facts within his knowledge or to answer inquiries respecting such facts, the law is if he undertakes to do so he must disclose the whole truth. [Citations] From the face of the complaint, it should have been reasonably apparent to defendants that her vast outlay of cash for the many hundreds of additional hours of instruction was not justified by her slow and awkward progress, which she would have been made well aware of if they had spoken the 'whole truth'.

* * *

It accordingly follows that the order dismissing plaintiff's last amended complaint with prejudice should be and is reversed.

CASE 12-3

The following case demonstrates the type of circumstances a party must show to be entitled to rescission of a contract on the grounds of economic duress.

AUSTIN INSTRUMENT, INC. v. LORAL CORPORATION
Court of Appeals of New York, 1971
29 N.Y.2d 124, 324 N.Y.S.2d 22

FULD, Chief Judge. The defendant, Loral Corporation, seeks to recover payment for goods delivered under a contract which it had with plaintiff Austin Instrument, Inc., on the ground that the evidence establishes, as a matter of law, that it was forced to agree to an increase in price on the items in question under circumstances amounting to economic duress.

In July of 1965, Loral was awarded a $6,000,000 contract by the Navy for the production of radar sets. The contract contained a schedule of deliveries, a liquidated damages clause applying to late deliveries and a cancellation clause in case of default by Loral. The latter thereupon solicited bids for some 40 precision gear components needed to produce the radar sets, and awarded Austin a subcontract to supply 23 such parts. That party commenced delivery in early 1966.

In May 1966, Loral was awarded a second Navy contract for the production of more radar sets and again went about soliciting bids. Austin bid on all 40 gear components but, on July 15, a representative from Loral informed Austin's president, Mr. Krauss, that his company would be awarded the subcontract only for those items on which it was low bidder. The Austin officer refused to accept an order for less than all 40 of the gear parts and on the next day he told Loral that Austin would cease deliveries of the parts due under the existing subcontract unless Loral consented to substantial increases in the prices provided for by that agreement -- both retroactively for parts already delivered and prospectively on those not yet shipped -- and placed with Austin the order for all 40 parts needed under Loral's second Navy contract. Shortly thereafter,

Austin did, indeed, stop delivery. After contacting 10 manufacturers of precision gears and finding none who could produce the parts in time to meet its commitments to the Navy, Loral acceded to Austin's demands; in a letter dated July 22, Loral wrote to Austin that "We have feverishly surveyed other sources of supply and find that because of the prevailing military exigencies, were they to start from scratch as would have to be the case, they could not even remotely begin to deliver on time.... Accordingly, we are left with no choice or alternative but to meet your conditions."

Loral thereupon consented to the price increases insisted upon by Austin under the first subcontract and the latter was awarded a second subcontract making it the supplier of all 40 gear parts for Loral's second contract with the Navy. Although Austin was granted until September to resume deliveries, Loral did, in fact, receive parts in August and was able to produce the radar sets in time to meet its commitments to the Navy on both contracts. After Austin's last delivery under the second subcontract in July, 1967, Loral notified it of its intention to seek recovery of the price increases.

On September 15, 1967, Austin instituted this action against Loral to recover an amount in excess of $17,750 which was still due on the second subcontract. On the same day, Loral commenced an action against Austin claiming damages of some $22,250 -- the aggregate of the price increases under the first subcontract -- on the ground of economic duress. The two actions were consolidated and, following a trial, Austin was awarded the sum it requested and Loral's complaint against Austin was dismissed on the ground that it was not shown that "it could not have obtained the items in question from other sources in time to meet its commitment to the Navy under the first contract." A closely divided Appellate Division affirmed.... There was no material disagreement concerning the facts; as Justice STEUER stated in the course of his dissent below, "the facts are virtually undisputed, nor is there any serious question of law. The difficulty lies in the application of the law to these facts."...

The applicable law is clear and, indeed, is not disputed by the parties. A contract is voidable on the ground of duress when it is established that the party making the claim was forced to agree to it by means of a wrongful threat precluding the exercise of his free will.... The existence of economic duress or business compulsion is demonstrated by proof that "immediate possession of needful goods is threatened"... or, more particularly, in cases such as the one before us, by proof that one party to a contract has threatened to breach the agreement by withholding goods unless the other party agrees to some further demand.... However, a mere threat by one party to breach the contract by not delivering the required items, though wrongful, does not in itself constitute economic duress. It must also appear that the threatened party could not obtain the goods from another source of supply and that the ordinary remedy of an action for breach of contract would not be adequate.

We find without any support in the record the conclusion reached by the courts below that Loral failed to establish that it was the victim of economic duress. On the contrary, the evidence makes out a classic case, as a matter of law, of such duress.

It must be remembered that Loral was producing a needed item of military hardware. Moreover, there is authority for Loral's position that nonperformance by a subcontractor is not an excuse for default in the main contract.... In light of all this, Loral's claim should not be held insufficiently supported because it did not request an extension from the Government.

Loral, as indicated above, also had the burden of demonstrating that it could not obtain the parts elsewhere within a reasonable time, and there can be no doubt that it met this burden. The 10 manufacturers whom Loral contacted comprised its entire list of "approved vendors" for precision gears, and none was able to commence delivery soon enough. As Loral was producing a highly sophisticated item of military machinery requiring parts made to the strictest engineering standards, it would be unreasonable to hold that Loral should have gone to other vendors, with whom it was either unfamiliar or dissatisfied, to procure the needed parts. As Justice STEUER noted in his dissent, Loral "contacted all the manufacturers whom it believed capable of making these parts", and this was all the law requires.

It is hardly necessary to add that Loral's normal legal remedy of accepting Austin's breach of the contract and then suing for damages would have been inadequate under the circumstances, as Loral would still have had to obtain the gears elsewhere with all the concomitant consequences mentioned above. In other words, Loral actually had no choice, when the prices were raised by Austin, except to take the gears at the "coerced" prices and then sue to get the excess back.

Austin's final argument is that Loral, even if it did enter into the contract under duress, lost any rights it had to a refund of money by waiting until July, 1967, long after the termination date of the contract, to disaffirm it. It is true that one who would recover moneys allegedly paid under duress must act promptly to make his claim known.... In this case, Loral delayed making its demand for a refund until three days after Austin's last delivery on the second subcontract. Loral's reason -- for waiting until that time -- is that it feared another stoppage of deliveries which would again put it in an untenable situation. Considering Austin's conduct in the past, this was perfectly reasonable, as the possibility of an application by Austin of further business compulsion still existed until all of the parts were delivered.

In sum, the record before us demonstrates that Loral agreed to the price increases in consequence of the economic duress employed by Austin. Accordingly, the matter should be remanded to the trial court for a computation of its damages.

CASE 12-4

In the following case, the court discusses the circumstances under which a party may be entitled to relief from a contract on the grounds of a unilateral mistake.

BALABAN-GORDON CO., INC. v. BRIGHTON SEW. DIST.
Appellate Division, New York (4th Dept.), 1973
41 A.D.2d 246; 342 N.Y.S.2d 435

SIMONS, Judge. This appeal questions the right of a contractor to withdraw its bid on a public construction contract because of a unilateral mistake in interpreting the engineers' specifications concerning equipment to be included in the bid price.

A bid is a binding offer to make a contract. It may be withdrawn in the case of unilateral mistake by the bidder where the mistake is known to the other party to the transaction and (1) the bid is of such consequence that enforcement would be unconscionable, (2) the mistake is material, (3) the mistake occurred despite the exercise of ordinary care by the bidder and (4) it is possible to place the other party in status quo....

In 1967 the appellant Brighton Sewer District No. 2 advertised for bids to construct two sewage treatment plants. Bids were received for the general construction, plumbing, heating and electrical work for each facility and bidders could bid each contract separately or in combination. Respondent Balaban-Gordon Company, Inc. was the lowest bidder on the general construction contract for both plants. Its total bid for the work was $2,249,700, $530,300 below the second bidder. It also bid on the plumbing contract. It was the high bidder for that job, its bid being $376,230 higher than the low bid of $687,770. The respondent's representatives, upon learning of the difference in the bids, checked with the appellant's engineers and re-examined their worksheets. They determined that they had incorrectly interpreted the specifications and had included the cost of several pieces of mechanical equipment in the bid for the plumbing contract which should have been in the bid for the general construction. The trial court has found this mistake was due to the bidder's negligence. The respondent

explained the error in detail at a conference with appellant's representatives and asked that its bid be withdrawn. The appellant insisted that the bid could not be withdrawn under General Municipal Law (§ 105) and demanded that respondent execute the contracts for general construction. When the respondent refused to do so, the appellant readvertised for bids and declared the respondent's bid bond forfeited. This action to rescind the bid and to cancel the bond followed. The trial court granted judgment for respondent, holding that it was entitled to rescind its mistaken bid notwithstanding its negligence.

If the bid may be rescinded, then the bid bond must be canceled because the municipality may not retain the proceeds either as a penalty or liquidated damages. If there is no legal obligation on the part of the contractor to fulfill its bid, it may not be held on the bid bond for its failure to do so....

It is apparent from the facts that there was a material mistake of serious consequence to the bidder from which it should be relieved if the appellant can be placed in status quo and if respondent's mistake is excusable. The mistake in computing the bid was "palpable", i.e., known to the other party because of the disparity in the bids and because of the prompt actual notice to appellant once the bids were opened and before the contract was awarded. Furthermore, the appellant's position has not been damaged. It could have awarded the contract to the second bidder. The election to rebid the job was its own and not required by any act of respondent. Appellant lost the bargain but that is not a compensable loss if the bid may be rescinded, because it was a bargain to which the appellant was never entitled. The case turns on whether this is the type of a mistake which justifies relief by rescission. Mistakes by definition reflect oversight or some lack of care and so the requirement that the mistake occur in the exercise of ordinary care may not be interpreted narrowly. The question is whether the mistake is of the variety considered excusable, and each case must be considered on its own facts....

The parties are in agreement that relief is available where the mistake is clerical or arithmetical.... In such a case, the mistaken bid does not express the true intention of the bidder. If he were to recompute the bid or if another person were to do so, the obvious error would be discovered and corrected. Its existence may be objectively determined. In those circumstances, there is said to be no meeting of the minds because the bid was one which the bidder never intended to make.

On the other hand, it is commonly recognized that a bidder will not be relieved from an error in a value judgment in estimating the requirements or costs necessary to fulfill a contract. Mistakes of this type are inherent business risks assumed by contractors in all bidding situations. If the specifics of the job were recalculated by the bidder, his bid would be the same, for these estimates do not involve oversights. They represent subjective judgments deliberately made with respect to the requirements of the job. Another person calculating the bid might or might not make the same "mistake", depending upon his mental evaluation of the work to be performed, but in any event, the minds of the bidder and the offeree meet because the bid is precisely what the bidder intends even though his judgment later proves faulty.

The appellant claims that the error must be considered one of these two types, either clerical and arithmetical, or an error of judgment, relief by rescission being available in the former case but not in the latter. Since the incorrect interpretation of the specifications was not clerical or arithmetical appellant claims that respondent should be held to the bid and liable for liquidated damages under its bid bond. Unfortunately, not all mistakes made by contractors are categorized so easily. Applying the reasoning of the two types of mistakes to the facts of this case illustrates the difficulty. If respondent's representatives were to recompute its bid, they doubtless would interpret the specifications the same way. In that sense, the bid accurately represented the contract respondent was willing to make and there was a meeting of the minds. Nevertheless, the error was objectively discoverable. Another contractor computing the bid would not, and in fact no others did, make the

same mistake in interpretation and in that sense the bid did not represent the bid intended because respondent was working under a misapprehension with respect to the particulars called for by the specifications. Reasonable care probably dictated that respondent should have asked the engineers to clarify the meaning of the ambiguous specifications (at least one other bidder did so), but respondent's failure to investigate should not prevent it from obtaining relief.

The case fits squarely within the factual pattern of *President & Council of Mount St. Mary's Coll. v. Aetna Cas. & Sur. Co.* There, the court granted relief by rescission to a bidder who, because of an error in interpreting the specifications, failed to include the cost of certain equipment in his bid. Although the error was the result of negligence by the bidder in not asking the architect for an interpretation of the specifications, relief was granted because the bidder's negligence was not "culpable". Similar analyses of the degree of the bidder's mistake, i.e., whether the bidder is "more" or "less" negligent, have been made in other cases.... When an effort is made to apply these tests, they are found to be elusive to say the least. The decisive factual question is whether the mistake is one the courts will excuse. Then, if the mistake concerns a material matter in an executory contract under circumstances where relief to the bidder results in no damage to the municipality but enforcement results in serious harm to the bidder, rescission will be granted. Manifestly, rescission may be allowed more readily for a mistake made by a bidder which is objectively established and which does not evolve from an inherent risk of business. Even though the mistake is the product of negligence on the part of the bidder, relief should be granted because the assurance exists from the objective proof that the transaction is free from mischief. This satisfies a fundamental purpose of the public bidding statutes.

The error in this case did not pertain to an evaluation of risks or estimation of requirements or costs by the bidder and the effect of the mistake was verifiable in much the same way as a clerical error, the impossibility of performance or an arithmetical error. That being the case, it should be excused and rescission granted. In these days of multi-million dollar construction contracts, the public interest requires stability in bidding of public contracts under rules that protect against chicane and overreaching. Nevertheless, little is to be gained if a contractor is forced to perform a contract at an extravagant loss or the risk of possible bankruptcy. If a mistake has been made under circumstances justifying relief, the municipality should not be allowed to enforce the bargain. Its remedy to avoid loss is to award the contract to the next bidder or assume the responsibility of rebidding.

The judgment granting respondent rescission of its bid and canceling the bond should therefore be affirmed.

Judgment unanimously affirmed, with costs.

CASE 12-5

The New York Statute of Frauds provides that the Statute of Frauds may be satisfied by a "note or memorandum" of the contract that is signed by the party against whom enforcement of the contract is sought. The following case answers several significant questions about what the note or memorandum must contain and whether it may be "pieced together" from several different documents.

CRABTREE v. ELIZABETH ARDEN SALES CORP.

Court of Appeals of New York, 1953
305 N.Y. 48

FULD, Judge. In September of 1947, Nate Crabtree entered into preliminary negotiations with Elizabeth Arden Sales Corporation, manufacturers and sellers of cosmetics, looking toward his employment as sales manager. Interviewed on September 26th, by Robert P. Johns, executive vice-president and general manager of the corporation, who had apprised him of the possible opening, Crabtree requested a three-year contract at $25,000 a year. Explaining that he would be giving up a secure well-paying job to take a position in an entirely new field of endeavor - which he believed would take him some years to master - he insisted upon an agreement for a definite term. And he repeated his desire for a contract for three years to Miss Elizabeth Arden, the corporation's president. When Miss Arden finally indicated that she was prepared to offer a two-year contract, based on an annual salary of $20,000 for the first six months, $25,000 for the second six months and $30,000 for the second year, plus expenses of $5,000 a year for each of those years, Crabtree replied that that offer was "interesting". Miss Arden thereupon had her personal secretary make this memorandum on a telephone order blank that happened to be at hand:

"EMPLOYMENT AGREEMENT WITH
NATE CRABTREE Date Sept 26-1947
At 681 - 5th Ave   6: PM
          * * *
Begin $20,000.
6 months $25,000.
6 months $30,000.
$5,000. - per year
Expense money
2 years to make good

Arrangement with Mr. Crabtree
By Miss Arden
Present Miss Arden
Mr. John
Mr. Crabtree
Miss OLeary"

A few days later, Crabtree 'phoned Mr. Johns and telegraphed Miss Arden; he accepted the "invitation to join the Arden organization", and Miss Arden wired back her "welcome". When he reported for work, a "pay-roll change" card was made up and initialed by Mr. Johns, and then forwarded to the payroll department. Reciting that it was prepared on September 30, 1947, and was to be effective as of October 22d, it specified the names of the parties, Crabtree's "Job Classification" and, in addition, contained the notation that "This employee is to be paid as follows:

"First six months of employment $20,000. per annum
     Next six months of employment 25,000. per annum
     After one year of employment 30,000. per annum
     Approved by RPJ [initialed]"

After six months of employment, Crabtree received the scheduled increase from $20,000 to $25,000, but the further specified increase at the end of the year was not paid. Both Mr. Johns and the comptroller of the corporation, Mr. Carstens, told Crabtree that they would attempt to straighten out the matter with Miss Arden, and, with that in mind, the comptroller prepared another "pay-roll change" card, to which his signature is appended, noting that there was to be a "Salary increase" from $25,000 to $30,000 a year, "per contractual arrangements with Miss Arden". The latter, however, refused to approve the increase and, after further fruitless discussion, plaintiff left defendant's employ and commenced this action for breach of contract.

At the ensuing trial, defendant denied the existence of any agreement to employ plaintiff for two years, and further contended that, even if one had been made, the statute of frauds barred its enforcement. The trial court found against defendant on both issues and awarded plaintiff damages of about $14,000, and the Appellate Division, two justices dissenting, affirmed. Since the contract relied upon was not to be performed within a year, the primary question for decision is whether there was a memorandum of its terms, subscribed by defendant, to satisfy the statute of frauds....

Each of the two payroll cards - the one initialed by defendant's general manager, the other signed by its comptroller - unquestionably constitutes a memorandum under the statute. That they were not prepared or signed with the intention of evidencing the contract, or that they came into existence subsequent to its execution, is of no consequence...; it is enough, to meet the statute's demands, that they were signed with intent to authenticate the information contained therein and that such information does evidence the terms of the contract. Those two writings contain all of the essential terms of the contract - the parties to it, the position that plaintiff was to assume, the salary that he was to receive - except that relating to the duration of plaintiff's employment. Accordingly, we must consider whether that item, the length of the contract, may be supplied by reference to the earlier unsigned office memorandum, and, if so, whether its notation, "2 years to make good", sufficiently designates a period of employment.

The statute of frauds does not require the "memorandum to be in one document. It may be pieced together out of separate writings, connected with one another either expressly or by the internal evidence of subject matter and occasion". Where each of the separate writings has been subscribed by the party to be charged, little if any difficulty is encountered. Where, however, some writings have been signed, and others have not - as in the case before us - there is basic disagreement as to what constitutes a sufficient connection permitting the unsigned papers to be considered as part of the statutory memorandum. The courts of some jurisdictions insist that there be a reference, of varying degrees of specificity, in the signed writing to that unsigned, and, if there is no such reference, they refuse to permit consideration of the latter in determining whether the memorandum satisfies the statute. That conclusion is based upon a construction of the statute which requires that the connection between the writings and defendant's acknowledgment of the one not subscribed, appear from examination of the papers alone, without the aid of parol evidence. The other position - which has gained increasing support over the years - is that a sufficient connection between the papers is established simply by a reference in them to the same subject matter or transaction. The statute is not pressed "to the extreme of a literal and rigid logic"... and oral testimony is admitted to show the connection between the documents and to establish the acquiescence, of the party to be charged, to the contents of the one unsigned.

The view last expressed impresses us as the more sound, and we now definitively adopt it, permitting the signed and unsigned writings to be read together, provided that they clearly refer to the same subject matter or transaction.

The language of the statute - "Every agreement... is void, unless... some note or memorandum thereof be in writing, and subscribed by the party to be charged", does not impose the requirement that the signed acknowledgment of the contract must appear from the writings alone, unaided by oral testimony. The danger of fraud and perjury, generally attendant upon the admission of parol evidence, is at a minimum in a case such as this. None of the terms of the contract are supplied by parol. All of them must be set out in the various writings presented to the court, and at least one writing, the one establishing a contractual relationship between the parties, must bear the signature of the party to be charged, while the unsigned document must on its face refer to the same transaction as that set forth in the one that was signed. Parol evidence to portray the circumstances surrounding the making of the memorandum - serves only to connect the separate documents and to show that there was assent, by the party to be charged, to the contents of the one unsigned. If that testimony does not convincingly connect the papers, or does not show assent to the unsigned paper, it is within the province of the judge to conclude, as a matter of law, that the statute has not been satisfied. True, the possibility still remains that, by fraud or perjury, an agreement never in fact made may occasionally be enforced under the subject matter or transaction test. It is better to run that risk, though, than to deny enforcement to all agreements, merely because the signed document made no specific mention of the unsigned writing. As the United States Supreme Court declared, in sanctioning the admission of parol evidence to establish the connection between the signed and unsigned writings. "There may be cases in which it would be a violation of reason and common sense to ignore a reference which derives its significance from such [parol] proof. If there is ground for any doubt in the matter, the general rule should be enforced. But where there is no ground for doubt, its enforcement would aid, instead of discouraging, fraud."...

Turning to the writings in the case before us - the unsigned office memo, the payroll change form initialed by the general manager Johns, and the paper signed by the comptroller Carstens - it is apparent, and most patently, that all three refer on their face to the same transaction. The parties, the position to be filled by plaintiff, the salary to be paid him, are all identically set forth; it is hardly possible that such detailed information could refer to another or a different agreement. Even more, the card signed by Carstens notes that it was prepared for the purpose of a "Salary increase per contractual arrangements with Miss Arden". That certainly constitutes a reference of sorts to a more comprehensive "arrangement," and parol is permissible to furnish the explanation.

The corroborative evidence of defendant's assent to the contents of the unsigned office memorandum is also convincing. Prepared by defendant's agent, Miss Arden's personal secretary, there is little likelihood that that paper was fraudulently manufactured or that defendant had not assented to its contents. Furthermore, the evidence as to the conduct of the parties at the time it was prepared persuasively demonstrates defendant's assent to its terms. Under such circumstances, the courts below were fully justified in finding that the three papers constituted the "memorandum" of their agreement within the meaning of the statute.

Nor can there be any doubt that the memorandum contains all of the essential terms of the contract. Only one term, the length of the employment, is in dispute. The September 26th office memorandum contains the notation, "2 years to make good". What purpose, other than to denote the length of the contract term, such a notation could have, is hard to imagine. Without it, the employment would be at will... and its inclusion may not be treated as meaningless or purposeless. Quite obviously, as the courts below decided, the phrase signifies that the parties agreed to a term, a certain and definite term, of two years, after which, if plaintiff did not "make good", he would be subject to discharge. And examination of other parts of the memorandum supports that construction. Throughout the writings, a scale of wages, increasing plaintiff's salary periodically, is set out; that type of arrangement is hardly consistent with the hypothesis that the employment was meant to be at will. The most that may be argued from defendant's standpoint is that "2 years to make good", is a cryptic and ambiguous statement. But, in such a case, parol evidence is admissible to explain its meaning. Having in mind the relations of the parties, the course of the negotiations and plaintiff's insistence upon security of employment, the purpose of the phrase - or so the trier of the facts was warranted in finding - was to grant plaintiff the tenure he desired.

CASE 12-6

The Statute of Frauds may be satisfied by a written a note or memorandum of the contract that is signed by the party against whom enforcement of the contract is sought. The following case considers whether the buyer's deposit check, which the seller endorsed and deposited, is sufficient to satisfy the Statute of Frauds for a contract for the sale of real property.

H. ROTHVOSS & SONS, INC. v. ESTATE OF NEER
Supreme Court of New York, Appellate Division, Third Department, 1988
139 A.D.2d 37; 530 N.Y.S.2d 331

MERCURE, Judge. Plaintiff seeks specific performance and money damages resulting from the alleged breach of a contract for the sale of real property by S. Hollis Neer, defendants' decedent and predecessor in title, to plaintiff. The complaint alleges the terms of the purported contract, that "[a]s evidence of plaintiff's good faith and intentions to carry out the contract" plaintiff's officer executed and delivered to Neer a check in the amount of $500 dated July 24, 1984, which check was endorsed and deposited by Neer, and that Neer died on October 30, 1985, prior to completion of the contract of sale. Annexed to the complaint is a detailed and unsigned contract for the sale of real property.

Defendants moved to dismiss the complaint on grounds that it failed to state a cause of action and was barred by the Statute of Frauds. In opposition thereto, plaintiff submitted the affidavit of its vice-president, Henry F. Rothvoss, Jr., in which he stated that the terms of the oral contract of sale with Neer were embodied in the unexecuted contract, that the contract was prepared by Neer's attorney, and that, as evidence of his good faith and "to insure that the contract would be carried out", he handed the $500 check to Neer. The check, annexed to the affidavit, contains the purported endorsement of Neer. The memo portion thereof contains the words "land on Rt 22" and "down payment". There is no dispute that the land in question is located on State Route 22 in the Town of Ancram, Columbia County.

Supreme Court denied the motion, finding that the canceled check, endorsed and thereby subscribed by Neer, together with the unexecuted contract, satisfied the Statute of Frauds and the provision that a "contract for * * * the sale, of any real property, or an interest therein, is void unless the contract or some note or memorandum thereof, expressing the consideration, is in writing, subscribed by the party to be charged" (General Obligations Law § 5-703 [2]). Defendants appeal.

We reverse. The action is barred by the Statute of Frauds, and the motion to dismiss should have been granted on that basis. Although the requisite memorandum may be pieced together out of several writings, some signed and others unsigned, and parol evidence may be resorted to in aid thereof, it is essential that the separate writings sought to be so employed clearly refer to the same subject matter or transaction. Additionally, in such case the signed writing must establish a contractual relationship between the parties. Here, the signed writing, the check, does not establish such a contractual relationship. Moreover, it does not contain even a general description of the land to be conveyed and fails to state the purchase price and other essential terms of sale, such as financing.

In *Mulford v Borg-Warner Acceptance Corp.*, this court rejected the contention that an endorsed check could establish the necessary contractual relationship. We conclude that just as the check notation "(new lease)" was insufficient to establish a tenancy involving all the provisions of a proposed unsigned lease, including the term, the words "land on Rt 22" and "down payment" noted on the check herein are insufficient to establish an agreement involving all the terms of a proposed unsigned contract of sale including the purchase price, terms of payment and description of property to be conveyed. Further, although plaintiff is the drawer of the check, the purchasers under the formal written contract of sale are plaintiff and two other individuals, August F. Corsini and Laura M. Corsini, thereby creating uncertainty as to the identity of the parties to the purported contract. Additionally, the $500 actually paid is not reflected in and bears no relationship to the claimed contract, which provides for a $15,000 down payment upon execution.

Nor would treatment of the $500 as partial payment of the purchase price remove the contract from the Statute of Frauds. "With respect to land contracts, part payment of the purchase price, or even full payment thereof, is not considered part performance of the contract, standing alone; such payment, to be sufficient, must be accompanied by other acts, such as possession, or possession and improvements." Clearly, the $500 check was nothing more than earnest money to show plaintiff's good intentions and was not intended to evidence a completed contract. Where, as here, the parties contemplate a formal, binding, written contract, which is never executed, there is no mutual assent and no contract.

Order reversed, on the law, with costs, motion granted and complaint dismissed.

Case 12-7

The following case illustrates the type of circumstances that may constitute "part performance" sufficient to satisfy the real property provision of the New York Statute of Frauds.

Schafer v. Albro
Appellate Division, New York (4th Dept.), 1996
233 A.D.2d 900, 649 N.Y.S.2d 260

Memorandum: Supreme Court properly denied that part of defendant's motion seeking partial summary judgment dismissing the cause of action alleging breach of a real estate contract between the parties. Although the alleged contract is not in writing or subscribed by plaintiffs (see, General Obligations Law § 5-703 [2]), plaintiffs allege in their verified complaint that they had possession of the property; made part payment of the purchase price to defendant and her husband; made extensive improvements to the property at a total cost of over $ 20,000; paid off the second mortgage in the amount of $ 25,733.76; and, from November 1, 1988 to February 1991, made the payments on the first mortgage. Plaintiffs have thereby raised an issue of fact whether they are entitled to specific performance of the contract based upon part performance (see, General Obligations Law § 5-703 [4] [Citations]).

* * *

CASE 13-1

This case involves an employment contract pursuant to which the employee must perform to the employer's satisfaction. The court discusses how satisfaction must be defined or measured.

APPELGATE v. MACFADDEN NEWSPAPER CORP.
Appellate Division, New York (1st Dept.), 1925
214 A.D. 221, 212 N.Y.S. 67

MERRELL, Judge. The action was brought to recover the sum of $12,000 damages alleged to have been sustained by the plaintiff by reason of his wrongful discharge by the defendant from its employ. The contract between the parties whereby the plaintiff was employed by the defendant was in writing. The defendant is a newspaper publishing corporation and employed the plaintiff "as Editor of the Saturday feature section and to have charge of the Rotogravure section" of the defendant's newspaper. The contract, a copy of which is annexed to the complaint, recites that "Whereas, Mr. Appelgate is an editor possessing unique and original ability," and the employer desired to secure his exclusive services, the said Appelgate desiring to secure and accept employment with the defendant, "First. The Employer does hereby employ the Employee to render his services as Editor of the Saturday feature section and to have charge of the Rotogravure Section of the newspaper to be published by the MacFadden Newspaper Publishing Corporation exclusively...." It is further provided "that the Employee will work for and devote his entire time, skill, attention and energy to the Employer exclusively," and that "it being conceded by the Employee that his services are special, unique and extraordinary." In the 4th paragraph of the contract it is provided: "Fourth. The Employee shall faithfully execute to the satisfaction of the Employer all instructions in respect to his duties given by his Employer."

The plaintiff alleges that the contract in question was entered into between the parties on July 28, 1924, and that pursuant thereto and on or about August 4, 1924, the plaintiff entered upon his duties as editor of the Saturday feature section and took charge of the rotogravure section of the newspaper published by the defendant, and continued to perform such duties until on or about November 7, 1924, and duly performed all the terms and conditions on the part of the plaintiff to be performed under the said agreement; that on or about said last-mentioned date the defendant wrongfully and without just cause therefor discharged the plaintiff to plaintiff's damage in the sum of $12,000.

A perusal of the contract discloses that the parties regarded the services of the plaintiff for which the defendant contracted as of the character commonly known as unique. The contract itself recites that "Mr. Appelgate is an editor possessing unique and original ability" Plaintiff was hired as "Editor of the Saturday feature section and to have charge of the Rotogravure Section" of the defendant's newspaper. There can be no doubt that the parties understood that the plaintiff was to render services involving "art, taste, fancy and judgment".

In a contract for services involving fancy, taste and judgment, the question whether the fancy, taste or judgment of the employer is arbitrary or unreasonable does not arise, the question being whether the claimed dissatisfaction was feigned or genuine.

In *Crawford v. Mail & Express Publishing Co.* the plaintiff was employed as an editor to write at least two columns a week on the progress of the world or other appropriate subjects for publication in The *Mail and Express*, and in his contract with the defendant agreed that his services would be satisfactory to the defendant, and that in case they were not he should receive one week's notice. In discussing the absence of limitation upon the exercise by the employer of its judgment as to what was satisfactory to it, the Court of Appeals said "But, on the part of the publishers of The *Mail & Express*, it is very clear that they did not intend to be bound for a period longer than his services proved satisfactory, and that they expressly reserved the right to discharge him upon a week's notice. It is also apparent from a reading of the contract that the employment was not intended to be that of an ordinary servant to perform work, labor and services of an ordinary business or of a commercial nature. He was not called upon to perform the work of an ordinary reporter, writing up the general news of the day, but contracted to prepare articles on the progress of the world or other appropriate subjects in the line of the policy of the paper for the purpose, as expressed, of promoting the general interests of the paper, of aiding in its circulation and the obtaining of advertisements, by improving the quality of its contents. The evident design was that the articles should be interesting and attractive, involving art, taste, fancy and judgment. There is no provision in the contract in any manner limiting the publishers in the exercise of their judgment as to what is satisfactory, but if his services are unsatisfactory for any reason they are given the right to terminate the employment upon a week's notice, at any time they so elect."

In *Diamond v. Mendelsohn* the contract required the employee to "perform the duties of foreman competently and energetically to the best of his abilities and complete satisfaction of his employers."

Mr. Justice CLARKE of this court, now its presiding justice, in writing in that case said: "There is no doubt that under the terms of this written contract it lay within the power of the defendants to discharge the plaintiff because he did not perform his duties to their complete satisfaction and that it would not be proper to submit to a jury the question whether they ought to have been satisfied."

It, therefore, seems very clear to me that the only question to be determined upon the trial was as to whether the dissatisfaction pleaded by the defendant as ground for the discharge of the plaintiff was real or feigned. If the dissatisfaction was a mere whim of the employer, then, of course, it was not justified in terminating the contract, but if, in fact, the defendant was dissatisfied with the special and unique services rendered by the plaintiff as editor, then the defendant was justified in discharging him. The contract with the plaintiff clearly involved personal taste, fancy and judgment, and when the employer became dissatisfied with the services of the character specified which its employee was to render, it had the right to discharge him and was not called upon to give reasons therefor.

The order appealed from should be reversed.

CASE 14-1

This case distinguishes between *material* and *trivial* breaches of contract and discusses the appropriate measure of damage for each kind of breach.

JACOB & YOUNG v. KENT
Court of Appeals of New York, 1921
230 N.Y. 239

CARDOZO, Judge. The plaintiff built a country residence for the defendant at a cost of upwards of $77,000, and now sues to recover a balance of $3,483.46, remaining unpaid. The work of construction ceased in June, 1914, and the defendant then began to occupy the dwelling. There was no complaint of defective performance until March, 1915. One of the specifications for the plumbing work provides that "all wrought iron pipe must be well galvanized, lap welded pipe of the grade known as 'standard pipe' of Reading manufacture." The defendant learned in March, 1915, that some of the pipe, instead of being made in Reading, was the product of other factories. The plaintiff was accordingly directed by the architect to do the work anew. The plumbing was then encased within the walls except in a few places where it had to be exposed. Obedience to the order meant more than the

substitution of other pipe. It meant the demolition at great expense of substantial parts of the completed structure. The plaintiff left the work untouched, and asked for a certificate that the final payment was due. Refusal of the certificate was followed by this suit.

The evidence sustains a finding that the omission of the prescribed brand of pipe was neither fraudulent nor willful. It was the result of the oversight and inattention of the plaintiff's subcontractor. Reading pipe is distinguished from Cohoes pipe and other brands only by the name of the manufacturer stamped upon it at intervals of between six and seven feet. Even the defendant's architect, though he inspected the pipe upon arrival, failed to notice the discrepancy. The plaintiff tried to show that the brands installed, though made by other manufacturers, were the same in quality, in appearance, in market value and in cost as the brand stated in the contract -- that they were, indeed, the same thing, though manufactured in another place. The evidence was excluded, and a verdict directed for the defendant. The Appellate Division reversed, and granted a new trial.

We think the evidence, if admitted, would have supplied some basis for the inference that the defect was insignificant in its relation to the project. The courts never say that one who makes a contract fills the measure of his duty by less than full performance. They do say, however, that an omission, both trivial and innocent, will sometimes be atoned for by allowance of the resulting damage, and will not always be the breach of a condition to be followed by a forfeiture. The decisions in this state commit us to the liberal view, which is making its way, nowadays, in jurisdictions slow to welcome it. Where the line is to be drawn between the important and the trivial cannot be settled by a formula. "In the nature of the case precise boundaries are impossible" (2 Williston on Contracts, sec. 841). The same omission may take on one aspect or another according to its setting. Substitution of equivalents may not have the same significance in fields of art on the one side and in those of mere utility on the other. Nowhere will change be tolerated, however, if it is so dominant or pervasive as in any real or substantial measure to frustrate the purpose of the contract. There is no general license to install whatever, in the builder's judgment, may be regarded as "just as good". The question is one of degree, to be answered, if there is doubt, by the triers of the facts and, if the inferences are certain, by the judges of the law. We must weigh the purpose to be served, the desire to be gratified, the excuse for deviation from the letter, the cruelty of enforced adherence. Then only can we tell whether literal fulfillment is to be implied by law as a condition. This is not to say that the parties are not free by apt and certain words to effectuate a purpose that performance of every term shall be a condition of recovery. That question is not here. This is merely to say that the law will be slow to impute the purpose, in the silence of the parties, where the significance of the default is grievously out of proportion to the oppression of the forfeiture. The

willful transgressor must accept the penalty of his transgression. For him there is no occasion to mitigate the rigor of implied conditions. The transgressor whose default is unintentional and trivial may hope for mercy if he will offer atonement for his wrong.

In the circumstances of this case, we think the measure of the allowance is not the cost of replacement, which would be great, but the difference in value, which would be either nominal or nothing. Some of the exposed sections might perhaps have been replaced at moderate expense. The defendant did not limit his demand to them, but treated the plumbing as a unit to be corrected from cellar to roof. In point of fact, the plaintiff never reached the stage at which evidence of the extent of the allowance became necessary. The trial court had excluded evidence that the defect was unsubstantial, and in view of that ruling there was no occasion for the plaintiff to go farther with an offer of proof. We think, however, that the offer, if it had been made, would not of necessity have been defective because directed to difference in value. It is true that in most cases the cost of replacement is the measure. The owner is entitled to the money which will permit him to complete, unless the cost of completion is grossly and unfairly out of proportion to the good to be attained. When that is true, the measure is the difference in value. Specifications call, let us say, for a foundation built of granite quarried in Vermont. On the completion of the building, the owner learns that through the blunder of a subcontractor part of the foundation has been built of granite of the same quality quarried in New Hampshire. The measure of allowance is not the cost of reconstruction. "There may be omissions of that which could not afterwards be supplied exactly as called for by the contract without taking down the building to its foundations, and at the same time the omission may not affect the value of the building for use or otherwise, except so slightly as to be hardly appreciable." The rule that gives a remedy in cases of substantial performance with compensation for defects of trivial or inappreciable importance, has been developed by the courts as an instrument of justice. The measure of the allowance must be shaped to the same end.

Case 14-2

A party seeking to recover damages for breach of contract must prove the existence and amount of such damages with reasonable certainty. The following case illustrates the difficulties faced by a plaintiff who seeks to recover damages for lost profits

SCHONFELD v. HILLIARD
U.S. Ct. App. 2d Cir., 2000
218 F.3d 164

McLAUGHLIN, C. J.

This case involves a closely-held cable television corporation that imploded just as it was about to launch its flagship channel. In 1988, brothers Russ and Les Hilliard formed International News Network, Inc. ("INN") to distribute a British news and information channel in the United States (the "Channel"). Prior to this ambitious venture, the Hilliard brothers owned small mid-western cable television companies with an aggregate of only 66,000 subscribers.

To secure large-scale expertise and prestige, INN brought in Reese Schonfeld, a founder and former President of Cable News Network ("CNN")-initially as a consultant, and later as a shareholder-to help INN negotiate with the British Broadcasting Corporation (the "BBC") for a programming license. INN also retained Daniels & Associates ("Daniels"), the nation's leading financial services company for the cable industry, to prepare a business plan and to drum up investors.

In February 1994, the Hilliards and Schonfeld executed a written Shareholders' Agreement whereby each became a one-third shareholder in INN in return for a $10,000 capital contribution. In addition, the Hilliards, who had each already lent $300,000 to INN, agreed to lend up to another $350,000 to INN if necessary to meet its obligations to the BBC. In lieu of a further cash contribution, Schonfeld agreed to invest his time and effort.

The Shareholders' Agreement confirmed the parties' understanding that INN itself would not operate the Channel. Instead, INN would invest in a yet-to-be-formed operating entity. INN's shareholders, if they chose, could increase their personal stakes in the Channel by making additional cash investments in the separate operating entity. The agreement said nothing about the percentage of profits that INN, or any other equity investor, would receive from the Channel's operation.

Although the Shareholders' Agreement provided for a two-member board of directors (one chosen by Schonfeld, the other by the Hilliards), no board members were formally designated. It appears, however, that Schonfeld assumed the three roles of director, President and CEO of INN. Russ Hilliard acted as the other director. Les Hilliard apparently played no role in INN, other than investor.

The final piece of the puzzle fell into place on March 4, 1994, when the BBC granted INN a 20-year exclusive license to distribute its news and information programming in a 24-hour format, commencing not later than February 1995 (the "March Supply Agreement"). The agreement provided for INN's assignment of the benefits and privileges of the agreement to the yet-to-be-formed operating entity upon written consent of the BBC, whose consent would not be unreasonably withheld. The BBC retained its right, however, to withhold consent to any delegation of INN's duties under the contract.

* * *

In October 1994, the FCC promulgated a new rule allowing cable operators to charge an increased per-channel monthly rate for up to six new channels as of January 1, 1995. To take advantage of this window of opportunity, INN asked the BBC to accelerate the launch date of the Channel.

INN and the BBC signed an "Interim Agreement," effective December 14, 1994, in which the BBC agreed to provide provisional programming as early as possible, and to develop an "Americanized" programming format to become available to INN no later than December 31, 1995 under a revised 20-year supply agreement (the "December Supply Agreement"). In consideration for the interim programming feed, INN agreed to pay the BBC approximately $20 million in installments beginning January 3, 1995. The BBC retained the right to terminate the Interim Agreement if, by January 31, 1995, INN had failed to get letters indicating an intent to carry the Channel from cable systems with an aggregate of at least 500,000 subscribers. The December Supply Agreement also: (1) capped INN's initial capital contribution to the operating entity at

15%; and (2) gave the BBC a non-dilutable 20% equity interest in the operating entity.

According to three witnesses-Richard Blumenthal (INN's attorney), Schonfeld and Mark Young (a representative of the BBC)-Russ Hilliard repeatedly promised orally that he and his brother would personally fund the Interim Agreement. These promises were allegedly made to induce Schonfeld and the BBC to abandon the March Supply Agreement and enter into the Interim and December Supply Agreements despite the fact that INN did not yet have the cash available to make the necessary payments to the BBC. Schonfeld and Blumenthal testified in depositions that the Hilliards said they planned to invest up to $20 million in the operating entity as financing for the BBC payments. However, there is no oral or written agreement memorializing the precise amount promised, or defining the liabilities and remedies of the parties in the event of the Hilliards' failure to fund.

By mid-January 1995, the Hilliards had provided none of the promised funding and INN was in default under the Interim Agreement. In February 1995, the parties met in New York to discuss the situation. Russ Hilliard did not deny that he and his brother had promised to fund the Interim Agreement. He claimed, however, that funding had been withheld because INN was having difficulty obtaining cable operator support. Rather than suing the Hilliards and INN for breach of contract, the BBC offered a chivalrous solution: in exchange for the dissolution of both the Interim and December Supply Agreements, the BBC agreed to release the Hilliards and INN from any and all claims arising out of their breach of the oral agreement and Interim Supply Agreement.

Schonfeld alleges that the Hilliards never really intended to fund the Interim Agreement themselves. He claims that, all along, they had been unsuccessfully attempting to get the money from William Bresnan, the CEO of Bresnan Communications (which is 80% owned by TCI Cable). Russ Hilliard has admitted in deposition testimony that: (1) the funds he had promised were supposed to come from Bresnan or TCI, not from himself and his brother; and (2) he knew the BBC would never have signed the Interim Agreement had it known the truth (i.e., would never have agreed to make the Interim Agreement contingent on funding from Bresnan or TCI).

In April 1995, Schonfeld commenced this diversity action in the United States District Court for the Southern District of New York . . . . Schonfeld alleged

derivative claims on behalf of INN for: . . . breach of contract . . . .

In a nutshell, Schonfeld alleged that the Hilliards induced him and INN to abandon the March Supply Agreement and enter into the Interim and December Supply Agreements by falsely representing their intention to personally fund the Interim Agreement. He alleged that the Hilliards' breach of this oral agreement to fund led directly to INN's breach of the Interim Agreement and subsequent loss of the December Supply Agreement.

* * *

To establish lost profit damages, Schonfeld relied on: (1) INN's Business Plan; . . . (3) the BBC's, the Hilliards' and Schonfeld's "belief" that the proposed operating entity would be profitable; and (4) the reports and deposition testimony of two damage experts-Donald Curtis and William Grimes.

* * *

. . . [T]he district court held that Schonfeld could not prove, with reasonable certainty, the existence or amount of damages for lost profits.

* * *

Finding Schonfeld's claims for lost asset damages to be nothing more than a "back door" attempt to recover lost profits, . . . the district court held that Schonfeld could not establish lost asset damages with reasonable certainty because the value of the supply agreements also depended on their ability to generate profits. In addition, the district court held that Schonfeld had failed to establish that the supply agreements were "recoverable assets." All expert testimony proffered to establish their market value was, therefore, excluded as irrelevant.

Finally, the court ruled that, as a matter of law, Schonfeld was not entitled to punitive damages.

Accordingly, the district court granted summary judgment . . . .

Plaintiff, Schonfeld, now appeals . . . .

* * *

DISCUSSION

* * *

I. Lost Profits

* * *

In an action for breach of contract, a plaintiff is entitled to recover lost profits only if he can establish both the existence and amount of such damages with reasonable certainty. [Citation] "[T]he damages may not be merely speculative, possible or imaginary." Although lost profits need not be proven with "mathematical precision," they must be "capable of measurement based upon known reliable factors without undue speculation." [Citations] Therefore, evidence of lost profits from a new business venture receives greater scrutiny because there is no track record upon which to base an estimate. [Citation] Projections of future profits based upon "a multitude of assumptions" that require "speculation and conjecture" and few known factors do not provide the requisite certainty. [Citation]

The plaintiff faces an additional hurdle: he must prove that lost profit damages were within the contemplation of the parties when the contract was made. [Citation] "The party breaching the contract is liable for those risks foreseen or which should have been foreseen at the time the contract was made." Where the contract is silent on the subject, the court must take a "common sense" approach, and determine what the parties intended by considering "the nature, purpose and particular circumstances of the contract known by the parties ... as well as what liability the defendant fairly may be supposed to have assumed consciously." [Citations]

Here, the district court concluded that the Channel was a new entertainment venture . . . . The operating entity's profits, the court noted, "were purely hypothetical, stemming from the sale of untested programming to a hypothetical subscriber base, sold to advertisers at a hypothetical price and supported by hypothetical investors and carriers." [Citation] After reviewing the seemingly endless list of assumptions upon which Schonfeld's expert relied in determining lost profits, the court held that Schonfeld could establish neither the existence nor the amount of lost profits with reasonable certainty. The court also concluded that lost profits were not within the contemplation of the parties. We fully agree with the district court's analysis.

* * *

Subject as they are to the changing whims and artistic tastes of the general public, claims for profits lost in unsuccessful entertainment ventures have received a chilly reception in the New York courts. [Citations] Curtis believes he adjusted his profit figures to take such factors into account by providing for a 25% variance on the projected cash flows of the operating entity. In his deposition, he stated that he chose the 25% variance based on his experience with the cable industry. However, Curtis failed to establish that this variance would adequately account for any inaccuracies in the revenue and expense assumptions discussed above as well as any changes in consumer demand for British-style news reporting.

Indeed, Curtis failed to account for the effects of any general market risks on the Channel's probability of success. These risks include: (1) the entry of competitors; (2) technological developments; (3) regulatory changes; or (4) general market movements. As the district court correctly noted, "[f]ailure to control for adverse market conditions allows the false inference that plaintiff's venture was an assured success." [Citation] Therefore, the court properly held that Schonfeld failed to establish a foundation for the existence of lost profits.

C. The Contemplation of the Parties

Finally, Schonfeld maintains that he adduced sufficient evidence to establish that liability for lost profits was within the parties' contemplation at the time the Hilliards promised to fund the Interim Agreement.

* * *

. . . Schonfeld is not seeking profits that would have accrued under the alleged oral agreement to fund, or even under the Interim Agreement. Rather, Schonfeld wants to recover lost profits that INN or a non-existent operating entity might have received from the operation of the Channel. Further, the profitability of the Channel was highly uncertain when the Hilliards promised to fund the Interim Agreement. Nor did they exercise "near exclusive control" over the profitability of the venture. In light of "the nature, purpose and particular circumstances of the contract known by the parties," by orally promising to provide up to $20 million to fund the Interim Agreement, the Hilliards cannot "be supposed to have assumed" liability for approximately $269 million in lost profits that might have been garnered in the future by a non-existent operating entity. [Citation].

* * *

For all the foregoing reasons, we affirm the district court's grant of summary judgment dismissing all claims insofar as they seek damages for lost profits.

Case 14-3

This case discusses the requirements for awarding the remedy of specific performance for a breach of contract and applies them to a failure to give screen credit for making a motion picture.

TAMARIND LITHOGRAPHY WORKSHOP, INC. v. SANDERS
Cal. Ct. App. Sec. Dist., 1983
143 Cal. App. 3d 571, 193 Cal. Rptr. 409

STEPHENS, J.

The essence of this appeal concerns the question of whether an award of damages is an adequate remedy at law in lieu of specific performance for the breach of an agreement to give screen credits. Our saga traces its origin to March of 1969, at which time appellant, and cross-complainant below, Terry Sanders (hereinafter "Sanders" or "appellant"), agreed in writing to write, direct and produce a motion picture on the subject of lithography for respondent, Tamarind Lithography Workshop, Inc. (hereinafter referred to as "Tamarind" or "respondent").

Pursuant to the terms of the agreement, the film was shot during the summer of 1969, wherein Sanders directed the film according to an outline/treatment of his authorship, and acted as production manager by personally hiring and supervising personnel comprising the film crew. Additionally, Sanders exercised both artistic control over the mixing of the sound track and overall editing of the picture.

After completion, the film, now titled the "Four Stones for Kanemitsu," was screened by Tamarind at its tenth anniversary celebration on April 28, 1970. Thereafter, a dispute arose between the parties concerning their respective rights and obligations under the original 1969 agreement. Litigation ensued and in January 1973 the matter went to trial. Prior to the entry of judgment, the parties entered into a written settlement agreement, which became the premise for the instant action. Specifically, this April 30, 1973, agreement provided that Sanders would be entitled to a screen credit entitled "A Film by Terry Sanders."

Tamarind did not comply with its expressed obligation pursuant to that agreement, in that it failed to include Sanders' screen credits in the prints it distributed. As a result a situation developed wherein Tamarind and co-defendant Wayne filed suit for declaratory relief, damages due to breach of contract, emotional distress, defamation and fraud. Sanders cross-complained, seeking damages for Tamarind's breach of contract, declaratory relief, specific performance of the contract to give Sanders screen credits, and defamation. Both causes were

consolidated and brought to trial on May 31, 1977. A jury was impaneled for purposes of determining damage issues and decided that Tamarind had breached the agreement and awarded Sanders $25,000 in damages.

The remaining claims for declaratory and injunctive relief were tried by the court. The court made findings that Tamarind had sole ownership rights in the film, that "both June Wayne and Terry Sanders were each creative producers of the film, that Sanders shall have the right to modify the prints in his personal possession to include his credits." All other prayers for relief were denied.

It is from the denial of appellant's request for specific performance upon which appellant predicates this appeal.

* * *

The availability of the remedy of specific performance is premised upon well established requisites. These requisites include: A showing by plaintiff of (1) the inadequacy of his legal remedy; (2) an underlying contract that is both reasonable and supported by adequate consideration; (3) the existence of a mutuality of remedies; (4) contractual terms which are sufficiently definite to enable the court to know what it is to enforce; and (5) a substantial similarity of the requested performance to that promised in the contract. [Citation]

It is manifest that the legal remedies available to Sanders for harm resulting from the future exhibition of the film are inadequate as a matter of law. The primary reasons are twofold: (1) that an accurate assessment of damages would be far too difficult and require much speculation, and (2) that any future exhibitions might be deemed to be a continuous breach of contract and thereby create the danger of an untold number of lawsuits.

There is no doubt that the exhibition of a film, which is favorably received by its critics and the public at large, can result in valuable advertising or publicity for the artists responsible for that film's making. Likewise, it is unquestionable that the non-appearance of an artist's name or likeness in the form of screen credit on a successful film can result in a loss of that valuable publicity. However, whether that loss of publicity is measurable dollar wise is quite another matter.

By its very nature, public acclaim is unique and very difficult, if not sometimes impossible, to quantify in monetary terms.

* * *

We return to the remaining requisites for Sanders' entitlement to specific performance. The need for our finding the contract to be reasonable and supported by adequate consideration is obviated by the jury's determination of respondent's breach of that contract. The requisite of mutuality of remedy has been satisfied in that Sanders had fully performed his obligations pursuant to the agreement (i.e., release of all claims of copyright to the film and dismissal of his then pending action against respondents). [Citation] Similarly, we find the terms of the agreement sufficiently definite to permit enforcement of the respondent's performance as promised.

In conclusion, the record shows that the appellant is entitled to relief consisting of the damages recovered, and an injunction against future injury.

CASE 25-1

Courts in a number of states have allowed at-will employees to bring claims for "wrongful discharge" under tort or contract theories. In the following case, the New York Court of Appeals considers – and rejects – a plaintiff's arguments that New York should recognize such causes of action.

Murphy v. American Home Products Corporation
Court of Appeals of New York, 1983
58 N.Y. 2d 293, 461 N.Y.S.2d 232, 448 N.E.2d 86

Jones, J. This court has not and does not now recognize a cause of action in tort for abusive or wrongful discharge of an employee; such recognition must await action of the Legislature. Nor does the complaint here state a cause of action for intentional infliction of emotional distress, for prima facie tort, or for breach of contract. These causes of action were, therefore, properly dismissed. . . .

Plaintiff, Joseph Murphy, was first employed by defendant, American Home Products Corp., in 1957. He thereafter served in various accounting positions, eventually attaining the office of assistant treasurer, but he never had a formal contract of employment. On April 18, 1980, when he was 59 years old, he was discharged.

Plaintiff claims that he was fired for two reasons: because of his disclosure to top management of alleged accounting improprieties on the part of corporate personnel and because of his age. As to the first ground, plaintiff asserts that his firing was in retaliation for his revelation to officers and directors of defendant corporation that he had uncovered at least $50 million in illegal account manipulations of secret pension reserves which improperly inflated the company's growth in income and allowed high-ranking officers to reap unwarranted bonuses from a management incentive plan, as well as in retaliation for his own refusal to engage in the alleged accounting improprieties. He contends that the company's internal regulations required him to make the disclosure that he did. He also alleges that his termination was carried out in a humiliating manner.

* * *

The complaint set up four causes of action. As his first cause of action, plaintiff alleged that his discharge "was wrongful, malicious and in bad faith" and that defendant was bound "not to dismiss its employees for reasons that are contrary to public policy". In his second cause of action, plaintiff claimed that his dismissal "was intended to and did cause plaintiff severe mental and emotional distress thereby damaging plaintiff". His third claim was based on an allegation that the manner of his termination "was deliberately and viciously insulting, was designed to and did embarrass and humiliate plaintiff and was intended to and did cause plaintiff severe mental and emotional distress thereby damaging plaintiff". In his fourth cause of action, plaintiff asserted that, although his employment contract was of indefinite duration, the law imposes in every employment contract "the requirement that an employer shall deal with each employee fairly and in good faith". On that predicate he alleged that defendant's conduct in stalling his advancement and ultimately firing him for his disclosures "breached the terms of its contract requiring good faith and fair dealing toward plaintiff and damaged plaintiff thereby". Plaintiff demanded compensatory and punitive damages.

[D]efendant moved on July 27, 1981 to dismiss the complaint on the grounds that it failed to state a cause of action and that the fourth cause of action was barred by the Statute of Frauds. Defendant contended that plaintiff was an at-will employee subject to discharge at any time, that New York does not recognize a tort action for abusive or wrongful discharge, and that the prima facie tort and intentional infliction of emotional distress claims were unavailable and insufficient.

On October 16, 1981, plaintiff served an amended complaint with his opposing papers on the motion. The amended complaint, among other things, added a fifth cause of action, alleging that plaintiff was denied advancement due to his age which constituted "illegal employment discrimination on the basis of age in violation of New York Executive Law § 296. "

Special Term denied defendant's motion to dismiss the wrongful discharge tort claim but granted the motion as to the causes of action for breach of contract, prima facie tort, intentional infliction of emotional distress, and age discrimination. Although the court noted that New York had not yet adopted the doctrine of abusive discharge, it declined to put plaintiff out of court before he had had opportunity by means of disclosure procedures to elicit evidence which might put his claim on firmer footing. Special Term held the cause of action for breach of contract barred by the Statute of Frauds. As to the second and third causes of action the court ruled that plaintiff's allegations as to the manner of his dismissal were not sufficient to support causes of action for intentional infliction of emotional distress or for prima facie tort. . . .

On cross appeals, the Appellate Division, modified, to the extent of granting the motion to dismiss the first cause of action, and otherwise affirmed the order of Special Term. The court noted that it does not appear that New York recognizes a cause of action for abusive discharge and that, in any event, plaintiff had failed to show the type of violation of penal law or public policy that has been held sufficient in other jurisdictions to support a cause of action for abusive discharge. According to the appellate court, plaintiff's charge that the corporation's records were not kept in accordance with generally accepted accounting principles appeared to involve a dispute over a matter of judgment as to the proper accounting treatment to be given the terms involved and not a dispute over false book entries. As to the other causes of action, the court ruled that Special Term had properly dismissed them either for failure to state a cause of action [and] failure to comply with the Statute of Frauds or, regarding the age discrimination claim, failure to assert it within the statutory time period . . . We modify the order of the Appellate Division from which plaintiff appeals by reinstating the fifth cause of action for age discrimination and otherwise affirm. [*The age discrimination claim was reinstated because the court below had applied the wrong statute of limitations.*]

With respect to his first cause of action, plaintiff urges that the time has come when the courts of New York should recognize the tort of abusive or wrongful discharge of an at-will employee. To do so would alter our long- settled rule that where an employment is for an indefinite term it is presumed to be a hiring at will which may be freely terminated by either party at any time for any reason or even for no reason . . . . Plaintiff argues that a trend has emerged in the courts of other States to temper what is perceived as the unfairness of the traditional rule by allowing a cause of action in tort to redress abusive discharges. He accurately points out that this tort has elsewhere been recognized to hold employers liable for dismissal of employees in retaliation for employee conduct that is protected by public policy. Thus, the abusive discharge doctrine has been applied to impose liability on employers where employees have been discharged for disclosing illegal activities on the part of their employers . . . , where employees have been terminated due to their service on jury duty . . . , and where employees have been dismissed because they have filed workers' compensation . . . . Plaintiff would have this court adopt this emerging view. We decline his invitation, being of the opinion that such a significant change in our law is best left to the Legislature.

Those jurisdictions that have modified the traditional at-will rule appear to have been motivated by conclusions that the freedom of contract underpinnings of the rule have become outdated, that individual employees in the modern work force do not have the bargaining power to negotiate security for the jobs on which they have grown to rely, and that the rule yields harsh results for those employees who do not enjoy the benefits of express contractual limitations on the power of dismissal. Whether these conclusions

B52

are supportable or whether for other compelling reasons employers should, as a matter of policy, be held liable to at-will employees discharged in circumstances for which no liability has existed at common law, are issues better left to resolution at the hands of the Legislature. In addition to the fundamental question whether such liability should be recognized in New York, of no less practical importance is the definition of its configuration if it is to be recognized.

Both of these aspects of the issue, involving perception and declaration of relevant public policy (the underlying determinative consideration with respect to tort liability in general, . . . are best and more appropriately explored and resolved by the legislative branch of our government. The Legislature has infinitely greater resources and procedural means to discern the public will, to examine the variety of pertinent considerations, to elicit the views of the various segments of the community that would be directly affected and in any event critically interested, and to investigate and anticipate the impact of imposition of such liability. Standards should doubtless be established applicable to the multifarious types of employment and the various circumstances of discharge. If the rule of nonliability for termination of at-will employment is to be tempered, it should be accomplished through a principled statutory scheme, adopted after opportunity for public ventilation, rather than in consequence of judicial resolution of the partisan arguments of individual adversarial litigants.

Additionally, if the rights and obligations under a relationship forged, perhaps some time ago, between employer and employee in reliance on existing legal principles are to be significantly altered, a fitting accommodation of the competing interests to be affected may well dictate that any change should be given prospective effect only, or at least so the Legislature might conclude.

For all the reasons stated, we conclude that recognition in New York State of tort liability for what has become known as abusive or wrongful discharge should await legislative action.

Plaintiff's second cause of action is framed in terms of a claim for intentional infliction of emotional distress. To survive a motion to dismiss, plaintiff's allegations must satisfy the rule set out in Restatement of Torts, Second, which we adopted in *Fischer v Maloney* . . ., that: "One who by extreme and outrageous conduct intentionally or recklessly causes severe emotional distress to another is subject to liability for such emotional distress" (§ 46, subd [1]). Comment *d* to that section notes that: "Liability has

been found only where the conduct has been so outrageous in character, and so extreme in degree, as to go beyond all possible bounds of decency, and to be regarded as atrocious, and utterly intolerable in a civilized community". The facts alleged by plaintiff regarding the manner of his termination fall far short of this strict standard. Further, in light of our holding above that there is now no cause of action in tort in New York for abusive or wrongful discharge of an at-will employee, plaintiff should not be allowed to evade that conclusion or to subvert the traditional at-will contract rule by casting his cause of action in terms of a tort of intentional infliction of emotional distress . . . .

Plaintiff's third cause of action was also properly dismissed. If considered, as plaintiff would have us, as intended to allege a prima facie tort it is deficient inasmuch as there is no allegation that his, discharge was without economic or social justification . . . . Moreover, we held in *James v Board of Educ.* . . ., which also involved the exercise of an unrestricted right to discharge an employee, that: "Plaintiff cannot, by the device of an allegation that the sole reason for the termination of his employment by these public officials acting within the ambit of their authority was to harm him without justification (a contention which could be advanced with respect to almost any such termination), bootstrap himself around a motion addressed to the pleadings". Nor does the conclusory allegation of malice by plaintiff here supply the deficiency. As with the intentional infliction of emotional distress claim, this cause of action cannot be allowed in circumvention of the unavailability of a tort claim for wrongful discharge or the contract rule against liability for discharge of an at-will employee.

Plaintiff's fourth cause of action is for breach of contract. Although he concedes in his complaint that his employment contract was of indefinite duration (inferentially recognizing that, were there no more, under traditional principles his employer might have discharged him at any time), he asserts that in all employment contracts the law implies an obligation on the part of the employer to deal with his employees fairly and in good faith and that a discharge in violation of that implied obligation exposes the employer to liability for breach of contract. Seeking then to apply this proposition to the present case, plaintiff argues in substance that he was required by the terms of his employment to disclose accounting improprieties and that defendant's discharge of him for having done so constituted a failure by the employer to act in good faith and thus a breach of the contract of employment.

No New York case upholding any such broad proposition is cited to us by plaintiff (or identified by our dissenting colleague), and we know of none. New York does recognize that in appropriate circumstances an obligation of good faith and fair dealing on the part of a party to a contract may be implied and, if implied will be enforced . . . . In such instances the implied obligation is in aid and furtherance of other terms of the agreement of the parties. No obligation can be implied, however, which would be inconsistent with other terms of the contractual relationship. Thus, in the case now before us, plaintiff's employment was at will, a relationship in which the law accords the employer an unfettered right to terminate the employment at any time. In the context of such an employment it would be incongruous to say that an inference may be drawn that the employer impliedly agreed to a provision which would be destructive of his right of termination. The parties may by express agreement limit or restrict the employer's right of discharge, but to imply such a limitation from the existence of an unrestricted right would be internally inconsistent. In sum, under New York law as it now stands, absent a constitutionally impermissible purpose, a statutory proscription, or an express limitation in the individual contract of employment, an employer's right at any time to terminate an employment at will remains unimpaired.

* * *

Accordingly, the fourth cause of action should have been dismissed for failure to state a cause of action. [*The Court notes that the courts below appear to have erred in dismissing this cause of action under the Statute of Frauds because the contract of employment was not one which, by its terms, could not have been performed within one year.*]

* * *

For the reasons stated, the order of the Appellate Division should be modified, with costs, to reinstate plaintiff's fifth cause of action for age discrimination.

Selected
New York
Statutes

SELECTED NEW YORK STATE STATUTES

NEW YORK GENERAL OBLIGATIONS LAW

§ 1-202. Definition

As used in this chapter, the term "infant" or "minor" means a person who has not attained the age of eighteen years. (eff. Sept. 1, 1974)

§ 3-101. When contracts may not be disaffirmed on ground of infancy

1. A contract made on or after September first, nineteen hundred seventy-four by a person after he has attained the age of eighteen years may not be disaffirmed by him on the ground of infancy.

* * *

3. A husband and wife, with respect only to real property they occupy or which they affirm they are about to occupy as a home, regardless of the minority of either or both and without limitation of the powers of any such person who is of full age, shall each have power (a) to enter into and contract for a loan or loans with a bank, trust company, ... savings bank or savings and loan association whose home office is located in this state, with any insurance company authorized to do business in this state, with the United States government and its agencies, with respect to such real property and take any other action and execute any other document or instrument to the extent necessary or appropriate to effect any such loan, provide security therefor, carry out or modify the terms thereof, and effect any compromise or settlement of any such loan or of any claim with respect thereto; (b) to receive, hold and dispose of such real property, make and execute contracts, notes, deeds, mortgages, agreements and other instruments necessary and appropriate to acquire such property; and (c) to dispose of such real property so acquired, and make and execute contracts, deeds, agreements and other instruments necessary and appropriate to dispose of such property.

Notwithstanding any contrary provision or rule of law, no such husband or wife shall have the power to disaffirm, because of minority, any act or transaction which he or she is hereinabove empowered to perform or engage in, nor shall any defense based upon minority be interposed in any action or proceeding arising out of any such act or transaction.

****

§ 3-102. Obligations of certain minors for hospital, medical and surgical treatment and care

An obligation incurred by a married minor for hospital, medical and surgical treatment and care for such minor or such minor's children shall not be voidable because of minority. For the purpose of this section only, subsequent judgment of divorce or annulment shall not alter the obligation previously incurred.

§ 3-112. Liability of parents and legal guardians having custody of an infant for certain damages caused by such infant

1. The parent or legal guardian, other than the state, a local social services department or a foster parent, of an infant over ten and less than eighteen years of age, shall be liable to any public officer, organization or authority, having by law the care and/or custody of any public property of the state or of any political subdivision thereof, or to any private individual or organization having by law the care, custody and/or ownership of any private property, for damages caused by such infant, where such infant has willfully, maliciously, or unlawfully damaged, defaced or destroyed such public or private property, whether real or personal, or, where such infant, with intent to deprive the owner and/or custodian of such property or to appropriate the same to himself or herself or to a third person, has knowingly entered or remained in a building and has wrongfully taken, obtained or withheld such public or private personal property from such building which personal property is owned or maintained by the state or any political subdivision thereof or which is owned or maintained by any individual, organization or authority, or where such infant has falsely reported an incident or placed a false bomb . . . . Such public officer, organization or authority, or private individual or organization, as the case may be, may bring an action for civil damages in a court of competent jurisdiction for a judgment to recover such damages from such parent or legal guardian other than the state or a local social services department or a foster parent. For the purposes of this subdivision, damages for falsely reporting an incident or placing a false bomb shall mean the funds reasonably expended by a victim in responding to such false report . . . . In no event shall such damages portion of a judgment authorized by this section, as described in

this subdivision, exceed the sum of five thousand dollars.

2. Notwithstanding the provisions of subdivision one of this section, prior to the entering of a judgment under this section in the sum total of five hundred dollars or more, the court shall provide such parent or legal guardian of such infant with an opportunity to make an application to the court based upon such parent's or legal guardian's financial inability to pay any portion or all of the amount of such sum total which is in excess of five hundred dollars . . .

3. It shall be a defense to an action brought under this section that restitution has been paid . . . . It shall also be a defense to an action brought under this section that such infant had voluntarily and without good cause abandoned the home of the parent or guardian and without good cause refused to submit to the guidance and control of the parent or guardian prior to and at the time of the occurrence of such damages or destruction. In no event shall it be a defense that the parent or legal guardian has exercised due diligent supervision over the activities of such infant, provided, however, that in the interests of justice, the court may consider mitigating circumstances that bear directly upon the actions of the parent or legal guardian in supervising such unemancipated infant.

§ 5-325. Garages and parking places

1. No person who conducts or maintains for hire or other consideration a garage, parking lot or other similar place which has the capacity for the housing, storage, parking, repair or servicing of four or more motor vehicles, as defined by the vehicle and traffic law, may exempt himself from liability for damages for injury to person or property resulting from the negligence of such person, his agents or employees, in the operation of any such vehicle, or in its housing, storage, parking, repair or servicing, or in the conduct or maintenance of such garage, parking lot or other similar place, and, except as hereinafter provided, any agreement so exempting such person shall be void.

2. Damages for loss or injury to property may be limited by a provision in the storage agreement limiting the liability in case of loss or damage by theft, fire or explosion and setting forth a specific liability per vehicle, which shall in no event be less than twenty-five thousand dollars, beyond which the person owning or operating such garage or lot shall not be liable; provided, however, that such liability may on request of the person delivering such vehicle be increased, in which event increased rates may be charged based on such increased liability.

§ 5-326. Agreements exempting pools, gymnasiums, places of public amusement or recreation and similar establishments from liability for negligence void and unenforceable

Every covenant, agreement or understanding in or in connection with, or collateral to, any contract, membership application, ticket of admission or similar writing, entered into between the owner or operator of any pool, gymnasium, place of amusement or recreation, or similar establishment and the user of such facilities, pursuant to which such owner or operator receives a fee or other compensation for the use of such facilities, which exempts the said owner or operator from liability for damages caused by or resulting from the negligence of the owner, operator or person in charge of such establishment, or their agents, servants or employees, shall be deemed to be void as against public policy and wholly unenforceable.

§ 5-332. Unsolicited and voluntarily sent merchandise deemed unconditional gift

1. No person, firm, partnership, association or corporation, or agent or employee thereof, shall, in any manner, or by any means, offer for sale goods, wares, or merchandise, where the offer includes the voluntary and unsolicited sending of such goods, wares, or merchandise not actually ordered or requested by the recipient, either orally or in writing. The receipt of any such goods, wares, or merchandise shall for all purposes be deemed an unconditional gift to the recipient who may use or dispose of such goods, wares, or merchandise in any manner he sees fit without any obligation on his part to the sender.
If after any such receipt deemed to be an unconditional gift under this section, the sender continues to send bill statements or requests for payment with respect thereto, an action may be brought by the recipient to enjoin such conduct, in which action there may also be awarded reasonable attorney's fees and costs to the prevailing party.

* * *

§ 5-401. Illegal wagers, bets and stakes

All wagers, bets or stakes, made to depend upon any race, or upon any gaming by lot or chance, or upon any lot, chance, casualty, or unknown or contingent event whatever, shall be unlawful.

§ 5-411. Contracts on account of money or property wagered, bet or staked are void

All contracts for or on account of any money or property, or thing in action wagered, bet or staked, as provided in section 5-401, shall be void.

§ 5-501. Rate of interest; usury forbidden

1. The rate of interest, as computed pursuant to this title, upon the loan or forbearance of any money, goods, or things in action, except as provided in subdivisions five and six of this section or as otherwise provided by law, shall be six per centum per annum unless a different rate is prescribed in section fourteen-a of the banking law. . . . [See below.]

§ 5-511. Usurious contracts void

1. All bonds, bills, notes, assurances, conveyances, all other contracts or securities whatsoever, . . . and all deposits of goods or other things whatsoever, whereupon or whereby there shall be reserved or taken, or secured or agreed to be reserved or taken, any greater sum, or greater value, for the loan or forbearance of any money, goods or other things in action, than is prescribed in section 5-501, shall be void, except that the knowingly taking, receiving, reserving or charging such a greater sum or greater value by a savings bank, a savings and loan association or a federal savings and loan association shall only be held and adjudged a forfeiture of the entire interest which the loan or obligation carries with it or which has been agreed to be paid thereon. If a greater sum or greater value has been paid, the person paying the same or his legal representative may recover from the savings bank, the savings and loan association or the federal savings and loan association twice the entire amount of the interest thus paid.

2. Except as provided in subdivision one, whenever it shall satisfactorily appear by the admissions of the defendant, or by proof, that any bond, bill, note, assurance, pledge, conveyance, contract, security or any evidence of debt, has been taken or received in violation of the foregoing provisions, the court shall declare the same to be void, and enjoin any prosecution thereon, and order the same to be surrendered and cancelled.

§ 5-513. Recovery of excess

Every person who, for any such loan or forbearance, shall pay or deliver any greater sum or value than is allowed to be received pursuant to section 5-501, and his personal representatives, may recover in an action against the person who shall have taken or received the same, and his personal representatives, the amount of the money so paid or value delivered, above the rate aforesaid.

§ 5-515. Borrower bringing an action need not offer to repay

Whenever any borrower of money, goods or things in action, shall begin an action for the recovery of the money, goods or things in action taken in violation of the foregoing provisions of this title, it shall not be necessary for him to pay or offer to pay any interest or principal on the sum or thing loaned; nor shall any court require or compel the payment or deposit of the principal sum or interest, or any portion thereof, as a condition of granting relief to the borrower in any case of usurious loans forbidden by the foregoing provisions of this title.

§ 5-521. Corporations prohibited from interposing defense of usury

1. No corporation shall hereafter interpose the defense of usury in any action . . . .

2. The provisions of subdivision one of this section shall not apply to a corporation, the principal asset of which shall be the ownership of a one or two family dwelling, where it appears either that the said corporation was organized and created, or that the controlling interest therein was acquired, within a period of six months prior to the execution, by said corporation of a bond or note evidencing indebtedness, and a mortgage creating a lien for said indebtedness on the said one or two family dwelling; . . . .

Any provision of any contract, or any separate written instrument executed prior to, simultaneously with or within sixty days after the delivery of any moneys to any borrower in connection with such indebtedness, whereby the defense of usury is waived or any such corporation is estopped from asserting it, is hereby declared to be contrary to public policy and absolutely void. . . .

§ 5-701. Agreements required to be in writing

a. Every agreement, promise or undertaking is void [unenforceable], unless it or some note or memorandum thereof be in writing, and subscribed by the party to be charged therewith, or by his lawful agent, if such agreement, promise or undertaking:

1. By its terms is not to be performed within one year from the making thereof or the performance of which is not to be completed before the end of a lifetime;

2. Is a special promise to answer for the debt, default or miscarriage of another person;

3. Is made in consideration of marriage, except mutual promises to marry;

* * *

§ 5-703. Conveyances and contracts concerning real property required to be in writing

1. An estate or interest in real property, other than a lease for a term not exceeding one year, or any trust or power, over or concerning real property, or in any manner relating thereto, cannot be created, granted, assigned, surrendered or declared, unless by act or operation of law, or by a deed or conveyance in writing, subscribed by the person creating, granting, assigning, surrendering or declaring the same, or by his lawful agent, thereunto authorized by writing. But this subdivision does not affect the power of a testator in the disposition of his real property by will; nor prevent any trust from arising or being extinguished by implication or operation of law, nor any declaration of trust from being proved by a writing subscribed by the person declaring the same.

2. A contract for the leasing for a longer period than one year, or for the sale, of any real property, or an interest therein, is void unless the contract or some note

selling/transfer — need to be in writing

rent land — oral lease — 1 year

[handwritten margin notes: "Promissory Estoppel → limited usage → charitable pledge agreement"]

or memorandum thereof, expressing the consideration, is in writing, subscribed by the party to be charged, or by his lawful agent thereunto authorized by writing.

3. A contract to devise real property or establish a trust of real property, or any interest therein or right with reference thereto, is void unless the contract or some note or memorandum thereof is in writing and subscribed by the party to be charged therewith, or by his lawfully authorized agent.

4. Nothing contained in this section abridges the powers of courts of equity to compel the specific performance of agreements in cases of part performance.

§ 5-1103. Written agreement for modification or discharge

An agreement, promise or undertaking to change or modify, or to discharge in whole or in part, any contract, obligation, or lease, or any mortgage or other security interest in personal or real property, shall not be invalid because of the absence of consideration, provided that the agreement, promise or undertaking changing, modifying, or discharging such contract, obligation, lease, mortgage or security interest, shall be in writing and signed by the party against whom it is sought to enforce the change, modification or discharge, or by his agent.

§ 5-1105. Written promise expressing past consideration

[handwritten margin note, rotated: "has to be in writing expressing past consideration"]

A promise in writing and signed by the promisor or by his agent shall not be denied effect as a valid contractual obligation on the ground that consideration for the promise is past or executed, if the consideration is expressed in the writing and is proved to have been given or performed and would be a valid consideration but for the time when it was given or performed.

§ 5-1107. Written assignment

An assignment shall not be denied the effect of irrevocably transferring the assignor's rights because of the absence of consideration, if such assignment is in writing and signed by the assignor, or by his agent.

§ 5-1109. Written irrevocable offer

Except as otherwise provided in section 2-205 of the uniform commercial code with respect to an offer by a merchant to buy or sell goods, when an offer to enter into a contract is made in a writing signed by the offeror, or by his agent, which states that the offer is irrevocable during a period set forth or until a time fixed, the offer shall not be revocable during such period or until such time because of the absence of consideration for the assurance of irrevocability. When such a writing states that the offer is irrevocable but does not state any period or time of irrevocability, it shall be construed to state that

the offer is irrevocable for a reasonable time.

§ 5-1113. Written or published promise or reward

A promise to pay a reward for return of lost or mislaid property is not unenforceable because of absence of consideration if the promise was made in writing or the promisor caused it to be published.

§ 15-303. Release in writing without consideration or seal

A written instrument which purports to be a total or partial release of all claims, debts, demands or obligations, or a total or partial release of any particular claim, debt, demand or obligation, or a release or discharge in whole or in part of a mortgage, lien, security interest or charge upon personal or real property, shall not be invalid because of the absence of consideration or of a seal.

§ 15-501. Executory accord

1. Executory accord as used in this section means an agreement embodying a promise express or implied to accept at some future time a stipulated performance in satisfaction or discharge in whole or in part of any present claim, cause of action, contract, obligation, or lease, or any mortgage or other security interest in personal or real property, and a promise express or implied to render such performance in satisfaction or in discharge of such claim, cause of action, contract, obligation, lease, mortgage or security interest.

2. An executory accord shall not be denied effect as a defense or as the basis of an action or counterclaim by reason of the fact that the satisfaction or discharge of the claim, cause of action, contract, obligation, lease, mortgage or other security interest which is the subject of the accord was to occur at a time after the making of the accord, provided the promise of the party against whom it is sought to enforce the accord is in writing and signed by such party or by his agent. If executed by an agent, any promise required by this section to be in writing which affects or relates to real property or an interest therein as defined in section 5-101 in any manner stated in subdivisions one or two of section 5-703 of this chapter shall be void unless such agent was thereunto authorized in writing.

3. If an executory accord is not performed according to its terms by one party, the other party shall be entitled either to assert his rights under the claim, cause of action, contract, obligation, lease, mortgage or other security interest which is the subject of the accord, or to assert his right under the accord.

§ 15-503. Offer of accord followed by tender

1. An offer in writing, signed by the offeror or by his agent, to accept a performance therein designated in satisfaction or discharge in whole or in part of any claim, cause of action, contract, obligation, or lease, or any mortgage or other security interest in personal or real property, followed by tender of such performance by the offeree or by his agent before revocation of the offer, shall not be denied effect as a defense or as the basis of an action or counterclaim by reason of the fact that such tender was not accepted by the offeror or by his agent.

2. If executed by an agent, any offer required by this section to be in writing which affects or relates to real property or an interest therein as defined in section 5-101 in any manner stated in subdivisions one or two of section 5-703 of this chapter shall be void unless such agent was thereunto authorized in writing.

§ 17-103. Agreements waiving the statute of limitation

1. A promise to waive, to extend, or not to plead the statute of limitation applicable to an action arising out of a contract express or implied in fact or in law, if made after the accrual of the cause of action and made, either with or without consideration, in a writing signed by the promisor or his agent is effective, according to its terms, to prevent interposition of the defense of the statute of limitation in an action or proceeding commenced within the time that would be applicable if the cause of action had arisen at the date of the promise, or within such shorter time as may be provided in the promise.

2. A promise to waive, to extend, or not to plead the statute of limitation may be enforced as provided in this section by the person to whom the promise is made or for whose benefit it is expressed to be made or by any person who, after the making of the promise, succeeds or is subrogated to the interest of either of them.

3. A promise to waive, to extend, or not to plead the statute of limitation has no effect to extend the time limited by statute for commencement of an action or proceeding for any greater time or in any other manner than that provided in this section, or unless made as provided in this section.

4. This section

    a. does not change the requirements or the effect with respect to the statute of limitation, of an acknowledgment or promise to pay, or a payment or part payment of principal or interest, or a stipulation made in an action or proceeding;

    b. does not affect the power of the court to find that by reason of conduct of the party to be charged it is inequitable to permit him to interpose the defense of the statute of limitation; and

    c. does not apply in any respect to a cause of action to foreclose a mortgage of real property or a mortgage of a lease of real property, or to a cause of action to recover a judgment affecting the title to or the possession, use or enjoyment of real property, or a promise or waiver with respect to any statute of limitation applicable thereto.

NEW YORK BANKING LAW

§ 14-a. Rate of interest; banking board to adopt regulations

1. The maximum rate of interest provided for in section 5-501 of the general obligations law shall be sixteen per centum per annum.

2. The rate of interest as so prescribed under this section shall include as interest any and all amounts paid or payable, directly or indirectly, by any person, to or for the account of the lender in consideration for the making of a loan or forbearance as defined by the banking board pursuant to subdivision three of this section.

NEW YORK CIVIL PRACTICE LAW AND RULES (C.P.L.R.)

§ 1411. Damages recoverable when contributory negligence or assumption of risk is established

In any action to recover damages for personal injury, injury to property, or wrongful death, the culpable conduct attributable to the claimant or to the decedent, including contributory negligence or assumption of risk, shall not bar recovery, but the amount of damages otherwise recoverable shall be diminished in the proportion which the culpable conduct attributable to the claimant or decedent bears to the culpable conduct which caused the damages.

§ 3002. Actions and relief not barred for inconsistency

* * *

(d) *Action on contract and to reform.* A judgment denying recovery in an action upon an agreement in writing shall not be deemed to bar an action to reform such agreement and to enforce it as reformed.

(e) *Claim for damages and rescission.* A claim for damages sustained as a result of fraud or misrepresentation in the inducement of a contract or other transaction, shall not be deemed inconsistent with a claim for rescission or based upon rescission. In an action for rescission or based upon rescission the aggrieved party shall be allowed to obtain complete relief in one action, including rescission, restitution of the benefits, if any, conferred by him as a result of the transaction, and damages to which he is entitled because of such fraud or misrepresentation; but such complete relief shall not include duplication of items of recovery.

§ 3004. Where restoration of benefits before judgment unnecessary

A party who has received benefits by reason of a transaction that is void or voidable because of fraud, misrepresentation, mistake, duress, infancy or incompetency, and who, in an action or by way of defense or counterclaim, seeks rescission, restitution, a declaration or judgment that such transaction is void, or other relief, whether formerly denominated legal or equitable, dependent upon a determination that such transaction was void or voidable, shall not be denied relief because of a failure to tender before judgment restoration of such benefits; but the court may make a tender of restoration a condition of its judgment, and may otherwise in its judgment so adjust the equities between the parties that unjust enrichment is avoided.

§ 7501. Effect of arbitration agreement

A written agreement to submit any controversy thereafter arising or any existing controversy to arbitration is enforceable without regard to the justiciable character of the controversy and confers jurisdiction on the courts of the state to enforce it and to enter judgment on an award. In determining any matter arising under this article, the court shall not consider whether the claim with respect to which arbitration is sought is tenable, or otherwise pass upon the merits of the dispute.

NEW YORK EDUCATION LAW

§ 281. Loans and extensions of credit to infants

A contract hereafter made by an infant after he has attained the age of sixteen years in relation to obtaining a loan or extension of credit from an institution of the university of the state of New York in connection with such infant's attendance upon a course of instruction offered by such institution, or from a bank, trust company, industrial bank or national bank whose principal office is in this state for the purpose of defraying all or a portion of the expenses of such infant's attendance upon a course of instruction in an institution of the university of the state of New York or any other institution for higher education without this state which is a member of or accredited by an accrediting agency recognized by the department, may not be disaffirmed by him on the ground of infancy.

§ 6501. Admission to a profession (licensing)

Admission to practice of a profession in this state is accomplished by a license being issued to a qualified applicant by the education department. To qualify for a license an applicant shall meet the requirements prescribed in the article for the particular profession . . . .

§ 6503. Practice of a profession

Admission to the practice of a profession (1) entitles the licensee to practice the profession as defined in the article for the particular profession, (2) entitles the individual licensee to use the professional title as provided in the article for the particular profession, and (3) subjects the licensee to the procedures and penalties for professional misconduct as prescribed in this article . . . .

§ 6512. Unauthorized practice a crime

1. Anyone not authorized to practice under this title who practices or offers to practice or holds himself out as being able to practice in any profession in which a license is a prerequisite to the practice of the acts, or who practices any profession as an exempt person during the time when his professional license is suspended, revoked or annulled, or who aids or abets an unlicensed person to practice a profession, or who fraudulently sells, files, furnishes, obtains, or who attempts fraudulently to sell, file, furnish or obtain any diploma, license, record or permit purporting to authorize the practice of a profession, shall be guilty of a class E felony. . . .

§ 6513. Unauthorized use of a professional title a crime

1. Anyone not authorized to use a professional title regulated by this title, and who uses such professional title, shall be guilty of a class A misdemeanor. . . .

NEW YORK PENAL LAW

§ 180.00 Commercial bribing in the second degree

A person is guilty of commercial bribing in the second degree when he confers, or offers or agrees to confer, any benefit upon any employee, agent or fiduciary without the consent of the latter's employer or principal, with intent to influence his conduct in relation to his employer's or principal's affairs.
Commercial bribing in the second degree is a class A misdemeanor.

§ 180.03 Commercial bribing in the first degree

A person is guilty of commercial bribing in the first degree when he confers, or offers or agrees to confer, any benefit upon any employee, agent or fiduciary without the consent of the latter's employer or principal, with intent to influence his conduct in relation to his employer's or principal's affairs, and when the value of the benefit conferred or offered or agreed to be conferred exceeds one thousand dollars and causes economic harm to the employer or principal in an amount exceeding two hundred fifty dollars.
Commercial bribing in the first degree is a class E felony.

§ 180.08 Commercial bribe receiving in the first degree

An employee, agent or fiduciary is guilty of commercial bribe receiving in the first degree when, without the consent of his employer or principal, he solicits, accepts or agrees to accept any benefit from another person upon an agreement or understanding that such benefit will influence his conduct in relation to his employer's or principal's affairs, and when the value of the benefit solicited, accepted or agreed to be accepted exceeds one thousand dollars and causes economic harm to the employer or principal in an amount exceeding two hundred fifty dollars.
Commercial bribe receiving in the first degree is a class E felony.

§ 190.40 Criminal usury in the second degree

A person is guilty of criminal usury in the second degree when, not being authorized or permitted by law to do so, he knowingly charges, takes or receives any money or other property as interest on the loan or forbearance of any money or other property, at a rate exceeding twenty-five per centum per annum or the equivalent rate for a longer or shorter period.
Criminal usury in the second degree is a class E felony.

NEW YORK ARTS AND CULTURAL AFFAIRS LAW

§ 35.03. Judicial approval of certain contracts for services of infants; . . . .

1. A contract made by an infant or made by a parent or guardian of an infant, or a contract proposed to be so made, under which (a) the infant is to perform or render services as an actor, actress, dancer, musician, vocalist or other performing artist, or as a participant or player in professional sports, or (b) a person is employed to render services to the infant in connection with such services of the infant or in connection with contracts therefor, may be approved by the supreme court or the surrogate's court as provided in this section where the infant is a resident of this state or the services of the infant are to be performed or rendered in this state. If the contract is so approved the infant may not, either during his minority or upon reaching his majority, disaffirm the contract on the ground of infancy or assert that the parent or guardian lacked authority to make the contract. A contract modified, amended or assigned after its approval under this section shall be deemed a new contract.

2. (a) Approval of the contract pursuant to this section shall not exempt any person from any other law with respect to licenses, consents or authorizations required for any conduct, employment, use or exhibition of the infant in this state, nor limit in any manner the discretion of the licensing authority or other persons charged with the administration of such requirements, nor dispense with any other requirement of law relating to the infant.

(b) No contract shall be approved which provides for an employment, use or exhibition of the infant, within or without the state, which is prohibited by law and could not be licensed to take place in this state.

(c) No contract shall be approved unless (i) the written acquiescence to such contract of the parent or parents having custody, or other person having custody of the infant, is filed in the proceeding or (ii) the court shall find that the infant is emancipated.

(d) No contract shall be approved if the term during which the infant is to perform or render services or during which a person is employed to render services to the infant, including any extensions thereof by option or otherwise, extends for a period of more than three years from the date of approval of the contract . . . .

NEW YORK CIVIL SERVICE LAW

§ 75-b. Retaliatory action by public employers
* * *

2. (a) A public employer shall not dismiss or take other disciplinary or other adverse personnel action against a public employee regarding the employee's employment because the employee discloses to a governmental body information: (i) regarding a violation of a law, rule or regulation which violation creates and presents a substantial and specific danger to the public health or safety; or (ii) which the employee reasonably believes to be true and reasonably believes constitutes an improper governmental action. "Improper governmental action" shall mean any action by a public employer or employee, or an agent of such employer or employee, which is undertaken in the performance of such agent's official duties, whether or not such action is within the scope of his employment, and which is in violation of any federal, state or local law, rule or regulation.

(b) Prior to disclosing information pursuant to paragraph (a) of this subdivision, an employee shall have made a good faith effort to provide the appointing authority or his or her designee the information to be disclosed and shall provide the appointing authority or designee a reasonable time to take appropriate action unless there is imminent and serious danger to public health or safety. For the purposes of this subdivision, an employee who acts pursuant to this paragraph shall be deemed to have disclosed information to a governmental body under paragraph (a) of this subdivision.
* * *

NEW YORK LABOR LAW

§ 201-d. Discrimination against the engagement in certain activities

1. Definitions. As used in this section:

a. "Political activities" shall mean (i) running for public office, (ii) campaigning for a candidate for public office, or (iii) participating in fund-raising activities for the benefit of a candidate, political party or political advocacy group;

b. "Recreational activities" shall mean any lawful, leisure-time activity, for which the employee receives no compensation and which is generally engaged in for recreational purposes, including but not limited to sports, games, hobbies, exercise, reading and the viewing of television, movies and similar material;
* * *

2. Unless otherwise provided by law, it shall be unlawful for any employer or employment agency to refuse to hire, employ or license, or to discharge from employment or otherwise discriminate against an individual in compensation, promotion or terms, conditions or privileges of employment because of:

a. an individual's political activities outside of working hours, off of the employer's premises and without use of the employer's equipment or other property, if such activities are legal, provided, however, that this paragraph shall not apply to persons whose employment is defined in paragraph six of subdivision (a) of section seventy-nine-h of the civil rights law, and provided further that this paragraph shall not apply to persons who would otherwise be prohibited from engaging in political activity pursuant to chapter 15 of title 5 and subchapter III of chapter 73 of title 5 of the USCA;

b. an individual's legal use of consumable products prior to the beginning or after the conclusion of the employee's work hours, and off of the employer's premises and without use of the employer's equipment or other property;

c. an individual's legal recreational activities outside work hours, off of the employer's premises and without use of the employer's equipment or other property; or

d. an individual's membership in a union or any exercise of rights granted under Title 29, USCA, Chapter 7 or under article fourteen of the civil service law.

§ 740. Retaliatory personnel action by employers; prohibition
* * *

2. Prohibitions. An employer shall not take any retaliatory personnel action against an employee because such employee does any of the following:

(a) discloses, or threatens to disclose to a supervisor or to a public body an activity, policy or practice of the employer that is in violation of law, rule or regulation which violation creates and presents a substantial and specific danger to the public health or safety or which constitutes health care fraud;

(b) provides information to, or testifies before, any public body conducting an investigation, hearing or inquiry into any such violation of a law, rule or regulation by such employer; or

(c) objects to, or refuses to participate in any such activity, policy or practice in violation of a law, rule or regulation.

3. Application. The protection against retaliatory personnel action provided by paragraph (a) of subdivision two of this section pertaining to disclosure to a public body shall not apply to an employee who makes such disclosure to a public body unless the employee has brought the activity, policy or practice in violation of law, rule or regulation to the attention of a supervisor of the employer and has afforded such employer a reasonable opportunity to correct such activity, policy or practice.

4. Violation; remedy. (a) An employee who has been the subject of a retaliatory personnel action in violation of this section may institute a civil action in a court of competent jurisdiction for relief as set forth in subdivision five of this section within one year after the alleged retaliatory personnel action was taken.

* * *

5. Relief. In any action brought pursuant to subdivision four of this section, the court may order relief as follows:

(a) an injunction to restrain continued violation of this section;

(b) the reinstatement of the employee to the same position held before the retaliatory personnel action, or to an equivalent position;

(c) the reinstatement of full fringe benefits and seniority rights;

(d) the compensation for lost wages, benefits and other remuneration; and

(e) the payment by the employer of reasonable costs, disbursements, and attorney's fees.

6. Employer relief. A court, in its discretion, may also order that reasonable attorneys' fees and court costs and disbursements be awarded to an employer if the court determines that an action brought by an employee under this section was without basis in law or in fact. * * *

§ 741 Prohibition; health care employer who penalizes employees because of complaints of employer violations.

2. Retaliatory action prohibited. Notwithstanding any other provision of law, no employer shall take retaliatory action against any employee because the employee does any of the following:

(a) discloses or threatens to disclose to a supervisor, or to a public body an activity, policy or practice of the employer or agent that the employee, in good faith, reasonably believes constitutes improper quality of patient care; or

(b) objects to, or refuses to participate in any activity, policy or practice of the employer or agent that the employee, in good faith, reasonably believes constitutes improper quality of patient care.

3. Application. The protection against retaliatory personnel action provided by subdivision two of this section shall not apply unless the employee has brought the improper quality of patient care to the attention of a supervisor and has afforded the employer a reasonable opportunity to correct such activity, policy or practice. This subdivision shall not apply to an action or failure to act described in paragraph (a) of subdivision two of this section where the improper quality of patient care described therein presents an imminent threat to public health or safety or to the health of a specific patient and the employee reasonably believes in good faith that reporting to a supervisor would not result in corrective action.

NEW YORK UNIFORM COMMERCIAL CODE

Section 1-207. Performance or Acceptance Under Reservation of Rights.

A party who with explicit reservation of rights performs or promises performance or assents to performance in a manner demanded or offered by   the other party does not thereby prejudice the rights reserved. Such words as "without prejudice," "under protest" or the like are sufficient.

Additional Problems

Chapter 4 Torts and Cyber Torts

1. Don Juan is so busy trying to get the attention of a young woman that he walks into a light pole and is knocked unconscious. Driver happens to be driving down the road and sees Don Juan's unfortunate incident. Driver is so amused by the incident that he takes his eyes off the road for a moment and nearly slams into the car ahead of him. Veering off the road to avoid an accident, Driver drives into a restaurant, breaking a large window. Noodle, who was enjoying a bowl of soup at that moment, is burned by the hot soup, which is knocked off the table and into Noodle's lap. Noodle sues the restaurant, Driver and Don Juan for negligence. As to each claim, what result? Explain.

Chapter 10 Agreement in Traditional and E-Contracts

1. Danforth Corporation entered into a written employment agreement with Eva on September 1, which provided in part that employment would commence on the following January 1 and "will continue for a period of time to be mutually agreed upon". One month before January 1, Danforth Corporation notified Eva that it had changed its mind and would not employ Eva. In Eva's action against Danforth for breach of contract, Danforth contends that there is no contract. Judgment for whom? Explain.

2. On April 15, Ramon wrote to Ivana offering to sell a piece of land that Ramon owned for $50,000. The letter, which was signed by Ramon, stated that the offer would expire on July 30.

On April 20, Ramon received a better offer from Lou. Ramon called Ivana and told her that he was withdrawing his offer to Ivana.

On April 25, Ivana called Ramon and told him that she was accepting Ramon's offer of April 15. Ramon said that it was too late to accept the offer.

In an action by Ivana against Ramon for breach of contract, judgment for whom? Explain.

3. On May 1, Esther, a retail wine seller, sent a letter to Samuel offering to buy 50 cases of Chateau Le Pew wine at $100 a case. The letter, which was signed by Esther, stated that it was a firm offer for 30 days. Samuel received the offer on May 2.

By May 10, however, the price of wine was dropping and Esther wrote to Samuel saying, "I am sorry but I hereby withdraw the offer." Samuel received this letter on May 12.

On May 15, Samuel called Esther and told her that he accepted Esther's offer of May 1. Esther claimed that the offer had been withdrawn and refused to accept delivery of the wine.

In an action by Samuel against Esther for breach of contract, judgment for whom? Explain.

4. On July 1, Stan, a steel manufacturer, telephoned Byron and offered to sell Byron six carloads of steel at $600 a ton. Byron said, "That's a lot of steel! Would you promise to keep your offer open for 10 days so that I can think about whether I can use that much?" Stan replied, "Sure. I promise to keep the offer open for 10 days."

On July 6, Stan sent a letter to Byron that stated, "I hereby revoke my offer of July 1." Byron received this letter on July 7.

On July 7, Byron called Stan and said that he was accepting Stan's offer of July 1. Stan refused to deliver the steel, claiming that he had validly revoked the offer.

In an action by Byron against Stan for breach of contract, judgment for whom. Explain?

5. Mira offered to sell Peter a parking lot for $75,000. The offer was in writing and signed by Mira and provided that any acceptance by Peter must be within 5 days. On the fourth day, Mira accepted a better offer from Dean and transferred the parking lot to Dean on that day. Unaware of this sale, Peter telephoned Mira on the fifth day and accepted Mira's offer. In an action by Peter against Mira for breach of contract, judgment for whom?

↳ revoked

offeree thinks there's still an offer

- Dean wins

6. Ty, a merchant, wrote to Marcus: "August 1, I offer to sell you one Model A Desktop Computer system, price $1,000. This is a firm offer for 30 days from the above date. (*Signed*) Ty."

(a) On August 10, Marcus received a letter from Ty: "I hereby revoke my offer of August 1."

On August 17, Marcus wrote to Ty: "I hereby accept your offer of August 1."

Is there a contract? Explain.

(b) Assume that Ty's offer stated that it was a firm offer for four months, and that on November 15, Marcus mailed an acceptance. Is there a contract? Explain.

(c) Assume that Ty's offer stated that it was a firm offer for four months, and that on November 14, Marcus received a letter from Ty, dated November 12: "I hereby revoke my offer of August 1." On November 15, Marcus mailed an acceptance. Is there a contract? Explain.

7. On March 1, Irina wrote a signed letter to Benito and offered to sell the piano in her home to Benito for $400, and stated that she would keep her offer open for 4 months. On April 1, Irina sold the piano to Tonya, her cousin, for $500, without informing Benito that she did so. On June 10, Benito wrote Irina stating that he accepted Irina's offer. Irina immediately notified Benito that she could not sell him the piano because she had already sold it to Tonya. Benito sues Irina for breach of contract. Judgment for whom? Explain.

8. On September 15, Preet wrote to Lila as follows: "I offer to sell you my farm, Blackacre, for $300,000, all cash, closing on November 1. Please advise as soon as possible. (Signed) Preet."

On October 1, Lila mailed her acceptance to Preet, unaware that Preet had died on September 30 When Lila learned of Preet's death on October 5, Lila insisted that the Estate of Preet nevertheless deliver the deed to Blackacre in exchange for Lila's certified check for $300,000. Xavier, the Executor of Preet's Estate, refused to do so.

(a) In an action by Lila against the Estate of Preet for breach of contract, judgment for whom? Explain.

(b) If Preet's offer was a valid irrevocable offer for 30 days, would your answer to (a) be different? Explain.

9. On October 1, Tsering received the following letter from Shoshanna: "I understand that you are interested in buying a pick-up truck, I will sell you mine for $10,000 all cash, and will have it ready for delivery to you on November 15. (*Signed*) Shoshanna."

Later that day Tsering telephoned Shoshanna and inquired: "Can I have 20 days to think over your offer?" Shoshanna replied: "O.K., you have an irrevocable option for 20 days. Write to me when you decide."

On October 6, Tsering wrote Shoshanna: "I am still very much interested in your offer. I'm a little short of cash at the moment and would like to know if you would consider taking $5,000 cash and my 30-day note for the other $5,000? (Signed) Tsering." Shoshanna did not reply.

On October 10, without Tsering's knowledge, Shoshanna sold and delivered the truck to Mario for $11,000 cash.

On October 15, Tsering wrote Shoshanna: "I have decided to accept your offer and will pay you $10,000 in cash when I pick up the truck on Nov.15. (Signed) Tsering." Shoshanna wrote back: "The truck is sold." Tsering sued Shoshanna for damages for breach of contract. Judgment for whom? Explain.

10. On May 1, Kodzo, a textile manufacturer, mailed to Bonnie, a merchant, a written and signed offer to sell 1,000 bolts of blue denim at $40 per bolt. Each bolt would contain 25 square yards. The offer stated that "it would remain open for 10 days from the above date (May 1) and that it would not be withdrawn prior to that date."

Two days later, Kodzo, noting a sudden increase in the price of blue denim, changed his mind. After making great personal efforts to contact Bonnie, Kodzo sent Bonnie a letter revoking the offer of May 1. The letter was mailed on May 4 and received by Bonnie on May 5. Bonnie chose to disregard the letter of May 4. Instead, she continued to watch the price of blue denim rise.

On May 9, Bonnie mailed a letter accepting the original offer. The letter was sent by mail and was properly addressed and contained the correct postage. However, it was not received by Kodzo until May 12, due to a delay in the mail. Bonnie demanded delivery of the goods according to the terms of the offer of May 1, but Kodzo has refused, claiming there is no contract

(a) Is there a contract? Explain.

(b) If Kodzo was not a merchant, would there be a contract? Explain.

11. Sara, a wholesale fruit dealer, sent the following letter to Bud, a fruit merchant: "Feb. 1, offer 1,000 boxes of Los Angeles, San Gabriel oranges, at $10.60 per box, F.O.B. Los Angeles: March delivery. Unless I receive your acceptance by 2 P.M. on Feb. 4, I will dispose of them elsewhere. (Signed Sara)." Sara's letter was received by Bud on Feb. 2, at 3 P.M.

At 1 P.M. on Feb. 2, Sara mailed Bud the following letter. "I regret to inform you that I am compelled to withdraw my offer dated Feb. 1." Sara's second letter was not received by Bud until Feb. 3.

Meanwhile at 5 P.M. on Feb. 2, Bud mailed the following letter to Sara: "I accept your offer dated Feb. 1. (Signed Bud)." Because of a severe snowstorm, which disrupted all means of communication, Bud's letter was not delivered to Sara until 4 P.M. on Feb. 4.

(a) Is there a contract between Sara and Bud? Explain.

(b) Assume that the words "Unless I receive your acceptance by 2 P.M. on Feb 4, I will dispose of them elsewhere" were not included in Sara's Feb. 1 letter to Bud. Is there a contract between Sara and Bud? Explain.

12. Mel offered to sell to Sue a ten-acre tract of commercial property for $750,000. Mel's signed letter indicated the offer would expire on March 1 at 3:00 P.M. and that any acceptance must be received in his office by that time.

On February 28, Sue decided to accept the offer and mailed an acceptance at 4:00 P.M. Sue indicated in her letter that in the event the acceptance did not arrive on time, she would assume there was a contract if she did not hear anything from Mel by March 10. The letter arrived on March 2. Mel never responded to Sue's letter.

In an action by Sue against Mel for breach of contract, judgment for whom? Explain.

13. On March 10, Lev sent a signed written offer to Boris to sell 3,000 tons of steel rails on certain specified terms. Boris received this letter on March 11. On March 25, Boris faxed his acceptance, which reached Lev at 3 P.M. on that day. On the same day, March 25, at 2 PM., Lev mailed Boris a revocation of his March 10 offer, which Boris received the following day. Is there a contract? Explain.

14. Seth, a manufacturer, sent to Belkys, a retail merchant, an offer to sell 100 television sets for $30,000, terms C.O.D. Belkys wrote to Seth: "I accept your offer, and will pay you 30 days after delivery. (Signed Belkys)." Seth tendered delivery of the TV sets to Belkys and demanded cash on delivery. Belkys refused to pay on delivery, and Seth withheld delivery. Seth then sued to recover damages for breach of contract.

(a) Judgment for whom? Explain.

(b) Assume that Belkys's letter read as follows: "I accept your offer provided that you agree that payment is due 30 days after delivery." Is there a contract if Seth made no reply? Explain.

Chapter 11 Consideration, Capacity and Legality

1. The chairman of the board of directors of Xerxes Corp. wrote a signed letter to Pablo, the president, who is 68 years old and planned to retire at the end of the year. "The corporation will pay you a pension of $100,000 a year for life if you retire as planned, and agree not to take another job in this industry." Pablo replied, "I promise to do as you wish." Two years later, Xerxes Corp. stopped the pension payments. Pablo sues Xerxes Corp. for the current installment.

(a) May he recover? Explain.

(b) Instead of the above letter, assume that at Pablo's retirement dinner, the chairman of the board of directors of Xerxes Corp., in his speech, said "In view of the fact that you have been faithful to Xerxes Corp. for 30 years and have resisted efforts of our competitors to hire you away from us, the corporation promises to pay you a pension of $100,000 a year for life." Pablo stood up and said, "I accept your pension promise with gratitude." Is Xerxes Corp.'s promise enforceable by Pablo and if not, what would be necessary to make it enforceable? Explain.

2. Alfalfa, a novice rock climber, decided to go on a very difficult climb. Half way up, he found himself in trouble. Darla, a more experienced climber, at great peril to herself, rescued Alfalfa from almost certain serious injury, if not death. Alfalfa was so grateful for what Darla had done that he promised to send her a check for $1,000. Alfalfa failed to send the check and Darla sues him for breach of contract. Judgment for whom? Explain.

3. Debbie owed Carlos $50,000 on a contract for the purchase of 200 air-conditioners on credit, the terms of payment stating "Payment due 60 days after delivery." Delivery was made on January 2. On March 10, Debbie met Carlos and told him, "I'm sorry I missed out on paying you what I owe you. Collections have been slow. If you give me until May 1, I'll pay you what I owe plus interest at 9%." Carlos said, "O.K. I'll give you until May 1." On March 15, Carlos changed his mind and sued Debbie for $50,000. Debbie contends that the debt is not due until May 1. Is Debbie's contention valid? Explain.

4. Benito borrowed $1,000 from Leslie at 5% interest and gave Leslie a promissory note for $1,050 payable in one year. The year having elapsed, Benito tendered a check for $900 with these words written on the back above the space where Leslie would endorse it: "I (Leslie) hereby accept the face amount of this check in complete satisfaction of the debt owed by Benito." Leslie cashed the check and now seeks to recover the balance from Benito. Is the entire debt discharged? Explain.

5. Aldo shipped 10 refrigerators to Rafael pursuant to a sales contract under which title to the goods and risk of loss would pass to Rafael upon delivery to Fleet Railroad. The agreed price was $5,000. When the refrigerators were delivered to Rafael, he found they were damaged. An estimate for repairing them showed it would cost up to $1,000, and an expert opinion was to the effect that they were defective when shipped. Rafael put in a claim to Aldo, which Aldo rejected. Rafael then wrote to Aldo, "I don't like to get into a dispute of this nature. I am enclosing my check for $4,000 in full payment of the shipment." Aldo did not reply, but he cashed the check and then sued Rafael for the $1,000 balance. May he recover? Explain.

6. In the previous problem, assume that there was no damage to the refrigerators and no dispute, but that Rafael did not pay. One month after payment was due, Rafael wrote to Aldo, "I'll pay you $4,000 if you will accept it in full payment." Aldo wrote back, "Since I have despaired of getting any more out of you, I'll take the $4,000 in full payment." Rafael paid the $4,000 and later, Aldo sued Rafael for the $1,000 balance. May he recover? Explain.

7. Eva and Maria entered into a written contract pursuant to which Eva was to render decorating services for Maria for a total price of $75,000. After the services had been performed, a good faith dispute arose between Eva and Maria over whether all of the services had been properly performed. Eva claimed that the full amount was due, but Maria argued that only $50,000 worth of services had been performed. After several weeks of argument, Maria sent a check for $60,000 to Eva on which Maria had written "payment in full for decorating services."

(a) Eva endorsed the check, without making any further notations on it, deposited it and sued Maria for the remaining $15,000 she claims is due. Judgment for whom? Explain.

(b) Instead of the facts in (a) assume that Eva wrote "under protest" on the check when she endorsed it and, after depositing it, sues Maria for $15,000. What result? Explain.

(c) Instead of the facts in (a) and (b), assume that Eva and Maria had a telephone conversation in which Eva agreed to take $60,000 in full satisfaction of Maria's obligation under the contract. Maria then sent the check, with a letter referencing the telephone conversation. Eva wrote "under protest" on the check, endorsed and deposited it, and then sued Maria for $15,000. What result? Explain.

8. Digna owed Cecelia $10,000 under a valid loan agreement. Payment was due on September 1. Digna informed Cecelia that she was unable to pay on September 1.

(a) Assume that on September 5, Cecelia orally agreed to accept $8,000 plus the transfer of Digna's stamp collection (which Cecelia admired) as payment in full, if Digna would do so by September 10. Digna did pay the $8,000 and transferred the stamp collection to Cecelia on September 8. The stamp collection had a market value of $1,000. On September 15, Cecelia sued Digna for the $1,000 balance Cecelia claims is due. How much, if anything, will Cecelia recover from Digna? Explain.

(b) Instead of the assumption in (a), assume that on September 5, Cecelia orally agreed to accept $9,000 in full payment of Digna's debt if Digna paid before September 10. Digna paid Cecelia $9,000 on September 8. On September 15, Cecelia sued Digna for $1,000. How much, if anything, will Cecelia recover from Digna? Explain.

(c) Would your answer to (b) be different if Cecelia agreed in a signed writing to accept $9,000 in full payment of Digna's debt? Explain.

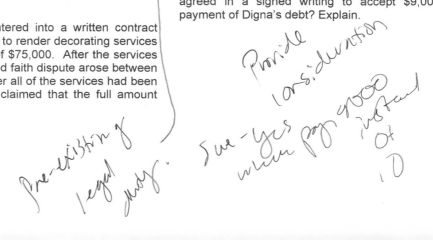

9. Camila, a building contractor, entered into a written agreement with Owen, the owner of 27 Y Street, to build a new wing on Owen's house for $90,000. After the work was one-half done, Camila complained about the rising cost of materials and stopped work. Owen said to Camila: "If you go ahead and finish the job, I'll pay you a bonus of $10,000." Camila agreed and finished the job. Camila then demanded payment of $100,000, but Owen refused to pay more than $90,000.

(a) How much may Camila collect from Owen? Explain.

(b) Assume that Camila wrote on the bottom of the written contract, "The agreed price for the above work is $100,000" and said to Owen: "I'll go ahead if you sign that," which Owen did. How much may Camila collect from Owen? Explain.

10. Armand was hired to work as the chef for the restaurant at Scallop's seaside resort for 3 months during the summer, under a written contract that provided that Armand would receive compensation of $50,000. During the first month, the guests were wildly enthusiastic about the quality of the food and Scallop's reservations for the resort and restaurant doubled. Noticing this, Armand felt he was entitled to share in Scallop's increased profits. During a conversation, Scallop promised to pay Armand a $20,000 bonus at the end of the summer if he continued to work under his contract. At the end of the three months, Scallop paid Armand $50,000 and refused to pay the $20,000 bonus he had promised. Armand sued Scallop for breach of contract. Judgment for whom? Explain.

11. In May, Mike, a 17-year-old college student, was introduced to Dover, the operator of a summer camp, through Excel Employment Agency. Mike and Dover entered into a written agreement whereby Dover hired Mike as a camp counselor during the summer vacation period at a salary of $2,000 per month. Mike also agreed in writing to pay Excel Employment Agency a certain commission for their services. In June, Mike discovered that he had failed one of his final exams, and decided that, instead of working, he would attend college during the summer session. Mike disaffirmed both contracts.

(a) What rights, if any, do Dover and Excel Employment Agency have against Mike? Explain.

(b) Would your answer to (a) be the same if, when he entered into the contracts, Mike had fraudulently misrepresented his age as 18? Explain.

12. The father of a 17-year-old daughter, Alicia, sent his daughter away to college, and paid Alicia's expenses for board, clothing and tuition.

(a) Assume that Alicia decided to occupy her spare time, and accordingly contracted to take a two-year correspondence course in computer repair with Careers Correspondence School. After Alicia became 18, she continued to receive the course materials for 6 months, did the correspondence lessons, used the books sent to her, and made six monthly payments. Then she notified Careers Correspondence School that she disaffirmed any further obligation under the contract. In an action by Careers Correspondence School against Alicia to recover the balance due under the contract, judgment for whom? Explain.

(b) Assume that while Alicia was 17, her father suffered financial reverses and Alicia and her father agreed that thereafter Alicia was on her own. In order to return to college, Alicia borrowed $25,000 from the college's Student Aid Fund to cover her expenses for the next year. The loan was payable at the end of 3 years. When Alicia became 18, she immediately notified the college that she disaffirmed the loan agreement. May the college enforce the loan agreement against Alicia? Explain.

13. On his 17th birthday, Alex received a deed to Blackacre, a tract of farmland, as a gift from his uncle. Alex cut down a number of trees suitable for making railroad ties. Alex sold Blackacre to Bertha for $100,000 and the felled timber to Carmen for $3,000. He spent the money and, immediately after his 18th birthday, notified Bertha and Carmen that he disaffirmed the respective contracts. In the meantime, however, Bertha had sold Blackacre to Marvin and Carmen had sold the timber to Ned. Is Alex entitled to recover:

(a) Blackacre from Marvin? Explain.

(b) the timber from Ned? Explain.

14. Bob, who was 17 years old, bought a used sports car for $12,000 from Ace Motors on the installment plan. He had already paid $3,000 on the car when he disaffirmed the contract on his 18th birthday. He offered to return the car and demanded the return of the $3,000 he had paid. The car is now worth only $8,000. What are the rights of the parties? Explain.

15. Ad and Bookem, an accounting firm operating nationally over a long period of years, with branch offices in all major cities and coverage of all major industrial areas in the United States, acquired the entire practice and goodwill of Sub and Div. another accounting firm operating nationally, with branch offices in all major cities. The price was to be paid in ten annual installments. The agreement contained a provision that provided that the five major partners of Sub and Div, both individually and as members of the accounting firm, were not to engage in practice anywhere in the United States for three years.
(a)   Is the provision enforceable? Explain.
(b)   Assuming the provision is enforceable, what remedies does Ad and Bookem have against any of the partners who breach the contract provision? Explain.

16. On February 1, Brad purchased the assets of Smalls, a small management-consulting firm based in Manhattan. Under their written agreement, Brad agreed to pay $80,000 a year for five years. The agreement required Smalls to transfer all of his assets and goodwill to Brad. Further, the agreement required Smalls not to compete with Brad for a period of five years within Manhattan, where the majority of Small's clients were located. Other clients of Smalls were located throughout New York State. Three months later, on May 1, Brad learned that Smalls had opened a management consulting firm three blocks from where Smalls' office had been located on February 1. What rights, if any, does Brad have against Smalls?

17. Dr. Livingston was the only oral dental surgeon in the village of Briarcliff Manor, New York, which has a population of 10,000. The nearest oral dental surgeon to Briarcliff Manor was 15 miles away. Dr. Livingston, who intended to retire that year, learned that Dr. Stanley, a recently licensed oral dental surgeon, intended to open her dental office in Briarcliff Manor within the next two months. Dr. Livingston persuaded Dr. Stanley to execute a contract with Dr. Livingston, which provided that Dr. Livingston would pay Dr. Stanley $50,000 if she would not open her dental office in Briarcliff Manor during the next six months. Seven months later, Dr. Livingston retired and Dr. Stanley immediately thereafter opened her dental office in Briarcliff Manor When Dr. Livingston refused to pay Dr. Stanley $50,000, she sued him for breach of contract. Judgment for whom? Explain.

18. OmniHealth, a national biotechnology firm, executed a three-year written employment contract with Edgar, who was to be in charge of the research and development division responsible for developing new drugs, at an annual salary of $350,000. At that time, OmniHealth was working on several different highly experimental drugs, trying to bring them to market. OmniHealth was anxious to protect its trade secrets and Edgar agreed in his employment contract that he would not work for any of OmniHealth's competitors anywhere in the United States for a period of one year after his employment terminated. At the end of the second year of Edgar's employment, Edgar resigned and promptly went to work for Technology, Inc. Technology, Inc. had known of Edgar's contract with OmniHealth, but persuaded Edgar to breach that contract and to become an employee of Technology, Inc.
(a)   What rights, if any, does OmniHealth have against Edgar? Explain.
(b   What rights, if any, does OmniHealth have against Technology, Inc.? Explain.

For problems 19 to 21, assume that the legal rate of interest in New York is 16%.

19. For each of the following transactions, explain whether the transaction is usurious and how much, if anything, the lender may recover.
(a)   Jack lends Bobby $1,000 and Bobby signs a promissory note for $1,160, payable in one year.
(b)   Jack lends Bobby $1,000 and Bobby signs a promissory note for $1,160, payable in three months.
(c)   Barry agrees to sell Lisa his valuable oil painting for $50,000 and to buy it back from her in three months for $75,000.

20. Devin had been down on his luck for years. Unable to pay his bills, Devin approached his best friend Craig for a loan. On January 1, 2009, Craig and Devin agreed in a signed writing that Craig would lend Devin $10,000. The terms of the loan agreement called for Devin to repay the loan, along with $3,250 in interest, on January 1, 2010.
    On December 31, 2009, Devin called Craig and advised that he would not repay the above loan.
(a)   In an action by Craig against Devin for money damages, judgment for whom?
(b)   In an action by Craig against Devin for equitable relief, judgment for whom?

21. Caleb and Dexter entered into a loan agreement on February 1. The agreement called for Caleb to lend Dexter $5,000, and in return Dexter was to pay off the loan in monthly installments of $900 for a period of six (6) months. In addition, the agreement also called for Dexter to pay Caleb a monthly $3.00 service fee on the loan. In fact, this fee did not relate to any services performed by Caleb either in connection with the loan, or in connection with the processing of Dexter's loan repayment checks.

After making the first two monthly installment payments, Dexter made no further payments to Caleb.

In an action by Caleb against Dexter, judgment for whom?

Chapter 12 Defenses to Contract Enforceability

[handwritten: Fraud and inducement]

1. Smith owned five acres of land in Wilton, New York, on which were two springs of mineral water and machinery to bottle the mineral water. Smith sold the real property to Brown for $300,000, representing that the water was natural mineral water and could be bottled or sold as it flowed from the ground. Smith also represented to Brown that the daily natural flow of water from the two springs was 4,200 gallons. Brown entered into possession and purchased and installed modern machinery for the bottling and distribution of the mineral water. He soon discovered that the water was not natural mineral water, but fresh water to which certain chemicals had been added. He also discovered that the daily flow did not exceed 160 gallons. By the time he discovered these facts, Brown had expended $75,000 for the installation of new machinery.
(a) Did Smith commit fraud? Explain. *[handwritten: Yes all 5 elem. or]*
(b) What remedy or remedies, if any, are available to Brown? Explain. *[handwritten: sue to rescind ; damage claim]*

2. On April 1, Santos, a dealer in mining stocks, sold to Burns, 10,000 shares of Alaska Uranium, Inc., at $5 per share, knowingly misrepresenting that Alaska Uranium, Inc. had proven uranium deposits in its Alaska properties. Burns paid Santos for the stock on April 1.

On April 15, on the advice of friends, Burns had the corporation investigated and found that it had never had any prospects of uranium, but that it had just discovered a copper vein on its property and was putting it into production. During the following February, Burns received and deposited a $100 check from Alaska Uranium, Inc. for its one cent per share dividend. One month later, Burns regretted his purchase.
(a) In an action by Burns against Santos to disaffirm the contract on the grounds of fraud, judgment for whom? Explain.
(b) In an action by Burns against Santos to recover damages based on fraud, judgment for whom? Explain.
(c) In an action by Burns against Alaska Uranium, Inc. to recover damages based on fraud, judgment for whom? Explain.

[handwritten: no reliance / false rep / knowingly / incuced? / justified and rely / damage / unhicked]

[handwritten: False representation]

3. On February 13, Mario purchased an engagement ring from John, a jeweler, for $5,000, relying upon John's representation that the ring was set with a genuine diamond. The next morning, Mario had the ring appraised by a gemologist and learned to his amazement that the center stone was not a genuine diamond, but rather a zircon, a cheap imitation that looked like a diamond but was worth only $50, and that the entire value of the ring was $200. Nevertheless, the next day, Mario gave the engagement ring to Gina, his fiancée, on Valentine's Day, as he had promised. One month later, Gina terminated her engagement to Mario and returned the ring to him. The following day, Mario decided to rescind his contract with John and to sue John for damages.
(a) Does Mario have the right to rescind his contract with John? Explain. *[handwritten: affirm]*
(b) Does Mario have the right to recover damages, from John and if so, how would the damages be computed? Explain. *[handwritten: Nope / damages yes]*

[handwritten: inducement]

4. Max Corporation, a well-known television manufacturer, had several odd lots of discontinued models, which it desired to clear out. Max, the president, invited Dharun, the owner of Dharun Discount Chain, to come in and examine the different models and make Max an offer for the entire lot. The sets were segregated from the regular inventory. Fifteen televisions that were not discontinued models were accidentally included in this segregated group by one of Max's employees. Dharun was unaware that Max did not intend to include the fifteen televisions in the group. Dharun made Max an offer of $10,000 for the entire lot. Unaware of his employee's error, Max accepted the offer. Max would not have accepted Dharun's offer if Max had known the fifteen current models had been included. Upon learning of the error, Max Corporation refused to perform and alleged mistake as a defense. Dharun Discount Chain sued Max Corporation for breach of contract. Judgment for whom? Explain.

[handwritten: sue for damages / dividend check - know fraud / affirm contract → cannot rescind]

[handwritten, right margin vertical: Qual ans / Qual ans / did we form the contract]

5. Cynthia was bequeathed an oil painting by her childless aunt. Cynthia was not favorably disposed toward the painting because it reminded her that her aunt had left her entire estate (except the painting) to the Society for the Prevention of Cruelty to Animals. When Cynthia's best friend, Beatrice, admired the painting, Cynthia offered to sell it to her for $10. Beatrice accepted, paid the $10 and took the painting. The painting was clearly an original and bore the signature, "Ad Schreyer," but neither Cynthia nor Beatrice had ever heard of the painter.

Several weeks later, Beatrice informed Cynthia that she had inquired about the artist and had learned that the painting was worth $15,000. On hearing this, Cynthia tendered $10 to Beatrice and demanded the return of the painting. Beatrice refused and Cynthia brought suit against Beatrice to recover the painting.

(a) Judgment for whom? Explain.

(b) Would your answer to (a) be the same if Beatrice had known, at the time she bought the painting, that Ad Schreyer was a famous artist and that the painting was far more valuable than Cynthia realized? Explain.

(c) Would your answer to (a) be the same if Beatrice had told Cynthia that Ad Schreyer was an amateur painter when Beatrice knew that Shreyer was a famous painter? Explain

6. Jorge is the owner of a 20-story office building undergoing renovation. A flooring contractor, Mikhail, came to the building to measure the job in preparation for making an offer. Mikhail mistakenly failed to include one of the floors, and his offer was thus 5% lower than it otherwise would have been. Jorge, who did not know of Mikhail's error, accepted Mikhail's offer. When Mikhail's workers came to start the job, they noticed the error. Mikhail now wants to avoid the contract. Will he be successful? Explain.

7. Aldo, an adult college student, went to Brentwood Department store to buy clothes. He selected two new suits and a coat for $950 and asked to open up a charge account. The credit manager was willing to open account but was concerned about payment. Aldo told the credit manager to call Franco, his father. On the telephone, Franco told the credit manager. "Go ahead, open the account for him. It will teach him to stand on his own feet if he has to pay his own bills. But don't worry, if Aldo doesn't pay you, I will." The clothes were given to Aldo and billed to Aldo. Aldo failed to pay. The store sues Franco who pleads the Statute of Frauds as a defense. Judgment for whom? Explain.

8. Assume in the previous question that the credit manager refused to open the account for Aldo, that he called Franco on the telephone, and Franco said. "I have an account with your store, give Aldo the clothes and charge them to my account. "The clothes were given to Aldo. Is Franco liable for payment if he pleads the Statute of Frauds as a defense? Explain.

9. Bo was the owner of Lot No. 1 on which he had built his home. Sadia owned the adjoining Lots No. 2 and 3, which were undeveloped, along with Lot No. 4 on which Sadia's home was located. Bo wished to acquire Lot No. 2 in order to protect his home site from crowding if Lot No. 2 should be sold to a stranger.

Meeting Sadia on the street on January 2, Bo explained his wish to acquire Lot No. 2 and offered to buy it from Sadia for $75,000 cash. Sadia agreed and promised to deliver a deed to Lot No. 2 in 4 weeks. Bo paid Sadia $1,000 as a deposit or down payment towards the purchase price of $75.000.

On February 1, Sadia told Bo that she had changed her mind. Bo demands that Sadia perform the contract. Sadia contends that if there is any contract, it is unenforceable.

(a) Was there an offer and acceptance sufficient to constitute a contract between Sadia and Bo? Explain.

b) In an action by Bo against Sadia for breach of contract, judgment for whom? Explain.

(c) Assume that on January 10, Bo sent to Sadia his check for $1,000 bearing the notation "On account of purchase price of Lot No. 2" and that Sadia cashed the check, but later refused to convey Lot No. 2. Would Bo's payment constitute sufficient part performance to enable Bo to enforce the contract against Sadia? Explain.

(d) If the contract is not enforceable, may Bo recover his $1,000? Explain.

(e) Assume that in addition to the payment, Bo, with Sadia's knowledge and consent, entered on Lot No. 2 and had it cleared of brush on January 20 at a cost of $150, but Sadia still refused to convey. Would Bo be entitled to obtain a decree of specific performance to compel Sadia to deliver a deed to Lot. No. 2 to Bo upon paying to Sadia the balance of $74,000? Explain.

(f) Would Bo be entitled to recover his $1,000 payment plus the $150 cost of clearing the land? Explain.

(g)   Assume that on March 1. Bo instituted a suit for specific performance and that Sadia denied she had agreed to sell. At the trial, the court decided that Bo was telling the truth. and ordered Sadia to execute and deliver to Bo a deed to Lot. No. 2 upon Bo paying the balance of $74,000.   Is Sadia entitled to have the decision reversed on appeal, if on the appeal Sadia raises for the first time the defense that her agreement was not in a writing signed by the party to be charged? Explain.

10.   Assume that in the preceding problem Sadia had sent to Bo a receipt for the $1,000 reading as follows: "January 11. Received from Bo $1,000 on account of $75,000 purchase price of Lot No. 2 at 27 Y Street. Albans, NY Closing in 4 weeks. (Signed) Sadia."
(a) Would Bo be entitled to a decree of specific performance against Sadia? Explain.
(b)   Assume that Sadia is willing to perform, but that Bo refuses. Would Sadia be entitled to damages against Bo? Explain.

11.   On September 15, Lubov agreed orally with Tim to lease a store to Tim in Manhattan at $5,000 per month for one year starting the following January 1.
(a) Is the oral agreement enforceable? Explain.

Assume that the oral lease was for three years, that Tim moved in on January 1, and paid the monthly rent for six months, and that Lubov then notified Tim to vacate.
(b)   Is the oral agreement enforceable by Tim for the balance of the three-year term? Explain.
(c)   Is the oral agreement enforceable by Tim for an additional six months? Explain.

12. On December 15, Lisa, a landlord, entered into an oral agreement with Tom to lease apartment 5W to Tom for one year starting on January 1, at a rental of $2,000 per month. On the same day Lisa hired Jarvis as superintendent of the building for a period of one year starting January 1 at a salary of $5,000 per month. On December 20, Lisa changed her mind and notified Tom and Jarvis that she would not rent to Tom or employ Jarvis.
(a)   In an action by Tom against Lisa, judgment for whom if Lisa pleads the Statute of Frauds as a defense? Explain.
(b)   In an action by Jarvis against Lisa judgment for whom if Lisa pleads the Statute of Frauds as a defense? Explain.

13.   (a)   On December 5, Alvin entered into an oral agreement with Courtney to perform certain advisory services for Courtney for a fee of $15,000 per month. The services were to commence on the following February 15, and to end on December 15. Is the agreement enforceable? Explain.
  (b) Also on December 5, Alvin entered into an oral agreement with Francine for Francine to do some remodeling and rewiring of Alvin's offices.   The agreement provided that Francine was to be paid $20,000 and was to complete all work no later than December 15 of the following year.   Is the agreement enforceable? Explain.

14. Bonnie, wishing to start her own business, borrowed $15,000 from Laura. Bonnie orally agreed to repay the loan in two years. Bonnie refused to pay when the loan became due. Laura sued Bonnie for breach of contract. Bonnie asserts the oral contract is unenforceable according to the Statue of Frauds. Judgment for whom? Explain.

15. Sven and Brent entered into an oral agreement under which Sven agreed to sell to Brent 8 used air-conditioners at $200 each, delivery at Brent's place of business ten days later; payment C.O.D. Brent refused to complete the purchase. Assume that Brent pleads the Statute of Frauds.
(a) If Sven sues Brent for breach of contract, judgment for whom? Explain.

(b) Would Sven be entitled to judgment if Sven can prove that Brent made a down payment of $200? Explain.

(c) Would Sven be entitled to judgment if Sven can prove
that Brent took 4 air-conditioners at the time the agreement was made? Explain.

16.   During the examination of the financial statements of the Wilbur Watch Company, the following problem was discovered. On January 16, Corey, one of Wilbur's salesmen, called upon Percy, the vice president of purchasing for Xenon Department Stores. He showed Percy the new line of plastic watches with large, bright-colored faces. Percy ordered 150 watches from $5 to $20 each at a total cost of $1,475. Delivery was to be made not later than March 15. Corey wrote the orders in his order book as Percy orally indicated the quantity of each watch he desired. Neither party signed anything.
    Corey promptly submitted the Xenon Department

Stores' order to the sales department of Wilbur Watch Company. The next day the order was recorded and a memorandum was sent to Xenon Department Stores, in care of Percy. The memorandum described the transaction, indicated the number and prices of the watches purchased and was signed by S.A. Williams, vice president of marketing. However, the total price and delivery terms were erroneously omitted.

Percy received the memo on January 20. He read it and placed it in his goods-on-order file.

On February 20, the market for plastic watches collapsed. Percy promptly notified Wilbur Watch Company by phone that Xenon Department Stores was not interested in the plastic watches and would refuse delivery. Wilbur Watch Company Store sued Xenon Department Stores to recover damages for breach of contract. Xenon Department Stores contends (1) there is no contract and (2) if there was a contract it is unenforceable under the Statute of Frauds Will Wilbur Watch Company prevail in its action against Xenon Department Stores? Explain.

17. On May 1, Study and Burrow, two college professors, entered into an oral contract under which Study agreed to sell his computer to Burrow for $1,300, with delivery and payment on May 15. On May 2, Study sent Burrow a signed letter confirming all the terms of their oral contract. Burrow received Study's letter on May 3 but never responded. On May 15, Study tendered delivery of the computer to Burrow, but Burrow refused to accept or pay for it, stating that he had changed his mind and did not need Study's computer. Study sues Burrow for breach of contract. Burrow pleads the Statute of Frauds as a defense.
(a) Judgment for whom? Explain.
(b) If Study and Burrow were merchants who sold computers, judgment for whom? Explain.

Chapter 13 Third Party Rights and Discharge

1. Salvador, who owned a retail shoe store, decided to sell the business. The assets of the business consisted of a one story building worth $100,000, merchandise worth $50,000, accounts receivable of $10,000, fixtures worth $30,000 and goodwill estimated at $50,000. He owed various wholesalers a total of $20,000 for shoes bought by him on credit.

Salvador offered to sell all of these assets to Byron for $220,000 cash, provided that Byron would also agree to assume payment of the $20,000 owed for merchandise. Byron agreed, and a written contract was executed by both parties. Upon payment of $220,000 by Byron, Salvador signed a deed and bill of sale for all the assets listed.

Charles, who is one of the wholesalers to whom Salvador owed $5,000, demanded that Salvador pay the $5,000 owed. Salvador informed him that Byron was to pay. Charles sued Salvador and Byron for payment.
(a) Byron defended on the ground that he had made no contract with Charles. Is the defense valid? Explain.
(b) Salvador defended on the ground that Byron had agreed to pay. Is the defense valid? Explain.

Assume that the court entered judgment against Salvador and Byron for $5,000 as a joint liability.
(c) If Salvador paid $2,500 and Byron paid $2,500, has either any claim against the other? Explain.
(d) Would your answer to (a) be the same if Byron had paid $240,000 for the assets but had not agreed to pay the $20,000 owed to Salvador's creditors. Explain.

2. In the previous question, assume that Salvador wished to make a present to his wife, Wilma, of one half of the sales value of the business, and that Byron agreed to pay for the business in two installments. Accordingly, the contract between Salvador and Byron provided that Byron would "pay $110,000 to Salvador upon taking over the store, and $110,000 to Wilma two years later." Wilma was not one of the parties to the contract. Two years have elapsed and Byron has not paid Wilma.
(a) Does Wilma have a cause of action against Byron for the $110,000 promised to her? Explain.
(b) Would the one year Statute of Frauds be a defense to Byron if the agreement between Salvador and Byron were oral? Explain. → Sal fully performed
no SOF

Donee (intended) → sue Byron

3. In question 1, assume that Salvador, on closing the contract with Byron, signed a document reading as follows: "May 1. For value received, I hereby transfer to Byron all of my right, title and interest in and to the following accounts receivable owed to me: (1) From Darren, $5,000 due June 1; (2) From Ellen, $2,000 presently due, and (3) From Fatima, $3,000 due July 1."
(a) If Darren paid Salvador $5,000 on June 3, without knowledge of the assignment, what are Byron's rights against Darren and Salvador?
(b) If Byron immediately notified Ellen of the assignment, and then Ellen paid Salvador the $2,000,

Indemnification

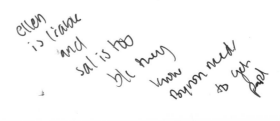
Ellen is liable and Sal is too (b/c they know) Byron needs to get paid

what are Byron's rights against Ellen and Salvador? Explain.

(c) If Byron notified Ellen of the assignment, but Ellen did not pay because she was insolvent, what are Byron's rights against Salvador?

(d) Assume that Byron notified Fatima of the assignment on June 15 and Fatima failed to pay on the due date. Byron then sued Fatima for $3,000, and Fatima interposed as a defense the fact that the goods sold to her by Salvador (the transaction from which her debt to Salvador arose) were defective, and worth only $1,000. What are Byron's rights against Fatima and Salvador?

(e) Assume that in (d), Fatima instead interposed as a defense the fact that she had paid the $3,000 on June 10 to Xavier, to whom Salvador had assigned the same debt on June 1. What are Byron's rights against Fatima, Xavier and Salvador? Explain *Sue Sal sue X*

(f) In (c) and (d) above, what steps could Byron have taken to ensure the collectability of the debts. Explain.

4. Tom sold goods to Gerard on 30 days credit for $10,000. The next day, Tom assigned this account receivable to Lou, who promptly notified Gerard in writing of the assignment. One week after receiving notice of the assignment from Lou, Gerard discovered that $2,000 of Tom's goods were defective and were worth only $500. Gerard promptly reported this information to Tom and Lou. Tom acknowledged that the defective goods were his fault but said that he could do nothing about it because he had already assigned the account receivable to Lou. Lou informed Gerard that he should pursue his claim with Tom, but should pay Lou the $10,000 due.

(a) What rights, if any, does Lou have against Gerard to recover the $10,000? Explain.

(b) Assume Lou agrees to accept $8,500 from Gerard, after deducting $1,500 for defective goods. What rights, if any, does Lou have against Tom? Explain. *Collects 1500 based on warranty*

5. Ed owned a company that cleaned swimming pools. He charged his customers $100 per month and billed them every two months. At the beginning of September, Ed had not yet collected for the months of July and August from his customer, Suzy, whose pool he had cleaned during that period.

On September 5, Ed spoke with Larry who was selling a used mountain bike. Larry said that he would sell the bike to Ed for $250. Ed accepted this offer, gave Larry $50 and a signed writing assigning to Larry the debt owed by Suzy.

The next day, Larry attempted to collect the $200 from Suzy. She refused to pay, telling Larry that she

was not prepared to pay anything because Ed had been adding the wrong chemicals to the water, causing her to suffer a severe skin rash. She only discovered the cause, she said, after seeing a doctor in mid-August. Larry sues both Suzy and Ed for $200.

(a) How much if anything, may Larry recover from Suzy? *Larry Sue Ed*

(b) How much, if anything, may Larry recover from Ed?

6. Abbott enters into a written signed contract with Costello to sell Costello 3,000 reels of comedy films for $60,000. Without the knowledge or consent of Costello, Abbott assigns his right to receive Costello's payment to Edgar, a creditor of Abbott.

Edgar gives notice of the assignment to Costello and demands payment of $60,000. Costello, however, contends that he has no obligation to pay Edgar because: (1) Costello never consented to the assignment and (2) in any event, 2,000 of the film reels are totally defective and, therefore, Costello only owes $20,000.

Assume that Costello's claim of defective reels is proven and that Edgar did not know of the defects at the time the assignment was made. What rights, if any, does Edgar have:

(a) against Costello? Explain. *Sue*
(b) against Abbott? Explain. *Both*

7. On January 10, Simpson sold her business to Bart for $250,000 under an executed contract that provided that Bart would pay Simpson's indebtedness to Homer, which was due on February 10.

On February 10, Simpson refused Homer's demand for payment, explaining that Bart has agreed to pay Homer and that Homer should look to Bart for payment.

The next day, Homer demanded payment from Bart, who refused to pay upon the grounds that: (1) Bart had no contract with Homer requiring Bart to pay Homer and (2) Homer cannot enforce the contract between Simpson and Bart because Homer gave no consideration.

(a) In an action by Homer against Bart, judgment for whom? Explain.

(b) In an action by Homer against Simpson, judgment for whom? Explain.

8. By contract dated May 1, Rob agreed to sell to Nancy, and Nancy agreed to buy from Rob, a certain house located at 10 Melbourne Road. At the time she signed the contact, Nancy transferred to Rob a deposit equal to 10% of the purchase price. The contract stated

that closing and transfer of the property would occur on or before July 15. Nancy's finances were such that she needed to obtain a loan to pay the full purchase price for the house. Pursuant to the terms of the contract, Nancy was to obtain financing for the house in an amount of $180,000. The contract stated that Nancy was to apply for such financing in good faith within 7 days of the signing of the contract. It further stated that if Nancy could not obtain $180,000 in financing from a bank, savings bank, or savings and loan association, then Nancy could cancel the contract and recover her deposit.

(a) On May 5, Nancy applied for the $180,000 loan in good faith, but on July 1, the bank notified her that she would only be allowed a loan of $50,000. Rob demands that Nancy close on the purchase and sale of the house on July 15 and Nancy sues Rob for return of her deposit. Judgment for whom? Explain.

(b) Assume instead that Nancy waits until July 1 to apply for a bank loan, and when she applies, she does not give complete or accurate information to the bank about her income or assets. On July 10, the bank denies Nancy's application for a loan. On July 15, Rob demands that Nancy close on the purchase and sale of the house and she demands return of her deposit. Rob sues Nancy for breach of contract. Judgment for whom?

9. Dacor, a famous interior decorator and music lover, ordered a custom made, state of the art, big screen entertainment center from High Tech Manufacturing. Dacor maintained a lavish apartment that he used as a showcase to impress his wealthy clientele. In making the contract, Dacor insisted that the center meet his personal approval, and the contract guaranteed personal satisfaction. Skilled craftsman worked for months on the center and even competitors of High Tech considered it one of the finest products ever produced. Dacor, however, was not satisfied. He did not like the finish and he did not find the picture and sound quality to be as outstanding as he wished. He therefore refused to accept the entertainment center unless it was refinished and substantial improvements were made in the picture and sound quality. High Tech, stating that the entertainment center was the best that could be made, refused to make the changes and sued Dacor for breach of contract. Judgment for whom? Explain.

10. Saul, a cotton merchant, had 50 bales of cotton in his warehouse. Brown, a prospective buyer, inspected the bales in the warehouse, and entered into a signed written contract with Saul to buy the bales at a price of $1,000 per bale. Delivery was to be made by Saul to Brown's factory in two weeks. Two days before the delivery date, Saul's warehouse and the cotton were destroyed by fire caused by lightning. Brown demanded that Saul deliver another 50 bales of similar grade cotton. Upon Saul's refusal, Brown sued Saul for breach of contract. Judgment for whom? Explain.

11. On May 1, Peters, a concert producer, executed two contracts. The first contract was with Selena, a world renowned singer, which provided that Selena was to perform a concert at Thomas's theater in Manhattan on July 4 for a fee of $200.000. The second contract was with Thomas, the owner of a theater in Manhattan, under which Peters rented Thomas's theater in Manhattan for the July 4 concert for a rental fee of $20,000. Peters sold out in advance all of the tickets for the concert and would have made a net profit on the concert of $100,000, after deducting the rental cost of the theater, Selena's fee and $20,000 for advertising expenses.

On July 2, Thomas' theater burned down due to lightning. Peters immediately notified Selena, canceled the July 4 concert and refunded the full purchase price of the tickets to those who had bought tickets. Selena insisted upon payment of her fee because she was ready, willing and able to perform and the fire was not her fault.

(a) In an action by Selena against Peters to recover her fee, judgment for whom? Explain.

(b) In an action by Peters against Thomas to recover Peters actual expenses or $20,000 for advertising the concert and his lost profits of $100,000, judgment for whom? Explain.

(c) How could the parties protect themselves from financial loss in this situation? Explain.

12. Nissan Corp., wishing to dispose of its surplus warehouse, offered it for sale for $500,000 cash. Belle informed Nissan that she would pay the price asked. A contract of sale was executed by the parties and Belle paid 10% of the price as a down payment to Nissan. The closing was set for 4 weeks later, at which time Belle was to pay the balance by certified check and Nissan was to deliver the deed. The contract provided that Nissan Corp. would retain the down payment as liquidated damages if Belle defaulted. When the time for the closing arrived, Belle told Nissan Corp that her arrangements to borrow the balance of the purchase price had not been completed and she requested an additional two weeks to complete the arrangements, Nissan Corp. refused and stated that it was cancelling the contract and retaining the down payment.

No breach materially

(a) Did Belle's failure to pay on time constitute a material breach of the contract? Explain.

(b) If Belle raises the money in two weeks, is she entitled to a decree of specific performance of the contract against Nissan Corp.? Explain. *Specific performance*

Assume that Nissan Corp. granted Belle an additional 6 weeks to raise the money, but notified her that it would grant no further extensions. At the end of 6 weeks, Belle had still been unable to raise the money, and Nissan Corp. notified her that it was cancelling the contract. A month later, Nissan Corp. sold the warehouse to Chin for $550,000.

(c) Is Belle now entitled to recover her $50,000 down payment? Explain. *No damage cause*

Assume that when Belle originally negotiated for the purchase, Nissan Corp. had little confidence in Belle's ability to raise the money. Accordingly, the parties agreed to a clause in the contract stating, "Time is of the essence in this contract." At the closing Nissan Corp was unable to tender clear title to Belle because the day before the State Tax Department had notified Nissan that an unpaid franchise tax constituted a lien on the warehouse. Nissan Corp. requested a delay of 3 days to pay the tax and satisfy the lien. Belle, who had reconsidered her bargain, refused any extension, tendered her certified check for the balance, and demanded that Nissan deliver clear title. When Nissan Corp. was unable to comply, Belle said she was cancelling the contract.

(d) Is Belle entitled to the return of her down payment? Explain.

(e) Is Nissan Corp. liable in damages to Belle for Belle's cost of conducting a title search? Explain. *Yes*

13. Camille, a builder, contracted to build a house for Alan, in accordance with the specifications prepared by Alan's architect, for a total price of $350,000, payable in stages as the work progressed. The final payment of $20,000 was to be made when Camille obtained a completion certificate from Alan's architect certifying that the work had been done according to the detailed specifications. Camille, as was customary in the industry, subcontracted out various parts of the work to sub-contractors who were specialists in excavation, brickwork, electricity, flooring and other trades. When the house was finished, Alan's architect refused to issue a certificate of completion because the flooring was done in maple, instead of oak, as was required by the specifications. The difference in value because of the variation was $3,000. It turned out that Dan, the flooring subcontractor, had deliberately used the maple flooring to reduce the cost of his contract with Camille and, therefore, to make a larger profit. Camille did not know of or consent to the substitution. Alan refused to make the final payment of $20,000. Camille, who had already paid Dan, refused to replace the floors with oak wood. Camille now sues Alan for $20,000.

(a) Has Camille committed a material breach of the contract? Explain.

(b) Are Alan's damages measured by the cost of removing the maple floors and replacing them with oak floors? Explain.

(c) Is Camille entitled to be paid $20,000 less the damages incurred by Alan? Explain.

(d) Does Camille have a claim for damages against Dan? If so, for how much? Explain.

Chapter 14 Breach and Remedies

1. On April 1, Conrad and Owen executed a contract under which Conrad agreed to build a specified house on Owen's land for $700,000. The contract provided that Owen was to make periodic payments to Conrad as different phases of construction were completed, with the last payment of $70,000 due 5 days after completion of the house. The contract further provided that the house was to be completed by August 1 and included the following provision: "If Conrad is late in completing the construction of the house, the purchase price is to be reduced by $3,000 for each and every day after August 1." Conrad constructed the house according to the contract, except that it was completed 5 days after August 1. Owen made all scheduled payments except for the final payment of $70,000. Although Owen could not prove any monetary damages caused by Conrad's delay, Owen offered to make a final payment of $55,000 to Conrad, after deducting $15,000 for the 5 day delay. Conrad rejected Owen's offer and sued Owen for $70,000. How much, if anything, will Conrad recover from Owen? Explain.

No harm

Liquidated Damages clause

2. Millie, a famous singer, entered into a contract to perform at Tanya's night club during the month of December. Tanya advertised that Millie would be performing at Tanya's nightclub and obtained many advance reservations from customers for the performance.

In November, Raisa, the owner of another nightclub, convinced Millie to breach her contract with Tanya and to perform at Raisa's nightclub instead during the month of December. On November 15, Millie told Tanya that she would not be available to perform at Tanya's nightclub as planned. When Tanya found out that Millie would be performing at Raisa's nightclub instead, Tanya became furious and immediately called her lawyer.

(a) Tanya sues Millie, demanding specific performance of the contract. Discuss.

(b) Tanya seeks an injunction against Millie, to stop her from performing at Raisa's nightclub during December. Discuss. *yes - stop singing*

(c) Tanya sues Millie for breach of contract and demands damages. What damages, if any, may Tanya recover? *expenses*

(d) Does Tanya have any action for damages against Raisa? Discuss.

Tortious interference w/ contracts

Chapter 25 Employment Law

Can't force to perform

1. Tom, Dick and Jane are employed by Atlantic Motors, a large chain of used car lots with several hundred employees. None of them was hired for a definite period of time and each has an excellent record of sales. On April 15, all of them were fired.

(a) Tom, who is 50, was told by his manager that he was being fired so that the company could "make room for some young faces on the sales force."

(b) Dick, who is 49, was fired because, on April 15, he had become frustrated with a prospective customer who was arguing about prices and had punched the customer in the nose.

(c) Jane was fired because she repeatedly refused invitations from Al, the sole owner of Atlantic, to spend weekends with him at his beach house. Al had warned Jane that she would be fired if she continued to reject his advances.

Discuss, separately, whether Tom, Dick or Jane has any claim against Atlantic Motors.

TITLE VII age

STUDY THIS

LANDMARK IN THE LAW

BEYOND OUR BORDERS